OXFORD UNITED

THE COMPLETE RECORD 1893-2009

OXFORD UNITED

THE COMPLETE RECORD 1893-2009

MARTIN BRODETSKY

DB PUBLISHING

First published in Great Britain in 2009 by
The Breedon Books Publishing Company Limited

This paperback edition published in Great Britain in 2013 by
DB Publishing an imprint of JMD Media Ltd.

ISBN 978-1-78091-145-8
Printed and bound in Great Britain by Marston Book Services Ltd, Oxfordshire

Contents

FOREWORD

Oxford has a worldwide reputation as a centre of academic excellence – but for me Oxford United Football Club has always represented the heartbeat of the city.

My Oxford connections run deep – I was born, educated and started on the journalistic road in the city with the *Mail* and *Times*. The Us have been my team since I watched them as Headington United in the Southern League, and I still have hundreds of old programmes and scrapbooks lovingly preserved in the attic.

As a TV Sports Presenter I have been extremely fortunate to get paid for watching amazing sporting achievements all over the globe – but I'm certain my best assignment was on Sunday 20 April 1986 when Oxford United outplayed Queen's Park Rangers in the last-ever Milk Cup Final at the old Wembley Stadium. At the end of the ITV show in '86 I threw impartiality out of the Wembley studio window and put on my Oxford hat complete with ox horns – it felt great even if it wasn't the smartest career move. Even though I knew it was unlikely that I would get another chance to introduce my team before a major Final at Wembley, in my darkest hours I couldn't imagine where the club would go over the next 20 years.

Supporting Oxford has been a truly moving experience – up, up and down, down, down. The club flourished when it had good leadership at the top, and in many ways you could argue we massively overachieved, but it's those memories which keep us turning up week in week out.

The football business today is very different to how it was in 1986 – but you have to believe it's still possible for Oxford United to thrive. 'What's happened to your club?' I'm always asked. This book has the answers. The story of Oxford United needs to be written by a genuine fan, and Martin Brodetsky has been that for 40 years. That means he has seen the Yellows run out at Old Trafford and Anfield, and more recently at the Dripping Pan at Lewes!

We had a grim period of lack of care at the top and we are living proof of how easy it is to slip down the Leagues. We all know how tough it is to get up off the floor and fight back to where we belong. We should be a Championship club. We have the facilities and a fantastic fan base – but as I write at the end of 2008 that feels like a distant dream. Oxford is a special club which has produced excellent managers and players and has some of the most tolerant and loyal supporters in the country. Patience and devotion have been sorely tested since Malcolm Shotton lifted the Milk Cup. I fervently hope that in a few years time Martin will have another golden chapter to write – covering the resurgence of Oxford United.

Come on you Yellows…

Jim Rosenthal, December 2008.

Introduction

All football clubs have histories that are unique, which comprise success, failure, struggle and progress. These, along with the people who are entwined within the stories, are what forge the characters of the clubs and make them what they are today. However, I think it is reasonable to claim that Oxford United's story is an extraordinary one, which is deserving of a wider audience than the club's incredibly loyal and long-suffering fanbase.

From their beginnings as a village team at the end of the 19th century, through its embracing of professionalism and its rise through the Football League to its decline of the last decade, Oxford United's story is one that would struggle to be taken seriously if it was presented as a work of fiction. The 'rise and fall' of United is a story that is yet to have an end, and hopefully the clause 'and rise again' can be tagged onto the end of the phrase. The many people who have been involved with the club, either with a direct influence or as loyal supporters, deserve nothing less.

I first watched Oxford in October 1969 when my brothers took me to a game against Millwall. That game ended 0–0, as did my second experience of United a few weeks later against Carlisle. However, far from being put off I was enraptured by the atmosphere, the large crowds and the fact that I was watching football live and in colour, even if there were no action replays. I bought my first season ticket in 1985, to coincide with the club's top-flight debut, even though I lived in Ilfracombe, 180 miles away. When I lived in Australia in the early 1990s I kept up to date with frequent calls to Clubcall, there being no internet back then. On my return to Oxford I was recruited to write for the fanzine *Raging Bull*, eventually becoming joint editor. I set up the *Rage Online* website (the fanzine had by now changed its name to *Rage On*) and was a founder member of both *FOUL* and *OxVox*. More recently I was involved in the creation of the *Ultimate Yellows* group, so I like to think of myself as more than just a passive spectator.

In writing this book I have drawn upon a number of other works detailing United's history: former chairman Vic Couling's 1983 self-published *Anatomy of a Football Club*; in 1985 John Ley wrote *Rags To Riches – The Rise And Rise Of Oxford United*; this was followed in 1989 by Andy and Roger Howland's excellent *Oxford United: A Complete Record 1893-1989*, which like this volume was published by Breedon Books, and which has been an invaluable resource for the last 20 years; in 1993 United published *Oxford's Hundred, Oxford United's Official Centenary Publication*; and three years later Geron Swann and Andrew Ward produced the extraordinary *The Boys From Up The Hill*, an oral history of the club with transcripts of interviews from players, managers, directors and supporters; Jon Murray added to United's visual history with his book on Oxford United in the *Images Of England* series in 1998; the Howlands produced *The Headington Years* in 2001, a partial update of their earlier work; and finally Chris Williams compiled *Lords Of The Manor* in 2005, consisting of interviews with former players and others.

These have all proven very informative and helpful, as have various matchday programmes, club handbooks, annual accounts, and minutes of United's AGMs and directors' meetings.

In addition to all the above, a number of others have given me much-needed assistance. Much of the statistical data was provided by my website *www.rageonline.co.uk* which was built by my web technician Ian Pearce, who has worked above and beyond the call of duty to add new features and repair broken bits at the drop of a panicky email. Much of the early data on the site was provided by Steve Merritt. I would also like to thank the *Oxford Mail* for permission to reproduce many of the photographs herein, especially Chris McDowell in their archive department, plus photographer Steve Daniels, who provided me with many original prints. All at Oxford United have been incredibly helpful, especially Communications Officer Chris Williams, Chairman Kelvin Thomas and General Manager Mick Brown, while the Centre for Oxfordshire Studies has also been an invaluable resource. Thanks also to Jim Rosenthal for penning the foreword and to Geron Swann, Graham Shirley, Reg Earl, John Masters, Percy Blake and Dave Nash for providing some old photographs and memorabilia. Also to Tony Rosser for permitting me access to extracts from his book *The Rise and Theft of a Family Business* (*www.family-business.info*) and Stephanie Jenkins, who runs the *www.headington.org.uk* local history website. Special thanks also to Michelle Harrison and my editor Jonathan Hoggard from Breedon Books for their help and understanding, as well as their much-needed flexibility. My apologies to anyone who has helped whom I've inadvertently left out.

My biggest thanks go to the people without whom Oxford United would not exist – the players, managers, directors, back-room staff and especially the supporters. Keep the yellow flag flying high!

Martin Brodetsky, April 2009.

Oxford United's History

The Early Years

Oxford United had very humble beginnings, starting life as a village side created 'for the welfare of the young men of the Parish' once the local cricket club's season was over. The village was Headington, which was subsumed into the Oxford city boundary in 1929, allowing it access to electricity and telephones for the first time. The football club was inaugurated at a meeting at the Britannia Inn on London Road on Friday 27 October 1893 by Windmill Road resident Doctor Robert Hitchings. Dr Hitchings was at that time the captain of Headington United Cricket Club, but the football club initially did not include the United suffix. At the time of the creation of Headington Football Club, the population of the village was a little over 3,000.

The first recorded match played by the new team took place on Saturday 25 November 1893 against Cowley Barracks, which was won 2–1 by the Army side. Less than two months after its formation, Headington FC was affiliated to the Oxford City Junior Association, joining the City Junior League the following season but playing friendlies for the first year of its existence. The second reported game took place on 13 January 1894 at home to Victoria, during which the 39-year-old Revd John Holford Scott-Tucker 'registered two goals by good rushes' despite the fact that 'the corners were only being about 27 yards from the goals'. Victoria pulled a goal back before half-time and in the second half they scored twice more to take the lead, 'but a good bit of play by Dr Hitchings made the scores equal, and though the remainder of the game was in the neighbourhood of the home goal, the visitors could not score' and the game finished 3–3. The Revd Scott-Tucker, born in Kirby Muxloe, Leicestershire, in 1854, was to be influential in the club's formative years, being for several seasons the club president.

The following Saturday the two clubs played the return game at Victoria's New Marston ground 'before a good attendance of spectators'. On this occasion 'Headington had to meet a much better team…than they did previously, and in consequence were beaten by six goals to nil.' The report in the following week's *Jackson's Oxford Journal* is the first time that the club is referred to as Headington United, but that appears to be an anomaly, and even the club's own reports continued to call it Headington AFC for many years. Despite the heavy defeat, the report says that 'one must not think that they were easily defeated…for they gave the Victoria a far better game than some clubs have in the League matches this year, and as this is their first season they have performed very creditably, and I hear that it is their intention of entering for the Junior League next season. If they should, a surprise may be in store for some of the city clubs, as they appear to have some good players.' Headington were to lose again the following Saturday, going down 5–0 at Clarendon Press after being 1–0 down at half-time. They lost the return game with Clarendon Press 1–0 the following Saturday, but on 10 March Headington won for the first time, beating Cherwell Rovers 6–0.

On 27 September 1894 the committee of the City Junior League met and placed Headington in A Division for the new season. In the run-up to the tournament Headington played two friendlies (that we know about), losing them both. First they lost 2–0 to St Peter-le-Bailey on 6 October, but as frequently happened in those days the side was not fully represented. The following Saturday Headington suffered their heaviest loss to date, going down 7–0 at Cowley St John, and it could have been worse had the Headington goalkeeper not had a good game. The Cowley goal was never threatened, 'and only one goal-kick was taken'. The club's first competitive game was played on 17 November 1894 against Clarendon Press. It should have been an away game, but because of flooding at the Press's Osney pitch it was played in Headington, 'on a fearfully heavy and uneven ground'. Clarendon Press dominated the first half and they hit the bar twice, but the score at the break was 0–0. The visitors took the lead shortly after half-time, after which Headington 'woke up a little' and started to get back into the game, but to no avail as the Press ran out 4–0 winners. On Headington's side 'Dr Hitchings and Dearlove seemed to be the pick, whilst their custodian saved some hot shots'. Headington then lost 6–0 at home to St Barnabas before, on 8 December 1894, the side won a competitive fixture for the first time, beating Wanderers' 2nd 2–1 at Osney, with the goals being scored by H. Knowles and F. Collett.

A 5–2 defeat at Cowley St John was followed by a 2–0 win over St Peter-Le-Bailey, with goals from Dr Hitchings and C. Jacobs. The club then lost their next two games, 4–1 at home to St Barnabas and 5–0 at Victoria, before the City Junior League was abandoned due to the large number of unfulfilled fixtures caused by bad weather. Headington's Annual General Meeting that summer, held at the New Schools on 27 July 1895, was the club's third (the first, presumably, being the meeting when the football club was inaugurated, but I can find no record of the second). There was 'an unusually large number of members and persons interested being present', and the Revd Scott-Tucker was unanimously re-elected president. The most momentous decision of the meeting was 'that the colours of the club should be orange and dark blue'. 'A vote of thanks was passed to Mrs Wootten for the use of her field last season', while the report of the meeting concluded, 'Judging by the attendance, and the interest taken in the business of the Meeting, our Football Club bids fair to be popular and ought to show some good results this season.'

There were some good results in the 1895–96 season, although the most impressive was in a friendly game when Headington beat City Temperance 12–0. This season the Headington second team also started to play a number of fixtures, with mixed results. For many years the official records of Oxford United dated the club's formation as 1896, and in April 1947 the club held a dinner in honour of their Jubilee. In Vic Couling's 1983 book *Anatomy of a Football Club* he states: 'Headington United Football Club, founded in 1896, had for three years previously played on Quarry Fields', while the club's official yearbook for the 1950–51 season states: '…from 1896 until 1929 the club was purely a village side and a good one at that', although it does then go on to state that to go back to the origins of the

The front and back of the medal presented to Frank Taylor for Headington's win over St Mary Magdalene in the Oxford City Junior League Cup Final on 16 March 1899. (courtesy: John Masters)

club 'it is necessary to turn back to about 1893 when a few ambitious young men got together a scratch team'. However, I can find nothing extant that would make 1896 appear a more significant season than any other with regards to the club's origins, and certainly far less important than 1893, although they did enter the Oxfordshire Junior Shield for the first time, losing 4–1 at Newland Cygnets after beating Dorchester 1–0 in the first round.

The earliest balance sheet I have seen dates from 27 July 1896. The season's income stood at £12 9s 1d, with the largest sums being the sale of caps and shirts to members (£3 10s 0d) and subscriptions of 42 members (£2 2s 0d). Expenditure included the purchase of caps and shirts (£3 9s 3d), ground rent (£1 10s 0d) and two new balls (£1 0s 6d). In addition, the club paid 16s for the printing of fixture cards and a 2s 6d affiliation fee to the Oxford City Junior Association. The club was left with a balance of £2 18s 5d.

Following another relatively uneventful season in 1896–97, Headington won their first silverware in 1897–98, qualifying for the Oxford City Junior League Cup Final by virtue of winning Division B and then beating St Mary Magdalene 1–0 in the Final at Oxford City's White House Road ground in a replay after a 1–1 draw. After the game, 'the Headingtonians marched off in triumph, singing with much gusto the refrain "Three cheers for the Orange and Blue."' The *Headington Parish Magazine* celebrated the win with the note 'We heartily congratulate our football team on winning the Junior League Cup this year. The greatest credit is due to each member of the eleven, and to the officers of the club for their pluck and *espirit de corps.* Perseverance and kindly feeling have worked the club up to its present state of efficiency. Long may the club flourish!' The season had also started off well, with an 11–0 friendly win over Oxford Cygnets' 2nd, with H. Knowles scoring eight of the goals.

On 3 October 1898 Headington beat Clarendon Press 4–0 in the opening ceremony of Headington's new ground at the Britannia Field. That season Headington again reached the City Junior League Cup Final, and again their opponents were St Mary Magdalene. For the second successive season the sides drew the first game, where 'the Headington contingent was particularly large, and nearly everyone donned the colours of their camp [orange and blue]'. Again Headington were triumphant in the replay, this time beating their opponents 3–0, with goals from H. Fletcher, H. Knowles and an own-goal by W. Couling. This successful season also saw the club reach the Final of the Oxon Junior Shield, where they faced Chipping Norton Swifts. The first game, at Oxford City's ground, was a 0–0 draw, but Chipping Norton won the replay 2–1 at Witney Town's ground. This replay was the first recorded instance of a football special train for the club, which was 'full to inconvenience'. However, this match was beset by controversy, as Headington later claimed that Chipping Norton had fielded two players 'Webb and Juffs, who are Gloucestershire men. These two men are prominent forwards of Moreton-in-the-Marsh team in the Cotswold League. Of course, this is deliberately in violation of bye-law 6'. The matter was referred to the Executive Council of the Oxfordshire FA, who ruled that the competition should be declared incomplete, refusing Headington's request to have another set of medals made for them, although permitting the club to have their own medals minted.

This was not the first time that the issue of ineligible players was to be faced by Headington, who had earlier that season been challenged by St Barnabas for fielding P. Gough in the second round of the County Junior Shield, 'as he had previously played twice for St Catherine's in the Inter-Collegiate Cup', which was a Senior competition. This claim was dismissed as St Barnabas failed to provide any evidence to back up their accusation, and their appeal to the English Football Council was also dismissed, causing them to forfeit the £2 deposit, because the Council ruled that it was a matter for the Oxfordshire Association alone. However, Cowley also submitted a claim against Headington in respect of the same player and, after the two clubs provided contradictory evidence, the game was ordered to be replayed. Headington had won the original fixture 4–2, but in the replay Cowley won 3–1, with the Headington club making a counter claim that one of the Cowley players, Arnold, was a senior.

For the 1899–90 season, Headington's application to join the second division of the Oxfordshire District League was accepted. Headington decided to withdraw from the City Junior League because a new rule was introduced that barred players from the League who had won two Junior Cup medals, and as Headington had won both the previous two seasons' Cups, almost all of their players held two medals. Headington did decide to play their second XI in the City Junior League, but for the first team a change of policy was likely: 'Up to the present Headington have, with one or two exceptions, included no one but natives of the village in the team, but under the circumstances it will in all probability be found necessary to receive a little outside help.' The *Oxford Chronicle* reported that 'Their admission to the League should prove a stepping-stone to higher things, and it is certain that no other club in Oxford would have a more popular success than the plucky Headingtonians.' Headington started the season well and were soon ahead in the table, but they fell away and eventually finished third. In the County Junior Shield, Headington beat Clarendon Press and then Victoria, but they were eliminated in the third round by Chipping Norton Swifts, who won 3–2. The second XI fared poorly in the City Junior League, and eventually they had to 'throw up the sponge' in January 1900 and scratch their remaining matches after they lost two men who were called-up to fight in the Boer War, leaving them unable to field a full team.

The war was to intervene again the following season, when Headington had to withdraw from the Oxfordshire District League because of the large number of players called-up to fight in South Africa, with 10 men on active service, including W.J. Smith, 'probably the finest back ever seen in junior football', who died while serving out there. Instead they re-entered the City Junior League, despite still having many players barred due to the two-medal rule. The 'team from over the hill' struggled to field a representative team but still performed creditably, including beating Oxford City Reserves 10–1. In the Oxfordshire

Junior Shield they beat Thame and Clarendon Press before losing 2–1 to St Mary Magdalene, while in the Senior Cup, which they entered for the first time, they lost 3–2 to Thame after a 1–1 draw. Headington were once again blighted by controversy when they fielded an ineligible player in their 2–2 home draw with Victoria in the City Junior League. For this offence the club had two points deducted and were also fined £1, the most extreme penalty that the Association was able to impose for this offence and the first time that they had inflicted it.

Headington were back in the Oxfordshire District League for the 1901–02 season, while the second team competed in the City Junior League. In the County Senior Cup the side reached the Final after receiving a bye in the first round, then beating Banbury Harriers 3–1 in the semi-final at home. The Final, against Culham College, was played at Oxford City's White House Ground on 15 March and ended in a goalless draw. The replay was at the same venue four days later, when the Collegians won 3–2, having been 3–0 up at one stage.

Headington managed only one game in the Oxfordshire District League in the 1902–03 season, beating College Servants 6–0 on 21 February 1903, and they were forced to scratch their other fixtures because of crowd trouble the following week during a 4–2 home defeat by Victoria in the City Junior League. On 4 October Headington had beaten Victoria 1–0, but the game was declared void after Victoria complained that Frank Chapman's registration was received half an hour after the deadline. At the rearranged game, on 28 February, Headington had to field a weakened side because the Association ruled that only those players who were eligible for the original game could play, so they were without five regulars. The Headington players were clearly out to avenge themselves: 'In the first minute or so a Victoria man was laid out in a manner that showed it was not unintentional, and for the rest of the game the visitors were knocked about in a manner that was really disgraceful. The ball was quite a secondary matter with some of the villagers…' The crowd, meanwhile, felt that Headington were being discriminated against by the referee, Mr J.T. Benson, being a Victoria old-boy, and they clearly felt that the visitors' fourth goal was offside, invading the pitch and surrounding the referee, who called time without restarting play. As a result, Headington's captain, C. Creese, and P. Tolley were suspended, and the club was forbidden from playing any matches within three miles of their ground for the rest of the season.

The following season there was another episode involving an ineligible player, but on this occasion it benefitted Headington. In the Oxfordshire Junior Shield second round Thame beat Headington 3–2 after a 2–2 draw at the Britannia Ground, but Headington protested against the inclusion of three of the Thame players, claiming that they had already played in Senior competitions. Although the case against two of the players was not upheld, that against F. Bunyon was proven and the Oxfordshire Football Council ordered that the game be replayed in Headington, with the home side winning the replay 1–0. Headington beat Bicester 2–1 in the third round, and in the semi-final they beat St Thomas' 3–1 in a replay after the first meeting had ended 1–1. The replay was to have been held at St Thomas's ground, but because it was flooded the game took place at Headington instead. In the Final Headington were beaten 2–0 by Caversham St John at the White House Ground on 12 March 1904.

The 1904–05 season proved to be something of a non-event for Headington, but in 1905–06 the side reached two Finals, losing them both. In the City Junior League the club won Division B, beating St Thomas' 2–1 in the deciding match at the White House Ground on 3 March 1906. The Final took place against College Servants at the same venue on 7 April, with the College team winning 2–0. The other Final that Headington reached was that for the Oxfordshire League Division Two. This was played against YMCA at St Thomas's ground in Grandpont on 28 April 1906, with the Young Men winning 2–1.

Headington did not apply for membership of the Oxfordshire District League for the following season, and instead they played in the City Junior League Division Two, with disastrous results, including an 11–1 defeat against College Servants' second team, their heaviest defeat since formation, and a 9–1 reverse at home to St Thomas'. The reserves fared no better, on one occasion losing 15–0 at Hannington Reserves in Cowley. In this season Headington were in trouble with the authorities for transgressing the rule stating that clubs should play in their club colours, instead turning up, as they did for their game against Cowley, in a 'medley of hues'. Results picked up in 1907–08 with a 10–1 win over Eagle Ironworks followed by a 10–0 win against Hearts of Oak. This season Headington played some of their home games at Highfield, as well as their more regular venue of the Britannia Field. A more significant event occurred at the start of the season, in September 1907, when the members of Strete Temperance formed themselves into Headington Quarry FC. There had been a previous incarnation of a Quarry club, formed in September 1899, who played a few seasons in the City Junior League Second Division, but they disbanded the year before. There was also a brief mention of a Headington Rovers some years earlier, but they seem to have vanished without trace.

For 1908–09 the side played in the Oxfordshire District League Division Two, finishing fourth. They returned to the Sandy Lane ground for the 1909–10 season, and it was at the start of this season that the United suffix began to be used regularly in newspaper reports. Previously, league tables and fixture lists had always referred to the side as just Headington, with occasional, rare, references to Headington United, but from the start of this season reports named the side as Headington United almost invariably, although it appears that there was no official announcement of any change. That season was another disappointing one for Headington, with the side failing to fulfil all their fixtures in the Oxfordshire District League, scratching most of their away games, and the first XI performed fairly modestly in the City Junior League Division One, although the reserves had a fine season in the City Junior League Second Division, finishing second behind Cowley St John and beating College Servants 11–1 in October.

At the start of the 1910–11 season Headington withdrew their second XI from the

A cartoon from the *Oxford Chronicle* celebrating Headington's giant-killing over Oxford City Reserves on 11 November 1911.

City Junior League as they were finding it impossible to secure sufficient players to run two teams. They were beaten in the first round of the County Junior Shield by neighbours Headington Quarry in front of 400 spectators, but they finished second in the Oxfordshire Junior League Division Two, with results including a 9–0 win against the YMCA at Grandpont and a 7–1 win against Thame II at the Moat Ground.

A significant event in the club's history occurred on 25 July 1911 at a meeting held in the Schoolroom, presided over by Mr W.H. Piggott, a member of the Oxfordshire Football Association Council. It was announced that in the coming season 'Headington and Headington Quarry clubs have decided to amalgamate, and will compete in local competitions under the title of "Headington United".' The meeting was well attended by representatives of both clubs, who were unanimous in the decision, 'and if the club goes on as it has begun, Headington should once more become a football stronghold in the district'. The club's president was Revd R. Curtler, with Archie Coppock elected first-team captain. The first game for this newly united club was a home friendly against Oxford YMCA at the Quarry Recreation Ground on 23 September, which Headington won 2–1. As an interesting aside, this season featured the first appearance of a new club named Oxford United, whose first game was a 4–1 friendly defeat by Woodstock on Thursday 28 September. They were to compete in the Thursday League, and indeed they won the League in their first two seasons.

In their first official season as Headington United, the club came to local prominence with a 3–2 friendly win over the Oxford City A team. City were without doubt the leading club in the county, competing in the Isthmian League, which was one of the foremost amateur leagues in the south of the country, and for the village team to beat the City A side was considered a real giantkilling. Headington also won their section of the City Junior League Division One, meeting Foresters in the Final at the White House Ground. A crowd of between 1,300 and 1,400 saw the two teams fight out a 0–0 draw, while there were around 1,000 present for the replay, at the same venue, which Foresters won 1–0.

One of the earliest known action photos from a Headington United game, from the *Oxford Journal Illustrated*, against Foresters FC in the Final of the Oxford City Junior League on 18 April 1912.

Headington's final game before World War One in the Oxfordshire Junior League Final against YMCA on 18 April 1914.

Headington continued to impress in the 1912–13 season, doing well in both the City Junior League and the Oxfordshire Junior League, although without reaching the Final of either. At the club's AGM on 21 August 1913 it was announced that 'an important step was taken in the amalgamation of the Highfield Club with Headington, in consequence of which a Thursday section will next season be run by the club'. In fact, the club fielded both a first and second XI in the Thursday League, with the first team competing in the First Division and the reserves in the division below. The Thursday teams were not too successful in their inaugural season, with the first XI finishing in fifth place (out of eight) and the reserves picking up the wooden spoon in their section. Ironically (with the benefit of hindsight), the first XI were beaten 3–2 by Oxford United. The Saturday teams were far more successful, with the first team reaching two Finals. In the Oxfordshire Junior Shield a fine run commenced with a 7–2 win over Thame A in the first round. In the second round Headington won 1–0 at Cowley, while in the next round the club played their first game against Witney Gordons, winning 2–0 in Witney to set up a semi-final tie at Banbury Harriers. This was easily won 3–0, meaning that Headington United were in the Final at the White House Ground against Oxford Institute. A crowd of 600 saw Headington outclass their opponents, winning 5–2. United also reached the Final of the Oxfordshire Junior League Second Division, having disposed of St Barnabas 4–3 in the semi-final, played on the ground of the College Servants in Osney. The Final, against YMCA, was also played at the White House Ground, but the 800 present saw a distinctly off-colour Headington side surrender meekly to lose 3–0.

The defeat to YMCA was Headington's last game for over four years, due to the intervention of World War One, which Britain declared at midnight on 4 August 1914. Initially there was some confusion as to how this would affect football competitions in Oxfordshire, with the OFA eventually suspending most competitions. Some clubs continued to play, notably Oxford City, but Headington United found it impossible to carry on, losing too many men who were called-up for active service, including their newly elected captain, O. Ward. This was doubly unfortunate for the side, as they were hoping to enter one of the county's Senior competitions for the first time, and they were 'prepared to take a new more private ground than the Rec' for the abandoned 1914–15 season.

The Headington United side before the 3–0 defeat by YMCA in the Oxfordshire Junior League Final, 18 April 1914.

The Headington Thursday League side that won the title in 1922.

Headington's first game after the war was a friendly against WRM in Cowley on 16 March 1919, which the home side won 6–2. There followed a series of friendlies, with Headington's first home game since 1914 being against Cowley which they won 5–1. At the club's AGM on 1 September 1919 it was unanimously agreed to revive the club, with Major William Lauriston Melville Lee elected as president. Major Melville Lee lived in Stoke House, Stoke Row, and was a secret agent for PMS2 (a secret branch of MI5 set up in 1916 to spy on the British Labour Movement) during the war. He maintained his links with MI5 and in 1917 he established and edited a journal called *Industrial Peace*, which circulated information on left-wing political organisations and individuals, which was printed in Oxford and published until 1928.

Headington's first first-team competitive game since the war was away to Wolvercote on 18 October 1919 and ended in an 8–0 win for United. This was in the Oxford City FA League First Division, the OFA having dropped the Junior distinction in a shake-up just weeks before war was declared. At the end of the season, United reached the OCFA League Final, losing 1–0 to Cowley at the White House Ground before a crowd of 2,000. Cowley and Headington were quickly becoming major rivals, with the Cowley club having beaten United 6–0 in Headington's first appearance in the Oxfordshire Charity Cup earlier in the season and by the same scoreline in the Oxfordshire Junior League. Cowley even produced a mickey-taking 'in memoriam' card to celebrate their OCFA Cup win, claiming that Headington had died after 'a severe bout of Cowleyitis'. Headington's reserves reached the semi-final of the OCFA Second Division Cup, losing 2–1 to St Frideswide at the Cowley Barracks Ground.

In the 1920–21 season Headington reached the Final of the County Junior Shield with a run that saw them beat Iffley 3–2, Balliol Old Boys 5–1, Morris Motors 2–1, Launton 5–1 and Goring 2–1. In the Final they met Oxford Gasworks, and after a 2–2 draw at the White

House, United lost the replay 2–1. Headington's goalkeeper for the Final, Knight, was forced to borrow a shirt from Oxford City FC, for which he had to pay sixpence, later repaid to him by the Headington board. In the Oxford City League Division Two the reserves had another successful season, this time going one better than the previous year and reaching the Final, after beating Oxford Gasworks II 4–1 in the semi-final at the Oxford University ground in Iffley Road. However, a crowd of 1,100 saw them lose 2–1 to St Thomas' in the Final at the White House Ground.

The 1921–22 season saw another important step in the development of Headington United, with the decision to enter the Oxfordshire Senior League. The club still retained a team in the county's Junior League and two sides in the Oxford City League, in addition to a Minors team, and they re-entered the Thursday League. The chief home matches were to be played on the Manor Road pitch, at virtually the same site as the Manor Ground was to be built on, while the Minors and other lesser games would continue to take place at the Quarry Recreation Ground.

Headington's first game with their new status was a 6–0 defeat at Stone's Athletic, one of the stronger teams from the Banbury area, but their first home game was a 3–0 win over Morris Motors. The side did well in their first season of Senior football, sitting in second place after the Christmas games following a sequence that included a 9–0 win over Banbury Harriers, in which Percy Drewitt scored the first eight goals, setting a new local record for successive goalscoring. The side finished the season in fourth place, but they also reached the Final of the Oxfordshire Senior Cup, meeting their old rivals Cowley at the White House Ground before a crowd of 3,200, a new competition record. Cowley won the game 2–1. The reserves side won their section of the Oxford City League Second Division but were beaten 3–0 in the semi-finals by Balliol Old Boys, while the Minors side won their section of the Minors League but were beaten 3–1 in the Final by St Frideswide.

For the 1922–23 season Headington moved to the Manor Park ground on Manor Road, which was otherwise known as the Paddock. This was a 'new and enclosed ground...an excellent playing pitch...and dressing-room accommodation is being provided, which will be a big improvement'. This season the club were also granted a new nickname, with the newspapers referring to them as 'The Hillmen'. The Minors team continued to play at Quarry Recreation Ground. This season also marked the club's first entry into the Amateur Cup, the country's leading non-League Cup competition, although United never made it past the local preliminary rounds. In their first season they beat St Frideswide 4–0 after a 2–2 draw at Botley Road and were then knocked out after a 6–1 defeat at

Percy Cooper, 1922. (courtesy: Reg Earl)

The Headington Minors side from 1922. (courtesy: Reg Earl)

Newbury. Headington finished eighth in the Oxfordshire Senior League, where mixed results included an 8–1 win over St Frideswide and a 9–1 defeat at Banbury Works. The club suffered a controversial exit in the Oxfordshire Charity Cup when, after the initial game at Manor Park had to be abandoned because of poor light, they refused to accept an Oxfordshire FA ruling that Morris Motors should host the replay and failed to turn up for the game – a misdemeanour for which United were fined £2 2s. Headington's junior team's reserves won their section of the Oxford City League Division Two, but they were knocked out 2–1 by YMCA in the semi-finals.

Headington finished fifth in the Oxfordshire Senior League in 1923–24 and reached the Final of the Oxfordshire Charity Cup, in which they were beaten 2–1 by Witney Town in front of 2,600 at the White House Ground. The club also reached the semi-finals of the Woodstock Charity Cup, in the only season in which they entered that competition, losing 2–1 to Oxford Railway Sports. Morris Motors eliminated Headington from both the Amateur Cup and the County Junior Shield. The following season Headington were making plans for another ground move, this time just down the road to the Manor Ground, where they were to remain for the next 76 years. A statement read: 'The club does not expect to be able to use the new ground this season, but

The Headington Thursday League side that won the title in 1924. (courtesy: Graham Shirley)

hopes are entertained that the Manor Park ground may be secured for one more winter whilst necessary work is being carried out on the new ground'. The 1924–25 season was a disappointing one for the Hillmen as they finished fifth in the Oxfordshire Senior League and were eliminated from the Senior Cup, Amateur Cup and the Oxfordshire Charity Cup in the early rounds. The Thursday team did win their League, however, winning all 10 of their games, and reaching the semi-finals of the Korebo Cup, while the Thursday League reserve side came joint top of the Second Division, losing the decider to Miranda from Abingdon.

Headington United moved to the Manor Road ground for the 1925–26 season, but because the cricket club, with whom they shared the ground, hadn't yet finished their fixtures, the football club played the first three games of the season away from home. They officially opened the Manor on 26 September 1925, with an Oxfordshire Senior League game against Deddington. The game kicked-off late because the visitors' coach broke down on the way, but eventually the club's president, Major Melville Lee, performed a ceremonious kick-off before Deddington won the game 2–1, E. Grain scoring Headington's first goal at their new ground. United's first win at the Manor did not arrive until 21 November, when Thame were beaten 8–2. Headington finished fourth in the Senior League and were knocked out of the Amateur Cup at the first attempt, going down 6–0 at Oxford City, who were still by far and away the top team in the county. The attendance for the game was estimated to be around 3,000. The side did reach the Final of the Chipping Norton Hospital Cup, but they were beaten 2–1 by Chipping Norton. Headington were running a number of teams again this season, and it was claimed that the club had more playing members than any other club outside Oxford. They were also one of the best supported clubs, and a measure of this can be seen when two boys, aged 13 and 15, walked and ran from Headington to Woodstock to watch the semi-final of the Chipping Norton Hospital Cup as they did not have enough money to pay for the bus, although they were given a lift home on the supporters' coach.

The highlight of the 1926–27 season was reaching the Final of the Chipping Norton Hospital Cup again, although this time Headington were beaten 3–0 by Bicester. Headington finished a lowly sixth (out of 11) in the Oxfordshire Senior League, and at the annual meeting of the Oxfordshire FA the club supported a proposal by St Frideswide to form an Oxford City Senior League because of the travelling expenses involved in a countywide competition, but the idea was shelved after it lost a vote by 10–2. At the Headington FC annual meeting the club chose to reduce the number of teams that it ran because they were without a second ground, although they did make occasional use of a ground at Barton End.

In 1927–28 the senior side did poorly in all competitions, finishing eighth out of 10 in the Senior League and being eliminated from the early rounds of all the Cups except the Chipping Norton Hospital Cup, in which they reached the semi-final before losing 6–1 to Thame. The Minor team, however, again won their League with a 100 per cent record and beat the Rest of the Minors League team 2–1 in the Championship match at the Manor. The following season was another disappointing one for the club, although they did reach the Final of the new Bradley Cup, which they lost 3–1 to Littlemore. This replaced the Chipping

Norton Hospital Cup, which had become a more local junior tournament due to new rules about travelling distances laid down by the OFA. By this time the club had withdrawn from the Thursday League and instead permitted Erratics FC to play at the Manor in that competition.

The 1929–30 season failed to herald a great turnaround of fortune for the club, although in their penultimate Oxfordshire Senior League game at Witney Town Reserves United's 5–3 win was the home side's first defeat in two years. Although they were eliminated from the Amateur Cup by Oxford City in the first qualifying round, the 3–0 scoreline was considered a great triumph for Headington, especially considering that the score was 0–0 with about quarter of an hour remaining. The reserves won the City Junior League Division One Final with a 2–1 win over East Oxford Corinthians at the White House, while the same opponents beat United in the Oxford Junior League City Final 3–2 at the Botley Road Recreation Ground. After that last defeat Headington supporters were condemned for threatening to throw the referee into the river and for other disturbing scenes, and an OFA investigation suspended Headington United committee member Mr Hall from football management for the whole of the 1930–31 season, while G. Mattock was suspended until October 1930.

These suspensions failed to prevent the 1930–31 season from being the club's most successful to date. Headington achieved a third-place finish in the Oxfordshire Senior League, with results including a 7–0 home win over YMCA and a 9–1 win against Bicester. United also reached two Cup Finals, bringing back some silverware to Headington in the process. In the Oxfordshire Senior Cup, United commenced their Cup run with a 7–0 win over Osberton Works. After eliminating Thame 2–1, United beat Henley Town 4–1 at Thame in the semi-final. In the Final they faced Oxford City's reserves at the White House Ground, but after holding the favourites to 3–3 at half-time, the City's superiority shone through and they eventually won 8–3 before a crowd of 3,000. Under a month later United were back at the White House, contesting the Oxfordshire Charity Cup Final against Witney. In their run to the Final United had beaten Gasworks 7–1, Henley Town 3–0 and Oxford City Reserves 1–0. Less than a week earlier Headington had been beaten 4–2 at Witney in an Oxfordshire Senior League game, but the Charity Cup Final was a far tenser affair. At the end of full-time there was no score, and in the first period of extra-time Witney took the lead, but Headington hit back with two goals from Frank Margetts to win their first Senior trophy. Earlier that same day Headington had a Senior League game at Bicester, in which they fielded a team of reserves and lost 4–0, this being the only League game in which United failed to score.

After the highs of the previous season, the 1931–32 campaign failed to live up to expectations, although United still achieved a fourth-place finish in the Senior League and they again reached the Final of the Oxfordshire Charity Cup, losing an exciting game 5–4 to Banbury Harriers at the White House. This season also featured United's first entry into the FA Cup, although they were eliminated in their first game in the extra preliminary round, going down 8–2 at home to Hounslow. Their Charity Cup campaign started with a bye, as holders, into the second round, where they beat Clarendon Press 9–3. They then beat their opponents from the previous season's Final, Witney, 3–0 in the semi-final at Osberton Road.

United achieved a hat-trick of Oxfordshire Charity Cup Final appearances in 1932–33, and they also reached the semi-final of the Senior Cup to make up for their disappointing League campaign, which saw them finish sixth. United's opponents in the White House Final were Bicester, and Frank Margetts was again Headington's hero, scoring the only goal of the game. In the Senior Cup semi-final United were beaten 4–3 by Cowley, at that time Oxford's second club behind City, competing in the Spartan League. United's FA Cup campaign was again doomed to failure, after their bye into the first preliminary round saw them lose 4–2 at home to Bicester in a replay, after a 2–2 draw. In the Amateur Cup Headington were thrashed 7–1 at home by Marlow.

Headington suffered a poor season in 1933–34, in which United finished eighth in the Senior League and were eliminated in the early rounds of all the Cup competitions in which they competed. The only bright note came from the reserves, who won the Oxfordshire Junior Shield, beating Banbury GWR 4–1 in the Final, played at Banbury. The gate receipts of £22 were a record for that competition, vindicating the OFA's decision to experiment with hosting the Final out of Oxford. The reserve team were also runners-up in their section of the Oxfordshire Junior League and reached the semi-final of the City Junior League, in which they were beaten 1–0 by Osney Town.

The first team fared little better the following season, although the reserves were again successful in the Oxfordshire Junior League, this time beating Cold Arbour 2–1 in the White House Final. The most significant event for local football, though, was the withdrawal of Cowley from the Spartan League. The East Oxford side were getting very poor gates and had amassed over £200 of debt, incurred mainly because of their travelling expenses. However, a new force was emerging in the county, as this was Banbury Spencer's first season of Senior football, joining the Oxfordshire Senior League, which they won at the first attempt, doing the double over Headington. Midway through the season they sought permission from the OFA to join the Birmingham Combination to take over Rugby's fixtures and field their reserves in the Senior League, but this was refused and Spencer had to wait until the following season before moving up another level.

In 1935 a new league was formed called the Oxfordshire Intermediate League, designed to be a compromise between Senior and Junior leagues, as the distinction between them was rapidly becoming eroded. Headington entered their reserve side into this new competition and the earliest known issue of a Headington programme dates from their first game, at home to Thame Reserves. The 1935–36 season was to prove Headington's most successful yet, as they finished second in the Senior League and won their first major silverware in the shape of the Oxfordshire

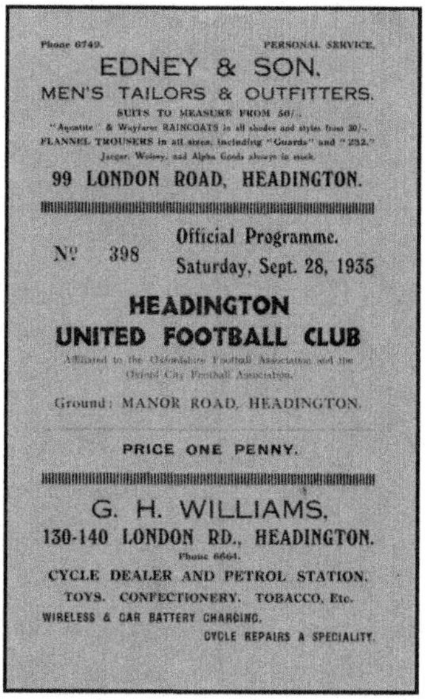

Phone 6749. PERSONAL SERVICE.

EDNEY & SON.

MEN'S TAILORS & OUTFITTERS.

SUITS TO MEASURE FROM 50/-.

"Aquatite" & Wayfarer RAINCOATS in all shades and styles from 30/-.

FLANNEL TROUSERS in all sizes, including "Guards" and "232."

Jaeger, Wolsey, and Alpha Goods always in stock.

99 LONDON ROAD, HEADINGTON.

No 398 Official Programme. Saturday, Sept. 28, 1935

HEADINGTON UNITED FOOTBALL CLUB

Ground: MANOR ROAD, HEADINGTON.

PRICE ONE PENNY.

G. H. WILLIAMS.

130-140 LONDON RD., HEADINGTON.

Phone 6664.

CYCLE DEALER AND PETROL STATION.

TOYS. CONFECTIONERY. TOBACCO, Etc.

WIRELESS & CAR BATTERY CHARGING.

CYCLE REPAIRS A SPECIALITY.

The front page of the earliest known Headington United programme, an Intermediate League reserves match against Thame Reserves on 28 September 1935.

Senior Cup, the 'Blue Riband' of local football. The season did not start too promisingly, with heavy defeats at Newbury and Marlow in the FA Cup and the Amateur Cup and three losses in the first four League games. However, from the start of December until the end of the season United lost just one League match, winning all the others. In the Senior Cup, Headington beat Henley Town, Old Oxford Citizens and Witney Town before facing Banbury Spencer in the Final at the White House Ground. The first game, on 13 April, ended 1–1 in front of a record crowd for the competition of 5,638, taking record receipts of £168. United won the replay 1–0 with a goal from Maurice Lonie before a crowd of more than 5,000, for which they were awarded a grant of £20 by the OFA. This capped a fine season, in which they also won the Bicester Charity Cup and the Wingfield Bradley Hospital Cup, and the reserves reached the semi-finals of the Oxfordshire Junior League and the Final of the Oxford City Junior League, losing 3–2 to Littlemore at the White House in the latter competition.

During the summer of 1936 Major Melville Lee stepped down as president of the club and he was replaced by Godfrey Elton, first Baron Elton of Headington. Lord Elton was a historian who lived at Greenways, 40 Manor Road (later Osler Road). At the same annual meeting, the committee decided not to enter the Bicester Charity Cup the following season due to the prohibitive travelling expenses involved.

In the 1936–37 season Headington failed to capitalise on their successes of the previous campaign. They were again eliminated from the FA Cup, Amateur Cup and Oxfordshire Charity Cup at the first attempt, and in the League they finished third. They reached the semi-finals of the Oxfordshire Senior Cup, where they were eliminated by Pressed Steel, who had also knocked them out of the FA Cup. In addition, United were beaten in the Finals of both the Wingfield-Bradley Hospital Cup and the Henley Hospital Cup. Headington were also forced to withdraw from the various Junior competitions they had entered because their Intermediate League fixtures did not provide enough vacant dates to fulfil their other commitments. However, the club's finances were extremely healthy, as despite a relatively poor season they took record gate receipts of over £78, and they could even afford to pay Cowley FC £27 4s 3d for their wooden stand.

On 4 September 1937 Headington won an FA Cup tie for the first time, beating Marlow 4–2 in the extra-preliminary round. This, however, was the only high point in the opening stages of the season, which saw them knocked out of the FA Cup in the next round and eliminated from the Oxfordshire Charity Cup and the Bradley Cup in the first round. They had a mini-run in the Amateur Cup, beating Osberton Radiators 6–3 after extra-time, with Jack Ramsden scoring an extra-time hat-trick in just three minutes, and Bicester Town 2–1 away, before Marlow avenged their FA Cup defeat by beating United 4–3. Things picked up slightly in the New Year, when the club reached the semi-finals of the Oxfordshire Senior Cup before being beaten 4–2 by Morris Motors at Witney. The end-of-season charge which took United to a second-placed finish in the League included a 9–1 win over Heyford RAF and a 7–3 win over Osberton Radiators. This latter game featured the inclusion of 14-year-old schoolboy Jimmy Smith, who scored one of the goals and was described as 'certainly no passenger' in the side. Smith would continue to play for Headington until September 1955. The reserves also finished second in the Oxfordshire Intermediate League.

The 1938–39 season was the club's most successful to date. They won the Oxfordshire Senior League at a canter, without defeat, and along their way to the title United beat Bicester RAF 8–0, Heyford RAF 7–0 (away) and both Thame and Chipping Norton 7–0. They also beat Banbury Harriers 16–1, with Charlie Machin scoring seven of the goals and goalkeeper Geoff Wyatt scoring from the penalty spot. United's unbeaten League performance was a new record for the competition, and the club also reached the Final of the Oxfordshire Senior Cup, which they lost 2–1 to Bicester Town before a White House crowd of 5,906. However, Headington got their revenge when they beat the same opponents 1–0 to win the Oxford Hospital Cup for the first time. United also won the Oxfordshire Charity Cup, beating Brize Norton No 2 Flying School 1–0 in the Final. The side's success was said to be down to the wonderful team spirit among the players, of whom three (Lonie, Wally Imms and Lones) were ever presents. The side's trainer, L. Parsons, was given a medal by the committee in recognition of his part in the club's exceptional performances. The only real disappointment in the season was the reserves, who had themselves gone unbeaten until 19 November but then fell away, and by February they were often unable to raise a team. This was in part attributed to a lack of interest on behalf of the club's Committee members, who much preferred to concentrate on the first team's successes. This was a record-breaking season for the club not just in terms of results, but in finances too, with gate receipts of £154 10s 11d leading to an end-of-season balance of just over £100 in the club's bank account.

There is no way of telling how successful this team might have been if it had been able to continue competing, but on 3 September 1939 Britain declared war on Germany, and as a result all competitive sport was immediately abandoned. This was just a week before the commencement of the 1939–40 season, and United had been drawn to play Oxford City at the White House in the extra-preliminary round of the FA Cup, but this game never went ahead, and indeed the FA Cup was postponed for the duration of the war. The Oxfordshire FA issued a statement saying that they had been officially informed by the FA that no competitive games could be played, but that teams could play friendly matches in their immediate vicinity provided the permission of the Chief Constable was obtained first. United played two friendlies, against Pressed Steel (2–2) and Oxford City (which they lost 4–0 at the White House before a crowd of 1,200, in a game where Lonie fractured his leg and then missed the rest of the season), before the OFA announced that they had been given permission by the FA for the recommencement of League football in the area.

The Oxfordshire Senior League was restarted, but with fewer sides than before and many new ones, largely representing the Forces or clubs such as Banbury Spencer and Morris Motors, who were previously in the Birmingham Combination and Spartan League respectively but had to switch because of the travelling constraints. Oxford City joined the Great Western Combination, which allowed them to play against decent opposition while keeping within the 50-mile travelling limit imposed by the government. These logistical problems, combined with the country's most severe winter for 45 years, meant that a lot of scheduled games were either abandoned or rearranged and this, coupled with sketchy newspaper coverage of the football results, means that records are sadly incomplete. These were not the only difficulties that clubs had to contend with; for example, Bert Nutt missed the first 10 minutes of United's 2–1 defeat at Oxford City Reserves because he had to register for National Service. Headington finished fourth in the League and reached the semi-finals of the Charity Cup (which they lost 5–3 to the Infantry Training Centre), the Senior Cup (2–1 to Oxford City Reserves) and the Oxford Hospital Cup (4–3 to Pressed Steel).

Because of the war there was some doubt over whether or not the 1940–41 season would take place, but the OFA eventually gave the go-ahead. The League was now even more disrupted, and again many scheduled games failed to be completed because of the travelling problems. Newspaper coverage was rarely comprehensive, making a proper assessment of results impossible. Headington's season opened with a 6–2 win over Benson RAF, in which Lonie played his first game since breaking his leg at the start of the previous campaign. United's League season was a disappointing one, the side finishing in seventh place, although they did reach the semi-final of the Charity Cup, losing to Brize Norton 6–5 after extra-time (3–3 at full-time). Just after Christmas, 17-year-old Brian Timms joined Wolverhampton Wanderers as a teenage trialist in August 1940 (all professional contracts and registrations had been officially cancelled due to the war). He failed to make the Wolves first team but played in two second-team friendlies. Headington's Minor team had a more successful season than the senior side, reaching the Final of the Oxford Minor Cup, losing 3–2 to St Barnabas at the White House Ground.

In 1941–42 the number of teams competing in the Senior League reduced to 11, most of them representing the Services. Headington were finding it difficult attracting good quality players, and the large number of high-scoring games throughout the League was a reflection of the lack of experienced players. When Headington beat Pressed Steel 5–1 in November, the average age of the United team was just 17 years. Despite this the club finished the season in third place and reached the Final of the Senior Cup, where they were beaten 2–1 by Oxford City at the White House before a crowd of over 2,500.

The following season was a poor one as far as Headington were concerned. The Oxfordshire Senior League was split into two sections, with United playing in Section A. Although the side opened the season with a 9–2 win over RASC Wallingford (with Westwood, a Halifax Town reserve, included in United's side) they only won four of their 11 games and ended the season in sixth place out of seven. In the Charity Cup they were knocked out by Milton (4–2) after beating Abingdon Services 3–1 in a replay following a 6–6 draw, and in the Senior Cup United beat Stanton Harcourt 7–1 before going out to Harwell 4–2.

In 1943–44 Headington again struggled to make any impression and ended the season in seventh place in the Senior League, with only nine teams entering the competition that season. Typical of the problems that sides faced in trying to play competitive football was the game at Abingdon Services on 11 March, when the home side could only muster nine players and Headington had only eight turning out. The game finished 2–2.

Headington showed a slight improvement in the 1944–45 season, finishing fourth out of 10 in the Senior League. One early impressive result was a 14–2 win over the MG Car Company, who included in their ranks former Headington player Jack Ramsden, who was home on leave. United also reached the semi-final of the Oxon Charity Cup, which they lost 8–0 to Bicester Services.

In the first post-war season United went some way towards recapturing their success of the last pre-war season. Although they lost their first game 8–1 at the newly reformed Banbury Spencer in the extra-preliminary round of the FA Cup, they followed that up with an 8–1 friendly win over Oxford City Reserves, whom they also beat in their next game, 7–4 in the first Oxfordshire Senior League fixture. This in turn was followed by an incredible 17–1 win over Didcot in the Senior League, although Didcot's team contained a number of former Prisoners of War who perhaps were not ready for the rigours of Senior football. Didcot withdrew from the League shortly afterwards, and the result was expunged from the League's records. An early exit to Marlow in the Amateur Cup failed to throw United off their stride, and they went unbeaten in the League until 26 January, when Oxford City Reserves got their revenge with a 4–1 win at the White House in front of 1,500 spectators. Headington then went on to win the Oxon Charity Cup, beating Brize Norton RAF 3–1 in the Final at the White House. At the same venue they knocked Morris Motors out of the Senior Cup 6–2 in the semi-final, watched by 2,300. In the Final they faced Oxford City, again at the White House, and a crowd of 6,788 saw City win 4–0. On the same day (Easter Monday), at the same ground, the Headington Minor side were beaten 3–0 by South Oxford in the Minor Cup Final. Meanwhile, United finished joint top of Section A of the Senior League, but Milton RAF won 4–2 after extra-time in the title decider, also at the White House, but before a more modest crowd of 600.

In July 1946 Oxfordshire football was shocked by the news that Banbury Spencer had decided to adopt professionalism. The implications of this were not lost on Headington United, who were one of the more ambitious clubs in the county. At the annual meeting, the first the club had held since 1941, the club secretary, S.W. Jacobs, resigned because of his duties as secretary of the Oxfordshire FA, to which post he had been elected in August 1945. The board offered him an honorarium of 10 guineas and appointed him as honorary treasurer. Another change, the significance of which would be far reaching, was the election of Vic Couling as club president. Couling was a local boxing promoter who was friends with United's trainer Tom Webb. Percy Cooper resigned from the club's committee and was elected as United's first honorary life vice-president. On 3 September the club called a public meeting at the Britannia Inn with the objective of forming a supporters' club. The meeting elected Billy Jewel as its first president, and Sid Toms as secretary, and the club's initial membership stood at 50.

The 1946–47 season saw the recommencement of the Oxfordshire Intermediate League and the Oxford City Junior League, and Headington entered clubs in both competitions. The season started well for United, with the opening game being a 3–2 win at the newly formed Bicester Town in the FA Cup extra-preliminary round. The following week United beat Moreton RAF 12–2, with Ray Mansell scoring seven of the goals. Unfortunately, like the win over Didcot the previous season, this was declared void after Moreton resigned from the League two weeks later. Charlie Machin, Headington's captain, injured his leg in this game and was forced to give up football on his doctor's advice, retiring to Blackpool to open a bed-and-breakfast business.

In the first preliminary round of the FA Cup United played the newly professional Banbury Spencer and beat them 3–2 at the Manor before a crowd of 2,094. Headington's young outside-right Joe Wilson afterwards signed pro forms with Spencer. United's Cup run continued with a 3–2 win at Aylesbury United, but they were eventually eliminated from the FA Cup at Uxbridge. On 16 November the void game against Moreton was compensated for when United beat RNAS Culham by the same score. This was bettered on 4 January, when United beat Thame 14–2 in the first round of the Oxfordshire Senior Cup. The bad winter meant that no football was played during February, and many games were not played. As a result, although the season lasted until mid-May, many results and the final table remain unknown.

Headington United were now hoping for a higher standard of football, and with this in mind they applied to join the Spartan League, but their application was initially refused so they opted to join the Reading and District Senior League, in which Morris Motors competed. However, United withdrew from this competition after their secretary, Arthur Harris, received a telegram informing him that United had been admitted to the Spartan League First Division after a vacancy arose. At the annual meeting Vic Couling claimed that the next season would mark the beginning of a new era in the club's history. The club remained in the Oxfordshire Senior League, but it was now the reserve team who played in this competition.

In their first season as a Spartan League Division One side, Headington started well, and by the time they beat Polytechnic on 22 March they were second in the table, just two points behind Berkhamsted and with a good chance of promotion. However, a run of three games without a win saw United drift away, and despite an 8–0 win away to Wycombe's Redford Sports in their final game, the side finished fifth. This disappointment, though, was compensated for by United's form in the Oxfordshire Senior Cup. A first-round 4–0 win over Pressed Steel was followed by a 4–1 win over Banbury Spencer Reserves at Bicester. This set up a Final at the University's Iffley Road ground against Oxford City. A crowd of 7,796 saw Jack Ramsden score the only goal as United lifted the trophy. This was replicated two months later in the Oxford Hospital Cup Final against City at the White House when Bill Pringle scored the winning goal in front of 6,500.

The decision to turn professional was taken at the club's Annual General Meeting on 15 July 1948, after Oxford City had rejected a similar proposal. At the post-match dinner following the Oxford Hospital Cup Herbert Smith, the OFA President, suggested that Headington, having twice beaten City, could now lay claim to be the premier club in Oxford. The City chairman, Brian Cox, allegedly replied that while Headington might be the best team for one day, City would always be the best team in Oxford. This comment apparently so irked United director Peter Smith that he immediately started to look into ways to make United the senior club in the city. Former Headington player Bert Nutt made the proposal, which was adopted by the members, to apply to join the Birmingham Combination or a similar professional league, although because of having to share the Manor with the cricket club, meaning the football pitch wasn't available for the whole season, it was decided to postpone the decision until a solution could be found. Treasurer S.W. Jacobs opposed the proposal, saying that the club should learn to walk before it could run and it should concentrate on getting into the Premier Division of the Spartan League before considering moving up to a higher class of football.

Headington were unable to replicate their success in the 1948–49 season, starting off slowly in the Spartan League and getting eliminated from the FA Cup by Banbury Spencer (3–1) in the preliminary round, and from the Amateur Cup (4–1) by Slough Town in the third preliminary round. Results in the League picked up slightly leading up to the New Year, and United recorded good wins against Pressed Steel and Osberton Radiators in the Oxfordshire Senior Cup. Meanwhile United, who had been granted associate membership of the Football Association, played a friendly on New Year's Day against Pegasus, the combined team of Cambridge and Oxford Universities; this was the two sides' first recorded meeting, which Pegasus won 3–2.

At an extraordinary general meeting on 1 February 1949 a resolution was passed, proposed by Vic Couling, which 'accepts the principle of entering professional football, and authorises [Headington United's] officials to take the necessary steps in this direction, if, and when, the opportunity arises'. This followed an article by Roy Peskett in the *Daily Mail*, in which he mentioned the Southern League's intention to form a Second Division, and which led Couling to meet with Arthur Mortimer, chairman of both Bath City and the Southern League, who encouraged Couling with his aspirations for United.

The Southern League management committee called a meeting of clubs interested in forming a new Second Division, held on 15 March 1949. Between 16 and 20 clubs sent representatives, including a club called Oxford Carpathians, represented by Professor George Keeton and comprising mostly Polish exiles from Aylesbury, who played at Oxford Stadium. Naturally this came as a shock to the Headington United representatives, who had never heard of the Carpathians before, but after the meeting the two clubs agreed that Oxford should make only one application and the Carpathians withdrew, while Professor Keeton joined the Headington United board. The meeting went very well and it looked likely that a Southern League Second Division of at least 14 clubs would proceed. However, a second meeting on 7 April, at which entries would be accepted, did not turn out so well, with a number of clubs dropping out with no explanation and others claiming that they were unable to resign from their current Leagues in time for the new Southern League season. This meant that only nine clubs were present at the meeting to decide the format of the new division. Nevertheless, the resolution to form a Second Division, proposed by United representative Vic Couling, was carried.

On the pitch, United's League form continued to fluctuate, with a run of four wins ending with Yiewsley completing the double over Headington. Oxford City earned their revenge for the previous season's defeats by beating United 2–1 in the semi-final of the Senior Cup, while United also lost in friendlies to West Ham Reserves (1–0) and Dutch touring side UVS Leyden (4–0), this being the club's first recorded meeting against overseas opposition. United's final Spartan League game was a 4–1 win at Chelsea Mariners, with Headington finishing fourth in the Division One Western Section. Oxford City then beat United 4–1 in the Final of the Oxon Benevolent Cup, with over 6,000 in attendance at the White House.

In preparation for impending professionalism, United started building work on new dressing rooms, but the club received a shock on the last day of April when the Southern League informed them that a couple of the prospective Division Two candidates had withdrawn at the last minute and they therefore had to postpone the idea of a Second Division. Headington, however, had not given up the idea of turning professional and joining the Southern League, and at the League's Annual General Meeting on 31 May 1949 Headington joined Weymouth, Llanelli and Uxbridge in applying for membership, along with the two teams who had finished bottom in 1948–49, Bedford Town and Chingford Town, who had to seek re-election. Headington were represented at the meeting by Couling, Peter Smith, Ron Coppock and Professor Keeton, who faced an anxious wait outside the Euston Hotel meeting room while the Southern League committee debated the policy for the following season. Eventually the committee agreed to Headington's proposal to extend the League from 22 to 24 clubs, and they then heard representation from each of the six clubs seeking entry. After this the committee voted as follows: Bedford Town 20, Weymouth 19, Chingford Town 17, Headington United 10, Llanelli 9, Uxbridge 3. So United made it by just one vote. In those days clubs had to arrange their own fixtures, and there followed strange scenes as the clubs bartered with each other trying to arrange favourable dates for games. It was later discovered that Hereford United had voted for Headington, instead of their original choice of Llanelli, because of a meeting between their director Jack Jones and Vic Couling at a Professional Boxing Promoters' Association meeting in London, both Jones and Couling being boxing promoters.

The Southern League Years

United were now confirmed as a professional club, but with no players, no manager, a half-built ground that would not be finished for another six months and no money. Many felt that Headington had pushed the boat out too soon and had stretched themselves too far, but the community rallied round, led by the fledgling supporters' club, and pitched in to help with the construction work. At the same time the club was given the option of purchasing the Cowley Airfield site (famous for being the last airfield from which Amy Johnson took off on her final flight), adjacent to a proposed new housing estate (Blackbird Leys) and the planned Eastern Bypass, between Garsington Road and Sandy Lane. However, this came at a bad time for the fledgling board and the current changes and financial constraints meant they had to reject the offer.

The new dressing rooms, with a stand above them, were built entirely by voluntary labour by supporters and local Headington people. To raise capital the club issued 400 shares at a price of £7 each. Headington United became a limited company on 5 July 1949, and the first meeting of the new company's directors took place on Monday 11 July at St Margaret's Road School. At that meeting, chaired initially by Syd Cox, Couling was elected the first chairman of the board, with Professor Keeton as vice-chairman and Edmund Gibbs as company secretary. Three of the club's directors, Percy Cooper, Ron Coppock and Frank Simmons, were former Headington United players. One of the directors, Peter Smith, reported that he had secured the services of Harry Thompson as player-coach with effect from 1 August at a salary of £550 per annum, plus a bonus of £2 a win and £1 a draw for the games in which he played. In addition, Thompson would receive a bonus dependent on

Harry Thompson in his playing days for Wolverhampton Wanderers.

where the team finished in the table. The contract was for two seasons, and accommodation was to be provided for the new coach. This first meeting was followed by an informal public meeting at the Quarry Gate pub in order to update members of the old club and to sell the initial tranche of shares. Future directors' meetings were held in Percy Cooper's sitting room at the British Workmen's Club in Old High Street.

On Tuesday 19 July, Oxford City players Cliff Nugent and Peter Sharman were interviewed by the board at their own request. The board warned the players of the consequences of giving up their amateur status and turning professional, but both players decided to sign on as part-time professionals. The players were to receive £3 per Southern League match, plus bonuses of £2 per win and £1 per draw. The first that Oxford City knew of the transfer was when they read about it in the *Oxford Mail.* Jack Casley was signed from Torquay United as a full professional, initially on a one-month trial, at the end of July at the wage of £6 per week plus bonuses. Further professionals were signed such as Norman Aldridge and David Scott from Northampton Town, Arthur Kay from Bury and Albert Brine from Wolverhampton Wanderers. These players, along with local amateurs such as Jack Ramsden, Jimmy Smith and Laurie Washington, gave Thompson a good basis for a first team, and trial matches were played to determine the team to start the Southern League campaign against Hastings United.

Now that United were a professional outfit, the reserves had no league, being barred from playing in all the local ones, so Professor Keeton exclaimed, 'Then we shall have to start one!' and, along with Dagenham, the club convened a meeting to found a new league, initially called the Home Counties League until that suggestion was rejected by the FA, then, after renaming in November 1949, the Metropolitan League, with Professor Keeton elected the first chairman. Just before the start of the season Syd Cox resigned from the board, feeling that his position as a sports journalist with the local papers gave him a conflict of interests as a board member of the major Oxford club.

Harry Thompson's duties included suggesting the team for the Southern League games, which would then be ratified by the board. Shortly afterwards the board formed an advisory sub-committee to assist Thompson with team selection, although Thompson retained the final say on players used for the first team, the reserves and the minor team. United's first match with their new status was away at Hastings United on 20 August. United were supported by 20 coachloads of Headington fans, along with many others who travelled in their own cars or by train. The Us conceded a goal in the first minute and

A cartoon from the *Oxford Times* illustrating Headington's application for Southern League membership in 1949.

eventually went 5–0 down before former United player Ray Mansell, playing his only game for the club before returning to Oxford City, from where he was on loan, scored United's first professional goal. Another goal, from Peter Roberts, made the final score 5–2. United then visited Colchester United, where they lost 4–1, before a 1–1 draw at Worcester City earned the club their first professional point on 1 September.

United's first win of the season came in the FA Cup extra-preliminary round, in which they beat Reading's Huntley & Palmer's 9–4, with Fred Tapping scoring four goals. This remains the highest-scoring first-team game. United's share of the gate money for this tie amounted to £98 1s 1d. A 3–1 defeat at Hereford United in the Southern League Cup was followed by the club's first home Southern League game – the delay was caused by Headington United Cricket Club, who were the main tenants of the Manor at that time, having to complete their fixtures. United lost the game 2–0 to Worcester City, watched by 3,500 spectators. United were then eliminated from the FA Cup in the preliminary round, former Spartan League opponents Hemel Hempstead beating Headington 3–1. United won their first game as a Southern League club on 22 September, beating Guildford City 4–2 at the Manor, with Jack Casley scoring a first-half hat-trick. Casley had played in goal during the opening-day defeat by Hastings. Peter Buchanan, who had played for Scotland during the war, was signed in time for this game at a fee of £12 per match. Buchanan was later selected for the Southern League Representative side. At this stage, all signings were negotiated by director P. Smith. Any illusions that the victory over Guildford was going to herald a turnaround in the side's fortunes were quickly dispelled, as they lost 6–0 at Barry Town in their next outing.

United achieved an exceptional result when they beat Merthyr Tydfil 2–1. The Welsh side had finished third the previous season and were destined to be the season's champions. This game, played on 8 October, marked the opening of the new Dressing Room stand and saw a new ground attendance record of 7,000, which was to be beaten three times during this first professional season. Headington then lost 2–0 at Bath before the fixture list threw up a run of five successive home matches. The first two, against Weymouth and Kidderminster Harriers, were lost 5–2 and 3–2, but the next three all resulted in wins for the Us, as Bedford Town were beaten 2–0, Exeter City Reserves lost 3–1 and Chingford Town were hammered 7–2, with Doug McPhee scoring a hat-trick.

The return match at Chingford, watched by just 350, was a 2–2 draw, before Kidderminster completed the double over United, winning 3–1 at Aggborough. Gloucester City visited the Manor and were despatched 5–0, and a 1–1 draw with Dartford was followed by United's first away win of the season as they completed the double over Bedford, winning 2–1 at the Eyrie. On Boxing Day a crowd of 8,163 set a new ground record as United beat Chelmsford City 2–1. Headington's first game of 1950 was an unsuccessful visit to Hereford, where the Bulls won 1–0, but the Us beat Hereford 2–0 in the return game, having earlier beaten Lovell's Athletic 1–0. After drawing 0–0 at Yeovil, United lost the next seven games. The first defeat of the sequence saw another ground attendance record when 9,000 watched Colchester win 3–2 at the Manor, after which United went down to their heaviest defeat of the season, losing 8–2 at eventual champions Merthyr. This sequence of defeats was ended with a 3–2 win at Lovell's, to complete the double over the Welsh outfit. In mid-March 1950, Headington paid a fee of £100 to sign Cyril Toulouse from Guildford City at a weekly wage of £8, with Toulouse signing an agreement not to leave the club before the end of the following season.

When Yeovil came to the Manor, the ground attendance record was broken for the fourth time, with 10,160 crammed in to watch the game. A home match against Gravesend was won 6–5, with Peter Buchanan scoring a hat-trick. Headington completed their first season as a professional club with a 3–2 win at Weymouth, a result which ensured that United did not need to seek re-election. Headington finished fourth from bottom, 11 points above bottom side Chingford but only two points above second-from-bottom Kidderminster. Both Chingford and Bedford were re-elected for the following season, while at the other end of the table Colchester and Gillingham were elected into Division Three South. They were replaced by Llanelli and Kettering Town. Headington's reserves finished fourth in the Metropolitan League, which was won by St Neots, while the minor team won the Oxon Minor League for the second successive season, with their campaign including wins over South Oxford of 17–0 at home and 16–0 away.

Percy Blake, training in front of the Cuckoo Lane end near to where the new Dressing Room stand was built in 1949. (courtesy: Percy Blake)

After the season Harry Thompson's position was changed from player-coach to player-manager, and his contract was extended for three years, while the club purchased the house at 41 Green Road for Thompson and his wife at a price of £2,750. One of the directors, H.F. Bradley, disapproved of Thompson's new role, feeling that he was not the right man to be a manager, and Bradley resigned at the next AGM. The selection advisory sub-committee was disbanded, and Thompson was empowered to sign players up to a maximum wage bill of £130 a week. Also during the close season the board agreed to enter the A team into the Oxon Senior League and to adopt Henley Town as the club's nursery side, while also agreeing with Abingdon Town to an interchange of players. United made two important signings during the summer, bringing in Vic Barney from Second Division Grimsby Town and Frank Ramshaw from Sunderland.

The 1950–51 season started slowly for Headington, who were knocked out of the Southern League Cup 4–2 at Bedford Town in the opening game, with new signing from Weymouth Ron Johnston scoring both of United's goals. In November Johnston was sold to Brighton & Hove Albion for £75. A 3–1 win over Bath City was followed by a 6–0 reverse at Merthyr Tydfil, who again went on to win the Championship. Headington then faced Kidlington in the FA Cup extra-preliminary round, with the Kidlington team agreeing to play the game at the Manor. United won 6–0, paying Kidlington £100 as their share of the gate receipts, but were beaten at home 4–3 by Slough Town in the preliminary round. Results then picked up following a 4–1 win at Chelmsford City on 14 October, and by the time United played Yeovil on 2 December the side were 12th in the table. The 1–1 draw with Yeovil was followed by a creditable 2–2 draw with Merthyr.

For some time Headington had been using floodlighting for training purposes, and the club arranged a friendly against the county's other professional club Banbury Spencer in

A selection card showing Percy Blake's call-up for a Metropolitan League reserves game against Millwall on 8 September 1951. (courtesy: Percy Blake)

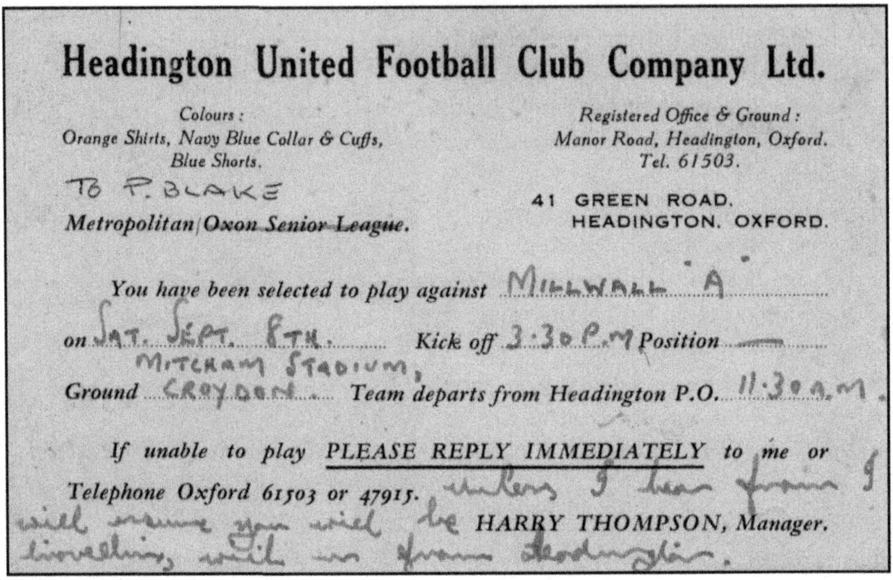
Headington United Football Club Company Ltd.

Colours:
Orange Shirts, Navy Blue Collar & Cuffs,
Blue Shorts.

Registered Office & Ground:
Manor Road, Headington, Oxford.
Tel. 61503.

TO P. BLAKE

Metropolitan/~~Oxon Senior League~~.

41 GREEN ROAD.
HEADINGTON. OXFORD.

You have been selected to play against MILLWALL "A"

on SAT. SEPT. 8TH. *Kick off* 3.30 P.M *Position* —

Ground MITCHAM STADIUM, CROYDON *Team departs from Headington P.O.* 11.30 a.m

If unable to play PLEASE REPLY IMMEDIATELY *to me or Telephone Oxford 61503 or 47915.* unless I hear from you I will assume you will be travelling with us from Headington.

HARRY THOMPSON, *Manager.*

Just before kick-off at an early floodlit match, possibly against Swindon Town. Note the special shiny shirt worn by Headington captain Frank Ramshaw.

aid of the Wingfield–Morris Orthopaedic Hospital (later renamed the Nuffield Orthopaedic Centre), after Oxford City had declined their invitation to play. The game was ratified by the Oxfordshire FA and took place on Monday 18 December, with a 7.30pm kick-off time. Wearing white shirts to show up better under the lights, Headington beat Banbury 3–0 in front of a crowd of 2,603 in a game heralded as the first one in the county to be played under artificial lights. However, they had to forgo the white ball they wanted to use in favour of a normal brown leather one because of the snow on the ground. Two days earlier, the Manor Ground hosted a representative match between the Metropolitan League and the Western League, the first time that the Manor had been chosen for a representative game. Included in the Metropolitan League side were Headington's David Johnston and Vic Moss, who was captain for the game, which the Metropolitan side won 3–1, Johnston being one of the scorers.

On Saturday 27 January Headington played a friendly at home to Gillingham, which United won 2–1. This was the first time that the team had beaten Football League opposition. So successful was the floodlighting experiment that further games were arranged before the equipment had to be returned to the Southern Electricity Board at the start of March, and Swindon were the next opponents. This match ended in a 0–0 draw, while the final floodlit friendly of the season was a 1–0 defeat by Northampton Town on 14 February. Meanwhile, Headington received £2,500, a Southern League record, when Cliff Nugent was sold to Cardiff City their original offer of £2,000 having been turned down.

After United's 4–1 home defeat by Chelmsford City on 24 March, Harry Thompson decided to end his playing career and he offered to resign as coach as a consequence. The board rejected this offer and instead appointed Thompson as manager on an annual contract. Meanwhile the supporters' club's offer to pay for the installation of permanent floodlighting, at a cost of £250, was accepted by the board. On 16 April the club played St Johnstone in a Festival of Britain game, with United winning 7–0, Bill Rowstron and Jimmy Smith both scoring hat-tricks. Headington ended the season with three successive victories, starting with a 3–1 win at Weymouth, who had beaten United 5–0 at the Manor earlier in the season. The final match was a 3–1 win at Dartford in which Sammy Chung scored twice. Chung was a local Abingdon boy whose father was Chinese. He made his first appearance after signing from Abingdon Town in the floodlit friendly game against Banbury, and he

Frank Ramshaw receives the Oxfordshire Professional Cup on 10 May 1952.

would later go on to manage Wolverhampton Wanderers. Chung was offered professional terms by the club but he turned them down, and in November 1951 he joined Reading as a part-time professional. Headington finished the season in seventh place, while the reserves also finished seventh in the Metropolitan League, but won the League Cup, beating Dagenham (who won the League) 1–0 with a goal from Chung.

The 1951–52 season was notable for United's exit from the FA Cup, after having beaten Wycombe Wanderers 3–2 in the second qualifying round. Wycombe put in a protest claiming that goalkeeper Colin McDonald was ineligible, and this was upheld. McDonald was registered with Burnley but was doing his National Service with the RAF at Moreton-in-Marsh. Burnley, after an approach from Harry Thompson, gave McDonald permission to play for Headington and he made his debut in the game at Yeovil in December 1950. However, in September 1951 Burnley informed Headington that they would not give permission for McDonald to play because he had told them that he was not prepared to re-sign for them. Harry Thompson and Peter Smith, together with McDonald, visited Burnley to try and reach an agreement, but none was forthcoming and so the club decided to continue playing McDonald as an amateur, a move which was ratified by the Oxfordshire FA. However, Burnley protested about the playing of McDonald to the FA, who set up a commission to deal with it. Eventually the FA Consultative Committee determined that McDonald had been played without Burnley's permission and Headington were therefore expelled from the FA Cup and fined £5 5s. McDonald would later to go on to play eight times for England.

In the Southern League, Headington finished 11th after some disappointing performances, Thompson describing the 1–0 Boxing Day defeat at Kettering as the worst of the season, with the team never looking like 'making a fight of it'. As a result, left-winger

Bobby Barker was immediately transferred to Worcester City in exchange for Arthur Haynes. The Metropolitan League side finished fourth and reached the League Cup Final, where they lost 1–0 to Spurs' A team, while the A team won the Oxfordshire Senior Cup, beating Chipping Norton 3–1 in the Final at the White House Ground. Because United had been unable to field their first team in the Senior Cup since turning professional, a new Oxfordshire Professional Cup was created between Headington and Banbury Spencer. Headington also played a number of floodlit friendlies against Football League opponents, recording wins against Watford (4–3) and Spurs (4–2) and drawing with Orient (2–2) and Brentford (0–0). United's pioneering of floodlit football led to the Southern League pre-empting the Football League by lifting its ban on floodlit League matches, and the first Southern League game to be played under lights was United's home game against Gravesend & Northfleet on 28 February.

After the season Headington made its first application for election to the Football League, but they were hampered by others' lack of knowledge of the club's location, and it was clear that the club needed to have Oxford in its name. At the club's annual meeting in November 1952 there was a lot of opposition to the club changing its name, and a proposal to call it Headington & Oxford FC was thrown out. Also at that meeting Professor Keeton resigned from the board and Ron Coppock was appointed vice-chairman.

The 1952–53 season was the club's most successful to date. For this season United changed from blue to black shorts and adopted a new club badge. United reached their furthest point yet in the FA Cup, getting knocked out 2–1 by Gillingham in the fourth qualifying round, and in both the Southern League Cup and the Southern League itself Headington United were triumphant. The FA Cup run started with an 8–0 hammering of Marlow in the preliminary round, followed by wins against Aylesbury United, Maidenhead and a 6–2 revenge win over Wycombe Wanderers before the defeat at Gillingham. In the Southern League Cup United beat Hastings United, Bath City, Worcester City and Guildford in the semi-final before meeting Weymouth in the Final, which was played over two legs. United lost the first game in Dorset 2–1 before beating the Terras 3–1 after extra-time in front of a crowd of 10,302 at the Manor. In the League, United had a storming run from 22 November, losing only three games in their last 30 matches before the end of the season.

Headington players celebrate a goal in front of the old Beech Road terrace (c.1952).

Headington United display the 1952–53 Southern League champions shield.

Headington finished with 58 points, the same as Merthyr Tydfil, but won the title with a superior goal average. Merthyr had won the Southern League in each of the previous three seasons, and they would also win it the following year.

The foundations for the success lay in the players whom Thompson had brought to the club, many from the Football League. These included goalkeeper Jack Ansell from Northampton Town, Ernie Hudson from East Fife, Ronnie Steel and Harry Yates, both from Darlington, and Arthur Turner from Charlton Athletic, along with Cheltenham's Norman Mills and Yeovil's Bobby Peart. These were in addition to players already at the club such as captain Frank Ramshaw, Cyril Toulouse, Jimmy Smith, Johnny Crichton and others of undoubted talent for this level. Headington also continued to perform well against Football League sides in their series of floodlit friendlies, recording wins over Fulham (3–1), Charlton (2–1) and QPR (1–0), and losing narrowly 3–2 to Wolverhampton Wanderers in a game watched by 10,180.

In 1953–54 Headington and Merthyr were again the two main challengers for the Southern League title, with United ahead on goal average in early March. However, Headington's poor run of results allowed the Welsh side to pull ahead, and a month later there was a 10-point gap between the sides. Merthyr more or less made sure of the title when they played Headington twice at the start of April, earning three points from the two games with a 0–0 draw at the Manor followed by a 2–1 win at Penydarren Park, but Headington recovered to finish second, nine points adrift of Merthyr. United retained the Southern League Cup, beating surprise finalists Lovell's Athletic 2–0 over two legs, with the first a 0–0 draw in Newport. Headington became only the second side to win the Cup in successive seasons, the first being Plymouth Argyle Reserves in the first two years of the Cup's existence in 1933 and 1934. The reserves also had success, winning the Metropolitan League Championship by one point from Hastings United, while the Headington A team finished sixth in the Hellenic League's inaugural season and reached the semi-final of the League Cup, losing 1–0 to Staines Town.

The Headington United amateur XI at the opening of Chipping Norton Town's new ground in 1953. (courtesy: Percy Blake)

However, it was in this season's FA Cup that United were to make their mark and receive national recognition for the first time. Because of their good run the previous season, Headington were excused from the preliminary round, and they entered the tournament in the first qualifying round, winning at Aylesbury. Home wins over Maidenhead and Chesham earned United an away tie at Wealdstone in the fourth qualifying round, United winning 3–0 to reach the first round proper for the first time. A win at Harwich & Parkeston set up a tie at the Den against Third Division South side Millwall. A crowd of 20,545 witnessed a thrilling 3–3 draw to bring the Lions back to Oxford, where a Ken Smith header put United into the third round. Headington had requested the FA to allow the replay to be played under floodlights but the request was denied, but it did serve to bring the issue of floodlit games to national attention. This was the club's first competitive victory against a side from the Football League, and United's reward was a visit to Third Division North side Stockport County. Three trainloads of supporters travelled from Oxford, along with many coaches and private cars, and the 15,650 crowd saw heroics from 'keeper Jack Ansell to ensure that the game ended goalless and earned the Us another prestigious, and lucrative, match at the

Frank Ramshaw receives the Southern League Cup from League chairman A.E. Mortimer in May 1954. Watching are club secretary Peter Smith (left) and manager Harry Thompson (second from left).

Ken Smith scores the goal that beat Millwall at the Manor on 17 December 1953.

Manor. This time the hero for Headington in their 1–0 win was Bob Peart, and the reward was a home game against First Division Bolton Wanderers.

Extensions were made to the ground by the addition of prefabricated terracing, despite Bolton's refusal to pay towards the cost, and large numbers of supporters assisted groundsman Les Bateman to clear snow from the pitch. A new ground record crowd of 16,670 crammed into the Manor to watch Nat Lofthouse's side win 4–2, although United's second-half display ensured that Bolton suffered a few nervous moments and drew praise from the national papers. The Cup run also brought United to the attention of the Football Association, and on 22 March United hosted the full England Amateur International XI in a floodlit match at the Manor, won 3–0 by Headington. This game also marked United's election to full membership of the FA. United's Cup run had earned them exemption from the early rounds, and they entered at the fourth qualifying round the following season.

The significant event of the summer of 1954 was the granting by Oxford City Council of permanent planning permission to develop the Manor as a football ground, despite the opposition of some local residents. This came in conjunction with the negotiation of a

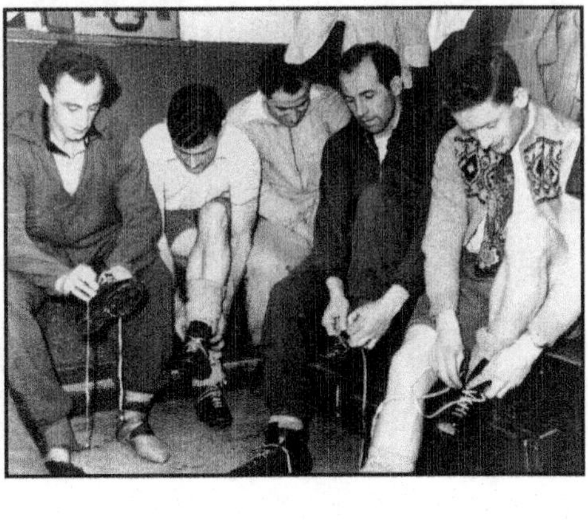

Headington United prepare for the Bolton game in 1954.

Headington United in 1954.

new 25-year lease on the ground with the Headington Sports Ground Company and the doubling of the number of entrances to four. Meanwhile, the club was again offered the Cowley Airfield site, and also a site in Marston, although this was known to be prone to flooding, but the board received professional advice to remain at the Manor given the new planning permission. The club also applied again for election to the Football League, but despite the FA Cup run and the floodlit friendlies against many League clubs, they received just one vote, thought to be from Cardiff City in appreciation for the sale of Cliff Nugent.

United started the 1954–55 season off well, with just one defeat in their first 10 League and Cup games, but between November and February the side won just two matches and slipped from second at the end of October to 12th by the time they drew 2–2 at eventual champions Yeovil on 12 February. United eventually finished 10th, but they were knocked out of the FA Cup in the first round at Norwich City and went out of the Southern League Cup in the first round at Gloucester City after a replay. New players joining the club included Welsh international Billy Rees, while United received £2,000 from Blackpool for former Sunderland centre-forward Ken Smith. The Headington A team won the Hellenic League Cup, beating Witney Town in the Final.

At the end of the season United released Ben Duncan, Bobby Craig, Johnnie Crichton, Ron Steel and Harry Yates following a dispute about the non-payment of appearance money, with the players refusing to play in the season's finale against Banbury Spencer in the Oxfordshire Professional Cup, which United won 5–4 on aggregate. Craig, Crichton and Yates all joined United's Southern League rivals Bedford Town. Their departures also enhanced the reputation of the club as having a large turnover of players, and this lack of stability was

The Headington United A team in April 1955, showing off the Hellenic League Cup.

exacerbated when two new arrivals, Geoff Denial and Bob Odell, were immediately conscripted to serve in the Forces at the time of the Suez Crisis. This was in part to blame for Headington's poor showing in the 1955–56 season, which saw the club finish in their lowest position since their first season in the Southern League, ending in 15th place and being knocked out of the FA Cup by Margate in the fourth qualifying round. The side had a better run in the Southern League Cup, reaching the semi-finals before being knocked out by Yeovil, while the reserves reached the Metropolitan League Cup Final, losing to Bedford Town 4–1 on aggregate, and the A team won the Hellenic League. In September 1955 Jimmy Smith played his last game for United, a 3–1 defeat at Chelmsford City, after which he retired through injury. Smith had first played for United as a 14-year-old 18 years earlier, and in his testimonial, held in October 1956, players turning out for the All-Star XI included Stanley Matthews and Ken Smith from Blackpool, Jimmy Bloomfield and former Oxford City player Cliff Holton from Arsenal, and former Headington players Cliff Nugent from Cardiff and Les Blizzard from Orient. After his recovery, Smith joined United's coaching staff.

Jimmy Smith.

Jimmy Smith with Stanley Matthews at Smith's testimonial on 17 October 1956.

Despite incurring losses, due in large part to the construction of a new stand on the Beech Road side going over budget because of the need to import the necessary steel from the Continent, United nevertheless purchased land adjoining the London Road, allowing a new entrance to be built on that side of the ground, which later superceded the Manor Road entrance as the main point of entry to the ground. Some of the costs were recovered by selling a portion of the land to the supporters' club for their new headquarters.

As in the previous season, United started the 1956–57 season in great form, and despite early elimination from the Southern League Cup, 6–1 on aggregate to Bedford Town, they reached November having lost just two League games and were at the top of the Division. However, just two wins in their next 12 games saw them slip away, and this sequence also included a 2–0 defeat at home to Guildford City in the fourth qualifying round of the FA Cup, which meant that United lost their preferential status and would have to start in the preliminary round the following season. United finished the season in ninth place, and neither the reserves nor the A team provided any silverware; although United did win the annual tussle with Banbury Spencer for the Oxfordshire Professional Cup.

The opening home game of the 1957–58 season against Cheltenham Town on 24 August marked the opening of the new Beech Road stand, which had taken two years to build, with FA treasurer Denis Follows wielding the ceremonial scissors. The supporters' club had donated £33,000 towards the costs of the stand, without which the construction would not have been possible. The season almost failed to start for United as it transpired that no one had registered any players with the Southern League, or with the Metropolitan and Hellenic

Headington fans showing their colours.

Leagues either. Harry Thompson rectified this, but the situation was a reflection of some of the turmoil behind the scenes, where chairman Vic Couling's position was starting to be challenged. Couling, who eventually stood down from the chair in November after the club's AGM, was to be replaced by vice-chairman Ron Coppock. At the annual meeting Peter Smith, who had been on the board since the club turned professional, failed to be re-elected.

The most notable of the new signings during the 1957 close season was that of Eddie McIlvenny from Waterford. His claim to fame was that he had been captain of the USA team that had beaten England 1–0 in the 1950 World Cup Finals in Belo Horizonte, Brazil. Although United's League form was indifferent, and they were again eliminated from the Southern League Cup at the first attempt (6–4 on aggregate by Chelmsford), the side did enjoy progress in the FA Cup to the fourth qualifying round. The run included wins over local sides Aylesbury United (3–0), Banbury Spencer (1–0) and Oxford City (2–0 before a White House crowd of 9,123). Marlow were also beaten (1–0) before Headington were eventually knocked out 2–0 at home to Margate. In the Southern League United finished ninth for the second successive season. The season was marred by injuries, with long-serving captain Frank Ramshaw ending his career following a 2–1 defeat at Bedford Town in February 1958, coincidentally the same opponents against whom he had played his first game for the club in August 1950.

The Southern League decided to enlarge to two divisions for the 1959–60 season, and so in 1958–59 the League was split into two regional sections in order to accommodate the new clubs, with the top 11 sides from each section forming the Southern League Premier Division and the rest comprising Division One. United were allocated to the north-western zone along with 17 other clubs, with a number of inter-zone friendly fixtures organised to make up the games. The start of the 1958–59 season also saw a reorganisation of the Football League, with the scrapping of the two regional Third Divisions and instead the

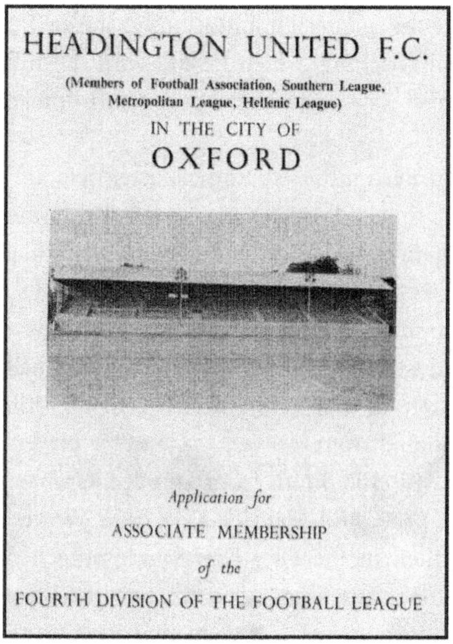

HEADINGTON UNITED F.C.

(Members of Football Association, Southern League, Metropolitan League, Hellenic League)

IN THE CITY OF

OXFORD

Application for

ASSOCIATE MEMBERSHIP

of the

FOURTH DIVISION OF THE FOOTBALL LEAGUE

Headington's application for the Football League in 1959.

creation of Division Four, which gave the club hope that election to the League might become easier. In readiness for this reorganisation United appointed Stan Aldous as player-coach (although he only played five games for United) from Orient, where he had been captain for the last seven seasons, to work alongside physical-fitness trainer Sam Gill, who had been brought in from the army at the start of the 1955–56 season.

United's opening to the season was exceptional, with five wins from the opening seven games. However, only two of those wins were in the Southern League, the remainder being a 4–0 aggregate defeat of Cheltenham in the Southern League Cup and a 7–0 demolition of Windsor & Eton in the FA Cup first qualifying round. United's League form deteriorated rapidly, however, and they lost the next seven Southern League matches, punctuated with some decent wins in the inconsequential Inter-Zone games and some good results in the FA Cup, including a 3–2 win against Oxford City, a 6–1 victory at Maidenhead, a 4–2 win at Wealdstone and a 3–2 defeat of Margate in the first round proper. This run ensured that for the next two seasons United would be exempt from having to compete in the competition until the fourth qualifying round. However, the Cup run only served to highlight the poor League form, and eventually, after a 4–0 defeat at Hastings United in an Inter-Zone game, Harry Thompson was dismissed. Thompson had been at the club for almost nine years, bringing unprecedented success, but he was a victim of that success as increasing amounts of money had to be spent on ground improvements at the expense of the playing budget.

While the board started to look for a successor to Thompson, Ron Coppock and fellow directors Tom Lees and Tony Padley took charge of team selection and playing arrangements, while Vic Couling took over secretarial duties. Under this arrangement the club's fortunes started to revive, and despite elimination from the FA Cup in the first round at Peterborough United (4–2), United won all five Southern League games while managed by the committee. Meanwhile, journalist John Ross informed Coppock of the availability of recently sacked Birmingham City manager Arthur Turner, and he was interviewed and, cautiously, accepted the post. Just two years previously Turner had led Birmingham to an FA Cup Final at Wembley, and he admitted that he had never heard of Headington and didn't know where it was until Ross told him. Before his interview Turner had already decided to reject any offer, but the friendliness of Coppock and the board was in direct contrast to his experiences at Birmingham and so he decided to accept the challenge 'against my will and better judgment'. Turner's first day of work was New Year's Day 1959, and he immediately identified that the club would not achieve success unless it had a fully professional playing staff. In order to accommodate the financial implications of this it was necessary to change the club's administration and coaching, which he did with the full backing of the board. Turner also increased players' wages and signing-on fees to make them commensurate with Football League teams.

On the playing field it took a bit of time for Turner's influence to make itself felt, and the side failed to win throughout January. But when they did register a victory, 2–1 at home to Barry Town, they went on to win the next five games, and at the end of the season they had another run of five straight wins which ensured that they finished the season in 10th place, just one above the lowest position to guarantee that they would be in the new Southern League Premier Division the following season. The margin of success was small indeed, as it came down to United's superior goal average over 12th-placed Merthyr Tydfil.

Turner's first signing was Cyril Beavon, who joined from Wolves, while other players brought in before the end of the season included Charlie Smith from Dundee, Graham Adams, for whom United paid Plymouth Argyle £750, and Maurice Kyle from Wolves. Meanwhile, at the start of April, Leeds United, then in the First Division, approached Turner to offer him the manager's job at Elland Road. The news was broken by the Press Association on 3 April, and a special directors' meeting was convened that evening to discuss the situation. After leaving the meeting for 20 minutes to consider his position, Turner returned to inform the board that he had decided to accept the Leeds offer. The board appointed Tony Padley to act as caretaker manager until a successor to Turner could be found. An emergency meeting was held on 11 April with representatives of the supporters' club also present, and it was decided that they should outbid Leeds' offer which, bearing in mind the relative status of the two clubs, was an extremely ambitious move. So impressed was Turner by this that he changed his mind about accepting the Leeds job and instead remained with Headington, claiming that 'I feel there is a future here and I want to be part of it'.

United were still continuing to chase the dream of League football, and to that aim Couling had been informed by both Sir Stanley Rous of the FA and Alan Hardacre, secretary of the Football League, that it would be essential to change the name of the club to Oxford. However, in order to do this the club would need the agreement of both the Oxfordshire FA and Oxford City FC. The application to change the club's name to Oxford United was unanimously approved by the OFA, but Oxford City objected and as a result the FA rejected the application. City's refusal to agree to United's proposed name change rankled in Headington and threatened to cause a rift in the city similar to that when United were looking at turning professional. The board of Headington United asserted their intention to pursue the matter 'at all angles and levels, unless it is established in the meantime that the name "Oxford" is copyright not only for marmalade, but football as well'. The club's programmes for the 1959–60 season reflected their disgruntlement, with the cover proclaiming simply 'United', as opposed to 'Headington United'.

During the summer of 1959 Turner signed Ron Atkinson from Aston Villa and his younger brother Graham, who was on Villa's groundstaff, as well as signing former Scotland international David Mathers on loan from Partick Thistle while he was working as an engineer in Oxford. He also brought in trainer Jack Shelton from Wolves, a former Walsall and Wolves player who had played in every position in his 400-plus first-team appearances for Walsall, including as goalkeeper, and who had captained Worcester City in their games against Headington United in the 1949–50 season. In addition, Turner introduced a new scouting system, utilising eight scouts around the country, and engaged new office staff. United did not lose a game until 7 November, when they went down 2–1 at Tonbridge, but several of those games were drawn, including a run of five straight draws. Two of those were 1–1 against Chelmsford City in both the home and away legs of the Southern League Cup qualifying round. As a result both sides went through to the first round, and, coincidentally, they met again in the second round, this time Chelmsford winning 1–0. Headington were knocked out of the FA Cup at Enfield (4–3), having won 3–2 at Cambridge City in the fourth qualifying round. At the start of November, Bath City and Headington were level on points, but the Twerton Park club gradually pulled away and they eventually won the League by a massive 13 points from Headington, who finished second. During this season Geoff Denial set two records that have yet to be broken: scoring in seven consecutive games and in nine consecutive away games. The reserves reached the Final of the Metropolitan League Cup, drawing 4–4 with Eastbourne United over two legs after beating Arsenal 2–1 in the semi-final.

One of the most significant events in the club's history occurred on 25 June 1960, when permission was finally obtained from the FA for the club to change their name to Oxford United. At one stage it looked like the club would be called Oxford and Headington United, but the eventual solution was that the company would continue to be called Headington United Football Club Company Ltd, but it would trade and be known as Oxford United Football Club. To go with the new name a competition was held among supporters to design a new badge. There were around 60 entries, and the winning one was chosen partly because of the background H behind the ox in a shield, in remembrance of the club's original name of Headington. The 1960–61 season also marked the official change in the club's colours from orange and blue to gold and black.

Hopes were high that Oxford, now with a nationally recognised moniker, would be elected to the Football League, but instead that honour went to Peterborough United of the Midland League, who were elected at the expense of Gateshead. Oxford received 10 votes, the highest of the unsuccessful non-League applicants.

Oxford started the new season with a 3–0 home win over Worcester City, and although Kettering Town won both legs of the Southern League Cup first round to knock United out 4–0 on aggregate, Oxford then went unbeaten until 17 December, when Worcester won 4–2. Included in that unbeaten run was a 9–0 win over Wisbech Town, in which Tony Jones scored five goals, which remains a club record victory since they turned professional in 1949. The run also included wins in the FA Cup at Brentwood & Warley of the Delphian League (4–0), Hendon (3–2 after a 2–2 draw), for which the highest home crowd of the season (10,600) was present, and Bridgewater Town (2–1) to set up a third-round trip to Filbert Street to face Leicester City. First Division City beat United 3–1 and went on to reach the Final, which they lost to double winners Tottenham Hotspur. After the Cup defeat, United lost only two more League games before the end of the season, eventually winning the Championship seven points ahead of second-placed Chelmsford City.

Goalkeeper Owen Medlock, signed from Swindon during the summer, was an ever present, and Tony Jones scored 38 goals, a new club record in the Southern League, beating Geoff Denial's record, set the previous season, by six goals. Bud Houghton, signed in March from Southend United, weighed in with 13 goals from just 14 games. Houghton had previously played under Arthur Turner at Birmingham. Another new player was Billy Simpson, a former Glasgow Rangers player and Northern Ireland international, signed from Partick Thistle. Simpson had been selected for Northern Ireland's squad for the 1958 World Cup in Sweden, but a late injury prevented him from playing during the Finals. Reflecting Turner's belief in youth players being the way forward, United featured just three regular players over 25 years old. As well as having the usual injuries to contend with, United also lost a number of players for part of the season because of National Service, with Ron Atkinson, Pat Quartermain and Ron Rivers all called-up in the final year of that institution.

United's reserve team finished fifth in the Metropolitan League and the A team finished fourth in the Hellenic League. United also entered the newly formed Wessex League for the under-18s, in which they finished fourth; a remarkable record considering that apart from Weymouth and United the rest of the clubs were Football League sides.

During the close season United made the significant step of purchasing the freehold of the Manor Ground from the Headington Sports Ground Company Ltd for the price of £10,000, thanks to a loan from Barclays Bank. Protective rights were granted to the adjacent bowls club, and the land previously used as an entrance to the football ground was transferred to the bowls club. This enabled the club to buy a strip of land alongside 15 Osler Road, which was converted into a new entrance. To raise the funds to buy the ground a bonus share issue was offered to existing shareholders.

The change of name to Oxford United, coupled with the winning of the Southern League Championship and a good FA Cup run, meant that United's latest application to join the Football League was received more favourably than previously. The club received

The Oxford United squad in 1961 in front of the Beech Road terrace.

Director Percy Cooper showing off the Southern League champions shield in 1961.
(courtesy: Reg Earl)

Oxford's 1961–62 Southern League Championship-winning team.

19 votes, comfortably ahead of any of the other non-League clubs but still some way behind the lowest of the League clubs.

United made a bit of a stuttering start to the 1961–62 season, yet again being knocked out of the Southern League Cup at the first hurdle, losing 6–2 on aggregate to Cambridge City. After winning the opening League game 3–0 at Weymouth, Oxford lost their first home game 2–0 to Guildford City. A slight recovery included a 7–2 win at King's Lynn, with Bud Houghton scoring a hat-trick, and after two successive away defeats United embarked on a run of 13 League games unbeaten, starting with an 8–0 win over Gravesend & Northfleet, although the side was eliminated from the FA Cup, losing 3–0 at Brentford in the first round after beating Salisbury City 3–2 in the fourth qualifying round. The final game of that unbeaten run was a 6–0 win at Clacton Town, and three weeks later, during which United failed to win in three games, they won 6–0 away again, this time completing an aggregate score of 14–0 against Gravesend. A run of seven consecutive wins followed shortly after, and on Good Friday United won 1–0 at second-placed Bath City to secure the title. The final three games of the season, all defeats, were inconsequential. Bud Houghton was top scorer with 43 goals, a record yet to be beaten, and he also retains the record for scoring in consecutive home games (12) and for scoring most home goals in a season (22).

It was not just United's League form that was impressive; the side played two games, against First Division Leicester and Third Division Coventry City, in testimonial games for Geoff Denial and Johnny Love, and won them both comfortably, beating Leicester 5–2 and Coventry 3–0, with both sides fielding their strongest line ups. United also played friendly games against Millwall (won 4–2) and Chelsea (drew 3–3), while also beating Hereford United 2–1 on aggregate to win the Hereford County Cup and Banbury Spencer 4–2 to win the Oxon Professional Cup for the 11th successive season (including 1952–53, when a 1–1 draw meant that the clubs shared the trophy). In addition, United beat Yeovil Town 2–0 to win the Southern League Challenge Cup, played between the Southern League champions and Cup winners.

In the Metropolitan League the reserves finished seventh, but extraordinarily scored 104 goals, while the A side finished seventh in the Hellenic League Premier Division. United finished third in the Wessex Youth League and also reached the fourth round of the FA Youth Cup, where they lost 7–0 to Chelsea.

It was no surprise, then, that Oxford's application to join the Football League was regarded optimistically at the Manor, especially given that Accrington Stanley had gone bankrupt and resigned from the Fourth Division after completing just 33 games, their results being expunged. The ballot to decide the membership of the Football League was held at the Café Royal in Regent Street, London, on 2 June 1962. Chester City, Doncaster Rovers and Hartlepools United were all re-elected with 46, 45 and 40 votes respectively. The final place was given to Oxford United, who received 27 votes. In little over 13 years United had gone from an amateur club to members of the Football League, and a civic reception was held in Oxford to celebrate the achievement. It cost United a £100 admission fee to join the League, and membership of the 92 would mean a higher wage structure, employment of a full-time secretary (Ken McCluskey), more expensive overnight stays for away games and a reduction in the reliance on voluntary assistance as befitting a more professional approach.

Into the League

United's first, historic, match as a League side was at Holker Street, Barrow, where goals from Brian 'Bud' Houghton and Graham Atkinson saw the Us go down 3–2 in front of a crowd of 6,569. As a memento of the occasion, the Barrow chairman presented the club with an engraved shield. Four days later, the club's first home game in the League was against Lincoln City, and Houghton and Alan Willey scored in a 2–1 win in front of a Manor crowd of 10,483. United supporters were ecstatic four days later when Oxford beat Hartlepools United 6–2 at the Manor.

Oxford then lost three consecutive away games, including going down 2–0 at Torquay United in the club's first-ever League Cup tie. In the defeat at Lincoln John Shuker made his first Oxford appearance. This was followed by a run of five successive draws, the last one of which, at home to Oldham, was watched by 10,676. The sequence was brought to a halt in the best possible way, a 5–1 home win over Newport County in which Tony Jones scored four goals. This was just a temporary relief, though, as Oxford failed to win any of their next six games.

This form was reversed when Oxford beat Chester City 3–0 at the Manor. Six days later, Oxford won 2–1 at York City to give the team their first away League victory. Just over a week later, United won 2–1 at Falmouth in the first round of the FA Cup. United also won 2–1 at Kings Lynn in the second round to set up a dream tie at Highbury against Arsenal.

The very poor winter of that year saw a major disruption to the football programme, and after twice being postponed it wasn't until 30 January that the game at Arsenal could go ahead, the Gunners beating the Us 5–1. The League programme did not resume for a further six weeks, and United greeted the resumption of games with three defeats on the trot. A 3–3 draw at home to Doncaster interrupted this run, which was then resumed with three more defeats in the next four games. This run meant that United dropped into the re-election zone.

United then embarked on a run of 10 games without defeat, starting with a 2–1 win over Bradford City, and which included a 4–1 win at Valley Parade, an Alan Willey hat-trick in a 3–0 home win over Mansfield and a 4–2 win over Darlington at the Manor. Because of the winter weather, this season went on almost to the end of May, and United's last win, on 11 May, was at home to Brentford, when in front of the Manor's biggest attendance of Oxford's League career so far, 11,247 saw the Bees beaten 2–1. The season was wrapped up with three successive away defeats.

United finished their inaugural League season in 18th place, three points above the re-election zone. The club was fifth in the Division's average attendance chart, with an average of 7,600 over the season. In the Metropolitan League the reserves finished second, behind Arsenal, losing just six games in the 32-match season.

Tony Jacques and Tony Buck made their first appearances for the first team in the autumn, while Colin Harrington joined from Wolves (where he was an amateur) in October, but he did not make his debut until April. Oxford paid a club record fee of £5,000 to Wolves for Maurice Kyle, who had been effectively on loan since February 1959. This record was beaten in December, when United signed Bernard Evans from Queen's Park Rangers for £5,500. At the end of the season a number of long-established United players left, with Graham Atkinson going (temporarily, as it turned out) to Cambridge United, initially on loan, and Owen Medlock moved to Chelmsford City. Geoff Denial, who had spent seven seasons at the Manor, moved to Wisbech Town. Ken McCluskey was brought in as the club's first full-time secretary, allowing Arthur Turner to concentrate on team management and giving the club an altogether more professional approach.

During the summer the club made extensive modifications to the Manor, building a new roofed terrace at the London Road end and installing a new floodlight system, with four pylons in the corners of the ground replacing the poles along the sides. This was all paid for by grants from the supporters' club, which also paid the balance due on the purchase of the Manor. Vic Couling invited John George Vanderbilt Henry Spencer-Churchill, then Marquess of Blandford, to become the club's president, which he did, and he remained president after becoming the Duke of Marlborough in 1972. At the club's AGM on 14 August the shareholders voted unanimously to change the name of the company from Headington United Football Club Company Ltd to Oxford United Football Club Company Ltd.

The 1963–64 season opened with a 2–0 win at Chester City, and a crowd of over 9,000 watched the first home game, a 1–0 defeat by Doncaster. For the second season United lost in the first round of the League Cup, losing 1–0 at home to Exeter, but it was in the FA Cup that the club came to national attention. United were favoured with home draws in every round, and in the early stages they routinely disposed of non-League sides Folkestone and Kettering, and Fourth Division Chesterfield. In the fourth round United were held to a 2–2 draw by Brentford, but in front of 26,000 Oxford won the replay 2–1 thanks to two goals from Bill Calder.

This earned United a fifth-round tie against Blackburn Rovers, who were second in the First Division at the time and featured Fred Pickering and international players such as Ron Clayton, Michael England and Bryan Douglas. Arthur Turner's strategy of man-marking Pickering and Douglas, Rovers' top scorers, worked, and United won 3–1 thanks to two Tony Jones goals and one from Bill Calder. Utilising temporary terracing, the attendance of 21,700 set a new ground record, and the win gave Oxford the distinction of becoming the first Fourth Division club to reach the FA Cup quarter-finals. United were again favoured with a home draw, this time against Preston North End, who were third in the Second Division. Despite the wave of optimism surrounding Oxford, on the day the side were outclassed and went down 2–1, with Jones scoring Oxford's goal. The ground record was again broken, with 22,750 at the game. This was the first Oxford game for which a 'pirate' programme was issued, and such was the level of interest that the *Sunday Mirror* awarded Oxford a special 'Giant Killers' Cup', while the Lord Mayor of Oxford gave the team a civic reception.

In the League, United were unable to replicate their Cup form, and the season ended with a run in which they won just two of their last 16 games, slipping from 11th on 8 February to a final place of 18th, the same as the previous season. United avoided having to seek re-election by just two points. The reserves finished fourth in their last season in the Metropolitan League, having had an application to join the Second Division of the Football Combination accepted.

United again broke their transfer record, paying £8,500 to Bury for Bill Calder in November. In December, £6,000 was spent on Keith Havenhand, from Derby. During the summer Arthur Turner brought in players such as Colin Booth and Rodney Smithson, but perhaps the most important signing was that of Ken Fish, a former South Africa international, as trainer. Fish, a strict disciplinarian, was to have a strong influence behind the scenes at the club for many years.

In 1964–65 United finally won a League Cup tie, beating Walsall 6–1 in a replay after a 1–1 draw, but they were knocked out at Fulham in the second round. The FA Cup highlights of the previous season failed to be repeated as they lost 1–0 at home to Mansfield in the first round. However, United's League campaign ensured that these disappointments were not too keenly felt as the side, in only their third season as a Football League club, earned promotion to the Third Division, finishing in fourth place. On 9 January, highlights of United's 1–0 win

Mascot Frank Kowalski and his son Eric before the FA Cup match against Blackburn Rovers on 15 February 1964.

The 1964–65 Oxford squad line up by positions.

over Tranmere were broadcast on the new BBC programme *Match of The Day*, becoming the first non-Division One game the programme had shown. At the final home game of the season, against Darlington, 12,866 watched as Cyril Beavon scored the winning penalty-kick, although promotion was not confirmed until the following Tuesday, when Doncaster beat Tranmere. On the way to promotion United beat Barrow 7–0 on 19 December, a result that was United's best League win in their 44 years as a Football League club. The promotion earned United their second civic reception in two seasons.

In the Football Combination United's reserves had an excellent first season, finishing fourth, three points behind champions Southampton, but for a long time leading the table. They opened the season with a 5–0 win over Swindon, and most of the home games produced crowds approaching 3,000 or more. The best attendance was 4,003 for the visit of Brighton in March, which United won 5–4.

United's first season in the Third Division was something of a slow-burner, and for a while it looked possible that the club would be immediately relegated back to the Fourth Division. However, although the season finished with four successive defeats, a good run of results in April ensured that the club finished in a comfortable 14th position, although both Cups were exited in the first round. The largest home crowd for a League game came when 16,074 saw United lose 3–0 to Swindon, while the 31,992 who were at Hull's Boothferry Park comprised the largest crowd to have watched an Oxford game so far. During the season, United paid £8,000 to Coventry City for Ken Hale and £4,000 to Chelsea for goalkeeper Jim Barron, who was Peter Bonetti's understudy. Sales included Alan Willey, for whom Millwall paid £5,000.

At the end of the season Tom Webb, the club's trainer and masseur, who had been at United since 1935 and had experienced their rise from the Oxfordshire Senior League into the Spartan League, the Southern League and the Football League, retired. The club organised a testimonial game for him against Luton Town, although that did not take place until May 1968. Meanwhile, more building work was undertaken at the Manor, with the Cuckoo Lane terracing extended, although plans to put a roof on it and to extend it over the Lane were scuppered after protests from the nearby hospital.

The 1966–67 season was another one of initial struggle for the club, with a first-round exit from the League Cup to Peterborough and inconsistent League form. An early high was a 6–1 win over Doncaster, but that was followed just three days later by a 3–1 home defeat at the hands of Reading. Two wins, over Grimsby and Workington, were followed by four successive defeats, and that was pretty much the pattern going into the New Year. Following elimination from the FA Cup in the second round to Southern League Bedford (1–0 after a 1–1 draw at the Manor), United won six straight League games to reach 10th place and allay any relegation fears. United's inconsistency returned and the side fell away to eventually finish in 16th place. Their final game of the season was at Ayresome Park, with Middlesbrough needing a win to ensure promotion to the Second Division, behind QPR. The crowd of 39,683 became the largest that United had played before, and Middlesbrough duly won 4–1.

George Kerr had been signed from Bury for £8,000 in a bid to revive the club's fortunes, but with just six goals in his 44 appearances he proved not to be the answer to the scoring problems. Tony Buck became United's first goalscoring substitute in the 2–1 League Cup first-round defeat at Peterborough. The reserves finished seventh in the Football Combination, while a mediocre season for the youth team led to the decision to leave the Hellenic League and instead join the South-East Counties League.

The 1967–68 season started slowly for United, and they did not win an away game until 16 March, when they beat Grimsby 1–0. Their home form was enough to ensure that they were ninth in the table before that game, largely thanks to a sequence of nine consecutive home wins between 9 September and 18 November. The win at Blundell Park sparked a run of six successive victories, at the end of which United were second in the table, just one point behind leaders Torquay United. The next game, on 12 April, was the home match against Swindon, and a new record for a League game was set when 17,836 crammed in to the Manor to watch a 0–0 draw. The season culminated with four consecutive victories, a sequence that took United to the top of the table and earned them the Championship with 57 points, just one ahead of Bury, and the lowest points total for the Third Division champions since it had stopped being regionalised. A crowd of 14,038 saw David Sloan score the goal that beat Southport 1–0 and ensure promotion to the Second Division, just six seasons after joining the Football League.

In the League Cup United had their most successful season yet by reaching the third round, when they were beaten 5–1 by QPR, for whom Alan Wilks scored all five goals. In the FA Cup United were knocked out of the competition by a Southern League side for the second year running, this time eventual champions Chelmsford City doing the damage. It took two replays before Chelmsford won 1–0 at neutral Brentford, the first occasion that United had been involved in a second replay, both drawn games ending 3–3.

At the start of the season United bought Mickey Bullock from Birmingham City for £10,000, a new club record, while Ken Skeen was signed from Swindon for £3,500. Tony Buck and Tony Jones both left for Newport County for £2,000 and £1,500 respectively. Buck had been the history-making first substitute, while Jones had joined in 1959 and made 358 appearances for the club.

Promotion was achieved with a number of players who had been with the club since their Southern League days, including captain Ron Atkinson, his brother Graham, Cyril

Beavon, Maurice Kyle and John Shuker, plus manager Arthur Turner. Ron Atkinson became the first player to captain a team from the Southern League to the Second Division. The implications for the club were immense, as they were now a full member of the Football League, with the voting rights that went with it, and would be exempt until the third round of the FA Cup. The finances would also be affected, with higher gates offset by increased wages and transfer fees. Another implication was the status of the Manor, which many felt was inadequate for the higher standard of football, despite ongoing improvements to the Beech Road stand and the Cuckoo Lane terracing and a complete overhaul of the floodlighting system. The local planning authority identified a 23-acre site (five times the area of the Manor) in Horspath Road. Although this was a tempting location, the hostile opposition from local residents and the subsequent about-turn in support from local councillors meant there would be too many difficulties, and the proposal was shelved.

Partly because of prohibitive transfer fees, Arthur Turner decided to give the players who had earned promotion their chance to impress in the Second Division. The side had a slow start, opening with a 1–1 home draw with Bolton Wanderers and then being knocked out of the League Cup at Brighton. A defeat and two draws followed before United won their first game, 2–0 at Carlisle. After another defeat, at Derby, Oxford gained their first home win, beating Fulham 1–0. It was after this game that an Oxford United player received a full international cap for the first time, with David Sloan being called-up to represent Northern Ireland for a friendly game against Israel in Tel Aviv. Also appearing for Northern Ireland as a substitute was Ray Gaston, who had just signed for United from Coleraine for a club-record fee of £12,500. Unfortunately Gaston failed to impress and he submitted a transfer request in September 1969, having scored only two goals, but no club was willing to meet United's valuation of £8,000 (although Glentoran offered to take him on a free transfer) and he went on a month's loan to Lincoln City with a view to a possible transfer. Also leaving the club was Mickey Bullock, who was sold for a record fee of £8,000 to Orient. He was replaced by Ron Clayton, whom United bought for £1,000 from Warley FC. Meanwhile, Graham Atkinson rejected a move to Walsall, who offered United £11,000, and Rodney Smithson turned down a move to Aldershot, who were willing to pay £5,000 for him. Aldershot did, however, sign John Lloyd for £3,250 in February. In March United almost signed Matt Tees from Charlton Athletic for a record-equalling £12,500, but the deal fell through because of Tees' excessive signing-on demands. In November, United appointed Jimmy Adam, from Stourbridge FC, as assistant trainer and coach, but he resigned in March after making adverse remarks to the press.

After winning the following game at Sheffield United, the Us embarked on a run of 13 games in which they won only one (1–0 at Birmingham City). This sequence was halted with a 2–1 win over Preston, but then followed by six consecutive League defeats, sandwiching an FA Cup third-round exit at Southampton in a replay. Present at the home game with Southampton was Robert Maxwell, who had requested two seats in the directors' box. The last of these defeats was a 5–0 reverse at Cardiff City, United's heaviest defeat of the season. On 16 January a special board meeting was convened, at which it was agreed that Arthur Turner should be made general manager, with a separate team manager to be appointed. A win over Huddersfield was followed by Preston reversing the scoreline at Deepdale, after which the board appointed the unproven Ron Saunders from Yeovil as team manager. Saunders was one of 30 applicants for the post. Although some board members were opposed to the sacking of Turner, the change had an immediate effect, as United lost just one of their next nine games and thereby ensured their safety from relegation. Oxford finished the season third from bottom, three points above second-from-bottom Bury.

The reserves had had a poor season in the Combination, losing eight of their first nine games (including an 8–0 defeat at Swindon in the opening fixture, watched by 3,647) and results did not get much better throughout the season. It was felt that the club needed to produce more home-grown players to counter high transfer fees, and that money could be saved by joining the London Mid-Week League. The club therefore resigned from the Combination. However, before the end of the season the resignation was rescinded with the hope that the reserves' fixtures could be moved to midweek.

In May 1969 Robert Maxwell, Labour MP for Buckingham, offered to loan the club £25,000 in additional capital. However, the club refused the offer, although they did write to Maxwell to thank him for his interest.

The club received a massive blow in the summer when Ron Saunders left to become manager of Norwich City, leaving the club without a manager for its pre-season preparations. Norwich had offered Saunders £5,000 a year with a three-year contract. United were unable to match the Norwich offer, but they did offer to increase Saunders' salary to £4,000 from his current £2,500 and give him a three-year contract with full control. Saunders initially accepted the Oxford offer, but Norwich then increased their offer to a level that Saunders found irresistible and he immediately accepted it. However, the board acted promptly to approach and recruit Gerry Summers, who had also been in the running for the job after Turner's dismissal. Summers had no previous managerial experience, but he was an FA qualified coach. Another disappointment came when the youth team failed to be re-elected into the South-East Counties League after performing poorly the previous season. However, both the Metropolitan League and the Hellenic League (both of which Oxford United helped found) offered the United A team a place, and the club eventually opted for the Metropolitan League. An innovation for the 1969–70 season was the introduction of the Manorettes, a group of 35 girls wearing a special uniform in club colours selling programmes and jackpot tickets.

The 1969–70 season began with three defeats in the first four League games, but form soon picked up and away wins at Birmingham City and Preston, and draws at Swindon and with Sheffield United and Middlesbrough saw the club comfortably in mid-table. Meanwhile the side's most successful League Cup run was under way. After routine wins over Northampton (2–0) and Bury (4–1) in the first two rounds, Oxford were drawn at home to Swindon in the third round. Swindon were the Cup holders, having surprisingly beaten Arsenal 3–1 in the previous season's Final, but a goal from David Sloan in front of a crowd of 18,193 earned the Us a tie at First Division Nottingham Forest in the fourth round. A goal from Ken Skeen was enough to give United their first away win in the competition and their first win at a First Division ground, and take United into the quarter-finals, where they faced Carlisle United. After a goalless draw at the Manor, Carlisle won the

Manorettes selling programmes on the Cuckoo Lane terrace. (courtesy: Jackie Duvall)

replay 1–0 from a penalty, with almost 1,000 people listening to a broadcast of the game at the Manor. United remained inconsistent in the League but won enough points that they were never in danger of relegation. In the final game of the season United beat promoted Blackpool 2–0 to finish in 15th place. In the FA Cup they went out in the third round, losing 3–2 at Stoke City after a goalless draw at the Manor.

In December Mick Brown was appointed as assistant trainer to Ken Fish on Gerry Summers' recommendation. Transfer activity was slow to start, although Brian Sherratt had left to join Barnsley on a free transfer in the summer. In October the club agreed a fee of £15,000 with Rotherham to sign Stephen Downes, but the player rejected the move, and it was not until mid-January that the first new player arrived, Brian Lewis joining from Luton Town for £9,000. At the end of the season Roy Pack, who had signed from Portsmouth on 13 May 1969, but who had never played for United because of injury, was released from his contract by mutual consent. In July Jim Barron, who had impressed during the League Cup game at the City Ground, was signed by Nottingham Forest for £30,000, after Oxford had rejected their initial offer of £22,500. United received only £27,000 from Forest, who claimed that Oxford had agreed to pay the £1,500 due to both the player and the Football League, a claim denied by United but which they could not prove to be untrue. Also in July, United agreed a fee of £15,000 with Sheffield Wednesday for the signature of Mike Prendergast, but again the deal fell through due to the player turning down the move. The following season Prendergast was Wednesday's top scorer.

On 21 April 1970 Ron Coppock resigned as chairman of the board. He had suffered with ill health for some time, but he had delayed his departure as he felt that the club was not in a stable enough state. Vice-chairman Peter Playford was elected to replace him. Also in April, Malcolm Gamlen replaced Ken McCluskey as the club secretary. It was at this time that Gerry Summers first mooted the idea of a change in the club's strip to a brighter yellow, with dark blue shorts and yellow socks, believing that it would add brightness to the appearance of the team. The board, however, preferred to retain the old gold and black that the club had worn since 1960.

United's reserves had finished 12th out of 15 in the Metropolitan League, but the club was unhappy with certain aspects of the League's administration and so decided to resign from the Metropolitan League and instead join a new mid-week league for youth players that was being set up by Northampton Town. United made a donation of £100 to the Metropolitan League as thanks for admitting the side at short notice after it was not re-elected to the South-East Counties League.

Nine games into the 1970–71 season, and with United having played three more games away than at home, Oxford were top of the Second Division, their highest placing ever. Up to 26 September United had lost just one game (4–0 at Luton) and had won 2–0 at Middlesbrough and 2–0 at Bolton. In addition, they had also knocked out First Division Wolves from the League Cup (1–0). A 1–1 draw with Norwich City allowed Leicester to displace the Us from top spot, and that was followed by elimination from the League Cup 3–1 at Carlisle. After this storming start United inevitably slipped away, and after beating Burnley 3–0 in the FA Cup United then failed to win in their next eight League games. Meanwhile they had eliminated Watford from the FA Cup (2–1) in a replay after drawing 1–1 at the Manor in a game where the wall at the front of the London Road end collapsed during a goalmouth scramble. There were seven minor injuries, including a broken leg. In the fifth round United drew 1–1 with Leicester City at Filbert Street, but they lost the replay 3–1 after extra-time before a Manor crowd of 17,948. After a 1–0 win at Hull, United drew six of their next seven games (beating Birmingham 1–0 in the other), as they eventually finished 14th. At the end of the season, on 9 May, United embarked on their first overseas tour, visiting Benidorm in Spain and playing three games, against CD Almoradi, Lorca CF and Atlético Orihuela.

On 23 September 1970 Mick Kearns played for the Republic of Ireland in a friendly game against Poland, coming on as a half-time substitute for Allan Kelly, and thus becoming the first Oxford-produced player to receive international honours. United made some significant signings during the season, with goalkeeper Roy Burton signing as a professional after a short trial in September. Derek Clarke joined from Wolves for £11,111 in October, and the following month Nigel Cassidy, a teammate of Kevin Keegan at Scunthorpe, joined for

Nigel Cassidy scoring his first goal for the club against Cardiff City on 5 December 1970.

£20,000. This was followed in February by the capture of Dave Roberts from Fulham for just £2,500, despite interest from Reading in Roberts' signature.

Shortly before the start of the 1971–72 season Watford asked for permission to speak to Gerry Summers about their vacant manager's job, but Summers said that he was not prepared to attend for interview as he was under contract to Oxford. Following the success of the previous campaign, the season started poorly for Oxford, who won just one of their first seven League games. United were eliminated from the League Cup by Stoke City in a replay, and Oxford were also eliminated from the FA Cup at the first hurdle, losing 3–0 to Liverpool before an 18,000 capacity crowd (the capacity of the ground had been reduced for this game). The attendance for the home game against Birmingham City on 31 March was 18,740, which was a new ground record for a Football League match. The season petered out for United after February, and the club won just two games in the last two months and scored 11 goals in the last 13 games to finish 15th.

The reserves, on the other hand, had an excellent season under Mick Brown's management. They finished second in the Combination and produced several high crowds, with 5,527 watching their game against eventual champions Tottenham Hotspur on 22 March. There were also attendances of 3,339 against Southampton on 29 December and 4,072 against Swansea the following week.

In August, Peter Playford was replaced as chairman by Bob Kearsey, a farmer from Charlbury, while on New Year's Day 1972 former chairman Ron Coppock died after a long illness. During the season the club also dismissed Arthur Turner, despite having already agreed with him a contract that would have taken him through to his retirement two years hence. The general manager post had failed to work properly, largely because the role was never clearly defined, and there was a fractious relationship between Turner and Gerry Summers, with the former resentful that the manager failed to seek his advice. It was a sad end to the career of one of the most important individuals in the club's history.

Another long-standing individual who left the club that season was captain Ron Atkinson, who moved to Kettering Town to become player-manager. John Shuker, in his testimonial year, replaced the Tank as captain. A significant addition to the staff was that of Fred Ford as chief scout and youth administrator. Ford had been manager of Swindon for the previous three years, winning the 1969 Anglo-Italian League Cup and the 1970 Anglo-Italian Cup. Before that he had managed both Bristol clubs, spending seven years at City.

At the AGM on 31 July 1972 a special resolution was passed restricting the number of shares that one individual could own to 3,000. When the club had turned professional in 1949, the old amateur club was wound up and replaced by Headington United Football Club Co Ltd, with 100 shares issued at £7 each, with individual holding restricted to three in order to prevent the club falling under the control of one or two unscrupulous people. This was gradually increased until, in 1952, 20,000 £1 shares were released and the restriction on individual holding was removed. Now, however, the board felt that outsiders Tony Rosser and Basil Terry were looking to take control by buying out people's shares, and so they voted to reintroduce the restriction. At the end of the meeting an election was held to fill four of the director posts, with seven candidates. The three unsuccessful candidates were Tony Rosser, Basil Terry and Geoff Coppock (son of former chairman Ron Coppock).

Oxford started the 1972–73 season very impressively, losing just one of their opening seven games. These included a 4–0 League win over Middlesbrough, a 4–0 League Cup win over Peterborough and a 2–2 draw with Manchester United in the second round of the League Cup. Oxford were leading 2–1 with goals from Roy Clayton and Ken Skeen before a 30-yard Bobby Charlton shot levelled the scores with five minutes remaining. Manchester United won the replay 3–1. The League form continued throughout the season, with impressive wins over Sunderland (5–1), Brighton (3–0) and Hull (5–2). In December Gerry Summers received the Manager of the Month award. In addition, on 24 February Oxford won 3–1 at the County Ground, the only occasion that United have won at Swindon. Goalscorers for the Us were Dave Roberts, Nigel Cassidy and Hugh Curran. Oxford finished the season with two consecutive wins to finish in eighth place, the club's best final position so far. This season also saw the Us enter the Anglo-Italian tournament, in which they played four games, at home to Torino and Como and away at Bologna and Roma. United won two and drew two of the games, including a 2–0 win at Stadio Olimpico against Roma with two goals from Hugh Curran. However, this was not enough for qualification to the semi-finals and so United's only competitive European venture ended with early elimination. Including a pre-season game against Guernsey, the two Anglo-Italian Cup games and a four-game post-season tour of Norway, United played seven games overseas this season and were undefeated in all of them.

The reserves had another successful season, finishing in fourth place in the Combination. Although the attendances did not quite reach the previous season's highs, there were still over 4,000 present for the visit of Bristol City, while QPR, Spurs and Arsenal all attracted over 2,300. In September United paid a club record £50,000, a huge sum by United's standards, for former Scotland international Hugh Curran from Wolves. Curran scored on his debut against Millwall and finished the season with 17 goals.

Just before the 1973–74 season, at the club's AGM on 1 August, a resolution was passed that increased the number of directors from eight to nine, and at the subsequent election Tony Rosser was voted onto the board. In the meantime Basil Terry had died of a heart attack, while Rosser had been instrumental in setting up the Summertown Stars boys' football club.

The season started badly for Oxford, now wearing an all-yellow strip for the first time, with just two wins in the first 14 games, which included a 5–0 defeat at Cardiff and elimination from the League Cup at the hands of Fulham (3–0 in a replay). United avenged the Ninian Park defeat by beating Cardiff 4–2 at the Manor, and they also beat Bristol City 5–0, but it was clear from the general form that a relegation battle was under way, especially now that the format of the League had been changed to three up, three down. A 5–2 home defeat by Manchester City in the FA Cup heralded a run of five League games without a win, but the side recovered and found themselves needing a point from the final game at Millwall. The match ended 0–0, with Millwall's Alf Wood missing an open goal in the closing minutes. United finished fifth from bottom, two points above relegated Crystal Palace, with Swindon Town in bottom place. The major signing this season was Max Briggs from Norwich City for £28,000, plus a further £2,000 after 20 appearances. Oxford also tried to sign Peter Eastoe from Wolves, but they were put off by the £100,000 asking price.

United were now negotiating with British Leyland to buy a site at Brasenose Driftway. Initially it was envisaged that this would be a shared facility with Oxford Stadium, but after vociferous local opposition the speedway element was dropped from the plans. The proposal was dependent on Leyland acquiring permission to buy and turn a site on Horspath Road into a car storage facility on the very site that United had just failed to move to after planning permission was refused. However, Leyland had second thoughts and decided not to sell, so Rosser prepared a plan to redevelop the Manor which would involve relocating the bowls club and buying out some Osler Road residents. However, news of the plans leaked out in the *Oxford Mail*, leading to strong opposition from the locals. This, compounded by a challenge to a number of directors from Geoff Coppock and David Meeson, led to six board members resigning en bloc. Chairman Bob Kearsey, vice-chairman Fred Waters, plus former chairmen Vic Couling and Peter Playford, along with former player Harold Kimber and Arthur Harris all stood down, issuing a statement about their dissatisfaction with the way the club's affairs were being handled, although they knew that their time was up as they had lost share control. This left a five-man board of David Meeson, Howard Atkins (company secretary of the Rosser Group), Geoff Coppock, co-optee Ron Russell (Rosser Group solicitor) and new chairman Tony Rosser in control of the club. Rosser, an avid United supporter, was a local housing developer, who had also recently started the country's first free newspaper, the *Oxford Journal*, in January 1973, and who saw the acquisition of United as an ideal vehicle for improving advertising sales in the *Oxford Journal* in direct competition with the *Oxford Mail*.

The new-look board was not averse to spending money to strengthen United, and in the close season they bought goalkeeper John Milkins from Portsmouth for £10,000, winger Brian Heron from Dumbarton for £22,000 and Andy McCulloch from Cardiff City for a club record £73,000, reducing Cardiff's asking price from £100,000. Off the pitch, John Tagholm was recruited to the new post of public relations officer from the Independent Broadcasting Authority. The board also negotiated a new mortgage on the Manor of £44,500, repayable over seven years, with the money realised being used to gut the Beech

A model showing what the Manor might have looked like if it had been redeveloped.

Oxford United's board and players in 1973.
(courtesy: Tony Rosser)

Road stand and install new dressing rooms, a players' lounge, a warm-up room, a board room, a new tunnel and converting the old dressing-room stand into the Manor Club. Leaving the club was Hugh Curran, who joined Bolton for £40,000 after Bristol City had offered £30,000 for him, while the long-serving Graham Atkinson and Ken Skeen left on free transfers.

United were unbeaten in the first six League games of the 1974–75 season, but a run of four consecutive defeats, including a 4–0 home reverse by Southampton, dropped the club from fourth in the table to 16th. Home form picked up, although United found it difficult to pick up points away from home, and on 8 February they welcomed Division Two leaders Manchester United to the Manor. The game coincided with Sir Matt Busby opening the new dressing rooms under the Beech Road, and to cap a good day a shot by Derek Clarke from 30 yards went in off the post to seal a special win for United, all covered by John Motson and the *Match of the Day* cameras. United won only one away game all season, 2–1 at Nottingham Forest on 31 August, but still managed to finish in 11th place thanks to their results at the Manor. They were eliminated from both Cups at the first attempt, losing 1–0 at Colchester in the League Cup and 3–1 at Leicester City in the FA Cup. The youth team, under Fred Ford's guidance, won the Midland Youth League.

During the season the new board introduced a ban on Radio Oxford's coverage of games because they thought that attendances could be increased. This caused a huge uproar involving the Football League Secretary Alan Hardaker, but United stuck to their guns and attendances did improve markedly, with over 11,000 attending the League game against Southampton. The club eventually caved in when other reporters threatened to boycott games in support of the BBC. Club secretary Derek Wright resigned, to be replaced by Southampton's assistant secretary Brian Truscott, while Company Secretary Edmund Gibbs, husband of Oxford's Lord Mayor Olive Gibbs and secretary since the company was formed in July 1949, also stood down. Another innovation introduced during the season was to have bands performing live before games on a temporary stage set up on the Beech Road terracing, adjacent to the new players' tunnel. Ace played before the Fulham game on 26 October, followed by Starry Eyed & Laughing, who played before the Hull game on 7 December, and Brinsley Schwarz, who played before the Cardiff match on 14 December. The experiment came to an abrupt end when neighbours complained about the noise.

During the season United were forced to sell Dave Roberts for £60,000 to Hull, and Hugh Curran for £40,000 to Bolton in order to offset financial losses. It was noted in the minutes of the club's AGM that players of this quality could have remained with the club had Gerry Summers sold transfer-listed players earlier in the season, as he had agreed. Coming into the club during the close season was Peter Houseman, who joined from Chelsea for £30,000. United changed their club strip for the following season, adopting bright yellow and royal blue thick striped shirts and royal blue shorts.

Sir Matt Busby and Tony Rosser at the opening of the new Beech Road dressing rooms on 8 February 1975. (courtesy: Tony Rosser)

The 1975–76 season started disastrously for United, with just one win (2–0 at home to Bolton) in the opening 12 games, leaving United bottom of the table. This run concluded with a 3–2 home defeat by Charlton after extra-time in the League Cup second round, second replay. The day after this game the board decided that Gerry Summers had to go. Chairman Tony Rosser was lobbied by former director Jack King to offer Ron Atkinson the job, and Atkinson clearly wanted the post, but assistant manager Mick Brown claimed that he would not be able to work under Atkinson and so Brown was offered the position instead. Ironically, Brown was later to work under Atkinson at both West Brom and Manchester United. Brown brought in Roger Hynd on loan from Birmingham and wanted to keep him as player-coach, but the board refused this request. Although Brown won his first two games in charge, his cause was not helped when Brian Heron broke his leg in the 1–0 win at Notts County on 11 October. That was the last win for eight games, and United then went from 6 December to 2 March without a win, including a 2–1 FA Cup third-round exit at Old Trafford, where Manchester United were awarded two controversial penalties. The club was virtually condemned to the drop at the 2–0 defeat at Blackpool on 21 February, in which Oxford became just the second club to have three players sent off in a game, as Peter Houseman, John Shuker and Mick Tait were all dismissed. A run of four successive victories lifted United to 20th place, but with just one win in the last five games Oxford were unable to sneak out of the relegation zone and ended in 20th position, third from bottom and condemned to their first relegation ever. Meanwhile, on 14 April, Brian Heron made his comeback in a reserve game against Fulham and promptly broke his leg again within five minutes of the game starting.

Off the field the club was suffering financially, with the chairman's company The Rosser Group having to loan United £40,000. The club's losses were partially offset by the sales of Andy McCulloch to Brentford for £30,000 in February. Company secretary Howard Atkins resigned and was replaced by Glyn Pritchard, the new Rosser Group / Free Newspapers company secretary. Another significant change in the boardroom had occurred earlier in the season, when Bill Reeves was appointed a director on 30 September, with Ron Russell standing down a week later. Despite the financial pressure, in May 1976 United turned down an offer of £50,000 from Carlisle United for Mick Tait.

Paul Bryant in April 1975, as Oxford's youth team won the Midland Youth League.

United's first season back in the Third Division did not start too encouragingly. After a mixed performance in the pre-season Kent Cup, the first couple of competitive games saw the club knocked out of the League Cup by Cambridge United, 2–1 on aggregate, followed by just two wins in the opening six League games. After beating Grimsby 5–2 on 18 September, United then went eight games without a win and found themselves fifth from bottom. Oxford were knocked out of the FA Cup in the first round by Southern League Kettering Town, for whom player-manager Derek Dougan scored the only goal in a replay at the Manor. Results picked up slightly, with United picking up points at home especially, and even though they did not win any of their last four games United still finished in 17th place, four points above relegated Reading.

The club suffered a devastating blow on Sunday 20 March 1977 when Peter Houseman was killed in a car crash on the Oxford by-pass. Also killed in the accident were Houseman's wife, Sally, and their two friends Alan and Janice Gillham, with six children orphaned as a result. They were on their way home from a dance at Cowley Workers Social Club, organised by the Oxford United Football and Supporters' Club Joint Fundraising Committee. On 2 April, after 534 appearances for the club, John Shuker played his last game for United in a 3–2 defeat at Peterborough, while at the other end of the scale, on 7 September, Jason Seacole became the youngest player to play for United in the Football League, aged 16 years and 149 days, when he came on as substitute for Billy Jeffrey in a 3–0 home defeat by Mansfield. Players leaving included Derek Clarke, who moved to Orient, and Mick Tait, who joined Carlisle for £65,000. In the close season Shuker, given a free transfer by United, tried unsuccessfully to sue the club for wrongful dismissal, and popular winger Brian Heron left to join Scunthorpe.

Behind the scenes there were further changes. Secretary Brian Truscott resigned to take up a similar position at his former club Southampton, and he was replaced by Jim Hunt, who had been treasurer and secretary of the Oxford United supporters' club. Truscott had also acted as company secretary since Edmond Gibbs' resignation, and these duties were now taken over by Glyn Pritchard, who was co-opted onto the board. The poor performances on the field led Tony Rosser to stand down as chairman on 4 October, although he remained a director, guaranteeing all club finances and continuing to hold share control, and Geoff Coppock took over the chair. Coppock and fellow director Dave Meeson resigned from the board on 4 January after Bill Reeves, an East Oxford dentist, bought Tony Rosser's shareholding and became chairman, with Rosser becoming vice-chairman, and one of Reeves' first moves was to co-opt author and sociologist Desmond Morris onto the board. United dropped their striped shirts for the next season but kept the bright yellow and royal blue colour scheme.

The 1977–78 season started with the return of Hugh Curran from Bolton, along with Brian Drysdale, a full-back signed from Bristol City, while Gary Briggs joined on loan from Middlesbrough in January. In the first game United put Rotherham to the sword, and they then beat Shrewsbury Town 3–0 in the first round, first leg of the League Cup, and going through 5–2 on aggregate, but they were knocked out by Bury 1–0 in a replay in the second round. League form started well, and after United had beaten Chester 4–1 on 24 September they were second, behind Colchester on goal average. On 29 October United lost 2–1 at

Cambridge, having been 1–0 up at half-time. After the game Cambridge supporters threw stones into the United supporters' enclosure, and despite injuries the watching police took no action. This led to a pitch invasion by the Oxford fans, who broke a crossbar and caused severe damage, and the disturbances continued on the journey back from Cambridge to Oxford. United supporter Mick Brown had decided to start an organised travel club, to be called the London Road Travel Club, and this was their first game. After a 1–0 win over Sheffield Wednesday on 12 November, United did not win again for 11 games, including elimination from the FA Cup in the first round at a Southern League club for the second season running, as Nuneaton Borough won 2–0. The sequence was halted with a 3–1 win over Bradford City on 21 January, and a month later United beat Hereford (3–0) and Wrexham (2–1) to win consecutive games for the only time that season. United ended the season in 18th place, just four points above relegated Port Vale.

At the start of the season the youth team was re-elected into the South-East Counties League, a decision that was vindicated when they reached the Final of the South-East Counties League Cup, losing 5–4 on aggregate to Tottenham Hotspur. Included in that side was Nick Merry, who was called-up to represent England Schoolboys against Scotland in May 1977.

There were significant changes on the board during the season. At the club's AGM in September 1977 Geoff Coppock was elected back onto the board, replacing long-term director Tom Lees, who became an honorary life vice-president. Peter Marsh joined in January, while Tony Rosser and Glyn Pritchard both resigned in February, the main reason being the retention by the board of Mick Brown as manager. Before leaving, Rosser and Pritchard set up a lottery system, broadcast live over Radio Oxford, which proved very successful, realising £4,000 net per week. Harold Kimber returned to the board in June 1978, while Jim Hunt took on Pritchard's company secretary duties in addition to his own club secretary work.

The 1978–79 season commenced with the permanent signing of Gary Briggs from Middlesbrough for £12,500. The fee was set at the first transfer tribunal, set up to determine transfer deals when two clubs were unable to reach an agreement. Briggs's case was the second to be heard by that first tribunal. Also signing were Kevin Brock, who had come up through the Oxford youth ranks and had already won England Schoolboy international honours. However, Mick Brown's attempts to bring Dave Roberts back to the club were unsuccessful. After knocking Cardiff out of the League Cup, winning both legs 2–1, United proceeded to lose their first three League games and were bottom of Division Three by the time they beat Exeter City on 16 September. In the meantime they had progressed to the third round of the League Cup by beating Plymouth 2–1 in Devon, although they were beaten 5–0 at the Manor by Nottingham Forest, the European champions, in the third round. After the Forest defeat United had a run of seven draws in the next eight games, after which they were knocked out of the FA Cup 4–2 at Colchester. United's form for the latter part of the season was steady, and the club finished the season in 11th place.

On 26 September United bought Gordon Hodgson from Mansfield for £35,000, and on 6 November Ray Graydon was signed from Washington Diplomats for £37,000. At the end of the season Hugh Curran's contract was terminated by mutual consent after a disappointing season in which injury meant that he played just four full games with one substitute appearance. John Doyle and Nick Merry were both released on 1 August 1979.

On 24 July manager Mick Brown asked to be released from his contract so that he could go to West Brom and work as assistant to Ron Atkinson. Bill Asprey was appointed as Brown's replacement, while Brian Sargent joined the club on 19 October as reserve-team coach, although he was released at the end of January when it was decided a more experienced person was required, and Roy Barry replaced him on 14 March. At the start of the season Joe Cooke was signed from Peterborough for £50,000, and in October David Brown joined for £40,000 from Middlesbrough.

The 1979–80 season did not start off too promisingly, with a 7–2 aggregate defeat by Reading in the first round of the League Cup, including a 5–1 home defeat. However, League form was good in the early stages and after four games United were second, having won three and drawn one. However, a run of 13 games with just one win saw the Us drop to 16th by Boxing Day. Included in this sequence was another embarrassing first-round FA Cup defeat, United losing 1–0 at Isthmian League Barking. United's home form was similar to that of relegated clubs Bury and Mansfield, and worse than third-from-bottom Southend, and it was only thanks to the away form that Oxford were able to finish as high as 17th, only two points above the relegation zone.

Asprey adopted a stringent regime when he took over, and this was reflected by a high turnover of players. In addition to those mentioned above, Malcolm Shotton and Tim Smithers arrived from Nuneaton Borough at a cost of £15,000 each, and Adrian O'Dowd joined on a free transfer from Aston Villa. Players leaving the club included Colin Duncan, who joined Gillingham for £50,000, Gary Watson, who was signed by Carlisle for £20,000 and Hugh McGrogan, who also joined Carlisle for £19,000. Jimmy Sweetzer joined Millwall for £15,000, Archie White moved to Heart of Midlothian for a similar fee and Banbury United paid £2,000 for Phil Emsden.

It was at the start of this season that a new club badge, designed by vice chairman Desmond Morris, was adopted. It was based on a Mycenaean bull design and was deliberately made easy to replicate. It still forms the basis of the club badge, 30 years later.

In 1980–81, despite reaching the third round of the League Cup, where they lost 1–0 at Preston, the side had an appalling start to the League season and did not win a home game until they beat Chester 1–0 on 15 November. Despite away wins at Chester, Newport, Hull and a 4–0 thrashing of Fulham, United found themselves fourth from bottom, just four points above bottom club Hull. After a run of four consecutive defeats, including a 3–0 reverse at Plymouth in the second round of the FA Cup, Bill Asprey was dismissed on 15 December, with Ian Greaves appointed on 23 December. The change had the desired effect, with United beating top-of-the-table Charlton Athletic 1–0 in Greaves' first game in charge on Boxing Day. The club then went through their final 13 games without defeat, setting a new club League record. United finished the season in 14th place. In the South-East Counties League, United's youth team finished in second place, and in the summer they won an International Youth Tournament in Saarbrücken, Germany.

At the start of the season Phil Lythgoe arrived from Norwich City for £15,000, while 17-year-old Mark Wright signed professional forms. Keith Cassells came from Watford on a free transfer in November, and Oxford paid £7,000 to Birmingham for Malcolm Page in February. John Milkins was released during the summer, Gordon Hodgson was sold to Peterborough for £8,000 and Andy Bodel went to Oxford City for £2,000. During the season Adrian O'Dowd joined Banbury on a free transfer on 20 October, and on 7 November Watford paid £100,000 for Les Taylor, a new club record.

Despite the sale of Taylor, the club accounts for the season showed a loss of £138,129 and the club's bank put restraints on their borrowing. This meant that no new players could be bought and the club had to look at ways of proving their viability.

The 1981–82 season started disastrously for United, with three consecutive defeats in the new Group Cup competition. This was an innovative tournament for lower-League clubs, with an experiment introduced in which sides could choose five substitutes, of whom two could be used during a match. The season proper had a much better start for the Us, with the first two games being won and progression in the Milk Cup, which was the new sponsor's name for the League Cup, at the expense of Brentford. After the Milk Cup win, United suffered three successive defeats, which left the club in 20th place. However, recovery was rapid and United went undefeated in the next nine League games, lifting the side up to fourth. On 31 October, for the home game against Lincoln City, United shirts bore their first sponsorship, with the *Sunday Journal*, owned by former chairman Tony Rosser's Free Newspapers Group, agreeing a deal to become shirt sponsors. The side beat Millwall 4–3 on aggregate in the second round of the Milk Cup before being beaten 1–0 at Goodison by First Division Everton. United then had the rare experience of beating non-League opposition in the FA Cup first round, winning 2–0 at Southern League Dover Athletic. In the second round United beat Aldershot 4–2 after a 2–2 draw, and they then won 2–0 at Bournemouth in the third round. United travelled to First Division Brighton for the fourth-round tie, and thanks to two goals from Peter Foley and another from Keith Cassells Oxford won 3–0, the single most impressive win that Oxford had achieved to that date.

United's next game was a 3–1 win at Walsall, after which Ian Greaves left to become manager of Wolverhampton Wanderers, giving no notice because he did not have a contract. Roy Barry stepped into the breach as caretaker manager, and one of his first games was at his former club Coventry City in the fifth round of the FA Cup. Oxford lost that match 4–0, but in the League United remained unbeaten under Barry's charge. On Tuesday 2 March Jim Smith was appointed manager, his first game being a 2–0 win at Bristol City. Smith was friends with Ron Atkinson, who introduced him to Oxford director Paul Reeves shortly before Smith's sacking by Birmingham City. The day after Smith's dismissal, Reeves phoned him to ask if he'd be interested in the Oxford job. After an interview Smith took the job and brought in Ray Graydon as his assistant.

After a brief wobble, United went unbeaten for 12 games and reached second place on 1 May after a 0–0 draw with Millwall, earning Jim Smith the Manager of the Month award for April. The run included a 5–0 win over Swindon on 7 April, followed by a 3–0 win at Reading. In the return game at Swindon, on 4 May, Oxford lost 3–2 after a controversial incident when a smoke bomb was thrown into the Oxford goalmouth, obscuring Roy Burton's view. However, the referee allowed play to continue and Swindon went on to score past the unsighted Burton. The resulting riots by Oxford fans made the national news that night. Oxford lost their last four games and finished fifth, seven points behind third-placed Fulham.

Players leaving the club included Keith Cassells and Mark Wright, who together joined Southampton for £115,000 each, jointly setting a new club record, while Trevor Hebberd's arrival from the Saints was a club-record buy, costing £80,000. George Lawrence arrived on loan from Southampton, and Ray Train joined from Watford for £10,000.

It was off the pitch that the most dramatic changes occurred for Oxford, as the club found themselves in financial dire straits. The club's lottery had collapsed, the club had lost £83,000 over the six months to the end of December, the Barclays overdraft limit of £150,000 had been exceeded by £31,000 and the Inland Revenue were owed £60,000 and were threatening distraint proceedings. At Christmas the bank informed the club that they had a fortnight to repay the overdraft or they would close down Oxford United FC, and they would not cash any cheques after 31 December. The father of Bob Oakes, club secretary Jim Hunt's assistant, held a high position in a company owned by local millionaire Robert Maxwell, who lived at Headington Hill Hall just a few hundred yards from the Manor, and he phoned Maxwell, who asked Reeves to call him. Although Maxwell was on holiday in the West Indies, he managed to forestall the bank. On his return he contacted former company secretary Edmund Gibbs, and after going through the figures Maxwell decided to inject £121,000 into the club, buying £4 shares for £1 each. After becoming chairman on 6 January and securing the future of the club, Maxwell invited Gibbs back onto the board, along with Les Town and Gary Whiting. Maxwell's first action after assuming control of the club was to change bank from Barclays to National Westminster. The club was just five days from liquidation before Maxwell took over. Three weeks after Maxwell became chairman, Peter Marsh resigned from the board, his last act as director being to appoint the London Road Club organiser Mick Brown as a youth liaison officer.

THE GLORY YEARS AND BEYOND

The 1982–83 season started with another experimental tournament in the Football League Trophy, in which any team scoring three or more goals in a game were awarded a bonus point. Although United earned a bonus with a 3–1 win at Aldershot, they were beaten at Reading and Bournemouth and so failed to qualify for the knock-out part of the competition. Undeterred, Oxford won their first four League games and also knocked Reading out of the Milk (League) Cup 4–0 on aggregate. Huddersfield then eliminated Oxford from the Milk Cup 2–1 on aggregate before United beat Folkestone Town, of the Southern League Southern Division, 5–2 in the first round of the FA Cup. This was the first of a run of eight successive wins for United, which included a 5–1 win at Leyton Orient, a 4–0 win over Isthmian League First Division outfit Worthing in the second round of the FA Cup, a 4–2 win over Bristol Rovers and finally a 3–0 win at Reading, which took Oxford to fifth in the table. The run was halted with a 1–1 home draw against Torquay United in the FA Cup third round, the Gulls winning the replay 2–1. This heralded a slight loss of form in the League, United winning just one of the next seven games before beating Bradford City 5–1.

By the time Oxford won 1–0 at Doncaster on 16 April the club were seventh, nine points beneath third-placed Newport County and with little chance of promotion. It was on this date the news broke that Robert Maxwell was going to merge Oxford United and Reading to form a new club called the Thames Valley Royals. Maxwell issued a statement saying 'Oxford United FC are to acquire Reading FC by an offer to purchase the whole of the issued share capital [73,000 shares] of Reading FC at a price of £3 a share, payable in cash. Mr Frank Waller [Reading's chairman] and his colleagues on the Reading FC board holding a majority of the shares have irrevocably accepted the offer and agreed to recommend it to the Reading shareholders'. The scheme, which had the support in principle of The Football League, was to involve the building of a new stadium at an unspecified site, and it would be funded by the sale of the Manor and Reading's Elm Park. It was envisaged that the team would be ready in time for the following season, with Jim Smith as manager and Maurice Evans, Reading's manager, as his assistant.

Inevitably, the scheme was met with a hostile reaction by supporters of both Oxford and Reading, although the *Oxford Mail* called it 'bold and enterprising'. On 18 April Maxwell exclaimed that unless Oxford and Reading merged and moved to a new stadium the club would cease to exist, and that attempts to stop the merger would be like 'trying to make the Thames run backwards'. At a meeting on 20 April the Oxford board, which had been unaware of Maxwell's plans before they were made public, unanimously supported the proposal, with the one alteration that the club should be called Thames Valley United instead. Oxford supporters started the Save Oxford Soccer campaign, while in Reading shareholders looked into mounting a legal challenge to the scheme. The Mayor of Didcot was keen for the new club to locate there, on a site originally intended for Didcot Town, although residents in the town objected, fearful of hooliganism.

United fans invade the pitch before the Wigan game on 23 April 1983 in protest against the proposed merger with Reading.

United fans prepare to march from the station to the Manor in protest against the proposed merger with Reading before the two teams met on 2 May 1983.

At United's home game with Wigan on 23 April, the SOS campaigners organised a peaceful sit-in on the Manor pitch, holding the game up for 33 minutes. The only time things turned sour was when Maxwell took his seat in the directors' box. United won the game 2–0, but that was secondary to the main events of the day, although Maxwell himself was unimpressed with the demonstration, calling it 'bloody disgrace'. On 2 May United had a home game against Reading before which Oxford supporters held a protest march, despite the game being moved to a morning kick-off. Maxwell went to Gloucester Green to confront the protestors, where he explained, to cries of 'Maxwell Out', that although he had sympathy with the protests, if it wasn't for him United would already have gone out of business. United lost the game 2–1, which finally ended their hopes of promotion, and the side finished fifth again.

Meanwhile, Maxwell continued talks with the City Council about a new site for the ground, but discussions broke down when the council expressed a preference for a site at Blackbird Leys, while Maxwell preferred a site in Marston. Councillor Albert Ramsay offered to negotiate with the Co-op over a site on the Botley Road, but this was denounced by Conservative councilors as vote-seeking, with local elections being due. With Labour returned to power, a spokesman for SOS, former Oxford director Peter Marsh, called on the council to take a controlling interest in the football club, calling it a valuable community resource.

However, it was in Reading that the merger idea eventually fell apart. It was discovered as early as 19 April that Reading chairman Frank Waller did not have a controlling share, and on 22 April he was handed an injunction preventing him from selling his shares to Maxwell until 3 May. The injunction was extended until 13 June, meaning that planning for the new season would have to proceed on the basis of two separate clubs, with the Football League requiring lists of retained players by 21 May. On 12 May the Reading board met and former player Roger Smee forced the resignations of Waller and fellow directors Leslie Davies and John Briggs, meaning that the merger plan was effectively over.

There had been quite a large turnover in players in the season, with Paul Berry, Billy Jeffrey, Jason Seacole and Ollie Kearns, among others, all released in the summer, while Roy Burton and Clive Morgan both had their contracts paid up by United later in the season. John Butcher, Gary Barnett, Steve Biggins, David Linney and Steve Aries arrived before the start of the season. They were joined during the course of the season by George Lawrence on a permanent deal, Steve Hardwick and Neil Whatmore.

Maxwell remained chairman of United, and despite the failure of the merger or the council in providing a new stadium site he did not close down the club. He was rewarded with the most successful season in United's history. Oxford did not lose in the 1983–84 season until 15 October, when Plymouth won 2–1 at Home Park. Meanwhile they had knocked Bristol City out of the Milk Cup 2–1 on aggregate, drawn 1–1 at Second Division Newcastle United in the second round first leg and stormed to the top of the Third Division. Oxford then won just one of their next six League games, but they came to national attention with their 2–1 defeat of Newcastle in the second leg. In the third round of the Milk Cup United were drawn away to another Division Two side, Leeds United, and again United held them to a draw, 1–1 at a fog-bound Elland Road. Before the replay,

Oxford beat Peterborough 2–0 in the first round of the FA Cup. United were rampant in their replay against Leeds, beating the Yorkshire side 4–1 to set up a home tie against Manchester United, who were managed by former Oxford player Ron Atkinson.

By the time Manchester came to the Manor, United were back on top of the Third Division, having beaten Newport 2–0. Mark Hughes scored for the visitors after 10 minutes of his debut, but Bobby McDonald equalised for United to set up a replay at Old Trafford. In the rematch, Kevin Brock scored direct from a free-kick, but Mike Duxbury equalised a minute later and the stage was set for a second replay. Manchester United chairman Martin Edwards offered to host the match at Old Trafford again, but Robert Maxwell refused the offer, and so the matter was decided on the toss of a coin, performed over the phone at League Headquarters. Maxwell won the toss and with it the right to hold the match at the Manor. In the 12 days leading up to the game, United knocked Reading out of the FA Cup second round 3–0, after a 1–1 draw, and also won 2–1 at Rotherham in the League. In the third game against Manchester United, Oxford went behind through a goal by Arthur Graham, but two minutes later George Lawrence headed an equaliser. In the first period of extra-time, Steve Biggins headed home to give United a 2–1 victory.

United continued to do well in the League, with a New Year's Eve 5–2 win over Orient earning Jim Smith the Bells Manager of the Month award, before disaster struck when Andy Thomas broke his leg at Exeter on 2 January. Nevertheless, United next knocked out Burnley from the FA Cup, although the coin-throwing antics of the London Road crowd left Burnley 'keeper Roger Hansbury needing treatment and led to the erection of a roof-high net in front of the stand. In the fifth round of the Milk Cup United welcomed Everton to the Manor. Oxford were leading 1–0 through Neil Whatmore and were on course for the semi-finals, but nine minutes from time a soft backpass from Brock was intercepted by Adrian Heath, who equalised. It has often been said that this was the goal that revitalised Everton's fortunes, as they went on to reach the Final of the Milk Cup and also win the FA Cup this season, although Steve Biggins missed an open goal in the last minute, which would have put Oxford through had he scored. Everton won the replay 4–1 at Goodison.

United's next game was a 2–1 win over Blackpool in the FA Cup fourth round, but the Us were knocked out by Sheffield Wednesday 3–0 in the fifth round. Oxford were the first side from the Third Division to have reached the fifth round of both the FA and League Cups in the same season. No one seemed to notice the defeat by Swindon in the Associate Members' Cup, as United's stunning League form saw them lose just one of their final 20 League matches; that was their only home defeat of the season, against Gillingham. Included in this sequence were 5–0 wins over Plymouth and Bolton. Promotion was assured before United won 2–1 at Leyton Orient, as nearest challengers Wimbledon lost at home to Gillingham. Meanwhile, Kevin Brock was called-up to represent the England under-21 team and Jim Smith was voted the Third Division Manager of the Season.

Players joining the club during the season included Crystal Palace's Paul Hinshelwood and Bobby McDonald from Manchester City. United set a new club transfer record by buying Peter Rhoades-Brown from Chelsea for £85,000, while just £5,000 less secured John Aldridge from Newport County. Another new signing was former Derby County and England defender Colin Todd, while Newcastle's John Trewick joined on loan. Peter Foley and Tim Smithers both left the club. In January Maurice Evans was sacked as Reading manager, and he joined Oxford United as chief scout and youth development officer.

During the season Robert Maxwell had tried to buy Manchester United, for which he had offered £10 million, but the bid had been rejected with Martin Edwards asking for £15 million. Meanwhile, he had cleared Derby County's debts and bought the Baseball Ground after Stuart Webb, chairman at Derby, had approached Maxwell looking for a way to save the financially troubled club. At Oxford he had co-opted Pat McGeough onto the board as finance director following the retirement of Edmund Gibbs. At the annual meeting in March, Desmond Morris did not stand for re-election, but both Ian Maxwell, one of Robert's sons, and Robert's daughter Ghislaine Maxwell, were elected to the board.

In the summer leading up to the start of the 1983–84 season Jim Smith signed Dave Langan on a free transfer from Birmingham. Smith had initially brought Langan to Birmingham for £300,000 from Derby, then a record signing for the Blues, but Langan's back trouble meant Ron Saunders, Smith's successor, released him. It was initially envisaged that Langan would be back-up to Paul Hinshelwood, but just before the first game of the season Hinshelwood went down with a stomach upset. Langan replaced him and did so well that he became a first-team regular. Another new signing was Northern Ireland international Billy Hamilton, who joined from Burnley for £95,000, another new club record.

The season started with United in fine form, winning the first game 3–0 at Huddersfield and losing just once in the League before December. They knocked Hereford United out of the Milk Cup 7–5 on aggregate in the first round and then eliminated Blackburn Rovers 4–2 on aggregate. After beating Hereford 5–3 at the Manor, United won five successive League games to go into second place. A 1–0 defeat at Manchester City dropped Oxford back to fourth but with a game in hand on the teams above them. On 31 October Oxford, who by now were top of the Division, met Arsenal, top of the First Division, in the Milk Cup third round at the Manor. Goals from Billy Hamilton and John Aldridge ensured that the sides were drawing 2–2 when Langan hit a long-range shot that Arsenal goalkeeper Pat Jennings could only palm into the net to give United a 3–2 win. United were still top when they visited Ipswich Town in the fourth round, but their form deserted them and United were beaten 2–1. The following week United were home to Leeds United, and in front of the *Match of the Day* cameras they were soon trailing 2–0, with Gary Briggs pulling a goal back just before half-time. A Billy Hamilton goal followed by a John Aldridge hat-trick secured a famous fight-back, but after the controversial sending-off of Peter Lorimer the Leeds fans in the Cuckoo Lane terrace started throwing coins onto the pitch, knocking Steve Hardwick unconscious. While the Oxford goalkeeper was receiving treatment the Leeds fans started dismantling the temporary TV gantry at the rear of the terrace and threw planks of wood onto the pitch. The following week, United were knocked off the top of the table when they lost 2–0 to bottom side Notts County.

United then beat Charlton Athletic 5–0 before losing in bizarre circumstances at Portsmouth in the run-up to Christmas. United were leading 1–0 through a Kevin Brock goal when a Portsmouth supporter dressed in a Santa Claus outfit ran onto the pitch. In the time added on for this stoppage Portsmouth's Alan Biley scored twice to give Pompey the lead. There was still time for Billy Hamilton to hit the bar, but United could not draw level and Portsmouth went second, with United now out of the promotion places. However, a Boxing Day 4–0 win over Cardiff City was followed three days later by a 5–0 win over Crystal Palace to send United back to second, three points behind Blackburn. At the end of 1984, United won the FIAT Uno Team of the Year Award.

A New Year's Day win at Middlesbrough was followed by a 2–0 FA Cup third-round win at Shrewsbury. Poor weather through January meant that the next game was in the FA Cup fourth round, when Blackburn won 1–0 at the Manor. A 1–0 win at Carlisle took United back to the top of the Division on goal difference, after which United went five games without a win, including their only home defeat of the season, 3–0 against Birmingham, dropping them back to fourth. This run came to a halt with a 4–0 win over Wimbledon, followed shortly by a 3–0 win against table-topping Manchester City, which took United back into second place, four points behind City but with three games in hand. After a 3–0 defeat at Barnsley, United won their next six games. The final game of that sequence saw Dave Langan score the goal that beat Shrewsbury 1–0 to guarantee United promotion to the top flight for the first time in the club's history. Three days later United lost 1–0 at Leeds, followed by two draws, which meant that the final game of the season, a 4–0 win over Barnsley, gave the club the Divisional Championship. Sadly, this achievement was overshadowed by a fire in the main stand at Bradford City the same day, in which 56 people died. The achievement of winning the Championships of third and second tiers in successive seasons has never been equalled, while John Aldridge's 34 League and Cup goals was a new record for United since they joined the Football League.

In the warm-up before the Blackburn FA Cup game Billy Hamilton injured his knee, causing him to miss the next five games, and after aggravating the injury in the defeat at Barnsley he missed the remainder of the season. As a replacement, United bought Jeremy Charles from QPR for £100,000, again breaking the club's transfer record. Also arriving was Arsenal winger Brian McDermott, while Paul Hinshelwood left for Millwall.

Just before the season started Ian Maxwell resigned from the board to become chairman of Derby County. His brother Kevin was appointed to the Oxford board on 28 May 1985. The big change, though, was Jim Smith leaving for QPR. After promotion had been achieved, Smith went to see Maxwell to negotiate a new contract, but discussions were interrupted when the news of the Heysel riots came through, the implications of which would be far-reaching for Oxford. At the rearranged meeting a few weeks later Maxwell made Smith an offer that the Oxford manager considered not good enough, and Maxwell invited Smith to talk to other clubs, which he did. QPR offered Smith more than he had asked Maxwell for, and so Smith left to manage the West London club. Meanwhile, United spent over a million pounds on ground work to bring it up to First Division standards, including redeveloping the whole Osler Road side.

Maxwell immediately tried to get Maurice Evans to take over from Smith, but Evans initially refused, agreeing to take the post purely as a caretaker. For the 1985–86 season United replaced the royal blue in their kit with navy blue. They drew their first game in the top flight 1–1 at West Bromwich Albion, with Bobby McDonald scoring the side's first Division One goal. In their first home game they welcomed Tottenham Hotspur to the

Manor. Losing 1–0 at half-time, a late equaliser from Jeremy Charles earned United a point. In the next game, United played Leicester City at the Manor, and with Trevor Hebberd pulling the strings Oxford won 5–0 for what turned out to be their best win in the top flight. In the wave of euphoria following this result, Maxwell persuaded Maurice Evans to become manager, although Evans refused to sign a contract. Four defeats in a row brought United back to earth, including a 3–0 reverse at Manchester United in front of 51,820, the largest crowd to have yet watched an Oxford game. Evans bought his first players, signing Wales international full-back Neil Slatter from Bristol Rovers for a record-equalling £100,000. This was beaten by the second signing, Ray Houghton coming from Fulham for £147,000. The run of defeats was halted with a 2–2 home draw against Liverpool, with United's equaliser being a long-range own-goal by Alan Kennedy.

United's first Cup success came in the next game, when they beat Shrewsbury 3–0 in the Full Members' Cup, followed shortly afterwards by a hard-fought Milk Cup second-round, first-leg win 2–1 over Northampton. After beating Manchester City 1–0 at the Manor, United drew 4–4 at Leicester then lost 2–0 at Everton before completing the job against Northampton, winning 2–0. A 2–1 win over Chelsea, lifted out of the ordinary by a superb Peter Rhoades-Brown volley against his former club, was followed by a 2–0 win at Fulham in the next round of the Full Members' Cup. United beat Newcastle 3–1 in the third round of the Milk Cup and then beat Stoke 1–0 in the semi-final of the Southern Section of the Full Members' Cup. After successive 2–1 defeats to West Ham and at Arsenal, Oxford beat Norwich City 3–1 in the fourth round of the Milk Cup. This was followed by a home game against Ipswich Town, in which United were 2–0 down at half-time and 3–0 down shortly afterwards. Oxford struck back, with John Aldridge scoring a hat-trick in 10 minutes and Neil Slatter scoring a late winner with his first goal for the club. This game was followed by United's participation in the *Daily Express* National Five-a-Side Championship at Wembley Arena, in which the Us beat Watford 1–0, West Ham 2–1 and Nottingham Forest 3–1 on their way to the Final, where they beat Arsenal 1–0 in a sudden-death penalty shoot-out after a 2–2 draw.

After a 1–1 draw at Nottingham Forest, United lost 4–1 at home to Chelsea in the Southern Section Final of the Full Members' Cup. A 5–1 defeat at Tottenham was followed by a 2–2 draw with West Brom, and then the Us won 1–0 at Stamford Bridge in the second leg of the Full Members' Cup Southern Section Final, to go out 4–2 on aggregate. Just before Christmas United broke their transfer record again, signing Spurs striker David Leworthy for £200,000. Leworthy made his debut in the Boxing Day game against Southampton, scoring twice as United won 3–0. The New Year started with a 3–1 defeat at QPR, after which Tottenham knocked United out of the FA Cup 2–1, after a 1–1 draw at the Manor. A run of four League defeats, including a home 3–1 defeat by Manchester United, sandwiched a 3–1 win over Portsmouth in the Milk Cup quarter-finals. The run ended with a 4–1 win over Chelsea at Stamford Bridge in which Peter Rhoades-Brown again scored against his former club, followed by another heavy away win, 3–0 at Manchester City. United then went to Villa Park for the first leg of the Milk Cup semi-final against Aston Villa. Two goals from John Aldridge, one a penalty, earned United a 2–2 draw in front of a crowd of 23,098, which was estimated to include approximately 7,000 Oxford fans. In the return game at the Manor

Robert Maxwell with the Milk Cup on the balcony of the Town Hall on 21 April 1986.

on 12 March, Les Phillips gave Oxford a second-half lead, which was extended by Jeremy Charles. Villa pulled a goal back towards the end, but United held on to earn their first trip to Wembley.

On 22 March United suffered their heaviest defeat since joining the Football League when Liverpool won 6–0 at Anfield. A week later Oxford drew 3–3 with their Milk Cup Final opponents QPR, during which Peter Rhoades-Brown tore his cartilage, which meant he would miss the Final. Three consecutive draws left United fourth from bottom of the First Division, one point above Villa. Defeat at West Ham dropped Oxford into the bottom three before they stepped out at Wembley on Sunday 20 April 1986 against Queen's Park Rangers, managed by Jim Smith. United had been allocated 30,346 tickets for the Final, but secretary Jim Hunt increased the number to almost 36,000 by purchasing tickets from northern clubs who were not interested in selling their allocation for a Cup Final between Oxford and QPR. The crowd of 90,396, the largest ever to watch United, saw a nervy first half in which Man of the Match Trevor Hebberd broke the deadlock five minutes before the break, beating Paul Barron at his near post. In the second half United were rampant, playing some glorious football. An interchange of passes between Hebberd and Ray Houghton climaxed with Houghton sidefooting home to double United's lead, and with just a few minutes remaining Barron parried a John Aldridge shot into the path of Jeremy Charles, whose winner brought the memorable pronouncement from TV commentator Barry Moore 'That's three, and that's victory!' After the game, United manager Maurice Evans sent long-serving physio Ken Fish up the steps to receive his winners' medal in an unprecedented gesture. This was the last Milk Cup, as the following season the sponsorship was taken over by Littlewoods.

After the greatest single day in the club's history, United still had to avoid relegation. They were not helped when relegation rivals Ipswich Town beat United 3–2 at Portman Road to leave Oxford three points adrift of fourth-from-bottom Leicester, although with a game in hand. On 30 April Everton visited the Manor, needing to win to maintain their title challenge against neighbours Liverpool. An 86th-minute goal by Les Phillips gave United a 1–0 win in front of an emotional and passionate home crowd. This lifted Oxford above Leicester on goal difference and left Everton five points behind Liverpool. On 3 May United lost 3–1 at home to Nottingham Forest to fall back into the relegation zone again, two points behind Ipswich, who had now played all their games while Oxford still had one match remaining, against seventh-placed Arsenal. United won 3–0, with a John Aldridge penalty and goals from Ray Houghton and Billy Hamilton, playing just his eighth game of the season, to earn survival and another season in the top flight.

During the season, six Oxford players were awarded full international caps, with Jeremy Charles and Neil Slatter called up to play for Wales, Billy Hamilton for Northern Ireland and Dave Langan, John Aldridge and Ray Houghton for the Republic of Ireland. In addition, Kevin Brock won another England Under-21 cap. United spent over £530,000 on new players during the season, although it was one of the free arrivals, Steve Perryman, who received an MBE for his services to football, and he was made new club captain at the end of the season, replacing Malcolm Shotton. Further ground improvements were made, with 420 seats added to the Osler Road side for home supporters. Oxford City Council gave the club a grant of £250,000 towards this and the previous year's expenditure, while the Football Grounds Improvement Trust granted United an additional £636,505 towards the work. As part of the condition of the City Council grant, United inaugurated the Oxford United Juniors scheme, which boasted over 600 members at the end of its first season.

Maxwell's ambitions to realise a new stadium for the club had not relented, and he submitted a planning application to develop a site at the Pear Tree roundabout, between North Oxford and Woodstock. The project was estimated to cost around £20 million for a 25,000 all-seater stadium and ancillary development and it received support in principle from Oxford City Council, although the site actually lay outside their jurisdiction, in Cherwell District. In June Kevin Maxwell was appointed deputy chairman of the club and at the same time Patrick Morrissey, managing director of Mirror Group Newspapers, was appointed to the board. Most of the old directors took this opportunity to resign, with Bill Reeves, Les Town, Geoff Coppock, John Devaney, Harold Kimber and Paul Reeves deciding not to seek re-election. This left a board consisting of three Maxwells (Robert, Kevin and Ghislaine), McGeough, Morrissey and Brian Dalton, the managing director who was appointed before the start of the 1985–86 season.

Because of the Heysel riots and the subsequent ban on English clubs playing in European competition, United were denied a place in the UEFA Cup in the 1986–87 season and so missed out on the possibility of facing Sporting Lisbon, Athletico Madrid, Werder Bremen, Barcelona, Inter Milan, Rangers or Sigma Olomouc. Instead, United had to make do with an opening-day trip to Watford, where they lost 3–0 and substitute Tony Obi played his only 15 minutes in an Oxford shirt. United eventually won in their fifth game of the season, 2–1 at Villa Park. On 24 September John Aldridge scored four goals as Gillingham were despatched 6–0 in the first leg of the second round of the Littlewoods Cup. A 3–2 home win over Charlton was followed by a 6–1 hammering at Sheffield Wednesday. United drew 1–1 at Gillingham in the second leg and then beat Coventry 2–0 before losing 4–0 to Liverpool at Anfield.

After beating Nottingham Forest 2–1, United beat Sheffield United 3–1 in the third round of the Littlewoods Cup, and on 8 November the side beat Manchester United 2–0 at the Manor, with Alex Ferguson taking charge of the Red Devils for the first time. On 15 November, following a 1–1 draw at QPR, Maurice Evans instructed the driver of the team coach not to wait for seven of the players who were late, and so the bus drove off without them. Included in the seven was leading scorer John Aldridge, who a few days later said he wanted a move to a 'bigger' club.

Ten days later Oxford, the holders, were eliminated from the Littlewoods Cup 1–0 at West Ham, thanks to a controversial Tony Cottee penalty. David Leworthy scored in the opening minute at home to his former club Spurs, but Oxford were beaten 4–2, and after losing 2–1 at Norwich, Oxford beat Luton 4–2. On 10 December United played in the Guinness Soccer Sixes at G-Mex in Manchester, beating Arsenal in the Final 2–1 with two goals in the last two minutes, from John Aldridge and Paul Swannock, in front of a capacity crowd of 5,500. United qualified for the Final by beating Manchester United 2–1 and then drawing 1–1 with Chelsea. Steve Hardwick was named Player of the Tournament. On New Year's Day United beat Southampton 3–1, but they were knocked out of the FA Cup in the third round 3–0 by Fourth Division Aldershot. The attendance of 2,034 reflected the tripling of the usual ticket price to £9, as the Shots tried to cash in on the visit of a First Division side.

United then lost 4–3 at Blackburn Rovers in the Full Members' Cup. After beating West Ham 1–0 at Upton Park, United went on a run of seven games without a win, which dropped them to 17th in the table, five points above Leicester in the relegation zone. A 2–1 win over Sheffield Wednesday was followed by a 3–2 defeat at Old Trafford, and despite beating Wimbledon 3–1, successive defeats at Spurs and against Norwich left Oxford in 18th place, four points above the relegation places with two games remaining. On 5 May United visited fifth-placed Luton, and despite that club's ban on away supporters a healthy United following saw the side win 3–2 with a last-minute Dean Saunders header and thus ensure safety from relegation. In the final match United drew 0–0 with Leicester, condemning the Foxes to the drop.

During the season John Aldridge secured his dream move to Liverpool for a new club record £775,000. Andy Thomas went to Newcastle for £100,000, Steve Perryman left for Brentford, Bobby McDonald went to Leeds, Mark Jones left, and both Billy Hamilton and Jeremy Charles retired through injury. Incoming were John Dreyer, Billy Whitehurst, who joined from Newcastle for £187,500, Dean Saunders, signed as Aldridge's replacement for £60,000 from Brighton, Martin Foyle, signed from Aldershot for £140,000, goalkeeper Peter Hucker from QPR and Arsenal's Tommy Caton. Saunders and Slatter were both capped by Wales during the season, as were the Irish triumvirate of Aldridge, Houghton and Langan.

On 31 May Robert Maxwell resigned the chairmanship of Oxford to take on the same role at Derby County, with his son Kevin assuming the chair at Oxford. Directors Geoff Coppock, John Devaney and Paul Reeves had all been re-appointed to the board after their previous resignations. The planning application for a new stadium at Pear Tree had been rejected by Cherwell District Council, and the club put in an appeal to the secretary of state for the environment, having already spent approximately £90,000 on the application.

United opened the 1987–88 season with a 4–2 win over newly promoted Portsmouth, a game which featured a rare double from Billy Whitehurst. Martin Foyle then scored in two successive 1–1 draws at Sheffield Wednesday and Wimbledon, before three consecutive defeats gave an indication of what the season ahead would hold. The sequence was ended with a 2–0 win over QPR, followed by a 1–1 draw at Mansfield in the Littlewoods Cup second round, first leg. Two League wins, 1–0 at Derby and 3–0 against Norwich, were followed by a 2–0 win against Mansfield in the second leg. After beating Charlton 2–1, United drew 0–0 at home to Leicester in the Littlewoods Cup third round, but they won the replay 3–2. On 7 November Oxford beat Coventry 1–0 to go ninth in the table. This would prove to be United's last League win of the season. It was followed by a 1–0 win over Crystal Palace in the Simod Cup, the new name for the Full Members' Cup, and shortly afterwards Oxford beat Wimbledon 2–1 in the fourth round of the Littlewoods Cup. After draws with Watford and at Everton, United lost their next six League games, the last being a 5–2 home defeat by Wimbledon to send United to fourth from bottom, one point above Portsmouth.

A 2–0 win over Leicester in the third round of the FA Cup was followed by elimination from the Simod Cup 1–0 at Reading, and after drawing 2–2 at Portsmouth, Oxford beat

Manchester United 2–0 in the Littlewoods Cup quarter-finals. This was followed 10 days later by Bradford City knocking the Us out of the FA Cup 4–2 and then an extraordinary 7–4 defeat at Luton which left United second from bottom. Luton were then the visitors to the Manor for the first leg of the Littlewoods Cup semi-finals. The game ended 1–1 thanks to Dean Saunders scoring a controversial penalty for United, but he also missed a second spot-kick. After two 0–0 draws at home to Tottenham and Derby, Oxford made the trip to Kenilworth Road for the second leg of the semi-final. However, in front of the live TV cameras United failed to perform and were beaten 2–0 by Luton, who went on to beat Arsenal 3–2 in the Final. A 1–1 draw at West Ham was followed by a 4–2 defeat at Norwich, after which Oxford drew 4–4 with Chelsea. After the draw with West Ham, Maurice Evans announced that he was relinquishing the manager's post, believing that the manager's position was made impossible by the new Freedom of Contract regulations, although he agreed to remain in charge until a successor was recruited, before returning to his previous post of chief scout and youth development officer. Journalist John Maddock, from the *Sunday People*, phoned Mark Lawrenson, who had just had to retire from playing for Liverpool with a ruptured Achilles, to inform him that Evans was about to stand down, so Lawrenson called Kevin Maxwell and arranged for an interview. Oxford were second from bottom, four points from safety. It was Lawrenson's first managerial post, and in his first game Oxford drew 0–0 at home to Arsenal. However, in their last eight games United could only pick up two more points and they eventually finished bottom of the table, 11 points from safety.

Lawrenson had brought in Brian Horton, former player-manager at Hull City, as his assistant to replace Ray Graydon, and he also had Maurice Evans's desk brought into his office so that he could use Evans's experience and advice. David Moss was also appointed to the coaching staff, with special responsibility for the youth team. At the end of the season Ken Fish, aged 74, retired from the club he joined in 1964. He was replaced by John Clinkard. Declining attendances led to the sale of players, with Ray Houghton leaving for Liverpool for a new club record £825,000. Malcolm Shotton left for Portsmouth for £70,000, to be replaced as club captain by Tommy Caton, Kevin Brock was sold to Jim Smith at QPR for £260,000, Dave Langan, Brian McDermott and Tony Obi left on free transfers, Reading bought Billy Whitehurst for £122,500 and John Trewick went for £30,000 to Birmingham. Joining the club were Gary Shelton from Sheffield Wednesday for £155,000, and the Watford pair of David Bardsley and Richard Hill for £265,000 and £260,000 respectively, Bardsley becoming the club's new record signing. This was beaten in February when centre-back Colin Greenall was signed from Bury for £285,000.

With United back in the Second Division, the 1988–89 season started off well for the Us, who were unbeaten and in sixth place after five games. In the Littlewoods Cup second round they were beaten 6–2 on aggregate by Bristol City, while on 5 October they drew 1–1 with Swindon in their first League meeting since the infamous 'smoke-bomb' game five and a half years earlier. On 22 October United were 10th after drawing 1–1 with Blackburn Rovers. After the game Dean Saunders, who had signed a new three-year contract at the start of the season, was called in to Mark Lawrenson's office to be told that Derby County's manager Arthur Cox wanted to speak to him. Despite promises from Kevin Maxwell that

Saunders would stay at Oxford until the end of the season, Robert Maxwell overruled him. Lawrenson persuaded Robert Maxwell to increase the offer from £750,000 to £1 million, and secretary Jim Hunt managed to add a 10 per cent sell-on clause. Lawrenson, who had accepted the inevitability of Saunders leaving at the end of the season, requested that the deal be delayed by a fortnight to enable him to buy a replacement before prices were inflated, but this was refused. The following Monday, Lawrenson requested a meeting with Kevin Maxwell, at which he intended to tender his resignation, but Maxwell pre-empted this and sacked Lawrenson for alleged breach of contract. Brian Horton was then offered the job, which he accepted with Lawrenson's blessing, and he promoted David Moss to be his assistant.

Before he left, Lawrenson had signed Mike Ford, Cardiff City's Player of the Year the previous season, for £150,000 and Phil Heath from Stoke for £80,000. He had also brought in Gary Smart from Wokingham for £22,500 and Jon Purdie from Wolves on a free transfer. He sold Trevor Hebberd to Derby for £300,000 after Hebberd had rejected an improved contract to stay, with £70,000 Mickey Lewis coming the other way as part of the deal. Lawrenson's final signing was Jimmy Phillips, a left-back from Glasgow Rangers bought because Ford injured his back on honeymoon just after signing for United. Phillips cost £160,000, and Lawrenson had to seek permission from Derby chairman Robert Maxwell (not Kevin, the Oxford United chairman) to spend the money. In September director John Devaney resigned after buying a considerable holding in Peterborough United.

Brian Horton's first game in charge of Oxford was a 1–0 defeat at Crystal Palace, and the club lost six of the next seven games, including being knocked out of the Simod Cup by Ipswich, as they suffered a reaction to the Saunders affair. Horton's first win came on 12 November, when United beat Birmingham 3–0. United beat Barnsley 2–0, and on Boxing Day the side recorded their best win of the season, winning 5–1 at Walsall with Richard Hill scoring four of the goals. United beat Sunderland 2–0 in the third round of the FA Cup after a 1–1 draw at Roker Park, but after beating Leeds 3–2 they lost the fourth-round tie 4–0 at Manchester United. A 3–0 defeat at Swindon saw the club drop to 19th place and a season that had started with United in contention for the Play-offs was rapidly becoming one where a second relegation might occur. A run of six games without defeat (although only one of them a win) inched the side up to 17th, and wins over Hull, Stoke and Bournemouth ensured that United would be safe, despite losing their last four games. The final game of the season was a 4–0 home defeat by Watford in which 18-year-old Joey Beauchamp made his debut, coming off the bench to replace Lee Nogan. United finished the season in 17th place.

Brian Horton's first signing was winger Paul Simpson, who cost £200,000 from Manchester City, and a further £250,000 was spent on Liverpool reserve striker John Durnin. Ceri Evans, a New Zealand international studying as a Rhodes Scholar, joined the side following a brief trial after being recommended by Richard Hill. Leaving the club were Gary Briggs, who moved to Blackpool, Dave Leworthy, signed by Reading, and Neil Slatter. Following a year's secondment to the club, Malcolm Elias joined permanently as the youth, schools and community officer. Jim Hunt, club secretary for the last 13 years, retired and joined the board, with Mick Brown replacing him. Oxford recorded the heaviest losses in their history in the year ending June 1989, with a negative balance of £559,117, resulting largely from a reduction in attendances, a lack of success in the Cups, increases in wages and less money coming down from the top clubs. The Maxwell family contributed £350,000 to the club to cover the deficit, but it was estimated that the club was losing £12,000 a week.

Oxford got off to a slow start in 1989–90, being surprisingly knocked out of the Littlewoods Cup by Fulham 5–4 on aggregate after winning the first leg 1–0 at Craven Cottage. Wins over Bradford City (2–1) and Newcastle (2–1) in September were United's only League victories before they beat Portsmouth 2–1 on 7 October, by which time United were 18th. A 0–0 draw at Leicester was followed by three defeats, including 3–0 at Swindon, before Oxford beat Stoke 3–0 and their neighbours Port Vale 2–1. United were beaten 3–2 by Luton in the newly renamed Zenith Data Systems (ZDS) Trophy (the erstwhile Full Members' Cup). United started December with consecutive 3–2 wins against Plymouth and at Newcastle, and, after winning 1–0 at Brighton on 30 December, they started the New Year with three successive wins, including 1–0 at Plymouth in the third round of the FA Cup. They were knocked out of the FA Cup in the next round, however, going down 1–0 at Southampton. League form continued to be up and down, with a 4–2 home defeat by Leeds and a 4–2 home win over Leicester being the highlights. After winning 2–1 at Stoke on 10 April, United were 12th, 10 points adrift of the Play-off places. However, they failed to win any of their remaining six games and slipped to a 17th-place finish.

New signings this season included David Penney for £175,000 from Derby and Steve Foster, the new club captain, from Luton for a similar amount. Mark Stein arrived from QPR, along with £200,000, as part of the deal that took David Bardsley to Loftus Road, while Steve McClaren came from Bristol City in exchange for Gary Shelton. Goalkeeper Paul Kee arrived from Ards and Les Robinson joined from Doncaster for £150,000. Joey Beauchamp signed as a new professional, while Chris Allen was a new first-year scholar. Leaving the club were Jimmy Phillips, who joined Middlesbrough for £250,000, Neil Slatter, who became a policeman, Peter Rhoades-Brown, who retired through injury, Sean Reck, who went to Wrexham, and Peter Hucker, who left for Millwall. Paul Kee's performances (he won the Player of the Month award in February) won him his first Northern Ireland cap.

In December Kevin Maxwell held the club's first fans' forum, which he pledged to hold twice a season. In January Patrick Morrissey resigned from the board. The Taylor Report, which arose from the Hillsborough tragedy in 1989, was published in January 1990. This resulted in the removal of fences from the Osler Road end and a new police control unit at the rear of the Cuckoo Lane terrace. The board took the decision not to convert terracing to seating as it was envisaged that this would be complied with when the club moved to a new stadium, and to do so would have reduced the capacity of the Manor to 7,500. The appeal against the rejection of the Pear Tree site was withdrawn in favour of a new application on Watlington Road, on land owned by the city council. Club losses for this financial year had more than doubled, to over £1.17 million, as attendances fell and costs rose.

The 1990–91 season started well for United as they beat Port Vale 5–2 in their opening game and then knocked Reading out of the League Cup, now renamed the Rumbelows Cup, 3–1 on aggregate. A run of 10 League games without a win saw United drop to second from bottom by 13 October. This run included a 4–2 home defeat by Swindon, with United 2–0 up at one stage. It also sandwiched a 2–0 Rumbelows Cup win at Port Vale, with the home leg ending 0–0. The run came to an end with a 3–0 win over Brighton in which Paul Simpson scored a hat-trick. On 31 October United beat West Ham 2–1 in the Rumbelows Cup third round, in which Jim Magilton scored his first goal for the club. Wins at Millwall (2–1) and over Bristol City (3–1) were followed by a 3–3 draw against Charlton Athletic, played at Selhurst Park, and then a 2–2 draw with Bristol City in the ZDS Trophy first round, with Oxford winning their first penalty shoot-out to advance to the second round.

After a 5–2 home defeat by Middlesbrough, Oxford were beaten 2–1 by Chelsea at the Manor in the Rumbelows Cup fourth round. United beat Portsmouth 1–0 in the second round of the ZDS Trophy. A Boxing Day 3–3 draw at Hull City was followed by a 3–1 win at Blackburn and a 2–1 win over Ipswich before the Us had to face Chelsea again, this time at Stamford Bridge in the FA Cup third round where Oxford won 3–1. At the end of January, Oxford were knocked out of two Cup competitions in the space of four days, losing 2–1 at Ipswich in the ZDS Trophy and then 4–2 at Spurs in the FA Cup fourth round, in which United were destroyed by a phenomenal performance from Paul Gascoigne in front of over 5,500 travelling fans. This was followed by a 5–1 win over Oldham and then, after a 3–1 defeat at Bristol City, United embarked on a 15-game unbeaten run. These games included a 0–0 draw at Swindon, a 2–1 win over West Ham and a 3–3 draw at Wolves in which Oxford were 3–0 down at half-time thanks to a Steve Bull hat-trick, and after Mark Stein had equalised United hit the crossbar. United also won 2–0 at promotion-chasing Sheffield Wednesday, where Ken Veysey saved a penalty when the game was goalless, and 3–0 at Brighton. United lost their last two games of the season to end in 10th place, and the final match, a 1–0 defeat at Filbert Street, ensured Leicester's survival at the expense of West Brom.

Paul Wanless and Mark Druce were among the YTS trainees taken on at the start of the season, while Andy Melville signed from Swansea for a tribunal-determined £275,000. Jim Magilton joined from Liverpool reserves for £100,000, while Ian Walker joined on loan from Spurs for two games, Ken Veysey was loaned by Torquay, signing permanently for £110,000 in October, and Lee Gardner came on loan from Aberdeen. Robbie Mustoe left for Middlesbrough for £375,000 and Colin Greenall joined Bury for £125,000. Magilton won his first cap for Northern Ireland in February.

If the previous season had started well for United, the 1991–92 season began disastrously. United set an unwanted club record by losing their first five games, gained their first point with a 2–2 draw against Millwall before finally winning, on 18 September, at home to Derby (2–0). This win did not herald a significant change of fortune for the Us, who lost their next game 2–1 at Bristol Rovers, hitherto the only side in the Division below Oxford. United beat Plymouth 3–2 before losing on penalties at Swindon, following a 3–3 draw, in the ZDS Trophy. Oxford were knocked out of the Rumbelows Cup by Portsmouth, 1–0 on aggregate, before beating Tranmere 1–0. Oxford then lost six of the next seven games, including a 4–3 defeat at Newcastle, with the only exception being a 3–2 win at Southend, to sink to second from bottom of Division Two, one point above Plymouth. After United lost 1–0 to Southend in a rare Boxing Day reverse, Oxford were bottom of the table, six points behind Brighton. This was followed two days later by the side's best win of the season so far, 3–0 against Sunderland, in which Joey Beauchamp, newly returned from a loan spell at Swansea, scored his first senior goal for the club. United opened the New Year by knocking Tranmere out of the FA Cup 3–1, but they were unable to win in their next four League games, including a 2–1 defeat at Swindon.

On 1 February Oxford beat fellow relegation candidates Newcastle United 5–2, with two goals from Steve Foster, before being knocked out of the FA Cup at home to Sunderland (3–2). After losing 2–1 at Leicester, Oxford had their best sequence of the season, remaining undefeated for five games, which included an extraordinary 5–3 win over Swindon. This run lifted United to third from bottom, just one point behind Plymouth and Watford. A 2–1 win over Play-off chasing Portsmouth and a 1–0 win against Wolves lifted United out of the relegation zone, but failure to win in their next five games, including a 3–1 defeat at Plymouth, dropped United back to third-bottom with just one game to play, away to John Aldridge's Tranmere Rovers. The final match of that sequence, a 1–1 home draw with Ipswich, gave the visitors the Second Division Championship. Oxford were one point behind Plymouth, two behind Newcastle and three adrift of Grimsby and Sunderland. There were 2,000 Oxford fans at Prenton Park to cheer on Oxford against Tranmere, and they were rewarded with a 2–1 win thanks to goals from John Durnin and Joey Beauchamp, aided by some excellent goalkeeping from Paul Kee and an overall battling team performance. John Aldridge, in scoring Tranmere's equaliser, equalled the club goalscoring record with 40 goals for the season. Oxford were still dependent on results elsewhere going their way, and with Grimsby and Newcastle both winning their games there followed an agonising wait for the result from Home Park, where Plymouth were playing Play-off hopefuls Blackburn in a game that was late to end. Eventually the news came through that a David Speedie hat-trick had earned Blackburn a 3–1 win, and United's fans and players celebrated an unlikely escape from relegation.

At the start of the season Steve McClaren was appointed coach for the youth team and reserves, while continuing to play for the first team. Among the season's intake of new trainees was Bobby Ford, while Chris Allen was one of four new professionals taken on. During the summer Alan Judge moved to Hereford and Richard Hill left for Kettering, both on free transfers, Martin Foyle joined Port Vale for £375,000 and scored twice against Oxford in the opening game of the season. Trevor Aylott joined from Birmingham on loan before joining permanently, while Mark Stein moved to Stoke, initially on loan before signing for £100,000. Other incoming loanees included Brett Williams from Nottingham Forest, John Keeley from Oldham and Gary Bannister from West Brom. Lee Nogan joined Watford for £275,000 in December, while Paul Simpson left for Derby for £500,000 in February. On 5 May United released skipper Steve Foster, who went to Brighton.

If this was a significant season for United on the pitch, there were even more momentous events taking place off it. On 5 November Robert Maxwell went missing from his yacht the *Lady Ghislaine* in the Canary Islands, and his body was found shortly afterwards by a local fisherman. Although Maxwell had left Oxford to take over at Derby, he was still the club's major shareholder, with 89.5 per cent of the club's shares. Kevin Maxwell remained as chairman, but with United estimated to be losing £12,000 a week there was uncertainty that the finances would be available to keep the club running. In

December, as the full extent of Robert Maxwell's financial status was becoming clearer, Kevin Maxwell announced that the family would no longer be able to support the club's losses. Director Paul Reeves resigned from the board on 15 November, with Jim Hunt following on 3 December, Albert Ramsay the following day and Geoff Coppock and Ghislaine Maxwell resigning two days later. This left Kevin Maxwell as the sole director. In March Pat McGeough was made managing director.

On 1 May it was announced that new buyers had been found for the club, and on 15 May it was revealed that the new owners were Jardine Matheson, an offshore trading company specialising in the energy business. Jardine Matheson, registered in the tax haven of Bermuda, were owners of Energy Holdings Ltd, who themselves controlled Biomass Recycling Ltd, the company named as the purchaser of Maxwell's shareholding. Pat McGeough was installed as United's new chairman, with Keith Cox, a Biomass director and solicitor, becoming the club's managing director. Also on the new-look board were Cox's partner in his legal firm Martin Clitheroe and Paul Lowe, a local solicitor. United also appointed an environmental director in the form of the Biomass managing director Tim Midgley, who took over as chairman from McGeough in June. It was Lowe's approach to Midgley that led to Biomass buying Maxwell's shares.

During the summer, United's plans to build a new stadium at Watlington Road were thrown out after an appeal, with the government inspector unhappy at the ancillary developments considered necessary by the club to fund the project. Because the stadium was located in the Green Belt, the planning application was subject to more stringent checks, and the inspector said that he felt the club had not considered all the available alternative sites in the area.

After the trauma of the previous season, 1992–93 started fairly quietly with a 2–1 win over Bristol Rovers and a 3–1 aggregate win over Swansea in the first round of the Coca-Cola Cup (the new name for the League Cup). United were beaten 3–1 by Swindon in the preliminary round of the new Anglo-Italian Cup and on 15 September they beat Cambridge United 3–0 at the Manor. Five days later United drew 2–2 at Swindon, with David Penney scoring a late spectacular equaliser in United's first League game to be televised live. United were beaten 4–2 on aggregate by Aston Villa in the second round of the Coca-Cola Cup, and they also lost 2–0 at Brentford in the Anglo-Italian tournament, which ensured that they would take no further part in that short-lived competition. After the second leg at Villa Park, United went seven games unbeaten to climb to 13th in the table. This run started with a 1–0 televised win at Derby, in which diminutive goalkeeper Paul Reece won the Man of the Match award in his third appearance. The run included United's highest-scoring League draw, 5–5 against Portsmouth, in which Oxford were 5–2 down and they were still two goals adrift in the final minute before a Jim Magilton penalty and Chris Allen's last-second header. The run climaxed with a 3–0 win at Southend and a 4–0 win over Luton, in which John Durnin scored all four goals, before United lost 5–3 at West Ham. Oxford ended 1992 with a 4–2 win over Newcastle United.

The New Year started with a 1–1 draw at Swansea in the FA Cup third round, followed by a 1–0 home defeat by Swindon before losing the replay to Swansea in a penalty shoot-out after a 2–2 draw. United then lost 4–0 at Tranmere before a 2–2 draw at Cambridge, enlivened by defender Mike Ford scoring two spectacular long-range goals. Wins against Millwall, Bristol Rovers and Wolves left United in 12th place, before a run of five consecutive defeats dropped the Us to 16th, just four points above the relegation zone. A 1–0 win over West Ham was followed by three more defeats, but a 1–0 win at Barnsley, United's first win at Oakwell, ensured the club's safety from relegation with three games still to play. United finished the season in 14th place.

There was only a small amount of pre-season transfer activity. Dave Collins joined on a free transfer from Liverpool, while Jon Narbett came from Hereford for £65,000 and Nick Cusack arrived from Darlington for £95,000. Meanwhile Peter Rhoades-Brown, playing non-League football, joined the club as football in the community officer. Paul Reece joined on a three-month deal after being released by Grimsby, Matt Murphy joined from Corby Town for £20,000, while Imre Varadi played on loan from Leeds United. In March United turned down a £1 million bid from Premier League Wimbledon for Joey Beauchamp.

In February Geoff Coppock was appointed as a 'special independent' director, with a remit to give fans a direct link to the board. A new company called Oxford United Recycling put in a tender for the metal recycling business of Unipart, the club's sponsors. A new video screen scoreboard was erected at the rear of the Cuckoo Lane end and smaller screens were installed in the roof of the London Road stand at a cost of £135,000. In July 1993 Midgley resigned from the board after failing to buy the club from Energy Holdings, spending £120,000 on an unrealistic proposal to relocate the club to Kidlington and opposition in the boardroom to his 'all or nothing' green policies.

United started their centenary season, 1993–94, with a 3–2 win over Portsmouth, but they then lost the next four games, including a 2–1 defeat at Bristol City in the Anglo-Italian Cup. United received a shock after their 3–2 home defeat by Watford on 28 August, when Brian Horton left for Manchester City, taking David Moss with him to be his assistant. Maurice Evans took charge, along with Steve McClaren, for the next two games as caretaker, before Denis Smith was appointed ahead of favourite Peter Withe, bringing in Malcolm Crosby as his assistant. His first game in charge was a 4–2 win over his previous employers, Bristol City. United lost the next four games, including elimination from the Anglo-Italian Cup against Portsmouth (2–0) and defeat at Tranmere in the first leg of the Coca-Cola Cup (5–1). On 16 October Oxford were beaten 6–1 at Southend, in which Shrimpers striker Tommy Mooney scored a hat-trick. Wins over Derby and Leicester were followed by a run of nine League games without victory, although they did beat Tranmere 2–0 in the FA Cup third round, to leave United second from bottom, two points behind Barnsley and Watford.

In the fourth round of the FA Cup United were held 2–2 at home by Premier League Leeds after Oxford were leading 2–0 at half-time. Before the replay United lost 3–0 at Luton, but at Elland Road the side put their League form to one side as they again stormed into a 2–0 lead. Leeds hit back with two late goals, and but for a splendid save by Phil Whitehead they would have won the tie, but in the second period of extra-time Jim Magilton lobbed Warren Feeney to give United a 3–2 win. In the League Oxford lost 4–0 at the Manor to Charlton before welcoming Chelsea in the FA Cup fifth round. Joey Beauchamp gave Oxford a first-half lead, but Chelsea hit back with two goals. Oxford were awarded a late penalty, but regular penalty-taker Jim Magilton had been transferred to Southampton before the game, so captain Mike Ford took responsibility, smashing the spot-kick against the bar. United's form picked up after this, and by the time they beat Wolves 4–0, in Graham Taylor's first game in charge on 4 April, they were out of the bottom three. However, a run of four games without a win plunged them back into the mire, and although they again pulled themselves out of the relegation zone by beating Sunderland 3–2, a 2–1 defeat at Derby meant they required an unlikely sequence of results to stay up on the last day of the season. Oxford did their bit by beating Notts County 2–1, with Beauchamp scoring a wonder goal, but with Birmingham and West Brom also winning Oxford were relegated in 23rd place, two points from safety.

Before the start of the season Ken Veysey had left for Exeter and the long-serving Les Phillips joined Northampton. John Durnin moved to Portsmouth for £200,000 and Andy Melville moved to Sunderland for £500,000 plus left-back Anton Rogan. Ceri Evans decided to quit professional football and act as a 'locum' doctor in London. During the season Jim Magilton joined Southampton for £600,000 while Paul Kee spent a month on loan at his former club Ards and later joined Reading on loan, Matt Murphy was loaned to Kettering, Nick Cusack went on loan to Wycombe and Dave Penney joined Swansea, initially on loan but signing permanently at the end of the season for £20,000. Alex Dyer joined on a free transfer from Charlton at the start of the season. At the end of September Phil Whitehead joined on loan from Barnsley, and that deal was made permanent for £75,000 at the start of November, at the same time that John Byrne joined from Millwall for £50,000 and four days later Matt Elliott signed from Scunthorpe for £150,000. On 21 February United signed Southampton striker Paul Moody for £60,000. Carl Saunders played on trial from Bristol Rovers, while Jimmy Carter came on loan from Arsenal, along with the unplayed Scott Marshall. In March Joey Beauchamp rejected a £1 million move to West Ham.

During the season Energy Holdings Ltd, run by the Jersey-based Alan Corbett, loaned the club £1.2 million in order to meet United's debts. This was on top of £1.1 million owed to the bank and another £1 million that appeared in the accounts as a loan from PH (US) Inc, one of Robert Maxwell's companies. Meanwhile, the club had identified a site on Sandy Lane, adjacent to a new Tesco supermarket, for a 15,000 all-seater stadium. At the end of the season an exhibition was hosted in the Museum of Oxford to celebrate the club's centenary year. One unpopular end-of-season move was to relocate the club shop from the corner of Osler Road and London Road to within the Score Sports shop further up London Road.

United got off to a flyer at the start of the 1994–95 season, remaining unbeaten until October and winning their first six games, including knocking Peterborough out of the Coca-Cola Cup 4–1 on aggregate. John Byrne scored a hat-trick in the opening 4–0 win over Hull, and Paul Moody replicated the feat in a 3–1 win at Cardiff. United drew 1–1 with Oldham in the first leg of the second round of the Coca-Cola Cup, and after beating Orient 3–2 they drew 2–2 with Bristol Rovers in the first round of the Auto Windscreens Shield, which was the sponsor's name for the Associate Members' Cup. United were top, a point clear of Huddersfield, when they visited Chester City, bottom of the table and without a win, on 1 October, but United were beaten 2–0. They were then eliminated from the Coca-Cola Cup with a 1–0 defeat at Oldham. After United drew 0–0 at Bournemouth in the Auto

Windcreens Shield the club suffered what could be considered its worst result since turning professional when the Us were knocked out of the FA Cup first round 2–0 at Marlow, then occupying the third-bottom place in the Isthmian League Premier Division (then called the Diadora League) and without a home win. John Caesar scored both goals. What made it worse for United was that Marlow were managed by old-boy Peter Foley and included in their side former players Les Phillips and Peter Rhoades-Brown, who was still United's community officer. Ceri Evans was also a Marlow player, but he missed this game with a knee injury.

After the Marlow debacle, United won their next four games, including a 2–1 victory at Brentford in the Auto Windscreens Shield second round, to go back to the top of the League. On Boxing Day United won 4–1 at Peterborough to go three points ahead of Birmingham. However, they lost the next game 2–0 at home to Wycombe in the sides' first League meeting, and that heralded a run of 10 games without a win, including five consecutive defeats and being knocked out of the Auto Windscreens Shield by Swansea City, to drop the Us to eighth. A 1–0 win over Chester was the first of six unbeaten games that took Oxford back to third, but with United winning just two of their last 10 games, they fell away to finish in seventh place.

Before the start of the season Joey Beauchamp completed his move to West Ham for £1 million. He played in one game for the Hammers, a friendly at Oxford City, before informing his new manager Harry Redknapp that he had made a mistake and wanted to leave. West Ham had no choice but to sell him, and he joined Swindon for £800,000. Gary Smart, Paul Kee and Jon Narbett left on free transfers. Arrivals included Dave Smith from Norwich for £100,000, and free transfers Stuart Massey from Crystal Palace and Steve Wood from Southampton. Paul Reece left for Notts County, to be replaced by Mark Deegan. Paul Powell was one of the new first-year trainees, along with Elliot Jackson. During the season David Rush joined from Sunderland for £100,000, and in February Phil Gilchrist arrived from Hartlepool for the same amount. Loan arrivals included Tony Dobson, Guy Butters, Jimmy Carter (again) and Lance Key. John Byrne left on a free transfer to join Brighton for personal reasons.

There was a significant move in United's ongoing search for a new ground, when Oxford City Council identified a site at Minchery Farm, between Blackbird Leys and Littlemore. This came after protests about the proposed site at Sandy Lane, not least from Tesco, who were worried about football fans using their car park. The City Council's planning committee voted to grant outline planning permission for the site on 12 April, with a scheduled opening date of summer 2007. This was ratified at a full council meeting at the start of May. At the end of March Formula 1 racing car designer Robin Herd bought out the Biomass 89.5 per cent shareholding to take over the club, keeping Keith Cox as managing director, while appointing Nick Harris and Geoff Coppock to the board. Denis Smith was promoted to the board and made director of football, while *Raging Bull* fanzine editor Ian Davies joined the backroom staff as club manager, taking on some of Keith Cox's duties.

The 1995–96 season was in some respects the mirror-image of the previous year, with United having a slow start but a great run at the end. Although Oxford were unbeaten at

Chris Allen scores in a 4–0 win over Stockport County on 28 February 1995.

home until a 2–1 defeat by Bristol Rovers on 30 September, away from home United did not record their first League win until the end of January, when they beat Burnley 2–0, by which time United were 14th in the table. In the Cups, United had beaten Hereford 5–2 on aggregate in the first round of the Coca-Cola Cup, but lost 3–2 on aggregate to QPR in the second round. In the Auto Windscreens Shield they beat Bristol City 3–0 in the first round and Barnet 3–2 in the second round, but they lost 2–1 at home to Chesterfield in the third round. In the FA Cup first round Oxford recorded their best result since election to the League when they beat Dorchester Town of the Southern League 9–1, with Paul Moody scoring a hat-trick past former United goalkeeper Ken Veysey. They beat Northampton Town 2–0 in the second round, drew 3–3 at Millwall in the third round, with Bobby Ford scoring direct from a corner in the final minute, before beating them 1–0 in the replay. United drew 1–1 at Premier League Nottingham Forest in the fourth round but lost the replay 3–0.

In the League, United had beaten Carlisle 4–0, lost 4–1 at home to Wycombe Wanderers and beaten Swansea City 5–1, but it was not until a 2–1 win at Carlisle, in which Matt Elliott scored with a 40-yard shot and Martin Aldridge grabbed a last-minute winner, that United turned around their away form. That match was the first of eight without defeat, including a 3–0 win over Swindon, in which the returned Joey Beauchamp scored against his former club, and a 5–0 win over Burnley, in which Paul Moody came off the bench with 15 minutes remaining and scored a hat-trick. A 4–2 defeat at Stockport, for which Matt Elliott was unavailable, was the only blot in United's run in, during which they went unbeaten for their last eight games, winning the last four. Significant results included a 1–0 win over top-of-the-table Blackpool, in which Joey Beauchamp scored a 35-yard volley, later described as the best goal seen at the Manor, a 3–0 win at Wycombe Wanderers, a 6–0 win over Shrewsbury, with all six goals being headers, and a 2–1 win away to Crewe which, because

Joey Beauchamp scores 'The best goal at the Manor': a 35-yard volley against leaders Blackpool on 6 April 1996. (courtesy: Steve Daniels)

it wasn't made all-ticket, saw the away end full an hour and a half before kick-off, with no home supporters yet in the ground. It was in this game that Oxford went above Blackpool into second place, with just one match remaining. The final game of the season, which United needed to win to guarantee promotion, was at home to Peterborough. After a nervy, goalless first half, Oxford eventually took the lead through a Giuliano Grazioli own-goal and went on to win 4–0 to return to the second flight. United's youth team also tasted success, beating Coventry City 3–2 on aggregate to lift the Southern Junior Floodlit Cup, and they also reached the South-East Counties League Cup Final, where they lost 2–1 to Spurs, and finished fourth in the South-East Counties League Division Two.

Mark Angel, Wayne Biggins and Tim Carter all arrived on free transfers during the summer, while Simon Marsh and Danny Cullip signed as professionals. Leaving were David Collins, Mark Deegan, Alex Dyer and Anton Rogan, while Paul Wanless was also released. Steve McClaren left to join Jim Smith at Derby County, to be replaced by former Stafford manager Mark Harrison. Joining during the season were Martin Aldridge from Northampton, Joey Beauchamp, for whom United paid just £75,000 only 14 months after selling him for £1 million, and Martin Gray, who signed from Sunderland for £100,000. Wayne Biggins moved on, as did Paul Milsom, who had made just one substitute appearance, while Chris Allen went on loan to Nottingham Forest.

Things started to move on the new stadium, with the City Council planning committee approving detailed planning permission on 17 November. In February, United appointed Taylor Woodrow to be the construction company, with the construction timetable announced at the start of April and work starting over the summer. Taylor Woodrow, through Cornhill Insurance Services, agreed to ensure that the necessary finances were raised to complete construction, and they introduced Stadivarios to the football club.

Paul Moody with the Oxfordshire Benevolent Trophy after scoring a hat-trick in a 3–2 win over West Ham United on 5 August 1995.

Les Robinson being presented with the Oxfordshire Benevolent Cup after a 2–1 win over Southampton on 8 August 1996.

Oxford United believed that Stadivarios, an Abingdon-based company whose chief executive was Patrick Nally and who were represented by former Oxford player Roy Pack, would inject £8 million as part of a stadium business partner programme. Additional funding was to come from the sale of the Manor and a grant from the Football Trust, but no contracts were signed with Stadivarios. In February the club shop moved back to its original location on the corner of Osler Road.

The 1996–97 season started with a defeat at QPR, but United then beat Southend 5–0 and knocked Norwich out of the Coca-Cola Cup 4–3 on aggregate, winning 3–2 at Carrow Road. In the second round Oxford beat Premier League Sheffield Wednesday 2–1 on aggregate, with former Wednesdayite Nigel Jemson scoring the winning goal at the Manor. Wins over Bradford City, Grimsby and Portsmouth were followed by six games without a win, including a 0–0 draw at Port Vale in the Coca-Cola Cup third round, to leave the Us in 16th place at the end of October. A 4–1 win over Stoke started a run of five successive victories, in which Oxford beat Port Vale 2–0 in the Coca-Cola Cup replay and won 3–2 against Manchester City at Maine Road. United drew 1–1 with Southampton in the Coca-Cola Cup fourth round, with former Saint Paul Moody scoring for Oxford. After a Martin Aldridge hat-trick helped beat Sheffield United 4–1 and took United to fifth place, United lost the replay at Southampton 3–2. United's 2–0 defeat at Watford in the FA Cup third round began a run of four defeats, including a live televised home reverse 4–1 against Manchester City. United also lost 4–1 at home to Crystal Palace. After losing 4–0 at champions-elect Bolton, Oxford beat Swindon 2–0 and ended the season with a 5–1 hammering over Barnsley, newly promoted to the Premiership. United finished the season in 17th place, a comfortable 11 points above the drop zone.

New signings in the summer included Darren Purse, who cost £100,000 from Orient, and Nigel Jemson, signed for £60,000 from Notts County. Paul Powell and Elliott Jackson signed professionally, while new trainees included Rob Folland, Simon Weatherstone and Tony Wright. In March Brian Wilsterman arrived from Belgian club Beerschot for £200,000 and former Leeds defender Chris Whyte joined from Orient. Notable departures before the season started included Chris Allen, signed by Forest for £450,000, and Steve Wood and Danny Cullip, who both left on free transfers. Mark Druce was signed by Rotherham for £50,000 after a successful loan spell there, while in January Matt Elliott joined Leicester City for £1.6 million, a new record sale by Oxford United.

Taylor Woodrow had erected the steelwork on the South, North and East Stand of the Minchery Farm ground, and put in most of the pre-cast concrete terracing units on the South Stand, as well as laid the foundations for the West Stand. However, they abandoned the site in November, having failed to receive payment for the work already carried out. The site for the stadium had initially been purchased by the City Council from Thames Water for £40,000, and a lot of preparatory work had to be done, including removing topsoil, contaminated as a result of sludge disposal from the nearby sewage farm and allowing archaeologists to study artefacts found on the site that related to the former priory adjacent to the site and the Roman pottery industry. The initial archaeological contractor went into liquidation, but further work was undertaken later.

In February 1997 the news broke that Oxford were considering linking with Italian giants Juventus, with Robin Herd claiming that Oxford would be sending its youngsters to Italy to learn the game and that Flavio Briatore's Benetton team, based in Enstone, would invest in Oxford. Briatore denied any knowledge of this, but nevertheless United had a football strip mocked up in Juventus's colours with the Oxford logos.

After beating Huddersfield at home in the opening game, and then knocking Plymouth out of the Coca-Cola Cup 7–3 on aggregate, the 1997–98 season started to go disastrously wrong for United, with four League defeats in succession. A 3–0 win over Wolves temporarily stopped the rot, as did a 6–2 aggregate win over York City in the Coca-Cola Cup second round. Tranmere Rovers were beaten on a penalty shoot-out in the third round, but after a 1–0 win over Ipswich the Us went eight games without a win, including elimination from the Coca-Cola Cup 2–1 at home by Ipswich. That run also included a 4–1 home defeat by Middlesbrough. After losing 4–1 at Swindon, United beat QPR 3–1 in a live TV game at which United supporters held up SOS cards, distributed by the fanzines, to show their support for the club. On Christmas Eve Denis Smith left for West Brom, to be replaced by Malcolm Crosby. Crosby's reign started with a 1–0 defeat at Wolves on Boxing Day, and Oxford were then knocked out of the FA Cup 4–0 by Leeds United and followed that with a 5–1 defeat at Huddersfield. After a 2–1 defeat at home to Charlton, which left the club fifth from bottom, Crosby resigned to join Smith at West Brom. Malcolm Shotton, formerly assistant manager at Barnsley, was appointed Oxford's new manager following a fans' campaign, led by Neil Wakefield and supported by the *Rage On* fanzine, to get the former United captain appointed.

Shotton's first game in charge was an emotional 1–0 win over Portsmouth, followed by a 3–1 win away to Nottingham Forest. Denis Smith's West Brom were beaten 2–1 at the Manor, and after losing 5–2 at Ipswich Oxford then went on a run of five games unbeaten, including a 2–0 win at Manchester City, a 5–1 win over Stoke and a 3–0 win over Reading. Oxford beat Swindon 2–1 before failing to win in their last four games, the last of which, 4–1 at Middlesbrough, saw the home side win promotion to the Premiership. Oxford finished the season in 12th place.

At the start of the 1997–98 season United's reserves played their home games at Witney Town's Marriotts Stadium, the deal having been arranged when it was thought that United would be moving to their new ground this season. In December the deal was scrapped and the reserves moved back to the Manor. New signings at the start of the season were Phil Whelan, who cost £170,000 from Middlesbrough, Christophe Remy and Nick Banger, while Jamie Cook signed as a professional. Paul Moody was sold to Fulham for £200,000. During the season Arjan Van Heusden joined on loan from Port Vale, O'Neill Donaldson came on loan from Sheffield Wednesday, Kevin Francis joined from Birmingham for £100,000 and Steve Davis arrived from Barnsley for £75,000. Bruce Grobbelaar, former Liverpool and Zimbabwe goalkeeper, signed for United, but he left after a week without playing a game. Leaving the club were Bobby Ford, who joined Sheffield United for £400,000, Nigel Jemson, who moved to Bury for £100,000, and Darren Purse, for whom Birmingham paid £500,000.

On 31 October 1997 Robin Herd stood down as chairman, ostensibly to concentrate on engineering projects he was running in the North East. Keith Cox reassumed his position as managing director, and shortly afterwards Maurice Evans was appointed to the board. At the time of Herd's resignation, the club owed Taylor-Woodrow £6 million for the work undertaken on the Minchery Farm site, untouched for almost a year, and the City Council was owed £1.9 million for the land on which the stadium was being built. The club was still losing approximately £15,000 a week and there was still uncertainty about a claim by the receivers looking into the affairs of the late Robert Maxwell, Arthur Anderson, over £5 million allegedly owed by the club.

The FOUL Years

The 1998–99 season began with Oxford making their record signing, buying Dean Windass from Aberdeen for £470,000. Despite Windass having a scoring debut in a 2–2 draw at Bristol City, United were unable to win for their first five League games, and the side was also eliminated from the League Cup, newly renamed the Worthington Cup, in the first round, losing 5–4 on aggregate to Luton after winning 3–2 at Kenilworth Road. United's first win was a 3–0 victory over Portsmouth on 6 September, after which they were beaten 4–1 at Swindon and then suffered a 7–0 defeat at Sunderland, United's heaviest margin of defeat since being beaten 8–1 at Banbury Spencer in September 1945. United bounced back from this humiliation with a 4–1 win over QPR and a Tuesday night 3–0 win over West Brom. This was followed by a run of seven games without a win, culminating with a 2–0 defeat at Watford in which United turned out in the host's away strip, leading to rumours that the club had been forced into administration and had its kit repossessed. In their next game United became the first team to win at Birmingham that season, and they won their next two games, including a 3–1 televised win at Norwich. Oxford then lost four games in a row, including a 7–1 defeat at the Manor by Birmingham, their worst home defeat since Boxing Day 1956. This match was on-loan goalkeeper Mike Salmon's only appearance for the club.

Some good news came with a 3–1 win at Crewe in the FA Cup third round, but by the time Chelsea came to visit in the fourth round Oxford were third from bottom. A crowd of 9,059, producing record gate receipts of £136,423, saw Oxford take the lead against Chelsea through Dean Windass, but with a couple of minutes remaining the visitors were awarded a controversial penalty by referee Mike Reed and scored it to take Oxford to a replay. Oxford again took the lead at Stamford Bridge, through Phil Gilchrist, but Chelsea were too strong and won 4–2, with prospective new owner Firoz Kassam watching from the stands. On 27 February United's home 0–0 draw against Sunderland was the first game to be televised by

Sky TV on a pay-per-view basis. Dean Windass scored twice as Oxford beat Swindon 2–0, but Oxford only won twice more in the 15 remaining games, beating Sheffield United 2–1 at Bramall Lane and then beating Stockport County 5–0 in the last game of the season. However, other results did not go Oxford's way, and they were relegated in 23rd place, three points from safety.

As well as Windass, United signed Danny Hill from Spurs and Andy Thomson from Southend on free transfers. Sam Ricketts and Dean Whitehead were among the new YTS intake. Hill left for Cardiff in November, while in a fire-sale United were forced to sell Phil Whitehead to West Brom for £250,000 and Simon Marsh to Birmingham for the same sum. Other free transfer signings were Canadian international Mark Watson who joined from Swedish side Osters, Paul Tait who signed from Birmingham, and goalkeeper Pal Lundin, a former teammate of Watson's, who joined in April. Loanees included Mark Warren and goalkeeper Paul Gerrard from Everton, who was altogether more successful than Salmon. Mike Ford rejoined Cardiff in August, Dave Smith left for Stockport in February, while Dean Windass was sold to Bradford City for £950,000, plus a further £50,000 after the Bantams were promoted to the Premier League. This sale enabled Oxford to pay Aberdeen the money owed for buying Windass.

The season was one of significant developments regarding the club ownership and the Minchery Farm project. On 1 August it was revealed that a consortium calling itself Grenoble Investments Ltd was in talks with Robin Herd about his 89.2 per cent shareholding. The company had been registered in the Bahamas on 2 January by an organisation named Fonsecca and was fronted by John Gunn, a former chairman of the British & Commonwealth Finance Group, which had gone into administration in 1990 after acquiring Atlantic Computers for £408 million in 1988. Gunn claimed that the consortium, whose sole representative was Martyn Deaner (a former oilman who was declared bankrupt after investing in Newbury Town, leading to the club's closure), was interested in the Minchery Farm site for the potential to develop adjacent land into a leisure complex, but if they were unable to do so they would just walk away. They did just this on 2 November, when they realised the full extent of United's financial problems, with the club £10 million in debt and requiring a further £15 million to complete the stadium.

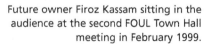

Future owner Firoz Kassam sitting in the audience at the second FOUL Town Hall meeting in February 1999.

Further problems emerged the following day with the news that the playing and non-playing staff had not been paid in October, leading to the players refusing to do any promotional work for the club. The following week the club's directors promised to continue funding, and Lloyds Bank agreed to extend the club's overdraft which, along with assistance from the Professional Footballers' Association, enabled the players to be paid. The backroom staff, who continued to go unpaid, received food parcels from members of the public and national newspapers. In response to the crisis, with local media speculating that it was only a matter of time before the club was put into administration, the *Rage On* fanzine called a meeting, held in the supporters' club, on 10 November for supporters interested in taking action to help save the club. At the meeting a group called FOUL (Fighting for Oxford United's Life) was formed, the name suggested by the *Yellow Fever* fanzine.

FOUL's first act was to hold a public meeting at the Oxford Town Hall, at which over 800 people were present, in order to raise awareness of the club's plight and to seek further input and ideas. FOUL was set up as a campaigning body, while simultaneously a totally separate organisation called SOUS (Save Oxford United Soccer) was formed with the express intent of raising funds for the club. Two initial awareness raising ideas were to try to get Malcolm Shotton voted BBC Sports Personality of the Year (he didn't win, but he received over 3,000 votes, leading to a special feature on *Football Focus*) and an attempt to create a Scarf of Unity by collecting scarves from as many different clubs as possible and stitching them together; the resulting scarf stretched all around the perimeter of the pitch at the Manor, and it was sent around the country to other clubs in danger of folding.

At the same time that negotiations were being held with the Grenoble Consortium, London Irish Rugby Club expressed an interest in taking over the project to complete a 12,000-seat stadium to replace their ground at Sunbury. At the time, the City Council believed that London Irish would have a better chance of completing the deal than Grenoble Investments. FOUL called a second public meeting at the Town Hall in February, at which Keith Cox and council leader John Tanner were due to be questioned. However, Cox resigned on 2 February after a Sunday newspaper ran a story that he was wanted for questioning in Florida about his alleged involvement in fraudulent land deals, although all charges were later dropped. There were a tense few days after Cox's resignation, with no one quite sure what was happening, but then Robin Herd announced that he had signed a heads of agreement with a potential new buyer, London hotelier Firoz Kassam. The open meeting went ahead despite Cox's resignation, and at an emotional event Kassam, who had been sitting quietly in the audience, came on stage and pledged to work with the City Council to save the club. Robin Herd, meanwhile, appointed Oxford solicitor David Bower as acting managing director.

Two weeks after the Town Hall meeting, Firoz Kassam offered the City Council a deal of a 20 per cent stake in the new stadium company in exchange for a deal on the adjoining land, which could then be sold to help finance the stadium construction. Crucial to this going ahead, and to the entire funding of the stadium project, was that planning permission be granted for a multiplex cinema. On 1 April Firoz Kassam completed the purchase of Robin Herd's shares, for which he paid £1 but also took on the club's mounting debts, estimated at £15 million. In May the Football Licensing Authority agreed special dispensation to allow United to remain at the Manor for another season, despite its crumbling concrete terracing and asbestos roofs.

Also in May, Firoz Kassam's company Firoka submitted the planning application for a multiplex cinema adjacent to the stadium site, while a few days later Kassam announced a Company Voluntary Arrangement (CVA) to cut the club's unsecured debts of approximately £9 million to 10p in the pound. This led to the resignation, in June, of the directors remaining from Robin Herd's time (Geoff Coppock, Nick Harris and Maurice Evans) while David Bower refused to join the board after a bust-up with Kassam. A new group of potential buyers made themselves known, consisting of ITV sports reporter Jim Rosenthal, David Bower, plus Chadlington residents George Bailey and Hamish Dewar, dubbed the 'Gang of Four' by the local media. Both this group and Kassam said that they would step down if they failed to receive the support of FOUL, whose committee met with both parties to ascertain their viability. FOUL came out in favour of Kassam, believing that the Gang of Four lacked Kassam's resources. True to their word, the Gang of Four withdrew their bid. In July a creditors' meeting approved the CVA, meaning that all unsecured creditors owed more than £1,000 would receive 10 per cent of what they were owed, while small creditors would receive the full amount. On 12 August 1999 Firoz Kassam was formally appointed as chairman. Before this, in May, Fenton Higgins and Ashwini Tawakley were appointed to the board.

The 1999–2000 season started well enough for United, with new signing Steve Anthrobus scoring the winner at Stoke in the opening game, followed by a 2–0 win at Southend in the Worthington Cup. After Anthrobus was sent off in the 1–0 defeat at Bristol Rovers, United completed the job against Southend, beating them 1–0 at the Manor to progress to the second round, in which they faced Everton. A 1–1 draw at the Manor was followed by Joey Beauchamp scoring the only goal at Goodison for an unlikely victory. After a run of four League games without a win, Oxford beat Bristol City 3–0 at the Manor, thanks to three goalkeeping mistakes. A run of five consecutive defeats saw United knocked out of the Worthington Cup 2–0 at Tranmere and plunged the club into the relegation zone. Malcolm Shotton and Mark Harrison were persuaded to leave by Firoz Kassam, with Mickey Lewis taking over as caretaker.

A 3–2 win over Conference club Morecambe in the FA Cup stopped the rot briefly, with none of the next 10 games ending in defeat. This sequence included a 2–1 win over Shrewsbury in an FA Cup second-round replay, after which Mickey Lewis was appointed first-team coach for the remainder of the season and Ray Harford came in as technical director. United also drew 1–1 at Nottingham Forest in the FA Cup third round and beat Luton 2–0 in the Auto Windcreens Shield first round. A 4–0 defeat at Bournemouth ended the run, and after a Boxing Day win over Cambridge United (1–0) United failed to win any of their next 10 games, apart from a penalty shoot-out win against Wycombe in the Auto Windcreens Shield second round, in which goalkeeper Pal Lundin scored the winning penalty. During this run United were beaten at home by Forest in the FA Cup replay and also lost at the Manor 5–0 to Bristol Rovers and 4–0 to Preston North End, after which Denis Smith returned to manage the club for a second time. In the meantime, six weeks after he arrived, Ray Harford walked out of the club having received no money and not being used. A 1–0 win at Wycombe provided some relief, and eventually Oxford's 2–0 win over Scunthorpe, combined with Cardiff's defeat at Gillingham the following midweek, ensured that Oxford finished fifth from bottom, one point above Cardiff.

In addition to Anthrobus, new players arriving in pre-season included Andre Arendse for £50,000 from Fulham, Derek Lilley from Leeds for £75,000 and Peter Fear from Wimbledon on a free transfer. Leaving were Christophe Remy, Brian Wilsterman, Martin Gray and Andy Thomson. Ross Weatherstone signed as a professional, while first-year scholars included Jamie Brooks, Chris Hackett, Simon King and Phil Wilson. Once the season had started, United signed Neil McGowan from Albion Rovers, Jamie Lambert on trial, Ben Abbey for £30,000, Richard Knight, Nigel Jemson (again) and Eddie Newton. Loanees included Craig Russell and Christian Edwards. After the game at Stoke, Phil Gilchrist was sold to Leicester for £500,000. Jamie Lambert left in December after being unable to agree terms. Chief scout Maurice Evans resigned in November to take up the same post at Reading. The club was shocked to learn of the death of former player Martin Aldridge in a car crash while on loan from Blackpool to Rushden & Diamonds, making the side's next match, at home to Blackpool, very poignant. The club's first manager Harry Thompson died in the same week.

In August 2000 United received outline planning permission for the multiplex cinema after a holding order was lifted. Pentith Development and British Rail Property applied for a judicial review into this decision, as they had earlier been denied planning permission to build a multiplex close to the Westgate Centre, in a much more central location. The application for a judicial review was rejected by the High Court in October, but Nick Pentith appealed against this decision and his appeal in March was upheld. In October the City Council agreed to the proposed land deal at Minchery Farm, finally signing the legally binding agreement in November, almost a year after it was agreed. Also in November, Kassam and Taylor-Woodrow reached a settlement that allowed the construction company to leave the project.

A date of 17 July was set for the hearing of the Pentith judicial review, but in the event it did not go ahead as Nick Pentith and the council reached an agreement over revised development plans for Oxpens Road and Pentith withdrew his application for a judicial review. Meanwhile, the Morrells Brewery revealed that a covenant on the Blackbird pub in Blackbird Leys meant that no other supplier could sell alcohol within half a mile of the pub on land which had been owned by the City Council when the covenant was awarded in 1962, within which distance the new stadium fell. As Morrells declared their intention to uphold the covenant, FOUL called for a boycott of Morrells pubs. The covenant had applied when the pub was owned by the City Council, but a summary judgement declared that the covenant could not be transferred with the land. Morrells appealed against this decision but again they were overruled, and with the brewery not taking the matter to the House of Lords this was another obstacle removed. One consequence of the Morrells episode was that the council withdrew from the deal to buy 20% of the stadium company.

Another potential obstacle to construction work restarting on the stadium concerned another covenant, this time on the land that Thames Water had sold to the council where the stadium and leisure complex were to be built, which stated that the land had to be used for recreational purposes. This had initially been settled by the High Court two years earlier, but the council had refrained from paying Thames Water compensation and were considering appealing against the decision. After intensive lobbying by FOUL, the council, now under the control of the Liberal Democrats, decided not to appeal but to come to a financial settlement. After a summer of successful legal fights, the club received approval from the Football Licensing Authority for another year at the Manor, due to the new stadium plans still progressing.

The 2000–01 season started with four consecutive League defeats, sandwiching a 1–0 win at Wolves in the Worthington Cup, but United lost the second leg 3–1 at the Manor to go out of the competition. After beating Bury 1–0, United took just one point from the next nine games, a run that included a 5–0 defeat at Millwall and 4–3 defeats at home to Wrexham and at Reading. After losing 1–0 at home to Bristol City, Denis Smith resigned, with Mike Ford taking over in a caretaker capacity. Ford's first game was a 2–1 defeat at Swindon. After the defeat at Reading, United announced David Kemp as their new manager, with Alan McLeary his assistant and Joe Kinnear as director of football. United won 1–0 at Macclesfield in the first round of the FA Cup before a run of four defeats, including a 4–1 reverse at Brentford in the LDV Vans Trophy (the new name for the Associate Members' Cup) and a 3–2 FA Cup second-round defeat at Chester after United were 2–0 up. United won just twice in their next 14 games, which included a 5–3 reverse at Wrexham and a 2–0 home defeat by Swindon.

At the end of January Joe Kinnear resigned, citing poor health, only to turn up as Luton's director of football three days later. United beat Rotherham 4–3 and then lost 4–3 at Bournemouth, with Phil Gray scoring after just 11 seconds to set a new record for Oxford since they joined the League. Relegation was confirmed on 7 April with a 1–0 home defeat by Oldham, with seven games still remaining. A 6–2 defeat at Bristol Rovers, who were also under threat of relegation, was marked by the curious sight of a number of Oxford fans cheering on the home team, in the vain hope that Rovers would stay up at Swindon's expense. A 3–1 home win over Swansea was enlivened by vigorous chants of 'Kemp Out' every time Oxford scored. The fans were granted their wish in time for the following match against Brian Horton's Port Vale, the final League game to take place at the Manor. With Mike Ford acting as caretaker, the game finished 1–1, Andy Scott scoring the last Oxford goal at the ground and Vale's Tony Naylor scoring the last goal on the ground in the 90th minute. The season ended with a 2–1 defeat at Notts County, leaving United in 24th place, 10 points below 23rd-placed Swansea, 25 points from safety and having conceded exactly 100 goals. On 13 May there was a farewell to the Manor evening, during which United's Milk Cup-winning team played against the QPR side from that day, and the final match at the Manor was the John Byles Memorial Cup Final between Garden City and Oxford City on 15 May.

Goalkeeper Jimmy Glass, famous for scoring the last-minute goal that kept Carlisle from relegation on 8 May 1999, had joined at the start of the season, as had Manny Omoyinmi, famous for playing for West Ham in the League Cup having already played for Gillingham in the same competition in the same season. Richard Knight signed permanently, Lee Jarman and Jon Richardson joined from Exeter, and John Robertson came from Ayr

United. Mike Ford returned to the club from Cardiff in September to become reserve-team coach. A number of senior professionals departed, including Andre Arendse, Steve Davis, Nigel Jemson, Pal Lundin, Les Robinson and Phil Whelan. New professionals were Chris Hackett, Sam Ricketts and Dean Whitehead. Leon Mike joined from Manchester City on loan, while Guy Whittingham joined on loan from Portsmouth, scoring in his only game for the club, away at Swindon. After Kemp's arrival Keith Brown joined on loan from Barnsley, Keith Andrews signed on loan from Wolves, while Phil Gray joined on a free transfer from Burnley. Wayne Hatswell was signed from Forest Green Rovers, Neil Cutler joined on loan from Aston Villa, Garry Monk joined on loan from Southampton and Andy Scott and Robert Quinn were both signed from Brentford for £75,000 each. In February Darren Patterson joined from York City and was made club captain. Youth player Jonathan Mills was sold to Southampton for £25,000, while £75,000 was realised by the sale of Derek Lilley to Dundee United.

In September 2000 planning permission for the leisure complex adjacent to the new stadium at Minchery Farm was granted, and the following week Firoz Kassam met with contractors Barr Construction. However, a deal with Barr failed to materialise, and on 19 October Kassam announced that Birse Construction were to complete the stadium in time for the start of the next season. At the end of October work started on making the site safe, and in November work started in earnest, including the demolition of a part of the South Stand that had become unsafe in the four years that the part-finished stadium had been unoccupied. In January 2001 Bill Smith was appointed associate director in order to help make executive decisions. In March Kassam announced that he had sold the Manor Ground, although he did not name the buyer until May, when he revealed that his own company, Firoka, had paid £6 million for the ground. This was enough to pay the secured creditors, including Alan Corbett, Robin Herd and the bank. The Acland Hospital submitted a planning application for a new hospital on the site, and St Andrew's School and Headington Library also expressed their interest in moving there. A year later, having secured planning permission for the site, Firoka sold the Manor to Nuffield Nursing Homes, the owners of the Acland Hospital, for £12 million, and the site was redeveloped into a private hospital called the Manor Hospital.

A final issue blocking the go-ahead to recommence construction on the leisure complex concerned landowner Les Wells, who owned land adjacent to the stadium site and who claimed he had a right of way across it. Wells, advised by former United chairman Tim Midgley, eventually settled for £1 million compensation from Firoz Kassam. In addition to the right of way claim, Les Wells was also pursuing a judicial review in an attempt to overturn the multiplex planning permission, disputing that a proper environmental impact assessment had been carried out. The case was due to go to the High Court in the first week of April, but it did not directly threaten the transfer of land from the City Council to Firoka and the stadium, although it did threaten the planning permission for the multiplex, which was required for its funding. Wells had indicated to FOUL that he would drop his legal actions if Kassam paid him enough money.

In 1996 Oxford United, under Keith Cox's control, had originally agreed to buy Wells' land for £380,000 and had already paid him a 10% deposit. Wells was now asking for over

£2 million for his land, which was far more than it was worth. At the end of March a payment was due to stadium developers Birse Stadia of approximately £1.5 million. A week before the payment was due Kassam made an ultimatum to Oxford City Council to agree to a settlement and transfer the land to his stadium company, otherwise the payment would not be made and development would stop. If this were to happen it would mean there would be no chance of United starting the new season at Minchery Farm. Eventually, £1 million was agreed between Wells and Kassam for the land adjacent to the stadium site, in return for which Wells withdrew all legal actions, but the final sticking point was the payment of the council's legal costs of around £60,000. FOUL eventually brokered a deal to split the costs between Wells and the City Council.

The Thames Water issue still needed to be settled. However, the council were able to finalise the legal agreement with Thames Water and, despite a late scare over Thames Water's legal costs, this was completed in time for the deadline. Meanwhile, Kassam paid the Headington Bowls Club £40,000 for an option to release the ground from a restrictive covenant, subject to meeting certain confidential conditions.

In May, Firoz Kassam announced that the new stadium would be called the Kassam Stadium, claiming it was a gesture of his commitment to the club. Mark Wright, who started his career with Oxford United before being sold to Southampton, was named the club's new manager, with Ted McMinn as his assistant. United requested that their first game of the 2001–02 season be away, in order to give them a few extra days to get the new ground ready, but the League denied this request and handed the Us an opening match at home to Rochdale. After failing in attempts to sign David Reeves from Cheltenham and Jim McIntyre from Reading, and holding unsuccessful talks with Neil Ruddock and Dean Saunders, Wright signed Martin Thomas from Brighton, as well as bringing in defenders Phil Bolland and Scott Guyett, whom he had managed at Southport, and spending £150,000 for Sam Stockley from Barnet. Meanwhile, the club was granted only a partial safety certificate for their pre-season friendly with Crystal Palace, meaning that the upper tier of the South Stand, including the directors' box and the executive boxes, would remain closed. United and Palace drew 1–1, with Paul Powell scoring Oxford's first goal at their new home and Oxford winning the following penalty shoot-out to lift the Oxford Benevolent Cup. After impressing in the Palace game, United signed triallist David Savage, although they had already released another triallist, former player John Dreyer.

However, United's League introduction to their new stadium was an unhappy one, losing their first game 2–1 to Rochdale after Jamie Brooks had equalised Matt Doughty's opener. The attendance was 8,842. United also lost their first floodlit game at the Kassam Stadium, beaten 2–1 by Gillingham in the first round of the Worthington Cup. The first win of the season came at Halifax (2–0), followed by the first win at the new ground, 3–2 over Rushden & Diamonds. After a 2–0 home defeat by Macclesfield, United spent £150,000 to bring Paul Moody back to the club from Millwall, with the striker scoring in his first game back, a 2–0 win over Southend. After United lost 2–0 at Northampton in the LDV Vans Trophy, they were beaten 1–0 at home by Scunthorpe on 20 October, during which referee Joe Ross sent Mark Wright to the stands. Wright was later reported by Ross for making racist remarks to the official. Although Wright denied the allegations, on 22 November, with United fourth from bottom of Division Four and knocked out of the FA Cup 1–0 at Mansfield, the Oxford board suspended him and, following a disciplinary hearing, Wright resigned on 30 November.

In the meantime, United had appointed Ian Atkins as director of football but, following Wright's departure, Atkins took over managerial duties, with Oxford beating Cheltenham 3–0 in his first match in charge. On Boxing Day a Kassam Stadium crowd of 11,121 saw United lose 2–1 to second-placed Luton Town. This was followed three days later by a 6–1 demolition of doomed Halifax Town, with Moody scoring a hat-trick. Goalkeeper Andy Woodman was signed from Colchester, but Oxford continued to struggle, winning just four games in the remainder of the season. On 23 February, in a 2–1 defeat by Exeter, Joey Beauchamp played his final game for United, scoring Oxford's goal with a spectacular volley. After beating Hull 1–0, United took just one point from their last six games to finish fourth from bottom, 11 points above relegated Halifax. The last game, a 2–1 defeat by Darlington, saw former Thame United striker Jefferson Louis coming on for his debut. In order to protect the new pitch, the reserves played their home games at Oxford City's Court Place Farm.

At the end of the season it was revealed that, despite receiving £12 million from the sale of the Manor to Nuffield Nursing Homes, Firoka still owed the City Council £494,000 for the land on which the Kassam Stadium had been built, although legal action was postponed while negotiations continued on the value of the Priory pub, which Kassam wanted to buy from the council. In August Kassam paid the council the money owed, plus £16,000 interest, after legal action was launched to recover the money. A car park extension was delayed when it was discovered that water voles, an endangered species, inhabited the part of Northfield Brook where a bridge was to be built. Meanwhile, Kassam tried to bring in Rugby Union side Wasps to groundshare, but they moved to Wycombe Wanderers instead, although the stadium was used to host the Parker Pen European Shield Final between Sale and Pontypridd. The stadium also hosted an Under-17 international tournament that summer, which featured England, Italy, Brazil and the Czech Republic.

The FOUL group officially disbanded on 15 November 2001, as the immediate future of the club appeared to be secure. They were replaced by a new group, a supporters' trust called OxVox, which was formally launched on 21 March 2002, becoming the 50th supporters' trust under the auspices of Supporters Direct, a government body that offers advice to new trusts.

During the summer United signed James Hunt from Northampton, defenders Scott McNiven and Matt Robinson, David Oldfield and striker Lee Steele, as well as bringing back former player Bobby Ford. Steve Basham joined from Preston just before the first game of the season. Scott Guyett, who had been released because he wanted to return to his native Australia, was signed by Chester City, now managed by Mark Wright. Oxford then received bad news when Jamie Brooks was taken into hospital suffering from the debilitating Guillain-Barré Syndrome. At the end of the previous season Brooks had won the Supporters' Player of the Year, the Players' Player of the Year, the Young Player of the Year, and the Sports Writers' Player of the Year, and was due to be offered a trial by Arsenal.

Jamie Brooks celebrates scoring in the first League game at the Kassam Stadium, against Rochdale, on 11 August 2001. (courtesy: Steve Daniels)

The 2002–03 season was notable for two Cup runs. In the Worthington Cup United won 1–0 at Bristol City in the first round and visited Premier League Charlton Athletic in the second round. A strong defensive performance earned the Us a 0–0 draw, and after extra-time produced no more goals Oxford won on a penalty shoot-out, the decisive spot-kick being scored by Jefferson Louis. In the third round, a Kassam Stadium gate of 12,177 saw United lose 3–0 to Aston Villa. United's FA Cup run started with a 2–0 win at Dover Athletic. Their second-round tie at home to Swindon Town was chosen by the BBC to be shown live, and with 11,655 in the ground Jefferson Louis was once more the hero, scoring the only goal. When Oxford were drawn at Arsenal in the third round, TV viewers saw Gunners fan Louis dance naked around the dressing room. United scored in the second minute at Highbury, but the goal was disallowed (wrongly) for offside and the home side went on to win 2–0, with Dennis Bergkamp scoring his 100th goal for Arsenal. Oxford's League campaign ended in disappointment, with the side just missing out on the Play-offs by one point, despite beating York 2–0 in the final game.

After the season finished Paul Powell was told that he would not be having his contract renewed, while goalkeeper Ian McCaldon was also released. New signings included Derek Townsley and strikers Julian Alsop and Mark Rawle. Paul McCarthy joined from Wycombe and Danny Brown arrived from Barnet. Dave Savage, the Supporters' Player of the Season, left for Bristol Rovers following his disparagement at not being offered a new contract. When the *Oxford Mail* reported this, reporter Jon Murray was banned from the stadium, although this was rescinded three months later. Bobby Ford left to join Bath City, while other former youth players Sam Ricketts and Simon King both moved on.

The 2003–04 season started well for Oxford, who went unbeaten in their first nine games, including winning 1–0 at Millwall in the first round of the League Cup, now renamed the Carling Cup. Oxford beat Swansea City 3–0, with all three goals coming in the last five minutes, and substitute Mark Rawle scored with his first touch on his debut, 17 seconds after coming on. The run ended with a 2–0 defeat at Doncaster, after which United were beaten 3–1 at home by Reading in the Carling Cup second round. A 1–0 defeat at Colchester in the first round of the FA Cup failed to halt Oxford's momentum in the League, and after winning 1–0 at Southend on 28 December Oxford were top of the Division, two points above Doncaster and four points above third-placed Hull. However, United lost momentum and after losing 4–2 at Hull Oxford dropped to third and gradually fell away from the title race. Oxford's promotion push was further disrupted when Firoz Kassam suspended manager Ian Atkins for allegedly talking to Bristol Rovers about a move there the following season. Atkins' last game for Oxford was, like his first, a win over Cheltenham. David Oldfield was appointed caretaker manager, but his only game in charge, at Mansfield, was abandoned at half-time because of high winds. On 22 March Graham Rix was appointed as Atkins' successor, initially on a temporary basis, and in his first game Oxford drew 0–0 with League-leaders Doncaster, with debutant goalkeeper Simon Cox winning the Man of the Match award. However, Rix failed to win any of his first nine games in charge, only breaking his duck with a 2–0 win over Rochdale in the final game of the season. This left Oxford finishing ninth, three points away from the Play-offs.

Dean Whitehead celebrates a goal against Bury on 21 February 2004. Celebrity Joan Collins was among the spectators for the 1–1 draw. (courtesy: Steve Daniels)

Despite this poor finish, Rix was surprisingly retained for the 2004–05 season. Tommy Mooney was the surprise signing at the start of the season, the former Swindon player joining on a free transfer, while Barry Quinn, who had a loan spell at the end of the previous season, was signed permanently. Also joining were Lee Bradbury from Walsall, Dave Mackay, Terry Parker, Leo Roget, David Woozley and Danny Morgan. A pre-season friendly against Chelsea, in their first game under Jose Mourinho's management, ended 1–1 and was watched by 11,282. The season started promisingly enough, with Oxford losing just the first of their opening eight League games, although they were knocked out of the Carling Cup 2–0 at home to Reading in the first round. This sequence came to a shuddering halt with a 6–1 defeat at Yeovil. A 3–0 win over Bury was followed by a penalty shoot-out defeat at home to Exeter in the LDV Vans Trophy, before United lost their next five games. A 1–0 win over Cheltenham was followed by a 4–0 defeat at Southend, in which goalkeeper Alan Judge became the oldest player to turn out for Oxford, aged 44 years and 176 days. A 2–1 defeat at Rochdale in the first round of the FA Cup signalled the end of Graham Rix's time at Oxford, with Darren Patterson appointed caretaker for the next three games. With the local media anticipating Chris Turner to be the new manager, Firoz Kassam surprised everyone with the announcement that the new manager was to be Ramon Díaz, a World Cup-winning player for Argentina and one of the most successful managers that country had produced. Díaz initially joined for six months.

The arrival of Díaz was brokered by Jean-Marc Goiran, a businessman from Monaco, where Kassam had relocated for tax reasons. Díaz brought with him a large team of backroom staff, including Goiran, Horacio Rodriguez as coach, Raoul Marcovic as his assistant, Dr Rafael Giuilietti, physical trainer Paolo Fernandez and translator Giulliano Iacoppi. The following day Brendon Cross, Bill Smith and Lord Faulkner of Worcester revealed that they were in talks with Kassam, representing a consortium interested in buying the club. All three men were former associate directors who had left the board in May 2004, after Kassam had asked them to invest £25,000 each to keep their positions.

Díaz's first game in charge was a 2–1 win over Cambridge United, in which Craig Davies was given his first start and scored. He then tried to sign defender Bruno Rodriguez but could not afford his wage demands, so his first signing was Doudou, a diminutive Congolese winger. Doudou played just one half for Oxford before returning to DRC for family reasons. Other players brought in by the new management included Mateo Corbo, Lucas Cominelli, Juan Pablo Raponi, Amine Karam and Ramon's son Emiliano. Behind the scenes things were not too rosy, though, as both Díaz and Rodriguez had to spend time away to sort out work permit issues, with David Oldfield taking charge for the games they missed. There was also growing friction between Goiran and Kassam, with Goiran claiming that he was looking to buy the club and Kassam claiming at the AGM in March that the club was not for sale. Talks between Kassam and the management team continued but broke down when Kassam refused to offer Díaz a contract for the following season, although it appeared at first that Rodriguez would be kept on as Díaz's replacement with a two-year contract. On 5 May relations broke down irrevocably, and at the last game of the season, at home to Chester on 7 May, there were extraordinary scenes as Díaz, Goiran and Rodriguez tried to gain access to the East Stand but were denied by stewards, acting under instruction from Kassam. David Oldfield took charge for the game, a 1–0 defeat, with Brian Talbot introduced to the crowd as the next manager for the following season.

Talbot's first signings were Chris Willmott from Northampton, and Stuart Gray and goalkeeper Billy Turley from his former club Rushden & Diamonds. Meanwhile, all the foreign players brought in by Díaz left the club, as did Paul Wanless and Danny Brown. Tommy Mooney was offered a new contract, but he rejected it and left for Wycombe. Lee Mansell arrived to replace the departing Dave Mackay, while Terry Parker had his contract

An exotic Oxford United bench for a 2–1 win against Southend United on 23 April 2005. From left: Bradie Clarke, Billy Beechers (hidden), Dr Rafael Giuilietti, Lee Molyneaux (partly hidden), Paolo Fernandez, Juan Pablo Raponi, Horacio Rodriguez, Giuliano Iacoppi, Emiliano Díaz. (courtesy: Steve Daniels)

cancelled after being sent to prison for 18 months for assault. Chris Hargreaves arrived from Brentford, Jude Stirling joined on a short-term contract, as did Rob Hughes after impressing while playing against United for Yeading during a pre-season friendly. Also during the summer, former FOUL chairman Steve Hanks was appointed as general manager.

United started the 2005–06 season looking reasonably comfortable, and after beating Carlisle 1–0 on 7 October they were sixth, although they had been eliminated from the Carling Cup 1–0 at Gillingham. Orient's visit in the LDV Vans Trophy resulted in a record low crowd for the Kassam Stadium, with just 1,521 turning up. In the FA Cup United were held to a 1–1 draw at Conference South Eastbourne Borough, but a Steve Basham hat-trick eased the Us into the second round. Eastbourne's Yemi Odubade impressed United enough for the club to sign him during the January transfer window for £15,000, and Talbot also raided his old club to sign Andy Burgess for £35,000 and John Dempster for £10,000, and he bought Tim Sills from Aldershot for £35,000. Also in January, Lee Bradbury left United after Talbot refused to play him, as his 25th League appearance would have triggered a clause in his contract offering him an automatic extension for the following season. Meanwhile Craig Davies was sold to Verona for £85,000 and Chris Hackett joined Hearts for £20,000.

Cheltenham knocked United out of both the FA Cup and the LDV Vans Trophy, after which the club went on a run of 10 games without a win, leaving them 18th and just five points above the relegation zone. At a fans' forum in February, Kassam claimed that he would not separate the club and stadium but would sell both as a package, if he sold at all. In March David Oldfield left the club after Talbot asked him not to be involved on match days, followed a few days later by Jon 'Woosie' Edmunds, the assistant physio. Steve Hanks also left the club. At the same time, Firoz Kassam was in talks with former youth-team player Nick Merry about selling the club, with Kassam initially refusing Merry's overtures and installing former directors Bill Smith and Brendon Cross to run the club on a day-to-day basis. Their first action was to sack Talbot and install youth-team coach Darren Patterson as manager until the end of the following season, with the intention to appoint Jim Magilton as Patterson's assistant.

Patterson's first game in charge was at home to Bristol Rovers, which United won 1–0. Before the game there was a demonstration outside the ground against Firoz Kassam, while simultaneously representatives from OxVox and other supporters held a meeting with Smith and Cross to put forward the fans' views. Meanwhile, Merry announced that he was withdrawing his bid for the club as Kassam was not prepared to accept his offer, adding caveats to the agreed price. At this time OxVox announced that they would be calling the ground the United Stadium in a protest against Kassam's continued intransigence. On 21 March Kassam sold Oxford United, but not the Kassam Stadium, to Woodstock Partners Ltd, a consortium fronted by Merry, for £1, with the consortium taking on the club's £2 million of debts. Jim Smith was installed as manager, with Patterson offered the option of returning to the youth-team role. Smith was also made a director, along with Kelvin Thomas, an associate of Merry's based in Florida. With the takeover concluded the day before the transfer deadline, Smith acted promptly to sign Scot Gemmill as player-coach and also brought in a number of loan players, including goalkeeper Andrea Guatelli and Liam Horsted from Portsmouth, Tcham N'Toya and Jay Smith. The first game under the new ownership was an emotional 1–0 win over Peterborough, with N'Toya scoring the winning goal. After defeat at Mansfield, his only appearance, Gemmill left for a coaching role in New Zealand. United lost the next two games, and despite beating Barnet 2–0 they failed to win any of their last four games and were relegated to the Conference, leaving the Football League 44 years after joining it. The final game, at home to Orient, was watched by a near-capacity 12,243, setting a new ground record, with Orient's 3–2 win sealing promotion for them as well as Oxford's demotion.

During the close season, Smith brought in a number of new players, the most significant of which was probably former Us defender Phil Gilchrist. Also joining were former Oxford trainee Eddie Odhiambo-Anaclet, Eddie Hutchinson, who rejected a deal with Swindon to sign for United, Gavin Johnson, Rob Duffy, Matt Day and Carl Pettefer. None of the players who had joined on loan at the end of the previous season were retained, while Eric Sabin retired and Supporters' Player of the Season Lee Mansell moved to Torquay, who had avoided relegation at Oxford's expense under their manager Ian Atkins. United announced that reserve games from next season would be played at Didcot Town's Loop Meadow. On 8 August 2006 a pre-season friendly against a Manchester United side that included Cristiano Ronaldo attracted a crowd of 11,463 to watch Oxford lose 4–1.

The 2006–07 season started spectacularly well for United, who set a new Conference record by going unbeaten in their first 19 games. By the time of their first League defeat, 1–0 at Gravesend & Northfleet, United led the table by five points from Dagenham & Redbridge. United were knocked out of the FA Cup in the first round, 2–1 at Wycombe, having beaten Dagenham & Redbridge 1–0 away in the fourth qualifying round, the first time that United had played at that stage of the competition since 1961. On Boxing Day a new record attendance for a Conference game of 11,065 saw a 0–0 draw with Woking at the Kassam Stadium. On New Year's Day an injury-ridden Oxford lost 2–1 at Exeter, allowing Dagenham to overtake them for the first time. An 11-game run without a win in the Conference left United seven points behind the Daggers, and Oxford remained in second place for the remainder of the season, although by the end they were ahead of Morecambe only on goal difference, with Dagenham 14 points ahead. This earned Oxford their first experience of the Play-offs. United won 1–0 at Exeter in the first leg, thanks to an own-goal by Andy Taylor, while Yemi Odubade and loanee Chris Zebroski missed good chances to extend the lead. In the second leg Odubade put United 2–0 ahead on aggregate, but goals from Lee Phillips and Adam Stansfield, combined with a glaring miss from Rob Duffy, took the tie to extra-time and then penalties. Oxford lost the penalty shoot-out, with Billy Turley and Zebroski both hitting the post.

In April Oxford released Jim Smith's assistant Andy Awford and reserve-team coach Shaun North, with Darren Patterson promoted in Awford's place. In May former coach Mickey Lewis was appointed to run the youth team, which, under Darren Patterson, won the Puma Youth Alliance League title without losing a game. The management team took the decision to withdraw the reserve team from competitive games following a disastrous season which had seen the side, comprising mainly first-team players recovering from injury or youth-team players gaining additional experience, gain just seven points in their

United fans unveil their giant flag at the Boxing Day game against Woking in 2006, the game producing a record crowd for a Conference fixture. (courtesy: Steve Daniels)

18 Pontins Holiday Combination games. During the season Rufus Brevett was signed to stand in for the injured Gavin Johnson, while Latvian international Kristaps Grebis was brought in on the recommendation of a contact of Jim Smith's. Luke Foster joined from Stalybridge after a short trial following a letter from his father to Jim Smith. Danny Rose joined on loan from Manchester United, where he had been captain of the reserves, while other players to feature included Martin Foster, Georges Santos and Michael Corcoran, whose loan deal expired just before the Play-offs started. In April 2007 the club held a fans' forum, in which Ian Lenagan, the main force behind WPL, informed attendees that director Kelvin Thomas was to return to Florida. A backroom reshuffle was also announced, with Ian's son Simon Lenagan becoming the club's youth and community general manager, while Mick Brown was promoted to the new position of general manager. It was also revealed that WPL had agreed a fee of £13 million with Firoz Kassam to buy the stadium and conference centre, and they were seeking partners to fund the enterprise.

New signings for the 2007–08 season included Alex Jeannin from Hereford, Gary Twigg and Joel Ledgister. Steve Basham left at the end of the season, while Danny Rose signed a one-year deal after being released by Manchester United and then rejected by Bristol Rovers, and Michael Corcoran also signed a permanent contract, with Phil Trainer signing from Moor Green.

The side had a less-than-impressive start to the season, and following a 5–0 reverse at Rushden on 1 November, live on TV, United stood 10th in the table. After this, Jim Smith took the decision to step down from team management, while remaining a director, and Darren Patterson took over. Patterson had a slow start, with Oxford being knocked out of

United fans welcome the team onto the pitch before playing Torquay United on 28 February 2009. (courtesy: Steve Daniels)

the FA Cup 3–0 at Southend in a second-round replay and also eliminated from the FA Trophy 1–0 at Tonbridge Angels. After an appalling January in which United earned just one point from five games, results picked up and Oxford won nine of their last 11 matches to climb from 15th to finish ninth. During the season United had used a record 41 players, many of whom were youth-teamers or short-term loanees. Big successes were Adam Murray from Macclesfield and Matt Green on loan from Cardiff, who scored 10 goals in 16 starts. Phil Gilchrist retired after the Rushden defeat. A new group was formed called Ultimate Yellows with the aim of improving the atmosphere at the Kassam Stadium.

After the season finished, Patterson was unable to retain the nucleus of the side that had finished so strongly, with Matt Green signing for Torquay on the morning that he was due to join Oxford, while he allowed Craig McAllister to leave for Exeter and did not sign left-back Michael Howard from Morecambe, opting instead to bring in Chris Carruthers from Bristol Rovers. With a restricted budget, Patterson brought in three players on season-long loans in strikers James Constable from Shrewsbury and Jamie Guy from Colchester, and winger Lewis Haldane from Bristol Rovers. Also joining were midfielder Joe Burnell from Northampton, and Rob Davies, Michael Husbands and Levi Reid on short-term contracts.

United had a poor start to the 2008–09 season, winning just one of their opening six games, a 6–3 win over Eastbourne Borough. Although home form picked up, on the road Oxford won just one League game (2–1 at Northwich Victoria) before the end of November. On 2 October Nick Merry resigned as chairman, although he remained on the board, and Kelvin Thomas returned from Florida to take over. Jim Smith retired from being a director on 10 November.

James Constable scores against Grays Athletic on 14 March 2009. (courtesy: Steve Daniels)

A 2–0 defeat at Torquay in the FA Cup second round, with the side languishing in 14th place, led Kelvin Thomas to end Patterson's time as manager, and Jim Smith returned in a caretaker capacity while a recruitment process was started. Smith's side was unbeaten in his four games in charge before the appointment of former Halifax manager Chris Wilder was announced. Wilder's first game was a Boxing Day defeat at Salisbury in which Sam Deering broke his leg, after which the side went unbeaten for nine Conference games and rose to seventh, just two points off the Play-offs. However, on 12 January it was revealed that Eddie Hutchinson, transfer-listed by Darren Patterson, had not been properly registered with the Conference and United were deducted five points and fined £500.

After the Salisbury defeat, United were unbeaten away from home and lost just two home games (plus an FA Trophy defeat by York). This run took the Us to the edge of the Play-offs, which they missed, on the last day of the season, by just four points, finishing seventh. United's reserves won the Oxfordshire Senior Cup, beating Banbury United 2–1 in the Final.

At the end of the season Chris Wilder signed a new three-year contract. Oxford signed Constable on a three-year deal for an undisclosed fee, and they also signed Kidderminster defender Mark Creighton for an undisclosed fee and signed 22-goal striker Jack Midson from Histon. The released list included three of the club's longest-serving players: Barry Quinn, Chris Willmott and Yemi Odubade, while Eddie Hutchinson and Matt Day were also let go. Constable won his third England C cap, and his second while at Oxford, on 19 May in the International Challenge Trophy Final, held at the Kassam Stadium. Belgium won the game 1–0.

Stadia History

Early Days (1893–1925)

For the club's first season (1893–94), home games were played at Quarry Recreation Ground. Although contemporary maps do not mark the site of the ground, it is reasonable to assume from later maps that this occupied the same site as the current recreation ground, between Margaret Road and Ramsay Road. There were some troublesome encounters between the inhabitants of Headington and the Quarry over use of this field as a football pitch, with Quarry youths chasing away those from Headington who had the audacity to try and play there: 'They used to come across – if you weren't pretty smart, your football would disappear pretty quick. They'd just take the ball away from you. P'raps about six or eight'd come running across, and if you kicked the ball where they were that ball just disappeared – they pinched the ball and went back towards Quarry.' (Jackson's *Oxford Journal*, 25 January 1898)

However, the field there was inadequate for football, with the corners only being about 27 yards from the goals.

The following season, the club's first as a League team, the club moved closer to their Headington roots, playing at Wootten's Field, part of the estate of the Wootten-Woottens of Headington House. This was to the east of Sandy Lane (now Osler Road) on the site where the Stephen Road development was later built.

The side played at Wootten's Field for four years before moving to Sandy Lane, which occupied virtually the same site as the Manor Ground. This was also part of the Headington House estate, and the club's tenure lasted until 1900 when the owner, Colonel Hoole, expressed his wish that his paddock should not be used by either the cricket or the football clubs while he was away in South Africa fighting in the Boer War. The club then moved to the other side of London Road to the Britannia Field, adjacent to the pub in which United were formed. The field occupied the area which is now the northern end of Lime Walk, which was built in 1914 and was originally used for stabling and grazing the horses of travellers staying at the Britannia Inn.

In 1909 the club returned to Sandy Lane for one season, before relocating back to Quarry Recreation Ground, where they remained until the end of World War One. The Headington Recreation Ground Committee, which was formed in 1913 with the express intent of purchasing land

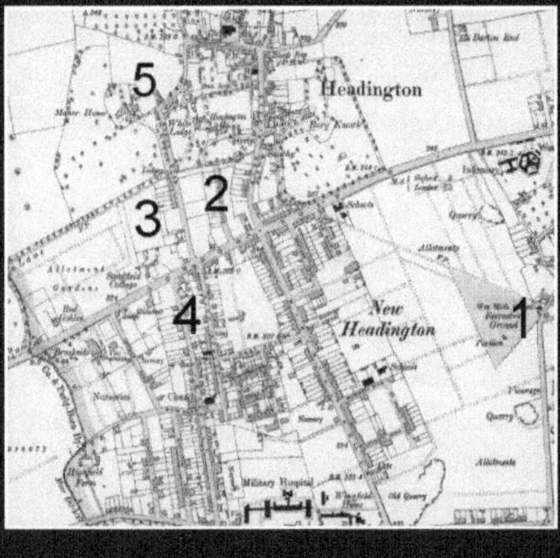

A map of Headington showing the approximate locations of Headington United's different grounds. 1: Quarry Recreation Ground, 2: Wootten's Field, 3: Sandy Lane; Mattock's Field; The Manor, 4: Britannia Field, 5: The Paddock.

for the use of the cricket and football clubs, bought the Sandy Lane site in 1918. This was then also known as Mattock's Field after owner George Mattock, the famous rose grower who lived in Rose Cottage, on the corner of Osler Road and London Road.

After another four years, in 1922, the club was forced to move again, due to the need to upgrade their changing facilities. The new ground was just a few hundred yards north of Mattock's Field, in the Paddock of the Manor House on land currently occupied by the J.R. Hospital. This ground was called either The Paddock or Manor Park. This was an enclosed ground with an excellent playing field and dressing-room accommodation.

In 1925 the Headington Sports Ground Ltd was founded with the aim of purchasing a permanent sports site for the village. It bought the Sandy Lane site, including the bowls club, from Mattock's Nursery, and the football club remained there for the next 76 years.

The Manor (1925–2001)

The *Oxford Times* of 18 September 1925 described the Manor Ground thus: 'This ground is splendidly situated and adapted for the game, being naturally high and dry, in addition to being also very convenient for visitors. Buses pass within 100 yards of the entrance. The playing pitch could hardly be better, and it is so enclosed as to allow all a comfortable view. There will be an enclosure on the pavilion side of the ground, which can be reached by way of Sandfield Road (off the London Road) entrance, as well as a main entrance to the ground, which will be in Manor Road. The charges for admission to all matches, except Amateur Cup and Senior Cup ties, will be: Enclosure, 6d; ground, 4d; ladies and boys, 2d. Season tickets will again be issued, 4s., including tax.'

The first game, at home to Deddington, kicked-off late at 4.10 because the visitors' bus broke down en route to the Manor. Headington president Major Melville Lee eventually ceremoniously kicked-off the game, which the visitors went on to win 2–1.

For the first couple of decades the site was shared with the Headington United Cricket Club, until they moved out in 1949. They initially played at the Cowley barracks before moving to their current home on Barton Road in 1954, thanks to inheriting some land bequeathed by Horace J. Bradley, a well-known local businessman and former United director, who resided at Barton End House.

The first major development at the Manor Ground occurred in 1946, when a stand purchased from Cowley FC was erected on the Osler Road side. It collapsed the following winter and was rebuilt with seats at the Cuckoo Lane end. Two years later the first terracing was built at the ground, stretching along the London Road end and a little up the Osler Road. It cost £100 to construct, with voluntary labour from the club's supporters.

As Headington United turned professional and entered the Southern League in 1949, £4,000 was spent on sunken terracing along the Osler Road, five rows of terracing on the Beech Road and London Road, a dressing room on the corner of the Beech Road and Cuckoo Lane, with 180 seats above, and adjacent to it an uncovered stewards' stand with toilets underneath. This again was all built by voluntary labour from among the supporters. The new stands increased the capacity of the ground from under 4,000 to around 12,000 and were officially opened on Good Friday 1949. Loudspeakers were also installed at the ground for the first time, again funded by the supporters' club. The following year a

A view of the Beech Road stand, showing the old floodlighting scaffold poles.

corrugated iron roof and backing was added to the Osler Road terracing. The club then erected rows of 18 floodlights on poles along the Beech and Osler Roads, and the first game to be played under them was against Banbury Spencer in a friendly on 18 December 1950.

With United playing Millwall in the FA Cup first round in 1953, the club built new terracing along the Beech Road over a period of four days, but the city engineer refused the club permission to use it. For the fourth-round tie against First Division Bolton Wanderers a large area of 15-step covered and seven-step uncovered terracing was built down the Beech Road, stretching from near the Dressing Room stand to the halfway line. From the halfway line to the corner of the London Road the remainder of this 22-step terrace was uncovered (except for a small temporary cover near the London Road end). A crowd of

The construction of the new London Road terrace, with the new floodlight pylon alongside the old scaffold pole lighting.

16,670 watched the match, setting a new ground record. Later that year United received planning permission to develop the ground as a permanent football stadium, which meant that they would not have to vacate the premises when their lease expired in 1959. As a result, the number of entrances to the Manor was doubled to four (utilising 16 turnstiles).

In 1955 the Bolton covered terrace was demolished and work commenced on a new 1,600 seat state-of-the-art stand to the rear of the Beech Road terracing. The following year the club purchased land from Sandfield Cottage, the home of Barbara Woodhouse, the famous dog trainer, and this enabled them to have direct access to London Road, which became the main entrance to the ground instead of Osler Road. In 1957 United opened a social club under the new Beech Road stand, which incorporated a gymnasium and offices, and which was officially opened by FA treasurer Denis Follows.

A hugely significant development occurred in 1961, when United put a deposit of £880 on the Manor Ground freehold to buy it from Headington Sports Ground Ltd. The purchase was completed a year later for £10,000, with a loan covered by the supporters'

Construction work underway on the new banked terrace at the Cuckoo Lane end of the Manor.

The Manor during the FA Cup quarter-final versus Preston North End, with the record attendance of 22,750 accommodated in temporary stands adjoining the Osler Road terrace (to the left of the photo) and the Beech Road terrace (in the top right corner).

club. The Osler Road entrance was moved from near the halfway line further towards the corner of London Road after the bowls club was given some land, and the club bought an access route to Osler Road and re-sited the Cuckoo Lane entrance. On 23 October 1961 a covenant was drawn up that stated the site could only be used as an open-air sports ground and that any buildings on the east side of the site (the Osler Road side) could not be higher than 26ft along the boundary of the site or 30ft in total. In 1962, with the club's election to the Football League, the Cuckoo Lane stand was dismantled and replaced by a dozen rows of terracing. The following year the 4,000 capacity London Road terrace was built and the 18 floodlight poles were replaced by four pylons, one at each corner of the ground.

For the Blackburn Rovers and Preston North End FA Cup games in 1964, a lot of temporary terracing was built down the Beech Road and Osler Road sides, leading to a still record crowd of 22,750 for the Preston quarter-final. In 1965 extensive terracing was built at the Cuckoo Lane end, making the ground capacity 19,000. For an FA Cup fourth-round tie against Watford in 1971, a gate of 17,814 saw a 1–1 draw. During a goalmouth scramble the wall at the front of the London Road end collapsed, with one spectator

The wall at the front of the London Road terrace collapsed during an FA Cup fourth-round tie against Watford on 23 January 1971.

Looking towards the London Road end from the Cuckoo Lane terrace.

breaking a leg.

The first season of crowd segregation was in 1973. The left side of the London Road end was devoted to visiting fans, with a head-high fence separating home and away supporters. The fence was extended to the roof in 1975 after clashes between opposing fans. The following season featured the first appearance of the dry moat at the front of the London Road end, and the ground was sectioned off to prevent supporters moving from stand to stand in a bid to combat hooliganism. The club also bought a house in Beech Road that they converted to a players' hostel, but by the end of 1975 the club closed it for financial reasons. In February 1975 new dressing rooms, offices, a board room, press box and a players' tunnel were opened under the Beech Road stand by Sir Matt Busby, manager of visiting Manchester United. The former Dressing Room stand was converted to the Manor social club at the start of the 1975–76 season, when the stewards' stand was covered and converted to seats. At the same time, United announced plans to become the first Football League club to install a synthetic all-weather pitch; although, needless to say, this never came to fruition.

In 1982 fences were erected at the front of the Cuckoo Lane, Osler Road and London Road terraces in response to increased violence between opposing sets of fans. Following a coin-throwing incident in an FA Cup tie against Burnley in January 1984, the fence at the front of the London Road was extended to the full height of the roof. With promotion to the top flight in 1985, the old Osler Road terracing was demolished and replaced with new terracing and a new roof as far as the halfway line. The remainder of the old terracing was replaced by two separate covered areas, one set aside for family terracing and the other (seated) for away supporters. The Beech Road terrace between the players' tunnel and the Cuckoo Lane was replaced by family seating, and a police observation post was constructed

The Beech Road shelf, with the police observation box at the back.

at the rear of the Cuckoo Lane terracing. The following year the family terracing on Osler Road was replaced by seats to become a family seating area.

In 1992, 10 years after it was erected, the fence at the front of the London Road terrace was removed. The same year United launched their unique 'Videowall', which consisted of a number of large screens joined together and mounted on the front of the police observation post behind the Cuckoo Lane terrace to form one large composite screen. In addition, two large-screen TVs were placed at the front of the roof above the London Road terrace.

Once planning permission had been granted for the Minchery Farm site, further development work came to a halt at the Manor and even standard maintenance work was often not carried out. For the last two seasons at the ground the club was only granted special dispensation to play there by the Football Licensing Authority because of the imminent move. The roofs of the London Road terrace and Beech Road stand were made of asbestos and failed to comply with current safety standards, while the terracing,

The Manor Club stand, formerly the Dressing Room stand, with the disabled enclosure in front.

especially on the Beech Road side, was starting to decay. Feasibility studies suggested that for the club to stay at the Manor would cost several million pounds of work and would result in a reduced all-seating capacity of just 2,803. After the 1989 Hillsborough Disaster increasingly stringent safety standards meant that the ground capacity was reduced on an almost annual basis, and by the time the club vacated the Manor the capacity was down to just 9,500.

The last League game at the Manor took place on 1 May 2001, a 1–1 draw against Port Vale. Andy Scott scored United's last goal at the ground. That same day, at Oxford United's Annual General Meeting, it was announced that one of chairman Firoz Kassam's companies, Firoka, was to buy the Manor from the football club for £6 million, while the covenant on the ground that was owned by the adjacent bowls club was settled for £44,000.

In November 2001, Firoka were granted permission to build a hospital and 87 flats on the site. Kassam then sold the Manor to the Nuffield Nursing Trust for £12 million. The ground was demolished almost immediately after the Kassam Stadium was opened, and building started in mid-2002 on the new Acland Hospital, which was renamed the Manor Hospital prior to its opening in 2004. A small piece of art at the hospital commemorates the football ground.

Looking Around

When Headington United turned professional and joined the Southern League in 1949 the search for a new stadium began in earnest. Between 1949 and 1953 discussions between the City Council and the club took place with regard to a new ground at either Court Place Farm at Marston (where Oxford City now play) or at Cowley Airfield (off Barns Road before it was converted into a housing estate in 1955). However, the club considered neither of these sites to be satisfactory as relocating conflicted with their plans to develop the Manor Ground to help their ambitions of Football League membership.

In July 1968, due to the increased problems of Football League membership (higher crowds and tighter safety regulations and ground requirements), the club was urged by the City Council's Planning Committee 'to make progress in relation to the possible move to the Horspath Road site'. This site, to the south of Horspath Road, had been the subject of discussions between United, the City Council and the County Council on various occasions since 1965. However, the County Council refused the application

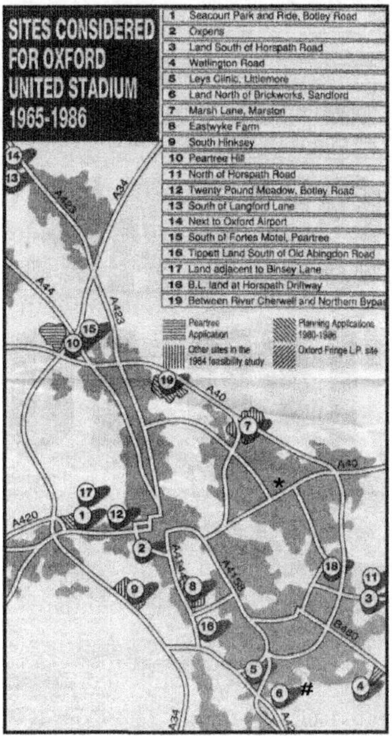

A diagram illustrating the various sites considered for Oxford United's relocation between 1965 and 1986. * = The Manor, # = Minchery Farm. (copyright *Oxford Mail*)

but suggested four alternative sites for consideration. These were north of Botley Road; south of Blackbird Leys at Watlington Road; south of Langford Lane, Kidlington; and north of Horspath Road. The site at Court Place Farm was subsequently added to the list. The Horspath Road site was outside the City Council boundary but on land owned by the City, who gave United permission to develop there. The club failed to follow this up.

The club also took the view that there was little point in considering detailed alternatives to the Manor Ground at that stage, because the viability of any move was being brought into doubt by the City Council's insistence that the Manor should be redeveloped only for residential use. An application for redevelopment into residential use, parking and ancillary shopping was withdrawn by the club in February 1971 due to opposition from the Council.

In August 1971 the city architect and planning officer prepared an exploratory report looking at 10 possible sites for relocation. Although the report was circulated to Oxfordshire and Berkshire county planning officers for their comments, none were forthcoming. The 10 sites were: 1) next to Oxford Airport at Langford Lane, Kidlington; 2) south of Fortes Motel at Pear Tree Roundabout; 3) Court Place Farm; 4) north of Horspath Road; 5) south of Horspath Road; 6) south of Blackbird Leys; 7) tipped land south of Old Abingdon Road; 8) Oxpens Recreation Ground; 9) Twenty Pound Meadow north of Botley Road; 10) land adjacent to Binsey Lane.

During the next two years United were involved in discussions with both the City Council and British Leyland, and in August 1973 the club submitted an outline planning application for a 25,000 capacity stadium, a multipurpose sports/entertainment centre and parking spaces for 500 cars on land owned by Leyland at Horspath Driftway. The City Council actually indicated that it was willing to grant planning permission for the proposal, but the secretary of state (Geoffrey Rippon) announced his intention to call in the application and hold a public enquiry. Following acrimony and then changes on the board of directors at United the club withdrew the application. This was probably the most feasible scheme which the club had come up with in regards to relocation but it was altered to a proposed £1.5 million, 22,000 capacity ground and sports complex at the Manor. This proposal never reached fruition.

In April 1980 South Oxfordshire District Council (SODC) consulted the City Council on an application by United, in association with Hotel Inns Limited, to develop approximately 67 acres between the River Cherwell and the northern bypass for a football stadium, sports centre, hotel, marina and hypermarket, with all the associated parking, accesses and landscaping. Although welcoming the club's initiative to move to a more suitable site, the council directed SODC to turn down the proposal due to its inappropriateness, as the proposed site was in the Green Belt and in the flood plain. The application was subsequently withdrawn.

Court Place Farm reared its head again in the early 1980s as United and Hotel Inns Ltd made a number of proposals for development. This site was owned by the City Council but was located within the boundaries of SODC. All these schemes included provision for a new stadium for United, together with a superstore of varying sizes (85,000 to 100,000sq ft), recreational facilities and parking. Some also included either a hotel or pub/restaurant and a petrol station. The County Council objected to the two proposals which actually reached the state of formal planning applications, although the City Council indicated that it had no objections in principle but it required various safeguards. SODC did not have a formal stance, but informally it voiced considerable opposition. Following revisions of the scheme, the City Council considered possible alternative sites at Oxpens Recreation Ground; south of Blackbird Leys; and at the Manor Ground itself. Its stated preference was for the site at Blackbird Leys adjacent to Watlington Road. It resolved not to sell the Marston site.

In November 1981 the City Council made representations on the Draft Fringe Local Plan, stating that 'an alternative site for a stadium for Oxford United could be considered in the area [south of Blackbird Leys]...' It was also during this period that Robert Maxwell became chairman of United (in January 1982), and in March 1982 the club notified the City Council of its withdrawal from the Hotel Inns scheme.

In May 1982 a scheme was submitted for planning permission, independent of the club, for a site north of Botley Road, partly in the City Council's area and partly in the Vale of White Horse. In March 1983 the applicants asked for the scheme to be held in abeyance pending discussions between themselves and United, and nothing was ever heard of it again.

In May 1983 the City Council considered seven alternative sites with a view to shortlisting some of them for more detailed evaluation. The seven, some of which were only included in order to be discarded, were at Red Barn Farm (in the parish of Gosford and Water Eaton, near Kidlington); land to the north of Botley Road; Oxpens Recreation Ground; land south of Horspath Road; land at Watlington Road; land behind Leys Clinic (where the University science park has been built, next to the Kassam Stadium); and land north of Sandford-on-Thames brickworks. It is noticeable how the same sites kept recurring, notably Horspath Road (north and south), Oxpens and Watlington Road. Of these seven possibilities, Botley Road, Oxpens and Watlington Road were the sites chosen for further study, and a detailed feasibility report was considered at the start of 1984 by the City Council; although Oxpens was rejected as being too small for the club's requirements.

Subsequently, the Council offered the club two options: either a rebuilding scheme at the Manor, with the Council donating £250,000 and the club agreeing to community use of the new facilities, or the Council making the land it owned at Watlington Road available on terms that included the club agreeing to make the new facilities available for community use providing United secured a package of stadium and commercial development for the site, with proven financial backing and planning permission. The club's architects rejected the possibility of redeveloping the Manor and reiterated the need for a new site.

The Oxford Fringe Local Plan was placed on formal deposit in December 1983 and it included an area of land adjacent to Watlington Road for the relocation of the club. The site was to be excluded from the Green Belt and no other development except a stadium was to be allowed on the site. However, the plan was never processed.

A year later Oxford United submitted four possible sites for development, at Marsh Lane, Marston (next to Court Place Farm); Eastwyke Farm on Abingdon Road; land at South Hinksey; and land at Pear Tree Hill. The club eventually selected Pear Tree from this list and in September 1986 it submitted a planning application for a 25,000 all-seater

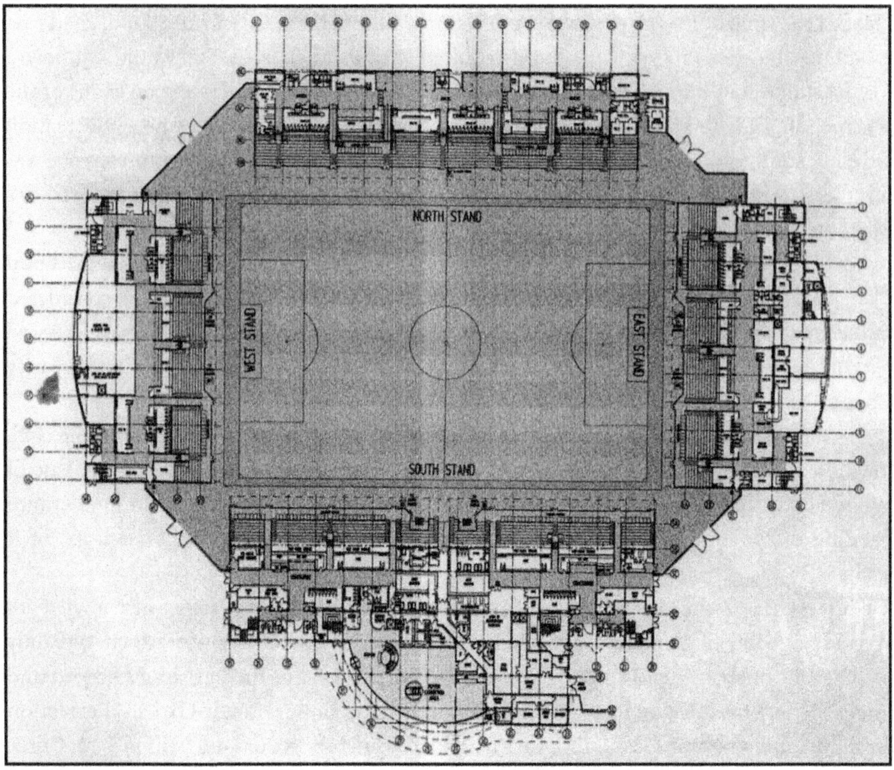

A schematic of the Minchery Farm stadium, showing the original plans for the ground, including the West Stand.

stadium with a leisure complex, 180,000sq ft of retailing and spaces for 5,000 cars. The City Council agreed in principle to support a move to this site but had reservations about the extent of the development, especially its effect on the proposed North Oxford bypass (which has still not been built), and the existing park and ride operation. Cherwell District Council refused the application on shopping, Green Belt and transport grounds and the subsequent appeal was withdrawn.

Oxfordshire County Council, which had opposed the Pear Tree application, then took the initiative and, after reviewing some 20 sites which had at one time or another been considered for possible relocation, it concluded that there was unlikely to be District Council support for any site other than the one at Watlington Road. The Council's conclusion included the remark that 'they could only support a recreational use in the Green Belt[...]without any associated commercial development'.

In April 1988 a revised scheme for the Pear Tree site was also refused planning permission by Cherwell and, later that year, the club embarked on a feasibility study of sites near Watlington Road at Guydens Farm (owned by the County Council) and at Great Leys Farm (owned by the City Council).

In 1989 the draft Central Oxfordshire Local Plan (South Oxfordshire) was published to succeed the Oxford Fringe Local Plan, and it continued to allocate the site for a stadium, but it now proposed to include the site in the Green Belt. The club welcomed the allocation but made the representation that it would need to fund the stadium with a commercial development. In response to this SODC excluded the stadium allocation from the deposited local plan, stating that there seemed little point in continuing with the allocation as the council had already clearly stated that they would oppose commercial or housing development in the area. Oxfordshire County Council and Oxford United lodged formal objections to this omission and the City Council lodged a holding objection.

In October 1990 the football club lodged a planning application for a 20,000 seat stadium with associated leisure and commercial facilities at Great Leys Farm. The club's arguments for the necessity of this development hinged on the Lord Justice Taylor Report, written as a result of the Hillsborough Disaster in 1989, becoming legislation, and they claimed that their 'special circumstances' were in line with the exceptions to restrictions on Green Belt development outlined in the Planning Policy Guidance note (PPG) 17. SODC's argument against the development were that 'planning law would have to be broken' for the stadium to be built, which was not true if the Department of Environment inspector agreed that the club did indeed have special circumstances and that 'all other practical options for location' had been exhausted.

However, despite United's managing director Pat McGeough claiming that 'We know there are no other new sites and we know the Watlington Road site is best', in June 1992 the government vetoed the plans because of its Green Belt location and vociferous objections from neighbours, not least from the nearby village of Garsington. This led United to consider a site between Oxford and Kidlington next to a grain silo, but which was also on Green Belt land, and a newly vacated brownfield site on the ring road by the Garsington Road roundabout. This was the site of the South Works of the Rover car plant, a windfall 46-acre planning gain that was bought by Arlington Securities, which was in the process of developing a business park on the site of the North Works. However, Arlington claimed that it was 'extremely unlikely that we would have countenanced or consummated an agreement with Oxford United. It would certainly contravene our master plan.' The site was later developed as an extension to the business park.

This was one of three sites under consideration by the club, the others being 'within the Oxford local authority area, with part of the land coming inside the Green Belt', and on land on the border of Oxford and another local authority area, which would have required planning permission for a change of use.

In December 1993, Oxford United announced its intention to seek planning permission to build a 15,000-seater stadium on Sandy Lane in Blackbird Leys, virtually opposite the Arlington South Works site. Again there was a lot of opposition to this proposal from residents of the estate and the owners of the nearby Tesco superstore, which was concerned about football fans using its car park. However, before the application was considered by the planning committee, a joint initiative between the City Council and the football club identified a site at Minchery Farm, between Blackbird Leys and Littlemore, for a new stadium complex on land then occupied by playing fields.

The Kassam Stadium (2001 onwards)

To say that the development of the new stadium at Minchery Farm was beset by problems would be to severely understate the case. It was initially planned that the stadium would have a capacity of 15,000, with flexibility to increase that to 23,000 by developing the corners. The plans included a stand-alone conference centre in the South Stand, while the East Stand would include a supporters' club, the main ticket office, club shop, club offices and a new Manor Club, with 500 'cinema-style' seats. Following the granting of planning permission in November 1995, construction began on 12 August 1996. One early decision that was to have far-reaching consequences in the future was to set up a separate company to fund the development of the stadium.

It quickly became clear that all was not well as work ceased just before Christmas 1996, when the contractors, Taylor Woodrow, downed tools with just the steel supports in place for the North Stand and the East Stand, while the South Stand also had the concrete terracing in place and just the footings had been laid for the West Stand.

Following a long series of protracted legal moves (details of which can be found in the general club history section), work recommenced on 20 November 2000 by newly appointed contractors Birse Stadia. On 8 May 2001 Firoz Kassam announced that the new stadium was to be called the Kassam Stadium, allegedly as a public gesture of his commitment to remain at the club for the long term, a move which was not popular among many United supporters. That same summer local newspaper the *Oxford Mail* sponsored the East Stand.

The first game at the new stadium was an Oxfordshire Benevolent Cup game against Crystal Palace on 4 August 2001. The match ended 1–1, with Paul Powell scoring for Oxford, and United won the resultant penalty shoot-out 5–4. Because of the delay in finishing the stadium, a safety certificate for the upper tier of the South Stand was refused

The Kassam Stadium under construction.

and so that part of the ground remained unused for the game; although it was deemed safe in time for the first League game at the ground, a Fourth Division match against Rochdale. United lost 2–1 before a crowd of 8,842, with Jamie Brooks scoring Oxford's equaliser.

The stadium has just three sides completed, with the West Stand remaining undeveloped as a cost-cutting exercise. The largest stand is the South Stand, which also contains the Quadrangle conference centre, the club offices, the main ticket office, the changing rooms, the boardroom, the directors' box and a row of 28 glass-fronted executive boxes that divide the stand into two tiers. The total capacity of the South Stand is 4,495. The lower tier includes the family section, while the upper tier contains the safety control post, the press area and a press room, which also doubles as the venue for Oxford Learning United, a scheme that offers lessons for local schoolchildren.

The East Stand, which is behind the goal, has a capacity of 2,879. Despite earlier plans to include a supporters' club and other facilities, these never came to fruition and so the stand contains a large void at the back where these were going to be located.

The North Stand is split into three sections. For most games the away supporters are confined to the west end of the stand, with home supporters at the east end, and the central section remains cordoned off. There is a ticket office at the west end for away fans. The capacity of this stand is 5,026.

Unlike the Manor Ground, where there were four floodlight pylons, all of The Kassam Stadium's lights are situated on top of the two stands at the side, with two levels of brightness possible: 1,000 lux or 800 lux. The lights on the North Stand are on pods to make them the same height as those on the two-tier South Stand.

The record crowd for a game at the stadium is currently 12,243. This was for United's final game of the 2005–06 season, when they lost 3–2 to Leyton Orient and consequently suffered relegation to the Conference. The ground also holds the record for the largest crowd to attend a Conference game, when 11,065 attended a 0–0 draw against Woking on Boxing Day 2006. On 24 July 2006 a sell-out crowd of 17,500 attended a pop concert by Elton John.

Summary

1893–94	Quarry Rec
1894–98	Wootten's Field
1898–1902	Sandy Lane
1902–09	Britannia Field
1909–10	Sandy Lane
1910–18	Quarry Rec
1918–22	Sandy Lane (Mattock's Field/Manor Ground)
1922–25	The Paddock
1925–2001	The Manor Ground
2001–date	The Kassam Stadium

Matches to Remember

19 March 1898

Headington 1 St Mary Magdalene 0

Oxford City Junior League Final replay (first trophy)

This game, played at Oxford City's White House Road ground in Grandpont, provided Headington with their first silverware. Headington qualified for the Final by virtue of winning the Oxford City Junior League Division B, playing eight games, winning seven and drawing one. Headington had scored 33 goals in the process and conceded just two. Headington's opponents, St Mary Magdalene, had a similarly impressive record in winning Division A, winning five and drawing one of their six matches. Although they had only scored 12 goals they had conceded just once.

The earliest known photograph of Headington FC, showing off their first silverware: the Oxford City Junior League Cup.

The first game, on Saturday 5 March, had ended in a 1–1 draw, with the Saints narrowly avoiding defeat. The replay was a close-fought affair, with neither side dominating in the first half. The Headington team was described as 'heavy and formidable', but it was their opponents who had the first attack and Gray in the Headington goal saved well. United then went on the attack but were unable to beat the Saints' 'keeper Couling, who saved three shots in quick succession. Headington were unable to keep the ball in play, disappointing the crowd with their frequent kicks into touch, while St Mary squandered the few opportunities that they were able to create with poor finishing.

The second half started in a similar fashion to the first, with Headington frequently putting the ball out of play. The Headington backs were quite happy to hoof the ball as far as they could, causing some in the crowd to shout their derision, while the St Mary front line received no service due to the reckless kicking of their colleagues. At one stage one of the Saints side shot towards his own goal and only good luck prevented Headington from taking the lead, earning a corner-kick instead. A Headington centre-forward then missed a sitter right in front of the goal. Headington were beginning to get the upper hand, but whenever they had sight of the St Mary goal they seemed to freeze and all their efforts went behind. Then St Mary started to get on top, but poor positioning from their forwards and poor kicking from the half-backs meant that they had nothing to show for their dominance. Headington had a couple of breakaway attacks, and on the second one the inside-right, H. Fletcher, scored the winner with only a few minutes remaining. However, Gray had to push one St Mary Magdalene shot away for a corner before the final whistle blew.

The Headington supporters were naturally jubilant at the result, giving a huge cheer when the referee blew the final whistle. Bicyclists were despatched to the village of Headington, where a bonfire was lit and fireworks set off. The evening culminated in a smoking concert held at the home of one of the club's founders, the Revd Scott-Tucker.

Headington: H. Gray, W.J. Smith, F. Taylor, W. Edney, W. Morris, P.S. Dearlove, J. Grimsley, H. Fletcher, H.R.E. Knowles, G. Fletcher, J. Fletcher.

20 August 1949

Hastings United 5 Headington United 2

Southern League (first game as a professional club)

At the end of the 1948–49 season Hastings had won nine out of their last 10 games, drawing the other, in a run that took them to 14th in the table. As a result, it was no surprise to many that Southern League newcomers Headington United lost 5–2 in their first competitive game as a professional football club, at Hastings' Elphinstone Road Stadium. The scoreline was a bit deceptive, however, because at one stage before half-time Headington were definitely on top and a draw looked a possibility. However, Hastings' third goal settled the issue beyond all doubt.

After a shaky start, the visiting team matched Hastings, except when it came to finishing in front of goal and several good opportunities were wasted through poor shooting. Headington's defence failed to combine well at the outset and in the early stages both Sid Stanton and Pete Sharman gave too much room to the Hastings inside men and the defence was often caught out of position. Up front, Ray Mansell worked very hard indeed, but he was always too slow to really trouble the opposing centre-half.

In the second half, mainly thanks to Fred Tapping, ably supported by Sharman, Headington repeatedly looked dangerous, and Henry Blake often threatened from the right when Stanton gave him through passes to run onto. Bert Kay, at inside-right, worked hard, but his finishing was poor. Peter Roberts, on the other hand, was a source of danger when moving with the ball, and from just such a move Headington netted their second goal.

Programme cover from United's first game in the Southern League, at Hastings United's Elphinstone Road ground.

During the closing stages of the game, when two quick goals were conceded, Headington were on top and gave an indication that when they settled down they would be a force to be reckoned with in the Southern League. The team had shown signs that they could become a good combination, but there were obvious weaknesses to be overcome and they needed a leader for the forward line with experience of League football, while the outside-left position also needed to be adequately filled. The goals from Hastings came courtesy of a Sammy Moore hat-trick and a Bernard Booth brace, while Mansell and Roberts were on the mark for the visitors.

This game marked a slow start by Headington to their inaugural Southern League campaign. They did not win their first League game until 22 September, when Jack Casley scored a hat-trick in a 4–2 win over Guildford City, and they did not pick up their first away win until 17 December, when they visited the Eyrie and beat Bedford Town 2–1.

Headington United: Scott, Aldridge, Brine, Stanton, Thompson (player-coach), Sharman, Blake, Kay, Mansell, Tapping, Roberts.

30 January 1954

Headington United 2 Bolton Wanderers 4

FA Cup fourth round (first competitive game against Division One opponents)

The visit of First Division Bolton Wanderers was the culmination of Headington United's epic FA Cup run that had seen them play nine games to get to the fourth-round stage. This was the first time that United had met a top-flight club in a competitive game, and they were up against the side that had been narrowly defeated by Blackpool in the famous 'Stanley Matthews' FA Cup Final the previous season and who were set to finish fifth in the First Division. On their way to the fourth round, Headington had been drawn at home just twice, against Maidenhead United, who they beat 4–0 after winning 2–1 at Aylesbury United in the first qualifying round, and against Chesham United, who they beat 2–0 in the third qualifying round. Those games were followed by wins at Wealdstone and Harwich & Parkeston, before United were drawn away to Millwall in the second round. That was the side's first competitive game against a Football League team and after an exciting 3–3 draw at the Den, Headington beat the Third Division South side 1–0 at the Manor. This earned them a visit to Stockport County of Division Three North. A superb goalkeeping display by Jack Ansell earned United a 0–0 draw, and Headington again won the replay 1–0.

United's Bobby Craig and Bolton's Nat Lofthouse tussle for the ball.

In the game against Bolton, Headington battled strongly and, even when three goals down, they did not give up hope. Having been 3–0 down, a 4–2 defeat was a fine achievement. Headington had had as much of the play as their opponents and, at times, they had the Bolton defenders kicking desperately into touch to keep them out.

Where Headington were clearly inferior was in their finishing. They failed to score from at least three excellent openings because the forwards got flustered and mishit their shots. Bolton, on the other hand, once they had got used to the slippery pitch, played coolly and confidently and took all their chances. Their wingers, Doug Holden and particularly Ray Parry, showed remarkable speed and agility, while, for the Us, Johnnie Crichton was outstanding. He used his speed to set in motion many Headington attacks and he was one of the best half-backs on the field. Ronnie Steel also worked magnificently on the right wing, as did Ernie Hudson and Ted Croker in the defence. However, this was truly a team performance and every player contributed a do-or-die performance.

Just how much Headington achieved by bringing a full First Division side to Oxford for the first time in the city's history was evident from the appearance of the packed ground, with a new 15-step covered terrace built along the Beech Road side, from the Dressing Room stand to the halfway line. There was a real Cup tie atmosphere in the ground, with cheerleaders in bright costumes, rattles, bells and hooters among the record crowd of 16,670 spectators, bringing in receipts of just over £3,000.

Headington United: Ansell, Ramshaw, Croker, Hudson, Craig, Crichton, Steel, Peart, Smith, Duncan, Maskell.

18 August 1962

Barrow 3 Oxford United 2

Division Four (first game as a Football League club)

Oxford United's first game as a Football League club ended with something of an anticlimax, as the side lost 3–2 on their first visit to Holker Street. This game was the culmination of a decade of applications to join the League, which eventually became reality after the resignation of Accrington Stanley the previous season as the Lancashire club finally succumbed to financial problems. Having won the Southern League for two successive seasons, and being widely regarded as the best non-League side around, the election of Oxford to succeed Accrington was always on the cards.

For 30 minutes of a thrill-packed struggle, an Oxford success seemed the only likely result. But they were playing against a side which had lost only three times at home the previous season, and with the atmosphere as electric as for any Cup tie, Barrow began to take the upper hand, although Oxford played well enough to deserve at least a draw. United took the lead in the 25th minute when Graham Atkinson was first to the rebound after a Bud Houghton shot was blocked. Just a minute later the hosts were level when Tommy Dixon scored. Seven minutes before the interval, Houghton headed home a Ray Colfar cross to give the Us a half-time lead.

Gordon Brown scores Barrow's winner.

However, it was Oxford's over-eagerness to succeed which partly brought about their downfall. When Barrow launched a final onslaught, Oxford, instead of continuing to play the same steady and sound defensive game which had been working so effectively, panicked. Everyone dropped back at once, with the result that there was no one to pick up the clearances and Barrow simply took the opportunities to pile in fresh attacks. A lucky goal in the 82nd minute, which many felt should not have stood after an infringement, put Barrow level and then, with three minutes left, came the final blow. The ball bobbled about just inside the penalty area and at least three Oxford players lunged in desperation to try and clear, but Gordon Brown, the Barrow inside-right, stabbed the ball home.

This game proved to Oxford United that Fourth Division football was vastly different from that in the Southern League. None of the Oxford players could be faulted for effort, though with Houghton at centre-forward, Peter Knight and Colfar on the wings, and Kevin Cornwell at inside-left all doing enough to show that they would cope well with the new standard. In defence, however, where Oxford did so well until those last eight minutes, there were moments when players were caught napping by the extra speed of the Fourth Division game.

Barrow manager Ron Staniforth said after the game, 'I was surprised at the speed and skill of Oxford's play. They really had us rattled until that final spell when they fell back and relied entirely on defence, which is usually fatal. I am quite sure they will do well, however, and predict here and now that Oxford will finish in the top six'.

Oxford United: Medlock, Beavon, Quartermain, R. Atkinson, Kyle, Jones, Knight, G. Atkinson, Houghton, Cornwell, Colfar.

15 February 1964

Oxford United 3 Blackburn Rovers 1

FA Cup fifth round

Most people expected that United were to be handed a lesson by Blackburn, who were second in the First Division at the time of this match. Instead, it was a day when the underdogs not merely overcame, but outsmarted and for lengthy periods outclassed and

Tony Jones celebrates scoring United's second goal against First Division Blackburn.

outplayed their more illustrious opponents, six-times winners of the trophy and strongly fancied to reach the Final again that season.

Apart from a short spell just after they scored midway through the second half, Blackburn were made to play second fiddle and look second-rate to opponents who sensed in the opening minutes that victory was a strong possibility.

United's opening goal by Tony Jones in the 14th minute provided the springboard, and Blackburn were totally incapable of checking the home team's unquenchable spirit and endeavour. Whenever Blackburn tried to increase the pace and impose themselves on the game, they found United one step ahead of them, and there were long periods when the visitors seemed completely bewildered by what was going on around them.

Blackburn's policy was immediately obvious: to feed Bryan Douglas. However, United were anticipating this and often two and sometimes even three or four men were in position to mark him; seldom can the former England winger have suffered such a frustrating afternoon. In the end it was not so much a case of Oxford watching Douglas, as Blackburn watching Jones, who was playing at inside-left. Jones easily managed to avoid challenges by Ronnie Clayton so that he was twice on hand to snap up half chances.

In a convincing team display, Maurice Kyle completely overshadowed the future England forward Fred Pickering, while Pat Quartermain crowned his splendid performance by determinedly fighting his way through on the left to provide the cross from which Bill Calder notched up Oxford's dramatic third goal on the stroke of time. Ron Atkinson's tackling was swift and strong, his distribution and control sure, not least when he swung the ball across for Bill Calder to lay on Jones's second goal. Calder began to get the better of centre-half Mike England in the second period, and although Harry Fearnley was initially at fault when Blackburn scored, failing to clear a corner, this was his only slip, and he had a quiet afternoon compared with Fred Else, who was peppered with shots from all angles. At the end, the Oxford fans showed their jubilation with an impromptu pitch invasion, carrying the players shoulder high from the field. In their short history as a professional football club, United had just achieved the pinnacle of their success to date.

Oxford United: Fearnley, Beavon, Quartermain, Atkinson, Kyle, Shuker, Knight, Longbottom, Calder, Jones, Harrington.

29 February 1964

Oxford United 1 Preston North End 2

FA Cup quarter-final (record attendance)

This was a record-breaking match for Oxford United. There were 22,750 packed into a specially modified Manor Ground, a record attendance for an Oxford home game before or since. In addition, it was the first time that a club from Division Four had reached the FA Cup quarter-finals. This historic game took place just two weeks after the impressive win over Blackburn Rovers, giving the excited Oxford fans barely time to recover their breath.

Alex Dawson puts Preston ahead with a hotly disputed goal.

Preston won the toss and Tommy Lawton chose to play the first half up the slope, thus robbing United of their preference for attacking the London Road end in the second half. The most critical moment came with Preston's hotly disputed opening goal in the eighth minute, which seemed to sap United's spirit for the rest of the half. United's defenders clamoured in vain for offside around referee David Smith when he pointed emphatically to the centre spot. Alex Dawson, jostled by Cyril Beavon, saw his shot bounce off Harry Fearnley and back on to his own knees before going into the net. Often in the first half almost everything United tried went wrong.

Despite Preston's clear supremacy in the first half, which may have led them into a degree of complacency, the Second Division side were subjected to almost unremitting pressure in the last 45 minutes. It was almost all United, as Bill Calder, Arthur Longbottom and Tony Jones all missed easy chances. United had many shots blocked, charged down or with no more than a hair's breadth from the target in the closing minutes. United were magnificent in defence but unconvincing in attack, where Longbottom struggled to get into the game and Calder failed to live up to the occasion. In the 76th minute Calder miscued completely when John Shuker set him up.

United's magnificent second-half recovery had deserved a replay at Deepdale. In the end, though, it was not to be, and it was Preston who set up a semi-final date against Swansea Town.

Oxford United: Fearnley, Beavon, Quartermain, Atkinson, Kyle, Shuker, Knight, Longbottom, Calder, Jones, Harrington.

24 February 1973

Swindon Town 1 Oxford United 3

Division Two

This game remains unique in United's history, being the only time that Oxford have won at Swindon Town's County Ground in 25 attempts. This would be a remarkable record against any team, but against the club's main local rivals it is in truth a source of embarrassment. Four years earlier United had earned their first win against Swindon when knocking the then holders out of the League Cup 1–0 in the third round, but they had to wait until the 1972–73 season to reclaim local bragging rights, doing the double over the Robins for the only time. Oxford had already beaten Swindon 1–0, through a goal by Nigel Cassidy, at the Manor in December by the time that they travelled away for the return game.

This win was United's first in seven attempts at the County Ground, and the first time they had scored more than once. It lifted United up to fourth place in the Second Division while compounding Swindon's relegation worries. Oxford looked cool and confident in the face of Swindon's frenetic opening, with Nigel Cassidy and Hugh Curran tormenting Frank Burrows and Ray Potter with darting runs and neat flicks. Oxford took the lead in the 38th minute, when Dave Roberts forced the ball past Peter Downsborough after a finely floated cross from the left wing by Steve Aylott. Colin Clarke and Roberts produced their best performances of the season to nullify the threat of Peter Noble and Ray Treacy in the Town attack, while Mick McGovern was denied by Roy Burton. A poor back pass allowed David

Hugh Curran celebrates scoring United's third, deep into injury time, at the County Ground.

Moss, later to become Oxford's assistant manager under Brian Horton, an opportunity, but Burton pulled off an amazing save to deny him, diving at the forward's feet. Swindon were so desperate for a goal that they lost their heads, while Oxford's John Evanson, John Fleming and Curran held on to the ball well, taking on their opponents and forcing them into errors.

In the 55th minute, from the third of three successive corners, Roberts rose and headed the ball down for Nigel Cassidy to neatly double Oxford's lead. However, United allowed Swindon back into the game nine minutes later, when substitute Roger Smart split the defence with a pass to Noble, whose header behind Dick Lucas allowed McGovern to charge in and beat Burton. Swindon started to mount the pressure for the next 10 minutes, but Clarke twice made saving headers from Noble. There was occasionally panic in the Us defence, but it held firm and in the fifth minute of injury time Curran collected a long pass from Evanson and cut inside two defenders, before beating Downsborough with a left-footed shot just inside the post for his first goal in three months.

Oxford United: Burton, Lucas, Shuker, Roberts, Clarke, Evanson, Sloan, Fleming, Curran, Cassidy, Aylott.

26 October 1983

Oxford United 2 Newcastle United 1

League Cup second round, second leg

Newcastle United, lying second in the Second Division, were the hot favourites to beat Oxford United and progress to the third round of the League Cup, despite Oxford having earned a 1–1 draw in the first leg at St James' Park thanks to a Steve Biggins goal. However, Oxford were top of the Third Division and had yet to be beaten at home. With the away end packed, the 13,040-strong crowd formed the biggest attendance seen at the Manor for five seasons, since United had lost 5–0 to Nottingham Forest in the same competition in October 1978.

Newcastle included such luminaries as Kevin Keegan, Peter Beardsley and Chris Waddle in their line up for their first visit to the Manor, while the referee was the notable Clive Thomas. United were kicking down the slope in the first half and were soon on the ascendency. The game was just 18 minutes old when Oxford took the lead, Neil Whatmore tapping in at the near post after a pinpoint cross from Kevin Brock. George Lawrence then brought a save out of Martin Thomas, before Oxford doubled their lead in the 32nd minute. Bobby McDonald and Brock combined to set up Andy Thomas on the left of the Newcastle penalty area, and Thomas controlled the ball and then curled a powerful shot past his namesake between the Newcastle posts to score a goal that has gone down in Oxford United folklore.

In the second half Oxford came close to increasing their lead when Lawrence set up Brock, who shot narrowly wide. Thomas then hit the bar after pouncing on a rebound and

Andy Thomas receives congratulations after scoring United's second goal.

it was clear that there was only going to be one winner, even though Malcolm Shotton had to clear the ball off the line from a Beardsley cross. However, United were reduced to 10 men when Gary Briggs, who had already been booked, fouled Keegan. With 10 minutes remaining, Keegan span and shot home a Beardsley cross to set up a nervous finale, but the defence held firm.

It was this game, probably more than any other, that set United on their way and initiated what were later called the Glory Years of the mid-1980s. The Cup-tie atmosphere under the floodlights and United's new-found reputation as Cup giant-killers were to rekindle Oxford's reputation and kick-started the good times of the next three or four seasons.

Oxford United: Hardwick, Fogg, McDonald, Thomas, Briggs, Shotton, Lawrence, Barnett, Whatmore, Hebberd, Brock. Sub: Jones for Whatmore.

19 December 1983

Oxford United 2 Manchester United 1

League Cup fourth-round second replay

Manchester United were top of the First Division, but in the two games against Oxford before this second replay, the Us had matched them. The first game, at the Manor, ended 1–1 with Bobby McDonald scoring for Oxford. Not many people fancied Oxford's chances of getting anything out of the replay at Old Trafford, but they reckoned without Kevin Brock's free-kick expertise and he gave United the lead in the second half. This lasted for just one minute before Frank Stapleton equalised, and Oxford held on through extra-time for a second replay. Initially Manchester United had offered to host the replay at Old Trafford, presumably believing that Oxford would jump at the chance of the extra revenue, but Robert Maxwell had other ideas and insisted that the League toss a coin to decide the venue. This was done via telephone from the League headquarters, and Maxwell won the toss to play at the Manor.

Oxford surprisingly elected to kick towards the London Road end in the first half, despite winning the toss, and they soon had the visitors on the back foot thanks to the pace of Brock, whose cross was narrowly missed by both Mick Vinter and Neil Whatmore. Steve Hardwick did well to save from Norman Whiteside, but most of the threat came from the home team, with Andy Thomas, Whatmore and George Lawrence all missing chances. However, it was the visitors who took the lead when an Arnold Muhren corner was flicked on by Whiteside and fired home by Arthur Graham. As in the first replay, the lead did not last long and Oxford were level two minutes later. Trevor Hebberd headed on a Brock corner, and McDonald's header was deflected onto the bar, bouncing down for Lawrence to score with a rare header.

Despite attacking up the slope in the second half, Oxford came out strongly and put the visitors under pressure. Thomas brought out a good save from Jeff Wealands and then Brock rounded the Manchester 'keeper only for his shot to be cleared off the line by Kevin Moran. Brock and Whatmore both brought further saves from Wealands, while Hardwick had to be alert to save from Stapleton. Wealands saved again from Vinter, while Hebberd volleyed just over and then brought another save from the beleaguered Wealands.

Steve Biggins wins a header.

With the scores still level at the end of 90 minutes, the tie went into extra-time again. Wealands had to save a long-range scorcher from Thomas before the goal came that settled the tie. Brock's corner found Hebberd, who returned the ball to the Oxford winger. From Brock's cross, Steve Biggins, on as a substitute for Whatmore, outjumped the visiting defenders and the ball looped over Wealands and dropped into the net, setting off scenes of mayhem among the home fans. There was no way back for Manchester United and Oxford claimed yet another notable scalp.

In the next round Oxford played Everton at the Manor, and United were just five minutes from a semi-finals appearance after McDonald had given them the lead. However, a misplaced back pass from Brock let in Adrian Heath for an equaliser, and Everton went on to win the replay 4–1.

Oxford United: Hardwick, Hinshelwood, McDonald, Thomas, Briggs, Shotton, Lawrence, Whatmore, Vinter, Hebberd, Brock. Sub: Biggins for Whatmore.

24 November 1984

Oxford United 5 Leeds United 2

Division Two

This Second Division game against Leeds was filled with incident, and it has gone down as a special game for United for a number of reasons, not all them found on the pitch. Oxford were top of the Division, having won the Third Division title the previous season, while Leeds were in the chasing pack, lying fifth. Oxford had not lost at home, they had won their nine previous home games and had already scored 45 goals in all competitions during the season. The Manor pitch was in a muddy condition, which was to influence the game, and the ground was packed, with a temporary TV gantry erected at the back of the Cuckoo Lane terrace.

Early in the game Trevor Hebberd let fly from 20 yards out and hit the post, while at the other end Dave Langan cleared off the line from an Andy Ritchie effort. On 18 minutes Tommy Wright burst through to put Leeds ahead, and 10 minutes later Wright crossed for Peter Lorimer to shoot home. Finding themselves 2–0 down after just 22 minutes was a shock, but Oxford managed to regroup and started to apply some pressure. Five minutes before half-time Gary Briggs was on the end of a Kevin Brock corner to powerfully head home and halve the arrears. This gave United's players and fans the confidence they needed to come out in the second half and take the game to the visitors.

Billy Hamilton scores United's equaliser against Leeds.

Billy Hamilton equalised two minutes after the restart when he chested down a Hebberd cross and shot in from a narrow angle, and five minutes later Oxford took the lead. John Aldridge released Brock down the right and then was on hand at the far post to head in from Brock's pinpoint cross. Just after the hour mark Aldridge scored again after latching onto a superb defence-splitting pass from Hamilton and taking the ball around David Harvey. Ten minutes later Aldridge and Lorimer clashed on the Osler Road touchline, and Lorimer was sent off. This incident sparked riots among the away fans, who dismantled the TV scaffolding and threw planks and other missiles onto the pitch. Steve Hardwick was felled by a coin thrown from the away end and the game was held up for several minutes. The stoppage failed to affect United negatively, and, with three minutes remaining, Aldridge completed his hat-trick when he headed in another Brock cross.

Oxford's home winning run was eventually increased to 13 games, and United scored 109 goals in all competitions that season. They also won the Division Two title on the final day of the season after beating Barnsley 4–0.

Oxford United: Hardwick, Langan, McDonald, Trewick, Briggs, Shotton, Rhoades-Brown, Aldridge, Hamilton, Hebberd, Brock.

20 April 1986

Oxford United 3 Queen's Park Rangers 0

Milk Cup Final

Ask any Oxford United fan above a certain age what their most memorable moment following the Yellows was and they will almost invariably answer: the game at Wembley where the Us won the Milk Cup on Sunday 20 April 1986. There were approximately 36,000 United fans among the crowd of 90,396, which remains the largest crowd ever to have watched United.

The game itself took a while to get going, and neither Oxford nor QPR were initially prepared to be very adventurous. Rangers were by far the favourites to lift the Milk Cup, which was in its final year before a change of sponsor, but they looked more overawed by the occasion than their more relaxed opponents. The first real incident occurred when John Aldridge was blocked by Steve Wicks, but United squandered the opportunity and neither goalkeeper was tested for long periods. Then, with five minutes to go before half-time, Aldridge sent Trevor Hebberd clear down the left. Hebberd reached the angle of the six yard box, checked onto his right foot to take the ball past Alan McDonald and then beat Paul Barron at his near post to give United a half-time lead.

The setback took the wind out of QPR's sails and United dominated the second half. Eight minutes after the break Oxford broke swiftly down the left, with Hebberd and Ray Houghton exchanging passes. After a neat interchange Houghton side-footed past Barron to double Oxford's lead. United should have made it three when Aldridge somehow side-footed wide with just Barron to beat, while Alan Judge had to make his first save of any note in the 73rd minute when he stretched to tip over a speculative long-range shot from Ian Dawes. Oxford were guaranteed victory with just four minutes remaining, as Hebberd, clear

Ray Houghton sidefoots home to give United a 2–0 lead.

Man of the Match, set up Aldridge, whose powerful shot could only be parried by Barron straight at Jeremy Charles, who was lurking three yards out. Charles made no mistake, leaving the ITV commentator with the memorable line, 'That's three, and that's victory'.

After the game the Oxford supporters cheered as Malcolm Shotton went up the famous steps to hold aloft the Milk Cup. Manager Maurice Evans displayed his characteristic generosity and humility when he sent up long-serving trainer Ken Fish to collect his winners' medal, while Oxford fans applauded their side's lap of honour and chanted to Jim Smith: 'You should have stayed at the Manor', recognising his part in building the victorious side. The only real regret was that substitute Andy Thomas was not given any time on the pitch to play at Wembley for the team he grew up with. The Oxford supporters were out again the following day to pack the city centre and applaud the side on its open-top bus tour and presentation on the town hall balcony.

Oxford United: Judge, Trewick, Langan, Briggs, Shotton, Phillips, Houghton, Hebberd, Brock, Aldridge, Charles.

5 January 1991

Chelsea 1 Oxford United 3

FA Cup third round

Oxford United had been floundering at the foot of the Second Division just a week before this Cup tie against First Division Chelsea and before the game no one had given the Us any hope of FA Cup advancement, but United gave a battling team performance that surprised

Jim Magilton scores United's third goal at Stamford Bridge.

their illustrious hosts and gave heart to the 1,500 away fans. Oxford simply outplayed, outfought and outmanoeuvred Chelsea all over the pitch. They were resolute and disciplined in defence, inventive and industrious in midfield, and fast and skilful in attack.

Early in the game Graham Stuart hit the post with a hopeful cross, but a combination of defenders Steve Foster and Andy Melville and goalkeeper Ken Veysey kept the Chelsea strikeforce of Kerry Dixon and Kevin Wilson at bay. Dave Beasant was called on to make instinctive saves to deny first Paul Simpson and then Lee Nogan, whose close-range header was parried away to Jim Magilton, only for his fierce drive to come back off the post. Oxford opened the scoring just four minutes before the interval, as Simpson launched a counter-attack down the left wing and floated a through ball to the unmarked Nogan, who shot high into the net past a bemused Beasant.

United had a scare at the start of the second half when a poor back pass from Les Phillips let in Dixon, but Veysey was equal to his powerful drive. That was a rare Chelsea attack though, as Oxford were clearly the better side on the day. Ten minutes into the second half the Us extended their lead when Steve McClaren's penetrating pass set Nogan free on the right. His long, low cross was met by John Durnin, who ran through to side-foot past the hesitant Beasant. Chelsea tried to take the game to Oxford after that, but left themselves vulnerable to the counter-attack, and when Durnin set up Simpson for a volley Beasant had to save at full stretch. McClaren then had to make a goalline clearance, but Chelsea scored their inevitable goal with just a quarter of an hour remaining. Magilton, on a counter-attack, lost possession just outside the Chelsea penalty area and Stuart's long clearance evaded Foster, leaving Dixon with just Veysey to beat, which he did with a powerful drive inside the far post. Chelsea's renewed hope was short-lived though, as five minutes later Phillips found Durnin on the wing. His perfect cross was met by Magilton, who controlled the ball before side-stepping Beasant and slotting home to send the United supporters wild with delight.

Oxford United: Veysey, Robinson, Smart, McClaren, Foster, Melville, Magilton, Phillips, Durnin, Nogan, Simpson.

2 May 1992

Tranmere Rovers 1 Oxford United 2

Division Two (avoiding relegation)

Oxford visited Prenton Park on the last day of the season needing a win to stay in the Second Division. However, even with the three points United were still reliant on results elsewhere going their way in order to avoid relegation.

Oxford were clearly the better team in the first half, which remained goalless only because Joey Beauchamp failed to convert any of his four clear-cut chances. Beauchamp gave Tranmere left-back Steve Mungall a difficult time with his trickery and pace, but when he was presented with goalscoring chances he either failed to get enough power into his shot or it went narrowly off target. At the other end, Paul Kee, so often the target of derision of the Oxford fans for his goalkeeping errors, pulled off a fine stop to deny Dave Martindale. The misery of the large contingent of travelling supporters was compounded at half-time with the news that Plymouth Argyle, Newcastle United and Grimsby Town were all leading. A combination of results that, if they remained the same, would leave United relegated.

Joey Beauchamp scores to keep United in the Second Division.

In the second half Tranmere forced United onto the defensive, and Kee was called on to make superb reaction saves from Kenny Irons and a blistering drive from Tony Thomas. Former Oxford hero John Aldridge shot wide after latching onto a huge kick from 'keeper Eric Nixon, who was so often a thorn in Oxford's side. Oxford seemed to be getting desperate as they hung on, but suddenly they took the lead. Gary Bannister, on loan from Nottingham Forest, anticipated an Ian Nolan back pass and ran forwards to intercept. He sent John Durnin on his way and the Oxford striker took the ball into the box and around the stranded Nixon to score. The joy of the Oxford supporters was quietened almost immediately though, as Tranmere rushed forward to equalise. Aldridge pounced on a loose ball and beat Kee with a precise left-footed strike. It was Aldridge's 40th goal of the season, equalling the Tranmere record, and afterwards no Oxford supporter begrudged him that honour.

Usually when Oxford let a lead slip they go on to lose, but on this occasion United refused to bow down and in their very next attack they restored the lead. Bannister and Mickey Lewis exchanged passes in midfield and Lewis set Beauchamp up with a penetrating pass. This time the Oxford-born winger made no mistake, slipping the ball under Nixon to make it 2–1. After this, United were content to soak up the Tranmere pressure. Kee made another superb save from a powerful cross-shot by Martindale, and then got to the ball just ahead of Aldridge from a dangerous Irons cross. The final whistle was greeted with delirium on the terraces, but the joy was soon tempered when the fans realised that they were not yet safe.

The game at Home Park between Plymouth and Blackburn had been delayed by 15 minutes, and so there followed an agonising wait for the full-time score to come through. The Oxford players came back out onto the pitch and stood in front of the packed away terrace, waiting to find out if they were to be condemned or saved. Finally, the news that every Oxford supporter wanted to hear came through. A David Speedie hat-trick had given Blackburn a 3–1 win to cement Rovers' place in the Play-offs. Plymouth were down and Oxford would be a Division Two club again the following season. Players, management and supporters cheered uncontrollably.

Oxford United: Kee, Smart, Ford, Lewis, Evans, Melville, Magilton, Beauchamp, Aylott, Durnin, Bannister.

3 November 1993

Oxford United 5 Portsmouth 5

Division Two

In this extraordinary game Oxford trailed first 3–0, then 4–1 and eventually 5–2, but two goals in the last 90 seconds rescued an unlikely point for United as they achieved one of their greatest comebacks in a game that has gone down in United legend. Quite how United gained a point is a mystery, as for all but 20 minutes of the game they were overrun and outclassed by a rampant Portsmouth side.

'Penalty' screams the overhead video wall as Jim Magilton scores United's fourth goal.

Portsmouth came at the Us from the off, throwing everything at them, and it took three splendid saves from Paul Reece to keep the scoreline respectable. Chris Allen had an early effort blocked, after which Pompey carved United apart at will. Oxford held out until the 17th minute, when Alan McLoughlin headed home off the underside of the bar. Three minutes later future Oxford player (for just one game) Guy Whittingham, whom Reece had denied three times, scored with a low shot into the corner. After 32 minutes United looked dead and buried when Mark Chamberlain's corner was unfortunately turned into his own goal by Ceri Evans. However, with virtually the first real United attack, Joey Beauchamp broke down the right wing. After his first cross was blocked his second reached John Durnin, whose header was parried by Alan Knight straight to Dave Penney, who drove the ball high into the roof of the net. Portsmouth then immediately restored their three-goal advantage when Whittingham was on the end of a cross to hit a deflected shot beyond Reece. But United hit back straight away, when an angled cross from Beauchamp reached Jim Magilton, who volleyed low past Knight to reduce the arrears.

Portsmouth continued to attack at the start of the second half, with Chamberlain having a shot blocked and McLoughlin shooting wide when faced with an almost open goal. Portsmouth did regain their three-goal lead when Chamberlain scored a superb goal, his rising shot going just inside the post, while the Oxford defence stood around admiringly. Many United fans had already left the ground in despair before Oxford got another goal back in the 73rd minute, after Kit Symons misdirected a header to John Durnin, who stretched to put the ball into the net.

Four minutes from time, Magilton scooped an easy-looking chance high over the bar after being set up by Beauchamp and it looked like that would be it for the Us. However, as the game moved towards injury time, Chris Allen cut inside the penalty area and was brought down by substitute Stuart Doling. Magilton, whose penalty-taking record for Oxford was phenomenal, converted the spot-kick to give Oxford a glimmer of hope, although only seconds remained. Pompey lost possession straight from the kick-off and the ball found its way back to Reece. The 'keeper hammered the ball forwards, Nick Cusack flicked it on and the ball fell to Durnin, who missed his kick completely. However, Beauchamp raced on to the loose ball and shot, but Knight stretched out to block it. The ball fell kindly for the unmarked Chris Allen, who easily headed home to the astonishment of the home supporters and the despair of the travelling fans. The final whistle blew as Portsmouth restarted the game.

Oxford United: Reece, Smart, Ford, Lewis, Evans, Melville, Magilton, Beauchamp, Penney, Durnin, Allen. Subs: Narbett for Lewis, Cusack for Penney.

8 April 1996

Oxford United 3 Wycombe Wanderers 0

Division Two

If ever a game reflected United's unstoppable charge towards automatic promotion in the second half of the 1995–96 season, it was this extraordinary win at Adams Park against a Wycombe side that Oxford had not yet beaten in the League.

The first half hour of the game was relatively quiet, but United eventually started to apply the pressure on their neighbours. Matt Murphy went close with a header from a corner, and then Matt Elliott, the powerhouse centre-half, neatly controlled a crossfield pass from Joey Beauchamp on his chest before driving powerfully straight at Sieb Dykstra. Three minutes before half-time Oxford made the breakthrough. Les Robinson beat Steve McGavin on the right and sent in an outswinging cross which just evaded Dykstra but was met by David Rush to head home.

Wycombe started the second half looking for an equaliser and it took an intervention from Robinson to take the ball off the toes of Steve Brown, and shortly afterwards McGavin's shot hit the top of the bar. However, that was all that Wycombe were able to muster and United came forward to take charge of the game again. Midway through the second half Denis Smith took Martin Aldridge off and brought on the towering Paul Moody. The Wycombe defenders were clearly preoccupied with marking this new threat and they left substitute Stuart Massey completely unmarked. Elliott flicked on Beauchamp's corner at the near post and Massey nodded home on the goalline. In the 75th minute Massey set Moody free in the inside-left position. With no Wycombe defenders closing him down, Moody charged forward before blasting the ball under Dykstra to send the away fans into raptures. Moody performed his trademark somersault, while Massey followed up to hang from the crossbar in delight. The resulting photograph became an iconic Oxford image and was even reproduced on T-shirts in celebration.

Paul Moody does a handstand and Stuart Massey hangs from the crossbar to celebrate Moody's goal.

The win left Oxford in third place, still seven points behind second-placed Blackpool but with a game in hand. United had beaten Blackpool 1–0 in the previous game with a Joey Beauchamp goal later described as the best ever scored at the Manor. They clearly had the momentum, but with just five games remaining automatic promotion was still a big ask.

Oxford United: Whitehead, Robinson, Ford, Smith, Elliott, Gilchrist, Rush, Lewis, Aldridge, Beauchamp, Murphy. Subs: Allen for Rush, Moody for Aldridge, Massey for Murphy.

4 May 1996

Oxford United 4 Peterborough United 0

Division Two (clinching promotion)

This game, which ensured that Oxford would take the second automatic promotion place to return to the second tier, encapsulated the very strange season that the match concluded. For the first few months United had been woeful, the nadir coming at Shrewsbury in October when United went down 2–0 and Denis Smith was on the verge of being sacked. However, the side slowly pulled themselves back from the brink, and once they had earned their first away win at Burnley at the end of January they started to mount an irresistible surge to promotion.

In this final game, United were poor in the first half, with nerves and tension obviously getting to the players. Normally United's home form, especially in the second half of the season, saw them strutting about with an arrogance that made them virtually unbeatable,

David Rush ensures promotion for United as they demolish Peterborough in the second half.

but at the start of this game they were subdued and withdrawn, and it was Peterborough who almost broke the deadlock when a dipping shot from Marcus Ebdon went close. At the other end, United were unable to finish the numerous chances that they created. Joey Beauchamp, a hero to United fans since his prodigal return from Swindon in October, missed three glorious chances, while others guilty of spurning opportunities were Stuart Massey, Paul Moody and David Rush. Peterborough had done their homework, putting three men on Matt Elliott when he went forwards for set pieces and closely marking wingers Massey and Beauchamp to cut off the crosses on which Moody and Rush thrived. In the first half United failed to muster a single corner.

Oxford's potency from corners was evident to all when they eventually earned a flag-kick seven minutes into the second half. Beauchamp delivered his usual near-post kick, but instead of Elliott flicking the ball on, it was Posh's Ken Charlery who got his head to the ball. His flick fell into the middle ground between 'keeper and defence, and Giuliano Grazioli headed into his own net. Suddenly, the tension evaporated. The crowd sensed victory and the players started displaying their usual form.

Oxford were almost made to pay when a free-kick from Mark Blount went close, but on 66 minutes United went 2–0 up. Rush crossed from the right, Massey hooked the ball back across the goal and Moody headed home at the far post. Two minutes later and another header put United 3–0 up; Phil Gilchrist's cross was flicked on by Rush and Elliott was there to loop the ball over Jon Sheffield. Four minutes later and the contest was over, as Mike Ford threaded a pass through the centre of Peterborough's forlorn defence and Rush nipped in to chip the ball over the diving Sheffield. Oxford saw out the game playing exhibition football, and at the final whistle they executed a well-deserved lap of honour, with Denis Smith famously sporting a tartan cap and wig and Stuart Massey uttering what was to become his catchphrase: 'Get in there!'

Oxford United: Whitehead, Robinson, Ford, Smith, Elliott, Gilchrist, Rush, Gray, Moody, Beauchamp, Massey. Sub: Lewis for Gray.

25 January 1999

Oxford United 1 Chelsea 1

FA Cup fourth round

With Oxford United in the midst of a financial crisis, with no owner and on the verge of folding, and sitting third from bottom of the second tier, an FA Cup tie against Premier League leaders Chelsea brought the club much-needed income as well as the glare of national publicity. No one gave United any hope of beating Gianluca Vialli's side. Chelsea featured £29 million worth of talent, including the likes of player-manager Vialli, Gianfranco Zola, Roberto Di Matteo and a teenage centre-back named John Terry.

Chelsea started the game well, impressing with their movement and passing, but they had to be aware of Oxford's counter-attacking, and Ed de Goey had to punch away a powerful header from Mark Watson after half an hour. Dean Windass then shot narrowly over from a free-kick four minutes later. United had youngster Elliott Jackson in goal, as their usual 'keeper Paul Gerrard was not permitted to play by his parent club, Everton. Jackson, just 21, had played 11 games for United, but this was only his third appearance of the season. He gave

Dean Windass (far right) heads United in front following a corner by Jamie Cook (far left).

a heroic performance, however, saving a Zola free-kick and going on to make several more vital stops. Oxford, without the suspended Joey Beauchamp, were matching their more illustrious visitors, who appeared to be suffering from complacency.

Oxford started the second half strongly, attacking down the slope towards the London Road end. They forced a succession of corners and Windass almost got on the end of a Les Robinson cross. In the 52nd minute United got the breakthrough their play had deserved when Windass met a Jamie Cook corner at the near post and headed home from close range. Chelsea were shell-shocked, while United were unrestrained. Kevin Francis and Cook both had excellent chances to score a second, but shot wide when well placed. Chelsea then won a corner, and in the ensuing scramble Francis lunged into a tackle on Vialli and the Chelsea player-manager went down. Referee Mike Reed, no stranger to controversy, pointed to the penalty spot, although television replays clearly showed that Francis had played the ball and made a good tackle. Franck Leboeuf scored the penalty, although Jackson, diving to his left, almost got to the ball.

Chelsea won the replay 4–2, although United had taken an early lead through Phil Gilchrist. The replay was Jackson's last appearance for Oxford, while watching from the stands was Firoz Kassam, who was close to completing his purchase of the club.

Oxford United: Jackson, Robinson, Watson, Gilchrist, Powell, Banger, Gray, Tait, Cook, Murphy, Windass. Subs: Remi for Banger, Francis for Murphy.

11 August 2001

Oxford United 1 Rochdale 2

League Two (first game at Minchery)

United might have had a new ground, a new manager, new players and a new kit, but the football was of the same poor standard that had been on offer for the previous four years or so, as Oxford capitulated to an ordinary Rochdale side.

The excuses were there to be made: there were five new players in the side, which obviously needed time to gel; the team desperately needed a new goalkeeper and a new striker to provide competition and to strengthen the first 11; Rochdale successfully disrupted the flow of the game, not allowing United to build up any rhythm; and the referee was poor. These truths failed to distract attention from the stark fact that Oxford simply failed to threaten, except on three or four occasions. It would have been nice to have started with a win at the new stadium, but perhaps it was just as well that United realised that the Fourth Division was not going to be the cakewalk that many had anticipated. Jamie Brooks scored Oxford's first competitive goal at the new ground, named after chairman Firoz Kassam, but it was in vain as the visitors struck back to take the points.

There were also one or two strange decisions made by new manager Mark Wright. Why was the inexperienced Sam Ricketts brought on for the obviously unfit Paul Powell instead of Joey Beauchamp, who looked distinctly disconsolate warming up along the touchline? It also seemed strange to replace Martin Thomas with Manny Omoyinmi, when Wayne Hatswell was having such a poor game at the back.

Jamie Brooks scores United's first goal at the Kassam Stadium.

This turned out to be just one typical game of a long, hard season, with United struggling to adapt to the new standard of the lower division. Mark Wright lasted less than four months before he was alleged to have racially abused referee Joe Ross and he eventually resigned to be replaced by Ian Atkins.

Oxford United: Knight, Guyett, Stockley, Bolland, Hatswell, Savage, Tait, Powell, Thomas, Scott, Brooks. Subs: Ricketts for Powell, Omoyinmi for Thomas.

8 December 2002

Oxford United 1 Swindon Town 0

FA Cup second round

It says a lot about Oxford supporters that this win over local rivals Swindon sticks in the mind more than the third-round tie at Highbury that followed, where Oxford played Arsenal, the Premiership title holders. This is because there was much more than progress in the FA Cup at stake for this game. This was an opportunity for United to restore some local pride against a Swindon side that was in a higher division and who had done the double over Oxford two seasons previously. Oxford had beaten Dover Athletic 2–0 at the Crabble in the first round to set up this tie and were sitting comfortably in mid-table in the basement division. Swindon were 18th in the division above Oxford and fighting against relegation.

United started the game nervously and were reliant on their back three to keep Swindon at bay in the early stages. However, United fashioned the first real scoring chance when Bart Griemink managed to block James Hunt's shot after a good run and cross down the left

James Hunt watches as Jefferson Louis' header evades the despairing dive of Bert Griemink.

from Dave Savage. Griemink saved again shortly afterwards when Jefferson Louis curled a shot that looked like it was going in at the near post before the Swindon 'keeper saved with his foot. At the other end, the visitors failed to trouble Andy Woodman and their only attacking threat came from a couple of free-kicks that went high and wide. Meanwhile, Savage headed just over from a Bobby Ford corner.

Oxford started the second half on top, with Louis breaking clear and creating a scramble in the Swindon penalty area. United then had a strong appeal for a penalty turned away following a handball as the home side continued to press. Swindon were forced to rely on breakaways and Danny Invincibile almost forced Woodman into his first save of the game after an hour. Five minutes later, United scored the goal that they had been threatening. Scott McNiven took a long throw from the right, Louis flicked the ball goalwards and Steve Basham distracted Griemink long enough for him to lose the flight of the ball, which crept over the line at the far post. United fans celebrated as though they had won the FA Cup. Swindon failed to be galvanized by this setback and it was Oxford who looked more likely to score again. McNiven's long-range shot went narrowly wide, and Basham's shot also went wide when he was well placed to score. Swindon failed to respond and United were through to the third round, with every Oxford player hailed as a hero.

Oxford were drawn to play at Arsenal and they were beaten 2–0 at Highbury, despite Basham having a goal wrongly ruled out for offside in just the second minute. That game was notable for Dennis Bergkamp scoring his 100th Arsenal goal.

Oxford United: Woodman, McNiven, Waterman, Crosby, Bound, Robinson, Hunt, Ford, Savage, Louis, Basham. Subs: Whitehead for Ford, Sall for Basham.

6 May 2006

Oxford United 2 Leyton Orient 3

League Two (relegation to the Conference)

Oxford United had given it their all, but they were left heartbroken as they were relegated from the Football League. United had battled back from behind before an injury-time goal from Lee Steele secured the win and promotion for the visitors. As the teams kicked-off the atmosphere was electric, with Oxford needing a win to stay up and Orient needing a win to get promotion.

The decision to start with Billy Turley had raised a few eyebrows, but after just five minutes he justified his selection with two fantastic saves. First he blocked a Craig Easton volley and then he tipped a shot from Steele onto the post. The nerves were starting to get to everybody when, roared on by the home fans, United scored the opener. Oxford pushed forward and won a 14th-minute free-kick, and Andy Burgess played in a wonderful ball and Eric Sabin scored from six yards. Unfortunately for United, just two minutes later Orient were back on level terms. Good work down the left from Wayne Corden created the space for the cross which was met by the head of Easton. The goal woke up the away side and efforts from Corden and Simpson went close to giving them the lead, although Sabin then wasted a glorious chance when he raced clear and fired over from six yards with just the 'keeper to beat. Despite the away side having the majority of possession, the United defence held firm and went into the break with the scores level.

With a sell-out record crowd, there were hundreds of fans hanging on the fences to try and watch the drama. The Us soaked up pressure early in the second half and only a fine block by the rock-solid Chris Willmott and then a reflex save from Turley from an

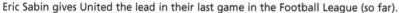

Eric Sabin gives United the lead in their last game in the Football League (so far).

Alexander header kept the scores level in the first five minutes. United were struggling to contain Orient and on 63 minutes they were almost crushed by Gary Alexander's goal. The striker ran clear onto a through ball from Steele and showed great calmness to lift the ball over the advancing Turley and send the away fans into raptures of delight. United were stunned, but two minutes later they were level again. The goal came from a Burgess free-kick which was met powerfully by skipper Chris Hargreaves. Goalkeeper Garner parried it, but Willmott was first to react and thumped his header into the net to spark huge celebrations among the home fans. Sabin had limped off just after Orient's second goal, to be replaced by top scorer Steve Basham, and on 73 minutes it took a flying save to keep Basham's header out from a Matt Robinson cross. Steele inadvertently blocked a goal-bound effort from Corden, thereby doing his former side a great favour. Oxford's task got even harder with six minutes remaining, as Willmott was sent off after a tussle with the booked Mackie. The game ended, predictably, with Steele tapping home from five yards after a breakaway. The final whistle sparked emotional scenes all round, but the sad fact was that after 44 years in the Football League United would once again have to get used to playing non-League football.

Oxford United: Turley, Mansell, Robinson, Quinn, Willmott, Dempster, Sabin, N'Toya, Burgess, Smith, Hargreaves. Subs: Brooks for Mansell, Basham for Sabin, Beechers for Smith.

8 May 2007

Oxford United 1 Exeter City 2

Conference Play-off semi-final (2–2 on aggregate, Oxford lost 4–3 on penalties)

United were condemned to another season of Conference football as they blew a two-goal aggregate lead to lose on penalties to Exeter City at the Kassam Stadium. In a performance that was a microcosm of Oxford's season, the side was in the driving seat following Yemi Odubade's low 29th-minute shot which Martin Rice failed to keep out. This gave the Us a 2–0 lead on aggregate, and, despite having been under the cosh for much of the preceding half hour, they looked like they were cruising to the Play-off Final at Wembley. However, doing things easily is not the United way, and five minutes before half-time their defending at set pieces undid them once again, as they failed to deal with a free-kick and Lee Phillips headed in unmarked at the far post.

The second half continued in the same vein, with Oxford still struggling to create much of a threat. However, an important moment came just after the hour mark when Dave Challinor shot over. Rob Duffy broke free and bore down on goal, Rice committed himself and all Duffy had to do was to steer the ball past the prone 'keeper to restore United's two-goal cushion. Instead, Oxford's leading scorer hit his shot tamely into Rice's midriff and the chance was gone. Less than 10 minutes later, United were ruing the miss as City substitute Adam Stansfield burst into the area and shot home from a narrow angle to level the aggregate scores. Odubade did get the ball in the net again for United, but his close-range header was ruled out for offside.

Yemi Odubade shoots home to give United a 2–0 aggregate lead in the Play-off semi-final, but Exeter struck back to level the score and then win the penalty shoot-out.

Extra-time saw the game become a more even contest, with both teams visibly tiring after the high-tempo opening 90 minutes. Both sides again had good chances to score, with Billy Turley again outstanding in the Oxford goal, while the referee denied United a blatant penalty for handball. And so the game went to a penalty shoot-out, which Oxford lost, again after holding the advantage, and at the end of the marathon tie United were still a non-League club.

Another Conference season would almost certainly mean reduced attendances at home and a smaller following away. Despite the failures of the season, the Us remained the biggest, and richest, club in the Conference the following season and started as the favourites for promotion.

Oxford United: Turley, Odhiambo-Anaclet, Day, Quinn, Gilchrist, Burgess, Foster, Hargreaves, Rose, Odubade, Zebroski. Subs: Duffy for Odhiambe-Anaclet, Pettefer for Foster, Johnson for Rose.

Top Players

John Aldridge

John Aldridge was the most prolific player ever to play for Oxford, scoring 90 goals in his 141 (including three substitute) appearances. He was signed from Newport County by Jim Smith for £78,000 towards the end of the 1983–84 Third Division Championship season, and he was instrumental in the club winning the Second Division Championship the following season, when he scored a club Football League record 34 goals in an unstoppable partnership with Billy Hamilton.

Aldridge was often compared to Liverpool striker Ian Rush, both for their similarity in looks and their similarity in goalscoring. He made his Oxford debut on 7 April 1984, coming on as a substitute in a 1–0 win at Walsall, and he made his full debut 13 days later, when he scored in a 5–0 demolition of Bolton Wanderers.

'Aldo' went on to score 31 goals in the club's first Division One season, although he also missed an open goal in the Milk Cup Final that season. Possibly his most memorable game was against Ipswich on 23 November 1985, when he scored a hat-trick to help turn a 3–0 deficit into a 4–3 victory. He scored three other hat-tricks for United and also hit four goals against Gillingham in a 6–0 League Cup win.

He was on 21 goals for the season in January 1987 when Liverpool paid £750,000 for him. He went on to score 50 goals in 83 games for the Reds. In September 1989 Real Sociedad paid £1 million for Aldridge and he continued his goalscoring exploits in Spain, hitting the back of the net 33 times in 63 appearances.

Two years later he joined Tranmere Rovers for £250,000, where he stayed as a player until May 1998 and scored 138 goals in 242 games. He became their manager in April 1996. He eventually left the Merseyside club in March 2001 and became a media pundit. While at United, Aldo won the first seven of his 25 caps for the Republic of Ireland.

Chris Allen

Chris Allen was a local lad, bought up in Blackbird Leys and brought through United's youth ranks. He made his debut on 1 October 1991 in a Zenith Data Systems Cup game at Swindon that ended 3–3, with United losing on penalties. Allen's League debut came on 8 February 1992, when he was brought on as a substitute in a 2–1 defeat at Leicester City, and he made his first start on 22 February in a 1–0 win over Cambridge United. Although Chris started off mainly on the bench, he soon forced his way into Brian

Horton's line up as a pacey left-winger. 'Chrissy' scored his first goal for the Us on April Fool's Day 1992, in a 2–1 defeat at Millwall.

In February 1996, after having impressed in a 1–1 draw at Nottingham Forest in the FA Cup, Chrissy was taken on loan by Forest, and after his return to the Manor he only made six more appearances, all as substitute. His final appearance for United was in a 1–1 home draw against Notts County on 16 April 1996. At the end of that season, Chrissy was signed by Nottingham Forest for £500,000. He was not too successful there, playing just 25 League games without scoring, and he later had spells at Luton and Cardiff on loan.

Port Vale signed Chris from Forest in 1999 but he played just five games for his new club, scoring once, before moving to Stockport County. He played 17 games for Stockport and then went to Brighton, where he did not get a game. His last professional club was Dover Athletic before he hung up his boots and became a fitness instructor back in Oxford. He joined North Leigh in the Hellenic League and combined playing for them with his duties as a youth coach at Oxford. In total, Chris played 179 games for United, scoring 17 goals.

Jack Ansell

William John Ansell, or 'Jack' as he liked to be known, was born in Newport Pagnell in 1921. A goalkeeper, he was playing for Bletchley Brickworks when Derby County realised his potential and made an offer for him. He did not join the Rams, however, and in January 1947 Northampton Town stepped in, offering terms and the chance for him to remain in his hometown, and he soon took over as the club's number-one 'keeper. A broken leg against Southend United in February 1951 ended a run of 105 consecutive League and Cup games, and when he returned to full fitness he found his way barred by the more experienced Alf Wood. In all, he made 147

first-team appearances for Northampton. Released in 1952, he joined Headington United and in three seasons helped the club win the Southern League Championship once and the Southern League Cup twice. He made his Headington debut on 23 August 1952, keeping a clean sheet in a 0–0 draw with Kidderminster Harriers.

Ansell was an excellent 'keeper and hardly missed a game. In three seasons with the Us he made 149 appearances, keeping 51 clean sheets. He starred in United's 1953–54 FA Cup run and almost single-handedly ensured that the team drew 0–0 at Stockport County to earn a third-round replay, which United won 1–0. His final game for United was on 20 April 1955, in a 2–0 home defeat by Gloucester City.

After leaving Headington, Jack went back to his roots and signed for Bletchley Town. He was also a keen cricketer and played into his 60s. He died in April 2008.

Graham Atkinson

Graham Atkinson was Ron Atkinson's younger brother; both joined United in 1959 from Aston Villa, where they were on the groundstaff while trying to break into the reserves. Graham scored United's first-ever League goal in a 3–2 defeat at Barrow on 18 August 1962. Intotal he scored 107 goals in 398 games. He is still United's top League goalscorer with 77 goals (five more than John Aldridge), and he is sixth in United's appearances table.

Graham's first game for United was on 2 September 1959, a 1–1 Southern League Cup draw with Chelmsford City. He had a brief loan spell at Cambridge United in 1963 before he was recalled by Oxford, who felt that they were missing his punch in attack. He featured regularly as the side climbed from the Fourth Division to reach the Second Division in 1968. Graham was

an outstanding midfielder, strong in defence, swift on the counter-attack and clinical in front of goal. He was granted a testimonial, against Coventry City in May 1973, but his last couple of seasons at Oxford were plagued by injuries and his goals dried up as he played an ever-deeper role. Graham left United at the end of the 1973–74 season to join his brother Ron, who was then manager of Kettering Town.

Ron Atkinson

'Big Ron' is possibly United's most famous player, although, it has to be said, for events after he left Oxford. He joined United in the summer of 1959 as an apprentice from Aston Villa, and before long he became the club's captain. Indeed, he became the first man to captain a club from non-League football to Division Two, a feat which was achieved in just seven years.

Atkinson was never a prolific goalscorer but did reach fifth on United's appearances table. 'Tank' (his nickname at United because of his indomitable midfield displays) made his United debut on 22 August 1959 in a 3–2 win at Weymouth. He went on to play 562 times for the side, 136 of them before election to the Football League. He scored 21 goals altogether, the first coming in a 1–1 draw at Chelmsford City in the Southern League Cup on 9 September 1959. His last game for Oxford was a 1–1 draw at Fulham on 12 October 1971.

Ron left United in 1971 to become player-manager at Kettering Town. He was so successful there that Cambridge United appointed him manager in November 1974, where further success led West Brom to appoint him as boss in 1977, where he was famous for his selection of several black players in the years before this was normal practice. Three years later he was appointed as Manchester United's manager, where he achieved yet more success before they sacked him for not being successful enough and appointed Alex Ferguson instead.

After Old Trafford, Ron returned to West Brom, then briefly managed Atletico Madrid before finishing his managerial career at Sheffield Wednesday. He went on to become a media pundit and his unusual use of English phraseology spawned its own language: Ronglish. He was suspended from ITV for uttering a racist comment without realising that he was still on air, and he was later reappointed by Kettering.

David Bardsley

David Bardsley was an exciting, attacking right-back. He joined Oxford from Watford for £265,000, which was then a record fee for United, in September 1987. He went on to make 94 appearances for the Yellows, scoring seven goals.

He started his career with Blackpool, for whom he played 45 games before moving to Watford for £150,000, when he was switched to right-back from right wing. He made 100 League appearances for the Hornets, scoring seven times. Bardsley had great pace, and could cross the ball while running. He was brought to Oxford to replace Dave Langan, another attacking right-back, and he proved immensely popular with United supporters.

He made his debut on 19 September 1987 in a 2–0 win over QPR and scored his first goal on 16 March 1988, in a 4–2 defeat at Norwich. His final game in an Oxford shirt was on 2 September 1989, in a 2–2 draw at Blackburn Rovers, before he left for QPR for £375,000 plus Mark Stein (who was valued at £125,000). After 296 games for the R's, with six goals to his credit, he left on a free transfer to return to Blackpool, where he played a further 64 League games. He then had a brief (two-game) spell at Northwich Victoria before setting up as a coach in the US.

Bardsley was capped twice for England while at QPR, to add to the England Youth caps that he earned while at Watford.

Jim Barron

Jim Barron is regarded by many Oxford supporters as one of the best goalkeepers to have played for the side. He arrived in March 1966 from Chelsea, where he had made one appearance as Peter Bonetti's deputy. His first game for United was on 8 April 1966 in a 2–0 home defeat by Hull City, and he went on to complete 165 games for the club, keeping 51 clean sheets. In 1970, after a string of impressive performances, he was sold to Nottingham Forest for £30,000. His final game for the Us was on 18 April 1970, when Oxford beat Blackpool, who had just won promotion to the First Division, 2–0 at the Manor.

Barron was the son of James Barron, who had played in goal for Blackburn Rovers and Darlington. As a youth he played for Newcastle West End and turned out for England Boys' Clubs against Ireland. He had the chance to sign for Newcastle United before signing professionally for Wolverhampton Wanderers, for whom he made eight appearances before he moved to Chelsea as understudy to Peter Bonetti. He played 155 games for Forest, after which he joined Swindon Town, where he made 79 appearances. He left the County Ground to go to America, playing 10 times for Connecticut Bicentennials in 1977. His final club was Peterborough United, for whom he played 21 times before retiring in 1981.

Barron formed part of an ex-Oxford contingent at West Brom, where he was a coach alongside manager Ron Atkinson and assistant manager Mick Brown, and he later became Atkinson's assistant. He performed a caretaker managerial role at Wolves in 1984, and four years later he took charge of Cheltenham Town for a season. More recently he was joint caretaker-manager at Birmingham City in 2001 and again at Northampton Town in 2006. He is currently first-team coach at Sixfields.

Steve Basham

Steve Basham joined United just before the 2002–03 season started, having turned down the offer of a new contract from Preston North End. Basham came with rave reviews from Preston, where he had established a reputation for himself as a top goalscorer before a broken leg robbed him of a regular first-team place, which he was never able to recover. 'Bash' failed to make too many appearances at the start of the 2002–03 season due to injury, but his finishing in those games he did play fully justified his signing. He found his scoring boots again at the end of the season and signed a new one-year contract before the start of the 2003–04 season. This was extended for a further year during the summer of 2004, thanks to Bash notching up over 30 appearances and thereby triggering an extension clause.

At the start of the 2004–05 season Basham found it difficult to break into the team, but he did feature at right wing for a few games. Later in the season, after the arrival of Ramon Diaz as manager, Basham started to forge a decent partnership with either Tommy Mooney or Craig Davies and he added to his goal tally. He signed a new two-year contract with United for the 2005–06 season but was released by Jim Smith at the end of the 2006–07 season, after missing the second half of the campaign following an injury received at Exeter, whom he joined after leaving United. He left United just one goal short of his 50th.

Basham scored on his Oxford debut at Darlington on 17 August 2002 and went on to play 189 games for the Us. His last game was on New Year's Day 2007, a 2–1 defeat at Exeter. His last goal for United came in a 1–1 draw with Grays Athletic in September 2006. He was the club's leading scorer in both 2003–04 and 2005–06.

Basham started his career with Southampton, for whom he played 20 games, scoring once, before loan moves to Wrexham and Preston. He then joined Preston on a permanent contract before his eventual move to Oxford. Basham was released by Exeter in May 2009.

Joey Beauchamp

In a poll run by United fanzine *Rage On*, Joey Beauchamp was voted Oxford United's Player of the '90s. The winger, who was born in Oxford and played for Summertown Stars as a youth, was signed by Oxford as a YTS trainee in 1987, making his debut on 13 May 1989 as a substitute against Watford. His pace, skill and ability to play to good effect on either wing made him an instant hero with the Oxford faithful, and the fact that he was local and supported the side as a child (he was even a ball boy for the 1986 Milk Cup Final) made him immensely popular.

Joey scored his first goal for the club on 28 December 1991 in a 3–0 win over

Sunderland, and he went on to score 77 goals in 428 appearances, spread over two separate spells with United. This puts him 10th in the Oxford appearances table and fifth in the all-time Oxford goalscoring chart.

Having made an impact in the Second Division, Joey was bought by West Ham United for £1 million after the end of the 1993–94 season, in which United suffered relegation. Typically, Joey scored a sensational goal in the final game against Notts County in what was thought to be his farewell appearance. However, Joey failed to settle at Upton Park, claiming that the move was a mistake, and he was sold to Swindon Town for £800,000 just six weeks later, having played just one game for the Hammers – a friendly at Oxford City. His stay at the County Ground was an unhappy one, and he lost his first-team place after falling out with manager Steve McMahon. Hearing that he was available, Denis Smith bought Joey back to the Manor for just £75,000, 16 months after he had left. On his return Joey immediately became a hero again and was quickly forgiven for joining Swindon when he scored the third goal in a 3–0 win over them. As United went on a promotion-winning run in 1996, Joey scored a supreme volley from 35 yards against Blackpool; a goal that was later voted the best Oxford goal at the Manor by supporters.

Joey's career was cut short by an injury to his big toe that failed to heal properly, and he left United on a sad note following a contractual dispute with chairman Firoz Kassam. In his last game for the club, against Exeter City at the Kassam Stadium, Joey scored another excellent goal with a volley from the edge of the penalty area. After leaving United Joey went on to play locally for Didcot Town and Abingdon Town, before ending up with Sunday League side Oxford Yellows.

Cyril Beavon

Cyril Beavon joined Headington United in January 1959 from Wolverhampton Wanderers, where he had played for the England Youth team against Hungary in 1956. Beavon was on the verge of breaking into Wolves' first team when the Molineux club decided to let him go, and Arthur Turner persuaded him to come to the Manor, where he quickly established himself as an uncompromising defender.

Beavon made his United debut at Gravesend & Northfleet on 21 January 1959 and went on to play 464 times for the side over the next 10 years. His final match was on 20 April 1969 against Sheffield United in the Second Division. Beavon is currently fifth in United's all-time appearances chart. Arthur Turner, for whom Beavon was his first signing for United, claimed that Cyril could have played at a much higher level, and he would have taken Beavon to Leeds United

with him had he taken the Elland Road job. Beavon was one of four regular players who featured for United in the Southern League and the rise up to the Second Division (along with the Atkinson brothers and Maurice Kyle).

After leaving Oxford Beavon joined Banbury United on a free transfer, staying with the Puritans for a season before going on to manage Bicester Town. Beavon's son Stuart played for United's youth team before joining Tottenham Hotspur and Reading, while his grandson, also called Stuart, had an unsuccessful trial with United before leaving Didcot Town for Weymouth and then Wycombe.

Gary Briggs

Gary Briggs earned himself the nickname 'Rambo' due to his solid and aggressive performances in the centre of Oxford's defence. He joined United from Middlesbrough (after a four-month loan spell) in July 1978 for £12,500, a fee settled

by the Football League's first tribunal sitting (Briggs' was the second case they heard). Briggs made his Oxford debut in a 3–2 home defeat by Cambridge United on 11 January 1978 and he went on to play 508 times for the club, scoring 22 goals. He scored in his last game for United, a 2–2 draw at Shrewsbury Town on 14 April 1989.

Briggs was arguably one of the most able central-defenders to have played for United, and he was present throughout the glory years in the mid-1980s. His partnership with Malcolm Shotton is often quoted by Oxford fans as the best defensive partnership seen at the club. He was granted a testimonial game against Swindon Town in August 1987. Briggs left Oxford for Blackpool on a free transfer and he played there for six seasons before joining Chorley. He played in United's Farewell to the Manor match and also in Peter Rhoades-Brown's testimonial game against Chelsea, on both occasions proving that he could still play as well as some of the younger players on show.

Kevin Brock

Kevin Brock was born in Bicester and signed for Oxford as a schoolboy. He made his debut for United on 1 September 1979, just eight days before his 17th birthday,

against Barnsley. He went on to make 305 appearances for the Yellows. While with Oxford Brock won four England Under-21 caps. Brock's final game for Oxford was on 9 May 1987, a 0–0 draw against Leicester that saw the Foxes get relegated from the First Division.

Brock was an accomplished wide midfielder and an integral part of the hugely successful Oxford side of the mid-1980s. After leaving Oxford he followed former United manager Jim Smith around, first to QPR, who paid Oxford £260,000 for him, and then to Newcastle United for £300,000 in December 1998. After a brief loan spell at Cardiff City Brock went to Banbury United and eventually became their manager, leading them from the Hellenic League to the Southern League Premier Division. He left the Puritans in some controversy, resigning after financial cuts, and went to the Hellenic League's Ardley United.

Brock's lasting legacy at Oxford is his infamous back-pass, made during a League Cup fifth-round tie against Everton on 18 January 1984. With Third Division United leading 1–0 with less than 10 minutes remaining, Brock's ball to Steve Hardwick was intercepted by Adrian Heath, who equalised. Everton won the replay and turned around their ailing fortunes.

Mickey Bullock

Mickey Bullock arrived at the Manor from Birmingham City in the summer of 1967. He had made his Birmingham debut when he was 16, scoring the winning goal in a 2–1 win against Manchester United. Oxford paid Birmingham almost £10,000 for Bullock, setting a new club record in the process. In his first season for United he was the club's leading scorer, with 16 goals in 50 games, as Oxford won promotion to Division Two for the first time.

Bullock, true to his name, was a big, strong centre-forward. He combined well with United's other forwards, notably Graham Atkinson and John Shuker, and his presence was enough of a distraction to defenders for others to take advantage. Bullock was less prolific in the higher division, however, and in October, after playing just 15 games and scoring twice, United sold him to Leyton Orient for £18,000.

He was with Orient until 1975, after which he went to Halifax, initially as a player, although after three years he hung up his boots and took over managerial duties. He was sacked in October 1984 and went on to manage Goole Town and then Ossett Town until 1991.

Roy Burton

Hailed by many who saw him as United's best-ever 'keeper, Roy Burton kept goal for United for 11 years, before leaving for Witney Town. Burton made his debut for Oxford on 20 November 1971 in a 2–0 defeat at Portsmouth, replacing Republic of Ireland international Mick Kearns. Previously, Burton had played in the Football Combination for United's reserves, having signed in 1969, and he became a full professional in September 1970 at the age of 19.

In March 1982 new manager Jim Smith took over from Ian Greaves, and the next season was Burton's last for United. He played the first 16 games before Smith replaced him with John Butcher, whom he had managed at Blackburn Rovers. Burton returned for one final game, on 28 December 1982, a 2–1 win over Newport County, before being released at the end of the season following the signing of Steve Hardwick for £20,000 from Newcastle United the previous February.

In all, Burton played 449 games for the Yellows, keeping a grand total of 132 clean sheets. He will be fondly remembered by United fans for his eccentric attire, as his shorts were often found wanting of elastic, exposing his rear end to the crowd behind the goal in the London Road end. He will also be remembered for some absolutely outstanding saves, many of which seemed impossible, especially given that he was just 5ft 9in tall. He was always bantering with the home supporters and will always be an Oxford legend. He is one of the most popular old boys when the stars of yesteryear gather for games.

John Byrne

John Byrne was signed by Denis Smith in November 1993 at the same time as Matt Elliott and Phil Whitehead, and he made his debut in a 2–2 draw at Millwall's New Den on 6 November. Byrne was a stylish, flamboyant striker, signed in a vain attempt to keep the club from relegation to Division Three. He was famous among Oxford fans for, among other things, his bull-horn goal celebration. He struck up an excellent partnership with Paul Moody before injury cut short his time at United. His last game was on 21 February 1995 at Rotherham United, before he returned to his home town of Brighton. Byrne played 66 games for United, scoring 19 goals. Rarely has United fielded a player with such flair, and he was an instant favourite with the Oxford fans.

Byrne started his career with York City in 1979, where he first played alongside, and was later managed by, Denis Smith. In

1984 he moved to QPR for £115,000, where he played on the losing side to Oxford in the 1986 Milk Cup Final. In 1988 he moved to Le Havre for £175,000, before a £120,000 move to Brighton in 1990. He met up again with Smith briefly in 1991 when he moved to Sunderland for £225,000. While at Roker Park he scored in every round of the club's FA Cup run except the Final, but a year later he was on the road again, joining Millwall for £250,000. He had a lengthy loan spell back at Brighton at the end of the 1993–94 season before his £50,000 move to Oxford United. After returning to Brighton from Oxford he played for the Seagulls for just over a year before eventually retiring and becoming a radio commentator. Byrne also won 23 caps for the Republic of Ireland, all coming before he joined Oxford, and scored four goals.

Jack Casley

Jack Casley was United's first full-time professional footballer. He signed in July 1949, initially on a one-month trial at a wage of £6 a week plus bonuses, before signing permanently for £7 a week plus £1 a week groundsman's fees. He came from Torquay United, his home-town club, whom he joined in June 1947. In his final game for Torquay he had played in goal because of an injury crisis, and his first game for Headington, on 27 August 1949, again saw him don the custodian's gloves, although he conceded four goals in a 4–2 defeat at Colchester United. In his next game for United, on 17 September 1949, he played up front as Headington lost 3–1 at Hemel Hempstead in an FA Cup preliminary-round tie. In the following match he scored the club's first Southern League hat-trick in a 4–2 win over Guildford City. These were Casley's only goals for the club.

The club initially decided to refrain from offering Casley a new contract at the end of the 1949–50 season, but after he agreed to reduce his winter wages to £3 a week they relented and he was re-signed.

Casley eventually played a total of 19 games for Headington, his final match being a 3–1 win at Dartford on 10 May 1951. After his early retirement, Casley

stayed on at United in a variety of roles, eventually becoming chief scout. In 2002 the club recognised his long service, presenting him with a special award.

Nigel Cassidy

Nigel Cassidy was a true 1970s icon for United, and his long hair and trademark moustache were distinctive even in an era of long hair and moustaches. He started his career with Lowestoft Town, and from there he moved to Norwich City in July 1967. His stay at Carrow Road was brief, and he made just four League appearances before he moved to Scunthorpe United, where he partnered Kevin Keegan. There is a common misperception that United went to Scunthorpe to buy Keegan but returned with Cassidy in error; however it was Cass in whom United were interested and they brought him to the Manor for £20,000 in November 1970, setting a new club transfer record.

Cassidy's first game was a 0–0 draw against Swindon Town on 21 November and he went on to play 135 games for United, scoring 34 goals. His first goal, on 5 December 1970, gave the Us a 1–0 win over Cardiff City, and he was also one of Oxford's scorers in their 3–1 win at Swindon on 24 February 1973. His final goal for the club was on 29 December 1973, in a 2–1 win over Aston Villa, while his last appearance was in a 3–0 home defeat by Millwall on 26 January 1974.

Cassidy was then sold to Third Division Cambridge United for £28,000. After a season at the Abbey he played for Denver Dynamos in the US before returning to Cambridge in 1975, but then an Achilles tendon injury forced him to retire. He stayed in the Oxford area, playing for Bicester Town before becoming player-manager of Banbury United, and he then retired to Cornwall to manage a pub. He died on 19 May 2008 after a short illness caused by an insect bite received while travelling abroad.

Colin Clarke

Colin Clarke joined Oxford United from Arsenal on a free transfer in July 1965. He had arrived at the Gunners from Scottish side Arthurlie Juniors but failed to get into the Arsenal first team. He made his debut for United as a 19-year-old centre-half in a 2–1 defeat at Workington on 11 February 1966 and went on to play 497 games for the club over the next 12 years. His final appearance was on 1 March 1978 in a 2–1 home win over Wrexham.

Although a commanding defender, Clarke also scored 26 goals for the club, and United only lost one of the games in

which Clarke scored. Clarke was prominent throughout the club's first seasons in the Second Division, playing alongside Dave Roberts in the side's most successful spells. He was eventually supplanted by Gary Briggs, and he was awarded a well-deserved testimonial against Norwich City in May 1977.

After finishing at Oxford, where many fans rate him as one of the best defenders to have played for the club, he went to play briefly in the US for Los Angeles Aztecs before joining Malcolm Allison's Plymouth Argyle. From there he went on to be player-manager of Kettering Town, who he took to second in the Conference, and then Corby Town before becoming youth-team manager of first Charlton Athletic and then Aston Villa. He then moved permanently to the US, becoming assistant men's soccer coach for the University of Tulsa.

Derek Clarke

Derek was one of the famous Clarke brothers, whose number included striker Allan, who played for Leicester City, Leeds United and England, and Frank, who achieved fame at Nottingham Forest. Derek began his career with Walsall, for whom he played six League games in 1967–68, scoring twice, before he moved to

Wolverhampton Wanderers. He made only five appearances for Wolves in two seasons before Oxford signed him for £11,500 on 2 October 1970. Derek made his United debut on 24 October in a 1–0 win at Sunderland, and he scored the first of his 40 goals for Oxford one week later when United beat Charlton Athletic 2–1 at the Manor.

Clarke was a stylish centre-forward, whose goals included the spectacular as well as the routine. One of his best goals came in a 2–1 win over Fulham at the Manor on 26 October 1974, when he curled the ball around the defenders and goalkeeper from the corner of the penalty area. He also scored a magnificent 30-yarder when Oxford beat Manchester United 1–0 in the Second Division on 8 February 1975. His last goal for the club was scored on 17 April 1976 in a 3–1 home defeat by Luton Town. His last appearance for United was as a substitute on 17 August 1976 in a 2–0 League Cup defeat at Cambridge United.

After leaving Oxford, Clarke spent three seasons at Leyton Orient, where he scored six goals in 36 games, and he had a brief, one-game loan spell at Carlisle United before injury forced him to retire.

Joe Cooke

Joe Cooke was born on the Leeward Island of Dominica, and he came to England as a child. He joined Bradford City as a schoolboy in July 1970 and made his debut as a 16-year-old in September 1971. In 1979 he joined Peterborough United and in August that year he moved to Oxford United for £50,000.

Joe started life at Oxford as a striker alongside Paul Berry, but loss of form led to him being played further back, alongside Gary Briggs in defence. He scored on his Oxford debut, a 2–2 draw at Hull City on 25 August 1979, and

eventually scored 13 goals for United. His last game was a 1–0 win over Millwall on 29 April 1981.

Cooke was a solid defender, and he was also United's first black captain. In June 1981 he was sold to Exeter City for £25,000, after which he returned to Bradford City where he played for three years before joining Rochdale and then Wrexham, where he finished his professional career in 1988, when he joined Liversedge.

Hugh Curran

Hugh Curran was a strong Scottish striker who had two spells at Oxford, although the first was undeniably his most successful. He started off as an apprentice with Manchester United, but his first professional club was Third Lanark in his native Glasgow, for whom he played nine games, scoring twice, in 1962–63. After a season with Corby Town he joined Millwall in March 1964 and was their top goalscorer in the following season, when they were promoted from the Fourth Division. In January 1966 he was signed by Norwich City, where he was voted the club's Player of the Year for 1968. In 1969 he moved to First Division Wolverhampton Wanderers, and he won five caps for Scotland while at Molineux. His last game for Wolves was the second leg

of the 1972 UEFA Cup Final which they lost to Tottenham Hotspur.

In September 1972 Oxford paid Wolves £50,000 and he soon forged a strong partnership with Nigel Cassidy. Curran was leading scorer in both the 1972–73 and 1973–74 seasons, with 17 and 14 goals respectively. His first game was on 16 September 1972 against Millwall, and Curran scored the first of his 43 goals in that match. He scored his only hat-trick for the club five games later, in a 5–1 win over Sunderland on 7 October, and he was also one of Oxford's scorers in their 3–1 win at the County Ground on the only occasion that United have won at Swindon Town.

Curran left Oxford for Bolton Wanderers in September 1974 for £40,000, but he returned to the Manor three years later. In 1979 Curran retired through injury and returned to Scotland to run his own hairdressing business. He later returned to Oxfordshire, where he managed pubs in Horton-cum-Studley and Islip for a while.

Geoff Denial

Geoff Denial joined Headington United from Sheffield United in 1955, but as a part-time professional he was available for conscription and was called-up to serve during the Suez Crisis of that year. He eventually made his Headington debut on 29 September 1956 against Exeter City Reserves in the Southern League, and he went on to play 199 matches for the club, scoring the first of his 51 goals against Banbury Spencer in a 1–0 win in the FA Cup first qualifying round on 21 September 1957.

Although as a 16-year-old Denial played for Oaksfold, the Sheffield Wednesday nursery side, he signed for Sheffield United aged 17. Denial made 16 appearances for the Blades prior to joining United, and he went on to become a

prominent part of the club's most successful Southern League years that saw them gain election to the Football League in 1962. Denial was made captain in 1959–60 after Frank Ramshaw left the club and he was the most senior player as the club entered the League; although he only played seven games in 1962–63.

Denial was a versatile player, filling a number of positions with equal success, although most usually as left wing-half. He was only a part-time player, working as a heating engineer the rest of the time. Denial was granted a testimonial match along with Johnny Love against Stoke City in February 1962, but it was cancelled and rearranged for the following month against Leicester City (with United winning 5–2) and then the duo had a second testimonial in April of that season against Coventry City, which United won 3–0. After leaving Oxford, Denial joined Rugby Town.

John Durnin

John Durnin joined Oxford from Liverpool in February 1989. He had joined Liverpool from youth side Waterloo Dock in 1986 but only managed two first-team performances for the Reds, both League Cup games. He then had a loan spell at West Bromwich Albion in 1988, scoring two goals in five games, before he sealed his move to Oxford for £225,000. He made his Oxford debut on 11 February 1989 in a 1–0 win over Portsmouth and he scored his first goal on 27 March 1989 as United beat Walsall 1–0.

Durnin quickly established a reputation at Oxford as a poacher, lethal in the six-yard box. He scored 47 goals for the club, including a brace against Swindon Town when Oxford beat them 5–3 in March 1992, and on 14 November 1992 Durnin scored all the goals as Oxford beat Luton Town 4–0 at the Manor. Durnin played 180 games for the Us and his final match was a 1–1 draw against Notts County on 1 May 1993.

In July 1993 Portsmouth paid Oxford £200,000 for Durnin. He made 207 appearances over almost seven seasons for Pompey, scoring 33 goals. He had loan spells at Blackpool and Carlisle United before joining the Cumbrians permanently in February 2000. At the end of the 2000–01 season he joined League new boys Kidderminster Harriers, and eight months later he left for Port Vale, managed by his former Oxford colleague Martin Foyle. In April 2003 Durnin joined Accrington Stanley, before retiring from the professional game in May 2004.

Matt Elliott

Matt Elliott is a true Oxford United legend and is possibly one of the club's greatest-ever players. He started his career with Leatherhead and Epsom & Ewell before joining Charlton Athletic in 1988 for £5,000. He played just one game at Charlton and in 1989 he moved to Torquay United for £10,000. He played 158 games for the Gulls and scored 20 goals in three seasons at Plainmoor before joining Scunthorpe United for £50,000 in June 1992 after a brief loan spell.

In November 1993 Oxford United paid Scunthorpe £150,000 for Elliott's services and he made his debut, along with Phil Whitehead and John Byrne, on 6 November in a 2–2 draw at Millwall, and he scored his first goal for the club the following week as United beat Derby County 2–0. Elliott was unable to prevent Oxford's relegation that season but he was instrumental in leading United to the top of the Third Division in the first half of the following season and United's promotion the season after, scoring and making a significant number of goals for a central-defender.

In total, Elliott scored 25 goals for Oxford in 181 appearances, including a superb 35-yard effort at Carlisle United in February 1996. Elliott's last game for Oxford was on 11 January 1997 in a 2–0 defeat at Bradford City, after which he was sold to Leicester City for a club record £1.6 million.

Although a couple of months earlier United had been in the Play-off positions, they were in mid-table by the time of Elliott's sale. However, many Oxford supporters still attribute the start of the club's decline to Elliott's departure. He stayed at Leicester for seven years, during which time he was called-up to play for Scotland, for whom he won 18 caps and scored one goal.

In 2004 Elliott had a 10-game loan spell at Ipswich Town, and in 2008 he became assistant manager at Hednesford Town.

Ceri Evans

Ceri Evans was an example of one of those rare footballers who fall into the lap of a club by chance. Evans was already an established New Zealand international when he arrived in Oxford to study as a Rhodes Scholar, and he gained a first-class honours degree in experimental psychology. He had played National

League Soccer for Nelson United in 1980–81, before playing for Christchurch United in 1982, Dunedin City the following year and then Christchurch again from 1984–87. With Christchurch Evans twice won the National League and was named Footballer of the Year in New Zealand.

Ceri signed for Oxford on the recommendation of Richard Hill, who had a spell in New Zealand after he left United, and he went on to play 135 times for the Us, making his debut as a substitute on 1 April 1989 in a 1–0 defeat at Leicester City. Evans was a towering centre-back, tough in the tackle, commanding in the air and calm on the ball. He was described by New Zealand defender Garry Lund as 'probably New Zealand's premier centre-back'.

Ceri won 85 New Zealand caps, two of them while with Oxford, and scored three goals for his country. Evans's final game for United was a 1–0 defeat by Charlton Athletic on 17 April 1993, after which he played for Marlow. He was injured when Marlow astonishingly beat Oxford United 2–0 in the FA Cup first round in November 1994. After finishing at Marlow Evans retired from football and became a forensic psychiatrist in Christchurch, New Zealand.

David Fogg

David Fogg was born in Dingle, Liverpool, and after leaving school he earned a living as an apprentice toolmaker. He was playing for local side Belvedere when he was spotted by Wrexham at the age of 17. However, he decided to finish his apprenticeship, and it was not until he was 21 that he joined the Welsh club, making his debut on 22 February 1971 in a 2–2 draw at Plymouth. He went on to make 176 appearances for Wrexham before he was released in the summer of 1976, when he joined Oxford. He played in both full-back positions with equal ability and also became Oxford's regular penalty taker for a while.

Fogg made his Oxford debut on 17 August 1976, in a League Cup defeat at Cambridge United. He went on to play 336 games for the Us over the next eight seasons, finally hanging up his boots after playing his last game on 5 February 1985, at Crystal Palace.

In his last two seasons at Oxford he only played six games, having lost his place to David Hinshelwood, who was himself replaced by Bobby McDonald. Although Fogg was never known as a goalscorer (he did not score once at Wrexham), he still managed to find the net 21 times for United. He scored his first in a 5–2 home win over Grimsby Town on 18 September 1976 and was also on target in the 5–0 win over Swindon Town on 7 April 1982. He was granted a testimonial against QPR on 7 May 1986.

After retiring, Fogg joined the Oxford coaching staff, managing the reserves side for a while. He went on to become youth-team coach at Everton before leaving after the resignation of manager Kevin Ratcliffe. He then moved on to Chester City, where he was instrumental in setting up their youth system, before he joined Shrewsbury Town as assistant manager in controversial circumstances, the Shrews being found guilty of making an illegal approach for Fogg.

Peter Foley

Peter Foley was spotted by Oxford manager Gerry Summers while playing for Bardwell Boys in the Bicester Boys' League Cup Final at the age of 14. He signed as an apprentice in September 1973, aged 16,

and a year later he became a full professional. He made his debut on 22 March 1975 in a 1–1 draw at Oldham Athletic, and he scored the first of his 90 Oxford United goals in a 3–3 League Cup draw at Charlton Athletic on 9 September 1975. In 1976–77 he was the side's leading scorer with 13 goals and the following season he struck 21 goals. He was selected to play four times for the Republic of Ireland youth team and won six caps at Under-21 level as well, captaining the side against Argentina and Yugoslavia in the Toulon tournament. He was selected to play for the full side in a friendly at Malta, but United needed him for a vital League game and so he had to withdraw from the squad.

West Brom manager Ron Atkinson offered United £100,000 for Foley, but United turned it down. He played 321 games in total for United. He went out on loan to Gillingham in February 1983 and at the end of that season he left Oxford for the now defunct Bulova FC (in Hong Kong), where he spent 15 months. Upon his return to England he joined Aldershot, where he played alongside Martin Foyle until injury ended his career. He later played for and managed Witney Town, and he then moved on to Brackley Town and then Marlow, whom he managed when they beat Oxford United 2–0 in the FA Cup first round in 1994. He followed this with spells as manager of Oxford City, Thame United, Didcot Town and, most recently, Ardley. Foley was granted a testimonial against Manchester United in May 1985.

Bobby Ford

Bobby Ford is one of those rare players who has played for United in two separate spells. The first time around he came through the ranks to become one of the club's most gifted midfielders of modern times. Ford made his first-team debut on 4

September 1993 in an Anglo-Italian Cup defeat at Bristol City. A few substitute appearances followed before he cemented his place in the starting line up in February 1994, coming in for the 3–2 FA Cup replay win at Leeds United. He scored his first goal for United on Boxing Day 1994, in a 4–1 win at Peterborough United.

He was transferred to Sheffield United for £400,000 in November 1997 when the club was desperate for cash, and he inevitably scored against Oxford when the clubs next met. Almost five years later, after 188 games and seven goals for the Blades, he returned to Oxford on a free transfer following a successful trial. His second spell at the Us was an unhappy one, as manager Ian Atkins's tactics of bypassing the midfield did not suit Ford's style of play. He lasted just one season, playing 41 games and scoring once before quitting the professional game, signing for Bath City and taking up plumbing.

In his two spells for the club Ford played a total of 190 games, during which he scored 12 times. His goals included a memorable solo effort straight from a kick-off in a League Cup defeat at Southampton and a long-range shot in a televised 3–0 win over Wolverhampton Wanderers at the Manor.

Mike Ford

Ford arrived at the club from Cardiff City in the summer of 1988 but he did not make his debut until 7 January 1989, when he came on as a substitute in a third-round FA Cup tie at Sunderland, which ended in a 1–1 draw. This was because Ford, who had won the Cardiff Player of the Season award the previous season, injured his back while on honeymoon in the summer.

Ford had arrived at Cardiff from Devizes Town, whom he joined after serving his apprenticeship at Leicester City. He played 167 times for the Bluebirds, scoring 13 goals, before Oxford paid £150,000 for his services.

Initially signed as a midfielder, Ford found his niche at left-back. He suffered numerous injuries at the club which severely limited his appearances. 'Fordy' was one of Oxford's most popular players, making 339 appearances for the side and scoring 22 goals, including a memorable brace, both from long range, at Cambridge. He was honoured with a testimonial against Manchester United in May 2000.

Ford returned to Cardiff in August 1998, spending two years at Ninian Park and playing 52 games, scoring once, before coming back to the Manor for his swan song in September 2000. He played just one game in his second spell, on 30 December 2000 in a home defeat by Bristol City. Ford went on to have a short spell as caretaker manager for Oxford after Denis Smith's departure and then became assistant manager at Oxford City.

Martin Foyle

On 26 March 1987 United paid Aldershot £140,000 for the services of Martin Foyle. He had played 206 games for the Shots and scored 44 goals after they signed him for £10,000 from Southampton, where he had played 14 games, scoring three times. He went on loan to Swedish side Munkfors from May to October 1982, and he also had a brief loan spell at Blackburn Rovers but failed to play any first-team games.

Foyle's Oxford debut came when he replaced Ray Houghton as a substitute in a 2–1 win over Sheffield Wednesday on 28 March. Foyle initially found games difficult to come by during the 1986–87 season, as Billy Whitehurst resisted attempts to replace him. Foyle scored his first goal for the Us in a 1–1 draw at Sheffield Wednesday on 18 August 1987. He carried on playing for the Yellows until the end of the 1990–91 season and altogether he clocked up 151 appearances and scored 44 times. His final appearance was a 1–0 defeat at Leicester on 11 May 1991 and his last goal was in a 3–0 win at Brighton, on 20 April, the fifth anniversary of United's Milk Cup Final triumph.

Foyle was an intelligent player, often bringing others into the game, and the partnership that he forged with Dean Saunders was memorable, if brief. Foyle joined Port Vale for £375,000 in the summer of 1991, becoming the Valiants' record signing. He played well over 500 games for Vale over the next nine seasons and scored 107 goals to become their record post-war goalscorer.

He was appointed Vale manager in February 2004 and he remained in that position until September 2007. Foyle later became assistant manager at Wrexham before, in November 2008, he was appointed manager of Conference side York City.

Phil Gilchrist

Phil Gilchrist started as a Nottingham Forest trainee in 1990 but he moved to Middlesbrough just over a year later without having played a game for Forest. He was at Ayresome Park for 11 months when he joined Hartlepool United on a free transfer, again without having played for Middlesbrough. He made 96 appearances for Pools.

Gilchrist's debut for United, after signing from Hartlepool for £100,000, was a 0–0 draw against Bristol Rovers on 18 February 1995. Gilly's arrival helped to steady the ship as Oxford had begun to plummet down the table, having topped the division on Boxing Day, but it was the following season, 1995–96, that Gilchrist's partnership with Matt Elliott was really forged as both players were virtual ever presents. After Elliott's departure in January 1998 Gilchrist stayed for a further two seasons, eventually leaving to rejoin Elliott at Leicester City, still in the Premiership, for £500,000, just after the first match of the 1999–2000 season by which time United were back in the third tier. Gilchrist's final match was a 2–1 win at Stoke's Britannia Stadium.

Gilchrist was with Leicester for 17 months, playing 51 times, before West Brom paid another £500,000 for him. He played 105 times for West Brom before a brief loan spell at Rotherham United turned into a permanent move. He had played a total of 51 games for Rotherham when Jim Smith brought Gilchrist back to

Oxford after the side's relegation to the Conference in the summer of 2006, and he immediately installed him as captain. In his second spell with the club Gilchrist made 44 appearances, to add to the 201 he had made earlier in his career, and he scored a total of 12 goals in both spells with United. After retiring from playing during the 2007–08 season, he joined Woking as assistant manager before becoming manager in October 2008. He was sacked on 2 April 2009, with Woking facing relegation.

Billy Hamilton

Billy Hamilton joined Oxford from Burnley, to whom United paid £95,000 plus Neil Whatmore, in the summer of 1984. He started his career with Belfast Scots but was spotted by Linfield, with whom he won the Ulster League and Cup double in 1978. In March that year QPR signed him for £25,000 and it was while with Rangers that Hamilton won his first Northern Ireland cap. He joined Burnley from Loftus Road for £55,000 in November 1979.

In 1982 Billy played in the World Cup Finals in Spain and he scored both goals in the 2–2 draw with Austria. He won 41 caps for Northern Ireland, scoring five goals. He made his Oxford debut in the first game of the 1984–85 season, a 3–0 win at Huddersfield. His first goal came in his next outing, a League Cup draw at Hereford, but he made a real mark in the second leg when he scored a hat-trick in a 5–3 victory.

It was during the 1984–85 season that Hamilton forged his strong partnership with John Aldridge. The two players appeared together in 31 matches, with Billy scoring 18 times, 10 of them in the Second Division. Both players scored two hat-tricks, with Billy's second trio coming in a 4–0 home win over Carlisle at the end of September. Billy was a tall target man, unbeatable in the air and with an unerring ability to find his teammates with his flicks and headers.

The following season, in Division One, Billy's time was even more blighted by injury than the previous campaign, and he managed only eight games, in which he scored three times. Two of those goals came in the early-season 5–0 thrashing of Leicester City, while the third came in the last game of the season, which United had to win to stay up, when they beat Arsenal 3–0. That was Billy's last goal for the club and he only played in two more matches before being forced to retire with the injury that had restricted his appearances the previous two seasons, his last game being a 2–0 win over Coventry City on 11 October 1986.

In total, Hamilton played just 41 games for United, scoring an incredible 20 goals. Hamilton was nicknamed 'Mushroom Billy' by United fans, because of his stated predilection for eating the wild mushrooms that grew at the Oxford training ground. After leaving Oxford, he had a testimonial game against a Northern Ireland XI that included George Best, and he went on to become player-manager of Limerick after doing a couple of months' scouting for United. After spells with Sligo Rovers and Coleraine he was signed by Distillery as player-manager in 1989 before eventually retiring in 1995.

Colin Harrington

Colin Harrington was an exciting left-winger who joined United in the club's last Southern League season; although he did not make his debut until 19 April 1963 in a 0–0 draw at Workington. The Bicester-born player had spent a couple of seasons on the books of Wolves, without playing a game, and when he was released Arthur Turner offered him a trial at United. Harrington went on to play 260 games for United, scoring the first of his 32 goals in a 2–0 win at Chester City on 24 August 1963.

Harrington is widely regarded as one of the fastest players to have played for the club and was given the nickname 'Flash' by his colleagues. He was also an excellent crosser of the ball with his left foot. When Gerry Summers became manager Harrington was sacrificed for a change in formation, and he played just twice in the 1970–71 season, making his final appearance for United on 10 March 1971 in a home defeat by Orient. That summer he moved to Mansfield Town, where he played 13 games before Ron Atkinson signed him for Kettering Town. He made 81 appearances for the Poppies, scoring 18 goals, after making his debut on 12 August 1972.

Trevor Hebberd

Hebberd joined United in March 1982 as part of the deal that took Mark Wright to Southampton. He had joined the Saints as a schoolboy in 1974 and made his first-team debut in 1976, going on to play 97 League games for them. He also had loan spells at Washington Diplomats, Leicester City and Bolton Wanderers before leaving for Oxford.

Hebberd made his United debut on 27 March in a 1–1 home draw against Chesterfield, and he went on to make 326 appearances, not one of them as substitute. At the Saints he was famous for his stamina and earned the nickname 'Nijinski' as a result. Although he found it difficult to settle after first joining the club, he became one of the side's most pivotal players, reaching his zenith with a Man of the Match performance in the 3–0 Milk Cup Final win over QPR on 20 April 1986.

The 1987–88 season was to be Hebberd's final campaign as an Oxford player before he was signed by Robert Maxwell's Derby County for £300,000. Hebberd scored three goals in his farewell season to take his Oxford total up to 43 goals. His last match for United was a 5–3 defeat at Nottingham Forest, a game in which he scored. Hebberd played over 80 games for Derby, and in 1991 he had a brief loan spell at Portsmouth before joining Chesterfield. After three seasons he joined Lincoln City, where he played for a season, and thence to Grantham Town.

Brian Heron

Brian Heron started his career with Ballieston before turning professional with Glasgow Rangers, for whom the Dumbarton-born left-winger played seven games. He left Rangers for Motherwell, along with Bobby Watson, in 1969 as part-exchange for Tom Forsyth. He played 75 games, scoring 20 goals, before leaving for Dumbarton in 1972. He scored 10 goals in 36 games for Dumbarton before Oxford signed him for just £20,000 in the summer of 1974.

Heron made his Oxford debut on 17 August 1974, scoring in a 1–1 draw with Cardiff City at Ninian Park. He initially linked up with Hugh Curran and Andy McCulloch in a three-man all-Scottish front line; however, he was troubled by

injuries throughout his Oxford career and as a result played a lot fewer games than he should. On 11 October 1975 Heron suffered a broken leg in a 1–0 win at Notts County and missed the next 17 months while recuperating. He played only four more games for Oxford, his final match coming on 9 April 1977 at Reading. In total he played 47 games for the club, scoring nine goals.

Heron was a flying winger and his impact on the side when he first joined was immediate, but after his injury United failed to find an adequate replacement and the side was relegated at the end of the 1975–76 season. He moved to Scunthorpe United on a free transfer and eventually played a further 25 matches for the Iron, scoring once, before retiring. At the end of 2007 Brian suffered a stroke and was left partially paralysed as a result.

Richard Hill

Richard Hill was an exciting striker who forged a reputation as a goalscorer at Northampton Town. United signed him at the same time as David Bardsley for

£235,000 from Watford on 18 September 1987. He scored his first Oxford goal the following day from a Bardsley cross in a 2–0 First Division home win over QPR. He scored again two weeks later, when United beat Norwich 3–0, but he only found the net once more in that relegation season – when Oxford famously lost 4–7 at Luton. Including substitute appearances, Hill played 31 times in his first season at Oxford.

The following season Hill was much more prolific and scored 10 goals, although he had to wait until 29 October before breaking his duck in a 3–4 defeat at Bradford City. His best game for United was on Boxing Day, when Oxford won 5–1 at Walsall with Hill scoring four. At the end of that season he left United and joined Kettering Town.

Hill was born in Hinckley, near Leicester, and City were his first professional club. After being released by the Foxes he went to New Zealand, before returning to play for Nuneaton Borough where he was spotted by Northampton. Watford bought him from the Cobblers for £257,500 but he only started twice for the Hornets and was played out of position in central midfield.

After he left Kettering, Hill played for Witney Town before moving into football management. He was assistant manager at Reading, and then joined John Gregory at Wycombe Wanderers. He then had a short stint as manager of Stevenage Borough, before spells as assistant at Gillingham and Northampton. He was assistant boss to Brian Little at Tranmere Rovers from 2003 until 2005, where he was linked briefly with the Oxford job following Graham Rix's departure. Instead he joined QPR as assistant to John Gregory once again. In February 2007 he was suspended by QPR and arrested for his part in an on-pitch brawl during a friendly with the Chinese Under-23 side, after which Hill was banned from football for three months. He was dismissed by Rangers in the summer of 2007 as a result of the brawl. Most recently, Hill played for Hellenic League Division One West side Clanfield 85 FC, where he is now coach.

Bud Houghton

Brian Houghton, to give him his proper name, joined Oxford in March 1961, choosing the Southern League side over a number of League clubs. He first played football at school in Surrey and was selected for Godalming School Association. When he left school he signed for St Wilfred's, a youth team in Bradford, and he joined Bradford Park Avenue as an amateur in 1955. He had played 28 times and scored seven goals when Arthur Turner signed him for Birmingham City in 1957. He only played four times (scoring once) for Birmingham before joining Southend United in 1959. At Roots Hall he scored an astonishing 32 goals from 68 games before Turner signed him again, this time for Oxford for a club record £2,000.

Houghton played 56 times for Oxford before they joined the Football League, scoring 55 goals. He made his debut on 4 March 1961, in a 1–1 draw at Cambridge City, and he scored his first two goals a week later in a 2–2 draw with Yeovil Town. While in the Southern League, Houghton scored 10 braces and four hat-tricks, and on 12 April 1961 he scored five in a 7–2 win over Boston United. He was unable to maintain that form in Division Four; although he scored in each of United's first three games as a League club. Altogether, Houghton scored 75 goals for the Us in 114 Southern League and Football League appearances. His last goal for the club was in a 2–0 win at Chester City on 24 August 1963 and his last match was on 8 October 1963, a 5–2 defeat at Bradford City.

After he left Oxford Houghton joined Lincoln City in October 1963 for £6,000, playing 54 games for the Red Imps over two seasons and scoring 22 goals. He later left Lincoln for Chelmsford City for whom he scored 73 goals in two seasons up to 1967.

Ray Houghton

When Ray Houghton joined Oxford United on 13 September 1985 for £147,000 he was new manager Maurice Evans's second signing for the club. Scottish-born Houghton started his career with West Ham United, signing as a professional in 1979, but he only made one substitute appearance in three years at Upton Park and so moved to Fulham in July 1982. Houghton made an impression as a hard-working midfielder at Craven Cottage, where he played 129 first-team games and scored 16 goals in three seasons.

Houghton's first game for Oxford was on 14 September 1985 in a 2–2 home draw with Liverpool, and he scored his first goal for the club four days later in a 3–0 Full Members' Cup win over Shrewsbury Town. He also scored an excellent goal in United's 3–0 Milk Cup Final win over QPR, capping a superb passing move with Trevor Hebberd, and a vital goal in Oxford's 3–0 win over Arsenal in the final game of the season which saw the club avoid relegation. In his two years with the club, Houghton played 105 games for United and scored 14

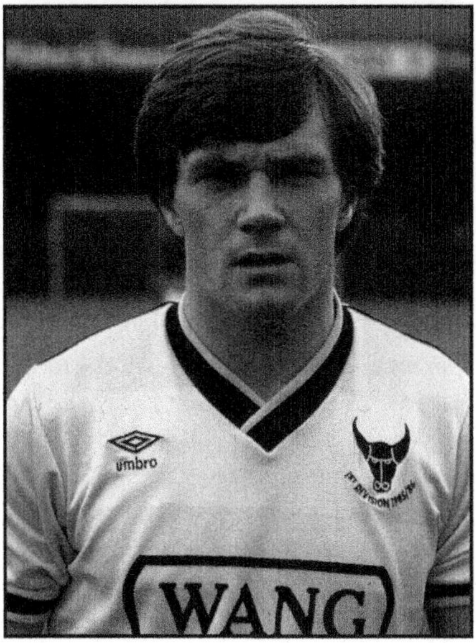

goals. His last game was a 2–1 home defeat by West Ham United before he joined John Aldridge at Liverpool for £825,000.

While at Oxford, Houghton won the first 12 of his 73 Republic of Ireland caps, often featuring alongside Dave Langan and John Aldridge in Jackie Charlton's side. His first goal was famously against England in the 1988 European Championships in West Germany. He also scored the winning goal against Italy in the 1994 US World Cup Finals in New York. He scored six international goals.

In five seasons with Liverpool Houghton played 202 games, scored 38 goals and won the League Championship in 1988 and 1990, and an FA Cup-winners' medal in 1989 and 1992. In July 1992 Aston Villa paid £900,000 for Houghton, and he was an unused substitute when the Villains won the League Cup in 1994. Houghton played 117 games for Villa, scoring 11 goals, before Crystal Palace paid £300,000 for him in March 1995. In two seasons with Palace he played 87 games, scoring eight goals. He then joined Reading in July 1997, playing 56 games and scoring once in his only season there. His final club before retiring to take up TV and radio punditry was Stevenage Borough, for whom he played just three games.

Peter Houseman

Peter Houseman is arguably one of the most famous players to have played for Oxford. Having joined Chelsea as an apprentice and signing professional forms in 1963, he scored in the 1970 FA Cup Final against Leeds United and won a European Cup-Winners' Cup medal with the Blues the following season when they beat Real Madrid in the Final. After Chelsea were relegated to Division Two in 1975 Oxford paid £35,000 for Houseman,

who had played 343 games and scored 39 goals for the Stamford Bridge side.

Houseman was a left-sided midfielder who made 72 appearances for Oxford, starting with a 1–1 draw at Carlisle United on 16 August 1975. Although he did not score in his time at the club, he created numerous goals for others with his accurate crosses from the left, resuming his original position after he had dropped back to left-back towards the end of his Chelsea career.

His last game for Oxford was a 1–0 home defeat by Crystal Palace on 19 March 1977. The following day Houseman, his wife Sally and their friends Alan and Janice Gillham were all killed in a car crash on the A40, near Oxford, on their way home to Witney. Both couples left three parentless children and a fund was established to raise money for the six orphans. A youth League in Oakley, Hampshire, where Houseman set up and coached a youth team, has been named after him.

Billy Jeffrey

Gerry Summers signed Billy Jeffrey as a schoolboy, and after becoming a regular for the reserves he made his first-team debut on 26 September 1973 in a 0–0 draw with Fulham, becoming the club's youngest League debutant in the process. During the next nine seasons, Jeffrey played 356 games for the Us, three of them as a substitute, and he became the side's captain following Les Taylor's departure to Watford in November 1980. He was also capped for Scotland at youth international level. Jeffrey's final game for United, before Jim Smith allowed him to leave on a free transfer to Blackpool, came on 11 May 1982 in a 1–0 defeat at Bristol Rovers.

Billy scored 26 goals for Oxford, the first coming in a 4–2 home win over Cardiff City on 24 October 1973. His final goal for the side was at Swindon Town the week before he left, although the

opposition won 3–2. After Blackpool, Jeffrey played for Northampton Town and Kettering Town before going into non-League management, initially for Irthlingborough Diamonds, becoming assistant to Roger Ashby when they merged with Rushden Town to become Rushden & Diamonds in 1992. He was also assistant to Brian Talbot at Nene Park. He later went on to manage Stamford and then Rugby Town until September 2008. He became Banbury United manager in March 2009.

Nigel Jemson

Nigel Jemson had two spells at Oxford, the first being much more successful than the second. He started his career at his home-town club Preston North End, making his debut as a substitute at the end of the 1985–86 season in which Preston finished second-bottom of the whole Football League. However, the following year Preston won promotion, with Jemson scoring in his first start. His strength and vision attracted the attention of bigger

clubs, and in 1988, after 40 games and 14 goals, Brian Clough paid £150,000 to take him to Nottingham Forest. He played 61 games for Forest and hit 20 goals, but it was his arrogance which earned him a reputation, with Clough claiming that Jemson was the only man in football with a bigger head than him.

Jemson scored the only goal as Forest beat Oldham to win the League Cup Final in 1990. He then had loan spells at Bolton Wanderers and back at Preston before Sheffield Wednesday paid £800,000 for him in September 1991. He spent three years at Hillsborough but he was a substitute as often as a starter, eventually playing 68 games for the Owls, scoring 11 goals. After a brief loan spell at Grimsby he joined Notts County for £300,000. Jemson failed to impress at County, however, and only played 19 games for the Meadow Lane club. He spent time on loan at Watford, Coventry and Rotherham, and it was at Millmoor that he had his best time, scoring nine goals in 19 games, including both goals when Rotherham beat Shrewsbury 2–1 in the Auto Windscreens Shield Final at Wembley.

He arrived at the Manor in the summer of 1996, signing from Notts County for £60,000, and made his debut on 17 August at QPR, where he scored in a 2–1 defeat. He played 82 games for United in the year and a half he was there and scored 33 goals, including the winner at Sheffield Wednesday in a League Cup game. His last goal for Oxford came in a home defeat to Charlton Athletic on 17 January 1998. His last game was in a 3–1 win at Nottingham Forest, after which he moved to Bury for £100,000. He only stayed at Gigg Lane until the end of that season, playing 32 games and scoring just once (against Oxford, typically), and from there he went to Ayr United on a free transfer.

Jemson was at Ayr for five months, scoring five times in 10 games before he returned to Oxford in January 2000. In his second spell with the club Jemson failed to score in any of his 18 games, from a 2–0 defeat at Oldham on 29 January until a 1–0 defeat at Millwall on 6 May. He left Oxford for Shrewsbury where he had a revival of fortunes, playing 127 games over the next three seasons. He scored 43 goals for the Shrews, including two as the fourth-tier side beat Everton in the FA Cup third round. Shrewsbury were relegated from the Football League at the end of 2002–03 and Jemson moved on to Ballymena in Northern Ireland. From there he moved to Ilkeston Town, where he eventually became player-manager and then manager, before he left in January 2008. In July 2008 Jemson became assistant player-manager at Halifax Town, becoming caretaker boss in April 2009 after which he played for Rainham.

Tony Jones

Tony Jones was born in Birmingham, and he joined Birmingham City as an amateur. In 1959 he joined Headington United and made his debut on 10 October in a 1–0 win at Poole Town. Over the next eight seasons Jones played 356 times for United, scoring exactly 100 goals, making him United's second-highest goalscorer since the club turned professional in 1949. His first goal came on 24 October 1959, in a 4–2 win at Yeovil Town. In addition to four hat-tricks, Jones also scored four goals in a Division Four 5–1 win over Newport County on 22 September 1962, Jones's first League goals, and he hit five goals in United's best professional win when they beat Wisbech Town 89–0 in the Southern League in December 1960. He also scored a brace in United's 3–1 win over First Division Blackburn Rovers in the FA Cup fifth round in 1964.

Jones was United's leading scorer in their Southern League Championship-

winning side of 1960–61 with 38 goals, but he often played wing-half as well as up front so even when he was not scoring goals he was an influential member of the team. He was made team captain when Ron Atkinson was injured at the start of 1967–68 season, although that proved to be his last campaign for the club. He left for Newport County, where he played 54 games and scored nine goals, and in 1969 he ended up with Witney Town. He died in 1990.

Alan Judge

Judge served his apprenticeship at Luton Town, where he signed professionally in 1979. He only made 11 appearances for the Hatters, however, and in the 1982–83 season he went on loan to Reading, where he also made 11 appearances. He then signed permanently for the Biscuitmen and played 77 games for the Elm Park side before joining Oxford, signing on Christmas Eve 1984, as cover for Steve Hardwick. He later spent some time on loan at Lincoln City, where he played twice.

It was almost a year before Judge, who was born on 14 May 1960, made his United debut at Stamford Bridge, in the Full Members' Cup Southern Section Final on 17 December 1985. Judge kept a clean sheet as United beat Chelsea 1–0. However, United had already lost the first leg 4–1 at the Manor and so they failed to progress to the national final. Hardwick came back into the side but by the end of February he was injured again, and Judge completed the season as first-choice 'keeper. He was later United's goalkeeper for the Milk Cup Final win over QPR on 20 April 1986.

At the end of the 1990–91 season Judge moved on to Hereford United, where he made 105 appearances in three seasons, before moving to Bromsgrove Rovers. He went on to play for Banbury United while also earning a living as a driving instructor.

After hanging up his boots Judge came back to United, by now at Minchery Farm, as goalkeeping coach, but on 18 March 2003 an injury to Andy Woodman saw Judge pressed into action against

Cambridge United at home, a game which United drew 1–1. That should have been the end of his playing career, but on 6 November 2004 he was again called upon to cover for Chris Tardif and Bradie Clarke for a match at Southend United. Judge's playing career ended ignominiously, as Oxford lost 4–0. Judge was 44 years, five months and 23 days old.

During his time at Oxford, Alan Judge played 102 games and kept 21 clean sheets. He forged a reputation as a great shot stopper, but was sometimes a bit less confident on crosses. He was not the tallest 'keeper around, but his 'Beatles-style' haircut ensured that he was very distinctive.

Maurice Kyle

Darlington-born Kyle is currently eighth in the list of all-time appearances for United. He joined Headington United in February 1959 as one of Arthur Turner's first signings, following Cyril Beavon from Wolverhampton Wanderers. Kyle was a part-timer at Wolves, playing for their nursery side Wath Wanderers and for Wolves' Central League side. He joined United on loan initially, but when Stan Cullis expressed no interest in taking him back to Birmingham he stayed at the Manor. When Oxford joined the Football League in 1962 his transfer had to be properly registered, and Oxford paid Wolves a then club record £5,000 for him.

Kyle made his United debut on 14 February 1959, in a 2–1 win over Barry Town. The centre-half went on to play 448 games for the side, 142 in the club's Southern League days and the remainder after their election to the Football League. His last game for the side was a Second Division game at Bolton Wanderers on 18 October 1969, which ended 1–1. Thus Kyle, along with Beavon and the Atkinson brothers, had played for United in the Southern League and three divisions of the Football League. Kyle also scored four goals for the Us, the first coming in an FA Cup second-round tie against Bridgewater Town which Oxford won 2–1. He also scored in a 3–1 win over Weymouth and 1–1 draws with Middlesbrough and Colchester United. All of his goals were scored at the Manor.

Kyle's nickname at Oxford was 'King', and his centre-half performances were indeed imperious. He stayed at Oxford despite attention from clubs in higher divisions, and after leaving the Manor he joined Southend United. He left them for Worcester City and thence to Bath City.

Dave Langan

Dave Langan joined Oxford United for the start of the club's Second Division Championship season in the summer of 1984. He joined from Birmingham City,

where Jim Smith had signed him from Derby County for £350,000, which was then a record for a full-back and a record for Birmingham. He had not played for the Blues for over a year because of injury but Smith was keen to bring him to Oxford, who he joined on a free transfer.

Langan had started his career with the Cherry Orchard youth club in Dublin before Derby brought him to England, and he made his debut for County in 1977 as a 19-year-old. He made over 150 first-team appearances before his move to Birmingham, where he played over 100 games. The first Oxford game in which he played was away to Huddersfield Town on 25 August 1984, which Oxford won 3–0. During that season 'Langy' became a United icon with his overlapping runs from right-back. The highlight of that first season was the famous 3–2 League Cup win over First Division leaders Arsenal, in which Langy scored the winning goal with a blistering shot from 35 yards that Pat Jennings could only palm into the Cuckoo Lane goal.

In that first top-flight season, Langan was injured in the New Year's Day defeat at QPR. He recovered in time to play in the Milk Cup Final win over the same opponents and then lost his regular starting place to John Trewick. His final match for United was a 5–2 home defeat by Luton Town on 15 September 1987, after which he moved to Bournemouth following a brief loan spell at Leicester City.

Langan's career ended at Peterborough United, cut short by injury brought on as a result of all the various cortisone injections he had in his knees throughout his career. He had several knee operations to try and repair the damage, and he also underwent two spinal fusion operations after cracking vertebrae, first at Birmingham and then at Peterborough. Langan is now registered disabled and has to take pain-killers regularly, and he works for Peterborough Council.

George Lawrence

'Chicken George', as he was affectionately known, signed for Oxford United from Southampton for £45,000 in November 1982, having already spent some time on loan at the club. He signed schoolboy forms for the Saints at the age of 15 in 1978, eventually turning professional two years later and making his debut in October 1981. After 10 games he was loaned to Oxford, playing his first game on 27 March 1982, scoring in a 1–1 draw with Chesterfield. He played 15 games and scored three goals up to the end of the 1982–83 season, before returning to Southampton. He endeared himself to Oxford supporters during his loan spell by scoring in the 5–0 win over Swindon. After he returned to Oxford he made his full debut on 4 December 1982, in United's 5–1 win at Leyton Orient, and Lawrence was again on the scoresheet.

In his second spell with the club Lawrence played 86 games and scored 24 goals. His wing play was exciting, if erratic, and he was famous for running out of play at the end of the pitch after storming runs that beat half the oppositions' defences. His last game for United was on Boxing Day 1984 when the Us beat Cardiff City 4–0, and he returned to Southampton in January 1985 and spent a further two years at the Dell, scoring 11 goals in 70 League games. In July 1987 Millwall paid £160,000 for him and he helped the Lions win Division Two and promotion to the First Division for the first time in their history. In 1989 he went to AFC Bournemouth for three seasons. After a summer spent with Mikkelin Palloilijat in Finland, Lawrence joined Portsmouth, where he made 14 substitute appearances. In 1993 he went to play for Maltese side Hibernians, where he won two consecutive League titles and the 1995 Player of the Year award. After a spell with Hednesford Town he turned his hand to sports therapy, and he then became a self-employed coach.

Mickey Lewis

Mickey Lewis played for Oxford for over 10 years, clocking up 351 appearances from his debut in a 1–1 draw at Leeds United on 27 August 1988 until his final match on 19 February 2000, a 2–1 win at Chesterfield. Lewis joined United from Derby County as part-exchange for Trevor Hebberd. Derby had signed him from West Bromwich Albion for £25,000 in November 1984. Lewis scored seven goals for United, the first securing a 1–0 win at Watford on 13 January 1990.

Lewis finished his playing career at Oxford and fulfilled a variety of other roles while at the club, including youth-team coach, caretaker manager, assistant manager and even, on one occasion at Blackpool, stand-in physiotherapist.

Although he had a brief spell playing for Banbury United before returning to Oxford, Lewis completed over 10 seasons for United, most recently as assistant manager to Darren Patterson and then Chris Wilder from November 2007. His playing days will be mainly remembered

for his ferocious tackling and his trademark 'airplane' arms, which will be forever associated with Mad Dog's tough playing style.

Johnny Love

Johnny Love was born in Eynsham, and before joining Headington United he played for Eynsham, Oxford City and the Wolverhampton Wanderers youth team. He also represented Oxford at both football and boxing, as well as being the Oxfordshire Youth Table Tennis champion.

Love made his Headington debut on 15 March 1955 in a 0–0 draw with Barry Town, and in his second season with the club he was selected to play for the England Youth team against Wales and Scotland.

Love was a speedy left-winger who commanded the attention of several League clubs, but United rebuffed all advances. He weighed in with a number of goals, scoring 45 in his time with the club, the first coming in a 3–1 win at Guildford

City on 21 September 1955. After that match he had to do his National Service in the West Indies and he did not feature again for United for almost two years, his next game coming on 24 August 1957 against Cheltenham Town. It is this gap which makes his appearance record all the more remarkable. In eight and a half seasons Love clocked up 309 games for United, of which 282 came before their election to the Football League – at that time a new club record. He scored on his League debut in a 2–1 defeat at Darlington on 1 September 1962, and his last game was on 20 September 1963, a 2–1 defeat at Carlisle United. He moved to Wellington Town the following month.

Jim Magilton

Magilton joined Oxford from Liverpool for £100,000, despite never having played a first-team game for the Reds. He made his Oxford debut on 3 October 1990 in a 2–0 defeat at West Ham United, and he went on to play 173 times for the Yellows, playing his last match in an FA Cup replay at Leeds on 9 February 1994, where 'Magic' scored an extra-time winner to set up a home fifth-round tie against Chelsea. Unfortunately United sold him to Southampton for £600,000 before that match, which United lost 2–1.

During his time at Oxford Magilton became regarded as one of the most creative midfielders to have played for the club, and he won the first 18 of his 52 Northern Ireland caps while at United and became Oxford's most-capped player. He scored for Northern Ireland on his debut in a 3–1 friendly win over Poland on 6 February 1991 and scored five international goals in total, the first four while with Oxford. Magilton played 156 games for the Saints, scoring 18 goals, before signing for Sheffield Wednesday for £1.6 million in September 1997. He played

just 30 times for the Owls in 18 months, before an 11-game loan spell with Ipswich Town, who he then joined permanently for £682,500. Over the next eight years Magilton played over 300 games for Ipswich and scored 20 goals, before he was appointed manager in 2006. Magilton was sacked by Ipswich on 22 April 2009 and appointed QPR's new manager on 3 June.

Bobby McDonald

Bobby McDonald arrived at United at the start of the 1983–84 Third Division Championship campaign. He arrived from Manchester City, with whom he had played in the previous season's FA Cup Final, after being released from his contract for a breach of discipline. Before playing at Maine Road he had played for Coventry City, whom he had joined from Aston Villa for £40,000. He had won a League Cup-winners' medal with the Villains and also won promotion with them from Division Two. Manchester City paid Coventry £250,000 for his signature in October 1980.

McDonald's first game for United was on 10 September 1983, a 2–2 home draw with Burnley. He scored three First Division goals in 1985–86, including a brace at Highfield Road as Oxford lost 5–2 to Coventry, but he was injured for the Milk Cup Final after receiving a knock at QPR on New Year's Day 1986. That was Bobby's last game for Oxford until 29 November that year.

Bobby proved himself to be a strong left-back, whose link-up play was a vital ingredient during the club's promotions from the Third Division to the First Division. Bobby scored a total of 21 goals in his 125 games for United, and his last match for the Yellows was on 20 January 1987, a 4–3 defeat at Ewood Park, as Blackburn Rovers eliminated United from the Full Members' Cup. He then moved to Leeds United, where he played for less than

a year before a short loan spell at Wolves. He joined VS Rugby in the summer of 1988 and then Burton Albion the following season. He later set up several youth academies and became a self-employed coach at a number of clubs.

Owen Medlock

Oxford United's first game as a Football League club was on 18 August 1962, a 3–2 defeat at Barrow. In goal on that historic occasion was one of United's more iconic goalkeepers, Owen Medlock. Although Medlock started his career at Chelsea in 1955, he joined Swindon Town in February 1959. Ten months later, after making three League appearances, he made the short trip to the Manor.

Medlock made his Headington United debut on 12 December 1959 in a 2–1 home win over Gravesend & Northfleet, and with them he won five of his first six games and drew the other. His first clean sheet for the club came in his sixth game, a 2–0 home win over Dartford, and Medlock went on to complete 24 games in his debut season,

keeping six clean sheets as United finished second in the Southern League. The following season Medlock was an ever present as the club, now renamed Oxford United, charged to the Southern League Championship title. The 1961–62 campaign was another Championship-winning season for United, although Medlock missed the middle part of the season due to injury. The following season, in Division Four, was Medlock's last at the club, and his appearances were frequently interrupted by injury and the good form of his replacement, Mike Richards.

Medlock's last six games for the club all ended in defeat, and in the close season he was given a free transfer to Chelmsford City, for whom he played until 1971. Medlock completed 133 appearances in total for United, of which 110 were while the side was in the Southern League. He kept 38 clean sheets in that time.

Andy Melville

Andy Melville started his career as an apprentice with his home-town club Swansea City, making his first appearance in 1986. He played 213 games for the Swans, initially as a midfielder, and scored 29 goals, before Oxford bought him for £275,000 in July 1990 to shore up their defence. He had already won his first four Wales caps but at Oxford he went on to be capped a further 11 times, and eventually he won 65 caps for his country, scoring three goals.

Melville made his Oxford debut on 25 August 1990 in a 5–2 win over Port Vale. The towering centre-back initially partnered former England international Steve Foster, but by the time he played his last game for United, a 1–0 win at Watford on 8 May 1993, he was the senior defender at the club having made 159 appearances for the Us. He also scored 15 goals for the club.

When Sunderland paid United £750,000 for him on 9 August 1993 he was widely regarded as the best signing made by Terry Butcher in his days as Sunderland manager. In the next five seasons he played 236 games for the Rokerites and scored 14 goals. Towards the end of his time in the North East he lost his place to Jody Craddock and was loaned out to Bradford City in February 1998, where he enjoyed a successful six-game spell. He stormed back to form in 1998–99 to lead Sunderland back to the Premiership and in the process won a recall to the Wales team for their Euro '96 qualifiers against Italy and Denmark.

In June 1999 he moved to Fulham on a free transfer and played 193 games, scoring four goals, before he was signed by West Ham United in January 2004. He made only 21 appearances for the Hammers, and had 15 games on loan to Nottingham Forest, before eventually retiring in August 2005.

Paul Moody

Paul Moody was a tall, powerful striker with a deceptive turn of pace. In his first spell at Oxford he became a legend at the club thanks to his goalscoring prowess. Unfortunately, in his second period with Oxford he failed to recapture the form that had made him a hero with United's fans.

Moody started his career at Fareham Town, but it was while at Waterlooville that he was spotted by Southampton, who signed him for £5,000 in 1991. He played just 14 games for the Saints and failed to find the net in any of them, although he fared slightly better in a loan spell at Reading in 1992, where he scored once in six matches. In February 1994 Oxford took a gamble and paid Southampton £60,000 for him. He made his Oxford debut on 26 February in a 1–0 win over Nottingham Forest, and he scored his first goal for the club on 12 March in a 2–1 defeat at home to Peterborough. The seven goals that he scored in his first season were not enough to prevent United being relegated to the Third Division.

Moody started the 1994–95 season spectacularly, scoring in the first three games, the third of which saw him strike a superlative hat-trick at Cardiff City which included one goal where he dribbled past five defenders before beating the 'keeper. He also scored three hat-tricks the following season, the first in the 9–1 FA Cup win over Dorchester Town and the last one in 12 minutes after coming off the bench in a 5–0 win over Burnley.

The 1995–96 season saw Moody at his best, although he celebrated his goals with a cartwheel that did not do his injured back any good. He played 151 games for Oxford, scoring 62 goals, before leaving the club, and he played his last game on 4 May 1997 in a 5–1 rout of newly promoted Barnsley. Fulham paid Oxford £200,000 for Moody, and in two seasons he played 49 games for the Cottagers, scoring 20 goals, before they sold him to Millwall for £140,000. In just over two years Moody played 69 games for the Lions and scored 27 goals.

By September 2001 United were in the bottom division and desperate for a goalscorer, so they paid £150,000 to Millwall to bring Moody back to Oxford, then in their first season at the Kassam Stadium. He scored on his debut in a 2–1 win over Southend United on 22 September and finished the season with 13 goals from 36 games. His last appearance for the Yellows was on 20 April 2002 in a 2–1 home defeat by Darlington. From Oxford he moved to Conference side Aldershot, and a year later he left to play for Gosport Borough, a club nearer his home.

Matt Murphy

Matt Murphy joined United from Corby Town in February 1993 for a fee of £20,000. After a spell in the reserves, the

rangy midfielder made his debut on 6 May 1993 in a 2–1 defeat at Newcastle United. Murphy suffered somewhat in that he could play in a variety of positions and so he often found himself on the bench. He was not blessed with the greatest of pace, but he could unlock defences with pinpoint passing and he possessed an aerial threat. Murphy also had an eye for goal, and in 1999–2000 he was the side's leading scorer with 17 goals. In his eight years at United Murphy scored 55 goals, including spectacular volleys at Cardiff and Reading. He made a total of 287 appearances for Oxford, his final game being a 2–1 defeat at Notts County on 5 May 2001.

Murphy left the club when new manager Mark Wright refused to offer him a new contract allegedly after receiving a derogatory letter from his agent. After leaving Oxford, Murphy signed for Bury, where he played just 10 games in his only season there. He had a slightly better time at Swansea City, scoring three goals in 14 appearances.

After leaving the Vetch, Murphy joined Ford Sports and netted 31 times for the Motormen during the 2003–04 campaign. He then left for Slough Town for the following season and from there went to Brackley Town, where he again topped the goalscoring tables. He moved to neighbours Banbury United in September 2007, and in March 2008 he was on his way again, joining Spalding United. In January 2009 Murphy became assistant manager at Long Buckby.

Cliff Nugent

Cliff Nugent was, along with Peter Sharman, the first player to be signed by Headington United upon the club turning professional in 1949. He started his career as an amateur with Sheffield United before joining the forces when he was 18 and ending up in Oxford. He was playing as an amateur with Oxford City when he approached the Headington United committee to request an interview, and he signed as a part-time professional, receiving £3 a match, with a win bonus of £2 and a draw bonus of £1.

Nugent made his Southern League debut on 22 October 1949 in a 5–2 defeat at home to Weymouth and went on to play 68 games for the club. The first of his 15 goals was scored on 12 November 1949 against Exeter City Reserves. In January 1951 Cardiff City offered £2,000 for Nugent, which was negotiated up to £2,500 by the time the move was completed on 14 February. This was a Southern League record fee. His last game for United was a 3–2 home defeat by Barry Town on 10 February 1951.

Nugent made his Cardiff debut in the 1951–52 season and established himself in the first team during the 1953–54 season. In seven years at Ninian Park, Nugent played 113 League games, scoring 19 goals. He then moved to Mansfield Town in 1958, making 53 League appearances in two years, finding the net seven times and from there went to Weymouth. He played 180 games for the Terras, was captain for a season and scored 37 goals before he joined Portland United as player-coach in 1965.

Jimmy Phillips

Jimmy Phillips started his career with Bolton Wanderers, his home-town club, signing in August 1983. He played 137 games for the Trotters, scoring two goals, before Glasgow Rangers paid £95,000 for him in March 1987. He was Rangers manager Graeme Souness's first signing, but he made just 33 appearances for Rangers before Oxford paid the Scottish giants £150,000 for him in August 1988.

Phillips made his Oxford debut on 27 August 1988 in a 1–1 draw at Leeds United. He was a solid, reliable left-back, putting in strong defensive performances and also scoring seven goals in his 89 appearances

for United. In his 19 months at the Manor, Phillips missed just three matches. His last match, on 13 March 1990, was a 1–0 defeat at Ipswich Town. Two days later Phillips joined Middlesbrough for £250,000. In his three seasons at Ayresome Park, Phillips played 88 games, scored eight goals and won promotion to the Premiership.

In July 1993 Phillips returned to Bolton, who paid 'Boro £250,000 for his signature. He completed eight more seasons with them, playing another 272 games and scoring six goals, twice winning promotion to the Premiership. In 2001 he hung up his boots and joined the Bolton backroom team, first as reserve-team manager and later as director of the Bolton Academy.

Les Phillips

Les Phillips began his career with Birmingham City, for whom he played 44 League games. After Phillips joined Oxford from Birmingham City on transfer-deadline day in March 1984, he found it difficult to break into Jim Smith's side. He made his debut on 24 March 1984, replacing Kevin Brock in a 5–0 win over Plymouth. At first, however, Brock was preferred in the centre alongside Hebberd, and Phillips made just six appearances in the 1983–84 season. The following season saw John Trewick selected ahead of Phillips, and again Les made just two starts in the Second Division Championship season. It was in 1985–86, Oxford's first season as a top-flight club, that Phillips got a regular run in the side, following an injury to Trewick after 11 games. He played in 42 games altogether, including, of course, the Milk Cup Final. Phillips scored five goals that season, his first goal for Oxford United coming in the 3–1 fourth-round Milk Cup win over Norwich City. He also scored in the next round, a 3–1 defeat of Portsmouth, and in the semi-final second leg when Aston Villa were beaten 2–1 to send the Us to Wembley. However, possibly his most memorable goal was the one that beat Everton at the Manor with just a few minutes remaining and which virtually ensured that the Toffees surrendered their title to Liverpool.

The following season Phillips missed the first two months through injury. He went on to play a further five seasons at the Manor, completing a total of 224 matches for Oxford and establishing himself as one of United's most consistent midfielders for decades. His final appearance was on 3 April 1993 in a 2–0 defeat at Brentford.

After leaving Oxford, Phillips went on to play 26 times for Northampton Town and then played for Marlow, and was in that team that beat Oxford 2–0 in the FA Cup on 13 November 1994. He finished his playing career at Banbury United, and in 2008 he became a scout for Oxford.

Paul Powell

Paul Powell was born in Wallingford and signed for Oxford in August 1994, after coming through the youth ranks and playing for the England Youth team. It was another 15 months before Powell made his first-team debut, coming on as a substitute in a 3–2 Auto Windscreens Shield win at

Barnet on 7 November 1995. He made his first start for the club on 20 January 1996 in a 1–0 defeat at Chesterfield, and he scored his first goal on 22 November 1997 in a 2–1 defeat at Norwich City. After a number of substitute appearances, Powell gained a regular place in the starting XI in January 1998 and went on to complete 202 appearances for the Yellows, scoring 23 goals.

Although his natural position was as a left-winger, Powell could also play in defence and was often used as a left-back, but that meant that his deadly crossing ability was seriously underused. In April 1988 Powell was called-up for the England Under-21 squad for a Toulon tournament but he had to withdraw due to illness. A number of higher League clubs were linked with moves for Powell, and United turned down bids from Premiership sides Bradford City and Newcastle United, with the latter offer alleged to be for £1 million.

Powell scored the first goal at the Kassam Stadium in a pre-season friendly against Crystal Palace on 4 August 2001, but he failed to get on with manager Mark Wright and it was not until Ian Atkins took over that he regained his place in the team. Unfortunately the later part of Powell's time at Oxford was blighted with injuries and rumours about his personal life, and he played his last game for the Us on 1 April 2003, a 0–0 draw with Carlisle United.

On 22 August 2003 Powell signed for Conference club Tamworth on a one-month trial, having earlier in the summer turned down a 12-month deal at Barnet and a lucrative offer to play in China. He turned out five times for the Lambs, scoring once. However, at the end of the trial Powell signed for his local side Didcot Town, making a goalscoring debut for them on 23 September 2003 against Brackley Town. He then joined Brackley briefly at the start of the 2004–05 season but after just nine games he returned to Didcot, where he has remained, despite a brief interlude with Hungerford Town in March 2008. Powell starred in Didcot's FA Vase Final win over AFC Sudbury at White Hart Lane in May 2005.

Pat Quartermain

Pat Quartermain was born in Garsington in 1937, and at the age of 16 he played for the Pressed Steel junior team and Headington United's juniors. He signed as an amateur for United in the 1955–56 season and made his debut against Exeter City Reserves in a 7–0 Southern League win on 24 September 1955. He played two further first-team games as an amateur before signing as a part-time professional.

Quartermain supplemented his footballing income by working as an apprentice toolmaker, but in 1958 he had to give up both to report for his National Service in Cyprus. Two years later he returned to his work and to Oxford United.

Originally a strong centre-half, Quartermain was switched to left full-back in November 1961, and he remained in that position for the remainder of his career. He became a full-time professional when United joined the Football League in 1962.

In the Southern League, Quartermain played 98 games for United, and after the club was elected to the League he completed a further 206 appearances, just one as substitute, playing his final match on 27 March 1967 at Leyton Orient. He failed to score in any of those games. He missed the final 10 games of the 1966–67 season through injury and was given a free transfer at the end of the season after which he joined Cambridge United. Pat Quartermain was given a testimonial match against Swindon Town on 24 May 1963.

Frank Ramshaw

Frank Ramshaw was signed for Headington United following a visit to Sunderland by then player-manager Harry Thompson. He joined the club at the same time as fellow Rokerite Vic Barney, although neither had played any first-team games for Sunderland.

Ramshaw, who could play at either half-back or full-back, initially received £7 a week for his services. He made his debut in a Southern League Cup qualifying round defeat at Bedford Town on 19 August 1950, and in his first season with the club he was selected to represent the Southern League. He was made club captain for the 1952–53 season and led the club to its first Southern League Championship. He also captained the side to two Southern League Cup wins and was skipper for the momentous FA Cup run in 1953–54.

Ramshaw was regarded as one of the best players to have represented United during its early Southern League years, and in October 1955 he was granted a testimonial game against an All-Star XI after just five seasons with the club. Ramshaw played 361 games for United, ending his time with the Us as it began, against Bedford Town, in a 2–1 defeat at the Eyrie on 1 February 1958. He had received an injury at Hereford at the end of August but continued to play on, despite being in pain, and was ruled out for the remainder of the season, and he eventually retired on the advice of a specialist at the age of 33, before the start of the following season. He scored just one goal for United, in a 3–1 win at Guildford City on 21 September 1955.

Billy Rees

Billy Rees was born in Blaengarw on 10 March 1924. His first side was Caernarvon Rovers, for whom he played while working in a coal mine. He signed for Cardiff City in 1944 and scored 74 goals in 83 wartime games for them, as well as playing for Wales in a wartime international against England in 1945. Once normal football resumed he helped Cardiff to promotion in the first post-war season. He was top scorer the following season, after which Tottenham Hotspur signed him in 1949 for

£14,000. He won the first of his four Wales caps, against Northern Ireland, just before he left Cardiff.

Rees made 101 League appearances for the Bluebirds in three years, scoring 33 goals, but he played just 11 games for Spurs, scoring three goals, after injuries led him to a loss of form. In 1950 Leyton Orient bought him for £14,500 and he spent six years at Brisbane Road. In 184 League games, Rees scored 58 goals for the O's.

Rees was signed by Headington initially as cover for injuries, but the inside-forward gave such good displays that he soon became a regular member of the first team. He made his debut on Boxing Day 1955, scoring in a 3–1 win over Kettering Town. He played 131 games for United and scored 60 goals, including a hat-trick in a 7–2 win over Barry Town in October 1957. His last game for United was on 30 March 1959 against Kidderminster Harriers. After leaving Headington he joined Kettering Town and then took up running a general store and working in a pharmaceutical factory as a plant operator, while keeping pigeons in his spare time. He lived in

Llangeinor near Bridgend until his death in a Cardiff hospital on 25 July 1996 after a sudden illness.

Dave Roberts

Rarely, if ever, can a better defender than Dave Roberts have pulled on the yellow shirt of Oxford United. He joined Fulham as an apprentice and played 22 games for them between 8 March 1969 and 1971. He joined United for £2,500 on 8 February 1971, making his debut as a substitute (his only appearance from the bench) 12 days later in a 3–0 defeat at Swindon Town. He made his full debut six days later in a 2–0 defeat at Charlton Athletic. Roberts went on to play 176 times for United, and became club captain in 1973. He scored eight goals for Oxford, his first on 28 August 1971 in a 2–1 win over Burnley, and he also scored in United's only win at the County Ground on 24 February 1973. His final appearance for the Yellows was on 8 February 1975, when Oxford beat Manchester United 1–0 in a Division Two game at the Manor.

Roberts was sold by United to Hull City for £70,000, for whom he played 86 times, and three years later he moved to Cardiff City for £50,000. He played 41 games for the Bluebirds. When he retired in 1981 he became coach to Cardiff's reserves after a brief interlude playing for Tsuen Wan in Hong Kong.

Roberts won his first full Wales cap on 23 March 1973 in a World Cup qualifying game against Poland, which Wales won 2–0. He won a further five caps for Wales while with United and went on to win 18 in total. He also won four caps for the Wales Under-23 side while with Oxford, despite having been born in Southampton.

Les Robinson

Robinson arrived at the club from Doncaster Rovers in March 1990, making his debut in the final game of the 1989–90 season, a 0–0 home draw with Port Vale. He started as a junior with Chesterfield in 1984, before joining Mansfield Town in October 1984. In two years he played just 16 games for the Stags before joining Stockport County. He had made 77

appearances while at Edgeley Park when he moved to Doncaster for £20,000 in March 1988. He played 96 games at Belle Vue and scored 13 goals before Oxford paid £150,000 for him.

Robinson started his career playing in central midfield but dropped deeper to become a very accomplished right-back. He suffered with two long-term injuries after his arrival, but he managed to overcome them to get a regular place in the side. He was later appointed club captain, a role in which he excelled with his committed tackling and organisational ability.

'Robbo' continued playing for the Us until the end of the 1999–2000 season, after which he went to Mansfield Town on a free transfer. His final Oxford game was a 1–0 defeat at Millwall on 6 May 2000. Despite clocking up 458appearances for Oxford over 10 seasons, and scoring six goals, Sir Les, as Robinson was named by the fans, was never granted a testimonial.

After 91 games with the Stags, Robinson turned down the opportunity to sign for Notts County and Tamworth, instead moving to Southern League Premier Division Hednesford Town in July 2002. In September 2003 he returned to Oxfordshire to play for Banbury United, before age and injury caught up with him and he retired in 2005.

Dean Saunders

Dean Saunders came to Oxford on a free transfer from Brighton on 12 March 1987. Saunders' first game for the Yellows came just two days later in a 3–1 home defeat by Liverpool in the First Division. Saunders missed the first few weeks of the following season, and his last game was on 22 October 1998, a 1–1 draw with Blackburn Rovers, after which Oxford boss Mark Lawrenson was informed by chairman Kevin Maxwell that Saunders had been

sold to Robert Maxwell's Derby County for £1 million. 'Deano' had played 73 times for United, scoring 33 goals.

Saunders started his career at Swansea City in 1982, playing 55 games and scoring 12 goals before he joined Brighton, after a brief loan spell at Cardiff City. He played 86 times for the Seagulls before Maurice Evans brought him to the Manor. After 131 games for Derby, for whom he scored 57 goals, Dean was bought for £2.9 million by Liverpool. He was at Anfield for just one season before Aston Villa paid £2.3 million for him, and three years later he moved to Turkey when Galatasaray paid £2.35 million. A year later Nottingham Forest brought him back to England, paying £1.5 million for his signature, and in December 1997 he left for no fee to join Sheffield United. He was with the Blades for almost exactly one year before he had a second spell abroad, this time joining Benfica for £500,000.

In August 1998 Saunders joined Bradford City on a free transfer before eventually hanging up his boots in May

2001, after making transfers worth over £10.6 million in total during his career. He became a coach at Bradford and then at Newcastle United. After his sacking by Newcastle he became Wales' assistant manager in June 2007, and in October 2008 Saunders was appointed manager of Conference side Wrexham. He won 75 caps for Wales, scoring 22 goals, making him the country's fourth-top scorer, and he won six of those caps while with Oxford.

Jason Seacole

Seacole became United's youngest-ever Football League player when he made his debut on 7 September 1976 at the age of just 16 years and 149 days in a 3–0 home defeat by Mansfield Town. He is also the youngest United player to start a game, on 2 October 1976 in a 1–1 draw with Tranmere Rovers, and he is also the youngest United player to score, with his first goal coming in a 4–2 win over Shrewsbury Town on 1 March 1977. Seacole came through the youth-team ranks at Oxford but suffered due to coming of age at a time when the club was at its lowest ebb for many years. He also

suffered through a serious injury that caused him to miss the whole of the 1978–79 season. He never regained his first-team place and made just a handful of appearances in the next two seasons before given a free transfer. Over the course of six seasons Seacole made 134 appearances for Oxford, scoring 26 goals.

Seacole was called-up for the England Youth squad to play in the 29th UEFA international tournament in Poland in May 1978. He later joined Witney Town after a brief spell on Swindon's books, where he did not play a game. He was with Witney for five years and in 1986 joined Wycombe Wanderers, with whom he won promotion to the Conference, and in December 1987 he rejoined Witney. He now plays cricket for Witney Swifts.

Malcolm Shotton

Shotton signed in the summer of 1980, Roy Barry signing him from part-time Nuneaton Borough, whom he had joined after having failed to get into Leicester

City's first team. His first game for United was a League Cup game at Southend United on 8 August 1980, which Oxford lost 1–0. Shotton's first goal came in the second leg of that League Cup tie, which was won 2–0 by the Us. Shotton (whose nickname for some reason was 'Sheeny') scored five League goals and two in the League Cup that season.

In 1982–83 Jim Smith took over from Ian Greaves and he initially expressed his consternation with the defensive pairing of Shotton and Gary Briggs, but the committed performances that they both consistently produced won him over and he soon put aside any thoughts of replacing them, and instead he built his incredibly successful side around them. This excellent partnership continued in United's first season as a top-flight club, with Shotton by now established as the club captain.

The next season, after a home defeat by Spurs in November 1986, Shotton suffered a long spell out of the side and only returned for the final game of the season. His next game for the club was a 1–1 draw at Wimbledon at the start of the following season, when he came off the bench to replace Trevor Hebberd. This, it turned out, was his final match for United; he joined Portsmouth for £70,000 after 338 first-team games and 15 goals for the Us. He later joined Huddersfield, Barnsley, Hull City and Ayr United, before ending his playing career back at Barnsley. He later returned to Oxford as manager in January 1998, hired by Keith Cox following a fans' campaign for his appointment, and he lifted the club from the danger of relegation to the Third Division to mid-table safety. Unfortunately he was unable to maintain this the following season and new chairman Firoz Kassam arranged for a mutual ending of his contract. He went on to coach at Loughborough College.

John Shuker

John Shuker was playing junior football in his native Manchester when an Oxford scout spotted him and he was invited to the Manor for a trial. He was signed as an amateur in 1960 and played for United's Metropolitan League side initially, mainly as an outside-left. He then moved to Oxford and took a job as a decorator. In June 1961 he became a part-time professional, becoming full time at Christmas 1961.

At the end of his first season with United Shuker was given a free transfer, but he won a last-minute reprieve following an excellent display at wing-half in an end-of-season friendly. Shuker made his first-team debut on 29 August 1962 at Lincoln City in a 1–0 defeat, playing at centre-forward. He was also played at inside-right and inside-left before he scored his first goal for the club in a 3–0 win over Chester City on 20 October 1962. That season, as well as scoring five League goals, he scored 17 goals for the reserves as they finished runners-up to Arsenal in the Metropolitan League.

Shuker continued to play in a number of different positions; he was a left-half while captaining the reserves in 1964–65 and later also played in defence, where he brought style and imagination to the role and still always looked to attack. He became captain of the first team after Ron Atkinson left in 1971 and again after Dave Roberts' departure in 1975. Shuker holds the United all-time appearance record, having played 534 games for the club. His last match was on 2 April 1977 in a 3–2 defeat by Peterborough United. He scored 47 goals in that time and was awarded a testimonial against Manchester City on 5 May 1972.

In 1977 Shuker was released and he sued the club for wrongful dismissal, but an industrial tribunal ruled in the club's favour. He later earned his FA coaching badges and in 2001 became manager of Witney Academy, formed from the ashes of Witney Town, until it folded the following year. He had earlier, in 2000, been appointed as director of football at Milton United.

Paul Simpson

Carlisle-born Paul Simpson was given his chance by Manchester City while still an apprentice, becoming one of their youngest debutants when, aged 16, he appeared on 2 October 1982 in a 3–2 win over Coventry City. He had a brief loan spell at Irish side Finn Harps before returning to City for the end of the 1984–85 season, during which time he scored six goals in 10 games to help City win promotion to the First Division. While at Maine Road Simpson won three England Under-18 caps and five England Under-21 caps, scoring in the 1987 Toulon Tournament.

After 155 games for City, in which he scored 50 goals, 'Simmo' joined Oxford United for £200,000 in October 1988.

Simpson's first game for United was a 4–2 defeat at home to Sunderland on 2 November 1988, and his first goal came three days later in a 3–2 defeat at West Brom. Over the next three and a half years Simpson went on to make 168 appearances for the Yellows and scored 50 goals, including two hat-tricks.

In his time at the Manor, Simmo proved to be an exciting, attacking winger, and he was immensely popular with the Oxford fans both for scoring goals and for his many assists. In his last game for the Us, on 15 February 1992, Simpson scored both goals in a 2–1 win at Brighton. Five days later Derby County paid Oxford £500,000 for him.

Simpson was at Derby for over five years, playing 225 games and scoring 57 goals. He then had loan spells at Sheffield United and Wolverhampton Wanderers before Wolves signed him permanently for £75,000 in November 1997. Simpson spent just under three years at Molineux, making 63 appearances (including eight while on loan from Derby) and scored seven goals (two of which came during his loan period).

Simpson played 10 games while on loan to Walsall, scoring once, and in August 2000 he moved on to Blackpool. He played 94 games for the Tangerines and scored 13 goals, helping the side win promotion via the Play-offs, before moving on to join Rochdale in March 2002. His nine appearances and six goals helped Rochdale into the Play-offs at the end of the 2001–02 season, but they lost to Rushden & Diamonds.

After the departure of John Hollins, Simpson was appointed player-manager at Rochdale. However, his playing form dropped with the pressure of management, and despite a good FA Cup run he was released by Rochdale after the side finished 19th in the Fourth Division. In July 2003 Simpson joined Carlisle United as a player, before taking over the management duties from Roddy Collins. By this time Carlisle were suffering a transfer embargo and were 15 points adrift at the foot of Division Four. Carlisle lost the first 12 matches in which he was in charge but he then fashioned a remarkable turnaround that almost saved the club from relegation to the Conference. However, they won promotion at the first attempt via the Play-offs, and the following season Carlisle reached the final of the Football League Trophy and won a second successive promotion. He was named League Two Manager of the Year and was statistically the best manager in the country.

In June 2006, after 157 games in charge, Simpson shocked the Cumbrians by joining Preston North End. He led Preston to the top of the Championship, their highest League placing for 55 years, before an alarming slump saw the side miss out on the Play-offs. Simpson was sacked in November 2007 and went to manage Shrewsbury Town in March 2008.

Ken Skeen

Ken Skeen was born in Cheltenham and was spotted by Swindon Town scouts while playing for a local Cheltenham side. He became a regular in Swindon's youth side until a camping accident left him with serious burns and out of the game for two seasons. However, salvation came when he was offered a chance to play for Southern League Trowbridge, and it was after playing in a pre-season friendly against Swindon in 1964 that the Robins signed him on again. He made his debut as a striker in a 3–1 defeat against Crystal Palace but initially found games hard to come by. He made only sporadic appearances over the next three seasons, and by the time he signed for Oxford for £3,500 in the summer of 1967 he had played just 22 games for Swindon, scoring six goals.

Skeen's first game for United was a 2–0 defeat at Shrewsbury on 19 August 1967 and he went on to play in every position except left-back. He even featured in goal against Bristol City after an injury to Roy Burton in December 1971. He made 270 appearances for United in a seven-year period, scoring 40 goals, including a brace in his second game for the club in a 3–1 League Cup win over Swansea.

He started at Oxford as an outside-right but moved to inside-right shortly

afterwards. After missing most of the start of the 1968–69 season Skeen returned at centre-forward, but he dropped into the midfield after the signings of Nigel Cassidy and Derek Clarke. Towards the end of his time with United, his versatility often saw him used as a substitute. His penultimate goal for the club came on 6 September 1972 in the 2–2 League Cup draw with Manchester United. His last appearance for Oxford was a 1–0 home defeat by Carlisle United on 23 April 1974, and he was released at the end of that season, going on to sign for his home-town club Cheltenham Town.

David Sloan

David Sloan was an exceptional right-winger; small and quick, he was a tenacious player with plenty of skill and a fierce shot. Sloan signed for Scunthorpe United from Irish club Bangor in November 1963, aged 22, after losing his job as a shipyard worker. While at Bangor he won two amateur international caps, both against England in 1962 and 1963, with Sloan scoring the winning goal in a 2–1 win in the latter game. He also won a youth international cap, also against England, in May 1960.

At Scunthorpe, Sloan won an Under-23 cap for Northern Ireland against Wales in February 1964. He made his League debut for the Iron at Swansea Town on 16 January 1964, scoring with a long-range shot, and he also scored in his next two matches. He played 136 games for the Iron and scored 42 goals before he signed for Oxford in February 1968. George Kerr went the other way, with his value of £7,000 supplemented by £2,500 in cash.

Sloan's arrival proved the catalyst for Oxford to win the Third Division Championship. His first game was on 24 February 1968 in a 1–1 draw at Reading, and he scored his first goal a month later in

a 2–1 win at Colchester United. He also scored in the next two games as United mounted their assault on the top of the table. It was Sloan's goal in the last game of the season, a 1–0 win over Southport on 11 May, that clinched the title for the Us.

The following season Sloan scored United's first goal in the Second Division after just six minutes of the opening game against Bolton Wanderers in a 1–1 draw. He also scored the club's first away goal in Division Two; although United lost 2–1 at Millwall. On 24 September 1969 Sloan scored the only goal with a diving header as United knocked out League Cup holders Swindon Town in the third round of the competition. He also became the first player on Oxford's books to win a full international cap, being called-up to play for Northern Ireland against Israel in Tel Aviv on 10 September 1968 in a game which Ireland won 3–2. He won his second cap in Seville against Spain on 11

November 1970, where he played alongside George Best as Northern Ireland lost 3–0.

Sloan made a total of exactly 200 appearances for United, his last match being the famous 3–1 win at the County Ground, the only time Oxford have won in Swindon, on 24 February 1973. Altogether he scored 33 goals for the club. At the end of the 1972–73 season Sloan moved to Walsall, having turned down a move to Aldershot and the opportunity of playing in New Zealand. He played 49 games and scored three goals for the Saddlers. He then turned down the option of a third year at Fellows Park, instead returning to Scunthorpe to become a steelworker. He still turned out for Bridlington for a while.

Gary Smart

Gary Smart was a right-back who played for Oxford for six seasons without scoring. He was born in Devon and lectured in PE at Abingdon College of Further Education. He initially played for Wokingham Town, playing in the side that reached the semi-finals of the FA Trophy in 1988.

Smart joined Oxford in July 1988 for £22,500 and made his debut in a 2–1 defeat at Bournemouth on 24 September 1988. He did not establish himself in the first team until coming on as a substitute against Ipswich Town in a Zenith Data Systems Cup first-round tie on 23 November 1988, after which he had a spell of 10 consecutive games. The following season he became the first-choice right-back and he gave some solid defensive performances. However, he rarely got forward and the Oxford supporters, who were used to overlapping full-backs, failed to warm to Smart.

Over the seasons Smart went on to complete 204 games for United, including the match at Tranmere Rovers when the club avoided relegation on the final day of the 1991–92 season. However, he was also an integral part of the side that, two years later, found itself relegated to the Third Division, and his last game for United came on 8 May 1994 in the 2–1 win over Notts County, the final match of that relegation season.

After his release by United, Smart moved to Stevenage Borough. He stayed at Broadhall Way for one season and he actually scored a goal, against Telford, in his 22 games. Smart's next club was Slough Town, where he again scored in his only League appearance, although he also played two FA Cup games. In 1998 Smart joined Oxford City as player-coach, replacing Kelvin Alexis, and in 2000 he moved to Windsor & Eton in the Isthmian League First Division.

Jim Smith

Jim Smith joined Headington United when they were still in the Oxfordshire Senior League, making his debut on 2 April 1938 at the age of 14 years and scoring in a 7–3 win over Osberton Radiators. He scored again three weeks later in a 3–1 win at

Banbury Harriers as United finished second in the League. Smith did not feature much in the first team before World War Two broke out in September 1939, but during the war, with many players called-up to serve in the forces, Smith became a regular.

After Headington United joined the Southern League, Smith opted to retain his amateur status. He missed the first five games of the club's first season at that level, coming back into the side for a 1–1 draw with Worcester City on 1 September 1949, in which he scored Headington's goal. Smith scored five goals in six games playing at outside-left, using his speed and his powerful shooting ability to full advantage. However, towards the end of the season he suffered an injury that saw him lose form. Smith was called-up for a trial with the England Amateur international side on 27 October 1951.

By the time that Smith ended his playing career he was the longest-serving amateur in the Southern League. His final game was on 3 September 1955 in a 3–1 defeat at Chelmsford City, although that was his only game since November 1954. Smith had played a total of 142 Southern League games, scoring 22 goals, and he had also captained the Oxfordshire FA. After he finished playing Smith became a coach at Headington United.

Rodney Smithson

In 1958 Rodney Smithson was taken on as an apprentice by Arsenal, having already received schoolboy representative honours in his native Leicester and a call-up to the England Youth side (in which John Milkins also featured). He turned professional in 1962 and signed with Oxford United in the summer of 1964, after making only two appearances for the Gunners. He did not immediately gain a place in the side;

however, after making his debut on 23 October 1965 in a 0–0 draw with Brighton, Smithson soon established a reputation as one of the best anchormen around, and by the time United reached Division Two in 1968 he was a regular in the side. Smithson was linked with a move to higher-placed clubs, but with his son Jeremy ill in hospital he opted to remain at the Manor.

During the 1972–73 season Smithson played only two games, and one of those was in the Anglo-Italian Tournament in a 1–1 draw with Torino. The following season he again appeared just twice (once as a substitute in a 1–0 win at Sheffield Wednesday, the other in the final game of the season, when a 0–0 draw at Millwall saved Oxford from relegation), and in his final season he played three games, his Oxford career ending on 5 November 1974 with a 3–0 defeat at Bristol City. This lack of first-team games meant that Smithson consolidated himself as captain of the reserves.

In total, Smithson played 180 games for the Us, scoring six goals. He was granted a testimonial against Swindon Town in May 1975. After leaving Oxford, Smithson went on to be player-manager of Witney Town.

Andy Thomas

Andy Thomas started his career with Oxford United, signing apprentice forms in May 1979. He performed outstandingly in the reserves and on 6 September 1980 he was rewarded with his first-team debut, coming off the bench in a 3–0 home defeat by Chesterfield. On 10 January 1981 Thomas made his first start for United, in a goalless draw at Rotherham. He established himself in the first team at the start of the 1981–82 season, but at the start of the following season he found himself used more and more as a substitute, and in the middle of the 1982–83 season he had short loan spells at Derby County, where

he made one appearance, and Fulham, where he played four games and scored two goals. He later became an important player for Jim Smith's side in 1983–84 and scored a stunning goal in the 2–1 League Cup win over Newcastle United on 26 October 1983.

However, Thomas's career took a turn for the worse on 2 January 1984 when, in a 3–1 defeat at Exeter City, he suffered a badly broken leg. He did not return to first-team action until coming on as a substitute in a 1–0 defeat at Leeds United on 27 April 1985. He returned to regular football at the start of the club's First Division campaign the following season; however, he suffered another injury in December and did not play again until he came off the bench in February, and he only played two more games for Oxford, both as substitute, in March.

Thomas's last game for United was on 22 March 1986 in the side's then record 6–0 defeat by Liverpool at Anfield. Thomas was on the bench for the Milk Cup Final at Wembley but did not get on the pitch, even when the team was winning 3–0. On 24 September 1986 Newcastle United came in for Thomas, who moved to St James' Park for £85,000 plus £25,000 after he had played 25 games.

In total Thomas played 150 games for United and scored 45 goals.

In two seasons Thomas played 31 League games for the Magpies, scoring six goals, before he moved to Bradford City for £80,000. He played 23 League games for the Bantams, finding the net five times, and from there he went to Plymouth Argyle, also for £80,000, in July 1989. In two seasons at Home Park, Thomas played 50 League games and scored 19 goals before retiring from professional football in July 1991 as a result of a serious back injury. After a brief spell at Thame United Thomas became the player-manager at Oxford City, and he led the side to the FA Vase Final at Wembley in 1995 which they lost 2–1 to Arlesey Town. He later managed Brackley Town.

Cyril Toulouse

Cyril Toulouse arrived at Headington United from Guildford City on 18 March 1950. He was born in Acton on Christmas Eve 1923 and signed for his first club, Brentford, in January 1946. He played 10 times for the Bees in his first season but was unable to prevent them from relegation to the Second Division. The following season he made three

appearances before being transferred to Tottenham Hotspur on 12 January 1947. Toulouse played just two games for Spurs before moving on to Guildford City.

Headington signed Toulouse for £150, at a wage of £8 per week, with Toulouse signing an agreement that he would not leave the club before the end of the 1950–51 season. In the event, however, Toulouse stayed with the club until the end of the 1953–54 season. He was a right wing-half; tall and described as 'unbeatable in the air'. He was also called the 'best pivot in the Southern League'. His debut for Headington was on 18 March 1950, in a 2–1 defeat by Tonbridge. He went on to complete 153 appearances for the Us, with his final game a 3–2 defeat at Llanelli on 26 April 1954.

Despite only being at the club for little over four seasons, Toulouse was granted a five-year testimonial, in accordance with Southern League rules, which was played against an 'All Star XI' on 20 September 1954. Toulouse scored 20 goals for United, including one against Weymouth in the Southern League Cup Final second leg on 27 April 1953, which United won 3–1 to take the trophy 4–3 on aggregate. His first goals for the club had come on 1 April 1950, when he scored a brace in a 3–1 win over Hastings United, and it was there where Toulouse went after leaving the Manor. He died in 1980.

Paul Wanless

A Banbury lad, Paul Wanless came through United's youth setup but was unable to establish himself in the side, playing just 39 games (of which only 14 saw him in the starting line up). He made his debut on 9 October 1991 in a 1–0 defeat by Portsmouth, and his first start came on 30 November 1991 in a 1–1 draw at Cambridge United. He scored one goal, in a 1–1 draw against Tranmere Rovers in the

League Cup second round, second leg on 5 October 1993. His last game for United before moving on to Lincoln City in the summer of 1995 was a 1–1 draw at Plymouth Argyle on 6 May 1995. He made just 10 appearances for Lincoln and had a couple of months on loan at Woking, before moving to Cambridge United in March 1996. He made 335 appearances for Cambridge, scoring 50 goals, and was appointed club captain before his surprising return to Oxford on 7 August 2003.

Wanless had started out with United as a forward, but by the time he returned to the club he had converted into a central midfielder, and it was there that he played his first game after his return on 9 August 2003 in a 1–0 win at Lincoln City. He was back at United for two seasons, during which time he scored six goals, and he ended his career playing as a makeshift centre-half, where he did an accomplished job.

There was a lot of dissatisfaction from the fans when he was released by Brian Talbot in the summer of 2005, having played his last game on 7 May 2005 in a 1–0 home defeat by Chester City. In total Wanless had played 106 games for the Us, scoring seven goals. After leaving Oxford Wanless signed for Conference outfit Forest Green Rovers, for whom he played 38 games and scored 10 goals, and he was made their caretaker manager after the club terminated the contract of Gary Owers in August 2006, with the club having lost all four of their opening games. Wanless led them for two games, both draws, before the appointment of Jimmy Harvey. He was released by Rovers in May 2007 and joined Llanelli as player-coach. He had played 15 games for the Welsh club, scoring twice, at the time of writing.

Dean Whitehead

'Deano' was one of United's rising stars, coming through the youth team and reserves to the first team. He gave strength

and vision to the midfield, where he played mostly on the right side, where his accurate crossing worked wonders. Whitehead would almost certainly have established himself in the United pantheon of home-grown greats, but he was signed by Sunderland before fully realising his potential at the Us.

Whitehead made his first-team debut on 7 December 1999, coming on as a substitute in a 2–0 win over Luton Town in the Auto Windscreens Shield. His first start was on 22 August 2000, when United beat Wolverhampton Wanderers 1–0 at Molineux in a League Cup first-round tie. He was never the greatest goalscorer, finding the net just nine times in his 136 games at Oxford. His first goal was on 1 September 2001 in a 3–2 win over Rushden & Diamonds. He also scored a wonderful goal against Chelsea in a pre-season friendly at the Kassam Stadium on 24 July 2002, striking a perfect free-kick that even had Chelsea star Gianfranco Zola congratulating him.

Whitehead's appearances under Ian Atkins were initially limited to covering for the more experienced regulars, but in the second half of the 2003–04 season he eventually made himself a regular in the midfield and was consistently United's best player. He was even captain for a day in United's final away game of the season at Macclesfield, which Oxford lost 2–1. His last appearance for United was a week later, when he scored in United's 2–0 win over Rochdale on 8 May 2004. Whitehead was signed on a three-year contract by Sunderland in the close season on a Bosman transfer. Because he was under 23 years old the Rokerites had to pay compensation to Oxford, with the fee determined by a tribunal. Sunderland were ordered to pay £150,000 plus the following – £15,000 every 10 appearances up to 50, £100,000 on promotion, £50,000 on his first competitive international appearance and 25 per cent of his fee should Sunderland sell him on. Although he was relegated in his first season on Teesside, Sunderland won promotion back to the Premiership at their first attempt. Whitehead then became a regular in the side and went on to captain Sunderland in the Premiership.

Phil Whitehead

Phil Whitehead is considered by many Oxford fans to be one of the club's best-ever goalkeepers. He played for United for almost exactly five years, during which time he cemented a reputation as not just a brilliant shot-stopper but also a commanding and resilient character, who forged an excellent rapport with the London Road crowd. Certainly he was aided by having a strong defence in front of him, featuring Matt Elliott and Phil Gilchrist, for a large proportion of his games.

Whitehead's career started at Halifax, where he played 52 games after making his debut in 1988. In March 1990 he was signed by near neighbours Barnsley for

£60,000 but they immediately loaned him back to the Shaymen for a further nine games. He also had loan spells at Scunthorpe (twice) and Bradford City, clocking up a further 30 games, meaning that he had only played 16 times for Barnsley when Oxford signed him for £75,000 in October 1993.

Whitehead made his United debut on 2 October, when Oxford drew 2–2 with Grimsby Town. He kept his first clean sheet for the Yellows eight days later, when Oxford beat Stoke City 1–0, but six days later he was on the receiving end of a 6–1 hammering at Southend United when Tommy Mooney scored a hat-trick. Nevertheless Whitehead was immediately established as Oxford's number one, replacing Paul Reece, but he was not able to prevent the Us being relegated to the Third Division.

Whitehead was immensely popular with the Oxford fans, and his impressive performances earned him the nickname 'God'. His last appearance for United was in a live TV game at Norwich City, which Oxford won 3–2. By this time the club was in dire financial straits and Whitehead was one of several players sold in order to bring in some much-needed income. He went to Second Division rivals West Brom for £250,000, where he played 28 games before being sold for the same amount to Reading just under a year later. He was with the Biscuitmen for almost four seasons, playing 108 games for them, and spent loan spells at both York City and Tranmere before joining Tamworth. He has also been goalkeeping coach at AFC Bournemouth.

Whitehead played 238 games for United in just over five years, keeping a remarkable 70 clean sheets in those games. His last appearance, and his only one at the Kassam Stadium, was when he kept goal in Peter Rhoades-Brown's testimonial against Chelsea Youth at the end of 2006–07.

Alan Willey

Alan Willey started out on the groundstaff of his home-town club, Exeter City. He then joined Bridgwater Town but after impressing in an FA Cup second-round tie at the Manor on 26 November 1960, which Oxford won 2–1, he was signed by United in the first week of December despite interest from other teams.

United paid £300 for the inside-forward, who made his Oxford debut on 11 March 1961 in a 2–2 home draw with Yeovil Town. That was his only appearance that season, but at the start of the following season Willey started getting regular outings, generally as an inside-left. His first goals for United came on 2 September 1961, when he scored twice as Oxford beat Tonbridge 4–1, and his most prolific game came 28 days later when he hit four goals as United beat Gravesend & Northfleet 8–0. The following season Willey scored United's first home League goal when the side beat Lincoln City 2–1 on 22 August

1962, and he then scored two in the following game as United beat Hartlepools 6–2. On 27 April 1963 he scored his only League hat-trick in a 3–0 home win over Mansfield Town. He scored 48 goals for United in 128 games, of which one, in September 1965 against Bristol Rovers, was as substitute.

Willey's final game for the Us was a 4–0 defeat at Shrewsbury Town on 5 February 1966. The following month he moved to Millwall, for whom he played six games in his first season and four games the following season. He then went to play for Durban City in South Africa, before returning to Oxfordshire to play for Banbury United.

Dean Windass

Dean Windass became Oxford's record signing when the club bought him from Aberdeen for £475,000 in the summer of 1998. He made his debut in the first game of the 1998–99 season at Bristol City on 8 August and he scored the first of his 18 Oxford goals in that 2–2 draw.

A Humberside boy, Windass began his career with North Ferriby before joining Hull City in 1991, where he played 176 games and scored 57 goals. He joined Aberdeen in December 1995 for £700,000 and played 95 games for the Dons, scoring 34 goals. While at Pittodrie he suffered the ignominy of being sent off three times in one game. Windass's stay at Oxford was not a particularly happy one, and although he finished the season as the side's leading scorer, when he heard that Bradford City were interested in signing him he lost interest in playing for United. His final game, on 3 March 1999 at QPR, featured a particularly uninterested performance and he joined Bradford for £950,000, rising to £1 million when the Bantams were promoted to the Premiership at the end of that season. The money received from

Windass's sale enabled United to pay Aberdeen for his signing, as the Scottish club had yet to receive any instalments from Oxford. He stayed at Bradford for almost exactly two years, playing 88 games and scoring 20 goals, including one against Liverpool that saved the club from relegation at the end of their first Premiership season.

Middlesbrough then paid £600,000 for Windass, but he played only 46 games for them over the next couple of years. He had loan spells at both Sheffield clubs before joining United on a free transfer in January 2003. At the end of the 2002–03 season he rejoined Bradford, where he stayed for the next four seasons, playing 155 games and scoring 66 goals. He spent the latter half of the 2006–07 season on loan to Hull City, scoring eight goals in 18 games, and he joined the Tigers permanently in the summer of 2007, for a fee of £150,000. He was still playing in the Premiership at the age of 38, although he spent some time on loan to Oldham. After his release by Hull in June 2009 Windass became Colin Todd's assistant at Darlington.

Managers

Harry Thompson (1949–58)

Mansfield-born Harry Thompson started his playing career with Mansfield Town Juniors, signing as a professional in 1932, but he joined Wolverhampton Wanderers in 1933 without ever having played a game for the Stags. After 69 League games and 16 goals, in 1937 Sunderland paid Wolves the then enormous sum of £7,500 for Thompson, who played as an inside-forward. He was at Roker Park when World War Two broke out, having played 11 games and scored once for Sunderland. During the war Thompson played for some top-class army teams as well as guesting for York City while on army duties at Marston Moor.

In 1946 the resumption of League football saw Thompson sign for Northampton Town on a part-time basis. In the following three seasons he played 38 League games for the Cobblers, scoring twice, after having switched to playing centre-half. During the summers Thompson coached Norwegian side Ranheim, based near Trondheim.

In July 1949 Headington United director Peter Smith reported to the club's first board meeting that he had secured the services of Harry Thompson as player-coach, with effect from 1 August 1949. Thompson was given a two-year contract and was to be paid £550 a year, plus a match bonus of £2 per win and £1 per draw while playing. In addition, he would receive an extra bonus depending on where the team finished in the Southern League. United were to provide Thompson with accommodation, and the club eventually bought a house for him in Green Road, Headington. Thompson's duties were to assemble a squad by recommending players to the board and to coach the players, with Mr Smith negotiating the contracts. Team selection was initially undertaken by a sub-committee, of which Thompson was a member.

At the end of the 1949–50 season Thompson was appointed player-manager, a decision that led board member H.F. Bradley to resign in protest, and he was empowered to sign his own players up to a maximum wage bill of £130 per week. The side had finished fourth from bottom in their inaugural Southern League season, during which Thompson had played 44 games before an injury at Gillingham on 5 April ended his season. The following season United fared much better, finishing seventh, with Thompson playing 21 games and scoring once, in a 3–2 win at Torquay United Reserves on 11 November 1950. His last game for the club was a 4–1 defeat at Chelmsford City on 24 March 1951, after which he decided to end his playing career. Thompson offered to resign if the club decided it wanted to appoint another player-manager, but the board instead appointed him manager on an annual contract, with effect from August 1951.

Under Thompson's guidance United went from strength to strength, winning the Southern League and Southern League Cup in 1952–53, and finishing second the following season while retaining the Southern League Cup and reaching the fourth round of the FA Cup. He was eventually sacked in November 1958 after the side had lost seven consecutive Southern League games. His last game as manager was a 1–0 defeat at Guildford City in the Southern League Inter-Zone Competition. After leaving Headington United, Harry worked for Morris Motors and then Pressed Steel in Cowley. He died on 29 January 2000, aged 84.

Thompson was described as a modest man, who was very fair, talked common sense and would drop players who played badly, telling them why and treating everyone, whether full-time, part-time or amateur, the same. Thompson was responsible, along with the board, for turning Headington from a part-time local team into a full-time professional side that became known nationally. He started from scratch with no players, but he managed to build up a team of good ball-players. He brought in players such as Geoff Denial, Johnny Love, Pat Quartermain and Frank Ramshaw, all of whom went on to have lengthy and distinguished careers with United.

Competition	*Games*	*W*	*D*	*L*	*F*	*A*
FA Cup	37	26	3	8	109	52
Southern League	394	168	77	149	708	641
Southern League Cup	38	16	9	13	67	53
Southern League Inter-Zone	4	2	0	2	7	10
Total	**473**	**212**	**89**	**172**	**891**	**756**

Arthur Turner (1958–69)

Arthur Turner was born on 1 April 1909 in Chesterton, a small former mining village on the edge of Newcastle-under-Lyme, Staffordshire. As a youth Turner played for Downings Tileries, the same team that produced Stoke City and Leeds United forward Freddie Steele. Chesterton was part of the Wolstanton United Urban District, and Turner's next club was Wolstanton PSA. He left them in 1929, joining West Bromwich Albion as an amateur, and he then left the following year for Stoke City, where he played as a centre-half and made seven League appearances in his debut season. Two seasons later Turner was an ever present and scored five goals as Stoke were

promoted to the First Division, and he continued as a regular for the Potters over the next four seasons, becoming Stoke's main penalty taker. By the time he moved to Birmingham City in 1938, Turner had played 290 League games for Stoke, scoring 17 goals, 10 of which came from the spot. His first season at Birmingham ended badly, with the Blues relegated to Division Two and Turner playing only 12 games. The following season Turner had played just two games before the season was halted early due to the outbreak of World War Two. During the war Turner played nearly 200 games for Birmingham, captaining them to the Championship of the Wartime Football League South. In the first post-war season Turner played 27 games for Birmingham, who finished third in the Second Division, just missing out on promotion, and reached the semi-final of the first post-war FA Cup.

In January 1948 Turner was appointed player-manager of Southport, where he played 28 League games. He played his last game in October 1948 when he left to become manager of Crewe Alexandra. He was at Crewe for three seasons before returning to Stoke to become assistant manager to Bob McGrory and then Frank Taylor. In November 1954 Turner left Stoke to become manager of Birmingham City, leading them to the Second Division Championship in his first season, and then to sixth in Division One the following season. Turner resigned in September 1958 after finding out from the press that Pat Beasley, who he thought was appointed as his assistant, had in fact been named as joint manager.

Turner joined Headington United on New Year's Day 1959, becoming manager without a contract. On 2 April 1959 Turner was approached by First Division Leeds United to become their manager. Turner initially accepted the Leeds offer, but when Headington matched their terms he decided to remain in Oxford and signed a permanent contract. During what remained of the 1958–59 season he managed to improve the side's results enough to ensure that they finished in the top half of the Southern League North Western Zone, thereby guaranteeing a place in the Southern League Premier Division the following season, albeit on goal average. The following season Headington were runners-up to Bath City, but in the next two seasons the club, now called Oxford United, won the Southern League Championship. In 1961–62 Accrington Stanley resigned from the Football League after going bankrupt and United were the obvious team to replace them.

The first season as a Football League club was one of consolidation, but the following season Oxford became the first Fourth Division side to reach the quarter-finals of the FA Cup, famously beating First Division Blackburn Rovers 3–1 in the fifth round before losing 2–1 to Preston North End. The following season United finished fourth in Division Four, earning promotion. Three seasons later Arthur Turner led United to the Third Division title and promotion to Division Two, just 10 seasons after becoming manager of a club in the bottom half of the Southern League.

Unfortunately United struggled in their first season in the second tier and Turner resigned from team duties, becoming general manager in January 1969. Turner's time at the club ended on a sour note, when he was sacked in the spring of 1972, having earlier been given a leave of absence, after United admitted that they could not afford to retain him, despite having promised him a job until his retirement.

After leaving Oxford, Turner remained involved in football, scouting for Rotherham United and Sheffield Wednesday. He died on 12 January 1994, aged 84.

Competition	*Games*	*W*	*D*	*L*	*F*	*A*
FA Cup	30	13	7	10	54	52
League Cup	11	3	1	7	14	19
League	306	112	83	111	439	410
Southern League	145	87	26	32	333	180
Southern League Cup	8	1	2	5	7	13
Southern League Inter-Zone	4	2	0	2	6	6
Total	**504**	**218**	**119**	**167**	**853**	**680**

Ron Saunders (1969)

Birkenhead-born Ron Saunders joined Everton as a junior and made three League appearances for the Toffees in 1954–55. The following season he joined Southern League side Tonbridge, but returned to the Football League with Gillingham in 1957. Centre-forward Saunders was at the Gills for two seasons, scoring 20 goals in his 49 League appearances, before he moved to First Division Portsmouth in 1958. His 21 goals from 36 games failed to prevent Pompey's relegation, however, and two seasons later they were relegated again to the Third Division, despite Saunders scoring 20 goals, adding to the 17 he had scored the previous season. Saunders continued his impressive goals return the following season, scoring 32 from 42 games as Portsmouth won the Division Three Championship. In 1964 Saunders moved to Watford, having played 236 League games and scored 145 goals. He was with Third Division Watford for one season, scoring 18 goals in his 39 games, before moving back up a division to join Charlton Athletic, where he played 65 games and scored 24 times.

On 17 April 1967 Saunders became player-manager of Yeovil Town in the Southern League, but he left to join Oxford United on 19 February 1969, doubling his salary to £80 a week and becoming the first person to move from managing a non-League club to a Second Division side.

When Saunders arrived at Oxford, United were bottom of Division Two with just 12 games of the season remaining. His first game in charge was a 1–1 draw at Bolton Wanderers, and over the next 11 games United lost only three and drew two to ensure their survival. They finished three points clear of relegated Bury, and eight points above Fulham. Considering Saunders' relative managerial inexperience this was a magnificent achievement and one that did not go unnoticed elsewhere. During the summer of 1969 Saunders moved to Norwich City, having been in charge at Oxford for just 12 matches.

During his first two seasons at Carrow Road, Norwich lingered in mid-table in Division Two, but in his third season Saunders led the Canaries to the Second Division title with an unbeaten home record. The following season Norwich survived in the First Division, finishing in 20th place. Norwich finished bottom the next season, but Saunders had already left the club in November 1973, taking over the reins at First Division Manchester City. He was in charge at Maine Road for less than six months before being sacked, having won just six out of 24 games. However, he was not out of work for long as he joined Aston Villa in the summer of 1974. In his first season in charge Saunders took Villa to second in Division Two, just three points behind Manchester United. Their first season in Division One saw Villa finish 16th, but without an away win, and in 1976–77 they finished fourth. In the next three seasons the Villains finished in the top half of the table and in 1980–81 Saunders led Villa to the First Division title after finishing four points above Ipswich Town. In February 1982, after more than 350 games in charge, Saunders left Villa to become manager of their arch-rivals Birmingham City.

Saunders' first two seasons at St Andrews were ones of struggle, with the Blues finishing in 16th and then 17th place. In the third season the Blues lost the struggle and finished 20th, the third relegation place. Saunders got Birmingham back into the top flight the following season, as they finished second in Division Two, two points behind Oxford United. However, Saunders resigned from Birmingham in January 1986 to join local rivals West Bromwich Albion, who were facing relegation. That season West Brom finished bottom of Division One, to go down along with Birmingham. He was sacked by West Brom in September 1987, with the Baggies struggling to avoid relegation to the Third Division. Saunders has not managed in football since leaving the Hawthorns.

Competition	*Games*	*W*	*D*	*L*	*F*	*A*
League	12	6	3	3	11	9
Total	**12**	**6**	**3**	**3**	**11**	**9**

Gerry Summers (1969–75)

Gerry Summers' first professional club was West Bromwich Albion, whom he joined from Erdington Albion in 1951. He made his debut as a wing-half in 1955, playing 20 games in his debut season for the First Division side. He played just twice the following season, after which he joined Second Division Sheffield United. At the end of his fourth season with the Blades, where he played 260 games, scoring four goals, they won promotion to the top flight and finished fifth in the First Division the following year. In April 1964 Summers moved to Hull City of Division Three. He played just one full season at Boothferry Park before moving to Walsall in October 1965. He played 31 games for

Walsall, scoring once, until he left Fellows Park in 1967. He then did some coaching at Wolves and was a coach on the staff of the FA before being appointed manager at the Manor in July 1969.

Summers' first game in charge was on 9 August 1969, a 2–1 home defeat by Huddersfield Town. During his first season he managed to consolidate the side in Division Two and also reached the quarter-finals of the League Cup, which they lost 1–0 at Carlisle United in a replay after a 0–0 draw at the Manor. In 1970–71 Summers took United to the top of the Second Division by the end of September, the highest the club had ever been. This was the season that Summers brought in some iconic players who were to carve their names in the United history books, such as Derek Clarke, Nigel Cassidy and Dave Roberts. However, United fell away from the top and ended the season in 14th place. The Us finished 15th the following season, but in 1972–73 they ended in their highest position yet, eighth in the Second Division. The following season was much tougher for United, who looked like they could go down until the final match of the season, a 0–0 draw at Millwall, left Oxford in 18th place and just two points above relegated Crystal Palace. The 1974–75 campaign was another relatively successful season for United. They finished 11th but for much of the season were higher than that, and they also notably beat champions Manchester United 1–0 at the Manor. In this season Summers was forced to sell Roberts to Hull, which was to set the club back almost irretrievably. Summers' big signing in the close season was Peter Houseman from Chelsea, but United made a poor start and were bottom by the end of September. As a result attendances fell, and because of the club's precarious financial situation Summers was dismissed. In total he had managed Oxford for 293 games, winning 93 and losing 111. His final game was a 3–2 home defeat by Charlton Athletic on 29 September 1975.

Three weeks after his dismissal Summers was appointed manager of Third Division Gillingham. In his six seasons with the Gills, his most successful was 1978–79 when they finished fourth, one point behind promoted Swansea City. He had 262 games in charge at Priestfield before being sacked at the end of the 1980–81 season. He went on to coach at West Bromwich Albion, Leicester City and Derby County, becoming youth development officer with the Rams until his retirement in October 1998.

Competition	*Games*	*W*	*D*	*L*	*F*	*A*
FA Cup	12	3	3	6	14	22
League Cup	20	7	6	7	26	25
League	261	83	80	98	255	302
Total	**293**	**93**	**89**	**111**	**295**	**349**

Mick Brown (1975–79)

Despite being in charge of Oxford United for four seasons, Mick Brown is not a name that supporters readily recall when listing United's most influential managers. United suffered relegation from Division Two at the end of his first season and then fought relegation to Division Four in the next two campaigns. However, there were mitigating circumstances and, in retrospect, Brown played an important role in building the foundations for those who followed.

Brown started his playing career as a full-back with Hull City, whom he had joined as a junior before becoming a professional in 1958. He played twice in his first season with the Tigers, who suffered relegation to Division Three at the end of the campaign. He played just six more games over the next two years

before, in July 1967, he joined Lincoln City. He played 38 Fourth Division games for the Red Imps and then moved to Southern League side Cambridge United.

It was from Cambridge that Gerry Summers recruited Brown to help Ken Fish with training Oxford's reserve and A teams in January 1970. Before the 1971–72 season Brown was made assistant manager, and when Summers was sacked in October 1975 Brown was made his successor. His first game, on 4 October, was a 2–1 win over Leyton Orient, and Brown's appointment led to a slight improvement in the team's results. They finished the season third from bottom but still in the relegation zone. This was United's first relegation.

Oxford initially struggled in the Third Division, finishing four points above the drop zone in each of the next two seasons. This was partly because Brown was forced to use many of United's youngsters as the club's financial situation worsened, and he also struggled through the sale of Derek Clarke, injury to Brian Heron and Peter Houseman's death in a car crash. In 1978–79 United finished in a more respectable 11th position, and at the end of that season Brown left to join Ron Atkinson at West Bromwich Albion as his assistant.

Atkinson and Brown (and goalkeeping coach Jim Barron) were at West Brom until June 1981, after which Brown went with Atkinson to Manchester United. As a management duo the pair enjoyed huge success, twice winning the FA Cup, reaching the semi-final of the European Cup-Winners' Cup and the League Cup Final, as well as finishing in the top four in each of the five years they were there. However, the absence of a League title led to the Old Trafford board dismissing Atkinson and Brown in November 1986. Three years later Brown became Phil Neal's assistant at Bolton Wanderers, where he remained until 1992, losing his job when Neal was sacked. In the summer of 1992 Brown was employed by the Pahang FA in Malaysia as a coach, and he then returned to England to become Coventry City's chief scout. Five years later Brown became Blackburn Rovers' chief scout and a year later he returned to Old Trafford to take up the same position for Manchester United. Upon reaching the age of 65 he was forcibly retired by the Manchester club, whereupon he rejoined West Brom as chief scout in 2005. Two years later Roy Keane took him to Sunderland to perform the same function.

Competition	*Games*	*W*	*D*	*L*	*F*	*A*
FA Cup	5	0	1	4	4	10
League Cup	11	5	3	3	14	15
League	171	49	56	66	194	224
Total	**187**	**54**	**60**	**73**	**212**	**249**

Bill Asprey (1979–80)

Wolverhampton-born Asprey joined Stoke City as a junior, signing as a full professional in September 1953. He had a slow start at Stoke, making just one appearance in his first season, three the next and nine the following season, before breaking into the first team and becoming a regular in the defence. Before leaving the Potters for Oldham Athletic in January 1966, Asprey had made 341 appearances and scored 26 goals, and in 1962–63 he was an ever present as Stoke won the Second Division Championship. In his first season at Third Division Oldham Asprey played 26 League games, scoring once. He went on to complete 80 League games and score four goals before signing for Port Vale in December 1967. He played 31 games for Vale without scoring, before hanging up his boots and joining the coaching staff at Sheffield Wednesday.

Between 1975 and 1978 Asprey was national coach in Rhodesia before joining Coventry City as Noel Cantwell's assistant. He did not stay long at Coventry, however, and joined Oxford United as a reserve-team coach in the 1978 close season. After Mick Brown left to join West Brom, Barry was promoted to the role of first-team manager, and he started in his new role with a League Cup game against Reading on 11 August 1979. It was not the most auspicious of beginnings as United were hammered 5–1 at the Manor before losing the second leg 2–1 at Elm Park. Brown's League management career got off to a better start, however, as the Us beat Rotherham United 5–1 at the Manor and then drew 2–2 at Hull City. Two more home wins followed, including a 4–0 revenge over Reading, before the wheels started to come off and United faced another relegation battle, eventually finishing the season 17th in Division Three. The following season started no better for Asprey and with crowds plummeting (United recording their lowest League attendance of 2,526 against Chester City in November 1980) Asprey was sacked following a 2–1 defeat at Millwall that left Oxford third from bottom of the Division, two points above bottom club Hull City.

After leaving the Manor, Asprey returned to Stoke as assistant to Richie Barker, becoming manager following Barker's dismissal in December 1983. He initially worked miracles to keep Stoke in the First Division, but the following season Stoke finished bottom, recording just 17 points, which at the time was a record low for the Division. With just over a month of the season left Asprey resigned through ill-health in April 1985, having already been suspended on full pay.

Competition

	Games	*W*	*D*	*L*	*F*	*A*
FA Cup	3	1	0	2	1	4
League Cup	7	2	0	5	8	12
League	71	19	20	32	74	93
Total	**81**	**22**	**20**	**39**	**83**	**109**

Ian Greaves (1980–82)

Oldham-born Ian Denzil Greaves started his playing career at Buxton before moving to Manchester United in May 1953. He was a 'Busby babe', one of a number of young players given a chance by Manchester United manager Matt Busby, although he was never a regular at Old Trafford. In his first season Greaves played just once, at full-back; although he played 15 League games in 1955–56, winning a League Champions' medal in the process. He played just three games the following season, and 12 the next. On 6 February 1958 many Manchester United players were killed or badly injured in the Munich Air Disaster, and it is possible that, but for an injury sustained before that fateful day, Greaves might also have been involved. However, the misfortune of others allowed him to secure a regular place in the first team and he went on to play 34 League games that season as the side finished second in the League and runners-up in the FA Cup. The following season he played just twice before, in December 1960, he moved on to Lincoln City. Greaves was at Sincil Bank for just five months, playing 11 games as Lincoln were relegated to the Third Division, before he moved back to Lancashire to play for Oldham Athletic. He played 22 games for the Latics in the next two seasons and finished his playing career at Altrincham.

In 1964 Greaves joined Huddersfield Town as a coach and became their manager in June 1968. He led the Second Division side to sixth position in his first season, and the following year they won the Division Two Championship to earn promotion to the First Division for the first time in their history. They finished 15th in their first season, but were relegated the next season after finishing in bottom place. Greaves remained in charge despite a second successive relegation, and the next season the Terriers finished 10th in Division Three. In October 1974 Greaves replaced Jimmy Armfield as Bolton Wanderers manager, and in his first season the side finished 10th in Division Two. The following two seasons Bolton finished fourth before, in 1977–78, Greaves led them to the Second Division title and promotion. As at Huddersfield, though, Greaves struggled in the top flight as Bolton finished 17th in their first season and were relegated in bottom place in 1979. With the side struggling en route to a second relegation, Greaves was sacked in January 1980. He then spent most of 1980 as assistant manager at Hereford United before joining Oxford United in December.

Greaves inherited a side that was second from bottom of the Third Division, with mounting debts, declining gates and a sub-standard playing staff. His first game, on Boxing Day 1980, saw United incredibly beat top-of-the-table Charlton Athletic 1–0, and the following day they followed this up with a 1–0 win at Reading. After a brief stutter, United went unbeaten in their last 13 games and they finished 14th in the table. In the 1981–82 season United had their most successful time for 15 years as they finished fifth in the Third Division and had decent runs in both Cup competitions, getting knocked out of the League Cup by First Division Everton and winning 3–0 at Division One side Brighton in the FA Cup. Throughout his time at Oxford Greaves had not signed a contract, and so it came as no great surprise when he left in February 1982 to take over at First Division Wolves. His last game in charge of Oxford was a 3–1 win at sixth-placed Walsall, which left United ninth in the table and still in the FA Cup.

When Greaves took charge at Molineux Wolves were struggling to remain in the top flight, and he was unable to save them from the drop. In August 1982 Wolves were taken over by a consortium headed by Derek Dougan, and Greaves was dismissed. He then left the game for a while before returning to manage Mansfield Town in January 1983. Relying mainly on a strong youth policy, Greaves took Mansfield up into the Third Division in 1986, and the following season the Stags won the Freight Rover Trophy Final, beating Bristol City on penalties at Wembley. He resigned in February 1989 and later had stints coaching at Bury and managing at non-League Emley, before embarking on scouting work for a number of clubs in the North West. Greaves died on 2 January 2009, aged 76.

Competition	*Games*	*W*	*D*	*L*	*F*	*A*
FA Cup	5	4	1	0	13	4
Football League Group Cup	3	0	0	3	2	7
League Cup	5	3	1	1	7	4
League	41	17	14	10	49	38
Total	**54**	**24**	**16**	**14**	**71**	**53**

Roy Barry (caretaker 1982)

Roy Barry was born on 19 September 1942. He started his playing career with Musselburgh Athletic Juniors before joining Heart of Midlothian in 1961. He

made his Hearts debut at centre-half in August 1961 and went on to play 178 games for the Edinburgh club before being sold to Dunfermline for £13,000 in September 1966. In April 1968 Barry was captain of the Pars when they beat Hearts 3–1 in the Scottish Cup Final. In October 1969 Coventry City paid £40,000 for Barry, who made 15 appearances in his first season for the Sky Blues. The following season Barry appeared only once before breaking his leg, but he went on to complete 83 appearances for Coventry, scoring twice, before Crystal Palace bought him for £45,000 in September 1973. He was at Palace for two seasons, playing 42 games and scoring once, before returning north of the border to sign for Hibernian. He was at Hibs for a season, playing 36 games, before moving to East Fife to become player-manager. He made 12 appearances over the next one and a half years, before retiring from playing.

After leaving East Fife, Barry worked for a time on the assembly line at the Leyland Triumph factory in Coventry, while also managing Nuneaton Borough on a part-time basis. He was appointed assistant to Bill Asprey at Oxford in March 1980, and when Ian Greaves left to manage Wolves, Barry stepped in as caretaker, although he made no secret of his desire to make the role permanent. Barry was in charge of Oxford for just seven games, including the 4–0 FA Cup fifth-round defeat at his former club Coventry. He started his reign with a 1–0 win over Reading on 3 February 1982, and ended it on 27 February with a 3–1 win over Chester City. After leaving Oxford, Barry left the game and worked in London for 25 years until his retirement in 2008.

Competition

	Games	*W*	*D*	*L*	*F*	*A*
FA Cup	1	0	0	1	0	4
League	6	3	3	0	8	4
Total	**7**	**3**	**3**	**1**	**8**	**8**

Jim Smith (1982–85)

James Michael Smith began his professional playing career when he signed for his home-town club Sheffield United as a trainee in January 1959, having previously played for Oaksfield. Smith never played for Sheffield's first team and he joined Fourth Division Aldershot in July 1961. He had four seasons at the Rec, playing 74 League games in midfield and scoring one goal, and in July 1965 he joined Halifax Town, also in Division Four. In his first season at the Shay Smith played 45 games, scoring four goals, and by the time he left for Lincoln City in March 1968 he had played 114 games for the Shaymen and had seven goals to his name. Smith played 54 League games at Lincoln in the next 15 months, and he then left to become player-manager at Boston United in the Northern Premier League in 1969.

In his first season at Boston Smith played 53 games and scored five goals as

his new club finished third. He played 45 games the next season, scoring 11 times, and secured a fourth-place finish, while in 1971–72 he played a further 52 games and found the net six times as he took the club up to second place. In his final season with the Pilgrims Smith played 19 games and scored one goal as Boston won the title. In addition to his player-manager duties Smith also had to find time to act as club secretary, run the club lottery, dig new drains, concrete the car park and decorate the boardroom. During his time at York Street Boston always finished in the top four and the side had gone unbeaten for almost 40 games of a run of 51 League games without defeat (a British professional record) when he left to join Colchester United in October 1972. Colchester were bottom of the Fourth Division when Smith joined, but he turned things around and won the divisional Manager of the Month award in his first month. At the end of the season Smith retired from playing, having managed eight games, as Colchester were re-elected to the Football League. The following season Smith turned Colchester around and the club finished third to earn promotion to Division Three, where the next season they finished 11th.

Smith's success at Colchester got him noticed by some bigger clubs, and in June 1975 he moved to Second Division Blackburn Rovers. But in March 1978 he became disillusioned with the lack of money available to strengthen the team and moved to Birmingham City. At the end of the following season Birmingham were relegated from Division One after finishing 21st, but Smith took them straight back up the following season with a third-place finish. After a mid-table finish the next season Birmingham were struggling once again and Smith was replaced by Ron Saunders. Within two days of leaving St Andrews, Smith was contacted by Oxford director Paul Reeves and had an interview lined up for the vacant Oxford post.

United were still in with a chance of promotion when Smith took over, and they won his first game 2–0 at Bristol City on 6 March 1982. United were in second place on 1 May, but they lost their last four games to finish fifth and miss out on promotion. This proved a blessing for Smith, who was able to rebuild the side. United finished fifth again the following season, but then Smith worked his magic and in 1983–84 the Us won the Third Division title at a canter, at the same time also becoming the first side from Division Three to reach the fifth round of both the FA Cup and League Cup in the same season. The following season United became the first team to win consecutive Third and Second Division titles as Smith took the Us into the top flight for the first time in the club's history. Smith was awarded the Bells Scottish Whisky Second Division Manager of the Season award. Sadly, Smith never managed Oxford in the First Division as he had a dispute with Maxwell about a pay rise, and that summer Smith moved to Queen's Park Rangers.

In his first season at Loftus Road Smith took QPR to the League (Milk) Cup Final, where they were beaten 3–0 by an Oxford side composed mostly of players who had played under Smith. Three seasons later, in December 1988, he moved to Newcastle United, who finished third in Division Two in Smith's first full season. On 26 March 1991 Smith resigned from Newcastle, claiming that the club was unmanageable, and he became manager of Portsmouth that June. He took them to the FA Cup semi-finals in 1992, and the following season they missed out on automatic promotion to the Premiership on goal difference, losing in the Play-offs. Two seasons later Smith was sacked from Fratton Park and then spent the next five months as chief executive of the League Managers' Association. In June 1995 Smith became manager of Derby County, pushing them towards promotion to the Premier League in his first full season. Derby fared well in their first three seasons, but the following two campaigns saw the side struggling against relegation and Smith resigned in October 2001. Three months later he became Roland Nilsson's assistant at Coventry City, but the whole management team was sacked just three months later. Later in 2002 Smith became Harry Redknapp's assistant at Portsmouth, but they both resigned after the appointment of a director of football who they considered to be a threat to their authority and control in team matters. Redknapp became the manager of Southampton and Smith was appointed his assistant a few weeks later, on 22 December 2004, having previously turned down the role of chief scout. However, when Southampton were relegated at the end of the season Smith's contract was not renewed due to cost-cutting.

In March 2006 Smith was part of a consortium with his neighbours and friends Nick Merry and Ian Lenagan, who together formed Woodstock Partners Ltd, a company named after the Oxfordshire village in which they all lived. They bought Oxford United from Firoz Kassam for £1, taking on the club's £2 million debts, and Smith, now a director of the club, was installed as manager. Oxford were 18th, seven points above the drop zone, with seven games to play. Unfortunately, Smith was unable to halt the club's slide and a 3–2 home defeat to Leyton Orient in the final game of the season consigned the club to relegation to the Conference after 44 years in the Football League. The next season Oxford set a Conference record by going unbeaten for their first 19 games; however, after their first defeat in November 2006 the club lost their way and eventually finished second to Dagenham & Redbridge. With just one automatic promotion place United had to take part in the Play-offs for the first time, but they lost on penalties to Exeter City in the semi-finals after leading 2–0 on aggregate.

The following season Oxford started disappointingly, and after a 5–0 televised defeat at Rushden & Diamonds Smith handed over the reins to Darren Patterson and resumed his directorial duties. Smith resigned as a director in November 2008, and after Patterson's dismissal, Smith took on the caretaker manager role until a successor was appointed. United went unbeaten during the four matches that Smith was in charge, including winning 3–1 at Mansfield Town live on TV, to reverse the side's decline and set things up for new boss Chris Wilder. Smith remains at the club in an advisory capacity.

Smith has gone down in Oxford United history as a legend. Arguably the club's most successful manager after Arthur Turner, Smith's three separate spells in charge of the club have all made their mark in one way or another.

Competition	*Games*	*W*	*D*	*L*	*F*	*A*
Associate Members' Cup	1	0	0	1	1	3
FA Cup	16	9	3	4	27	15
Football League Trophy	3	1	0	2	4	6
League Cup	21	10	8	3	36	26
League + Conference	231	114	64	53	377	235
FA Trophy	5	2	2	1	6	4
Total	**277**	**136**	**77**	**64**	**451**	**289**

Maurice Evans (1985–88)

Didcot-born Evans signed for Reading aged just 16, joining Elm Park as a groundstaff junior. He played his first game for Reading in the 1955–56 season, in the Third Division South, and he soon became a regular wing-half for the Biscuitmen. In his 12 seasons at the club Evans played 459 games, and it is a measure of his character that he was not booked once during that time. While at Reading Evans completed his National Service, during which he won representative honours for the army, and

on his return to Elm Park he was also selected to represent the Third Division South in a game against the Third Division North.

In 1967 Evans left Reading and became player-manager at Andover Town, but the following year he joined Shrewsbury Town as a player-coach before becoming their manager in 1972. The Shrews were relegated in 1974 and Evans left Gay Meadow to return to Reading as a coach and assistant to Charlie Hurley. When Hurley left in 1977 Evans was appointed as his replacement, initially as a caretaker, and the following season Evans led Reading to the Fourth Division Championship and was awarded the divisional Manager of the Year award. Reading were relegated back to Division Four in 1983, after four seasons in the Third Division, and Evans was sacked in January 1984 after Roger Smee became chairman, despite the Biscuitmen being in third place.

After his departure from Elm Park Evans joined Oxford United, initially as chief scout and youth development officer. Following Jim Smith's departure Evans took over as caretaker manager, but after a successful start to their first season in the First Division, with United drawing their opening two games and then thrashing Leicester City 5–0, Evans became the side's permanent manager, although he refused to sign a contract. Using the side that Smith had built, with the addition of Ray Houghton, Evans led Oxford to their first major honour, a 3–0 triumph over Smith's QPR in the Milk Cup Final at Wembley. At this game Evans demonstrated his humility by sending long-serving trainer Ken Fish up the famous steps to receive Evans' winners' medal in his stead. However, he always faced a struggle to keep United in the top flight, especially given the injury to Billy Hamilton and the departures of Houghton and John Aldridge to Liverpool, and in March 1988, with United having just been eliminated from the League Cup semi-finals by Luton Town and not having won a League game since a 1–0 win over Coventry City on 7 November (when Oxford reached ninth in the First Division), Evans resigned. His last game in charge of Oxford was a 0–0 draw at Charlton Athletic on 26 March.

Despite stepping down from the job of team manager, Evans remained at the Manor and became the club's general manager, and again he found himself as chief scout and youth development officer. In 1993, following the departure of Brian Horton, Evans briefly became caretaker manager, looking after team affairs for just two games before Denis Smith was appointed. Oxford lost both matches. In January 1998 Evans was appointed to the board of directors, but on 5 November 1999 he resigned and rejoined Reading as chief scout, having felt frozen out by the club after Fenton Higgins was appointed director of football and manager Malcolm Shotton stopped asking Evans for his advice. On 18 August 2000 Evans died of a heart attack, aged 63.

Competition	*Games*	*W*	*D*	*L*	*F*	*A*
FA Cup	5	1	1	3	6	10
Full Members' Cup	6	4	0	2	11	8
League Cup	20	13	5	2	41	17
League	117	27	35	55	147	215
Simod Cup	2	1	0	1	1	1
Total	**150**	**46**	**41**	**63**	**206**	**251**

Mark Lawrenson (1988)

Mark Lawrenson's first club was Preston North End, his home-town team, whom he joined when he was 17 years old in 1974. Two years later he won the first of

his 39 Republic of Ireland caps. That same season he won Preston's Player of the Year award. In the summer of 1977 Brighton paid Preston £100,000 for Lawrenson, who had made 73 League appearances for the Deepdale club, scoring two goals. 'Lawro' played 152 League games for Brighton, scoring five goals, including 39 games in the club's 1978–79 promotion-winning season to the First Division. In the summer of 1981 financial problems led to Brighton having to sell Lawrenson to Liverpool for £900,000. Lawro was at Anfield for seven seasons, during which time he consolidated his place in the Ireland side and established himself as a Liverpool legend. He won five League Championship medals and two runners'-up medals, plus a European Cup-winners' medal, an FA Cup-winners' medal, three League Cup-winners' medals, two Charity Shield-winners' medals and a number of runners'-up medals in all the above competitions plus the World Club Championship in 1985. Lawrenson had played 332 games for Liverpool, scoring 18 goals, before he damaged his Achilles tendon in a career-ending injury in his final title-winning season in 1988.

When Lawrenson was appointed as Oxford's manager after the resignation of Maurice Evans, Oxford's fanzine *Raging Bull* claimed that he was a player-manager who could no longer play and had never before managed. Lawrenson was indeed a surprise choice by Oxford and he arrived to find the club in a state of disarray. Oxford were second from bottom of the First Division, having not won a League game for almost five months, and, in addition, they had just been knocked out of the League Cup at the semi-final stage and morale was rock bottom. His first game, at home to Arsenal on 30 March 1988, ended in a 0–0 draw, but that was as good as it got for the rest of the season and Lawrenson did not see Oxford score until 23 March, when a Dean Saunders penalty rescued a point in a 1–1 draw with Everton. By that time United's relegation had already been confirmed and that was the last point they won before finishing bottom of the table. The following season Lawrenson started to halt the decline and consolidate in mid-table in the Second Division; however, just after United had drawn 1–1 with Blackburn Rovers to leave the Us 10th in the table, he was told by chairman Kevin Maxwell that United had sold striker Dean Saunders to Derby County, managed by Kevin's father Robert Maxwell, for £1 million. He was then sacked by United (allegedly by Robert, not Kevin, Maxwell) in order to pre-empt his resignation.

After playing a handful of games for Thame United, and two games for Barnet, Lawrenson went to America to coach Tampa Bay Rowdies, whom he took to the American Professional Soccer League title. On 6 September 1989 Lawrenson became manager of Fourth Division Peterborough United. His success there was limited and he left in November 1990 after the chairman ordered him to drop five first-team players because they could not afford to pay them the agreed appearance money. Lawro then had a brief spell in charge of Corby Town in the Beazers Home League, and in 1992–93 he played for Chesham United. He had by now turned his attention to the media, with a brief hiatus when he became Kevin Keegan's defensive coach at Newcastle United, becoming a regular for the BBC both on television and radio. He still occasionally played football, turning out for Oxford City for 21 games between 4 December 1993 and 7 May 1994.

Competition	*Games*	*W*	*D*	*L*	*F*	*A*
League Cup	2	0	0	2	2	6
League	21	4	8	9	22	34
Total	**23**	**4**	**8**	**11**	**24**	**40**

Brian Horton (1988–93)

Brian Horton was born in Hednesford in 1949 and after a brief spell with Walsall's youth team he joined his home-town club, Hednesford Town. In July 1970 Port Vale signed Horton and he spent six years as a midfielder at Vale Park, playing 236 League games and scoring 33 goals. To the disappointment of Vale fans he was sold to Brighton in March 1976 for £30,000, and it was at the Goldstone Ground that he played alongside Lawrenson. At the end of his first full season Brighton were promoted to the Second Division and two years later they achieved promotion to the top flight. Horton left Brighton after five full seasons, having played 217 League games and scored 33 goals. Luton Town signed him in August 1981 and in his first season at Kenilworth Road he captained the Hatters to the Second Division title. After two seasons in the top flight, and having played 118 games with eight goals, he moved to Boothferry Park to become player-manager at Hull City in July 1984. In his first season Hull finished third in Division Three and were promoted, with Horton playing in 22 League games. Horton continued to play sporadically for the next two seasons, eventually hanging up his boots after playing 38 League games for the Tigers. After a good start to the 1987–88 season Hull started slipping down the table, and on 13 April Horton was sacked.

Horton's former teammate at Brighton, Mark Lawrenson, brought him to the Manor as his assistant in June 1988, and when Lawro was sacked in October, Horton, who had offered to resign in support of Lawrenson, was appointed manager with Lawro's blessing. Horton's first game was a 1–0 defeat at Crystal Palace on 25 October, which began a run of four successive defeats and just one win in the next eight matches. Horton's first signing was Paul Simpson, whose arrival was pivotal to the team's fortunes. Oxford finished 17th in Division Two at the end of

Horton's first season and in the same position the following year. Fortunes improved in 1990–91 as United finished in 10th place and beat First Division Chelsea 3–1 at Stamford Bridge in the FA Cup third round, but the following season was one of struggle which culminated in a dramatic last-day escape from relegation with a 2–1 win at Tranmere Rovers. The next season Horton again steadied the ship as United finished a respectable 10th, but the 1993–94 season had only just started when Manchester City surprised everyone by offering Horton the manager's job at Maine Road to replace Peter Reid. Horton's final game in charge of Oxford was a 3–1 defeat at West Bromwich Albion on 21 August 1993.

At the end of Horton's first season with City the team finished 16th in the Premier League, having been bottom in February. The following season City started off well, and they were sixth at the start of December, but a run in which they won just four of their remaining 25 League games saw them finish 17th, just four points above the drop zone, and Horton was sacked. He was then appointed manager of Huddersfield Town, taking them to eighth in the second tier (then called Division One) in his first season. The following season, though, Huddersfield only just avoided relegation, finishing in 20th place, and he was sacked in September 1997 after a disappointing start to the season. Five months later, Horton was appointed manager of Third Division Brighton, but he failed to make much of an impact at his former club, who finished second from bottom. Things improved the following season, but in January 1999 Horton left Brighton to become manager of Port Vale. They survived the drop in his first season at the club, finishing 21st in Division One, but the following season they finished just one place above bottom side Swindon Town and dropped to Division Two. In 2001 Port Vale won the LDV Vans Trophy at the Millennium Stadium, beating Brentford in the Final. In his sixth season as manager at Vale Park, Horton left by mutual consent after it was revealed that the board was considering reducing his contract as a cost-cutting measure. In April 2004 he was appointed manager of Division Three side Macclesfield Town. Horton was able to keep the struggling side away from relegation with a 20th-placed finish, and the following season he took them into the Play-offs, where they lost to Lincoln City in the semi-finals. They finished 17th the following season, but in 2006–07 the Silkmen failed to win any of their first 12 games and Horton was sacked with the side bottom of the League. On 23 May 2007 Horton was appointed assistant manager to Phil Brown at Hull City, and the following season the side won promotion to the Premiership for the first time.

Competition	*Games*	*W*	*D*	*L*	*F*	*A*
FA Cup	11	4	2	5	17	18
League Cup	14	6	2	6	17	15
League	220	67	60	93	294	320
Simod Cup	1	0	0	1	2	3
ZDS Trophy	5	2	0	3	9	10
Total	**251**	**79**	**64**	**108**	**339**	**366**

Maurice Evans (caretaker 1993)

(See previous entry)

Denis Smith (1993–97)

Denis Smith was an uncompromising centre-half in his playing days and became a Stoke City legend in the process. He was born on 19 November 1947 in Stoke-on-Trent and joined Stoke in 1964 after leaving school, becoming a professional

two years later and making his debut in 1968–69. Over the next 14 years Smith played 407 League games for the Potters, scoring 29 goals. In March 1982 he had a seven-game loan spell at York City, scoring once, before joining the Minstermen permanently in August that year. Smith played 30 games in his first season at Bootham Crescent, scoring four goals, before being appointed manager of the club the following season.

York finished seventh in Division Four in Smith's first season, but the following year he took the club to the title and promotion to the Third Division while becoming the first club in the country to achieve 100 points in a season. The following year York beat Arsenal in the FA Cup and held Liverpool to a draw before losing the replay at Anfield. By the time Smith moved to Sunderland in 1987 he had been in charge of 258 York games. In Smith's first season at Roker Park he guided the club to the Third Division title with a record 101 points, and two seasons later Sunderland reached the Play-offs where they were beaten by Swindon Town. However, Swindon were found guilty of financial irregularities and were demoted to Division Three, with Sunderland promoted to the First Division in their place. Sunderland struggled in the top flight and were relegated on the last day of their first season. The following season Sunderland failed to make an impact and with the club in danger of relegation Smith was sacked in December 1991 and replaced by his assistant, Malcolm Crosby. He had been in charge of the Rokerites for 229 games.

In March 1992 Smith became manager of Bristol City, but he resigned the following May having been unable to forge a decent working relationship with player-coach Russell Osman and unable to get on with the board.

Smith next applied for the vacant Oxford United post and was appointed in September 1993. His first game, against former club Bristol City, ended in a 4–2 win for United and was a stormy affair, with Smith confronting City's new boss Osman in the tunnel after the game and blaming him for getting David Penney sent off. At the end of Smith's first season, Oxford were relegated to Division Three. The next season United started strongly and were three points clear at the top on Boxing Day, after winning 4–1 at Peterborough United. However, in the next game United were beaten 2–0 at home by Wycombe Wanderers and that started a run of nine League games without a win, after which United slipped out of contention for the Play-offs. In addition, the club had arguably the worst result in its professional history up to that point, losing 2–0 at Marlow in the FA Cup first round on 13 November 1994. The following season was the opposite of the last, with Oxford starting slowly but having a storming finish to claim automatic promotion in second place behind Swindon Town. Considering that

United did not win their first away game until 30 January and were 13th in mid-February, 12 points behind second-placed Crewe Alexandra, this was a fantastic achievement. In 1996–97 United finished 17th, but the following season was another one of underachievement. With Oxford in 16th place following a 2–0 win at Tranmere Rovers, and the club under severe financial restraints, Smith resigned on Christmas Eve 1997, after 240 games in charge.

A few days after leaving Oxford, Smith was appointed manager of West Brom. The Baggies finished 10th in Smith's first season, 12th the following year and in July 1999 he was sacked. Smith was then out of work until February 2000, when he then applied for the vacant job at Oxford United following Malcolm Shotton's departure. His first match back in charge was on 5 February, a 1–0 home defeat by Bristol City as Oxford battled relegation. They eventually secured Second Division safety with a 2–0 win over Scunthorpe United in the penultimate game of the season. United started the following season with four successive League defeats, and they were without a win in their first seven League games. The fans were disgruntled and after a home defeat by Brentford on 26 August they made their displeasure known. Smith strode over to the London Road end and held an impromptu fans' forum on the pitch. However, this was not enough to save him and, with United at the bottom of the division, Smith resigned after a 1–0 home defeat by Bristol City on 30 September 2000.

Over a year later Smith was appointed manager of Wrexham. Although the Welsh side were relegated at the end of that campaign, Smith took them straight back up to Division Two the following season. A mid-table finish in 2003–04 was followed by another relegation to the newly renamed League Two (fourth tier) as Smith was hamstrung by chairman Alex Hamilton, who was trying to get the club evicted from the Racecourse Ground so he could sell it. In order to avoid paying the club's creditors, Hamilton had it put into administration, becoming the first club to be docked 10 points under new League rules. Despite relegation, Wrexham went on to win the LDV Vans Trophy. They finished 13th in League Two the next season, and in January 2007, with Wrexham in danger of relegation to the Conference, Smith was sacked. He was once again linked with the Oxford job following Darren Patterson's dismissal in December 2008, and spent a lot of time promoting his autobiography *Just One of Seven*, which was published in October 2008.

Competition	*Games*	*W*	*D*	*L*	*F*	*A*
Auto Windscreens Shield	7	3	2	2	12	9
FA Cup	12	5	3	4	24	18
League Cup	26	13	7	6	42	33
League	231	87	50	94	307	308
Total	**276**	**108**	**62**	**106**	**385**	**368**

Malcolm Crosby (1997–98)

Although born in South Shields on 4 July 1954, Malcolm Crosby started his playing career as an apprentice with Aldershot. He joined the Shots in 1971, making his debut that same season, coming on as a substitute. He became a professional at the end of that season and made just one appearance as the Shots won promotion to Division Three. It was not until the 1974–75 season that he became established as a regular in the Aldershot midfield, and he went on to make 294 League appearances, scoring 23 goals, before joining York City in November

1981. At York he played an important role in their record-breaking promotion season in 1983–84, and he played 103 League games, scoring four goals, for the Minstermen before Denis Smith, who became York boss in 1982, made Crosby his assistant. Crosby's managerial career was, for a long time, to be inextricably linked with Smith's. Crosby also had a brief loan spell at Wrexham in September 1984, playing five games and scoring once. After leaving York he went to Kuwait for two years to do some coaching.

When Smith moved to Roker Park to become Sunderland's manager in 1987 Crosby followed him as youth team coach, before becoming reserve coach and then first-team coach. He even played a few reserve games for Sunderland in the Central League. After Smith's sacking in 1991 Crosby was appointed caretaker manager while a replacement was sought. This took longer than anticipated, and in the meantime Crosby led Second Division Sunderland to the 1992 FA Cup Final, which they lost 2–0 to Liverpool. As a result Crosby was offered the manager's job; however, the following season Sunderland continued to struggle in the League and in February 1993 Crosby was sacked.

When Denis Smith was appointed manager of Oxford in September 1993, his first act was to bring in Crosby as his assistant. When Smith resigned in 1997 Crosby was appointed manager, with his first game in charge a 1–0 defeat at Wolves on Boxing Day. After five games, which yielded just one point, Crosby decided that management was not for him and he stepped down to become first-team coach. His final game was a 2–1 home defeat by Charlton Athletic on 17 January 1998.

Almost immediately, Smith invited Crosby to become his assistant at West Brom and Crosby left for the Hawthorns. However, on 11 June 1999 the opportunity arose for Crosby to become Jim Smith's assistant at Premiership side Derby County as a replacement for Ray Harford. Crosby had been recommended to Smith by former Oxford player Steve McClaren, then assistant manager at Manchester United. On 15 February 2000 Crosby parted company with Derby with the agreement of Jim Smith, after a poor season saw the Rams languishing close to the Premier League relegation zone. On 4 May 2000 Crosby was appointed coach at Swindon Town, despite attempts by Denis Smith, then back at Oxford, to lure him back to the Manor. Crosby was initially under Roy Evans at the County Ground, but after Evans' resignation in December 2001 Crosby took over the first-team affairs for one game before Steve King was appointed and Crosby became his assistant. Crosby was at Swindon for four years before joining Middlesbrough as reserve coach in 2004, becoming Gareth Southgate's assistant two years later.

Competition	*Games*	*W*	*D*	*L*	*F*	*A*
FA Cup	1	0	0	1	0	4
League	4	0	1	3	3	9
Total	**5**	**0**	**1**	**4**	**3**	**13**

Malcolm Shotton (1998–99)

Malcolm Shotton initially joined Oxford as a player from Nuneaton Borough in the summer of 1980, having previously been on the books of Leicester City, and by the time United experienced their 'Glory Years' of the mid-1980s towering centre-half Shotton was the club captain. In August 1987 Shotton, who was nicknamed Sheeny, was sold to Portsmouth for £70,000. He played just 12 games for Pompey before Huddersfield paid £20,000 for him in February 1988. His time at Huddersfield was only slightly longer as he played 18 games for the Terriers, scoring one goal, before moving to Barnsley in September 1988. He had a longer time at Oakwell, playing 74 games and scoring six goals before Hull City paid £35,000 for him in February 1990. Shotton played 65 games for the Tigers, scoring two goals, before he moved north of the border to Ayr United. In his 22 months at Somerset Park, Shotton made 83 appearances and scored three goals before returning to Barnsley in July 1994. In the 1994–95 season he played 11 games for the Tykes and scored one goal, in his final match, against Sunderland, after which he retired from playing and became Barnsley's reserve team coach and assistant to Danny Wilson.

In January 1998, to popular acclaim, Shotton was appointed manager of Oxford United, having earlier claimed that this would be his 'dream job'. He was the first ex-Oxford player to become manager of the club, following a campaign for his appointment led by Oxford supporter Neil Wakefield and supported by Oxford's fanzine *Rage On*. At the time of his appointment Oxford were fifth from the bottom of Division One, having just lost 2–1 at home to Charlton Athletic. Shotton's first game in charge was at home to Portsmouth, who were bottom of the table, and Oxford won 1–0. They followed this up with a 3–1 win at Nottingham Forest, and by the end of the season Shotton had steered the side to 12th place. The following season was a disappointing one as the club suffered financial problems that led to its near demise. The club was forced to sell its best players just to survive, and for two months in October and November the backroom staff, including Shotton and his assistant Mark Harrison, went unpaid, while the players had to be paid by a loan from the Professional Footballers' Association. Unsurprisingly, results suffered and United fell to their two worst defeats since turning professional in 1949, with a 7–0 defeat at Sunderland followed three months later by a 7–1 home defeat by Birmingham City. The one chink of light came when Oxford were handed a home draw against Chelsea in the fourth round of the FA Cup, but with United leading 1–0 and with less than five minutes remaining, Chelsea were awarded a controversial penalty to take the tie to a replay, which they won 4–2. Although Oxford won the final game of the season 5–0 against Stockport County, results elsewhere ensured that they had already been relegated. United started the following season badly, and on 25 October, following a 1–0 home defeat by Luton Town, which left United fourth from bottom of Division Two, Shotton and Harrison left the club after coming to an agreement with chairman Firoz Kassam.

In June 2000, Shotton's former Huddersfield teammate Chris Hutchings was appointed manager of Bradford City, and his first move was to bring in Shotton as first-team coach following Terry Yorath's departure. However, after a run of 10 games without a win, plunging City to second from bottom of the Premiership, Hutchings and Shotton were both dismissed. Shotton then dropped out of professional football, becoming director of football of Loughborough University's football team for several years.

Competition	*Games*	*W*	*D*	*L*	*F*	*A*
FA Cup	3	1	1	1	6	6
League Cup	5	3	0	2	7	7
League	79	22	20	37	89	113
Worthington Cup	2	1	1	0	2	1
Total	**89**	**27**	**22**	**40**	**104**	**127**

Mickey Lewis (caretaker 1999–2000)

Birmingham-born Mickey Lewis started his playing days as an apprentice with West Brom, signing professional forms in February 1982. After playing 33 games for the Baggies he moved to Derby County for £25,000 in November 1984, but he played just 50 games between then and August 1988, scoring one goal, when he moved to Oxford as part of the deal that took Trevor Hebberd to the Baseball Ground.

Lewis, a tenacious midfielder who earned the nickname 'Mad Dog', made his Oxford debut on 27 August 1988 in a 1–1 draw at Leeds United, and he went on to play 351 games for the Us over the next 12 years, making his final appearance as a substitute in a 2–1 win over Chesterfield on 19 February 2000. This last appearance was an anomaly though, as Lewis had effectively retired from playing at the end of the 1995–96 season. He then became United's youth-team coach before being recalled to first-team duty in August 1999 as the result of an injury crisis. This came to an end in October 1999, after the 1–0 defeat by Luton Town that signalled the end of Malcolm Shotton's management, and Lewis was appointed caretaker manager. In that 1999–2000 season Lewis had played in defence and in midfield, he had run the reserves, the youth team, driven the team bus to take the club's young players to matches and even acted as physio in that season's game at Blackpool. Lewis's first game in charge of the first team was a 3–2 first-round FA Cup win over Conference side Morecambe, in which Ben Abbey scored in the final minute, his only goal for the club. Lewis looked after the team for over three months, a period which culminated in a 4–0 home defeat by Preston North End, after which Denis Smith was reappointed as manager. Lewis remained in charge of the youth team and continued adding his experience to United's reserves. In his time as manager Lewis proved himself to be popular with the players and the fans, but it was probably because he was too popular that he failed to land the job permanently, as he seemed reluctant to drop under-performing players. He was also tactically inexperienced, failing to alter his preferred tactics of playing nice passing football when a more direct style was sometimes required. Lewis was appointed Denis Smith's assistant manager and acted as caretaker for a 1–1 draw with Cambridge United when Smith was hospitalised with a blood infection. After Smith's resignation in October 2000, Lewis then acted as assistant to caretaker manager Mike Ford.

Lewis, who did not have a contract, was sacked by United in November 2000 while on loan to Banbury United, with whom he was playing on a non-contract basis. He played just one game for the Puritans, in a 2–1 defeat at Corby Town in September, before joining Oxford City as player-coach, eventually giving up the playing side to become assistant manager. While at Court Place Farm, Lewis also became head coach to the Oxford University football team, leading them to three consecutive Varsity successes. Lewis left City in December 2003 following the resignation of manager Paul Lee. In January 2004 Lewis became coach at Slough Town in Ryman League Division One, and in July 2005 he became David Penney's assistant at Doncaster Rovers, leading the reserves to their League title. On 30 August 2006 Lewis and Penney both left Doncaster and Lewis returned to Oxford. He became a van driver while returning to coach Oxford University, and at the same time he also coached at Southern League Abingdon United and worked with Oxford United's Under-11s. On 10 May 2007 he became youth-team coach at the Kassam Stadium, replacing Darren Patterson who had stepped up to become Jim Smith's assistant. When Patterson replaced Smith as first-team manager in November 2007, Lewis was made his assistant, continuing in that role after Chris Wilder's appointment in December 2008.

Competition	*Games*	*W*	*D*	*L*	*F*	*A*
Auto Windscreens Shield	3	2	0	1	3	3
FA Cup	5	2	2	1	9	9
League	14	3	5	6	11	25
Total	**22**	**7**	**7**	**8**	**23**	**37**

Denis Smith (2000)

(See previous entry)

Mike Ford (caretaker 2000)

Bristol-born Mike Ford began his playing career at Leicester City, where he had joined as an apprentice before signing as a professional in February 1984. He did not make a first-team appearance for the Foxes and moved to Devizes Town in June 1984. Just three months later he was signed by Cardiff City, for whom he went on to make 167 appearances, scoring 13 goals. In the 1987–88 season Ford was Cardiff's Player of the Season, and Oxford bought him for £150,000 in June 1988. In

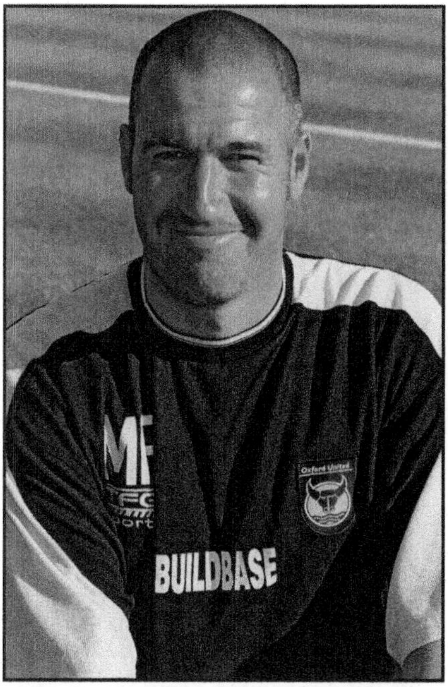

the following 10 years he played 338 games for the Us, scoring 22 goals. Ford played in a variety of positions, starting as a midfielder, then moving to become a central-defender before converting to left-back. In August 1998 he rejoined Cardiff, where he stayed for two seasons, playing 65 matches and scoring one FA Cup goal. In May 2000 Ford announced that he was retiring from playing after receiving a back injury.

At the start of August 2000 Ford returned to Oxford United, ostensibly as reserve and youth-team coach. He played in just one first-team game, on 30 September, which United lost 1–0 to Bristol City. This was Denis Smith's last match in charge of United, and Ford was immediately chosen to act as caretaker manager while a replacement was sought. Ford's first game was a local derby at Swindon Town, for which he drafted in Guy Whittingham on loan from Portsmouth. Whittingham scored United's goal in a 2–1 defeat and was immediately recalled by his home club. Ford had six games in charge in which United picked up just one point, before David Kemp was appointed in November and Ford was made youth-team coach. When Kemp and his assistant Alan McLeary were sacked at the end of April 2001, Ford was again made caretaker manager for United's last two games of the season. Ford was still unable to find a win, earning a point against Port Vale in United's final match at the Manor and then losing 2–1 at Notts County. Ford then became reserve-team coach after Mark Wright became manager.

Following Wright's resignation and the appointment of Ian Atkins in November 2001, Ford was made Atkins' assistant. On 11 February 2003 Ford was sacked by United and a week later he joined Ryman League First Division club Thame United as a player. In August 2003 Ford signed for Didcot Town, managed by Peter Foley, in the Cherry Red Records Hellenic League Premier Division. At the end of the 2003–04 season Ford then moved to Brackley Town, newly promoted to the Dr Martens League Division One West, as player-coach, becoming player-manager in October 2004. At the start of November 2006 Ford became assistant manager and coach at Oxford City, having by now given up playing entirely.

Competition	*Games*	*W*	*D*	*L*	*F*	*A*
League	8	0	2	6	10	18
Total	**8**	**0**	**2**	**6**	**10**	**18**

David Kemp (2000–01)

Harrow-born David Kemp had a fairly peripatetic footballing career, beginning his playing days at Harrow Borough before moving to Maidenhead United and then on to Slough Town. He signed for Crystal Palace in April 1975. As a forward,

Kemp scored 10 League goals in 35 Division Three games for Palace before Third Division Portsmouth signed him in November 1976. Kemp was leading goalscorer in his first season and for the following season as well, despite moving to Carlisle United in March 1978. He scored 30 goals in 64 League games at Fratton Park. Carlisle were also in the Third Division and Kemp played 61 League games for the Cumbrians, scoring 22 goals, before Plymouth Argyle paid a club record £75,000 for him in September 1979. Kemp scored 39 goals in 84 League games for Argyle, plus two goals in nine games while on loan to Gillingham and one goal in his three loan games at Brentford, before he crossed the Atlantic in June 1982. His first club in the NASL was Edmonton Drillers, for whom he played 16 games, scoring seven goals. The following season he played for Seattle Sounders, where he scored nine goals in 20 games, and the next season he joined Oklahoma City Stampede of the United Soccer League, where he played 28 games.

Kemp's first job as a manager was with Swedish side Norrköping in 1985. The following year he joined the coaching staff at Wimbledon, before becoming manager of Plymouth Argyle in March 1990. In 1992, after little success at Home Park he left Plymouth to become manager of Conference team Slough Town, and at the end of the 1992–93 season he joined Crystal Palace as assistant manager to Alan Smith. He then followed Smith to Wycombe Wanderers at the start of the 1995–96 season, leaving at the start of the following season to become John Docherty's assistant at Millwall. His next post, in 1998, was as first-team coach at Wimbledon, under Joe Kinnear, before he returned to Millwall as first-team coach. Tony Pulis appointed Kemp in the same capacity at Portsmouth in December 1999.

Kemp was appointed Oxford manager at the end of October 2000, where he again met up with Kinnear, who was director of football at the Manor. His first game in charge was a 1–0 home defeat by Bristol Rovers, and despite two successive away wins in the next two games things went downhill and United were relegated to the bottom flight with seven games still to play. Following protests by Oxford United fans, including incessant chants of 'Kemp out' during his final game, a 3–1 win over Swansea City, Kemp was sacked by United with two games left of the 2000–01 season. Kemp's side had won just seven out of 31 games and had lost 21 matches.

After leaving Oxford Kemp was appointed chief scout at Leicester City in December 2001. Pulis made him first-team coach at Stoke City in August 2004, but he left the club the following June after Pulis was dismissed. He rejoined Pulis as assistant manager at Plymouth in

September 2005, leaving in August 2006. That October he returned to Stoke as assistant manager, and he stayed at the Britannia as Stoke won promotion to the Premier League in 2008.

Competition

	Games	W	D	L	F	A
FA Cup	2	1	0	1	3	3
League	28	6	3	19	38	60
LDV Vans	1	0	0	1	1	4
Total	**31**	**7**	**3**	**21**	**42**	**67**

Mike Ford (caretaker 2001)

(See previous entry)

Mark Wright (2001)

Mark Wright was born in Dorchester-on-Thames in Oxfordshire on 1 August 1963. He played his first game for Oxford United on 13 December 1980, aged 17, in a 3–0 FA Cup second-round defeat at Plymouth Argyle. His next appearance was not until 17 October 1982, when he played in a 1–0 win over Bristol City. He went on to complete 12 games for United, making his final appearance in a 2–1 defeat at Lincoln City on 20 March 1982. He was then sold to Southampton, along with Keith Cassells, with their joint value determined as £230,000 (£115,000 each, a record fee for Oxford), with Trevor Hebberd and George Lawrence coming the other way. In Wright's first full season for Southampton he was voted the club's Player of the Year, and the following season he earned his first England cap. In August 1987 Derby County paid a club record fee of £760,000 for the tall central-defender. He had played 222 games for the Saints, scoring 11 goals. At Derby, Wright was made captain, but financial problems following the departure of Robert Maxwell led to the club being relegated to Division Two at the end of the 1990–91 season, and after 171 games for Derby, with 10 goals, Wright joined Liverpool in July 1991 for £2.5 million. Wright played for Liverpool until he retired in the summer of 1998. He had played 210 games and scored nine goals. He had also won 45 England caps and had scored one goal in the game against Egypt in the 1990 World Cup in Italy, becoming the only home-grown Oxford player to have represented England.

Wright took over as manager of Conference side Southport halfway through the 1999–2000 season. They were second from bottom when Wright arrived, and he led them back up to seventh place. The following season the Sandgrounders spent most of the time in the top three, eventually finishing fourth, after which Wright took over from David Kemp at Oxford United just after the season finished, giving him time to rebuild the newly relegated side. Wright immediately brought the central-defensive duo of Phil

Bolland and Scott Guyett from Southport and by the time the side kicked-off in Division Four there were five new faces in the team, including captain Martin Thomas. Oxford lost that historic game 2–1 to Rochdale, and Wright's first season went from bad to worse as the side struggled to adapt to his defensive tactics, despite the arrival of former Oxford hero striker Paul Moody in September. On 20 October United lost 1–0 at home to Scunthorpe, with two Oxford players and Wright being sent off by referee Joe Ross. In the aftermath Wright was accused of making racist remarks to Ross, and United, looking for an excuse to rid themselves of their manager, suspended him on full pay pending an investigation, while Ian Atkins was appointed director of football. Wright then resigned, followed shortly afterwards by his assistant Ted McMinn.

Two months later, on 9 January 2002, Wright was appointed manager of Conference side Chester City. In his first full season Chester reached the Play-off semi-finals, where they lost to Doncaster Rovers. The following season Wright led them to the title and a return to the Football League. However, just two days before the start of the following season, Wright resigned from Chester following allegations that he was having an affair with a player's wife. After being out of the game for a whole season, Wright became manager of Peterborough United. He was at London Road from May 2005 until January 2006, at which point he was sacked for gross misconduct after allegedly making a racist comment to a member of staff; an allegation that Wright strenuously denied. A month later Wright rejoined Chester and saved the side from relegation to the Conference. Just before the final game of the 2006–07 season Wright was sacked as Chester struggled just above the relegation zone. To the surprise of many, he was again reappointed to the Chester post by Steve Vaughan in November 2008, joining on a non-contract basis. On 22 June 2009 Mark Wright quit his post at Chester seven weeks after they were relegated back to the Conference.

Competition	*Games*	*W*	*D*	*L*	*F*	*A*
FA Cup	1	0	0	1	0	1
League Cup	1	0	0	1	1	2
League	19	4	7	8	17	22
LDV Vans	1	0	0	1	0	2
Total	**22**	**4**	**7**	**11**	**18**	**27**

Ian Atkins (2001–04)

Birmingham-born Atkins' first club was Shrewsbury Town, whom he joined in 1973 upon leaving school. He turned professional two years later and went on to stay with the Shrews until 1982. He made 279 appearances for the Shropshire club, scoring 58 goals, including 17 in his final season at the club in 1981–82. He then moved on to First Division Sunderland, who signed him in August 1982 for £80,000. In the next two seasons Atkins

played 77 games for the Rokerites, scoring six goals, having by now turned from a midfielder into a defender. In November 1984 Everton paid £70,000 for him, but he failed to break into the Toffees' first team, playing just seven games and scoring one goal. He moved to Ipswich Town for £100,000 in September 1985, and he established himself at Portman Road, playing 77 games and scoring three goals in the following three seasons. However, by the time that Birmingham City paid £50,000 for him in March 1988, Ipswich had been relegated to Division Two. Atkins played 93 games for the Blues and suffered relegation to the Third Division with them in 1989. He scored six goals before moving to Colchester United as player-manager in 1990.

Atkins took Colchester to second place in the Conference, which was not quite enough to earn promotion, and he returned to St Andrews in July 1991 as player-assistant manager. Atkins played eight games for Birmingham before he moved to Cambridge United as player-manager in December 1992. He played just two games for Cambridge, who were relegated from Division One (second tier) at the end of that season, and in May 1993 he was sacked. He returned to Sunderland as a player but failed to make the first team, and in January 1994 he went to Doncaster Rovers, for whom he played seven games. After spells with Solihull Borough and Redditch United, Atkins went to manage Northampton Town in October 1994. In 1997 he took Northampton into the Second Division, via the Play-offs, and the following season Northampton again reached the Play-off Final, but this time they were beaten by Grimsby Town. In 1998–99 Northampton were relegated back to the bottom flight, and in October 1999 Atkins resigned. He became boss of Chester City in January 2000, but he was unable to save them from relegation to the Conference and he resigned in the 2000 close season. He became manager of Carlisle United in June 2000 and helped them avoid relegation to the Conference, despite having few resources at his disposal. In July 2001 Atkins became assistant manager to Alan Cork at Cardiff City, but when Mark Wright was suspended by Oxford United in November 2001 he was appointed as director of football at the Kassam Stadium, while also taking charge of the first team.

Atkins' first game in charge of Oxford was a highly encouraging 3–0 win over high-flying Cheltenham Town, but although the side improved they still finished 21st in the bottom division. The following season Oxford were challenging for promotion for much of the time, but were unable to put together a consistent run and ended up finishing eighth, just behind Lincoln City who occupied the final Play-off place. Oxford had a mini-FA Cup run, beating Swindon Town 1–0 in the second round before narrowly losing to Arsenal at Highbury. They also beat Premiership club Charlton Athletic on penalties at the Valley in the second round of the League Cup. United looked much stronger in the 2003–04 season, and by the turn of the year the side was top of the table. However, they were overtaken by Hull City and, following a 4–2 defeat at the KC Stadium, United started to slip out of contention.

In March 2004 Atkins was controversially suspended by Firoz Kassam, allegedly for speaking to Bristol Rovers about their managerial vacancy. Atkins was out of contract at the end of that season and negotiations for a new contract had not yet started. Atkins' final game as Oxford manager was, like his first, a home win over Cheltenham Town on 17 March 2004; this time United won 1–0.

Atkins earned a reputation as a dour, defensive manager while at Oxford, whose preferred long-ball tactics worked initially but once found out by opponents quickly failed, and his critics also claimed he had no Plan B to back it up. This profile rather unfairly ignores the fact that he was probably United's most successful manager since Denis Smith's first spell in charge.

After being sacked by Oxford, Atkins took over at Bristol Rovers on 26 April 2004, but he was sacked in September the following year after a poor start to the season. In April 2006 Atkins took over at Torquay United, with the club bottom of the League, five points adrift and with just six games remaining. But Atkins took the Gulls on a magnificent run, the outcome of which saw Torquay safe for another season while condemning Oxford to relegation to the Conference. He remained with Torquay until he was replaced by Lubos Kubik in November 2007, after which he did some work in the media before being appointed European scout by Sunderland.

Competition	*Games*	*W*	*D*	*L*	*F*	*A*
FA Cup	4	2	0	2	2	3
League Cup	5	3	0	2	3	6
League	110	43	33	34	141	117
LDV Vans	2	0	0	2	2	4
Total	**121**	**48**	**33**	**40**	**148**	**130**

Graham Rix (2004)

Graham Rix joined Arsenal in 1974, initially as an apprentice but he signed as a professional the following season. He scored on his debut in April 1977 and played 464 games as a left-winger for the Gunners, becoming captain in 1983, and scoring 51 goals. In 1980 Rix made his debut for England and had won 17 caps by

the time of his last appearance in 1984. He lost his place in the Arsenal team because of injury, and after playing six games on loan to Brentford in 1987 he was released. He went to France to play for Caen, where he played 89 games and scored nine goals, and then to Le Havre, for whom he made 12 appearances. He then moved to Scotland to play for Dundee where he played 14 games and scored two goals.

In 1993 Rix joined Chelsea as youth-team coach, but an injury crisis led to his recall as a player and he played one game against Arsenal in 1995. In 1996 Ruud Gullit made him assistant manager and he remained in that position when Gianluca Vialli became manager. In March 1999 Rix was convicted of having sex with a 15-year-old girl and he spent six months of a 12-month sentence in prison. Upon his release he rejoined Chelsea, again as assistant manager, and after Vialli was sacked in September 2000 Rix had a brief spell as caretaker manager before he also left the club. He became manager of Portsmouth in February 2001, but just over a year later he was sacked.

Following Ian Atkins' suspension in March 2004, Rix was hired by United until the end of that season. His first game in charge was on 27 March and was a 0–0 draw against leaders Doncaster Rovers. Surprisingly, after the end of the season Rix was offered a proper contract, despite the side only winning once in the nine games he was in charge. However, United fared little better at the start of the following season and Rix was relieved of his duties in November 2004 after a run of eight defeats in nine games. His last game was a 2–1 defeat at Rochdale in the FA Cup on 13 November. Rix had managed Oxford for 29 matches. However, he was not sacked but instead was made director of football, a position he held until he eventually left the club in March 2005.

In November 2005 Rix was appointed manager of Hearts, where he remained until March 2006, taking charge of just 19 games. He is currently coaching for the Glenn Hoddle Academy in southen Spain

Competition	*Games*	*W*	*D*	*L*	*F*	*A*
FA Cup	1	0	0	1	1	2
League Cup	1	0	0	1	0	2
League	26	6	7	13	19	35
LDV Vans	1	0	0	1	2	2
Total	**29**	**6**	**7**	**16**	**22**	**41**

Darren Patterson (caretaker 2004)

Darren Patterson started his playing career at West Brom, whom he joined in July 1988, but he left for Wigan Athletic in April 1989 without playing a game for the Baggies. Over the next three years Patterson played 124 games for Wigan, scoring 10 goals, which earned him a £225,000 move to Crystal Palace in July 1992. However, Patterson did not play for Palace until the 1994–95 season, by which time the club was in the Premiership. 'Patto' played 32 games for the London club, including their FA Cup semi-final defeat by Manchester United, during which he was sent off for fighting along with Roy Keane. He scored one goal in his time at Selhurst Park before Luton Town paid £230,000 for Patterson, who had earned his first Northern Ireland cap in 1994. In his three seasons at Kenilworth Road Patterson made 66 appearances without getting on the score sheet. He also had a two-game loan spell at Preston North End. In July 1998 he joined Dundee United, where he played 38 games and scored one goal. In May 2000, after injuries had curtailed his first-team chances, he left Tannadice Park by mutual consent and in December he signed a three-month contract with York City.

Towards the end of his contract, on 14 February 2001, Patterson joined Oxford United.

Patterson was signed for Oxford by David Kemp, for whom he had played while at Palace, and he was Kemp's first signing as Oxford boss. Patto's first game for United was a 3–1 defeat at Bury on 17 February 2001, and he went on to play 20 games for the Us. He finally hung up his boots on 1 April 2002 after a 1–0 defeat to his previous side, York City. Injury had cut short his playing career and at the end of the 2002–03 season Patterson left the club, his contract having come to an end. After featuring in a couple of pre-season friendlies Patterson returned to Oxford on 3 September 2002 as youth-team coach, and on 14 November 2004 Patterson was appointed caretaker manager after Graham Rix had been relieved of his managerial duties. Patterson was in charge for three games before Argentinian Ramon Díaz was announced as the new manager. United won one of the three, at Chester City, and lost the other two games. After Díaz's arrival Patterson returned to coaching the youth team. In March 2006, after David Oldfield's departure, Patterson looked after the reserve team, and just a week later when Brian Talbot was sacked he was placed in charge of the first team and given a contract until the end of the following season. His first game was a 1–0 win over Bristol Rovers on 20 March, and relegation-threatened United drew their next two games before Nick Merry was installed as chairman and brought in Jim Smith as manager, with Patterson returning to his former job as youth-team coach.

In December 2006 Patterson was interviewed by Brentford for their managerial vacancy and he was offered the job, but he turned it down ostensibly because of contractual issues. In 2006–07 he guided the youth team to the Puma Youth Alliance South West Conference title without losing a game, and in April 2007 Smith appointed him assistant manager following the departures of Andy Awford and Shaun North. In November 2007, after a poor run of results led to Smith stepping down as manager, Patterson was appointed to the post. His first game in charge was a 3–1 win over Northwich Victoria in the first round of the FA Cup. After a dip in form United's results picked up and they finished the season winning nine of their last 11 games to finish ninth. The 2008–09 season started badly for United, with two successive defeats and only two wins in their first 10 games. Although home form was good, Oxford struggled on the road and, with finances tight, a 2–0 defeat at Torquay United in the FA Cup on 29 November 2008 led to Patterson's dismissal. In May 2009 it was reported that Patterson was to be named as Bristol Rovers' head of youth from 1 July.

Competition	*Games*	*W*	*D*	*L*	*F*	*A*
FA Cup	7	3	2	2	8	7
League + Conference	54	23	10	21	63	56
FA Trophy	2	0	1	1	0	1
Setanta Shield	2	0	0	2	1	3
Total	**65**	**26**	**13**	**26**	**72**	**67**

Ramon Díaz/Horacio Rodriguez (2004–05)

Ramon Díaz was born in La Rioja, Argentina, on 29 August 1959, and he joined River Plate in 1978. He played in the same Argentina Under-20 side as Diego Maradona, winning the World Youth Cup in 1979 where they both scored in the final against the Soviet Union. He played for Argentina in the 1978 World Cup, scoring against Brazil. He made his River Plate debut on 13 August 1978 and played 123 games, scoring 57 goals, before leaving for Napoli in the Italian Serie A. He had one season at Napoli, scoring three times in 27 games, and then spent three seasons at US Avellino, where he played 78 games and scored 23 goals. In 1986 he moved to Fiorentina, where he scored 17 goals in 53 games over two seasons. His final Italian club was Inter Milan, for whom he played 33 games with a return of 12 goals as he helped them win the Scudetto. In 1989 he signed for AS Monaco, who were managed by Arsene Wenger, playing 60 games over two seasons and scoring 24 goals. He returned to River Plate in 1991, and over the next two seasons he played 52 games and scored 27 goals. His final club was Yokohama Marinos in Japan, where he spent two seasons, playing 75 games and scoring 52 goals.

In 1995 Díaz was appointed River Plate's manager and over the next five years he won the Libertadores Cup and five Argentinian Championships. Díaz, who was being tipped to become the Argentina coach, resigned as River Plate coach in 2002 in protest at club president David Pintado's austerity drive following the collapse of the Argentine economy.

In 2004, Monaco businessman Jean-Marc Goiran introduced Díaz to Firoz Kassam, and the eventual upshot was that Díaz agreed to come to Oxford United to manage the team. It was to the astonishment of just about everyone connected with football when this was announced. Díaz was one of the most successful managers and players in the world, and his arrival was totally unexpected. It was thought that Díaz was promised 10 per cent of shares in the club should he achieve promotion in the six months he was given, while Goiran claimed that Díaz took the job in order to establish a foothold in English football. Díaz brought with him a team of backroom staff, including Horacio Rodriguez, his former assistant at River Plate, and four others from their time at River Plate: Raul Marcovich, a coach; Pablo Fernandez, a physical trainer who worked with Saudi Arabia's 1994 World Cup squad; Rafael Giulietti, a doctor; and Giuliani Iacoppi, a translator.

Díaz's first game in charge was at home to Cambridge United on 11 December 2004 which United won 2–1. Results certainly improved for Oxford that season but they came nowhere near to challenging for promotion, finishing in 15th place. Díaz was absent for many of the 25 games for which he was nominally the manager, with the team being coached mainly by Rodriguez and, on a couple of occasions, David Oldfield. This led to speculation that Díaz was working in the country illegally, although nothing was ever announced, and Rodriguez was also absent for a fortnight in March 2005 to sort out the paperwork to allow him to stay in the country. The Argentine reign ended abruptly and in controversy when talks about a new contract for Díaz broke down at the end of April and he returned to France; although at the time it was announced that Rodriguez would remain. However, at United's last game of the season, at home to Chester City, Kassam took the extraordinary step of refusing to allow Díaz or any of his contingent to pay for admission to the stadium, leading to a fracas in the car park outside the ground while the game was being played.

In 2007 Díaz was appointed head coach of Argentine side San Lorenzo, leading them to the Championship in his first season. In 2008 he moved to Mexican side Club America, where he was given a contract estimated to be worth $3.5 million a year; a far cry from the work he did at Oxford. He was sacked by America in February 2009.

Competition

	Games	W	D	L	F	A
League	25	10	7	8	35	38
Total	**25**	**10**	**7**	**8**	**35**	**38**

David Oldfield (2005)

Australian-born midfielder David Oldfield was playing for North Buckinghamshire village side Stoke Goldington when he was spotted by Luton Town, for whom he signed professional terms at the age of 18 in 1986. He had played just 39 games for Luton, scoring eight goals, when Manchester City paid £600,000 for him in March 1989. He was at Maine Road for only 10 months, making 30 appearances and scoring nine times, before Leicester City signed him for £150,000 in January 1990. He stayed with the Foxes for four and a half seasons, playing 221 games and scoring 32 goals, with a brief 17-game (and six-goal) spell on loan at Millwall, before Luton Town bought him back for £150,000 in July 1995. He played 139 games for Luton, scoring 25 goals, before moving on to Stoke City in the summer of 1998. Oldfield played 74 games for Stoke, scoring just seven times, before leaving for Peterborough United in March 2000.

Oldfield was at London Road for 15 months, playing 96 games and scoring five goals before he joined Oxford United, after a trial, in August 2002.

Oldfield's first game for Oxford was in the opening fixture of 2002–03 against Bury on 10 August, which United won 2–1. When Mike Ford left United in February 2003, Oldfield assisted manager Ian Atkins with the coaching. At the end of the 2002–03 season Oldfield was out of contract but was eventually re-signed as player-coach in time for the start of the following season. Oldfield's last match for United was a 1–1 draw at Kidderminster Harriers on 30 August 2003, after which injury prevented him from playing for the first team again and instead he was made assistant manager to Atkins. After Atkins was dismissed Oldfield was appointed caretaker manager, but the only game for which he was in charge, away to Mansfield on 20 March 2004, was abandoned at half-time with the score 0–0 and therefore does not feature in official records. Oldfield's reputation as a coach was demonstrated when he was kept on by Rix and then Ramon Díaz. In March 2005, when both Díaz and his assistant Horacio Rodriguez were absent, Oldfield took charge of team affairs for draws at Scunthorpe United and against Leyton Orient. Following the departure of Díaz, Oldfield took charge of the team for the final game of the 2004–05 season, a 1–0 home defeat by Chester City. However, on 6 March 2006 Oldfield left United after being frozen out by manager Brian Talbot, who had told him that he did not want Oldfield to be involved on match days.

Oldfield signed for Conference side Stafford Rangers at the start of the 2006–07 season. He played 23 games as player-assistant manager before signing for Tamworth on 30 November 2007, making his debut the following day. Just four days after signing for the Lambs, Oldfield left to become manager of Brackley Town. In the summer of 2008 Oldfield left to become reserves and Under-18s manager at Peterborough United.

Competition	*Games*	*W*	*D*	*L*	*F*	*A*
League	1	0	0	1	0	1
Total	**1**	**0**	**0**	**1**	**0**	**1**

Brian Talbot (2005–06)

Brian Talbot was a much-travelled midfielder, who started his career with his home-town club, Ipswich Town, joining as an apprentice in 1968. In 1971 he spent two seasons on loan with Toronto Metros before returning to Portman Road. He went on to play 227 games for Ipswich, with whom he won the 1978 FA Cup. He was also capped five times for England while at Ipswich. In January 1979 he was signed by Arsenal for £450,000 and at the end of that first season he scored at Wembley as Arsenal beat Manchester United 3–2 in the FA Cup Final. The following season Talbot played 70 games for Arsenal, setting a new club record, and

by the time he left Highbury in June 1985 he had made 327 appearances and scored 49 goals. While at Arsenal Talbot won his sixth, and last, England cap. In 1984 Talbot was elected chairman of the Professional Footballers' Association, a position he held for four years. After leaving Arsenal, Talbot signed for Watford for £150,000, playing 48 League games and scoring eight goals before a move to Stoke City in 1986, and he played 54 League games and scored five goals before he joined West Bromwich Albion as player-manager in November 1988. He stayed with West Brom for just over two years, leaving in January 1991 after West Brom were beaten 4–2 by non-League Woking in the FA Cup; he had played 74 games for the Baggies. After a short five-game spell with Fulham, he ended an incident-packed career with 11 games at Aldershot in March 1991, before joining Sudbury Town.

In 1993 Talbot went to Malta to manage Hibernians, with whom he won the Maltese Premier League in 1993 and 1994, before returning to England to become a coach at Conference side Rushden & Diamonds in 1996. He became manager in the summer of 1999 and, using chairman Max Griggs's money, he won the title and took the club into the Football League in 2001. They reached the Play-offs the following season but lost in the Final to Cheltenham Town. However, in 2003 they were crowned Third Division champions. Rushden started well the next season but started to slip down the table as Griggs reduced his investment and in March 2004 Talbot left and went to manage Oldham Athletic. He secured Oldham's place in Division Two at the end of the 2003–04 season, but after 55 games in charge Talbot left the club at the end of February 2005.

Talbot was unveiled as Oxford United's manager before the final game of the 2004–05 season, and he took charge of his first game at the start of the following season, a 1–1 draw at Grimsby Town on 6 August. The season started well and Oxford were sixth by the start of October. However, a slump soon set in and Talbot made a number of dubious decisions, such as stopping playing Lee Bradbury after mid-January so that it failed to trigger a clause in his contract allowing him an automatic extension the following season. With striker Craig Davies leaving for Verona and Chris Hackett allowed to leave for Millwall, the side got progressively weaker and, after a 2–1 defeat at Stockport County on 11 March 2006, Oxford were third from bottom of League Two and just one point above the relegation zone. Talbot was sacked three days later, and Oxford were relegated on the last day of the season.

In April 2006, Talbot received a phone call from Mark Sciriha, chairman of Maltese club Marsaxlokk, offering him the manager's job. Talbot accepted and in his first season he led the club to the Maltese Championship for the first time. In December 2008 Patrick Curmi was appointed coach of Marsaxlokk, with Talbot becoming technical director and adviser to the club's president.

Competition	*Games*	*W*	*D*	*L*	*F*	*A*
FA Cup	5	1	1	3	6	10
FA Cup	4	1	2	1	6	4
League Cup	1	0	0	1	0	1
League	35	8	13	14	34	46
LDV Vans	3	2	0	1	3	3
Total	**43**	**11**	**15**	**17**	**43**	**54**

Darren Patterson (2006)

(See previous entry)

Jim Smith (2006–07)

(See previous entry)

Darren Patterson (2007–08)

Jim Smith (caretaker 2008)

Chris Wilder (2008–)

Chris Wilder was born in Stocksbridge, near Sheffield, and started his career at Southampton, for whom he signed as a trainee in 1982. He was released by the Saints in 1986 and in August that year he signed for Sheffield United. Wilder played 112 games for the Blades, scoring just one goal over six seasons, and he also had short loan spells at Walsall, Charlton Athletic (twice) and Leyton Orient. In July 1992 Rotherham United paid £50,000 for him and he spent the next three and a half years at Millmoor. He played 158 games for the Millers, scoring 12 goals, before joining Notts County for £130,000 in January 1996. He played 53 games for the Magpies before Bradford City bought him for £150,000 in March 1997. Wilder was at Valley Parade for exactly a year, playing 45 games for the Bantams, after which he rejoined Sheffield United. He played 14 games and also had loan spells at Northampton Town and Lincoln City, before leaving in August 1999. Wilder's next club was Brighton, where he spent two months and played 13 games. He then joined Halifax Town on 22 October 1999, going on to play 58 games and scoring one goal in the next two seasons. In July 2002 Wilder became manager of Halifax, who had just been relegated to the Conference. In his 312 games in charge of the Shaymen, he guided Halifax to the Conference Play-off Final in 2006, where they lost to Hereford in extra-time. He was always battling against the club's financial problems, and in June 2008 the club were demoted three divisions to Unibond Division One North after failing to get a Company Voluntary Arrangement passed

after they had entered administration. As a result Wilder resigned from Halifax and joined League Two side Bury as assistant manager to Alan Knill.

Wilder was the first manager to be appointed by Oxford United following a proper recruitment and interview process since Denis Smith's first stint in 1993. The criteria that the board insisted upon included proven success at Conference level, experience of having success in the League, experience of finding and developing players and being able to work within financial constraints. Wilder may not have had much experience of success in the Football League, but he met all the other criteria. He was appointed in December 2008, and his first game was a 2–1 defeat at Salisbury City on Boxing Day. At the end of his first season Wilder had taken United to within touching distance of the Play-offs, after which he signed a new three-year contract.

Competition	*Games*	*W*	*D*	*L*	*F*	*A*
FA Trophy	1	0	0	1	1	2
Conference	23	16	4	3	42	18
Total	**24**	**16**	**4**	**4**	**43**	**20**

1949-50

Southern League

Manager: Harry Thompson

Did you know that?

This was United's first season as a professional club, and Harry Thompson's first season as player-coach. The club was made a limited company on 5 July 1949.

Jack Casley, the club's first full-time professional player, played in goal in his first game for the club and at centre-forward for his second game. He scored a hat-trick against Guildford City on 22 September, his only goals for United.

In August, United paid £1,000 for Bert Kay from Bury, a record fee for the club, beating the £750 paid to Northampton Town for Norman Aldridge in July.

The 13 goals in the 9–4 win over Huntley & Palmer's in the FA Cup extra-preliminary round, the club's first home game as a professional outfit, remains the largest number of goals scored in a first-team game.

The 7,000 who attended the match against Merthyr Tydfil on 8 October set a new ground record. This was beaten on 26 December, when 8,163 watched the match against Chelmsford, which in turn was beaten when 9,000 attended the match against Colchester on 4 February. On 7 April this was beaten again when 10,160 watched the match against Yeovil.

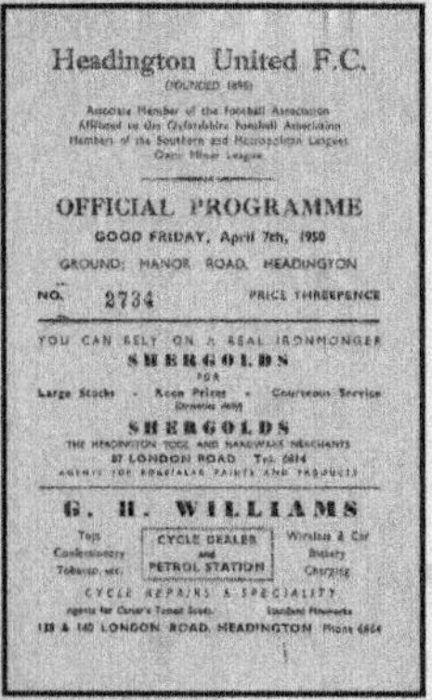

Match No.	Date		Opponents	Result	(F-A)	Scorers	At
1	20/08/1949	A	Hastings United	L	2-5	Mansell, Roberts	
2	27/08/1949	A	Colchester United	L	1-4	Blake	
3	01/09/1949	A	Worcester City	D	1-1	J Smith	
4	15/09/1949	H	Worcester City	L	0-2		
5	22/09/1949	H	Guildford City	W	4-2	Casley (3), Buchanan	
6	24/09/1949	A	Barry Town	L	0-6		
7	29/09/1949	H	Cheltenham Town	W	2-1	J Smith, Buchanan	
8	01/10/1949	H	Torquay United Reserves	L	0-1		
9	08/10/1949	H	Merthyr Tydfil	W	2-1	J Smith, Stephens	
10	15/10/1949	A	Bath City	L	0-2		
11	22/10/1949	H	Weymouth	L	2-5	J Smith (2)	
12	29/10/1949	H	Kidderminster Harriers	L	2-3	Roberts (2)	
13	05/11/1949	H	Bedford Town	W	2-0	Potter (og), J Smith	
14	12/11/1949	H	Exeter City Reserves	W	3-1	J Smith, Nugent, Roberts	
15	19/11/1949	H	Chingford Town	W	7-2	J Smith (2), McPhee (3), Buchanan, Roberts	
16	26/11/1949	A	Chingford Town	D	2-2	J Smith, Nugent	
17	03/12/1949	A	Kidderminster Harriers	L	1-3	J Smith	
18	10/12/1949	H	Gloucester City	W	5-0	J Smith, McPhee, Buchanan (2), Roberts	
19	15/12/1949	H	Dartford	D	1-1	McPhee	
20	17/12/1949	A	Bedford Town	W	2-1	Kay, McPhee	
21	24/12/1949	A	Dartford	L	0-2		
22	26/12/1949	H	Chelmsford City	W	2-1	Stanton, Roberts	
23	27/12/1949	A	Chelmsford City	L	0-5		
24	07/01/1950	A	Hereford United	L	0-1		
25	14/01/1950	H	Lovell's Athletic	W	1-0	Kay	
26	21/01/1950	H	Hereford United	W	2-0	Kay, McPhee	
27	28/01/1950	A	Yeovil Town	D	0-0		
28	04/02/1950	H	Colchester United	L	2-3	J Smith, Buchanan	
29	11/02/1950	A	Merthyr Tydfil	L	2-8	Johnston, Roberts	
30	25/02/1950	H	Bath City	L	1-2	Buchanan (pen)	
31	04/03/1950	A	Exeter City Reserves	L	0-1		
32	11/03/1950	A	Torquay United Reserves	L	0-2		
33	15/03/1950	A	Tonbridge	L	1-2	Howse	
34	18/03/1950	H	Tonbridge	L	1-2	Tapping	
35	23/03/1950	A	Lovell's Athletic	W	3-2	Howse (2), Buchanan	
36	25/03/1950	H	Barry Town	L	1-3	Buchanan	
37	29/03/1950	A	Gravesend & Northfleet	D	1-1	Nugent	
38	01/04/1950	H	Hastings United	W	3-1	Nugent, Toulouse (2)	
39	05/04/1950	A	Gillingham	L	0-2		
40	07/04/1950	H	Yeovil Town	D	1-1	Buchanan	
41	08/04/1950	A	Gloucester City	D	0-0		
42	17/04/1950	H	Gravesend & Northfleet	W	6-5	Kay, J Smith, Jenkins, Buchanan (3) (1 pen)	
43	22/04/1950	H	Gillingham	L	1-3	Kay	
44	26/04/1950	A	Cheltenham Town	L	2-4	Kay, Toulouse	
45	29/04/1950	A	Guildford City	L	0-1		
46	06/05/1950	A	Weymouth	W	3-2	Nugent (2), Toulouse	

FA Cup

xPre	03/09/1949	H	Huntley & Palmer's	W	9-4	Kay (2), J Smith, Tapping (4), Roberts (2)	
Pre	17/09/1949	A	Hemel Hempstead	L	1-3	Buchanan	

Southern League Cup

R1	10/09/1949	A	Hereford United	L	1-3	Tapping	

Total appear

Total

Brine	Stanton	Thompson	Sharman	Blake	Kay	Mansell	Tapping	Roberts	Casley	Quinlan	Woodward	Carr	Smith, J	Buchanan	Edwards	Stephens	Washington	Hale	Nugent	Wilson	McPhee	Gregory	Howse	Johnston	Amphlett	Jenkins	Toulouse	Young	Potts	Bidois	Davidson	Hall
3	4	5	6	7	8	9	10	11																								
3	4	5	6	7	8		9	10	1	11																						
3	4	5	6	7	8			10			1	9	11																			
3	4	5	6	11	8			10			1			7	9																	
3	4	5	6		8				9		1		11	7		10																
3	4	5	6		8				9		1		11			10	7															
	4	5	6		8				9		1		11	7		10		2														
3	4	5	6		8		10		9		1		11	7																		
3	4	5	6		8				9		1		11	7		10																
3	4	5	6	7	8				9		1		11			10																
3	4	5	6		8				9		1		11			10			7													
3	4	5			8		9	10	6		1		11						7													
	4	5						10					9	7				2	11	6	8											
	4	5						10					9	7				2	11	6	8	3										
	4	5	6					10					9	7				2	11		8											
	4	5						10					9	7				2	11	6	8											
	4	5						10					9	7				2	11	6	8											
3	4	5						10					9	7					11	6	8											
3		5	6					10	1				9	7					11	4	8											
3	4	5			9			10						7					11	6	8											
	4	5	6	7	10								9					2	11		8											
3	4	5	6		8			10					9	7					11													
3	4	5		7				10	1			9							11	6	8											
	4	5	6					10					9	7				2	11		8											
	4	5	6		10								9	7				2	11		8											
	4	5	6		10								9	7				2	11		8											
	4	5	6					10	9					7					11		8	3										
	4	5	6										9	7					11		8	3	10									
	4	5	6					8					9						7			3	10	11								
	4	5	6				3						9	7					11		8			10								
	4	5					6	10					9						11					7	3	8						
	4	5			8		6						9	7					11						3	10						
	4	5					6				1		9	7					11		8		10		3							
		5					10						9	7					11	4					3		6	8				
	6	5							1					8					11				9	10	3		4		7			
	6	5							1					8					11				9	10	3		4		7			
	6	5					3		7		1			8					11				9	10			4					
	6	5					3						9	8					11					10			4		7			
		5						7	9		1			8					11					10	3		4			6		
	6						3						9	7					11		8			10			4				5	
	6						3	10			1		9	7					11		8						4				5	
	6				8		3				1		9	7					11							10	4				5	
	6				8		3						9	7					11							10	4				5	
	6				8		3				1			7					11		9					10	4				5	
		7			10		3							8					11							6	4				5	7
		6			8		3							7					11				9			10	4				5	

Brine	Stanton	Thompson	Sharman	Blake	Kay	Mansell	Tapping	Roberts	Casley	Quinlan	Woodward	Carr	Smith, J	Buchanan	Edwards	Stephens	Washington	Hale	Nugent	Wilson	McPhee	Gregory	Howse	Johnston	Amphlett	Jenkins	Toulouse	Young	Potts	Bidois	Davidson	Hall
3	4	5	6	7	8		9	10			1		11																			
3	4	5	6				9	11	7		1			8		10																

Brine	Stanton	Thompson	Sharman	Blake	Kay	Mansell	Tapping	Roberts	Casley	Quinlan	Woodward	Carr	Smith, J	Buchanan	Edwards	Stephens	Washington	Hale	Nugent	Wilson	McPhee	Gregory	Howse	Johnston	Amphlett	Jenkins	Toulouse	Young	Potts	Bidois	Davidson	Hall
3	4	5	6	7		11	8	10			1	9																				

Brine	Stanton	Thompson	Sharman	Blake	Kay	Mansell	Tapping	Roberts	Casley	Quinlan	Woodward	Carr	Smith, J	Buchanan	Edwards	Stephens	Washington	Hale	Nugent	Wilson	McPhee	Gregory	Howse	Johnston	Amphlett	Jenkins	Toulouse	Young	Potts	Bidois	Davidson	Hall
19	44	44	25	9	24	2	21	24	17	1	19	3	34	36	1	7	1	10	36	9	20	4	7	9	7	7	13	1	3	1	7	1
	1			1	8	1	6	10	3				15	14		1			6		7		3	1		1	4					

League Table

	P	W	D	L	F	A	Pts
Merthyr Tydfil	46	34	3	9	143	62	71
Colchester United	46	31	9	6	109	51	71
Yeovil Town	46	29	7	10	104	45	65
Chelmsford City	46	26	9	11	121	64	61
Gillingham	46	23	9	14	92	61	55
Dartford	46	20	9	17	70	65	49
Worcester City	46	21	7	18	85	80	49
Guildford City	46	18	11	17	79	73	47
Weymouth	46	19	9	18	80	81	47
Barry Town	46	18	10	18	78	72	46
Exeter City Reserves	46	16	14	16	73	83	46
Lovell's Athletic	46	17	10	19	86	78	44
Tonbridge	46	16	12	18	65	76	44
Hastings United	46	17	8	21	92	140	42
Gravesend & Northfleet	46	16	9	21	88	81	41
Torquay United Reserves	46	14	12	20	80	89	40
Bath City	46	16	7	23	61	78	39
Gloucester City	46	14	11	21	72	101	39
Hereford United	46	15	8	23	74	76	38
Cheltenham Town	46	13	11	22	75	96	37
Headington United	46	15	7	24	72	97	37
Bedford Town	46	12	11	23	63	79	35
Kidderminster Harriers	46	12	11	23	64	108	35
Chingford Town	46	10	6	30	63	151	26

1950-51

Southern League

Manager: Harry Thompson

Did you know that?

On 18 December, United became the first professional club to play a match under floodlights, when they beat Banbury Spencer 3–0 in a friendly in front of 2,603. Sammy Chung made his United debut in that game. United also played floodlit games against Swindon Town (the first recorded game against Swindon) and Northampton Town. Both games were watched by over 7,000 spectators.

In the floodlit match against Northampton, Chung became the first substitute used by United.

On 14 February Cliff Nugent was sold to Cardiff City for £2,500, a Southern League record at the time.

In the summer of 1950 Les Bateman was appointed groundsman at the Manor, a position he was to hold until 1985.

Harry Thompson's final game as a player was on 24 March, when he was injured at Chelmsford City.

Match No.	Date		Opponents	Result	(F-A)	Scorers
1	26/08/1950	H	Bath City	W	3-1	R Johnston (2), Nugent
2	30/08/1950	A	Merthyr Tydfil	L	0-6	
3	09/09/1950	H	Gravesend & Northfleet	D	3-3	R Johnston (2), Kay
4	13/09/1950	H	Kettering Town	L	2-3	Nugent, Toulouse
5	21/09/1950	A	Hereford United	L	1-3	R Johnston
6	23/09/1950	H	Torquay United Reserves	W	4-3	Barney, Kay (2), Nugent
7	27/09/1950	H	Kidderminster Harriers	L	1-2	Nugent
8	30/09/1950	A	Guildford City	L	0-3	
9	05/10/1950	H	Dartford	W	5-1	Johnston, Toulouse (pen), Buchanan (3)
10	07/10/1950	H	Guildford City	L	1-3	Tapping
11	11/10/1950	A	Exeter City Reserves	L	1-5	Rowstron
12	14/10/1950	A	Chelmsford City	W	4-1	Rowstron (3), Nugent
13	28/10/1950	A	Cheltenham Town	W	3-2	Kay, Rowstron (2)
14	04/11/1950	H	Lovell's Athletic	D	2-2	Kay (2)
15	11/11/1950	A	Torquay United Reserves	W	3-2	Rowstron (2), Thompson
16	18/11/1950	H	Weymouth	L	0-5	
17	25/11/1950	A	Barry Town	W	3-0	Nugent, Elliott (2)
18	02/12/1950	H	Yeovil Town	D	1-1	Rowstron
19	09/12/1950	H	Merthyr Tydfil	D	2-2	Duncan, Rowstron
20	16/12/1950	A	Gravesend & Northfleet	D	0-0	
21	23/12/1950	A	Kettering Town	D	1-1	Elliott
22	25/12/1950	H	Bedford Town	W	2-0	Aldridge, Rowstron
23	26/12/1950	A	Bedford Town	W	4-1	Duncan, Rowstron (3)
24	30/12/1950	H	Hereford United	W	2-1	Rowstron (2)
25	06/01/1951	A	Kidderminster Harriers	W	5-1	Duncan (3), Rowstron, Nugent
26	13/01/1951	A	Yeovil Town	W	4-1	Barney, Rowstron (2), Elliott
27	20/01/1951	A	Hastings United	L	2-5	Barney, Elliott
28	03/02/1951	A	Bath City	D	1-1	Barney
29	10/02/1951	H	Barry Town	L	2-3	Barney, Rowstron
30	17/02/1951	H	Worcester City	W	2-1	Dutton (og), Barney
31	24/02/1951	H	Gloucester City	W	2-0	Duncan, Barney
32	03/03/1951	A	Llanelli	L	1-2	Chung
33	10/03/1951	H	Exeter City Reserves	W	2-0	Duncan (2)
34	23/03/1951	H	Tonbridge	D	0-0	
35	24/03/1951	H	Chelmsford City	L	1-4	Rowstron
36	26/03/1951	A	Tonbridge	D	1-1	Quinlan
37	07/04/1951	H	Cheltenham Town	L	1-2	Rowstron
38	14/04/1951	A	Lovell's Athletic	D	1-1	Rowstron
39	19/04/1951	A	Gloucester City	L	0-2	
40	24/04/1951	H	Llanelli	D	1-1	Duncan
41	26/04/1951	A	Worcester City	L	1-4	D Johnston
42	28/04/1951	A	Weymouth	W	3-1	J Smith (2), Elliott
43	05/05/1951	H	Hastings United	W	3-1	Barney (2), Rowstron
44	10/05/1951	A	Dartford	W	3-1	Duncan, Chung (2)

FA Cup

xPre	02/09/1950	H	Kidlington	W	6-0	Barney, R Johnston, Kay, Nugent (2), Toulouse
Pre	16/09/1950	H	Slough Town	L	3-4	Barney (2), Buchanan

Southern League Cup

Q1	19/08/1950	A	Bedford Town	L	2-4	R Johnston (2)

Total appear

Total

Tapping	Toulouse	Thompson	Davidson	Buchanan	Kay	Johnston, R	Barney	Nugent	Stanton	Casley	Jenkins	Woodward	Aldridge	Bidois	Rowstron	Smith, J	Elliott	Duncan	McDonald	Blake	Chung	Carr	Quinlan	Johnston, D	Crichton
3	4	5	6	7	8	9	10	11																	
3	4	5	6	7	8	9	10	11																	
3	4	5		7	8	9	10	11	6																
3	4	5	6		8	9		11		7	10														
3		6	5	7	8	9	10	11				1		4											
		6	5	7	8	9	10	11				1	3	4											
		6	5	7	8	9	10	11				1	3	4											
	5	6		7		10	8	11				1	3	4	9										
	5			7	8	9	10	11	6			1	3	4											
3	5			7	8	9	10	11	6			1				4									
3	5			7	8		10	11	6			1		4	9										
3	5	4			8		10	11				1			9	6	7								
3	5	4			8		10	11				1	2		9	6	7								
3	5	4			8		10	11				1			9	6	7								
	5	4			8		10	11				1	3		9	6	7								
	5	4					8	11				1	3		9	6	7	10							
	5	4			8		10	11				1	3		9	6	7								
	5	4			8		10	11					3		9	6	7		1						
	5						8	11					3	4	9	6	7	10	1						
	5						8	11					3	4	9	6	7	10	1						
	5						8	11					3	4	9	6	7	10	1						
	5						8	11					3	4	9	6	7	10	1						
	5						8	7			4	1	3		9	6		10		11					
	5						8	11			4	1	3		9	6	7	10							
	5						8	11			4	1	3		9	6	7	10							
	5						8	11			4		3		9	6	7	10	1						
	5						8	11			4	1	3		9	6	7	10							
	5						8	11			4		3		9	6	7	10	1						
	5						8	11			4		3		9	6	7	10	1						
	5						8				4		3		9	6	7	10	1		11				
	5						8				4		3		9	6	7	10	1			11			
	5						8				4		3			6	7	10	1		9	11			
	5	11					8				4		3			6	7	10	1		9				
	5						8				4		3			6	7	10	1		9		11		
	5	6					8				4		3		9	11	7	10	1						
	5						8				4		3		9	6	7	10	1				11		
	5				10		8				4		3		9	6	7	11	1						
	5						8						3	4	9	6	7	10	1			11			
	5						8				6		3	4	9	11	7	10	1						
	5						8				6		3	4		11	7	10	1		9				
	5						8		4		6		3			11	7		1		9			10	
	5						8		4		6		3			11	7	10	1		9				
	5						8		4				3		9	11	7	10	1						6
	5						8			3	4					11	7	10	1		9				6

Tapping	Toulouse	Thompson	Davidson	Buchanan	Kay	Johnston, R	Barney	Nugent	Stanton	Casley	Jenkins	Woodward	Aldridge	Bidois	Rowstron	Smith, J	Elliott	Duncan	McDonald	Blake	Chung	Carr	Quinlan	Johnston, D	Crichton
3	4	5	6	7	8	9	10	11																	
3	4	5	6	7	8	9	10	11																	

Tapping	Toulouse	Thompson	Davidson	Buchanan	Kay	Johnston, R	Barney	Nugent	Stanton	Casley	Jenkins	Woodward	Aldridge	Bidois	Rowstron	Smith, J	Elliott	Duncan	McDonald	Blake	Chung	Carr	Quinlan	Johnston, D	Crichton
3	4	5	6	7	8	9	10	11																	

Tapping	Toulouse	Thompson	Davidson	Buchanan	Kay	Johnston, R	Barney	Nugent	Stanton	Casley	Jenkins	Woodward	Aldridge	Bidois	Rowstron	Smith, J	Elliott	Duncan	McDonald	Blake	Chung	Carr	Quinlan	Johnston, D	Crichton
13	44	20	9	13	20	13	46	32	7	2	21	17	34	13	28	34	32	26	23	1	8	3	2	1	2
1	3	1		4	7	9	12	9					1		24	2	6	10			3		1	1	

League Table

	P	W	D	L	F	A	Pts
Merthyr Tydfil	44	29	8	7	156	66	66
Hereford United	44	27	7	10	110	69	61
Guildford City	44	23	8	13	88	60	54
Chelmsford City	44	21	12	11	84	58	54
Llanelli	44	19	13	12	89	73	51
Cheltenham Town	44	21	8	15	91	61	50
Headington United	44	18	11	15	84	83	47
Torquay United Reserves	44	20	6	18	93	79	46
Exeter City Reserves	44	16	12	16	90	94	44
Weymouth	44	16	12	16	82	88	44
Tonbridge	44	16	12	16	79	87	44
Gloucester City	44	16	11	17	81	76	43
Yeovil Town	44	13	15	16	72	72	41
Worcester City	44	15	11	18	69	78	41
Bath City	44	15	10	19	66	73	40
Dartford	44	14	11	19	61	70	39
Bedford Town	44	15	9	20	64	94	39
Gravesend & Northfleet	44	12	14	18	65	83	38
Kettering Town	44	13	11	20	87	87	37
Lovell's Athletic	44	12	13	19	81	93	37
Kidderminster Harriers	44	13	9	22	58	103	35
Barry Town	44	13	7	24	54	104	33
Hastings	44	11	6	27	91	143	28

1951-52

Southern League

Manager: Harry Thompson

Did you know that?

Headington United were disqualified from the FA Cup for fielding an ineligible player after beating Wycombe Wanderers 3–2 in the third qualifying round. The player was goalkeeper Colin McDonald, who was registered with Burnley but played for Headington while stationed at Moreton-in-Marsh for his National Service. Headington believed that Burnley had given permission for McDonald to play in the FA Cup, but Burnley denied this. McDonald went on to play eight games for England.

The game against Gravesend & Northfleet on 28 February was the first Southern League game to be played under floodlights.

At the end of the season Headington lodged their first application for election to the Football League, but they failed to receive any votes.

Match No.	Date		Opponents	Result	(F-A)	Scorers	At
1	18/08/1951	H	Worcester City	W	2-0	Crichton, Chung	
2	23/08/1951	A	Gloucester City	D	1-1	Crichton (pen)	
3	25/08/1951	H	Llanelli	W	4-0	Chung (3), Sheridan	
4	01/09/1951	A	Hastings United	W	2-0	Barney, Chung	
5	08/09/1951	H	Cheltenham Town	W	1-0	Barney	
6	22/09/1951	H	Dartford	W	2-0	Rowstron, Barker	
7	06/10/1951	H	Yeovil Town	L	0-3		
8	20/10/1951	A	Llanelli	L	2-3	Jefferies, Barney (pen)	
9	27/10/1951	H	Gloucester City	W	2-0	Jefferies, Chung	
10	03/11/1951	H	Merthyr Tydfil	D	0-0		
11	10/11/1951	A	Exeter City Reserves	L	3-4	Harrower (og), Barney (2) (1 pen)	
12	17/11/1951	H	Barry Town	W	3-1	Jefferies, Elliott, Toulouse	
13	24/11/1951	H	Chelmsford City	W	3-0	Duncan, Barney, Toulouse	
14	01/12/1951	A	Gravesend & Northfleet	D	2-2	Duncan, Elliott	
15	08/12/1951	H	Hastings United	W	2-0	Duncan, Rowstron	
16	15/12/1951	H	Bedford Town	D	0-0		
17	22/12/1951	A	Kidderminster Harriers	L	0-3		
18	24/12/1951	H	Kettering Town	W	2-1	Rowstron, Barker	
19	26/12/1951	A	Kettering Town	L	0-1		
20	29/12/1951	A	Hereford United	L	0-2		
21	05/01/1952	H	Hereford United	L	0-2		
22	12/01/1952	A	Worcester City	L	0-1		
23	19/01/1952	A	Merthyr Tydfil	L	2-3	Haynes, Rowstron	
24	26/01/1952	H	Tonbridge	W	2-0	Barney (pen), Rowstron	
25	02/02/1952	A	Dartford	W	1-0	Barney (pen)	
26	09/02/1952	H	Lovell's Athletic	D	1-1	Barney (pen)	
27	16/02/1952	A	Weymouth	L	0-2		
28	23/02/1952	H	Exeter City Reserves	D	1-1	Crichton	
29	28/02/1952	H	Gravesend & Northfleet	W	4-3	Crichton, Jefferies, McKeown (2)	
30	01/03/1952	A	Bath City	L	0-2		
31	08/03/1952	H	Weymouth	D	0-0		
32	12/03/1952	A	Tonbridge	W	4-0	Jefferies, McKeown (2), Butler	
33	15/03/1952	H	Kidderminster Harriers	D	0-0		
34	20/03/1952	A	Bedford Town	L	0-5		
35	22/03/1952	A	Chelmsford City	L	3-4	Haynes, Barney, McKeown	
36	03/04/1952	A	Lovell's Athletic	L	0-1		
37	05/04/1952	A	Barry Town	L	1-5	Sheridan	
38	11/04/1952	H	Guildford City	D	1-1	Toulouse	
39	14/04/1952	A	Guildford City	D	0-0		
40	23/04/1952	H	Bath City	W	2-0	Jenkins, Butler	
41	24/04/1952	A	Yeovil Town	W	1-0	McKeown	
42	26/04/1952	A	Cheltenham Town	D	1-1	Butler	

FA Cup

Pre	15/09/1951	H	Oxford City	D	2-2	Crichton (2) (1 pen)
Pre r	19/09/1951	A	Oxford City	W	3-0	Barney, Rowstron, Barker
1Q	29/09/1951	H	Chesham United	W	5-2	Barney (2), Barker, Sheridan (2)
2Q	13/10/1951	H	Wycombe Wanderers	W	3-2	Barker, Chung (2)

Southern League Cup

Q 1L	29/08/1951	H	Bedford Town	W	2-1	Duncan (2)
Q 2L	06/09/1951	A	Bedford Town	D	0-0	
R1	03/10/1951	H	Guildford City	D	2-2	Barney, Rowstron
r	17/10/1951	A	Guildford City	L	0-1	

Total appeara

Total

Craig	Crichton	Toulouse	Smith, J	Sheridan	Barney	Chung	Duncan	Barker	Hall	Rowstron	Jenkins	O'Sullivan	Jefferies	Ashton	Elliott	Bidois	Haynes	Aldridge	Clinkaberry	Tallant	McKeown	Carpenter	Butler
3	4	5	6	7	8	9	10	11															
3	4	5	6	7	8	9	10	11															
3	4	5	6	7	8	9	10	11															
3	4	5	6	7	8	9	10	11	2														
3	4	5	6	7	8		10	11		9													
3	6	5		7	8		10	11		9	4												
	6	5		7	8		10	11	3	9	4												
3	4	5	6	7	8	9		11				1	10										
3	6	5		7	8	9		11			4		10	1									
3	4	5	6	7	8	9		11					10	1									
3	4	5	6	7	8	9	10	11						1									
3	6	9	5		8		10				4		11	1	7								
3	6	9	5		8		10				4		11	1	7								
3	6	9	5		8		10				4		11	1	7								
3	6		5		8		10			9			11	1	7	4							
3	6		5		8		10			9			11	1	7	4							
3		5	6	7	8		10	11		9				1		4							
3	6		5	7	8		10	11		9	4			1									
3	6	4	5	7	8		10	11		9				1									
3	6	5			8		10			9	4		11	1	7								
3	6	5					10			9	4		11	1	7		8						
3		5		7	8		6		2	9			11	1			10						
3		5		8	4		6			9			11	1	7		10						
3		5		7	8		6			9			11	1			10	2					
3	10	5		7	8		6		2	9			11	1									
3	10	5		7	8		6		2				11	1			9						
3	4	5	9	7	8		6						11	1			10						
3	10	5			8		6		2	9	7		11	1									
3	8	5					6						11				10	2	1	7	9		
3	8	5					6			9			11	1			10	2		7			
3	8	5		7	10		6						11	1				2			9		
3	4	5		7	10		6						11								9	1	8
3	4	5		7	10		6						11	1							9		8
3	4	5		7	10		6						11								9	1	8
3	4	5			10		6		7				11	1			8				9		
3	4	5			10		6						11	1	7						9		8
3	4	5		8	10		6				7		11	1							9		
3	4	5	11		10		6		7					1							9		8
3	6	5		7	8		10				4		11	1							9		
3	6		5	7	4		10				11			1							9		8
3	6	8	5	11	4		10							1	7						9		
3	6		5	11	4		10							1	7						9		8

Craig	Crichton	Toulouse	Smith, J	Sheridan	Barney	Chung	Duncan	Barker	Hall	Rowstron	Jenkins	O'Sullivan	Jefferies	Ashton	Elliott	Bidois	Haynes	Aldridge	Clinkaberry	Tallant	McKeown	Carpenter	Butler
3	4	5	6	7	8	9	10	11															
3	6	5		7	8		10	11		9	4												
	6	5		7	8		10	11	3	9	4												
3	4	5	6	7	8	9	10	11															

Craig	Crichton	Toulouse	Smith, J	Sheridan	Barney	Chung	Duncan	Barker	Hall	Rowstron	Jenkins	O'Sullivan	Jefferies	Ashton	Elliott	Bidois	Haynes	Aldridge	Clinkaberry	Tallant	McKeown	Carpenter	Butler
3	4	5	6	7	8	9	10	11	2														
3	4	5	6	7	8	9		11					10										
	6	5		7	8		10	11	3	9	4												
3	6	5		7	8			11		9		1	10			4							

Craig	Crichton	Toulouse	Smith, J	Sheridan	Barney	Chung	Duncan	Barker	Hall	Rowstron	Jenkins	O'Sullivan	Jefferies	Ashton	Elliott	Bidois	Haynes	Aldridge	Clinkaberry	Tallant	McKeown	Carpenter	Butler
47	46	45	25	37	47	12	45	22	11	20	16	2	29	31	11	4	9	4	1	2	13	2	7
	6	3		4	14	8	5	5		7	1		5		2		2				6		3

League Table

	P	W	D	L	F	A	Pts
Merthyr Tydfil	42	27	6	9	128	60	60
Weymouth	42	22	13	7	81	42	57
Kidderminster Harriers	42	22	10	10	70	40	54
Guildford City	42	18	16	8	66	47	52
Hereford United	42	21	9	12	80	59	51
Worcester City	42	23	4	15	86	73	50
Kettering Town	42	18	10	14	83	56	46
Gloucester City	42	19	8	15	68	55	46
Lovell's Athletic	42	18	10	14	87	68	46
Bath City	42	19	6	17	75	67	44
Headington United	42	16	11	15	55	53	43
Bedford Town	42	16	10	16	75	64	42
Barry Town	42	18	6	18	84	89	42
Chelmsford City	42	15	10	17	67	80	40
Dartford	42	15	9	18	63	65	39
Tonbridge	42	15	6	21	63	84	36
Yeovil Town	42	12	11	19	56	76	35
Cheltenham Town	42	15	4	23	59	85	34
Exeter City Reserves	42	13	7	22	76	106	33
Llanelli	42	13	6	23	70	111	32
Gravesend & Northfleet	42	12	7	23	68	88	31
Hastings United	42	3	5	34	41	131	11

1952-53

Southern League

Manager: Harry Thompson

Did you know that?

Headington won the Southern League Cup for the first time, beating Weymouth 4–3 on aggregate, after extra-time, in a two-legged Final.

Headington won the Southern League title on goal average from Merthyr Tydfil.

The ground attendance record was broken when 10,180 saw United play Wolverhampton Wanderers in a floodlit friendly game on 23 February.

During this season Headington United lodged an unsuccessful application with the FA to change their name to Oxford United.

Match No.	Date		Opponents	Result	(F-A)	Scorers	A
1	23/08/1952	H	Kidderminster Harriers	D	0-0		
2	27/08/1952	H	Hereford United	W	4-1	Yates, Mills (2), Mitchell	
3	30/08/1952	A	Gravesend & Northfleet	L	0-1		
4	06/09/1952	H	Lovell's Athletic	W	1-0	Mills	
5	16/09/1952	H	Bedford Town	W	4-3	J Smith (2), Mitchell, Toulouse	
6	20/09/1952	H	Exeter City Reserves	W	3-2	Turner, J Smith, Mills	
7	04/10/1952	A	Barry Town	L	3-5	Turner, Yates, Mills	
8	18/10/1952	A	Guildford City	L	0-1		
9	01/11/1952	A	Dartford	W	3-0	Steel, Mills (2)	
10	15/11/1952	A	Bath City	D	2-2	Yates, Mills	
11	22/11/1952	H	Gravesend & Northfleet	L	1-2	Yates	
12	29/11/1952	A	Weymouth	D	1-1	Crichton	
13	06/12/1952	H	Yeovil Town	W	3-2	Duncan, Steel, Mills	
14	13/12/1952	A	Gloucester City	W	7-1	Crichton, Duncan, Steel (2), Yates (3)	
15	20/12/1952	A	Hereford United	W	2-1	Crichton (pen), Duncan	
16	24/12/1952	A	Kettering Town	W	2-1	Mills, Mitchell	
17	26/12/1952	H	Kettering Town	D	0-0		
18	27/12/1952	A	Cheltenham Town	W	5-1	Yates, Maskell, Mitchell (3)	
19	03/01/1953	A	Hastings United	D	1-1	Yates	
20	10/01/1953	A	Yeovil Town	D	2-2	Mitchell (2)	
21	17/01/1953	H	Weymouth	D	0-0		
22	24/01/1953	A	Llanelli	W	1-0	Duncan	
23	31/01/1953	H	Bath City	W	3-0	Turner, Mills (2)	
24	07/02/1953	A	Tonbridge	W	1-0	Crichton (pen)	
25	14/02/1953	H	Dartford	W	2-1	Turner, Toulouse	
26	21/02/1953	A	Worcester City	W	3-1	J Smith, Mills, Mitchell	
27	05/03/1953	H	Worcester City	D	1-1	Yates	
28	07/03/1953	A	Merthyr Tydfil	L	0-1		
29	14/03/1953	H	Barry Town	D	1-1	Yates	
30	18/03/1953	A	Chelmsford City	W	3-2	Yates, Toulouse (2)	
31	21/03/1953	A	Exeter City Reserves	L	1-2	Mills	
32	26/03/1953	H	Tonbridge	W	3-1	Steel, Mitchell, Toulouse	
33	28/03/1953	H	Chelmsford City	W	4-0	Steel (2), Yates, Mitchell	
34	30/03/1953	H	Merthyr Tydfil	D	2-2	Steel, Mitchell	
35	03/04/1953	H	Guildford City	D	2-2	James (og), Duncan	
36	04/04/1953	H	Cheltenham Town	W	5-1	Duncan (2), Peart, Steel, Maskell	
37	06/04/1953	A	Kidderminster Harriers	W	3-1	Crichton, Duncan, Maskell	
38	11/04/1953	A	Lovell's Athletic	W	3-2	Steel, Mills, Toulouse	
39	16/04/1953	A	Bedford Town	L	2-4	Fisher (og), Peart	
40	23/04/1953	H	Llanelli	D	1-1	Peart	
41	29/04/1953	H	Gloucester City	W	6-0	Peart, Yates (3), Mitchell (2)	
42	02/05/1953	H	Hastings United	W	2-0	Peart, Steel	

FA Cup

Pre	13/09/1952	A	Marlow	W	8-0	Turner (3), Crichton (2) (1 pen), Steel, Mitchell (2)
1Q	27/09/1952	H	Aylesbury United	W	4-2	Turner (3), Steel
2Q	11/10/1952	H	Maidenhead United	W	2-0	Yates, Mitchell
3Q	25/10/1952	H	Wycombe Wanderers	W	6-2	Turner (2), Steel, Yates, Mills (2)
4Q	08/11/1952	A	Guildford City	L	1-2	Mills

Southern League Cup

Q 1L	03/09/1952	H	Hastings United	D	1-1	Duncan
Q 2L	10/09/1952	A	Hastings United	D	1-1	Turner
R1	01/10/1952	H	Bath City	W	2-1	Yates, Mills
R2	16/10/1952	H	Worcester City	W	5-1	Turner, Duncan, Yates (2), Mills
SF	28/02/1953	H	Guildford City	W	3-1	Steel, Yates, Mills
F 1L	08/04/1953	A	Weymouth	L	1-2	Turner
F 2L	27/04/1953	H	Weymouth	W	3-1	Peart, Mills, Toulouse

Total appear

Total

Craig	Crichton	Toulouse	Duncan	Steel	Yates	Mitchell	Mills	Thomas	Smith, R	Smith, J	Maskell	Turner	Hudson	Potter	Peart
3	4	5	6	7	8	9	10	11							
3	4	5	6	7	8	9	10	11							
3	4	5	6	7	8	9	10	11							
	4	5		7	8	9	10		3	6	11				
	4	5	6	7		8	10		3	11		9			
	4	5	6	7		8	10		3	11		9			
	4	5	6	7	8		10		3		11	9			
5	4		6	7	8		10		3		11	9			
5	4			7	8		10		3		11	9	6		
5			6	7	8	9	10		3		11		4		
5	4		6	7	8		10		3		11	9			
5	4		11	7		8	10		3			9	6		
5	4		11	7	8	9	10		3				6		
5	4		11	7	8	9	10		3				6		
5	4		11	7	8	9	10		3				6		
5	4		11	7	8	9	10		3				6		
5	4		11	7	8	9	10			3			6		
5	3		4	7	8	9	10				11		6		
5	4		11	7	8	9	10		3				6		
5	4		11	7	8	9	10						6	3	
5	4		11	7	8	9	10						6	3	
5	6	4	11	7		8	10					9		3	
5	6	4	11	7		8	10					9		3	
5	6	4	11	7		8	10					9		3	
		4	11	7	8		10		3	5		9	6		
5	4			7	8	9	10			11			6	3	
5			6	7	8		10			11		9	4	3	
5			6	7	8		10					9	4	3	11
5		4	6	7	8	9	10			11				3	
5		4	11	7	8	9	10						6	3	
5		4	11	7	8	9	10						6	3	
5	6	4	11	7	8	9	10							3	
5	6	4	11	7	8	9	10							3	
5	6	4	11	7	8	9	10							3	
5	6	4	11	7	8	9	10							3	
5	6	4	10	7							11	9		3	8
5	6	4	10	7		9			3		11				8
5	6	4	10	7			8		3		11				9
5	6	4	10	7		9			3		11				8
5	6	4	10	7			8		3		11			2	9
5	6	4	11	7	8		10							3	9
5	6	4	11	7	8		10							3	9

Craig	Crichton	Toulouse	Duncan	Steel	Yates	Mitchell	Mills	Thomas	Smith, R	Smith, J	Maskell	Turner	Hudson	Potter	Peart
	4	5	6	7		8	10		3	11		9			
	4	5	6	7	8		10		3	11		9			
5	4		6	7	8	9	10		3		11				
5	4		6	7	8		10		3		11	9			
3	4	5	6	7	8		10				11	9			

Craig	Crichton	Toulouse	Duncan	Steel	Yates	Mitchell	Mills	Thomas	Smith, R	Smith, J	Maskell	Turner	Hudson	Potter	Peart
3	4	5	6	7	8	9	10				11				
	4	5		7		8	10	11	3	6		9			
	4	5	6	7	8		10	11	3			9			
5	4		6	7	8		10		3		11	9			
5		4		7	8	9	10			11			6	3	
5	6	4	10	7	8						11	9		3	
5	6	4		7	8		10				11			3	9

Craig	Crichton	Toulouse	Duncan	Steel	Yates	Mitchell	Mills	Thomas	Smith, R	Smith, J	Maskell	Turner	Hudson	Potter	Peart
45	46	34	48	54	41	35	50	5	26	12	19	22	19	22	9
	7	7	10	15	22	17	22			4	3	15			6

League Table

	P	W	D	L	F	A	Pts
Headington United	42	23	12	7	93	50	58
Merthyr Tydfil	42	25	8	9	117	66	58
Bedford Town	42	24	8	10	91	61	56
Kettering Town	42	23	8	11	88	50	54
Bath City	42	22	10	10	71	47	54
Worcester City	42	20	11	11	100	66	51
Llanelli	42	21	9	12	95	72	51
Barry Town	42	22	3	17	89	64	47
Gravesend & Northfleet	42	19	7	16	83	77	45
Gloucester City	42	17	9	16	50	79	43
Guildford City	42	17	8	17	64	60	42
Hastings	42	18	5	19	75	66	41
Cheltenham Town	42	15	11	16	70	89	41
Weymouth	42	15	10	17	70	75	40
Hereford United	42	17	5	20	76	73	39
Tonbridge	42	12	9	21	62	88	33
Lovell's Athletic	42	12	8	22	68	81	32
Yeovil Town	42	11	10	21	75	99	32
Chelmsford City	42	12	7	23	58	92	31
Exeter City Reserves	42	13	4	25	71	94	30
Kidderminster Harriers	42	12	5	25	54	85	29
Dartford	42	6	5	31	40	121	17

1953-54

Southern League

Manager: Harry Thompson

Did you know that?

United's FA Cup second-round game with Millwall was the first time that the club had met a Football League side in a competitive match.

The ground attendance record was broken again when 16,670 watched the FA Cup fourth-round tie against Bolton Wanderers, whose side included Nat Lofthouse.

Ted Croker, who was later to become the secretary of the Football Association, joined United from Kidderminster Harriers.

In addition to winning the Southern League Cup for the second successive season, United's reserves won the Metropolitan League for the first time.

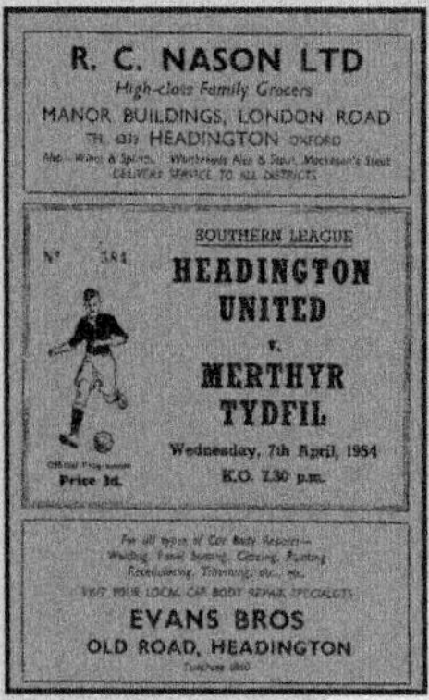

Match No.	Date		Opponents	Result	(F-A)	Scorers	At
1	19/08/1953	H	Hastings United	W	2-0	Yates, Mills	
2	22/08/1953	A	Bath City	W	3-2	K Smith (3)	
3	26/08/1953	H	Chelmsford City	W	5-0	Steel, Mills (3), Mitchell	
4	29/08/1953	H	Hereford United	W	3-1	Yates, Mills (2)	
5	05/09/1953	A	Worcester City	L	0-1		
6	12/09/1953	H	Gloucester City	W	2-0	K Smith, Hudson	
7	16/09/1953	A	Chelmsford City	W	2-0	Peart, Mitchell	
8	19/09/1953	A	Cheltenham Town	W	2-1	K Smith, Bradley	
9	03/10/1953	A	Barry Town	L	1-3	Peart	
10	14/10/1953	H	Gravesend & Northfleet	W	4-1	K Smith, Craig (pen), Crichton, McGarrity	
11	17/10/1953	A	Lovell's Athletic	W	1-0	Mitchell	
12	31/10/1953	A	Bedford Town	W	2-0	Toulouse (2)	
13	02/11/1953	H	Exeter City Reserves	W	1-0	K Smith	
14	14/11/1953	A	Kidderminster Harriers	L	1-2	McGarrity	
15	28/11/1953	A	Dartford	D	1-1	Craig (pen)	
16	02/12/1953	H	Yeovil Town	W	4-3	Craig (pen), Peart, Steel, Mills	
17	05/12/1953	H	Weymouth	D	2-2	K Smith, Maskell	
18	19/12/1953	H	Bath City	W	3-1	K Smith (2), Crichton	
19	26/12/1953	A	Kettering Town	W	2-0	K Smith, Bradley	
20	28/12/1953	H	Kettering Town	L	0-2		
21	02/01/1954	A	Hereford United	L	1-3	Mills	
22	16/01/1954	H	Worcester City	W	1-0	Maskell	
23	23/01/1954	A	Gloucester City	L	1-2	K Smith	
24	06/02/1954	H	Cheltenham Town	W	3-0	Steel (3)	
25	10/02/1954	H	Guildford City	W	1-0	Steel	
26	13/02/1954	A	Hastings United	L	1-2	Craig (pen)	
27	20/02/1954	H	Barry Town	D	0-0		
28	27/02/1954	A	Gravesend & Northfleet	W	1-0	Crichton	
29	06/03/1954	H	Lovell's Athletic	D	0-0		
30	13/03/1954	A	Exeter City Reserves	D	0-0		
31	20/03/1954	H	Bedford Town	W	3-1	Steel, Mills, Toulouse	
32	27/03/1954	A	Yeovil Town	L	0-4		
33	03/04/1954	H	Kidderminster Harriers	D	0-0		
34	07/04/1954	H	Merthyr Tydfil	D	0-0		
35	12/04/1954	A	Merthyr Tydfil	L	1-2	Bradley	
36	14/04/1954	A	Guildford City	D	2-2	Crombie, Bradley	
37	16/04/1954	H	Tonbridge	W	3-0	Craig (pen), Burton, Bradley	
38	17/04/1954	H	Dartford	D	1-1	Crichton	
39	19/04/1954	A	Tonbridge	L	0-3		
40	24/04/1954	A	Weymouth	W	1-0	Yates	
41	26/04/1954	A	Llanelli	L	2-3	Charles, Mills	
42	01/05/1954	H	Llanelli	W	5-0	K Smith, Duncan, Charles (2), McGarrity	
FA Cup							
1Q	26/09/1953	A	Aylesbury United	W	2-1	K Smith, Duncan	
2Q	10/10/1953	H	Maidenhead United	W	4-0	K Smith, Craig (pen), Peart, Mills	
3Q	24/10/1953	H	Chesham United	W	2-0	McGarrity (2)	
4Q	07/11/1953	A	Wealdstone	W	3-0	K Smith, Middleton, Steel	
R1	21/11/1953	A	Harwich & Parkeston	W	3-2	Craig (pen), Duncan, Steel	
R2	12/12/1953	A	Millwall	D	3-3	Peart, Steel, Maskell	
r	17/12/1953	H	Millwall	W	1-0	K Smith	
R3	09/01/1954	A	Stockport County	D	0-0		
r	14/01/1954	H	Stockport County	W	1-0	Peart	
R4	30/01/1954	H	Bolton Wanderers	L	2-4	K Smith, Peart	
Southern League Cup							
Q 1L	02/09/1953	H	Kettering Town	L	1-2	Mitchell	
Q 2L	10/09/1953	A	Kettering Town	W	3-2	Yates (2), Mills	
R1	17/02/1954	H	Bedford Town	W	7-0	Craig, Crichton (3), Peart (2), Steel	
R2	24/02/1954	H	Gravesend & Northfleet	W	3-1	Chambers (og), Lewis (og), Steel	
SF	01/04/1954	H	Guildford City	D	1-1	Yates	
r	10/04/1954	A	Guildford City	W	1-0	Bradley	
F 1L	21/04/1954	A	Lovell's Athletic	D	0-0		
F 2L	28/04/1954	H	Lovell's Athletic	W	2-0	Steel, Yates	

Total appear

Total

Croker	Crichton	Craig	Hudson	Steel	Yates	Peart	Mills	Maskell	Smith, K	Mitchell	Duncan	Bradley	McGarrity	Potter	Smith, J	Toulouse	Parker	Middleton	Milliner	Clinkaberry	Charles	Burton	Crombie	Howlett	Johnston	Humpston	Jones
3	4	5	6	7	8	9	10	11																			
3	4	5	6	7	8		10	11	9																		
3	4	5	6	7	8		10	11		9																	
3	4	5	6	7	8		10	11		9																	
3	4	5	6	7	8			11	9		10																
3	4	5	6	7			10		9			11	8														
	4	5	6			8				9	11	7	10	3													
	4	5	6	7			10		9		11		8	3													
	4	5	6	7		8			9		10			3	11												
3	6	5		7					9	8	11		10			4											
3	6	5	4	7					9	8	11		10														
2	6	5	4	7							11		8			9	3	10									
2	6	5	4	7							11		10		3	9			8								
2	6	5	4	7					9	8	11		10				3										
2	6	5	4	7			10		9		11				3	8											
3	6	5	4	7			10		9		11					8											
3	6	5		7				11	9		10		8			4											
3	6		4			8			9		10	11			5	7											
3	6	5	4	7		8			9		10	11															
3	6	5		7		8			9		10	11				4											
3	4	5		7			10		9		11		8		6					1							
3	4					8		11	9		10	7			5	6											
	6	5		7		8		11	9		10				4		3										
3	6	5	4	7		8		11	9		10																
3	6	5	4	7		8		11			10						2				9						
3	6	5	4	7		8		11			10					9											
3	8	5	4	7		9	10				11				6												
3	8	5	4	7		9	10				11				6												
3	8	5	4	7		9	1				11				6												
3		5	4	7		9	10				11				6						8						
3	8	5	4	7			10	11							6	9											
3	6			7	8		10	11	9		4				5												
	4	5		7	8	10		11			6					9	3										
	4	5		7		8		11	9						6		3					10					
	4	5	6	7		8			9			11					3					10					
3	6	5	4	7					9		8	11											10				
3	4	5		7					9		8	11			6							10					
3	4	5		7					9		8				6							10		11			
2						9	10	11			8			6		5	3				7				4		
3	4	5			8						11				6						7	10	9				
						9	10	11			7				2		3				8				4	1	5
3	4	5					10		9		11		8		6						7						

Croker	Crichton	Craig	Hudson	Steel	Yates	Peart	Mills	Maskell	Smith, K	Mitchell	Duncan	Bradley	McGarrity	Potter	Smith, J	Toulouse	Parker	Middleton	Milliner	Clinkaberry	Charles	Burton	Crombie	Howlett	Johnston	Humpston	Jones
	4	5	6	7		8		11	9		10			3													
3	6	5		7		8	10		9		11					4											
3	6	5	4	7				11	9	8			10														
2	6	5	4	7				11	9				10		3			8									
2	6	5	4	7					9		10	11			3	8											
3	6	5	4	7		8		11	9		10																
3	6	5	4	7		8		11	9		10																
3	6	5	4	7		8		11	9		10																
3	6	5	4	7		8		11	9		10																
3	6	5	4	7		8		11	9		10																

Croker	Crichton	Craig	Hudson	Steel	Yates	Peart	Mills	Maskell	Smith, K	Mitchell	Duncan	Bradley	McGarrity	Potter	Smith, J	Toulouse	Parker	Middleton	Milliner	Clinkaberry	Charles	Burton	Crombie	Howlett	Johnston	Humpston	Jones
3	4	5	6	7	8		10	11		9																	
3	4	5	6	7	8		10	11		9																	
3		5	4	7	8	9	10				11				6												
3	8	5	4	7			10		9		11				6												
3	4			7	8			11	9		6				5								10				
	4	5		7	8				9			11			6		3					10					
3	4	5				10			9		11				6	7						8					
3	4	5		7	8				9		11				6							10					

Croker	Crichton	Craig	Hudson	Steel	Yates	Peart	Mills	Maskell	Smith, K	Mitchell	Duncan	Bradley	McGarrity	Potter	Smith, J	Toulouse	Parker	Middleton	Milliner	Clinkaberry	Charles	Burton	Crombie	Howlett	Johnston	Humpston	Jones
50	56	54	40	52	14	29	23	28	40	9	47	11	13	5	27	17	10	2	1	1	6	8	3	1	2	1	1
	7	8	1	13	7	9	12	3	17	4	3	6	5		1	3		1			3	1	1				

League Table

	P	W	D	L	F	A	Pts
Merthyr Tydfil	42	27	8	7	97	55	62
Headington United	42	22	9	11	68	43	53
Yeovil Town	42	20	8	14	87	76	48
Bath City	42	17	12	13	73	67	46
Kidderminster Harriers	42	18	9	15	62	59	45
Weymouth	42	18	8	16	83	72	44
Barry Town	42	17	9	16	108	91	43
Bedford Town	42	19	5	18	80	84	43
Gloucester City	42	16	11	15	69	77	43
Hastings United	42	16	10	16	73	67	42
Kettering Town	42	15	12	15	65	63	42
Hereford United	42	16	9	17	66	62	41
Llanelli	42	16	9	17	80	85	41
Guildford City	42	15	11	16	56	60	41
Gravesend & Northfleet	42	16	8	18	76	77	40
Worcester City	42	17	6	19	66	71	40
Lovell's Athletic	42	14	11	17	62	60	39
Tonbridge	42	15	9	18	85	91	39
Chelmsford City	42	14	10	18	67	71	38
Exeter City Reserves	42	11	13	18	61	72	35
Cheltenham Town	42	11	12	19	56	83	34
Dartford	42	6	13	23	42	89	25

1954-55

Southern League

Manager: Harry Thompson

Did you know that?

Striker Ken Smith was sold to Blackpool for £2,000 in December.

A player dispute concerning appearance money if a player was unable to return after injury, led to five players rejecting terms at the end of the season and refusing to play in the Oxfordshire Professional Cup Final, which United won 5–4 on aggregate against Banbury Spencer.

In the Hellenic League, Headington United beat champions Witney Town in the League Cup Final.

Match No.	Date		Opponents	Result	(F-A)	Scorers	At
1	21/08/1954	H	Bedford Town	W	2-1	Wilson, Yates	
2	25/08/1954	A	Gravesend & Northfleet	W	1-0	Craig (pen)	
3	28/08/1954	A	Weymouth	W	3-1	K Smith, Steel, Yates	
4	04/09/1954	A	Barry Town	L	0-1		
5	11/09/1954	H	Merthyr Tydfil	W	4-0	K Smith (3), Yates	
6	15/09/1954	H	Cheltenham Town	W	5-0	K Smith, Craig (pen), Wilson, Yates (2)	
7	18/09/1954	A	Kidderminster Harriers	D	0-0		
8	25/09/1954	H	Yeovil Town	W	3-0	Wilson, Yates (2)	
9	02/10/1954	A	Llanelli	L	1-3	Bain	
10	09/10/1954	H	Hastings United	W	8-2	K Smith (4), Wilson, Bain, Yates (2)	
11	16/10/1954	A	Dartford	W	4-1	K Smith, Steel (2), Yates	
12	23/10/1954	H	Gravesend & Northfleet	W	4-1	K Smith (3), Wilson	
13	30/10/1954	A	Guildford City	L	0-2		
14	13/11/1954	A	Bath City	L	0-4		
15	04/12/1954	H	Exeter City Reserves	L	1-4	Yates	
16	11/12/1954	A	Lovell's Athletic	L	2-3	Yates, Johnston	
17	14/12/1954	H	Kettering Town	D	1-1	Bain	
18	18/12/1954	A	Bedford Town	D	0-0		
19	27/12/1954	A	Kettering Town	L	1-5	Varney	
20	28/12/1954	H	Tonbridge	W	2-1	Varney (2)	
21	01/01/1955	H	Weymouth	L	1-2	Varney	
22	22/01/1955	A	Merthyr Tydfil	L	0-1		
23	29/01/1955	A	Cheltenham Town	L	1-2	Johnston	
24	05/02/1955	H	Kidderminster Harriers	W	2-1	Varney (2)	
25	12/02/1955	A	Yeovil Town	D	2-2	Bain, Yates	
26	19/02/1955	H	Llanelli	W	5-1	Wilson, Crichton, Varney, Yates, Skull	
27	26/02/1955	A	Chelmsford City	L	1-2	Morley (og)	
28	05/03/1955	H	Dartford	D	1-1	Skull	
29	12/03/1955	A	Tonbridge	L	1-2	Clarke	
30	15/03/1955	H	Barry Town	D	0-0		
31	19/03/1955	H	Guildford City	D	0-0		
32	23/03/1955	H	Chelmsford City	W	4-1	Yates, Nicklas (2), Skull	
33	26/03/1955	A	Gloucester City	L	0-2		
34	02/04/1955	H	Bath City	W	2-0	Yates (2)	
35	08/04/1955	H	Hereford United	W	3-1	Nicklas (2), Skull	
36	09/04/1955	A	Hastings United	L	1-5	Crichton (pen)	
37	11/04/1955	A	Hereford United	L	1-2	Skull	
38	16/04/1955	H	Worcester City	W	7-0	Crichton (2) (2 pens), Varney, Yates (2), Skull (2)	
39	20/04/1955	H	Gloucester City	L	0-2		
40	23/04/1955	A	Exeter City Reserves	W	2-0	Walter (og), Skull	
41	28/04/1955	A	Worcester City	L	2-3	Crichton, Yates	
42	30/04/1955	H	Lovell's Athletic	W	4-2	Duncan (2), Varney, Yates	

FA Cup

4Q	06/11/1954	H	Tonbridge	W	1-0	Yates
R1	20/11/1954	A	Norwich City	L	2-4	K Smith, Yates

Southern League Cup

Q 1L	01/09/1954	A	Cheltenham Town	D	2-2	K Smith, Bain
Q 2L	08/09/1954	H	Cheltenham Town	W	3-1	Wilson, Steel, Yates
R1/1	27/10/1954	H	Gloucester City	D	0-0	
R2/2	06/12/1954	A	Gloucester City	L	1-2	Yates

Total appear

Total

Croker	Hudson	Craig	Crichton	Steel	Yates	Smith, K	Wilson	Bain	Duncan	Smith, J	Humpston	Nicklas	Clinkaberry	Parker	Johnston	Burton	Bennett	Varney	Farr	Skull	Clarke	Love	Jackson	Wood	Otter	Mumford
3	4	5	6	7	8	9	10	11																		
3		5	4	7	8	9	10	11	6																	
3		5	4	7	8	9	10	11	6																	
3		5	4	7	8	9	10	11	6																	
3		5	4	7	8	9	10	11		6																
3		5	4	7	8	9	10	11		6	1															
3		5	4	7	8	9	10	11		6	1															
3		5	4	7	8		10	11		6	1	9														
3		5	4	7	8	9	10	11		6	1															
3		5	4	7	8	9	10	11		6			1													
3		5		7	8	9	10	11	4	6			1													
3		5		7	8	9	10	11	4	6																
2		5	6		8		7	11				9		3	4	10										
3	4	5	6		8	9	7	11	10																	
2	6	5		7	8	9		11	10					3	4											
2	6	5		7	8			11	10					3	4	9										
2		5	6		8		7	11						3	4	9	10									
2		5	6		8		7	11						3	4	9	10									
2		5	6	7	8			11						3	4		10	9								
5		2	6	7	8			11						3	4		10	9								
5		2	6	7	8		10	11						3	4			9								
3		5		7	8		10	11	6						4				9							
3		5	6	7			8	11	10						4				9							
3	6	5			8			11	10						4			9		7						
5	6	3			8		10	11							4			9		7						
5		3	6		8		10	11							4			9		7						
5		3	6		8		10	11							4				9	7						
5			6		8		10	11						3	4				9	7						
5			6		8		10	11						3	4					7	9					
5		9	6		8		10							3	4					7		11				
5		9	6		8		10	11						3	4					7						
5	6				8		10	11				9		3	4					7						
5	6				8		10	11				9		3	4					7						
3		5	6		8		10	11				9			4					7						
3		5	6		8		10	11				9			4					7						
		5	6		8				10			9		3						7			4	11		
	4	5			8			11				9		3	6			10		7					1	
		5	6		8			11	10			3			4			9		7					1	
		5	6	7	8				10			3			4			9						11		
		5	6		8			11	10			3						9		7			4		1	
	6	5	10		8			11				3			4					7					1	9
		5	6		8			11	10			3						9		7			4		1	

Croker	Hudson	Craig	Crichton	Steel	Yates	Smith, K	Wilson	Bain	Duncan	Smith, J	Humpston	Nicklas	Clinkaberry	Parker	Johnston	Burton	Bennett	Varney	Farr	Skull	Clarke	Love	Jackson	Wood	Otter	Mumford
3		5	4	7	8	9		11	10	6																
3	4	5	6	7	8	9	10	11																		

Croker	Hudson	Craig	Crichton	Steel	Yates	Smith, K	Wilson	Bain	Duncan	Smith, J	Humpston	Nicklas	Clinkaberry	Parker	Johnston	Burton	Bennett	Varney	Farr	Skull	Clarke	Love	Jackson	Wood	Otter	Mumford
2		5	4	7	8	9	10	11	6					3												
3		5	4	7	8	9	10	11	6																	
2		5			8			11	6			7		3	4	9	10									
2	6	5	4	7	8	9		11	10					3												

Croker	Hudson	Craig	Crichton	Steel	Yates	Smith, K	Wilson	Bain	Duncan	Smith, J	Humpston	Nicklas	Clinkaberry	Parker	Johnston	Burton	Bennett	Varney	Farr	Skull	Clarke	Love	Jackson	Wood	Otter	Mumford
41	12	44	37	25	47	18	33	45	21	9	4	14	2	19	27	5	5	11	4	18	1	1	3	2	5	1
		2	5	4	25	15	7	5	2			4			2			9		8	1					

League Table

	P	W	D	L	F	A	Pts
Yeovil Town	42	23	9	10	105	66	55
Weymouth	42	24	7	11	105	84	55
Hastings United	42	21	9	12	94	60	51
Cheltenham Town	42	21	8	13	85	72	50
Guildford City	42	20	8	14	72	59	48
Worcester City	42	19	10	13	80	73	48
Barry Town	42	16	15	11	82	87	47
Gloucester City	42	16	13	13	66	54	45
Bath City	42	18	9	15	73	80	45
Headington United	42	18	7	17	82	62	43
Kidderminster Harriers	42	18	7	17	84	86	43
Merthyr Town	42	17	8	17	97	94	42
Exeter City Reserves	42	19	4	19	67	78	42
Lovell's Athletic	42	15	11	16	71	68	41
Kettering Town	42	15	11	16	70	69	41
Hereford United	42	17	5	20	91	72	39
Llanelli	42	16	7	19	78	81	39
Bedford Town	42	16	3	23	75	103	35
Tonbridge	42	11	8	23	68	91	30
Dartford	42	9	12	21	55	76	30
Chelmsford City	42	11	6	25	73	111	28
Gravesend & Northfleet	42	9	9	24	62	97	27

1955-56

Southern League

Manager: Harry Thompson

Did you know that?

New signings at the start of the season included Pat Quartermain, who was to remain with United until 1967, and Welsh international Billy Rees.

Jim Smith, who had played first-team football for Headington for 20 years, made his final appearance on 3 September, at Chelmsford City.

In the Hellenic League, Headington's A team won the Championship, in only their third season of existence.

United bought land adjoining the London Road, allowing a new entrance to the ground and a new base for the supporters' club's headquarters.

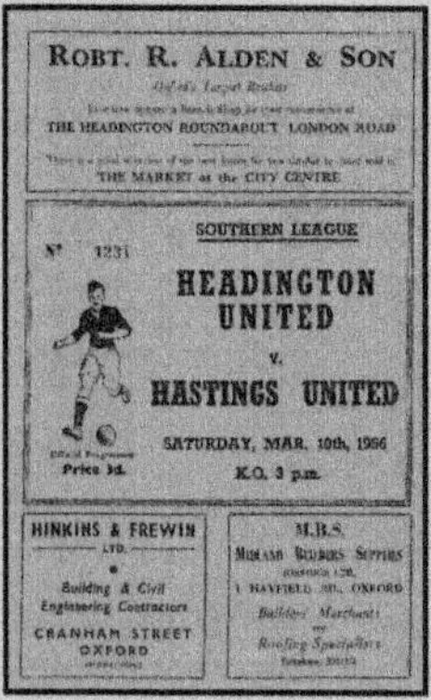

Match No.	Date		Opponents	Result	(F-A)	Scorers	At
1	20/08/1955	A	Gloucester City	L	0-2		
2	24/08/1955	H	Guildford City	L	0-3		
3	27/08/1955	H	Worcester City	D	1-1	Adams	
4	03/09/1955	A	Chelmsford City	L	1-3	Adams	
5	17/09/1955	A	Yeovil Town	L	2-4	Varney, Killip	
6	21/09/1955	A	Guildford City	W	3-1	Love, Ramshaw, Smillie	
7	24/09/1955	H	Exeter City Reserves	W	7-0	Eele (2), Doherty, Adams (2), Smillie (2)	
8	01/10/1955	A	Barry Town	L	1-2	Eele	
9	08/10/1955	H	Cheltenham Town	W	2-1	Smillie (2)	
10	15/10/1955	A	Lovell's Athletic	W	2-0	Collins (2)	
11	22/10/1955	H	Llanelli	W	3-1	Collins, Bain, Smillie	
12	29/10/1955	A	Hastings United	L	0-1		
13	10/11/1955	H	Tonbridge	W	1-0	Barley	
14	12/11/1955	A	Bath City	L	1-2	Adams	
15	26/11/1955	A	Cheltenham Town	L	0-4		
16	01/12/1955	H	Hereford United	D	1-1	Skull	
17	03/12/1955	H	Weymouth	D	3-3	Nielson, Smillie, Skull	
18	10/12/1955	A	Gravesend & Northfleet	L	0-4		
19	17/12/1955	H	Gloucester City	L	0-2		
20	24/12/1955	A	Worcester City	L	0-4		
21	26/12/1955	H	Kettering Town	W	3-1	Rees, Phillips, Smillie	
22	27/12/1955	A	Kettering Town	L	2-4	Rees (2)	
23	31/12/1955	H	Chelmsford City	W	3-1	Rees, Adams, Smillie	
24	14/01/1956	A	Kidderminster Harriers	D	3-3	Dawks (og), Rees, Bain	
25	21/01/1956	H	Yeovil Town	W	3-2	Phillips (2), Smillie	
26	28/01/1956	H	Merthyr Tydfil	W	5-3	Rees, Adams, Smillie (3)	
27	04/02/1956	A	Exeter City Reserves	L	2-3	Doherty, Smillie (pen)	
28	08/02/1956	H	Bedford Town	W	3-2	Rees, Adams, Phillips	
29	11/02/1956	H	Barry Town	W	3-2	Rees, Adams, Smillie	
30	18/02/1956	A	Bedford Town	L	2-4	Rees (2)	
31	25/02/1956	H	Lovell's Athletic	L	1-2	Adams	
32	03/03/1956	A	Llanelli	W	4-0	Rees, Phillips (2), Smillie (pen)	
33	10/03/1956	H	Hastings United	W	3-0	Rees, Adams, Smillie (pen)	
34	14/03/1956	H	Kidderminster Harriers	W	5-2	Rees, Phillips, Smillie (3)	
35	17/03/1956	A	Hereford United	W	3-2	Rees, Smillie (2)	
36	24/03/1956	H	Bath City	W	3-0	Rees, Mulgrew, Smillie (pen)	
37	30/03/1956	H	Dartford	L	1-3	Adams	
38	31/03/1956	A	Tonbridge	D	1-1	Phillips	
39	14/04/1956	A	Weymouth	L	0-6		
40	21/04/1956	H	Gravesend & Northfleet	L	1-2	Phillips (pen)	
41	23/04/1956	A	Dartford	L	1-2	Phillips	
42	28/04/1956	A	Merthyr Tydfil	D	2-2	Adams, Murray	

FA Cup

4Q	05/11/1955	H	Margate	L	2-4	Adams, Murray	

Southern League Cup

Q 1L	31/08/1955	H	Worcester City	W	3-0	Skull (3)	
Q 2L	05/09/1955	A	Worcester City	L	0-2		
R1	17/11/1955	H	Kidderminster Harriers	W	4-0	Smale (og), Eele, Smillie, Skull	
R2	07/01/1956	H	Kettering Town	W	3-2	Rees, Phillips, Smillie	
SF	20/03/1956	H	Yeovil Town	L	1-3	Phillips	

Total appear

Total

Lewis	Johnston	Capper	Doherty	Skull	Killip	Nielson	Adams	Bain	Cairney	Gillies	Eele	Jackson	Varney	Murray	Mulgrew	Smith, J	Smillie	Collins	Hall	Hudson	Harper	Otter	Love	Quartermain	Barley	Wood	Rees	Phillips	Hill	Dean	Bidois
3	4	5	6	7	8	9	10	11																							
3	4	5		7		9		11	6	8	10																				
3		6		7			10				9	4	5	8	11																
3		5		7			10					4			11	6	7	8													
					8		10	11					9	4			7		3	5	6										
	4		3				10				9			8			7			5	6	1	11								
	4		3				10	11			9			8			7				6	1		5							
	4		3				10	11			9			8			7				6	1		5							
			3				10	11	4		9			8			7				6	1		5							
			3	7			10	11						8				9			6	1		5	4						
			3				10	11						8			7	9			6	1		5	4						
2		6	3				10	11						8			7	9				1		5	4						
	8	5	3				10	11			9						7					1		6	4						
3		5	6	8			10	11			9						7					1			4						
3		5	6	8			10	11			9						7								4						
3				9		8	10							4	11		7							5	6						
3				9		8	10	11						4			7					1		5	6						
3				9			10	11			8			4			7							5	6						
	4		3	9		8	10	11					6				7							5							
	4		3				10				9		8				7			6		1		5		11					
	4		3				10	11									7			6		1		5			8	9			
	4		3				10										7			6		1		5		11	8	9			
	4		3				10	11									7			6		1		5			8	9			
	4		3				10	11									7			6		1		5			8	9			
	4		3				10	11									7			6		1		5			8	9			
	4		3				10	11									7			6		1		5			8	9			
	4		3				10	11									7			6		1		5			8	9			
	4		3				10	11									7			6		1		5			8	9			
	4		3				10	11									7				6	1		5			8	9			
	4		3				10	11									7			6		1		5			8	9			
			3				10	11									7			4	6			5			8	9			
3							10	11									7			4	6			5			8	9			
3							10	11									7			4	6			5			8	9			
3							10	11									7			4	6			5			8	9			
3							10								11		7			4	6			5			8	9			
							10						3		11		7			4	6	1		5			8	9			
3							10	11									7			4	6			5			8	9	1		
			3				8	11									7			4	6				5			9	1	10	
	4		3				8	11									7				6			5				9	1	10	
			3				10	11									7			4	6			5				9	1	8	
2	8		3	7			11													5	6	1							9		10
			3				10	11									7			6	8			5				9	1		4

Lewis	Johnston	Capper	Doherty	Skull	Killip	Nielson	Adams	Bain	Cairney	Gillies	Eele	Jackson	Varney	Murray	Mulgrew	Smith, J	Smillie	Collins	Hall	Hudson	Harper	Otter	Love	Quartermain	Barley	Wood	Rees	Phillips	Hill	Dean	Bidois
		6	3				10	11						8			7	9				1		5	4						

Lewis	Johnston	Capper	Doherty	Skull	Killip	Nielson	Adams	Bain	Cairney	Gillies	Eele	Jackson	Varney	Murray	Mulgrew	Smith, J	Smillie	Collins	Hall	Hudson	Harper	Otter	Love	Quartermain	Barley	Wood	Rees	Phillips	Hill	Dean	Bidois
3		5	6				10				8				11		7	9							4						
3				9			10			6				4	11		7			5					8						
3		5	6	8			10	11			9						7					1			4						
	4		3				10										7	11		6		1		5			8	9			
							10						3		11		7			4	6			5			8	9			

Lewis	Johnston	Capper	Doherty	Skull	Killip	Nielson	Adams	Bain	Cairney	Gillies	Eele	Jackson	Varney	Murray	Mulgrew	Smith, J	Smillie	Collins	Hall	Hudson	Harper	Otter	Love	Quartermain	Barley	Wood	Rees	Phillips	Hill	Dean	Bidois
19	21	11	33	14	2	5	47	35	2	2	13	2	6	14	8	1	43	7	1	26	21	26	1	35	14	2	19	24	5	4	1
			2	6	1	1	14	2			4		1	2	1		25	3					1		1		16	12			

League Table

	P	W	D	L	F	A	Pts
Guildford City	42	26	8	8	74	34	60
Cheltenham Town	42	25	6	11	82	53	56
Yeovil Town	42	23	9	10	98	55	55
Bedford Town	42	21	9	12	99	69	51
Dartford	42	20	9	13	78	62	49
Weymouth	42	19	10	13	83	63	48
Gloucester City	42	19	9	14	72	60	47
Lovells Athletic	42	19	9	14	91	78	47
Chelmsford City	42	18	10	14	67	55	46
Kettering Town	42	16	11	15	105	86	43
Exeter City Reserves	42	17	9	16	75	76	43
Gravesend & Northfleet	42	17	8	17	79	75	42
Hereford United	42	17	7	18	90	90	41
Hastings United	42	15	10	17	90	73	40
Headington United	42	17	6	19	82	86	40
Kidderminster Harriers	42	14	7	21	86	108	35
Llanelli	42	14	6	22	64	98	34
Barry Town	42	11	11	20	91	108	33
Worcester City	42	12	9	21	66	83	33
Tonbridge	42	11	11	20	53	74	33
Bath City	42	7	10	25	43	107	24
Merthyr Town	42	7	10	25	52	127	24

1956-57

Southern League

Manager: Harry Thompson

Did you know that?

A crowd of over 10,000 saw Headington beat an All-Star XI, including Stanley Matthews, in a testimonial for former player Jim Smith on 17 October.

New signings included Les Blizzard, who had made over 200 appearances for Leyton Orient, and Geoff Denial, who was to go on to make 162 full appearances in the Southern League, and exactly 200 appearances altogether for United, despite missing 10 games this season after being called-up for the army during the Suez Crisis.

Johnny Love missed the entire season after being called-up for National Service in the West Indies.

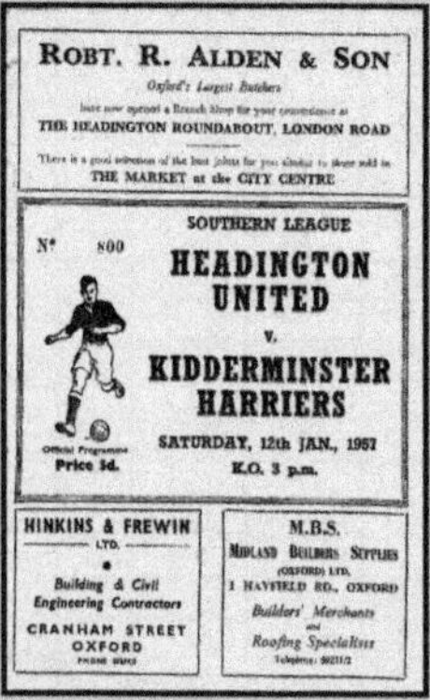

Match No.	Date		Opponents	Result	(F-A)	Scorers	A
1	18/08/1956	H	Yeovil Town	W	2-0	Phillips, Smillie	
2	22/08/1956	A	Dartford	D	3-3	Dean, Rowden (2)	
3	25/08/1956	A	Worcester City	W	3-0	Budgett (og), Taylor, Dean	
4	01/09/1956	H	Lovell's Athletic	W	3-0	Taylor, Phillips (2)	
5	08/09/1956	A	Exeter City Reserves	W	3-1	Rees, Phillips (2)	
6	15/09/1956	H	Gloucester City	W	2-0	Dean, E Adams	
7	19/09/1956	H	Tonbridge	W	3-2	Rees, Phillips, McLain	
8	22/09/1956	A	Yeovil Town	W	4-2	Dean, E Adams, Phillips, Smillie	
9	26/09/1956	H	Dartford	L	1-3	Smillie	
10	29/09/1956	H	Exeter City Reserves	W	3-2	Taylor, Rees, Phillips	
11	01/10/1956	A	Kidderminster Harriers	W	1-0	Phillips	
12	06/10/1956	H	Hastings United	W	2-1	Harper, Phillips	
13	13/10/1956	A	Gravesend & Northfleet	L	0-2		
14	20/10/1956	H	Weymouth	D	1-1	Harper	
15	27/10/1956	A	Bath City	W	3-0	Taylor, Dean, Phillips	
16	10/11/1956	A	Merthyr Tydfil	L	1-5	McLain	
17	24/11/1956	A	Hereford United	L	0-3		
18	01/12/1956	H	Barry Town	W	3-0	D Adams, Dean, Eele	
19	08/12/1956	A	Guildford City	W	1-0	Phillips	
20	22/12/1956	H	Worcester City	L	0-1		
21	25/12/1956	A	Bedford Town	L	1-2	Phillips	
22	26/12/1956	H	Bedford Town	L	0-6		
23	05/01/1957	H	Hereford United	L	1-2	Rees	
24	12/01/1957	H	Kidderminster Harriers	D	2-2	Dean, Rees	
25	19/01/1957	A	Gloucester City	L	0-2		
26	23/01/1957	H	Cheltenham Town	D	1-1	Collins	
27	26/01/1957	A	Barry Town	W	1-0	Rees	
28	02/02/1957	H	Llanelli	W	4-2	Rees, E Adams, McLain (2)	
29	16/02/1957	A	Hastings United	W	2-0	Rees, McLain	
30	23/02/1957	H	Gravesend & Northfleet	L	2-3	E Adams, Johnston	
31	02/03/1957	A	Weymouth	L	0-1		
32	09/03/1957	H	Bath City	D	2-2	Harper, Rees	
33	14/03/1957	A	Lovell's Athletic	L	0-1		
34	16/03/1957	A	Kettering Town	L	1-3	Smillie	
35	23/03/1957	H	Merthyr Tydfil	W	2-1	Eele, Bidois	
36	30/03/1957	A	Cheltenham Town	L	1-2	McLain	
37	06/04/1957	H	Kettering Town	L	0-1		
38	13/04/1957	A	Llanelli	D	1-1	Odell	
39	19/04/1957	A	Chelmsford City	W	1-0	E Adams	
40	20/04/1957	H	Guildford City	L	0-2		
41	22/04/1957	H	Chelmsford City	W	2-0	Dean, Rees	
42	01/05/1957	A	Tonbridge	D	1-1	Bowie	

FA Cup

4Q	03/11/1956	H	Guildford City	L	0-2	

Southern League Cup

R1/1	29/08/1956	H	Bedford Town	D	1-1	E Adams
R1/2	06/09/1956	A	Bedford Town	L	0-5	

Total appear

Total

Ramshaw	McLain	Odell	Harper	Smillie	Rees	Phillips	Forrester	Taylor	Dean	Rowden	Adams, E	Hudson	Denial	Parker	Fraser	Collins	Quartermain	Adams, D	Johnston	Eele	Blizzard	Bowie	Parsons	Bidois	Otter
3	4	5	6	7	8	9	10	11																	
3	4	5	6		8		11		7	9	10														
3	4	5	6		8	9		11	7		10														
3	4		6	7	8	9		11			10	5													
3	4	5	6		8	9		11	7		10														
3	4		6	11	8	9			7		10	5													
3	4		6	11	8	9			7		10	5													
3	4	5	6	11	8	9			7		10														
3	4	5	6	11	8	9			7		10														
2	4	5	6	7	8	9		11			10		3												
2		5	6	7		8					11	4		3	9	10									
2	8	5	6	7		9		11			10	4		3											
2	4	5	6	7	8	9		11			10						3								
2	4	5	6	7	10	9		11			8		3												
2	4	5	6		8	9		11	7				3					10							
2	8	5	6		10			11	7			4					3	9							
2			6	11		8	10		7			5							4	9					
3			4			8	10		7			6					5	9		11					
3				7		8	10					4					5	9		11	6				
3				7	9	8					10						5		4	11	6				
3			8		9	7		11			10	5							4		6				
3			9	11	8	7					10	5							4		6				
2		5	6		8			11	7		10		3						4		9				
2		5		7	8	9			11			6	3						10		4				
2		5		7	8				11		10	4	3							9	6				
2		5		7	8				11		10	4	3			9					6				
2		5	10	7	8						11	4	3			9					6				
2	9	5	6	7	8				11		10	4	3												
2	9	5	6	7	8				11		10	4	3												
2	9	5	6	7	8						11	4	3									10			
2	9	5	6	7	8						11	4	3									10			
2		5	4	7	9				11				6									10	3	8	
2	4	5		7					11				3							9	6	10		8	
2		5	4	7	8								6					9		11		10	3		
2		5	4	7									6		9					11		10	3	8	
2	8	5	4	7			10						6		9					11			3		
2		5	4	7	8						11		6							9		10	3		
2		5	4		9				7		11		6									10	3	8	
2			4						7		11		6				5				9	10	3	8	
2		5	4		9				7		11		6									10	3	8	
2		5	4		9				7		11		6									10	3	8	
2		5		7	8				11			6	3			9					4	10			1

Ramshaw	McLain	Odell	Harper	Smillie	Rees	Phillips	Forrester	Taylor	Dean	Rowden	Adams, E	Hudson	Denial	Parker	Fraser	Collins	Quartermain	Adams, D	Johnston	Eele	Blizzard	Bowie	Parsons	Bidois	Otter
2	4	5	6	7	8	9		11					3					10							

Ramshaw	McLain	Odell	Harper	Smillie	Rees	Phillips	Forrester	Taylor	Dean	Rowden	Adams, E	Hudson	Denial	Parker	Fraser	Collins	Quartermain	Adams, D	Johnston	Eele	Blizzard	Bowie	Parsons	Bidois	Otter
3	4	5	6		8	9		11	7		10														
3	4	5	6	7	8	9		11			10														

Ramshaw	McLain	Odell	Harper	Smillie	Rees	Phillips	Forrester	Taylor	Dean	Rowden	Adams, E	Hudson	Denial	Parker	Fraser	Collins	Quartermain	Adams, D	Johnston	Eele	Blizzard	Bowie	Parsons	Bidois	Otter
45	24	35	38	32	36	24	6	15	25	1	31	20	24	2	3	4	6	6	6	10	12	12	9	7	1
	6	1	3	4	10	13		4	8	2	6					1		1	1	2		1		1	

League Table

	P	W	D	L	F	A	Pts
Kettering Town	42	28	10	4	106	47	66
Bedford Town	42	25	8	9	89	52	58
Weymouth	42	22	10	10	92	71	54
Cheltenham Town	42	19	15	8	73	46	53
Gravesend & Northfleet	42	21	11	10	74	58	53
Lovell's Athletic	42	21	7	14	99	84	49
Guildford City	42	18	11	13	68	49	47
Hereford United	42	19	8	15	96	60	46
Headington United	42	19	7	16	64	61	45
Gloucester City	42	18	8	16	74	72	44
Hastings United	42	17	9	16	70	58	43
Worcester City	42	16	10	16	81	80	42
Dartford	42	16	10	16	79	88	42
Chelmsford City	42	16	9	17	73	85	41
Tonbridge	42	14	12	16	74	65	40
Yeovil Town	42	14	11	17	83	85	39
Bath City	42	15	8	19	56	78	38
Exeter City Reserves	42	10	10	22	52	89	30
Merthyr Tydfil	42	9	11	22	72	95	29
Kidderminster Harriers	42	7	10	25	60	83	24
Barry Town	42	6	11	25	39	84	23
Llanelli	42	5	8	29	39	123	18

1957-58

Southern League

Manager: Harry Thompson

Did you know that?

New signings at the start of the season included Eddie McIlvenny from Waterford. McIlvenney had been the captain of the USA team that had beaten England 1–0 in the World Cup Finals in Brazil.

On 24 August the new Beech Road stand was opened by FA treasurer Denis Follows. The supporters' club had contributed over £33,000 to the funding of the stand.

Chairman Vic Couling, who had been chairman since August 1949, resigned on 27 November because of ill-health. He was succeeded by Ron Coppock.

Headington United received two votes for election to the Football League at the League's AGM.

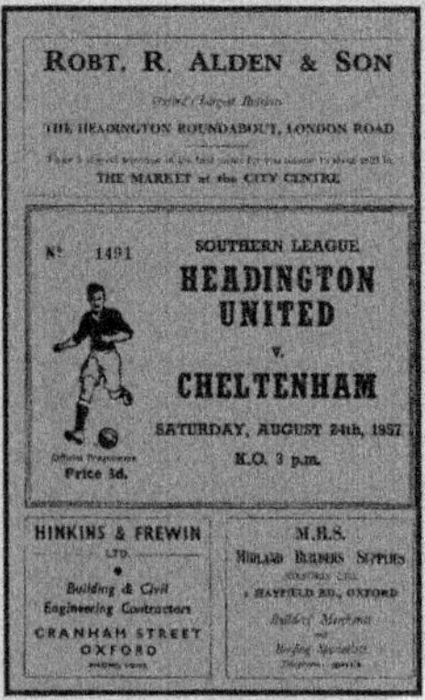

Match No.	Date		Opponents	Result	(F-A)	Scorers	At
1	24/08/1957	H	Cheltenham Town	W	2-0	Rees, Gibson	
2	28/08/1957	H	Tonbridge	W	5-2	Gibbs, Cross (3), Gibson	
3	31/08/1957	A	Hereford United	L	0-3		
4	14/09/1957	A	Bath City	L	0-5		
5	18/09/1957	A	Tonbridge	W	3-1	Cross (2) (1 pen), McCall	
6	28/09/1957	H	Chelmsford City	L	2-3	Eele, Odell	
7	30/09/1957	A	Worcester City	L	0-4		
8	09/10/1957	H	Barry Town	W	7-2	Cross (2), Rees (3), Denial (2)	
9	12/10/1957	A	Exeter City Reserves	W	3-2	McCall (2), Cotton	
10	23/10/1957	H	Hastings United	D	1-1	Cross	
11	26/10/1957	A	Weymouth	L	1-2	McCall	
12	09/11/1957	A	Kettering Town	L	3-4	Harper, Odell, Gibson	
13	16/11/1957	H	Gloucester City	W	3-1	Leach, Cross, Gibson	
14	20/11/1957	H	Lovell's Athletic	W	2-1	Rees, McCall	
15	23/11/1957	A	Lovell's Athletic	L	1-2	Cross	
16	27/11/1957	H	Bedford Town	L	1-2	Love	
17	30/11/1957	H	Worcester City	W	2-1	Denial, McCall	
18	07/12/1957	A	Poole Town	D	1-1	Cross	
19	14/12/1957	H	Guildford City	W	4-1	Love, Cross (2) (1 pen), Denial	
20	21/12/1957	A	Cheltenham Town	L	2-4	Hyde (og), Rees	
21	25/12/1957	A	Kidderminster Harriers	W	3-1	Love, Cross, Rees	
22	26/12/1957	H	Kidderminster Harriers	W	3-0	Love (2), Cross	
23	28/12/1957	H	Hereford United	W	2-1	Cross (pen), Rees	
24	04/01/1958	A	Merthyr Tydfil	L	2-3	Cross, Rees	
25	11/01/1958	A	Barry Town	W	3-2	Love, Denial, Gibson	
26	18/01/1958	H	Bath City	W	4-1	Cross (2), Rees (2)	
27	25/01/1958	H	Merthyr Tydfil	W	5-0	Lowe (og), Leach, Cross (2) (1 pen), Gibson	
28	01/02/1958	A	Bedford Town	L	1-2	Denial	
29	08/02/1958	A	Chelmsford City	L	1-3	Love	
30	19/02/1958	H	Gravesend & Northfleet	D	1-1	Cross	
31	22/02/1958	H	Exeter City Reserves	D	1-1	Cross	
32	01/03/1958	A	Dartford	L	1-3	Cross	
33	08/03/1958	H	Weymouth	W	3-1	Harper, Rees, Dean	
34	15/03/1958	A	Hastings United	D	2-2	Eele, Dean	
35	22/03/1958	H	Kettering Town	D	1-1	Dean	
36	26/03/1958	H	Dartford	L	3-4	Cotton (3)	
37	29/03/1958	A	Gloucester City	W	3-2	Cross, Gibson, Cotton	
38	07/04/1958	H	Yeovil Town	D	1-1	Leach	
39	19/04/1958	H	Poole Town	W	4-3	Leach (2), Rees, McCall (pen)	
40	26/04/1958	A	Guildford City	L	1-3	Leach	
41	28/04/1958	A	Gravesend & Northfleet	L	1-3	Leach	
42	03/05/1958	A	Yeovil Town	L	1-2	Gibson	

FA Cup

Pre	07/09/1957	H	Aylesbury United	W	3-0	Cross, Gibson, McCall
1Q	21/09/1957	H	Banbury Spencer	W	1-0	Denial
2Q	05/10/1957	A	Oxford City	W	2-0	Rees, McCall
3Q	19/10/1957	H	Marlow	W	1-0	Denial
4Q	02/11/1957	H	Margate	L	0-2	

Southern League Cup

Q 1L	04/09/1957	A	Chelmsford City	L	1-2	Rees
Q 2L	11/09/1957	H	Chelmsford City	L	3-4*	Cross, Gibson, Cotton
R1	08/01/1958	A	Guildford City	L	0-2	

* Headington qualified on goal average

Total appear

Total

Leach	Harper	Odell	Pembery	Gibson	Rees	Cross	Gibbs	Love	Otter	Denial	Cotton	McCall	Quartermain	McIlvenny	Eale	Simpson	Dean	Bidois	Peters	Youngman	Norris
3	4	5	6	7	8	9	10	11													
3	4	5	6	7	8	9	10	11													
3	4	5	6	7	8	9	10	11	1												
3	4	5		7		9	10			6	8	11									
3	4	5			8	9		11	1	10		7	6								
3		5			8			11	1	10		7	6	4	9						
3	4	5						11	1	10	9	7	6			8					
6	4	5		7	8	9			1	10	2	11									
6	4	5		7	8	9			1	10	2	11									
6	4			7		9	8		1	10	2	11	5								
6	4	5			8	9			1	10	2	11					7				
6	4	5		7	8	9				10	2	11									
6	4			7	10	9		11	1	5	2							8			
6	4			7	8	9		11	1	5	2	10									
6	4			7	9	8		11	1	5	2	10									
6	4	5		7	8	9		11		10	2										
6	4	5				9	8	11		10	2	7									
6	4	5		7	8	9		11		10				2							
6	4	5		7	8	9		11		10				2							
6	4	5		7	8	9		11		10	2										
6	4	5			8	9		11		10	2	7									
6	4	5		7	8	9		11			2	10									
6	4	5		7	8	9		11			2	10									
6	4	5		7	8	9		11			2	10									
6	4			7	8	9		11		10			5	2							
6	4			7	8	9		11		10			5	2							
6	4			7	8	9		11		10			5	2							
6	4			7	8	9		11		10			5	2							
6	4			7	8			11		10	3	9	5	2							
6	4		3		8	9		11		10	7		5	2					1		
6	4		3		8	9		11		10		7	5	2					1		
6	4		3		10	9		11		8		7	5	2							
10	4		3	7	9			11		6			5	2			8				
10	4		3	7				11		6			5	2	9		8				
10	6		3	7		9		11					5	2			8	4			
10	6		3	7				11			9		5	2				4		8	
6	4		3	8		7		11	1	5	9			2	10						
6	4		3	7		8		11			9		5	2	10				1		
10	4		3	7	8			11		6		9	5	2					1		
10	4		3	7	8			11		6		9	5	2					1		
10	4	5	3	7	8			11		6		9		2					1		
6	4	5	10	7	8			11		3				2					1		9

3	4	5		7	8	9	10			2		11				6					
3	4	5			8	9		11	1	10			6			7					
6	4	5		7	8	9			1	10	2	11									
6	4	5		7	8	9			1	10	2	11		3							
6	4	5		7	8	9			1	10	2	11									

3	4	5	6	7	8	9	10		1			11									
3	4	5	6	7		9		11			8	10									
6	4	5				9		11		10	7	8	9	2							

50	49	30	18	39	39	40	8	39	17	39	27	29	21	23	4	3	4	3	7	1	1
7	2	2		10	15	27	1	7		8	6	9			2		3				

League Table

	P	W	D	L	F	A	Pts
Gravesend & Northfleet	42	27	5	10	109	71	59
Bedford Town	42	25	7	10	112	64	57
Chelmsford City	42	24	9	9	93	57	57
Weymouth	42	25	5	12	90	61	55
Worcester City	42	23	7	12	95	59	53
Cheltenham Town	42	21	10	11	115	66	52
Hereford United	42	21	6	15	79	56	48
Kettering Town	42	18	9	15	99	76	45
Headington United	42	18	7	17	90	83	43
Poole Town	42	17	9	16	82	81	43
Hastings United	42	13	15	14	78	77	41
Gloucester City	42	17	7	18	70	70	41
Yeovil Town	42	16	9	17	70	84	41
Dartford	42	14	9	19	66	92	37
Lovell's Athletic	42	15	6	21	60	83	36
Bath City	42	13	9	20	65	64	35
Guildford City	42	12	10	20	58	92	34
Tonbridge	42	13	7	22	77	100	33
Exeter City Reserves	42	12	8	22	60	94	32
Barry Town	42	11	9	22	72	101	31
Kidderminster Harriers	42	10	10	22	60	101	30
Merthyr Town	42	9	3	30	69	137	21

1958-59

Southern League North-West Zone

Manager: Harry Thompson then Arthur Turner

Did you know that?

Harry Thompson was sacked on 26 November, after a run of 10 games that yielded only four points and with the club knocked out of the Southern League Cup by Dartford. The team was managed by a committee of board members until Arthur Turner, recently sacked by First Division Birmingham City, took over on New Year's Day.

Three months after starting with Headington, Turner was approached by First Division Leeds United, then without a manager, to become their new boss. After a hastily convened board meeting, United topped Leeds' offer and Turner stayed in Oxford.

Arthur Turner's first signing was Wolves' Cyril Beavon, who went on to make over 460 appearances for the Us, the fifth-highest number. Turner also signed Maurice Kyle, who played almost 450 games for United.

Headington's 10th-place finish in the Southern League North-West Zone was just enough for them to earn entry into the following season's Southern League Premier Division, on goal average.

In the summer of 1959, United bought the Manor from the Manor Ground Company for £10,000.

Headington polled seven votes in their bid to join the Football League.

Match No.	Date		Opponents	Result	(F-A)	Scorers
1	23/08/1958	A	Hereford United	L	1-2	Jackson
2	30/08/1958	H	Boston United	W	5-2	Williams (og), Rees, Dickson (3)
3	06/09/1958	H	Wellington Town	W	3-0	Jackson, Rees, Dickson
4	13/09/1958	A	Merthyr Tydfil	L	1-3	Jackson
5	27/09/1958	A	Barry Town	L	4-5	Leach, Gibson (3)
6	01/10/1958	H	Cheltenham Town	L	0-1	
7	11/10/1958	A	Rugby Town	L	1-4	Jackson
8	25/10/1958	A	Gloucester City	L	1-2	Rees
9	06/11/1958	H	Burton Albion	L	2-3	Jackson, Dickson
10	08/11/1958	A	Worcester City	L	0-2	
11	29/11/1958	H	Wisbech Town	W	5-1	Rees (2), Gibson (2), Dickson
12	13/12/1958	H	Rugby Town	W	5-0	Love (2), Rees, Gibson, Dickson
13	20/12/1958	H	Hereford United	W	2-1	Rees, Gibson
14	26/12/1958	H	Corby Town	W	7-3	Love, Neilson (og), Morris (og),Jackson, Rees (2), Dickson
15	27/12/1958	A	Corby Town	W	6-2	Jackson (2), Rees (2), Gibson (2)
16	03/01/1959	A	Boston United	L	1-2	Gibson
17	17/01/1959	A	Wellington Town	D	3-3	Love, Denial (pen), Dickson
18	31/01/1959	H	Merthyr Tydfil	L	0-1	
19	07/02/1959	A	Cheltenham Town	L	1-5	Rees
20	14/02/1959	H	Barry Town	W	2-1	Love, Denial (pen)
21	21/02/1959	A	Bath City	W	3-2	Rees, Gibson, Dickson
22	25/02/1959	H	Lovell's Athletic	W	2-1	Jackson, Denial
23	28/02/1959	H	Gloucester City	W	3-1	Jackson, Gibson, Dickson
24	07/03/1959	A	Lovell's Athletic	D	1-1	Love
25	14/03/1959	H	Worcester City	L	0-1	
26	21/03/1959	A	Nuneaton Borough	D	2-2	Rees, Thomson
27	30/03/1959	A	Kidderminster Harriers	L	0-2	
28	31/03/1959	H	Nuneaton Borough	L	1-3	Shields
29	04/04/1959	A	Wisbech Town	W	3-1	Denial (pen), Gibson, Thomson
30	11/04/1959	H	Kettering Town	W	2-0	Harper, Gibson
31	18/04/1959	A	Burton Albion	W	2-1	Thomson, Gibson
32	22/04/1959	H	Bath City	W	1-0	Jackson
33	25/04/1959	H	Kidderminster Harriers	W	4-0	Jackson (2), Gibson, Dickson
34	27/04/1959	A	Kettering Town	L	2-3	Beavon, Adams

Southern League Inter-Zone Competition

1	08/10/1958	A	Tonbridge	W	4-3	Love, Gibson, Dickson (2)
2	22/10/1958	H	Guildford City	W	3-2	Love, Jackson (2)
3	22/11/1958	A	Guildford City	L	0-1	
4	26/11/1958	A	Hastings United	L	0-4	
5	10/01/1959	H	Hastings United	L	1-2	Rees
6	21/01/1959	A	Gravesend & Northfleet	L	0-3	
7	18/02/1959	H	Gravesend & Northfleet	W	2-0	Rees, Dickson
8	04/03/1959	H	Tonbridge	W	3-1	Boulton, Gibson (2)

FA Cup

1Q	20/09/1958	H	Windsor & Eton	W	7-0	Leach, Gibson, Dickson (2), Jackson (3)
2Q	04/10/1958	H	Oxford City	W	3-2	Jackson (2), Dickson
3Q	18/10/1958	A	Maidenhead United	W	6-1	Dickson (2), Leach (2), Jackson, Denial (pen)
4Q	01/11/1958	A	Wealdstone	W	4-2	Love, Jackson, Dickson (2)
R1	15/11/1958	H	Margate	W	3-2	Jackson, Rees, Dickson
R2	06/12/1958	A	Peterborough United	L	2-4	Rees (2)

Southern League Cup

Q 1L	03/09/1958	A	Cheltenham Town	W	2-0	Dickson (2)
Q 2L	10/09/1958	H	Cheltenham Town	W	2-0	Dickson (2)
R1	19/11/1958	A	Dartford	L	0-2	

Total appear

Total

McDonald	Harper	Quartermain	Cross	Gibson	Rees	Jackson	Holder	Love	Denial	Stables	Dickson	Aldous	Peters	Oldham	Leach	Wilkie	Styles	Beavon	Smith, C	Adams	Kyle	Otter	Boulton	Thomson	Shields	Clark	Vickers
3	4	5	6	7	8	9	10	11																			
3	4		6		8	9		11	5	7	10																
3	4		6		8	9		11	5	7	10																
3	4		6	8		9		11		7	10	5															
3	4		6	7		9		11	5		10		1	2	8												
3	4		6	7		9		11	5		10		1		8												
3			4	7	8	9		11	5		10				6												
	4			7	8	9		11	5		10	2			6	3											
	4			7	8	9		11	5		10				6	3											
	4			7	8	9		11	5		10				6	3											
3			4	7	8	9		11	5		10				6	2											
3			4	7	9	8		11	5		10				6	2											
3			4	7	9	8		11	5		10				6	2											
3			4	7	9	8		11	5		10				6	2											
3			4	7	9	8		11	5		10				6	2											
3			4	7	9	8		11	5		10				6	2											
3				7	9	8		11	5		10				6	2	4										
			4	7	9		8	11	5						6	2		3	10								
		5		7	9	8		11			10				6	2	4	3									
				7	9	8		11	6		10						4	2		3	5						
			4	7	9	8		11	6		10							2		3	5	1					
			4	7	9	8		11	6		10							2		3	5	1					
			4	7		8		11	6		10							2		3	5	1	9				
			4	7	8			11	6		10							2		3	5	1	9				
			4	7		8		11	6		10							2		3	5	1	9				
			4		9			11	6		8							2		3	5	1	7	10			
					8			11	6								4	2		3	5	1	7	10	9		
			4	7				11	6		8		1					2		3	5			10	9		
	4			7				11	6		8		1					2		3	5			10		9	
	4			7		8		11	6		10		1					2		3	5			9			
	4			7		9		11	6		8		1					2		3	5			10			
	4			7		9		11	6		8		1					2		3	5			10			
	4			7		9		11	6		8		1					2		3	5			10			
	4			7		9		11	6		8		1					2		3	5			10			

McDonald	Harper	Quartermain	Cross	Gibson	Rees	Jackson	Holder	Love	Denial	Stables	Dickson	Aldous	Peters	Oldham	Leach	Wilkie	Styles	Beavon	Smith, C	Adams	Kyle	Otter	Boulton	Thomson	Shields	Clark	Vickers
3			4	7	8			11	5		10				6											9	
3	4			7	8	9		11	5		10				6												
3			4		8	9		11	5	7	10				6	2											
3			4	7	8	9		11	5		10				6	2											
3			4	7	9			11	5		10				6	2											8
				7	9	8		11	5		10				6	2	4	3									
			4	7	9	8		11	6		10							2		3	5	1					
			4	7		8		11	6		10							2		3	5	1	9				

McDonald	Harper	Quartermain	Cross	Gibson	Rees	Jackson	Holder	Love	Denial	Stables	Dickson	Aldous	Peters	Oldham	Leach	Wilkie	Styles	Beavon	Smith, C	Adams	Kyle	Otter	Boulton	Thomson	Shields	Clark	Vickers
3	4		6	7		9		11			10	5	1	2	8												
3	4		6	7	8	9		11	5		10																
3				7	8	9		11	5		10			4	6												
	4			7	8	9		11	5		10	2			6	3											
	4			7	8	9		11	5		10				6	3											
3			4	7	8	9		11	5		10				6	2											

McDonald	Harper	Quartermain	Cross	Gibson	Rees	Jackson	Holder	Love	Denial	Stables	Dickson	Aldous	Peters	Oldham	Leach	Wilkie	Styles	Beavon	Smith, C	Adams	Kyle	Otter	Boulton	Thomson	Shields	Clark	Vickers
3	4		6		8	9		11	5	7	10																
3	4		6		8	9		11		7	10	5															
	4			7	8	9		11	5		10				6	3											

McDonald	Harper	Quartermain	Cross	Gibson	Rees	Jackson	Holder	Love	Denial	Stables	Dickson	Aldous	Peters	Oldham	Leach	Wilkie	Styles	Beavon	Smith, C	Adams	Kyle	Otter	Boulton	Thomson	Shields	Clark	Vickers
25	23	2	32	44	37	43	2	51	46	6	48	5	10	3	27	20	5	20	1	17	17	9	6	9	2	2	1
	1			20	19	23		9	5		27				4			1		1			1	2	1		

League Table

	P	W	D	L	F	A	Pts
Hereford United	34	22	5	7	80	37	49
Kettering Town	34	20	7	7	83	63	47
Boston United	34	18	8	8	73	47	44
Cheltenham Town	34	20	4	10	65	47	44
Worcester City	34	19	4	11	74	47	42
Bath City	34	17	5	12	89	62	39
Wellington Town	34	15	9	10	74	58	39
Nuneaton Borough	34	17	5	12	76	66	39
Wisbech Town	34	16	5	13	77	54	37
Headington United	34	16	3	15	76	61	35
Barry Town	34	15	5	14	64	67	35
Merthyr Tydfil	34	16	3	15	54	59	35
Gloucester City	34	12	6	16	50	65	30
Corby Town	34	10	8	16	59	79	28
Lovell's Athletic	34	10	3	21	51	70	23
Rugby Town	34	7	6	21	45	93	20
Kidderminster Harriers	34	7	3	24	42	94	17
Burton Albion	34	3	3	28	41	104	9

1959-60

Southern League Premier Division

Manager: Arthur Turner

Did you know that?

At the end of this season the FA overruled Oxford City's opposition to Headington's proposed name change, and they became Oxford United FC.

Joining the club in pre-season were Ron and Graham Atkinson, both previously with Aston Villa. Graham became the club's youngest debutant since it became professional in 1949. He was 16 years and 108 days old.

Bath City's 13-point lead over runners-up Headington United was a record margin for the Southern League.

Geoff Denial's 32 goals made him United's record goalscorer in a season. His record of scoring in seven consecutive games has yet to be beaten by a United player, as has his record of scoring in nine consecutive away games.

Headington received ten votes for election to the Southern League, but it was Peterborough United who were elected in place of Gateshead.

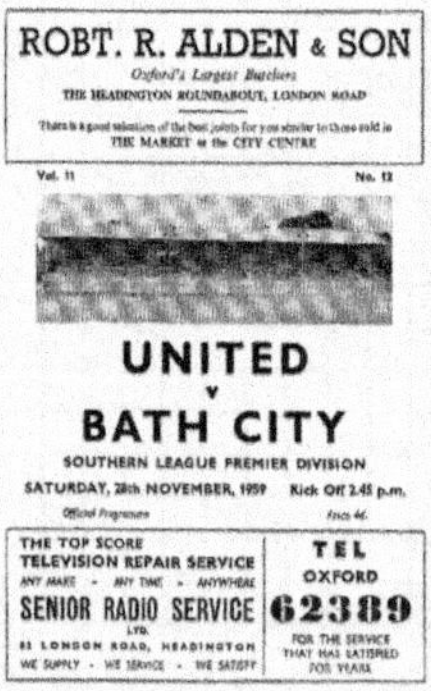

Match No.	Date		Opponents	Result	(F-A)	Scorers
1	22/08/1959	A	Weymouth	W	3-2	Love, Thomson, McInnes
2	26/08/1959	H	Wisbech Town	W	4-1	Love, Denial (pen), Gibson, Thomson
3	29/08/1959	H	Hereford United	D	1-1	Love
4	05/09/1959	A	Kettering Town	D	1-1	McInnes
5	12/09/1959	H	Chelmsford City	D	0-0	
6	16/09/1959	A	Wisbech Town	W	2-1	Love, Denial
7	19/09/1959	A	Chelmsford City	W	2-1	Rivers, Denial
8	21/09/1959	A	Cambridge City	W	3-2	Rivers, Denial, Thomson
9	26/09/1959	H	Cheltenham Town	W	1-0	R Atkinson
10	03/10/1959	A	Worcester City	D	1-1	Denial
11	10/10/1959	A	Poole Town	W	1-0	Denial
12	17/10/1959	H	King's Lynn	W	3-2	Brown (og), Denial, Dickson
13	24/10/1959	A	Yeovil Town	W	4-2	Jones, Donnelly, Denial, Thomson
14	07/11/1959	A	Tonbridge	L	1-2	Denial
15	21/11/1959	A	Bedford Town	L	2-3	Smith, Thomson
16	28/11/1959	H	Bath City	W	3-1	Jones, Denial (2)
17	05/12/1959	A	Boston United	L	1-2	Dickson
18	12/12/1959	H	Gravesend & Northfleet	W	2-1	Love, Thomson
19	19/12/1959	H	Weymouth	D	1-1	Denial
20	26/12/1959	H	Barry Town	W	2-1	Denial, Dickson
21	28/12/1959	A	Barry Town	W	6-2	Jones (2), Dolman (og), Denial (3)
22	02/01/1960	A	Hereford United	W	3-2	Smith, Grieve, Dickson
23	09/01/1960	H	Dartford	W	2-0	Veitch (og), Dickson
24	23/01/1960	H	Hastings United	W	1-0	Grieve
25	30/01/1960	A	Dartford	L	0-2	
26	06/02/1960	H	Cambridge City	W	3-2	Denial (3)
27	20/02/1960	H	Worcester City	L	2-3	Denial (2)
28	24/02/1960	A	Cheltenham Town	L	1-6	Love
29	27/02/1960	H	Poole Town	W	3-0	Denial (2), Dickson
30	05/03/1960	A	King's Lynn	L	1-2	Smith
31	12/03/1960	H	Yeovil Town	W	2-0	G Atkinson, Denial
32	19/03/1960	A	Hastings United	L	0-1	
33	26/03/1960	H	Tonbridge	W	4-1	Smith, Denial, Grieve, Dickson
34	30/03/1960	H	Kettering Town	L	1-3	R Atkinson
35	09/04/1960	H	Bedford Town	D	2-2	Jones, Thomson
36	11/04/1960	A	Nuneaton Borough	L	0-4	
37	15/04/1960	A	Wellington Town	W	1-0	Grieve
38	16/04/1960	A	Bath City	L	0-3	
39	18/04/1960	H	Wellington Town	W	3-0	Denial (2) (1 pen), Thomson
40	23/04/1960	H	Boston United	D	1-1	Dickson
41	27/04/1960	H	Nuneaton Borough	D	1-1	Thomson
42	30/04/1960	A	Gravesend & Northfleet	W	3-1	Rivers (2), Denial

FA Cup

4Q	31/10/1959	A	Cambridge City	W	3-2	Denial (3)
R1	14/11/1959	A	Enfield	L	3-4	Rivers, Denial (pen), Mathers

Southern League Cup

Q 1L	02/09/1959	H	Chelmsford City	D	1-1	G Atkinson
Q 2L	09/09/1959	A	Chelmsford City	D	1-1	R Atkinson
R1	25/11/1959	H	Hereford United	W	3-0	Jones, B Smith, Thomson
R2	13/01/1960	A	Chelmsford City	L	0-1	

Total appear

Total

Adams	Atkinson, R	Kyle	Denial	Flood	Thomson	McInnes	Dickson	Love	Gibson	Feehan	Harper	Aries	Shields	Mathers	Rivers	Atkinson, G	Jones	Smith, B	Donnelly	McDonald	Medlock	Selby	Grieve	Doughty	Shipperley	Puffett	Quartermain	McLaughlin
3	4	5	6	7	8	9	10	11																				
3	4	5	6		8	9	10	11	7																			
3	4	5	6		8	9	10	11	7																			
3	4	5				9	10	11	7	1	6	8																
3	7	5	6		9	7	10	11		1	4																	
3	4	5	8		7		10	11		1	6		9															
3	8	5	9				10	11		1	4			6	7													
3	4	5	9		8		10	11		1	6				7													
3	8	5	9				10	11		1	4			6	7													
3	4	5	9		7	8	10	11		1				6														
3		5	9		8		10	11	7	1				6			4											
3		5	10		7		8	11		1				6			4	9										
3		5	10		7			11		1				6			4	9	8									
3	4	5	10		7		8	11		1				6				9										
	4		5		10			11		1				6	7		8	9		3								
	4	5	9		7		10	11		1				6			8			3								
	4	5	9		7		10	11		1				6			8			3								
3	4		5		7		10	11						6			8	9			1							
3	4	5	9		7		10	11						6			8				1							
3	4	5	9		7		10	11						6			8				1							
11	4	5	9				10							6			8				1	3	7					
3	4		5		11		10							6			8	9			1		7					
3	4	5	9		11		10							6			8				1		7					
3	4	5	9				10							6			8	11			1		7					
	4		5				10	11						6			8	9			1	3	7					
3	4	5	9		11		10							6			8				1		7					
3	4	5	9				10	11						6			8				1		7					
3	4	5	9		7		10	11						6		8					1							
3	4	5	10		7		8	11					9	6							1							
3	4		5		7		10	11						6			8	9			1							
	4	5	9		11		10							6		8					1		7	3				
3	4	5	9		11		10		7					6		8					1							
3	4	5	10				8		7					6				9			1				11			
3	4						10		7			8		6				9			1				11	5		
3	4		5		9		10	11						6			8						7					
3	4		5		9		10	11	7								8			6								
3	4	5	10		9		8	11	7					6							1							
3	4	5	10		9		8	11	7					6							1							
3	4	5	10		9		8	11	7					6							1							
3	4	5	10		9		8	11	7					6							1							
3	4		9		7		10	11						6		8					1						5	
3	4	5	9		11		10		7					6	8						1							

Adams	Atkinson, R	Kyle	Denial	Flood	Thomson	McInnes	Dickson	Love	Gibson	Feehan	Harper	Aries	Shields	Mathers	Rivers	Atkinson, G	Jones	Smith, B	Donnelly	McDonald	Medlock	Selby	Grieve	Doughty	Shipperley	Puffett	Quartermain	McLaughlin
3	4	5	10		7		8	11		1				6				9										
3	4	5	10		7			11		1				6	8			9										

Adams	Atkinson, R	Kyle	Denial	Flood	Thomson	McInnes	Dickson	Love	Gibson	Feehan	Harper	Aries	Shields	Mathers	Rivers	Atkinson, G	Jones	Smith, B	Donnelly	McDonald	Medlock	Selby	Grieve	Doughty	Shipperley	Puffett	Quartermain	McLaughlin
3	5		6			9	10	11	7	1						8												4
3	8	5	6			9	10	11		1	4		7															
	4		5		7		10	11		1				6			8	9		3								
3	4	5	9		8		10	11									6				1		7					

Adams	Atkinson, R	Kyle	Denial	Flood	Thomson	McInnes	Dickson	Love	Gibson	Feehan	Harper	Aries	Shields	Mathers	Rivers	Atkinson, G	Jones	Smith, B	Donnelly	McDonald	Medlock	Selby	Grieve	Doughty	Shipperley	Puffett	Quartermain	McLaughlin
42	45	37	46	1	37	8	45	38	14	19	7	2	3	37	6	5	21	14	1	5	24	2	10	1	2	1	1	1
	3		32		10	2	8	6	1					1	5	2	6	5	1				4					

League Table

	P	W	D	L	F	A	Pts
Bath City	42	32	3	7	116	50	67
Headington United	42	23	8	11	78	61	54
Weymouth	42	22	9	11	93	69	53
Cheltenham Town	42	21	6	15	82	68	48
Cambridge City	42	18	11	13	81	72	47
Chelmsford City	42	19	7	16	90	70	45
Bedford Town	42	21	3	18	97	85	45
King's Lynn	42	17	11	14	89	78	45
Boston United	42	17	10	15	83	80	44
Wisbech Town	42	17	10	15	81	84	44
Yeovil Town	42	17	8	17	81	73	42
Hereford United	42	15	12	15	70	74	42
Tonbridge	42	16	8	18	79	73	40
Hastings United	42	16	8	18	63	77	40
Wellington Town	42	13	11	18	63	78	37
Dartford	42	15	7	20	64	82	37
Gravesend & Northfleet	42	14	8	20	69	84	36
Worcester City	42	13	10	19	72	89	36
Nuneaton Borough	42	11	11	20	64	78	33
Barry Town	42	14	5	23	78	103	33
Poole Town	42	10	8	24	69	96	28
Kettering Town	42	9	10	23	60	90	28

1960-61

Southern League Premier Division

Manager: Arthur Turner

Did you know that?

In March, United signed Bud Houghton from Southend United for £2,000, a record fee for United. Houghton was to score 75 goals in just over two years, taking him to sixth place in United's top goalscorer chart. Other new signings during the season included Alan Willey and John Shuker.

Houghton scored nine goals in a week in April to ensure that United won the Southern League title.

Tony Jones scored 38 goals to become the side's new record goalscorer for a season.

United's 9–0 win against Wisbech is the club's biggest win since turning professional.

Oxford United received 19 votes in their campaign for election to the Football League. This was a record for a Southern League club.

Match No.	Date		Opponents	Result	(F-A)	Scorers
1	20/08/1960	H	Worcester City	W	3-0	Knight, Simpson, Dickson
2	25/08/1960	A	Romford	D	0-0	
3	27/08/1960	A	Folkestone Town	W	4-0	Simpson, Shipperley (2), McIntosh
4	03/09/1960	H	Wellington Town	W	3-0	Jones (3)
5	10/09/1960	A	Wisbech Town	W	1-0	Denial
6	14/09/1960	H	Romford	W	3-1	Denial, McIntosh (2)
7	17/09/1960	H	Hereford United	D	0-0	
8	21/09/1960	A	Dartford	W	3-1	Jones, Simpson, McIntosh
9	24/09/1960	A	King's Lynn	D	0-0	
10	01/10/1960	H	Guildford City	W	2-1	Knight, Dickson
11	08/10/1960	A	Bath City	D	1-1	Beavon (pen)
12	15/10/1960	H	Cambridge City	W	2-1	Jones, Luke
13	29/10/1960	H	Clacton Town	W	5-1	Jones, Knight, Love, McIntosh (2)
14	12/11/1960	H	Hastings United	W	3-2	Knight, Love, McIntosh
15	19/11/1960	A	Gravesend & Northfleet	W	1-0	Jones
16	03/12/1960	A	Cheltenham Town	W	2-0	McIntosh, Dickson
17	07/12/1960	H	Tonbridge	W	1-0	R Atkinson
18	10/12/1960	H	Wisbech Town	W	9-0	Jones (5), Knight, Luke (2), McIntosh
19	17/12/1960	A	Worcester City	L	2-4	Jones, Harris
20	24/12/1960	A	Bedford Town	L	1-2	Luke
21	26/12/1960	H	Bedford Town	W	3-2	Jones (2), McIntosh
22	31/12/1960	H	Folkestone Town	W	6-1	Jones (3), Love, Luke, McIntosh
23	21/01/1961	H	Dartford	D	1-1	McIntosh
24	28/01/1961	A	Boston United	W	5-1	Jones (3), Luke (2)
25	04/02/1961	A	Hereford United	D	2-2	Love, Luke
26	11/02/1961	H	King's Lynn	W	1-0	Denial
27	18/02/1961	A	Guildford City	L	0-2	
28	25/02/1961	H	Bath City	L	0-2	
29	04/03/1961	A	Cambridge City	D	1-1	McIntosh
30	06/03/1961	A	Chelmsford City	W	2-0	Denial, McIntosh
31	11/03/1961	H	Yeovil Town	D	2-2	Houghton (2)
32	18/03/1961	A	Clacton Town	W	3-0	Houghton, Jones (2)
33	20/03/1961	A	Wellington Town	W	2-0	Jones (2)
34	25/03/1961	H	Chelmsford City	W	3-0	Jones (2), Knight
35	31/03/1961	H	Weymouth	W	3-1	Jones (2), Kyle
36	01/04/1961	A	Tonbridge	D	1-1	McIntosh
37	03/04/1961	A	Weymouth	L	0-3	
38	08/04/1961	H	Gravesend & Northfleet	W	8-2	Houghton (3), Jones (2), Shipperley, Denial, McIntosh
39	12/04/1961	H	Boston United	W	7-2	Houghton (5), Jones, Knight
40	15/04/1961	A	Hastings United	W	3-2	Houghton, Love, McIntosh
41	22/04/1961	H	Cheltenham Town	W	2-1	Jones, Knight
42	26/04/1961	A	Yeovil Town	D	3-3	Houghton, Jones, Love

FA Cup

4Q	22/10/1960	A	Brentwood & Warley	W	4-0	Jones, Love, Mann (og), Denial
R1	05/11/1960	A	Hendon	D	2-2	Jones, Luke
r	09/11/1960	H	Hendon	W	3-2	Jones, Love, McIntosh
R2	26/11/1960	H	Bridgewater Town	W	2-1	Kyle, Dickson
R3	07/01/1961	A	Leicester City	L	1-3	Jones

Southern League Cup

R1/1	29/08/1960	A	Kettering Town	L	0-3	
R1/2	07/09/1960	H	Kettering Town	L	0-1	

Total appear

Total

Tether	Atkinson, R	Kyle	Denial	Knight	McIntosh	Simpson	Dickson	Love	Mathers	Adams	Shipperley	Jones	Luke	Titcombe	Quartermain	Harris	Munro	Houghton	Willey
3	4	5	6	7	8	9	10	11											
3	4	5	10	7	8	9		11	6										
	4	5		7	8	9	10		6	3	11								
3	4	5		7	8	9			6		11	10							
	4	5	9	7	8			11	6	3		10							
	4	5	10	7	8	9		11	6	3									
	4	5	10	7	8	9		11	6	3									
		5	10	7	8	9			6	3	11	4							
	4	5	9	7	8				6	3	11	10							
	4	5		7	8	9	10			3	11	6							
	4	5		7	8	9		11	6	3		10							
	4	5		7	8			11	6	3		10	9						
	4	5		7	8			11	6	3		10	9						
	4			7	8			11	6	3		10	9	5					
	4	5		7			10	11	6	3		8	9						
	4	5		7	8		10	11		3		6	9						
	4	5		7	8		10	11		3		6	9						
	4	5		7	8					3		10	9		6	11			
	4	5		7	8					3		10	9		6	11			
	4	5		7	8					3		10	9		6	11	2		
	4	5	6	7	8			11		3		10	9						
	4	5	6	7	8			11		3		10	9						
	4	5	6	7	8			11		3		10	9						
3	4	5	6	7	8			11				10	9						
3	4	5	6	7	8			11				10	9						
3	4		6	7	8			11				10	9	5					
3	4	5	6	7	8			11				10	9						
3	4	5			8			11			10	6	9			7			
3	4		6	7	8			11				10		5				9	
3	4	6	10	7	8			11						5				9	
3	4		6	7	8			11						5				9	10
3	4	6		7	8			11				10		5				9	
3	4	6		7	8			11				10		5				9	
3	4	6		7	8			11				10		5				9	
3	4	6		7	8			11				10		5				9	
3	4	6		7	8			11				10		5				9	
3	4	6		7	8			11				10		5				9	
3	4		6	7	8						11	10		5				9	
3	4	6		7	8			11				10		5				9	
3	4	6		7	8			11				10		5				9	
3	4	6		7	8			11				10		5				9	
3		6	4	7	8			11				10		5				9	

Tether	Atkinson, R	Kyle	Denial	Knight	McIntosh	Simpson	Dickson	Love	Mathers	Adams	Shipperley	Jones	Luke	Titcombe	Quartermain	Harris	Munro	Houghton	Willey
	4	5	9	7	8			11	6	3		10							
	4	5		7	8			11	6	3		10	9						
	4	5		7	8			11	6	3		10	9						
	4	5		7	8		10	11	6	3			9						
	4	5	6	7	8			11		3		10	9						

Tether	Atkinson, R	Kyle	Denial	Knight	McIntosh	Simpson	Dickson	Love	Mathers	Adams	Shipperley	Jones	Luke	Titcombe	Quartermain	Harris	Munro	Houghton	Willey
	4	5		7	8	9	10		6	3	11								
3	4	5		7	8	9		11	6			10							

Tether	Atkinson, R	Kyle	Denial	Knight	McIntosh	Simpson	Dickson	Love	Mathers	Adams	Shipperley	Jones	Luke	Titcombe	Quartermain	Harris	Munro	Houghton	Willey
23	47	44	21	48	48	11	8	39	19	26	8	40	21	16	3	4	1	14	1
	1	2	6	8	18	3	4	8			3	38	9			1		13	

League Table

	P	W	D	L	F	A	Pts
Oxford United	42	27	10	5	104	43	64
Chelmsford City	42	23	11	8	91	54	57
Yeovil Town	42	23	9	10	109	54	55
Hereford United	42	21	10	11	83	67	52
Weymouth	42	21	9	12	78	63	51
Bath City	42	18	14	10	74	52	50
Cambridge City	42	16	12	14	101	71	44
Wellington Town	42	17	9	16	66	68	43
Bedford Town	42	18	7	17	94	97	43
Folkestone Town	42	18	7	17	75	86	43
King's Lynn	42	13	16	13	68	66	42
Worcester City	42	15	11	16	69	69	41
Clacton Town	42	15	11	16	82	83	41
Romford	42	13	15	14	66	69	41
Guildford City	42	14	11	17	65	66	39
Tonbridge	42	16	6	20	79	85	38
Cheltenham Town	42	15	7	20	81	82	37
Gravesend & Northfleet	42	15	7	20	75	101	37
Dartford	42	13	11	18	57	90	37
Hastings United	42	8	9	25	60	99	25
Wisbech Town	42	9	6	27	58	112	24
Boston United	42	6	8	28	61	123	20

1961-62

Southern League Premier Division

Manager: Arthur Turner

Did you know that?

Bud Houghton beat Tony Jones' goalscoring record set the previous season by scoring 43 League and Cup goals. This has yet to be beaten for United.

Houghton set two other goalscoring records, scoring in 12 consecutive home games, and scoring in 22 home games overall.

In the bid to replace Accrington Stanley, who had resigned from the Football League, the League's Associate members gave Oxford 27 votes, 15 more than the runner-up, Wigan Athletic, and one more than all the other candidates combined. At the following day's Football League AGM, Oxford polled 39 votes, with runners-up Wigan receiving five votes. This was the biggest winning margin by a newcomer.

Match No.	Date		Opponents	Result	(F-A)	Scorers	At
1	19/08/1961	A	Weymouth	W	3-0	Houghton, Jones, Love	
2	26/08/1961	H	Guildford City	L	0-2		
3	02/09/1961	H	Tonbridge	W	4-1	Jones, Love, Willey (2)	
4	09/09/1961	A	King's Lynn	W	7-2	Houghton (3), Jones, Knight, Willey (2)	
5	11/09/1961	A	Worcester City	W	3-1	Houghton, Love, Willey	
6	16/09/1961	H	Cambridge United	D	2-2	G Atkinson, Knight	
7	20/09/1961	H	Worcester City	W	5-0	G Atkinson, Houghton, Knight, Willey (2)	
8	23/09/1961	A	Kettering Town	L	2-3	Knight, Willey	
9	28/09/1961	A	Bedford Town	L	0-1		
10	30/09/1961	H	Gravesend & Northfleet	W	8-0	G Atkinson (2), Houghton, Love, Willey (4)	
11	03/10/1961	A	Cambridge City	W	2-1	Beavon (pen), Willey	
12	14/10/1961	H	Folkestone Town	W	3-1	G Atkinson, Love, Willey	
13	28/10/1961	H	Bexley Heath & Welling	W	6-0	R Atkinson, Houghton (2), Willey (2), Nekrews (og)	
14	11/11/1961	H	King's Lynn	W	1-0	Houghton	
15	18/11/1961	A	Romford	W	6-3	Houghton (3), Knight, Love, Willey	
16	02/12/1961	A	Chelmsford City	D	1-1	Houghton	
17	09/12/1961	H	Yeovil Town	W	2-1	Beavon (pen), Houghton	
18	16/12/1961	H	Weymouth	W	4-1	Houghton (2), Love, Willey	
19	26/12/1961	H	Hereford United	W	2-0	G Atkinson, Houghton	
20	10/01/1962	A	Guildford City	D	1-1	Bisset (og)	
21	20/01/1962	H	Bedford Town	W	4-2	Houghton (2), Willey (2)	
22	27/01/1962	A	Clacton Town	W	6-0	G Atkinson (2), Jones, Knight, Love, Willey	
23	03/02/1962	A	Cambridge United	L	1-2	Houghton	
24	07/02/1962	H	Clacton Town	D	2-2	Houghton (2)	
25	10/02/1962	H	Cheltenham Town	D	1-1	Houghton	
26	17/02/1962	A	Gravesend & Northfleet	W	6-0	G Atkinson (3), Houghton (2), Knight	
27	22/02/1962	A	Hereford United	L	1-2	Knight	
28	24/02/1962	H	Merthyr Tydfil	W	3-0	Houghton (2), Knight	
29	03/03/1962	A	Folkestone Town	W	4-1	Houghton (2), McIntosh (2)	
30	10/03/1962	H	Chelmsford City	W	2-0	Houghton, Jones	
31	14/03/1962	A	Cheltenham Town	W	2-1	G Atkinson, Knight	
32	17/03/1962	A	Bexley Heath & Welling	W	4-1	G Atkinson (2), Houghton (2)	
33	24/03/1962	H	Wellington Town	W	1-0	Houghton	
34	28/03/1962	A	Tonbridge	W	3-2	Houghton (2), Willey	
35	02/04/1962	A	Wellington Town	L	1-3	G Atkinson	
36	07/04/1962	H	Romford	W	4-0	G Atkinson, Jones, Knight (2)	
37	09/04/1962	A	Merthyr Tydfil	W	3-0	Houghton, Jones, Knight	
38	14/04/1962	H	Kettering Town	W	3-0	G Atkinson, Houghton, Jones	
39	20/04/1962	A	Bath City	W	1-0	Love	
40	21/04/1962	H	Cambridge City	L	0-1		
41	23/04/1962	H	Bath City	L	1-3	Willey	
42	28/04/1962	A	Yeovil Town	L	3-4	G Atkinson (2), Houghton	

FA Cup

4Q	21/10/1961	H	Salisbury City	W	3-2	Houghton (3)
R1	04/11/1961	A	Brentford	L	0-3	

Southern League Cup

Q1/1	29/08/1961	A	Cambridge City	L	2-3	Houghton, Jones
Q1/2	06/09/1961	H	Cambridge City	L	0-3	

Total appear

Total

Tether	Atkinson, R	Kyle	Jones	Knight	McIntosh	Houghton	Luke	Love	Willey	Denial	Quartermain	Atkinson, G	Jacques	Beeby	Cullen	Johnstone	Bottoms	Cornwell
3	4	5	6	7	8	9	10	11										
3	4	5	6	7	8	9		11	10									
3	4	5	6	7	8			11	10	9								
3	4	5	6	7		9	8	11	10									
3		4	6	7		9		11	10		5	8						
3	4	5	6	7		9		11	10			8						
3		6	4	7		9		11	10		5	8						
3	4	6	8	7		9		11	10		5							
3	4	5		7		9		11	10			8	6					
3	4	5	6	7		9		11	10			8						
	4	5	6	7		9		11	10			8		3				
	4	5	6	7				11	10	9		8		3				
	4	5	6	7	8	9		11	10					3				
	4	5	6	7	8	9		11				10		3				
	4	5	6	7		9		11	10			8		3				
	4	5	6	7		9		11	10		3	8			1			
	4	5	6	7		9		11	10		3	8			1			
	4	5	6	7		9		11	10		3				1	8		
	4	5	6	7		9		11	10		3	8			1			
	4	5	6	7		9		11		10	3	8			1			
	4	5	6	7	8	9		11	10		3				1			
	4	5	6	7		9		11	10		3	8			1			
	4	5	6	7		9		11	10		3	8			1			
	4	5	6	7		9		11	10		3	8			1			
	4	5	6	7	8	9		11	10		3							
	4		6	7		9		11		5	3	8					10	
	4	5	6	7		9		11			3	8					10	
	4	5	6	7		9		11			3	8					10	
	4	5	6	7	8	9		11		10	3							
	4	5	10	7		9		11		6	3	8						
	4	5		7	10	9		11		6	3	8						
	4	5	6	7		9		11			3	8						10
	4	5	10	7		9		11		6	3	8						
	4	5	6	7		9		11	10		3	8						
	4	5	6	7		9		11	10		3	8						
	4	5	10	7		9		11		6	3	8						
	4	5	10	7		9		11		6	3	8						
	4	5	10	7		9		11		6	3	8						
	4	5	10	7		9		11		6	3	8						
	4	5		7				11	9	6	3	8						10
	4	5	10	7		9			11	6	3	8						
	4	5		7		9			11	6	3	8					10	

Tether	Atkinson, R	Kyle	Jones	Knight	McIntosh	Houghton	Luke	Love	Willey	Denial	Quartermain	Atkinson, G	Jacques	Beeby	Cullen	Johnstone	Bottoms	Cornwell
	4	5	6	7	8	9		11	10					3				
	4	5	6	7	8	9		11	10					3				

Tether	Atkinson, R	Kyle	Jones	Knight	McIntosh	Houghton	Luke	Love	Willey	Denial	Quartermain	Atkinson, G	Jacques	Beeby	Cullen	Johnstone	Bottoms	Cornwell
3	4	5	10	7		9		11	8	6								
3	4		6	7			8	11	9		5	10						

Tether	Atkinson, R	Kyle	Jones	Knight	McIntosh	Houghton	Luke	Love	Willey	Denial	Quartermain	Atkinson, G	Jacques	Beeby	Cullen	Johnstone	Bottoms	Cornwell
12	44	44	42	46	11	42	3	44	31	16	31	33	1	7	9	1	4	2
	1		9	13	2	43		9	23			19						

League Table

	P	W	D	L	F	A	Pts
Oxford United	42	28	5	9	118	46	61
Bath City	42	25	7	10	102	69	57
Guildford City	42	24	8	10	79	49	56
Yeovil Town	42	23	8	11	97	59	54
Chelmsford City	42	19	12	11	74	60	50
Weymouth	42	20	7	15	80	64	47
Kettering Town	42	21	5	16	90	84	47
Hereford United	42	21	2	19	81	68	44
Cambridge City	42	18	8	16	70	71	44
Bexleyheath & Welling	42	19	5	18	69	75	43
Romford	42	15	9	18	62	69	39
Cambridge United	42	13	12	17	76	78	38
Wellington Town	42	14	10	18	75	78	38
Gravesend & Northfleet	42	17	4	21	59	92	38
Bedford Town	42	16	5	21	73	79	37
Worcester City	42	15	7	20	51	64	37
Merthyr Tydfil	42	13	11	18	62	80	37
Clacton Town	42	13	10	19	74	91	36
Tonbridge	42	10	14	18	71	92	34
King's Lynn	42	12	8	22	59	74	32
Folkestone Town	42	12	6	24	64	103	30
Cheltenham Town	42	9	7	26	48	86	25

1962-63

Division Four

Manager: Arthur Turner

Did you know that?

Oxford paid Wolves a club record fee of £5,000 for Maurice Kyle, who had been effectively on loan to United since joining in February 1959.

In December this was beaten when United paid QPR £5,500 for centre-forward Bernard Evans.

Ken McCluskey became the club's first full-time secretary, allowing Arthur Turner to concentrate on his managerial duties.

United's first season as a Football League club saw well-established players Graham Atkinson, Owen Medlock and Geoff Denial all leave at the end of the campaign.

In the summer of 1963 work began on building a new stand at the London Road end of the ground, while new floodlight pylons replaced the old scaffold poles.

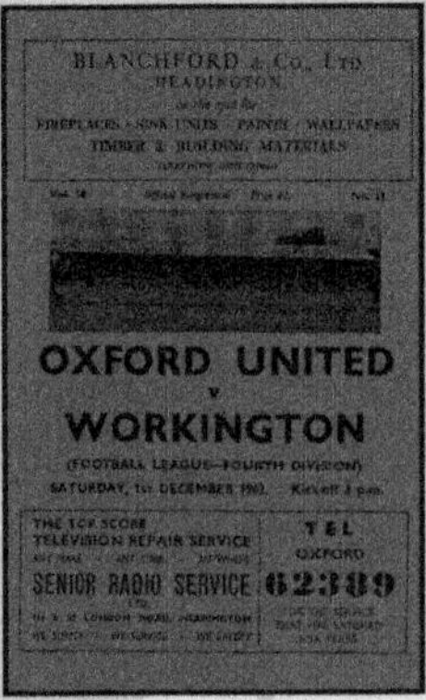

Match No.	Date		Opponents	Result	(F-A)	Scorers	A
1	18/08/1962	A	Barrow	L	2-3	G Atkinson, Houghton	
2	22/08/1962	H	Lincoln City	W	2-1	Houghton, Willey	
3	25/08/1962	H	Hartlepools United	W	6-2	Colfar, Houghton (2), Knight, Willey (2)	
4	29/08/1962	A	Lincoln City	L	0-1		
5	01/09/1962	A	Darlington	L	1-2	Love	
6	05/09/1962	H	Torquay United	D	1-1	Willey	
7	08/09/1962	H	Southport	D	0-0		
8	12/09/1962	A	Torquay United	D	2-2	G Atkinson, Houghton	
9	15/09/1962	A	Aldershot	D	0-0		
10	19/09/1962	H	Oldham Athletic	D	1-1	Houghton	
11	22/09/1962	H	Newport County	W	5-1	Houghton, Jones (4)	
12	26/09/1962	A	Oldham Athletic	L	0-2		
13	29/09/1962	A	Doncaster Rovers	L	2-4	Houghton, Jones	
14	03/10/1962	H	Stockport County	D	1-1	Ricketts (og)	
15	06/10/1962	H	Gillingham	L	2-3	Houghton, Jones	
16	08/10/1962	A	Stockport County	D	1-1	Colfar	
17	13/10/1962	A	Crewe Alexandra	L	2-3	Colfar, Houghton	
18	20/10/1962	H	Chester City	W	3-0	Cornwell (2), Shuker	
19	26/10/1962	A	York City	W	2-1	Houghton, Willey	
20	10/11/1962	A	Rochdale	L	1-2	Knight	
21	17/11/1962	H	Chesterfield	D	0-0		
22	01/12/1962	H	Workington	W	2-1	Jones, Knight	
23	08/12/1962	A	Mansfield Town	L	2-3	Love (2)	
24	15/12/1962	H	Barrow	W	4-1	R Atkinson, Cornwell, Jones, Knight	
25	22/12/1962	A	Hartlepools United	W	2-1	G Atkinson (2)	
26	09/03/1963	A	Chester City	L	1-2	Shuker	
27	11/03/1963	A	Tranmere Rovers	L	0-3		
28	16/03/1963	H	York City	L	0-2		
29	20/03/1963	H	Doncaster Rovers	D	3-3	Evans, Love, Bratt (og)	
30	23/03/1963	A	Brentford	L	0-4		
31	30/03/1963	H	Exeter City	L	0-3		
32	04/04/1963	H	Tranmere Rovers	D	2-2	Bowstead, Houghton	
33	06/04/1963	A	Chesterfield	L	0-1		
34	12/04/1963	H	Bradford City	W	2-1	Bowstead, Houghton	
35	13/04/1963	H	Rochdale	D	0-0		
36	15/04/1963	A	Bradford City	W	4-1	R Atkinson, Beavon, Cornwell (2)	
37	19/04/1963	A	Workington	D	0-0		
38	27/04/1963	H	Mansfield Town	W	3-0	Willey (3)	
39	01/05/1963	H	Aldershot	D	1-1	Houghton	
40	04/05/1963	H	Darlington	W	4-2	Houghton, Jones, Shuker, Willey	
41	08/05/1963	A	Exeter City	D	1-1	Houghton	
42	11/05/1963	H	Brentford	W	2-1	R Atkinson, Shuker	
43	15/05/1963	H	Crewe Alexandra	D	0-0		
44	18/05/1963	A	Southport	L	2-4	Shuker, Darvell (og)	
45	20/05/1963	A	Gillingham	L	1-2	Love	
46	23/05/1963	A	Newport County	L	0-1		

FA Cup

R1	04/11/1962	A	Falmouth	W	2-1	G Atkinson, Houghton
R2	24/11/1962	A	King's Lynn	W	2-1	Houghton, Jones
R3	30/01/1963	A	Arsenal	L	1-5	Jones

League Cup

R1	03/09/1962	A	Torquay United	L	0-2	

Total appear

Total

Quartermain, Pat	Atkinson, R	Kyle	Jones	Knight	Atkinson, G	Houghton	Cornwell	Colfar	Willey	Shuker	Love	Richards	Denial	Jacques	Buck	Bowstead	Evans	Higgins	Bryan	Harrington
3	4	5	6	7	8	9	10	11												
3	4	5	6	7	8	9		11	10											
3	4	5	6	7	8	9		11	10											
3	4	5	6	7		8		11	10	9										
3	4	5	6	7		9			10	8	11									
3	4	5	6	7	8	9		11	10											
3	4	5	6	7		9		11	8			1	10							
3	4	5	6	7	8	9		11	10			1								
3	4	5	6	7	8	9		11	10			1								
3	4	5	10	7	8	9					11	1	6							
3	4	5	10	7	8	9					11	1	6							
3	4	5	10	7	8	9					11	1	6							
3	4	5	10	7	8	9		11				1		6						
3	4	5	6	7	8	9					11	1			10					
3	4	5	10	7		9		11				1	6		8					
3	4	5	6	7	8	9		11		10		1								
3	4	5	6	7		9		11		10		1				8				
3	4	5	6	7		9	8	11		10										
3	4	5	6	7		9	8	11	10											
3	4	5	6	7	8	9		11	10											
3	4	5	6	7	8	9	10	11												
3	4	5	10	7		9					11		6			8				
3	4	5	6	7	8	10					11						9			
3	4	5	6	7	8	9	10				11									
3	4	5	6	7	8	9	10				11									
3	4	5	6	7		10				8	11						9			
3	4	5	6	7		9	8	11	10			1								
3	4	5	6	7		9	8		10		11	1								
3	4	5	10	7		8					11	1		6			9			
3		5	4	7		8				10	11			6			9			
3	4	5	10		8	9			7		11			6						
3	4	5	6	7		10					11	1				8	9			
3	4	6		7		10					11	1				8	9	5		
3	6	5		7		9			10		11	1				8			4	
3	6	5		7					10		11	1			8		9		4	
3	4	5	6	7			8		10	9	11	1								
3	4	5	6	7			8		10	9		1								11
3	4	5	6	7		9			10	8		1								11
3	4	5	6	7		8			10	9	11	1								
3	4	5	6	7		8			10	9	11	1								
3	4	5		7		8	9		10	6		1								11
3	4	5		7		8			10	9		1		6						11
3	4	5		7		8			10	9		1		6						11
3	4			7		8			10	9		1		6				5		11
3	4	5	6	7					10	8	11						9			
3	4	5	6	7		8			10	9	11									

Quartermain, Pat	Atkinson, R	Kyle	Jones	Knight	Atkinson, G	Houghton	Cornwell	Colfar	Willey	Shuker	Love	Richards	Denial	Jacques	Buck	Bowstead	Evans	Higgins	Bryan	Harrington
3	4	5	6	7	8	9		11	10											
3	4	5	10	7		9		11	8				6							
3	4	5	6	7	8	10					11						9			

Quartermain, Pat	Atkinson, R	Kyle	Jones	Knight	Atkinson, G	Houghton	Cornwell	Colfar	Willey	Shuker	Love	Richards	Denial	Jacques	Buck	Bowstead	Evans	Higgins	Bryan	Harrington
3	4	5	6	7	8	9			10		11									

Quartermain, Pat	Atkinson, R	Kyle	Jones	Knight	Atkinson, G	Houghton	Cornwell	Colfar	Willey	Shuker	Love	Richards	Denial	Jacques	Buck	Bowstead	Evans	Higgins	Bryan	Harrington
50	49	49	43	49	21	46	11	19	29	18	25	27	7	7	3	5	9	2	2	6
	3		11	4	5	18	5	3	9	5	5					2	1			

League Table

	P	W	D	L	F	A	Pts
Brentford	46	27	8	11	98	64	62
Oldham Athletic	46	24	11	11	95	60	59
Crewe Alexandra	46	24	11	11	86	58	59
Mansfield Town	46	24	9	13	108	69	57
Gillingham	46	22	13	11	71	49	57
Torquay United	46	20	16	10	75	56	56
Rochdale	46	20	11	15	67	59	51
Tranmere Rovers	46	20	10	16	81	67	50
Barrow	46	19	12	15	82	80	50
Workington	46	17	13	16	76	68	47
Aldershot	46	15	17	14	73	69	47
Darlington	46	19	6	21	72	87	44
Southport	46	15	14	17	72	106	44
York City	46	16	11	19	67	62	43
Chesterfield	46	13	16	17	70	64	42
Doncaster Rovers	46	14	14	18	64	77	42
Exeter City	46	16	10	20	57	77	42
Oxford United	46	13	15	18	70	71	41
Stockport County	46	15	11	20	56	70	41
Newport County	46	14	11	21	76	90	39
Chester	46	15	9	22	51	66	39
Lincoln City	46	13	9	24	68	89	35
Bradford City	46	11	10	25	64	93	32
Hartlepools United	46	7	11	28	56	104	25

1963-64

Division Four

Manager: Arthur Turner

Did you know that?

United became the first club from Division Four to reach the FA Cup quarter-finals, beating Blackburn Rovers, second in the First Division, 3–1 in the fifth round.

The Blackburn game set a new ground attendance record of 21,700. This was beaten for the quarter-final tie against Preston North End, which was watched by 22,750, a figure that has not been exceeded.

Bud Houghton played his last game for Oxford in October, before joining Lincoln City for £6,000. Also leaving the club in October were Johnny Love and Bernard Evans.

In November, United paid a new club record transfer fee of £8,500 for centre-forward Bill Calder, from Bury. Keith Havenhand joined from Derby County for £6,000 the following month.

Match No.	Date		Opponents	Result	(F-A)	Scorers
1	24/08/1963	A	Chester City	W	2-0	Harrington, Houghton
2	28/08/1963	H	Doncaster Rovers	L	0-1	
3	31/08/1963	H	York City	D	4-4	R Atkinson, Colfar, Willey (2)
4	07/09/1963	A	Barrow	D	1-1	Harrington
5	10/09/1963	A	Doncaster Rovers	W	1-0	Cornwell
6	14/09/1963	H	Rochdale	D	1-1	Jones
7	18/09/1963	H	Brighton & Hove Albion	L	1-3	Longbottom
8	20/09/1963	A	Carlisle United	L	1-2	Evans
9	27/09/1963	A	Workington	L	1-2	Cornwell (pen)
10	01/10/1963	A	Brighton & Hove Albion	L	1-2	Cornwell (pen)
11	05/10/1963	H	Newport County	W	2-1	Knight (2)
12	08/10/1963	A	Bradford Park Avenue	L	2-5	Evans, Harrington
13	12/10/1963	H	Halifax Town	D	2-2	Harrington, Knight
14	16/10/1963	H	Bradford Park Avenue	W	2-1	Cornwell, Knight
15	18/10/1963	A	Tranmere Rovers	W	3-1	Atkinson, Knight, Willey
16	21/10/1963	A	Stockport County	D	0-0	
17	26/10/1963	H	Darlington	W	5-0	Harrington, Longbottom (4)
18	30/10/1963	H	Stockport County	W	1-0	Willey
19	02/11/1963	A	Hartlepools United	L	1-2	Cornwell
20	09/11/1963	H	Exeter City	L	0-2	
21	23/11/1963	H	Gillingham	W	3-1	R Atkinson, Knight, Longbottom
22	30/11/1963	A	Lincoln City	L	2-3	Calder, Linnecor (og)
23	14/12/1963	H	Chester City	W	2-1	Calder, Jones
24	21/12/1963	A	York City	W	2-0	Harrington, Havenhand
25	26/12/1963	H	Torquay United	W	1-0	Willey
26	28/12/1963	A	Torquay United	D	0-0	
27	11/01/1964	H	Barrow	D	0-0	
28	18/01/1964	A	Rochdale	D	0-0	
29	01/02/1964	H	Carlisle United	L	1-2	Longbottom
30	08/02/1964	H	Workington	W	2-1	Calder, Longbottom
31	22/02/1964	A	Halifax Town	L	1-3	Calder
32	02/03/1964	A	Newport County	L	0-1	
33	07/03/1964	A	Darlington	L	0-3	
34	11/03/1964	H	Bradford City	D	1-1	Hartland
35	14/03/1964	H	Hartlepools United	W	5-1	Calder, Harrington, Hartland (2), Longbottom
36	21/03/1964	A	Exeter City	L	2-3	Calder, Longbottom
37	27/03/1964	A	Chesterfield	D	0-0	
38	28/03/1964	H	Aldershot	D	1-1	Calder
39	30/03/1964	H	Chesterfield	L	1-2	Longbottom
40	11/04/1964	H	Lincoln City	W	2-0	Calder, Knight
41	13/04/1964	A	Southport	D	1-1	Longbottom
42	15/04/1964	A	Gillingham	L	0-2	
43	18/04/1964	A	Bradford City	L	1-2	Calder
44	22/04/1964	A	Aldershot	L	0-2	
45	25/04/1964	H	Southport	D	0-0	
46	29/04/1964	H	Tranmere Rovers	L	0-2	

FA Cup

R1	16/11/1963	H	Folkestone Town	W	2-0	Longbottom, Peplow (og)
R2	07/12/1963	H	Kettering Town	W	2-1	Calder, Longbottom
R3	04/01/1964	H	Chesterfield	W	1-0	Willey
R4	25/01/1964	H	Brentford	D	2-2	Calder, Willey
r	28/01/1964	A	Brentford	W	2-1	Calder (2)
R5	15/02/1964	H	Blackburn Rovers	W	3-1	Calder, Jones (2)
QF	29/02/1964	H	Preston North End	L	1-2	Jones

League Cup

R1	04/09/1963	H	Exeter City	L	0-1	

Total appear

Total

Beavon	Atkinson, R	Kyle	Jones	Knight	Shuker	Houghton	Willey	Harrington	Quartermain	Colfar	Longbottom	Higgins	Cornwell	Evans	Love	Richards	Bryan	Bowstead	Fearnley	Hartland	Calder	Havenhand	Buck	Fahy
3	4	5	6	7	8	9	10	11																
2	4	5	6	7	8	9	10	11	3															
2	4	5	6			9	10	11	3	7	8													
3		5	6		4	9	7	11			8	2	10											
3		5	6		4	9	10	11			7	2	8											
3		5	6		4	9	10	11			7	2	8											
3	4	5	6	7		10					8			9	11									
3	4	5	6	7		10					8			9	11	1								
3	6	5	10	7		9		11					8			1	4							
2	4	5	6	7				11	3				10	9		1		8						
2	4	5	6	7		10		11	3					9				8	1					
2	4	5	6	7		10		11	3					9				8	1					
2	4	5	6	7	10			11	3				9						1	8				
2	4	5	6	7			10	11	3				9						1	8				
2	4	5	6	7			10	11	3		8		9						1					
2	4	5	6	7			10	11	3		8		9						1					
2	4	5	6	7			10	11	3		8		9						1					
2	4	5	6	7			10	11	3		8		9						1					
2	4	5	6	7			10	11	3		8		9						1					
	4	5	6	7			10	11	3		8		9						1					
2	4	5	6	7			10	11	3		8								1		9			
2	4	5	6	7	11		10		3		8								1		9			
2	4	5	6	7			10	11	3		8								1		9			
2	4	5	6	7			10	11	3										1		9	8		
2	4	5	6	7			10	11	3										1		9	8		
2	4	5	6	7			10	11	3										1		9	8		
2	4	5	6	7			10	11	3										1		9	8		
2	4	5	6	7			10	11	3										1		9	8		
2		5	4	7	6		10	11	3		8								1		9			
2	4	5	6	7			10	11	3		8								1		9			
2	4	5	10	7	6			11	3										1		9	8		
2	4	5	6	7				11	3		8		10						1		9			
2	4	5	10	7	6			11	3		8								1		9			
2	4	5	10	7	6			11	3											8	9			
2	4		6	7				11	3		8	5								10	9			
2	4	5	6	7				11	3		8									10	9			
2	4	5	6	7			10	11	3		8										9			
2		5	6	7			10	11	3		8									4	9			
2	4	5	6					11	3		9									10		8	7	
2	4	5	10	7				11	3		8									6	9			
2	4	5	10	7				11	3		8									6	9			
2	4	5	10	7				11	3		8									6	9			
2	4	5	10		6		8	11	3												7			9
2	4	5	6	7			10	11	3		8										9			
2	4	5	6				10	11	3		8		7								9			
2	4	5	6	7			10	11	3		8										9			

Beavon	Atkinson, R	Kyle	Jones	Knight	Shuker	Houghton	Willey	Harrington	Quartermain	Colfar	Longbottom	Higgins	Cornwell	Evans	Love	Richards	Bryan	Bowstead	Fearnley	Hartland	Calder	Havenhand	Buck	Fahy
3	4	5	6	7			9	11			8								1	10				
2	4	5	6	7			10	11	3		8								1		9			
2	4	5	6	7			10	11	3										1		9	8		
2		5	4		6		7	11	3		10								1		9	8		
2		5	4	7	6		10	11	3		8								1		9			
2	4	5	10	7	6			11	3		8								1		9			
2	4	5	10	7	6			11	3		8								1		9			

Beavon	Atkinson, R	Kyle	Jones	Knight	Shuker	Houghton	Willey	Harrington	Quartermain	Colfar	Longbottom	Higgins	Cornwell	Evans	Love	Richards	Bryan	Bowstead	Fearnley	Hartland	Calder	Havenhand	Buck	Fahy
2	4	5	6	7		9	10	11	3		8													

Beavon	Atkinson, R	Kyle	Jones	Knight	Shuker	Houghton	Willey	Harrington	Quartermain	Colfar	Longbottom	Higgins	Cornwell	Evans	Love	Richards	Bryan	Bowstead	Fearnley	Hartland	Calder	Havenhand	Buck	Fahy
53	47	53	54	46	16	12	35	51	46	1	37	4	15	5	2	3	1	3	30	11	31	9	1	1
	3		5	7		1	7	7		1	14		5	2						3	14	1		

League Table

	P	W	D	L	F	A	Pts
Gillingham	46	23	14	9	59	30	60
Carlisle United	46	25	10	11	113	58	60
Workington	46	24	11	11	76	52	59
Exeter City	46	20	18	8	62	37	58
Bradford City	46	25	6	15	76	62	56
Torquay United	46	20	11	15	80	54	51
Tranmere Rovers	46	20	11	15	85	73	51
Brighton & Hove Albion	46	19	12	15	71	52	50
Aldershot	46	19	10	17	83	78	48
Halifax Town	46	17	14	15	77	77	48
Lincoln City	46	19	9	18	67	75	47
Chester	46	19	8	19	65	60	46
Bradford Park Avenue	46	18	9	19	75	81	45
Doncaster Rovers	46	15	12	19	70	75	42
Newport County	46	17	8	21	64	73	42
Chesterfield	46	15	12	19	57	71	42
Stockport County	46	15	12	19	50	68	42
Oxford United	46	14	13	19	59	63	41
Darlington	46	14	12	20	66	93	40
Rochdale	46	12	15	19	56	59	39
Southport	46	15	9	22	63	88	39
York City	46	14	7	25	52	66	35
Hartlepools United	46	12	9	25	54	93	33
Barrow	46	6	18	22	51	93	30

1964-65

Division Four

Manager: Arthur Turner

Did you know that?

On 19 December United achieved their record victory in the Football League, beating Barrow 7–0 in front of the season's lowest home attendance of 5,201.

New signings for the start of the season included Rodney Smithson and Colin Booth, for whom United paid Doncaster Rovers £7,500. Also arriving was trainer Ken Fish, previously at Birmingham City. Graham Atkinson returned to Oxford from Cambridge United in December.

Leaving the club were Peter Knight, who joined Reading for £5,000, and Keith Havenhand.

Oxford achieved promotion to the Third Division on the final day of the season, thanks to Doncaster's win over Tranmere.

Match No.	Date		Opponents	Result	(F-A)	Scorers	A
1	22/08/1964	H	Crewe Alexandra	W	4-2	Calder (3), Longbottom	
2	25/08/1964	A	Brighton & Hove Albion	D	0-0		
3	29/08/1964	A	Barrow	D	1-1	Paton	
4	04/09/1964	H	Hartlepools United	W	3-0	Booth, Longbottom, Morris	
5	09/09/1964	A	Lincoln City	W	2-0	Booth, Calder	
6	12/09/1964	A	Rochdale	D	3-3	Booth (2), Havenhand	
7	16/09/1964	H	Lincoln City	W	2-0	Calder (pen), Havenhand	
8	19/09/1964	H	Millwall	L	0-2		
9	26/09/1964	A	Bradford City	L	1-2	Calder	
10	28/09/1964	A	Stockport County	D	0-0		
11	03/10/1964	H	Chester City	W	3-2	Booth, Calder, Hartland	
12	07/10/1964	H	Stockport County	W	2-0	Calder, Knight	
13	10/10/1964	H	Halifax Town	W	1-0	R Atkinson	
14	12/10/1964	A	York City	L	1-2	Calder	
15	17/10/1964	A	Notts County	D	0-0		
16	21/10/1964	H	York City	W	2-0	Harrington, Hartland	
17	24/10/1964	H	Chesterfield	W	1-0	Booth	
18	26/10/1964	A	Darlington	L	0-2		
19	31/10/1964	A	Doncaster Rovers	D	2-2	Fahy, Jones	
20	07/11/1964	H	Aldershot	D	0-0		
21	21/11/1964	H	Southport	D	1-1	Booth	
22	28/11/1964	A	Wrexham	D	1-1	Hartland	
23	12/12/1964	A	Crewe Alexandra	D	2-2	G Atkinson, Booth	
24	19/12/1964	H	Barrow	W	7-0	G Atkinson, R Atkinson, Booth (3), Harrington, Willey	
25	26/12/1964	A	Newport County	W	3-0	Booth (2), Morris	
26	02/01/1965	A	Hartlepools United	D	1-1	G Atkinson	
27	09/01/1965	H	Tranmere Rovers	W	1-0	Beavon (pen)	
28	16/01/1965	H	Rochdale	D	2-2	G Atkinson (2)	
29	23/01/1965	A	Millwall	D	2-2	Booth, Willey	
30	30/01/1965	A	Bradford Park Avenue	L	0-1		
31	06/02/1965	H	Bradford City	W	3-1	G Atkinson, Booth (2)	
32	13/02/1965	A	Chester City	L	1-2	G Atkinson	
33	17/02/1965	H	Newport County	W	4-1	Calder (3), Willey	
34	20/02/1965	A	Halifax Town	W	3-1	G Atkinson (2), Booth	
35	27/02/1965	H	Notts County	W	4-0	G Atkinson, Booth (2), Harrington	
36	06/03/1965	A	Chesterfield	L	1-2	G Atkinson	
37	13/03/1965	H	Doncaster Rovers	W	1-0	G Atkinson	
38	20/03/1965	A	Aldershot	L	1-4	Beavon	
39	27/03/1965	H	Bradford Park Avenue	W	3-0	Fahy (3)	
40	31/03/1965	H	Brighton & Hove Albion	D	2-2	Fahy (2)	
41	03/04/1965	A	Southport	W	3-0	Booth (3)	
42	09/04/1965	H	Wrexham	W	4-0	Fahy, Jones (3)	
43	17/04/1965	A	Tranmere Rovers	W	4-2	Fahy, Jones (2), Morris	
44	19/04/1965	H	Torquay United	W	3-0	Booth, Fahy, Jones	
45	21/04/1965	A	Torquay United	D	1-1	Fahy	
46	24/04/1965	H	Darlington	W	1-0	Beavon (pen)	

FA Cup

R1	14/11/1964	H	Mansfield Town	L	0-1	

League Cup

R1	02/09/1964	A	Walsall	D	1-1	Harrington
r	07/09/1964	H	Walsall	W	6-1	R Atkinson, Calder (4) (2 pens), Havenhand
R2	23/09/1964	A	Fulham	L	0-2	

Total appear

Total

Quartermain	Atkinson, R	Kyle	Jones	Morris	Booth	Calder	Longbottom	Harrington	Beavon	Paton	Knight	Havenhand	Rouse	Hartland	Shuker	Fahy	Willey	Hyde	Atkinson, G	Buck
3	4	5	6	7	8	9	10	11												
3	4	5	6	7	8	9	10	11	2											
3	4	5	6	7	8	9		11	2	10										
3	4	5	6	7	8	9	10	11	2											
3	4	5	6		10	9		11	2		7	8								
3	4	5	6		10	9		11	2		7	8								
3	4	5	6		10	9		11	2		7	8	1							
3	4	5	6		10	9		11	2		7	8	1							
3	4	5	6	7	10	9	8	11	2		8									
3	4	5	6	11	10	9			2		7			8						
3	4	5	6		8	9		11	2		7			10						
3	4	5	6		8	9		11	2		7			10						
3	4	5	6		8	9		11	2		7			10						
3	4	5	6		8	9		11	2		7				10					
3	4	5	6		8	9		11	2		7				10					
3	4	5	6	7	8	9		11	2					10						
3	4	5	6	7	8			11	2					10		9				
3	4	5	6	7	10			11	2			8					9			
3	4	5	6	7	8				2					10		9		11		
3	4	5	6	7	10			11		8						9				
3	4	5	6	7	8				2					10			9	11		
3	4	5	6	7	10				2					8	11		9			
3	4	5	6	7	8				2						11		9		10	
3	4	5	6	7	8			11	2								9		10	
3	4	5	6	7	8			11	2								9		10	
3	4	5	6	7	8			11	2								9		10	
3	4	5	6		8	9		11	2								7		10	
3	4	5	6		8	9		11	2								7		10	
3	4	5	6	7	8			11	2								9		10	
3	4	5	6	7	8			11	2								9		10	
3	4	5	6	7	8				2								9	11	10	
3	4	5	6		8			11	2								9	7	10	
3	4	5	6		8	9		11	2								7		10	
3	4	5	6		8	9		11	2								7		10	
3	4	5	6		8	9		11	2								7		10	
3	4	5	6		8	9		11	2								7		10	
	4	5	10			9		11	3						6				8	7
	4	5	6	7	8	9		11	3										10	
3	4	5	6	7	8			11	2							9			10	
3	4	5	6	7	8			11	2							9			10	
3	4	5	10	7	8			11	2						6	9				
3	4	5	10	7	8			11	2						6	9				
3	4	5	10	7	8			11	2						6	9				
3	4	5	10	7	8			11	2						6	9				
3	4	5	10	7	8			11	2						6	9				
3	4	5	10	7	8			11	2						6	9				

Quartermain	Atkinson, R	Kyle	Jones	Morris	Booth	Calder	Longbottom	Harrington	Beavon	Paton	Knight	Havenhand	Rouse	Hartland	Shuker	Fahy	Willey	Hyde	Atkinson, G	Buck
3	4	5	6	7												9	8	11		10

Quartermain	Atkinson, R	Kyle	Jones	Morris	Booth	Calder	Longbottom	Harrington	Beavon	Paton	Knight	Havenhand	Rouse	Hartland	Shuker	Fahy	Willey	Hyde	Atkinson, G	Buck
3	4	5	6	7	8	9	10	11	2											
3	4	5	6		10	9		11	2		7	8								
3	4	5	6	7	10	9		11	2			8								

Quartermain	Atkinson, R	Kyle	Jones	Morris	Booth	Calder	Longbottom	Harrington	Beavon	Paton	Knight	Havenhand	Rouse	Hartland	Shuker	Fahy	Willey	Hyde	Atkinson, G	Buck
48	50	50	50	32	48	27	5	43	47	2	11	7	2	9	11	12	18	5	18	2
	3		7	3	23	16	2	4	3	1	1	3		3		10	3		12	

League Table

	P	W	D	L	F	A	Pts
Brighton & Hove Albion	46	26	11	9	102	57	63
Millwall	46	23	16	7	78	45	62
York City	46	28	6	12	91	56	62
Oxford United	46	23	15	8	87	44	61
Tranmere Rovers	46	27	6	13	99	56	60
Rochdale	46	22	14	10	74	53	58
Bradford Park Avenue	46	20	17	9	86	62	57
Chester	46	25	6	15	119	81	56
Doncaster Rovers	46	20	11	15	84	72	51
Crewe Alexandra	46	18	13	15	90	81	49
Torquay United	46	21	7	18	70	70	49
Chesterfield	46	20	8	18	58	70	48
Notts County	46	15	14	17	61	73	44
Wrexham	46	17	9	20	84	92	43
Hartlepools United	46	15	13	18	61	85	43
Newport County	46	17	8	21	85	81	42
Darlington	46	18	6	22	84	87	42
Aldershot	46	15	7	24	64	84	37
Bradford City	46	12	8	26	70	88	32
Southport	46	8	16	22	58	89	32
Barrow	46	12	6	28	59	105	30
Lincoln City	46	11	6	29	58	99	28
Halifax Town	46	11	6	29	54	103	28
Stockport County	46	10	7	29	44	87	27

1965-66

Division Three

Manager: Arthur Turner

Did you know that?

The club laid on it first Football Special train for the trip to Exeter City on 11 December, with over 200 fans taking advantage.

A record crowd for a League game at the Manor was achieved when 16,074 saw United beaten 3–0 by Swindon Town on 29 January.

Alan Willey became United's first substitute in a competitive game when he replaced Tony Jones at Bristol Rovers on 18 September.

Alan Willey was sold to Millwall for £5,000, while Oxford paid £8,000 to Coventry City for Ken Hale and £4,000 to Chelsea for goalkeeper Jim Barron.

The crowd of 31,992 at Boothferry Park on 11 April was the largest to have watched an Oxford United game.

Trainer Tom Webb, who had been at the club since 1935, retired at the end of the season.

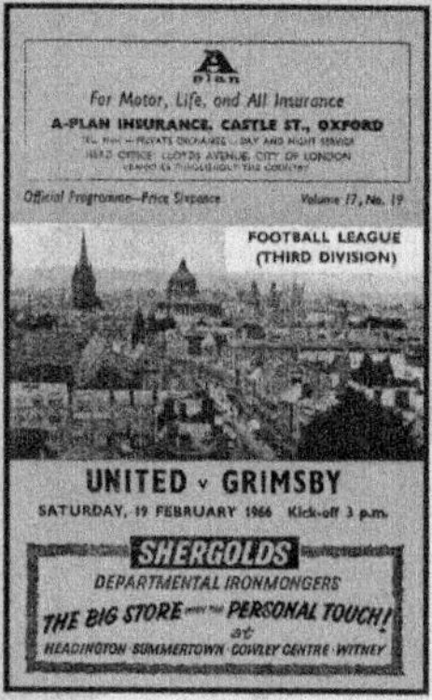

Match No.	Date		Opponents	Result	(F-A)	Scorers	A
1	21/08/1965	A	Swindon Town	D	0-0		
2	25/08/1965	H	Southend United	W	3-2	Fahy (2), Jones	
3	28/08/1965	H	Shrewsbury Town	L	0-1		
4	04/09/1965	A	Grimsby Town	D	1-1	Jones	
5	11/09/1965	H	Brentford	W	2-0	Jones, Shuker	
6	14/09/1965	A	Bournemouth & Boscombe A	D	1-1	Beavon	
7	18/09/1965	A	Bristol Rovers	L	1-3	Jones	
8	25/09/1965	H	York City	W	4-1	G Atkinson, Harrington (2), Willey	
9	01/10/1965	A	Reading	W	1-0	Travers (og)	
10	09/10/1965	H	Mansfield Town	W	4-1	G Atkinson, Harrington, Spelman (pen), Willey	
11	16/10/1965	A	Queen's Park Rangers	W	3-2	Jones, Shuker (2)	
12	23/10/1965	H	Brighton & Hove Albion	D	0-0		
13	30/10/1965	A	Scunthorpe United	W	2-1	G Atkinson, Jones	
14	03/11/1965	H	Bournemouth & Boscombe A	W	2-1	Shuker, Willey	
15	06/11/1965	H	Watford	L	1-2	G Atkinson	
16	20/11/1965	H	Gillingham	L	0-4		
17	22/11/1965	A	Southend United	L	1-2	Jones	
18	27/11/1965	A	Millwall	L	0-2		
19	11/12/1965	A	Exeter City	W	2-1	G Atkinson, Calder	
20	18/12/1965	H	Queen's Park Rangers	L	1-3	R Atkinson	
21	27/12/1965	H	Walsall	W	7-1	G Atkinson (3), Calder, Harrington, Morris, Willey	
22	01/01/1966	A	Mansfield Town	W	4-1	G Atkinson (2), Calder (2)	
23	08/01/1966	H	Oldham Athletic	D	3-3	G Atkinson, Willey (2)	
24	29/01/1966	H	Swindon Town	L	0-3		
25	05/02/1966	A	Shrewsbury Town	L	0-4		
26	11/02/1966	A	Workington	L	1-2	R Atkinson	
27	19/02/1966	H	Grimsby Town	W	2-0	G Atkinson (2)	
28	26/02/1966	A	Brentford	L	1-5	Harrington	
29	05/03/1966	H	Workington	L	0-2		
30	08/03/1966	A	Brighton & Hove Albion	L	0-2		
31	12/03/1966	H	Bristol Rovers	W	1-0	Hale	
32	18/03/1966	A	York City	W	4-1	G Atkinson, Fahy (2), Morris	
33	26/03/1966	H	Reading	W	2-0	G Atkinson, Hale	
34	02/04/1966	A	Watford	D	1-1	Buck	
35	08/04/1966	H	Hull City	L	0-2		
36	09/04/1966	H	Peterborough United	W	1-0	Buck	
37	11/04/1966	A	Hull City	L	1-2	G Atkinson	
38	16/04/1966	A	Gillingham	W	2-1	Hale, Morris	
39	23/04/1966	H	Millwall	W	3-1	Buck, Shuker (2)	
40	27/04/1966	H	Swansea Town	D	2-2	G Atkinson, Morris	
41	30/04/1966	A	Peterborough United	W	3-2	G Atkinson, Shuker (2)	
42	04/05/1966	A	Walsall	D	1-1	Shuker	
43	07/05/1966	H	Exeter City	L	0-1		
44	17/05/1966	A	Swansea Town	L	2-3	G Atkinson, Morris	
45	21/05/1966	A	Oldham Athletic	L	0-3		
46	28/05/1966	H	Scunthorpe United	L	0-3		

FA Cup

R1	13/11/1965	H	Port Vale	D	2-2	Spelman (pen) Calder
R1r	15/11/1965	A	Port Vale	L	2-3	Poole (og), Calder

League Cup

R1	01/09/1965	H	Millwall	L	0-1	

Total appear
Sub appear
Total

Quartermain	Atkinson, R	Kyle	Shuker	Morris	Atkinson, G	Fahy	Jones	Harrington	Booth	Spelman	Hyde	Willey	Smithson	Higgins	Sherratt	Calder	Bryan	Clarke	Hale	Buck	Lloyd	Barron
3	4	5	6	7	8	9	10	11														
3	4	5		7	10	9	6	11	8													
3	4	5		7	10	9	6	11	8													
3	4	5	6		8	9	10			7	11											
3	4	5	6		8	9	10	11		7												
3	4	5	6		8	9	10	11		7												
3	4	5	6		8	9	**10**	11		7		12										
3	4	5	6		8		10	11		7		9										
3	4	5	6		8		10	11		7		9										
3	4	5	6		8		10	11		7		9										
3	4	5	6		8		10	11		7		9										
3	5		6		8		10	11		7		9	4									
3	4		6	7	8		10	11				9		5								
3	4		6		8		10	11		7		9		5								
3	4		6		8		10	11		7		**9**		5	1	12						
3	5		6		10		4	11	8	7					1	9						
3	4		6	7	8	9	10	11						5			2					
3	4		6	7	8	9	10	11						**5**						12		
5	4		10		8		6	11			7					9	2					
5	4		10		8		6	11			7					9	2					
5	4			7	10		6	11				8				9	2					
5	4		12	7	10		6	11				8				9	2					
5	4			7	10		6	11				8				9	2					
3	4	5		7	10		6	11				8				9						
5	4		6		10			11		7		8				9	2					
3	4	5		7	8		10	11							1	9	2	6				
3	4	5	6		8		10	11			7				1	9	2					
3	4	5	6		8		10	11			7				1	9	2					
3	4	5	11		10					7					1	9	2	6	8			
3	4	5	11		10					7					1	9		6	8			
3	4	5		7	10	9	6	**11**		12					1				8			
3	4	5		7	10	9	6	11							1				8			
3	4	5		7	10		6	11							1				8	9		
	4	5		7	10		6	11							1				8	9	3	
	4	5		7	10		6	11											8	9	3	1
	4	5	6	7			10	11											8	9	3	1
	4	5	11	7	10		6												8	9	3	1
	4	5	11	7	10		6												8	9	3	1
	4	5	11	7	10		6												8	9	3	1
	4	5	11	7	10		6												8	9	3	1
	4	5	11	7	10		6												8	9	3	1
	4	5	11	7	10		6												8	9	3	1
	4	5	11	7	10		6												8	9	3	1
	4	5	9	7	10		6	11											8		3	1
3	4	5	9	7	10		6	11											8			1
	4	5		7	10		6	11											8	9	3	1

Quartermain	Atkinson, R	Kyle	Shuker	Morris	Atkinson, G	Fahy	Jones	Harrington	Booth	Spelman	Hyde	Willey	Smithson	Higgins	Sherratt	Calder	Bryan	Clarke	Hale	Buck	Lloyd	Barron
3	6		10				8	11		7			5			9	4					
3	5		6		10		4	11	8	7						9						

Quartermain	Atkinson, R	Kyle	Shuker	Morris	Atkinson, G	Fahy	Jones	Harrington	Booth	Spelman	Hyde	Willey	Smithson	Higgins	Sherratt	Calder	Bryan	Clarke	Hale	Buck	Lloyd	Barron
3	4	5	6		8	9	10	11		7												

Quartermain	Atkinson, R	Kyle	Shuker	Morris	Atkinson, G	Fahy	Jones	Harrington	Booth	Spelman	Hyde	Willey	Smithson	Higgins	Sherratt	Calder	Bryan	Clarke	Hale	Buck	Lloyd	Barron
37	49	34	36	27	47	12	46	39	4	18	5	13	2	5	11	15	12	3	18	12	12	12
			1							1		1				1				1		
	2		9	5	19	4	7	5		2		6				6			3	3		

League Table

	P	W	D	L	F	A	Pts
Hull City	46	31	7	8	109	62	69
Millwall	46	27	11	8	76	43	65
Queen's Park Rangers	46	24	9	13	95	65	57
Scunthorpe United	46	21	11	14	80	67	53
Workington	46	19	14	13	67	57	52
Gillingham	46	22	8	16	62	54	52
Swindon Town	46	19	13	14	74	48	51
Reading	46	19	13	14	70	63	51
Walsall	46	20	10	16	77	64	50
Shrewsbury Town	46	19	11	16	73	64	49
Grimsby Town	46	17	13	16	68	62	47
Watford	46	17	13	16	55	51	47
Peterborough United	46	17	12	17	80	66	46
Oxford United	46	19	8	19	70	74	46
Brighton & Hove Albion	46	16	11	19	67	65	43
Bristol Rovers	46	14	14	18	64	64	42
Swansea Town	46	15	11	20	81	96	41
Bournemouth & Boscombe A	46	13	12	21	38	56	38
Mansfield Town	46	15	8	23	59	89	38
Oldham Athletic	46	12	13	21	55	81	37
Southend United	46	16	4	26	54	83	36
Exeter City	46	12	11	23	53	79	35
Brentford	46	10	12	24	48	69	32
York City	46	9	9	28	53	106	27

1966-67

Division Three

Manager: Arthur Turner

Did you know that?

New signings included Ricky George, later to find fame with Hereford United, and George Kerr, who was signed for £8,000 from Bury.

United's final match of the season, at Ayresome Park, was watched by 39,683, the largest crowd that United had played in front of.

Tony Buck became the club's first goalscoring substitute in the League Cup tie at Peterborough United, after coming on for John Evanson.

At the end of the season United withdrew from the Hellenic League and instead joined the South-East Counties League.

Match No.	Date		Opponents	Result	(F-A)	Scorers
1	20/08/1966	H	Bournemouth & Boscombe A	D	1-1	Morris
2	27/08/1966	A	Swansea Town	W	1-0	Buck
3	03/09/1966	H	Middlesbrough	D	1-1	Kyle
4	06/09/1966	A	Doncaster Rovers	L	1-2	Buck
5	10/09/1966	A	Shrewsbury Town	L	0-1	
6	17/09/1966	H	Colchester United	D	1-1	Kyle
7	24/09/1966	A	Bristol Rovers	L	1-2	Hale
8	28/09/1966	H	Doncaster Rovers	W	6-1	G Atkinson, Beavon, Hale (2), Jones, Morris
9	01/10/1966	H	Reading	L	1-3	G Atkinson
10	08/10/1966	A	Mansfield Town	D	1-1	Morris
11	15/10/1966	H	Grimsby Town	W	3-1	Calder (2), Kerr
12	19/10/1966	H	Workington	W	3-0	Calder, Hale, Kerr
13	22/10/1966	A	Walsall	L	0-2	
14	29/10/1966	H	Peterborough United	L	0-3	
15	05/11/1966	A	Torquay United	L	0-1	
16	12/11/1966	H	Brighton & Hove Albion	L	1-2	Shuker
17	16/11/1966	A	Workington	D	0-0	
18	19/11/1966	A	Darlington	W	2-1	Harrington, Morris
19	03/12/1966	A	Watford	L	0-2	
20	10/12/1966	H	Swindon Town	D	0-0	
21	17/12/1966	A	Bournemouth & Boscombe A	D	0-0	
22	26/12/1966	H	Gillingham	D	1-1	Jones
23	27/12/1966	A	Gillingham	L	1-3	Kerr
24	31/12/1966	H	Swansea Town	L	2-3	Beavon, Harrington
25	14/01/1967	H	Shrewsbury Town	W	2-1	G Atkinson, Jones
26	21/01/1967	A	Colchester United	W	2-1	G Atkinson, Jones
27	04/02/1967	H	Bristol Rovers	W	4-1	G Atkinson (2), Morris (2)
28	11/02/1967	A	Reading	W	2-1	Jones (2)
29	18/02/1967	H	Scunthorpe United	W	2-1	Jones, Kerr (pen)
30	25/02/1967	H	Mansfield Town	W	2-1	G Atkinson, Jones
31	04/03/1967	A	Grimsby Town	L	0-1	
32	10/03/1967	A	Scunthorpe United	D	2-2	G Atkinson, Jones
33	18/03/1967	H	Walsall	L	1-2	G Atkinson
34	24/03/1967	H	Orient	D	0-0	
35	25/03/1967	A	Peterborough United	W	3-2	G Atkinson, Buck, Harrington
36	27/03/1967	A	Orient	L	1-2	Harrington
37	01/04/1967	H	Torquay United	D	2-2	G Atkinson, Jones
38	08/04/1967	A	Brighton & Hove Albion	L	0-2	
39	12/04/1967	H	Oldham Athletic	W	3-1	Harrington, Jones (2)
40	15/04/1967	H	Darlington	W	3-2	G Atkinson, Jones, Morris
41	22/04/1967	A	Queen's Park Rangers	L	1-3	G Atkinson
42	25/04/1967	A	Oldham Athletic	D	1-1	Hale
43	29/04/1967	H	Watford	D	0-0	
44	06/05/1967	A	Swindon Town	L	0-3	
45	13/05/1967	H	Queen's Park Rangers	W	2-1	Shuker (2)
46	16/05/1967	A	Middlesbrough	L	1-4	Harrington

FA Cup

R1	26/11/1966	A	Yeovil Town	W	3-1	G Atkinson, Harrington, Kerr
R2	11/01/1967	H	Bedford Town	D	1-1	G Atkinson
r	16/01/1967	A	Bedford Town	L	0-1	

League Cup

R1	24/08/1966	A	Peterborough United	L	1-2	Buck

Total appea

Sub appea

Total

Quartermain	Atkinson, R	Kyle	Jones	Morris	Hale	Atkinson, G	Evanson	Shuker	Buck	George	Kerr	Harrington	Lloyd	Calder	Clarke	Higgins	Sherratt	Smithson
3	4	5	6	7	8	**9**	10	11	12									
3	4	5	6	7	8			10	9	11								
3	4	5	6	7	8			10	**9**	11					12			
3	4	5	6		8	10		11	9	7								
3	4	5	6		8			11	9	7	10							
3	4	5	6	7	10				9	11	8							
3	4	5	6	7	8	10					9	11						
3	4	5	6	7	8	10					9	11						
3	4	5	6	7	8	10					9	11						
	4	5	6	7	10			11	9		8		3					
	4	5	6	7	10						8	11	3	9				
	4	5	6	7	10						8	11	3	9				
	4	5	6	7	10						8	11	3	9				
	4	5	6	7	10						8	11	3	9				
2		5	4		8	10		7			9	11	3		6			
2	4	5	10		8			11			9	7	3		6			
3	4	5	10	9	8						7	11			6			
3	4	5	10	9	8			12			7	**11**			6			
3		5	4	9	8	10	12	6			7	11						
		5	10	7	8	12		6			9	11	3		4			
3	4			7	8	10		6			9	11				5		
3	4		10	7	8			6			9	11				5		
3	4		7	12	**8**	10		6			9	11				5		
	4		7		8	10		6	9			11	3			5		
3	4	5	10	7	8	9		12				**11**			6		1	
	4	5	10	7		9			8			11			6	2	1	
	4	5	10	7		9		3	12		8	**11**			6		1	
	4	5	10	7		9		3			8	11			6		1	
	4	5	10	7		9		3			8	11			6		1	
	4	5	10	7		9		3	12		8	11			**6**		1	
	6	5	10	7		9		3			8	11					1	4
	4	5	10	7		9		3			8	11			6		1	
12	4	5	10	7		9		3			**8**	11			6		1	
3	4	5	10			9			8	**7**		11			6		1	12
3		5	10	7		8			9			11			6		1	4
3	4	5	10			8	7		9			11			6		1	12
	4	5	10	7		8			9			11	3		6		1	
	4	5	10	7	**8**	9			12			11	3		6		1	
	6	5	8	7		9						11	3		10		1	4
	6	5	8	7		9						11	3		10		1	4
	6	5	10	7	8	9						11	3		4		1	
	6	5	10		8	9	7					11	3				1	4
	4	5	10		8	9	7					11	3		6		1	
		5	10		8	9		6			7	11	3		4		1	
	4	5			10	9		11			8	7	3		6		1	
	4	5			10	9		11			8	7	3		6		1	

Quartermain	Atkinson, R	Kyle	Jones	Morris	Hale	Atkinson, G	Evanson	Shuker	Buck	George	Kerr	Harrington	Lloyd	Calder	Clarke	Higgins	Sherratt	Smithson
3		5	4	9	8	10		6			7	11						
3		5	6		8	10		11	9			7			4		1	
3	6	5	10			9		8		7		11			4		1	

Quartermain	Atkinson, R	Kyle	Jones	Morris	Hale	Atkinson, G	Evanson	Shuker	Buck	George	Kerr	Harrington	Lloyd	Calder	Clarke	Higgins	Sherratt	Smithson
3	4	5	6	7			**10**	8	12			11		9				

Quartermain	Atkinson, R	Kyle	Jones	Morris	Hale	Atkinson, G	Evanson	Shuker	Buck	George	Kerr	Harrington	Lloyd	Calder	Clarke	Higgins	Sherratt	Smithson
25	43	46	47	35	34	35	5	28	13	7	30	43	19	5	27	5	24	5
1				1		1	1	2	5						1			2
		2	13	7	5	15		3	4		5	7		3				

League Table

	P	W	D	L	F	A	Pts
Queen's Park Rangers	46	26	15	5	103	38	67
Middlesbrough	46	23	9	14	87	64	55
Watford	46	20	14	12	61	46	54
Reading	46	22	9	15	76	57	53
Bristol Rovers	46	20	13	13	76	67	53
Shrewsbury Town	46	20	12	14	77	62	52
Torquay United	46	21	9	16	73	54	51
Swindon Town	46	20	10	16	81	59	50
Mansfield Town	46	20	9	17	84	79	49
Oldham Athletic	46	19	10	17	80	63	48
Gillingham	46	15	16	15	58	62	46
Walsall	46	18	10	18	65	72	46
Colchester United	46	17	10	19	76	73	44
Orient	46	13	18	15	58	68	44
Peterborough United	46	14	15	17	66	71	43
Oxford United	46	15	13	18	61	66	43
Grimsby Town	46	17	9	20	61	68	43
Scunthorpe United	46	17	8	21	58	73	42
Brighton & Hove Albion	46	13	15	18	61	71	41
Bournemouth & Boscombe A	46	12	17	17	39	57	41
Swansea Town	46	12	15	19	85	89	39
Darlington	46	13	11	22	47	81	37
Doncaster Rovers	46	12	8	26	58	117	32
Workington	46	12	7	27	55	89	31

1967-68

Division Three

Manager: Arthur Turner

Did you know that?

In the close season United signed Mickey Bullock from Birmingham City for £10,000, a new club record. Also joining were Ken Skeen for £3,500 from Swindon, and Barry Thornley.

Tony Jones left the club for Newport County for £1,500 after making 388 appearances for the Us. Tony Buck also joined Newport, for £2,000.

The FA Cup tie against Chelmsford remains the only occasion that United have had to play a second replay at a neutral ground.

A new Manor League attendance record was set when 17,836 saw United draw 0–0 with Swindon Town on Good Friday, 12 April.

Winning the Third Division title meant that Oxford became the first club to rise from non-League through two divisions in just six seasons.

Match No.	Date		Opponents	Result	(F-A)	Scorers	A
1	19/08/1967	A	Shrewsbury Town	L	0-2		
2	26/08/1967	H	Bury	W	5-4	G Atkinson, Bullock (pen), Jones (2), Thornley	
3	02/09/1967	A	Bournemouth & Boscombe A	L	1-2	G Atkinson	
4	06/09/1967	H	Bristol Rovers	L	0-2		
5	09/09/1967	H	Colchester United	W	3-1	Bullock, Hale (2)	
6	16/09/1967	A	Peterborough United	D	1-1	Clarke	
7	23/09/1967	H	Mansfield Town	W	2-0	Hale (pen), Kerr	
8	26/09/1967	A	Bristol Rovers	D	1-1	Bullock	
9	30/09/1967	A	Watford	L	0-2		
10	04/10/1967	H	Oldham Athletic	W	3-1	Bullock, Jones, Smithson	
11	07/10/1967	H	Reading	W	2-0	Jones, Skeen	
12	14/10/1967	A	Torquay United	D	1-1	Shuker	
13	21/10/1967	H	Grimsby Town	W	2-1	Clarke, Skeen	
14	24/10/1967	A	Oldham Athletic	L	1-3	G Atkinson	
15	28/10/1967	A	Gillingham	L	1-2	G Atkinson	
16	04/11/1967	H	Walsall	W	4-0	Bullock (2), Clarke, Shuker	
17	11/11/1967	A	Northampton Town	D	1-1	Shuker	
18	15/11/1967	H	Bournemouth & Boscombe A	W	3-2	Clarke, Shuker, Skeen	
19	18/11/1967	H	Orient	W	2-0	G Atkinson, Thornley	
20	24/11/1967	A	Tranmere Rovers	D	1-1	Shuker	
21	02/12/1967	H	Stockport County	D	2-2	Shuker (2)	
22	16/12/1967	H	Shrewsbury Town	D	2-2	G Atkinson, Shuker	
23	23/12/1967	A	Bury	D	1-1	Hale	
24	26/12/1967	A	Scunthorpe United	D	1-1	Hale	
25	30/12/1967	H	Scunthorpe United	L	2-3	Clarke, Evanson	
26	20/01/1968	H	Peterborough United	W	3-1	G Atkinson, Bullock, Thornley	
27	27/01/1968	A	Brighton & Hove Albion	D	0-0		
28	03/02/1968	A	Mansfield Town	L	0-1		
29	10/02/1968	H	Watford	W	1-0	Bullock	
30	16/02/1968	A	Southport	L	0-1		
31	24/02/1968	A	Reading	D	1-1	Chapman (og)	
32	02/03/1968	H	Torquay United	W	2-0	G Atkinson, Clarke	
33	09/03/1968	A	Barrow	L	0-3		
34	16/03/1968	A	Grimsby Town	W	1-0	Evanson	
35	23/03/1968	H	Gillingham	W	3-0	G Atkinson, Bullock, Harrington	
36	25/03/1968	A	Colchester United	W	2-1	Harrington, Sloan	
37	29/03/1968	A	Walsall	W	1-0	Sloan	
38	03/04/1968	H	Barrow	W	3-1	Clarke, Shuker, Sloan	
39	06/04/1968	H	Northampton Town	W	1-0	Bullock	
40	12/04/1968	H	Swindon Town	D	0-0		
41	13/04/1968	A	Orient	L	0-1		
42	16/04/1968	A	Swindon Town	D	1-1	G Atkinson	
43	20/04/1968	H	Tranmere Rovers	W	1-0	Skeen	
44	26/04/1968	A	Stockport County	W	4-0	Bullock (2), Clarke, Harrington	
45	04/05/1968	H	Brighton & Hove Albion	W	2-0	G Atkinson, Bullock	
46	11/05/1968	H	Southport	W	1-0	Sloan	

FA Cup

R1	09/12/1967	A	Chelmsford City	D	3-3	Clarke, Shuker, Wilson (og)
r	13/12/1967	H	Chelmsford City	D	3-3	G Atkinson, Bullock, Skeen
r2	18/12/1967	N	Chelmsford City	L	0-1	

League Cup

R1	23/08/1967	H	Swansea Town	W	3-1	Bullock, Skeen (2)
R2	13/09/1967	H	Preston North End	W	2-1	G Atkinson, Skeen
R3	10/10/1967	A	Queen's Park Rangers	L	1-5	Bullock

Total appear
Sub appear
Total

Shuker	Atkinson, R	Kyle	Jones	Skeen	Bullock	Atkinson, G	Kerr	Harrington	Beavon	Clarke	Thornley	Smithson	Hale	Buck	Barron	Lloyd	Higgins	Evanson	Sloan	Hatch	Fursdon
3	4	5	6	7	8	9	10	11													
3		5	6	7	9	10	**8**		2	4	11					12					
3	4	5	10	7	8	9			2	6	11										
3		5		7	9	8	10		2	6	11	4									
3		5		7	9	8			2	6	11	4	10								
3		5		7		8	12		2	6	**11**	4	10	9							
3		5		7	9		8	11	2	6		4	10								
3		5		7	9	10	8		2	6		4	11								
3		5		7	9	8	10		2	6		4	11								
		5	10	7	9				2	6	11	4	8		1	3					
		5	10	7	9				2	6	11	4	8		1	3					
11		5	10	7	9				2	6		4	8			3					
11		5	10	7	9				2	6		4	8		1	3					
11		5		7	9	10			2	6		4	8		1	3					
3	4	5	6	7	9	10		11	2				**8**		1	12					
10	4	5		7	9	8			2	6	11				1	3					
10	4			7	9	8			2	6	11				1	3	5				
10	4			7	9	8			2	6	11				1	3	5				
10	4			7	8	9			2	6	11				1	3	5				
10	4			7	9	8			2	6	11		12		1	3	**5**				
10	4			7	9	8			2	6	11	5			1	3					
3	4		10	7	9	8			2	6	11	5									
	4	5		7	9	8			3	6		2	10		1			11			
	4	5		7	9	8			3	6		2	10		1			11			
	4	5		7	9	8			3	6		2	10		1			11			
3	4	5		7	9	10	8		**2**	6	11		12		1						
3	4	5		7	9	10	8	11	2	6					1						
3	4	5		7	9	10	8	11	2	6					1						
3	6	5		7	9		8		2	10	11	4			1						
3	4	5		7	9	10	8		2	6	11				1						
11	4	5		12	9	8			**2**	6		10			1	3			7		
10	4	5			8	9				6	11	2			1	3			7		
6	4	5			9	10				8	11	2			1	3			7		
10	4	5			9			11		6		2			1	3		8	7		
6	4	5		12	9	8		11				2			1	3		**10**	7		
6	4	5		8	9	10		**11**							1	3			7	12	
10	4	5			9	8		11		6		2			1	3			7		
10	4	5			9	8		11		6		2			1	3			7		
10	4	5			9	8		11		6		2			1	3			7		
10	4	5			9	8		11		6		2			1	3			7		
10	4	5		8	9	12		**11**		6		2			1	3			7		
	4	5		8	9	10		11		6		2			1	3			7		
12	4	5		8	**9**	10		11		6		2			1	3			7		
	4	5		8	9	10		11		6		2			1	3			7		
	4	5		8	9	10		11		6		2			1	3			7		
	4	5		8	9	10		11		6		2			1	3			7		

Shuker	Atkinson, R	Kyle	Jones	Skeen	Bullock	Atkinson, G	Kerr	Harrington	Beavon	Clarke	Thornley	Smithson	Hale	Buck	Barron	Lloyd	Higgins	Evanson	Sloan	Hatch	Fursdon
10	4		3	7	9	8			2	6		5						11			
3	4			7	9	8			2	6	11	5	10								
11	4	5	12	**7**	9	8			2	6			10								3

Shuker	Atkinson, R	Kyle	Jones	Skeen	Bullock	Atkinson, G	Kerr	Harrington	Beavon	Clarke	Thornley	Smithson	Hale	Buck	Barron	Lloyd	Higgins	Evanson	Sloan	Hatch	Fursdon
3		5	6	7	9	10	8	11	2	4											
3		5		7		8	9		2	6	11	4	10								
		5	10	7	9				2	6	11	4	8			3					

Shuker	Atkinson, R	Kyle	Jones	Skeen	Bullock	Atkinson, G	Kerr	Harrington	Beavon	Clarke	Thornley	Smithson	Hale	Buck	Barron	Lloyd	Higgins	Evanson	Sloan	Hatch	Fursdon
41	37	44	12	43	50	43	13	19	36	48	22	36	18	1	35	28	4	6	16	0	1
1			1	2		1	1						2			2				1	
10			4	8	16	13	1	3		9	3	1	5					2	4		

League Table

	P	W	D	L	F	A	Pts
Oxford United	46	22	13	11	69	47	57
Bury	46	24	8	14	91	66	56
Shrewsbury Town	46	20	15	11	61	49	55
Torquay United	46	21	11	14	60	56	53
Reading	46	21	9	16	70	60	51
Watford	46	21	8	17	74	50	50
Walsall	46	19	12	15	74	61	50
Barrow	46	21	8	17	65	54	50
Peterborough United	46	20	10	16	79	67	50
Swindon Town	46	16	17	13	74	51	49
Brighton & Hove Albion	46	16	16	14	57	55	48
Gillingham	46	18	12	16	59	63	48
Bournemouth & Boscombe A	46	16	15	15	56	51	47
Stockport County	46	19	9	18	70	75	47
Southport	46	17	12	17	65	65	46
Bristol Rovers	46	17	9	20	72	78	43
Oldham Athletic	46	18	7	21	60	65	43
Northampton Town	46	14	13	19	58	72	41
Orient	46	12	17	17	46	62	41
Tranmere Rovers	46	14	12	20	62	74	40
Mansfield Town	46	12	13	21	51	67	37
Grimsby Town	46	14	9	23	52	69	37
Colchester United	46	9	15	22	50	87	33
Scunthorpe United	46	10	12	24	56	87	32

1968-69

Division Two

Manager: Arthur Turner then Ron Saunders

Did you know that?

David Sloan became the first Oxford United player to earn a full international cap, when appearing for Northern Ireland against Israel on 10 September 1968.

United paid a new club record fee of £12,500 for Ray Gaston three days earlier. Gaston came on as a substitute for his only Northern Ireland cap in the same game that Sloan made his debut.

Mickey Bullock was sold to Orient for £18,000. John Lloyd went to Aldershot for £4,000. Cyril Beavon made his 500th Oxford United appearance before joining Banbury United.

In February, Arthur Turner was made general manager, with Ron Saunders becoming team manager.

A record home League attendance of 17,939 watched United lose 2–0 to Brian Clough's Derby County on 22 March.

The A team finished bottom of the South-East Counties League and joined the Metropolitan League after failing to gain re-election.

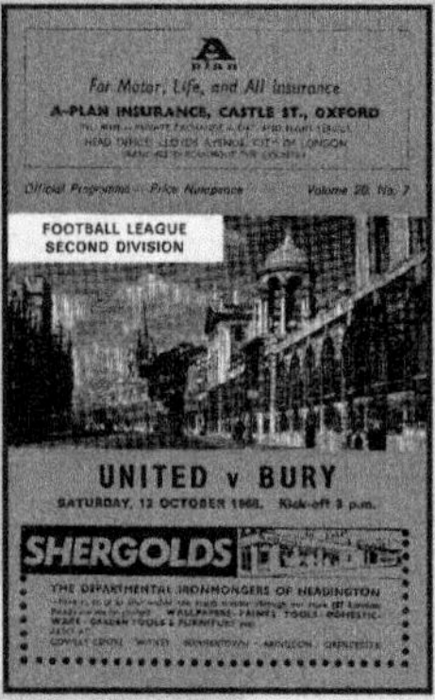

Match No.	Date		Opponents	Result	(F-A)	Scorers	A
1	10/08/1968	H	Bolton Wanderers	D	1-1	Sloan	
2	17/08/1968	A	Millwall	L	1-2	Sloan	
3	21/08/1968	H	Blackpool	D	0-0		
4	24/08/1968	H	Hull City	D	1-1	Harrington	
5	27/08/1968	A	Carlisle United	W	2-0	G Atkinson, Bullock	
6	31/08/1968	A	Derby County	L	0-2		
7	07/09/1968	H	Fulham	W	1-0	Evanson	
8	14/09/1968	A	Sheffield United	W	2-1	G Atkinson, Shuker	
9	18/09/1968	A	Blackburn Rovers	L	0-1		
10	21/09/1968	H	Bristol City	D	0-0		
11	28/09/1968	A	Aston Villa	L	0-2		
12	05/10/1968	A	Portsmouth	L	0-3		
13	09/10/1968	H	Carlisle United	L	0-1		
14	12/10/1968	H	Bury	D	2-2	Bullock (pen), Gaston	
15	19/10/1968	A	Charlton Athletic	L	0-1		
16	26/10/1968	H	Middlesbrough	L	2-4	R Atkinson, Gaston	
17	02/11/1968	A	Birmingham City	W	1-0	G Atkinson	
18	09/11/1968	H	Crystal Palace	L	0-2		
19	16/11/1968	A	Norwich City	D	1-1	Clarke	
20	23/11/1968	H	Cardiff City	L	0-2		
21	30/11/1968	A	Huddersfield Town	L	1-2	Thornley	
22	07/12/1968	H	Preston North End	W	2-1	Clarke, Skeen	
23	14/12/1968	A	Bury	L	1-3	Sloan	
24	21/12/1968	H	Charlton Athletic	L	0-1		
25	11/01/1969	H	Birmingham City	L	1-2	G Atkinson	
26	24/01/1969	A	Middlesbrough	L	0-2		
27	01/02/1969	H	Norwich City	L	0-2		
28	08/02/1969	A	Cardiff City	L	0-5		
29	15/02/1969	H	Huddersfield Town	W	3-0	Skeen (2), Sloan	
30	22/02/1969	A	Preston North End	L	1-2	G Atkinson	
31	01/03/1969	A	Bolton Wanderers	D	1-1	Shuker	
32	05/03/1969	H	Portsmouth	W	3-1	Harrington (2), Shuker	
33	08/03/1969	H	Millwall	W	1-0	Shuker	
34	14/03/1969	A	Hull City	D	0-0		
35	22/03/1969	H	Derby County	L	0-2		
36	26/03/1969	A	Crystal Palace	D	1-1	Sloan	
37	29/03/1969	A	Fulham	W	1-0	Shuker	
38	04/04/1969	H	Blackburn Rovers	W	2-1	Shuker (2) (1 pen)	
39	05/04/1969	H	Aston Villa	W	1-0	Shuker	
40	07/04/1969	A	Blackpool	L	0-1		
41	12/04/1969	A	Bristol City	L	0-2		
42	20/04/1969	H	Sheffield United	W	1-0	Harrington	

FA Cup

R3	04/01/1969	H	Southampton	D	1-1	Sloan
r	08/01/1969	A	Southampton	L	0-2	

League Cup

R1	14/08/1968	A	Brighton & Hove Albion	L	0-2	

Total appear
Sub appear
Total

Lloyd	Atkinson, R	Smithson	Shuker	Sloan	Skeen	Bullock	Atkinson, G	Harrington	Kyle	Clarke	Evanson	Hatch	Lucas	Beavon	Gaston	Crook	Jones	Higgins	Thornley	Fursdon
3	4	5	6	7	**8**	9	10	11			12									
12	4	6	3	7		9	8		5	**10**	11									
3	4		10	7		9	8	11	5	6										
3	4			7		9	8	11	5	6	10									
3	4			7		9	8	11	5	6		10								
3	4			7		9	8	11	5	6		10	12							
	4		3	7		9	8	11	5	6	10		2							
	4	12	**10**	7		9	8		5	6	11		2	3						
	4			7			8	11	5	6	10		2	3	9					
	4			7		12	8	11	5	6	**10**		2	3	9					
	4		11	7		10	8		5	6			2	3	9					
	4	8	3	7		9		11	5	6				12		**10**				
	6	4	3	7		9		11	5						8		10			
12	6	4	3	7		8		**11**	5						9		10			
	6	4	3	7		9		11			12				**8**		10	5		
	4	12	10	7				11		6				3	9		**8**	5		
	4		3	7			10	11		6			2	12	9		**8**	5		
	4		3	7			10	11		6		5	2		9		8			
3	4		2	7	8		9	11		6	10							5		
3	4		2	7	8			11		6	10				9			5		
	4		3	7	9		10			6							8	5	11	
	4		**10**	7	8		9	11		6				3				5		12
	4	10		7	8		9	11		6				3				5		
3	4			7	8		9	11		6	10							5		
3	6	4		7	8		9	11		5	10	12	**2**							
	6	4	3	7	8		9	11		5	10							2		
	4	5	3	7	**11**		8			6	10				9			2	12	
	4	2	3	7	12		8	11		6	**10**				9			5		
3	6	4	10	7	9		8			5				2					11	
	6	4	10	7	9		8	12		5				2					**11**	
	4	5	9	7	8		10	11		6				2						
	4	6	8	7	9		10	11		5				2						
	4	6	8	7	9		10	**11**		5				2				12		
	4	6	8	7	**9**		10	11		5				2				12		
	4	6	8	7	9		10	11		5				2						
	4	6	8	7	9		10	11		5				2				12		
	4	6	8	7	**9**		10	11		5				2				12		
	4	6	8	7	9		10	11		5				2						
	4	6	8	7	**9**		10	11		5				3			12	2		
	4	6	8	7	9		10	11		5				2				3		
	4		8	7	9		10	11		5		12		2				**6**		
	4	6	8	7	9		10	11		5				2				12		

Lloyd	Atkinson, R	Smithson	Shuker	Sloan	Skeen	Bullock	Atkinson, G	Harrington	Kyle	Clarke	Evanson	Hatch	Lucas	Beavon	Gaston	Crook	Jones	Higgins	Thornley	Fursdon
	4		3	7	8		9	11	5	6	10			12				**2**		
	4	2	3	7	8		9	11	**5**	6	10				12					

Lloyd	Atkinson, R	Smithson	Shuker	Sloan	Skeen	Bullock	Atkinson, G	Harrington	Kyle	Clarke	Evanson	Hatch	Lucas	Beavon	Gaston	Crook	Jones	Higgins	Thornley	Fursdon
3	4	5	6	7		9	8	11			10									

Lloyd	Atkinson, R	Smithson	Shuker	Sloan	Skeen	Bullock	Atkinson, G	Harrington	Kyle	Clarke	Evanson	Hatch	Lucas	Beavon	Gaston	Crook	Jones	Higgins	Thornley	Fursdon
11	45	26	37	45	26	14	39	38	15	40	16	3	8	21	12	1	7	16	3	0
2		2			1	1		1			2	2	1	3	1		1	5	1	1
	1		8	6	3	2	5	4		2	1				2				1	

League Table

	P	W	D	L	F	A	Pts
Derby County	42	26	11	5	65	32	63
Crystal Palace	42	22	12	8	70	47	56
Charlton Athletic	42	18	14	10	61	52	50
Middlesbrough	42	19	11	12	58	49	49
Cardiff City	42	20	7	15	67	54	47
Huddersfield Town	42	17	12	13	53	46	46
Birmingham City	42	18	8	16	73	59	44
Blackpool	42	14	15	13	51	41	43
Sheffield United	42	16	11	15	61	50	43
Millwall	42	17	9	16	57	49	43
Hull City	42	13	16	13	59	52	42
Carlisle United	42	16	10	16	46	49	42
Norwich City	42	15	10	17	53	56	40
Preston North End	42	12	15	15	38	44	39
Portsmouth	42	12	14	16	58	58	38
Bristol City	42	11	16	15	46	53	38
Bolton Wanderers	42	12	14	16	55	67	38
Aston Villa	42	12	14	16	37	48	38
Blackburn Rovers	42	13	11	18	52	63	37
Oxford United	42	12	9	21	34	55	33
Bury	42	11	8	23	51	80	30
Fulham	42	7	11	24	40	81	25

1969-70

Division Two

Manager: Gerry Summers

Did you know that?

Ron Saunders left to join Norwich City in the close season and he was replaced by Gerry Summers.

United reached the quarter-finals of the League Cup for the first time, losing 1–0 at Carlisle United in a replay after a 0–0 draw at the Manor.

A post-season testimonial for Ron Atkinson, Maurice Kyle and Cyril Beavon attracted 5,630 spectators. The trio had played 1,468 games between them in all first-team competitions.

In April, Ron Coppock stood down as chairman, to be replaced by Peter Playford.

Match No.	Date		Opponents	Result	(F-A)	Scorers
1	09/08/1969	H	Huddersfield Town	L	1-2	G Atkinson
2	16/08/1969	A	Birmingham City	W	3-1	G Atkinson (2), Skeen
3	23/08/1969	H	Portsmouth	L	0-2	
4	26/08/1969	A	Charlton Athletic	L	0-1	
5	30/08/1969	A	Preston North End	W	1-0	Skeen
6	06/09/1969	H	Watford	W	2-1	Clarke, Skeen
7	13/09/1969	A	Swindon Town	D	0-0	
8	17/09/1969	H	Sheffield United	D	0-0	
9	20/09/1969	H	Middlesbrough	D	1-1	G Atkinson
10	27/09/1969	A	Norwich City	L	0-2	
11	04/10/1969	H	Millwall	D	0-0	
12	08/10/1969	H	Birmingham City	W	2-0	Shuker (2)
13	11/10/1969	A	Hull City	L	1-3	Sloan
14	18/10/1969	A	Bolton Wanderers	D	1-1	Sloan
15	25/10/1969	H	Aston Villa	D	2-2	Skeen, Sloan
16	01/11/1969	A	Leicester City	L	1-2	Shuker
17	08/11/1969	H	Carlisle United	W	1-0	Harrington
18	11/11/1969	A	Bristol City	L	0-2	
19	15/11/1969	H	Cardiff City	D	1-1	Shepherd
20	22/11/1969	A	Blackpool	L	0-1	
21	29/11/1969	H	Blackburn Rovers	W	1-0	Skeen
22	06/12/1969	A	Queen's Park Rangers	W	2-1	Harrington, Skeen
23	13/12/1969	H	Swindon Town	D	0-0	
24	20/12/1969	A	Watford	L	0-2	
25	10/01/1970	A	Middlesbrough	L	0-2	
26	17/01/1970	H	Norwich City	W	1-0	Thompson
27	24/01/1970	A	Portsmouth	L	1-2	Skeen
28	31/01/1970	A	Millwall	D	0-0	
29	07/02/1970	H	Hull City	D	0-0	
30	18/02/1970	H	Preston North End	W	3-1	Lewis, Sloan, Thompson (pen)
31	21/02/1970	A	Carlisle United	D	1-1	Lewis
32	24/02/1970	A	Huddersfield Town	L	0-1	
33	28/02/1970	H	Bolton Wanderers	W	3-1	Skeen, Sloan (2)
34	14/03/1970	A	Blackburn Rovers	L	0-2	
35	18/03/1970	H	Bristol City	W	2-0	Lewis (2)
36	21/03/1970	H	Queen's Park Rangers	D	0-0	
37	27/03/1970	H	Leicester City	L	0-1	
38	28/03/1970	A	Cardiff City	D	0-0	
39	31/03/1970	A	Aston Villa	D	0-0	
40	04/04/1970	H	Charlton Athletic	D	1-1	Skeen
41	15/04/1970	A	Sheffield United	L	1-5	Clayton
42	18/04/1970	H	Blackpool	W	2-0	Clayton, Hatch

FA Cup

R3	03/01/1970	H	Stoke City	D	0-0	
r	07/01/1970	A	Stoke City	L	2-3	G Atkinson, Skeen

League Cup

R1	13/08/1969	H	Northampton Town	W	2-0	G Atkinson, Jones
R2	03/09/1969	H	Bury	W	4-1	Skeen (2), Sloan (2)
R3	24/09/1969	H	Swindon Town	W	1-0	Sloan
R4	15/10/1969	A	Nottingham Forest	W	1-0	Skeen
QF	29/10/1969	H	Carlisle United	D	0-0	
r	04/11/1969	A	Carlisle United	L	0-1	

Total appear
Sub appear
Total

Smithson	Clarke	Gladwin	Hatch	Atkinson, G	Way	Skeen	Shuker	Evanson	Kyle	Sloan	Jones	Atkinson, R	Shepherd	Harrington	Thompson	Clayton	Lewis	Clinch	Kearns
3	4	5	**6**	7	8	9	10	11		12									
4	6	3		8		9			5	7	10	11							
4	**6**	3		9		8		12	5	7	11	10							
4	6		3	8		9		12	5	7	**10**	11							
4	6		12	8		9	3		5	7	**10**	11							
4	6			8		9	3		5	7	10	11							
4	6			8		9	3		5	7	10	11							
4	6			8		9	3		5	7	10	11							
4	6			8		9	3		5	7	10	11							
4	6			8		9	3		5	7	10	11							
4	6			8		9	3		5	7	12	11	**10**						
4	5	3		8		9	6			7	12	11	10						
4	5	3		8		9	6			7	12	**11**	10						
6	4	3		8		9	11		5	7			10						
4	5	3		8		9	6			7		11	10						
4	5	3		8		9	6			7		11	10						
4	5	3		8		9	6			**7**		10	12	11					
4	5	3		8		9	**6**	7				10		11	12				
4	5	3		8		9	**6**	7				10	12	11					
4	5	3		8		9	6	7				10		11	12				
4	5	3		8		9						11	7	10	6				
4	5	3		8		9						11	7	10	6				
4	5	3		8		9				7		11		10	6				
4	5	3			12	8	**10**	7				11			6	9			
4	5			8		9	3					11	7	10	6				
4	5					9	3			7		11		10	6		8		
4	5			10		**9**	3			7		11		12	6		8		
4	5			8		9	3					11		10	6		7		
4	5			8		9	3					11		10	6		7		
4	5			8		9	3			7		11			6		10		
4	5			8		9	3			7		11			6		10		
4	6			8		**9**	3			7		11		12			10	5	
4	5		3	8	6	9				7		11					10		
4	5	2		10		9	3			7		11			6	8			
4	5	3		8		9				7		11			6		10		
4	5			10		9	3			**7**		11			6	12	8		
4	5			8		9	3					11			6	7	10		1
4	5			**10**		9	3	8				11		12	6	7			1
4	5				8	9	3	9				11			6	7			1
4						9	3	8				11			6	7	10	5	
4			5	8		9	3	9				11			6	7			
4			5			9	3	8		7		11			6	10			

Smithson	Clarke	Gladwin	Hatch	Atkinson, G	Way	Skeen	Shuker	Evanson	Kyle	Sloan	Jones	Atkinson, R	Shepherd	Harrington	Thompson	Clayton	Lewis	Clinch	Kearns
4	5			8		9	3			12		11	**7**	10	6				
4	5			8		9	3			12		11	7	10	6				

Smithson	Clarke	Gladwin	Hatch	Atkinson, G	Way	Skeen	Shuker	Evanson	Kyle	Sloan	Jones	Atkinson, R	Shepherd	Harrington	Thompson	Clayton	Lewis	Clinch	Kearns
4	6	3		10		9			5	7	11	8							
3	8			7		10	5		4	9	11	6							
4	6			8		9	3		5	7	10	11							
4	6			8		9	3		5	7		11	10						
4	5	3		8		9	6			7		11	10						
4	5	3		8		9	6			7		11	**10**	12					

Smithson	Clarke	Gladwin	Hatch	Atkinson, G	Way	Skeen	Shuker	Evanson	Kyle	Sloan	Jones	Atkinson, R	Shepherd	Harrington	Thompson	Clayton	Lewis	Clinch	Kearns
50	47	21	5	45	3	50	41	10	15	33	12	48	14	13	22	8	12	2	3
			1		1			2		3	3			4	2	1			
	1		1	6		13	3			9	1		1	2	2	2	4		

League Table

	P	W	D	L	F	A	Pts
Huddersfield Town	42	24	12	6	68	37	60
Blackpool	42	20	13	9	56	45	53
Leicester City	42	19	13	10	64	50	51
Middlesbrough	42	20	10	12	55	45	50
Swindon Town	42	17	16	9	57	47	50
Sheffield United	42	22	5	15	73	38	49
Cardiff City	42	18	13	11	61	41	49
Blackburn Rovers	42	20	7	15	54	50	47
Queen's Park Rangers	42	17	11	14	66	57	45
Millwall	42	15	14	13	56	56	44
Norwich City	42	16	11	15	49	46	43
Carlisle United	42	14	13	15	58	56	41
Hull City	42	15	11	16	72	70	41
Bristol City	42	13	13	16	54	50	39
Oxford United	42	12	15	15	35	42	39
Bolton Wanderers	42	12	12	18	54	61	36
Portsmouth	42	13	9	20	66	80	35
Birmingham City	42	11	11	20	51	78	33
Watford	42	9	13	20	44	57	31
Charlton Athletic	42	7	17	18	35	76	31
Aston Villa	42	8	13	21	36	62	29
Preston North End	42	8	12	22	43	63	28

1970-71

Division Two

Manager: Gerry Summers

Did you know that?

Jim Barron joined Nottingham Forest for £35,000, with United bringing in Roy Burton as a replacement.

On 26 September Oxford headed the Second Division table for the first time.

United broke their transfer-fee record when signing Nigel Cassidy for £20,000 from Scunthorpe United. Other incoming players included Derek Clarke, who joined from Wolves for £11,500, and Fulham's Dave Roberts, who cost £2,500.

Mick Kearns' cap for the Republic of Ireland in their 2–1 defeat by Poland on 23 September 1970 was the first cap earned by a home-grown Oxford player.

At the end of the season, Bob Kearsey replaced Peter Playford as chairman of the board.

Match No.	Date		Opponents	Result	(F-A)	Scorers	A
1	15/08/1970	A	Millwall	W	2-1	C Clarke, Sloan	
2	22/08/1970	H	Sheffield Wednesday	D	1-1	G Atkinson	
3	29/08/1970	A	Middlesbrough	W	2-0	Skeen (2)	
4	01/09/1970	A	Luton Town	L	0-4		
5	05/09/1970	H	Leicester City	W	1-0	Smithson (pen)	
6	12/09/1970	A	Birmingham City	D	1-1	Clayton	
7	19/09/1970	H	Watford	W	2-1	Clayton, Skeen	
8	21/09/1970	A	Blackburn Rovers	D	0-0		
9	26/09/1970	A	Bolton Wanderers	W	2-0	R Atkinson, Smithson	
10	03/10/1970	H	Norwich City	D	1-1	G Atkinson	
11	10/10/1970	A	Bristol City	W	4-0	G Atkinson, Evanson (2), Smithson (pen)	
12	17/10/1970	H	Millwall	L	2-3	R Atkinson, Sloan	
13	21/10/1970	H	Queen's Park Rangers	L	1-3	Shuker	
14	24/10/1970	A	Sunderland	W	1-0	G Atkinson	
15	31/10/1970	H	Charlton Athletic	W	2-1	D Clarke, Skeen	
16	07/11/1970	A	Carlisle United	L	2-3	Skeen, Sloan	
17	14/11/1970	H	Hull City	L	0-3		
18	21/11/1970	H	Swindon Town	D	0-0		
19	28/11/1970	A	Sheffield United	L	0-3		
20	05/12/1970	H	Cardiff City	W	1-0	Cassidy	
21	12/12/1970	A	Portsmouth	L	0-1		
22	19/12/1970	A	Sheffield Wednesday	D	1-1	Sloan	
23	09/01/1971	H	Blackburn Rovers	W	2-1	Cassidy, Sloan	
24	16/01/1971	A	Queen's Park Rangers	L	0-2		
25	30/01/1971	H	Sheffield United	L	1-2	Smithson (pen)	
26	06/02/1971	A	Cardiff City	L	0-1		
27	20/02/1971	A	Swindon Town	L	0-3		
28	26/02/1971	A	Charlton Athletic	L	0-2		
29	06/03/1971	H	Sunderland	D	0-0		
30	10/03/1971	H	Orient	L	0-1		
31	13/03/1971	A	Hull City	W	1-0	D Clarke	
32	20/03/1971	H	Carlisle United	D	1-1	Smithson	
33	24/03/1971	H	Portsmouth	D	1-1	G Atkinson	
34	27/03/1971	A	Leicester City	D	0-0		
35	03/04/1971	H	Middlesbrough	D	2-2	D Clarke, Skeen	
36	09/04/1971	H	Birmingham City	W	1-0	Cassidy	
37	10/04/1971	A	Orient	D	0-0		
38	12/04/1971	A	Norwich City	D	1-1	Sloan	
39	17/04/1971	H	Bristol City	W	1-0	D Clarke	
40	24/04/1971	A	Watford	L	1-2	Clayton	
41	28/04/1971	H	Luton Town	W	2-1	Cassidy, D Clarke	
42	01/05/1971	H	Bolton Wanderers	D	1-1	Lucas	

FA Cup

R3	11/01/1971	H	Burnley	W	3-0	G Atkinson, Cassidy, Skeen
R4	23/01/1971	H	Watford	D	1-1	Skeen
r	27/01/1971	A	Watford	W	2-1	Clarke, Skeen
R5	13/02/1971	A	Leicester City	D	1-1	Lucas
r	17/02/1971	H	Leicester City	L	1-3	R Atkinson

League Cup

R2	09/09/1970	H	Wolverhampton Wanderers	W	1-0	Lucas
R3	06/10/1970	A	Carlisle United	L	1-3	Clayton

Total appea
Sub appea
Total

Shuker	Smithson	Clarke, C	Thompson	Sloan	Atkinson, G	Skeen	Clayton	Atkinson, R	Lewis	Evanson	Clarke, D	Cassidy	Way	Roberts	Harrington	Jones
3	4	5	6	7	8	9	10	11								
3	4	5	**6**	7	8	9	10	11	12							
3	4	5	6	7	8	9	10	11								
3	4	5	6	7	8	9	10	11								
3	4	5	6	7	8	9	10	11								
3	4	5	6	7	8	**9**	10	11		12						
3	4	5	6	7	8	9	10	11								
3	4	5	6	7	8	9	10	11								
3	4	5	6	7	8	9	10	11								
3	4	5	6	7	8	9	10	11								
3	4	5	6	7	8	9	10			11						
3	6	5	**4**	7	8	9	10	12		11						
3	4	5		7	8	9	10	11		6						
3	4	5		7	8	9		11		6	10					
3	4	5		7	8	9		11		6	10					
3	**4**	5	12	7	8	9		11		6	10					
3	4	5	6	7	8	9		11	12		**10**					
3	4	5	6	7	8	9		11				10				
3	4	5	6	7		9		11			12	10	**8**			
3	4	5	6	7	8	9		11				10				
3	4	5	6	7	8	9		11				10				
3	4	5		7	8	9		11		6		10				
3	4	5		7	8	9		11		6		10				
3	4	5		7	8	9		11		6		10				
3	4	5		7	8	9		**11**		6		10	12			
3	4	5		7	8	9		11		6		10				
3	**4**	5		7	8	9	10			6			11	12		
3		5		7	8			11		6	9	10		4		
3		5	**8**	12		9		11		6		10		4	7	
3		5			8	9		11		6	10			4	7	
3		5	7		8	9		11		6	10			4		
3	4	5	7		8	9		11		6	10					
3		5		7	8	9		11		6	10			4		
3		5		12	8	10		11		7	9			4		**6**
3		5		7	8	12		11		6	9	10		**4**		
3		5			8	9		11		6	7	10		4		
3		5			8	9	7	11		6		10		4		
3		5		10	8	9	7			6		10		4		
3		5			8	11	7			6	9	10		4		
3		5		12	8		7	11		6	9	10		4		
3		5			8	9		11		6	7	10		4		
3		5		12	**8**	9		11		6	7	10		4		

Shuker	Smithson	Clarke, C	Thompson	Sloan	Atkinson, G	Skeen	Clayton	Atkinson, R	Lewis	Evanson	Clarke, D	Cassidy	Way	Roberts	Harrington	Jones
3	4	5		7	8	9		11		6		10				
3	4	5		7	8	**9**		11		6		10			12	
3	4	5		7	8	9		11		6		10				
3	4	5		7	8	9		11		6		10				
3	4	5		7	8	9		11		6		10				

Shuker	Smithson	Clarke, C	Thompson	Sloan	Atkinson, G	Skeen	Clayton	Atkinson, R	Lewis	Evanson	Clarke, D	Cassidy	Way	Roberts	Harrington	Jones
3	4	5	6	7	8	9	10	11								
3	4	5	6	7	8	9	10	**11**		12						

Shuker	Smithson	Clarke, C	Thompson	Sloan	Atkinson, G	Skeen	Clayton	Atkinson, R	Lewis	Evanson	Clarke, D	Cassidy	Way	Roberts	Harrington	Jones
49	35	49	22	38	47	46	20	44	0	32	16	24	2	14	2	1
			1	4		1		1	2	2	1		1	1	1	
1	5	2		6	6	9	4	3		2	5	5				

League Table

	P	W	D	L	F	A	Pts
Leicester City	42	23	13	6	57	30	59
Sheffield United	42	21	14	7	73	39	56
Cardiff City	42	20	13	9	64	41	53
Carlisle United	42	20	13	9	65	43	53
Hull City	42	19	13	10	54	41	51
Luton Town	42	18	13	11	62	43	49
Middlesbrough	42	17	14	11	60	43	48
Millwall	42	19	9	14	59	42	47
Birmingham City	42	17	12	13	58	48	46
Norwich City	42	15	14	13	54	52	44
Queen's Park Rangers	42	16	11	15	58	53	43
Swindon Town	42	15	12	15	61	51	42
Sunderland	42	15	12	15	52	54	42
Oxford United	42	14	14	14	41	48	42
Sheffield Wednesday	42	12	12	18	51	69	36
Portsmouth	42	10	14	18	46	61	34
Orient	42	9	16	17	29	51	34
Watford	42	10	13	19	38	60	33
Bristol City	42	10	11	21	46	64	31
Charlton Athletic	42	8	14	20	41	65	30
Blackburn Rovers	42	6	15	21	37	69	27
Bolton Wanderers	42	7	10	25	35	74	24

1971-72

Division Two

Manager: Gerry Summers

Did you know that?

Departures from the Manor included 63-year-old former manager Arthur Turner, despite previous assurances that he would have a job until his retirement, and Ron Atkinson, who left to become player-manager at Kettering Town.

Another League attendance record was broken, as 18,740 watched United lose 1–0 to Birmingham City.

Former chairman Ron Coppock died on New Year's Day, after a long illness.

Match No.	Date		Opponents	Result	(F-A)	Scorers
1	14/08/1971	H	Orient	D	1-1	Sloan
2	21/08/1971	A	Hull City	L	0-1	
3	28/08/1971	H	Burnley	W	2-1	Cassidy, Nigels
4	01/09/1971	H	Luton Town	D	1-1	D Clarke
5	04/09/1971	A	Preston North End	L	0-1	
6	11/09/1971	H	Millwall	L	1-2	R Atkinson
7	18/09/1971	A	Norwich City	L	2-3	Cassidy, Thompson
8	25/09/1971	H	Sheffield Wednesday	W	1-0	Lucas
9	29/09/1971	H	Queen's Park Rangers	W	3-1	Cassidy (2), Sloan
10	02/10/1971	A	Birmingham City	D	0-0	
11	09/10/1971	H	Middlesbrough	D	0-0	
12	12/10/1971	A	Fulham	D	1-1	C Clarke
13	16/10/1971	A	Orient	D	1-1	D Clarke
14	23/10/1971	H	Sunderland	W	2-0	Cassidy, Clayton
15	30/10/1971	A	Carlisle United	L	1-2	Cassidy
16	06/11/1971	H	Swindon Town	D	1-1	C Clarke
17	13/11/1971	A	Charlton Athletic	L	0-3	
18	20/11/1971	A	Portsmouth	L	0-2	
19	27/11/1971	H	Blackpool	W	3-1	Cassidy (2), Roberts
20	11/12/1971	H	Bristol City	D	0-0	
21	18/12/1971	H	Preston North End	W	2-0	Aylott, Skeen
22	27/12/1971	A	Watford	W	1-0	D Clarke (pen)
23	01/01/1972	H	Norwich City	L	0-2	
24	08/01/1972	A	Burnley	D	1-1	Dobson (og)
25	22/01/1972	A	Queen's Park Rangers	L	2-4	Cassidy (2)
26	29/01/1972	H	Fulham	W	1-0	Evanson
27	05/02/1972	A	Luton Town	W	2-1	G Atkinson, Skeen
28	12/02/1972	A	Sunderland	L	0-3	
29	19/02/1972	H	Carlisle United	W	3-1	Cassidy (2), Ross (og)
30	26/02/1972	A	Swindon Town	L	0-4	
31	04/03/1972	H	Charlton Athletic	W	2-1	Clayton, Sloan
32	11/03/1972	A	Middlesbrough	L	1-2	Sloan
33	18/03/1972	H	Hull City	D	2-2	Clayton, Evanson
34	21/03/1972	A	Cardiff City	D	1-1	C Clarke
35	25/03/1972	A	Millwall	L	0-2	
36	31/03/1972	H	Birmingham City	L	0-1	
37	01/04/1972	H	Watford	D	0-0	
38	03/04/1972	A	Sheffield Wednesday	D	0-0	
39	08/04/1972	H	Portsmouth	D	2-2	D Clarke, Sloan
40	15/04/1972	A	Blackpool	L	0-2	
41	22/04/1972	H	Cardiff City	W	1-0	Thompson
42	29/04/1972	A	Bristol City	L	2-4	Cassidy, D Clarke (pen)

FA Cup

R3	15/01/1972	H	Liverpool	L	0-3	

League Cup

R2	08/09/1971	H	Millwall	W	1-0	Skeen
R3	05/10/1971	H	Stoke City	D	1-1	Evanson
r	18/10/1971	A	Stoke City	L	0-2	

Total appear
Sub appear
Total

Shuker	Roberts	Clarke, C	Evanson	Sloan	Atkinson, G	Skeen	Clarke, D	Atkinson, R	Cassidy	Thompson	Clayton	Way	Aylott	Smithson	Fleming	Hatch	Burton
3	4	5	6	7	8	**9**	10	11	12								
3	4	5	6	7	8	9	10	11									
3	4	5	6	7	8		9	11	10								
3	4	5	6	7	8	12	9	11	**10**								
3	4	5	**6**	7	8	12	9	11	10								
3	4	5		7	8	6	9	11	10								
3	4	5			8	9	7	11	**10**	6	12						
3	4	5		7	8	6		11	10		9						
3	4	5	6	7		8		11	10		9						
3	4	5	6	7		8		11	10		9						
3	4	5	8	7					10	6	9	2	11				
3	4	5	6		8		7	11	**10**		9	2	12				
3	4	5	6	7	8		10				9	2	11				
3		5	8				7		10	6	9		11	4			
3		5	6				8		10		9		7	4	11		
		5	6				7		10		9		11	4	8	3	
3		5				**6**	7		10	12	9		11	4	8		
3	4	5	6	7	8		10		9				11				1
3	4	5	**6**		8	7	9		10			2	11		12		1
3	4	5	6			**7**	9		10		12		11		8		1
3	4	5		7		6	9		10				11		8		
3	4	5		7		6	9		10				11		8		
3		5	12	7		8	9		10				11	4	**6**		
3		5	**6**	12		8	9		10			2	11	4	**7**		
3		5	6		8	7			10		9	2	11	4			
3		5	6		8	7			10		9	2	11	4			1
3		5	6		8	7			10		9	2	11	4			1
3	4	5	**6**	12	8	7			10		9	2	11				1
3	4	5		7	8				10	6	9		11				1
3	4	5		7	8				10	6	9		11				1
3	4	5	12	7		8			10	**6**	9		11				1
3	4	5	12	7		8			10	**6**	9		11				1
3	4	5	8	7		12			10	**6**	9		11				1
3	4	5	8	7		6			10		9		11				1
3	4	5	6	7		8	12		10		**9**		11				1
3	4	5	8	7		6	12		10		**9**		11				1
3	4	5		7	8	12	9		10	**6**					11		1
3	4			7	8	6	9		10					5	11		1
3	4			7	8	6	9		10					5	11		1
3	4			7	8	6	9		10				11	5			1
3	4			7	8		9		10	6			11	5			1
3	4			7	8	12	9		10	**6**			11	5			1

3		5	6	12		7	9		10			2	11	4	**8**		

3	4	5		7	8	6	9	11	10								
3	4	5	6	7		8		11	10		9	2					
3	4	5	6	7	**8**	12	10				9		11				

45	36	41	28	32	26	29	29	13	42	11	24	11	30	15	12	1	20
			3	3		6	2		1	1	2		1		1		
	2	3	3	5	1	3	5	1	13	2	3		1				

League Table

	P	W	D	L	F	A	Pts
Norwich City	42	21	15	6	60	36	57
Birmingham City	42	19	18	5	60	31	56
Millwall	42	19	17	6	64	46	55
Queen's Park Rangers	42	20	14	8	57	28	54
Sunderland	42	17	16	9	67	57	50
Blackpool	42	20	7	15	70	50	47
Burnley	42	20	6	16	70	55	46
Bristol City	42	18	10	14	61	49	46
Middlesbrough	42	19	8	15	50	48	46
Carlisle United	42	17	9	16	61	57	43
Swindon Town	42	15	12	15	47	47	42
Hull City	42	14	10	18	49	53	38
Luton Town	42	10	18	14	43	48	38
Sheffield Wednesday	42	13	12	17	51	58	38
Oxford United	42	12	14	16	43	55	38
Portsmouth	42	12	13	17	59	68	37
Orient	42	14	9	19	50	61	37
Preston North End	42	12	12	18	52	58	36
Cardiff City	42	10	14	18	56	69	34
Fulham	42	12	10	20	45	68	34
Charlton Athletic	42	12	9	21	55	77	33
Watford	42	5	9	28	24	75	19

1972-73

Division Two

Manager: Gerry Summers

Did you know that?

In November, Roy Clayton was sold to Ron Atkinson's Kettering for £8,000, a non-League record.

United paid a club record transfer fee to capture Hugh Curran from Wolves for £50,000 in September.

In March, United won 3–1 at Swindon Town to complete the double. This remains the only time that Oxford have won at the County Ground.

United's eighth-place finish was their best yet, and was to remain so until 1985.

Dave Roberts earned his first international cap, playing for Wales in a World Cup qualifying 2–0 win over Poland on 28 March.

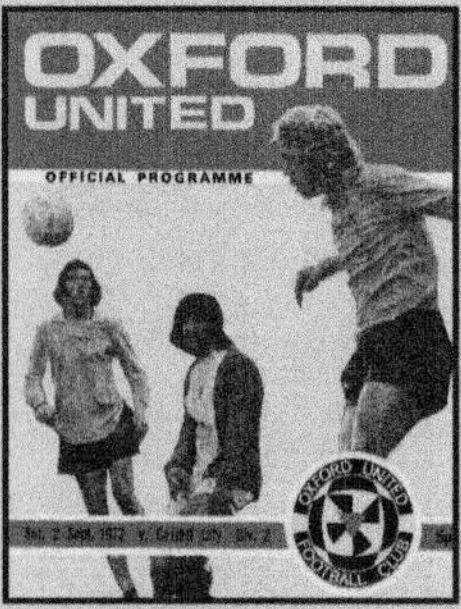

Match No.	Date		Opponents	Result	(F-A)	Scorers	A
1	12/08/1972	A	Orient	D	1-1	Skeen	
2	19/08/1972	H	Middlesbrough	W	4-0	Cassidy, D Clarke (2), Evanson	
3	26/08/1972	A	Nottingham Forest	L	1-2	Skeen	
4	30/08/1972	A	Luton Town	W	1-0	Cassidy	
5	02/09/1972	H	Cardiff City	W	2-1	Aylott, Cassidy	
6	09/09/1972	A	Huddersfield Town	L	0-2		
7	16/09/1972	H	Millwall	W	2-1	Cassidy, Curran	
8	20/09/1972	H	Sheffield Wednesday	W	1-0	Curran	
9	23/09/1972	A	Brighton & Hove Albion	D	2-2	Curran (2)	
10	27/09/1972	A	Portsmouth	L	0-1		
11	30/09/1972	H	Preston North End	L	0-2		
12	07/10/1972	H	Sunderland	W	5-1	Cassidy, Curran (3), Sloan	
13	14/10/1972	A	Blackpool	L	1-2	D Clarke	
14	21/10/1972	H	Bristol City	L	0-2		
15	27/10/1972	A	Hull City	W	1-0	Curran	
16	04/11/1972	H	Portsmouth	L	1-3	Curran	
17	11/11/1972	A	Sheffield Wednesday	W	1-0	Bray	
18	18/11/1972	A	Carlisle United	L	1-2	Bray	
19	25/11/1972	H	Aston Villa	W	2-0	Bray, Curran	
20	02/12/1972	A	Queen's Park Rangers	D	0-0		
21	09/12/1972	H	Fulham	D	0-0		
22	16/12/1972	H	Swindon Town	W	1-0	Cassidy	
23	23/12/1972	A	Burnley	D	1-1	Cassidy	
24	26/12/1972	H	Brighton & Hove Albion	W	3-0	Bray, Gough (2)	
25	30/12/1972	A	Middlesbrough	L	0-1		
26	06/01/1973	H	Nottingham Forest	W	1-0	Winfield (og)	
27	19/01/1973	A	Cardiff City	L	0-2		
28	27/01/1973	H	Huddersfield Town	W	2-0	Curran, Evanson	
29	10/02/1973	A	Millwall	L	1-3	Shuker (pen)	
30	17/02/1973	H	Orient	W	2-1	Evanson, Sloan	
31	24/02/1973	A	Swindon Town	W	3-1	Cassidy, Curran, Roberts	
32	03/03/1973	A	Sunderland	L	0-1		
33	10/03/1973	H	Blackpool	L	0-1		
34	17/03/1973	A	Bristol City	D	0-0		
35	23/03/1973	H	Hull City	W	5-2	D Clarke (2), Curran, Fleming, Hatch	
36	31/03/1973	A	Aston Villa	L	1-2	Roberts	
37	07/04/1973	H	Queen's Park Rangers	W	2-0	Curran (2) (1 pen)	
38	14/04/1973	A	Fulham	L	0-2		
39	20/04/1973	H	Burnley	L	0-2		
40	21/04/1973	H	Carlisle United	D	1-1	Cassidy	
41	24/04/1973	A	Preston North End	W	1-0	Fleming	
42	28/04/1973	H	Luton Town	W	2-1	Cassidy, Roberts	

FA Cup

R3	13/01/1973	A	York City	W	1-0	Gough
R4	03/02/1973	H	Queen's Park Rangers	L	0-2	

League Cup

R1	16/08/1972	H	Peterborough United	W	4-0	C Clarke, D Clarke (2), Sloan
R2	06/09/1972	H	Manchester United	D	2-2	Clayton, Skeen
r	12/09/1972	A	Manchester United	L	1-3	Bray

Anglo-Italian Cup

Int Grp	21/02/1973	A	Bologna (Italy)	D	0-0	
Int Grp	28/03/1973	H	Torino (Italy)	D	1-1	D Clarke
Int Grp	04/04/1973	A	Roma (Italy)	W	2-0	Curran (2)
Int Grp	02/05/1973	H	Como (Italy)	W	1-0	Roberts

Total appear
Sub appear
Total

Shuker	Roberts	Clarke, C	Skeen	Sloan	Evanson	Clarke, D	Cassidy	Aylott	Atkinson, G	Clayton	Fleming	Smithson	Bray	Curran	Gough	Thompson	Hatch	Thomas	Lowe	Light
3	4	5	6	7	8	9	10	11												
3	4	5	8	7	6	9	10	11												
3	4	5	8	7	**6**	9	10	11		12										
3	4	5		7	6	9	10	11	**8**		12									
3	4	5		7	6	**9**	10	11	8			12								
3	4	5	8	7	6		10	11		**9**			12							
3	4	5	8	7	6		10	11						9						
3	4	5	8	7	6		10	11						9						
3	4	5	8	7	6		10	11			12			**9**						
3	4	5	8	7	6	9	10	11												
3	4	5	8	**7**	6		10	11						9						
3	4	5	8	7	6	12	**10**	11						9						
3	4	5	8	7	6	10		11						9						
3	4	5	8	7	**6**	10		11					12	9						
3	4	5	8	7	6		10	11						9						
3	4	5	**8**	7	6		10	11					12	9						
3	4	5	7		6			11			8		10	9						
3	4	5	**7**	12	6			11			8		10	9						
3	4	5			6	8		11			7		10	9						
3	4	5		8	6			11			7		10	9						
3	4	5		7	6	**10**	12	11			8			9						
3	4	5		**7**	6		12	11			8		10	9						
3	4	5	9		6	10	11				8				7	12				
	4	5	11		6		9				8		10		7		3			
	4	5	8		6		9	12			**7**		10		11		3			
	4	5	7		6		10				8			9	11		3			
	4	5	11		6		9				**8**		12	10	7		3			
3	4	5	11		6		10				8			9	7					
3	4	5			6	11					7		10	9		8				
3	4	5	11	7	6		9				8			10						
3	4	5		7	6		10	11			8			9						
3	4	**5**			6	12	9	11			8			10	7			1		
3	4		12		6		9	**11**			8			10	7			1	5	
3	4		6				9	11			8			10	7			1	5	
	4		6			7	9	11			8			10			3	1	5	
3	4		**8**		6	9	11				7			10	12			1	5	
3	4	8			6		10	12			7			11	9				5	
3	4	9			6		10				8			11	7				5	
	4	5	11		6	7	9				8			10			3			
3	4	5			6		9		8		7			11	10					
3	4	5			**6**	10	9	12	11		8				7					2
3	4	5	12			8	9	11	6					10	**7**					2

3	4	5	11		6		9				8			10	7
3	4	5	11		6	12	9				**8**			10	7

3	4	5	8	7	6	9	10	11											
3	4	5	8	7	6		10	11		9									
3	4	5	8	7	6		10	11					9						

3	4	**5**		7	6		9	11			8			10					12
			11		6	7	9				8	4		10			3	1	5
3	4	11			6	**9**					8		12	10	7				5
3	4	5				8	9		11		6			10	7				

44	50	46	33	25	47	21	41	32	6	2	31	1	9	37	18	1	7	6	8	2
			2	1		3	2	3		1	2	1	5		1	1			1	
1	4	1	3	3	3	8	10	1		1	2		5	17	3		1			

League Table

	P	W	D	L	F	A	Pts
Burnley	42	24	14	4	72	35	62
Queen's Park Rangers	42	24	13	5	81	37	61
Aston Villa	42	18	14	10	51	47	50
Middlesbrough	42	17	13	12	46	43	47
Bristol City	42	17	12	13	63	51	46
Sunderland	42	17	12	13	59	49	46
Blackpool	42	18	10	14	56	51	46
Oxford United	42	19	7	16	52	43	45
Fulham	42	16	12	14	58	49	44
Sheffield Wednesday	42	17	10	15	59	55	44
Millwall	42	16	10	16	55	47	42
Luton Town	42	15	11	16	44	53	41
Hull City	42	14	12	16	64	59	40
Nottingham Forest	42	14	12	16	47	52	40
Orient	42	12	12	18	49	53	36
Swindon Town	42	10	16	16	46	60	36
Portsmouth	42	12	11	19	42	59	35
Carlisle United	42	11	12	19	50	52	34
Preston North End	42	11	12	19	37	64	34
Cardiff City	42	11	11	20	43	58	33
Huddersfield Town	42	8	17	17	36	56	33
Brighton & Hove Albion	42	8	13	21	46	83	29

1973-74

Division Two

Manager: Gerry Summers

Did you know that?

For the first time United produced detailed proposals for a move from the Manor, with Brasenose Driftway identified as the new location.

Changing rooms and dugouts were built in the Beech Road stand, with the former Dressing Room stand becoming the Manor Club.

The Manor witnessed live electric music for the first time, with bands Ace, Starry Eyed & Laughing, and Brinsley Schwarz playing before three home games, until neighbours complained about the noise.

Blackpool bought John Evanson for £40,000, with Oxford using £30,000 to replace him with Max Briggs from Norwich City. United also sold Nigel Cassidy to Cambridge United for £28,000.

An end-of-season upheaval saw six board members resign, including chairman Bob Kearsey and former chairman Vic Couling. Tony Rosser became the club's new chairman.

Match No.	Date		Opponents	Result	(F-A)	Scorers	A
1	25/08/1973	A	Hull City	D	0-0		
2	01/09/1973	H	Nottingham Forest	W	1-0	Cassidy	
3	08/09/1973	A	Aston Villa	L	0-2		
4	12/09/1973	A	Cardiff City	L	0-5		
5	15/09/1973	H	Sunderland	L	0-1		
6	19/09/1973	H	Notts County	W	2-1	D Clarke, Roberts	
7	22/09/1973	A	Carlisle United	L	1-2	Curran	
8	26/09/1973	H	Fulham	D	0-0		
9	02/10/1973	A	Notts County	D	0-0		
10	06/10/1973	A	Portsmouth	L	1-2	Cassidy	
11	13/10/1973	H	Crystal Palace	D	1-1	Curran	
12	20/10/1973	A	Swindon Town	L	0-1		
13	24/10/1973	H	Cardiff City	W	4-2	Cassidy, D Clarke (2), Jeffrey	
14	27/10/1973	H	Orient	D	1-1	Curran	
15	03/11/1973	A	Bolton Wanderers	L	1-2	Cassidy	
16	10/11/1973	H	Middlesbrough	L	0-2		
17	17/11/1973	H	Preston North End	D	1-1	Curran	
18	24/11/1973	A	Sheffield Wednesday	W	1-0	Curran	
19	08/12/1973	A	West Bromwich Albion	L	0-1		
20	15/12/1973	H	Blackpool	D	2-2	Curran (2) (1 pen)	
21	22/12/1973	A	Fulham	L	1-3	D Clarke	
22	26/12/1973	H	Bristol City	W	5-0	G Atkinson (2), Cassidy, C Clarke, Curran	
23	29/12/1973	H	Aston Villa	W	2-1	G Atkinson, Cassidy	
24	01/01/1974	A	Nottingham Forest	D	1-1	D Clarke	
25	12/01/1974	A	Sunderland	D	0-0		
26	19/01/1974	H	Hull City	D	1-1	Gough	
27	26/01/1974	H	Millwall	L	0-3		
28	02/02/1974	A	Blackpool	L	0-2		
29	17/02/1974	A	Crystal Palace	L	0-2		
30	23/02/1974	H	Portsmouth	W	3-0	Aylott, Curran, Gough	
31	02/03/1974	A	Bristol City	D	0-0		
32	10/03/1974	A	Orient	D	1-1	Hoadley (og)	
33	17/03/1974	H	Swindon Town	D	1-1	Curran	
34	23/03/1974	A	Middlesbrough	L	0-1		
35	30/03/1974	H	Bolton Wanderers	L	0-2		
36	06/04/1974	H	Sheffield Wednesday	W	1-0	Curran	
37	12/04/1974	H	Luton Town	D	1-1	Curran	
38	13/04/1974	A	Preston North End	D	0-0		
39	16/04/1974	A	Luton Town	W	1-0	Skeen	
40	20/04/1974	H	West Bromwich Albion	W	1-0	Aylott	
41	23/04/1974	H	Carlisle United	L	0-1		
42	27/04/1974	A	Millwall	D	0-0		

FA Cup

R3	05/01/1974	H	Manchester City	L	2-5	G Atkinson, Curran (pen)

League Cup

R2	10/10/1973	H	Fulham	D	1-1	Curran
r	16/10/1973	A	Fulham	L	0-3	

Total appear
Sub appear
Total

Shuker	Roberts	Clarke, C	Evanson	Fleming	Atkinson, G	Clarke, D	Curran	Cassidy	Bray	Skeen	Gough	Aylott	Lowe	Jeffrey	Light	Flay	Smithson	Briggs
3	4	5	6	7	8	9	10	11										
3	4	5	6	7	8	9	10	11										
3	4	5	**6**	7	8	9		10	11	12								
3	4	5		8	11	10		9		**6**	7	12						
3	4	5		**7**	**8**	9		10	11	12		6						
3	4	5		8	11	7	10	9				6						
3	4	5	6	8	12	7	10	9				**11**						
3	4		**8**		12	7	10	9		6			5	11				
3	4	6		12		7	10	9		8			5	**11**				
3	4	11				7	10	9		6			5	8				
3	4		6	8		7	10	9		11	12		5		2			
	4		6		**7**	9	10			11	12		5	8	2	3		
3	4		6			7	10	9		11			5	8	2			
3	4		6			7	10	9		11			5	8	2			
3	4		6			7	10	9		11	12		5	**8**	2			
3	4	5	6		8	11		10		12	9			**7**				
3	4	5	6		8	9	11	10						7				
3	4	5	6	10	8		11	**9**		7							12	
3	4	5	6	8	10	9	11			7								
3	4	5	6	7	8	10	11			9								
3	4	5	6		8	9	11			7		12		**10**				
3	4	5	6		8	7	10	9				11						
3	4	5	**6**		8	7	10	9		12		11						
3	4	5	6		8	7	10	9				11						
3	4	5		6	8	7	10	**9**		12		11			2			
3	4	5		**6**	8	9	10			12	7	11			2			
3	4	5	12		8	9		10		**6**	7	11			2			
3	**4**	5	6	12		9			8	10	7	11			2			
3	4	5	**6**		8	9	10			12	7	11			2			
3	4	5			8	9	10				7	11			2			6
3	4	5			8	9	10				7	11			2			6
3	4	5			8	10	9				7	11			2			6
3	4	5			8	10	9				7	11			2			6
3	4	5			8	10	9			12	**7**	11			2			6
3	4	5			8	7	9		10	12		**11**			2			6
3	4	5		8		7	**9**		12		10	11			2			6
3	4	5		8	11	**9**	10		12		7				2			6
3	4	5		8	**10**		9		12	7		11			2			6
3	4	5		8			9		10	7		11			2			6
3	4	5		7			9		10	8		11			2			6
3	4	5		8			9		10	7		11			2			6
3	4	5		7		11	9				10				2		8	6

3	4	**5**	6		8	7	10	9		12		11						

3	4		6	8		7	10	9		11			5		2			
	4		6			7	10	9		11	8		5		2	3		

43	45	37	24	21	29	40	39	25	7	21	15	23	10	10	25	2	1	13
			1	2	2				3	10	3	2					1	
	1	1			4	5	14	6		1	2	2		1				

League Table

	P	W	D	L	F	A	Pts
Middlesbrough	42	27	11	4	77	30	65
Luton Town	42	19	12	11	64	51	50
Carlisle United	42	20	9	13	61	48	49
Orient	42	15	18	9	55	42	48
Blackpool	42	17	13	12	57	40	47
Sunderland	42	19	9	14	58	44	47
Nottingham Forest	42	15	15	12	57	43	45
West Bromwich Albion	42	14	16	12	48	45	44
Hull City	42	13	17	12	46	47	43
Notts County	42	15	13	14	55	60	43
Bolton Wanderers	42	15	12	15	44	40	42
Millwall	42	14	14	14	51	51	42
Fulham	42	16	10	16	39	43	42
Aston Villa	42	13	15	14	48	45	41
Portsmouth	42	14	12	16	45	62	40
Bristol City	42	14	10	18	47	54	38
Cardiff City	42	10	16	16	49	62	36
Oxford United	42	10	16	16	35	46	36
Sheffield Wednesday	42	12	11	19	51	63	35
Crystal Palace	42	11	12	19	43	56	34
Preston North End	42	9	14	19	40	62	31
Swindon Town	42	7	11	24	36	72	25

1974-75

Division Two

Manager: Gerry Summers

Did you know that?

United broke their club transfer fee record again with the signing of Andy McCulloch for £70,000 from Cardiff City. They also paid £20,000 to Dumbarton for Brian Heron and £10,000 to Portsmouth for John Milkins.

Graham Atkinson, the only surviving player from Southern League days, left to join his brother Ron at Kettering. Hugh Curran was sold to Bolton Wanderers for £50,000, while Dave Roberts left to join Hull City for £70,000.

United's 1–0 win over Manchester United was the first time that Oxford had beaten the Red Devils, and the game featured Hugh McGrogan making his debut.

Match No.	Date		Opponents	Result	(F-A)	Scorers	A
1	17/08/1974	A	Cardiff City	D	1-1	Heron	
2	24/08/1974	H	York City	W	3-1	Curran, Roberts, Swallow (og)	
3	31/08/1974	A	Nottingham Forest	W	2-1	McCulloch (2)	
4	07/09/1974	H	Oldham Athletic	W	1-0	Heron	
5	14/09/1974	A	Millwall	D	0-0		
6	17/09/1974	A	York City	D	1-1	Heron	
7	21/09/1974	H	Orient	L	1-2	McCulloch	
8	25/09/1974	H	Southampton	L	0-4		
9	28/09/1974	A	West Bromwich Albion	L	0-3		
10	05/10/1974	A	Sunderland	L	0-2		
11	12/10/1974	H	Sheffield Wednesday	W	1-0	Bray	
12	19/10/1974	A	Notts County	L	1-4	Heron	
13	23/10/1974	H	Bristol City	W	2-0	Heron, Sims	
14	26/10/1974	H	Fulham	W	2-1	D Clarke (2)	
15	02/11/1974	A	Manchester United	L	0-4		
16	05/11/1974	A	Bristol City	L	0-3		
17	09/11/1974	H	Portsmouth	W	1-0	McCulloch	
18	16/11/1974	A	Blackpool	D	0-0		
19	23/11/1974	H	Bristol Rovers	W	2-1	Aylott, McCulloch	
20	30/11/1974	A	Aston Villa	D	0-0		
21	07/12/1974	H	Hull City	W	3-1	C Clarke, D Clarke, Light	
22	14/12/1974	H	Cardiff City	W	1-0	DClarke (pen)	
23	21/12/1974	A	Bolton Wanderers	L	1-3	Bray	
24	26/12/1974	H	Millwall	W	3-1	Aylott, Gough, Heron	
25	28/12/1974	A	Norwich City	L	0-1		
26	11/01/1975	A	Hull City	L	0-1		
27	18/01/1975	H	Aston Villa	L	1-2	D Clarke	
28	25/01/1975	H	Norwich City	W	2-1	Heron, Shuker (pen)	
29	01/02/1975	A	Portsmouth	L	1-2	McCulloch	
30	08/02/1975	H	Manchester United	W	1-0	D Clarke	
31	15/02/1975	A	Bristol Rovers	L	0-1		
32	22/02/1975	H	Blackpool	D	0-0		
33	28/02/1975	H	Nottingham Forest	D	1-1	Jeffrey	
34	15/03/1975	H	West Bromwich Albion	D	1-1	Shuker (pen)	
35	18/03/1975	A	Southampton	L	1-2	Aylott	
36	22/03/1975	A	Oldham Athletic	D	1-1	McGrogan	
37	29/03/1975	H	Bolton Wanderers	W	2-1	D Clarke, Shuker (pen)	
38	31/03/1975	A	Orient	D	1-1	D Clarke	
39	12/04/1975	H	Sunderland	W	1-0	C Clarke	
40	19/04/1975	A	Sheffield Wednesday	D	1-1	McCulloch	
41	22/04/1975	A	Fulham	D	0-0		
42	26/04/1975	H	Notts County	L	1-2	McCulloch	

FA Cup

R3	03/01/1975	A	Leicester City	L	1-3	D Clarke

League Cup

R1	20/08/1974	A	Colchester United	L	0-1	

Total appea
Sub appear
Total

Shuker	Roberts	Clarke, C	Briggs	Heron	Fleming	McCulloch	Jeffrey	Curran	Aylott	Clarke, D	Light	Smithson	Gough	Sims	Flay	Bray	Duncan	Burton	McGrogan	Lowe	Tait	Foley	Taylor
3	4	5	6	7	8	9	10	11															
3	4	5	6	11	**8**	9		10	7	12													
3	4	5	6	7		10	8		11	9													
3	4	5	6	11		10	8	12	7	**9**	2												
3	4	5	6	11	12	10	**8**		7	9	2												
3	4	5	6	11	12	10	**8**		7	9	2												
3	4	5	6	11		10	8		7	9	2												
3	4	5	6	11		**10**	8		7	9	2		12										
3		5	6		12		**8**		7	9	2	4	10	11									
3	4	5	6		8				11	9	2	**7**		10		12							
6	4	5		11	8				7	10	2				3	9							
6	4	5	12	11	8				7	9	2				**3**	10							
3	4	5	6	**11**	8				7	9	2			10		12							
3	4	5	6	11	8				7	9	2			10									
3	4	5	6	**11**	8	10			7	9	2			12									
3	4		6		8	10			7	9	2	5		11									
3	4	5	6			**10**			7	9	2		12	11			8						
3	4	5	6			8	10		7	9	2						11						
3	4	5	6	11		**10**			7	9	2					12	8						
3	4	5	6	11					7	9	2					10	8						
3	4	5	6	11		10			7	9	2						8						
3	4	5	6	11		10			7	9	2						8	1					
3	4	5	6	11		10			7		2					9	8	1					
3	4	5	6	11		**10**			7		2		12			9	8	1					
3	4	5	6	11					7		2		10			9	8	1					
3	4	5	6	11					8	9	2					10	7	1					
3	4	5	6	11					7	9	2		**10**			12	8	1					
3	4	5		11		10	8		6	9	2						7	1					
3	**4**	5	12	11		10	6		7	9	2						8	1					
3	4	5				10	6		7	9	2						8	1	11				
3		5				10	6		7	9							8	1	11	4			
3		5		11		10	6		7	9							8	1			4		
3		5		11	7	10	6			9	2						8	1			4		
3		5		11	**8**	10	6			9	2						7	1	12		4		
3		5				10	6		7	9	2						8	1	11		4		
3		5					6		11	9	2						8		7	4		10	
3		5		12			6		10	9	2						8		**7**	4		11	
3		5	8	11		10	6		12	9	**2**									4			7
3		5		**11**		8	6		10	9							7		12	4			2
3		5	12			**8**	6		10	9	2								7	4			11
3		5		11			6		7	9	2		10							4			8
3		5		12		10	6			9	2						**8**		7	4			11

Shuker	Roberts	Clarke, C	Briggs	Heron	Fleming	McCulloch	Jeffrey	Curran	Aylott	Clarke, D	Light	Smithson	Gough	Sims	Flay	Bray	Duncan	Burton	McGrogan	Lowe	Tait	Foley	Taylor
3		5	6	11					7	9	2					10	8	1		4			

Shuker	Roberts	Clarke, C	Briggs	Heron	Fleming	McCulloch	Jeffrey	Curran	Aylott	Clarke, D	Light	Smithson	Gough	Sims	Flay	Bray	Duncan	Burton	McGrogan	Lowe	Tait	Foley	Taylor
3	4	5	6	11	**8**	9	7	10	12														

Shuker	Roberts	Clarke, C	Briggs	Heron	Fleming	McCulloch	Jeffrey	Curran	Aylott	Clarke, D	Light	Smithson	Gough	Sims	Flay	Bray	Duncan	Burton	McGrogan	Lowe	Tait	Foley	Taylor
44	30	43	28	32	12	30	25	3	38	38	37	3	4	6	2	8	24	15	7	9	4	2	5
			3	2	3			1	2	1			3	1		4			2				
3	1	2		7		8	1	1	3	9	1		1	1		2			1				

League Table

	P	W	D	L	F	A	Pts
Manchester United	42	26	9	7	66	30	61
Aston Villa	42	25	8	9	79	32	58
Norwich City	42	20	13	9	58	37	53
Sunderland	42	19	13	10	65	35	51
Bristol City	42	21	8	13	47	33	50
West Bromwich Albion	42	18	9	15	54	42	45
Blackpool	42	14	17	11	38	33	45
Hull City	42	15	14	13	40	53	44
Fulham	42	13	16	13	44	39	42
Bolton Wanderers	42	15	12	15	45	41	42
Oxford United	42	15	12	15	41	51	42
Orient	42	11	20	11	28	39	42
Southampton	42	15	11	16	53	54	41
Notts County	42	12	16	14	49	59	40
York City	42	14	10	18	51	55	38
Nottingham Forest	42	12	14	16	43	55	38
Portsmouth	42	12	13	17	44	54	37
Oldham Athletic	42	10	15	17	40	48	35
Bristol Rovers	42	12	11	19	42	64	35
Millwall	42	10	12	20	44	56	32
Cardiff City	42	9	14	19	36	62	32
Sheffield Wednesday	42	5	11	26	29	64	21

1975-76

Division Two

Manager: Gerry Summers then Mick Brown

Did you know that?

At the start of the season United paid £35,000 to Chelsea for Peter Houseman.

On 21 February United had three players, Peter Houseman, Mick Tait and captain John Shuker, sent off at Blackpool.

Gerry Summers was sacked at the end of September, being replaced by Mick Brown. Brown signed Roger Hynd on loan from Birmingham, but Hynd returned when the board refused to allow him to become player-coach. Brown had no coach until the end of 1977–78.

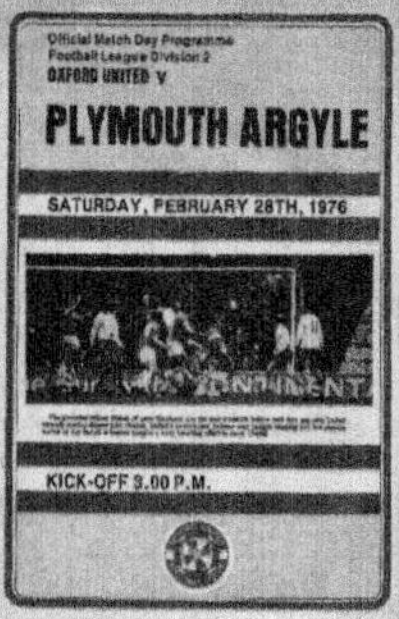

Match No.	Date		Opponents	Result	(F-A)	Scorers	A
1	16/08/1975	A	Carlisle United	D	1-1	Tait	
2	20/08/1975	H	Bolton Wanderers	W	2-0	D Clarke, Gibbins	
3	23/08/1975	H	Sunderland	D	1-1	D Clarke	
4	27/08/1975	A	Chelsea	L	1-3	McGrogan	
5	29/08/1975	A	Charlton Athletic	L	1-2	Tait	
6	06/09/1975	H	Fulham	L	1-3	D Clarke	
7	12/09/1975	A	Bristol City	L	1-4	Tait	
8	20/09/1975	H	Nottingham Forest	L	0-1		
9	27/09/1975	A	York City	L	0-2		
10	04/10/1975	H	Orient	W	2-1	D Clarke, Heron	
11	11/10/1975	A	Notts County	W	1-0	D Clarke	
12	18/10/1975	H	Blackburn Rovers	D	0-0		
13	25/10/1975	A	Plymouth Argyle	L	1-2	Tait	
14	01/11/1975	H	Hull City	L	2-3	Foley, McGrogan	
15	08/11/1975	A	Oldham Athletic	D	1-1	Tait	
16	12/11/1975	H	West Bromwich Albion	L	0-1		
17	15/11/1975	H	Blackpool	L	1-3	Shuker (pen)	
18	22/11/1975	A	Blackburn Rovers	D	0-0		
19	29/11/1975	A	Portsmouth	W	2-0	Tait (2)	
20	06/12/1975	H	Bristol Rovers	W	2-1	McCulloch, Tait	
21	13/12/1975	A	Sunderland	L	0-1		
22	20/12/1975	H	Carlisle United	D	0-0		
23	26/12/1975	A	Luton Town	L	2-3	Jeffrey, Shuker	
24	27/12/1975	H	Southampton	L	1-2	Tait	
25	10/01/1976	H	Bristol City	D	1-1	C Clarke	
26	17/01/1976	A	Fulham	D	1-1	Foley	
27	07/02/1976	H	Chelsea	D	1-1	Tait	
28	14/02/1976	H	Oldham Athletic	D	1-1	Foley	
29	21/02/1976	A	Blackpool	L	0-2		
30	25/02/1976	A	West Bromwich Albion	L	0-2		
31	28/02/1976	H	Plymouth Argyle	D	2-2	Tait (2)	
32	02/03/1976	A	Bolton Wanderers	W	1-0	Briggs	
33	06/03/1976	A	Hull City	L	0-2		
34	13/03/1976	H	Notts County	W	2-1	Aylott, C Clarke	
35	20/03/1976	H	Portsmouth	W	1-0	Foley	
36	27/03/1976	A	Bristol Rovers	W	1-0	Gibbins	
37	03/04/1976	H	York City	W	1-0	D Clarke	
38	10/04/1976	A	Nottingham Forest	L	0-4		
39	16/04/1976	H	Charlton Athletic	W	1-0	Lowe	
40	17/04/1976	H	Luton Town	L	1-3	D Clarke	
41	19/04/1976	A	Southampton	L	1-2	Shuker (pen)	
42	24/04/1976	A	Orient	L	1-2	Jeffrey	

FA Cup

R3	03/01/1976	A	Manchester United	L	1-2	D Clarke

League Cup

R2	09/09/1975	A	Charlton Athletic	D	3-3	Aylott, Foley, Jeffrey
r	16/09/1975	H	Charlton Athletic	D	1-1	Heron
r2	29/09/1975	H	Charlton Athletic	L	2-3	Jeffrey, Lowe

Total appear
Sub appear
Total

Shuker	Lowe	Clarke, C	Jeffrey	Houseman	Tait	Clarke, D	Gibbins	Heron	Aylott	McGrogan	Milkins	Bodel	Duncan	Foley	Taylor	Briggs	Hynd	McCulloch
3	4	5	6	7	8	9	10	11										
3	4	5	6	7	8	9	10	11	2									
3	4	5	6	7	**8**	9	10	11	2	12								
3	4	5	6	11	8	9	10		2	7								
3	4	5	6	11	8	9	10			7	1							
3	**4**	5	6	11	8	9	10		2	7	1			12				
3		5	6		12	9			11	7	1	4	8	**10**				
3	4	5		**10**	8	9		11	7	12					2	6		
3	4	5	6		12	9		11	7				**8**	10	2			
3		5	6	7		9		11	8					10	2		4	
3		5	6	7	12	9		**11**	8					10	2		4	
3		5	**6**	7	8	9			11	12				10	2		4	
3		5	**6**	7	8	9			11	12				10	2		4	
3		5	6	7	8	9			**11**	12				10	2		4	
3	4	5	6	7	8	9			11					10	2			
3	4	5	6	7	8		12		**9**	11				10	2			
3	4	5	6	7	10	9			11					8	2			
3	5		6	7	10	9			11	12		4		**8**	2			
3	4	5	6	**7**	8	9			11					12	2			10
3	4	5	6	7	8	9			11						2			10
3		5	6	7	8	9			11			4			2			10
3	4	5	6	7	8	**9**			11					12	2			10
3	4	5	6	7	11				8					9	2			10
3	4	5	**6**	7	11	9			8					12	2			10
3	4	5	**11**	7		9			8					12	2	6		10
3	4	5		7	11	9			12					8	**2**	6		10
3	4	5		7	11	9								8	2	6		10
3	4	5		7	11	9								8	2	6		10
3	4	5		7	11	9			12					8	2	**6**		10
	4	5	7			9	12		3				**11**	8	2	6		10
3	4	**5**	6	7	10	9	12						11	8	2			
3	4	5		7	11	9	10		8						2	6		
	4	5	7			9	10		3				11	8	2	6		
3	4	5		7		9	10		11					8	2	6		
3	4	5		7	11	9	10							8	2	6		
3	4	5		7	11	9	10							8	2	6		
3	4	5	7		11	9	10		12					**8**	2	6		
3	4	5		7	11	9	10							8	2	6		
3	4	5		7	11	9	10							8	2	6		
3	4	5		7	11	9	**10**		12					8	2	6		
3	4	5		8	10	9			11	**7**				12	2	6		
3	4	5	11	7	10		9							8	2	6		

Shuker	Lowe	Clarke, C	Jeffrey	Houseman	Tait	Clarke, D	Gibbins	Heron	Aylott	McGrogan	Milkins	Bodel	Duncan	Foley	Taylor	Briggs	Hynd	McCulloch
3	4	5	6	7		9			8						2	11		10

Shuker	Lowe	Clarke, C	Jeffrey	Houseman	Tait	Clarke, D	Gibbins	Heron	Aylott	McGrogan	Milkins	Bodel	Duncan	Foley	Taylor	Briggs	Hynd	McCulloch
3		5	6			9			11	7	1	4	8	10				
3	4	5	6	7		9		11	2				8	10				
3	4	5	**6**	7	12	9		11	8					10	2			

Shuker	Lowe	Clarke, C	Jeffrey	Houseman	Tait	Clarke, D	Gibbins	Heron	Aylott	McGrogan	Milkins	Bodel	Duncan	Foley	Taylor	Briggs	Hynd	McCulloch
44	38	45	33	40	34	43	16	9	32	7	4	4	7	30	37	19	5	13
					4		3		4	6				6				
3	2	2	4		12	8	2	2	2	2				5		1		1

League Table

	P	W	D	L	F	A	Pts
Sunderland	42	24	8	10	67	36	56
Bristol City	42	19	15	8	59	35	53
West Bromwich Albion	42	20	13	9	50	33	53
Bolton Wanderers	42	20	12	10	64	38	52
Notts County	42	19	11	12	60	41	49
Southampton	42	21	7	14	66	50	49
Luton Town	42	19	10	13	61	51	48
Nottingham Forest	42	17	12	13	55	40	46
Charlton Athletic	42	15	12	15	61	72	42
Blackpool	42	14	14	14	40	49	42
Chelsea	42	12	16	14	53	54	40
Fulham	42	13	14	15	45	47	40
Orient	42	13	14	15	37	39	40
Hull City	42	14	11	17	45	49	39
Blackburn Rovers	42	12	14	16	45	50	38
Plymouth Argyle	42	13	12	17	48	54	38
Oldham Athletic	42	13	12	17	57	68	38
Bristol Rovers	42	11	16	15	38	50	38
Carlisle United	42	12	13	17	45	59	37
Oxford United	42	11	11	20	39	59	33
York City	42	10	8	24	39	71	28
Portsmouth	42	9	7	26	32	61	25

1976-77

Division Three

Manager: Mick Brown

Did you know that?

On 4 October Tony Rosser resigned as chairman, being replaced by Geoff Coppock, son of former chairman, Ron. Coppock himself stood down on 4 January to be replaced by Bill Reeves, while Desmond Morris was co-opted onto the board.

On 20 March Peter Houseman, his wife and two friends were killed in a car crash that left six orphaned children.

John Shuker's Oxford career came to an end after 534 appearances, second only to Ron Atkinson, while Derek Clarke left for Orient.

Jason Seacole became the youngest player to play a League game for the club, aged 16 years and 149 days. It is a record that still stands.

Match No.	Date		Opponents	Result	(F-A)	Scorers	A
1	21/08/1976	A	Brighton & Hove Albion	L	2-3	Tait (2)	
2	28/08/1976	A	Chester City	W	3-1	Houseman, McGrogan, Loska (og)	
3	04/09/1976	H	Preston North End	D	2-2	C Clarke, Tait	
4	07/09/1976	H	Mansfield Town	L	0-3		
5	11/09/1976	A	Rotherham United	D	1-1	Shuker (pen)	
6	18/09/1976	H	Grimsby Town	W	5-2	C Clarke, Fogg, Foley, Tait, Harding (og)	
7	25/09/1976	A	York City	L	1-2	Tait	
8	02/10/1976	H	Tranmere Rovers	D	1-1	Jeffrey	
9	09/10/1976	A	Crystal Palace	D	2-2	Foley (2)	
10	16/10/1976	H	Bury	D	2-2	Bodel, Foley	
11	23/10/1976	A	Peterborough United	L	0-2		
12	26/10/1976	H	Lincoln City	L	1-2	Bodel	
13	30/10/1976	A	Shrewsbury Town	L	0-1		
14	02/11/1976	A	Walsall	D	2-2	Tait (2)	
15	06/11/1976	H	Portsmouth	W	2-1	Tait (2)	
16	13/11/1976	A	Northampton Town	L	0-1		
17	27/11/1976	H	Port Vale	D	0-0		
18	04/12/1976	A	Wrexham	D	1-1	Jeffrey	
19	11/12/1976	H	Gillingham	W	3-1	Houseman, Jeffrey, Tait	
20	18/12/1976	H	Sheffield Wednesday	D	1-1	Foley	
21	27/12/1976	A	Swindon Town	L	0-1		
22	29/12/1976	H	Reading	W	1-0	Foley	
23	01/01/1977	A	Portsmouth	D	1-1	Foley (pen)	
24	08/01/1977	H	Chesterfield	W	3-2	Bodel, Foley, Taylor	
25	22/01/1977	H	Brighton & Hove Albion	W	1-0	Lowe	
26	29/01/1977	A	Gillingham	D	1-1	Tait	
27	05/02/1977	H	Chester City	W	2-0	Bodel, Jeffrey	
28	07/02/1977	A	Mansfield Town	L	0-3		
29	12/02/1977	A	Preston North End	L	1-2	Lowe	
30	19/02/1977	H	Rotherham United	L	1-2	Jeffrey	
31	26/02/1977	A	Grimsby Town	W	2-1	Jeffrey, Taylor	
32	01/03/1977	H	Shrewsbury Town	W	4-2	Foley, Jeffrey (2), Seacole	
33	05/03/1977	H	York City	L	0-2		
34	11/03/1977	A	Tranmere Rovers	D	1-1	Foley	
35	19/03/1977	H	Crystal Palace	L	0-1		
36	26/03/1977	A	Bury	L	1-2	Seacole	
37	02/04/1977	H	Peterborough United	L	2-3	Bodel, Seacole	
38	08/04/1977	H	Swindon Town	D	0-0		
39	09/04/1977	A	Reading	L	0-2		
40	12/04/1977	H	Walsall	D	0-0		
41	16/04/1977	A	Lincoln City	W	1-0	Foley	
42	23/04/1977	H	Northampton Town	W	1-0	C Clarke	
43	30/04/1977	A	Port Vale	L	1-2	Bodel	
44	04/05/1977	A	Chesterfield	L	0-2		
45	07/05/1977	H	Wrexham	D	2-2	Foley, Dwyer (og)	
46	14/05/1977	A	Sheffield Wednesday	L	0-2		

FA Cup

R1	20/11/1976	A	Kettering Town	D	1-1	Foley	
r	23/11/1976	H	Kettering Town	L	0-1		

League Cup

R1/1	14/08/1976	H	Cambridge United	W	1-0	Tait	
R1/2	17/08/1976	A	Cambridge United	L	0-2		

Total appear
Sub appear
Total

Shuker	Bodel	Clarke, C	Briggs	McGrogan	Houseman	Foley	Tait	Duncan	Jeffrey	Fogg	Seacole	Milkins	Lowe	Heron	White	Berry	Aleksic	Kingston	Clarke, D
3	4	5	**6**	7	8	9	10	11	12										
3	4	5		7	8	9	10	**11**	6	12									
3	4	5		7	**8**	9	10	11	6	12									
3	4	5	8	7		9	10	11	**6**		12								
3	4	5	6	7	8	9	10	11											
	4	5	6	7	8	9	10	11		3									
12	4	5	6	7		9	**10**	11	8	3									
	4	5	6	7		9		10	8	3	11								
3	4	5	6	7		9		11	8		10								
	4	5	6	7		9	10	11	8	3									
3	4	5	6	7		9	10	11	**8**		12								
3	4	5	6	7	8	9	**10**	11			12	1							
3	4	5	6	7	8	9	10	11				1							
3	4	5		**7**	8	9	10	11	6	2	12	1							
3	4	5		7	8	9	10	11	6	2		1							
3	4	5		**7**	8	9	10	11	6	2	12	1							
3	4	5		7	8	9		11	6	2	10	1							
3	4	5	7		8	9	10	11	6	2		1							
3	4	5	7		8	9	10	11	6	2									
3	4	5	7		8	9	10	11	6	2									
3	4		7	12	**8**	9	10	11	6	2			5						
3	4	5	7		8	9	10	11	6	2									
3	4	5	7		8	9	10	11	6	2									
3	4	5	7	12	8	9	10	11		2									
3	4		7		8	9	10	11	6	2			5						
3	4		7		8	9	10	11	6	2			5						
3	4		7		8	9		11	6	2	10		5						
3	4		7		8	9		11	6	2	10		5						
3	4				8	9		11	6	2	10		5						
3	4				8	9		11	6	2	10		5						
3	4			12	8	9		**11**	6	2	10		5						
	4		8	7		**9**		11	6	3	10		5	12					
	4		7	**11**	8	9		12	6	3	10		5						
	4		7		8	9		11	6	3	10		5						
	4		**7**	12	8	9		11	6	3	10		5						
3	4			**7**		9		11	6	2	10		5			12			
3	4					9		10	6	2	8		5	11		12			
	4	5	9			9		11	6	3	**10**			7		12			
	4	5	**9**			9		11	6	3	10			7		12			
	4	5	9			**7**		11	6	3	10					8			
	4	5	7	12		8		11	6	3	**10**					9			
	4	5	7	12		9		11	6	3	**10**					8			
	4	5	8	7		9		11	6	3						10			
	4	5	8	7		9		11	6	3						10			
	4	5	8	7		9		11	6	3					10				
	4	5	**8**	7		9		11	6	3					10			12	

Shuker	Bodel	Clarke, C	Briggs	McGrogan	Houseman	Foley	Tait	Duncan	Jeffrey	Fogg	Seacole	Milkins	Lowe	Heron	White	Berry	Aleksic	Kingston	Clarke, D
3	4	5		7	8	9	10	11	6	2		1							
3	4	5		7	8	9	10	11	6	2		1							

Shuker	Bodel	Clarke, C	Briggs	McGrogan	Houseman	Foley	Tait	Duncan	Jeffrey	Fogg	Seacole	Milkins	Lowe	Heron	White	Berry	Aleksic	Kingston	Clarke, D
3	4	5	6	7	8	9	10	11									1		
	4	5	6	7	8	9	10	**11**		3							1		12

Shuker	Bodel	Clarke, C	Briggs	McGrogan	Houseman	Foley	Tait	Duncan	Jeffrey	Fogg	Seacole	Milkins	Lowe	Heron	White	Berry	Aleksic	Kingston	Clarke, D
32	50	36	37	28	32	50	27	49	42	40	19	9	14	3	2	5	2	0	0
										2	5			1		4		1	1
											3		2						

League Table

	P	W	D	L	F	A	Pts
Mansfield Town	46	28	8	10	78	42	64
Brighton & Hove Albion	46	25	11	10	83	40	61
Crystal Palace	46	23	13	10	68	40	59
Rotherham United	46	22	15	9	69	44	59
Wrexham	46	24	10	12	80	54	58
Preston North End	46	21	12	13	64	43	54
Bury	46	23	8	15	64	59	54
Sheffield Wednesday	46	22	9	15	65	55	53
Lincoln City	46	19	14	13	77	70	52
Shrewsbury Town	46	18	11	17	65	59	47
Swindon Town	46	15	15	16	68	75	45
Gillingham	46	16	12	18	55	64	44
Chester	46	18	8	20	48	58	44
Tranmere Rovers	46	13	17	16	51	53	43
Walsall	46	13	15	18	57	65	41
Peterborough United	46	13	15	18	55	65	41
Oxford United	46	12	15	19	55	65	39
Chesterfield	46	14	10	22	56	64	38
Port Vale	46	11	16	19	47	71	38
Portsmouth	46	11	14	21	53	70	36
Reading	46	13	9	24	49	73	35
Northampton Town	46	13	8	25	60	75	34
Grimsby Town	46	12	9	25	45	69	33
York City	46	10	12	24	50	89	32

1977-78

Division Three

Manager: Mick Brown

Did you know that?

Oxford United's youth team reached the South East Counties League Cup Final.

In March Colin Clarke left for Los Angeles Aztecs, having played 497 games for the club.

Hugh Curran returned from Bolton, and Brian Drysdale signed from Bristol City. In January Gary Briggs was signed on loan from Middlesbrough.

Nick Merry joined the club as an apprentice.

The attendance of 3,113 for the Cambridge United game on 11 January 1978 was the lowest at the Manor for a Football League fixture.

Match No.	Date		Opponents	Result	(F-A)	Scorers
1	20/08/1977	H	Rotherham United	L	2-3	Seacole, Taylor
2	22/08/1977	A	Wrexham	D	2-2	Fogg, Foley
3	27/08/1977	A	Bradford City	W	3-2	Berry, Foley, Jeffrey
4	03/09/1977	H	Preston North End	W	1-0	Curran
5	10/09/1977	A	Gillingham	L	1-2	McGrogan
6	14/09/1977	H	Lincoln City	W	1-0	Curran
7	17/09/1977	A	Carlisle United	D	2-2	Foley, Taylor
8	24/09/1977	H	Chester City	W	4-1	Foley (3) (1 pen), Taylor
9	28/09/1977	H	Portsmouth	D	0-0	
10	01/10/1977	A	Hereford United	L	1-2	Duncan
11	04/10/1977	A	Peterborough United	L	0-1	
12	08/10/1977	H	Tranmere Rovers	W	1-0	Taylor
13	14/10/1977	A	Colchester United	D	1-1	Foley
14	22/10/1977	H	Plymouth Argyle	W	2-1	Bodel, Curran
15	29/10/1977	A	Cambridge United	L	1-2	Curran
16	05/11/1977	A	Exeter City	L	1-2	Curran
17	12/11/1977	H	Sheffield Wednesday	W	1-0	Taylor
18	19/11/1977	A	Walsall	L	1-2	McGrogan
19	03/12/1977	H	Shrewsbury Town	D	1-1	Foley
20	10/12/1977	A	Bury	L	2-3	Foley (pen), Seacole
21	16/12/1977	A	Tranmere Rovers	L	1-4	Seacole
22	26/12/1977	H	Swindon Town	D	3-3	Foley (2), Stott
23	27/12/1977	A	Port Vale	D	1-1	Stott
24	31/12/1977	H	Exeter City	D	0-0	
25	02/01/1978	A	Chesterfield	L	0-3	
26	11/01/1978	H	Cambridge United	L	2-3	Foley, Jeffrey
27	14/01/1978	A	Rotherham United	L	0-2	
28	21/01/1978	H	Bradford City	W	3-1	Curran, Foley (2)
29	04/02/1978	H	Gillingham	D	1-1	Seacole
30	11/02/1978	H	Carlisle United	D	0-0	
31	21/02/1978	A	Preston North End	L	2-3	Curran, Duncan
32	25/02/1978	H	Hereford United	W	3-0	Curran, Foley, Seacole
33	01/03/1978	H	Wrexham	W	2-1	Curran, Foley
34	08/03/1978	A	Lincoln City	L	0-1	
35	11/03/1978	H	Colchester United	W	3-0	Curran (2) (1 pen), Jeffrey
36	18/03/1978	A	Plymouth Argyle	L	1-2	Bodel
37	25/03/1978	H	Port Vale	D	1-1	Foley
38	27/03/1978	A	Swindon Town	L	2-3	Foley, Seacole
39	01/04/1978	H	Chesterfield	D	1-1	Seacole
40	04/04/1978	A	Portsmouth	W	2-0	Seacole, Taylor (og)
41	08/04/1978	A	Sheffield Wednesday	L	1-2	G Briggs
42	12/04/1978	A	Chester City	L	1-3	Fogg (pen)
43	15/04/1978	H	Walsall	W	3-1	Bodel, Foley, Seacole
44	22/04/1978	A	Shrewsbury Town	L	0-1	
45	26/04/1978	H	Peterborough United	D	3-3	G Briggs, Duncan, Taylor
46	29/04/1978	H	Bury	D	0-0	

FA Cup

R1	26/11/1977	A	Nuneaton Borough	L	0-2	

League Cup

R1/1	13/08/1977	H	Shrewsbury Town	W	3-0	Foley, McGrogan (2)
R1/2	16/08/1977	A	Shrewsbury Town	D	2-2	Foley, Seacole
R2	31/08/1977	H	Bury	D	1-1	White
r	05/09/1977	A	Bury	L	0-1	

Total appear
Sub appear
Total

Drysdale	Bodel	Clarke	Jeffrey	McGrogan	Duncan	Foley	Seacole	Taylor	Berry	Curran	Briggs, M	Kingston	Milkins	Doyle	Stott	Briggs, G	White
3	4	5	6	7	8	9	10	11									
3	4	5	6	**7**	11	9	10	8	12								
3	4	5	6		11	9	10	8	7								
3	4	5	6	7	11	9	10	8		12							
	4	5	6	7	11	9	12	2		10	**8**						
	4	5	6	7	11	9		8		10		2					
	4	5	6	7	11	9		8		10		2					
	4	5	6	**7**	11	9	12	8		10		2					
	4	5	6	**7**	11	9	12	8		10		2					
	4	5	6	7	11	9		8		10		2					
	4	5	6	**7**	11	9	12	8		10		2					
	4	5	6	**7**	11	9		8	12	10		2					
	4	5	6		11	9		8	7	10		2					
	4	5	6	7	11	9		8		10		2					
	4	5	6	7	11	9		8		10		2					
	4	5	6	7		9	12	11		10	**8**	2					
	4	5	6	7	11		9	8		10		2					
	4	5	6	7	11		9	2	8	10							
	4	5	6		11	9	7	8		10			1	2			
	4	5	**6**	12	7	9	10	8		11			1	2			
	4	5	6	12	11	9	7	8		**10**		1	2				
3		5	6	7	11	9	10	8					1		4		
3	4		6		**11**	9	10	8	7	12			1		5		
3	4		**6**	7	11	9	10	8		12			1		5		
3	4				11	9	7	8	6	10			1		5		
3			6		11	9	7	8		10			1		5	4	
3		5	6		11	9	10	8	**7**	12						4	
3		5	6		11	9	8	7		**10**						4	12
3		5	6		11	9	8	7		10						4	
3		5	6		11	9	7	8		10						4	
3		5	6	7	11		9	8		**10**						4	12
3		5	6	12	**11**	9	7	8		10						4	
		5		7	**11**	9		8	6	10		2				4	12
	5		6	**7**	11	9	10	8				2				4	12
	5		6	12	11	9	7	8		**10**		2				4	
	5		6		11	9	7	8		10		2				4	
	5		6	12	11	9	**7**	8		10		2				4	
	5		6		11	9	7	8		10		2				4	
	5		**6**	11	11	9	7	10				2				4	12
	5		6	7	11	9	10	8				2				4	
	5		6	7	11	9	10	8				2				4	
	5		6	**7**	11	9	10	8				2				4	12
	5		6	7	11	9	10	8				2				4	
	5		6	**7**	11	9	10	8				2			4		12
	5		6		11	9	10	8				2				4	7
	5		6		11	9	10	8				2				4	7

Drysdale	Bodel	Clarke	Jeffrey	McGrogan	Duncan	Foley	Seacole	Taylor	Berry	Curran	Briggs, M	Kingston	Milkins	Doyle	Stott	Briggs, G	White
	4	5	6	12	11	9	7	2	**8**	10							

Drysdale	Bodel	Clarke	Jeffrey	McGrogan	Duncan	Foley	Seacole	Taylor	Berry	Curran	Briggs, M	Kingston	Milkins	Doyle	Stott	Briggs, G	White
3	4	5	10	7		**9**	12	8		11	6						
3	4	5	6	7		9	12	11		**10**	8						
3	4	5	6		11	9	10	7	**8**								12
	4	**5**	6	7	11	9	10	2			8						12

Drysdale	Bodel	Clarke	Jeffrey	McGrogan	Duncan	Foley	Seacole	Taylor	Berry	Curran	Briggs, M	Kingston	Milkins	Doyle	Stott	Briggs, G	White
18	42	34	49	30	48	48	36	51	9	32	5	26	8	3	6	20	2
				6			7		2	4							9
	3		3	4	3	21	10	6	1	11					2	2	1

League Table

	P	W	D	L	F	A	Pts
Wrexham	46	23	15	8	78	45	61
Cambridge United	46	23	12	11	72	51	58
Preston North End	46	20	16	10	63	38	56
Peterborough United	46	20	16	10	47	33	56
Chester	46	16	22	8	59	56	54
Walsall	46	18	17	11	61	50	53
Gillingham	46	15	20	11	67	60	50
Colchester United	46	15	18	13	55	44	48
Chesterfield	46	17	14	15	58	49	48
Swindon Town	46	16	16	14	67	60	48
Shrewsbury Town	46	16	15	15	63	57	47
Tranmere Rovers	46	16	15	15	57	52	47
Carlisle United	46	14	19	13	59	59	47
Sheffield Wednesday	46	15	16	15	50	52	46
Bury	46	13	19	14	62	56	45
Lincoln City	46	15	15	16	53	61	45
Exeter City	46	15	14	17	49	59	44
Oxford United	46	13	14	19	64	67	40
Plymouth Argyle	46	11	17	18	61	68	39
Rotherham United	46	13	13	20	51	68	39
Port Vale	46	8	20	18	46	67	36
Bradford City	46	12	10	24	56	86	34
Hereford United	46	9	14	23	34	60	32
Portsmouth	46	7	17	22	41	75	31

1978-79

Division Three

Manager: Mick Brown

Did you know that?

Gary Briggs' permanent transfer to Oxford from Middlesbrough for £12,500 was decided at the Football League's first transfer tribunal.

Bill Asprey joined from Coventry City to become Mick Brown's first coach.

Gordon Hodgson, from Mansfield, and Ray Graydon, from Washington Diplomats, both joined for £30,000 each. Hugh Curran and Max Briggs both retired through injury.

A new lowest crowd record was set when just 2,913 were at the Southend United game, the first time a Football League match at the Manor was watched by fewer than 3,000 people.

The attendance of 1,381 at Tranmere Rovers on 16 February was the lowest crowd to watch Oxford United in the Football League.

Match No.	Date		Opponents	Result	(F-A)	Scorers	A
1	19/08/1978	A	Blackpool	L	0-1		
2	23/08/1978	H	Shrewsbury Town	L	0-1		
3	26/08/1978	H	Swansea City	L	0-2		
4	02/09/1978	A	Chesterfield	D	1-1	Duncan	
5	09/09/1978	H	Bury	D	0-0		
6	11/09/1978	A	Southend United	L	0-2		
7	16/09/1978	H	Exeter City	W	3-2	Duncan, Foley (2)	
8	23/09/1978	A	Watford	L	2-4	Bodel, McGrogan	
9	27/09/1978	H	Mansfield Town	W	3-2	Fogg (pen), Foley, Seacole	
10	30/09/1978	A	Hull City	W	1-0	Foley	
11	07/10/1978	H	Tranmere Rovers	D	0-0		
12	14/10/1978	A	Peterborough United	D	1-1	Seacole	
13	17/10/1978	A	Sheffield Wednesday	D	1-1	Seacole	
14	21/10/1978	H	Chester City	D	0-0		
15	28/10/1978	H	Gillingham	D	1-1	McGrogan	
16	04/11/1978	A	Brentford	L	0-3		
17	11/11/1978	H	Chesterfield	D	1-1	Bodel	
18	18/11/1978	A	Swansea City	D	1-1	Seacole	
19	02/12/1978	H	Rotherham United	W	1-0	Foley	
20	09/12/1978	A	Lincoln City	D	2-2	Foley, Hodgson	
21	26/12/1978	H	Colchester United	W	2-0	Foley, Graydon	
22	30/12/1978	H	Walsall	W	2-1	Fogg, Seacole	
23	20/01/1979	A	Exeter City	L	0-2		
24	27/01/1979	H	Watford	D	1-1	Foley	
25	10/02/1979	H	Hull City	W	1-0	Foley	
26	16/02/1979	A	Tranmere Rovers	L	0-1		
27	20/02/1979	A	Plymouth Argyle	W	1-0	Berry	
28	24/02/1979	H	Peterborough United	L	0-2		
29	03/03/1979	A	Chester City	L	1-4	Seacole	
30	07/03/1979	H	Southend United	D	0-0		
31	10/03/1979	A	Gillingham	L	1-2	McGrogan	
32	20/03/1979	A	Bury	D	1-1	Duncan	
33	24/03/1979	A	Shrewsbury Town	D	0-0		
34	28/03/1979	H	Blackpool	W	1-0	Seacole	
35	31/03/1979	H	Carlisle United	W	5-1	Berry (2), McGrogan, Sweetzer, Tait (og)	
36	04/04/1979	H	Brentford	L	0-1		
37	07/04/1979	A	Rotherham United	D	0-0		
38	11/04/1979	H	Plymouth Argyle	W	3-2	Berry, Graydon (2) (1 pen)	
39	14/04/1979	A	Colchester United	D	1-1	Taylor	
40	16/04/1979	H	Swindon Town	L	0-1		
41	21/04/1979	A	Walsall	W	1-0	Seacole	
42	25/04/1979	H	Sheffield Wednesday	D	1-1	White	
43	28/04/1979	H	Lincoln City	W	2-1	Jeffrey, Smith (og)	
44	02/05/1979	A	Swindon Town	L	0-2		
45	05/05/1979	A	Carlisle United	W	1-0	Graydon	
46	14/05/1979	A	Mansfield Town	D	1-1	Graydon	

FA Cup

R1	25/11/1978	A	Colchester United	L	2-4	Foley, Seacole

League Cup

R1/1	12/08/1978	A	Cardiff City	W	2-1	Foley, Taylor
R1/2	16/08/1978	H	Cardiff City	W	2-1	Duncan, Fogg (pen)
R2	30/08/1978	H	Plymouth Argyle	D	1-1	Seacole
r	05/09/1978	A	Plymouth Argyle	W	2-1	Seacole, Sweetzer
R3	04/10/1978	H	Nottingham Forest	L	0-5	

Total appear
Sub appear
Total

Fogg	Briggs	McIntosh	Jeffrey	McGrogan	Taylor	Foley	Curran	Duncan	Kingston	Seacole	Stott	Sweetzer	Bodel	White	Hodgson	Watson	Graydon	Berry	Milkins
3	4	5	6	**7**	8	9	10	11		12									
3	4	5	6	7	8	9		11	2	10									
3	4	5	6	**7**	8	9		11	2	10		12							
3	4		6	7	8	9	12	11	2	10	**5**								
3	4		6	7	2	9		11		10			5	8					
3	4		6	7	2	9		11		10			5	8					
3	4		6	7	8	9		11		10	5								
3	4		6	7	8	**9**		11		10		12	5						
3	4		6	7	8	9		**11**		10		12	5						
3	4		6	7	8	9				10			5	12	11				
2		5	6	**7**	8	9				11			4	12	10	3			
2		5	6		8	9		7		10			4		11	3			
2		5	6		8	9		7		10			4		11	3			
2		5	**6**	12	8	9		7		10			4		11	3			
2		5		6	8	9		7		10			4		11	3			
2	4	5	12	6	8	9		7		10					11	3			
	4		6	7	2	9		8		10			5		11	3			
3	4		6		2	9		8		11			5		10		7		
3	4		6		2	9		11		10			5		8		7		
3	4		6		2	9		8		10			5		11		7		
3	4		6		2	9		8		10			5		11		7		
3	4		6		2	9		8		10			5		**11**		7	12	
3	4	2			6	9		8		10			5		11		7		
3	4	2			6	9		8		**10**			5		11		7	12	
3	4	2			6	9		8		**10**			5		11		7	12	
3	5	2	**7**		6			8		10		12	4		11			9	
3	4	2	7		8			6		10			5		11			9	
3	4	**2**	12		6	9		11		7			5		10			8	1
3	4	**2**	6	12	8			7		10			5		11			9	
3	4	2	6	7	8			11		10			5					9	
3	4		8	7	2			6		**10**		12	5		11			9	
3	4		8	7	2			6		10		12	5		11			**9**	
3	4		6	7	2			8		10			5		11			9	
3	4		8	7	2			6		10			5		11			9	
3	4		8	7	2			11		10		12	5		6			9	
3	4		8	7	2			6		10		12	5		11			9	
3	4		8		2			6		10			5		11		7	9	
3	4		8		2			6		10			5		11		7	9	
3	4		8	12	2			6		10			5		11		7	**9**	
3	4		8		2	9		6		10			5	12	**11**		7		1
3	4	2	6		8	9		11		10			5				7		1
3	4	2	6		8			11		10			5	12			7	**9**	1
3	**4**	2	6		8	12				10			5	11			7	9	1
3		4	8		2	9		6		10			5		11		7		1
2		4	8		11	9		6		10			5	12		3	**7**		1
	4	2	6		8	9		11		10			5			3	7		

Fogg	Briggs	McIntosh	Jeffrey	McGrogan	Taylor	Foley	Curran	Duncan	Kingston	Seacole	Stott	Sweetzer	Bodel	White	Hodgson	Watson	Graydon	Berry	Milkins
3	4		6		2	9		8		10			5		11		7		

Fogg	Briggs	McIntosh	Jeffrey	McGrogan	Taylor	Foley	Curran	Duncan	Kingston	Seacole	Stott	Sweetzer	Bodel	White	Hodgson	Watson	Graydon	Berry	Milkins
3	4	5	6	**7**	8	9	10	11		12									
3	4	5	6	7	8	9	10	11											
3	4		6	7	8	9		11	2	10	5								
3	4		6	7	2	**9**		11		10		8	5	12					
2	4	5	6	7	8	9	**10**			11				12		3			

Fogg	Briggs	McIntosh	Jeffrey	McGrogan	Taylor	Foley	Curran	Duncan	Kingston	Seacole	Stott	Sweetzer	Bodel	White	Hodgson	Watson	Graydon	Berry	Milkins
50	45	26	46	26	52	37	4	48	4	49	3	1	42	3	32	10	19	16	7
			2	3		1	1			2		8		7				3	
3			1	4	2	11		4		11		2	2	1	1		5	4	

League Table

	P	W	D	L	F	A	Pts
Shrewsbury Town	46	21	19	6	61	41	61
Watford	46	24	12	10	83	52	60
Swansea City	46	24	12	10	83	61	60
Gillingham	46	21	17	8	65	42	59
Swindon Town	46	25	7	14	74	52	57
Carlisle United	46	15	22	9	53	42	52
Colchester United	46	17	17	12	60	55	51
Hull City	46	19	11	16	66	61	49
Exeter City	46	17	15	14	61	56	49
Brentford	46	19	9	18	53	49	47
Oxford United	46	14	18	14	44	50	46
Blackpool	46	18	9	19	61	59	45
Southend United	46	15	15	16	51	49	45
Sheffield Wednesday	46	13	19	14	53	53	45
Plymouth Argyle	46	15	14	17	67	68	44
Chester	46	14	16	16	57	61	44
Rotherham United	46	17	10	19	49	55	44
Mansfield Town	46	12	19	15	51	52	43
Bury	46	11	20	15	59	65	42
Chesterfield	46	13	14	19	51	65	40
Peterborough United	46	11	14	21	44	63	36
Walsall	46	10	12	24	56	71	32
Tranmere Rovers	46	6	16	24	45	78	28
Lincoln City	46	7	11	28	41	88	25

1979-80

Division Three

Manager: Bill Asprey

Did you know that?

Mick Brown left in July to become Ron Atkinson's assistant at West Brom. He was succeeded by Bill Asprey.

Players arriving included Joe Cooke from Peterborough for £50,000 and goalkeeper David Brown for £40,000 from Middlesbrough, but Colin Duncan left for Gillingham for £60,000. Nick Merry was released in August.

On 2 February just 2,871 were at the Mansfield Town game, setting another new low-crowd record. This was beaten on 19 March when 2,603 watched United beat Wimbledon 4–1.

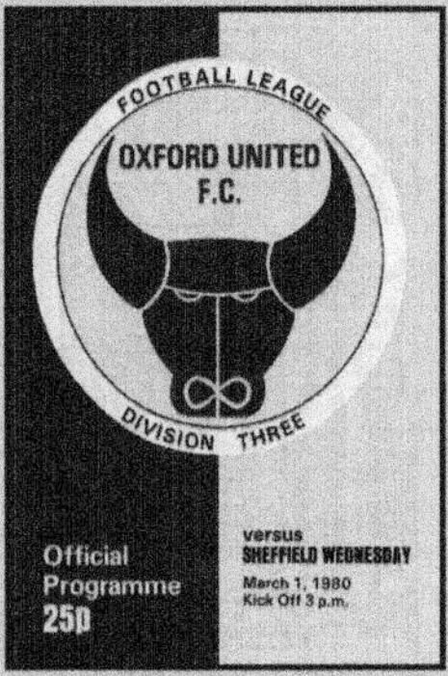

Match No.	Date		Opponents	Result	(F-A)	Scorers	A
1	18/08/1979	H	Rotherham United	W	5-1	Berry (2), Foley, Hodgson, Jeffrey	
2	25/08/1979	A	Hull City	D	2-2	Berry, Cooke	
3	01/09/1979	H	Barnsley	W	1-0	Berry	
4	08/09/1979	H	Reading	W	4-0	Berry, Fogg, Graydon (2) (1 pen)	
5	15/09/1979	A	Mansfield Town	L	0-1		
6	18/09/1979	A	Plymouth Argyle	D	1-1	Berry	
7	22/09/1979	H	Bury	W	3-1	Briggs, Cooke, Graydon (pen)	
8	29/09/1979	A	Sheffield United	L	1-3	Graydon (pen)	
9	06/10/1979	A	Chesterfield	D	2-2	Cooke, Stott	
10	10/10/1979	H	Brentford	L	0-2		
11	13/10/1979	H	Millwall	L	1-2	Cooke	
12	20/10/1979	A	Sheffield Wednesday	D	2-2	Hodgson, Jeffrey	
13	23/10/1979	A	Gillingham	L	0-4		
14	27/10/1979	H	Carlisle United	W	1-0	Berry	
15	31/10/1979	H	Plymouth Argyle	D	1-1	Foley	
16	03/11/1979	A	Rotherham United	W	2-0	Foley (2)	
17	07/11/1979	H	Gillingham	D	1-1	Berry	
18	10/11/1979	H	Chester City	L	0-1		
19	17/11/1979	A	Exeter City	D	0-0		
20	01/12/1979	H	Grimsby Town	L	0-1		
21	08/12/1979	A	Blackburn Rovers	L	1-2	Graydon	
22	15/12/1979	A	Brentford	D	1-1	Foley	
23	26/12/1979	A	Southend United	D	1-1	Foley	
24	29/12/1979	H	Hull City	W	3-0	Berry (2), Foley	
25	05/01/1980	A	Blackpool	W	2-1	Taylor (2)	
26	12/01/1980	H	Colchester United	L	0-2		
27	26/01/1980	A	Barnsley	L	0-2		
28	02/02/1980	H	Mansfield Town	W	3-1	Cooke (2), Fogg	
29	06/02/1980	H	Swindon Town	D	2-2	Brock, Taylor	
30	09/02/1980	A	Bury	W	2-1	Foley, McGrogan	
31	16/02/1980	H	Sheffield United	D	1-1	Brock	
32	23/02/1980	A	Millwall	L	0-3		
33	01/03/1980	H	Sheffield Wednesday	L	0-2		
34	08/03/1980	A	Carlisle United	D	2-2	Berry (2)	
35	14/03/1980	H	Chesterfield	L	1-2	Berry	
36	19/03/1980	H	Wimbledon	W	4-1	Jeffrey, McGrogan, O'Dowd, Taylor	
37	22/03/1980	A	Chester City	L	0-1		
38	26/03/1980	A	Reading	L	0-2		
39	29/03/1980	H	Exeter City	W	2-0	Foley (pen), Taylor	
40	05/04/1980	H	Southend United	W	1-0	Berry	
41	07/04/1980	A	Swindon Town	D	1-1	Foley	
42	12/04/1980	H	Blackpool	L	0-2		
43	15/04/1980	A	Wimbledon	W	3-1	Cooke, McGrogan, Taylor	
44	19/04/1980	A	Grimsby Town	L	0-2		
45	26/04/1980	H	Blackburn Rovers	L	0-1		
46	02/05/1980	A	Colchester United	L	0-2		

FA Cup

R1	24/11/1979	A	Barking	L	0-1	

League Cup

R1/1	11/08/1979	H	Reading	L	1-5	Foley
R1/2	15/08/1979	A	Reading	L	1-2	Foley

Total appear
Sub appear
Total

Fogg	Briggs	Stott	Jeffrey	Graydon	Duncan	Foley	Berry	Hodgson	McGrogan	Cooke	Brock	Taylor	White	Brown	Watson	Doyle	Bodel	O'Dowd	Kingston	Jones
3	4	5	6	7	8	**9**	10	11	12											
3	4	5	6	7	8	**9**	12	11		10										
3	4	5	**6**	7	8		9	11		10	12									
3	4	5	6	7	8		9	11		10										
3	4	5	6	7	**8**		9	11		10	12									
3	4	5	6	7	8		9	11	12	**10**		2								
3	4	5	6	7	8		9	11		10										
3	4	5	6	7	8		9	11		10		2								
3	4	5	6	7	8	12	**9**	11		10		2								
3	4	5	6	7	8	**9**	12	11		10		2								
3	4	**5**	6	7	8		9	11		10		2	12							
	4	5	6	12	8	9		11		**10**		2	7	1	3					
	4		6		8	9		11		10		2	7	1	3					
3	4	5	6	7	8		9	11		10		2								
3	4	5	6	7	8	12	9	**11**		10		2								
3	4	5	6	7	8	9	10	11				2								
3	4	5	6	7	8	**9**	10	11				2								
3	4	5	6	7	8	**9**	10			12	11									
3	4	5	6		**8**	9	7	11	12	10										
3	4	5		7	8			11		10	6		9			2				
3	4		6	7	8			11		10	9			1		2				
	4		6	12	8	**9**	10	11		5		7		1		2				
	4		6		8	9	10	11		5		7		1		2				
	4		6		8	9	10	11		5		7		1	3	2				
	4		6		8	9	10			5		7		1	11	2				
	4		6		8	9	10					7	12	1	**11**	2	5			
	4		6		11	9	10			5		8		1	7	2				
2	4		6				10		11	9	8	7		1	3					
2	4		6				10		11	9	8	7		1	3					
2	4		6			12	9		11	10	**8**	7		1	3					
2	4		6			9	10		11	5	8	7		1	3					
2	4		6			9	**10**	12	11	5	8	7		1	3					
2	4		6			9		11		5	8	7		1	3			10		
2	4		6				9	11		5	8	7		1		3		10		
3	4		6				**9**	11		5	8	7		1		2		10		
3	4		6				9	11	7	5	8	2						10		
3	4		6				9	11	7	5	8	2						**10**		
3	4			12			9	11	**7**	5		8						10	2	
	4		6			10	9		7	5	11	8			3					12
	4		6			10	9		7	5	11	8			3				12	
12	4		6			10	9	11	7	5		8			**3**				2	
3	4		6			10	9	**11**	7	5		8							2	12
3	4		6			**10**	9	11	7	5		8						12	2	
3	4		6			**10**	9	11	7	5		8						12	2	
3	4		6			**10**	9	11	7	5	12	8							2	
3	4		6			10	9	11	**7**	5	12	8		1			2			

Fogg	Briggs	Stott	Jeffrey	Graydon	Duncan	Foley	Berry	Hodgson	McGrogan	Cooke	Brock	Taylor	White	Brown	Watson	Doyle	Bodel	O'Dowd	Kingston	Jones
3	4	5	6	12	8		9	11	**7**	10										

Fogg	Briggs	Stott	Jeffrey	Graydon	Duncan	Foley	Berry	Hodgson	McGrogan	Cooke	Brock	Taylor	White	Brown	Watson	Doyle	Bodel	O'Dowd	Kingston	Jones
3	**4**		6	7	8	9	10	11									5		2	
3		5	6	7	8	9	10	11											2	

Fogg	Briggs	Stott	Jeffrey	Graydon	Duncan	Foley	Berry	Hodgson	McGrogan	Cooke	Brock	Taylor	White	Brown	Watson	Doyle	Bodel	O'Dowd	Kingston	Jones
38	48	21	47	20	30	28	42	38	17	42	15	36	3	18	15	10	3	6	8	0
1				4		3	2	1	3	1	4		2					2	1	2
2	1	1	3	5		12	14	2	3	7	2	6						1		

League Table

	P	W	D	L	F	A	Pts
Grimsby Town	46	26	10	10	73	42	62
Blackburn Rovers	46	25	9	12	58	36	59
Sheffield Wednesday	46	21	16	9	81	47	58
Chesterfield	46	23	11	12	71	46	57
Colchester United	46	20	12	14	64	56	52
Carlisle United	46	18	12	16	66	56	48
Reading	46	16	16	14	66	65	48
Exeter City	46	19	10	17	60	68	48
Chester	46	17	13	16	49	57	47
Swindon Town	46	19	8	19	71	63	46
Barnsley	46	16	14	16	53	56	46
Sheffield United	46	18	10	18	60	66	46
Rotherham United	46	18	10	18	58	66	46
Millwall	46	16	13	17	65	59	45
Plymouth Argyle	46	16	12	18	59	55	44
Gillingham	46	14	14	18	49	51	42
Oxford United	46	14	13	19	57	62	41
Blackpool	46	15	11	20	62	74	41
Brentford	46	15	11	20	59	73	41
Hull City	46	12	16	18	51	69	40
Bury	46	16	7	23	45	59	39
Southend United	46	14	10	22	47	58	38
Mansfield Town	46	10	16	20	47	58	36
Wimbledon	46	10	14	22	52	81	34

1980-81

Division Three

Manager: Bill Asprey then Ian Greaves

Did you know that?

On 15 November United recorded their lowest home crowd for a Football League game, with just 2,526 in attendance for a 1–0 win over Chester City.

With United 22nd in the table after 25 games, Bill Asprey was sacked in December, to be replaced by Ian Greaves. His first game was a win over table-topping Charlton Athletic.

Malcolm Shotton arrived from Nuneaton for £15,000, and Mark Wright made his Oxford United debut.

The £100,000 that Watford paid for Les Taylor was a new club record.

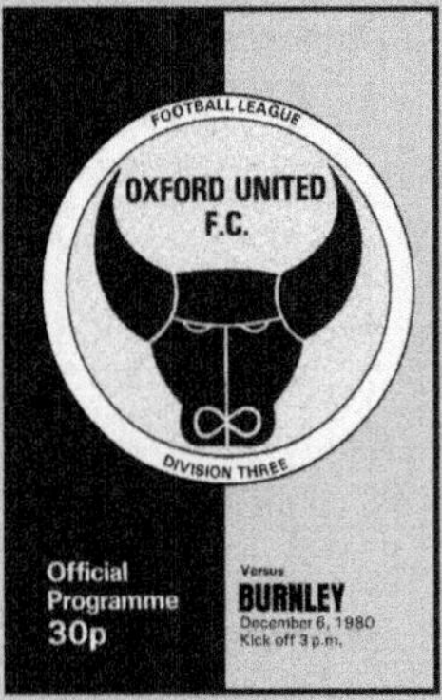

Match No.	Date		Opponents	Result	(F-A)	Scorers	A
1	16/08/1980	A	Chester City	W	1-0	Brock	
2	20/08/1980	H	Exeter City	L	1-2	Shotton (pen)	
3	23/08/1980	A	Sheffield United	L	0-1		
4	30/08/1980	H	Plymouth Argyle	D	0-0		
5	06/09/1980	H	Chesterfield	L	0-3		
6	13/09/1980	A	Newport County	W	1-0	Brock	
7	16/09/1980	A	Swindon Town	L	0-1		
8	20/09/1980	H	Carlisle United	L	1-2	Lythgoe	
9	27/09/1980	A	Gillingham	D	1-1	Lythgoe	
10	01/10/1980	H	Swindon Town	D	0-0		
11	04/10/1980	A	Hull City	W	1-0	Brock	
12	08/10/1980	H	Huddersfield Town	L	0-2		
13	11/10/1980	H	Walsall	D	1-1	Cooke	
14	18/10/1980	A	Fulham	W	4-0	Brock (2), Jeffrey, Lythgoe	
15	21/10/1980	A	Barnsley	D	1-1	Briggs	
16	25/10/1980	H	Portsmouth	L	1-2	Cooke	
17	29/10/1980	H	Rotherham United	D	1-1	Shotton (pen)	
18	01/11/1980	A	Brentford	L	0-3		
19	04/11/1980	A	Huddersfield Town	L	0-2		
20	08/11/1980	H	Blackpool	L	0-2		
21	12/11/1980	A	Exeter City	D	1-1	Foley	
22	15/11/1980	H	Chester City	W	1-0	Cooke	
23	29/11/1980	A	Colchester United	L	0-3		
24	06/12/1980	H	Burnley	L	0-2		
25	20/12/1980	A	Millwall	L	1-2	Cooke	
26	26/12/1980	H	Charlton Athletic	W	1-0	Berry	
27	27/12/1980	A	Reading	W	1-0	Cooke	
28	10/01/1981	A	Rotherham United	D	0-0		
29	17/01/1981	H	Colchester United	W	2-1	Jeffrey, Shotton	
30	24/01/1981	A	Plymouth Argyle	L	0-3		
31	31/01/1981	H	Sheffield United	W	2-0	Foley, Thomas	
32	07/02/1981	H	Newport County	L	0-1		
33	14/02/1981	A	Chesterfield	L	1-2	Foley	
34	21/02/1981	H	Gillingham	D	1-1	Shotton	
35	28/02/1981	A	Carlisle United	D	0-0		
36	07/03/1981	H	Hull City	D	1-1	Cooke	
37	14/03/1981	A	Walsall	W	3-0	Cassells, Foley, Jones	
38	21/03/1981	H	Fulham	W	2-0	Seacole, Shotton (pen)	
39	24/03/1981	H	Barnsley	D	1-1	Cassells	
40	29/03/1981	A	Portsmouth	D	1-1	Cassells	
41	04/04/1981	H	Brentford	D	1-1	Fogg (pen)	
42	12/04/1981	A	Blackpool	D	1-1	Foley	
43	18/04/1981	H	Reading	W	2-1	Page, Smithers	
44	21/04/1981	A	Charlton Athletic	D	0-0		
45	29/04/1981	H	Millwall	W	1-0	Smithers	
46	02/05/1981	A	Burnley	D	1-1	Smithers	

FA Cup

R1	22/11/1980	H	Aldershot	W	1-0	Foley
R2	13/12/1980	A	Plymouth Argyle	L	0-3	

League Cup

R1/1	08/08/1980	A	Southend United	L	0-1	
R1/2	13/08/1980	H	Southend United	W	2-0	Foley, Shotton
R2/1	26/08/1980	A	Chesterfield	L	1-3	Lythgoe
R2/2	03/09/1980	H	Chesterfield	W	3-0	Brock, Lythgoe, Shotton (pen)
R3	23/09/1980	A	Preston North End	L	0-1	

Total appea
Sub appear
Total

Smithers	Jeffrey	Briggs	Shotton	Brock	Taylor	O'Dowd	Foley	Seacole	Burton	Jones	Kingston	Lythgoe	Cooke	Berry	Thomas	Graydon	McIntosh	Cassells	Doyle	Page	Wright
3	4	5	6	7	8	9	10	**11**			12										
3	4	5	6	7	8	**9**	10	11				12									
3	**4**	2	6	7	8		10	12				11	5	9							
3	4	5	6	7	8		**10**	12	1			11	9								
3	**4**	2	6	7	8		9		1	10		11	5		12						
	4		6	7	8		9		1	10	2	11	5								
	4		6	7	8		9		1	10	2	11	5								
	4		6	7	8		**9**		1	10	2	11	5	12							
	4	2	6	7	8		9		1			11	5	10							
	4	2	6	7	8		9		1			11	5	10							
	4	2	6	7	8				1	10		11	5	9							
	4	2	6	7	8		10		1	12		11	5	9							
	4	2	6	7	8				1	9		11	5	**10**		12					
	4	2	6	7	8				1	10		11	5	9							
	4	2	6	7	**8**		12		1	10		11	5	9							
	4	2	6	7	8		12		1	**10**		11	5	9							
	4	2	6	7	8		10		1			**11**	5	9		12					
	4	2	6		8				1	10	12	11	5	**9**			7				
12	4	5	**6**		8				1	10	2	11	9				7				
2	4	5	6	7			10		1				9	11			8				
	4	5		7			10		1		2		9	11			6	8			
	4	5		7			10		1		2		9	11			6	8			
12	4	5		7			10		1	9	2	**11**					6	8			
12	4	5	6	7			10		1	9	2	11						8			
11	4	5	6	12					1	7			9	10			2	8			
11	4	5	6				8		1	7			9	10			2				
11	4	5	6				8		1	7			9	10			2				
11	4	5	6				8		1	7				10	9				2		
11	4	5	6				8		1	7				10	9				2		
11	4	6					10		1	7		12	5	8	**9**				2		
11	4	6					8		1	7		10	5		9				2		
11	4	6					8		1	7		10	5		9			12	**2**		
11	4	6		12			8		1	**7**			5		9			10	2		
11	**4**	6	5				8		1	7				9	12				2	10	
11		5	6	4			8		1	7				9				10	2		
11	4	5		10			8		1	7			6	9					2		
	4	5	6				8		1	7			**10**	9				12	2	11	
9	4	5	6				8	12	1	7				11				**10**	2		
9	4	5	6				8	12	1	7				**11**				10	2		
9	4	5	6				8	12	1	7				**11**				10	2		
2	4	5	6				8	**11**	1	7					9	12		10			
9	4	5	6				8		1	7								10	2	11	
9	4	5	6				8		1	7								10	2	11	
9	4	5	6				8		1	7								10	2	11	
9	4		6				8		1	7			5					10	2	11	
9	4	5	6				8		1	7								10	2	11	

Smithers	Jeffrey	Briggs	Shotton	Brock	Taylor	O'Dowd	Foley	Seacole	Burton	Jones	Kingston	Lythgoe	Cooke	Berry	Thomas	Graydon	McIntosh	Cassells	Doyle	Page	Wright
	4	5		7			10		1		2	11		9			6	8			
3	4	2	6	7					1			11	9			10		8			5

Smithers	Jeffrey	Briggs	Shotton	Brock	Taylor	O'Dowd	Foley	Seacole	Burton	Jones	Kingston	Lythgoe	Cooke	Berry	Thomas	Graydon	McIntosh	Cassells	Doyle	Page	Wright
3	4	2	6	7	8		10	11					5	**9**							
3	4	2	6	7	8	9	10	11					5								
3	4	2	6	7	8		10					11	5	9							
3	4	2	6	7	8		9		1	10		11	5								
	4		6	7	8		9		1	**10**	2	11	5	12							

Smithers	Jeffrey	Briggs	Shotton	Brock	Taylor	O'Dowd	Foley	Seacole	Burton	Jones	Kingston	Lythgoe	Cooke	Berry	Thomas	Graydon	McIntosh	Cassells	Doyle	Page	Wright
32	52	48	44	31	24	3	44	5	47	37	10	26	36	30	7	1	10	18	18	7	1
3				2			2	5		1	2	2		2	2	3		2			
3	2	1	7	6			7	1		1		5	6	1	1			3		1	

League Table

	P	W	D	L	F	A	Pts
Rotherham United	46	24	13	9	62	32	61
Barnsley	46	21	17	8	72	45	59
Charlton Athletic	46	25	9	12	63	44	59
Huddersfield Town	46	21	14	11	71	40	56
Chesterfield	46	23	10	13	72	48	56
Portsmouth	46	22	9	15	55	47	53
Plymouth Argyle	46	19	14	13	56	44	52
Burnley	46	18	14	14	60	48	50
Brentford	46	14	19	13	52	49	47
Reading	46	18	10	18	62	62	46
Exeter City	46	16	13	17	62	66	45
Newport County	46	15	13	18	64	61	43
Fulham	46	15	13	18	57	64	43
Oxford United	46	13	17	16	39	47	43
Gillingham	46	12	18	16	48	58	42
Millwall	46	14	14	18	43	60	42
Swindon Town	46	13	15	18	51	56	41
Chester	46	15	11	20	38	48	41
Carlisle United	46	14	13	19	56	70	41
Walsall	46	13	15	18	59	74	41
Sheffield United	46	14	12	20	65	63	40
Colchester United	46	14	11	21	45	65	39
Blackpool	46	9	14	23	45	75	32
Hull City	46	8	16	22	40	71	32

1981-82

Division Three

Manager: Ian Greaves, Roy Barry (caretaker), then Jim Smith

Did you know that?

Robert Maxwell invested £121,000 in January, in order for the club to honour its financial commitments, and took over from Bill Reeves as chairman.

Ian Greaves resigned in February to take the vacant post at Wolves, with Roy Barry appointed as caretaker manager. In March, Jim Smith was appointed manager, and he appointed Ray Graydon to take over from Barry as first-team coach.

United's 3–0 win at First Division Brighton was the best win in 22 years by a club from the bottom two divisions against a top-flight side.

Mark Wright and Keith Cassells were sold to Southampton in a deal worth £230,000 (£115,000 each, both new club records), while Trevor Hebberd's arrival from the Saints for £80,000 was a new record fee for United.

The away game at Swindon was controversial; with Swindon scoring the opening goal after a smoke bomb had been thrown into the Oxford penalty area impairing Roy Burton's view of the game. The resulting riots by Oxford supporters were featured on national TV.

Match No.	Date		Opponents	Result	(F-A)	Scorers	A
1	29/08/1981	A	Plymouth Argyle	W	1-0	Cassells	
2	05/09/1981	H	Huddersfield Town	W	1-0	Foley	
3	12/09/1981	A	Newport County	L	2-3	Cassells, Shotton	
4	19/09/1981	H	Walsall	L	0-1		
5	23/09/1981	H	Portsmouth	L	0-2		
6	26/09/1981	A	Carlisle United	L	1-2	Shotton	
7	29/09/1981	A	Millwall	W	2-1	Cassells, Jones	
8	03/10/1981	H	Fulham	W	2-0	Foley, Thomas	
9	10/10/1981	A	Chester City	D	2-2	Cassells, Jones	
10	17/10/1981	H	Bristol City	W	1-0	Cassells (pen)	
11	21/10/1981	H	Bristol Rovers	D	1-1	Cassells	
12	24/10/1981	A	Southend United	W	1-0	Thomas	
13	31/10/1981	H	Lincoln City	D	1-1	Thomas	
14	04/11/1981	A	Exeter City	W	2-1	Thomas (2)	
15	07/11/1981	A	Chesterfield	D	2-2	Briggs, Thomas	
16	14/11/1981	H	Brentford	L	1-2	Foley	
17	28/11/1981	H	Preston North End	W	3-0	Cassells (2) (1 pen), Foley	
18	05/12/1981	A	Burnley	L	1-2	Brock	
19	09/01/1982	A	Huddersfield Town	L	0-2		
20	30/01/1982	A	Walsall	W	3-1	Cassells, Foley, Thomas	
21	03/02/1982	H	Reading	W	1-0	Jones	
22	06/02/1982	H	Newport County	D	1-1	Thomas	
23	09/02/1982	A	Portsmouth	D	1-1	Thomas	
24	20/02/1982	H	Carlisle United	W	2-1	Thomas (2)	
25	23/02/1982	A	Fulham	D	0-0		
26	27/02/1982	H	Chester City	W	3-1	Cassells, Jeffrey, Smithers	
27	06/03/1982	A	Bristol City	W	2-0	Kearns, Shotton	
28	13/03/1982	H	Southend United	L	0-2		
29	17/03/1982	H	Exeter City	D	0-0		
30	20/03/1982	A	Lincoln City	L	1-2	Thomas	
31	23/03/1982	A	Doncaster Rovers	D	1-1	Seacole	
32	27/03/1982	H	Chesterfield	D	1-1	Lawrence	
33	31/03/1982	H	Gillingham	D	1-1	Kearns	
34	03/04/1982	A	Brentford	W	2-1	Foley, Hebberd	
35	07/04/1982	H	Swindon Town	W	5-0	Fogg (pen), Foley, Lawrence, Shotton, Thomas	
36	10/04/1982	A	Reading	W	3-0	Brock (2), Jeffrey	
37	12/04/1982	H	Doncaster Rovers	W	3-1	Brock, Fogg, Thomas	
38	17/04/1982	H	Burnley	D	0-0		
39	20/04/1982	A	Wimbledon	W	3-2	Hebberd, Lawrence, Leslie (og)	
40	24/04/1982	A	Preston North End	D	2-2	Brock, Kearns	
41	28/04/1982	H	Plymouth Argyle	W	1-0	Kearns	
42	01/05/1982	H	Millwall	D	0-0		
43	04/05/1982	A	Swindon Town	L	2-3	Fogg (pen), Jeffrey	
44	08/05/1982	A	Gillingham	L	1-2	Lawrence	
45	11/05/1982	A	Bristol Rovers	L	0-1		
46	15/05/1982	H	Wimbledon	L	0-3		

FA Cup

R1	21/11/1981	A	Dover Athletic	W	2-0	Smithers, Thomas
R2	15/12/1981	A	Aldershot	D	2-2	Cassells (2)
r	30/12/1981	H	Aldershot	W	4-2	Cassells (3), Thomas
R3	02/01/1982	A	AFC Bournemouth	W	2-0	Cassells, Thomas
R4	23/01/1982	A	Brighton & Hove Albion	W	3-0	Cassells, Foley (2)
R5	13/02/1982	A	Coventry City	L	0-4	

League Cup

R1/1	02/09/1981	H	Brentford	W	1-0	Cassells
R1/2	15/09/1981	A	Brentford	W	2-0	Foley, Whitehead (og)
R2/1	06/10/1981	A	Millwall	D	3-3	Cassells (2), Thomas
R2/2	28/10/1981	H	Millwall	W	1-0	Cassells
R3	11/11/1981	A	Everton	L	0-1	

Football League Group Cup

Grp	15/08/1981	H	Aldershot	L	0-1	
Grp	19/08/1981	H	Watford	L	2-4	Cassells, Fogg
Grp	22/08/1981	A	Reading	L	0-2	

Total appear
Sub appear
Total

Fogg	Jeffrey	Briggs	Shotton	Jones	Foley	Cassells	Page	Smithers	Kearns	Thomas	Lythgoe	Kingston	Wright	Brock	Berry	Seacole	Train	Lawrence	Hebberd
3	4	5	6	7	8	9	10	11											
3	4	5	6	7	8	9	10	11											
3	4	5	6	**7**	8	9	10	11		12									
3	4	5	6	7	**8**	9	10	11			12								
3	**4**	5	6	7		9		11	8	10	12								
3	4	5	6	7		9	10	11	12	**8**									
3	4	5	6	7	8	9		11		10									
3	4	5	6	7	8	9		11		10		2							
3	4	5	6	**7**		9		11	8	10	12								
3	4		6	**7**	8	9		11	12	10			5						
3		5	6	7	8	9	4	11		10									
3		5	6	7	8	9	4	11		10									
3	4	5	6	**7**	8			11	9	10				12					
3	4	5	6	7	8	9		11		10									
3	4	5	6	7	8	9		11		10									
3	4	5	6	**7**	8	9		11		10				12					
3	4	5	6	12	8	9		11		**10**				7					
3	4	5	6	10	8	9		11		12				7					
3	4	5	**6**		8	9		11		10			12		7				
3	4	5	6		8	9		11	12	10				7					
3	4	5		7	8	9		11		10			6						
3	4	5		7	8	9		11		10			6						
3	4	5		7	8	9		11		10			6						
3	4	5			8	9		11		10			6	7					
3	4	5			8	9		11		10			6	7					
3	4	5			8	9		11		10			6	7					
3	4	5	6		8	**9**			12	10				7		11			
3	4	5	6		8	**9**		11	12	10				7					
3		5	6					11	9	10	8		12	7	4				
3		5	6					11	9	10	**8**	12	2	7	4				
2	**4**	5	6					3	9	10		12		7	8	11			
2		5	6					3	8					10		11	4	7	9
2		5	6					3	8	12				10		**11**	4	7	9
2	11	5	6		8			3						10			4	7	9
2	**11**	5	6		8			3		12				10			4	7	9
2	11	5	6		8			3						10			4	7	9
2	11	5	6		**8**			3		12				10			4	7	9
2	11	5	6		8			3		12				10			4	7	9
2		5	6		**8**			3	12	11				10			4	7	9
2		5	6					3	8	11				10			4	7	9
2		5	6		8			3	12	11				10			4	**7**	9
2		5	6		8			**3**	12	11				10			4	7	9
2	11	5	6		8				12					10			4	7	9
2	11	5	6		8			**3**		12				10			4	7	9
2	11	5	6		8			3		12				**10**			4	7	9
12		5	6		8			3		11				10			4	**7**	9

Fogg	Jeffrey	Briggs	Shotton	Jones	Foley	Cassells	Page	Smithers	Kearns	Thomas	Lythgoe	Kingston	Wright	Brock	Berry	Seacole	Train	Lawrence	Hebberd
3	4	5	6	7	8	9		11		10									
3	4	5	6	7	**9**	9		11		10				12					
	4	5	6	11		9		3		10	7				8				
	4	5	6	11		9		3		10	7				8				
3	4	5	6	7	8	9		11		10									
3	4	5			8	9		11	12	10			6	**7**					

Fogg	Jeffrey	Briggs	Shotton	Jones	Foley	Cassells	Page	Smithers	Kearns	Thomas	Lythgoe	Kingston	Wright	Brock	Berry	Seacole	Train	Lawrence	Hebberd
3	4	5	6	7	8	9	10	11											
3	4	5	6	7	8	9		11			10								
3	4	5	6	7	**8**	9		11	12	10									
3	4	5	6	7	8	**9**		11	12	10									
3	4	5	6	7	**8**	9		11		10				12					

Fogg	Jeffrey	Briggs	Shotton	Jones	Foley	Cassells	Page	Smithers	Kearns	Thomas	Lythgoe	Kingston	Wright	Brock	Berry	Seacole	Train	Lawrence	Hebberd
3	4	5	6	**7**	8	10	11	9				13				12			
3	4	5	6	**7**		10	11	9	8			2		13		12			
3	4	5	6	7	8	12	10	11	**9**			2		13					

Fogg	Jeffrey	Briggs	Shotton	Jones	Foley	Cassells	Page	Smithers	Kearns	Thomas	Lythgoe	Kingston	Wright	Brock	Berry	Seacole	Train	Lawrence	Hebberd
57	49	59	53	33	48	40	11	58	11	40	5	3	9	27	6	4	15	15	15
1				1		1			12	8	3	3	2	6		2			
4	3	1	4	3	10	22		2	4	18				5		1		4	2

League Table

	P	W	D	L	F	A	Pts
Burnley	46	21	17	8	66	45	80
Carlisle United	46	23	11	12	65	50	80
Fulham	46	21	15	10	77	51	78
Lincoln City	46	21	14	11	66	40	77
Oxford United	46	19	14	13	63	49	71
Gillingham	46	20	11	15	64	56	71
Southend United	46	18	15	13	63	51	69
Brentford	46	19	11	16	56	47	68
Millwall	46	18	13	15	62	62	67
Plymouth Argyle	46	18	11	17	64	56	65
Chesterfield	46	18	10	18	57	58	64
Reading	46	17	11	18	67	75	62
Portsmouth	46	14	19	13	56	51	61
Preston North End	46	16	13	17	50	56	61
Bristol Rovers	46	18	9	19	58	65	61
Newport County	46	14	16	16	54	54	58
Huddersfield Town	46	15	12	19	64	59	57
Exeter City	46	16	9	21	71	84	57
Doncaster Rovers	46	13	17	16	55	68	56
Walsall	46	13	14	19	51	55	53
Wimbledon	46	14	11	21	61	75	53
Swindon Town	46	13	13	20	55	71	52
Bristol City	46	11	13	22	40	65	46
Chester	46	7	11	28	36	78	32

1982-83

Division Three

Manager: Jim Smith

Did you know that?

George Lawrence, who had been at the club on loan from Southampton the previous season, was signed for £45,000. United also paid Wrexham £25,000 for Mick Vinter, Birmingham the same amount for Neil Whatmore, and Newcastle £20,000 for Steve Hardwick.

On 16 April, chairman Robert Maxwell announced that Oxford were to be merged with Reading to form the Thames Valley Royals, under Jim Smith, playing home games alternating between the Manor and Elm Park until a new ground could be built, probably at Didcot. Both sets of fans protested, to Maxwell's bemusement, and the deal was eventually scuppered when Roger Smee became Reading's chairman in place of the supportive Frank Waller.

United's 5–1 win at Orient was the side's record away win since joining the Football League.

Match No.	Date		Opponents	Result	(F-A)	Scorers	A
1	28/08/1982	A	Gillingham	W	1-0	Barnett	
2	04/09/1982	H	AFC Bournemouth	W	2-0	Thomas, Vinter	
3	08/09/1982	H	Doncaster Rovers	W	3-0	Biggins, Brock, Thomas	
4	11/09/1982	A	Preston North End	W	2-1	Hebberd, Thomas	
5	18/09/1982	H	Portsmouth	D	1-1	Briggs	
6	25/09/1982	A	Huddersfield Town	L	0-2		
7	28/09/1982	A	Chesterfield	W	2-1	Brock, Hebberd	
8	02/10/1982	H	Cardiff City	D	2-2	Brock, Fogg	
9	09/10/1982	A	Millwall	L	1-2	Thomas	
10	16/10/1982	H	Walsall	W	4-2	Brock, Fogg (pen), Shotton, Whatmore	
11	20/10/1982	H	Brentford	D	2-2	Fogg (pen), Whatmore	
12	23/10/1982	A	Wrexham	D	1-1	Vinter	
13	30/10/1982	H	Exeter City	D	1-1	Whatmore	
14	03/11/1982	A	Bradford City	L	2-3	Whatmore (2)	
15	06/11/1982	H	Sheffield United	D	0-0		
16	13/11/1982	A	Plymouth Argyle	L	1-2	Fogg	
17	04/12/1982	A	Orient	W	5-1	Foley (2), Lawrence, Smithers, Vinter	
18	18/12/1982	A	Wigan Athletic	W	1-0	Foley	
19	27/12/1982	H	Bristol Rovers	W	4-2	Foley (2), Grant, Lawrence	
20	28/12/1982	A	Newport County	W	2-1	Hebberd (2) (1 pen)	
21	01/01/1983	H	Southend United	W	1-0	Vinter	
22	03/01/1983	A	Reading	W	3-0	Lawrence (2), Vinter	
23	15/01/1983	H	Gillingham	D	1-1	Lawrence	
24	22/01/1983	A	Portsmouth	L	0-1		
25	29/01/1983	H	Preston North End	W	3-2	Smithers, Vinter (2)	
26	01/02/1983	A	AFC Bournemouth	L	0-2		
27	05/02/1983	H	Huddersfield Town	D	1-1	Barnett (pen)	
28	12/02/1983	A	Cardiff City	L	0-3		
29	26/02/1983	A	Walsall	L	0-1		
30	02/03/1983	H	Bradford City	W	5-1	Thomas, Vinter, Whatmore (3)	
31	05/03/1983	H	Wrexham	W	2-0	Vinter, Whatmore	
32	12/03/1983	A	Exeter City	L	1-3	Lawrence	
33	16/03/1983	H	Lincoln City	W	1-0	Whatmore	
34	19/03/1983	A	Sheffield United	L	2-3	Jones, Vinter	
35	22/03/1983	A	Brentford	D	1-1	Hebberd	
36	26/03/1983	H	Plymouth Argyle	D	1-1	Hebberd (pen)	
37	02/04/1983	H	Newport County	L	0-3		
38	05/04/1983	A	Bristol Rovers	W	1-0	Hebberd	
39	09/04/1983	H	Orient	D	2-2	Hebberd (2)	
40	16/04/1983	A	Doncaster Rovers	W	1-0	Hebberd	
41	23/04/1983	H	Wigan Athletic	W	2-0	Lawrence, Thomas	
42	27/04/1983	H	Millwall	W	1-0	Fogg (pen)	
43	30/04/1983	A	Lincoln City	D	1-1	Lawrence	
44	02/05/1983	H	Reading	L	1-2	Whatmore	
45	07/05/1983	H	Chesterfield	W	1-0	Lawrence	
46	13/05/1983	A	Southend United	W	2-1	Thomas, Whatmore	
FA Cup							
R1	20/11/1982	H	Folkestone Town	W	5-2	Fogg (pen), Foley (2), Shotton, Vinter	
R2	11/12/1982	H	Worthing	W	4-0	Foley, Hebberd, Vinter (2)	
R3	08/01/1983	H	Torquay United	D	1-1	Foley	
r	12/01/1983	A	Torquay United	L	1-2	Fogg (pen)	
League Cup							
R1/1	01/09/1982	A	Reading	W	2-0	Barnett, Fogg (pen)	
R1/2	15/09/1982	H	Reading	W	2-0	Thomas, Vinter	
R2/1	05/10/1982	A	Huddersfield Town	L	0-2		
R2/2	27/10/1982	H	Huddersfield Town	W	1-0	Biggins	
Football League Trophy							
	14/08/1982	A	Reading	L	1-2	Hebberd	
	17/08/1982	A	Aldershot	W	3-1	Foley (2), Thomas	
	21/08/1982	A	AFC Bournemouth	L	0-3		

Total appear

Sub appear

Total

Linney	Brock	Briggs	Shotton	Barnett	Biggins	Vinter	Hebberd	Train	Thomas	Jones	Foley	Whatmore	Butcher	Grant	Lawrence	Smithers	Donovan	Hardwick	Attley	McIntosh
3	4	5	6	7	8	9	10	**11**	12											
2	7	5	6	8	**9**	10	11	4	12											
2	7	5	6	8	10	9	11	**4**	12											
2		5	6	8	**10**	9	11	4	12	7										
2	7	5	6	8	12	**9**	11	4	10											
2	**7**	5	6	8	10		11	4	9	12										
2	7	5	6	8	10	9	11	4												
2	7	5	6	8	**10**	9	11	4	12											
2	8	5	6	7			11	4	9		10									
2	7	5	6	8			11	4			10	9								
2	7	5	6	8		12	11	4			**10**	9								
2	**7**	5	6	8		10	11	4	12			9	1							
2	7	5	6	**8**		9	11	4	12			10	1							
2	7	5	6			9	11		4	8	12	10	1	3						
2	7		6			9	5		11	8		10	1	3						
2	7		6			9	5		**11**	8	12	10	1	3						
2	12		6			**9**	10	4			8		1	3	7	11				
2	4		6	12		11	8				10		1	5	**7**	9				
2	4		6			9	10				8		1	3	7	11				
2	4		6			9	10	11		12	8				7	3				
2	4		6			9	10	11			8		1		7	3				
2			6	11		9	10	12		4	**8**		1		7	3				
		5	6	12		9	**10**	4			8		1	3	7	11				
	10	5	6	12		9		4			**8**		1	3	7	11				
	10	5	6			9		4		12	8		1	3	**7**	11				
	10		6		5	9		4		7			1	3		11	8			
		5	6	10		9		4		7	12		1	3		11	8			
2		5	6			9		4	10	12			1	**3**	7	11	8			
2		5	6			9	10	**4**	12	7		8		3		11		1		
2	7	5	6			9	10	4	11			8		3				1		
2	7	5	6			9	10	4	11			8		3				1		
	7	5	6			9	10	4	**11**	12		8		3	2			1		
		5	6			9	10	4		11		8			7	3		1	2	
	12	5	6			9	10	**4**		11		8			7	3		1	2	
	12	5	6			9	10			7		8		**3**	4	11		1	2	
	11	5	6		12	9	10			7		8			**4**	3		1	2	
	4	5	6	11		9	10			12		8			7	3		1	**2**	
	11	5	6			9	10	4		7		8		3				1		2
	11	5	6	12		9	10	4		7		8		3				1		2
	11	5	6			9	10	4		7		**8**		3		12		1		
	11	5	6	4		9			8	7					10	3		1		
	11	5	6	4		9			8	7					10	3		1		
	11	5	6			9	4		8	7		12			10	3		1		
	11	5	6			**9**	4		12	7		8			10	3		1		
		5	6			9	4	7	11			8			10	3		1		
		5	6			9	10	4	11	12		8			7	**3**		1		

Linney	Brock	Briggs	Shotton	Barnett	Biggins	Vinter	Hebberd	Train	Thomas	Jones	Foley	Whatmore	Butcher	Grant	Lawrence	Smithers	Donovan	Hardwick	Attley	McIntosh
2	**7**		6			9	10	4		12	8		1	3		11				
2		5	6			9	10	4			8		1		7	11				
2	4		6	11		9	10				8		1		7	3				
2	11		6	4		9	10	12			8		1		7	3				

Linney	Brock	Briggs	Shotton	Barnett	Biggins	Vinter	Hebberd	Train	Thomas	Jones	Foley	Whatmore	Butcher	Grant	Lawrence	Smithers	Donovan	Hardwick	Attley	McIntosh
2	7	5	6	8	9	10	11	4												
2	7	5	6	8		9	11	4	10											
2	7	5	6			9	11	**4**	12	8	10									
2	7	5	6	8	10	9	11	**4**	12				1							

Linney	Brock	Briggs	Shotton	Barnett	Biggins	Vinter	Hebberd	Train	Thomas	Jones	Foley	Whatmore	Butcher	Grant	Lawrence	Smithers	Donovan	Hardwick	Attley	McIntosh
2	7	5	6	11	9	8	10	4	13					**3**		12				
12	4	5	6			8	11		10	7	9		1	**3**		13				
12	4	5	6	7	13	9	10		11		8			**3**						

Linney	Brock	Briggs	Shotton	Barnett	Biggins	Vinter	Hebberd	Train	Thomas	Jones	Foley	Whatmore	Butcher	Grant	Lawrence	Smithers	Donovan	Hardwick	Attley	McIntosh
35	44	45	57	25	11	53	50	40	18	21	19	22	22	24	25	28	3	18	5	2
2	3			4	3	1		2	12	8	3	1				3				
	4	1	2	3	2	14	12		9	1	11	12		1	9	2				

League Table

	P	W	D	L	F	A	Pts
Portsmouth	46	27	10	9	74	41	91
Cardiff City	46	25	11	10	76	50	86
Huddersfield Town	46	23	13	10	84	49	82
Newport County	46	23	9	14	76	54	78
Oxford United	46	22	12	12	71	53	78
Lincoln City	46	23	7	16	77	51	76
Bristol Rovers	46	22	9	15	84	58	75
Plymouth Argyle	46	19	8	19	61	66	65
Brentford	46	18	10	18	88	77	64
Walsall	46	17	13	16	64	63	64
Sheffield United	46	19	7	20	62	64	64
Bradford City	46	16	13	17	68	69	61
Gillingham	46	16	13	17	58	59	61
Bournemouth	46	16	13	17	59	68	61
Southend United	46	15	14	17	66	65	59
Preston North End	46	15	13	18	60	69	58
Millwall	46	14	13	19	64	77	55
Wigan Athletic	46	15	9	22	60	72	54
Exeter City	46	14	12	20	81	104	54
Orient	46	15	9	22	64	88	54
Reading	46	12	17	17	64	79	53
Wrexham	46	12	15	19	56	76	51
Doncaster Rovers	46	9	11	26	57	97	38
Chesterfield	46	8	13	25	43	68	37

1983-84

Division Three

Manager: Jim Smith

Did you know that?

United became the second team from the bottom two divisions to reach the fifth rounds of both the FA Cup and the League Cup.

The venue for the fourth-round second replay was decided on the toss of a coin, performed over the phone, after Robert Maxwell declined Manchester United's offer to play the game at Old Trafford.

Peter Rhoades-Brown was signed from Chelsea for £85,000, a new club record. Other important arrivals included John Aldridge for £80,000 from Newport County, Colin Todd, Bobby McDonald and Paul Hinshelwood.

United won the Third Division Championship without playing, when Wimbledon lost at home to Gillingham on Easter Monday.

Match No.	Date		Opponents	Result	(F-A)	Scorers	A
1	27/08/1983	H	Lincoln City	W	3-0	Biggins, Lawrence, Whatmore	
2	03/09/1983	A	Wigan Athletic	W	2-0	Briggs, Vinter	
3	07/09/1983	A	Scunthorpe United	D	0-0		
4	10/09/1983	H	Burnley	D	2-2	Lawrence, Thomas	
5	17/09/1983	A	Gillingham	W	3-2	Barnett, Biggins, Hebberd	
6	24/09/1983	H	Millwall	W	4-2	Barnett, Jones, Lawrence (2)	
7	28/09/1983	H	Walsall	W	6-3	Barnett (2), Lawrence (2), Thomas (2)	
8	01/10/1983	A	Preston North End	W	2-1	Biggins, Thomas	
9	08/10/1983	H	Brentford	W	2-1	Biggins (2)	
10	15/10/1983	A	Plymouth Argyle	L	1-2	Lawrence	
11	19/10/1983	H	Bradford City	W	2-0	Hebberd (2) (1 pen)	
12	22/10/1983	A	AFC Bournemouth	L	1-2	Barnett	
13	29/10/1983	H	Hull City	D	1-1	Lawrence	
14	01/11/1983	A	Wimbledon	L	1-3	Thomas	
15	05/11/1983	H	Sheffield United	D	2-2	Barnett, Biggins	
16	12/11/1983	A	Port Vale	W	3-1	Hebberd (2) (1 pen), Thomas	
17	26/11/1983	H	Newport County	W	2-0	Thomas, Vinter	
18	02/12/1983	A	Southend United	W	1-0	Biggins	
19	17/12/1983	A	Rotherham United	W	2-1	Whatmore (2)	
20	26/12/1983	H	Bristol Rovers	W	3-2	Brock, Vinter (2)	
21	27/12/1983	A	Bolton Wanderers	L	0-1		
22	31/12/1983	H	Orient	W	5-2	Brock, Hebberd (2) (2 pens), Vinter (2)	
23	02/01/1984	A	Exeter City	L	1-3	Barnett	
24	14/01/1984	A	Lincoln City	D	2-2	Hebberd, Vinter	
25	04/02/1984	H	Preston North End	W	2-0	Hebberd, Vinter	
26	11/02/1984	A	Millwall	L	1-2	Cusack (og)	
27	15/02/1984	H	Wimbledon	W	2-0	McDonald, Morris (og)	
28	25/02/1984	H	AFC Bournemouth	W	3-2	Biggins, Brock, Rhoades-Brown	
29	28/02/1984	A	Hull City	W	1-0	Vinter	
30	03/03/1984	A	Bradford City	D	2-2	Biggins, Rhoades-Brown	
31	06/03/1984	A	Sheffield United	W	2-1	Biggins (2)	
32	10/03/1984	H	Port Vale	W	2-0	McDonald (pen), Rhoades-Brown	
33	14/03/1984	H	Gillingham	L	0-1		
34	17/03/1984	A	Brentford	W	2-1	Biggins, Hebberd	
35	24/03/1984	H	Plymouth Argyle	W	5-0	Biggins (3), McDonald (2) (2 pens)	
36	27/03/1984	A	Burnley	D	1-1	Jones	
37	31/03/1984	H	Scunthorpe United	W	1-0	Shotton	
38	07/04/1984	A	Walsall	W	1-0	Rhoades-Brown	
39	14/04/1984	H	Southend United	W	2-1	Biggins (2)	
40	20/04/1984	H	Bolton Wanderers	W	5-0	Aldridge, Biggins, Briggs, Hebberd, McElhinney (og)	
41	21/04/1984	A	Bristol Rovers	D	1-1	Aldridge	
42	28/04/1984	A	Newport County	D	1-1	Aldridge	
43	02/05/1984	H	Wigan Athletic	D	0-0		
44	05/05/1984	H	Exeter City	D	1-1	Briggs	
45	07/05/1984	A	Orient	W	2-1	Aldridge, Vinter	
46	12/05/1984	H	Rotherham United	W	3-2	Biggins, Lawrence, Vinter	

Fogg	Thomas	Briggs	Shotton	Lawrence	Whatmore	Biggins	Hebberd	Brock	Grant	Vinter	McDonald	Barnett	Jones	Train	Trewick	Rhoades-Brown	Todd	Phillips	Aldridge	Butcher
3	4	5	6	7	8	9	10	11												
	4	**5**	6	7	8	9	10	11	3	12										
	4	5	6	7	**8**	12	10	11	3	9										
	4	5	6	7		9	10	11		8	3									
	4	5	6	7		9	10	11			3	**8**	12							
	4	5	6	7		**9**	10	11			3	8	12							
	4	5	6	7		9	10	11			**3**	8	12							
	4	5	6	7		9	10	11			3	8								
	4	5	6	7		9	10	11			3	8								
	4	5	6	7		9	10	11			3	8								
	4	5	6	7		9	10	11			3	8								
	4	5	6	7		9	10	11			3	8	12							
2	4	5	6	7	9		10	11			3	8								
	4	5	6	7	**9**		10	11			3	8	12							
	4		6		9	12	10	**11**		8	3	7	5							
	4	5	6	7		8	10	11		9	3									
	4	5	6	7		8	10	11		9	3									
	4	5	6			8	10	11		9	3	**7**	12							
	4	5		7	12	8	10	11		9	3	**6**								
	4	5	6	7		8	10	11		9	3									
	4	5	6	**7**	12	8	10	11		9	3									
	4	5	6	7	8		10	11	3	9										
	4	5	6		8	12	10	11	3	9		7								
		5	6	7		8	10	11		9	3			4						
		5	6	7		12	8	10		9	3				4	**11**				
		5	6	7		12	8	10		9	3				4	**11**				
		5	6	7		11	8	10		**9**	3				4	12				
		5	6	7	**9**	8	10	4			3	12				11				
			6	7	8		10	4		9	3					11	5			
		12	6	7	9	8	10	4			3					**11**	5			
		12	6	7		8	10	4		9	3					**11**	5			
		5		7		8	10	4			3	9				11	6			
		5		7		8	10	4			3	9	12			11	6			
		5	2			8	10	4			3	9	7			11	6			
			6			8	10	**4**		9	3		7			11	5	12		
			6			8	10	4		9	3		7			**11**	5	12		
			6			8	10	4		9	3		7			11	5			
			6			8	10	4		**9**	3		7			11	5		12	
			6			8	10	4		9	3		7			11	5			
		5	6			8	10	**4**			3		7			11		12	9	
			6			8	10	4		**9**	3		7				5	11	12	
		5	6			8	10	4			3		7			11			9	
		5	6	7		**8**	10				3		4			11		12	9	
3		5	6	7		12	10	4				8	11						9	
		5	6	**2**		12	10	4		8			7			11		3	9	
		5	6	7		8	10	4		9	3					**11**			12	

League Table

	P	W	D	L	F	A	Pts
Oxford United	46	28	11	7	91	50	95
Wimbledon	46	26	9	11	97	76	87
Sheffield United	46	24	11	11	86	53	83
Hull City	46	23	14	9	71	38	83
Bristol Rovers	46	22	13	11	68	54	79
Walsall	46	22	9	15	68	61	75
Bradford City	46	20	11	15	73	65	71
Gillingham	46	20	10	16	74	69	70
Millwall	46	18	13	15	71	65	67
Bolton Wanderers	46	18	10	18	56	60	64
Orient	46	18	9	19	71	81	63
Burnley	46	16	14	16	76	61	62
Newport County	46	16	14	16	58	75	62
Lincoln City	46	17	10	19	59	62	61
Wigan Athletic	46	16	13	17	46	56	61
Preston North End	46	15	11	20	66	66	56
Bournemouth	46	16	7	23	63	73	55
Rotherham United	46	15	9	22	57	64	54
Plymouth Argyle	46	13	12	21	56	62	51
Brentford	46	11	16	19	69	79	49
Scunthorpe United	46	9	19	18	54	73	46
Southend United	46	10	14	22	55	76	44
Port Vale	46	11	10	25	51	83	43
Exeter City	46	6	15	25	50	84	33

1983-84

Cont.

Manager: Jim Smith

FA Cup

Match No.	Date		Opponents	Result	(F-A)	Scorers	A
R1	19/11/1983	H	Peterborough United	W	2-0	Biggins, McDonald	
R2	10/12/1983	A	Reading	D	1-1	Biggins	
r	14/12/1983	H	Reading	W	3-0	Brock, McDonald, Vinter	
R3	07/01/1984	A	Burnley	D	0-0		
r	11/01/1984	H	Burnley	W	2-1	Lawrence, Scott (og)	
R4	28/01/1984	H	Blackpool	W	2-1	McDonald (2) (2 pens)	
R5	18/02/1984	H	Sheffield Wednesday	L	0-3		

League Cup

Match No.	Date		Opponents	Result	(F-A)	Scorers	A
R1/1	12/09/1983	A	Bristol City	W	1-0	Thomas	
R1/2	31/08/1983	H	Bristol City	D	1-1	Brock	
R2/1	05/10/1983	A	Newcastle United	D	1-1	Biggins	
R2/2	26/10/1983	H	Newcastle United	W	2-1	Thomas, Whatmore	
R3	09/11/1983	A	Leeds United	D	1-1	Vinter	
r	23/11/1983	H	Leeds United	W	4-1	Biggins, Brock, McDonald, Vinter	
R4	30/11/1983	H	Manchester United	D	1-1	McDonald	
r	07/12/1983	A	Manchester United	D	1-1	Brock	
r2	19/12/1983	H	Manchester United	W	2-1	Biggins, Lawrence	
R5	18/01/1984	H	Everton	D	1-1	McDonald	
r	24/01/1984	A	Everton	L	1-4	Hinshelwood	

Associate Members' Cup

Match No.	Date		Opponents	Result	(F-A)	Scorers	A
R1	22/02/1984	H	Swindon Town	L	1-3	Bailie (og)	

Total appea
Sub appea
Tota

Fogg	Thomas	Briggs	Shotton	Lawrence	Whatmore	Biggins	Hebberd	Brock	Grant	Vinter	McDonald	Barnett	Jones	Train	Trewick	Rhoades-Brown	Todd	Phillips	Aldridge	Butcher	Gibson
	4	5	6	7		8	10	11		9	3										
	4	5	6	7		8	10	11		9	3		12								
	4	5	**6**	7	12		10	11		9	3	8									
		5	6	7	**8**	12	10	11		9	3	4									
		5	6	7		8	10	11		9	3	4									
		5	6	7	8			10		9	3				4	11					
		5	6	7	12	8	10	4		9	3					**11**					

Fogg	Thomas	Briggs	Shotton	Lawrence	Whatmore	Biggins	Hebberd	Brock	Grant	Vinter	McDonald	Barnett	Jones	Train	Trewick	Rhoades-Brown	Todd	Phillips	Aldridge	Butcher	Gibson
	4	5	6	7		9	10	11		**8**	3	12									
	4	5	6	7	8	9	10	11	3	12											
	4	5	6	7		9	10	11			3	8									
2	4	5	6	7	**9**		10	11			3	8	12								
	4		6	**7**		9	10	11		8	3	12	5								
	4	5	6	7		8	10	11		9	3										
	4	5	6	7		**8**	10	11		9	3		12								
	4	5	6	7		8	10	11		9	3										
	4	5	6	7	**8**	12	10	11		9	3										
		5	6	7	12	8	**10**	11		9	3			4							
		5	6	7		8		11		9	3	**10**		12	4						

Fogg	Thomas	Briggs	Shotton	Lawrence	Whatmore	Biggins	Hebberd	Brock	Grant	Vinter	McDonald	Barnett	Jones	Train	Trewick	Rhoades-Brown	Todd	Phillips	Aldridge	Butcher	Gibson
		5	6		8	9	10				3	7	12	4		11				1	13

Fogg	Thomas	Briggs	Shotton	Lawrence	Whatmore	Biggins	Hebberd	Brock	Grant	Vinter	McDonald	Barnett	Jones	Train	Trewick	Rhoades-Brown	Todd	Phillips	Aldridge	Butcher	Gibson
4	35	54	62	52	17	49	63	63	5	40	57	25	14	3	5	22	12	2	5	1	
		2			5	9				2		3	11	1		1		4	3		1
	9	3	1	11	4	24	11	7		14	11	7	2			4			4		

1984-85

Division Two

Manager: Jim Smith

Did you know that?

United became the first (and so far only) club to win the third tier and second tier Championships in successive seasons.

Ian Maxwell resigned from the Oxford United board to become chairman of Derby County.

Another club-record transfer fee was set in August, when Billy Hamilton was signed from Burnley for £95,000. This was beaten in February, when United paid QPR £100,000 for Jeremy Charles. Other new signings included Dave Langan from Birmingham City and Brian McDermott from Arsenal.

In Oxford United's 1,000th League game, United beat Crystal Palace 5–0 in the last match of 1984.

At the end of 1984, United were named FIAT Uno Team of the Year.

United's goal difference of +48 was the best in the whole Football League this season.

The PFA's Second Division team included six Oxford United players: Aldridge, Briggs, Hamilton, Hebberd, Langan and Shotton.

John Aldridge's 30 League goals was the best return for an Oxford striker since the club joined the Football League.

Jim Smith was named the Bell's Whisky Second Division Manager of the Season.

To celebrate promotion to the First Division, the Osler Road side of the ground was redeveloped, with a new roof and a new seated area at the Cuckoo Lane end.

Match No.	Date		Opponents	Result	(F-A)	Scorers	A
1	25/08/1984	A	Huddersfield Town	W	3-0	Aldridge, Hebberd, Burke (og)	
2	01/09/1984	H	Portsmouth	D	1-1	Stanley (og)	
3	08/09/1984	A	Wimbledon	W	3-1	Aldridge, Brock, McDonald	
4	15/09/1984	H	Fulham	W	3-2	Aldridge (2), Hamilton	
5	19/09/1984	H	Wolverhampton Wanderers	W	3-1	Aldridge (2), Biggins	
6	22/09/1984	A	Grimsby Town	W	2-1	Rhoades-Brown, Robinson (og)	
7	29/09/1984	H	Carlisle United	W	4-0	Aldridge, Hamilton, Hebberd, Rhoades-Brown	
8	06/10/1984	A	Manchester City	L	0-1		
9	13/10/1984	H	Brighton & Hove Albion	W	2-1	Aldridge, Biggins	
10	20/10/1984	H	Sheffield United	W	5-1	Aldridge (pen), Hebberd, Lawrence (2), Rhoades-Brown	
11	27/10/1984	A	Birmingham City	D	0-0		
12	03/11/1984	H	Blackburn Rovers	W	2-1	Hamilton (2)	
13	10/11/1984	A	Shrewsbury Town	D	2-2	Aldridge (2)	
14	17/11/1984	A	Oldham Athletic	D	0-0		
15	24/11/1984	H	Leeds United	W	5-2	Aldridge (3), Briggs, Hamilton	
16	01/12/1984	A	Notts County	L	0-2		
17	08/12/1984	H	Charlton Athletic	W	5-0	Aldridge, Lawrence, Briggs, Hebberd, McDonald (pen)	
18	22/12/1984	A	Portsmouth	L	1-2	Brock	
19	26/12/1984	H	Cardiff City	W	4-0	Aldridge (2), Hamilton (2)	
20	29/12/1984	H	Crystal Palace	W	5-0	Aldridge, Hamilton (2), McDonald (2)	
21	01/01/1985	A	Middlesbrough	W	1-0	Hebberd	
22	02/02/1985	A	Carlisle United	W	1-0	Brock	
23	05/02/1985	A	Crystal Palace	L	0-1		
24	19/02/1985	A	Fulham	L	0-1		
25	23/02/1985	A	Blackburn Rovers	D	1-1	Brock	
26	02/03/1985	H	Birmingham City	L	0-3		
27	09/03/1985	A	Sheffield United	D	1-1	Charles	
28	13/03/1985	H	Wimbledon	W	4-0	Aldridge (2), McDermott, Shotton	
29	16/03/1985	A	Brighton & Hove Albion	D	0-0		
30	23/03/1985	H	Manchester City	W	3-0	Aldridge (2) (1 pen), Hebberd	
31	30/03/1985	H	Grimsby Town	W	1-0	Rhoades-Brown	
32	02/04/1985	A	Barnsley	L	0-3		
33	06/04/1985	A	Cardiff City	W	2-0	Aldridge, Charles	
34	08/04/1985	H	Middlesbrough	W	1-0	Charles	
35	13/04/1985	A	Wolverhampton Wanderers	W	2-1	Briggs, Brock	
36	17/04/1985	H	Huddersfield Town	W	3-0	Aldridge, McDermott, McDonald	
37	20/04/1985	H	Oldham Athletic	W	5-2	Aldridge (3), Brock, McDonald	
38	24/04/1985	H	Shrewsbury Town	W	1-0	Langan	
39	27/04/1985	A	Leeds United	L	0-1		
40	04/05/1985	H	Notts County	D	1-1	Thomas	
41	07/05/1985	A	Charlton Athletic	D	3-3	Aldridge, Briggs, Curbishley (og)	
42	11/05/1985	H	Barnsley	W	4-0	Aldridge (2), Charles, McDonald	

FA Cup

R3	05/01/1985	A	Shrewsbury Town	W	2-0	Aldridge, McDermott
R4	30/01/1985	H	Blackburn Rovers	L	0-1	

League Cup

R1/1	29/08/1984	A	Hereford United	D	2-2	Hamilton, Hebberd
R1/2	05/09/1984	H	Hereford United	W	5-3	Aldridge (2), Hamilton (3)
R2/1	25/09/1984	A	Blackburn Rovers	D	1-1	Rhoades-Brown
R2/2	10/10/1984	H	Blackburn Rovers	W	3-1	Hamilton (3)
R3	31/10/1984	H	Arsenal	W	3-2	Aldridge, Hamilton, Langan
R4	20/11/1984	A	Ipswich Town	L	1-2	Brock

Total appear
Sub appear
Total

McDonald	Trewick	Briggs	Shotton	Jones	Aldridge	Hamilton	Hebberd	Brock	Rhoades-Brown	Biggins	Hinshelwood	Lawrence	Phillips	Barnett	McDermott	Fogg	Charles	Spearing	Thomas
3	4	5	6	7	8	9	10	11	12										
3	4	5	6		8	9	10	11	7										
3	4	5	6		8	9	10	11	**7**	12									
3	4	5	6		8	9	10	11	**7**	12									
3	4	5	6		8	9	10	11	**7**	12									
3	4	5	**6**	12	8	9	10		7	11									
3	4	5	6		8	9	10	11	7	12									
3	4	5	6		8	9	10	**11**	7	12	2								
	4	5	6		8	9	10		11	12	3	**7**							
3	4	5	6		8	9	10		11			7							
3	4	5	6		8	9	10	12	**11**			7							
3	4	5	6		8	9	10	11	12			**7**							
3	4	5	6	12	8		10	11	**9**				7						
3	4	5	6		8		10	11	9				7						
3	4	5	6		8	9	10	11	7										
3	4	5	6		8	9	10	**11**	7				12						
3	4	5	6		8	9	10	11				**7**		12					
3	4	5	6		8	9	10	11				7							
3	4	5	6		8	9	10	11				7							
3	4	5	6	12	8	9	10	11	**7**										
3	4	5	6	12	8	9	10	11							**7**				
	4	5	6	9	8		10	11							7	3			
	4	5	6	12	8		10	11						**9**	7	3			
3	4	5	6		8		10	11	12						7		9		
	4	5	**6**		8		10	11	12						7		9	3	
	4	5	6		8		10	11	12						**7**		9	3	
	12	5	6		8	9	10	11	7								**4**	3	
	4	5	6	9	8		10	11	**7**						12			3	
	4	5	6	7	8	9	10		11									3	
3	4	5	6		8	9	10	7	11										
3	4	5	6	9	8		10	7	11						12		**2**		
3	4	5	6		8	9	10	**7**	11						12		2		
3	4	5	6	12	8		10	**7**							11		9		
3	4	5	6	12	8		10		11						**7**		9		
3	4	5	6	12	8		10	11							7		**9**		
3	4	5	6	9	8		10	11	12						**7**				
3	4	5	6	**9**	8		10	11	12						7				
3	4	5	6	9	8		10	11	12						7				
3	4	5	6	9	8		10	11	**7**										12
3	4	5	6	**9**	8		10	11							7				12
3	4	5	6		8		10	11							12		9		7
3	4	5	6		8		10	11							7		**9**		12

3	4	5	6		8	9	10	11							7				
3	4	5	6	12	8	**9**	10	11							7				

	4	5	6	7	8	9	10	11			3								
3	4	5	6		8	9	10	11	7										
3	4	5	6		8	9	10		7	11									
3	4	5	6		8	9	10		11	12		7							
3	4	5	6		8	9	10	11				7							
3	4	5	6		8	9	10	11	**7**				12						

41	49	50	50	11	50	31	50	42	27	2	3	9	2	1	16	2	11	5	1
	1			9				1	8	7			2	1	4				3
7		4	1		34	17	7	7	5	2		3			3		4		1

League Table

	P	W	D	L	F	A	Pts
Oxford United	42	25	9	8	84	36	84
Birmingham City	42	25	7	10	59	33	82
Manchester City	42	21	11	10	66	40	74
Portsmouth	42	20	14	8	69	50	74
Blackburn Rovers	42	21	10	11	66	41	73
Brighton & Hove Albion	42	20	12	10	54	34	72
Leeds United	42	19	12	11	66	43	69
Shrewsbury Town	42	18	11	13	66	53	65
Fulham	42	19	8	15	68	64	65
Grimsby Town	42	18	8	16	72	64	62
Barnsley	42	14	16	12	42	42	58
Wimbledon	42	16	10	16	71	75	58
Huddersfield Town	42	15	10	17	52	64	55
Oldham Athletic	42	15	8	19	49	67	53
Crystal Palace	42	12	12	18	46	65	48
Carlisle United	42	13	8	21	50	67	47
Charlton Athletic	42	11	12	19	51	63	45
Sheffield United	42	10	14	18	54	66	44
Middlesbrough	42	10	10	22	41	57	40
Notts County	42	10	7	25	45	73	37
Cardiff City	42	9	8	25	47	79	35
Wolverhampton W	42	8	9	25	37	79	33

1985-86

Division One

Manager: Maurice Evans

Did you know that?

On 11 June Jim Smith resigned as manager after Robert Maxwell refused a request for a wage increase. He was replaced, initially in a caretaker capacity, by chief scout Maurice Evans.

United's second home game in the top flight, in which they recorded their first win, was to remain their record victory in the First Division, beating Leicester City 5–0. After the game Evans accepted the manager's position permanently, but he refused to sign a contract. He eventually put pen to paper following survival from relegation in the season's final game.

United's record transfer fee of £100,000 was equalled with Evans' first signing, Neil Slatter from Bristol Rovers. This was beaten in September, when Ray Houghton was signed from Fulham for £147,000, and again in December, when £200,000 was paid to Tottenham for striker David Leworthy.

The 3–0 defeat by Manchester United at Old Trafford on 7 September was watched by 51,820, the biggest crowd to watch Oxford at that point, and still the biggest for a League match.

The 90,396 who watched United beat QPR 3–0 in the Milk Cup Final at Wembley is the largest crowd United have ever played in front of. This was the biggest winning margin of the League Cup since the Final began to be played at Wembley, 20 years previously.

United's 6–0 defeat at Anfield was their worst defeat since joining the Football League, and their equal worst since turning professional in 1949.

United won the National Daily Express Five-a-Side Championship at Wembley Arena, beating Arsenal on penalties in the Final.

Match No.	Date		Opponents	Result	(F-A)	Scorers	A
1	17/08/1985	A	West Bromwich Albion	D	1-1	McDonald	
2	21/08/1985	H	Tottenham Hotspur	D	1-1	Charles	
3	24/08/1985	H	Leicester City	W	5-0	Charles, Hamilton (2), Hebberd, Trewick (pen)	
4	26/08/1985	A	Birmingham City	L	1-3	Aldridge	
5	31/08/1985	H	Sheffield Wednesday	L	0-1		
6	03/09/1985	A	Coventry City	L	2-5	McDonald (2)	
7	07/09/1985	A	Manchester United	L	0-3		
8	14/09/1985	H	Liverpool	D	2-2	Aldridge, Kennedy (og)	
9	21/09/1985	A	Newcastle United	L	0-3		
10	28/09/1985	H	Manchester City	W	1-0	Trewick (pen)	
11	02/10/1985	A	Leicester City	D	4-4	Aldridge (2), Thomas, Trewick (pen)	
12	05/10/1985	A	Everton	L	0-2		
13	12/10/1985	H	Luton Town	D	1-1	Hebberd	
14	19/10/1985	H	Chelsea	W	2-1	Aldridge, Rhoades-Brown	
15	26/10/1985	A	Watford	D	2-2	Houghton, Rhoades-Brown	
16	02/11/1985	A	Aston Villa	L	0-2		
17	09/11/1985	H	West Ham United	L	1-2	Aldridge	
18	16/11/1985	A	Arsenal	L	1-2	Charles	
19	23/11/1985	H	Ipswich Town	W	4-3	Aldridge (3), Slatter	
20	01/12/1985	A	Nottingham Forest	D	1-1	Thomas	
21	07/12/1985	A	Tottenham Hotspur	L	1-5	Aldridge	
22	14/12/1985	H	West Bromwich Albion	D	2-2	Aldridge (pen), Charles	
23	26/12/1985	H	Southampton	W	3-0	Aldridge, Leworthy (2)	
24	01/01/1986	A	Queen's Park Rangers	L	1-3	Leworthy	
25	11/01/1986	H	Manchester United	L	1-3	Leworthy	
26	18/01/1986	A	Sheffield Wednesday	L	1-2	Slatter	
27	25/01/1986	H	Coventry City	L	0-1		
28	01/02/1986	H	Birmingham City	L	0-1		
29	08/02/1986	A	Chelsea	W	4-1	Aldridge, Charles, Hebberd, Rhoades-Brown	
30	01/03/1986	A	Manchester City	W	3-0	Charles, Aldridge (2)	
31	15/03/1986	A	Luton Town	W	2-1	Charles, Aldridge (pen)	
32	19/03/1986	H	Newcastle United	L	1-2	Aldridge	
33	22/03/1986	A	Liverpool	L	0-6		
34	29/03/1986	H	Queen's Park Rangers	D	3-3	Aldridge (2) (2 pens),Houghton	
35	01/04/1986	A	Southampton	D	1-1	Aldridge	
36	05/04/1986	H	Aston Villa	D	1-1	Charles	
37	09/04/1986	H	Watford	D	1-1	Aldridge	
38	12/04/1986	A	West Ham United	L	1-3	Houghton	
39	26/04/1986	A	Ipswich Town	L	2-3	Phillips, Aldridge	
40	30/04/1986	H	Everton	W	1-0	Phillips	
41	03/05/1986	H	Nottingham Forest	L	1-2	Charles	
42	05/05/1986	H	Arsenal	W	3-0	Aldridge (pen), Hamilton, Houghton	
FA Cup							
R3	04/01/1986	H	Tottenham Hotspur	D	1-1	Slatter	
r	08/01/1986	A	Tottenham Hotspur	L	1-2	Aldridge	
League Cup							
R2/1	25/09/1985	H	Northampton Town	W	2-1	Rhoades-Brown, Houghton	
R2/2	07/10/1985	A	Northampton Town	W	2-0	Aldridge (2)	
R3	30/10/1985	H	Newcastle United	W	3-1	Hebberd, Thomas (2)	
R4	20/11/1985	H	Norwich City	W	3-1	Aldridge, Phillips, Thomas	
R5	22/01/1986	H	Portsmouth	W	3-1	Briggs, Phillips, Slatter	
SF L1	04/03/1986	A	Aston Villa	D	2-2	Aldridge (2) (1 pen)	
SF L2	12/03/1986	H	Aston Villa	W	2-1	Charles, Phillips	
Final	20/04/1986	N	Queen's Park Rangers	W	3-0	Charles, Hebberd, Houghton	
Full Members' Cup							
R3	18/09/1985	H	Shrewsbury Town	W	3-0	Briggs, Charles, Houghton	
R4	22/10/1985	A	Fulham	W	2-0	Thomas (2)	
Sth SF	06/11/1985	A	Stoke City	W	1-0	Aldridge	
Sth F L1	04/12/1985	H	Chelsea	L	1-4	Aldridge (pen)	
Sth F L2	17/12/1985	A	Chelsea	W	1-0	Hebberd	

Total appea
Sub appea
Total

McDonald	Trewick	Briggs	Shotton	Jones	Aldridge	Hamilton	Hebberd	Brock	Charles	Thomas	McDermott	Barnett	Houghton	Slatter	Phillips	Rhoades-Brown	Judge	Leworthy	Perryman
3	4	5	6	7	8	**9**	10	11	12										
3	4	5	6	**7**		9	10	11	12	8									
3	4	5	6			9	10	**11**	7	8	12								
3	4	5	6		8		10	11	9	**7**	12								
3	4	5	6		8	9	10	11	**7**	12									
3	4	5	6		**8**		10	11	9		7	12							
3	**4**	5	6		8		10	11	9		7	12							
3	4	5	6		8		10	**11**	9				7			12			
3	4	5	6		8		10	11	**9**				7			12			
	4	5	6		8		10	11		9			7	3					
	4	5	6		8		10	11	12	9			7	3					
		5	6		8		10	**11**	9	12			7	3	4				
		5	6		8		10		12	**9**			7	3	4	11			
		5	6		8		10			9			7	3	4	11			
		5	6				10		8	9			7	3	4	11			
		5	6		8		10			9			7	3	4	11			
	4	5	6		8		10	12	9				7	3		**11**			
	4	5	6		8		10		9				7	3	**11**	12			
	4		6		8		5			9			7	3	**10**	11			
3	4		6		8		11			9			7	5	10				
3	4	5	6		8		11		**9**	9			7	2	10	12			
3		5	6		8		10	11	9				7		4				
3		5	6		8		10	11					7		4		1	9	
3	12	5	6		8			11					7	10	4		1	9	
	2		6	**7**	8		10		5				11	3	4	12	1	9	
	2		6	12	8		10	11	**5**				7	3	4		1	9	
	2	5	6	12	8		10	**11**					7	3	4		1	9	
	2	5	6		8		10	11		12			7	3	**4**		1	9	
	2	5	6		8		10			9			7	3	4	11	1		
	2	5	6		8		10		9				7	**3**	4	11	1		
	2	5	6		8		10		**9**	12			7	3	4	11	1		
	2	5	6		8		10						7	**3**	4	11	1	9	
	3	**5**	6		8		10		9	12			7			11			
	3	5	6		8		10	12	9				7			**11**	1		4
	2	5	6		8		10		9				7	3	4		1		11
	3	5	6		8		10	12	**9**				7		4		1		11
	3	5	6		8	9	10						7		4		1		11
	3	5	6		8	**9**	10		12				7		4		1		11
	3	5	6		8		10	12	**9**				7		4		1		11
	3	5	6		8	9	10						7		4		1		11
	3	**5**	6		8		10	12	9				7		4		1		11
	3	5	6	4	8	9	10						7				1		11

McDonald	Trewick	Briggs	Shotton	Jones	Aldridge	Hamilton	Hebberd	Brock	Charles	Thomas	McDermott	Barnett	Houghton	Slatter	Phillips	Rhoades-Brown	Judge	Leworthy	Perryman
	2	5	6		8		10	11					7	3	4		1	9	
	2	5	6		8		10	11					7	3	**4**	12	1	9	

McDonald	Trewick	Briggs	Shotton	Jones	Aldridge	Hamilton	Hebberd	Brock	Charles	Thomas	McDermott	Barnett	Houghton	Slatter	Phillips	Rhoades-Brown	Judge	Leworthy	Perryman
3	4	**5**	6		8		10		9		7	12	11						
		5	6		8		10	11		9			7	3	4				
	12	5	6				10		9	8			7	3	**4**	11			
	4		6	12	8		5	7		9				3	10	11			
	2	5	6	12	8		10	11	**9**				7	3	4		1		
	2	5	6		8		10		9				7	3	4	11	1		
	2	5	6		8		10		9				7	3	4	11	1		
	3	5	6		8		10	11	9				7		4		1		

McDonald	Trewick	Briggs	Shotton	Jones	Aldridge	Hamilton	Hebberd	Brock	Charles	Thomas	McDermott	Barnett	Houghton	Slatter	Phillips	Rhoades-Brown	Judge	Leworthy	Perryman
3	4	5	6		8		10	11	**9**				7			12			
12			6		8		10		5	9			7	3	**4**	11			
	12	5	6		8		10		13	9			7	3	4	**11**			
3	12	5	6	13	8		10			9			7	3	**4**	11			
	2	5	6	12	8		10	11	**9**				7	3	4		1		

McDonald	Trewick	Briggs	Shotton	Jones	Aldridge	Hamilton	Hebberd	Brock	Charles	Thomas	McDermott	Barnett	Houghton	Slatter	Phillips	Rhoades-Brown	Judge	Leworthy	Perryman
17	44	51	57	4	52	8	55	26	31	19	2	0	49	34	41	20	26	9	9
1	4			6				5	6	5	2	2			1	7			
3	3	2			31	3	5		12	7			7	4	5	4		4	

League Table

	P	W	D	L	F	A	Pts
Liverpool	42	26	10	6	89	37	88
Everton	42	26	8	8	87	41	86
West Ham United	42	26	6	10	74	40	84
Manchester United	42	22	10	10	70	36	76
Sheffield Wednesday	42	21	10	11	63	54	73
Chelsea	42	20	11	11	57	56	71
Arsenal	42	20	9	13	49	47	69
Nottingham Forest	42	19	11	12	69	53	68
Luton Town	42	18	12	12	61	44	66
Tottenham Hotspur	42	19	8	15	74	52	65
Newcastle United	42	17	12	13	67	72	63
Watford	42	16	11	15	69	62	59
Queen's Park Rangers	42	15	7	20	53	64	52
Southampton	42	12	10	20	51	62	46
Manchester City	42	11	12	19	43	57	45
Aston Villa	42	10	14	18	51	67	44
Coventry City	42	11	10	21	48	71	43
Oxford United	42	10	12	20	62	80	42
Leicester City	42	10	12	20	54	76	42
Ipswich Town	42	11	8	23	32	55	41
Birmingham City	42	8	5	29	30	73	29
West Bromwich Albion	42	4	12	26	35	89	24

1986-87

Division One

Manager: Maurice Evans

Did you know that?

Oxford received a record fee when they sold John Aldridge to Liverpool for £775,000. Andy Thomas was sold to Newcastle United for £100,000, while Steve Perryman left for Brentford, Bobby McDonald joined Leeds, and Jeremy Charles and Billy Hamilton retired through injury.

United paid £187,000 to Newcastle for Billy Whitehurst, plus £180,000 to Arsenal for Tommy Caton, £100,000 to QPR for Peter Hucker, £140,000 to Aldershot for Martin Foyle, and £60,000 to Brighton for Dean Saunders.

United won the Guinness Soccer Six competition at G-Mex in Manchester, beating Arsenal 2–1 in the Final.

At the end of the season, Robert Maxwell stood down as chairman to take over from his son Ian at Derby County. His other son, Kevin, was installed as Oxford United chairman.

Match No.	Date		Opponents	Result	(F-A)	Scorers	A
1	23/08/1986	A	Watford	L	0-3		
2	25/08/1986	H	Chelsea	D	1-1	Briggs	
3	30/08/1986	H	West Ham United	D	0-0		
4	02/09/1986	A	Everton	L	1-3	Houghton	
5	06/09/1986	A	Aston Villa	W	2-1	Aldridge, Leworthy	
6	13/09/1986	H	Manchester City	D	0-0		
7	20/09/1986	A	Arsenal	D	0-0		
8	27/09/1986	H	Charlton Athletic	W	3-2	Aldridge (2) (1 pen), Hebberd	
9	04/10/1986	A	Sheffield Wednesday	L	1-6	Aldridge	
10	11/10/1986	H	Coventry City	W	2-0	Aldridge (2) (1 pen)	
11	18/10/1986	A	Liverpool	L	0-4		
12	25/10/1986	H	Nottingham Forest	W	2-1	Aldridge, Houghton	
13	01/11/1986	A	Newcastle United	D	0-0		
14	08/11/1986	H	Manchester United	W	2-0	Aldridge (pen), Slatter	
15	15/11/1986	A	Queen's Park Rangers	D	1-1	Houghton	
16	22/11/1986	H	Tottenham Hotspur	L	2-4	Briggs, Leworthy	
17	29/11/1986	A	Norwich City	L	1-2	Aldridge	
18	06/12/1986	H	Luton Town	W	4-2	Aldridge (3), Brock	
19	14/12/1986	A	Leicester City	L	0-2		
20	20/12/1986	H	Aston Villa	D	2-2	Aldridge (pen), Briggs	
21	26/12/1986	A	Wimbledon	D	1-1	Aldridge	
22	27/12/1986	H	Queen's Park Rangers	L	0-1		
23	01/01/1987	H	Southampton	W	3-1	Aldridge (pen), Houghton, Whitehurst	
24	03/01/1987	A	Manchester City	L	0-1		
25	24/01/1987	H	Watford	L	1-3	Houghton	
26	07/02/1987	A	West Ham United	W	1-0	Leworthy	
27	10/02/1987	A	Chelsea	L	0-4		
28	14/02/1987	H	Everton	D	1-1	Trewick (pen)	
29	25/02/1987	H	Arsenal	D	0-0		
30	07/03/1987	A	Nottingham Forest	L	0-2		
31	14/03/1987	H	Liverpool	L	1-3	Caton	
32	20/03/1987	A	Coventry City	L	0-3		
33	24/03/1987	A	Charlton Athletic	D	0-0		
34	28/03/1987	H	Sheffield Wednesday	W	2-1	Dreyer, Saunders	
35	04/04/1987	A	Manchester United	L	2-3	Caton, Duxbury (og)	
36	11/04/1987	H	Newcastle United	D	1-1	Dreyer	
37	18/04/1987	A	Southampton	L	0-3		
38	20/04/1987	H	Wimbledon	W	3-1	Saunders (2), Whitehurst	
39	25/04/1987	A	Tottenham Hotspur	L	1-3	Saunders	
40	02/05/1987	H	Norwich City	L	0-1		
41	05/05/1987	A	Luton Town	W	3-2	Hebberd, Saunders (2)	
42	09/05/1987	H	Leicester City	D	0-0		

FA Cup

R3	10/01/1987	A	Aldershot	L	0-3	

League Cup

R2/1	24/09/1986	H	Gillingham	W	6-0	Aldridge (4), Houghton, Weatherley (og)
R2/2	07/10/1986	A	Gillingham	D	1-1	Aldridge
R3	29/10/1986	H	Sheffield United	W	3-1	Aldridge, Briggs, Slatter
R4	18/11/1986	A	West Ham United	L	0-1	

Full Members' Cup

R3	20/01/1987	A	Blackburn Rovers	L	3-4	Leworthy, Whitehurst (2)

Total appear
Sub appear
Total

Trewick	Phillips	Briggs	Shotton	Houghton	Aldridge	Charles	Hebberd	Perryman	Obi	Slatter	Leworthy	Reck	Parks	Dreyer	Hamilton	Whitehurst	Brock	Hardwick	McDonald	Mustoe	McDermott	Caton	Rhoades-Brown	Saunders	Foyle	Hucker
3	4	5	6	**7**	8	9	10	11	12																	
3	4	5	6	7	8	9	10	11																		
3	4	5	6	7	8	9	10	11																		
3	4	5	6	7	8	9	10	**11**		12																
3	4	5		7	8	9	10	**11**		6	12															
3	4	5	6	7	8	9	10	**11**			12															
3	4	5	6	7	8	9	10			11																
3	4	5	6	7	8		10			11	9															
3	4	5		7	8		10	6		11	**9**	12														
4		5		7	8		10	11		3			1	6	9											
11	4	5		7	8		10			3		12	1	6		**9**										
	4	5		7	8		10			6	9		1	3			11									
9	4	5		7	8		10			6			1	3			11									
10	4	5	6	7	8					3	9		1				11									
10	4	5	6	7	8					3	9						11	1								
	4	5	6	7	8					3	9	10				12	11	1								
	4	5			8						**7**	**10**		6		9	11	1	3	12						
4		5		7	8		10							6		9	11	1	3							
4		5		7	8		10				9			6			**11**	1	3		12					
4	12	5		7	8		10				9			6			11	1	**3**							
3	4	5		7	8		10							6		**9**	11	1	12							
3	4	5		7	8		10							6		9	11	1								
	4	5		7	8		10							6		9	11	1	3							
		5		7	8		10					4		6		9	11	1	3							
3		5		7	8		10					4		6		9	11	1								
4		5		7			10				8			3		9	11	1				6				
4	12	5		7			10				8			**3**		9	11	1				6				
3	4	5		7			10				8					9	11	1				6				
3	4	5		7			10				8					9	11	1				6				
3	4	5		7			10				8						11	1			12	**6**	9			
3	**4**	5		7			10				8						11	1		2		6	12	9		
3	4	5		7			10									9	11	1				6		8		
	4	5		7			10							3		9	11	1				6		8		
	4	5		**7**			10							3		9	11	1				6		8	12	
	4	5					10				12			3		9	11	1				6		7	8	
5	4			7			10			2				3			11	1				6	12	8	9	
	4	5					10			2				3		7	11	1				6	12	8	**9**	
	4	5		7			10							3		9	11					6		8		1
5	4			7			10			12				3		9	11					6		8		1
	4	5		**7**			10			12				3			11			9		6		8		1
9	**4**	5					10			3				12			11					6	7	8		1
9		5	4				10			3				12			11					6	**7**	8		1

Trewick	Phillips	Briggs	Shotton	Houghton	Aldridge	Charles	Hebberd	Perryman	Obi	Slatter	Leworthy	Reck	Parks	Dreyer	Hamilton	Whitehurst	Brock	Hardwick	McDonald	Mustoe	McDermott	Caton	Rhoades-Brown	Saunders	Foyle	Hucker
10				7	**8**		5				12	4		6		9	11	1	3							

Trewick	Phillips	Briggs	Shotton	Houghton	Aldridge	Charles	Hebberd	Perryman	Obi	Slatter	Leworthy	Reck	Parks	Dreyer	Hamilton	Whitehurst	Brock	Hardwick	McDonald	Mustoe	McDermott	Caton	Rhoades-Brown	Saunders	Foyle	Hucker
3	**4**	5	6	7	8	9	10			11	12						13									
11	4	5		7	8		10			3	12	13		6	**9**											
10	4	5	12	7	8					6	9			**3**			11	1								
	4	**5**	6	7	8					3	9	10		12			11	1								

Trewick	Phillips	Briggs	Shotton	Houghton	Aldridge	Charles	Hebberd	Perryman	Obi	Slatter	Leworthy	Reck	Parks	Dreyer	Hamilton	Whitehurst	Brock	Hardwick	McDonald	Mustoe	McDermott	Caton	Rhoades-Brown	Saunders	Foyle	Hucker
4		5		7			10				8			6		9	11	1	3							

Trewick	Phillips	Briggs	Shotton	Houghton	Aldridge	Charles	Hebberd	Perryman	Obi	Slatter	Leworthy	Reck	Parks	Dreyer	Hamilton	Whitehurst	Brock	Hardwick	McDonald	Mustoe	McDermott	Caton	Rhoades-Brown	Saunders	Foyle	Hucker
36	37	45	13	43	30	8	42	8	0	19	18	6	5	27	2	21	35	27	8	2	0	17	3	12	3	5
	2		1						1	3	6	3		3		1	1		1	1	2		3		1	
1		4		6	21		2			2	4			2		4	1					2		6		

League Table

	P	W	D	L	F	A	Pts
Everton	42	26	8	8	76	31	86
Liverpool	42	23	8	11	72	42	77
Tottenham Hotspur	42	21	8	13	68	43	71
Arsenal	42	20	10	12	58	35	70
Norwich City	42	17	17	8	53	51	68
Wimbledon	42	19	9	14	57	50	66
Luton Town	42	18	12	12	47	45	66
Nottingham Forest	42	18	11	13	64	51	65
Watford	42	18	9	15	67	54	63
Coventry City	42	17	12	13	50	45	63
Manchester United	42	14	14	14	52	45	56
Southampton	42	14	10	18	69	68	52
Sheffield Wednesday	42	13	13	16	58	59	52
Chelsea	42	13	13	16	53	64	52
West Ham United	42	14	10	18	52	67	52
Queen's Park Rangers	42	13	11	18	48	64	50
Newcastle United	42	12	11	19	47	65	47
Oxford United	42	11	13	18	44	69	46
Charlton Athletic	42	11	11	20	45	55	44
Leicester City	42	11	9	22	54	76	42
Manchester City	42	8	15	19	36	57	39
Aston Villa	42	8	12	22	45	79	36

1987-88

Division One

Manager: Maurice Evans then Mark Lawrenson

Did you know that?

Maurice Evans resigned in March following United's elimination from the League Cup at the semi-finals stage by Luton Town and after poor League form had left the club without a win since 7 November. He was succeeded by Mark Lawrenson, who had just retired from playing at Liverpool.

The record signing fee was broken three times this season. First, in September Richard Hill joined from Watford for £260,000. Almost immediately afterwards, United paid Watford a further £265,000 for David Bardsley. In February, Oxford paid Gillingham £285,000 for Colin Greenall. Other newcomers included Gary Shelton from Sheffield Wednesday for £155,000. Joey Beauchamp, a ball-boy at the 1986 Wembley Milk Cup Final, was a first-year YTS signing.

United's record sale was broken again when Liverpool paid £825,000 for Ray Houghton. Kevin Brock was sold to QPR for £260,000, Billy Whitehurst joined Reading for £122,500, Portsmouth paid £70,000 for Malcolm Shotton, and John Trewick left for Birmingham for £30,000.

Match No.	Date		Opponents	Result	(F-A)	Scorers	A
1	15/08/1987	H	Portsmouth	W	4-2	Caton, Langan, Whitehurst (2)	
2	18/08/1987	A	Sheffield Wednesday	D	1-1	Foyle	
3	22/08/1987	A	Wimbledon	D	1-1	Foyle	
4	01/09/1987	A	Tottenham Hotspur	L	0-3		
5	05/09/1987	H	Luton Town	L	2-5	Foyle, Slatter	
6	12/09/1987	A	Liverpool	L	0-2		
7	19/09/1987	H	Queen's Park Rangers	W	2-0	Hill, Houghton	
8	26/09/1987	A	Derby County	W	1-0	Slatter	
9	03/10/1987	H	Norwich City	W	3-0	Foyle, Hill, Slatter	
10	10/10/1987	A	Arsenal	L	0-2		
11	17/10/1987	H	West Ham United	L	1-2	Saunders	
12	24/10/1987	H	Charlton Athletic	W	2-1	Foyle, Saunders	
13	31/10/1987	A	Chelsea	L	1-2	Hebberd	
14	07/11/1987	H	Coventry City	W	1-0	Saunders (pen)	
15	14/11/1987	A	Southampton	L	0-3		
16	21/11/1987	H	Watford	D	1-1	Phillips	
17	28/11/1987	A	Everton	D	0-0		
18	05/12/1987	H	Newcastle United	L	1-3	Saunders (pen)	
19	12/12/1987	A	Manchester United	L	1-3	Saunders	
20	19/12/1987	H	Nottingham Forest	L	0-2		
21	26/12/1987	H	Liverpool	L	0-3		
22	28/12/1987	A	Queen's Park Rangers	L	2-3	Rhoades-Brown, Saunders	
23	02/01/1988	H	Wimbledon	L	2-5	Foyle, Saunders (pen)	
24	16/01/1988	A	Portsmouth	D	2-2	Briggs, Saunders	
25	06/02/1988	A	Luton Town	L	4-7	Saunders (pen), Foyle, Hill, Phillips,	
26	13/02/1988	H	Tottenham Hotspur	D	0-0		
27	20/02/1988	H	Derby County	D	0-0		
28	05/03/1988	A	West Ham United	D	1-1	Phillips	
29	16/03/1988	A	Norwich City	L	2-4	Bardsley, Hebberd	
30	19/03/1988	H	Chelsea	D	4-4	Foyle, Rhoades-Brown, Saunders (2)	
31	26/03/1988	A	Charlton Athletic	D	0-0		
32	30/03/1988	H	Arsenal	D	0-0		
33	02/04/1988	A	Coventry City	L	0-1		
34	04/04/1988	H	Southampton	D	0-0		
35	09/04/1988	A	Watford	L	0-3		
36	13/04/1988	H	Sheffield Wednesday	L	0-3		
37	23/04/1988	H	Everton	D	1-1	Saunders (pen)	
38	30/04/1988	A	Newcastle United	L	1-3	Phillips	
39	02/05/1988	H	Manchester United	L	0-2		
40	07/05/1988	A	Nottingham Forest	L	3-5	Foyle (2), Hebberd	

FA Cup

R3	09/01/1988	H	Leicester City	W	2-0	Foyle, Saunders
R4	30/01/1988	A	Bradford City	L	2-4	Rhoades-Brown, Saunders (pen)

League Cup

R2/1	23/09/1987	H	Mansfield Town	D	1-1	Saunders
R2/2	06/10/1987	A	Mansfield Town	W	2-0	Saunders, Charles (og)
R3	28/10/1987	H	Leicester City	D	0-0	
r	04/11/1987	A	Leicester City	W	3-2	Saunders, Shelton (2)
R4	18/11/1987	H	Wimbledon	W	2-1	Phillips, Saunders
R5	20/01/1988	H	Manchester United	W	2-0	Briggs, Saunders
SF/1	10/02/1988	H	Luton Town	D	1-1	Saunders (pen)
SF/2	28/02/1988	A	Luton Town	L	0-2	

Simod Cup

R1	11/11/1987	H	Crystal Palace	W	1-0	Saunders (pen)
R2	13/01/1988	A	Reading	L	0-1	

Total appea
Sub appea
Total

Slatter	Shelton	Briggs	Caton	Houghton	Foyle	Whitehurst	Hebberd	Rhoades-Brown	Dreyer	Trewick	Shotton	Reck	Saunders	Mustoe	Phillips	Bardsley	Hill	Hardwick	Judge	Greenall	Nogan	Denton	McDonagh	Leworthy
3	4	5	6	7	8	9	10	11	12															
2	4	5	6	7	8	9	10		3	11														
2	4	5	6	7	8	9	**10**		3	11	12													
2	4	5	6	7	8	9	10		3	**11**			12											
5			6	7	8	9	10	13	3			**4**	11	12										
2	4	5	6	7	8	9	10		3				**11**		12									
5	4		6	7	**8**	9	10		3				12			2	11							
5	4		6	7	8		10		3				9			2	11	1						
5	4		6	7	8				3				9		10	2	11	1						
5	**4**		6	7	8	13	11	12	3				9		10	2								
5	4		6	7	**8**	12	11		3				9		10	2	13							
5	**4**		6		8		7	12	3				9		10	2	11							
5	4		6		8		7	11	3				9		10	2								
5	4		6			8	7	11	3				9	12	10	2								
5	**4**		6		13	8	7	11	3				9		10	2	12							
5	4		6			8	7	11	3				9		10	2								
	4		6			8	7	11	3				9		10	2	5							
	4		6		12	8	7	11	3				9		10	2	**5**							
	4		6			8	7	11	3				9		10	2	5							
	4		6		12	8	7	11	3				9	13	10	2	5							
	4		6			8	7	11	3				9	12	10	2	**5**							
	4		6		11	8	7	12	3				9	**5**	10	2								
	4		6		8	5	7	11	3				9		10	2								
	4	5	6		8		7	**11**	3				9		10	2	12	1						
	4	5	**6**		8	12	7	11					9	13	10	2	3	1						
		5	6		8		7	11	3				9		10	2	4		1					
		5	6		8		7	11	3				9		10	2	4		1					
	4	5			8		7	12	3				9		10	2	11		1	**6**				
	4	5	6		8		7	12	3				9		10	2	**11**		1					
		5	**6**		8		7	11	3			12	9	10		2			1	4				
	4	**5**			8		7		3				9	11	10	2	12			6				
	4	5			8		7	11	**3**				9	10		2	12			6				
	4	5			**8**		7	11					9	10		2	3			6	12			
	4	**5**	12				7	11					9	10	3	2	13			6	8			
	4	5	12				7	**11**					9	10	3	2	13			6	8			
	4	5	12		8		7	11					9	10	3	2	13			6				
			5		8		7	11	3				9	10	4	2			1	6				
			5		8		7	11	**3**				9	10	4	2	12		1	6		13		
			5		8		7	**11**	3				9	10	4	2			1	6		12		
			5		8		7	11	3				9	10	4	2			1	6				

Slatter	Shelton	Briggs	Caton	Houghton	Foyle	Whitehurst	Hebberd	Rhoades-Brown	Dreyer	Trewick	Shotton	Reck	Saunders	Mustoe	Phillips	Bardsley	Hill	Hardwick	Judge	Greenall	Nogan	Denton	McDonagh	Leworthy
	4	5	6		8		7	11	3				9		**10**	2	12	1						
	4	5	6		8	12	7	11					9		10	2	**3**	1						

Slatter	Shelton	Briggs	Caton	Houghton	Foyle	Whitehurst	Hebberd	Rhoades-Brown	Dreyer	Trewick	Shotton	Reck	Saunders	Mustoe	Phillips	Bardsley	Hill	Hardwick	Judge	Greenall	Nogan	Denton	McDonagh	Leworthy
5	4		6	7	8	**9**	10		3				12			2	11							
5	4		6	7	8			12	3				9		10	2	**11**							
5	**4**		6		8	12	7	13	3				9		10	2	11							
3	4		5			8	7	11	6				9		10	2								
5	4		6			8	7	11	3				9		10	2								
	4	5	6		**8**	12	7	11	3				9		10	2			1					
	4	5	6		8		7	11	3				9		10	2	12		1					
	12	5	6		8		7	11	3				9		10	2	**4**		1					14

Slatter	Shelton	Briggs	Caton	Houghton	Foyle	Whitehurst	Hebberd	Rhoades-Brown	Dreyer	Trewick	Shotton	Reck	Saunders	Mustoe	Phillips	Bardsley	Hill	Hardwick	Judge	Greenall	Nogan	Denton	McDonagh	Leworthy
	4	**5**	6			8	7	11	3				9		10	2	12							
			6		8		7	11	3				9	4		2	**10**		1		12		5	

Slatter	Shelton	Briggs	Caton	Houghton	Foyle	Whitehurst	Hebberd	Rhoades-Brown	Dreyer	Trewick	Shotton	Reck	Saunders	Mustoe	Phillips	Bardsley	Hill	Hardwick	Judge	Greenall	Nogan	Denton	McDonagh	Leworthy
21	42	24	45	13	39	21	50	34	45	3	0	1	46	13	39	46	21	6	13	12	2	0	1	0
	1		3		3	6		8	1		1	1	3	5	1		12				2	2		1
3	2	2	1	1	11	2	3	3					21		5	1	3							

League Table

	P	W	D	L	F	A	Pts
Liverpool	40	26	12	2	87	24	90
Manchester United	40	23	12	5	71	38	81
Nottingham Forest	40	20	13	7	67	39	73
Everton	40	19	13	8	53	27	70
Queen's Park Rangers	40	19	10	11	48	38	67
Arsenal	40	18	12	10	58	39	66
Wimbledon	40	14	15	11	58	47	57
Newcastle United	40	14	14	12	55	53	56
Luton Town	40	14	11	15	57	58	53
Coventry City	40	13	14	13	46	53	53
Sheffield Wednesday	40	15	8	17	52	66	53
Southampton	40	12	14	14	49	53	50
Tottenham Hotspur	40	12	11	17	38	48	47
Norwich City	40	12	9	19	40	52	45
Derby County	40	10	13	17	35	45	43
West Ham United	40	9	15	16	40	52	42
Charlton Athletic	40	9	15	16	38	52	42
Chelsea	40	9	15	16	50	68	42
Portsmouth	40	7	14	19	36	66	35
Watford	40	7	11	22	27	51	32
Oxford United	40	6	13	21	44	80	31

1988-89

Division Two

Manager: Mark Lawrenson then Brian Horton

Did you know that?

In October, Dean Saunders was sold to Robert Maxwell's Derby County for £1 million, a new club record. The deal, and the manner in which it was conducted, led to Mark Lawrenson threatening to resign, causing Kevin Maxwell to sack him. Brian Horton, appointed Lawrenson's assistant in June, became the new manager.

Other major sales included Trevor Hebberd, who also joined Derby, for £300,000, and John Dreyer to Luton for £140,000.

New signings included Mickey Lewis, who arrived from Derby for £100,000 as part of the Hebberd deal, Phil Heath from Stoke for £80,000, Jimmy Phillips from Glasgow Rangers for £150,000, Paul Simpson (Horton's first signing) from Manchester City for £200,000, and John Durnin from Liverpool for £250,000. In addition, Ceri Evans, an Oxford student and a New Zealand international, joined after a successful trial.

Match No.	Date		Opponents	Result	(F-A)	Scorers	At
1	27/08/1988	A	Leeds United	D	1-1	Foyle	
2	29/08/1988	H	Hull City	W	1-0	Saunders	
3	03/09/1988	H	Brighton & Hove Albion	W	3-2	Greenall, Heath, Saunders	
4	10/09/1988	A	Chelsea	D	1-1	Leworthy	
5	17/09/1988	H	Leicester City	D	1-1	Shelton	
6	20/09/1988	A	Oldham Athletic	L	0-3		
7	24/09/1988	A	AFC Bournemouth	L	1-2	Mustoe	
8	01/10/1988	H	Shrewsbury Town	W	4-1	J Phillips, Foyle, Saunders, Mustoe	
9	05/10/1988	H	Swindon Town	D	1-1	Saunders	
10	08/10/1988	A	Portsmouth	L	1-2	Bardsley	
11	15/10/1988	A	Ipswich Town	W	2-1	J Phillips, Foyle	
12	22/10/1988	H	Blackburn Rovers	D	1-1	Bardsley	
13	25/10/1988	A	Crystal Palace	L	0-1		
14	29/10/1988	H	Bradford City	L	3-4	Foyle, Hill, Phillips	
15	02/11/1988	H	Sunderland	L	2-4	Foyle (2)	
16	05/11/1988	A	West Bromwich Albion	L	2-3	Foyle, Simpson	
17	12/11/1988	H	Birmingham City	W	3-0	Bardsley, Foyle (2)	
18	19/11/1988	H	Plymouth Argyle	L	0-1		
19	26/11/1988	A	Manchester City	L	1-2	Hill	
20	03/12/1988	H	Barnsley	W	2-0	J Phillips, Simpson	
21	10/12/1988	A	Watford	D	1-1	Bardsley	
22	26/12/1988	A	Walsall	W	5-1	Foyle, Hill (4)	
23	31/12/1988	A	Stoke City	L	0-1		
24	02/01/1989	H	Chelsea	L	2-3	Foyle, Hill	
25	14/01/1989	A	Sunderland	L	0-1		
26	21/01/1989	H	Leeds United	W	3-2	Foyle, L Phillips, Simpson	
27	05/02/1989	A	Swindon Town	L	0-3		
28	11/02/1989	H	Portsmouth	W	1-0	L Phillips	
29	21/02/1989	A	Blackburn Rovers	L	1-3	Simpson	
30	25/02/1989	H	Ipswich Town	D	1-1	Hill	
31	01/03/1989	H	Crystal Palace	W	1-0	Bardsley	
32	04/03/1989	A	Birmingham City	D	0-0		
33	11/03/1989	H	West Bromwich Albion	D	1-1	Foyle	
34	15/03/1989	A	Bradford City	D	0-0		
35	18/03/1989	H	Oldham Athletic	D	1-1	L Phillips	
36	25/03/1989	A	Brighton & Hove Albion	L	1-2	Foyle	
37	27/03/1989	H	Walsall	W	1-0	Durnin	
38	01/04/1989	A	Leicester City	L	0-1		
39	04/04/1989	A	Hull City	W	2-1	Durnin, Mustoe	
40	08/04/1989	H	Stoke City	W	3-2	Durnin, Hill (2)	
41	15/04/1989	A	Shrewsbury Town	D	2-2	Briggs, Greenall	
42	22/04/1989	H	AFC Bournemouth	W	3-1	Simpson (3)	
43	29/04/1989	H	Manchester City	L	2-4	Bardsley, Simpson	
44	01/05/1989	A	Barnsley	L	0-1		
45	06/05/1989	A	Plymouth Argyle	L	1-3	Ford	
46	13/05/1989	H	Watford	L	0-4		

FA Cup

R3	07/01/1989	A	Sunderland	D	1-1	Hill
r	11/01/1989	H	Sunderland	W	2-0	Hill (2)
R4	28/01/1989	A	Manchester United	L	0-4	

League Cup

R2/1	28/09/1988	H	Bristol City	L	2-4	Saunders (2)
R2/2	11/10/1988	A	Bristol City	L	0-2	

Simod Cup

R1	23/11/1988	H	Ipswich Town	L	2-3	Foyle, Hill

Total appear
Sub appear
Total

Phillips, J	Lewis	Hill	Greenall	Heath	Foyle	Saunders	Mustoe	Rhoades-Brown	Shelton	Purdie	Leworthy	Smart	Briggs	Phillips, L	Judge	Reck	Slatter	Simpson	Durnin	Ford	Evans	Nogan	Beauchamp
3	4	5	6	7	8	9	10	**11**	12														
3	4	5	6	7	8	9	10	**11**	12														
3	4	5	6	7	8	9	**10**		11	12													
3	4	5	6	7	8		10	13	**11**	9	12												
3	4	5	6	7	8		10		11	12	**9**												
3	4	5	6	7	8	9	**10**		11	12				13									
	4		6	7	8	9	13	12	11			3	5	10									
3		5	6		8	9	10	11		7				4	1								
3		12	6		8	9	**10**	11		7			5	4	1								
3		12	6		8	9	10	**11**		7			5	4	1								
3		12	6		8	9	10						**5**	4	1	7	11						
3			6		8	9	**10**			12			5	4	1	7	11						
3		9	6		8		10			12			5	4	1	**7**	11					13	
3		10	6	**11**	8				12		9		5	4	1		2						
3		**10**	6	13	8		12				9		5	4	1		2	11					
3	10		6	12	8		13						5	4	1	7	**11**	9					
3	10		6		8		11		5	12			5		1	**7**		9					
3	10	12	6	13	8		4			11			5		1	**7**		9					
3		9	6		8				10			7	5	4	1			11					
3	5	9	6		8				10			7		4	1			11					
3	5	9	6		8		12		10			7		4	1			**11**					
3	5	9	6		8				10			7		4	1			11					
3	5	9	6	12	8				10		13	7		**4**	1			11					
3	5	9	6	13	8		4		10		12	7						**11**					
3	5	9	6		8				10		12	7			1		4	**11**		13			
3	5	9	6		8				10					**4**	1		7	11		12			
3	5	9	6		8				10		12			4	1		7	**11**		13			
3	5	11	6		8									4			2		9	10			
3	5	**11**			8				13			2		4			6	12	9	10			
3	5	11			8				12			2		4			6		9	**10**			
3	5	11			8				10			2		4			6		9				
3	5	11	6		8		12		9					4			2		10				
3	5	7	6		8		9							4			2	11	10				
3	5	11	6		8		9							4			2	7	10				
3	5	7	6	13	8		9					12		4			**2**	11	10				
3	5	11	6		8		9		4		12						2	7	**10**				
3	5		6		8		9		4								2	7	10	11			
3		12	6		8		9		4								2	7	10	**11**	5		
3	5	11	6		8		9		4			2	7						10				
3	5	11	6		**8**		9		4		12	2	7						10				
3	5	**11**	6				9		4		12		7				2	8	10				
3	5		6	12			**9**		4			11					2	8	10				
3	5		6				9		4		12	**11**					2	8	10				
3	5	11					9		4								2	8	10		6		
3	5	11		13			9		4								**2**		10	12	6	8	
3	5	12							4			2			1			8	10	**11**	6	9	13
3	5	9		12	**7**		4		10			7			1		6	11		13			
3	5	9			8		4		10			7			1		6	11					
3	5	9	6						10	8				4	1		7	11					
		5	6	**7**	8	9	10	11		12		3		4									
3		12	6	13	8	9	10	**11**		7			5	4	1								
3	10	13	6	7	8		**4**				9	12	5		1			11					
50	40	37	44	10	45	12	33	7	31	7	4	19	17	28	25	6	28	28	19	6	4	2	0
		8		10			5	2	5	7	9	2		1				1		5		1	1
3		14	2	1	15	6	3		1		1		1	4				8	3	1			

League Table

	P	W	D	L	F	A	Pts
Chelsea	46	29	12	5	96	50	99
Manchester City	46	23	13	10	77	53	82
Crystal Palace	46	23	12	11	71	49	81
Watford	46	22	12	12	74	48	78
Blackburn Rovers	46	22	11	13	74	59	77
Swindon Town	46	20	16	10	68	53	76
Barnsley	46	20	14	12	66	58	74
Ipswich Town	46	22	7	17	71	61	73
West Bromwich Albion	46	18	18	10	65	41	72
Leeds United	46	17	16	13	59	50	67
Sunderland	46	16	15	15	60	60	63
Bournemouth	46	18	8	20	53	62	62
Stoke City	46	15	14	17	57	72	59
Bradford City	46	13	17	16	52	59	56
Leicester City	46	13	16	17	56	63	55
Oldham Athletic	46	11	21	14	75	72	54
Oxford United	46	14	12	20	62	70	54
Plymouth Argyle	46	14	12	20	55	66	54
Brighton & Hove Albion	46	14	9	23	57	66	51
Portsmouth	46	13	12	21	53	62	51
Hull City	46	11	14	21	52	68	47
Shrewsbury Town	46	8	18	20	40	67	42
Birmingham City	46	8	11	27	31	76	35
Walsall	46	5	16	25	41	80	31

1989-90

Division Two

Manager: Brian Horton

Did you know that?

New captain Steve Foster joined from Luton for £175,000, the same price that Oxford paid to Derby for Dave Penney's signature. United also paid Doncaster £150,000 for Les Robinson.

QPR paid £200,000 plus Mark Stein for David Bardsley. Middlesbrough paid £250,000 for Jimmy Phillips.

Steve McClaren, who later became England manager, joined on a free transfer from Bristol City.

Match No.	Date		Opponents	Result	(F-A)	Scorers	A
1	19/08/1989	A	Plymouth Argyle	L	0-2		
2	26/08/1989	H	Watford	D	1-1	Durnin	
3	02/09/1989	A	Blackburn Rovers	D	2-2	Foyle, Hendry (og)	
4	09/09/1989	H	Bradford City	W	2-1	Mustoe, Simpson	
5	13/09/1989	H	Newcastle United	W	2-1	Mustoe, Ranson (og)	
6	16/09/1989	A	West Bromwich Albion	L	2-3	Durnin, Foyle	
7	23/09/1989	H	Ipswich Town	D	2-2	Durnin, Penney	
8	27/09/1989	A	Leeds United	L	1-2	Stein	
9	30/09/1989	H	AFC Bournemouth	L	1-2	Stein	
10	07/10/1989	H	Portsmouth	W	2-1	Durnin (pen), J Phillips	
11	14/10/1989	A	Leicester City	D	0-0		
12	17/10/1989	A	Swindon Town	L	0-3		
13	21/10/1989	H	Barnsley	L	2-3	Durnin, Stein	
14	28/10/1989	A	West Ham United	L	2-3	Mustoe, Stein	
15	01/11/1989	H	Stoke City	W	3-0	Durnin, Foster, Mustoe	
16	04/11/1989	A	Port Vale	W	2-1	Durnin, Ford	
17	11/11/1989	H	Oldham Athletic	L	0-1		
18	18/11/1989	H	Hull City	D	0-0		
19	25/11/1989	A	Middlesbrough	L	0-1		
20	02/12/1989	H	Plymouth Argyle	W	3-2	Evans, J Phillips, Simpson	
21	09/12/1989	A	Newcastle United	W	3-2	Evans, J Phillips, Simpson	
22	16/12/1989	H	Wolverhampton Wanderers	D	2-2	Mustoe, Stein	
23	26/12/1989	A	Sunderland	L	0-1		
24	30/12/1989	A	Brighton & Hove Albion	W	1-0	Stein	
25	01/01/1990	H	Sheffield United	W	3-0	Simpson (2), Stein	
26	13/01/1990	A	Watford	W	1-0	Lewis	
27	20/01/1990	H	Blackburn Rovers	D	1-1	Penney	
28	10/02/1990	H	West Bromwich Albion	L	0-1		
29	17/02/1990	A	Bradford City	W	2-1	Mustoe, Stein	
30	24/02/1990	H	Middlesbrough	W	3-1	Durnin (2), Simpson	
31	03/03/1990	A	Hull City	L	0-1		
32	06/03/1990	A	AFC Bournemouth	W	1-0	Durnin	
33	10/03/1990	H	Leeds United	L	2-4	Durnin, Simpson	
34	13/03/1990	A	Ipswich Town	L	0-1		
35	17/03/1990	A	Portsmouth	L	1-2	Foster	
36	21/03/1990	H	Leicester City	W	4-2	Durnin, Mustoe, Stein, Walsh (og)	
37	24/03/1990	H	Swindon Town	D	2-2	Foster (2)	
38	31/03/1990	A	Barnsley	L	0-1		
39	07/04/1990	H	West Ham United	L	0-2		
40	10/04/1990	A	Stoke City	W	2-1	Simpson (2)	
41	14/04/1990	A	Sheffield United	L	1-2	Durnin	
42	16/04/1990	H	Sunderland	L	0-1		
43	21/04/1990	A	Wolverhampton Wanderers	L	0-2		
44	25/04/1990	H	Brighton & Hove Albion	L	0-1		
45	01/05/1990	A	Oldham Athletic	L	1-4	Ford	
46	05/05/1990	H	Port Vale	D	0-0		

FA Cup

R3	06/01/1990	A	Plymouth Argyle	W	1-0	Simpson
R4	27/01/1990	A	Southampton	L	0-1	

League Cup

R1/1	23/08/1989	A	Fulham	W	1-0	Foyle
R1/2	30/08/1989	H	Fulham	L	3-5	Durnin, Simpson (2)

ZDS Trophy

R1	08/11/1989	H	Luton Town	L	2-3	Durnin, J Phillips

Total appea
Sub appea
Total

Phillips, J	Phillips, L	Foster	Greenall	Penney	Mustoe	Foyle	Durnin	Simpson	Ford	Smart	Lewis	McClaren	Slatter	Judge	Stein	Evans	Heath	Byrne	Nogan	Beauchamp	Kee	Muttock	Robinson	Jackson
3	4	5	6	7	**8**	9	10	11	12	13														
3		5	6	7		9	10	11			4	8												
3	8		5	7		9	10	11			4		6											
3			5	7	12	9	10	11		2	4	**8**	6	1										
3			5	7	8	9	10	11		2	4		6	1										
3			5	7	8	9	10	**11**	13	2	4		6	1	12									
3			5	7	8	9	**10**	11	13	2	4		6	1	12									
3			5	**7**	8	9	10	11			4	2	6	1	12									
3			5	12	8	9	**10**	11	13		4	2	6		7									
3				7	8	**9**	12	11		2	4		6		10	5								
3			9	7	8			11		2	4		6		10	5								
3			6	**7**	8		9	11			4		2		10	5	12							
3					8		9		11	2	4	**6**			10	5	7	12						
3		5	6		7		9	12	8	2	4			1	10		**11**							
3		5	6		7		**9**	12	8	2	4	13		1	10		11							
3		5	6		7		9		8	2	4			1	10		11							
3		5	6	13	7		9	12	8	2	4			1	10		**11**							
3		5		13	7				12	2	4	8		**1**	10	6			9	11				
3		5			7		9			2	4	8			10	6			**11**	12	1			
3		5		9	**7**		12	13		2	4	8			10	6				11	1			
3		5					9	11		2	4	8			10	6	7				1			
3		5			8		9	11	6	2	4				10		7				1			
3		5			**8**		9	11	13	2	4	12			10	6	7				1			
3		5					9	11		2	4	8			10	6	7				1			
3		5					9	11		2	4	8			10	6	7				1			
3		5					9	11		2	4	8			10	6	7				1			
3		5		12			**9**	11		2	4	8			10	6	7				1			
3		5		**9**	13			11	6	2	4	8			10		7		12		1			
3		5			7		9	11	6	2	4	8			10						1			
3		5			7		9	11	6	2	4	8			10						1			
3		5		13	7		9	11	6	2	4	**8**			10		12				1			
3		5		8	7		9	11	6	2	4				10						1			
3		5		**8**	7		9	11	6	2	4				10		12				1			
3		5		8	7		9	11	6	2	4				10						1			
		5		**8**	7		9	11	6	2	4				10	3	12				1			
		5		12	**8**		9	11	3	2	4				10	6	7				1			
		5			8		9	11	3	2	4				10	6	7				1			
		5		13	8		9	11	3	2	4				10	6	12	**7**			1			
		5			8	12	9	11	3	2	4				10	6	**7**				1			
		5		7	8		9	11	3	2	4			1	10	6								
	13	5		7	8		9	**11**	3	2	4			1	10	6			12					
	12	5		**7**	8		9	11	3	2	4			1	10	6								
	7	5			8		12	11	3	2	4	13		1	10	6						**9**		
	8	5		13	7		9	11	3	2	**4**	12		1	10	6								
	8	5			**7**	12	9	11	3	2	4			1	10	6								
	8	5		13		9		11	3		**4**	12		1	10			7					2	6

Phillips, J	Phillips, L	Foster	Greenall	Penney	Mustoe	Foyle	Durnin	Simpson	Ford	Smart	Lewis	McClaren	Slatter	Judge	Stein	Evans	Heath	Byrne	Nogan	Beauchamp	Kee	Muttock	Robinson	Jackson
3		5					9	11		2	4	8			10	6	7				1			
3		5		9				11		2	4	8			10	6	**7**		12		1			

Phillips, J	Phillips, L	Foster	Greenall	Penney	Mustoe	Foyle	Durnin	Simpson	Ford	Smart	Lewis	McClaren	Slatter	Judge	Stein	Evans	Heath	Byrne	Nogan	Beauchamp	Kee	Muttock	Robinson	Jackson
3		5	6	7		9	10	11	8		4													
3		**5**	6	7		9	10	11	12		4	8												

Phillips, J	Phillips, L	Foster	Greenall	Penney	Mustoe	Foyle	Durnin	Simpson	Ford	Smart	Lewis	McClaren	Slatter	Judge	Stein	Evans	Heath	Byrne	Nogan	Beauchamp	Kee	Muttock	Robinson	Jackson
3		5	6		7		9		**8**	2	4	12		1	10		11							

Phillips, J	Phillips, L	Foster	Greenall	Penney	Mustoe	Foyle	Durnin	Simpson	Ford	Smart	Lewis	McClaren	Slatter	Judge	Stein	Evans	Heath	Byrne	Nogan	Beauchamp	Kee	Muttock	Robinson	Jackson
39	6	40	18	23	37	13	43	42	27	42	50	20	10	18	41	26	19	2	2	2	23	1	1	1
	2			9	2	2	3	4	7	1		6			3		5	1	3	1				
4		4		2	7	3	15	12	2		1				9	2								

League Table

	P	W	D	L	F	A	Pts
Leeds United	46	24	13	9	79	52	85
Sheffield United	46	24	13	9	78	58	85
Newcastle United	46	22	14	10	80	55	80
Swindon Town	46	20	14	12	79	59	74
Blackburn Rovers	46	19	17	10	74	59	74
Sunderland	46	20	14	12	70	64	74
West Ham United	46	20	12	14	80	57	72
Oldham Athletic	46	19	14	13	70	57	71
Ipswich Town	46	19	12	15	67	66	69
Wolverhampton W	46	18	13	15	67	60	67
Port Vale	46	15	16	15	62	57	61
Portsmouth	46	15	16	15	62	65	61
Leicester City	46	15	14	17	67	79	59
Hull City	46	14	16	16	58	65	58
Watford	46	14	15	17	58	60	57
Plymouth Argyle	46	14	13	19	58	63	55
Oxford United	46	15	9	22	57	66	54
Brighton & Hove Albion	46	15	9	22	56	72	54
Barnsley	46	13	15	18	49	71	54
West Bromwich Albion	46	12	15	19	67	71	51
Middlesbrough	46	13	11	22	52	63	50
Bournemouth	46	12	12	22	57	76	48
Bradford City	46	9	14	23	44	68	41
Stoke City	46	6	19	21	35	63	37

1990-91

Division Two

Manager: Brian Horton

Did you know that?

The attendance of 1,055 for the game against Portsmouth in the ZDS Trophy is the lowest home crowd for a first-team competitive game.

Significant purchases included Jim Magilton from Liverpool, for £100,000, and Andy Melville, who joined from Swansea for £275,000.

Sales included Robbie Mustoe to Middlesbrough for £375,000 and Colin Greenall to Bury for £125,000.

Match No.	Date		Opponents	Result	(F-A)	Scorers
1	25/08/1990	H	Port Vale	W	5-2	Foster (2), Simpson, Stein (2)
2	01/09/1990	A	Notts County	L	1-3	L Phillips
3	08/09/1990	H	West Bromwich Albion	L	1-3	Foyle
4	15/09/1990	A	Oldham Athletic	L	0-3	
5	18/09/1990	A	Plymouth Argyle	D	2-2	Foyle, Stein
6	22/09/1990	H	Swindon Town	L	2-4	Foyle, Penney
7	29/09/1990	H	Wolverhampton Wanderers	D	1-1	Simpson
8	03/10/1990	A	West Ham United	L	0-2	
9	06/10/1990	A	Barnsley	L	0-3	
10	13/10/1990	H	Newcastle United	D	0-0	
11	20/10/1990	H	Brighton & Hove Albion	W	3-0	Simpson (3)
12	24/10/1990	A	Bristol Rovers	L	0-1	
13	27/10/1990	A	Watford	D	1-1	Stein
14	03/11/1990	H	Leicester City	D	2-2	Foyle, Simpson
15	07/11/1990	A	Millwall	W	2-1	Foster, Foyle
16	10/11/1990	H	Bristol City	W	3-1	Foyle, Simpson (2)
17	17/11/1990	A	Charlton Athletic	D	3-3	Magilton, Nogan, Mortimer (og)
18	24/11/1990	H	Middlesbrough	L	2-5	Nogan, Stein
19	01/12/1990	A	Portsmouth	D	1-1	Durnin
20	15/12/1990	A	Port Vale	L	0-1	
21	22/12/1990	H	Sheffield Wednesday	D	2-2	Simpson (2)
22	26/12/1990	A	Hull City	D	3-3	Durnin, Magilton, Stein
23	29/12/1990	A	Blackburn Rovers	W	3-1	Durnin, Foster, Nogan
24	01/01/1991	H	Ipswich Town	W	2-1	Durnin, Magilton
25	12/01/1991	H	Notts County	D	3-3	Durnin, Melville, Stein
26	19/01/1991	A	West Bromwich Albion	L	0-2	
27	02/02/1991	H	Oldham Athletic	W	5-1	Foyle, Lewis, Magilton (2), Nogan
28	16/02/1991	H	Charlton Athletic	D	1-1	Foyle
29	23/02/1991	A	Bristol City	L	1-3	Nogan
30	27/02/1991	H	Millwall	D	0-0	
31	02/03/1991	H	Portsmouth	W	1-0	Melville
32	05/03/1991	A	Swindon Town	D	0-0	
33	09/03/1991	A	Middlesbrough	D	0-0	
34	13/03/1991	H	West Ham United	W	2-1	Durnin, Simpson
35	16/03/1991	A	Wolverhampton Wanderers	D	3-3	Melville, Simpson, Stein
36	23/03/1991	H	Barnsley	W	2-0	Ford, Foyle
37	30/03/1991	H	Hull City	W	1-0	Durnin
38	01/04/1991	A	Sheffield Wednesday	W	2-0	Durnin, Simpson
39	06/04/1991	H	Blackburn Rovers	D	0-0	
40	10/04/1991	A	Newcastle United	D	2-2	Simpson (2)
41	13/04/1991	A	Ipswich Town	D	1-1	Simpson
42	17/04/1991	H	Plymouth Argyle	D	0-0	
43	20/04/1991	A	Brighton & Hove Albion	W	3-0	Durnin, Evans, Foyle
44	27/04/1991	H	Bristol Rovers	W	3-1	Magilton, Simpson
45	04/05/1991	H	Watford	L	0-1	
46	11/05/1991	A	Leicester City	L	0-1	
FA Cup						
R3	05/01/1991	A	Chelsea	W	3-1	Durnin, Magilton, Nogan
R4	26/01/1991	A	Tottenham Hotspur	L	2-4	Foyle (2)
League Cup						
R1/1	28/08/1990	A	Reading	W	1-0	Simpson
R1/2	05/09/1990	H	Reading	W	2-1	Foster (2)
R2/1	24/09/1990	A	Port Vale	W	2-0	Foyle (2)
R2/2	10/10/1990	H	Port Vale	D	0-0	
R3	31/10/1990	H	West Ham United	W	2-1	Foyle, Magilton
R4	28/11/1990	H	Chelsea	L	1-2	Melville
ZDS Trophy						
R1	21/11/1990	H	Bristol City	W	2-2*	Magilton, Nogan
R2	12/12/1990	H	Portsmouth	W	1-0	Magilton
R3	22/01/1991	A	Ipswich Town	L	1-2	Foster

*3-2 on pens

Total appear
Sub appear
Total

Ford	Phillips, L	Foster	Melville	Evans	Lewis	Foyle	Stein	Simpson	Kee	Jackson	Penney	Nogan	Smart	Walker	McClaren	Durnin	Magilton	Beauchamp	Veysey	Byrne	Gardner
3	4	5	6	7	8	9	10	11													
3	4	5	6		8	9	10	11	1	**7**	12										
3	4	5	6	7	8	9	10	11	1												
3	4	5	6		8	9	10	11	1	**7**		12									
3	4	**5**	6		8	9	10	11	1		7		12								
3	4		6		8	9	10	11	1		7	12	**5**								
3	4		6		8	9	10	11		5				1	**7**	12					
3	4		6		**8**	9	10	11		5	12			1			7				
3	4	5	6	13	8		10	11			9					12	7				
	4	5	6	3		9	8	11									7	10			
	4	5	6	3		9	8	11	1								7	10			
		5	6	3	4	9	8	11	1			12					7	**10**			
		5	6	3	4	9	8	11	1			10					7				
		5	6	3	4	9	8	11	1			10					7				
		5	6		4	9	8	11	1			10					7				
	12	5	6	3	4	9	8	11	1			**10**	3				7				
		5	6	3	4	9	8	11	1			10					7				
		5	6	3	4	9	8	11	1			10					7				
		5	6		**4**	9	8	11			12	10	3			13	7		1		
		5	6	3	4		**8**	11			12	10				9	7		1		
8		5	6	3	4			11			12	10			13	9	7		1		
		5	6	3			**8**	11			12	10			4	9	7		1		
	8	5	6					11				10	3		4	9	7		1		
	8	5	6					11				10	3		4	9	7		1		
	8	5	6				12	11				10	3		4	9	7		1		
	8	5	6				12	11				10	3		**4**	9	7		1		
	8	5	6		9	4		11				10	3				7		1		
	8	5	6		9	4	12	11				10	3				7		1		
13	8	5	6		**9**	4	12	11				10	3				7		1		
3	8	5	6		9	4		**11**				10				12	7		1		
3	8	5	6		**9**	4		11				10				12	7		1		
3	8	5	6		9	4		11				**10**				12	7		1		
3	8	5	6		9	4		11								10	7		1		
3	8	5	6		9	4		11								10	7		1		
3	8	5	6		9	**4**	12	11								10	7		1		
3		5	6		4	9		11								10	7		1	8	
3		5	6		4	9		11								10	7		1	8	
3		5	6		4	9		11				8				10	7		1		
3		5	6		4	9	12	11				**8**				10	7		1		
3		5	6		4		9	11				**8**				10	7		1		12
3		5	6		4		9	11				8	2			10	**7**		1		12
3			6	5		10	9	11				8	2					7	1		4
3			6	5		7	9	11				8	2			10			1		4
3			6	5		7	**9**	11				8				10	4				12
3			6	5		7	9	11				8				**10**	4				12
3			6			7	9	11		13		8	5			**10**	4				12

Ford	Phillips, L	Foster	Melville	Evans	Lewis	Foyle	Stein	Simpson	Kee	Jackson	Penney	Nogan	Smart	Walker	McClaren	Durnin	Magilton	Beauchamp	Veysey	Byrne	Gardner
	8	5	6					11				10	3		4	9	7		1		
	8	5	6			4	12	11				**10**	3			9	7		1		

Ford	Phillips, L	Foster	Melville	Evans	Lewis	Foyle	Stein	Simpson	Kee	Jackson	Penney	Nogan	Smart	Walker	McClaren	Durnin	Magilton	Beauchamp	Veysey	Byrne	Gardner
3	4	5	6	7	8	9	10	11	1												
3	4	5	6		8	9	10	11	1	7											
3	4		6		8	9		11		5	7			1	10						
	4	5	6	3		9		11				12	13			**8**	7	10			
		5	6	3	4	9	**8**	11	1		12	10					7				
		5	6		4	9	8	11				10	3				7		1		

Ford	Phillips, L	Foster	Melville	Evans	Lewis	Foyle	Stein	Simpson	Kee	Jackson	Penney	Nogan	Smart	Walker	McClaren	Durnin	Magilton	Beauchamp	Veysey	Byrne	Gardner
	9		6	3	**4**		8	11			12	10	5				7	13	1		
	4	5	6	3	12	9	**8**	11				10				13	7		1		
	8	5	6			12		11				10	3		**4**	9	7		1		

Ford	Phillips, L	Foster	Melville	Evans	Lewis	Foyle	Stein	Simpson	Kee	Jackson	Penney	Nogan	Smart	Walker	McClaren	Durnin	Magilton	Beauchamp	Veysey	Byrne	Gardner
30	33	47	57	22	40	44	34	57	16	6	4	36	19	3	9	24	45	5	31	2	2
1	1			1	1	1	7			1	8	4	2		1	7		1			5
1	1	7	4	1	1	15	8	18			1	7				10	10				

League Table

	P	W	D	L	F	A	Pts
Oldham Athletic	46	25	13	8	83	53	88
West Ham United	46	24	15	7	60	34	87
Sheffield Wednesday	46	22	16	8	80	51	82
Notts County	46	23	11	12	76	55	80
Millwall	46	20	13	13	70	51	73
Brighton & Hove Albion	46	21	7	18	63	69	70
Middlesbrough	46	20	9	17	66	47	69
Barnsley	46	19	12	15	63	48	69
Bristol City	46	20	7	19	68	71	67
Oxford United	46	14	19	13	69	66	61
Newcastle United	46	14	17	15	49	56	59
Wolverhampton W	46	13	19	14	63	63	58
Bristol Rovers	46	15	13	18	56	59	58
Ipswich Town	46	13	18	15	60	68	57
Port Vale	46	15	12	19	56	64	57
Charlton Athletic	46	13	17	16	57	61	56
Portsmouth	46	14	11	21	58	70	53
Plymouth Argyle	46	12	17	17	54	68	53
Blackburn Rovers	46	14	10	22	51	66	52
Watford	46	12	15	19	45	59	51
Swindon Town	46	12	14	20	65	73	50
Leicester City	46	14	8	24	60	83	50
West Bromwich Albion	46	10	18	18	52	61	48
Hull City	46	10	15	21	57	85	45

1991-92

Division Two

Manager: Brian Horton

Did you know that?

On 9 December the Maxwell family withdrew all financial support to the club following the death of Robert Maxwell on 5 November. All 28 professional players were put on the transfer list. All four directors apart from chairman Kevin Maxwell resigned.

Players sold included Lee Nogan to Watford for £275,000 and Paul Simpson to Derby for £500,000. Martin Foyle had already left to join Port Vale for £375,000 in June, and Mark Stein had gone to Stoke for £100,000.

United needed to win at Tranmere on the last day of the season, while hoping that results elsewhere went their way. Oxford won 2–1, and there then followed an agonising wait for the other scores. In the end, a David Speedie hat-trick for Blackburn relegated Plymouth and saved Oxford.

Match No.	Date		Opponents	Result	(F-A)	Scorers
1	17/08/1991	A	Port Vale	L	1-2	Magilton
2	24/08/1991	H	Grimsby Town	L	1-2	Magilton
3	31/08/1991	A	Sunderland	L	0-2	
4	04/09/1991	H	Middlesbrough	L	1-2	Nogan
5	07/09/1991	A	Wolverhampton Wanderers	L	1-3	Nogan
6	14/09/1991	H	Millwall	D	2-2	Aylott, Melville
7	18/09/1991	H	Derby County	W	2-0	Aylott, Penney
8	21/09/1991	A	Bristol Rovers	L	1-2	Penney
9	28/09/1991	H	Plymouth Argyle	W	3-2	Nogan, Penney, Simpson
10	05/10/1991	A	Ipswich Town	L	1-2	Magilton
11	12/10/1991	H	Tranmere Rovers	W	1-0	Aylott
12	19/10/1991	A	Newcastle United	L	3-4	Durnin, Ford, Lewis
13	23/10/1991	H	Charlton Athletic	L	1-2	Magilton
14	26/10/1991	H	Leicester City	L	1-2	Simpson
15	30/10/1991	A	Southend United	W	3-2	Simpson (2), Stein
16	02/11/1991	H	Barnsley	L	0-1	
17	06/11/1991	A	Watford	L	0-2	
18	09/11/1991	A	Portsmouth	L	1-2	Magilton
19	16/11/1991	H	Bristol City	D	1-1	Simpson
20	23/11/1991	H	Brighton & Hove Albion	W	3-1	Magilton, Nogan, Simpson
21	30/11/1991	A	Cambridge United	D	1-1	Nogan
22	07/12/1991	H	Blackburn Rovers	L	1-3	Melville
23	26/12/1991	H	Southend United	L	0-1	
24	28/12/1991	H	Sunderland	W	3-0	Aylott, Beauchamp, Durnin
25	08/01/1992	A	Charlton Athletic	D	2-2	Beauchamp, Durnin
26	11/01/1992	A	Grimsby Town	L	0-1	
27	18/01/1992	H	Port Vale	D	2-2	Beauchamp, Lewis
28	28/01/1992	A	Swindon Town	L	1-2	Magilton
29	01/02/1992	H	Newcastle United	W	5-2	Aylott, Durnin, Foster (2), Simpson
30	08/02/1992	A	Leicester City	L	1-2	Melville
31	15/02/1992	A	Brighton & Hove Albion	W	2-1	Simpson (2)
32	22/02/1992	H	Cambridge United	W	1-0	Melville
33	29/02/1992	A	Blackburn Rovers	D	1-1	Durnin
34	07/03/1992	H	Swindon Town	W	5-3	Beauchamp (2), Durnin (2), Magilton (pen)
35	11/03/1992	H	Watford	D	0-0	
36	14/03/1992	A	Barnsley	L	0-1	
37	21/03/1992	H	Portsmouth	W	2-1	Aylott, Beauchamp
38	28/03/1992	A	Bristol City	D	1-1	Bannister
39	01/04/1992	A	Millwall	L	1-2	Allen
40	04/04/1992	H	Wolverhampton Wanderers	W	1-0	Penney
41	11/04/1992	A	Derby County	D	2-2	Lewis, Magilton (pen)
42	15/04/1992	A	Middlesbrough	L	1-2	Magilton
43	18/04/1992	H	Bristol Rovers	D	2-2	Lewis, Magilton
44	20/04/1992	A	Plymouth Argyle	L	1-3	Bannister
45	25/04/1992	H	Ipswich Town	D	1-1	Magilton
46	02/05/1992	A	Tranmere Rovers	W	2-1	Beauchamp, Durnin

FA Cup

R3	04/01/1992	H	Tranmere Rovers	W	3-1	Beauchamp, Magilton (pen), Vickers (og)
R4	05/02/1992	H	Sunderland	L	2-3	Penney, Simpson

League Cup

R2/1	24/09/1991	A	Portsmouth	D	0-0	
R2/2	09/10/1991	H	Portsmouth	L	0-1	

ZDS Trophy

R1	01/10/1991	A	Swindon Town	L*	3-3	Melville, Simpson (2)

* 3-4 on pens

Total appea
Sub appea
Total

Ford	Jackson	Foster	Melville	Magilton	Stein	Nogan	Penney	Simpson	Durnin	Byrne	Evans	Phillips, L	Lewis	Kee	Smart	Aylott	Beauchamp	Harris	Druce	Keeley	McClaren	Wanless	Allen	Williams	Bannister
3	4	5	6	7	8	9	**10**	11	12																
3		5	6	7	**8**	4	10	11	9	12	13														
3		5		7	**8**	9	10	11	12		6	4													
3		5	6	7		9		11	10			4	8												
3		5	6	7		9	12	11	10			4	**8**		13										
		5	6	7		10	12	11				4	**8**	1	3	9									
		5	6	7		10	8	11				4		1	3	9									
		5	6	7		10	8	**11**	12			4		1	3	9									
		5	6	7		10	8	11				**4**			3	9	12								
		5	6	7		10	**8**	11					4		3	9	12								
		5	6	7		10		11	8				4		3	9									
2		5	6	7		10		11	8				4		3	9									
3		5	6	7	12	**10**		11	8				4		2	9									
3		5	6	7	8	10		12					4	1	2	9		**11**							
		5	6	7	**8**	10		11					4	1	3	9			12						
		5	6	7	8	**10**		11			13		4	1	3	9			12						
		5	6	7		10		11			8		4		3	9				1					
		5	6	7		10		11	12				4		3	9				1	**9**				
		5	6	7		10		11					4		3	9				1	8				
		5	6	7		**10**		11	12				4		3	9				1	8				
		5	6	7		10		11	12				4		3	**9**				1		8			
			6	7		10		11	12		5		4		3	**9**	13			1		8			
			6	7				11	10		5		4		3	9	8								
			6	7				11	10		5		4		3	9	8								
			6	7				11	10		5		4		3	9	8								
			6	7				11	10		5		4		3	9	**8**					12			
			6	7			12	11	10		5		4		3	9	8					13			
	12		6	7			2	11	10		5		4		**3**	9	8					13			
	3	2	6				7	11	10		5		4			9	8								
	3		6					11	10		5		4				8				7	**9**	12		
	3		6	7				11	10		5		4			9	8								
			6	7					10		5		4		3	9	8						11		
			6	7					10		5		4		2	9	8						11	3	
			6	7			12		10		5		4		2	**9**	8						11	3	
			6	7			12		10		5		4		2	**9**	8						11	3	
			6	7			12		10		5		4		2	9	8						**11**	3	
			6	7					10		5		4		2	9	8						**11**	3	12
			6	7			11		**10**		5		4		2	9	8							3	12
			6	7			**10**		13		5		4		2	9	8						11	3	12
			6	7			3		10		5		4		2		8						11		9
			6	7			3		10		5		4		2		8						11		9
			6	7			3		10		5		4		2		8						11		9
			6	7			3		**10**		5		4		2	12	8						11		9
			6	7			3		12		5		4		2	9	8						**11**		10
			6	7			3		9		5		4	1	2	12	8						**11**		10
3			6	7					10		5		4	1	2	9	8								11

Ford	Jackson	Foster	Melville	Magilton	Stein	Nogan	Penney	Simpson	Durnin	Byrne	Evans	Phillips, L	Lewis	Kee	Smart	Aylott	Beauchamp	Harris	Druce	Keeley	McClaren	Wanless	Allen	Williams	Bannister
	3		6	7				11	10		5		4		2	9	8								
	3	2	6				7	11	**10**		5		4			9	8						12		

Ford	Jackson	Foster	Melville	Magilton	Stein	Nogan	Penney	Simpson	Durnin	Byrne	Evans	Phillips, L	Lewis	Kee	Smart	Aylott	Beauchamp	Harris	Druce	Keeley	McClaren	Wanless	Allen	Williams	Bannister
		5	6	7		10	8	11				4	9	1	3										
		5	6	7		10		11	9		**8**		4		3		12					13			

Ford	Jackson	Foster	Melville	Magilton	Stein	Nogan	Penney	Simpson	Durnin	Byrne	Evans	Phillips, L	Lewis	Kee	Smart	Aylott	Beauchamp	Harris	Druce	Keeley	McClaren	Wanless	Allen	Williams	Bannister
			6	7		10	8	11			5		4		13	9	**3**						12		

Ford	Jackson	Foster	Melville	Magilton	Stein	Nogan	Penney	Simpson	Durnin	Byrne	Evans	Phillips, L	Lewis	Kee	Smart	Aylott	Beauchamp	Harris	Druce	Keeley	McClaren	Wanless	Allen	Williams	Bannister
9	6	25	50	48	6	25	20	35	31	0	31	8	45	9	41	38	27	1	0	6	4	3	13	7	7
	1				1		6	1	9	1	2				2	2	4		2			4	3		3
1		2	5	13	1	5	5	12	8				4			6	8						1		2

League Table

	P	W	D	L	F	A	Pts
Ipswich Town	46	24	12	10	70	50	84
Middlesbrough	46	23	11	12	58	41	80
Derby County	46	23	9	14	69	51	78
Leicester City	46	23	8	15	62	55	77
Cambridge United	46	19	17	10	65	47	74
Blackburn Rovers	46	21	11	14	70	53	74
Charlton Athletic	46	20	11	15	54	48	71
Swindon Town	46	18	15	13	69	55	69
Portsmouth	46	19	12	15	65	51	69
Watford	46	18	11	17	51	48	65
Wolverhampton W	46	18	10	18	61	54	64
Southend United	46	17	11	18	63	63	62
Bristol Rovers	46	16	14	16	60	63	62
Tranmere Rovers	46	14	19	13	56	56	61
Millwall	46	17	10	19	64	71	61
Barnsley	46	16	11	19	46	57	59
Bristol City	46	13	15	18	55	71	54
Sunderland	46	14	11	21	61	65	53
Grimsby Town	46	14	11	21	47	62	53
Newcastle United	46	13	13	20	66	84	52
Oxford United	46	13	11	22	66	73	50
Plymouth Argyle	46	13	9	24	42	64	48
Brighton & Hove Albion	46	12	11	23	56	77	47
Port Vale	46	10	15	21	42	59	45

1992-93

Division One

Manager: Brian Horton

Did you know that?

During the summer, recycling firm BioMass, owned by Jersey-based businessman Alan Corbett, bought United.

A planning consent for a new stadium on Watlington Road was turned down by the Department of the Environment because it was in the Green Belt.

United paid £65,000 to Hereford for Jon Narbett, £95,000 to Darlington for Nick Cusack and £20,000 to Corby for Matt Murphy.

Match No.	Date		Opponents	Result	(F-A)	Scorers	A
1	15/08/1992	H	Bristol Rovers	W	2-1	Beauchamp, Penney (pen)	
2	22/08/1992	A	Millwall	L	1-3	Penney	
3	29/08/1992	H	Wolverhampton Wanderers	D	0-0		
4	05/09/1992	A	Grimsby Town	D	1-1	Durnin	
5	12/09/1992	H	Sunderland	L	0-1		
6	15/09/1992	H	Cambridge United	W	3-0	Allen, Magilton (pen), Penney	
7	20/09/1992	A	Swindon Town	D	2-2	Melville, Penney	
8	25/09/1992	H	Tranmere Rovers	L	1-2	Magilton	
9	03/10/1992	H	Birmingham City	D	0-0		
10	11/10/1992	A	Derby County	W	1-0	Durnin	
11	17/10/1992	H	Barnsley	D	0-0		
12	24/10/1992	A	Notts County	D	1-1	Cusack	
13	31/10/1992	H	Watford	D	1-1	Magilton (pen)	
14	03/11/1992	H	Portsmouth	D	5-5	Allen, Durnin, Magilton (2) (1 pen), Penney	
15	07/11/1992	A	Southend United	W	3-0	Durnin (2), Penney	
16	14/11/1992	H	Luton Town	W	4-0	Durnin (4)	
17	21/11/1992	A	West Ham United	L	3-5	Durnin, Magilton, Melville	
18	28/11/1992	A	Brentford	L	0-1		
19	13/12/1992	H	Leicester City	D	0-0		
20	19/12/1992	A	Charlton Athletic	D	1-1	Ford	
21	26/12/1992	A	Bristol City	D	1-1	Beauchamp	
22	28/12/1992	H	Newcastle United	W	4-2	Cusack, Durnin, Magilton (2) (1 pen)	
23	09/01/1993	H	Swindon Town	L	0-1		
24	15/01/1993	A	Tranmere Rovers	L	0-4		
25	23/01/1993	A	Cambridge United	D	2-2	Ford (2)	
26	30/01/1993	H	Millwall	W	3-0	Beauchamp (2), Magilton (pen)	
27	06/02/1993	A	Bristol Rovers	W	1-0	Melville	
28	09/02/1993	A	Sunderland	L	0-2		
29	20/02/1993	A	Wolverhampton Wanderers	W	1-0	Beauchamp	
30	23/02/1993	H	Grimsby Town	L	0-1		
31	27/02/1993	H	Derby County	L	0-1		
32	06/03/1993	A	Birmingham City	L	0-1		
33	09/03/1993	A	Luton Town	L	1-3	Cusack	
34	13/03/1993	H	Southend United	L	0-1		
35	20/03/1993	A	Peterborough United	D	1-1	Beauchamp	
36	23/03/1993	H	West Ham United	W	1-0	Melville	
37	27/03/1993	A	Portsmouth	L	0-3		
38	03/04/1993	H	Brentford	L	0-2		
39	07/04/1993	A	Leicester City	L	1-2	Ford	
40	10/04/1993	H	Bristol City	W	2-0	Beauchamp, Druce	
41	17/04/1993	H	Charlton Athletic	L	0-1		
42	20/04/1993	H	Peterborough United	W	2-1	Magilton (pen), Melville	
43	24/04/1993	A	Barnsley	W	1-0	Melville	
44	01/05/1993	H	Notts County	D	1-1	Magilton	
45	06/05/1993	A	Newcastle United	L	1-2	Cusack	
46	08/05/1993	A	Watford	W	1-0	Allen	

FA Cup

R3	02/01/1993	A	Swansea City	D	1-1	Cusack
r	12/01/1993	H	Swansea City	L*	2-2	Beauchamp, Magilton (pen)

* 4-5 on pens

League Cup

R1/1	18/08/1992	H	Swansea City	W	3-0	Allen (2), Cusack
R1/2	25/08/1992	A	Swansea City	L	0-1	
R2/1	23/09/1992	H	Aston Villa	L	1-2	Beauchamp
R2/2	07/10/1992	A	Aston Villa	L	1-2	Cusack

Anglo-Italian Cup

Pre	01/09/1992	H	Swindon Town	L	1-3	Magilton
Pre	29/09/1992	A	Brentford	L	0-2	

Total appear

Sub appea

Total

Ford	Collins	Evans	Melville	Phillips, L	Beauchamp	Cusack	Penney	Durnin	Allen	Lewis	Magilton	Reece	Robinson	Narbett	Wanless	Varadi	Jackson	Keeble	Druce	Murphy
3	4	5	6	7	8	9	10	11												
3	4	5	6	7	8	9	10	**11**	12	13										
3		5	6		8	9	**10**	11	12	4	7									
3		5	6		8	9	**10**	11	12	4	7									
3		5	6		8	**9**	12	10	11	4	7									
3	12	5	6		**8**		9	10	11	4	7									
3		5	6	12	8		9	10	**11**	4	7									
	3	5	6	13	8	12	9	10	**11**	4	7									
11	3	5	6	7		**8**	9	10	12	4		1								
3		5	6	11		8	9	10		4	7	1								
3		5	6		11	8	**9**	10	12	4	7	1								
3		5	6		11	**8**	9	10		4	7	1	12							
3		5	6		11	**8**	9	10	12	4	7	1								
3		5	6		8	12	**9**	10	11	4	7	1		13						
3		5	6		8		9	10	**11**	4	7	1		12						
3		5	6		8	12	**9**	10	11	4	7	1								
3		5	6		8	12	9	**10**	11	4	7	1								
3		5	6		8	12	**9**	10	11	4	7	1								
3		5	6		8	10	**9**		11	4	7	1			12					
3		5	6		8	10	9		11	4	7	1								
3		5	6		8	10	**9**	11	12	4	7	1								
		5	6		8	9		10	11	4	7	1	3							
13		5	6		8	**9**	12	10	11	4	7	1	3							
3		5	**6**		8	9	13	12	11	4	7	1	10							
3		5	6		8	**9**		10		4	7	1		11		12				
3		5	6		8			10		4	7	1		11		9				
3		5	6		8		12	10		4	7	1		11		**9**				
3		5	6		8		12	10	13	4	7	1		11		**9**				
3		5	6		8	9		**10**		4	7	1		11		12				
3		5			8	**9**	12	10	13	4	7	1	6	11						
3		5	6		8	**9**	10	12	13	4	7	1	11							
3		5	6		8	**9**	10	12	13	4	7	1	11							
3		5	6		8	9	10			4	7	1	11							
3		5		4	8	9			12		7	1	2	11			**6**	10		
3		5	6	4	8	9		10		7		1	2	11						
3		5	6	7	8	9		10		4		1	2	11						
3		5	6	4	8	9		10		11	7	1	2							
3		5	6	**4**	8	9		10	13	11	7	1	2						12	
3	4	5	6		8	9					7			11					10	
3	4	5	6		8	9	12				7			11					**10**	
3	4	5	6		8	9	12				7			**11**	13				10	
3	5		6		8			10	11	4	7	1			9					
3	5		6		8	13	12	10	11	4		1	7		**9**					
3	5		6		8	12		10		4	7	1	11		**9**					
3	5		6		8	12	13		11	4	7	1			**9**					10
3	5		6		8	12			11	4	7	1	13		**9**					10

Ford	Collins	Evans	Melville	Phillips, L	Beauchamp	Cusack	Penney	Durnin	Allen	Lewis	Magilton	Reece	Robinson	Narbett	Wanless	Varadi	Jackson	Keeble	Druce	Murphy
		5	6		8	9		10	11	4	7	1	3							
3		5	6		8	**9**	12	10	11	4	7	1								

Ford	Collins	Evans	Melville	Phillips, L	Beauchamp	Cusack	Penney	Durnin	Allen	Lewis	Magilton	Reece	Robinson	Narbett	Wanless	Varadi	Jackson	Keeble	Druce	Murphy
3	4	5	6	7	8	**9**	10	11	12	13										
3		5	6		8	9	10			4	7			11						
	3	5	6		8		9	10	11	4	7									
11	**3**	5	6	7		8	9	10	12	4		1								

Ford	Collins	Evans	Melville	Phillips, L	Beauchamp	Cusack	Penney	Durnin	Allen	Lewis	Magilton	Reece	Robinson	Narbett	Wanless	Varadi	Jackson	Keeble	Druce	Murphy
3		5	6		8	**9**	10	11	12	4	7									
	3	5	6	7	8	12	**9**	10	13	4				11						

Ford	Collins	Evans	Melville	Phillips, L	Beauchamp	Cusack	Penney	Durnin	Allen	Lewis	Magilton	Reece	Robinson	Narbett	Wanless	Varadi	Jackson	Keeble	Druce	Murphy
48	16	49	52	12	51	36	29	41	21	47	45	38	15	14	5	3	1	1	3	2
1	1			2		10	11	3	17	2			2	2	2	2			1	
4			6		9	7	6	11	5		13								1	

League Table

	P	W	D	L	F	A	Pts
Newcastle United	46	29	9	8	92	38	96
West Ham United	46	26	10	10	81	41	88
Portsmouth	46	26	10	10	80	46	88
Tranmere Rovers	46	23	10	13	72	56	79
Swindon Town	46	21	13	12	74	59	76
Leicester City	46	22	10	14	71	64	76
Millwall	46	18	16	12	65	53	70
Derby County	46	19	9	18	68	57	66
Grimsby Town	46	19	7	20	58	57	64
Peterborough United	46	16	14	16	55	63	62
Wolverhampton W	46	16	13	17	57	56	61
Charlton Athletic	46	16	13	17	49	46	61
Barnsley	46	17	9	20	56	60	60
Oxford United	46	14	14	18	53	56	56
Bristol City	46	14	14	18	49	67	56
Watford	46	14	13	19	57	71	55
Notts County	46	12	16	18	55	70	52
Southend United	46	13	13	20	54	64	52
Birmingham City	46	13	12	21	50	72	51
Luton Town	46	10	21	15	48	62	51
Sunderland	46	13	11	22	50	64	50
Brentford	46	13	10	23	52	71	49
Cambridge United	46	11	16	19	48	69	49
Bristol Rovers	46	10	11	25	55	87	41

1993-94

Division One

Manager: Brian Horton, Maurice Evans (caretaker), then Denis Smith

Did you know that?

Just days into the new season, Brian Horton left to become Manchester City's new manager. After a brief gap he was replaced by Denis Smith.

Immediately after beating Leeds United in the FA Cup Jim Magilton, scorer of the winning goal, signed for Southampton for £600,000. John Durnin joined Portsmouth for £200,000, and Andy Melville left for Sunderland for £500,000 plus Anton Rogan.

Denis Smith signed three key players in November, with John Byrne joining from Millwall for £50,000, Phil Whitehead from Barnsley for £75,000 after a loan spell, and Matt Elliott signed from Scunthorpe for £150,000. In February, Paul Moody joined from Southampton for £60,000.

United were relegated on the final day of the season. Despite beating Notts County 2–1, wins for Birmingham and West Brom condemned the Us to the drop.

Match No.	Date		Opponents	Result	(F-A)	Scorers	A
1	14/08/1993	H	Portsmouth	W	3-2	Allen, Magilton, Symons (og)	
2	21/08/1993	A	West Bromwich Albion	L	1-3	Robinson	
3	28/08/1993	H	Watford	L	2-3	Beauchamp, Robinson	
4	31/08/1993	A	Bolton Wanderers	L	0-1		
5	11/09/1993	H	Bristol City	W	4-2	Allen, Dyer, Magilton (2) (1 pen)	
6	18/09/1993	A	Peterborough United	L	1-3	Rogan	
7	25/09/1993	A	Tranmere Rovers	L	0-2		
8	02/10/1993	H	Grimsby Town	D	2-2	M Ford, Magilton (pen)	
9	10/10/1993	H	Stoke City	W	1-0	Penney	
10	16/10/1993	A	Southend United	L	1-6	Penney	
11	20/10/1993	A	Nottingham Forest	D	0-0		
12	23/10/1993	H	Luton Town	L	0-1		
13	30/10/1993	A	Charlton Athletic	L	0-1		
14	02/11/1993	H	Barnsley	D	1-1	Cusack	
15	06/11/1993	A	Millwall	D	2-2	Beauchamp, Cusack	
16	13/11/1993	H	Derby County	W	2-0	Elliott, Magilton	
17	20/11/1993	A	Leicester City	W	3-2	Cusack, Dyer, Rogan	
18	28/11/1993	A	Notts County	L	1-2	Elliott	
19	04/12/1993	H	Millwall	L	0-2		
20	11/12/1993	H	Bolton Wanderers	L	0-2		
21	18/12/1993	A	Portsmouth	D	1-1	Beauchamp	
22	27/12/1993	H	Crystal Palace	L	1-3	Dyer	
23	28/12/1993	A	Wolverhampton Wanderers	L	1-2	Elliott	
24	01/01/1994	H	Middlesbrough	D	1-1	Byrne	
25	03/01/1994	A	Birmingham City	D	1-1	Dyer	
26	11/01/1994	H	Sunderland	L	0-3		
27	15/01/1994	H	Southend United	W	2-1	Cusack (2)	
28	22/01/1994	A	Stoke City	D	1-1	Beauchamp	
29	05/02/1994	A	Luton Town	L	0-3		
30	12/02/1994	H	Charlton Athletic	L	0-4		
31	26/02/1994	H	Nottingham Forest	W	1-0	Dyer	
32	05/03/1994	A	Watford	L	1-2	Cusack	
33	12/03/1994	H	Peterborough United	L	1-2	Moody	
34	15/03/1994	A	Bristol City	W	1-0	Byrne	
35	19/03/1994	H	Tranmere Rovers	W	1-0	Beauchamp	
36	26/03/1994	A	Grimsby Town	L	0-1		
37	29/03/1994	H	Birmingham City	W	2-0	Byrne, Moody (pen)	
38	02/04/1994	A	Crystal Palace	L	1-2	Byrne	
39	04/04/1994	H	Wolverhampton Wanderers	W	4-0	Byrne, Elliott, Moody, Venus (og)	
40	09/04/1994	A	Middlesbrough	L	1-2	Moody (pen)	
41	12/04/1994	H	West Bromwich Albion	D	1-1	Moody	
42	16/04/1994	A	Barnsley	L	0-1		
43	23/04/1994	H	Leicester City	D	2-2	Elliott, Moody	
44	26/04/1994	A	Sunderland	W	3-2	Allen, Moody (2) (1 pen)	
45	30/04/1994	A	Derby County	L	1-2	Byrne	
46	08/05/1994	H	Notts County	W	2-1	Beauchamp, Byrne	

FA Cup

R3	08/01/1994	H	Tranmere Rovers	W	2-0	Byrne, Elliott
R4	29/01/1994	H	Leeds United	D	2-2	Dyer, Elliott
r	09/02/1994	A	Leeds United	W	3-2	Allen, Byrne, Magilton
R5	19/02/1994	H	Chelsea	L	1-2	Beauchamp

League Cup

R2/1	21/09/1993	A	Tranmere Rovers	L	1-5	Beauchamp
R2/2	05/10/1993	H	Tranmere Rovers	D	1-1	Wanless

Anglo-Italian Cup

Pre	04/09/1993	A	Bristol City	L	1-2	M Ford
Pre	14/09/1993	H	Portsmouth	L	0-2	

Total appear

Sub appea

Total

Ford, M	Lewis	Collins	Rogan	Magilton	Beauchamp	Dyer	Robinson	Allen	Cusack	Reece	Narbett	Druce	Penney	Whitehead	Wanless	Ford, B	Keeble	Elliott	Byrne	Jackson	Saunders	Moody	Carter
3	4	5	6	7	8	9	10	11															
3	4	5	6	7	8	9	**10**	11	12														
3	4	5	6	7	8	9	10	**11**				12											
3	4	5		7	8	9	10	12		1	6	**11**											
3	4	13	6	7	**8**	12	5	11	9	1			10										
	4	3	6	7	**8**	9	5	11		1			10		12								
3	4	2	6	7	8	**9**	5	11		1		12	10										
3	4	2	6	7	8	**9**	5	11				12	10	1	13								
3	4	2	6	7	8		5	11				**9**	10	1	13	12							
3	4	2	6	**7**	8		5	11				9	10	1	13	12							
3	4	2	6	7	8	12	5	11					10	1	**9**								
3	4	2	6	7	8	**9**	5	11					10	1			12						
3	4	2	6	7	8	12	5	11	**9**			13	10	1									
3	4	2	6	7	**8**	12	5	11	9			13	10	1									
3	4	12	6	7	8		**5**	11	9				13	1				2	10				
3	4		6	7	8		5	11	9				12	1				2	**10**				
3	4	13	6	7	**8**	12	5	11	9					1				2	10				
3	4	5	6	7	8	12		**11**	9					1				2	10				
	4	13	6	7	8	12	5	**11**	9					1				2	10	3			
	4	5	6	7	8	3		11	9			12	**10**	1				2					
	4	5	6	7	8	3		11	9			13	**10**	1				2		12			
3	4		6	7	**8**	11	5	12	9					1				2	10		13		
3	4		6	7	8	11	5		9					1				2	10				
3	4		6	7	8	11	5					12		1				2	10		**9**		
3	4		6	7	8	11	5	13				12		1				2	**10**		9		
3	4		6	7	8	11	5	13	**9**					1				2	10		12		
3	4		6	7	8	**11**	5	12	9					1				2	10				
3	4		6	7	8	11	5	13	**9**					1				2	10		12		
3	4		6	7	8	11	5	12	**9**				13	1				2	10				
3	7		6		8		5	9	12				**11**	1		4		2	10				
3	7	12			8	6		11				13		1		4		2	10			**9**	
3	7	6				12		**11**	10			13		1		4		2	8			9	
3	7	13			8	6		11	**10**					1		4		2	12			9	
3	7				8	6		11						1		4		2	10			9	
3	7				8	6		11						1		4		2	10			9	
3	7				12	6		11						1		4		2	**10**			9	8
3	7				13	6		11				12		1		4		2	**10**			9	8
3	7				9	6	4	**11**						1	12			2	10				8
3	7				11	6	4	12						1	13			2	10			9	**8**
3	7				11	6	4	12						1	13			2	10			9	**8**
3	7				11	6	4	8						1				2	10			9	
	7	3			11	6	4	12				13		1		**8**		2	10			9	
3	7				11	6	4	8				12		1				2	**10**			9	
3	7				11		4	**10**				6		1		8		2	12			9	
3	7	12			11		4	10				6		1		**8**		2	13			9	
3	7	12			11		4	**10**						1		8		2	6			9	

Ford, M	Lewis	Collins	Rogan	Magilton	Beauchamp	Dyer	Robinson	Allen	Cusack	Reece	Narbett	Druce	Penney	Whitehead	Wanless	Ford, B	Keeble	Elliott	Byrne	Jackson	Saunders	Moody	Carter
3	4		6	7	8	11	5	12	9					1				2	**10**				
3	4		6	7	8	**11**	5	13	9				12	1				2	10				
3	12		6	7	8	11	5	9	13					1		**4**		2	10				
3	7		6		8	11	**5**	9	13					1		4		2	10				
3	4		6	7	8	9	5	11		1		12	**10**		13								
3	4	2	6	7	8		5	11		1		**9**	10		13	12							
3	4	6			8	9		11	5	1	12	13			10	**4**							
3	4	12	6	7	8	9	5	11			10				13								
49	53	20	36	35	51	37	43	40	21	7	2	6	15	43	2	15	0	36	31	1	2	15	5
	1	9			2	8		12	4		1	16	4		10	3	1		3	1	3		
2			2	6	8	6	2	4	6				2		1			7	9			8	

League Table

	P	W	D	L	F	A	Pts
Crystal Palace	46	27	9	10	73	46	90
Nottingham Forest	46	23	14	9	74	49	83
Millwall	46	19	17	10	58	49	74
Leicester City	46	19	16	11	72	59	73
Tranmere Rovers	46	21	9	16	69	53	72
Derby County	46	20	11	15	73	68	71
Notts County	46	20	8	18	65	69	68
Wolverhampton W	46	17	17	12	60	47	68
Middlesbrough	46	18	13	15	66	54	67
Stoke City	46	18	13	15	57	59	67
Charlton Athletic	46	19	8	19	61	58	65
Sunderland	46	19	8	19	54	57	65
Bristol City	46	16	16	14	47	50	64
Bolton Wanderers	46	15	14	17	63	64	59
Southend United	46	17	8	21	63	67	59
Grimsby Town	46	13	20	13	52	47	59
Portsmouth	46	15	13	18	52	58	58
Barnsley	46	16	7	23	55	67	55
Watford	46	15	9	22	66	80	54
Luton Town	46	14	11	21	56	60	53
West Bromwich Albion	46	13	12	21	60	69	51
Birmingham City	46	13	12	21	52	69	51
Oxford United	46	13	10	23	54	75	49
Peterborough United	46	8	13	25	48	76	37

1994-95

Division Two

Manager: Denis Smith

Did you know that?

Formula 1 racing car designer Robin Herd bought out Biomass to become Oxford's new owner and chairman.

United were granted planning permission to build a new stadium at Minchery Farm on a site identified by the City Council.

Oxford started the season looking likely to make an immediate return to the Second Division, and were three points clear at the top of the table on Boxing Day. However, a poor second half to the season left the Us missing out on the Play-offs.

Local star Joey Beauchamp was sold to West Ham United for £1 million. He played just one game for the Hammers, a friendly at Oxford City, before moving to Swindon Town for £800,000. Dave Penney was sold to Swansea City for £20,000.

David Smith was signed from Norwich City for £100,000, the same fee that United paid to Sunderland for David Rush, and to Hartlepool for Phil Gilchrist.

Match No.	Date		Opponents	Result	(F-A)	Scorers	A
1	13/08/1994	H	Hull City	W	4-0	Byrne (3), Moody	
2	20/08/1994	A	Cardiff City	W	3-1	Moody (3)	
3	27/08/1994	H	Cambridge United	W	1-0	Moody (pen)	
4	30/08/1994	A	Bradford City	W	2-0	Moody (2)	
5	03/09/1994	A	Huddersfield Town	D	3-3	Druce, Moody (pen), Rogan	
6	10/09/1994	H	Birmingham City	D	1-1	Moody (pen)	
7	13/09/1994	H	Crewe Alexandra	W	2-1	Byrne (2)	
8	17/09/1994	A	Brighton & Hove Albion	D	1-1	Moody	
9	24/09/1994	H	Leyton Orient	W	3-2	Elliott, Moody, Rush	
10	01/10/1994	A	Chester City	L	0-2		
11	08/10/1994	H	Plymouth Argyle	W	1-0	Byrne	
12	15/10/1994	A	Swansea City	W	3-1	Byrne, Elliott, Moody	
13	22/10/1994	A	Wrexham	L	2-3	Moody	
14	29/10/1994	H	Shrewsbury Town	D	0-0		
15	01/11/1994	H	Blackpool	W	3-2	Byrne, Elliott, Rush	
16	05/11/1994	A	Stockport County	W	2-0	Moody (2)	
17	19/11/1994	H	Rotherham United	W	2-1	Moody (2)	
18	26/11/1994	A	AFC Bournemouth	W	2-0	Butters, Byrne	
19	10/12/1994	H	Cardiff City	W	1-0	Murphy	
20	17/12/1994	A	Hull City	L	1-3	Elliott	
21	26/12/1994	A	Peterborough United	W	4-1	B Ford, Murphy, Rush (2)	
22	27/12/1994	H	Wycombe Wanderers	L	0-2		
23	31/12/1994	A	Brentford	L	0-2		
24	02/01/1995	H	York City	L	0-2		
25	14/01/1995	A	Bristol Rovers	L	2-3	Druce (2)	
26	28/01/1995	A	Shrewsbury Town	D	1-1	Byrne	
27	04/02/1995	H	AFC Bournemouth	L	0-3		
28	11/02/1995	A	Blackpool	L	1-2	Rush	
29	18/02/1995	H	Bristol Rovers	D	0-0		
30	21/02/1995	A	Rotherham United	D	1-1	Murphy	
31	25/02/1995	H	Chester City	W	1-0	Gilchrist	
32	28/02/1995	H	Stockport County	W	4-0	Allen, Lewis, Murphy, Rush (pen)	
33	04/03/1995	A	Leyton Orient	D	1-1	Moody	
34	07/03/1995	H	Huddersfield Town	W	3-1	Elliott, Moody, Murphy	
35	11/03/1995	A	Cambridge United	W	2-1	Rush (2)	
36	18/03/1995	H	Bradford City	W	1-0	Moody	
37	21/03/1995	A	Birmingham City	L	0-3		
38	25/03/1995	H	Brighton & Hove Albion	D	0-0		
39	01/04/1995	A	Crewe Alexandra	L	2-3	Allen, Moody	
40	04/04/1995	H	Wrexham	D	0-0		
41	08/04/1995	H	Brentford	D	1-1	Dyer	
42	15/04/1995	A	Wycombe Wanderers	L	0-1		
43	17/04/1995	H	Peterborough United	W	1-0	Moody	
44	22/04/1995	A	York City	W	2-0	Murphy (2)	
45	30/04/1995	H	Swansea City	L	1-2	Rush	
46	06/05/1995	A	Plymouth Argyle	D	1-1	B Ford	

FA Cup

R1	13/11/1994	A	Marlow	L	0-2	

League Cup

R1/1	16/08/1994	H	Peterborough United	W	3-1	Massey, Moody (pen), Robinson
R1/2	23/08/1994	A	Peterborough United	W	1-0	Dyer
R2/1	20/09/1994	H	Oldham Athletic	D	1-1	Ford
R2/2	04/10/1994	A	Oldham Athletic	L	0-1	

AWS Shield

R1	27/09/1994	H	Bristol Rovers	D	2-2	Moody (2)
R1	08/11/1994	A	AFC Bournemouth	D	0-0	
R2	03/12/1994	A	Brentford	W	2-1	Murphy
R3	10/01/1995	H	Swansea City	L	1-2	B Ford

Total appear
Sub appear
Total

Ford, M	Dyer	Elliott	Rogan	Massey	Smith	Moody	Byrne	Allen	Druce	Deegan	Lewis	Cusack	Ford, B	Murphy	Marsh	Rush	Collins	Butters	Wanless	Dobson	Carter	Key	Wood	Gilchrist
3	4	5	**6**	7	8	9	10	11			12	13												
3	4	5	**6**	7	8	9	10	11			12													
3	4	5	6	7	8	9	**10**	11	12															
3	4	5	6	7	8	9		11	10															
3	4	5	6	7	8	9		11	**10**				12											
3	4	5	6	7	8	9		11	**10**					12										
3	4	5	6	7	8	**9**	10	11	12		13													
3		5		7	8	9	10	11		1	4				6									
3		5		7	8	**9**	10	11			4				6	12								
3	**6**	5		7	8	9	10	11			4					12								
3	4	5	6	7	8	**9**	10	11			13					12								
3	4	5	6	7	8	9	10	**11**			13					12								
3	4	5	6	7	8	9	10				12	13	**11**											
3	4	5	**6**	7	8	9	10				12		11			13								
	4	5		**7**	8	9	10						11		6	12	3							
	4	5		7	8	9	10				12		**11**		6	13		3						
	4	5			8	9	10	**7**			6		11			12		3						
	4	5			8	**9**	10		12		6		11			13		3	7					
	4	5			8	9	10		13		3		11	**7**		12			6					
	4	5			8	9	10		13		3		**11**	7		12				6				
	4	5	13		8		10				3		11	12		9				6	**7**			
	4	5	13		8	12	10				3		**11**			9				6	7			
	4	5			8	9	**10**				3		11	12					13	6	7			
	4	5			8	9		13			**3**			7	11	10				6	12			
	4	5	6		8			11	9	1			7	12	3	10			13					
	4	5	6		8	9	10	11	13		12		**7**				3					1		
	4	5	6		8	9	**10**	11	12				7			13						1	3	
	12	5	6		8	13	10	**11**			4		7			9						1	3	
	11	5			8		10				4			7	3	9						1		6
	11	5			8	12	**10**	13			4			7	3	9						1		6
	3	5			8	9		11			4			7		10						1		6
	3	5		12	8			11	9		4			7		10			13					6
3		5			8	12		11	9		4			7		**10**								6
		5	3		8	12		11	**9**		4			7		10								6
	12	5	3		8	9		**11**	13		4			7		10								6
	13	5	3		8	12		11	**9**		4			7		10								6
	13	5	3		8	12		11	**9**		4			7		10								6
	11	5	3		8	9		13	12		4			**7**		10								6
	13	5	3	7	**8**	9		11			4			12		10								6
	13	5	3	7	**8**	9		11			4		12			10								6
	10	5	3	**7**	8	9		11			4		12											6
12	**10**	5	3			9		11			4		7			8			13					6
12		5	**3**			9		11			4		7	8		10			13					6
		5	3			9		11			4		7	8		10								6
13			3	12		9		11			4		7	**8**		10			5					6
		5		9	13			11			4		7	8		10	3		12					**6**

Ford, M	Dyer	Elliott	Rogan	Massey	Smith	Moody	Byrne	Allen	Druce	Deegan	Lewis	Cusack	Ford, B	Murphy	Marsh	Rush	Collins	Butters	Wanless	Dobson	Carter	Key	Wood	Gilchrist
	4	5		7	8	9	10						11		**6**	12	3							

Ford, M	Dyer	Elliott	Rogan	Massey	Smith	Moody	Byrne	Allen	Druce	Deegan	Lewis	Cusack	Ford, B	Murphy	Marsh	Rush	Collins	Butters	Wanless	Dobson	Carter	Key	Wood	Gilchrist
3	**4**	5	6	7	8	9	10	11	12															
3	4	5	6	7	8	9	10	**11**			12													
3		5		7	8	**9**	10	11	12		4				6									
3	4	5		7	8	9	10	11							**6**	12								

Ford, M	Dyer	Elliott	Rogan	Massey	Smith	Moody	Byrne	Allen	Druce	Deegan	Lewis	Cusack	Ford, B	Murphy	Marsh	Rush	Collins	Butters	Wanless	Dobson	Carter	Key	Wood	Gilchrist
3	6	5		7	8	9	**10**	11		1	4					12								
					8				**7**	1	4		11	12	6	10	5	3	9					
	4	5			**8**		10				3		11	7		9			12				3	
	4	5	6		8			11	9	1			7	12	3	10								

Ford, M	Dyer	Elliott	Rogan	Massey	Smith	Moody	Byrne	Allen	Druce	Deegan	Lewis	Cusack	Ford, B	Murphy	Marsh	Rush	Collins	Butters	Wanless	Dobson	Carter	Key	Wood	Gilchrist
20	39	53	30	26	50	40	32	38	11	5	34		24	18	13	25	5	4	4	5	3	6	3	18
3	6		2	2	1	7		3	11		10	2	3	7		15			7		1			
1	2	5	1	1		24	10	2	3		1		3	8		9		1						1

League Table

	P	W	D	L	F	A	Pts
Birmingham City	46	25	14	7	84	37	89
Brentford	46	25	10	11	81	39	85
Crewe Alexandra	46	25	8	13	80	68	83
Bristol Rovers	46	22	16	8	70	40	82
Huddersfield Town	46	22	15	9	79	49	81
Wycombe Wanderers	46	21	15	10	60	46	78
Oxford United	46	21	12	13	66	52	75
Hull City	46	21	11	14	70	57	74
York City	46	21	9	16	67	51	72
Swansea City	46	19	14	13	57	45	71
Stockport County	46	19	8	19	63	60	65
Blackpool	46	18	10	18	64	70	64
Wrexham	46	16	15	15	65	64	63
Bradford City	46	16	12	18	57	64	60
Peterborough United	46	14	18	14	54	69	60
Brighton & Hove Albion	46	14	17	15	54	53	59
Rotherham United	46	14	14	18	57	61	56
Shrewsbury Town	46	13	14	19	54	62	53
Bournemouth	46	13	11	22	49	69	50
Cambridge United	46	11	15	20	52	69	48
Plymouth Argyle	46	12	10	24	45	83	46
Cardiff City	46	9	11	26	46	74	38
Chester City	46	6	11	29	37	84	29
Leyton Orient	46	6	8	32	30	75	26

1995-96

Division Two

Manager: Denis Smith

Did you know that?

In a mirror image of the previous campaign, United started slowly but embarked on a storming run at the end of the season to clinch the second automatic promotion place on the last day. United did not win a League game away from home until 30 January.

Big signings were the return of Joey Beauchamp from Swindon for £75,000 and the signing of Martin Gray from Sunderland for £100,000.

United's 9–1 win over Dorchester Town in the first round of the FA Cup was their biggest win since joining the Football League, and the second-biggest winning margin since turning professional.

Joey Beauchamp's long-range volley in the 1–0 win over Blackpool was later voted United's best-ever goal at the Manor. In the 6–0 win over Shrewsbury all the goals came from headers. The 5–0 win over Burnley included a 15-minute substitute appearance from Paul Moody, during which he scored a hat-trick.

United's youth team beat Coventry City 3–2 on aggregate to win the Southern Junior Floodlit Cup.

Match No.	Date		Opponents	Result	(F-A)	Scorers
1	12/08/1995	H	Chesterfield	W	1-0	Allen
2	19/08/1995	A	Brentford	L	0-1	
3	26/08/1995	H	Rotherham United	D	1-1	Ford
4	30/08/1995	A	Swindon Town	D	1-1	Moody
5	03/09/1995	H	York City	W	2-0	Biggins (pen), Elliott
6	09/09/1995	A	Hull City	D	0-0	
7	12/09/1995	A	Walsall	D	2-2	Gilchrist, Rush
8	16/09/1995	H	Carlisle United	W	4-0	B Ford, Gilchrist, Murphy, Rush
9	23/09/1995	A	Swansea City	D	1-1	B Ford
10	30/09/1995	H	Bristol Rovers	L	1-2	Allen
11	07/10/1995	H	Stockport County	W	2-1	Gilchrist, Moody
12	14/10/1995	A	Wrexham	L	1-2	Elliott
13	21/10/1995	H	Wycombe Wanderers	L	1-4	Smith
14	28/10/1995	A	Blackpool	D	1-1	Rush
15	31/10/1995	A	Shrewsbury Town	L	0-2	
16	04/11/1995	H	Bristol City	W	2-0	Angel, Murphy
17	18/11/1995	A	Peterborough United	D	1-1	M Ford
18	25/11/1995	H	Crewe Alexandra	W	1-0	Rush
19	09/12/1995	H	Swansea City	W	5-1	Elliott (2), Moody (3)
20	16/12/1995	A	Bristol Rovers	L	0-2	
21	23/12/1995	A	Bradford City	L	0-1	
22	26/12/1995	H	AFC Bournemouth	W	2-0	B Ford, Massey
23	13/01/1996	H	Brentford	W	2-1	Aldridge (2)
24	20/01/1996	A	Chesterfield	L	0-1	
25	30/01/1996	A	Burnley	W	2-0	Allen, Massey
26	03/02/1996	A	Rotherham United	L	0-1	
27	10/02/1996	H	Brighton & Hove Albion	D	1-1	Elliott
28	17/02/1996	H	Walsall	W	3-2	Aldridge (2), Moody (pen)
29	20/02/1996	A	York City	L	0-1	
30	24/02/1996	A	Carlisle United	W	2-1	Aldridge, Elliott
31	27/02/1996	H	Hull City	W	2-0	Rush (2)
32	02/03/1996	A	AFC Bournemouth	W	1-0	Beauchamp
33	09/03/1996	H	Bradford City	W	2-0	Aldridge, Moody
34	12/03/1996	A	Brighton & Hove Albion	W	2-1	Murphy (2)
35	16/03/1996	A	Notts County	D	1-1	Rush
36	19/03/1996	H	Swindon Town	W	3-0	Aldridge, Beauchamp, Elliott
37	23/03/1996	H	Burnley	W	5-0	Aldridge, Beauchamp, Moody (3)
38	30/03/1996	A	Stockport County	L	2-4	Aldridge, Beauchamp
39	02/04/1996	H	Wrexham	D	0-0	
40	06/04/1996	H	Blackpool	W	1-0	Beauchamp
41	08/04/1996	A	Wycombe Wanderers	W	3-0	Massey, Moody, Rush
42	16/04/1996	H	Notts County	D	1-1	Moody (pen)
43	20/04/1996	A	Bristol City	W	2-0	Moody, Rush
44	23/04/1996	H	Shrewsbury Town	W	6-0	Beauchamp, Massey, Moody (2), Murphy, Rush
45	27/04/1996	A	Crewe Alexandra	W	2-1	Beauchamp, Moody
46	04/05/1996	H	Peterborough United	W	4-0	Elliott, Moody, Rush, Grazioli (og)
FA Cup						
R1	11/11/1995	H	Dorchester Town	W	9-1	Beauchamp, B Ford, M Ford, Moody (3), Rush, Wood (2)
R2	02/12/1995	H	Northampton Town	W	2-0	Massey, Moody
R3	06/01/1996	A	Millwall	D	3-3	B Ford, Massey, Moody
r	16/01/1996	H	Millwall	W	1-0	Massey
R4	07/02/1996	A	Nottingham Forest	D	1-1	Massey
r	13/02/1996	H	Nottingham Forest	L	0-3	
League Cup						
R1/1	15/08/1995	A	Hereford United	W	2-0	Biggins (pen), Murphy
R1/2	22/08/1995	H	Hereford United	W	3-2	Allen, Moody, Smith
R2/1	19/09/1995	H	Queen's Park Rangers	D	1-1	Allen
R2/2	03/10/1995	A	Queen's Park Rangers	L	1-2	Robinson
AWS Shield						
R1	26/09/1995	H	Bristol City	W	3-0	Murphy, Rush (2)
R1	07/11/1995	A	Barnet	W	3-2	Moody, Murphy, Pardew (og)
R2	28/11/1995	H	Colchester United	L	1-2	Angel

Total appea

Sub appea

Total

Ford, M	Smith	Elliott	Wood	Rush	Biggins	Moody	Ford, B	Allen	Gilchrist	Massey	Murphy	Angel	Lewis	Beauchamp	Marsh	Whitehead	Aldridge	Powell	Druce	Gray	Milsom
3	4	5	6	7	8	9	10	11			12	13									
3	4	5		12	8	9		11	6	7	13		10								
3	4	5		7	8	9	13	11	6		10	12									
3	4	5		7	8	9	10	11	6		12										
3	4	5		7	8	9	10	11	6		13	12									
3	4	5		7	8	9	10	11	6	12	13										
3	4	5		7		9	10	11	6	8	13	12									
3	4	5		7		9	10	11	6	8	12										
3	4	5		7			10	11	6	8	9	12									
3	4	5		7		12	10	11	6	8	9	13									
3	4	5		7		9	10	11	6		12	13		8							
3	4	5		7	13	9	10	11	6		2			8	12						
3	4	5		7	12	9	10	11	6		13	14		8		1					
3	4	5	6	7	9		10	12		8	13	11				1					
3	4	5	12	7	9	13	10		6	8		11		14		1					
3	4	5		7		9	10		6	8	13	11		12		1					
3	4	5	2	7		9	10		6	8	12	11				1					
3	4	5	2	7		9	10		6	8	12	11		13		1					
3	4	5	2	7		9	10		6	8		11		12		1					
3	4	5	2	7		9	10		6	8	13	11		12		1					
3		5	2	7		9	10		6	8	4	11		13		1					
3	4	5		7		9	10	13	6	8		11				1	12				
3	4	5				9		13	6	8		11	12	7		1	10		14		
	4	5		7		9	10		6	8			12	11		1	13	3	14		
	4	5		7		9	10	13	6	8				11	3	1			12		
13	4	5	6	7		9	10	12		8				11	3	1			14		
3	4	5	6	7		9	10	13		8	14			11		1			12		
3	4	5				12	10		6	8		11	14	13		1	9		7		
3	4	5		12		7	10	13	6	8		11				1	9				
3	4	5		7					6	8	14	11	13	10		1	9	12			
3	4	5		7		13	12		6	8		11	14	10		1	9				
3	4	5		7		12			6	8	14	11	13	10		1	9				
3	4	5		7		13			6		14	11	8	10	12	1	9				
3	4	5		7		13			6		11		8	10	12	1	9		14		
3	4	5		7					6	8	11		13	10		1	9		12		
3	4	5		7		14			6	8	11		12	10		1	9	13			
3	4	5		7		12			6	8	11	14	13	10		1	9				
3	4		5	7		14		13	6	8	11		12	10		1	9				
3	4	5		7		14			6		11	12	13	10		1	9			8	
3	4	5		7		9		12	6		11		13	10		1	14			8	
3	4	5		7		14		13	6	12	11		8	10		1	9				
3	4	5				11		13	6	7	12		8	10		1	9			14	
3	4	5		7		9			6	11				10		1				8	
3	4	5		7		9			6	11	13	14	12	10		1				8	
3	4	5		7		9			6	11	12		13	10		1				8	
3	4	5		7		9			6	11			12	10		1				8	

3	4	5	2	7		9	10		6	8	13	11		12		1					
3	4	5	2			9	10		6	8	7	11		12		1					
3	4	5		7		9	10	12	6	8		11				1	13				
	4	5		13		9	10	12	6	8		11			3	1	7				
3	4	5	6			9	10	11		8	12			7		1					
3	4	5		12		9	10		6	8	7	13	7	11		1	14				

3	4	5			8	9	10	11	6	7	12										
3	4	5		7	8	9		11	6		10	12			13						
3	4	5		7	9		10	11	6	8	12										
3	4	5		7	13	9	10	11	6		8				12						

3	4	5		7			10	11	6	8	9	13									12
3	4	5		7	14	9	10		6		8	11		13		1		12			
3	4	5	2	7		9	0		6	8	13	11		12		1		14			

55	58	58	14	49	11	41	38	19	54	43	19	22	5	27	3	42	16	1	1	6	0
1			1	4	4	12	2	13		2	26	14	15	11	5		5	4	7	1	1
3	2	8	2	14	2	24	5	5	3	8	8	2		8			9				

League Table

	P	W	D	L	F	A	Pts
Swindon Town	46	25	17	4	71	34	92
Oxford United	46	24	11	11	76	39	83
Blackpool	46	23	13	10	67	40	82
Notts County	46	21	15	10	63	39	78
Crewe Alexandra	46	22	7	17	77	60	73
Bradford City	46	22	7	17	71	69	73
Chesterfield	46	20	12	14	56	51	72
Wrexham	46	18	16	12	76	55	70
Stockport County	46	19	13	14	61	47	70
Bristol Rovers	46	20	10	16	57	60	70
Walsall	46	19	12	15	60	45	69
Wycombe Wanderers	46	15	15	16	63	59	60
Bristol City	46	15	15	16	55	60	60
Bournemouth	46	16	10	20	51	70	58
Brentford	46	15	13	18	43	49	58
Rotherham United	46	14	14	18	54	62	56
Burnley	46	14	13	19	56	68	55
Shrewsbury Town	46	13	14	19	58	70	53
Peterborough United	46	13	13	20	59	66	52
York City	46	13	13	20	58	73	52
Carlisle United	46	12	13	21	57	72	49
Swansea City	46	11	14	21	43	79	47
Brighton & Hove Albion	46	10	10	26	46	69	40
Hull City	46	5	16	25	36	78	31

1996-97

Division One

Manager: Denis Smith

Did you know that?

Building work commenced on the Minchery Farm stadium, with a completion date set for the summer of 1997. However, by Christmas Taylor-Woodrow had left the site because of unpaid bills and all work ceased, leaving the skeletons of three stands (the construction of the fourth stand was shelved at an early stage to reduce costs).

United paid fees for Darren Purse (£100,000 from Orient), Nigel Jemson (£60,000 from Notts County) and Brian Wilsterman (£200,000 from Beerschot).

The £1.6 million that Leicester City paid for Matt Elliott remains United's record sale. Fees were also received for Chris Allen (£450,000 from Nottingham Forest), Mark Druce (£50,000 from Rotherham) and David Rush (£80,000 from York City).

United's FA Cup game at Watford was called off minutes before kick-off because of a frozen pitch. The rearranged game was delayed after the floodlights failed and had to be repaired by an Oxford supporter who was an electrician.

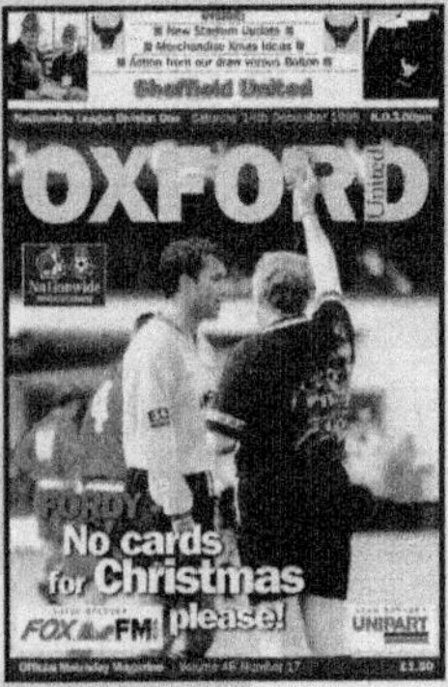

Match No.	Date		Opponents	Result	(F-A)	Scorers	A
1	17/08/1996	A	Queen's Park Rangers	L	1-2	Jemson	
2	24/08/1996	H	Southend United	W	5-0	Beauchamp (2), Jemson (2), Rush	
3	27/08/1996	H	Norwich City	L	0-1		
4	31/08/1996	A	Port Vale	L	0-2		
5	08/09/1996	A	Reading	L	0-2		
6	10/09/1996	H	Wolverhampton Wanderers	D	1-1	Ford	
7	14/09/1996	H	Bradford City	W	2-0	Jemson, Moody	
8	21/09/1996	A	Grimsby Town	W	2-0	Jemson, Handyside (og)	
9	28/09/1996	H	Portsmouth	W	2-0	Beauchamp, Ford	
10	01/10/1996	A	Tranmere Rovers	D	0-0		
11	12/10/1996	A	Swindon Town	L	0-1		
12	15/10/1996	A	Barnsley	D	0-0		
13	18/10/1996	H	Birmingham City	D	0-0		
14	26/10/1996	A	Charlton Athletic	L	0-2		
15	29/10/1996	H	Stoke City	W	4-1	Aldridge, Angel, Gray, Jemson	
16	02/11/1996	H	Ipswich Town	W	3-1	Elliott, Jemson, Mowbray (og)	
17	13/11/1996	A	Manchester City	W	3-2	Beauchamp, Elliott, Jemson	
18	16/11/1996	H	Huddersfield Town	W	1-0	Elliott	
19	19/11/1996	H	Bolton Wanderers	D	0-0		
20	23/11/1996	A	Oldham Athletic	L	1-2	Jemson	
21	30/11/1996	H	Charlton Athletic	L	0-2		
22	07/12/1996	A	Crystal Palace	D	2-2	Jemson, Massey	
23	14/12/1996	H	Sheffield United	W	4-1	Aldridge (3), Jemson	
24	21/12/1996	A	West Bromwich Albion	D	3-3	Elliott, Jemson, Murphy	
25	26/12/1996	A	Wolverhampton Wanderers	L	1-3	Gray	
26	28/12/1996	H	Reading	W	2-1	Beauchamp, Murphy	
27	11/01/1997	A	Bradford City	L	0-2		
28	18/01/1997	H	Tranmere Rovers	W	2-1	Aldridge, Jemson (pen)	
29	28/01/1997	A	Portsmouth	L	1-2	Angel	
30	02/02/1997	H	Manchester City	L	1-4	Moody	
31	07/02/1997	A	Stoke City	L	1-2	Moody	
32	15/02/1997	H	Oldham Athletic	W	3-1	Jemson, Purse, Graham (og)	
33	22/02/1997	A	Ipswich Town	L	1-2	Gabbiadini	
34	01/03/1997	H	Crystal Palace	L	1-4	Marsh	
35	04/03/1997	A	Huddersfield Town	L	0-1		
36	08/03/1997	H	West Bromwich Albion	W	1-0	Murphy	
37	15/03/1997	A	Sheffield United	L	1-3	Gilchrist	
38	18/03/1997	H	Grimsby Town	W	3-2	Aldridge, M Ford, Gilchrist	
39	22/03/1997	A	Southend United	D	2-2	Aldridge, Jemson	
40	29/03/1997	H	Queen's Park Rangers	L	2-3	Jemson (pen), Moody	
41	31/03/1997	A	Norwich City	D	1-1	Massey	
42	05/04/1997	H	Port Vale	L	0-2		
43	12/04/1997	A	Bolton Wanderers	L	0-4		
44	19/04/1997	H	Swindon Town	W	2-0	Aldridge, Massey	
45	26/04/1997	A	Birmingham City	L	0-2		
46	04/05/1997	H	Barnsley	W	5-1	Beauchamp (2), Ford, Jemson (2) (1 pen)	

FA Cup

R3	21/01/1997	A	Watford	L	0-2	

League Cup

R1/1	20/08/1996	H	Norwich City	D	1-1	Jemson
R1/2	03/09/1996	A	Norwich City	W	3-2	Aldridge, Elliott, M Ford
R2/1	18/09/1996	A	Sheffield Wednesday	D	1-1	Moody
R2/2	24/09/1996	H	Sheffield Wednesday	W	1-0	Jemson
R3	22/10/1996	A	Port Vale	D	0-0	
r	05/11/1996	H	Port Vale	W	2-0	Jemson (2)
R4	26/11/1996	H	Southampton	D	1-1	Moody
r	18/12/1996	A	Southampton	L	2-3	B Ford, Jemson

Total appear
Sub appear
Total

Ford, M	Smith	Elliott	Gilchrist	Rush	Ford, B	Aldridge	Jemson	Beauchamp	Murphy	Moody	Angel	Massey	Gray	Jackson	Purse	Marsh	Gabbiadini	Wilsterman	Whyte	Phillips	Weatherstone
3	4	5	6	7	8	9	10	11	12	13	14										
3	4	5	6	13	7	14	10	11		9		8	12								
3	4	5	6	12	7	13	10	11		9		8	14								
3	4	5	6	10	7	13		11		9	14	12	8								
3	4	5	6		7	14		11	12	9	13	10	8								
3	4	5	6		7	9	10	11	13	12	14		8								
3	4	5	6		7	9	10	13		14	11		8		12						
3	4	5	6		7	13	10	11	12	9			8								
3	4	5	6		7	13	10	11	12	9			8		14						
3	4	5	6		7		10	11	12	9			8	1	2						
3	4		6	13	7		10	11	12	9		14	8		5						
3	4	5	6	9			10	11		12		7	8								
3	4	5		13			10	11	12	9		7	8		6						
3	4	5		13			10	11	14	9	12	7	8		6						
3	4	5		13		9	10	11		12	7		8		6						
3	4	5		14		9	10	11		13	7	12	8		6						
3	4	5	6	13		9	10	11			7	12	8		14						
3	4	5	6	14		9	10	11		13	7	12	8		2						
3	4	5	6	13		9	10	11		14	7	12	8		2						
3	4	5	6		13	9	10	11		12	7	14	8		2						
3	4	5	6	9			10	11	14	13	7	12	8		2						
3	4	5	6		9	7	10	11		13		12	8		2						
3	4	5		13	9	7	10	11	12				8		6						
3	4	5			9	7	10	11	12	13		14	8		6						
3	4	5			9		10	11		7	13	12	8		6						
3	4	5			9		10	11	12	7			8			6					
3	4	5	6		9		10	11	13	7		12	8		14						
3	4		6		9	7	10	11	12	13			8		5						
3	4		6		9		10	11	2	13	7	12	8		5						
3	4		6		12		10	11	14	13	7		8			5	9				
3	4		6		12	13	10	11		14	7		8		5		9				
	4		6		14		10	11		13	12	7	8		5	3	9				
	4		6		11		10	13	12		14	7	8		5	3	9				
3	4		6		11		10	12	14				8		5	13	9	7			
3	4		6		11		10		9		7		8		5	14			2	13	
	4		6		11	9	10	13	12		7		8		5	3			2		
	4		6		11	9	10	13	12		7		8		5	3			2		
3	4		6		11	12	10	7	13	9			8						5		
3	4		6			13	10	7	12	9		11	8	1	14				5		
3	4		6			13	10	7	12	9		11	8	1					5		
3	4		6			13	10	12	7	9		11	8		5						
3	4		6			9	10	14	12		7	11	8		5						13
3			6		7		10	14	4	9	13	11	8		12				5		
3	4		6		7	8	10	11		13		12	8						5		
3	4		6		7	9	10	13	8	12		11							5		
3	4		6		7	12	10	11		9		8							5		

Ford, M	Smith	Elliott	Gilchrist	Rush	Ford, B	Aldridge	Jemson	Beauchamp	Murphy	Moody	Angel	Massey	Gray	Jackson	Purse	Marsh	Gabbiadini	Wilsterman	Whyte	Phillips	Weatherstone
3	4		6		9	7	10	11	13	12		14	8		5						

Ford, M	Smith	Elliott	Gilchrist	Rush	Ford, B	Aldridge	Jemson	Beauchamp	Murphy	Moody	Angel	Massey	Gray	Jackson	Purse	Marsh	Gabbiadini	Wilsterman	Whyte	Phillips	Weatherstone
3	4	5	6	13	7	9	10	11		12		8									
3	4	5	6		7	13		11		9	14	10	8		12						
3	4	5	6		7	9	10	11	13	12		14	8								
3	4	5	6		7	13	10	11	12	9			8								
3	4	5					10	11		9		7	8		6						
3	4	5		13		9	10	11			7	12	8		6						
3	4	5	6		12	9	10	11	13	14	7		8		2						
3	4	5			9	9	10	11		13		12	8		6						

Ford, M	Smith	Elliott	Gilchrist	Rush	Ford, B	Aldridge	Jemson	Beauchamp	Murphy	Moody	Angel	Massey	Gray	Jackson	Purse	Marsh	Gabbiadini	Wilsterman	Whyte	Phillips	Weatherstone
51	54	34	44	4	35	24	52	45	5	22	17	18	49	3	30	6	5	1	10	0	0
				13	5	14		9	28	24	10	18	2		7	2				1	1
5		5	2	1	1	9	23	7	3	6	2	3	2		1	1	1				

League Table

	P	W	D	L	F	A	Pts
Bolton Wanderers	46	28	14	4	100	53	98
Barnsley	46	22	14	10	76	55	80
Wolverhampton W	46	22	10	14	68	51	76
Ipswich Town	46	20	14	12	68	50	74
Sheffield United	46	20	13	13	75	52	73
Crystal Palace	46	19	14	13	78	48	71
Portsmouth	46	20	8	18	59	53	68
Port Vale	46	17	16	13	58	55	67
Queen's Park Rangers	46	18	12	16	64	60	66
Birmingham City	46	17	15	14	52	48	66
Tranmere Rovers	46	17	14	15	63	56	65
Stoke City	46	18	10	18	51	57	64
Norwich City	46	17	12	17	63	68	63
Manchester City	46	17	10	19	59	60	61
Charlton Athletic	46	16	11	19	52	66	59
West Bromwich Albion	46	14	15	17	68	72	57
Oxford United	46	16	9	21	64	68	57
Reading	46	15	12	19	58	67	57
Swindon Town	46	15	9	22	52	71	54
Huddersfield Town	46	13	15	18	48	61	54
Bradford City	46	12	12	22	47	72	48
Grimsby Town	46	11	13	22	60	81	46
Oldham Athletic	46	10	13	23	51	66	43
Southend United	46	8	15	23	42	86	39

1997-98

Division One

Manager: Denis Smith, Malcolm Crosby (caretaker) then Malcolm Shotton

Did you know that?

On 31 October Robin Herd resigned as chairman after sinking almost all of his fortune into the club. CEO Keith Cox assumed Herd's duties while searching for a new buyer.

Denis Smith resigned in December to take over at West Brom, to be succeeded by his assistant manager, Malcolm Crosby. He resigned in January to join Smith, and United appointed Malcolm Shotton as manager following a concerted campaign by Oxford supporters.

United paid £170,000 for Phil Whelan from Middlesbrough, £100,000 to Birmingham for Kevin Francis and £75,000 to Barnsley for Steve Davis.

United received £200,000 from Fulham for Paul Moody, £400,000 from Sheffield United for Bobby Ford, £100,000 from Bury for Nigel Jemson and £500,000 from Birmingham for Darren Purse.

Match No.	Date		Opponents	Result	(F-A)	Scorers
1	09/08/1997	H	Huddersfield Town	W	2-0	Aldridge, Jemson (pen)
2	16/08/1997	A	Charlton Athletic	L	2-3	Jemson (pen), Purse
3	23/08/1997	H	Nottingham Forest	L	0-1	
4	30/08/1997	A	Portsmouth	L	1-2	B Ford
5	02/09/1997	A	Sunderland	L	1-3	Angel
6	07/09/1997	H	Wolverhampton Wanderers	W	3-0	Beauchamp (2), B Ford
7	13/09/1997	A	Reading	L	1-2	Jemson
8	20/09/1997	H	Sheffield United	L	2-4	Jemson (2)
9	27/09/1997	H	Bradford City	D	0-0	
10	04/10/1997	A	West Bromwich Albion	W	2-1	Banger, Purse
11	11/10/1997	A	Stockport County	L	2-3	Aldridge, Purse
12	18/10/1997	H	Ipswich Town	W	1-0	Smith
13	21/10/1997	H	Middlesbrough	L	1-4	Purse
14	25/10/1997	A	Birmingham City	D	0-0	
15	01/11/1997	H	Manchester City	D	0-0	
16	04/11/1997	A	Stoke City	D	0-0	
17	08/11/1997	A	Crewe Alexandra	L	1-2	M Ford
18	15/11/1997	H	Bury	D	1-1	Banger
19	22/11/1997	A	Norwich City	L	1-2	Powell
20	29/11/1997	H	Port Vale	W	2-0	Beauchamp, Jemson
21	06/12/1997	A	Swindon Town	L	1-4	M Ford
22	12/12/1997	H	Queen's Park Rangers	W	3-1	Beauchamp (2), Jemson
23	20/12/1997	A	Tranmere Rovers	W	2-0	Massey, Robinson
24	26/12/1997	A	Wolverhampton Wanderers	L	0-1	
25	28/12/1997	H	Sunderland	D	1-1	Jemson (pen)
26	10/01/1998	A	Huddersfield Town	L	1-5	Gray
27	17/01/1998	H	Charlton Athletic	L	1-2	Jemson
28	24/01/1998	H	Portsmouth	W	1-0	Beauchamp
29	31/01/1998	A	Nottingham Forest	W	3-1	Beauchamp (2), Weatherstone
30	07/02/1998	A	Sheffield United	L	0-1	
31	21/02/1998	A	Bradford City	D	0-0	
32	24/02/1998	A	Ipswich Town	L	2-5	Donaldson (pen), Francis
33	28/02/1998	H	Stockport County	W	3-0	Davis, Donaldson, Francis
34	17/02/1998	H	West Bromwich Albion	W	2-1	Francis, Gilchrist
35	03/03/1998	H	Crewe Alexandra	D	0-0	
36	07/03/1998	A	Manchester City	W	2-0	Beauchamp, Cook
37	14/03/1998	H	Stoke City	W	5-1	Beauchamp, Francis (2), Murphy (2)
38	17/03/1998	H	Reading	W	3-0	Beauchamp (2), Gray
39	21/03/1998	A	Bury	L	0-1	
40	28/03/1998	H	Norwich City	W	2-0	Beauchamp (pen), Francis
41	04/04/1998	A	Port Vale	L	0-3	
42	11/04/1998	H	Swindon Town	W	2-1	Francis, Gilchrist
43	13/04/1998	A	Queen's Park Rangers	D	1-1	Davis
44	18/04/1998	H	Tranmere Rovers	D	1-1	Cook
45	25/04/1998	H	Birmingham City	L	0-2	
46	03/05/1998	A	Middlesbrough	L	1-4	Banger

FA Cup

R3	03/01/1998	A	Leeds United	L	0-4	

League Cup

R1/1	12/08/1997	H	Plymouth Argyle	W	2-0	Purse, Logan (og)
R1/2	26/08/1997	A	Plymouth Argyle	W	5-3	Beauchamp (2), Jemson, Murphy, Purse
R2/1	16/09/1997	H	York City	W	4-1	Aldridge, Beauchamp (2), Robinson
R2/2	23/09/1997	A	York City	W	2-1	Aldridge, Banger
R3	14/10/1997	H	Tranmere Rovers	W*	1-1	Beauchamp
R4	18/11/1997	H	Ipswich Town	L	1-2	Beauchamp

* 6-5 on pens

Total appea
Sub appea
Tota

Ford, M	Robinson	Whelan	Gilchrist	Ford, B	Smith	Banger	Jemson	Beauchamp	Aldridge	Purse	Angel	Massey	Gray	Jackson	Marsh	Wilsterman	Murphy	Stevens	Cook	Powell	Van Heusden	Weatherstone	Donaldson	Francis	Davis	Rose	Wright
3	4	5	6	7	8	9	10	11	12	13	14																
3	4		5	7	8	9	10	11	12	6		2	13														
	4			7	8		10	11		5	13			1	3	6	9	12	14								
	4	12		7	8		10	11	14	5	3					6	9			13							
	4	6	12	7	8	9	10	11	13	5	3						14										
	4	6	12	7	8		10	11	9	5	3	13							14								
	5	6	3	7	8	14	10	11	9		4	13		1		12											
	4	14	6	7	8	12	10	11	9	5	3	13		1													
3	4	5	12	7	8	9	10	11	13	6	14										1						
3	4	5	7		8	9		11	10	6	12					13					1						
3	4		6	13	8	9		11	10	5	12					7	14				1						
	6			7	8	9		11	10	4	3					5	12				1						
	4			7	8	9		11	10	5	3		13			6	14			12	1						
	4		2	7	8	9		11	12	5	3		14			6	10			13	1						
3	4		2	7	8	9	10	11	13	5						6	12				1						
3	4		2	7	8	9	10	11	12	5						6	13				1						
3	4		2	7	8	9	10	11	14		13		5			6	12				1						
3	4		2	7	8	9	10	11		5						6	12			13	1						
3	4		6	7		9	10			5	11	8	2				12			13	1						
3	4				8	12	10	11	9	5	13	7	2			6	14										
3	4		14		8		10	11	9	5	13	7	2			6	12										
3	4		6		8	13	10	11	9	5		7	2														
3	4		6		8		10	11	9	5		7	2														
3	4		6		8		10	11	9	5	13	7	2			12											
3	4		6		8		10	11	9	5		7	2						12								
	4		6		8		10	11		5		7	2			12			13	9							
	4		6		8		10	11	13	5		7			14	12	3		2	9							
	2		6		8		10	11		5	13	7	4		3	12	9					14					
	2		6		8		10	11		5			4			3	13		7			12	9				
	2		6		8			11	13	5			4			3	14		12	7		10	9				
3	2		6		8			11			12		4			5				7		13	10	9			
3	2		6		8			11					4						12	7		13	10	9	5		
3	2		6		8			11				7	4			12							10	9	5		
3	2		6		8			11			12		4			13				7		14	10	9	5		
	2		6		8			11				7	4	3			13		12			10		9	5		
	2		6		8			11				7	4	3					10	12		13		9	5		
	2		6		8	13		11					4	3			7		10	12				9	5		
	2		6		8	14		11					4	3		13	10		7	12				9	5		
	2		6		8	13		11					4	3			7		10	12				9	5		
	2		6		8	12		11					4	3			7		13	10				9	5		
	2		6		8	9		11			13		4	3			7		10			14			5	12	
	2		6			8		11			13		4	3			7		10			12		9	5		
	2		6		13	8		11					4	3			7		12	10				9	5		
6	2				3	8							4				7		11	10		12		9	5		13
6	2				8	12		11					4	3			7		13	10				9	5		
	2		6		8	12		11					4	3			7		13	10				9	5		

Ford, M	Robinson	Whelan	Gilchrist	Ford, B	Smith	Banger	Jemson	Beauchamp	Aldridge	Purse	Angel	Massey	Gray	Jackson	Marsh	Wilsterman	Murphy	Stevens	Cook	Powell	Van Heusden	Weatherstone	Donaldson	Francis	Davis	Rose	Wright
3	4		6		8		10	11		5	13	7	2						12	9							

Ford, M	Robinson	Whelan	Gilchrist	Ford, B	Smith	Banger	Jemson	Beauchamp	Aldridge	Purse	Angel	Massey	Gray	Jackson	Marsh	Wilsterman	Murphy	Stevens	Cook	Powell	Van Heusden	Weatherstone	Donaldson	Francis	Davis	Rose	Wright
3	4		6	7	8	9	10	11	12	5																	
	3			8	4		10	11	9	7	13			1	6	5	12										
	4		6	7	8	12	10	11	9	5	3			1													
	4	2	6	7	8	9	10	11	14	5	13	12		1	3												
	4		6	7	8	9		11	10	5	3						12				1						
3	4		6	7	8	9	10	11		5			2				12			13	1						

Ford, M	Robinson	Whelan	Gilchrist	Ford, B	Smith	Banger	Jemson	Beauchamp	Aldridge	Purse	Angel	Massey	Gray	Jackson	Marsh	Wilsterman	Murphy	Stevens	Cook	Powell	Van Heusden	Weatherstone	Donaldson	Francis	Davis	Rose	Wright
25	53	7	41	23	50	22	30	51	16	34	11	15	30	6	15	16	15	0	9	12	13	2	6	15	15	0	0
		2	4		1	11			13	1	17	4	3		1	9	17	1	12	10		9				1	1
2	2		2	2	1	4	10	19	4	6	1	1	2				3		2	1		1	2	7	2		

League Table

	P	W	D	L	F	A	Pts
Nottingham Forest	46	28	10	8	82	42	94
Middlesbrough	46	27	10	9	77	41	91
Sunderland	46	26	12	8	86	50	90
Charlton Athletic	46	26	10	10	80	49	88
Ipswich Town	46	23	14	9	77	43	83
Sheffield United	46	19	17	10	69	54	74
Birmingham City	46	19	17	10	60	35	74
Stockport County	46	19	8	19	71	69	65
Wolverhampton W	46	18	11	17	57	53	65
West Bromwich Albion	46	16	13	17	50	56	61
Crewe Alexandra	46	18	5	23	58	65	59
Oxford United	46	16	10	20	60	64	58
Bradford City	46	14	15	17	46	59	57
Tranmere Rovers	46	14	14	18	54	57	56
Norwich City	46	14	13	19	52	69	55
Huddersfield Town	46	14	11	21	50	72	53
Bury	46	11	19	16	42	58	52
Swindon Town	46	14	10	22	42	73	52
Port Vale	46	13	10	23	56	66	49
Portsmouth	46	13	10	23	51	63	49
Queen's Park Rangers	46	10	19	17	51	63	49
Manchester City	46	12	12	22	56	57	48
Stoke City	46	11	13	22	44	74	46
Reading	46	11	9	26	39	78	42

1998-99

Division One

Manager: Malcolm Shotton

Did you know that?

Keith Cox's attempt to sell United to a consortium called Grenoble Investment Ltd was scuppered after head of the consortium, John Gunn, discovered the state of United's finances. Following this news United's back-room staff went unpaid for two months, and members of the public delivered food parcels to the club. The players were paid by an emergency loan from the PFA.

A supporters' pressure group called FOUL (Fighting for Oxford United's Life), and a fundraising group called SOUS (Save Oxford United's Soul), were formed. Keith Cox resigned as managing director in February. Following a meeting at the Town Hall, called by FOUL, and meetings with the City Council to reach a cut-price deal at Minchery Farm, Firoz Kassam bought Oxford United for £1.

In June, Maurice Evans, Geoff Coppock and Nick Harris resigned from the board after a takeover involving David Bower, George Bailey, Jim Rosenthal and Hamish Dewar failed. A Company Voluntary Arrangement (CVA) was agreed in July, slashing United's unsecured debt to just £900,000.

At the start of the season Oxford paid a club record £475,000 to Aberdeen for Dean Windass. However, the Dons did not receive their money until after Windass had been sold to Bradford City for £950,000 in March.

A fire-sale of the players resulted in Phil Whitehead joining West Brom for £250,000 and Simon Marsh going to Birmingham for the same amount.

In the FA Cup, United were within a few minutes of beating Chelsea at the Manor before referee Mike Reed awarded the visitors a controversial penalty. United were leading 1–0 in the replay at Stamford Bridge, but eventually lost 4–2.

The 7–0 defeat at Sunderland and the 7–1 home defeat by Birmingham were both records: United's worst defeat since turning professional in 1949, and United's worst home defeat in the same period.

Match No.	Date		Opponents	Result	(F-A)	Scorers
1	08/08/1998	A	Bristol City	D	2-2	Murphy, Windass
2	15/08/1998	H	Wolverhampton Wanderers	L	0-2	
3	22/08/1998	A	Crystal Palace	L	0-2	
4	29/08/1998	H	Grimsby Town	D	0-0	
5	31/08/1998	A	Barnsley	L	0-1	
6	06/09/1998	H	Portsmouth	W	3-0	Marsh, Windass (2) (1 pen)
7	09/09/1998	A	Swindon Town	L	1-4	Banger
8	12/09/1998	H	Ipswich Town	D	3-3	Banger, Thomson, Windass
9	19/09/1998	A	Sunderland	L	0-7	
10	26/09/1998	H	Queen's Park Rangers	W	4-1	Beauchamp, Murphy, Thomson, Windass
11	29/09/1998	H	West Bromwich Albion	W	3-0	Beauchamp, Marsh, Powell
12	03/10/1998	A	Huddersfield Town	L	0-2	
13	10/10/1998	H	Tranmere Rovers	L	1-2	Windass
14	17/10/1998	A	Bolton Wanderers	D	1-1	Thomson
15	20/10/1998	A	Bury	L	0-1	
16	24/10/1998	H	Sheffield United	L	0-2	
17	31/10/1998	H	Crewe Alexandra	D	1-1	Windass
18	07/11/1998	A	Watford	L	0-2	
19	14/11/1998	A	Birmingham City	W	1-0	Murphy
20	21/11/1998	H	Port Vale	W	2-1	Powell, Windass (pen)
21	29/11/1998	A	Norwich City	W	3-1	Thomson, Wilsterman, Windass
22	05/12/1998	H	Bradford City	L	0-1	
23	12/12/1998	H	Birmingham City	L	1-7	Windass
24	19/12/1998	A	Stockport County	L	0-2	
25	26/12/1998	H	Crystal Palace	L	1-3	Windass
26	28/12/1998	A	Portsmouth	D	2-2	Banger (2)
27	09/01/1999	H	Bristol City	D	0-0	
28	16/01/1999	A	Grimsby Town	L	0-1	
29	30/01/1999	H	Barnsley	W	1-0	Windass
30	06/02/1999	A	Wolverhampton Wanderers	D	1-1	Windass
31	13/02/1999	H	Swindon Town	W	2-0	Windass (2) (1 pen)
32	20/02/1999	A	Ipswich Town	L	1-2	Remy
33	27/02/1999	H	Sunderland	D	0-0	
34	03/03/1999	A	Queen's Park Rangers	L	0-1	
35	06/03/1999	A	West Bromwich Albion	L	0-2	
36	09/03/1999	H	Huddersfield Town	D	2-2	Beauchamp, Cook
37	13/03/1999	H	Watford	D	0-0	
38	20/03/1999	A	Crewe Alexandra	L	1-3	Thomson
39	26/03/1999	A	Sheffield United	W	2-1	Banger, Thomson
40	03/04/1999	H	Bolton Wanderers	D	0-0	
41	05/04/1999	A	Tranmere Rovers	D	2-2	Gilchrist, Weatherstone
42	10/04/1999	H	Bury	L	0-1	
43	17/04/1999	A	Port Vale	L	0-1	
44	24/04/1999	H	Norwich City	L	2-4	Francis, Wilsterman
45	01/05/1999	A	Bradford City	D	0-0	
46	09/05/1999	H	Stockport County	W	5-0	Beauchamp, Gilchrist, Murphy, Powell, Thomson

FA Cup

R3	02/01/1999	A	Crewe Alexandra	W	3-1	Murphy (2), Windass
R4	25/01/1999	H	Chelsea	D	1-1	Windass
r	03/02/1999	A	Chelsea	L	2-4	Gilchrist, Windass (pen)

League Cup

R1/1	11/08/1998	A	Luton Town	W	3-2	Murphy (2), Weatherstone
R2/2	18/08/1998	H	Luton Town	L	1-3	Whelan

Total appear
Sub appear
Total

Marsh	Gray	Davis	Gilchrist	Banger	Windass	Thomson	Murphy	Beauchamp	Weatherstone	Smith	Powell	Hill	Remy	Whelan	Cook	Wilsterman	Wright	Rose	Jackson	Salmon	Gerrard	Watson	Warren	Tait	Francis	Lundin	Williams
3	4	*5*	6	7	8	**9**	10	11	12	13	14																
3	**4**	5	6	7	8		*10*	11	12	9	14	13															
14	4	*5*	6	13	8		10		9		3	**11**	7	12													
3	4		6	**9**	8	12	10	11			7	13		5	14												
3	4		6	13	8	12	**10**	11			7	14		5	9												
3	**4**		6		8	13	10	11			7	12		5	9												
3	4			**7**	8	12	10	11		13	6			5	9												
3	4			9	10	13		11		8	**7**	12		5		6											
3	4		6		10	9		11		8	7			5													
3	4		6		*10*	9	13	11		8	**7**	12		5	14												
3	4		6		10	9	13	11		8	**7**			5	12												
3	4		6		10	**9**	12	11		8	7			5	14	13											
3	4		6		10	**9**	12	11		8	7	13		5													
3	4		6		10	9	11			8	12		**7**			5											
3	4		6		10	9	11	13		8	12			**7**		5											
3	4				10		9	11		**8**	7			6	13	5	12										
3			6	12	10	**9**		11		8	7					5	4										
	4			**10**		9	7	12		8	3	13		5	14		11	*6*									
3	4		6		10	9	**7**			8	11					5	12										
3	4		6	12	10	**9**	7	11		8	2				13	5											
3	4		6	12	10	**9**	7			8	11					5											
3	4		6		10	9	**7**	12		8	11					5			1								
	4		6	13	10	9	12	11		8	3		**7**			5				1							
			6	13	10	*9*	11	14		8	3			4		5		12			1	7					
					10	9	11	12		8	3		7		14	13	**4**				1	5	6				
				9	10	14	8	11		12	3		7			13	**4**				1	5	6				
			6	9	10		8	11			3		7								1	5	4				
	4		6	9	10		11		13				**7**		12						1	5	3	8			
	4		6	7	10		**9**				3				11						1	5		8	12		
	4		6	7	10		8	11			3		13			12					1	**5**			9		
	4		6		10	13	12	11			3		2		**7**						1	5		8	9		
	4			12	10		**8**	11			3		7			6		13			1	5			9		
	4		6	**7**	10	12	13	11			3										1	5		8	9		
	4		6	7	10	13	12	11					**3**								1	5		8	9		
	4		6	14		10	13	11			**3**		12		*7*						1	5		8	9		
	4		6			10	9	11			3				**7**						1	5		8	12		
	4		6	13		10	9	11			3				**7**						1	5		8	12		
			6	**7**		10	4		9		3				11			12			1	5		8	13		
	4		6	7		**10**	11		12		3										1	5		8	9		13
	4		6	7		**10**	11				3											5		8	9	1	12
	4		6	7		**10**	11	13	12		3											5		8	9	1	
	4		6	**7**		10	12	11	13		3											5		8	9	1	
	4		6	7		12	10	**11**	13		3											5		8	9	1	
	4		**6**	7		14	*10*	11	9		3					12						5		8	13	1	
	4		6	7		12	10	11	**9**		3											5		8	13	1	
	4		6	**7**		13	*10*	11	14		3				12							5		8	9	1	
				9	10	13	8	11		12	3		7			5	**4**		1			6					
	4		6	**7**	10		9				3		12		11				1			5		8	13		
	4		6	7	10		9	14			3		12		*11*				1			5		8	13		
3	4		6	7	**8**		10	11	14	12	13					5		9									
3			6	**7**	8	*9*	10	11	13	4		12		5	14												
22	43	3	43	27	38	26	38	34	4	20	43	1	11	15	11	14	5	2	4	1	16	26	4	19	12	7	0
1				10		14	10	7	10	5	5	9	4	1	11	5	2	3							8		2
2			3	5	18	7	8	4	2		3		1	1	1	2										1	

League Table

	P	W	D	L	F	A	Pts
Sunderland	46	31	12	3	91	28	105
Bradford City	46	26	9	11	82	47	87
Ipswich Town	46	26	8	12	69	32	86
Birmingham City	46	23	12	11	66	37	81
Watford	46	21	14	11	65	56	77
Bolton Wanderers	46	20	16	10	78	59	76
Wolverhampton W	46	19	16	11	64	43	73
Sheffield United	46	18	13	15	71	66	67
Norwich City	46	15	17	14	62	61	62
Huddersfield Town	46	15	16	15	62	71	61
Grimsby Town	46	17	10	19	40	52	61
West Bromwich Albion	46	16	11	19	69	76	59
Barnsley	46	14	17	15	59	56	59
Crystal Palace	46	14	16	16	58	71	58
Tranmere Rovers	46	12	20	14	63	61	56
Stockport County	46	12	17	17	49	60	53
Swindon Town	46	13	11	22	59	81	50
Crewe Alexandra	46	12	12	22	54	78	48
Portsmouth	46	11	14	21	57	73	47
Queen's Park Rangers	46	12	11	23	52	61	47
Port Vale	46	13	8	25	45	75	47
Bury	46	10	17	19	35	60	47
Oxford United	46	10	14	22	48	71	44
Bristol City	46	9	15	22	57	80	42

1999-2000

Division Two

Manager: Malcolm Shotton, Mickey Lewis (caretaker) then Denis Smith

Did you know that?

Following Firoka's receipt of outline planning permission for a new multiplex cinema at Minchery Farm, rival developers Pentith Ltd and British Rail Properties sought a judicial review into the planning processes. This was rejected by the High Court in October, but overturned on appeal in March. The City Council agreed to a deal with Firoka for the land at Minchery Farm.

Malcolm Shotton and coach Steve Harrison left by mutual consent in October, with Mickey Lewis becoming caretaker manager. Ray Harford joined the club as a technical director in November, but he left six weeks later after a dispute about his expenses. In February, Denis Smith returned to the club as manager.

Fees were paid for Derek Lilley (£75,000 from Leeds), Andre Arendse (£50,000 from Fulham) and Ben Abbey (£30,000 from Crawley).

United received £500,000 from Leicester City for Phil Gilchrist, the only player sold during the season.

Match No.	Date		Opponents	Result	(F-A)	Scorers	A
1	07/08/1999	A	Stoke City	W	2-1	Anthrobus, Murphy	
2	14/08/1999	H	Cardiff City	L	2-3	Murphy (2) (1 pen)	
3	21/08/1999	A	Bristol Rovers	L	0-1		
4	28/08/1999	H	Oldham Athletic	W	1-0	Murphy (pen)	
5	30/08/1999	A	Blackpool	D	1-1	Lilley	
6	04/09/1999	H	Wycombe Wanderers	D	0-0		
7	11/09/1999	H	Gillingham	L	1-2	Cook	
8	18/09/1999	A	Wrexham	L	0-1		
9	25/09/1999	A	Luton Town	L	2-4	Lilley, Powell	
10	02/10/1999	H	Bristol City	W	3-0	Beauchamp (2), Lilley	
11	09/10/1999	H	Millwall	L	1-3	Murphy (pen)	
12	16/10/1999	A	Brentford	L	0-2		
13	19/10/1999	A	Scunthorpe United	L	0-1		
14	23/10/1999	H	Luton Town	L	0-1		
15	02/11/1999	H	Colchester United	D	1-1	Lambert	
16	07/11/1999	A	Reading	W	2-1	Murphy, Folland	
17	13/11/1999	H	Bury	D	1-1	Lambert	
18	23/11/1999	A	Notts County	W	1-0	Warren (og)	
19	27/11/1999	A	Chesterfield	D	0-0		
20	04/12/1999	H	Stoke City	D	1-1	Beauchamp	
21	18/12/1999	A	AFC Bournemouth	L	0-4		
22	26/12/1999	H	Cambridge United	W	1-0	Murphy	
23	28/12/1999	A	Burnley	L	2-3	Anthrobus, Whelan	
24	03/01/2000	H	Wigan Athletic	L	1-2	Cook	
25	15/01/2000	A	Cardiff City	D	1-1	Murphy	
26	22/01/2000	H	Bristol Rovers	L	0-5		
27	29/01/2000	A	Oldham Athletic	L	0-2		
28	01/02/2000	H	Preston North End	L	0-4		
29	05/02/2000	H	Blackpool	L	0-1		
30	12/02/2000	A	Wycombe Wanderers	W	1-0	Beauchamp	
31	19/02/2000	H	Chesterfield	W	2-1	Fear, Lilley	
32	26/02/2000	H	Wrexham	L	1-4	Edwards, Christian	
33	04/03/2000	A	Gillingham	L	0-1		
34	07/03/2000	H	Reading	L	1-3	Powell	
35	11/03/2000	A	Colchester United	W	2-1	S Weatherstone, Whelan	
36	14/03/2000	A	Preston North End	L	1-3	Murphy	
37	18/03/2000	H	Notts County	L	2-3	Powell (2) (1 pen)	
38	21/03/2000	A	Bury	W	2-1	Cook, Lilley	
39	25/03/2000	A	Cambridge United	L	0-2		
40	01/04/2000	H	AFC Bournemouth	W	1-0	Lilley	
41	08/04/2000	A	Wigan Athletic	L	0-2		
42	15/04/2000	H	Burnley	L	1-2	Murphy	
43	22/04/2000	H	Brentford	D	1-1	Lilley	
44	24/04/2000	A	Bristol City	D	2-2	Davis, Powell	
45	29/04/2000	H	Scunthorpe United	W	2-0	Murphy, Powell	
46	06/05/2000	A	Millwall	L	0-1		
FA Cup							
R1	30/10/1999	H	Morecambe	W	3-2	Lilley, Powell, Abbey	
R2	20/11/1999	A	Shrewsbury Town	D	2-2	Murphy, Folland	
r	30/11/1999	H	Shrewsbury Town	W	2-1	Murphy (2)	
R3	10/12/1999	A	Nottingham Forest	D	1-1	Powell	
r	08/01/2000	H	Nottingham Forest	L	1-3	Powell	
League Cup							
R1/1	10/08/1999	A	Southend United	W	2-0	Beauchamp, Murphy	
R1/2	24/08/1999	H	Southend United	W	1-0	Murphy	
R2	14/09/1999	H	Everton	D	1-1	Murphy	
r	22/09/1999	A	Everton	W	1-0	Beauchamp	
R3	12/10/1999	A	Tranmere Rovers	L	0-2		
AWS Shield							
R1	07/12/1999	H	Luton Town	W	2-0	Powell (2) (2 pens)	
R2	11/01/2000	H	Wycombe Wanderers	W*	1-1	Powell (pen)	
R3	25/01/2000	A	Brentford	L	0-2		

*5-3 on pens

Total appea
Sub appea
Total

Powell	Weatherstone, S	Watson	Gilchrist	Murphy	Tait	Anthrobus	Lilley	Beauchamp	Folland	Davis	Banger	Cook	Whelan	McGowan	Lundin	Lambert	Lewis	Fear	Abbey	Weatherstone, R	Francis	Knight	Jemson	Shepheard	Russell	Edwards	Newton	Hackett	Whitehead
3	4	5	6	7	8	9	**10**	11	12																				
3	12	5		4	8	9	10	11		6	**7**	13																	
3	4	5		7	8	9	10	11		13	14		*6*	12															
4	9	5		8	7	10	*11*	6	3		14	13		12	1														
3	*9*	4		8	7	10	11	6	13				5	12	1	14													
3	*10*	4		10	7		11	6	12			13	**5**		1	8	14												
4	14	5		10	7		*11*	6	3			13		12	1	8		10											
4				*8*	7	10	13	6	**2**			12		11	1	14	5	9											
4		13		9	*8*	11	14	7	**2**	6		12					5	10											
4		5		8		9	11	6	3			12			1	**10**		7	13										
4				7		9	11	6	3	5					1	**10**		8	12										
3		4		9	7	10	11	6		5						12		**8**	13										
3		4		9	7	10	11	6		5		12				**8**		13											
3		6		9	8	13	11	7		4				12		13	5	10											
4		5		8			**10**	7	3			12	6			11		9	13										
		5		8			10	11	4				6	3	1	**9**			12	7									
		4		8	7		**9**	6	3			12	5	11	1	10			13										
		4		9	8	12	**10**	7	3	5			6	11	1														
		4		9	8	12	**10**	7	3	5			6	11	1			13											
		4		7		9	10	6	3				5	11	1	13		12		8									
14		5		8			9	**7**	2	4		10	6	11	1			13			12								
4				8		13	**9**	7	3	5		10	6	11							12								
				7		9	**10**	5	2	4		12	6	11						8									
4		5		8		9	10	7	3			11	6																
5				9	8	10	12	7	3	4		**11**	6		1														
3				8	7	*9*	13	6		4		10	5	11				12	14			1							
3		4		7	6	**8**	9					13	5	*11*	1				12				10	14					
3		4		9	7			8				11	5		1			12					10	**6**					
3	13	4		8	7	14	10	6	12				5		1			**9**					*11*						
3				7	5	13		7		4			6		**1**			9				12	11		10				
3				8	**6**	12	14	7		4			5		1		13	9					10		*11*				
3	8			7		**9**	13	5				12			1			6					11		10	4			
3	12	4		8	6		13	**7**					5					9					10		11				
3		4		9	7		13	8					6		12						14		10		*11*	5			
4	**9**	5		8	6	13	*11*					12	7		1								10		14	3			
4	**9**	5		8	6	14	10					12	7						13			1	*11*			3			
3	9	5		8	7	13	10					12	6						14			1	*11*			**4**			
3	**8**	4		7	6	9	10			12		11	5									1							
3	8	**4**		7	5	9	10			12		11	6									1	13						
3	13	4		7	6	9	10			12		*11*	**5**									1	14				8		
4	12	3		8	6		9			5		11										1	**10**				7	13	
4		5		8	6	9	10					**11**	3									1	12				7		
4	13	5		8	6	14	9			3		12		11								1	*10*				**7**		
4	13	3		7	6	9	10		14	5		12		*11*								1					8		
4	8			7		9	10	12		3			5	11								1	13				6		
3	**8**			7		9	10		14	4			5	*11*								1	12				6	13	

4		5		8			11	7	**3**				6	12		10		9	13										
		4		8	7	12	**9**	6	2			13	5	11	1	10													
3		4		9	8	10	*11*	7	13	6		12	5		1	14													
12		4		7		*9*	10	6	**3**			14	5	11	1			13		8									
3		4		8		10	9	7	**2**			11	5		1						12								

3	13	4		8	7	9	10	6		5	12	**11**																	
3	4	5		7	*8*	9	10	11	6			13		12	1		14												
4				9	7		11	8	**3**	5		13		12			6	10											
3				8	9	**10**	12	5	11	6							7	4											
4				8	11	10	13	6	**2**	5		12	6					9											

3	8					9		**5**				10	4	11	1			6	13	7									12
9		**3**		8	6	11		14		12		10	4		1			2			*13*			5					
				7	6		9	12	3			10	4	11	1				13	**8**				5					

49	15	42	1	58	43	34	45	44	26	25	1	16	40	19	29	10	5	19	0	6	0	12	13	3	5	5	7	0	0
2	9	1				12	10	3	7	5	3	25		8	1	6	3	7	13		5	1	5	1	1			2	1
12	1			17		2	7	6	2	1		3	2			2		1	1							1			

League Table

	P	W	D	L	F	A	Pts
Preston North End	46	28	11	7	74	37	95
Burnley	46	25	13	8	69	47	88
Gillingham	46	25	10	11	79	48	85
Wigan Athletic	46	22	17	7	72	38	83
Millwall	46	23	13	10	76	50	82
Stoke City	46	23	13	10	68	42	82
Bristol Rovers	46	23	11	12	69	45	80
Notts County	46	18	11	17	61	55	65
Bristol City	46	15	19	12	59	57	64
Reading	46	16	14	16	57	63	62
Wrexham	46	17	11	18	52	61	62
Wycombe Wanderers	46	16	13	17	56	53	61
Luton Town	46	17	10	19	61	65	61
Oldham Athletic	46	16	12	18	50	55	60
Bury	46	13	18	15	61	64	57
Bournemouth	46	16	9	21	59	62	57
Brentford	46	13	13	20	47	61	52
Colchester United	46	14	10	22	59	82	52
Cambridge United	46	12	12	22	64	65	48
Oxford United	46	12	9	25	43	73	45
Cardiff City	46	9	17	20	45	67	44
Blackpool	46	8	17	21	49	77	41
Scunthorpe United	46	9	12	25	40	74	39
Chesterfield	46	7	15	24	34	63	36

2000-01

Division Two

Manager: Denis Smith, Mike Ford (caretaker), David Kemp, then Mike Ford (caretaker)

Did you know that?

Pentith and British Rail withdrew their request for a judicial review into the granting of planning permission for a cinema at Minchery Farm, and the High Court ruled that a covenent held by Morrells restricting the sale of alcohol at the new stadium did not apply if the City Council no longer owned the land. In November, Birse Stadia took on the stadium construction, and building recommenced after three years. Kassam paid £1 million to Les Wells to settle a right-of-way dispute. Oxford City Council agreed to transfer the stadium land to Kassam's company after Kassam threatened not to pay Birse £1.5 million if they refused. In May it was announced that the new ground would be called the Kassam Stadium.

Smith resigned at the end of September, following a home defeat by Bristol City and with United bottom of the table. Mike Ford was appointed caretaker manager. On 1 November United announced the appointment of David Kemp as manager, with Joe Kinnear as director of football, and Alan McLeary as assistant manager. At the end of January Kinnear quit, claiming ill-health, to be appointed Luton's manager three days later. Kemp and McLeary were sacked at the end of April, with United already relegated, with Ford appointed caretaker for the season's final two matches – including the last game at the Manor.

United's last competitive game at the Manor, where they moved to in 1925, was a 1–1 draw with Port Vale, Andy Scott scoring for Oxford.

Phil Gray's goal in the defeat at Bournemouth was United's fastest League goal, after just 11 seconds.

United bought Andy Scott and Rob Quinn from Brentford for £75,000 each. Derek Lilley was sold to Dundee United for £75,000 and youth player Jonathon Mills was sold to Southampton for £25,000.

Match No.	Date		Opponents	Result	(F-A)	Scorers	A
1	12/08/2000	H	Peterborough United	L	0-1		
2	19/08/2000	A	Port Vale	L	0-3		
3	26/08/2000	H	Brentford	L	0-1		
4	29/08/2000	A	Walsall	L	2-3	Beauchamp (2)	
5	02/09/2000	H	Cambridge United	D	1-1	Jarman	
6	08/09/2000	A	Wycombe Wanderers	L	1-3	Tait	
7	13/09/2000	A	Stoke City	L	0-4		
8	16/09/2000	H	Bury	W	1-0	Cook	
9	23/09/2000	A	Millwall	L	0-5		
10	30/09/2000	H	Bristol City	L	0-1		
11	08/10/2000	A	Swindon Town	L	1-2	Whittingham	
12	14/10/2000	H	Wrexham	L	3-4	Beauchamp, Tait, McGregor (og)	
13	17/10/2000	H	Luton Town	D	0-0		
14	21/10/2000	A	Rotherham United	L	1-3	Lilley	
15	24/10/2000	H	Wigan Athletic	L	0-2		
16	28/10/2000	A	Reading	L	3-4	Lilley, Richardson, Viveash (og)	
17	04/11/2000	H	Bristol Rovers	L	0-1		
18	11/11/2000	A	Swansea City	W	2-1	Beauchamp, Andrews	
19	25/11/2000	H	Notts County	L	2-3	Murphy (2)	
20	02/12/2000	A	Oldham Athletic	L	2-3	Gray (pen), Innes (og)	
21	16/12/2000	H	Northampton Town	W	3-1	Anthrobus, Murphy, Hackett	
22	22/12/2000	A	Colchester United	L	2-3	Beauchamp, Gray	
23	26/12/2000	H	AFC Bournemouth	L	1-2	Fear	
24	01/01/2001	A	Brentford	L	0-3		
25	13/01/2001	H	Walsall	W	2-1	Gray (2)	
26	27/01/2001	H	Colchester United	L	0-1		
27	30/01/2001	A	Peterborough United	L	2-4	Murphy, Fear	
28	10/02/2001	H	Wycombe Wanderers	L	1-2	Hackett	
29	17/02/2001	A	Bury	L	1-3	Beauchamp	
30	20/02/2001	H	Stoke City	D	1-1	Patterson	
31	24/02/2001	H	Millwall	L	0-2		
32	03/03/2001	A	Bristol City	D	0-0		
33	06/03/2001	A	Wrexham	L	3-5	Murphy, Powell, Gray (pen)	
34	10/03/2001	H	Swindon Town	L	0-2		
35	24/03/2001	H	Rotherham United	W	4-3	Scott, Quinn, Omoyinmi (2)	
36	27/03/2001	A	Cambridge United	L	0-1		
37	31/03/2001	A	Northampton Town	W	1-0	Tait	
38	03/04/2001	A	AFC Bournemouth	L	3-4	Quinn, Gray (2) (1 pen)	
39	07/04/2001	H	Oldham Athletic	L	0-1		
40	10/04/2001	A	Luton Town	D	1-1	Scott	
41	14/04/2001	A	Wigan Athletic	L	2-3	Beauchamp, Scott	
42	17/04/2001	H	Reading	L	0-2		
43	21/04/2001	A	Bristol Rovers	L	2-6	Scott, Richardson	
44	28/04/2001	H	Swansea City	W	3-1	Murphy, Brooks, Omoyinmi	
45	01/05/2001	H	Port Vale	D	1-1	Scott	
46	05/05/2001	A	Notts County	L	1-2	Folland	

FA Cup

R1	18/11/2000	A	Macclesfield Town	W	1-0	Gray
R2	09/12/2000	A	Chester City	L	2-3	Murphy, Gray

League Cup

R1/1	22/08/2000	A	Wolverhampton Wanderers	W	1-0	Murphy
R1/2	05/09/2000	H	Wolverhampton Wanderers	L	1-3	Shepheard

LDV Vans

R1	05/12/2000	A	Brentford	L	1-4	Anthrobus

League Table

	P	W	D	L	F	A	Pts
Millwall	46	28	9	9	89	38	93
Rotherham United	46	27	10	9	79	55	91
Reading	46	25	11	10	86	52	86
Walsall	46	23	12	11	79	50	81
Stoke City	46	21	14	11	74	49	77
Wigan Athletic	46	19	18	9	53	42	75
Bournemouth	46	20	13	13	79	55	73
Notts County	46	19	12	15	62	66	69
Bristol City	46	18	14	14	70	56	68
Wrexham	46	17	12	17	65	71	63
Port Vale	46	16	14	16	55	49	62
Peterborough United	46	15	14	17	61	66	59

	P	W	D	L	F	A	Pts
Wycombe Wanderers	46	15	14	17	46	53	59
Brentford	46	14	17	15	56	70	59
Oldham Athletic	46	15	13	18	53	65	58
Bury	46	16	10	20	45	59	58
Colchester United	46	15	12	19	55	59	57
Northampton Town	46	15	12	19	46	59	57
Cambridge United	46	14	11	21	61	77	53
Swindon Town	46	13	13	20	47	65	52
Bristol Rovers	46	12	15	19	53	57	51
Luton Town	46	9	13	24	52	80	40
Swansea City	46	8	13	25	47	73	37
Oxford United	46	7	6	33	53	100	27

Total appear
Sub appear
Total

…stone, S	Richardson	Robertson	Jarman	McGuckin	Murphy	Powell	Tait	Fear	Omoyinmi	Lilley	Beauchamp	Anthrobus	McGowan	Cook	Shepheard	Whitehead	Hackett	Folland	Busby	Glass	Ford	Mike	Ricketts	Whittingham	Brooks	Linighan	Brown	Andrews	Gray	Cutler	Hatswell	Weatherstone, R	Monk	Quinn	Scott	Patterson	Wilson	King	Holder
	3	4	*5*	6	7	8	9	**10**	11	12	13	14																											
	2	3		4	5	6	7	**8**	11	*10*	12	13	9	14																									
	3	2	4		**5**	6	8		11	13		10			7	9	12																						
	2	3	4		13	**5**	7		11	14	*9*	10			6	8		12																					
	3	2	4	5			6		11		8	10	9			7																							
	3	2	4		6		7	13		11	8	*10*	9	14	5				12																				
	2	3	13	4	5		6		10	14	8	*11*	**9**			7		12		1																			
	3	2		4	5		6		**11**	9	7	10	8	12																									
	3	2	12	**4**	5		6		*11*	9	7	10	8	14								13																	
	3	2	5				6	13	**10**	11	8			12		7					4	9																	
	2	14	4		5		**6**			10	8		*9*			7						13	3	11	12														
	2	13	4		*5*		6		14	11	8	12	9	**10**		7							3																
	2	12	4				**6**		13	11	8		9	10		7							3			5													
	3	2			7					11	12		9	10	6	**8**							13			5													
	3	2	13		8			9		11	12			*10*	*7*		14						5			6													
	3	**2**	5		7			8		11		10	9					12								6													
	3	4	12		6	7		**8**	14	10	9	11					13									5													
	2	3			6			7		11	9															5	4	8	10										
	2	3	12		7					11	9						13									6	5	8	10										
	2	**3**			6	13		*7*	14	*11*	9															5	4	8	10		12								
	2		4		6						9	11					7									5		8	10	1	3								
	2		4		6	12		8			9	11					7									**5**			10	1	3								
	3				6	12		8	11		9						7									5			10	1	4	2							
	2		4		6	**7**		9			10	11				12	8									5				1	3								
	2	3			6						9						7												10	1	5		4	8	11				
		2	**5**		6			12			9						7												10	1	4		3	8	11				
		2	**5**	12	6			7	13		*9*						14												10	1	4		3	8	11				
	2				5				12		**9**					7	6												10	1	4		3	8	11				
	2				**6**		14				8	13				12	11												9	1	5		3	7	10	4			
	2	3			6		12				9						**7**												10	1	5			8	11	4			
	2	3			6		12				**9**					13	7												10	1	5			8	11	4			
	3	2			6	**7**	8				12					9													10		5				11	4			
	3	2			6	7	8					12				9													10		5				**11**	4			
	4	2			6	*9*	*7*	12	13		14	**11**				8													10		5					3			
	2	3				**7**	8		11		12												4								6			9	10	5			
	2	3				**7**	8		11		12												4								6			9	10	5			
	2	3				**7**	8		11		12												4						13		6			9	10	5			
	2	3			12	*7*	8				13												**4**						11		6			9	10	5			
	3	2			13		7				8						12						**4**						11		6			9	10	5			
	3	2			7	8	**9**	12			13												4						11		6				10	5			
	2	3			7			8			9												4						11		6				10	5			
	2	3			7	12		8	14		9	13											**4**						*11*		6				10	5			
	2				6			7	10		8					13							3						14		5				9	4	12		
		2			5	**6**			11		8					7									10	12					4				9	3			
		2			5		14		*11*		8					7		13							10						4				9	3		**6**	12
		2			5	14					9					8		**6**							*11*						4			13	10	3	1	7	12
	3	2	6		7			8		11	9															5	4		10										
	2		4		6			8	12		9	**11**				13	7									5	3		10										
	3	**2**	4		*7*	5	8		*11*	13	14	10			6	9		12																					
	3	2	4		13		6		11	*14*	8	10	**9**		5	*7*		12																					
	3	2			7				11		9	12					13			1			**4**				5	8	10		6								
	46	41	19	6	41	16	24	16	19	16	36	16	12	4	7	18	11	1	0	2	1	1	14	1	3	14	6	5	24	11	27	1	5	12	21	18	1	2	0
		3	5	1	3	5	4	5	9	5	12	7		5		5	7	5	1			2	1		1	1			2		1		1				1		2
	2		1		8	1	3	2	3	2	7	2		1	1		2	1						1	1			1	9				2	5	1				

2001-02

Division Three

Manager: Mark Wright then Ian Atkins

Did you know that?

Former player Mark Wright was appointed as manager in June, with Ted McMinn as his assistant, but he was suspended in November after allegations that he had made racist remarks to referee Joe Ross, with Ian Atkins appointed director of football, becoming manager after Wright resigned. McMinn left immediately afterwards.

The first competitive game at United's new ground was a 2–1 defeat by Rochdale, with Jamie Brooks scoring Oxford's goal. The attendance was 8,842, but this was bettered on Boxing Day, when 11,121 were at the game against Luton. The season's lowest attendance was 4,964 for the visit of Macclesfield.

United paid £150,000 to Barnet for Sam Stockley, and a similar fee to Millwall to bring Paul Moody back to Oxford. The only player sold for a fee was Phil Bolland, who joined Mark Wright at Chester City for £15,000.

In November, the Bishop of Oxford performed a blessing ceremony at the new ground, which the *Sun* newspaper claimed was an exorcism in order to rid the stadium of a gypsy curse, made when a band of travellers was evicted from the site in order for the ground to be built.

At the end of the season the Minchery Farm stadium hosted an under-17s international tournament, featuring England, Italy, Brazil and the Czech Republic. In addition to the football, the stadium hosted the semi-final of Rugby Union's Parker Pen Trophy, between Pontypridd and London Irish.

Supporters' campaigning group FOUL was wound up following the successful move into the new stadium. A new group, called OxVox, was launched in March, becoming the 50th Supporters' Trust.

United's youth team won the Football League Youth Alliance South West Conference Under-19 title.

After a 52-year association with the club, chief scout Jack Casley, United's first full professional player, announced his retirement.

Homegrown striker Jamie Brooks won Players' Player of the Year, Young Player of the Year, the Guy Salmon Player of the Year, the Oxfordshire Media and Sports Writers' Player of the Year and the Supporters' Player of the Year. At the end of the season Brooks almost lost his life when contracting Guillain Barré Syndrome.

In May, the demolition of the Manor commenced, in readiness for the building of a private hospital on the site.

Match No.	Date		Opponents	Result	(F-A)	Scorers
1	11/08/2001	H	Rochdale	L	1-2	Brooks
2	18/08/2001	A	Swansea City	D	0-0	
3	25/08/2001	H	Shrewsbury Town	L	0-1	
4	27/08/2001	A	Halifax Town	W	2-0	Scott, Gray
5	01/09/2001	H	Rushden & Diamonds	W	3-2	Whitehead, Thomas, Bolland
6	08/09/2001	A	Luton Town	D	1-1	Scott
7	15/09/2001	A	Exeter City	L	2-3	Brooks, Thomas (pen)
8	18/09/2001	H	Macclesfield Town	L	0-2	
9	22/09/2001	H	Southend United	W	2-0	Moody, Ricketts
10	25/09/2001	A	Kidderminster Harriers	D	0-0	
11	29/09/2001	A	Bristol Rovers	D	1-1	Omoyinmi
12	06/10/2001	H	Plymouth Argyle	D	1-1	Moody (pen)
13	13/10/2001	A	Lincoln City	L	0-1	
14	20/10/2001	H	Scunthorpe United	L	0-1	
15	23/10/2001	H	Carlisle United	D	1-1	Brooks
16	27/10/2001	A	Hartlepool United	W	1-0	Moody
17	03/11/2001	H	York City	D	2-2	Brooks (2)
18	10/11/2001	A	Darlington	L	0-1	
19	20/11/2001	A	Leyton Orient	L	0-3	
20	24/11/2001	H	Cheltenham Town	W	3-0	Moody, Powell, Brooks
21	01/12/2001	A	Hull City	L	0-3	
22	15/12/2001	H	Mansfield Town	W	3-2	Morley, Gray (2)
23	22/12/2001	A	Torquay United	D	3-3	Moody, Crosby, Omoyinmi
24	26/12/2001	H	Luton Town	L	1-2	Scott
25	29/12/2001	H	Halifax Town	W	6-1	Moody (3) (1 pen), Savage, Scott, Omoyinmi
26	08/01/2002	A	Shrewsbury Town	L	0-1	
27	12/01/2002	H	Swansea City	W	2-1	Moody, Scott
28	19/01/2002	A	Rochdale	D	1-1	Moody
29	22/01/2002	H	Torquay United	D	1-1	Moody (pen)
30	26/01/2002	A	Plymouth Argyle	L	2-4	Powell, Morley
31	02/02/2002	H	Bristol Rovers	D	0-0	
32	05/02/2002	A	Rushden & Diamonds	L	1-2	Morley
33	09/02/2002	A	Scunthorpe United	L	0-1	
34	16/02/2002	H	Lincoln City	W	2-1	Scott (pen), Gray
35	23/02/2002	H	Exeter City	L	1-2	Beauchamp
36	26/02/2002	A	Macclesfield Town	W	1-0	Powell
37	02/03/2002	A	Southend United	D	2-2	Powell (pen), Scott
38	05/03/2002	H	Kidderminster Harriers	D	1-1	Brooks
39	09/03/2002	A	Mansfield Town	L	1-2	Moody (pen)
40	16/03/2002	H	Hull City	W	1-0	Brooks
41	23/03/2002	A	Carlisle United	L	1-2	Brooks
42	30/03/2002	H	Hartlepool United	L	1-2	Moody
43	01/04/2002	A	York City	L	0-1	
44	06/04/2002	H	Leyton Orient	D	1-1	Scott
45	13/04/2002	A	Cheltenham Town	L	0-2	
46	20/04/2002	H	Darlington	L	1-2	Brooks

FA Cup

R1	17/11/2001	A	Mansfield Town	L	0-1	

League Cup

R1	21/08/2001	H	Gillingham	L	1-2	Scott

LDV Vans

R1	16/10/2001	A	Northampton Town	L	0-2	

Total appea
Sub appea
Tota

Stockley	Bolland	Hatswell	Savage	Tait	Powell	Thomas	Scott	Brooks	Ricketts	Omoyinmi	McCaldon	Beauchamp	Gray	Whitehead	Folland	Quinn	Richardson	Moody	Hackett	Douglas	Morley	Crosby	Bound	Woodman	Maddison	Patterson	Waterman	King	Louis
3	4	5	6	7	**8**	9	10	11	12	13																			
2	4	5	8			11	10	9	6		1	7																	
3	4	5		11		7	8	**9**	*6*		1	12	10	13	14														
3	4	5		**8**		9	11	13	6		1		10	7		12													
3	4	5	8			9	10	14	6		1		*11*	7	12	13	2												
2	4	5	8			9	10		6		1		11	7															
2	**4**	5	8			10		9	6	13	1		11	7			12												
3	4	5	6		7	*8*	9		13	11	1		**10**	14	12														
3	4	6	8			10	**9**		5		1		12	7				11											
3	4	6	8			9			5	10	1			7				11											
3	4	6	8			9			5	10	1			7				11											
3	4	6	9	**8**		12			5	11	1			7				10											
4		10	7		12	11		13	*5*	**9**	1			6	14		3	8											
3	10	4	6		7			*8*	13	**9**	1			5	14			11	12										
13	4		7		8			9	*5*	12	1			6	14		3	10		**11**									
4	5		8		*9*			**10**	14		1			6	12	7	2	11		13									
2	4		7		8			9	5	**11**	1			13	14	6	3	10		12									
3	5		7		8			**9**		11	1			6	13		4	10	12										
3	*4*	5	7		8	10		9			1			6	13		14	**11**		12									
3	4	5	8		9			**10**	13		1			7			6	11	12										
6	4	5	8		9		**10**		13	12	1		14	7			2	*11*											
3		6	8		9		10			12	1		13			7	2	11			4	5							
3		**6**	8		9		10			12	1		13	14		7	2	*11*			4	5							
2		**6**	8		9		10			12	1		*11*	13		7	3	14				4	5						
3			8		9		10	14	**6**	12	1		13	7			2	*11*				4	5						
2			8		**9**		10	13	6	12	1			7			3	11				4	5						
3				13	9		10		6		1		14	8		7	2	*11*			4	5							
2			8	7	9		10			12			*11*	6		13		14			3	4	5	1					
2			8		9		10		12	13				6		7		11			3	4	5	1					
			8		9		10		5	12			11	**7**		6		13			2	3	4	1					
2		6	8		9					11				12		7		10	13		3	4	5	1					
2			8		9					11				13		7		10	12		3	5	6		4				
			8		**9**		13		12	*11*			10	7			3		14		2	5	6	1	4				
			8		9		10		12				11	7		13			6		2	**4**	5	1	3				
			8		9		10		5			**6**	*11*	13		7		14	12		2		4	1	3				
3			8		9		10		12					7				**11**			4		6	1	5				
2			**8**		9		10							7		12		11			3	5	6	1	4				
2				8	9		10	13						7			**3**	11			12	4	6	1	5				
2			8	7	9		10	13						12				11			**3**	5	6	1	4				
2			8	7	9			10					14	**6**				*11*	12		13	3	5	1	4				
2			8	**7**	9			*10*					11	12				14	13		3	4	5			6			
2			8	9	13		12	10			1							11	6			3	5		**4**		7		
2			8	9	13		14	10			1		*11*						6			12	4		**3**	5	7		
14			7	8	**9**		13	10						*5*				11	4			2	3	1			6	12	
			7	8	*9*		10	11	5									14	13		2	3	4	1			**6**		
2			8		*9*		12	10						7				11	**6**			3	4	1			14	5	13

Stockley	Bolland	Hatswell	Savage	Tait	Powell	Thomas	Scott	Brooks	Ricketts	Omoyinmi	McCaldon	Beauchamp	Gray	Whitehead	Folland	Quinn	Richardson	Moody	Hackett	Douglas	Morley	Crosby	Bound	Woodman	Maddison	Patterson	Waterman	King	Louis
3	4	5	7		8			**9**		11	1			6				10	12										
3	4	5	7	8		9	10		6		1	12	**11**	14	13														
2	4	5	8		12			9	**6**	10	1			7	11				13										
42	23	24	45	14	34	14	26	20	21	13	31	2	15	32	1	11	16	30	5	1	16	22	22	15	11	2	4	1	0
2				1	4	1	5	7	10	12		2	7	11	11	5	2	6	12	3	2	1					1	1	1
	1		1		4	2	9	10	1	3		1	4	1				13			3	1							

League Table

	P	W	D	L	F	A	Pts
Plymouth Argyle	46	31	9	6	71	28	102
Luton Town	46	30	7	9	96	48	97
Mansfield Town	46	24	7	15	72	60	79
Cheltenham Town	46	21	15	10	66	49	78
Rochdale	46	21	15	10	65	52	78
Rushden & Diamonds	46	20	13	13	69	53	73
Hartlepool United	46	20	11	15	74	48	71
Scunthorpe United	46	19	14	13	74	56	71
Shrewsbury Town	46	20	10	16	64	53	70
Kidderminster Harriers	46	19	9	18	56	47	66
Hull City	46	16	13	17	57	51	61
Southend United	46	15	13	18	51	54	58
Macclesfield Town	46	15	13	18	41	52	58
York City	46	16	9	21	54	67	57
Darlington	46	15	11	20	60	71	56
Exeter City	46	14	13	19	48	73	55
Carlisle United	46	12	16	18	49	56	52
Leyton Orient	46	13	13	20	55	71	52
Torquay United	46	12	15	19	46	63	51
Swansea City	46	13	12	21	53	77	51
Oxford United	46	11	14	21	53	62	47
Lincoln City	46	10	16	20	44	62	46
Bristol Rovers	46	11	12	23	40	60	45
Halifax Town	46	8	12	26	39	84	36

2002-03

Division Three

Manager: Ian Atkins

Did you know that?

Despite winning the season's final game against York City, United missed out on the Play-offs because of a missed penalty by Torquay United at Lincoln City.

Goalkeeper Alan Judge, who had played in United's Milk Cup-winning side of 1986, became the club's oldest player when starting in the 1–1 draw with Cambridge United.

There were reports that rugby union side Bristol Shoguns were going to groundshare with Oxford United because their ground did not meet the required standard for the Union Premiership. However, their relegation from the Premiership put an end to any deal.

Following United's derby win over Swindon in the FA Cup, TV cameras in the dressing room captured Jefferson Louis dancing naked after the Us were drawn to play the team he supported, Arsenal.

The attendance of 12,177 for the League Cup game against Aston Villa set a new ground record. A new low crowd for the stadium was 4,547 for the visit of Rochdale.

Match No.	Date		Opponents	Result	(F-A)	Scorers
1	10/08/2002	H	Bury	W	2-1	Crosby (pen), Omoyinmi
2	13/08/2002	A	Wrexham	L	0-1	
3	17/08/2002	A	Darlington	W	1-0	Basham
4	24/08/2002	H	Southend United	L	0-1	
5	27/08/2002	A	AFC Bournemouth	D	1-1	Basham
6	31/08/2002	H	Hartlepool United	L	0-1	
7	07/09/2002	H	Torquay United	D	2-2	Powell, Omoyinmi
8	14/09/2002	A	Boston United	W	3-1	Powell, Scott (2)
9	17/09/2002	A	Leyton Orient	W	2-1	Scott (pen), Crosby
10	21/09/2002	H	Hull City	D	0-0	
11	28/09/2002	A	York City	W	1-0	Gordon
12	05/10/2002	H	Scunthorpe United	L	0-1	
13	12/10/2002	H	Swansea City	W	1-0	Louis
14	19/10/2002	A	Cambridge United	D	1-1	Scott
15	26/10/2002	H	Shrewsbury Town	D	2-2	Louis, Scott
16	29/10/2002	A	Macclesfield Town	L	1-2	Louis
17	02/11/2002	A	Carlisle United	L	0-1	
18	09/11/2002	H	Rochdale	W	2-0	Basham, Hunt
19	30/11/2002	H	Lincoln City	W	1-0	Crosby (pen)
20	14/12/2002	A	Bristol Rovers	W	2-0	Louis, Robinson
21	21/12/2002	H	Exeter City	D	2-2	Steele, Bound
22	26/12/2002	H	AFC Bournemouth	W	3-0	Whitehead, Oldfield, Hunter
23	28/12/2002	A	Rushden & Diamonds	W	2-0	Savage, Oldfield
24	14/01/2003	H	Darlington	D	1-1	Basham
25	18/01/2003	A	Hartlepool United	L	1-3	Barron (og)
26	21/01/2003	A	Southend United	L	1-2	Basham
27	25/01/2003	H	Rushden & Diamonds	W	3-0	Savage (2), Crosby (pen)
28	28/01/2003	A	Kidderminster Harriers	W	3-1	Scott, Basham, Hinton (og)
29	04/02/2003	H	Wrexham	L	0-2	
30	08/02/2003	A	Rochdale	L	1-2	Savage
31	22/02/2003	A	Torquay United	W	3-2	Scott, Steele (2)
32	01/03/2003	H	Boston United	W	2-1	B Ford, Crosby
33	04/03/2003	H	Leyton Orient	L	0-2	
34	08/03/2003	A	Hull City	D	0-0	
35	15/03/2003	A	Shrewsbury Town	W	2-1	Waterman, Louis
36	18/03/2003	H	Cambridge United	D	1-1	Louis
37	22/03/2003	H	Macclesfield Town	L	0-1	
38	25/03/2003	A	Bury	D	1-1	McNiven
39	28/03/2003	A	Swansea City	L	2-3	Scott (2)
40	01/04/2003	H	Carlisle United	D	0-0	
41	05/04/2003	A	Lincoln City	W	1-0	Scott
42	12/04/2003	H	Kidderminster Harriers	W	2-1	Omoyinmi, McCarthy
43	19/04/2003	A	Exeter City	D	2-2	Scott, Crosby (pen)
44	21/04/2003	H	Bristol Rovers	L	0-1	
45	26/04/2003	A	Scunthorpe United	L	0-2	
46	03/05/2003	H	York City	W	2-0	Basham (2)

FA Cup

R1	16/11/2002	A	Dover Athletic	W	1-0	Oldfield
R2	08/12/2002	H	Swindon Town	W	1-0	Louis
R3	04/01/2003	A	Arsenal	L	0-2	

League Cup

R1	10/09/2002	A	Bristol City	W	1-0	Hunt
R2	01/10/2002	A	Charlton Athletic	W*	0-0	
R3	06/11/2002	H	Aston Villa	L	0-3	

* 6-5 on pens

LDV Vans

R1	22/10/2002	H	AFC Bournemouth	L	2-3	Waterman, Crosby (pen)

Total appear
Sub appear
Total

Waterman	Crosby	Bound	Robinson	Whitehead	Hunt	Oldfield	Omoyinmi	Savage	Ford	Basham	Scott	Ricketts	Hackett	Viveash	Powell	Gordon	Louis	Hunter	Sall	Steele	Edwards	Judge	McCarthy	Foley
3	4	5	6	7	8	9	10	11	12	13	14													
3	4	5	6	7	8	9	10	11	14	13	12													
3	4	5	6	14	7	8		11		10	9	12	13											
3	4	5	6		7	8	14	11	12	10	9		13											
11	4	3	5	6	8	7		10	12	9	13													
	4	3	5		8	7	13	11	6	10	9		12											
	4		6	7	9	8	14	11	5		10			3	13		12							
	5	4			9	7	12	11	6		10			3	8		13							
	4	3			7	6		11	10		9			5	8									
	5	3			9	8	12	11	6		10			4	7		13							
	4	3	6		8	9	10	11	7					5	12	13								
	4	3	6		7	12	14	11	8		10			5	13	9								
	4	3	5	6	8	12	10	11	7				13			9	14							
	5	4	6		7	8		11			10		12	3	13		9							
	5	4	6	12	7	14		10			9		11	3		13	8							
	5	4	6		7	8		11			10		14	3		13	9	12						
3	4		6		7			11		13	10		12	5	14	8	9							
14	4	3	6	7	9	8		11		10				5	13		12							
3	4	5	6	13	8	9		11	7	10					14		12							
3	4	5	6	9					8	11	14	13					10	7	12					
3	4	5	6		8			10	7	11	14		12				9			13				
3	4	5	6	14	9	12			8	11	13						10	7						
3	4	5	6	14		9		11	8	10	12						13	7						
2	3	4	6	7		13		10	8	11							9	5		12				
	4	5	7	13		12		10	6	11	14						9	8			2			
3	4	5	6		8	12		10	7	11	9										13			
	5	4	6		8			10		11	9						12	7			2			
13	5	4	6		8	12		10		11	9							7			2			
	5	4			7			10	13	11	9				8		14	6		12	2			
	5	4	6		8			10	13	11	9						12	7		14	2			
3	4	5	6		8			10	7	11	9						13	12		14				
3	4	5	6		8			10	7	11	9							13		12				
2	3	4	6		8			10	7	11	9		14				13	5		12				
3	4	5	6		8			11	7	9	13						12			10				
3	4	5	6	12	7	8		10	11								14	13		9				
3	4	5	6		8			10	7	12					13		9			11		1		
3	4	5	6		8		12	10	7	11			14		13		9							
3	4	5	6		8			10	7	11	9						12							13
	4	3	6		8		12	10	7	11	9						13						5	14
	3		5		7		13	11			10				12		9	6					4	8
3	4	6	7					11	8		9						12	13					5	10
3	5	5	7	13			12	11	8		9		14										4	10
3	4	5	7	14			13	11	8		9						12	6						10
3	4	5	6		9	8	13	11	7	14	10						12							
3	5		6		11	8	14	10	7	13	9						12						4	
3	4		6	7	9	13			8	11	10						12						5	

Waterman	Crosby	Bound	Robinson	Whitehead	Hunt	Oldfield	Omoyinmi	Savage	Ford	Basham	Scott	Ricketts	Hackett	Viveash	Powell	Gordon	Louis	Hunter	Sall	Steele	Edwards	Judge	McCarthy	Foley
6	4	5	3	8	9	10	13	7		11							12							
3	5	4	6	12	8			10	7	11							9		13					
3	4	5	6			9		11	8	10	13						14	7		12				

Waterman	Crosby	Bound	Robinson	Whitehead	Hunt	Oldfield	Omoyinmi	Savage	Ford	Basham	Scott	Ricketts	Hackett	Viveash	Powell	Gordon	Louis	Hunter	Sall	Steele	Edwards	Judge	McCarthy	Foley
	5	4	6		8	7		10	7		11			2	12									
	4	5	3		8	10	13	7	8		11			6	12		14							
	4	5	3	8	8		13	7		11			14	6		12	10							

Waterman	Crosby	Bound	Robinson	Whitehead	Hunt	Oldfield	Omoyinmi	Savage	Ford	Basham	Scott	Ricketts	Hackett	Viveash	Powell	Gordon	Louis	Hunter	Sall	Steele	Edwards	Judge	McCarthy	Foley
9	4	5	14	13		12		7		11			2	6	3		10	8						

Waterman	Crosby	Bound	Robinson	Whitehead	Hunt	Oldfield	Omoyinmi	Savage	Ford	Basham	Scott	Ricketts	Hackett	Viveash	Powell	Gordon	Louis	Hunter	Sall	Steele	Edwards	Judge	McCarthy	Foley
31	53	48	48	11	44	23	4	50	35	30	31	0	2	15	5	3	15	14	0	3	5	1	6	4
2			1	11		10	16		6	6	10	2	12		12	4	24	5	2	8	1			2
2	7	1	1	1	2	3	3	4	1	8	11				2	1	7	1		3			1	

League Table

	P	W	D	L	F	A	Pts
Rushden & Diamonds	46	24	15	7	73	47	87
Hartlepool United	46	24	13	9	71	51	85
Wrexham	46	23	15	8	84	50	84
Bournemouth	46	20	14	12	60	48	74
Scunthorpe United	46	19	15	12	68	49	72
Lincoln City	46	18	16	12	46	37	70
Bury	46	18	16	12	57	56	70
Oxford United	46	19	12	15	57	47	69
Torquay United	46	16	18	12	71	71	66
York City	46	17	15	14	52	53	66
Kidderminster Harriers	46	16	15	15	62	63	63
Cambridge United	46	16	13	17	67	70	61
Hull City	46	14	17	15	58	53	59
Darlington	46	12	18	16	58	59	54
Boston United	46	15	13	18	55	56	54
Macclesfield Town	46	14	12	20	57	63	54
Southend United	46	17	3	26	47	59	54
Leyton Orient	46	14	11	21	51	61	53
Rochdale	46	12	16	18	63	70	52
Bristol Rovers	46	12	15	19	50	57	51
Swansea City	46	12	13	21	48	65	49
Carlisle United	46	13	10	23	52	78	49
Exeter City	46	11	15	20	50	64	48
Shrewsbury Town	46	9	14	23	62	92	41

2003-04

Division Three

Manager: Ian Atkins then Graham Rix

Did you know that?

United started the season strongly and were top of the table in January; however, they lost momentum and in March, with Oxford just outside the automatic promotion places, Ian Atkins was placed on gardening leave after allegedly speaking to Bristol Rovers about moving there the following season. He was replaced by Graham Rix, who failed to win any of his first eight games, and United finished the season outside the Play-offs.

Youth-team player Dexter Blackstock joined Southampton without having played for Oxford's first team. The fee, determined by a tribunal, was £275,000.

The attendance of 2,510 for the visit of Rushden & Diamonds in the LDV Vans Trophy was a new low crowd record for the Kassam Stadium.

Match No.	Date		Opponents	Result	(F-A)	Scorers
1	09/08/2003	A	Lincoln City	W	1-0	Basham
2	16/08/2003	H	Hull City	W	2-1	Basham (2)
3	23/08/2003	A	Scunthorpe United	D	1-1	Crosby (pen)
4	25/08/2003	H	Swansea City	W	3-0	Crosby (pen), Rawle, Alsop
5	30/08/2003	A	Kidderminster Harriers	D	1-1	Rawle
6	06/09/2003	H	Southend United	W	2-0	Wanless, Basham
7	13/09/2003	H	Mansfield Town	D	1-1	Wanless
8	16/09/2003	A	Cheltenham Town	D	0-0	
9	20/09/2003	A	Doncaster Rovers	L	0-2	
10	27/09/2003	H	Northampton Town	W	3-0	Whitehead, Basham (2)
11	01/10/2003	H	Torquay United	W	1-0	Alsop
12	04/10/2003	A	Boston United	D	1-1	Louis
13	11/10/2003	H	Yeovil Town	W	1-0	Basham
14	18/10/2003	A	Bury	W	4-0	Whitehead (2), Basham (2)
15	21/10/2003	A	York City	D	2-2	Hackett, Brass (og)
16	25/10/2003	H	Bristol Rovers	D	0-0	
17	01/11/2003	H	Darlington	W	3-1	Wanless, Whitehead, Rawle
18	15/11/2003	A	Cambridge United	D	1-1	Rawle
19	22/11/2003	H	Macclesfield Town	W	3-1	Wanless, Hunt, Alsop
20	29/11/2003	A	Rochdale	W	2-1	Basham, Alsop
21	13/12/2003	H	Carlisle United	W	2-1	Crosby (pen), Robinson
22	20/12/2003	A	Huddersfield Town	D	1-1	Rawle
23	26/12/2003	H	Leyton Orient	W	2-1	Crosby (pen), Alsop
24	28/12/2003	A	Southend United	W	1-0	Rawle
25	06/01/2004	A	Swansea City	D	0-0	
26	10/01/2004	H	Lincoln City	D	0-0	
27	17/01/2004	A	Hull City	L	2-4	Basham, Bound
28	31/01/2004	H	Kidderminster Harriers	W	2-1	Basham, McCarthy
29	07/02/2004	A	Leyton Orient	L	0-1	
30	11/02/2004	H	Scunthorpe United	W	3-2	Wanless, Steele, Rawle
31	14/02/2004	A	Yeovil Town	L	0-1	
32	21/02/2004	H	Bury	D	1-1	Whitehead
33	28/02/2004	A	Bristol Rovers	D	1-1	Rawle
34	03/03/2004	H	York City	D	0-0	
35	06/03/2004	H	Huddersfield Town	L	0-1	
36	13/03/2004	A	Carlisle United	L	0-2	
37	17/03/2004	H	Cheltenham Town	W	1-0	Crosby (pen)
38	27/03/2004	H	Doncaster Rovers	D	0-0	
39	03/04/2004	A	Northampton Town	L	1-2	Basham
40	06/04/2004	A	Mansfield Town	L	1-3	Whitehead
41	09/04/2004	H	Boston United	D	0-0	
42	12/04/2004	A	Torquay United	L	0-3	
43	17/04/2004	A	Darlington	L	0-2	
44	24/04/2004	H	Cambridge United	D	2-2	Louis, McCarthy
45	01/05/2004	A	Macclesfield Town	L	1-2	Hunt
46	08/05/2004	H	Rochdale	W	2-0	Whitehead, Basham

FA Cup

R1	08/11/2003	A	Colchester United	L	0-1	

League Cup

R1	12/08/2003	A	Millwall	W	1-0	Basham
R2	24/09/2003	H	Reading	L	1-3	Louis

LDV Vans

R1	15/10/2003	H	Rushden & Diamonds	L	0-1	

Total appea
Sub appea
Tota

Townsley	Crosby	Robinson	Bound	Wanless	Brown	Ashton	Basham	Alsop	Hackett	Whitehead	Oldfield	Hunt	Scott	Rawle	Waterman	McCarthy	Louis	Steele	Foran	Omoyinmi	Quinn	Cox	Pitt	Walker	Winters
3	4	5	6	7	8	9	10	11	12	13															
7	4	6	5	8	9	3	11	10		13	12														
7	3	6	4	8		2	11	10		14	13	9	12												
6	2	9	3	8	7	4	11	10		14		13		12											
7	4	6	5	8	9	3	10				11	13		12											
8	3	6	4	7	9	5	11	10				13		12	14										
7	4	6	5	8	9	3	10			13			14	11	12										
7	4	6	5	8		3	10		13	9		12	14	11											
7	4	6	5	8		3		11	12	9		13	10	14											
12		6	5	8		3	10	11		7		9	13			4	14								
		6	5	8		3	10	11		7		9				4	12								
		6	5	8		3	10		13	7		9	11	14		4	12								
13	12	6	5	8		3	10			7		9		14		4	11								
	4	6	5	8		3	10		14	7		9			13	12	11								
	4	6	5	8		3	10	11	12	7		9			14		13								
	4	6	5	8		3	10	11	12	7		9													
	4	6	5	8		3	10	11	12	7		9		13											
	4	6	5	8		3	10	14	13	7		9		12			11								
	4	6	5	8		3	10	11	12	7		9			14		13								
	4	6		8	9	2	10	11		7					3	5									
	4	6	12	8		3	10	11		7		9				5	13								
	4	6	5	8		13	10	11		7		9		12		3									
	4	6	5	8			10	11		7		9		12		3		13							
	4	6	5	8		12	10	11		7		9		13		3									
	4	6	5	8		12	10			7		9		13		3	11								
	4	6	3	8			10			9		7		13		5	11		12						
	4	6	5	8			10			7		9		12		3	13		11						
	4	6	13	8		3	10			7		9		14		5		12	11						
	4	6		8		3	10			7		9		12		5	14	13	11						
	4	6	14	7		3	9	10		12		8		11		5		13							
	4	6		7		3	10	11	12	13		8		9		5		14							
	4	6		8		3		11		7		9		12		5	13	10		14					
	4	6	5	8				11		7		9		10		3	12	13							
	4	6	5					11	12	8		9		14	13	3		10			7				
	4	6	5					10	12	7		9		11		3	13	14			8				
	4	6	5					11	13	7		9		10		3	14	12			8				
	4	6	5				10	11		7		9			12	3					8			13	
	3	5		8			11	12	6	7		9		13	2	4						1	10		
	3	5		8		14	10	13	6	7					2	4		12				1	9	11	
	3	5		8		4	11		6	7		9		10	2							1	12		
	3		12		5	4	11		6	7		8		13				14					9	10	
	3		5	7	9	4	10		13	6		8		11	2								12		
	4		5	8	6		10		13	7		9				3		12					14	11	
	3								6	7		8		11	2	4	12	13		10			9		
				5	2				6	7		8		13		4	11	10		14	12	1	9		
	2		5		9		10	11		6		8				4	14	12			7	1			13

Townsley	Crosby	Robinson	Bound	Wanless	Brown	Ashton	Basham	Alsop	Hackett	Whitehead	Oldfield	Hunt	Scott	Rawle	Waterman	McCarthy	Louis	Steele	Foran	Omoyinmi	Quinn	Cox	Pitt	Walker	Winters
	4		5	8		9	10	11	13	7		9		12	3		14								

Townsley	Crosby	Robinson	Bound	Wanless	Brown	Ashton	Basham	Alsop	Hackett	Whitehead	Oldfield	Hunt	Scott	Rawle	Waterman	McCarthy	Louis	Steele	Foran	Omoyinmi	Quinn	Cox	Pitt	Walker	Winters
7	3	6	4	9	10	5	11			8	12														
9	4	6	5			3		10	12	7		8	14	11			13								

Townsley	Crosby	Robinson	Bound	Wanless	Brown	Ashton	Basham	Alsop	Hackett	Whitehead	Oldfield	Hunt	Scott	Rawle	Waterman	McCarthy	Louis	Steele	Foran	Omoyinmi	Quinn	Cox	Pitt	Walker	Winters
7	4	6	5		9	3			11						8		10			12					

Townsley	Crosby	Robinson	Bound	Wanless	Brown	Ashton	Basham	Alsop	Hackett	Whitehead	Oldfield	Hunt	Scott	Rawle	Waterman	McCarthy	Louis	Steele	Foran	Omoyinmi	Quinn	Cox	Pitt	Walker	Winters
12	45	43	37	40	14	34	40	28	7	40	1	38	2	11	8	28	7	3	3	1	5	5	5	3	0
2	1		4			4		3	18	7	3	5	5	22	7	1	16	13	1	3	1		3	1	1
	5	1	1	5			15	5	1	7		2		8		2	3	1							

League Table

	P	W	D	L	F	A	Pts
Doncaster Rovers	46	27	11	8	79	37	92
Hull City	46	25	13	8	82	44	88
Torquay United	46	23	12	11	68	44	81
Huddersfield Town	46	23	12	11	68	52	81
Mansfield Town	46	22	9	15	76	62	75
Northampton Town	46	22	9	15	58	51	75
Lincoln City	46	19	17	10	68	47	74
Yeovil Town	46	23	5	18	70	57	74
Oxford United	46	18	17	11	55	44	71
Swansea City	46	15	14	17	58	61	59
Boston United	46	16	11	19	50	54	59
Bury	46	15	11	20	54	64	56
Cambridge United	46	14	14	18	55	67	56
Cheltenham Town	46	14	14	18	57	71	56
Bristol Rovers	46	14	13	19	50	61	55
Kidderminster Harriers	46	14	13	19	45	59	55
Southend United	46	14	12	20	51	63	54
Darlington	46	14	11	21	53	61	53
Leyton Orient	46	13	14	19	48	65	53
Macclesfield Town	46	13	13	20	54	69	52
Rochdale	46	12	14	20	49	58	50
Scunthorpe United	46	11	16	19	69	72	49
Carlisle United	46	12	9	25	46	69	45
York City	46	10	14	22	35	66	44

2004-05

League Two

Manager: Graham Rix, Darren Patterson (caretaker), Ramon Diaz, then David Oldfield (caretaker)

Did you know that?

On 14 November, after losing nine of the previous 10 games, Graham Rix was removed as manager and replaced by Darren Patterson, acting as caretaker. Three weeks later Firoz Kassam astonished everyone by announcing Ramon Díaz as the new manager, along with a backroom team that included Horacio Rodriguez as coach. At the end of the season, after negotiations for a contract extension failed, Kassam banned Díaz and the rest of the team, including Jean-Marc Goiran, the deal-broker, from the ground for the final game of the season, for which David Oldfield took charge.

In June 2004, Sunderland signed Dean Whitehead for a fee determined by a tribunal of £150,000 initially, plus £100,000 after Sunderland were promoted, plus £75,000 after 50 appearances, plus a 25% sell-on clause.

The arrival of Díaz saw an influx of foreign players at United, headed by Uruguayan Mateo Corbo, plus Argentinians Lucas Cominelli and Juan Pablo Raponi (as well as Díaz's sons Emiliano and Michael), and Frenchman Amine Karam.

There were only 1,842 spectators for the LDV Vans Trophy game against Exeter City, a new low crowd record for the Kassam Stadium.

Alan Judge broke his own record, again becoming the oldest player to play for the club when turning out in the 4–0 defeat at Southend United. He was 44 years and 176 days old.

Match No.	Date		Opponents	Result	(F-A)	Scorers	A
1	07/08/2004	A	Boston United	L	0-1		
2	11/08/2004	H	Mansfield Town	W	1-0	Mooney	
3	14/08/2004	H	Scunthorpe United	D	1-1	Mooney	
4	21/08/2004	A	Leyton Orient	D	0-0		
5	28/08/2004	H	Shrewsbury Town	W	2-0	Bradbury, Mooney	
6	30/08/2004	A	Notts County	W	1-0	Bradbury (pen)	
7	03/09/2004	A	Wycombe Wanderers	D	1-1	Roget	
8	11/09/2004	H	Rushden & Diamonds	D	0-0		
9	18/09/2004	A	Yeovil Town	L	1-6	Hand	
10	25/09/2004	H	Bury	W	3-1	Basham, Scott (og), Mooney	
11	02/10/2004	A	Bristol Rovers	L	0-2		
12	10/10/2004	H	Darlington	L	1-2	Woozley	
13	16/10/2004	H	Lincoln City	L	0-1		
14	19/10/2004	A	Northampton Town	L	0-1		
15	23/10/2004	A	Macclesfield Town	L	0-1		
16	30/10/2004	H	Cheltenham Town	W	1-0	Mooney	
17	06/11/2004	A	Southend United	L	0-4		
18	20/11/2004	H	Rochdale	L	0-1		
19	27/11/2004	A	Chester City	W	3-1	Basham, Robinson, E'Beyer	
20	08/12/2004	H	Swansea City	L	0-1		
21	11/12/2004	H	Cambridge United	W	2-1	Mooney, Davies	
22	17/12/2004	A	Grimsby Town	D	1-1	Mooney	
23	26/12/2004	A	Rushden & Diamonds	D	3-3	Hackett, Bradbury, Davies	
24	28/12/2004	H	Kidderminster Harriers	L	0-2		
25	01/01/2005	H	Wycombe Wanderers	W	2-1	Brooks, Basham	
26	03/01/2005	A	Bury	D	0-0		
27	08/01/2005	A	Darlington	D	1-1	Brooks	
28	15/01/2005	H	Yeovil Town	W	2-1	Mooney, Davies	
29	22/01/2005	A	Kidderminster Harriers	W	3-1	Hackett, Basham, Davies	
30	29/01/2005	H	Bristol Rovers	W	3-2	Bradbury (pen), Roget, Davies	
31	05/02/2005	A	Lincoln City	L	0-3		
32	12/02/2005	H	Northampton Town	L	1-2	Mooney	
33	19/02/2005	A	Cheltenham Town	W	1-0	Mooney	
34	26/02/2005	A	Cambridge United	L	1-2	Basham	
35	05/03/2005	H	Grimsby Town	L	1-2	Cominelli	
36	12/03/2005	A	Mansfield Town	W	3-1	Hackett (2), Basham	
37	19/03/2005	H	Boston United	W	2-0	Basham (2)	
38	25/03/2005	A	Scunthorpe United	D	1-1	Mooney	
39	28/03/2005	H	Leyton Orient	D	2-2	Basham, Mooney	
40	02/04/2005	A	Shrewsbury Town	L	0-3		
41	06/04/2005	H	Macclesfield Town	D	1-1	Wanless	
42	09/04/2005	H	Notts County	W	2-1	Mooney (2) (2 pens)	
43	15/04/2005	A	Swansea City	L	0-1		
44	23/04/2005	H	Southend United	W	2-1	Mooney, Davies	
45	30/04/2005	A	Rochdale	L	1-5	Robinson	
46	07/05/2005	H	Chester City	L	0-1		

FA Cup

R1	13/11/2004	A	Rochdale	L	1-2	Bradbury

League Cup

R1	25/08/2004	H	Reading	L	0-2	

LDV Vans

R1	29/09/2004	H	Exeter City	L*	2-2	Winters, Hand

*1-3 on pens

Total appea

Sub appea

Total

Ashton	Roget	Robinson	Hackett	Wolleaston	Wanless	Brown	Mooney	Bradbury	Louis	Parker	Basham	Molyneaux	Quinn	Alsop	Hand	Winters	Davies	Woozley	Cox	E'Beyer	Rawle	Togwell	Judge	Clarke	Brooks	Morgan	Doudou	Corbo	Cominelli	Beechers	Raponi	Diaz	Burton	Karam
3	4	5	**6**	7	8	9	10	11	12	13																								
3	4	5	**6**	7	8	13	11	10		*9*	12	14																						
4		5	14	7		*8*	11	10		12	13	3	**6**	9																				
5	4	3	6	11	9		7	8			13	12	*11*	14																				
3	**4**	5		8		9	11	10			6	12			7	13																		
3	4	9		8			11	**10**		5	6				7		12																	
3	4	**9**		7			11			5	6			10	8	12																		
3		9		7			11			5	6	**4**		*10*	8	13	14	12																
3	4	*9*		7			11	10		5	6	12		13	8					14														
	3	9	12	7	13		11	10		**5**	6				8			4																
	3	5	6	12	8		11	10			**9**				7			4																
	3	5	6	12	8		11	**10**			9		13		7			4																
	3	5	6	**9**	8		11				10		13		7			4			12													
	3	5	6	8			*11*	14			**10**		9		7			4	13		12													
3	**4**	5	14				11	10			6		7		8				1	*9*	13	12												
5	4	6	13				**11**	9			10		8						1	7	12	3												
5	4	6	13		14		11	10			*9*		8							**7**	12	3	1											
4	3	5	6		7			11			10		8				12			9		2			13									
4	3	5			8		**11**	10			9		7				12			6														
4	3	5	13		8		*11*	10			9		7				14			**6**					12									
	3	5	6	12			*10*	8					7				**11**	4			13			1	9	14								
	3	5	**6**	14	12		*10*	7					8				11	4						1	9	13								
	3	5	**6**	14			10	8				12	7				11	4		13				1	*9*									
	3	5	6	**8**	12			10					7				11	4							9	13								
	3	5	6	12			10	8			13	14	7				*11*	4							**9**									
4	3	5		**8**	14		11	*9*			10	6	7												13		12							
3	4	5			7		11	8			14	6					*10*	12		13					9									
4	3	9			**8**		10	6			14	12	7				*11*			13								5						
4	3	9	**6**				10	7			14		8				*11*								12			5	13					
4	3	9	*6*				**10**	8			13		7				11								14			5	12					
4	3	9	**6**				11	8					7				10											5	13	12				
	3	5	**6**				10	9			13		7				11								12			4	8					
3		5	6		12		10	**8**			14		7				*11*											4	13		9			
4	3		6				**10**	8			11		7				12	5													9			
3		5	6		12		11				*10*		7				14											4	8		9	13		
3	4	9	10					6			*11*		7				14											5	**8**		13	12		
4	3	5	**6**				10	9			*11*		7				12												8		13	14		
4	3	5	**6**		13		11	9			10	12	7																8					
4	3	5	6				11	13			10	2	7																**8**	12	9			
3		5	6		4		*11*	8			10	12	7				13												14		9			
		5	6		3		*11*	**9**			10		7				14											4	8		12	13		
		5	9		**3**		11				10		7				12											4	*8*		13	6		14
		5	11		3			9			10		7				13							12				4	*8*			6		14
3		5	**6**		4		*11*	9				12	7				10												8		13	14		
		5	6		3		11	**9**			10		7			12	13											4	8					
		9	6		4		*11*	8			10	3	7				13											5		14			12	

Ashton	Roget	Robinson	Hackett	Wolleaston	Wanless	Brown	Mooney	Bradbury	Louis	Parker	Basham	Molyneaux	Quinn	Alsop	Hand	Winters	Davies	Woozley	Cox	E'Beyer	Rawle	Togwell	Judge	Clarke	Brooks	Morgan	Doudou	Corbo	Cominelli	Beechers	Raponi	Diaz	Burton	Karam
		5	13		8		**11**	10			9		7					4		6		3			12									
3	4	5		8	7	*9*	11	10		14	**6**															12							13	
		5	13	7	14		10	**11**			6	3			8	9	12	4																
31	36	48	31	16	20	4	45	42	0	6	32	7	35	3	12	1	13	13	2	7	0	4	1	3	6	0	0	13	11	0	5	2	0	0
			8	6	9	1		2	1	3	10	10	2	2		4	16	2	1	4	6	1		1	7	4	1		5	3	5	5	2	2
	2	2	4		1		15	5			9				2	1	6	1		1					2				1					

League Table

	P	W	D	L	F	A	Pts
Yeovil Town	46	25	8	13	90	65	83
Scunthorpe United	46	22	14	10	69	42	80
Swansea City	46	24	8	14	62	43	80
Southend United	46	22	12	12	65	46	78
Macclesfield Town	46	22	9	15	60	49	75
Lincoln City	46	20	12	14	64	47	72
Northampton Town	46	20	12	14	62	51	72
Darlington	46	20	12	14	57	49	72
Rochdale	46	16	18	12	54	48	66
Wycombe Wanderers	46	17	14	15	58	52	65
Leyton Orient	46	16	15	15	65	67	63
Bristol Rovers	46	13	21	12	60	57	60
Mansfield Town	46	15	15	16	56	56	60
Cheltenham Town	46	16	12	18	51	54	60
Oxford United	46	16	11	19	50	63	59
Boston United	46	14	16	16	62	58	58
Bury	46	14	16	16	54	54	58
Grimsby Town	46	14	16	16	51	52	58
Notts County	46	13	13	20	46	62	52
Chester City	46	12	16	18	43	69	52
Shrewsbury Town	46	11	16	19	48	53	49
Rushden & Diamonds	46	10	14	22	42	63	44
Kidderminster Harriers	46	10	8	28	39	85	38
Cambridge United	46	8	16	22	39	62	30

2005-06

League Two

Manager: Brian Talbot, Darren Patterson then Jim Smith

Did you know that?

On 10 March Firoz Kassam announced that he was withdrawing from a hands-on role at the club and would be a non-executive chairman. He brought in Bill Smith and Brendon Cross as executive managers. Their first act was on 14 March, when they sacked Brian Talbot with United third from bottom. They appointed youth-team manager Darren Patterson as boss and gave him a one-and-a-half year contract. However, the takeover of the club by WPL meant that Patterson lasted less than three weeks in the post.

Woodstock Partners Ltd (WPL), headed by Ian Lenagan and fronted by former youth-team player Nick Merry, bought United from Firoz Kassam for £1 (plus £2 million of debt) in March, although Kassam continued to own the stadium. Merry immediately installed fellow director Jim Smith as manager, but the Oxford legend was unable to prevent the side from being relegated from the Football League for the first time since joining it in 1962.

In January, Hellas Verona paid £85,000 for Craig Davies, and Hearts paid £20,000 for Chris Hackett. Lee Bradbury was released after Brian Talbot refused to continue playing him so that a contract clause offering him an automatic extension was not invoked. Andy Burgess and John Dempster were signed from Rushden for £35,000 and £10,000 respectively. Yemi Odubade arrived from Eastbourne Borough for £15,000, with Tim Sills joining from Aldershot for £35,000.

United were relegated on the last day of the season after losing 3–2 at home to Orient, who won automatic promotion as a result. The 12,243 in attendance set a new ground record. A new low crowd record was set when the same side visited in the LDV Vans Trophy, with just 1,521 at the game.

Match No.	Date		Opponents	Result	(F-A)	Scorers
1	06/08/2005	A	Grimsby Town	D	1-1	Hargreaves
2	10/08/2005	H	Torquay United	W	1-0	Bradbury
3	13/08/2005	H	Wycombe Wanderers	D	2-2	Hackett, Morgan
4	20/08/2005	A	Lincoln City	L	1-2	Davies
5	27/08/2005	H	Stockport County	D	1-1	Roget
6	02/09/2005	A	Shrewsbury Town	L	0-2	
7	10/09/2005	H	Rushden & Diamonds	D	2-2	Roget, Sabin
8	13/09/2005	A	Bristol Rovers	D	1-1	Hackett
9	17/09/2005	A	Darlington	W	2-1	Davies, Sabin
10	24/09/2005	H	Bury	W	2-1	Bradbury (pen), Mansell
11	27/09/2005	A	Rochdale	W	1-0	Quinn
12	01/10/2005	A	Barnet	D	0-0	
13	07/10/2005	H	Carlisle United	W	1-0	Basham
14	14/10/2005	A	Northampton Town	L	0-1	
15	22/10/2005	H	Boston United	D	0-0	
16	29/10/2005	A	Leyton Orient	L	0-1	
17	12/11/2005	H	Wrexham	L	0-3	
18	19/11/2005	A	Carlisle United	L	1-2	Bradbury
19	26/11/2005	H	Grimsby Town	L	2-3	Basham (pen), Fitzgerald
20	06/12/2005	A	Cheltenham Town	W	2-1	Basham, Sabin
21	10/12/2005	A	Torquay United	D	3-3	Bradbury (pen), Sabin (2)
22	16/12/2005	H	Lincoln City	L	0-1	
23	26/12/2005	H	Notts County	W	3-0	Basham, Quinn, Sabin
24	31/12/2005	H	Mansfield Town	L	1-2	Bradbury
25	02/01/2006	A	Chester City	W	1-0	Basham
26	07/01/2006	H	Shrewsbury Town	L	0-3	
27	10/01/2006	A	Peterborough United	D	0-0	
28	14/01/2006	A	Macclesfield Town	D	1-1	Basham
29	21/01/2006	H	Darlington	L	0-2	
30	28/01/2006	A	Rushden & Diamonds	L	0-3	
31	04/02/2006	H	Rochdale	D	1-1	Ashton
32	15/02/2006	H	Macclesfield Town	D	1-1	E'Beyer
33	18/02/2006	H	Cheltenham Town	D	1-1	Basham (pen)
34	25/02/2006	A	Wycombe Wanderers	L	1-2	Odubade
35	11/03/2006	A	Stockport County	L	1-2	Sills
36	15/03/2006	H	Bristol Rovers	W	1-0	Basham (pen)
37	18/03/2006	A	Notts County	D	0-0	
38	21/03/2006	A	Bury	D	1-1	Burgess
39	25/03/2006	H	Peterborough United	W	1-0	N'Toya
40	01/04/2006	A	Mansfield Town	L	0-1	
41	08/04/2006	H	Chester City	L	0-1	
42	15/04/2006	H	Barnet	W	2-0	N'Toya (2)
43	17/04/2006	A	Boston United	L	0-1	
44	22/04/2006	H	Northampton Town	L	1-3	Willmott
45	29/04/2006	A	Wrexham	D	1-1	N'Toya (pen)
46	06/05/2006	H	Leyton Orient	L	2-3	Willmott, Sabin

FA Cup

R1	05/11/2005	A	Eastbourne Borough	D	1-1	Basham
r	16/11/2005	H	Eastbourne Borough	W	3-0	Basham (3) (1 pen)
R2	03/12/2005	A	Cheltenham Town	D	1-1	Sabin
r	13/12/2005	H	Cheltenham Town	L	1-2	Basham

League Cup

R1	23/08/2005	A	Gillingham	L	0-1	

LDV Vans

R1	18/10/2005	A	Brentford	W*	1-1	Roget
R2	23/11/2005	H	Leyton Orient	W	1-0	Sabin
R3	20/12/2005	A	Cheltenham Town	L	1-2	Mansell

*4-3 on pens

Total appea
Sub appea
Total

Willmott	Ashton	Robinson	Hackett	Quinn	Hargreaves	Gray	Bradbury	Basham	Hughes	Davies	Morgan	Stirling	Roget	Campbell	Sabin	Griffin	E'Beyer	Fitzgerald	Roach	Tardif	Burgess	Dempster	Odubade	Brooks	Weedon	Sills	Goodhind	Guatelli	Smith	N'toya	Horsted	Gemmill	Beechers
3	4	5	6	7	8	**9**	10	11	12	13																							
3	4	5	6	7	8	9	11	**10**		12																							
3	4	5	6	7	8	9	**10**	13		11	12																						
3	**4**	5	6	7	8	9	*10*		13	11	14	12																					
	4	5	6	7	8	9		12		10	**11**	13	3																				
	3	5	6	7	8	**9**	*11*	10	12				4	13	14																		
	4	5	6		8	9	12			13		**2**	3	10	11																		
3		5	6	7	8	**9**	12			13			4	10	11																		
3	2	9	5	7			8			12			4	**10**	11																		
3	4	9	**5**	6			8	13		11		12	2		10																		
4	2	5		7			8	9		11			3		10																		
4	2	5		7			8	9		10			3		11																		
4	2	8	9	6			7	11					3		10																		
4	**3**	6	9	7				8		11			5	12	10																		
3	4	9	5	7			8	**10**		12			2		11																		
4	**2**	5	6	8	13		9	14		*11*		12	3		10																		
3	4	9	12	**6**	7		8	10		14			2		*11*	13																	
4		5	6	7	8		13	10		11		3				**9**	12																
4		5	6	7	8			13					3		**10**	9		11	12														
4	13	5		7	8		6	10		12			**3**		11	9																	
4	2	5		7	8		6	**10**		12			3		11	9																	
4	2	5	12	7	8					9			3		11			10															
4	3	5	9	8			12	10				2			11		**6**		13	1													
4	3	5	9	8			6	*10*				**2**	12		11			14	13	1													
4	3	5		8			6	10				2			11	9				1													
	4	5	6	8			7	10		13		**2**	3		11	9	12			1													
4	2	5		7	8			10					3		11	9				1													
3	2	5		7	8			11					4		10	**9**			13	1	12												
5	7	3		**4**	8			10					6		9		12		13	1	11												
5	7			4	8			12											9	1	3	6	**10**	11	13								
	7	3		4	8			10					6							1	9				5	11							
12	5	3		4	8			10					6				7				**9**					11							
13	5	3		4	8	9		10					6				7			**1**			14			11							
13	5	3		**4**	8	9		10					6								7		14			11	12						
9	5	3			8			10													7		6			11	4						
5		3		7	8			10					6										**9**	12		11	4						
5		3		7	8			10					6										**9**	12		11	4						
5		3		7	8								6								9		12	**10**		11	4						
5		3		7	8			14					6								**9**			12		*11*		1	4	10	13		
5		3		7	8			*11*														6		**3**		14	12	1	4	10	9	13	
5		3		7	8			*11*							10						9	6				13		1	**4**	14	12		
5		3		7	8			*11*					6		9						14			12		13			**4**	10			
5	4	**3**		7	8			12					6		9						13			*11*						10	14		
4		3		7	8			12					5		**9**						11	6	13							10			
5		3		7	8			*11*							9					12	4	6				14		**1**	13	10			
5		3		4	11			13							7						9	6		12					*10*	8			14

3	2	5		7	8		9	11					4		10																		
4		5	6	7	8		13	10		9		12	**3**		11																		
4		5		7	8		6	**10**		12			3		11	9																	
4		5	6	7			8	10		12			3		11	**9**	13																

		5	13	7		8	**6**	14	9	*11*	10	3	4							1													12

4		5	6	7			8	10	**9**	11		2	3							1													12
4		5	**6**	7	8		13	10					3		11	9	12																
4		5	13	7				14		12		2	3		10	9	**6**		*11*	1													

45	33	52	23	52	38	11	23	36	2	13	2	9	40	3	34	12	4	2	2	13	12	6	4	4	1	9	4	4	5	7	1	0	0
3	1		4		1		6	12	3	13	2	5	1	2	1	1	5	1	5	1	3		4	5	1	4	2		1	1	3	1	3
2	1		2	2	1		5	13		2	1		3		9		1	1			1		1			1				4			

League Table

	P	W	D	L	F	A	Pts
Carlisle United	46	25	11	10	84	42	86
Northampton Town	46	22	17	7	63	37	83
Leyton Orient	46	22	15	9	67	51	81
Grimsby Town	46	22	12	12	64	44	78
Cheltenham Town	46	19	15	12	65	53	72
Wycombe Wanderers	46	18	17	11	72	56	71
Lincoln City	46	15	21	10	65	53	66
Darlington	46	16	15	15	58	52	63
Peterborough United	46	17	11	18	57	49	62
Shrewsbury Town	46	16	13	17	55	55	61
Boston United	46	15	16	15	50	60	61
Bristol Rovers	46	17	9	20	59	67	60
Wrexham	46	15	14	17	61	54	59
Rochdale	46	14	14	18	66	69	56
Chester City	46	14	12	20	53	59	54
Mansfield Town	46	13	15	18	59	66	54
Macclesfield Town	46	12	18	16	60	71	54
Barnet	46	12	18	16	44	57	54
Bury	46	12	17	17	45	57	53
Torquay United	46	13	13	20	53	66	52
Notts County	46	12	16	18	48	63	52
Stockport County	46	11	19	16	57	78	52
Oxford United	46	11	16	19	43	57	49
Rushden & Diamonds	46	11	12	23	44	76	45

2006-07

Football Conference

Manager: Jim Smith

Did you know that?

Oxford set a new Conference record by going unbeaten in their opening 19 games. They were overtaken at the top by Dagenham & Redbridge on New Year's Day.

United set a new Conference attendance record when 11,065 attended the Boxing Day draw with Woking.

When United met Exeter City in the Play-off semi-finals at the end of the season, it was Oxford's first appearance in any Play-offs.

United's youth team, under Darren Patterson, won the Youth Alliance South West Conference title without losing a game.

In April, Patterson was promoted to assistant manager following the dismissal of Andy Awford and reserve-team coach Shaun North.

Match No.	Date		Opponents	Result	(F-A)	Scorers	A
1	12/08/2006	H	Halifax Town	W	2-0	Burgess, Duffy (pen)	
2	15/08/2006	A	Dagenham and Redbridge	W	1-0	Odubade	
3	18/08/2006	A	Burton Albion	W	2-1	Duffy (2) (1 pen)	
4	26/08/2006	H	Northwich Victoria	W	5-1	Basham, Odubade, Duffy, Pettefer, Johnson	
5	28/08/2006	A	Weymouth	D	1-1	Hargreaves	
6	01/09/2006	H	St Albans City	W	2-1	Odubade, Day	
7	09/09/2006	A	Morecambe	W	3-0	Gilchrist, Basham, Burgess	
8	12/09/2006	H	Exeter City	W	1-0	Basham	
9	16/09/2006	H	Grays Athletic	d	1-1	Basham	
10	18/09/2006	A	Crawley Town	W	1-0	Day	
11	23/09/2006	A	Stafford Rangers	W	1-0	Duffy	
12	30/09/2006	H	York City	W	2-0	Burgess, Duffy	
13	03/10/2006	H	Southport	D	2-2	Duffy (2) (2 pens)	
14	06/10/2006	A	Forest Green Rovers	W	5-1	Hargreaves, Odubade, Duffy (3)	
15	10/10/2006	A	Kidderminster Harriers	D	0-0		
16	14/10/2006	H	Altrincham	D	1-1	Day	
17	20/10/2006	A	Cambridge United	W	3-0	Hargreaves, Odubade (2)	
18	04/11/2006	H	Aldershot	W	2-0	Burgess (2) (1 pen)	
19	18/11/2006	A	Ebbsfleet United	L	0-1		
20	25/11/2006	H	Tamworth	W	2-1	Day, Duffy (pen)	
21	02/12/2006	A	Stevenage Borough	D	2-2	Hargreaves, Duffy	
22	09/12/2006	A	Rushden & Diamonds	L	0-1		
23	26/12/2006	H	Woking	D	0-0		
24	30/12/2006	H	Crawley Town	D	1-1	Duffy	
25	01/01/2007	A	Exeter City	L	1-2	Burgess (pen)	
26	06/01/2007	H	Morecambe	D	0-0		
27	20/01/2007	A	Grays Athletic	D	2-2	Duffy (2) (1 pen)	
28	23/01/2007	A	Woking	L	0-1		
29	29/01/2007	H	Rushden & Diamonds	L	0-1		
30	03/02/2007	H	Cambridge United	D	1-1	Odhiambo-Anaclet	
31	10/02/2007	A	Aldershot	D	1-1	Odubade	
32	17/02/2007	H	Ebbsfleet United	W	1-0	Duffy	
33	24/02/2007	A	Tamworth	W	3-1	Odubade, Odhiambo-Anaclet, Duffy (pen)	
34	03/03/2007	H	Stevenage Borough	W	2-0	Day, Odhiambo-Anaclet	
35	06/03/2007	A	Southport	W	1-0	Rose	
36	10/03/2007	H	Forest Green Rovers	L	0-2		
37	13/03/2007	H	Kidderminster Harriers	L	0-1		
38	17/03/2007	A	Altrincham	W	3-0	Robinson, Odhiambo-Anaclet, Corcoran	
39	21/03/2007	A	Halifax Town	D	1-1	Robinson	
40	26/03/2007	H	Dagenham and Redbridge	D	2-2	Odubade (2)	
41	31/03/2007	H	Burton Albion	D	0-0		
42	07/04/2007	A	Northwich Victoria	L	0-1		
43	09/04/2007	H	Weymouth	W	4-1	Quinn, Hargreaves, Robinson, Zebroski	
44	14/04/2007	A	St Albans City	W	2-0	Odubade, L Foster	
45	21/04/2007	H	Stafford Rangers	W	2-0	Daniel (og), Zebroski	
46	28/04/2007	A	York City	L	0-1		
POSF	04/05/2007	A	Exeter City	W	1-0	Taylor (og)	
POSF	08/05/2007	H	Exeter City	L*	1-2	Odubade	

*3-4 on pens

FA Cup

4Q	28/10/2006	A	Dagenham and Redbridge	W	1-0	Duffy (pen)
R1	11/11/2006	A	Wycombe Wanderers	L	1-2	Johnson

FA Trophy

R1	16/12/2006	A	Lewes FC	D	0-0	
r	09/01/2007	H	Lewes FC	W	1-0	Duffy (pen)
R2	13/01/2007	H	Halifax Town	D	2-2	Robinson, Rose
r	16/01/2007	A	Halifax Town	L	1-2	Duffy

Total appea

Sub appea

Total

Day	Quinn	Gilchrist	Johnson	Hutchinson	Dempster	Pettefer	Burgess	Duffy	Odubade	Hargreaves	Basham	Willmott	Robinson	Brevett	Slabber	Tardif	Kennet	Gunn	Santos	Rose	Grebis	Coombes	Corcoran	Foster, M	Foster, L	Zebroski	Beechers
3	4	5	6	**7**	8	9	10	*11*	12	13	14																
3	4	5	6	**7**	8	9	10	11	13	12																	
2		3	5	12	**4**	9	8	11	13	7	10																
12	4	5	**6**	13		7	9	*11*	14	8	10	3															
12	4	5	6	13		7	9	11	14	8	*10*	3															
12	3	4	**9**	14		6	8	*11*	13	7		2	10														
12	4	5		8	13	7	9		14		*10*	3	11	6													
4	3			**7**	12	6	8		13		10	2	11	9													
	4	5		8		7	9		12		10	3	11	6													
5	4				12	7	9	13	14	8	10	3	*11*	**6**													
5	4			13	**8**	7		11	12	9	10	3		6													
12	4	5		8	13	7	9	*11*	14		10	3		**6**													
12	4	**5**		8		7	9	11	14	13	*10*	3		6													
6	4	5			13	7	9	11	12	8	**10**	3															
12	4	5		14		7	9	11	13	8	*10*	3		**6**													
6	4	5			3	7	9	11	10	8																	
13	4	5		14	12	7	9		11	8	10	3		6													
	4	5	12	13		7	9	*11*	10	8	14	3		**6**													
12	4	5	14			7	9		13	8	10	3		**6**	*11*												
5	4		6	**7**		12	9	11	13	8		3			10												
3	8	5	6		14	7	10	11	13	9		4				12											
12	**4**	5	6		3	7	9	11	13	8	10				14												
3	4	5		*12*	**8**	7	9	11	13	14	10			6													
3	4	5	*6*		13	7	9	11	10	8	14			12													
3	4	**5**	14		10	7	9			8	*11*			6			13	12									
12	4	**5**	6			7	9	11	10										3	8							
12	4	5				7		11	13	8				6					3	9	10						
2	4	5	6		13	7		11	12	8			14						3	9	10						
	4	5	12				9	11	14				13	**6**		1		3		8	*10*	7					
	2	4	12				14	10	11	8			13	**5**		1				*9*			3	7			
		4	5				13	*10*	6	8			11			1		12		9	14		3	7			
	2	4	5			12	13	*11*	10	8			14							9			3	7			
12	**2**	4	5				13	*10*	11	8			14							9			3	7			
2		4	5			12	9	10	11				13							8			3	**7**			
2	13	4	5				9	*10*	11	14			12							8			3	7			
2		4	**5**				9	10	11	12			13							8			3	7			
		4				7	13	*10*		14			11	5						9			2	**8**	3		
12	4		6			13	14		*11*	8			10							9			3	7	5		
	5					7				8			10	6						9			3		4	11	
	3	4	5			**7**	9	14	10	13			12							8					2	*11*	
12	5		**14**				*6*	11	9	8										13			3	7	4	10	
2	4					**6**		13	10	8			*11*	5						9			3	7		14	
13	3	4	**5**						10	8			14							*9*			2	7	12	11	
2	4	5	**6**			7	13		*10*	8			14							9			3		12	11	
5	4		14			7	6	**10**	12	9													3	8	2	11	
8	5		*6*	13		7		10	12					14		1				9			4		3	11	
3	4	5					6	13	10	8				12						9				7		11	
3	4	5	14			13	6	12	10	8										*9*				7		11	

Day	Quinn	Gilchrist	Johnson	Hutchinson	Dempster	Pettefer	Burgess	Duffy	Odubade	Hargreaves	Basham	Willmott	Robinson	Brevett	Slabber	Tardif	Kennet	Gunn	Santos	Rose	Grebis	Coombes	Corcoran	Foster, M	Foster, L	Zebroski	Beechers
3	4	5		12		7	**9**	11	13	8	10			6													
14	4	5	12	**9**	13	7			11	8	10	3		*6*													

Day	Quinn	Gilchrist	Johnson	Hutchinson	Dempster	Pettefer	Burgess	Duffy	Odubade	Hargreaves	Basham	Willmott	Robinson	Brevett	Slabber	Tardif	Kennet	Gunn	Santos	Rose	Grebis	Coombes	Corcoran	Foster, M	Foster, L	Zebroski	Beechers
	3	5	*9*	7	4	13	14	11	10	8	12			6													
4	3		8		2	7	**9**	10	6				11	5													
5	4		6			7		11	9	12			**10**						3	8							
13	4					**7**		10	9	6			11	5					3	8							12

Day	Quinn	Gilchrist	Johnson	Hutchinson	Dempster	Pettefer	Burgess	Duffy	Odubade	Hargreaves	Basham	Willmott	Robinson	Brevett	Slabber	Tardif	Kennet	Gunn	Santos	Rose	Grebis	Coombes	Corcoran	Foster, M	Foster, L	Zebroski	Beechers
26	48	41	26	10	10	39	36	38	26	36	19	18	13	24	2	4	0	1	5	23	3	1	16	15	7	9	0
18	1		9	11	10	6	8	5	26	9	4		11	3	1	1	1	2		1	1				2	1	1
5	1	1	2			1	6	21	12	5	4		4							2			1		1	2	

League Table

	P	W	D	L	F	A	Pts
Dagenham & Redbridge	46	28	11	7	93	48	95
Oxford United	46	22	15	9	66	33	81
Morecambe	46	23	12	11	64	46	81
York City	46	23	11	12	65	45	80
Exeter City	46	22	12	12	67	48	78
Burton Albion	46	22	9	15	52	47	75
Gravesend & Northfleet	46	21	11	14	63	56	74
Stevenage Borough	46	20	10	16	76	66	70
Aldershot	46	18	11	17	64	62	65
Kidderminster Harriers	46	17	12	17	43	50	63
Weymouth	46	18	9	19	56	73	63
Rushden & Diamonds	46	17	11	18	58	54	62
Northwich Victoria	46	18	4	24	51	69	58
Forest Green Rovers	46	13	18	15	59	64	57
Woking	46	15	12	19	56	61	57
Halifax Town	46	15	10	21	55	62	55
Cambridge United	46	15	10	21	57	66	55
Crawley Town	46	17	12	17	52	52	53
Grays Athletic	46	13	13	20	56	55	52
Stafford Rangers	46	14	10	22	49	71	52
Altrincham	46	13	12	21	53	67	51
Tamworth	46	13	9	24	43	61	48
Southport	46	11	14	21	57	67	47
St Albans City	46	10	10	26	57	89	40

2007-08

Football Conference

Manager: Jim Smith then Darren Patterson

Did you know that?

Jim Smith stood down as manager to concentrate on his directorial duties after United were thrashed 5–0 at Rushden, live on TV. He was replaced by assistant manager Darren Patterson.

There were just 1,508 in attendance for the FA Trophy game against Tonbridge Angels. This was the lowest crowd to watch a first-team competitive game at the Kassam Stadium.

United's end-of-season run saw them win nine of their last 11 games.

Billy Turley's 19 clean sheets set a new club record.

United used 41 players during the season, a new club record.

Match No.	Date		Opponents	Result	(F-A)	Scorers
1	11/08/2007	H	Forest Green Rovers	W	1-0	Twigg (pen)
2	16/08/2007	A	Cambridge United	L	1-2	Twigg
3	19/08/2007	A	Burton Albion	W	2-1	Odubade, Twigg
4	25/08/2007	H	Stafford Rangers	W	2-1	Trainer (2)
5	27/08/2007	A	Stevenage Borough	D	0-0	
6	01/09/2007	H	Halifax Town	D	1-1	Duffy
7	04/09/2007	H	Exeter City	D	2-2	Duffy (2) (2 pens)
8	08/09/2007	A	Altrincham	W	3-1	Odubade, Day, Shaw
9	11/09/2007	A	Grays Athletic	D	0-0	
10	15/09/2007	H	Aldershot	L	2-3	Jeannin, Shaw
11	20/09/2007	A	Histon	L	0-1	
12	25/09/2007	H	Salisbury City	W	2-1	Odubade, Duffy (pen)
13	30/09/2007	H	York City	D	1-1	Corcoran
14	06/10/2007	A	Droylsden	L	1-3	Odubade
15	11/10/2007	H	Torquay United	D	3-3	Odubade (2), Hutchinson
16	14/10/2007	A	Farsley Celtic	W	1-0	Trainer
17	20/10/2007	H	Woking	D	0-0	
18	01/11/2007	A	Rushden & Diamonds	L	0-5	
19	17/11/2007	H	Ebbsfleet United	D	0-0	
20	24/11/2007	A	Kidderminster Harriers	W	2-0	Barnes, Green
21	08/12/2007	A	Northwich Victoria	L	0-1	
22	26/12/2007	H	Crawley Town	W	1-0	Trainer
23	29/12/2007	H	Kidderminster Harriers	D	0-0	
24	01/01/2008	A	Crawley Town	L	0-2	
25	05/01/2008	H	Altrincham	W	4-0	Duffy (2) (1 pen), Fisher, McAllister
26	08/01/2008	H	Weymouth	L	0-1	
27	12/01/2008	A	Salisbury City	L	1-3	Odubade
28	20/01/2008	A	Exeter City	L	0-2	
29	26/01/2008	H	Grays Athletic	D	0-0	
30	29/01/2008	A	Aldershot	L	0-1	
31	09/02/2008	H	Histon	W	3-0	Green (2), Howard
32	16/02/2008	H	Droylsden	W	1-0	Quinn
33	01/03/2008	A	Forest Green Rovers	D	0-0	
34	04/03/2008	H	Cambridge United	L	1-2	Green
35	08/03/2008	H	Burton Albion	L	0-3	
36	15/03/2008	A	Stafford Rangers	W	1-0	Green
37	22/03/2008	A	Halifax Town	W	3-0	Santos Gaia (og), Murray (pen), Richards
38	24/03/2008	H	Stevenage Borough	W	2-1	Trainer, Green
39	29/03/2008	H	Northwich Victoria	L	0-1	
40	05/04/2008	A	Weymouth	W	1-0	Trainer
41	08/04/2008	A	Torquay United	L	2-3	Murray (pen), McAllister
42	12/04/2008	H	Farsley Celtic	W	5-1	Odubade, Trainer, Green (2), Murray (pen)
43	15/04/2008	A	York City	W	1-0	Odhiambo-Anaclet
44	19/04/2008	A	Woking	W	2-1	Odubade, Trainer
45	22/04/2008	H	Rushden & Diamonds	W	1-0	Odubade
46	26/04/2008	A	Ebbsfleet United	W	3-1	Trainer, Green (2)

FA Cup

4Q	27/10/2007	A	Merthyr Tydfil	W	2-1	Rhodes (2)
1	10/11/2007	H	Northwich Victoria	W	3-1	Odubade (pen), Odhiambo-Anaclet, Jeannin
2	01/12/2007	H	Southend United	D	0-0	
2R	11/12/2007	A	Southend United	L	0-3	

FA Trophy

1	15/12/2007	H	Tonbridge	D	0-0
1R	18/12/2007	A	Tonbridge	L	0-1

Setanta Shield

4	22/12/2007	A	Aldershot	L	0-1

League Table

	P	W	D	L	F	A	Pts
Aldershot	46	31	8	7	82	48	101
Cambridge United	46	25	11	10	68	41	86
Torquay United	46	26	8	12	83	57	86
Exeter City	46	22	17	7	83	58	83
Burton Albion	46	23	12	11	79	56	81
Stevenage Borough	46	24	7	15	82	55	79
Histon	46	20	12	14	76	67	72
Forest Green Rovers	46	19	14	13	76	59	71
Oxford United	46	20	11	15	56	48	71

	P	W	D	L	F	A	Pts
Grays Athletic	46	19	13	14	58	47	70
Ebbsfleet United	46	19	12	15	65	61	69
Salisbury City	46	18	14	14	70	60	68
Kidderminster Harriers	46	19	10	17	74	57	67
York City	46	17	11	18	71	74	62
Crawley Town	46	19	9	18	73	67	60
Rushden & Diamonds	46	15	14	17	55	55	59
Woking	46	12	17	17	53	61	53
Weymouth	46	11	13	22	53	73	46

Total appea

Sub appea

Tota

	P	W	D	L	F	A
Northwich Victoria	46	11	11	24	52	78
Halifax Town	46	12	16	18	61	70
Altrincham	46	9	14	23	56	82
Farsley Celtic	46	10	9	27	48	86
Stafford Rangers	46	5	10	31	42	99
Droylsden	46	5	9	32	46	103

Gnohere	Quinn	Day	Jeannin	Hutchinson	Standing	Trainer	Duffy	Ledgister	Pettefer	Twigg	Corcoran	Foster	Odubade	Rose	Shaw	Tardif	Robinson	Willmott	Gilchrist	Bailey	Rhodes	St Aimee	Fisher	Collins	Benjamin	Clarke	Green	Barnes	Taylor	Murray	McAllister	Weedon	Howard	Richards	Blackwood	Hand	Sample	Warrell
3	4	5	6	7	**8**	9	10	*11*	12	13			14																									
5	4	3	6	7		9	*11*		**8**	10		12	13				14																					
	4	5	6	**7**		9		13	12	10	3	8	*11*				14																					
	4	5	6	7	**8**	9	14			10	3		*11*	12			13																					
12	4	5	6	7		9	14		8	*11*	3		10	13																								
	4	5	6			8	**11**		7		3	13	14	9	*10*		12																					
	4	5	6		7	9	*10*				3		13	8	11	12	14																					
5	4	2	6	**7**		8	10		12		3		9	14	*11*	1	13																					
5	4	2	6	7	12	**9**	13		8		3		10		*11*		14																					
5	4	2	6	14		8	10		7		3		13		9		*11*																					
5	4	3	6	**7**	12	9	14						10	13	8		*11*																					
	3	4	9	6		8	11				2		10	12	**7**																							
	3	4	8	6		7	*11*		13	14	2		10		9			12																				
5	8	**2**	6	7		9			12	13		3	10		11			4																				
		12	6	7		9			8		3	**2**	10					4	5	11	13																	
		13	5	12		8			6			2	10	9				3	4	**7**	*11*		14															
	3	5	9	13	12	8			6			2	10					**4**		7	*11*		14															
	10	5	*9*			8			12			2	14					3	**4**	7	11	6	13															
	3		9	6		8	12		7			4	10									*11*	14	2	13													
	3		5	8		9			7	14		4	10					12								2	*11*	13										
	3	8	5	7				14		9	12	4	13													2	10	*11*										
	3	**2**	5	8		9	11	6	7	13		4	10													12												
	3		5	8		9	10	**6**	7		4		11													2		13	12									
	3	8	5	7		9	14	*11*	6		13	4	10													**2**			12									
		2	5			8	*11*	9	12		3	4	**6**										14			13				7	10							
	3	**2**	5			8	10	6	14		4		9										13			12				**7**	*11*							
	7		5	12		*9*	11		6		3	4	10										14			2				8		13						
		3	12			8	11	13	7			4		9									*10*		14	2						**5**						
	3			14		8						4	**9**	12												2	10		13	7			5	*11*				
	3	12		7		9						4	14	13												**2**	*10*			8			5	11				
	3	2		7								4	6										13			12	10			8			**5**	11	9			
	3	2		8								4	14	13													*10*			7	12		5	11	9			
	3											4														2	13			8	10		5	11	9	7	12	
	3	2										4	12														11			8	10		5	13	9	7		
	3					**9**						4	9	12												2	*10*			7	11		5	14	13	6		
	3	2				**9**						4		12													10			8	13		5	11		7		
	3	2				9						4											13				**10**			7	12		5	11		8		
	3	2				9						4		12													11			7	13			10	5	8		
	3	2				9						4	13														10			8	14		5	*11*	12	**7**		
	3	4				9							12													2	**10**			7	13		5	11		8		
	3	2				9						4	12														**10**			8	11		5	13		7		
	3	2		8		**9**						4	10	12													14			7	*11*		5	13				
	4	5				9							**10**													3	11			7	13		6	12		8		
	3	4		14		9							10	12												2	13			7	*11*		**5**			8		
	3	2				**9**						4	10	12													13			7	11		5			8		
	3	2				9						**4**	10	13												12	*11*			7	14		5			8		
	7				14	8			12		3	2	10	*9*				4		6	11		13									**5**						
	4	**2**	6			9			8			5	10							7		11	13	3														
	3		5	7		8		13		**9**		4	12													2	10	11										
	3	**5**		7		8	13	6		9		4	10										14			2		*11*				12						
	3		5	8		9	*11*	6	7	13		4	10	**12**												2		14										
	3	12	6	7		8	11		**6**	9		4	14										13			2		*10*										1
	8	2	5				10	6	7		3	4	11	**9**														12	13									1
7	49	39	32	26	3	47	17	9	19	8	17	36	33	6	9	1	2	6	3	6	4	3	1	2	0	17	17	4	0	21	9	2	17	10	5	13	0	2
1		4	1	6	4		7	4	9	6	2	2	15	16		1	7	2			1		13		2	5	4	4	4		8	2		5	2		1	
	1	1	2	1		9	6			3	1		11		2						2		1				10	1		3	2		1	1				

2008-09

Football Conference

Manager: Darren Patterson, then Jim Smith (caretaker) then Chris Wilder

Did you know that?

On 2 October Kelvin Thomas took over as chairman following Nick Merry's resignation.

After being knocked out of the FA Cup by Torquay United, Darren Patterson was dismissed. Jim Smith took over for four games while a replacement was recruited, with Chris Wilder taking up the post just before Christmas.

At the start of January it was announced that Oxford were to be deducted points for fielding an unregistered player. Midfielder Eddie Hutchinson had been placed on the transfer list at the start of the season and had not been registered with the Conference. United were eventually docked five points.

The 383 present at the Forest Green Rovers game in the Setanta Shield formed the third-lowest crowd to have watched United in a competitive first-team game for which records exist, and the lowest attendance since Oxford left the Southern League.

Match No.	Date		Opponents	Result	(F-A)	Scorers
1	08/08/2008	A	Barrow	L	0-3	
2	12/08/2008	H	Weymouth	L	0-1	
3	16/08/2008	H	Eastbourne Borough	W	6-3	Pullen (own goal), Quinn, Hutchinson, Constable (2), Reid
4	21/08/2008	A	Wrexham	L	0-2	
5	25/08/2008	H	Woking	D	0-0	
6	30/08/2008	A	Ebbsfleet United	D	1-1	Reid
7	02/09/2008	A	Northwich Victoria	W	2-1	Constable (2)
8	06/09/2008	H	Kettering Town	D	1-1	Odubade
9	13/09/2008	A	Kidderminster Harriers	L	0-1	
10	20/09/2008	H	Crawley Town	L	1-2	Odubade (pen)
11	23/09/2008	H	Cambridge United	W	3-1	Murray, Guy, Haldane
12	27/09/2008	A	Lewes FC	L	1-2	Burnell
13	04/10/2008	H	Rushden & Diamonds	W	2-1	Quinn, Trainer
14	09/10/2008	A	Torquay United	D	1-1	Trainer
15	12/10/2008	A	Altrincham	L	0-1	
16	18/10/2008	H	Burton Albion	W	2-1	Trainer, Constable (pen)
17	01/11/2008	H	York City	W	1-0	Odubade (pen)
18	15/11/2008	A	Grays Athletic	L	0-2	
19	22/11/2008	A	Histon	L	2-5	Willmott, Hutchinson
20	25/11/2008	H	Kidderminster Harriers	W	1-0	Constable (pen)
21	04/12/2008	A	Mansfield Town	W	3-1	Constable, Guy, Deering
22	09/12/2008	A	Weymouth	D	2-2	Robinson (own goal), Day
23	20/12/2008	H	Stevenage Borough	D	1-1	Constable
24	26/12/2008	A	Salisbury City	L	1-2	Deering
25	28/12/2008	H	Ebbsfleet United	W	5-1	Odubade, Trainer, Fisher, Constable, Haldane
26	01/01/2009	H	Salisbury City	W	2-0	Constable, Sappleton
27	17/01/2009	H	Altrincham	W	1-0	Constable
28	20/01/2009	H	Forest Green Rovers	W	2-1	Odubade, Constable
29	24/01/2009	A	Crawley Town	W	1-0	Murray
30	29/01/2009	A	Cambridge United	D	1-1	Murray
31	01/02/2009	H	Lewes FC	W	2-1	Foster, Murray
32	14/02/2009	H	Barrow	W	3-0	Odubade, Farrell, Haldane
33	21/02/2009	H	Mansfield Town	W	1-0	Nelthorpe
34	28/02/2009	H	Torquay United	L	0-2	
35	07/03/2009	A	Forest Green Rovers	D	3-3	Murray, Constable (2) (2 pens)
36	14/03/2009	H	Grays Athletic	W	4-1	Constable (2), Chapman, Sandwith
37	03/03/2009	A	Eastbourne Borough	W	3-0	Murray, Farrell, Clist
38	19/03/2009	A	Kettering Town	W	2-1	Willmott, Nelthorpe
39	24/03/2009	A	Rushden & Diamonds	W	3-1	Constable (2) (1 pen), Clist
40	28/03/2009	A	Stevenage Borough	D	1-1	Constable
41	04/04/2009	H	Histon	W	2-1	Constable (2)
42	07/04/2009	A	York City	D	0-0	
43	11/04/2009	H	Wrexham	W	1-0	Constable
44	13/04/2009	A	Woking	W	2-0	Murray, Clist
45	17/04/2009	A	Burton Albion	W	1-0	Chapman
46	26/04/2009	H	Northwich Victoria	L	1-2	Constable

FA Cup

4Q	25/10/2008	H	Hayes & Yeading United	W	2-0	Constable, Guy
1	08/11/2008	H	Dorchester Town	D	0-0	
1R	18/11/2008	A	Dorchester Town	W	3-1	Odubade, Trainer, Constable
2	29/11/2008	A	Torquay United	L	0-2	

FA Trophy

1	13/12/2008	A	AFC Sudbury	W	2-0	Guy
2	13/01/2009	H	York City	L	1-2	Constable

Setanta Shield

3	04/11/2008	A	Forest Green Rovers	L	1-2	Hutchinson

Total appear
Sub appea
Total

Quinn	Foster	Carruthers	Davies	Murray	Burnell	Haldane	Odubade	Constable	Willmott	Reid	Husbands	Cole	Day	Fisher	Deering	Hutchinson	Guy	Osborne	Evans	Turley	Trainer	Taylor	Groves	Sappleton	Chapman	Killock	Nelthorpe	Batt	Farrell	Clist	Sandwith	Dobson
3	4	5	**6**	7	8	9	*10*	11	12	13	14																					
3	4	5		7	8	9	*10*	11		**6**	13	1	2	13	14																	
3	4	5		7	**8**	6	11	10		9		1	2		13	12																
3	4	**5**		7		9	11	*10*	13	6		1	2	14	12	8																
4		5		8		*9*	6	10	3	13		1	**2**		14	7	11															
3	4	9		6	**7**	13	10	14	2	12		1				8	*11*															
3		9		7	8	12		10	2	5						6	**11**	4														
3		**5**		8	7	9	13	10	2	6					12		11	4														
3		13		7	8	9	14	10	2	5					12		*11*	4	**6**													
2				7	8	6	11		3						13		14	4	*9*	**1**	10											
	3	5		7	8	13	**6**	10		12							11	4		1	9											
	3	5		7	8	13	**6**	*10*							14	12	11	4		1	9											
3	4	5		7	8	11	6		12								10			1	9											
3	4	5		7	8	6	11	13							12		**10**			1	9											
3	4	5		7	8	**6**	10								13	12	*11*			1	9	14										
3	4	5		7		**6**	13	10							9		11			1	8	12										
	4	5		7		**9**	13	11	3				2		6	12	10			1	8											
3		5		7	8	11	13	*10*	4				2		**6**	12	14			1	9											
	4	5		7			13	11	3				2		6	8	10			**1**	9											
	4	5		7		**9**	11	10					3		6	8	13			1	12											
	4	**6**		8	2		13	11	3				5		12	7	10			1	9											
	4			7	2	13	12	11	3				5		8	**6**	10			1	9											
	4			7	2	6	13	10	3				5		8	12	11			1	**9**											
	4			7	2	9	13	11	**3**				5	12	6		10			1	*8*											
	4			7		*11*	**6**	10	3				5	12		8				1	9	13	14									
	4			7		**6**		11	3				5			8	*10*		12	1	9	14		13								
	4	12		8	7	6	*11*	10	**3**				14							1				13	2	5	9					
	4			7	8	**6**	14	10	3				13			12				1				*11*	2	5	9					
	4	6		9		13	7	11	3							12				1				14	8	**5**	*10*	2				
	4	5		10	8	**6**	12	11	3							13				1					7		9	2				
	4	5		10		6	12		3				13			**8**				1					7		9	2	11			
	4	5		10		6	12	11	3											1					7		*9*	**2**	13	8		
	4	5		7			12	10	3											1					6		**9**	2	11	8		
	4	5		7		13	14	11	**3**											1					6		9	2	*10*	8	12	
		5		7		9	12	10	3				2			**8**				1					6				11		4	
	4	13		**8**		10	6	11	3											1					9			2	12	7	5	
	4	5		7		10	*6*	11	3							12				1					9			**2**	14	8	13	
	4	13		14		**6**		10	3							12				1					7		9	2	*11*	8	5	
	4	5		**8**		12	**6**	*11*	3							13				1					7		10	2	14	9		
	4	**5**		8		6	13	11	3											1					7		*10*	2	12	9	14	
	4			8		**6**	13	10	3							12				1					2		9		11	7	5	
	4				9	6	13	11	3							12				1					7		10	2		**8**	5	
	4			8		10	6	11	**3**											1					7		12	2	13	9	5	
	4	9		7		13	14	*10*	3							12				1					**6**			2	11	8	5	
	4			7		6	12	11	3							13				1					8		*10*	**2**	14	9	5	
	3	**5**		6		9	11	10												1					7		12	2	13	8	4	

Quinn	Foster	Carruthers	Davies	Murray	Burnell	Haldane	Odubade	Constable	Willmott	Reid	Husbands	Cole	Day	Fisher	Deering	Hutchinson	Guy	Osborne	Evans	Turley	Trainer	Taylor	Groves	Sappleton	Chapman	Killock	Nelthorpe	Batt	Farrell	Clist	Sandwith	Dobson
	4	5		7		**6**	14	10	3						9		*11*			1	8	13										12
		5		7	2	*11*	12	10	3				4		6	8	13			1	**9**											14
	4	5		7		**9**	13	10					3		6	8	11			1	12											
	4	5		7		9	10	11					3		6	8				1		13	12									

Quinn	Foster	Carruthers	Davies	Murray	Burnell	Haldane	Odubade	Constable	Willmott	Reid	Husbands	Cole	Day	Fisher	Deering	Hutchinson	Guy	Osborne	Evans	Turley	Trainer	Taylor	Groves	Sappleton	Chapman	Killock	Nelthorpe	Batt	Farrell	Clist	Sandwith	Dobson
	4	**6**		8	2	12	13	*10*	3				5		9	7	11			1	14											
	3	13			12	9	6	10					4			7				1				11	8	5						

Quinn	Foster	Carruthers	Davies	Murray	Burnell	Haldane	Odubade	Constable	Willmott	Reid	Husbands	Cole	Day	Fisher	Deering	Hutchinson	Guy	Osborne	Evans	Turley	Trainer	Taylor	Groves	Sappleton	Chapman	Killock	Nelthorpe	Batt	Farrell	Clist	Sandwith	Dobson
		5			7	9	10	*11*	4				2			3	13		12	1	8	14	**6**									

Quinn	Foster	Carruthers	Davies	Murray	Burnell	Haldane	Odubade	Constable	Willmott	Reid	Husbands	Cole	Day	Fisher	Deering	Hutchinson	Guy	Osborne	Evans	Turley	Trainer	Taylor	Groves	Sappleton	Chapman	Killock	Nelthorpe	Batt	Farrell	Clist	Sandwith	Dobson
15	44	37	1	49	25	40	24	47	38	6	0	5	21	0	13	18	21	6	2	44	19	0	1	2	21	4	14	16	7	14	9	0
		5		1	1	10	26	2	3	4	2		3	4	11	16	5		2		3	7	2	3			2		8		3	2
2	1			8	1	3	7	26	2	2			1	1	2	3	4				5			1	2		2		2	3	1	

League Table

	P	W	D	L	F	A	Pts
Burton Albion	46	27	7	12	81	52	88
Cambridge United	46	24	14	8	65	39	86
Histon	46	23	14	9	78	48	83
Torquay United	46	23	14	9	72	47	83
Stevenage Borough	46	23	12	11	73	54	81
Kidderminster Harriers	46	23	10	13	69	48	79
Oxford United	46	24	10	12	72	51	77
Kettering Town	46	21	13	12	50	37	76
Crawley Town	46	19	14	13	77	55	70
Wrexham	46	18	12	16	64	48	66
Rushden & Diamonds	46	16	15	15	61	50	63
Mansfield Town	46	19	9	18	57	55	62
Eastbourne Borough	46	18	6	22	58	70	60
Ebbsfleet United	46	16	10	20	52	60	58
Altrincham	46	15	11	20	49	66	56
Salisbury City	46	14	13	19	54	64	55
York City	46	11	19	16	47	51	52
Forest Green Rovers	46	12	16	18	70	76	52
Grays Athletic	46	14	10	22	44	64	52
Barrow	46	12	15	19	51	65	51
Woking	46	10	14	22	37	60	44
Northwich Victoria	46	11	10	25	56	75	43
Weymouth	46	11	10	25	45	86	43
Lewes	46	6	6	34	28	89	24

SEASON SUMMARY

	HOME						AWAY						OVERALL								
Season	P	W	D	L	F	A	P	W	D	L	F	A	P	W	D	L	F	A	Pts	Div	Pos
2008–09	23	16	3	4	42	20	23	8	7	8	30	31	46	24	10	12	72	51	77	Conf	7
2007–08	23	10	8	5	32	21	23	10	3	10	24	27	46	20	11	15	56	48	71	Conf	9
2006–07	24	11	9	4	34	18	24	12	6	6	34	17	48	23	15	10	68	35	84	Conf	2
2005–06	23	7	7	9	25	30	23	4	9	10	18	27	46	11	16	19	43	57	49	4	23
2004–05	23	11	4	8	29	24	23	5	7	11	21	39	46	16	11	19	50	63	59	4	15
2003–04	23	14	8	1	34	13	23	4	9	10	21	31	46	18	17	11	55	44	71	4	9
2002–03	23	9	7	7	26	20	23	10	5	8	31	27	46	19	12	15	57	47	69	4	8
2001–02	23	8	7	8	34	28	23	3	7	13	19	34	46	11	14	21	53	62	47	4	21
2000–01	23	5	4	14	23	34	23	2	2	19	30	66	46	7	6	33	53	100	27	3	24
1999–2000	23	6	5	12	24	38	23	6	4	13	19	35	46	12	9	25	43	73	45	3	20
1998–99	23	7	8	8	31	30	23	3	6	14	17	41	46	10	14	22	48	71	44	2	23
1997–98	23	12	6	5	36	20	23	4	4	15	24	44	46	16	10	20	60	64	58	2	12
1996–97	23	14	3	6	44	26	23	2	6	15	20	42	46	16	9	21	64	68	57	2	17
1995–96	23	17	4	2	52	14	23	7	7	9	24	25	46	24	11	11	76	39	83	3	2
1994–95	23	13	6	4	30	18	23	8	6	9	36	34	46	21	12	13	66	52	75	3	7
1993–94	23	10	5	8	33	33	23	3	5	15	21	42	46	13	10	23	54	75	49	2	23
1992–93	23	8	7	8	29	21	23	6	7	10	24	35	46	14	14	18	53	56	56	2	14
1991–92	23	10	6	7	39	30	23	3	5	15	27	43	46	13	11	22	66	73	50	2	21
1990–91	23	10	9	4	41	29	23	4	10	9	28	37	46	14	19	13	69	66	61	2	10
1989–90	23	8	7	8	35	31	23	7	2	14	22	35	46	15	9	22	57	66	54	2	17
1988–89	23	11	6	6	40	34	23	3	6	14	22	36	46	14	12	20	62	70	54	2	17
1987–88	20	5	7	8	24	34	20	1	6	13	20	46	40	6	13	21	44	80	31	1	21
1986–87	21	8	8	5	30	25	21	3	5	13	14	44	42	11	13	18	44	69	46	1	18
1985–86	21	7	7	7	34	27	21	3	5	13	28	53	42	10	12	20	62	80	42	1	18
1984–85	21	18	2	1	62	15	21	7	7	7	22	21	42	25	9	8	84	36	84	2	1
1983–84	23	17	5	1	58	22	23	11	6	6	33	28	46	28	11	7	91	50	95	3	1
1982–83	23	12	9	2	41	23	23	10	3	10	30	30	46	22	12	12	71	53	78	3	5
1981–82	23	10	8	5	28	18	23	9	6	8	35	31	46	19	14	13	63	49	71	3	5
1980–81	23	7	8	8	20	24	23	6	9	8	19	23	46	13	17	16	39	47	43	3	14
1979–80	23	10	4	9	34	24	23	4	9	10	23	37	46	14	13	19	57	61	41	3	17
1978–79	23	10	8	5	27	20	23	4	10	9	17	30	46	14	18	14	44	50	46	3	11
1977–78	23	11	10	2	38	21	23	2	4	17	26	46	46	13	14	19	64	67	40	3	17
1976–77	23	9	8	6	34	29	23	3	7	13	21	36	46	12	15	19	55	65	39	3	18
1975–76	21	7	7	7	23	25	21	4	4	13	16	34	42	11	11	20	39	59	33	2	20
1974–75	21	14	3	4	30	19	21	1	9	11	11	32	42	15	12	15	41	51	42	2	11
1973–74	21	8	8	5	27	21	21	2	8	11	8	25	42	10	16	16	35	46	36	2	18
1972–73	21	14	2	5	36	18	21	5	5	11	16	25	42	19	7	16	52	43	45	2	8
1971–72	21	10	8	3	28	17	21	2	6	13	15	38	42	12	14	16	43	55	38	2	15
1970–71	21	8	8	5	23	23	21	6	6	9	18	25	42	14	14	14	41	48	42	2	14
1969–70	21	9	9	3	23	13	21	3	6	12	12	29	42	12	15	15	35	42	39	2	15
1968–69	21	8	5	8	21	23	21	4	4	13	13	32	42	12	9	21	34	55	33	2	20
1967–68	23	18	3	2	49	20	23	4	10	9	20	27	46	22	13	11	69	47	57	3	1
1966–67	23	10	8	5	41	29	23	5	5	13	20	37	46	15	13	18	61	66	43	3	16
1965–66	23	11	3	9	38	33	23	8	5	10	32	41	46	19	8	19	70	74	46	3	14

Season	HOME P	W	D	L	F	A	AWAY P	W	D	L	F	A	OVERALL P	W	D	L	F	A	Pts	Div	Pos
1964–65	23	18	4	1	54	13	23	5	11	7	33	31	46	23	15	8	87	44	61	4	4
1963–64	23	10	7	6	37	27	23	4	6	13	22	35	46	14	13	19	59	62	41	4	18
1962–63	23	10	10	3	44	27	23	3	5	15	26	44	46	13	15	18	70	71	41	4	18
1961–62	21	15	3	3	58	17	21	13	2	6	60	29	42	28	5	9	118	46	61	SLP	1
1960–61	21	17	3	1	67	20	21	10	7	4	37	23	42	27	10	5	104	43	64	SLP	1
1959–60	21	13	6	2	42	21	21	10	2	9	36	40	42	23	8	11	78	61	54	SLP	2
1958–59	17	12	0	5	44	19	17	4	3	10	32	42	34	16	3	15	76	61	35	SL	10
1957–58	21	13	5	3	57	28	21	5	2	14	33	54	42	18	7	17	90	82	43	SL	9
1956–57	21	10	4	7	36	32	21	9	3	9	28	29	42	19	7	16	64	61	45	SL	9
1955–56	21	13	3	5	52	32	21	4	3	14	30	54	42	17	6	19	82	86	40	SL	15
1954–55	21	14	4	3	59	21	21	4	3	14	23	41	42	18	7	17	82	62	43	SL	10
1953–54	21	14	6	1	43	12	21	8	3	10	25	31	42	22	9	11	68	43	53	SL	2
1952–53	21	12	8	1	48	20	21	11	4	6	45	30	42	23	12	7	93	50	58	SL	1
1951–52	21	12	7	2	32	13	21	4	4	13	23	40	42	16	11	15	55	53	43	SL	11
1950–51	22	9	6	7	42	39	22	9	5	8	42	44	44	18	11	15	84	83	47	SL	7
1949–50	23	12	2	9	51	40	23	3	5	15	21	57	46	15	7	24	72	97	37	SL	21

Against Other Clubs

Opponent	Home P	W	D	L	F	A	Away P	W	D	L	F	A	Total P	W	D	L	F	A
AFC Bournemouth	13	8	1	4	24	17	15	4	4	7	14	21	28	12	5	11	38	38
AFC Sudbury	0	0	0	0	0	0	1	1	0	0	2	0	1	1	0	0	2	0
Aldershot	8	3	3	2	11	8	9	1	3	5	7	15	17	4	6	7	18	23
Altrincham	3	2	1	0	6	1	3	2	0	1	6	2	6	4	1	1	12	3
Arsenal	4	2	2	0	6	2	5	0	1	4	2	11	9	2	3	4	8	13
Aston Villa	10	4	3	3	14	14	9	1	3	5	6	13	19	5	6	8	20	27
Aylesbury United	2	2	0	0	7	2	1	1	0	0	2	1	3	3	0	0	9	3
Banbury Spencer	1	1	0	0	1	0	0	0	0	0	0	0	1	1	0	0	1	0
Barking	0	0	0	0	0	0	1	0	0	1	0	1	1	0	0	1	0	1
Barnet	1	1	0	0	2	0	2	1	1	0	3	2	3	2	1	0	5	2
Barnsley	11	6	3	2	19	7	11	1	2	8	2	14	22	7	5	10	21	21
Barrow	5	4	1	0	17	2	5	0	2	3	4	11	10	4	3	3	21	13
Barry Town	11	6	3	2	24	14	11	4	0	7	23	31	22	10	3	9	47	45
Bath City	14	10	1	3	30	14	13	4	3	6	15	26	27	14	4	9	45	40
Bedford Town	16	10	4	2	37	24	16	3	2	11	19	35	32	13	6	13	56	59
Bexley Heath & Welling	1	1	0	0	6	0	1	1	0	0	4	1	2	2	0	0	10	1
Birmingham City	13	4	3	6	11	17	13	3	6	4	8	12	26	7	9	10	19	29
Blackburn Rovers	13	6	4	3	16	12	12	1	6	5	13	18	25	7	10	8	29	30
Blackpool	14	6	3	5	15	15	13	1	4	8	7	17	27	7	7	13	22	32
Bologna (Italy)	0	0	0	0	0	0	1	0	1	0	0	0	1	0	1	0	0	0
Bolton Wanderers	11	4	4	3	16	12	10	2	3	5	8	14	21	6	7	8	24	26
Boston United	7	4	3	0	17	6	7	2	1	4	11	9	14	6	4	4	28	15
Bradford Park Avenue	2	2	0	0	5	1	2	0	0	2	2	6	4	2	0	2	7	7
Bradford City	13	9	2	2	26	11	14	4	4	6	19	20	27	13	6	8	45	31
Brentford	15	5	5	5	17	18	21	6	2	13	15	42	36	11	7	18	32	60
Brentwood & Warley	0	0	0	0	0	0	1	1	0	0	4	0	1	1	0	0	4	0
Bridgewater Town	1	1	0	0	2	1	0	0	0	0	0	0	1	1	0	0	2	1

Opponent	Home						Away						Total					
	P	W	D	L	F	A	P	W	D	L	F	A	P	W	D	L	F	A
Brighton & Hove Albion	14	7	4	3	22	13	16	5	5	6	18	18	30	12	9	9	40	31
Bristol City	21	12	6	3	35	15	21	6	7	8	22	28	42	18	13	11	57	43
Bristol Rovers	21	10	6	5	31	27	20	4	5	11	17	29	41	14	11	16	48	56
Burnley	9	4	2	3	15	10	8	1	5	2	9	9	17	5	7	5	24	19
Burton Albion	4	1	1	2	4	7	4	4	0	0	7	3	8	5	1	2	11	10
Bury	16	7	8	1	28	18	15	3	5	7	17	20	31	10	13	8	45	38
Cambridge City	4	2	0	2	5	7	5	3	1	1	11	9	9	5	1	3	16	16
Cambridge United	15	7	5	2	22	14	14	2	5	7	15	20	28	9	10	9	37	34
Cardiff City	12	8	2	2	21	12	12	3	4	5	10	21	24	11	6	7	31	33
Carlisle United	20	9	7	4	28	13	21	4	5	12	22	31	41	13	12	16	50	44
Charlton Athletic	17	7	3	7	23	23	17	1	8	8	15	27	34	8	11	15	38	50
Chelmsford City	15	9	3	3	38	18	16	6	3	7	26	29	31	15	6	10	64	47
Chelsea	9	1	4	4	14	19	8	3	1	4	13	16	17	4	5	8	27	35
Cheltenham Town	20	14	3	3	38	13	21	8	4	9	32	41	41	22	7	12	70	54
Chesham United	2	2	0	0	7	2	0	0	0	0	0	0	2	2	0	0	7	2
Chester City	12	8	1	3	19	8	13	5	1	7	18	21	25	13	2	10	37	29
Chesterfield	14	7	4	3	17	13	13	1	5	7	10	20	27	8	9	10	27	33
Chingford Town	1	1	0	0	7	2	1	0	1	0	2	2	2	1	1	0	9	4
Clacton Town	2	1	1	0	7	3	2	2	0	0	9	0	4	3	1	0	16	3
Colchester United	10	4	2	4	15	12	12	3	2	7	13	23	22	7	4	11	28	35
Como (Italy)	1	1	0	0	1	0	0	0	0	0	0	0	1	1	0	0	1	0
Corby Town	1	1	0	0	7	3	1	1	0	0	6	2	2	2	0	0	13	5
Coventry City	3	2	0	1	3	1	4	0	0	4	2	13	7	2	0	5	5	14
Crawley Town	3	1	1	1	3	3	3	2	0	1	2	2	6	3	1	2	5	5
Crewe Alexandra	6	3	3	0	8	4	7	2	1	4	13	15	13	5	4	4	21	19
Crystal Palace	9	3	1	5	11	14	8	0	3	5	6	13	17	3	4	10	17	27
Dagenham & Redbridge	1	0	1	0	2	2	2	2	0	0	2	0	3	2	1	0	4	2
Darlington	9	5	1	3	19	12	9	3	1	5	7	13	18	8	2	8	26	25
Dartford	11	4	4	3	20	16	12	5	2	5	20	18	23	9	6	8	40	34
Derby County	5	2	1	2	4	3	5	2	1	2	5	6	10	4	2	4	9	9
Doncaster Rovers	7	4	2	1	16	6	7	2	2	3	8	11	14	6	4	4	24	17
Dorchester Town	2	1	1	0	9	1	1	1	0	0	3	1	3	2	1	0	12	2
Dover Athletic	0	0	0	0	0	0	2	2	0	0	3	0	2	2	0	0	3	0
Droylsden	1	1	0	0	1	0	1	0	0	1	1	3	2	1	0	1	2	3
Eastbourne Borough	2	2	0	0	9	3	2	1	1	0	4	1	4	3	1	0	13	4
Ebbsfleet United	17	11	3	3	55	26	16	6	4	6	20	20	33	17	7	9	75	46
Enfield	0	0	0	0	0	0	1	0	0	1	3	4	1	0	0	1	3	4
Everton	5	1	4	0	5	4	6	1	1	4	3	10	11	2	5	4	8	14
Exeter City	17	3	6	8	17	23	15	3	4	8	17	26	32	6	10	16	34	49
Exeter City Reserves	9	6	2	1	22	11	9	3	1	5	15	18	18	9	3	6	37	29
Falmouth	0	0	0	0	0	0	1	1	0	0	2	1	1	1	0	0	2	1
Farsley Celtic	1	1	0	0	5	1	1	1	0	0	1	0	2	2	0	0	6	1
Folkestone Town	4	4	0	0	16	4	2	2	0	0	8	1	6	6	0	0	24	5
Forest Green Rovers	3	2	0	1	3	3	4	1	2	1	8	5	7	3	2	2	12	9
Fulham	11	6	3	2	16	12	13	4	4	5	11	13	24	10	7	7	27	25
Gillingham	17	4	7	6	27	24	17	3	3	11	15	29	34	7	10	17	42	53
Gloucester City	11	8	1	2	25	6	11	2	2	7	14	18	22	10	3	9	39	24
Grays Athletic	3	1	2	0	5	2	3	0	2	1	2	4	6	1	4	1	7	6
Grimsby Town	13	6	2	5	22	17	13	4	4	5	11	12	26	10	6	10	33	29
Guildford City	16	6	5	5	24	25	16	3	3	10	10	22	32	9	8	15	34	47
Halifax Town	6	3	3	0	14	6	6	3	1	2	11	7	12	6	4	2	25	13
Hartlepool United	5	3	0	2	15	6	5	2	1	2	6	7	10	5	1	4	21	13
Harwich & Parkeston	0	0	0	0	0	0	1	1	0	0	3	2	1	1	0	0	3	2

Opponent	Home						Away						Total					
	P	W	D	L	F	A	P	W	D	L	F	A	P	W	D	L	F	A
Hastings United	13	10	2	1	32	11	13	3	3	7	17	29	26	13	5	8	49	40
Hayes & Yeading United	1	1	0	0	2	0	0	0	0	0	0	0	1	1	0	0	2	0
Hemel Hempstead	0	0	0	0	0	0	1	0	0	1	1	3	1	0	0	1	1	3
Hendon	1	1	0	0	3	2	1	0	1	0	2	2	2	1	1	0	5	4
Hereford United	17	12	3	2	37	17	17	4	2	11	21	35	34	16	5	13	58	52
Histon	2	2	0	0	5	1	2	0	0	2	2	6	4	2	0	2	7	7
Huddersfield Town	13	8	2	3	20	9	13	1	2	10	9	25	26	9	4	13	29	34
Hull City	21	10	8	3	31	18	21	6	6	9	17	26	42	16	14	12	48	44
Huntley & Palmer's	1	1	0	0	9	4	0	0	0	0	0	0	1	1	0	0	9	4
Ipswich Town	10	4	4	2	20	17	10	1	1	8	12	21	20	5	5	10	32	38
Kettering Town	17	6	4	7	22	21	15	4	3	8	23	33	32	10	7	15	45	54
Kidderminster Harriers	18	8	6	4	29	16	17	7	5	5	26	20	35	15	11	9	55	36
Kidlington	1	1	0	0	6	0	0	0	0	0	0	0	1	1	0	0	6	0
Kings Lynn	3	3	0	0	5	2	4	2	1	1	10	5	7	5	1	1	15	7
Leeds United	5	3	1	1	16	11	6	1	2	3	6	11	11	4	3	4	22	22
Leicester City	13	4	6	3	19	13	14	2	4	8	16	25	27	6	10	11	35	38
Lewes FC	2	2	0	0	3	1	2	0	1	1	1	2	4	2	1	1	4	3
Leyton Orient	17	7	6	4	27	22	16	3	7	6	16	18	33	10	13	10	43	40
Lincoln City	14	9	2	3	18	8	14	4	3	7	14	18	28	13	5	10	32	26
Liverpool	4	0	1	3	3	11	3	0	0	3	0	12	7	0	1	6	3	23
Llanelli	7	5	2	0	23	6	7	2	1	4	12	12	14	7	3	4	35	18
Lovell's Athletic	11	7	3	1	19	9	11	4	3	4	14	13	22	11	6	5	33	22
Luton Town	17	5	5	7	25	26	15	6	2	7	23	34	32	11	7	14	48	60
Macclesfield Town	5	1	2	2	5	6	6	2	1	3	5	6	11	3	3	5	10	12
Maidenhead United	2	2	0	0	6	0	1	1	0	0	6	1	3	3	0	0	12	1
Manchester City	7	2	2	3	9	13	6	3	0	3	9	6	13	5	2	6	18	19
Manchester United	8	4	2	2	11	9	8	0	1	7	6	23	16	4	3	9	17	32
Mansfield Town	15	9	2	3	25	15	14	4	2	8	18	20	28	13	4	11	43	35
Margate	3	1	0	2	5	8	0	0	0	0	0	0	3	1	0	2	5	8
Marlow	1	1	0	0	1	0	2	1	0	1	8	2	3	2	0	1	9	2
Merthyr Tydfil	11	6	4	1	25	10	12	2	1	9	16	35	23	8	5	10	41	45
Middlesbrough	13	3	5	5	19	23	13	2	1	10	8	21	26	5	6	15	27	44
Millwall	25	12	4	9	29	27	24	4	8	12	27	45	49	16	12	21	56	72
Morecambe	2	1	1	0	3	2	1	1	0	0	3	0	3	2	1	0	6	2
Newcastle United	9	5	2	2	19	13	8	1	3	4	11	17	17	6	5	6	30	30
Newport County	7	4	1	2	14	8	7	3	1	3	9	7	14	7	2	5	23	15
Northampton Town	9	7	0	2	16	7	8	2	1	5	5	8	17	9	1	7	21	15
Northwich Victoria	4	2	0	2	9	5	3	1	0	2	2	3	7	3	0	4	11	8
Norwich City	12	5	2	5	15	14	12	2	3	7	17	24	24	7	5	12	32	38
Nottingham Forest	12	4	1	7	8	19	12	3	5	4	14	19	24	7	6	11	22	38
Notts County	13	6	4	3	26	18	13	3	5	5	9	15	26	9	9	8	35	33
Nuneaton Borough	2	0	1	1	2	4	3	0	1	2	2	8	5	0	2	3	4	12
Oldham Athletic	14	7	5	2	28	15	14	0	4	10	8	29	28	7	9	12	36	44
Oxford City	2	1	1	0	5	4	2	2	0	0	5	0	4	3	1	0	10	4
Peterborough United	15	9	1	5	27	17	15	4	5	6	21	25	30	13	6	11	48	42
Plymouth Argyle	16	8	7	1	26	14	18	5	3	10	22	34	34	13	10	11	48	48
Poole Town	2	2	0	0	7	3	2	1	1	0	2	1	4	3	1	0	9	4
Port Vale	13	5	7	1	19	11	13	3	2	8	12	20	26	8	9	9	31	31
Portsmouth	28	16	6	6	45	31	25	2	8	15	22	38	53	18	14	21	67	69
Preston North End	13	8	2	3	22	16	12	4	2	6	13	16	25	12	4	9	35	32
Queen's Park Rangers	14	6	3	5	24	20	14	2	3	9	16	30	28	8	6	14	40	50
Reading	18	11	0	7	29	23	19	8	2	9	23	23	37	19	2	16	52	46
Rochdale	8	2	4	2	9	7	9	2	3	4	11	16	17	4	7	6	20	23

Opponent	Home						Away						Total					
	P	W	D	L	F	A	P	W	D	L	F	A	P	W	D	L	F	A
Roma (Italy)	0	0	0	0	0	0	1	1	0	0	2	0	1	1	0	0	2	0
Romford	2	2	0	0	7	1	2	1	1	0	6	3	4	3	1	0	13	4
Rotherham United	9	5	2	2	20	14	9	2	4	3	7	9	18	7	6	5	27	23
Rugby Town	1	1	0	0	5	0	1	0	0	1	1	4	2	1	0	1	6	4
Rushden & Diamonds	8	4	2	2	11	7	7	2	1	4	9	15	15	6	3	6	20	22
Salisbury City	3	3	0	0	7	3	2	0	0	2	2	5	5	3	0	2	9	8
Scunthorpe United	9	4	1	4	11	12	9	1	5	3	7	10	18	5	6	7	18	22
Sheffield United	13	6	4	3	24	14	12	3	1	8	13	25	25	9	5	11	37	39
Sheffield Wednesday	15	7	4	4	13	15	14	3	7	4	14	19	29	10	11	8	27	34
Shrewsbury Town	17	9	4	4	32	16	17	2	6	9	13	27	34	11	10	13	45	43
Slough Town	1	0	0	1	3	4	0	0	0	0	0	0	1	0	0	1	3	4
Southampton	7	2	3	2	9	9	8	0	1	7	5	17	15	2	4	9	14	26
Southend United	17	11	2	4	23	10	17	7	3	7	21	28	34	18	5	11	44	38
Southport	5	1	4	0	4	3	5	2	1	2	7	6	10	3	5	2	11	9
St Albans City	1	1	0	0	2	1	1	1	0	0	2	0	2	2	0	0	4	1
Stafford Rangers	2	2	0	0	4	1	2	2	0	0	2	0	4	4	0	0	6	1
Stevenage Borough	3	2	1	0	5	2	3	0	3	0	3	3	6	2	4	0	8	5
Stockport County	10	7	3	0	22	5	10	2	4	4	12	12	20	9	7	4	34	17
Stoke City	9	5	4	0	19	7	10	3	2	5	9	15	19	8	6	5	28	22
Sunderland	15	5	4	6	19	16	14	2	2	10	6	26	29	7	6	16	25	42
Swansea City	14	7	1	6	28	18	12	3	5	4	13	13	26	10	6	10	41	31
Swindon Town	28	9	12	7	36	31	25	1	7	17	19	49	53	10	19	24	55	80
Tamworth	1	1	0	0	2	1	1	1	0	0	3	1	2	2	0	0	5	2
Tonbridge	15	12	2	1	33	11	14	5	4	5	22	20	29	17	6	6	55	31
Torino (Italy)	1	0	1	0	1	1	0	0	0	0	0	0	1	0	1	0	1	1
Torquay United	12	5	6	1	18	12	14	1	7	6	17	26	26	6	13	7	35	38
Torquay United Reserves	2	1	0	1	4	4	2	1	0	1	3	4	4	2	0	2	7	8
Tottenham Hotspur	4	0	3	1	4	6	5	0	0	5	5	17	9	0	3	6	9	23
Tranmere Rovers	17	9	5	3	20	14	15	4	4	7	17	29	32	13	9	10	37	43
Walsall	14	10	2	2	40	16	14	6	4	4	23	16	28	16	6	6	63	32
Watford	19	3	10	6	17	25	19	4	4	11	14	32	38	7	14	17	31	57
Wealdstone	0	0	0	0	0	0	2	2	0	0	7	2	2	2	0	0	7	2
Wellington Town	4	4	0	0	10	0	4	2	1	1	7	6	8	6	1	1	17	6
West Bromwich Albion	11	4	4	3	13	11	11	1	2	8	11	24	22	5	6	11	24	35
West Ham United	7	3	1	3	7	8	7	1	1	5	8	15	14	4	2	8	15	23
Weymouth	16	5	6	5	27	26	16	7	3	6	23	26	32	12	9	11	50	52
Wigan Athletic	4	1	1	2	3	4	4	2	0	2	5	5	8	3	1	4	8	9
Wimbledon	7	5	0	2	17	11	6	3	2	1	12	9	13	8	2	3	29	20
Windsor & Eton	1	1	0	0	7	0	0	0	0	0	0	0	1	1	0	0	7	0
Wisbech Town	3	3	0	0	18	2	3	3	0	0	6	2	6	6	0	0	24	4
Woking	3	0	3	0	0	0	3	2	0	1	4	2	6	2	3	1	4	2
Wolverhampton Wanderers	11	5	4	2	17	10	10	3	2	5	11	16	21	8	6	7	28	26
Worcester City	15	9	2	4	34	12	14	3	2	9	16	29	29	12	4	13	50	41
Workington	4	3	0	1	7	4	4	0	2	2	2	4	8	3	2	3	9	8
Worthing	1	1	0	0	4	0	0	0	0	0	0	0	1	1	0	0	4	0
Wrexham	11	4	3	4	15	16	11	0	5	6	12	20	22	4	8	10	27	36
Wycombe Wanderers	9	4	2	3	16	16	7	2	1	4	8	9	16	6	3	7	24	25
Yeovil Town	15	9	4	2	28	20	15	5	4	6	30	34	30	14	8	8	58	54
York City	17	9	4	4	29	18	17	8	3	6	20	15	34	17	7	10	49	33

Top Scorers

Season Top Scorers

Season	Name	Goals
2008–09	James Constable	26
2007–08	Yemi Odubade	11
2006–07	Robert Duffy	21
2005–06	Steve Basham	13
2004–05	Tommy Mooney	15
2003–04	Steve Basham	15
2002–03	Andy Scott	11
2001–02	Paul Moody	11
2000–01	Phil Gray	9
1999–2000	Matt Murphy	17
1998–99	Dean Windass	18
1997–98	Joey Beauchamp	19
1996–97	Nigel Jemson	23
1995–96	Paul Moody	24
1994–95	Paul Moody	24
1993–94	John Byrne	9
1992–93	Jim Magilton	13
1991–92	Jim Magilton	13
1990–91	Paul Simpson	18
1989–90	John Durnin	15
1988–89	Martin Foyle	15
1987–88	Dean Saunders	21
1986–87	John Aldridge	21
1985–86	John Aldridge	31
1984–85	John Aldridge	34
1983–84	Steve Biggins	24
1982–83	Mick Vinter	14
1981–82	Keith Cassells	22
1980–81	Peter Foley	7
	Malcolm Shotton	7
1979–80	Paul Berry	14

Season	Name	Goals
1978–79	Peter Foley	11
	Jason Seacole	11
1977–78	Peter Foley	21
1976–77	Peter Foley	13
1975–76	Mick Tait	12
1974–75	Derek Clarke	9
1973–74	Hugh Curran	14
1972–73	Hugh Curran	17
1971–72	Nigel Cassidy	13
1970–71	Ken Skeen	9
1969–70	Ken Skeen	13
1968–69	John Shuker	8
1967–68	Mick Bullock	16
1966–67	Graham Atkinson	15
1965–66	Graham Atkinson	19
1964–65	Colin Booth	23
1963–64	Bill Calder	14
1963–64	Arthur Longbottom	14
1962–63	Bud Houghton	18
1961–62	Bud Houghton	43
1960–61	Tony Jones	38
1959–60	Geoff Denial	32
1958–59	Joe Dickson	27
1957–58	Jack Cross	27
1956–57	Lionel Phillips	13
1955–56	Jimmy Smillie	25
1954–55	Harry Yates	25
1953–54	Ken Smith	17
1952–53	Harry Yates	22
1952–53	Norman Mills	22
1951–52	Vic Barney	14
1950–51	Bill Rowstron	24
1949–50	Jim Smith	15

Top Scorers (League)

Name	Goals
Graham Atkinson	97
Tony Jones	89
John Aldridge	72
Peter Foley	71
Bud Houghton	69
Joey Beauchamp	63
Paul Moody	63
Billy Rees	52
John Shuker	46
Alan Willey	46
John Durnin	44
Steve Basham	43
Geoff Denial	43
Paul Simpson	43
Johnny Love	40
Harry Yates	40
Hugh Curran	39
Matt Murphy	38
Trevor Hebberd	37
Martin Foyle	36

Top Scorers (all competitions)

Name	Goals
Graham Atkinson	107
Tony Jones	100
John Aldridge	90
Peter Foley	90
Joey Beauchamp	77
Bud Houghton	75
Paul Moody	75
Billy Rees	60
Matt Murphy	55
Harry Yates	54
Geoff Denial	51
Paul Simpson	50
Steve Basham	49
Alan Willey	48
John Durnin	47
John Shuker	47
Johnny Love	45
Andy Thomas	45
Martin Foyle	44
Hugh Curran	43

Hat-Tricks

Name	Goals	Date	Opponents
Bud Houghton	5	12 April 1961	Boston United
Tony Jones	5	10 December 1960	Wisbech Town
John Durnin	4	14 November 1992	Luton Town
Richard Hill	4	26 December 1988	Walsall
John Aldridge	4	24 September 1986	Gillingham
Bill Calder	4	7 September 1964	Walsall
Arthur Longbottom	4	26 October 1963	Darlington
Tony Jones	4	22 September 1962	Newport County
Alan Willey	4	30 September 1961	Gravesend & Northfleet
Ken Smith	4	9 October 1954	Hastings United
Fred Tapping	4	3 September 1949	Huntley & Palmer's
Robert Duffy	3	6 October 2006	Forest Green Rovers
Steve Basham	3	16 November 2005	Eastbourne Borough
Paul Moody	3	29 December 2001	Halifax Town
Martin Aldridge	3	14 December 1996	Sheffield United
Paul Moody	3	23 March 1996	Burnley
Paul Moody	3	9 December 1995	Swansea City
Paul Moody	3	11 November 1995	Dorchester Town
Paul Moody	3	20 August 1994	Cardiff City
John Byrne	3	13 August 1994	Hull City
Paul Simpson	3	20 October 1990	Brighton & Hove Albion
Paul Simpson	3	22 April 1989	AFC Bournemouth
John Aldridge	3	6 December 1986	Luton Town
John Aldridge	3	23 November 1985	Ipswich Town

John Aldridge	3	20 April 1985	Oldham Athletic
John Aldridge	3	24 November 1984	Leeds United
Billy Hamilton	3	10 October 1984	Blackburn Rovers
Billy Hamilton	3	5 September 1984	Hereford United
Steve Biggins	3	24 March 1984	Plymouth Argyle
Neil Whatmore	3	2 March 1983	Bradford City
Keith Cassells	3	30 December 1981	Aldershot
Peter Foley	3	24 September 1977	Chester City
Hugh Curran	3	7 October 1972	Sunderland
Graham Atkinson	3	27 December 1965	Walsall
Tony Jones	3	9 April 1965	Wrexham
Colin Booth	3	3 April 1965	Southport
John Fahy	3	27 March 1965	Bradford
Bill Calder	3	17 February 1965	Newport County
Colin Booth	3	19 December 1964	Barrow
Bill Calder	3	22 August 1964	Crewe Alexandra
Alan Willey	3	27 April 1963	Mansfield Town
Graham Atkinson	3	17 February 1962	Gravesend & Northfleet
Bud Houghton	3	18 November 1961	Romford
Bud Houghton	3	21 October 1961	Salisbury City
Bud Houghton	3	9 September 1961	Kings Lynn
Bud Houghton	3	8 April 1961	Gravesend & Northfleet
Tony Jones	3	28 January 1961	Boston United
Tony Jones	3	31 December 1960	Folkestone Town
Tony Jones	3	3 September 1960	Wellington Town
Geoff Denial	3	6 February 1960	Cambridge City
Geoff Denial	3	28 December 1959	Barry Town
Geoff Denial	3	31 October 1959	Cambridge City
Dave Gibson	3	27 September 1958	Barry Town
Jimmy Jackson	3	20 September 1958	Windsor & Eton
Joe Dickson	3	30 August 1958	Boston United
Fred Cotton	3	26 March 1958	Dartford
Billy Rees	3	9 October 1957	Barry Town
Jack Cross	3	28 August 1957	Tonbridge
Jimmy Smillie	3	14 March 1956	Kidderminster Harriers
Jimmy Smillie	3	28 January 1956	Merthyr Tydfil
John Skull	3	31 August 1955	Worcester City
Ken Smith	3	23 October 1954	Gravesend & Northfleet
Ken Smith	3	11 September 1954	Merthyr Tydfil
Johnnie Crichton	3	17 February 1954	Bedford Town
Ronnie Steel	3	6 February 1954	Cheltenham Town
Norman Mills	3	26 August 1953	Chelmsford City
Ken Smith	3	22 August 1953	Bath City
Harry Yates	3	29 April 1953	Gloucester City
Bobbie Mitchell	3	27 December 1952	Cheltenham Town
Harry Yates	3	13 December 1952	Gloucester City
Arthur Turner	3	27 September 1952	Aylesbury United
Arthur Turner	3	13 September 1952	Marlow
Sammy Chung	3	25 August 1951	Llanelly
Ben Duncan	3	6 January 1951	Kidderminster Harriers
Bill Rowstron	3	26 December 1950	Bedford Town
Bill Rowstron	3	14 October 1950	Chelmsford City
Peter Buchanan	3	5 October 1950	Dartford
Peter Buchanan	3	17 April 1950	Gravesend & Northfleet
Doug McPhee	3	19 November 1949	Chingford Town
Jack Casley	3	22 September 1949	Guildford City

Biggest Victories

Result	Opponent	Date	Venue	Competition
9–0	Wisbech Town	10 December 1960	Home	Southern League Premier
9–1	Dorchester Town	11 November 1995	Home	FA Cup
8–0	Ebbsfleet United	30 September 1961	Home	Southern League Premier
8–0	Marlow	13 September 1952	Away	FA Cup
7–0	Barrow	19 December 1964	Home	League
7–0	Windsor & Eton	20 September 1958	Home	FA Cup
7–0	Exeter City Reserves	24 September 1955	Home	Southern League
7–0	Worcester City	16 April 1955	Home	Southern League
7–0	Bedford Town	17 February 1954	Home	Southern League Cup
6–0	Shrewsbury Town	23 April 1996	Home	League
6–0	Gillingham	24 September 1986	Home	League Cup
7–1	Walsall	27 December 1965	Home	League
6–0	Ebbsfleet United	17 February 1962	Away	Southern League Premier
6–0	Clacton Town	27 January 1962	Away	Southern League Premier
6–0	Bexley Heath & Welling	28 October 1961	Home	Southern League Premier
8–2	Ebbsfleet United	8 April 1961	Home	Southern League Premier
8–2	Hastings United	9 October 1954	Home	Southern League
6–0	Gloucester City	29 April 1953	Home	Southern League
7–1	Gloucester City	13 December 1952	Away	Southern League
6–0	Kidlington	2 September 1950	Home	FA Cup

Biggest Defeats

Result	Opponent	Date	Venue	Competition
0–7	Sunderland	19 September 1998	Away	League
1–7	Birmingham City	12 December 1998	Home	League
0–6	Liverpool	22 March 1986	Away	League
0–6	Bedford Town	26 December 1956	Home	Southern League
0–6	Weymouth	14 April 1956	Away	Southern League
0–6	Merthyr Tydfil	30 August 1950	Away	Southern League
2–8	Merthyr Tydfil	11 February 1950	Away	Southern League
0–6	Barry Town	24 September 1949	Away	Southern League
0–5	Rushden & Diamonds	1 November 2007	Away	League
1–6	Yeovil Town	18 September 2004	Away	League
0–5	Millwall	23 September 2000	Away	League
0–5	Bristol Rovers	22 January 2000	Home	League
1–6	Southend United	16 October 1993	Away	League
1–6	Sheffield Wednesday	4 October 1986	Away	League
0–5	Nottingham Forest	4 October 1978	Home	League Cup
0–5	Cardiff City	12 September 1973	Away	League
0–5	Cardiff City	8 February 1969	Away	League
1–6	Cheltenham Town	24 February 1960	Away	Southern League
0–5	Bath City	14 September 1957	Away	Southern League
0–5	Bedford Town	6 September 1956	Away	Southern League Cup

Top 20 Appearances

Name	Apps (excl. Subs)
Ron Atkinson	559
John Shuker	529
Gary Briggs	506
Colin Clarke	496
Cyril Beavon	461
Les Robinson	454
Roy Burton	449
Maurice Kyle	448
Graham Atkinson	394
Joey Beauchamp	376
Frank Ramshaw	361
Tony Jones	357
Billy Jeffrey	353
Malcolm Shotton	336
David Fogg	331
Trevor Hebberd	326
Mike Ford	322
Mickey Lewis	319
Johnny Love	312
Peter Foley	306

Consecutive Appearances

Player	Consec apps	Start date
Cyril Beavon	138	15 February 1969
Tony Jones	132	16 December 1967
Malcolm Shotton	123	9 May 1987
Ron Atkinson	121	12 October 1971
Les Taylor	120	15 December 1979
Johnny Love	112	18 September 1963
Jim Barron	112	4 April 1970
Roy Burton	107	28 December 1982
John Shuker	107	26 March 1977
David Fogg	106	2 February 1985
Trevor Hebberd	105	10 October 1987
Paul Simpson	100	30 October 1991
Steve Hardwick	98	30 January 1988
Ken Skeen	97	13 April 1974
Frank Ramshaw	94	23 October 1957
Peter Knight	93	28 September 1964
Colin Clarke	89	14 January 1978
Andy Melville	84	20 March 1993
Rodney Smithson	84	5 November 1974
David Bardsley	83	22 April 1989

Top 20 Home Attendances

Attendance	Opponent	Result	Score	Date	Comp
22,750	Preston North End	Lost	1–2	29 February 1964	FA Cup
21,700	Blackburn Rovers	Won	3–1	15 February 1964	FA Cup
18,740	Birmingham City	Lost	0–1	31 March 1972	League
18,193	Swindon Town	Won	1–0	24 September 1969	League Cup
18,000	Liverpool	Lost	0–3	15 January 1972	FA Cup
17,964	Carlisle United	Drew	0–0	29 October 1969	League Cup
17,948	Leicester City	Lost	1–3	17 February 1971	FA Cup
17,939	Derby County	Lost	0–2	22 March 1969	League
17,836	Swindon Town	Drew	0–0	12 April 1968	League
17,814	Watford	Drew	1–1	23 January 1971	FA Cup
17,177	Manchester United	Drew	2–2	6 September 1972	League Cup
17,072	Aston Villa	Won	1–0	5 April 1969	League
17,010	Burnley	Won	3–0	11 January 1971	FA Cup
16,741	Leicester City	Lost	0–1	27 March 1970	League
16,670	Bolton Wanderers	Lost	2–4	30 January 1954	FA Cup
16,196	Birmingham City	Won	1–0	9 April 1971	League
16,074	Swindon Town	Lost	0–3	29 January 1966	League
16,057	Queen's Park Rangers	Lost	0–2	3 February 1973	FA Cup
15,815	Manchester United	Won	1–0	8 February 1975	League
15,686	Stoke City	Drew	0–0	3 January 1970	FA Cup

Top 20 Away Attendances

Attendance	Opponent	Result	Score	Date	Comp
51,820	Manchester United	Lost	0–3	7 September 1985	League
47,754	Manchester United	Lost	0–4	28 January 1989	FA Cup
42,266	Liverpool	Lost	0–2	12 September 1987	League
41,500	Manchester United	Lost	0–4	2 November 1974	League
41,082	Manchester United	Lost	1–2	3 January 1976	FA Cup
39,683	Middlesbrough	Lost	1–4	16 May 1967	League
39,222	Sunderland	Lost	0–1	3 March 1973	League
37,861	Liverpool	Lost	0–6	22 March 1986	League
35,432	Arsenal	Lost	0–2	4 January 2003	FA Cup
35,412	Liverpool	Lost	0–4	18 October 1986	League
34,802	Leicester City	Drew	1–1	13 February 1971	FA Cup
34,709	Manchester United	Lost	1–3	12 December 1987	League
34,567	Sunderland	Lost	0–7	19 September 1998	League
32,443	Manchester United	Lost	2–3	4 April 1987	League
32,106	Chelsea	Lost	2–4	3 February 1999	FA Cup
31,992	Hull City	Lost	1–2	11 April 1966	League
31,759	Birmingham City	Drew	0–0	2 October 1971	League
31,665	Tottenham Hotspur	Lost	2–4	26 January 1991	FA Cup
31,011	Everton	Lost	1–4	24 January 1984	League Cup
30,228	Middlesbrough	Lost	1–4	3 May 1998	League

Transfers (£100,000 plus)

Transfers paid

£470,000	Dean Windass (Aberdeen)	1998–99
£285,000	Colin Greenall (Gillingham)	1987–88
£275,000	Andy Melville (Swansea City)	1990–91
£265,000	David Bardsley (Watford)	1987–88
£260,000	Richard Hill (Watford)	1987–88
£250,000	John Durnin (Liverpool)	1988–89
£200,000	Brian Wilsterman (Beerschot)	1996–97
£200,000	Paul Simpson (Manchester City)	1988–89
£200,000	David Leworthy (Tottenham Hotspur)	1985–96
£187,000	Billy Whitehurst (Newcastle United)	1986–87
£180,000	Tommy Caton (Arsenal)	1986–87
£175,000	Steve Foster (Luton Town)	1989–90
£175,000	Dave Penney (Derby County)	1989–90
£170,000	Phil Whelan (Middlesbrough)	1997–98
£155,000	Gary Shelton (Sheffield Wednesday)	1987–88
£150,000	Sam Stockley (Barnet)	2001–02
£150,000	Paul Moody (Millwall)	2001–02
£150,000	Matt Elliott (Scunthorpe United)	1993–94
£150,000	Les Robinson (Doncaster Rovers)	1989–90
£150,000	Jimmy Phillips (Glasgow Rangers)	1988–89
£147,000	Ray Houghton (Fulham)	1985–86
£140,000	Martin Foyle (Aldershot)	1986–87
£110,000	Ken Veysey (Torquay United)	1990–91
£100,000	Kevin Francis (Birmingham City)	1997–98
£100,000	Darren Purse (Leyton Orient)	1996–97
£100,000	Martin Gray (Sunderland)	1995–96
£100,000	David Smith (Norwich City)	1994–95
£100,000	David Rush (Sunderland)	1994–95
£100,000	Phil Gilchrist (Hartlepool United)	1994–95
£100,000	Jim Magilton (Liverpool)	1990–91
£100,000	Mickey Lewis (Derby County)	1988–89
£100,000	Peter Hucker (Queen's Park Rangers)	1986–87
£100,000	Neil Slatter (Bristol Rovers)	1985–86
£100,000	Jeremy Charles (Queen's Park Rangers)	1984–85

Transfers received

£1,600,000	Matt Elliott (Leicester City)	1996–97
£1,000,000	Joey Beauchamp (West Ham United)	1994–95
£1,000,000	Dean Saunders (Derby County)	1998–99
£1,000,000	Dean Windass (Bradford City)	1998–99
£825,000	Ray Houghton (Liverpool)	1987–88
£775,000	John Aldridge (Liverpool)	1986–87
£600,000	Jim Magilton (Southampton)	1993–94
£500,000	Phil Gilchrist (Leicester City)	1999–2000
£500,000	Darren Purse (Birmingham City)	1997–98
£500,000	Andy Melville (Sunderland)	1993–94
£500,000	Paul Simpson (Derby County)	1991–92

£450,000	Chris Allen (Nottingham Forest)	1996–97
£400,000	Bobby Ford (Sheffield United)	1997–98
£375,000	Martin Foyle (Port Vale)	1991–92
£375,000	Robbie Mustoe (Middlesbrough)	1990–91
£300,000	Trevor Hebberd (Derby County)	1998–99
£300,000	Lee Nogan (Watford)	1991–92
£275,000	Dexter Blackstock (Southampton)	2003–04
£260,000	Kevin Brock (Queen's Park Rangers)	1987–88
£250,000	Phil Whitehead (West Bromwich Albion)	1998–99
£250,000	Simon Marsh (Birmingham City)	1998–99
£250,000	Jimmy Phillips (Middlesbrough)	1989–90
£200,000	Paul Moody (Fulham)	1997–98
£200,000	John Durnin (Portsmouth)	1993–94
£200,000	David Bardsley (Queen's Park Rangers)	1989–90
£150,000	Dean Whitehead (Sunderland)	2004–05
£140,000	John Dreyer (Luton Town)	1988–89
£125,000	Colin Greenall (Bury)	1990–91
£122,500	Billy Whitehurst (Reading)	1987–88
£115,000	Keith Cassells (Southampton)	1981–82
£115,000	Mark Wright (Southampton)	1981–82
£100,000	Nigel Jemson (Bury)	1997–98
£100,000	Mark Stein (Stoke City)	1991–92
£100,000	Tommy Caton (Charlton Athletic)	1988–89
£100,000	Andy Thomas (Newcastle United)	1986–87
£100,000	Les Taylor (Watford)	1980–81

INTERNATIONALS

Player	Country	Caps	Total Caps	Goals	Opponents
Aldridge, John	Eire	7	69		26 March 1986 Wales 0–1; 23 April 1986 Uruguay 1–1; 25 May 1986 Iceland 2–1; 27 May 1986 Czechoslovakia 1–0; 10 September 1986 Belgium 2–2 European Championship Gp 7; 15 October 1986 Scotland 0–0 European Championship Gp 7; 12 November 1986 Poland 0–1.
Arendse, Andre	South Africa	11	67		30 September 1999 Saudi Arabia 0–0 Afro–Asian Nations Cup; 27 November 1999 Sweden 1–0; 23 January 2000 Gabon 3–1 African Nations Cup; 27 January 2000 DR Congo 1–0 African Nations Cup; 6 February 2000 Ghana 1–0 African Nations Cup; 10 February 2000 Nigeria 0–2 African Nations Cup; 12 February 2000 Tunisia 2–2 African Nations Cup; 28 May 2000 Malta 1–0; 3 June 2000 USA 0–4 US Cup; 7 June 2000 Mexico 2–4 US Cup; 11 June 2000 Ireland 1–2 US Cup.
Burgess, Andy	England C	2	8	1	25 May 2007 Scotland 3–0* 4-Nations; 27 May 2007 Wales 3–0 4-Nations.
Charles, Jeremy	Wales	2	19		26 March 1986 Ireland 1–0; 10 June 1986 Finland 1–1 European Championship Gp 6.
Constable, James	England C	2	4	1	12 November 2008 Italy 2–2* International Challenge Trophy; 19 May 2009 Belgium 0–1 International Challenge Trophy Final.
Davies, Craig	Wales	2	5		17 August 2005 Slovenia 0–0; 7 September 2005 Poland 0–1 World Cup Qualifier.
Day, Matt	England C	1	1	1	16 September 2008 Bosnia & Herzegovina 2–6*.
Evans, Ceri	New Zealand	7	85		12 May 1991 Australia 0–1 Southern Cross Cup; 15 May 1991 Australia 1–2 Southern Cross Cup; 3 June 1991 England 0–1; 8 June 1991 England 0–2; 27 June 1992 Vanuatu 4–1 World Cup qualifier; 1 July 1992 Vanuatu 8–0 World Cup Qualifier.
Foster, Luke	England C	1	1		16 September 2008 Bosnia & Herzegovina 2–6.
Francis, Kevin	St Kitts and Nevis	2	2		3 April 1998 Dominica 1–2 Shell Caribbean Cup; 5 April 1998 Guadeloupe 2–1 Shell Caribbean Cup.
Gray, Phil	Northern Ireland	2	26		28 February 2001 Norway 0–4; 24 March 2001 Czech Republic 0–1 World Cup Qualifier.
Hamilton, Billy	Northern Ireland	6	41		12 September 1984 Romania 3–2 World Cup qualifier; 27 March 1985 Spain 0–0; 23 April 1986 Morocco 2–1; 3 June 1986 Algeria 1–1 World Cup finals; 7 June 1986 Spain 1–2 World Cup finals; 12 June 1986 Brazil 0–3 World Cup finals.
Houghton, Ray	Eire	12	73		26 March 1986 Wales 0–1; 23 April 1986 Uruguay 1–1; 25 May 1986 Iceland 2–1; 27 May 1986 Czechoslovakia 1–0; 10 September 1986 Belgium 2–2 European Championship Gp 7; 15 October 1986 Scotland 0–0 European Championship Gp 7; 12 November 1986 Poland 0–1; 18 February 1987 Scotland 1–0 European Championship Gp 7; 29 April 1987 Belgium 0–0 European Championship Gp 7; 28 May 1987 Luxembourg 2–0 European Championship Gp 7; 9 September 1987 Luxembourg 2–1 European Championship Gp 7; 14 October 1987 Bulgaria 2–0 European Championship Gp 7.
Kearns, Mick	Eire	1	18		23 September 1970 Poland 1–2.
Kee, Paul	Northern Ireland	7	9		27 March 1990 Norway 2–3; 12 October 1990 Yugoslavia 0–2 European Championship Qualifier; 17 October 1990 Denmark 1–1 European Championship Qualifier; 14 November 1990 Austria 0–0 European Championship Qualifier; 5 February 1991 Poland 3–1; 27 March 1991 Yugoslavia 4–1 European Championship Qualifier; 1 May 1991 Faroe Islands 1–1 European Championship Qualifier.

Player	Country	Caps	Total Caps	Goals	Opponents
Langan, Dave	Eire	11	25		1 May 1985 Norway 0–0 World Cup qualifier; 26 May 1985 Spain 0–0; 2 June 1985 Switzerland 3–0 World Cup qualifier; 26 March 1986 Wales 0–1; 23 April 1986 Uruguay 1–1; 10 September 1986 Belgium 2–2 European Championship Gp 7; 15 October 1986 Scotland 0–0 European Championship Gp 7; 12 November 1986 Poland 0–1; 23 May 1987 Brazil 1–0; 28 May 1987 Luxembourg 2–0 European Championship Gp 7; 9 September 1987 Luxembourg 2–1 European Championship Gp 7.
Magilton, Jim	Northern Ireland	18	52	4	5 February 1991 Poland 3–1*; 27 March 1991 Yugoslavia 1–4 European Championship Gp 4; 1 May 1991 Faroe Islands 1–0 European Championship Gp 4; 11 September 1991 Faroe Islands 5–0 European Championship Gp 4; 16 October 1991 Austria 2–1 European Championship Gp 4; 13 November 1991 Denmark 1–2 European Championship Gp 4; 19 February 1992 Scotland 0–1; 28 April 1992 Lithuania 2–2 World Cup qualifier; 2 June 1992 Germany 1–1; 9 September 1992 Albania 3–0* World Cup qualifier; 18 November 1992 Denmark 0–1 World Cup qualifier; 17 February 1993 Albania 2–1* World Cup qualifier; 31 March 1993 Ireland 0–3 World Cup qualifier; 25 May 1993 Lithuania 1–0 World Cup qualifier; 2 June 1993 Latvia 2–1* World Cup qualifier; 8 September 1993 Latvia 2–0 World Cup qualifier; 13 October 1993 Denmark 0–1 World Cup qualifier; 17 November 1993 Ireland 1–1 World Cup qualifier.
Melville, Andy	Wales	11	65		1 May 1991 Iceland 1–0; 30 May 1991 Poland 0–0; 5 June 1991 Germany 1–0 European Championship Gp 5; 11 September 1991 Brazil 1–0; 16 October 1991 Germany 1–4 European Championship Gp 5; 13 November 1991 Luxembourg 1–0 European Championship Gp 5; 20 May 1992 Romania 1–5 World Cup qualifier; 30 May 1992 Holland 0–4; 7 June 1992 Japan 1–0 Kirin Japan Cup; 28 April 1993 Czech Republic 1–1 World Cup qualifier; 6 June 1993 Faroe Islands 3–0 World Cup qualifier.
Roberts, Dave	Wales	6	17		28 March 1973 Poland 2–0; 15 May 1973 England 0–3 British Championships; 19 May 1973 Northern Ireland 0–1 British Championships; 11 May 1974 England 0–2 British Championships; 14 May 1974 Scotland 0–2 British Championships; 4 September 1974 Austria 1–2 European Championship Gp 2.
Saunders, Dean	Wales	6	75	2	23 March 1988 Yugoslavia 1–2*; 27 April 1988 Sweden 1–4; 1 June 1988 Malta 3–2; 4 June 1988 Italy 1–0; 14 September 1988 Holland 0–1 World Cup qualifier; 19 October 1988 Finland 2–2* World Cup qualifier.
Slatter, Neil	Wales	12	22	2	16 October 1985 Hungary 0–3; 25 February 1986 Saudi Arabia 2–1*; 10 May 1986 Canada 0–2; 19 May 1986 Canada 3–0; 10 September 1986 Finland 1–1* European Championships Gp 6; 29 April 1987 Czechoslovakia 1–1 European Championships Gp 6; 9 September 1987 Denmark 1–0 European Championships Gp 6; 14 October 1987 Denmark 0–1 European Championships Gp 6; 11 November 1987 Czechoslovakia 0–2 European Championships Gp 6; 1 June 1988 Malta 3–2; 4 June 1988 Italy 1–0 ; 8 February 1989 Israel 3–3.
Sloan, David	Northern Ireland	2	2		10 September 1968 Israel 3–2; 11 July 1970 Spain 0–3 European Championships Gp 4.

Player	Country	Caps	Total Caps	Goals	Opponents
Watson, Mark	Canada	12	78	1	27 April 1999 Northern Ireland 1–1; 2 June 1999 Guatemala 2–0 Canada Cup; 4 June 1999 Iran 0–1 Canada Cup; 6 June 1999 Ecuador 1–2 Canada Cup; 9 July 1999 Saudi Arabia 0–2; 13 February 2000 Costa Rica 2–2 Gold Cup; 15 February 2000 South Korea 0–0 Gold Cup; 20 February 2000 Mexico 2–1 Gold Cup; 24 February 2000 Trinidad & Tobago 1–0* Gold Cup; 27 February 2000 Colombia 2–0 Gold Cup; 16 July 2000 Trinidad & Tobago 0–2 World Cup qualifier; 23 July 2000 Panama 0–0 World Cup; 15 August 2000 Mexico 0–2 World Cup qualifier; 3 September 2000 Trinidad & Tobago 0–4 World Cup qualifier.

Under-23 (Appearances made while at Oxford United)

Ray Gaston	Northern Ireland	1			

Under-21 (Appearances made while at Oxford United)

Kevin Brock	England	4			
Chris Allen	England	2			
Simon Marsh	England	1			
Craig Davies	Wales	4			
Anthony Wright	Wales	3			
Rob Folland	Wales	1			
Adam Chapman	Northern Ireland	1			
Peter Foley	Ireland	6			

HEADINGTON OLD RESULTS

Date	Competition	Opponents	Venue	Score	Scorers	Attendance
1893–94						
25 November	Friendly	Cowley Barracks		1–2		
13 January	Friendly	Victoria	H	3–3	Scott-Tucker 2, Hitchings	
20 January	Friendly	Victoria	A	0–6		
10 February	Friendly	Clarendon Press	A	0–5		
17 February	Friendly	Clarendon Press		0–1		
10 March	Friendly	Cherwell Rovers		6–0		
1894–95						
6 October	Friendly	St Peter-le-Bailey		0–2		
13 October	Friendly	Cowley St John	A	0–7		
17 November	City Junior League A Division	Clarendon Press	H	0–4		
24 November	City Junior League A Division	St Barnabas	H	0–6		
8 December	City Junior League A Division	Wanderers 2nd	A	2–1	H. Knowles, F. Collett	
15 December	City Junior League A Division	Cowley St John	A	2–5		
5 January	City Junior Cup	St Peter-le-Bailey	H	2–0	Hitchings, Jacobs	
26 January	City Junior League A Division	St Barnabas		1–4		
2 March	City Junior Cup	Victoria		0–5		
1895–96						
19 October		St Kenelm's School	H	4–0		
26 October	City Junior League A Division	Cowley Barracks	H	2–2		
2 November	City Junior League A Division	Victoria	A	0–5		
9 November	City Junior League A Division	St Paul's	H	1–3		
16 November	City Junior League A Division	Cowley	A	1–4		
23 November	City Junior League A Division	YMCA	H	2–0		
30 November	Friendly	City Temperance	H	12–0		
7 December		Iffley		4–0		
21 December	City Junior League A Division	Cowley	H	0–2		200
11 January	City Junior League A Division	Clarendon Press	H	2–0		
25 January	City Junior League A Division	Cowley Barracks	A	5–1		
1 February	City Junior League A Division	St Paul's	A	5–2	H. Knowles 2, Fletcher 2, Collett	
8 February	Annual encounter	Culham College 2nd	A	2–2		
15 February	City Junior League A Division	Victoria	H	0–5		
22 February	City Junior League A Division	YMCA	A	0–1		
14 March	City Junior League A Division	Clarendon Press	A	0–2		
1896–97						
10 October	City Junior League B Division	Oxford United College Servants*		walk-over	*OUCS scratched	
17 October	City Junior Cup	Cowley St John	H	6–1		
24 October	County Junior Cup	Dorchester	A	1–0		
7 November	County Junior Cup	Newland Cygnets	A	1–4	Longford	
21 November	City Junior League B Division	Victoria Res	H	2–5	Knowles, H. Fletcher	
12 December	City Junior Cup	St Mary Magdalene	H	0–1	ABANDONED	
19 December	City Junior Cup	St Barnabas	A	0–3		
2 January	City Junior Cup	St Barnabas	H	1–1	Roberts	
9 January	City Junior Cup	Victoria Res	H*	2–2	H. Fletcher 2 *Should have been away!	
16 January	City Junior Cup	St Mary Magdalene	H	1–2	Rearranged	
30 January	Friendly	Old Wesleyans	H	1–0		
27 February	Annual encounter	Culham College		2–3	H. Knowles 2	
1897–98						
9 October	City Junior League B Division	Victoria Res		1–1	H. Knowles	
16 October		Cygnets 2nd	H	11–0	H. Knowles 8, Grimsley, B Edney	
23 October	City Junior League B Division	St Paul's	H	6–0	H. Knowles 5	
30 October		St Kenelm's	H	2–2		
6 November	City Junior League B Division	City Temperance		5–1	H. Knowles 3, H. Fletcher, W. Morris	

Date	Competition	Opponents	Venue	Score	Scorers	Attendance
13 November	Junior Shield	Clarendon Press		0–2		
20 November	City Junior League B Division	Oxford Institute	H	10–0		
18 December	City Junior League B Division	Victoria Res	A	1–0	Knowles	
27 January		Nomads	A	0–0		
29 January	City Junior League B Division	St Paul's		walk-over		
5 February	Annual encounter	Culham College 2nd	H	5–0		
19 February	City Junior League B Division	Temperance		2–0	H. Fletcher, G. Fletcher	
5 March	City Junior League Final	St Mary Magdalene	City Ground	1–1	G. Fletcher	
19 March	City Junior League Final replay	St Mary Magdalene	City Ground	1–0	Knowles	
1898–99						
24 Septmeber		Oxford City A	A	5–1	Ashmore 3, Knowles 2	
1 October	Opening of new ground	Clarendon Press	H	4–0	J. Fletcher, B. Edney, G. Fletcher 2	
	Friendly	United College Servants		4–2		
15 October	City Junior League A Division	St Barnabas	H	4–1	B. Edney 2, Grimsley 2	
29 October*	City Junior League A Division	Cowley Juniors	A	7–0	Knowles 6	
*Game ordered to be replayed as Headington fielded an ineligible player						
5 November		Clarendon Press	A	1–3		
12 November	Annual encounter	Culham College 2nd	H	9–1		
3 December	County Junior Shield	St Barnabas	A	1–0	J. Fletcher	
10 December		Witney Adult School	H	3–2		
17 December	Friendly	Oxford City A	H	1–2		
24 December		Cowley	H	3–3		
7 January	City Junior League A Division	Cowley	H	4–2	E. Knowles, H. Knowles 2, G. Fletcher	
21 January	City Junior League A Division	Cowley Juniors		walk-over		
28 January	County Junior Shield	Bicester	A	2–2	Grimsley, H. Knowles	
4 February	County Junior Shield	Bicester	H	0–0	ABANDONED	320
11 February*	County Junior Shield	Bicester	H	1–0	Knowles *rearranged game	
15 February	City Junior League A Division	Victoria	H	4–1	H. Fletcher 2, Knowles, J. Fletcher	
25 February	Oxfordshire Shield	Henley II	H	2–0	J. Fletcher, Grimsley	over 300
4 March*	City Junior League A Division	Cowley	A	1–3	Knowles *replayed game	
6 March	City Junior League A Division	Victoria	A	1–1	G. Fletcher	
11 March	City Junior League Final	St Mary Magdalene	City Ground	0–0	Grey saved pen	
16 March	City Junior League Final replay	St Mary Magdalene	City Ground	3–0	H. Fletcher, H. Knowles, Couling og	750
18 March	Oxfordshire Shield Final	Chipping Norton Swifts	City Ground	0–0		
1 April*	Oxfordshire Shield Final replay	Chipping Norton Swifts	Witney Ground	1–2		
*Competition declared incomplete because Chipping Norton fielded 2 ineligible players						
1899–1900						
14 October	Oxford & District League Div 2	Oxford Temperance	A	5–0	Knowles 3, J. Fletcher, G. Fletcher	
21 October	Oxford & District League Div 2	Culham College 2nd	H	1–2		
21 October	City Junior League B	Clarendon Press 2nd	A	0–4		
4 November	Oxford & District League Div 2	Banbury Britannia 2nd	H	4–1	G. Fletcher, H. Fletcher, J. Fletcher, Bolton	
4 November	City Junior League B	College Servants	A	0–10		
11 November	County Junior Shield	Clarendon Press 2nd	A	1–0	Hodgkins	
2 December	County Junior Shield	Victoria	H	3–2	Creese, Morris, G. Fletcher	
30 December	Oxford & District League Div 2	Oxford City 2nd	A	0–0		
30 December	City Junior League B	Victoria	A	–	Headington scratched	
5 January	Oxford & District League Div 2	Abingdon 2nd	H	3–0	J. Fletcher, Bolton 2 (1 pen)	
12 January	Oxford & District League Div 2	Oxford City 2nd	H	3–3	J. Fletcher, Ashmore 2	
19 January	County Junior Shield	Chipping Norton Swifts	A	2–3	own goal, unknown	
26 January	Oxford & District League Div 2	Abingdon 2nd	A	0–1		
3 March	Oxford & District League Div 2	Oxford Temperance	H	2–2	Grimsley, Knowles	
10 March	Oxford & District League Div 2	Culham College 2nd	A	1–4		
1900–01						
12 October	Friendly	SS Philip and James	H	5–2	H. Fletcher 2, Clinkard, Wakelin, Harris,	
19 October	City Junior League A Division	Oxford Temperance	A	3–1	Dawson, Bateman, Packford	
26 October	Friendly	Victoria	H	3–0	Taylor, Wakelin, Clinkard	
2 November	County Shield	Thame	A	3–2	Grimsley, Fletcher, Clinkard	

Date	Competition	Opponents	Venue	Score	Scorers	Attendance
9 November	City Junior League A Division	City A	A	0–2		
16 November	County Shield	Clarendon Press	H	1–0	Bateman	200
30 November	County Shield	St Mary Magdalene	H*	0–0	*at Sandy Lane	
7 December	County Shield	St Mary Magdalene	A	1–3	Clinkard	
15 December	City Junior League A Division	Oxford Temperance	H	0–2		
21 December	City Junior League A Division	Clarendon Press	A	0–1		
26 December	Friendly	Cowley Barracks	H	2–1	Wakelin, Jacobs	
29 December	City Junior League A Division	College Servants	H	1–0	Grimsley	
5 January	City Junior League A Division	Victoria	H	0–5		
12 January	City Junior League A Division	City Res	H	10–1	Wakelin 4, G. Fletcher, Jacobs, Bateman, J. Fletcher, Packford, Ashmore	
9 February	Oxfordshire Senior Cup	Thame	A	1–1	Ashmore	
16 February	City Junior League A Division	Clarendon Press	H	1–1	Wakelin	
22 February	Oxfordshire Senior Cup	Thame	H	2–3	Ashmore 2	
2 March	City Junior League A Division	College Servants*	A	walk-over	*College Servants scratched	
2 March	Friendly	College Servants	A	2–0	Packford, Wakelin	
16 March	City Junior League A Division	Victoria	H	2–2	Stow, Packford	

1901–02

Date	Competition	Opponents	Venue	Score	Scorers	Attendance
12 October	Oxford & District League Div 2	SS Philip and James	H	1–1	G. Fletcher	
19 October	City Junior League B Division	Victoria	H	3–0	Wakelin, Clinkard, Bateman	
26 October	Oxford & District League Div 2	Culham College II	H	0–0		
2 November	County Junior Shield*	Victoria	A	5–1	Clinkard 3, Trinder 2 *Reserves match	
16 November	City Junior League B Division	Victoria	A	1–1	Bateman	
16 November	Oxford & District League Div 2	Abingdon II	H	3–0	Prescott 2, Philcox	
16 November	County Junior Shield	Culham College II	A	1–1	Packford	
23 November	County Junior Shield	Culham College II	A	0–2		
23 November	City Junior League B Division	St Thomas' II	H	7–3		
30 November	City Junior League B Division	Central Night School	H	2–1	Wakelin, Bateman	
7 December	Oxford & District League Div 2	Victoria	A	4–0	Bateman 2, Wakelin, Levett	
14 December	City Junior League B Division	Clarendon Press	A	2–1	Organ 2	
28 December	Oxford & District League Div 2	College Servants	H	5–0	Clinkard 4, Bateman	
4 January	City Junior League B Division	St Barnabas	A	2–0	Stow, Packford	
11 January	City Junior League B Division	St Mary Magdalene	H	0–0		
18 January	City Junior League B Division	St Barnabas	H	1–2	Packford	
25 January	City Junior League B Division	St Mary Magdalene	A	1–3	Clinkard	
15 February	Friendly	Culham College II	A	1–3	Packford	
22 February	County Senior Cup semi-final	Banbury Harriers	H	3–1	Ashmore 2, Rose	
8 March	Oxford & District League Div 2	Victoria	H	3–1	Ashmore, Rose, Organ	
15 March	County Senior Cup Final	Culham College	White House	0–0		600 to 700
19 March	County Senior Cup Final replay	Culham College	White House	2–3	Packford, Wakelin	250
29 March	Oxford & District League Div 2	SS Philip and James	A	1–2		
12 April	Oxford & District League Div 2	St Barnabas	A	1–2		

1902–03

Date	Competition	Opponents	Venue	Score	Scorers	Attendance
27 September	Friendly	Temperance	A	1–4	Bateman	
4 October*	City Junior League B Division	Victoria	H	1–0		
*Game declared void because Chapman not registered for Headington						
25 October	City Junior League B Division	YMCA	A	7–1	Packford 3, Tolly, Stow, Bateman, Ingram	
1 November	County Junior Shield	Thame	A	2–1	Packford, Tolly	
15 November	County Junior Shield	Culham College	H	4–0	Packford 4	
22 November	City Junior League B Division	SS Philip and James	A	6–0	Ingram 2, Packford 2, Bateman, Tolly	
29 November	County Junior Shield	Bicester	H	2–2	Chapman, Creese (pen)	
13 December	County Junior Shield	Bicester	A	0–5		
27 December	City Junior League B Division	St Mary Magdalene	A	3–1	Chapman, Prescott, Packford	
3 January	City Junior League B Division	Victoria	A	1–1		
10 January	Friendly	Oxford City reserves	H	0–0		
31 January	County Senior Cup preliminary round	Culham College	H	0–2		
14 February	City Junior League B Division	SS Philip and James	H	2–1		
21 February	Oxford and District League Div 2	College Servants	A	6–0	G. Fletcher, Packford, J. Fletcher, Bateman, Tolley, Ingham	
28 February	City Junior League B Division	Victoria	H	2–4	Bateman, Tolley	

Date	Competition	Opponents	Venue	Score	Scorers	Attendance
1903–04						
3 October	Friendly	Temperance	A	1–3		
10 October	Oxford and District League Div 2	Clarendon Press	H	4–1	Tolley 2, Stow 2	
17 October	Oxford and District League Div 2	Culham College II	H	3–1	Merry, Stow, Packford	
24 October	Oxford and District League Div 2	Culham College II	A	2–1	Jacobs, Stow	
31 October	City Junior League A Division	Victoria	H	2–4	Packford, Stow	
7 November	City Junior League A Division	SS Philip and James Reserves	H	5–1		
14 November*	Oxfordshire Junior Shield second round	Thame	H	2–2		
*Game declared void after Thame fielded ineligible player						
21 November*	Oxfordshire Junior Shield second-round replay	Thame	A	2–3	Creese, Packford *Replayed game	
28 November	City Junior League A Division	St Thomas	H	2–2	Bateman, Packford	
5 December	Oxfordshire Junior Shield second-round replay	Thame	H	1–0	Stow	
12 December	Oxfordshire Junior Shield third round	Bicester	H	2–1	Stringer, Stow	
19 December	City Junior League A Division	YMCA	H	3–1	Tolley, Chapman	
2 January	City Junior League A Division	YMCA	A	0–1		
16 January	City Junior League A Division	Victoria	A	2–2	Stringer, Bateman	
23 January	City Junior League A Division	St Thomas	A	0–4		
6 February	Oxfordshire Junior Shield semi Final	St Thomas	H	1–1	Merry	
13 February	Oxfordshire Junior Shield semi Final replay	St Thomas	H	3–1	Creese 2 (2 pens), Bateman	
27 February	Oxford and District League Div 2	Clarendon Press	H	5–1	Tolley 3, Stow, Stringer	
5 March	City Junior League A Division	SS Philip and James Reserves	A	0–1		
12 March	Oxfordshire Junior Shield Final	Caversham St John's	White House	0–2		400
26 March	Oxford and District League Div 2	St Thomas	A	4–0	Merry, Wiltshire, Grimsley, Edney	
16 April	Friendly	YMCA	H	3–0	Dean og, Tolley	
23 April	Oxford and District League Div 2	Victoria	Temperance ground	0–3		
1904–05						
8 October	City Junior League Div 1	Cowley	H	4–3		
15 October	Oxfordshire County Shield first round	Victoria	H	4–3		
22 October	City Junior League Div 1	Wolvercote	H	1–1	Pettipher	
29 October	Oxfordshire County Shield second round	College Servants	H	3–3	Cull 2 + pen	
5 November	Oxfordshire County Shield second-round replay	College Servants	A	2–2		
12 November	Oxfordshire County Shield second round second replay		College Servants	H	2–5	Ponting, Stringer
19 November	City Junior League Div 1	St Frideswide	H	6–1		
3 December	City Junior League Div 1	Victoria	H	1–4	Ponting	
10 December	Oxfordshire League Div 2	Victoria	A	0–0		
17 December	Oxfordshire League Div 2	St Thomas	A	1–1	Thomas	
23 December*	City Junior League Div 1	St Barnabas	A			
*Headington no show. Game ordered to be replayd						
30 December	City Junior League Div 2	Victoria	A	0–6		
7 January	City Junior League Div 3	St Frideswide	A	1–4	Cull	
14 January	City Junior League Div 4	St Barnabas	H	4–5	Cull 2, Bateman, Pettifer	
21 January	City Junior League Div 5	Cowley	A	0–1		
28 January	City Junior League Div 6	Wolvercote	A	–	Headington no show	
4 February	Oxfordshire League Div 2	Culham College II	A	5–2	Bateman, Cull 2, Webb 2	
11 February	Oxfordshire League Div 2	Culham College II	H	5–0	Cull 3, Webb, Bateman	
25 February	Oxfordshire League Div 2	St Thomas	H	4–0	Bateman 2, Cull, og	
11 March	Oxfordshire League Div 2	Hinksey	A	0–2		
18 March	Oxfordshire League Div 2	Wolvercote	A	2–0	Cull, Crease (pen)	
25 March	Oxfordshire League Div 2	Victoria	H	1–3	Cull	
8 April	Oxfordshire League Div 2	Hinksey	H	1–6		
22 April	Friendly	Headingley	H	4–6	Headingley winners of Aston League	
Birmingham						
1905–06						
7 October	City Junior League B Division	St Thomas		4–1	Garth 2, Thomas, Cull	
14 October	County Shield first round	Bicester Reserves	A	0–0		
21 October	County Shield first round	Bicester Reserves	H	3–0	Cull 2, Bateman	
28 October	Oxfordshire League Div 2	St Frideswide	H	3–2	Cull, Stringer, Creese (pen)	
4 November	City Junior League B Division	Post Office	A	3–0	Jacobs, Cull, Creese (pen)	

Date	Competition	Opponents	Venue	Score	Scorers	Attendance
11 November	County Shield third round	SS Philip and James	H	3–0	Stringer 2, Pettyfer	
25 November	City Junior League B Division	St Thomas	A	1–3	Merry	
2 December	County Shield fourth round	Dorchester	A	0–4		
16 December	City Junior League B Division	Oxford Institute	H	3–2		
23 December	Oxfordshire League Div 2	Hannington	H	7–1	Packford 4, Webb 2, Merry	
30 December	City Junior League B Division	St Frideswide	H	6–0	Pettypher 3, Thomas 2, Webb	
27 January	Oxfordshire League Div 2	Hannington	A	3–0	Pettypher, Bateman, Merry	
3 February	Oxfordshire League Div 2	Culham	A	3–2		
17 February	City Junior League B Division	St Frideswide	A	3–0	Bateman, Pettypher, Ing	
24 February	City Junior League B Division	Oxford Institute	A	walk-over		
3 March	City Junior League B Division Decider	St Thomas	White House	2–1	Webb, Thomas	
24 March	Oxfordshire League Div 2	St Frideswide	A	2–2		
7 April	City Junior League Final	College Servants	White House	0–2		
21 April	Oxfordshire League Div 2	St Thomas	H	6–2	G. Fletcher 2, Stringer, J. Fletcher 2, Pettypher	
28 April	Oxfordshire League Div 2 Final	YMCA	St Thomas ground	1–2	G. Fletcher	

1906–07

Date	Competition	Opponents	Venue	Score	Scorers	Attendance
28 September	Friendly	Cowley St John	A	5–3		
6 October	City Junior League Div 2	Cowley	H	0–3		
13 October	County Junior Shield first round	Thame St Mary's	A	0–6		
10 November	City Junior League Div 2	St Thomas	A	0–6		
17 November	City Junior League Div 2	College Servants II	A	1–11		
24 November		Hannington	H	1–1		
31 November		Summertown	A	1–3		
8 December	City Junior League Div 2	Clarendon Press	A	–		Headington scratched
22 December	City Junior League Div 2	St Thomas	H	1–9		
5 January		Oxford Institute	H	4–1		
19 January	City Junior League Div 2	Clarendon Press	H	3–3		
9 February	City Junior League Div 2	Cowley	H	2–1		
23 February	City Junior League Div 2	College Servants II	H	0–3		

1907–08

Date	Competition	Opponents	Venue	Score	Scorers	Attendance
12 October	City Junior League Div 2	Oxford Institute II	H	3–1		
19 October	Friendly	Wesley Memorial	H	1–3		
26 October	City Junior League Div 2	St Frideswide II	H	0–2		
2 November	City Junior League Div 2	Eagle Ironworks	H	10–1		
9 November	City Junior League Div 2	Hearts of Oak	H	8–0	Bateman (pen), Merry 2, Jacobs 2	
16 November	City Junior League Div 2	Hannington II	A	0–3		
30 November	City Junior League Div 2	Wesley Memorial	H	5–0		
21 December	City Junior League Div 2	St Frideswide II	A	8–2		
28 December*	Friendly	YMCA	H	3–0		
*game abandoned due to injury to YMCA player						
4 January	City Junior League Div 2	YMCA II	A	0–1		
11 January	City Junior League Div 2	Oxford Institute II	H	0–4		
18 January	Friendly	Headington Quarry	H	3–0		
1 February	City Junior League Div 2	Hannington II	H	1–1		
8 February	City Junior League Div 2	Hearts of Oak	A	–		Headington scratched
15 February	City Junior League Div 2	YMCA II	H	0–9		
22 February	City Junior League Div 2	Wesley Memorial	A*	–		
*Headington showed up at their own ground, match ordered to be replayed						
18 April	Friendly	Headingley	H	6–4	Kelly 3, Fletcher, Stow, Wiltshire	

1908–09

Date	Competition	Opponents	Venue	Score	Scorers	Attendance
10 October	Friendly	St Frideswide	H	3–0	Cull 3	
24 October	Oxfordshire Junior Shield first round	Thame St Mary's	H	5–1	Webb 2, Cull, Talmage, Pettyfer	
31 October	Oxfordshire League Div 2	Cowley Barracks	A	0–2		
7 November	Oxfordshire Junior Shield second round	Dorchester	A	0–4		
28 November	Oxfordshire League Div 2	Radley	A	2–0	Fletcher, Pettyfer	
5 December	Oxfordshire League Div 2	Dorchester	A	0–4		
19 December	Oxfordshire League Div 2	Thame Victoria	H	4–1	Talmage 3, J. Fletcher	

Date	Competition	Opponents	Venue	Score	Scorers	Attendance
26 December	Friendly	Oxford Institute	H	2–0	Wiltshire, Cousins	
2 January	Friendly	Headington Quarry	A	3–2	Pettyfer 2, Wiltshire	
9 January	Oxfordshire League Div 2	Radley	H	3–2	Pettyfer 2, J. Fletcher	
16 January	Oxfordshire League Div 2	Cowley Barracks	H	2–3	Talmage 2	
23 January	Oxfordshire League Div 2	Dorchester	H	0–2		
30 January	Oxfordshire League Div 2	Thame Victoria	H	0–5		
6 February	Friendly	Culham College	H	0–1		
20 February	Oxfordshire League Div 2	Abingdon Reserves	A	3–1	G. Fletcher 2, Currill	
27 February	Oxfordshire League Div 2	Abingdon Reserves	H	3–3		
1909–10						
18 September	Friendly	Cowley Barracks	A	1–0	Cull	
25 September	Friendly	Oxford Institute	H	6–2		
2 October	City Junior League Div 1	Holy Trinity	A	0–1		
9 October	Oxfordshire District League Div 2	Cowley Barracks	A	1–2		
16 October	City Junior League Div 1	Oxford Institute	A	1–8	Stow	
23 October	County Junior Shield second round	Cowley	A	0–1		
30 October	City Junior League Div 1	College Servants	A	2–4		
6 November	Oxfordshire District League Div 2	Radley	H	1–1	Cooper	
13 November	City Junior League Div 1	Holy Trinity	H	1–1	Pettyfer	
26 December	Friendly	Mr W. Herbert's XI	H	3–1		
1 January	City Junior League Div 1	College Servants	H	4–0	E. Jacobs, King, Pettyfer, Walker	
12 February	Oxfordshire District League Div 2	Thame St Mary's	H	2–3	Talmage 2	
19 February	Oxfordshire District League Div 2	Dorchester	A	–	Headington scratched	
5 March	City Junior League Div 1	YMCA	H	3–3	Cooper, Phillips, Hemmings	
12 March	City Junior League Div 1	Oxford Institute	H	2–2	Cooper, E. Jacobs	
26 March	Oxfordshire District League Div 2	Dorchester	H	0–2		
1910–11						
1 October	City Junior League Div 1	Cowley & Church Army Press	A	1–3		
8 October	County Junior Shield first round	Headington Quarry	A	0–3		400
15 October	City Junior League Div 1	Wolvercote	A	3–2		
29 October	City Junior League Div 1	College Servants	A	0–3		
5 November	Oxfordshire League Div 2	YMCA	H	1–1		
12 November	City Junior League Div 1	Cowley Press	H	1–2		
19 November	Oxfordshire League Div 2	Watlington	H	3–0		
10 December	Oxfordshire League Div 2	Cowley Press	H	4–0	King 2, Webb, Bateman	
17 December	City Junior League Div 1	Cowley St John	A	0–8		
24 December	Oxfordshire League Div 2	College Servants	H	2–2	Phillips 2	
31 December	City Junior League Div 1	College Servants	H	2–1	King (pen), Webb	
14 January	City Junior League Div 1	Cowley St John	H	0–3		
21 January	Oxfordshire League Div 2	College Servants	A	0–0		
28 January	Oxfordshire League Div 2	Thame II	H	1–0		
4 February	Oxfordshire League Div 2	Cowley	A	3–4	King, Phillips, Webb	
11 February	Oxfordshire League Div 2	YMCA	A	9–0	Bateman 2, Webb 2, Jacobs 2, Morris, Phillips, Currill	
25 February	Oxfordshire League Div 2	Thame II	A	7–1	Yeomans 5, King, Morris	
25 March	Oxfordshire League Div 2	Watlington	A	4–1	King, H. Jacobs, Yeomans 2	100
1911–12						
23 September	Friendly	YMCA	H	2–1	Payne 2	
30 September	City Junior League Div 1	Summertown	H	1–1	own-goal	
7 October	Oxfordshire Junior Shield first round	Cowley	H	0–1		
14 October	City Junior League Div 1	New Marston	A	0–6		
21 October	Oxfordshire Junior League Div 2A	Bicester Reserves	H	4–0	Burke, Webb, Phillips, Cooper	
4 November	Oxfordshire Junior League Div 2A	Cowley St John	H	2–1	Phillips, Cooper	
11 November	Friendly	Oxford City A	H	3–2	Burke, Phillips 2	
18 November	City Junior League Div 1	Summertown	A	3–0	Phillips, Burke, Cooper	
25 November	Oxfordshire Junior League Div 2A	Thame A	H	3–0	Coppock, Burke, Cooper	
2 December	City Junior League Div 1	Clarendon Press	H	3–0	Burke 2, Webb	

Date	Competition	Opponents	Venue	Score	Scorers	Attendance
9 December	Oxfordshire Junior League Div 2A	Bicester Reserves	A	1–1	Phillips	
16 December	City Junior League Div 1	YMCA	H	6–0	Currill 2, Phillips 2, own-goal, Webb	
30 December	City Junior League Div 1	New Marston	H	1–0	Cooper	500
6 January	City Junior League Div 1	YMCA	A	4–0	Cooper 2, Webb 2	
13 January	Oxfordshire Junior League Div 2A	Thame A	A	4–1	Phillips 3, Burke	
27 January	City Junior League Div 1	Clarendon Press	A	3–1	Phillips, Cooper, Wells	
10 February	Oxfordshire Junior League Div 2A	Cowley St John	A	2–1	Phillips, Cooper	
17 February	Oxfordshire Junior League Div 2A	Littlemore	H	1–3	own-goal	
23 March	Oxfordshire Junior League Div 2A	Littlemore	A	0–0		
8 April	City Junior League Div 1 Final	Foresters	White House	0–0		1,300–1,400
18 April	City Junior League Div 1 Final replay	Foresters	White House	0–1		1,000
1912–13						
16 September	Friendly	Depot LI	A	1–5		
30 September	City Junior League Div 1	College Servants	A	1–4		
5 October	Oxfordshire Junior Shield	Thame A	A	4–5	A. Phillips 2, Vallis, J. Phillips	
2 November	City Junior League Div 1	YMCA	A	3–0	A. Phillips, J. Phillips	
16 November	City Junior League Div 1	College Servants	H	3–1	Coppock, Cooper, Morris	
23 November	Oxfordshire Junior League	Thame A	H	4–1	Coppock, Phillips, Morris 2	
30 November	City Junior League Div 1	Oxford Institute	A	1–4	Trafford	
7 December	Oxfordshire Junior League	Littlemore	H	2–0	Phillips, own-goal	
21 December*	City Junior League Div 1	Littlemore	A	0–1	*Match abandoned after ball 'collapsed'	
28 December	City Junior League Div 1	Depot LI	A	1–3	A. Phillips	
4 January	City Junior League Div 1	Oxford Institute	H	0–2		
11 January	Oxfordshire Junior League	Dorchester	H	4–1	Smith, Trafford 2, Morris	
18 January	City Junior League Div 1	YMCA	H	4–1	Phillips, Badger 2, Morris	
25 January	Oxfordshire Junior League	Dorchester	A	1–1	Phillips	
1 February	Oxfordshire Junior League	Cowley	H	3–1	Morris, Badger 2	
15 February	City Junior League Div 1	Depot LI	H	1–3	Phillips	
22 February	Oxfordshire Junior League	Littlemore	A	2–1	Badger, Lusty (own-goal)	
1 March	Oxfordshire Junior League	Cowley	A	1–5	Smith	
8 March	Oxfordshire Junior League	Depot LI	A	2–4	Anstey, Bateman	
15 March	Oxfordshire Junior League	Depot LI	H	0–2		
22 March	Friendly	Headingley	H	0–3		
30 March	Friendly	Cowley	H	2–0	Phillips (pen), Anstey	
1913–14						
20 September	Friendly	Marston	H	11–0		
27 September	City Junior League Div 1 A	Oxford Institute	H	0–1		
4 October	Oxfordshire Junior Shield first round	Thame A	H	7–2	J. Phillips, Anstey 2, Morris, A. Phillips, Gray 2	
11 October	City Junior League Div 1 A	YMCA	H	6–1	Morris 2, J. Phillips 2, Anstey, A. Phillips	
25 October	Oxfordshire Junior Shield second round	Cowley	A	1–0		
1 November	Oxfordshire Junior League Div 2	Church Army Press	A	2–2	McDermott, A. Phillips	
8 November	Oxon Charity Cup	Witney Town	A	1–0	J. Phillips	
15 November	Oxfordshire Junior Shield third round	Witney Gordons	A	2–0	Anstey, Morris	
22 November	City Junior League Div 1 A	College Servants	A	2–3	A. Phillips, Anstey	
6 December	City Junior League Div 1 A	YMCA	A	3–0	A. Phillips 2, Morris	
13 December	Oxon Charity Cup	Witney Swifts	A	1–1	A. Phillips	
20 December	Oxon Charity Cup replay	Witney Swifts	H	0–2		500
25 December	Oxfordshire Junior League Div 2	Thame A	H	3–0	A. Phillips 2 (1 pen), Harley	
26 December	Oxfordshire Junior League Div 2	Thame A	A	5–1	Morris, Harley 2, Smith, J. Phillips	
27 December	City Junior League Div 1 A	Oxford Institute	A	2–5	A. Phillips, Cooper	
3 January	Oxfordshire Junior Shield semi-final	Banbury Harriers	A	3–0	Smith, Morris, A. Phillips	
3 January	Friendly	Wolvercote United	A	1–6		
10 January	City Junior League Div 1 A	Church Army Press	A	1–2	Horwood	
17 January	Oxfordshire Junior League Div 2	Cowley	H	2–0	Morris, A. Phillips	
24 January	Oxfordshire Junior League Div 2	Littlemore	A	1–5	Smith	
31 January	Oxfordshire Junior League Div 2	Littlemore	H	3–1	A. Phillips 2, J. Phillips	
7 February	City Junior League Div 1 A	East Oxford United	H	walk-over EOU scratched		
14 February	Oxfordshire Junior League Div 2	Church Army Press	H	4–0	Smith, Badger (own-goal), McDermott, J. Phillips	

Date	Competition	Opponents	Venue	Score	Scorers	Attendance
21 February	Oxfordshire Junior Shield Final	Oxford Institute	White House	5–2	A. Phillips 2, McDermott 2, Morris	600
28 February	Oxfordshire Junior League Div 2	Depot LI	A	4–1	A. Phillips 2 (1 pen), McDermott, Smith	
7 March	Oxfordshire Junior League Div 2	Depot LI	H	walk-over Depot LI scratched		
21 March*	Oxfordshire Junior League Div 2	Dorchester	A	1–1	Smith	
*Dorchester scratched return game						
11 April	Oxfordshire Junior League semi-final	St Barnabas	College Servants ground	4–3	McDermott 2, A. Phillips 2	
18 April	Oxfordshire Junior League Final	YMCA	White House	0–3		800

1918–19

Date	Competition	Opponents	Venue	Score	Scorers	Attendance
15 March	Friendly	WRM	A	2–6	Shepherd, Drewitt	
28 March	Friendly	Cowley	A	2–1	Badger, Drewitt	
12 April	Friendly	Cowley	H	5–1	Smith 3, Washington, Phillips	
18 April	Friendly	East Oxford	H	7–0	Drewitt 4, Smith, Phillips, Washington	
19 April	Friendly	Cowley	H	5–2	Smith, Phillips 2, Drewitt, Morris	
26 April	Friendly	Cowley Barracks	A	2–1	Drewitt, own-goal	

1919–20

Date	Competition	Opponents	Venue	Score	Scorers	Attendance
4 October	Friendly	Clarendon Press	A	4–2	Drewitt 2, own-goal, Morris	
4 October	Oxford City FA League Div 2	Morris Motors	A	2–2		
18 October	Oxford City FA Div 1	Wolvercote	A	8–0	Phillips, Drewitt 3, Webb 4	
18 October	Oxford City FA League Div 2	Wolvercote II	H	7–1	Tolley, Sherlock 3, L. Coppock, V. Coppock, Shepherd	
25 October	County Junior Shield first round	Cowley	A	0–6		
25 October	Oxford City FA League Div 2	19th Boy Scouts	H	11–2	Badger 4, Ward 3, Morris 2, Smith, Phillips	
1 November	Oxon Junior League A	Littlemore	A	5–0	Coppock, Smith 2, Badger 2	
8 November	Oxford City FA Div 1	United Trades	A	2–1	Shepherd, Phillips	
15 November	Oxford City FA League Div 2	19th Boy Scouts	H	2–1	Goodgame, Parker	
29 November	Oxon Charity Cup	Cowley	H	0–6		500
6 December	Oxford City FA Div 1	Wolvercote	H	6–0	Webb, Washington 3, Smith 2	
13 December	Oxford City FA League Div 2	Balliol Club	H	3–1	Sherlock, V. Coppock, Creed	
20 December	Oxon Junior League A	YMCA	H	7–0	Webb 4, Tolley, Phillips, Morris	
20 December	Oxford City FA League Div 2	Balliol Boys	A	1–1		
25 December	Oxford City FA Div 1	Littlemore	A	2–0	Drewitt, Washington	
26 December	Oxford City FA Div 1	Littlemore	H	walk-over Littlemore failed to show		
10 January	Oxford City FA League Div 2	YMCA	A	7–0	Grain, Webb, Creed, Sherlock	
24 January	Oxon Junior League A	Dorchester	A	1–1	Webb	
31 January	Oxford City FA League Div 2	Summertown	H	1–1	Creed	
7 February	Oxford City FA Div 1	Oxford Trades	H	6–0	Martin 2, Morris, Phillips 2, Creed	
14 February	Friendly	Morris Motors	H	5–1	Coppock 2, Webb, Badger, Creed	
21 February	Oxon Junior League A	Dorchester	H	6–1	Creed 2, Webb 3, Badger	
28 February	Oxon Junior League A	Cowley	H	3–0	Webb 2, Creed	
6 March	Oxon Junior League A	Depot OBLI	H	1–0	Grain	
13 March	Friendly	Warneford	A	3–1	Webb, Creed, Morris	
27 March	Friendly	Hagbourne	A	5–3	Webb, Creed 2, Martin, Badger (pen)	
3 April	Oxon Junior League A	Cowley	A	1–2	Webb	
5 April	Oxford City FA Div 1 Final	Cowley	White House	0–1		2,000
17 April	Oxon Junior League semi-final	St Frideswide	Cowley Barracks	1–3*	Creed *aet	
24 April	Friendly	Hagbourne	H	1–3	Webb	

1920–21

Date	Competition	Opponents	Venue	Score	Scorers	Attendance
25 September	Oxford City League Div 1	Clarendon Press	A	3–5		
2 October	Oxford City League Div 1	Railway Sports Club	H	5–2	Grain, Drewitt, Sawyer, Webb, Smith	
9 October	County Junior Shield first round	Iffley	H	3–2	Wood (own-goal), Webb, Drewitt	
16 October	Oxon Charity Cup preliminary round	Depot OBLI	A	0–1		
23 October	Oxford City League Div 1	Territorials	A	9–0		
30 October	County Junior Shield second round	Balliol Old Boys	H	6–1	Drewitt 2, Grain 3	
6 November	Oxford City League Div 1	St Frideswide	H	0–1	Match abandoned	
13 November	Oxon Junior League section 5	Morris Motors	H	6–1	Grain 4, Drewitt 2	
20 November	County Junior Shield third round	Morris Motors	H	2–1	Drewitt, Grain	
27 November	Oxford City League Div 1	Botley St Lawrence	H	8–1		

Date	Competition	Opponents	Venue	Score	Scorers	Attendance
11 December	County Junior Shield fourth round	Launton	H	5–1	Drewitt 2, Webb, Grain 2	
18 December	Oxford City League Div 1	Clarendon Press	H	5–0	Grain 2, Sawyer, Drewitt 2	
25 December	Oxon Junior League section 5	Cowley	A	1–3	Creed	
26 December	Oxon Junior League section 5	Cowley	H	1–2	Grain	
8 January	Oxon Junior League section 5	Littlemore	H	2–0	Sawyer, Grain	
22 January	County Junior Shield semi-final	Goring	White House	2–1	Drewitt, Webb	
5 February	Oxon Junior League section 5	Littlemore	A	2–1		
12 February	Oxford City League Div 1	St Frideswide	H	1–3		
19 February	Oxon Junior League section 5	Dorchester	A	5–0		
26 February	Oxon Junior League section 5	Morris Motors	A	walk-over	Morris Motors scratched	
26 February	Friendly	Morris Motors	A	6–1	Drewitt 2, Webb 2, Grain, Sawyer	
12 March	Oxford City League Div 1	St Frideswide	H	2–2	Webb, Grain	
26 March	Oxford city league Div 2 semi-Final	Oxford Gasworks	Iffley Road	4–1	Adams 2 (1 pen), L. Coppock, V. Coppock	600
7 April	County Junior Shield Final	Oxford Gasworks	White House	2–2	Grain, Creed	2,000
16 April	Oxford City League Div 2 Final	St Thomas	White House	1–2	Adams	1,100
1921–22						
17 September	Oxfordshire Senior League	Banbury Stone's Athletic	A	0–6		
17 September	Oxford City League Div 1	Morris Motors	H	2–2		
24 September	Oxfordshire Senior League	Morris Motors	H	3–0	Phillips, Herman	
1 October	Oxfordshire Senior League	Bicester	A	2–3		
1 October	Oxford City League Div 1	Post Office	H	8–0		
8 October	Oxfordshire Senior League	Banbury GWR	H	3–0	Herman, Ing, Adams	
8 October	Oxford City League Div 1	Post Office	A	2–3		
15 October	Oxfordshire Senior League	Chipping Norton	H	2–0		
22 October	Oxfordshire Senior League	Oxford Gasworks	A	1–0	Spindler	
29 October	County Junior Shield first round	Thame A	H			
5 November	Oxfordshire Senior League	Banbury Stone's Athletic	H	2–0	Ing 2	
12 November	Oxon Charity Cup first round	Oxford Gasworks	A	0–1		
19 November	Oxfordshire Senior League	Bicester	H	4–0		
19 November	County Junior Shield second round	Littlemore	A	1–1		
26 November	Oxfordshire Senior League	Morris Motors	A	1–1	Goodgame	
26 November	County Junior Shield second-round replay	Littlemore	H	2–3		
3 December	Oxfordshire Senior League	St Frideswide	H	0–1		
10 December	Oxfordshire Senior League	St Frideswide	A	0–0		
17 December	Oxfordshire Senior League	Banbury Harriers	H	3–0		
24 December	Oxfordshire Senior League	Banbury Harriers	H	9–0	Drewitt 8, Ing	
24 December	Oxford City League Div 1	YMCA	A	2–1	Grain, Holland	
26 December	Oxfordshire Senior League	Deddington	A	0–0		
26 December	Oxfordshire Junior League	Cowley	H	2–2		
27 December	Oxfordshire Senior League	Deddington	H	2–0	Nutt, Drewitt	
7 January	Oxfordshire Senior League	Bloxham	H	4–0		
14 January	Oxfordshire Senior League	Thame	A	1–3		
14 January	Oxford City League Div 1	Victoria	H	4–2		
4 February	Oxfordshire Senior Cup first round	Culham College	A	0–0		
11 February	Oxfordshire Senior Cup first-round replay	Culham College	H	1–0		
11 February	Oxford City League Div 1	Oxford Railway Sports	A	1–2		
18 February	Oxfordshire Senior League	Banbury Works	A	1–4		
18 February	Oxford City League Div 1	Oxford Railway Sports	H	2–4		
25 February	Oxfordshire Senior Cup second round	Deddington	A	5–1	Coppock, Goodgame, Drewitt, Adams 2	
4 March	Oxfordshire Senior League	Thame	H	6–1	Spindler 2, V. Coppock, Cadwell (own-goal), Drewitt 2	
4 March	Oxfordshire Junior League	Littlemore	H	0–3		
18 March	Oxfordshire Senior League	Bloxham	A	0–2		
25 March	Oxfordshire Senior League	Banbury GWR	A	1–6		
25 March	Minor League Final	St Frideswide	White House	1–3		
1 April	Oxfordshire Senior Cup semi-final	Oxford Gasworks	White House	4–1	Adams 3, Ing	
8 April	Oxfordshire Junior League	Morris Motors	A	1–5		
15 April	Oxfordshire Senior Cup Final	Cowley	White House	1–2	Adams	
24 April	Oxfordshire Senior League	Cowley	A	0–1		

Date	Competition	Opponents	Venue	Score	Scorers	Attendance
27 April	Oxfordshire Senior League	Oxford Gasworks	H	3–1		
29 April	Oxfordshire Senior League	Banbury Harriers	A	2–2		
1 May	Oxfordshire Senior League	Cowley	H	0–2		
1922–23						
2 September	Oxfordshire Senior League	Banbury Harriers	A	2–5	Coppock, Drewett	
16 September	Oxfordshire Senior League	St Frideswide	A	2–3	Spindler, Adams	
16 September	Oxfordshire Junior League	Cowley	H	1–3		
23 September	Oxfordshire Senior League	Bicester	A	1–8	Grain	
30 September	Amateur Cup first preliminary round	St Frideswide	A	2–2	Baskerville, Adams	
7 October	Amateur Cup first preliminary round replay	St Frideswide	H	4–0	Adams, Spindler, Vallis, Durran	
7 October	County Junior Shield	Littlemore	H	0–8		
14 October	Amateur Cup second preliminary round	Newbury	A	1–6	Durran	
14 October	Oxford City League Div 1	Botley United	A	6–2	Surman 2, Grain 2, Arnold 2	
21 October	Oxon Charity Cup preliminary round	St Frideswide	H	2–0	Richards, Drewett	
28 October	Oxfordshire Senior League	St Frideswide	H	8–1	Richards 5, Durran 2, Spindler	
4 November	Oxfordshire Senior League	Bicester	H	1–3	Durran	
4 November	Oxford City League Div 1	Post Office	A	2–6	Shepherd 2	
11 November	Oxon Charity Cup first round	Culham College	H	4–1		
18 November	Oxfordshire Junior League	Baldon	A	3–1	Grain 2, Shepherd	
25 November	Oxfordshire Senior League	Banbury Works	A	1–9	Durran	
25 November	Oxford City League Div 1	Balliol Old Boys	H	1–0		
2 December	Oxon Charity Cup second round	Morris Motors	H	0–0	Abandoned due to poor light	
9 December	Oxon Charity Cup second round	Morris Motors	A	walk-over	Headington scratched	
16 December	Oxfordshire Senior League	Banbury GWR	H	2–2	Jeffs, Adams	
23 December	Oxfordshire Senior League	Banbury GWR	A	2–7	Baskerville	
25 December	Oxfordshire Senior League	Thame	H	4–1	Jeffs 2, Durran 2	
25 December	Oxfordshire Junior League	Littlemore	A	0–4		
26 December	Oxfordshire Senior League	Thame	A	1–2	Richards	
30 December	Oxfordshire Senior League	Banbury Harriers	H	5–2	Nutt, Jeffs 2, Richards 2	
6 January	Oxfordshire Senior Cup first round	St Frideswide	H	0–0		
13 January	Oxfordshire Senior Cup first-round replay	St Frideswide	A	3–3		
20 January	Oxfordshire Senior League	Witney Town	A	1–2		
20 January	Friendly	Post Office	H	3–0		
27 January	Oxfordshire Senior Cup second replay	St Frideswide	Morris Motors	0–1		
27 January	Oxford City League Div 1	Post Office	H	1–3		
10 February	Oxfordshire Senior League	Morris Motors	A	4–1	White (own-goal), Adams, Spindler, Jeffs	
17 February	Oxfordshire Senior League	Cowley	A	0–8		
24 February	Oxford City League Div 1	Post Office	H	1–1		
10 March	Oxfordshire Senior League	Cowley	H	0–6		
17 March	Oxfordshire Senior League	Morris Motors	H	2–2	Adams, Spindler	
24 March	Oxfordshire Senior League	Banbury Works	H	4–0	Adams 2, Vallis, Durran	
30 March	Oxfordshire Senior League	Chipping Norton	H	7–1	Durran 2, Warland 2, Adams 2, Vallis	
31 March	Oxford City League Div 2 semi-final	YMCA	Cowley	1–2	Hewlett	
2 April	Oxfordshire Senior League	Chipping Norton	A	2–0	Ing (pen), Wormold	
7 April	Oxfordshire Senior League	Witney Town	H	0–2		
20 April	Oxfordshire Senior League	Banbury Stone's Athletic	H	6–1		
28 April	Oxfordshire Senior League	Banbury Stone's Athletic	A	2–5		
1923–24						
1 September	Oxfordshire Senior League	Thame	A	2–1	Warland, Spindler	
8 September	Oxfordshire Senior League	Banbury Stone's Athletic	A	2–5		
15 September	Oxfordshire Senior League	Banbury Stone's Athletic	H	3–3	Higginson, Henwood, Warland	
22 September	Oxfordshire Senior League	Bicester	A	3–2	Henwood, Cozens 2	
29 September	Amateur Cup first preliminary round	Witney Town	H	2–1	Higginson, Henwood	
6 October	Oxfordshire Senior League	Banbury GWR	H	1–1	Higginson	
6 October	County Junior Shield first round	Post Office	A	6–0		
13 October	Amateur Cup second preliminary round	Morris Motors	A	0–2		
13 October	Oxfordshire Junior League	Wolvercote	H	4–2		
18 October	Friendly	Harefield Institute	A	2–2		

Date	Competition	Opponents	Venue	Score	Scorers	Attendance
20 October	Oxon Charity Cup preliminary round	Henley Town	H	2–0	Henwood, Boyt	
27 October	Oxfordshire Senior League	Chipping Norton	A	1–1	Warland	
27 October	County Junior Shield second round	Morris Motors	H	1–2		
3 November	Oxfordshire Senior League	Oxford Railway Sports	A	1–2	Henwood	
10 November	Oxon Charity Cup second round	Oxford Railway Sports	A	2–0	Henwood 2	
17 November	Oxfordshire Senior League	Banbury Works	H	6–2	Durran 2, Warland, Spindler, Hudson, Higginson	
24 November	Woodstock Charity Cup first round	Corporation	H	1–0	Hounslow	
1 December	Oxfordshire Senior League	Bicester	H	2–0	Jeffs (pen), Hudson	
15 December	Oxfordshire Senior League	Banbury Works	A	2–3	King, Warland	
29 December	Oxon Charity Cup semi-final	Thame	Cowley	1–1	Spindler	
5 January	Oxon Charity Cup semi-final replay	Thame	Cowley	2–0	Higginson, Henwood	
12 January*	County Senior Cup first round	Thame	A	1–2	Higginson	
*Game ordered replayed because Thame fielded ineligible player						
19 January	Oxfordshire Senior League	Cowley	H	1–2	Henwood	
26 January	County Senior Cup first round	Thame	A	3–2	Henwood 2, own-goal	
26 January	Oxfordshire Junior League	Post Office	H	1–1		
2 February	County Senior Cup second round	Morris Motors	H	1–1	Henwood	
9 February	County Senior Cup second-round replay	Morris Motors	A	0–3		
16 February	Oxfordshire Senior League	Railway Sports	H	5–0	Hudson 2, Spindler, Durran 2	
23 February	Oxfordshire Senior League	Chipping Norton	H	6–2	Higginson 3, Henwood 2, Durran	
8 March	Oxon Charity Cup Final	Witney Town	White House	1–2	Durran	2,600
15 March	Oxfordshire Senior League	Witney Town	H	2–1	Smith, Cozens	
22 March	Oxfordshire Senior League	Morris Motors	H	1–1	Ing	
29 March	Oxfordshire Senior League	Morris Motors	A	2–2	Warland, Ing (pen)	
5 April	Oxfordshire Senior League	Witney Town	A	1–2		
12 April	Oxfordshire Senior League	St Frideswide	H	2–2		
18 April	Oxfordshire Senior League	Thame	H	4–3		
19 April	Oxfordshire Senior League	Banbury Harriers	A	2–0	Hounslow, Cozens	
21 April	Oxfordshire Senior League	Banbury Harriers	H	3–0		
24 April	Woodstock Charity Cup second round	Post Office	A	3–0	Durran 3	
3 May	Oxfordshire Senior League	Banbury GWR	A	walk-over Banbury scratched		
10 May	Woodstock Charity Cup semi-final	Railway Sports	A	1–2	Sawyer (pen)	

1924–25

Date	Competition	Opponents	Venue	Score	Scorers	Attendance
6 September	Oxfordshire Senior League	Witney Town	A	2–0	Spindler 2	
13 September	Oxford City League Div 1	Post Office	H	3–2		
20 September	Oxfordshire Senior League	Banbury Stone's Athletic	A	2–5		
27 September	Amateur Cup preliminary round	Abingdon Town	A	1–2	Hudson	
27 September	Oxfordshire Junior League	Post Office	A	1–6		
4 October	Oxfordshire Junior Shield first round	Iffley	H	4–1	Grain, Fletcher 2, Hudson	
11 October	Oxfordshire Senior League	Banbury Works	H	6–0	Cozens, Hudson 2, Durran 2, Smith	
18 October	Oxfordshire Senior League	Chipping Norton	H	4–3	Brown 2, Cozens, Grain	
18 October	Oxford City League Div 1	Cowley	A	5–3	Smith 3, Coppock, Fletcher	
25 October	Oxfordshire Junior Shield second round	Clarendon Press	H	1–2	Coppock	
1 November	Oxfordshire Senior League	Banbury Works	A	4–0	Grain, Cozens, Ing, Hudson	
1 November	Oxford City League Div 1	Sandford	H	4–0		
8 November	Oxon Charity Cup first round	Morris Motors	A	0–3		
22 November	Oxfordshire Senior League	Railway Sports	H	3–0	Grain 2, Cozens	
29 November	Oxford City League Div 1	Cowley	H	5–0	Fletcher 2, Hudson 2, Shepherd	
13 December	Oxford City League Div 1	Marston		1–3		
13 December	Friendly	YMCA	H	2–1	Grain, Hudson	
20 December	Oxfordshire Senior League	Morris Motors	A	0–3		
25 December	Friendly	Morris Motors	H	2–2		
26 December	Friendly	Bicester	A	3–6		
27 December	Oxfordshire Senior League	Bicester	H	4–3		
3 January	Oxfordshire Senior Cup first round	Morris Motors	H	1–6	Grain	
17 January	Oxfordshire Senior League	Bicester	A	3–2	Fletcher, Hudson, Grain	
24 January	Oxfordshire Senior League	Witney Town	H	3–3	Grain 2, Sawyer (pen)	
7 February	Oxfordshire Senior League	Cowley	H	2–0	Grain, Durran	

Date	Competition	Opponents	Venue	Score	Scorers	Attendance
14 February	Oxfordshire Senior League	Railway Sports	A	1–2		
21 February	Oxfordshire Junior League	Wolvercote	H	4–2	Coppock	
28 February	Oxfordshire Senior League	Morris Motors	H	5–1	Durran, Lee, Fletcher 3	
7 March	Friendly	Oxford City Casuals	H	4–2	Fletcher, James, Durran, Warland	
14 March	Oxfordshire Senior League	Banbury Harriers	A	1–2	Durran	
19 March	Thursday Korebo Cup semi-final	YMCA		1–3	Fisher	
21 March	Oxfordshire Senior League	St Frideswide	H	1–4	Hudson	
26 March	Thursday Div 2 decider	Miranda		1–6		
4 April	Oxfordshire Senior League	Banbury Stone's Athletic	H	1–2	Fletcher	
11 April	Oxfordshire Senior League	Banbury Harriers	H	7–0	Higginson 2, Douglas, Fletcher, Hudson 2, Grain	
11 April	Oxfordshire Junior League Deciding tie	Wolvercote	New Rec, Botley Road	2–3		
18 April	Oxfordshire Senior League	Chipping Norton	A	1–3	Hall	
25 April	Oxfordshire Senior League	St Frideswide	A	1–8		
2 May	Oxfordshire Senior League	Cowley	H	5–1		

1925–26

Date	Competition	Opponents	Venue	Score	Scorers	Attendance
5 September	Oxfordshire Senior League	Banbury Harriers	A	2–4	Higginson, Fletcher	
12 September	Oxfordshire Senior League	Banbury Stone's Athletic	A	3–3		
19 September	Oxfordshire Senior League	Chipping Norton	A	4–2	Lee, Douglas 2, own-goal	
26 September	Oxfordshire Senior League	Deddington	H	1–2	Grain First game at the Manor	
3 October	Chipping Norton Hospital Cup first round	Cowley	H	4–4	Blundell, Douglas 3	
10 October	Amateur Cup first qualifying round	Oxford City	A	0–6		3,000
17 October	Oxon Charity Cup first round	Henley Town	H	3–3	Grain 2, Spindler	
24 October	Oxon Charity Cup first-round replay	Henley Town	A	3–1	Grain, Spindler, Douglas	
24 October	Eynsham Institute Cup	Marston	A	1–5		
31 October	Oxfordshire Senior League	Thame	A	1–2	Douglas	
14 November	Oxon Charity Cup second round	Thame	H	3–5	Douglas, Spindler, Grain	
21 November	Oxfordshire Senior League	Thame	H	8–2	Douglas 2, Spindler 2, Neal 2, Vallis, Grain	
28 November	Oxfordshire Senior League	St Frideswide	A	1–4	Spindler	
28 November	Eynsham Institute Cup	Freeland	A	0–5		
5 December	Oxfordshire Senior League	Chipping Norton	H	2–2	Grain, Noble	
12 December	Oxfordshire Senior League	Cowley	A	3–1	Noble, Douglas 2	
2 January	Oxfordshire Senior League	Cowley	H	4–2	Noble 3, Warland	
9 January	Oxfordshire Senior Cup first round	Cowley	A	1–3	Douglas	
23 January	Chipping Norton Hospital Cup	Bloxham	H	8–1	left–winger, Douglas, Spindler 3, Grain 3	
30 January	Oxfordshire Senior League	Morris Motors	A	7–2	Grain, Noble, Douglas 4, Sawyer	
13 February	Oxfordshire Senior League	Morris Motors	H	3–4	Spindler, Sawyer 2 (1 pen)	
27 February	Chipping Norton Hospital Cup semi-final	Chipping Norton	Woodstock	5–2	Neal, Douglas, Spindler 2, Grain	
13 March	Oxfordshire Senior League	Banbury Stone's Athletic	H	7–3	Spindler 2, Douglas 3, Grain, Douglas (own-goal)	
20 March	Friendly	Oxford City reserves	H	3–0	Grain, Douglas, Spindler	
27 March	Oxfordshire Senior League	St Frideswide	H	0–1		
3 April	Oxfordshire Senior League	Banbury Harriers	A	5–3		
5 April	Chipping Norton Hospital Cup Final	Chipping Norton	A	1–2	Spindler	
10 April	Oxfordshire Senior League	Bicester	H	7–0		
17 April	Oxfordshire Senior League	Deddington	A	3–5	Webb, Grain, Spindler	
1 May	Oxfordshire Senior League	Bicester	H	2–0		

1926–27

Date	Competition	Opponents	Venue	Score	Scorers	Attendance
28 August	Friendly	Cowley	A	0–3		
4 September	Oxfordshire Senior League	Banbury Harriers	A	5–0	Price, Grain, Collins, Douglas 2	
11 September	Oxfordshire Senior League	Bicester	A	0–2		
18 September	Oxfordshire Senior League	Banbury Stone's Athletic	H	0–3		
25 September	Oxfordshire Senior League	Cowley	H	3–1		
2 October	Oxfordshire Senior League	Bicester	H	2–2		
9 October	Amateur Cup first qualifying round	Abingdon	H	3–1	Higginson, Douglas, Price	
9 October	Oxfordshire Junior Shield first round	Thame A	A	1–0	Finch	
16 October	Oxon Charity Cup first round	Thame	A	0–2		
23 October	Amateur Cup second qualifying round	Newbury	A	0–7		
30 October	Oxfordshire Senior League	Banbury Harriers	H	5–1	Hall 2, Collins, Lee, own-goal	

Date	Competition	Opponents	Venue	Score	Scorers	Attendance
30 October	Oxfordshire Junior Shield second round	Watlington	A	4–0		
13 November	Oxfordshire Senior League	Morris Motors	H	1–2*	*according to Howlands	
20 November	Oxfordshire Senior League	Morris Motors	A	2–4		
20 November	Oxfordshire Junior Shield third round	Tetsworth		6–3		
27 November	Chipping Norton Hospital Cup	YMCA	H	7–4		
4 December	Oxfordshire Senior League	Littlemore	H	8–3		
11 December	Oxfordshire Junior Shield fourth round	YMCA	A	0–4		
18 December	Oxfordshire Senior League	Brackley	A	2–7		
31 December	Oxfordshire Junior Shield	Summertown	A	0–8		
1 January	Oxfordshire Senior League	Cowley	A	5–1		
15 January	Oxfordshire Senior League	Littlemore	A	4–3		
29 January	Oxfordshire Senior Cup second round	Morris Motors	A	1–7		
12 February	Oxfordshire Senior League	Thame	A	3–4		
19 February	Chipping Norton Hospital Cup semi-final	Brackley	Chipping Norton	3–1	Hone (own-goal), Hall 2	
26 February	Oxfordshire Senior League	Chipping Norton	H	6–1	Mathews 4, Haney (own-goal), Hall	
5 March	Oxfordshire Senior League	Banbury Stone's Athletic	A	1–3		
2 April	Oxfordshire Senior League	Brackley	H	2–4		
9 April	Oxfordshire Senior League	Thame	H	2–6		
16 April	Oxfordshire Senior League	Deddington	H	7–1		
18 April	Chipping Norton Hospital Cup Final	Bicester	Chipping Norton	0–3		
23 April	Oxfordshire Senior League	Chipping Norton	A	4–1		
30 April	Oxfordshire Senior League	Deddington	A	5–3		

1927–28

Date	Competition	Opponents	Venue	Score	Scorers	Attendance
10 September	Oxfordshire Senior League	Morris Motors	A	3–9		
17 September	Oxfordshire Senior League	Banbury Harriers	H	3–4		
24 September	Oxfordshire Senior League	Littlemore	H	2–7		
1 October	Oxfordshire Senior League	YMCA	H	3–2		
8 October	Amateur Cup first preliminary round	Windsor & Eton	A	1–6		
15 October	Oxon Charity Cup first round	YMCA	H	2–4	Spindler, Higginson	
22 October	Oxfordshire Senior League	Chipping Norton	H	8–2	Spindler 4, Stone 2, Webb, Cooper (pen)	
29 October	Oxfordshire Senior League	Brackley	A	1–2		
26 November	Oxfordshire Senior League	Chipping Norton	A	0–2		
3 December	Oxfordshire Senior League	YMCA	H	3–4		
10 December	Oxfordshire Senior League	Thame	A	1–2		
7 January	Oxfordshire Senior Cup first round	Henley Town	H	3–0		
14 January	Oxfordshire Senior League	Banbury Stone's Athletic	H	1–4	Douglas	
21 January	Oxfordshire Senior League	Banbury Harriers	A	6–5	Webb 3, Douglas 3	
28 January	Oxfordshire Senior Cup second round	Morris Motors	H	2–3	Spindler, Jaycock	
11 February	Oxfordshire Senior League	Thame	H	6–2		
18 February	Chipping Norton Hospital Cup	YMCA	H	2–0	Douglas 2	
25 February	Oxfordshire Senior League	Littlemore	A	2–1		
3 March	Oxfordshire Senior League	Brackley	H	2–1	Webb, Boyt	
10 March	Oxfordshire Senior League	Morris Motors	H	1–2	Hall	
17 March	Oxfordshire Senior League	Bicester	H	0–0		
24 March	Oxfordshire Senior League	Banbury Stone's Athletic	A	2–3		
7 April	Oxfordshire Senior League	Thame	A	1–6	Douglas	
9 April	Chipping Norton Hospital Cup semi-final	Thame		1–6		
14 April	Minor League	Rest of Minors League	H	2–1		
21 April	Oxfordshire Senior League	Bicester	A	1–5		

1928–29

Date	Competition	Opponents	Venue	Score	Scorers	Attendance
8 September	Friendly	YMCA	A	2–4		
15 September	Oxfordshire Senior League	Banbury Stone's Athletic	A	2–6	Webb, Spindler	
22 September	Oxfordshire Senior League	YMCA	H	1–0	Webb	
29 September	Oxfordshire Senior League	YMCA	A	6–2	Hathaway, Garrett 3, Webb, Spindler	
6 October	Amateur Cup preliminary round	Caversham St Andrews	A	1–4		
13 October	Oxon Charity Cup first round	Thame	A	1–5		
27 October	Oxfordshire Senior League	Witney	A	4–6	Garrett 2, Douglas 2	
3 November	Oxfordshire Senior League	Banbury Harriers	H	8–0	Douglas 5, Garrett 3	

Date	Competition	Opponents	Venue	Score	Scorers	Attendance
17 November	Oxfordshire Senior League	Thame	A	1–6		
24 November	Oxfordshire Senior League	Witney	H	1–2		
1 December	Oxfordshire Senior League	Banbury Stone's Athletic	H	3–1	Douglas 2 (1 pen), Howes	
8 December	Oxfordshire Senior League	Brackley	A	5–9		
22 December	Oxfordshire Senior League	Bicester	A	1–2		
29 December	Oxfordshire Senior League	Morris Motors	A	2–4	Douglas, Webb	
19 January	Oxfordshire Senior League	Littlemore	A	1–0	Douglas	
26 January	Oxfordshire Senior Cup second round	Henley Town	A	1–3	Webb	
2 February	Oxfordshire Senior League	Brackley	H	1–5	Douglas	
9 February	Oxfordshire Senior League	Banbury Harriers	A	2–2	Douglas, Webb	
23 February	Bradley Cup	Eynsham	A	4–1		
9 March	Oxfordshire Senior League	Bicester	H	1–5	Howes	
16 March	Oxfordshire Senior League	Thame	H	2–2	Wormold, Webb	
23 March	Oxfordshire Senior League	Morris Motors	H	0–1		
30 March	Bradley Cup semi-final	Thame	H	3–1		
13 April	Oxfordshire Senior League	Littlemore	H	5–0		
20 April	Bradley Cup Final	Littlemore	H	1–3	Webb	

1929–30

14 September	Oxfordshire Senior League	Brackley	A	4–3	Green 2, Webb, Jones	
21 September	Oxfordshire Senior League	Banbury Harriers	H	3–2	Milner, Godfrey (own-goal), Green	
5 October	Oxfordshire Senior League	Heyford RAF	A	1–3		
12 October	Amateur Cup first qualifying round	Oxford City	A	0–3		
19 October	Oxon Charity Cup first round	Morris Motors	H	2–2	Webb 2	
26 October	Oxon Charity Cup first-round replay	Morris Motors	A	3–1	Jones 3	
2 November	Oxfordshire Senior League	YMCA	H	1–2	Schulz	
9 November	Oxon Charity Cup second round	Bicester	A	1–2	Stokes	
16 November	Oxfordshire Senior League	Bicester	A	1–5	Higginson	
23 November	Oxfordshire Senior League	Stones Athletic	H	3–2	Webb, Jones, Morris	
30 November	Oxfordshire Senior League	Littlemore	A	5–0	Schulz, Morris, Webb 3	
7 December	Oxfordshire Senior League	Morris Motors	H	1–2	Green	
14 December	Oxfordshire Senior League	Thame	A	4–1		
27 December	Oxfordshire Senior League	Bicester	H	1–4	Webb (pen)	
4 January	Oxfordshire Senior Cup first round	Henley Town	H	6–0	Webb 2, Schulz 3, Jones	
11 January	Oxfordshire Senior League	Morris Motors	A	6–1	Morris 4, Webb 2	
18 January	Oxfordshire Senior League	Thame	H	3–4	Webb 2, Jones	
25 January	Oxfordshire Senior Cup second round	Oxford City reserves	H	0–4		
1 February	Oxfordshire Senior League	Littlemore	A	3–1	Morris, Jones, Gibbs	
8 February	Oxfordshire Senior League	Stones Athletic	A	6–4		
15 February	Oxfordshire Senior League	Heyford RAF	H	4–0	Morris 2, Gibbs, Jones	
22 February	Oxfordshire Senior League	Brackley	H	7–1	Gibbs 5, Webb 2	
1 March	Oxfordshire Senior League	YMCA	A	4–1	Webb, Gibbs 2, Schulz	
22 March	Oxfordshire Senior League	Bicester RAF	H	7–4	Gibbs 3, Slaymaker 2, Webb (pen)	
5 April	City Junior League Div 1 semi-final	University Press	Botley Road Rec	2–1	Ricketts, Milner	
12 April	Oxfordshire Senior League	Witney	H	1–5	Webb	
12 April	Oxon Junior Shield Final	Dorchester	White House	0–5		
19 April	Oxfordshire Senior League	Witney	A	5–3	Webb 2, Gibbs 2 (1 pen), Jones	
19 April	City Junior League Div 1 Final	East Oxford Corinthians	White House	2–1	Slaymaker, Washington	
26 April	Oxfordshire Senior League	Banbury Harriers	A	1–3	Gibbs	
1 May	Oxford Junior League City Final	East Oxford Corinthians	Botley Road Rec	2–3	Milne, Slaymaker	

1930–31

13 September	Oxfordshire Senior League	Heyford RAF	H	3–1		
20 September	Oxfordshire Senior League	Stones Athletic	A	2–0	F. Webb, B. Webb	
27 September	Oxfordshire Senior League	Morris Motors	A	3–2	Douglas, Schultz, Webb	
4 October	Oxfordshire Senior League	Bicester RAF	A	4–1	Douglas 4	
11 October	Oxon Charity Cup first round	Gasworks	H	7–1	Douglas 2, Gibbs, Webb	
25 October	Oxfordshire Senior League	Heyford RAF	H	4–4	Douglas 4	
1 November	Oxfordshire Senior League	Banbury Harriers	H	4–1		
8 November	Oxon Charity Cup second round	Henley Town	H	3–0	Morris 2, Webb	

Date	Competition	Opponents	Venue	Score	Scorers	Attendance
15 November	Oxfordshire Senior League	Osberton Works	A	2–3	Jones, Gibbs	
22 November	Oxfordshire Senior League	Morris Motors	H	2–1	Douglas, Schultz	
6 December	Oxfordshire Senior League	Thame	A	1–0	Douglas	
13 December	Oxon Charity Cup semi-final	Oxford City Reserves	H	1–0	Webb	
20 December	Oxfordshire Senior League	Osberton Works	H	2–3	Douglas 2	
3 January	Oxfordshire Senior Cup first round	Osberton Works	H	2–0	Gibbs, Jones	200
10 January	Oxfordshire Senior League	Thame	H	1–2	Douglas	
17 January	Oxfordshire Senior League	YMCA	H	7–0	Gibbs 2, Webb, Douglas 2, Jones, Coppock	
24 January	Oxfordshire Senior Cup second round	Thame	H	2–1	Margetts 2	
7 February	Oxfordshire Senior League	Littlemore	H	4–0	Margetts, Webb, Schultz, Jones	
14 February	Oxfordshire Senior Cup semi-final	Henley Town	Thame	4–1	Douglas, Schultz 2, Lock	
21 February	Oxfordshire Senior League	Banbury Harriers	A	5–2	Margetts 4, Douglas	
28 February	Oxfordshire Senior League	Witney	H	3–3	Douglas 2 (2 pens), Margetts	
7 March	Oxfordshire Senior League	Littlemore	A	4–5	Douglas, Milner, Jones 2	
14 March	Oxfordshire Senior League	Brackley	H	4–4	Coppock, Jones, Margetts, Douglas	
4 April	Oxfordshire Senior League	Brackley	A	2–3		
6 April	Oxfordshire Senior Cup Final	Oxford City Reserves	White House	3–8	Webb, Douglas, Jones	3,000
11 April	Oxfordshire Senior League	Stones Athletic	H	3–0	Douglas, Margetts, Webb	
25 April	Oxfordshire Senior League	Bicester	H	9–1	Margetts, Schultz 2, Bradbury 3, Douglas 2, Surman	
28 April	Oxfordshire Senior League	Witney	A	2–4	Margetts, Douglas	
2 May	Oxon Charity Cup Final	Witney	White House	2–1*	Margetts 2	*aet, 0–0 at full time
2 May	Oxfordshire Senior League	Bicester	A	0–4		
1931–32						
5 September	FA Cup extra preliminary round	Hounslow	H	2–8		
12 September	Oxfordshire Senior League	Brackley	A	4–0	Margetts, Webb, Jones 2	
19 September	Oxfordshire Senior League	Bicester	H	7–2	Margetts 6, Webb	
26 September	Amateur Cup preliminary round	Osberton Works	A	4–5	Margetts 2, Hooper, Douglas	200
3 October	Oxfordshire Senior League	Banbury Harriers	A	1–3	Jones	
17 October	Oxfordshire Senior League	Brackley	H	6–0	Jones 2, Margetts 2, Hooper, Schultz	
31 October	Oxfordshire Senior League	Littlemore	H	3–1	Margetts 2, Schultz	
7 November	Oxfordshire Senior League	Banbury Stone's Athletic	H	5–1	Margetts 3, Schultz, Webb	
14 November	Oxon Charity Cup second round	Clarendon Press	H	9–3	Webb, Hooper, Schultz 4, Lock, Jones 2, Douglas, Margetts	
21 November	Oxfordshire Senior League	Thame	A	1–2	Hooper	
28 November	Oxfordshire Senior League	Cowley	A	2–0	Margetts, Jones	
12 December	Oxon Charity Cup semi-final	Witney	Osberton Road	3–0	Douglas, Margetts, Jones	
19 December	Oxfordshire Senior League	Cowley	H	5–0	Douglas, Jones, Hooper, James, Margetts	
2 January	Oxfordshire Senior League	Witney	H	0–2		
9 January	Oxfordshire Senior League	Banbury Stone's Athletic	A	6–2	Douglas 3, Gibbs, Margetts, Wharton	
16 January	Oxfordshire Senior Cup first round	Thame	H	2–2	Schultz, Hooper	
23 January	Oxfordshire Senior Cup first-round replay	Thame	A	0–2		
30 January	Oxfordshire Senior League	Heyford RAF	H	5–1	Margetts 3 (1 pen), Milner, Jones	
6 February	Oxfordshire Senior League	Bicester	A	0–3		
13 February	Oxfordshire Senior League	Morris Motors II	A	1–0	Margetts	
20 February	Oxfordshire Senior League	Littlemore	A	5–3	Margetts, Douglas 2, Milner 2	
5 March	Oxfordshire Senior League	Heyford RAF	A	4–0		
12 March	Oxfordshire Senior League	Witney	A	0–2		
19 March	Oxfordshire Senior League	Morris Motors II	H	5–1	Milner 3, Margetts 2	
26 March	Oxfordshire Senior League	Osberton Works	H	5–4	Douglas 3, Schultz, Margetts	
2 April	Oxfordshire Senior League	Banbury Harriers	H	4–2	Schultz, Margetts, Milner, Douglas	
16 April	Bradley Cup	Abingdon Town	H	5–2	Margetts 3, Douglas 2 (1 pen)	
18 April	Oxfordshire Senior League	Thame	H	1–4	Hooper	
23 April	Oxfordshire Senior League	Osberton Works	A	8–0	Douglas 3, Louch, Milner 3, Margetts	
7 May	Oxon Charity Cup Final	Banbury Harriers	White House	4–5	Douglas 2, Milner, Schultz, Margetts	
1932–33						
10 September	Oxfordshire Senior League	Heyford RAF	A	4–2	Margetts 3, Jones	
17 September	FA Cup preliminary round	Bicester	A	2–2	Margetts 2	

Date	Competition	Opponents	Venue	Score	Scorers	Attendance
22 September	FA Cup preliminary round	Bicester	H	2–4	Lock, Webb (pen)	
1 October	Oxfordshire Senior League	Osberton Works	H	1–3	Jones	
8 October	Amateur Cup first qualifying round	Littlemore	A	4–2	Jones, Webb 2, Milner	
15 October	Oxon Charity Cup first round	Littlemore	H	8–3	Gibbs, Webb 4 (1 pen), Sawyer, Barker, Ballard	
22 October	Amateur Cup second qualifying round	Marlow	H	1–7	Webb	
12 November	Oxon Charity Cup second round	Old Oxford Citizens	H	6–3	Webb 2, Graham, Jones, Slaymaker, Margetts	
29 November	Bradley Cup	Osberton Works	A	1–4	Margetts	
5 November	Oxfordshire Senior League	Thame	H	1–4	Webb	
19 November	Oxfordshire Senior League	Witney	H	1–2	Margetts	
26 November	Oxfordshire Senior League	Banbury Stone's Athletic	H	5–0	Margetts 2, Webb, Graham, Hall	
10 December	Oxfordshire Senior League	Banbury Harriers	H	8–1	Webb 4, Hall 2, Margetts 2	
17 December	Oxon Charity Cup semi-final	Thame	A	3–2	Hall, Margetts, Webb	
24 December	Oxfordshire Senior League	Thame	A	0–4		
31 December	Oxfordshire Senior League	Stephen Reiss	H	3–0	Webb, Margetts, Washington	
7 January	Oxfordshire Senior League	Heyford RAF	H	2–3	Margetts 2	
14 January	Oxfordshire Senior Cup first round	Littlemore	A	3–1	Hall, Webb, Graham	
28 January	Oxfordshire Senior League	Cowley II	H	3–0	Sawyer, Jones, Margetts	
4 February	Oxfordshire Senior Cup second round	Osberton Works	H	4–1	Webb 2, Dodd	500
11 February	Oxfordshire Senior League	Littlemore	A	0–2		
18 February	Oxfordshire Senior League	Bicester	H	1–0	Douglas	
4 March	Oxfordshire Senior Cup semi-final	Cowley II	Morris Motors	3–4	Vowles, Margetts 2	800
11 March	Oxfordshire Senior League	Osberton Works	A	3–4	Douglas, Dodd, Ballard	
18 March	Oxfordshire Senior League	Morris Motors II	H	4–2	Vowles 2, Douglas, Graham	
1 April	Oxfordshire Senior League	Banbury Stone's Athletic	A	3–2	Ballard, Vowles 2	
8 April	Oxfordshire Senior League	Bicester	A	1–3	Dodd	
15 April	Oxon Charity Cup Final	Bicester	White House	1–0	Margetts	
15 April	Oxfordshire Senior League	Stephen Reiss	A	2–2	Abbott, Surman	
17 April	Oxfordshire Senior League	Witney	A	1–6	Dodd	
22 April	Oxfordshire Senior League	Littlemore	H	5–2	Margetts 2, Dodd, Douglas, Vowles	
29 April	Oxfordshire Senior League	Banbury Harriers	A	5–1	Margetts 3, Douglas, Vowles	

1933–34

Date	Competition	Opponents	Venue	Score	Scorers	Attendance
9 September	Oxfordshire Senior League	Stephen Reiss	A	6–0	Margetts 2, Dodd 2, Jones, Vowles	
30 September	Oxfordshire Senior League	Banbury Harriers	H	1–3		
7 October	Amateur Cup first preliminary round	Witney Town	H	2–0	Pitts, Jones	
14 October	Oxon Charity Cup first round	Henley Town	H	4–4		
21 October	Amateur Cup second preliminary round	Marlow	H	0–3		
28 October	Oxon Charity Cup second round	Henley Town	A	2–7		
4 November	Oxfordshire Senior League	Heyford RAF	A	0–7		
11 November	Oxfordshire Senior League	Chipping Norton	A	1–4	Pitts	
18 November	Oxfordshire Senior League	Bicester	H	5–1	Pitts 2	
25 November	Oxfordshire Senior League	Witney Town	A	1–5	Margetts	
2 December	Oxfordshire Senior League	Osberton Works	H	3–2		
9 December	Oxfordshire Senior League	Pressed Steel	A	2–0		
23 December	Oxfordshire Senior League	Thame	A	2–6	Margetts, Webb (pen)	
30 December	Oxfordshire Senior League	Littlemore	H	8–2	Walton (own-goal), Taylor (own-goal), Margetts 3, Pitts 3	
6 January	Oxfordshire Senior League	Witney Town	H	2–1	Martin, Margetts	
13 January	Oxfordshire Senior Cup first round	Littlemore	A	2–3	Martin, Webb	
20 January	Oxfordshire Senior League	Littlemore	A	3–2	Dodds, Vowles, Margetts	
27 January	Oxfordshire Senior League	Thame	H	5–5	Dodds, Margetts 2, Graham 2	
3 February	Oxfordshire Senior League	Stephen Reiss	H	4–0	Vowles, Martin, Sawyer, Margetts	
10 February	Oxfordshire Senior League	Pressed Steel	H	2–2	Margetts 2	
17 February	Oxfordshire Senior League	Morris Motors II	A	6–3	Vowles, 3, Margetts, Webb, Martin	
3 March	Oxfordshire Senior League	Banbury Harriers	A	2–2	Margetts, Martin	
17 March	Oxfordshire Senior League	Heyford RAF	H	0–6		
31 March	Oxfordshire Senior League	Littlemore	H	2–4		
31 March	Oxon Junior Shield Final	Banbury GWR	A	4–1	Hooper 3, Douglas	
7 April	Oxfordshire Senior League	Bicester	A	2–5	A.J. Douglas, R.E. Douglas	
14 April	Oxfordshire Senior League	Chipping Norton	H	5–2	Surman 2, Webb, Washington, Douglas	

Date	Competition	Opponents	Venue	Score	Scorers	Attendance
1934–35						
1 September	FA Cup extra preliminary round	Civil Service	H	0–3		
8 September	Oxfordshire Senior League	Chipping Norton Church Army	A	3–4		
15 September	Oxfordshire Senior League	Osberton Radiators	H	1–2	Margetts	
29 September	Oxfordshire Senior League	Pressed Steel	H	7–3	Margetts 3, Jones 3, Lonie	
6 October	Amateur Cup first preliminary round	Slough	H	2–8	Washington, Jones	
13 October	Oxfordshire Senior League	Bicester	H	2–0	Margetts, Lonie	
20 October	Oxon Charity Cup first round	Pressed Steel	H	3–0	Jones, Lonie, Douglas	
27 October	Oxfordshire Senior League	Pressed Steel	A	0–2		
3 November	Bradley Cup	Osberton Radiators	H	3–0	Lonie, Margetts 2	
10 November	Oxfordshire Senior League	Banbury Harriers	H	6–2	Lonie 3, Margetts, Pitts, Jones	
17 November	Oxon Charity Cup second round	Cowley	H	1–3	Margetts	
24 November	Oxfordshire Senior League	Thame	A	0–0		
1 December	Oxfordshire Senior League	Witney Town	H	1–2	Jones	
8 December	Oxfordshire Senior League	Heyford RAF	A	2–7		
15 December	Friendly	Old Oxford Citizens	H	3–4		
25 December	Oxfordshire Senior League	Cowley	H	2–0		
29 December	Oxfordshire Senior League	Osberton Radiators	A	3–2	Jones, White, Lonie	
5 January	Oxfordshire Senior League	Thame	H	5–1	Morris, White 2, Jones 2	
12 January	Oxfordshire Senior Cup first round	Oxford City Reserves	H	4–3	Jones, Margetts 3	
26 January	Oxfordshire Senior League	Witney Town	A	1–3		
2 February	Oxfordshire Senior League	MG Sports	H	1–2	E Webb	
9 February	Oxfordshire Senior Cup second round	Cowley	H	1–1	Margetts	600
16 February	Oxfordshire Senior Cup second-round replay	Cowley	A	0–3		500
23 February	Oxfordshire Senior League	Bicester	A	2–0	Margetts, White	
2 March	Oxfordshire Senior League	Heyford RAF	H	2–5	Webb 2	
30 March	Oxfordshire Senior League	Banbury Spencer	H	0–2		
6 April	Oxfordshire Senior League	Banbury Harriers	A	0–2		
19 April	Oxfordshire Senior League	Cowley	A	3–4	Margetts 3	
20 April	Oxfordshire Senior League	Banbury Spencer	A	4–6	Jones, Webb, Margetts, Douglas	
27 April	Oxfordshire Senior League	Chipping Norton Church Army	H	4–0	A.J. Douglas 3, R.E. Douglas	
4 May	Oxfordshire Junior League Final	Cold Arbour	White House	2–1	Surman, Burch	
1935–36						
7 September	FA Cup extra preliminary round	Newbury Town	A	2–6		
14 September	Oxfordshire Senior League	Chipping Norton CA	A	7–2	Lonie 3, Margetts, Cooper, E. Webb 2	
21 September	Oxfordshire Senior League	Bicester	H	0–3		
28 September	Amateur Cup preliminary round	Marlow	A	2–8		
19 October	Oxfordshire Senior League	Morris Motors II	H	2–3		
26 October	Bicester Charity Cup	St Albans United		2–0	Harrop 2	
9 November	Oxfordshire Senior League	Oxford City Casuals	A	3–1	Milner 2, Jones	
16 November	Oxon Charity Cup second round	Cowley	A	2–3	Rusling, Jones	
23 November*	Oxfordshire Senior League	Witney Town	A	4–2	Margetts, Lonie, Milner, Jones*Abandoned	
due to bad light						
30 November	Oxfordshire Senior League	Witney Town	A	0–6	replayed game	
7 December	Oxfordshire Senior League	Pressed Steel	H	5–3	Jones 2, Lonie, Margetts 2	
21 December	Oxfordshire Senior League	Osberton Radiators	H	4–0	Lonie, Jones 3	
25 December	Oxfordshire Senior League	Cowley	H	3–2		
28 December	Oxfordshire Senior League	Thame	A	5–0	Nutt, Jones 2, Lonie 2	
4 January	Oxfordshire Senior League	Banbury Harriers	H	1–0	Jones	
11 January	Oxfordshire Senior League	Bicester	A	1–4	Milner	
25 January	Oxfordshire Senior Cup first round	Henley Town	H	8–4	Margetts 5, Milner 3	
1 February	Oxfordshire Senior League	Thame	H	4–2	Rusling, Margetts 2, Milner	
8 February	Oxfordshire Senior Cup second round	Old Oxford Citizens	H	5–1	Margetts 4 (1 pen), Milner	
15 February	Oxfordshire Senior League	Chipping Norton CA	H	5–1	Margetts 2, Horwood 2	
28 February	Oxfordshire Senior League	Banbury Harriers	A	5–2	Margetts 3, Milner, Lonie	
7 March	Oxfordshire Senior Cup semi-final	Witney Town	Bicester	3–2	Milner, Jones 2	
14 March	Bicester Charity Cup semi-final	Wolvercote	Bicester	2–0	R.E. Douglas 2	
21 March	Oxfordshire Senior League	Pressed Steel	A	3–1	Margetts 2, Lonie	
4 April	Oxfordshire Senior League	Witney Town	H	5–4	Lonie 2, Goodchild, Faulkner, White	

Date	Competition	Opponents	Venue	Score	Scorers	Attendance
10 April	Oxfordshire Senior League	Cowley	A	3–1	Margetts 2, Lonie	
13 April	Oxfordshire Senior Cup Final	Banbury Spencer	White House	1–1	Jones	5,638
13 April	Oxford City Junior League Div 1 Final	Littlemore	White House	2–3	Morris, Hooper	
18 April	Oxfordshire Senior League	Osberton Radiators	A	3–0	Milner, Margetts (pen), Lonie	
23 April	Bicester Charity Cup Final	Bicester	A	2–3	Margetts 2 (1 pen)	
2 May	Oxfordshire Senior Cup Final replay	Banbury Spencer	White House	1–0	Lonie	5,000
1936–37						
5 September	FA Cup extra prelimary round	Pressed Steel	H	3–3	Margetts (pen), Carr 2	
12 September	Oxfordshire Senior League	Osberton Radiators	H	1–4	Margetts (pen)	
14 September	FA Cup extra preliminary round replay	Pressed Steel	A	1–6	Carr	
19 September	Oxfordshire Senior League	Oxford City Casuals	H	8–1	Ramsden 2, Oliver 2, Jones 2, White 2	
26 September	Amateur Cup preliminary round	Banbury Spencer	A	1–4	Oliver	
3 October	Oxfordshire Senior League	Pressed Steel	A	3–1	Lonie, Margetts, Ramsden	
10 October	Oxfordshire Senior League	Heyford RAF	A	5–1	Margetts 2, Oliver, Lonie, Ramsden	
17 October	Oxfordshire Senior League	Thame	H	7–5	Jones 4, Ramsden, own-goal, Lonie	
24 October	Oxfordshire Senior League	Pressed Steel	H	2–2	Ramsden (pen), Jones	
31 October	Oxon Charity Cup first round	Cowley	H	1–4	Ramsden	
7 November	Oxfordshire Senior League	Witney	A	3–4	Ramsden 2, White	
14 November	Oxfordshire Senior League	Cowley	A	3–2	Jones, White, Lonie	
5 December	Oxfordshire Senior League	Oxford City Casuals	H	7–3	Margetts 5, Jones, White	
12 December	Oxfordshire Senior League	Witney	H	3–1	Lonie, Margetts 2	
19 December	Oxfordshire Senior League	Bicester RAF	A	2–0	Margetts, Lonie	
25 December	Oxfordshire Senior League	Banbury Spencer A	A	5–3	Jones, Lonie 2, White, Faulkner (pen)	
2 January	Oxfordshire Senior League	Bicester Town	A	4–1	Margetts 3, Jones	
9 January	Oxfordshire Senior Cup first round	Morris Motors	H	2–1	Ramsden, Margetts (pen)	
16 January	Oxfordshire Senior League	Osberton Radiators	A	0–2		
23 January	Oxfordshire Senior League	Abingdon RAF	H	3–1	Margetts 2, Jones	
30 January	Oxfordshire Senior Cup second round	Henley Town	H	6–4	Ramsden 3, Douglas 2, Margetts	
6 February	Oxfordshire Senior League	Heyford RAF	H	2–2	Douglas 2 (1 pen)	
13 February	Oxfordshire Senior League	Bicester RAF	H	8–1	Margetts, Ramsden, White 2, Bowell 3, Jones	
20 February	Oxfordshire Senior League	Bicester Town	H	3–4	White, Lonie, Harris (own-goal)	
27 February	Oxfordshire Senior Cup semi-final	Pressed Steel	Morris Motors	0–4		
6 March	Oxfordshire Senior League	Cowley	H	1–5	White	
13 March	Oxfordshire Senior League	Banbury Harriers	A	2–3	Harris, Margetts	
26 March	Oxfordshire Senior League	Banbury Spencer A	H	6–1	Nutt 2, White 2, Margetts, Lonie	
3 April	Oxfordshire Senior League	Abingdon RAF	A	5–0	Margetts 2, Milner, Lonie, White	
17 April	Oxfordshire Senior League	Thame	A	4–2	Margetts 2, Milner, Lonie	
22 April	Bradley Cup semi-final	Cowley		2–1		
24 April	Oxfordshire Senior League	Banbury Harriers	H	7–1	Margetts 5, Lonie	
1 May	Henley Hospital Cup Final	Henley Town	A	1–2	Margetts	
	Bradley Cup Final	Osberton Radiators		0–2		
1937–38						
4 September	FA Cup extra preliminary round	Marlow	H	4–2	Sansom 3, Lonie	
11 September	Oxfordshire Senior League	Pressed Steel	H	0–0		
18 September	FA Cup preliminary round	Osberton Radiators	H	1–2	Sansom	
25 September	Amateur Cup extra qualifying round	Osberton Radiators	A	6–3*	Sansom 2, Lonie, Ramsden 3	*aet, 3–3 at full time.
2 October	Oxfordshire Senior League	Pressed Steel	A	3–6	Lonie, Imms, Sansom	
9 October	Amateur Cup first preliminary round	Bicester Town	A	2–1	Sansom, Lonie	
16 October	Oxfordshire Senior League	Bicester Town	A	6–2	Margetts 3, Lonie, Imms, Jones	
23 October	Amateur Cup second preliminary round	Marlow	A	3–4	Margetts 2	
27 October	Bradley Cup	Abingdon RAF		1–6		
30 October	Oxfordshire Senior League	Banbury Harriers	H	2–0	Imms, Webb	
6 November	Oxon Charity Cup first round	Oxford City Reserves	H	0–1		
13 November	Oxfordshire Senior League	Chipping Norton	H	3–2	Nutt 2, Jones	
20 November	Oxfordshire Senior League	Banbury Spencer A	H	4–1	Margetts, Faulkner, Ramsden, Lonie	
27 November	Oxfordshire Senior League	Witney	H	1–3	Harrop	
4 December	Oxfordshire Senior League	Abingdon RAF	A	1–2	Oliver	

Date	Competition	Opponents	Venue	Score	Scorers	Attendance
11 December	Oxfordshire Senior League	Thame	H	6–3	Machin, Nutt 2, Faulkner (pen), Imms, Lonie	
18 December	Oxfordshire Senior League	Heyford RAF	A	2–2	Currill, Nutt	
1 January	Oxfordshire Senior League	Witney	A	6–4	Margetts 2, Oliver 2, Ramsden, Jones	
8 January	Oxfordshire Senior Cup first round	Old Oxford Citizens	H	5–1	Lonie, Margetts 4	
15 January	Oxfordshire Senior League	Cowley	H	7–0	Nutt 2, Oliver, Ramsden, Margetts 3	
22 January	Oxfordshire Senior League	Bicester RAF	A	1–0	Lonie	
29 January	Oxfordshire Senior Cup second round	Henley Town	H	3–0	Oliver, Faulkner (pen), Machin	
5 February	Oxfordshire Senior League	Chipping Norton	A	3–0	Margetts 3	
12 February	Oxfordshire Senior League	Heyford RAF	H	9–1	Nutt 3, Ramsden, Lonie 2, Oliver, Margetts 2	
19 February	Oxfordshire Senior League	Abingdon Town	A	2–0	Nutt, Margetts	
26 February	Oxfordshire Senior Cup semi-final	Morris Motors	Witney	2–4	Nutt, Lonie	
5 March	Oxfordshire Senior League	Thame	A	3–0	Harrop 2, Lonie	
12 March	Oxfordshire Senior League	Bicester RAF	H	2–0	Ramsden, Nutt	
19 March	Oxfordshire Senior League	Banbury Spencer A	A	1–0	Nutt	
26 March	Oxfordshire Senior League	Bicester Town	H	2–4	Ramsden 2	
2 April	Oxfordshire Senior League	Osberton Radiators	H	7–3	W Jones, Ramsden, Nutt, Machin 3, Smith	
16 April	Oxfordshire Senior League	Cowley	A*	2–1	Nutt, Ramsden *played at Headington	
23 April	Oxfordshire Senior League	Banbury Harriers	A	3–1	Smith, Nutt, Lonie	
27 April	Oxfordshire Senior League	Abingdon RAF	H	3–3		
1938–39						
3 September	FA Cup extra preliminary round	Osberton Radiators	A	5–2	Nutt 2, Irving 3	
10 September	Amateur Cup extra preliminary round	Redford Sports	A	3–2	Irving, Ramsden 2	
17 September	FA Cup preliminary round	Henley Town	A	5–2	Imms, Irving 3, Ramsden	
24 September	Amateur Cup preliminary round	Wallingford	A	2–3	Ramsden 2	
1 October	FA Cup preliminary round	Windsor & Eton	H	2–3	Lonie, Machin	
8 October	Oxfordshire Senior League	Banbury Harriers	A	4–0	Irving 2, Imms 2	
15 October	Oxfordshire Senior League	Bicester RAF	H	8–1	Machin 5, Lonie, Imms, Ramsden	
22 October	Oxfordshire Senior League	Pressed Steel	A	2–1	Machin, Ramsden	
29 October	Oxfordshire Senior League	Heyford RAF	H	5–0	Machin, Lonie 3, Imms	
5 November	Oxon Charity Cup first round	Thame	H	8–0	Machin 2, Nutt, Lonie, Imms, Ramsden 3	
12 November	Oxfordshire Senior League	Banbury Spencer A	H	3–1	Machin, Lonie, Ramsden	
19 November	Oxfordshire Senior League	Chipping Norton	A	3–1	Tack, Graham, Lonie	
26 November	Oxon Charity Cup second round	Henley Town	H	6–2	Lovegrove (own-goal), Nutt 2, Machin 2, Ramsden	
3 December	Oxfordshire Senior League	Witney Town	A	2–0	Machin (pen), Lonie	
10 December	Oxfordshire Senior League	Harwell RAF	H	6–1	Nutt 2, Imms, Ramsden, Machin, Graham	
17 December	Oxon Charity Cup semi-final	Oxford City Reserves	Morris Motors	1–1	Lonie	700
31 December	Oxon Charity Cup semi-final replay	Oxford City Reserves	Morris Motors	8–1	Machin 5, Ramsden 2, Timms	
7 January	Oxfordshire Senior Cup first round	Morris Motors	A	6–2	Machin, Nutt 2, Ramsden 2, Jones	
14 January	Oxfordshire Senior League	Heyford RAF	A	7–0	Machin 2, Imms 2, Nutt, Tack, Lonie	
21 January	Oxfordshire Senior League	Banbury Harriers	H	16–1	Machin 8, Wyatt (pen), Ramsden 3, Lonie, Imms 2, Nutt	
28 January	Oxfordshire Senior Cup second round	Henley Town	H	4–1	Machin, Lonie, Ramsden (pen), Imms	1,000
4 February	Oxfordshire Senior League	Thame	A	3–0	Machin, Ramsden, Imms	
11 February	Oxfordshire Senior League	Witney Town	H	4–0	Machin 2, Ramsden, Talbot (own-goal)	
18 February	Oxfordshire Senior League	Banbury Spencer A	A	2–1	Ramsden, Imms	
25 February	Oxfordshire Senior Cup semi-final	Oxford City Reserves	Morris Motors	1–0	Machin	1,200
11 March	Oxfordshire Senior League	Abingdon RAF	A	2–2		
18 March	Oxfordshire Senior League	Thame	H	7–0	Ramsden 3, Lonie, Imms 2, Machin	
25 March	Oxfordshire Senior League	Pressed Steel	H	4–2	Jones, Ramsden, Machin 2	1,200
1 April	Oxfordshire Senior League	Harwell RAF	A	4–0	Lonie 2, Nutt 2	
10 April	Oxfordshire Senior Cup Final	Bicester Town	White House	1–2		5,906
15 April	Oxfordshire Senior League	Chipping Norton	H	7–0	Machin 2, Imms 2, Ramsden, Hudson 2	
19 April	Oxfordshire Senior League	Osberton Radiators	H	4–1		
22 April	Oxon Charity Cup Final	Brize Norton No 2 Flying School	White House	1–0	Machin	2,000
24 April	Oxfordshire Senior League	Bicester Town	H	5–0	Lonie 2, Nutt, Ramsden, Machin	1,000+
29 April	Oxfordshire Senior League	Abingdon RAF	H	10–2	Machin 4, Ramsden 3, Imms 2, Hudson	
1 May	Oxfordshire Senior League	Bicester Town	A	5–3	Machin 2, Ramsden 2	
3 May	Oxfordshire Senior League	Bicester RAF	A	6–1	Machin 3, Ramsden 2, Imms	

Date	Competition	Opponents	Venue	Score	Scorers	Attendance
6 May	Oxfordshire Senior League	Brize Norton No 2 Flying School	A	3–1		
13 May	Oxford Hospital Cup Final	Bicester Town	White House	1–0	Lonie	
1939–40						
16 September	Friendly	Pressed Steel	H	2–2	Machin, Ramsden (pen)	
30 September	Friendly	Oxford City	A	0–4		
7 October	Oxfordshire Senior League	Morris Motors	H	1–3	Garland (own-goal)	
14 October	Oxfordshire Senior League	Osberton Radiators	H	7–2	Ramsden 4, Machin, Hudson 2	
21 October	Oxfordshire Senior League	Bicester	H	6–0	Nutt 2, Imms, Ramsden 2, unknown	
28 October	Oxfordshire Senior League	Pressed Steel A	H	5–0	Hudson 2, Machin, Nutt, Imms	
4 November	Oxon Charity Cup first round	Brize Norton	H	5–3	Imms, Ramsden 2, Machin 2	
25 November	Oxon Charity Cup second round	Pressed Steel	H	4–3	Machin, Ramsden, Lones, Pooley	
2 December	Oxfordshire Senior League	Thame	H	5–2	3 unknown, Imms, Machin	
9 December	Oxon Charity Cup semi-final	Infantry Training Centre Services XI	Morris Motors	3–5	Machin, Imms, Phipps (pen)	
16 December	Oxfordshire Senior League	Bicester RAF	A	4–2		
23 December	Friendly	Oxford City	A	1–4	Pooley	
25 December	Oxfordshire Senior League	Cowley	H			
13 January	Oxfordshire Senior League	Morris Motors	A	4–2	Ramsden 2, Sansom 2	
10 February	Oxfordshire Senior Cup second round	Cowley	H	4–2	Ramsden 2, Machin 2	300
24 February	Oxfordshire Senior Cup semi-final	Oxford City Reserves	A	1–2	Machin	
2 March	Oxfordshire Senior League	Brize Norton	H			
9 March	Oxfordshire Senior League	Oxford City Reserves	A	1–2	Ramshaw	
23 March	Oxfordshire Senior League	Cowley	A			
25 March	Oxfordshire Senior League	Bicester	A	1–6	Machin	
30 March	Oxfordshire Senior League	Services XI	A	1–0	Ramsden	
6 April	Oxfordshire Senior League	Thame	A	4–2	Saw, 3 unknown	
8 April	Oxfordshire Senior League	Oxford City Reserves	H	4–2	Saw, Machin, Ramsden, Martin	
11 April	Oxfordshire Senior League	Banbury Spencer	H	3–2	Ramsden 2, Hewlett	
13 April	Oxfordshire Senior League	Banbury Spencer	A	0–3		
2 May	Oxfordshire Senior League	Services XI	H			
4 May	Oxfordshire Senior League	Brize Norton	A			
11 May	Oxfordshire Senior League	Pressed Steel A	A	2–6		
18 May	Friendly	RAF XI		8–5		
1 June	Oxford Hospital Cup semi-final	Pressed Steel	White House	3–4	Ramsden 2, Machin	
1940–41						
7 September	Oxfordshire Senior League	Benson RAF A	H	6–2	Machin 4, Smith 2	
14 September	Oxfordshire Senior League	Brize Norton B	A			
21 September	Oxfordshire Senior League	Banbury Spencer	H	3–4	Morris, Green, Machin	
28 September	Oxfordshire Senior League	Heyford RAF	A			
5 October	Oxfordshire Senior League	Benson RAF B	H	7–4	Machin 4, Timms, Ramsden 2	
12 October	Oxfordshire Senior League	Brize Norton B	H			
19 October	Oxfordshire Senior League	Heyford RAF	H	6–2	Donaldson 2, Timms 3, Morris	
26 October	Oxfordshire Senior League	Harwell Services	A			
2 November	Oxfordshire Senior League	Osberton Radiators	H			
16 November	Oxfordshire Senior League	Abingdon Services	A	4–4		
23 November	Oxfordshire Senior League	Infantry Training Centre A	H			
7 December	Oxfordshire Senior League	Pressed Steel	H			
14 December	Oxfordshire Senior League	Osberton Radiators	A	4–4	Machin, Timms 2, Ramsden	
21 December	Oxfordshire Senior League	Oxford City Reserves	H	6–1	Ramsden 2, Smith 3, Mortimer	
28 December	Oxfordshire Senior League	Oxford City Reserves	A	2–3	Mortimer, Timms	
1 February	Oxford Charity Cup semi-final	Brize Norton	H	5–6*	Smith, Saw 2, Mortimer, Lonie	*aet, 3–3 at full time.
15 March	Oxfordshire Senior League	Abingdon Services	H	2–1	Mortimer, Dear	
5 April	Oxfordshire Senior League	Harwell Services	H	2–4	Machin 2	
12 April	Oxfordshire Senior League	Pressed Steel	H	7–1		
26 April	Minor Cup Final	St Barnabas	White House	2–3	Harper 2	

Date	Competition	Opponents	Venue	Score	Scorers	Attendance
1941–42						
13 September	Oxfordshire Senior League	Abingdon Services	H	7–6	Ramsden 3, Harper 3, Smith	
20 September	Oxfordshire Senior League	Harwell RAF	H	5–4	Smith 3, Dear, Nutt	
27 September	Oxfordshire Senior League	Brize Norton Services	A	won		
4 October	Oxfordshire Senior League	Oxford City Reserves	A	1–3	Dear	
11 October	Oxfordshire Senior League	Heyford RAF	A	2–1		
18 October	Oxfordshire Senior League	Brize Norton Services	H	5–5		
25 October	Oxfordshire Senior League	Infantry Training Centre	A	1–4	Spiers	
1 November	Oxfordshire Senior League	Pressed Steel	H	5–1		
8 November	Oxon Charity Cup first round	Abingdon Services	H	2–8		
22 November	Oxfordshire Senior League	Milton Services	H	5–6		
6 December	Oxfordshire Senior League	Kidlington Services	A	3–2	Machin 2, Smith	
13 December	Oxfordshire Senior League	Abingdon Services	A	4–0		
25 December	Oxfordshire Senior League	Oxford City Reserves	H	0–3		
10 January	Oxfordshire Senior League	Benson Services	A	1–2		
17 January	Oxfordshire Senior League	Oxford City Reserves	H	8–1	Walker 3, Goddard 3, Smith 2	
31 January	Oxfordshire Senior Cup second round	Kidlington Services	H	7–6	Dear 2, Machin 2, Walker, Goddard, Nutt	
14 February	Oxfordshire Senior League	Infantry Training Centre	H	2–0		
28 February	Oxfordshire Senior Cup semi-final	Heyford RAF	White House	3–2		
21 March	Oxfordshire Senior League	Benson Services	H	1–2	Smith	
28 March	Oxfordshire Senior League	Heyford RAF	H	5–0	Goddard, Smith 3, Simmonds	
4 April	Oxfordshire Senior League	Kidlington Services	H	8–2	Blake 5, Machin 2, Smith	
6 April	Oxfordshire Senior Cup Final	Oxford City	White House	1–2	Blake	
1942–43						
12 September	Oxfordshire Senior League	RASC Wallingford	H	9–2	Spiers 4, Blake 2, Ansell, Machin, Edser	
19 September	Oxfordshire Senior League	Harwell RAF	H	8–0	Blake 2, Edser 2, Simmonds 2, Taylor 2	
3 October	Oxfordshire Senior League	Abingdon Services	A	2–5		
16 October	Friendly	Pressed Steel	H	5–0		
24 October	Oxfordshire Senior League	Benson Services	H	6–4	Spiers 3, Machin, Simmonds, Edser	
7 November	Oxon Charity Cup first round	Abingdon Services	A	6–6		
14 November	Oxon Charity Cup first-round replay	Abingdon Services	H	3–1		
28 November	Oxon Charity Cup second round	Milton Services	A	2–4		
25 December	Oxfordshire Senior League	Pressed Steel	H	5–4		
16 January	Oxfordshire Senior Cup first round	Stanton Harcourt	H	7–1		
23 January	Oxfordshire Senior Cup second round	Harwell RAF	H	2–4	Alder, Machin	
13 February	Oxfordshire Senior League	Abingdon Services	H	1–5		
26 April	Oxfordshire Senior League	Pressed Steel	H	1–0		
1943–44						
18 September	Oxfordshire Senior League	Oxford City Reserves	A	2–4	Machin, Gordon	
2 October	Oxfordshire Senior League	Harwell RAF	A	1–1		
16 October	Oxfordshire Senior League	Benson Services	H	3–1	Law 2, Nutt	
6 November	Oxon Charity Cup first round	Osberton Radiators	H	3–2		
27 November	Oxon Charity Cup second round	Pressed Steel	H	3–5		
1 January	Oxfordshire Senior League	Osberton Radiators	H	3–1	Watkins, Nutt, Graham	
22 January	Oxfordshire Senior Cup first round	Abingdon Services	A	1–2	Watkins	
5 February	Oxfordshire Senior League	Oxford City Reserves	H	3–4	Gordon, Jones, Phipps	
26 February	Oxfordshire Senior League	Abingdon Services	A	0–5		
11 March	Oxfordshire Senior League	Abingdon Services	A	2–2	Forrester, Law	
25 March	Oxfordshire Senior League	Pressed Steel	A	2–4	Law, Bagnell	
1 April	Oxfordshire Senior League	Osberton Radiators	A	6–3	Law 4, Nutt, Nash	
8 April	Oxfordshire Senior League	Milton Services	H	2–6	Bagnall, Machin	
15 April	Oxfordshire Senior League	Harwell RAF	H	2–2	Machin, Kenniar	
29 April	Oxfordshire Senior League	Pressed Steel	H	0–3		
1944–45						
23 September	Oxfordshire Senior League	GWR Sports	H	3–3	McHimmings, Anderson 2	
30 September	Oxfordshire Senior League	SMD Signals	A	2–0	Machin	
7 October	Oxfordshire Senior League	MG Car Company	H	14–2	Harrop 2, Arnold 3, Nutt 3, Machin 3, Green 2, Evans	

Date	Competition	Opponents	Venue	Score	Scorers	Attendance
14 October	Oxfordshire Senior League	Abingdon Services	A	4–2	Harrop 3, Machin	
21 October	Oxfordshire Senior League	Osberton Radiators	A	4–2	Machin, Nutt 2, unknown	
4 November	Oxfordshire Senior League	Harwell	A	3–1		
11 November	Oxon Charity Cup first round	GWR Sports	H	8–0	Nutt 3, Machin 2, Arnold (pen), Green	
18 November	Oxfordshire Senior League	Oxford City Reserves	A	1–6	Nutt	
25 November	Oxon Charity Cup second round	Oxford City Reserves	H	3–2	Machin 2, Harrop	
2 December	Oxfordshire Senior League	Milton	H	0–5		
9 December	Oxfordshire Senior League	Benson	H	2–1	Nutt, Green	
6 January	Oxfordshire Senior Cup first round	Osberton Radiators	A	8–1		
13 January	Oxon Charity Cup semi-final	Bicester Services	Morris Motors	0–8		
20 January	Oxfordshire Senior Cup second round	Abingdon Services	H	0–4		
24 February	Oxfordshire Senior League	Abingdon Services	H	0–3		
3 March	Oxfordshire Senior League	Osberton Radiators	H	9–0	Parker 4, Green 2, Jones 2, Belson	
10 March	Oxfordshire Senior League	Harwell	H	4–3	Green, Strange 2, Parker	
7 April	Oxfordshire Senior League	SMD Signals	H	2–2	Wilson, Bevan	
14 April	Oxfordshire Senior League	Pressed Steel	H	2–0	Nutt, Strange	
21 April	Oxfordshire Senior League	Oxford City Reserves	H	4–1	own-goal, Strange, Phipps, Harrop	

1945–46

1 September	FA Cup preliminary round	Banbury Spencer	A	1–8	Ayris	
8 September	Friendly	Oxford City Reserves	H	8–1		
15 September	Oxfordshire Senior League	Oxford City Reserves	H	7–4	Wilson 2, Green 2, Belson, Nutt, Lewis	
22 September	Oxfordshire Senior League	Didcot	H	17–1	Parker 6, Green 4, Wilson 2, Gordon 2, Machin, Fletcher (own-goal)	
29 September	Amateur Cup preliminary round	Pressed Steel	A	4–1	Parker 2, Green, Wilson	
6 October	Oxfordshire Senior League	GWR Sports	A	5–2		
13 October	Amateur Cup second qualifying round	Windsor & Eton	H	3–1	Nutt, Machin, own-goal	1,000
20 October	Oxfordshire Senior League	Ashhurst Hospital	A	3–1	Nutt 2, Ayris 2, Machin	
27 October	Amateur Cup third qualifying round	Marlow	H	5–3*	*aet Match abandoned because of bad light	
3 November	Amateur Cup third qualifying round	Marlow	A	2–6	Bowles, Green	
10 November	Oxon Charity Cup first round	Pressed Steel	H	6–2	Green 3, Machin, Nutt, unknown	
17 November	Oxfordshire Senior League	GWR Sports	H	6–1	Machin 3, Nutt, Ayris 2	
24 November	Oxfordshire Senior League	RNAS Culham	H	5–2	Nutt 2, Machin, Green 2	
8 December	Oxon Charity Cup second round	Benson	A	draw		
15 December	Oxon Charity Cup second-round replay	Benson	H	6–0	Ayris, Green, Blake 4	
22 December	Oxon Charity Cup semi-final	Brize Norton MU	H	6–1	Green 3, Wilson, Nutt, Blake	
5 January	Oxfordshire Senior Cup first round	Osberton Radiators	A	3–0	Phipps (pen), Wilson, Machin	
19 January	Oxfordshire Senior Cup second round	Henley Town	A	4–1		
26 January	Oxfordshire Senior League	Oxford City Reserves	A	1–4	Ayris	1,500
2 February	Oxfordshire Senior League	Benson	A	6–2		
9 February	Oxfordshire Senior Cup third round	Banbury Spencer	H	3–1	Ramsden (pen), Green, Phillips	1,000+
23 February	Oxon Charity Cup Final	Brize Norton RAF	White House	3–1	Ramsden, Ayris, Phillips	
2 March	Oxfordshire Senior Cup semi-final	Morris Motors	White House	1–1	Ramsden (pen)	
16 March	Oxfordshire Senior League	RNAS Culham	H	13–0	Ramsden 6, Phillips 3, Green, Wilson, Brain, own-goal	
30 March	Oxfordshire Senior Cup semi-final replay	Morris Motors	White House	6–2	Ayris 3, Ramsden (pen), Phillips, Cooney	2,300
6 April	Oxfordshire Senior League	Milton RAF	H	3–3	Phillips, England, Ramsden	
13 April	Oxfordshire Senior League	Milton RAF	A	3–3	Washington, own-goal, Blake	
22 April	Oxfordshire Senior Cup Final	Oxford City	White House	0–4		6,788
22 April	Minor Cup Final	South Oxford	White House	0–3		
25 April	Oxfordshire Senior League	Benson RAF	A	2–1	Green 2	
29 April	Oxfordshire Senior League Decider	Milton RAF	White House	2–4	after extra time	600
		Brize Norton RAF	H	walk-over	Headington awarded both points	
		Brize Norton RAF	A	walk-over	Headington awarded both points	

1946–47

7 September	FA Cup extra preliminary round	Bicester Town	A	3–2	Green, Mansell, Lewis	
14 September	Oxfordshire Senior League	Moreton RAF	H	12–2	Jenkins, Ramsden, Green 2, Mansell 7, Washington	
21 September	FA Cup preliminary round	Banbury Spencer	H	3–2	Drury, Green, Lewis	2,094

Date	Competition	Opponents	Venue	Score	Scorers	Attendance
28 September	Amateur Cup first preliminary round	Henley Town	A	5–1	Lewis 2, Green 2, Ramsden	
5 October	FA Cup second preliminary round	Aylesbury United	A	3–2	Lewis 2, Green	
12 October	Amateur Cup second preliminary round	Marlow	A	0–2		
19 October	FA Cup third preliminary round	Uxbridge	A	2–5	Mathews, Smith	2,000+
26 October	Oxfordshire Senior League	MPRD	H	3–1	Lewis 2, Mansell	
2 November	Oxon Charity Cup first round	RAOC	H	2–2		
9 November	Oxon Charity Cup first-round replay	RAOC	H	7–0		
16 November	Oxfordshire Senior League	RNAS	H	12–2	Dear 4, Machin 3, Green 2, Mansell 3	
23 November	Oxfordshire Senior League	Brize Norton RAF	A	1–3	Mansell	
30 November	Oxon Charity Cup second round	Brize Norton RAF	A	3–1	Dear 2, Green	
7 December	Oxfordshire Senior League	Bicester Town	H	0–3		
14 December	Oxon Charity Cup third round	Osberton Radiators	H	7–4	Green 2, Dear 2, Blake, Smith, Machin 2	
25 December	Oxfordshire Senior League	St Frideswide	H	6–1	Mansell 2, Green 2, Smith, Dear	
4 January	Oxfordshire Senior Cup first round	Thame	H	14–2	Machin 4, Green 3, Mansell 3, Ramsden 2, Dear 2	
11 January	Oxfordshire Senior League	Thame	A	5–0		
18 January	Oxfordshire Senior League	Osberton Radiators	H	0–1		500
25 January	Oxfordshire Senior Cup second round	Banbury Spencer A	A	0–1		
15 March	Oxon Charity Cup semi-final	Oxford City Reserves	Morris Motors	2–5	Mansell, Smith	
29 March	Oxfordshire Senior League	Brize Norton RAF	H	3–4	Thompson 2, Downer	
5 April	Oxfordshire Senior League	Thame	H	5–1	England, Smith, Gass, Green, Mansell	
7 April	Oxfordshire Senior League	St Frideswide	H	2–5	Watkins, Mansell	
12 April	Oxfordshire Senior League	Osberton Radiators	A	2–0		
19 April	Oxfordshire Senior League	Benson RAF	H	7–3		
26 April	Oxfordshire Senior League	Royal Naval School of Music	H	3–1	Mansell 2, Gass	
3 May	Oxfordshire Senior League	Bicester Town	A	2–4	Green, Smith	
6 May	Oxfordshire Senior League	Royal Naval School of Music	A	4–6		
10 May	Oxfordshire Senior League	MPRD	A	3–5		
21 May	Oxfordshire Senior League	Pressed Steel Reserves	A	3–0		
1947–48						
30 August	Spartan League	Marlow	A	1–2	Mansell	
6 September	Spartan League	Chelsea Mariners	H	7–1	Smith 2, Currill 2, Blake, Mansell 2	2,000+
10 September*	Spartan League	Hazell's	A	8–1		
*Hazell's resigned from the league after this game and the result was void						
13 September	Spartan League	Leighton United	A	1–1	Mansell	
20 September	FA Cup preliminary round	Wallingford	H	4–0	Blake, Mansell, Smith 2	
27 September	Amateur Cup extra preliminary round	Abingdon	H	5–2	Blake 2, Currill, Merritt, Smith	
4 October	FA Cup first preliminary round	Southall	A	1–2	Mansell	
11 October	Amateur Cup first preliminary round	Aylesbury	A	2–0	Blake, Mansell	
18 October	Spartan League	Leighton United	H	12–0	Smith 4, Mansell 2, Currill, 5 unknown	
25 October	Amateur Cup second preliminary round	Huntley & Palmer's	H	2–3	Smith, Mansell	3,000
8 November	Spartan League	Amersham	A	1–2	Mansell	
8 November	Oxon Charity Cup first round	St Frideswide	H	4–3	Osegood 3, Jones	
15 November	Spartan League	Marlow	H	3–1	Mansell 2, Blake	1,000
22 November	Spartan League	Wycombe Redfords	H	1–0	Harper	
22 November	Oxon Charity Cup second round	Bicester	A	1–1	Harrop	
29 November	Oxon Charity Cup second-round replay	Bicester	H	0–6		
6 December	Spartan League	Berkhamsted Town	H	4–1	Harper, Blake, Mansell, Currill	
13 December	Spartan League	Hemel Hempstead	A	5–3	Harper 2, 3 unknown	
20 December	Spartan League	Polytechnic	A	1–1	Currill	
27 December	Spartan League	Berkhamsted Town	A	2–2	Harper, Smith	
3 January	Spartan League	Hemel Hempstead	H	3–2	Mansell 2, Harper	2,000
10 January	Spartan League	Yiewsley	H	4–3	own goal, Blake, Mansell, Currill	2,000+
24 January	Oxfordshire Senior Cup second round	Pressed Steel	H	4–0	Harper 2, Ramsden, Mansell	1,500
31 January	Spartan League	Amersham	H	5–1	Currill, Tallent 2, Harper 2	1,000
7 February	Spartan League	Willesden	H	3–0	Mansell 2, Currill	
21 February	Oxfordshire Senior Cup semi-final	Banbury Spencer Res	Bicester	4–1	Smith, Harper 3	
28 February	Spartan League	Yiewsley	A	0–2		
6 March	Spartan League	Chelsea Mariners	A	4–1	Harper, Blake 2, Mansell	

Date	Competition	Opponents	Venue	Score	Scorers	Attendance
13 March	Spartan League	Slough Centre	H	1–5	Blake	
20 March	Spartan League	Polytechnic	H	3–1	Prescott (own-goal), Currill, Washbrook	
26 March	Spartan League	Henley Town	H	3–1	Harper 2, Mansell	3,000
29 March	Oxfordshire Senior Cup Final	Oxford City	Iffley Road	1–0	Ramsden	7,796
3 April	Oxford Hospital Cup semi-final	Osberton Radiators	H	5–0	Smith 2, Lee (pen), Pringle, Harper	1,800
3 April	Spartan League	Henley Town	A	4–5	Harris 2, Lee 2 (1 pen)	
10 April	Spartan League	Slough Centre	A	1–1	Pringle	
15 April	Spartan League	Willesden	A	1–1	Mansell	
17 April	Spartan League	Wycombe Redfords	A	8–0	Harper 4, Mansell 3, 1 unknown	
8 May	Oxford Hospital Cup Final	Oxford City	White House	1–0	Pringle	6,474
1948–49						
14 August	Friendly	Abingdon Town	A	2–2		
28 August	Spartan League	Slough Centre	A	2–8	Jeacock 2	
1 September	Spartan League	Henley Town	A	6–0	Warner (own-goal), Washington, Smith, Jeacock 2, Blake	
4 September	FA Cup extra preliminary round	Osberton Radiators	H	4–2	Jeacock 2, Bracegirdle, Pimm	
11 September	Spartan League	Berkhamsted	A	1–3	Jeacock	
18 September	FA Cup preliminary round	Banbury Spencer	H	1–3	Jeacock	3,000
25 September	Spartan League	Hemel Hempstead	A	2–3	Blake, Allsop (own-goal)	
2 October	Spartan League	Amersham	H	5–0	Jeacock 2, Currill, Bracegirdle, Blake	
9 October	Amateur Cup second Preliminary round	Wallingford	A	6–1	Bracegirdle 2, Jeacock 3, Blake	
16 October	Amateur Cup third preliminary round	Slough Town	H	1–4	Blake	
23 October	Spartan League	Marlow	A	1–2	Blake	
30 October	Spartan League	Polytechnic	A	3–0	Mansell 3	
6 November	Spartan League	Luton Amateurs	H	5–2	Blake, Mitchell, A. Smith (own-goal), Mansell 2	
6 November	Oxon Charity Cup first round	Kidlington	A	3–2	Jeacock 3	
13 November	Spartan League	Leighton United	H	3–0	Smith 2, Blake	
20 November	Spartan League	Henley Town	H	5–3	Blake, Mansell 3, Smith	
20 November	Oxon Charity Cup second round	Bicester	A	2–4	Harris, Pimm	
27 November	Spartan League	Chelsea Mariners	H	7–0	Washington, Mitchell, Currill, Blake, Mansell, J. Smith 2	
4 December	Spartan League	Lyons Club	A	6–0	Blake 2, Currill, Mansell 3	
11 December	Spartan League	Hemel Hempstead	H	2–3	Blake, Currill	
18 December	Spartan League	Rickmansworth	A	4–3	Smith, Mitchell, Mansell 2	
27 December	Friendly	Oxfordshire Thursday XI	H	5–3	Smith 3, Mansell, Blake	
1 January	Friendly	Pegasus	A	2–3	Mansell, Mitchell	
8 January	Oxfordshire Senior Cup first round	Pressed Steel	A	5–1	Mitchell, Mansell 2, Blake, Smith	
15 January	Spartan League	Amersham	A	6–0	Mansell 5, Blake	
22 January	Friendly	London University	H	2–1	Blake, Bishop	
29 January	Oxfordshire Senior Cup second round	Osberton Radiators	H	4–1	Mansell 2, Blake, Washington	
5 February	Spartan League	Luton Amateurs	A	1–2	Mansell	
12 February	Spartan League	Leighton United	A	2–3	Blake 2	
19 February	Spartan League	Rickmansworth	H	4–2	Mitchell 2, Mansell, Smith	1,500
26 February	Spartan League	Lyons Club	H	6–2	Bossino (own-goal), Blake 2, Smith, Owen, Mitchell	
5 March	Henley Charity Cup first round	Didcot	A	3–4	Blake, Mansell 2	
12 March	Spartan League	Polytechnic	H	3–1	Currill, Mitchell, Mansell	
19 March	Spartan League	Berkhamsted	H	3–0	Mansell 2, Robson	
26 March	Spartan League	Yiewsley	A	1–5	Blake	
2 April	Spartan League	Yiewsley	H	1–2	Blake	
9 April	Spartan League	Slough Centre	H	1–1	Currill	
15 April	Friendly	West Ham United A	H	0–1		
16 April	Spartan League	Marlow	H	3–2	Ramsden, Spiers, Owen	
18 April	Oxfordshire Senior Cup semi-final	Oxford City	Iffley Road	1–2	Washington	7,064
23 April	Friendly	UVS Leyden	Iffley Road	0–4		
4 May	Spartan League	Chelsea Mariners	A	4–1	Owen 2, Cassell 2	
10 May	Oxon Benevolent Cup semi-final	Bicester	White House	6–0	Owen 3, Blake 2, Mansell	2,500
14 May	Oxon Benevolent Cup Final	Oxford City	White House	1–4	Blake	6,000+
14 May	Minor Cup Final	Balliol Boys		1–1		

FRIENDLIES

Date	Opponent	Venue	F–A	Scorers	Att
1949–50					
27 August	Abingdon Town	A	3–3		
26 November	London University	H	2–0		
18 February	Tottenham Hotspur Reserves	H	4–1	Nugent, Johnson, Buchanan, Smith	
18 February	London University	A		Score unknown	
10 April	Portsmouth Reserves	H	4–2	McPhee, Roberts 2, Jenkins	
23 May	Witney Town	A		Score unknown	
1950–51					
18 November	Abingdon Town	A	4–2	Chung 3, unknown	
18 December	Banbury Spencer	H	3–0	(First match under floodlights at the Manor)	2,603
30 December	Croydon Rovers	A	1–1		
27 January	Gillingham	H	2–1	(First win over League opposition)	
31 January	Swindon Town	H	0–0	(First meeting with Swindon Town)	7,000
14 February	Northampton Town	H	0–1		7,000
28 February	Millwall	H	0–0		
31 March	Royal Air Force	H	1–3		
16 April	St Johnstone	H	7–0	(Festival of Britain Challenge) Rowstron 3, Smith 3, Barney	
2 May	Brentford	H	1–1	Smith	
14 May	Royal Ixelles Belgium	H	1–1	(Festival of Britain at Iffley Road) Smith	10,000
1951–52					
7 November	Cardiff City	H	1–3		
21 November	Royal Air Force XI	H	2–3	Elliott, Barney (pen)	6,053
5 December	Watford	H	4–3		
9 January	Tottenham Hotspur	H	4–2		
30 January	Northampton Town	H	0–3		
13 February	Colchester United	H	0–1		
27 February	The Army	H		Score unknown	
27 March	Leyton Orient	H	2–2	Crichton, McKeown	
16 April	Brentford	H	0–0		
1952–53					
16 September	Witney Town	A	4–1	(Annual Feast) Stewart 2, Blake 2	600
20 September	Army XI	A	–	(Played at Wheatley)	
19 November	Fulham	H	3–1		
6 January	Charlton Athletic	H	2–1		
9 February	Queen's Park Rangers	H	1–0		
23 February	Wolverhampton Wanderers	H	2–3		10,180
12 March	Harrow	H	4–1	Thomas, Maskell 2, Peart	
1953–54					
28 October	Rest of Southern League	H	0–1	(Southern League Championship)	
22 March	England Amateur International XI	H	3–0	Toulouse 2, Crombie	8,000
12 April	Oxford City	A	1–2	(Smith Memorial Cup) McGarrity (pen)	
1954–55					
23 October	Chippenham Town	A	1–4		
28 October	Southern League Representative XI	H		Score unknown	
30 October	Oxford University	H	2–3		
10 November	Merthyr Tydfil	H	2–4	(Southern League Cup Holders v Champions)	
15 January	Tottenham Hotspur Reserves	H	0–4		
18 January	Queen's Park Rangers	H	2–1	Yates 2	
19 January	Swindon Town	H	1–2	Yates	

Date	Opponent	Venue	F–A	Scorers	Att
16 February	Swindon Town	A	0–1		1,786
1 March	Aldershot	H	2–0	Skull, Yates	
7 March	US Dunkerquoise	H	8–0	Yates, Nicklas, own-goal, Johnstone, Skull 2, Crichton, Mumford	
30 March	Crystal Palace	H	0–2		
4 April	IFK Stockholm	H	5–1	Crichton 2, Nicklas 2, Duncan	
1955–56					
28 September	Brentford	H	3–1	Bain, Smillie, Eele	
12 October	All Star XI	H	3–3	(Frank Ramshaw testimonial) Collins 2, Angell (own-goal)	6,000
10 March	Trowbridge	A	3–3		
7 April	Notts County	H	1–0	(Midlands v Southern League) Adams	
1956–57					
17 October	All Star XI	H	4–2	(Jim Smith testimonial) Phillips, Taylor	10,000
17 February	Watford	A	1–1	Bowie	
20 February	Fulham	H		Score unknown	
2 April	Queen's Park Rangers	H	2–3	Adams, Rees	
1957–58					
15 February	Bedford Town	H	0–2		
19 March	Peterborough United	H	2–1	Cross, Stafford (own-goal)	
1958–59					
17 September	South Africa	H	2–2	Love 2 (1 pen)	7,000
24 January	Swindon Town	H	1–2	Jackson	
13 April	Airdrieonians	H	3–2	Dickson, Jackson, Beavon	
1959–60					
21 October	Lincoln City	H	2–4	Love, Denial	3,523
4 November	Notts County	H	2–2	Smith 2	3,800
18 November	Charlton Athletic	H	0–2		
22 February	Plymouth Argyle	H	4–1	Denial, Dickson, R. Atkinson, G. Atkinson	4,000
21 March	Swindon Town	H	0–1		
28 March	Brentford	H	0–1		
5 April	Port Vale	H	2–3	Dickson 2	2,095
1960–61					
1 May	Southend United	A	1–1	(Dave Robinson Testimonial) Houghton	3,267
5 May	Scunthorpe United	H	1–2	Beavon	4,000
13 May	Oxford City	H	5–1	(Oxfordshire Benevolent Cup Final)	3,250
1961–62					
23 August	Yeovil Town	H	2–0	(Southern League Challenge) Knight, McIntosh	
25 November	Millwall	H	4–3	Love, Knight, G. Atkinson, R. Atkinson	
13 January	Chelsea	H	3–3	Houghton, Love, Beavon	
28 February	Banbury Spencer	H	4–2	(Oxon Professional Cup)	
7 March	Hereford United	A	0–1	(Hereford County Cup first leg)	
19 March	Leicester City	H	5–2	(Geoff Denial and Johnny Love testimonial) Houghton 3, Jones, G. Atkinson	6,525
4 April	Coventry City	H	3–0	(Geoff Denial and Johnny Love testimonial) unknown, Houghton, G. Atkinson	
3 May	Hereford United	H	2–0	(Hereford County Cup second leg) Beavon, Knight	
4 May	Bury	H	0–2		
8 May	Thame United	H	4–0	(Oxon Benevolent Cup) Houghton 2, G. Atkinson, Cornwell	
12 May	Oxford City	H	3–0	(Oxon Benevolent Cup Final) Knight 3	
1962–63					
7 August	Southend United	H	2–3	(Trial) Willey, Love	3,145
11 August	Southend United	A	2–2	(Trial) Houghton, G. Atkinson	

Date	Opponent	Venue	F–A	Scorers	Att
6 March	Cambridge United	H	2–0	(Southern League Challenge) Jones, Evans	
24 May	Swindon Town	H	1–2	(Pat Quartermain testimonial) Shuker	5,719
1963–64					
13 August	Northampton Town	H	1–1	(Trial) Willey	5,656
17 August	Reading	H	3–1	(Trial) Willey, Jones 2	4,698
21 August	Reading	A	1–3	(Trial) Shuker	
24 September	Watford	H	1–4	Jones	3,442
6 January	Oxford City	A	1–2	Bowstead	
9 April	Spandauer Sport Verein	H	3–1	Houghton, Longbottom, Calder	3,968
9 May	Oxford City	H	5–1	(Oxfordshire Benevolent Cup Final) Longbottom 3, Hartland, Harrington	5,374
1964–65					
12 August	Watford	H	1–1	(Trial) Calder	4,704
15 August	Northampton Town	H	2–2	(Trial) Jones, Harrington	
21 November	Clifton Hampden	A	3–0	(Pavilion opening) Buck, Crook 2	
28 November	Swansea Town Reserves	H		Score unknown	
3 December	Southend United	H	2–1	Morris, Shuker	1,927
12 December	Bristol City Reserves	H	0–4		
3 March	Hereford United	H	3–0	(Herefordshire Senior Cup Final, first leg) Morris, Harrington, Calder	1,669
17 March	Hereford United	A	2–3	(Herefordshire Senior Cup Final, second leg) Buck, Jones	2,965
26 April	Grimsby Town	H	2–0	(General testimonial fund) R. Atkinson, Booth	2,003
29 April	Southampton	H	1–0	(General testimonial fund) Fahy	5,321
1965–66					
7 August	Derby County	H	2–2	(Trial) Booth, Morris	5,159
14 August	Southampton	H	1–2	Clarke	1,539
3 December	Tranmere Rovers	A	2–1	Calder 2	2,116
20 April	Valkeakosken Haka	H	6–1	G. Atkinson 2, Buck 2, Jones, Morris	1,982
12 May	Hereford United	A	3–1	(Herefordshire Senior Cup Final) Shuker, Morris, Harrington	1,779
1966–67					
6 August	Rotherham United	H	3–0	(Trial) Morris, Hale 2	2,806
8 August	Bristol City	H	1–4	(Trial) Hale (pen)	2,164
12 August	Aldershot	A	1–0	(Public practice) Calder	
13 August	Birmingham City	H	1–1	(Trial) Hale	4,193
16 August	Bristol City	A	0–2		
12 October	Leicester City	H	1–3	(Oxfordshire Benevolent Cup Final) Calder	5,806
1967–68					
5 August	Aldershot	H	0–3		3,623
7 August	Aston Villa	H	2–3	Bullock, Jones	5,363
12 August	Aldershot	A	2–2	Bullock (pen), Buck	2,146
15 August	Oxford City	A	3–0	Buck, Evanson, Clarke	
6 January	Crewe Alexandra	A	4–2	Bullock, Skeen 2, Hale	1,402
29 January	British Olympic XI	H	1–0	(Representative) G. Atkinson	2,490
22 April	Crystal Palace	H	1–1	(Oxfordshire Benevolent Cup Final) Thornley	2,237
17 May	Luton Town	H	2–3	(Tom Webb testimonial) Shuker, Clarke	6,342
1968–69					
29 July	Luton Town	A	0–3		6,659
31 July	Greenock Morton	H	2–3	Shuker, Bullock	3,826
3 August	Southampton	H	0–3		6,726
1969–70					
26 July	Coventry City	H	2–1	(Trial) Skeen 2	5,008
28 July	Wolverhampton Wanderers	H	1–5	(Trial) Sloan	3,555

Date	Opponent	Venue	F–A	Scorers	Att
30 July	Bournemouth	A	0–1	(Public practice)	2,521
4 August	Asante Kotoko	H	2–0	(Trial) Clarke, Shuker	4,391
12 September	Oxford City	A	1–2	Rex	
10 April	All Star XI	H	2–3	(Ron Atkinson, Maurice Kyle, and Cyril Beavon testimonial) Sloan, Evanson	5,630
20 April	Crystal Palace	H	0–1	(Oxfordshire Benevolent Cup Final)	
6 May	Swindon Town	A	2–0	(Clanfield Cup, at Clanfield) Sloan, Evanson	1,500
1970–71					
1 August	Manchester City	H	4–1	Sloan 2, G. Atkinson, Clayton	7,830
1 August	Oxford City	A	3–4	Way, Fleming, Harrington	
4 August	Hendon	A	2–2	McDonald, Lewis	
4 August	Chesterfield	A		Score unknown	
8 August	Aldershot	A	3–0	Clayton 2, Skeen	2,395
9 November	Great Britain Olympic XI	H	0–1	(Olympic trial)	1,600
15 March	Swindon Town	H	–	(Ron Atkinson, Maurice Kyle, and Cyril Beavon testimonial)	
4 May	Wimbledon	A	3–1	(Les Henley testimonial) Sloan, D. Clarke 2 (2 pens)	1,038
5 May	Walsall Wood	A	4–1	D. Clarke 2, Sloan, Clayton	2,000
6 May	Swindon Town	A	1–1	(Clanfield Cup, at Clanfield) Swindon won on pens	
7 May	All Star XI	H	1–2	(Ron Atkinson, Maurice Kyle, and Cyril Beavon testimonial) Evanson	6,096
16 May	Lorca CF (Spain)	A	2–0	G. Atkinson 2	
18 May	Atletico Orihuela (Spain)	A	1–0	G. Atkinson	
23 May	CD Almoradi (Spain)	A	3–1	Evanson, D. Clarke, G. Atkinson	
1971–72					
31 July	Walsall	A	3–1	D. Clarke, C. Clarke, G. Atkinson	2,218
2 August	Bohemians (Prague)	H	1–1	D. Clarke	3,515
7 August	Brentford	A	4–2	Skeen 2, G. Atkinson, Sloan	3,220
9 August	Hayes	A	1–0	Cassidy	
10 April	Chelmsford City	A	2–1	(Testimonial) D. Clarke (pen), Smithson (pen)	2,000
15 April	Oxford City	A	0–4	(–71 Smith Memorial Cup Final)	
18 April	Banbury United	H	1–0		
19 April	Great Britain Universities/Colleges XI	H	1–0		
2 May	Crystal Palace	H	2–0	(Oxfordshire Benevolent Cup Final) D. Clarke 2	891
3 May	Swindon Town	H	2–2	Thompson, Clayton (United won 4–3 on pens)	
5 May	Manchester City	H	2–4	(John Shuker testimonial)	
1972–73					
29 July	Aldershot	A	1–2	Smithson	1,000
1 August	Wolverhampton Wanderers	H	0–0		
4 August	Guernsey	A	10–0	Allen (own-goal), Cassidy 3, Clarke, Sloan 2, Herpe (own-goal), Clayton, Evanson	1,300
7 August	Ipswich Town	H	1–0	Aylott	2,000
7 May	Coventry City	H	1–2	(Graham Atkinson testimonial) G. Atkinson (pen)	4,191
10 May	Adger Kretslag (Norway)	A	3–0		
13 May	Sandefjord (Norway)	A	7–1		
15 May	Grue (Norway)	A	4–1	Curran 3	
17 May	Stromgodset (Norway)	A	3–2		
1973–74					
11 August	Aldershot	A	2–1	Fleming, Curran	3,022
14 August	Southampton	H	2–0	Fleming, Cassidy	2,016
18 August	Hereford United	A	0–0		4,626
3 May	Leicester City	H	2–1	(Ken Fish testimonial match) unknown, Jeffrey	2,833
6 May	Watford	A	1–0	(Clanfield Cup, at Clanfield) Curran	

Date	Opponent	Venue	F–A	Scorers	Att
1974–75					
3 August	Lincoln City	A	1–1		1,045
7 August	Ipswich Town	H	1–5		
10 August	Reading	A	0–2		
2 October	SC Bonn	H	3–1	Sims 2, Bodell	926
12 November	Yeovil Town	A	0–1		
30 April	Rushden Town	A	4–0	(Brian Thompson testimonial) McGrogan, D. Clarke, Jeffrey, Berry	
2 May	Swindon Town	H	2–2	(Rodney Smithson testimonial)	
5 May	Oxford City	H	2–1	(Oxfordshire Benevolent Cup Final)	
9 May	Gillingham	N	4–2	(Sahara Summer Cup, Sourse, Tunisia) McGrogan 2, Jeffrey, Shuker (pen)	
12 May	Peterborough United	N	1–3	(Sahara Summer Cup Final)	
1975–76					
2 August	Brentford	A	5–1	Shuker (pen), Heron 2, Gibbins, Houseman	1,420
8 August	Banbury United	A		Score unknown	
9 August	Royal Antwerp	H	1–2	Jeffrey	2,250
11 August	Derby County	H	1–1	Heron	2,206
12 August	Thame United	A	4–2		
30 April	Witney Town	H	5–1	(Oxfordshire Benevolent Cup Final) Bailey (own-goal), Foley, Gibbins, Tait, Houseman	663
3 May	Oxford City	A	4–0	(Eric Metcalfe testimonial) Tait, Gibbins, C. Clarke, Taylor (pen)	
1976–77					
31 July	Portsmouth	H	2–2	(Kent Cup)	1,868
3 August	Luton Town	H	2–1	(Kent Cup)	1,484
7 August	Watford	A	0–3	(Kent Cup)	
10 August	Wolverhampton Wanderers	H	0–4		1,623
3 April	Witney Town	A	1–0	(Charity match, combined Oxford United and Swindon Town team)	
25 April	Chelsea	H	1–3	(Charity match, in aid of Houseman–Gillham Children's Fund) Earle	7,015
23 May	Norwich City	H	2–2	(Colin Clarke testimonial match) Forbes (own-goal), Jeffrey	2,372
1977–78					
30 July	Watford	A	0–3		2,134
3 August	Birmingham City	H	0–1		2,483
6 August	Kettering Town	A	3–1		760
1978–79					
29 July	Aldershot	A	1–3		1,448
5 August	Luton Town	H	2–2		2,003
7 August	Wokingham Town	A		Score unknown	
9 August	Southampton	H	0–1		2,505
22 January	Guernsey	A	1–1	(At Corbetts Field) Taylor	
6 February	Denmark under-21	H	2–0	Berry, Fogg (pen)	804
1979–80					
28 July	Torquay United	A	1–3		1,094
1 August	Notts County	H	1–3		
4 August	Tottenham Hotspur	H	2–1		
6 August	Wolverhampton Wanderers	H	1–1		
29 January	West Bromwich Albion	H	0–1	(Les Bateman testimonial)	1,437
21 April	Norwich City	H	1–1	(Roy Burton testimonial) Burton (pen)	2,363
5 May	Oxford City	A	4–0	(John Woodley testimonial)	800
7 May	Kidlington	A	2–1	(Dressing Rooms opening)	753
1980–81					
30 July	Wrexham	H	0–0		995
2 August	Crystal Palace	H	1–4		1,672

Date	Opponent	Venue	F–A	Scorers	Att
1981–82					
10 August	Oxford City	A	5–1	Fogg 2 (1 pen), Allen (own-goal), Foley, Seacole	1,100
27 September	Swindon Town	N	3–2	(Charity match at Marriotts Close)	
27 January	Abingdon United	A	3–0	Thomas 2, Briggs	500
1982–83					
7 August	Coventry City	H	2–2	Thomas 2 (1 pen)	2,028
9 August	Wokingham Town	A	0–1		300
10 August	Nuneaton Borough	A	3–0	Biggins, Barnett, Vinter	444
12 August	Wantage Town	A	3–0	Carroll, Simpson, Morgan	
19 May	Thame United	A	4–1	Lawrence, Thomas 2, Spittle	300
1983–84					
6 August	Yeovil Town	A	2–0	Brock, own-goal	500
8 August	Southampton	H	4–5	Hinshelwood, Thomas, Vinter, own-goal	2,721
10 August	Boston United	A	3–3	Shotton, Biggins, Lawrence	711
10 August	Aylesbury United	A	0–4		
12 August	Wantage Town	A	1–2	Berry	
13 August	Worcester City	A	4–3	Biggins 2, Thomas, Barnett	580
14 August	Shamrock Rovers	A	2–2	Thomas, Biggins	400
16 August	Sligo Rovers	A	4–0	Whatmore 2, Lawrence 2	500
20 August	Watford	H	4–3	Thomas 2, Briggs, Lawrence	2,378
14 May	Reading	A	1–3	(Steve Hetzke testimonial) Phillips	1,229
16 May	Chelsea	H	2–1	(Battle Of The Champions, Division 3 Champions v Division 2 Champions) Lawrence, Aldridge	4,441
18 May	West Bromwich Albion	H	3–3	(Billy Jeffrey testimonial match) Aries, Jeffrey, Jones	1,660
1984–85					
4 August	North Berks League XI	A	10–0	Brock 2, Biggins 2, Barnett 2, Jones 2, Hinshelwood, McDonald (pen)	500
4 August	Wantage Town	A	5–0	Rhoades-Brown 2, Aldridge, Hicks, Vinter	
6 August	Southampton	H	0–3		2,753
8 August	Bath City	A	0–1		210
10 August	Forest Green Rovers	A	1–2		
11 August	Cambridge United	H	2–1	(Oxfordshire Benevolent Cup Final) Trewick, Fallon (own-goal)	1,029
13 August	Worcester City	A	2–0	Biggins, Jones	750
14 August	Hayes	A	0–1		
17 August	Brackley Town	A	2–0	(Stand opening)	
18 August	Reading	H	4–2	(NSPCC Centenary Appeal Match) Brock 2, McDonald (pen), Vinter	1,587
13 May	Farnborough Town	A	7–2	(Ted Pearce testimonial match) Barnett 3, Thomas 2, Brock, Aries	1,500
14 May	Manchester United XI	H	1–1	(Peter Foley testimonial match) Langan	2,438
1985–86					
29 July	Wallingford Town	A	1–1	(Compensation game for sale of John Dreyer) Reck	296
31 July	Halifax Town	A	5–1	Hamilton 2, Trewick, Aldridge, Rhoades-Brown	627
3 August	Bath City	A	3–0	McDonald, Pratt (own-goal), Jones	497
5 August	Farnborough Town	A	5–3		
7 August	Brighton & Hove Albion	H	1–1	(Oxfordshire Benevolent Cup Final) Briggs (Oxford lost 5–4 on penalties)	2,531
10 August	Brentford	A	2–4		
10 August	Basingstoke Town	A	3–0	(Hugh Batty Appeal Fund)	
19 December	Exmouth	A	7–1	(Floodlight opening) Jones, Hebberd, Aldridge 4, Obi	618
1 May	Harrow Borough	A	8–1	Leworthy 4, Jenkins 2, McDermott, unknown	
7 May	Queen's Park Rangers	H	2–2	(Dave Fogg testimonial) Thomas, Fogg	1,408
16 May	Bulgaria	A	0–5		30,000
18 May	Septemvriisk Slava (Bulgaria)	A	2–1		

Date	Opponent	Venue	F–A	Scorers	Att
1986–87					
24 July	Constanta (Romania)	A	0–1		
25 July	Varna Spartak (Bulgaria)	A	2–3	Aldridge 2	
29 July	Tring Town	A	1–4	own-goal	
31 July	Cheltenham Town	A	3–3	Thomas, Jones, Leworthy	
2 August	Oxford City	A	3–1		
2 August	March Town United	A	10–0	Thomas 4, Aldridge 3, Obi 2, Swannock	
6 August	Abertillary Town	A	1–2	Seymour (own-goal)	
7 August	Wokingham Town	A	1–0	Obi	300
9 August	Brentford	A	2–1	Swannock, Rhoades-Brown	1,144
12 August	Stoke City	H	2–2	(Oxfordshire Benevolent Cup Final) Langan, Thomas (United won on penalties)	
17 August	Derry City	A	1–1	Obi	10,000
30 September	Merthyr Tydfil	A	2–2	Hebberd, Leworthy	1,300
14 October	Exeter City	A	2–0	(Peter Hatch Benefit) Leworthy 2	772
8 December	Truro City	A	3–0	(Keith Solomon Memorial Shield and floodlight opening) Leworthy 2, Nogan	1,500
28 January	Bermuda National XI	A	5–2	(Bermuda Invitational Tournament) Whitehurst, Houghton, Leworthy, McDermott, Trewick	
30 January	Malmo	A	0–1	(Bermuda Invitational Tournament Final)	
11 February	Wokingham Town	A	1–1	Swan	
11 March	Northern Ireland XI	H	6–4	(Billy Hamilton testimonial) Hamilton 3, Langan, Phillips, Brock	5,875
12 May	Aylesbury United	A	1–2	(Keith Baker testimonial match) Tully	
14 May	Abingdon Town	A	1–2	(Paul Griffiths and Kurt Douglas testimonial match) Nogan	
1987–88					
24 July	Edsbro (Sweden)	A	4–0	Rhoades-Brown, Whitehurst 2, Mustoe	1,000
25 July	Beaconsfield United	A	2–3	Yamanaki, own-goal	
26 July	Skarblacka (Sweden)	A	9–1	Shelton, Saunders 4, Brock, Whitehurst 2, Reck	
28 July	Brommapojkarna (Sweden)	A	1–1	Whitehurst	
28 July	Amersham	A	1–1	Nogan	
30 July	Trosa (Sweden)	A	11–0	Foyle 4, Saunders 3, Reck 2, Brock, Whitehurst	
1 August	Hofors (Sweden)	A	9–1	Whitehurst 3, Rhoades-Brown, Houghton, Foyle, Saunders, Brock, own-goal	
1 August	Brackley Town	A	4–1	Amaning, Nogan 2, Farrell	
4 August	Newbury Town	A	1–1	(Centenary Match) Beauchamp	
5 August	Swindon Town	H	1–3	(Gary Briggs testimonial) Shotton	4,536
7 August	Birmingham City	A	2–1	Houghton 2	1,464
10 August	Bournemouth	H	4–0	(Oxfordshire Benevolent Cup Final)	
14 December	Thame United	A	4–2	Rhoades-Brown, Reck 2, Mustoe	
9 May	Oxford City	A	4–3	(Dale Thorn benefit) Mustoe 2, Nogan, Foyle	300
1988–89					
5 August	Kettering Town	A	3–2	Rhoades-Brown, Massey (own-goal), Hill	800
7 August	Limerick City	A	2–1	Shelton, Saunders	
9 August	Cardiff City	A	2–0	Saunders 2	
9 August	Milton Keynes Wolves	A	3–1		
11 August	Swansea City	A	1–1	Saunders (pen)	870
15 August	Derby County	H	1–1	(Oxfordshire Benevolent Cup Final) Saunders (Oxford won 3–1 on pens)	1,718
17 August	Fulham	A	0–1		854
19 August	Southend United	A	1–1	Foyle	1,295
17 April	Welton Rovers	A	7–1	(Official opening of floodlights)	
1989–90					
26 July	Flackwell Heath	A	8–0	Durnin 3, Hill, Mustoe, Evans, Shelton, Phillips	
29 July	Aylesbury United	A	3–0		
31 July	Coventry City	A	3–0	McDonnell 2, Smart	
1 August	Tranmere Rovers	A	1–0		
4 August	Supermarine	A	3–0	Keeble, Jackson, McDonnell	
5 August	Crewe Alexandra	A	1–3		

Date	Opponent	Venue	F–A	Scorers	Att
7 August	Reading	A	1–2		
8 August	Hungerford Town	A	1–1	Lewis	
9 August	Nuneaton Borough	A	3–0		
12 August	Luton Town	H	1–2	(Oxfordshire Benevolent Cup Final)	
14 August	Hednesford Town	A	4–0	Nogan, McDonnell, Waters, Evans	
16 August	Carterton Town	A	12–1	Evans 4, Beauchamp 4, McDonnell 2, Ford 2	
1990–91					
23 July	Blackpool	A	1–1	(Isle of Man Football Festival) Simpson	
25 July	Isle Of Man	A	7–1	(Isle of Man Football Festival) McClaren, Durnin 5, Simpson	
28 July	Motherwell	A	1–3	(Isle of Man Football Festival Final) Durnin	
1 August	Wootton Bassett Town	A	6–0	Beauchamp 3, Byrne 2, Allen	
4 August	North Leigh	A	3–0	(Official opening of Eynsham Park) Byrne, Penney, Muttock	
7 August	Andover	A	3–0	Durning, Foyle, Stein	
10 August	Carterton Town	A	5–2	Nogan 2, Jackson, Muttock, Byrne	
11 August	Cheltenham Town	A	2–0	Foyle, Stein	
13 August	Buckingham Town	A	0–3		
14 August	Brentford	A	1–1	Simpson	
15 August	Gloucester City	A	2–2	Nogan 2	
17 August	Coventry City	H	0–1	(Oxfordshire Benevolent Cup Final)	
1991–92					
27 July	Merthyr Tydfil	A	3–0		
27 July	Cirencester Town	A	2–0	Muttock, Keeble	
30 July	Farnborough Town	A	1–0	Muttock	
31 July	Stafford Rangers	A	2–1	Magilton, Peney	
3 August	Saint Mirren	A	0–1		1,200
3 August	Wantage Town	A			
6 August	Clydebank	A	2–1	Stein, Simpson	450
8 August	Thame United	A	4–0	Muttock, McDonnell 2, Wanless	
9 August	Coventry City	H	1–3	(Oxfordshire Benevolent Cup Final) Stein	1,839
10 August	Worthing	A	2–1	Allen, Durnin	
1992–93					
22 July	Chepstow Town	A	8–0	Keeble 2, Druce, Penney, Ford, Collins, Beauchamp, Holmes	
25 July	Farnborough Town	A	1–1	Penney	
27 July	Bashley	A	5–2	Beauchamp 2, Collins, Keeble, Penney	
29 July	Halesowen Town	A	2–0	Magilton, Druce	
1 August	Wimbledon	H	1–0	Magilton	
4 August	Cardiff City	A	5–1	Magilton, Beauchamp, Cusack, Penney 2	
8 August	Norwich City	H	1–2	(Oxfordshire Benevolent Cup Final)	
10 August	Milton United	A	3–0	Narbett 2 (1 pen), Phillips	
1993–94					
21 July	Brantham Athletic	A	3–0	Wanless, Cusack, Holmes	
23 July	Corby Town	A	1–0	(Elwyn Roberts and David Hofbauer testimonial)	
26 July	Wimborne Town	A	4–0	Lewis, Allen, Wallbridge, Penney	
28 July	Dunstable	A	2–0		300
29 July	Evesham United	A	2–1	Wallbridge, Druce	
30 July	Hereford United	A	5–0	(Herefordshire Senior Cup Final)	
31 July	Berkhamsted Town	A	3–0	Murphy 2, Penney	
2 August	Yeovil Town	A	4–0		
3 August	Newbury Town	A	1–3		
4 August	Exeter City	A	0–2		
5 August	Basingstoke Town	A	0–1		
7 August	Queen's Park Rangers	H	0–2	(Official Centenary match and Oxfordshire Benevolent Cup Final)	2,517
9 August	Oxford City	A	1–3	(Opening match at Court Place Farm)	

Date	Opponent	Venue	F–A	Scorers	Att
1994–95					
21 July	Moreton Town	A	1–0	Massey	295
23 July	Aylesbury United	A	2–2	Byrne, Allen	350
25 July	Devizes Town	A	2–1	Murphy 2	
27 July	Woking	A	0–0		811
30 July	Cheltenham Town	A	1–2	Collins	401
1 August	Aston Villa	H	3–3	(Ken Fish benefit match) Byrne, Ford, Allen	4,620
3 August	Kettering Town	A	2–1	Byrne, Murphy	
6 August	Wimbledon	H	2–3	(Oxfordshire Benevolent Cup Final) Moody 2	1,944
8 August	Milton United	H	6–0	Wanless 2 (1 pen), Druce, Robinson, Murphy, unknown	
1995–96					
18 July	Evesham United	A	2–0	Smith 2	250
22 July	Worcester City	A	1–1	Hick (own-goal)	418
26 July	Thame United	A	3–2	Moody, Angel 2	693
28 July	Woking	A	0–3		958
1 August	Northampton Town	A	1–0	Murphy	2,208
4 August	Abingdon Town Youth	A	6–0		110
5 August	West Ham United	H	3–2	(Oxfordshire Benevolent Cup Final) Moody 3	3,569
8 August	Milton United	A	5–0		
1996–97					
23 July	Evesham United	A	6–0		600
27 July	Dorchester Town	A	2–0		
30 July	Wokingham Town	A	3–1		
31 July	Newbury Town	A	5–0		250
3 August	Rushden and Diamonds	A	2–1		
6 August	Watford	A	0–1		
8 August	Southampton	H	2–1	(Oxfordshire Benevolent Cup Final)	4,500
10 August	Didcot Town	A	3–1		
12 August	Milton United	A	1–1		
1997–98					
18 July	Newcastle Town	A	4–0	Ford, Angel 3	
19 July	Redditch United	A	5–1	Aldridge 4, S. Weatherstone	235
22 July	Aldershot	A	4–1	Ford 2, Massey, Cook	1,008
23 July	Newbury Town	A	0–3		225
25 July	Derby County	H	3–3	(Maurice Evans testimonial match) Beauchamp, Rowett (own-goal), Kozluck (own-goal)	3,424
29 July	Tottenham Hotspur	H	2–3	(Bill Halsey Memorial Cup Final)	8,024
30 July	Evesham United	A		Score unknown	
2 August	Hereford United	A	0–1		1,346
2 August	Stratford	A	5–0	Aldridge 2, Folland 2, S. Weatherstone	
4 August	Milton United	A	2–2		
5 August	Basingstoke Town	A		Score unknown	
1998–99					
21 July	Yeovil Town	A	3–0	Marsh, Davis, S. Weatherstone	
23 July	Tiverton Town	A	3–3	Murphy 2, Windass	
25 July	Exeter City	A	0–0		856
28 July	Mansfield Town	A	2–1	Thomson, Murphy	
29 July	AFC Newbury	A	0–3		150
31 July	Panionios	H	3–1	(Bill Halsey Memorial Cup Final) Banger, Mitsiopoulos (own-goal), Gilchrist	3,080
3 August	Oxford City	A	1–0	Thomson	
5 August	Milton United	A	7–1	S. Weatherstone 3, Jones, Folland 3	
12 August	North Leigh	A	3–0	(Opening of new dressing rooms) Wright, S. Weatherstone, Cook	

Date	Opponent	Venue	F–A	Scorers	Att
1999–2000					
19 July	Ayr United	A	0–1		
20 July	Brackley Town	A	0–2		364
21 July	Saint Mirren	A	1–0	Cook	
24 July	Blyth Spartans	A	3–1	Murphy, Anthrobus, Beauchamp	
28 July	Derby County	H	1–0	Anthrobus	3,077
30 July	Walsall	H	1–3	(Bill Halsey Memorial Cup Final) Anthrobus	1,533
3 August	Egham Town	A	1–1		
2000–01					
19 July	Havant & Waterlooville	A	6–0	Omoyinmi, Powell, Hackett, Lilley, Whitehead, McGowan	
22 July	Gosport Borough	A	2–0	Murphy, Omoyinmi	
25 July	Birmingham City	H	0–3	(Bill Halsey Memorial Cup Final)	
26 July	Banbury United	A	1–1	Ricketts	308
28 July	Chelsea	H	1–4	Jacobsen	4,521
29 July	Crawley	A	0–0		
1 August	Hereford United	A	1–1	McGuckin	
5 August	Slough Town	A	1–1	Powell (pen)	500
7 August	Milton United	A	2–0	Cook 2	
15 August	Wantage Town	A	4–0	Cook 2, Blake, Mills	400
2001–02					
17 July	Brackley Town	A	2–0	Beauchamp, Scott	400
19 July	Didcot Town	A	1–0	Tait	739
21 July	Oxford City	A	5–0	Scott 2, Guyett, Brooks, Richardson	
24 July	Woking	A	0–1		
28 July	Banbury United	A	0–1		
28 July	Farnborough Town	A	2–1	Whitehead, Omoyinmi	
29 July	Thame United	A	2–1	Powell, Hedger	
31 July	Kingstonian	A	4–2	Andy Scott 3, Beauchamp	
4 August	Crystal Palace	H	1–1	(Bill Halsey Memorial Cup Final and first match at the Kassam Stadium) Powell (United won 5–4 on pens)	7,000+
14 August	Oxford City	A	4–2	Folland, Holder 2, Okoli	
6 December	Millwall	H	1–1	(at Iffley Road) Whitehead	
18 March	Banbury United	A	1–0	Winters	
13 March	Oxford University	A	4–0	Omoyinmi, Hackett, Gray, Ross (own-goal)	
2002–03					
13 July	Oxford City	A	1–0	Omoyinmi	700
15 July	Thame United	A	1–1	Louis	556
20 July	Derby County	A	0–1		
23 July	Moor Green	A	1–1	Louis (pen)	
24 July	Chelsea	H	1–3	Whitehead	6,856
25 July	Nuneaton Borough	A	1–2	Roget	300
28 July	Leicester City	H	0–0		2,081
30 July	Aylesbury United	A	1–0	Hackett	250
2 August	Southampton	H	3–3	(Bill Halsey Memorial Cup Final) Savage, Svennson (own-goal), Whitehead (Southampton won 5–3 on pens)	3,000
4 August	Studley	A	0–2		200
5 August	Didcot Town	A	2–1	King, Sylla	453
7 August	Birmingham City	A	1–3	Emblen	
14 August	Northampton Town	H	2–0	(Played at Didcot) Steele, Brownlie	
4 November	Reading	A	1–4	(played at Didcot) Blackstock	
19 December	Northampton Town	H	0–2		

Date	Opponent	Venue	F–A	Scorers	Att
2003–04					
12 July	Walsall	A	1–4	(Played at Lilleshall) Blackstock	
12 July	Thame United	A	1–3	Beechers	200
15 July	Oxford City	A	4–0	Crosby (pen), Widdrington, Scott, Hackett	660
16 July	Wantage	A	2–1	Van Dommele 2	675
19 July	Chipping Norton	A	2–0	Beechers, O'Sullivan	135
20 July	Tottenham Hotspur	H	0–3		6,277
23 July	Farnborough Town	A	1–1	Townsley	365
26 July	Coventry City	H	0–0	(Bill Halsey Memorial Cup Final)	2,808
29 July	Aldershot	A	3–0	Scott 2, Crosby (pen)	976
31 July	Nuneaton Borough	A	1–2	McCargo	414
2 August	Moor Green	A	3–1	Townsley 3	250
3 August	Hellenic League XI	A	0–4		100
6 August	Studley	A	5–0	Alexis 2, Ciampoli, O'Sullivan, Beechers	
17 September	Wycombe Wanderers	H	3–1	Garner, Watson 2	
18 November	Oxford City	A	3–2	Hackett, Rawle, Brandish	
2 December	Rushden and Diamonds	A	1–0	Omoyinmi	
5 December	Swindon Town	H	0–1		
15 December	Northampton Town	H	0–1		
24 January	Derby County	A	0–1		
26 January	Hereford United	H	3–0	Steele, Basham 2	
30 March	Reading	A	2–0	Ashton, Louis	
2004–05					
10 July	Oxford City	A	4–1	Roget, Alexis, E'Beyer, Bradbury (pen)	1,054
13 July	Shepshed Dynamo	A	5–2	E'Beyer, Garner, Morgan 3	
17 July	Chipping Norton Town	A	2–1	Winters, Roberts	65
17 July	Chelsea	H	1–1	Mooney	11,282
20 July	Ipswich Town	H	1–5	Basham	2,493
21 July	Banbury United	A	1–1	Astwood	320
28 July	Watford	H	0–2		1,842
31 July	Bournemouth	H	2–2	Mooney 2	1,413
21 September	Luton Town	H	2–2	Hackett, own-goal	
18 January	Wycombe Wanderers	H	1–1	Trialist	
22 March	Cardiff City	H	1–2	Raponi	
2005–06					
8 July	Swindon Town	A	3–0	Bradbury, Davies, Beavon	
9 July	Ardley United	A	1–0	Beechers	180
16 July	Milton United	A	3–2	Beechers 2, Smith (own-goal)	140
16 July	Yeading	A	0–2		200
19 July	Oxford City	A	4–1	Ashton, Hackett, Bradbury, Davies	1,076
20 July	Carterton Town	A	2–1	Meade 2	100
23 July	Aylesbury United	A	4–0	Stirling, Ashton, Hackett, Quinn	605
25 July	Brackley Town	A	0–2		325
27 July	Brighton & Hove Albion	H	4–1	Robinson, Willmott, Hackett, Bradbury	1,680
30 July	Leicester City	H	1–3	Morgan	2,129
2 August	Worcester City	A	1–0	Beechers	
2006–07					
19 July	Didcot Town	A	3–1	Quinn, Kennet, Odubade	1,220
26 July	Eastleigh	A	2–1	Odubade 2	435
29 July	Chesterfield	H	1–3	Duffy	1,378

Date	Opponent	Venue	F–A	Scorers	Att
31 July	Banbury United	A	0–3		800
4 August	Portsmouth	H	0–0		3,178
5 August	Abingdon Town	A	5–0	Weedon, Beechers, Odubade 3	220
8 August	Manchester United XI	H	1–4	Duffy	11,463
9 August	Oxford City	A	3–1	Willmott, Basham, Beechers	300
30 April	Chelsea	H	2–4	(Peter Rhoades-Brown testimonial) Patterson, Rhoades-Brown	5,130
2007–08					
21 July	Didcot Town	A	3–1	Odubade, Duffy 2	1,183
24 July	Eastleigh	A	1–0	Twigg	449
28 July	Carterton Town	A	2–0	Dzviti, Deering	
28 July	AFC Bournemouth	H	2–1	Trainer, Odubade	1,202
30 July	Luton Town	H	1–2	Jeannin	1,406
1 August	Oxford City	A	0–0		702
3 August	Wycombe Wanderers	H	1–1	Quinn	1,691
4 August	Abingdon United	A	1–1	Fisher	
6 August	Birmingham City	H	1–0	Hutchinson	2,497
2 October	Milton United	A	1–1	Standing	
22 January	North Leigh	A	3–1	Taylor 2, Jeannin	
30 January	Milton United	A	1–2	Fisher	
5 February	Abingdon United	A	1–1	(Michael Alexis benefit match) Blackwood	
26 February	Witney United	A	2–0	McAllister, Hutchinson	628
11 March	Kidlington	A	3–0	Fisher 2, Taylor	
1 April	Royal Navy	A	2–0	Odubade 2	
28 April	Kettering Town	A	4–3	(Brett Solkhon testimonial) Rose, Quinn, Trainer, Taylor	550
2008–09					
8 July	Oxford City	A	1–0	Constable	853
12 July	Brackley Town	A	1–2	Haldane	726
15 July	Banbury United	A	4–0	Guy 2, Constable, Reid	
19 July	Abingdon Town	A	9–1	(Luke Beauchamp testimonial) Hutchinson 2, Groves, Fower 2, Hodgkins 2, Manny, Woodley	200
19 July	Maidenhead United	A	3–1	Haldane (2), Guy (pen)	401
22 July	Bath City	A	1–0	Odubade	
24 July	Kidlington	A	2–3	Dobson, Fower	
26 July	Manchester United XI	H	2–2	Odubade, Guy	6,027
29 July	St Neots Town	A	2–5	Taylor, Fower	
29 July	Wycombe Wanderers	H	1–1	Guy	1,510
31 July	Milton United	A	3–0	Taylor, Deering, Hutchinson	
2 August	Cheltenham Town	H	2–1	Guy 2	1,174
4 August	Portsmouth	H	1–2	Fisher	4,956
7 August	Old Woodstock Town	A	1–2	Fower	
9 September	Brentford	A	1–2	Bowerman	
17 September	Kidlington	A	0–3		
16 December	Milton United	A	2–3	Fisher, Fower	
14 January	Didcot Town	A	1–1	Fisher	
26 January	Didcot Town	A	0–3		
18 April	Kidlington	A	2–0	Taylor 2	

OUFC Reserves Results

Metropolitan League

Season	Comp	Date	Opponents	Venue	Result	Score
1949–50	Friendly	27 August 1949	Abingdon Town	A	D	3–3
		10 September 1949	West Ham B	H	D	2–2
		17 September 1949	Dagenham Town	H	D	2–2
		24 September 1949	Chipperfield Town	H	W	7–4
		1 October 1949	Chingford Town Res	A	W	3–2
		8 October 1949	Hove FC	A	W	10–1
		15 October 1949	Dickinson-Apsley FC	H	W	4–2
		22 October 1949	Dickinson-Apsley FC	A	W	4–2
		5 November 1949	St Neots and District	A	D	2–2
		12 November 1949	Dagenham Town	A	L	1–3
	Friendly	26 November 1949	London University	H	W	2–0
		3 December 1949	Twickenham	H	W	6–2
		10 December 1949	Callendars Athletic	A	L	2–6
		17 December 1949	Chingford Town Res	H	W	4–1
	Cup	24 December 1949	Hove FC	H	W	9–0
	Oxon Senior Cup	27 December 1949	Marston United	H	W	5–2
		31 December 1949	Dagenham Town	H	W	7–0
		7 January 1950	Twickenham	H	W	2–0
	Oxon Senior Cup sf	28 January 1950	Oxford City	H	W	2–1
	Friendly	18 February 1950	London University	A	L	
	Cup	4 March 1950	St Neots and District	H	L	0–2
	Oxon Senior Cup Final	11 March 1950	Pegasus	Ox City	L	0–3
		8 April 1950	Callendars Athletic	H	D	1–1
		15 April 1950	Chipperfield Town	A	W	2–0

Metropolitan League

Season	Comp	Date	Opponents	Venue	Result	Score
1950–51		19 August 1950	Chipperfield	H	W	10–1
		26 August 1950	Dunstable Town	A	W	4–0
		30 August 1950	Luton Town A	H	W	2–1
		2 September 1950	Hove United	A	L	1–4
		9 September 1950	Vickers	A	D	2–2
		23 September 1950	Croydon Rovers	A	W	4–0
		30 September 1950	Dickinson (Apsley)	H	W	3–2
		7 October 1950	Chipperfield	A	W	1–0
		14 October 1950	Chingford	H	D	2–2
		21 October 1950	Dickinson (Apsley)	A	L	2–3
		28 October 1950	Brighton & Hove Albion A	H	L	0–1
		4 November 1950	Leatherhead	A	L	2–3
		11 November 1950	Callendars Athletic	H	W	5–1
	Friendly	18 November 1950	Abingdon Town	A	W	4–2
		25 November 1950	Leatherhead	H	W	2–1
		2 December 1950	Callendars Athletic	A	W	3–1
		16 December 1950	Brighton & Hove Albion A	A	L	1–3
	ML Cup	23 December 1950	Vickers	H	W	4–1
		26 December 1950	Dunstable Town	H	W	7–3
	Friendly	30 December 1950	Croydon Rovers	A	D	1–1
	ML Cup	6 January 1951	St Neots	H	W	2–1
		13 January 1951	Luton Town A	H	L	0–2
		20 January 1951	Twickenham	H	L	1–2

		27 January 1951	Vickers Armstrong	A	L	0–3
		3 February 1951	Hastings United	H	W	5–0
		10 February 1951	Chingford	A	W	4–1
		24 February 1951	Dagenham	A	D	4–4
		3 March 1951	Croydon Rovers	H	W	2–0
		17 March 1951	St Neots	H	L	0–5
	ML Cup	26 March 1951	Chingford Town	H	W	4–0
		31 March 1951	Twickenham	A	D	3–3
		7 April 1951	St Neots	A	L	2–4
	ML Cup Final	14 April 1951	Dagenham	H	W	1–0
		19 April 1951	Windsor & Eton	H	W	5–0
		28 April 1951	Dagenham	H	L	1–4
		2 May 1951	Windsor& Eton	A	L	0–7
		5 May 1951	Hastings United	A		
		12 May 1951	Hove United	H	Not played	

Metropolitan League

Season	**Comp**	**Date**	**Opponents**	**Venue**	**Result**	**Score**
1951–52		25 August 1951	Windsor & Eton	A	D	2–2
		1 September 1951	Luton Town A	H	W	6–3
		8 September 1951	Millwall A	A	W	2–1
		29 September 1951	Dunstable	A	W	3–2
		6 October 1951	Twickenham	A	L	1–2
		20 October 1951	Brighton & Hove Albion A	H	W	6–1
		27 October 1951	Tonbridge	A	D	1–1
		10 November 1951	Hastings United	H	W	3–2
		17 November 1951	Callendars Athletic	A	W	7–2
		1 December 1951	Luton Town	H	W	4–0
		15 December 1951	Hastings United	A		
		22 December 1951	Callendars Athletic	H	W	2–1
		26 December 1951	Dunstable	H	W	3–1
		29 December 1951	Horsham	A	D	1–1
	Oxon Senior Cup	5 January 1952	Bicester Town	A	W	4–1
	ML Cup	12 January 1952	Horsham	H	D	1–1
	Oxon Senior Cup	19 January 1952	Kirtlington	H	D	1–1
	Oxon Senior Cup	26 January 1952	Kirtlington	A	W	5–4
		2 February 1952	Tottenham Hotspur A	H	L	1–3
		16 February 1952	Windsor & Eton	H	W	6–2
		23 February 1952	Horsham	A	W	2–1
		1 March 1952	Vickers Armstrong	H	W	5–2
		8 March 1952	Skyways	A	L	2–4
		15 March 1952	Hastings United	A	D	2–2
	ML Cup sf	22 March 1952	Luton Town A	H	D	1–1
	Oxon Senior Cup sf	29 March 1952	Dorchester	A	W	1–0
		11 April 1952	Brighton & Hove Albion A	A	L	2–8
	Oxon Senior Cup final	14 April 1952	Chipping Norton	N	W	3–1
		19 April 1952	Twickenham	H	L	1–4
		21 April 1952	Tottenham Hotspur A	A	L	2–6
		26 April 1952	Horsham	H	D	1–1
			Tottenham Hotspur A	A	L	0–1
			Millwall A	H	W	4–1
		3 May 1952	Skyways	H	W	3–0
		5 May 1952	Tonbridge	H	D	2–2
	Oxon Professional Cup	10 May 1952	Banbury Spencer	H	W	5–4

Metropolitan League

Season	Comp	Date	Opponents	Venue	Result	Score
1952–53		30 August 1952	Vickers Armstrong	H	W	1–0
		3 September 1952	Newbury	A	W	1–0
		6 September 1952	Vickers Armstrong	A	D	2–2
		10 September 1952	Newbury	H	L	1–3
		13 September 1952	Tottenham Hotspur A	H	W	2–0
	Friendly	16 September 1952	Witney Town	A	W	4–1
		4 October 1952	Tonbridge	H	D	2–2
		11 October 1952	Tottenham Hotspur A	A	L	0–3
	ML Cup	18 October 1952	Brighton & Hove Albion A	H	W	2–1
		25 October 1952	Horsham	A	W	5–2
		1 November 1952	Windsor & Eton	H	L	1–2
		8 November 1952	Tonbridge	A	L	2–5
	ML Cup	15 November 1952	Haywards Heath	A	L	0–1
		22 November 1952	West Ham United A	A	W	5–2
		29 November 1952	Hastings United	H	D	3–3
		6 December 1952	Brighton & Hove Albion A	A	W	4–1
		13 December 1952	Luton Town A	H	W	1–0
		20 December 1952	Dunstable Town	H	D	1–1
		26 December 1952	Dunstable Town	A		
		27 December 1952	Hastings United	A	L	2–6
		3 January 1953	Windsor & Eton	A	L	0–1
	Professional Cup	10 January 1953	Tonbridge	H	L	0–2
		17 January 1953	Southwick	A		
		24 January 1953	Luton Town A	A	D	1–1
	Oxon Senior Cup	7 February 1953	Littlemore	H	W	6–1
		14 February 1953	haywards Heath	A	L	1–4
	Oxon Senior Cup	16 February 1953	Kirtlington	H	W	6–2
		21 February 1953	Twickenham	H	W	4–0
	Oxon Senior Cup	7 March 1953	Morris Motors	N	W	2–1
		21 March 1953	Horsham	H	D	0–0
		3 April 1953	Callendars Athletic	A	W	3–1
	Oxon Senior Cup final	6 April 1953	Witney Town	N	L	1–2
		11 April 1953	Brighton & Hove Albion A	H	W	2–0
		18 April 1953	Haywards Heath	H	L	0–1
		25 April 1953	Callendars Athletic	H	W	4–0
		30 April 1953	West Ham United A	H		
	Oxon Professional Cup	2 May 1953	Banbury Spencer	A	D	1–1
	Oxon Professional Cup	9 May 1953	Banbury Spencer	H	D	1–1

Metropolitan League

Season	Comp	Date	Opponents	Venue	Result	Score
1953–54		22 August 1953	Chelsea	H	L	0–4
		29 August 1953	Tonbridge	A	L	1–3
		2 September 1953	Newbury	A	W	2–1
		5 September 1953	Vickers	H	W	3–0
		9 September 1953	Windsor & Eton	H	W	7–0
		12 September 1953	Hastings United	A	L	2–3
		14 September 1953	Luton Town	H	W	5–1
		19 September 1953	Gravesend	H	W	2–0
		23 September 1953	Newbury Town	H	W	4–1
		26 September 1953	Guildford City	H	W	3–0
		3 October 1953	Tottenham Hotspur A	H	W	1–0
		10 October 1953	Gravesend	A	L	0–3

		17 October 1953	Horsham	H	W	2–1
		24 October 1953	Windsor & Eton	A	L	1–2
		7 November 1953	West Ham United A	H	W	4–0
		14 November 1953	Dartford	H	W	4–3
		21 November 1953	Tonbridge	H	L	2–3
		28 November 1953	Southwick	H	W	5–2
	ML Cup	5 December 1953	Windsor & Eton	A	D	3–3
	ML Cup	10 December 1953	Windsor & Eton	H	W	5–0
		19 December 1953	Dunstable Town	A	W	5–3
		26 December 1953	Brighton & Hove Albion	H	L	2–4
		2 January 1954	Tonbridge	H	L	0–6
		16 January 1954	Guildford City	A	D	2–2
	ML Cup	23 January 1954	Tottenham Hotspur A	H	D	2–2
		6 February 1954	Brighton & Hove Albion	A	W	4–1
		13 February 1954	Dartford	A	W	1–0
		20 February 1954	Horsham	A	L	1–2
		27 February 1954	Haywards Heath	A	W	4–0
	ML Cup	3 March 1954	Tottenham Hotspur A	H	W	2–1
		6 March 1954	Southwick	A	W	3–0
		20 March 1954	Tottenham Hotspur A	A	W	3–0
	ML Cup	27 March 1954	Hastings United	A	L	1–5
		3 April 1954	West Ham United A	A	W	3–1
		10 April 1954	Hastings United	H	W	3–0
		14 April 1954	Dunstable Town	H	W	5–0
		16 April 1954	Vickers	A	D	0–0
		17 April 1954	Luton Town	H	W	3–1
		24 April 1954	Haywards Heath	H	W	2–1
		29 April 1954	Chelsea	H	W	4–0
	Oxfordshire Professional Cup	5 May 1954	Banbury Spencer	H	W	2–1
	Oxfordshire Professional Cup	8 May 1954	Banbury Spencer	A	W	2–1

Metropolitan League

Season	Comp	Date	Opponents	Venue	Result	Score
1954–55		21 August 1954	Wokingham Town	A	W	3–1
		25 August 1954	Newbury Town	H	L	1–2
		28 August 1954	Wokingham Town	H	L	1–3
		1 September 1954	Newbury Town	A	L	0–1
	Challenge Cup	4 September 1954	West Ham United	H	W	2–1
		15 September 1954	Chelsea	H	D	3–3
		18 September 1954	Brighton & Hove Albion	H	L	0–1
		8 September 1954	Windsor & Eton	H	L	0–1
		25 September 1954	Vickers	A	L	1–2
	Professional Cup	2 October 1954	Hastings United	H	L	0–1
		9 October 1954	Hastings United	A	L	1–3
		16 October 1954	Dartford	H	L	0–1
	Friendly	23 October 1954	Chippenham Town	A	L	1–4
	Friendly	30 October 1954	Oxford University	H	L	2–3
		6 November 1954	Dunstable Town	A	L	0–3
		13 November 1954	West Ham United	H	W	4–0
		20 November 1954	Horsham	A	L	0–5
		27 November 1954	Luton Town	H	L	2–4
		11 December 1954	Vickers	H	W	5–0
		18 December 1954	Gravesend & Northfleet	H	L	0–1
		27 December 1954	Haywards Heath	H	L	0–2
		28 December 1954	Tonbridge	A	L	1–2

		1 January 1955	Haywards Heath	A	W	3–1
		8 January 1955	Windsor & Eton	A	W	1–0
	ML Cup	22 January 1955	Guildford City	H	W	2–0
		5 February 1955	Guildford City	H	D	1–1
	ML Cup	12 February 1955	Tonbridge	H	W	4–1
		19 February 1955	Chelsea	A		
		26 February 1955	Luton Town	H	L	1–6
		5 March 1955	Dartford	A	W	1–0
		12 March 1955	Tonbridge	H		
	ML Cup sf	19 March 1955	Windsor & Eton	A	L	2–3 aet
		26 March 1955	Horsham	H	D	1–1
		9 April 1955	Dunstable Town	H	W	4–0
	Smith Memorial Cup	18 April 1955	Oxford City	H	D	1–1
		23 April 1955	Tonbridge	H	L	0–1
	Smith Memorial Cup	25 April 1955	Oxford City	A	W	2–1
		30 April 1955	West Ham United	H	W	4–0
	Oxon Professional Cup	7 May 1955	Banbury Spencer		D	2–2
	Oxon Professional Cup	14 May 1955	Banbury Spencer		W	5–2

Metropolitan League

Season	Comp	Date	Opponents	Venue	Result	Score
1955–56		20 August 1955	Chelsea	H	L	0–2
		27 August 1955	Wokingham Town	A	W	5–1
		31 August 1955	Newbury Town	A	W	2–1
		3 September 1955	Guildford City	H	W	2–0
		8 September 1955	Bedford Town	A	W	2–1
		10 September 1955	West Ham United	H	W	4–1
		14 September 1955	Newbury Town	H	W	5–0
		17 September 1955	Gravesend & Northfleet	H	W	3–0
		21 September 1955	Bedford Town	H	L	0–1
		24 September 1955	Guildford City	A	W	6–0
		1 October 1955	Brighton & Hove Albion	H	W	4–0
	League Challenge Cup	8 October 1955	Horsham	A	W	6–0
		15 October 1955	Hastings United	H	L	2–3
		22 October 1955	Gravesend & Northfleet	A	L	1–3
		5 November 1955	Brighton & Hove Albion	A	W	2–0
		12 November 1955	Luton Town	H	W	2–0
		19 November 1955	West Ham United	H	W	7–0
		26 November 1955	Wokingham Town	H	W	6–0
		3 December 1955	Tonbridge	H	L	0–1
	MLC	10 December 1955	Gravesend & Northfleet	H	W	5–2
		17 December 1955	Horsham	A	L	0–4
		24 December 1955	Windsor & Eton	H	W	9–1
		26 December 1955	Dunstable Town	A	W	5–3
		27 December 1955	Dunstable Town	H	W	5–2
		7 January 1956	Heywards Heath	A	L	2–4
	MLC	14 January 1956	West Ham United	H	W	3–0
	Professional Cup	19 January 1956	Dartford	H	W	2–1
		4 February 1956	Luton Town	H	W	6–1
		18 February 1956	Dartford	H	W	3–1
	Professional Cup	25 February 1956	Chelsea	A	L	0–3
	Friendly	10 March 1956	Trowbridge	A	D	3–3
	MLC	17 March 1956	Hastings United	H	W	5–3
		30 March 1956	Horsham	H	W	7–1
		14 April 1956	Tonbridge	H	W	4–1

	MLC Final first leg	21 April 1956	Bedford Town	A	L	0–3
	Marriott Cup sf	23 April 1956	Witney & District XI		W	5–2
	MLC Final second leg	28 April 1956	Bedford Town	H	D	1–1
		30 April 1956	Dartford	A	L	0–1
		1 May 1956	Haywards Heath	H	W	9–1
	Smith Memorial Cup Final	2 May 1956	Bicester Town	H	W	3–0
	Marriott Cup Final	3 May 1956	OU Centaurs	Witney	W	1–0
	Oxon Professional Cup	8 May 1956	Banbury Spencer	H	W	4–1
	Oxon Professional Cup	12 May 1956	Banbury Spencer	A	D	1–1

Metropolitan League

Season	Comp	Date	Opponents	Venue	Result	Score
1956–57		18 August 1956	Horsham	A	W	3–1
		22 August 1956	Dartford	H	W	4–1
		25 August 1956	West Ham United	H	L	2–3
		27 August 1956	Luton Town	A	W	3–2
		1 September 1956	Newbury Town	A	L	0–1
		8 September 1956	Guildford City	H	D	2–2
		15 September 1956	Bedford Town	A	W	3–2
		19 September 1956	Tonbridge	A	L	0–2
	ML Cup	22 September 1956	Bedford Town	H	L	0–3
		29 September 1956	Eastbourne United	A	L	2–4
		6 October 1956	Hastings United	A	L	1–9
	Professional Cup	13 October 1956	Brighton & Hove Albion	H	L	2–4
		27 October 1956	Chelsea	H	W	3–1
		3 November 1956	Guildford City	A	W	2–1
		10 November 1956	Luton Town	H	L	1–2
		24 November 1956	West Ham United	H	W	2–1
		1 December 1956	Haywards Heath	A	L	2–5
		8 December 1956	Brighton & Hove Albion	H	W	5–0
		15 December 1956	Dunstable Town	H	W	3–1
		22 December 1956	Chelsea	A	L	1–3
		29 December 1956	Newbury Town	H	W	3–1
		5 January 1957	Brighton & Hove Albion	A	D	2–2
		12 January 1957	Crawley Town	A	W	2–1
		19 January 1957	Haywards Heath	H	W	3–0
		26 January 1957	Windsor & Eton	A	L	2–3
		9 February 1957	Windsor & Eton	H	L	1–2
		16 February 1957	Hastings United	H	D	1–1
		23 February 1957	Wokingham Town	A	L	1–2
		27 February 1957	Wokingham Town	H	W	4–0
		16 March 1957	Horsham	H	W	4–0
		30 March 1957	Crawley Town	H	D	0–0
		6 April 1957	Dartford	A	L	1–3
		13 April 1957	Eastbourne United	H	L	2–4

Metropolitan League

Season	Comp	Date	Opponents	Venue	Result	Score
1957–58		24 August 1957	Crawley	A	W	2–1
		28 August 1957	Dartford	A	L	2–3
		31 August 1957	Fulham	H	W	2–1
		4 September 1957	Chelsea	H	L	1–2
		9 September 1957	Luton Town	A	L	1–5
		14 September 1957	West Ham United	H	L	2–3

		18 September 1957	Tonbridge	H	L	1–2
		21 September 1957	Bedford Town	A	L	1–6
		28 September 1957	Brighton & Hove Albion	A	W	2–1
		2 October 1957	Didcot Town	A	W	4–1
	Professional Cup	5 October 1957	Tonbridge	H	L	2–5
		12 October 1957	Bedford Town	H	W	6–0
		19 October 1957	Haywards Heath	A	L	0–7
	League Cup	26 October 1957	Luton Town	H	W	4–0
		2 November 1957	Hastings United	A	L	2–3
		9 November 1957	Brighton & Hove Albion	H	W	2–0
		23 November 1957	Windsor & Eton	H	W	2–1
		30 November 1957	Windsor & Eton	A	L	1–2
		7 December 1957	Newbury Town	H	D	2–2
		14 December 1957	Guildford City	A	W	1–0
		21 December 1957	Luton Town	H	W	4–1
		26 December 1957	Newbury Town	A	L	1–2
	Professional Cup	4 January 1958	Tonbridge	A	L	1–2
		11 January 1958	Didcot Town	H	W	2–1
		1 February 1958	Dunstable	H	L	2–3
		8 February 1958	Chelsea	H	L	1–2
		15 February 1958	tonbridge	A	D	3–3
		1 March 1958	Dartford	H	W	7–3
	Challenge Cup	15 March 1958	Guildford City	H	D	2–2
	Challenge Cup	22 March 1958	Guildford City	A	L	0–1
		29 March 1958	Eastbourne United	H	L	1–4
		4 April 1958	Dunstable	A	L	0–2
		5 April 1958	Haywards Heath	H	W	2–0
		10 April 1958	West Ham United	H	W	4–2
		12 April 1958	Crawley	H	W	2–1
		14 April 1958	Hastings United	H	W	4–1
		19 April 1958	Eastbourne United	A	W	2–0
	Marriott Cup sf	21 April 1958	OU Centaurs	H	W	3–2
		26 April 1958	Guildford City	H	W	3–1
		1 May 1958	Fulham	H	L	0–3
	Marriott Cup Final	2 May 1958	Witney Town	A	W	2–1

Metropolitan League

Season	**Comp**	**Date**	**Opponents**	**Venue**	**Result**	**Score**
1958–59		23 August 1958	Brighton & Hove Albion	H	W	4–2
		30 August 1958	Guildford City	A	L	1–3
		3 September 1958	Newbury Town	A	D	2–2
		6 September 1958	Bedford Town	A	W	2–1
		13 September 1958	Dunstable	H	D	1–1
		17 September 1958	Newbury Town	A	L	2–6
		20 September 1958	Chelsea	A	L	0–5
		27 September 1958	Tonbridge	H	L	2–3
	Challenge Cup	11 October 1958	Hastings United	H	L	2–3
		18 October 1958	Dunstable	A	L	1–3
		22 October 1958	Didcot Town	A	D	1–1
	Professional Cup	25 October 1958	West Ham United	H	L	0–3
		1 November 1958	Tonbridge	A	L	2–7
		8 November 1958	Bedford Town	H	W	4–0
		15 November 1958	Arsenal	A	L	2–7
		22 November 1958	Guildford City	H	L	0–4
		29 November 1958	Hastings United	A	W	2–1

		6 December 1958	Fulham	H	D	0–0
		13 December 1958	Haywards Heath	A	W	4–3
		20 December 1958	Brighton & Hove Albion	A	L	1–3
		27 December 1958	Didcot Town	H	D	3–3
		3 January 1959	Arsenal	H	L	0–7
		17 January 1959	Dartford	H	D	1–1
		24 January 1959	Crawley Town	A	D	0–0
		7 February 1959	Eastbourne United	H	W	3–0
		21 February 1959	Windsor & Eton	H	L	1–2
		28 February 1959	Luton Town	A	W	1–0
		7 March 1959	West Ham United	H	W	6–3
		14 March 1959	Crawley Town	A	L	2–3
		21 March 1959	Hastings United	H	W	2–0
		27 March 1959	Luton Town	H	D	1–1
		30 March 1959	West Ham United	H	W	5–1
		4 April 1959	Fulham	H	D	4–4
		11 April 1959	Eastbourne United	A	W	4–1
		18 April 1959	Haywards Heath	H	W	3–1
		25 April 1959	Dartford	A	W	4–1
		27 April 1959	Chelsea	H	L	2–5
		2 May 1959	Windsor & Eton	H	D	2–2

Metropolitan League

Season	Comp	Date	Opponents	Venue	Result	Score
1959–60		22 August 1959	Haywards Heath	H	D	1–1
		26 August 1959	Newbury Town	A	L	0–10
		29 August 1959	Crawley Town	A	W	2–1
		3 September 1959	Didcot Town	H	W	3–2
		5 September 1959	Guildford City	H	W	2–0
		12 September 1959	Chelsea	A	W	2–1
		16 September 1959	Didcot Town	A	L	3–4
		19 September 1959	Eastbourne United	H	W	3–2
		24 September 1959	Newbury Town	H	W	5–1
	Challenge Cup	3 October 1959	West Ham United	H	W	3–1
	Professional Cup	10 October 1959	Luton Town	H	L	2–6
		17 October 1959	Bedford Town	A	L	1–2
		24 October 1959	Chelsea	H	W	4–1
		31 October 1959	Fulham	H	W	3–2
	Challenge Cup	7 November 1959	Chelsea	H	W	4–1
		14 November 1959	Hastings United	H	W	4–2
		21 November 1959	Bedford Town	H	L	1–2
		5 December 1959	Tonbridge	H	L	3–5
		12 December 1959	Arsenal	A	L	1–7
		19 December 1959	Dunstable Town	A	D	1–1
		26 December 1959	Eastbourne United	A	W	2–1
		2 January 1960	Canterbury	H	L	0–3
		9 January 1960	Dartford	A	L	1–3
		16 January 1960	Haywards Heath	A	L	2–5
		23 January 1960	Tonbridge	A	D	1–1
		30 January 1960	Dartford	H	W	6–2
		6 February 1960	Luton Town	A	L	3–4
		20 February 1960	Canterbury	A	L	0–5
		27 February 1960	Hastings United	A	D	3–3
		5 March 1960	Windsor & Eton	H	W	3–2
		12 March 1960	Guildford City	A	D	1–1

Season	Comp	Date	Opponents	Venue	Result	Score
		19 March 1960	Brighton & Hove Albion	H	L	0–3
	Challenge Cup	2 April 1960	Arsenal	H	W	2–1
		15 April 1960	Crawley Town	H	W	4–1
	Challenge Cup F first leg	16 April 1960	Eastbourne United	H	L	1–2
		21 April 1960	Dunstable Town	H	W	2–1
	Challenge Cup F first leg	23 April 1960	Eastbourne United	A	W	3–2
		30 April 1960	Arsenal	H	L	0–1
		5 May 1960	Fulham	H	W	4–1
		7 May 1960	Windsor & Eton	A		

Metropolitan League

Season	Comp	Date	Opponents	Venue	Result	Score
1960–61		20 August 1960	Crawley Town	A	W	3–0
		25 August 1960	Didcot Town	H	W	3–1
		27 August 1960	West Ham United	H	D	1–1
		3 September 1960	Dartford	A	L	2–3
		7 September 1960	Newbury Town	A	D	1–1
	Challenge Cup	10 September 1960	Luton Town	H	L	1–2
		14 September 1960	Didcot Town	A	L	1–2
		17 September 1960	Metropolitan Police	A	W	1–0
		22 September 1960	Newbury Town	H	W	5–3
		24 September 1960	Dunstable Town	H	W	3–2
		1 October 1960	St Neots Town	A	L	2–5
		8 October 1960	Luton Town	H	W	2–0
		15 October 1960	Brighton & Hove Albion	A	W	5–0
		22 October 1960	Bedford Town	H	W	2–1
		29 October 1960	Haywards Heath	A	W	6–2
		5 November 1960	Brighton & Hove Albion	H	W	8–0
		12 November 1960	Hastings United	A	D	1–1
	Professional Cup	19 November 1960	Tonbridge	H	W	7–1
		26 November 1960	Tonbridge	A	L	1–4
		3 December 1960	Arsenal	H	L	3–5
		10 December 1960	Luton Town	A	L	0–4
		17 December 1960	St Neots Town	H	W	2–0
		24 December 1960	Tonbridge	H	W	8–1
		26 December 1960	Bedford Town	A	W	3–2
		31 December 1960	Dunstable Town	A	L	1–4
		7 January 1961	Eastbourne United	A	D	2–2
		14 January 1961	Dartford	H	W	4–1
		4 February 1961	Guildford City	H	W	2–0
		11 February 1961	Guildford City	A	L	2–4
		18 February 1961	Eastbourne United	H	D	2–2
		4 March 1961	Hastings United	H	W	5–1
	Professional Cup	1 April 1961	Arsenal	H	L	0–2
		6 April 1961	Metropolitan Police	H	W	5–1
		8 April 1961	Arsenal	A	L	0–8
		15 April 1961	West Ham United	H	W	5–2
		29 April 1961	Crawley Town	H	W	9–1

Metropolitan League

Season	Comp	Date	Opponents	Venue	Result	Score
1961–62		19 August 1961	Bexley Heath & Welling	H	W	9–1
		23 August 1961	Didcot Town	A	W	6–2
		26 August 1961	Guildford City	A	L	2–3
		30 August 1961	Newbury Town	A	W	3–2

	Professional Cup	2 September 1961	Bedford Town	A	L	2–3
		9 September 1961	West Ham United	H	W	8–2
		16 September 1961	Crawley Town	A	L	4–0
	Professional Cup	23 September 1961	Bedford Town	H	W	3–1
		27 September 1961	Newbury Town	H	L	1–2
		7 October 1961	Arsenal	H	L	1–3
	Challenge Cup	17 October 1961	Arsenal	A	W	3–2
		21 October 1961	Rainham Town	A	W	3–1
		28 October 1961	Metropolitan Police	A	W	6–2
		4 November 1961	Crawley Town	H	W	4–1
	Professional Cup	7 November 1961	Arsenal	A	L	0–3
		11 November 1961	Dartford	A	L	1–4
		15 November 1961	Didcot Town	H	L	1–2
		18 November 1961	Woodford Town	H	W	10–2
	Professional Cup	22 November 1961	Arsenal	H	L	0–1
		25 November 1961	Bexley Heath & Welling	A	L	1–2
		2 December 1961	Rainham Town	H	W	5–2
		9 December 1961	Eastbourne United	A	D	3–3
		21 December 1961	Guildford City	H	L	1–2
		26 December 1961	St Neots Town	A	W	3–1
		20 January 1962	Bedford Town	A	W	4–3
		27 January 1962	West Ham United	A	D	2–2
	Challenge Cup	3 February 1962	St Neots Town	H	W	3–1
		10 February 1962	Woodford Town	A	D	1–1
		17 February 1962	Eastbourne United	H	W	3–0
		3 March 1962	Dartford	H	L	3–5
		17 March 1962	Metropolitan Police	H	L	2–3
		24 March 1962	Arsenal	A	L	0–4
		31 March 1962	Brighton & Hove Albion	A	L	1–2
		5 April 1962	St Neots Town	H	W	3–1
	Challenge Cup	7 April 1962	Didcot Town	A	L	2–4
		9 April 1962	Bedford Town	H	W	4–1
		14 April 1962	Tonbridge	A	W	4–3
		20 April 1962	Brighton & Hove Albion	H	D	1–1

Metropolitan League

Season	Comp	Date	Opponents	Venue	Result	Score
1962–63		18 August 1962	St Neots	H	W	3–0
		25 August 1962	Crawley Town	A	L	2–5
		29 August 1962	Didcot Town	A	W	3–1
	Professional Cup	1 September 1962	Gravesend	H	W	5–0
		15 September 1962	West Ham	A	L	0–2
		22 September 1962	Kettering	A	D	1–1
		26 September 1962	Didcot Town	H	W	4–0
		29 September 1962	Tonbridge	H	W	7–1
		6 October 1962	Guildford City	A	W	5–1
	Challenge Cup	13 October 1962	Rainham Town	H	W	2–1
		27 October 1962	Kettering	H	L	0–2
		3 November 1962	Bedford Town	H	W	3–1
	Challenge Cup	10 November 1962	Arsenal A	H	L	0–1
		17 November 1962	Dartford	A	D	1–1
		8 December 1962	Crawley Town	H	W	3–1
	Professional Cup	15 December 1962	Gravesend	A	W	2–0
		22 December 1962	Gravesend	H	W	3–0

		26 December 1962	Arsenal A	H	W	2–1
		2 March 1963	Woodford Town	A	W	3–0
	Professional Cup	6 March 1963	Guildford City	A	W	3–0
		9 March 1963	Bexleyheath	H	D	1–1
	Professional Cup	13 March 1963	Guildford City	H	W	4–0
		16 March 1963	Bedford Town	A	L	2–3
		23 March 1963	Guildford City	H	W	4–0
		30 March 1963	Eastbourne	A	W	4–1
		6 April 1963	Eastbourne	H	W	1–0
		9 April 1963	Bexleyheath	A	W	1–0
		13 April 1963	St Neots	A	W	3–1
		15 April 1963	Woodford Town	H	W	4–0
		20 April 1963	Dartford	H	W	3–2
	Professional Cup	22 April 1963	Kettering	H	L	1–2
		27 April 1963	Metropolitan Police	A	W	2–0
	Professional Cup	30 April 1963	Kettering	A	W	2–0
		2 May 1963	Tonbridge	A	W	2–1
	Professional Cup Final	4 May 1963	Dartford	A	L	1–2
		6 May 1963	Gravesend	A	W	2–0
	Professional Cup Final	9 May 1963	Dartford	H	D	1–1
		11 May 1963	Rainham Town	A	W	2–0
		15 May 1963	Arsenal A	A	L	0–2
		18 May 1963	Rainham Town	H	W	3–1
		20 May 1963	Metropolitan Police	H	W	2–1
		21 May 1963	West Ham	A	L	1–6

Football Combination

Season	**Comp**	**Date**	**Opponents**	**Venue**	**Result**	**Score**
1963–64		24 August 1963	Bexley United	H	W	5–2
		31 August 1963	Tottenham Hotspur A	A	W	2–0
		7 September 1963	Romford	H	D	1–1
		14 September 1963	Bedford Town	A	W	2–1
		21 September 1963	West Ham A	H	W	5–0
	Challenge Cup	28 September 1963	Ramsgate	H	W	6–0
		2 October 1963	Kettering	H	W	7–1
		5 October 1963	Chelmsford City	A	L	2–4
		12 October 1963	Cambridge City	A	L	0–2
		16 October 1963	Kettering	A	D	2–2
		19 October 1963	Cambridge City	H	L	2–3
	Professional Cup	26 October 1963	Hastings United	A	L	1–2
		2 November 1963	Dartford	H	W	3–0
		9 November 1963	Woodford Town	A	D	1–1
		16 November 1963	West Ham A	A	D	2–2
		23 November 1963	St Neots	A	W	4–3
		30 November 1963	Charlton Athletic Reserves	H	L	1–2
		21 December 1963	Tonbridge	H	W	10–0
		28 December 1963	Crawley	H	D	1–1
	Challenge Cup	4 January 1964	Rainham	A	L	1–2
		11 January 1964	Romford	A	D	1–1
	Professional Cup	15 January 1964	Hastings United	H	W	3–2
		18 January 1964	Arsenal A	H	W	2–0
		25 January 1964	Tonbridge	A	W	4–2
		1 February 1964	Rainham	A	D	2–2
	Professional Cup	4 February 1964	Hastings United	A	L	0–1

Season	Comp	Date	Opponents	Venue	Result	Score
		8 February 1964	Metropolitan Police	A	W	4–3
		22 February 1964	Woodford Town	H	D	2–2
		29 February 1964	Arsenal A	A	L	1–2
		7 March 1964	Eastbourne	H	W	4–1
		21 March 1964	Rainham	H	W	7–1
		27 March 1964	Chelmsford City	H	D	1–1
		28 March 1964	Dartford	A	W	8–0
		30 March 1964	Crawley	A	D	0–0
		4 April 1964	Metropolitan Police	H	L	0–1
		8 April 1964	Charlton Athletic Reserves	A	W	5–1
		11 April 1964	Eastbourne	A	W	2–0
		15 April 1964	Guildford	H	W	1–0
		18 April 1964	Tottenham Hotspur A	H	W	2–1
		20 April 1964	St Neots	H	D	2–2
		22 April 1964	Bedford Town	H	D	2–2
		27 April 1964	Guildford City	A	D	1–1
		29 April 1964	Bexley United	A	W	3–1

Football Combination

Season	Comp	Date	Opponents	Venue	Result	Score
1964–65		26 August 1964	Swindon	H	W	5–0
		2 September 1964	Leyton Orient	A	W	2–1
		9 September 1964	Southampton	H	W	2–1
		12 September 1964	Millwall	H	W	3–2
		19 September 1964	Queen's Park Rangers	A	D	0–0
		23 September 1964	Brentford	A	W	1–0
		26 September 1964	Birmingham	H	W	3–0
		29 September 1964	Bristol Rovers	A	D	1–1
		14 October 1964	Aldershot	H	W	2–1
		26 October 1964	Southend	A	W	3–2
		4 November 1964	Coventry	H	W	5–0
		18 November 1964	Southend	H	W	2–1
		25 November 1964	Southampton	A	L	1–2
		1 December 1964	Millwall	A	W	3–1
		5 December 1964	Bournemouth	H	W	2–0
		8 December 1964	Swindon	A	W	3–2
		16 December 1964	Leyton Orient	H	L	2–3
		23 December 1964	Notts County	A	W	3–0
		26 December 1964	Brentford	H	W	4–1
		6 January 1965	Charlton Athletic	H	W	4–1
		9 January 1965	Aldershot	A	L	0–2
		20 January 1965	Bournemouth	A	L	0–3
		27 January 1965	Reading	A	W	3–0
		30 January 1965	Luton	A	D	0–0
		2 February 1965	Watford	A	L	0–2
		13 February 1965	Queen's Park Rangers	H	W	4–0
		20 February 1965	Notts County	H	D	1–1
		23 February 1965	Coventry	A	L	0–7
		6 March 1965	Luton	H	L	1–3
		10 March 1965	Reading	H	W	2–1
		24 March 1965	Brighton	H	W	5–4
		31 March 1965	Birmingham	A	W	1–0
		6 April 1965	Brighton	A	L	0–3
		16 April 1965	Watford	H	L	1–2
		17 April 1965	Bristol Rovers	H	L	0–4
		24 April 1965	Charlton Athletic	A	L	0–1

Football Combination

Season	Comp	Date	Opponents	Venue	Result	Score
1965–66		21 August 1965	Aldershot	A	L	0–1
		4 September 1965	Bournemouth	H	D	0–0
		7 September 1965	Bournemouth	A	W	3–0
		11 September 1965	Southend	A	L	1–2
		15 September 1965	Bristol Rovers	H	W	2–0
		18 September 1965	Luton Town	H	W	3–1
		25 September 1965	Brentford	A	D	2–2
		2 October 1965	Birmingham City	H	L	0–2
		9 October 1965	Colchester United	A	W	3–2
		16 October 1965	Watford	H	L	0–2
		23 October 1965	Brighton and Hove Albion	A	L	0–1
		30 October 1965	Queen's Park Rangers	H	L	0–2
		6 November 1965	Mansfield Town	A	W	3–0
		20 November 1965	Notts County	A	W	5–0
		27 November 1965	Millwall	H	D	1–1
		1 December 1965	Reading	A	L	1–2
		11 December 1965	Colchester United	H	D	0–0
		28 December 1965	Bristol Rovers	A	L	0–4
		1 January 1966	Brighton and Hove Albion	H	W	3–0
		8 January 1966	Queen's Park Rangers	A	W	2–1
		15 January 1966	Mansfield Town	H	D	2–2
		5 February 1966	Gillingham	A	W	4–3
		12 February 1966	Leyton Orient	H	W	2–1
		22 February 1966	Watford	A	W	1–0
		26 February 1966	Southend United	H	W	4–2
		2 March 1966	Leyton Orient	A	D	1–1
		9 March 1966	Gillingham	H	W	3–1
		12 March 1966	Luton Town	A	W	2–1
		16 March 1966	Aldershot	H	W	4–0
		19 March 1966	Brentford	H	L	0–2
		26 March 1966	Birmingham City	A	D	1–1
		30 March 1966	Bristol City	H	L	0–3
		2 April 1966	Notts County	H	W	3–1
		9 April 1966	Bristol City	A	L	1–2
		11 April 1966	Charlton Athletic	A	L	0–9
		16 April 1966	Reading	H	L	1–3
		30 April 1966	Charlton Athletic	H	D	1–1
		9 May 1966	Millwall	A	D	1–1

Football Combination

Season	Comp	Date	Opponents	Venue	Result	Score
1966–67	Cup	20 August 1966	Birmingham City	A	D	2–2
	Cup	24 August 1966	Walsall	H	W	4–2
	Cup	27 August 1966	Birmingham City	H	L	0–2
		31 August 1966	Walsall	A	W	3–2
	Cup	7 September 1966	Mansfield Town	A	W	2–1
	Cup	10 September 1966	Mansfield Town	H	W	3–1
	Cup	17 September 1966	Notts County	A	W	4–3
	Cup	24 September 1966	Notts County	H	D	2–2
		8 October 1966	Mansfield Town	H	W	3–1
		22 October 1966	Brighton	H	W	1–0
		5 November 1966	Walsall	H	L	1–4
		12 November 1966	Mansfield Town	A	W	5–2

		19 November 1966	Cardiff City	H	W	2–1
		22 November 1966	Birmingham City	A	L	1–2
		26 November 1966	Brighton	A	L	1–3
		7 December 1966	Notts County	A	L	0–2
		17 December 1966	Brentford	H	D	0–0
		31 December 1966	Bournemouth	A	W	1–0
		14 January 1967	Norwich City	A	L	0–1
		18 January 1967	Cardiff City	A	L	1–2
		21 January 1967	Bristol City	H	L	0–4
		11 February 1967	Swansea Town	H	W	2–0
		25 February 1967	Walsall	A	L	0–4
		4 March 1967	Notts County	H	W	2–1
		15 March 1967	Birmingham City	H	W	2–1
		21 March 1967	Brentford	A	D	0–0
		25 March 1967	Bournemouth	H	L	0–1
		27 March 1967	Bristol Rovers	H	D	1–1
		28 March 1967	Swansea Town	A	L	1–3
		8 April 1967	Norwich City	H	D	1–1
		15 April 1967	Bristol City	A	L	2–3
		2 May 1967	Bristol Rovers	A	D	1–1

Football Combination

Season	Comp	Date	Opponents	Venue	Result	Score
1967–68		19 August 1967	Bournemouth	H	W	5–0
		26 August 1967	Norwich	A	L	1–4
		2 September 1967	Crystal Palace	H	L	0–3
		16 September 1967	Bristol Rovers	A	L	2–3
		20 September 1967	Bournemouth	A	L	1–2
		27 September 1967	Fulham	H	L	0–2
		30 September 1967	Crystal Palace	H	W	1–0
		7 October 1967	Bristol City	A	L	1–3
		14 October 1967	Brighton	H	W	2–0
		18 October 1967	Bournemouth	A	L	0–2
		25 October 1967	Cardiff City	A	D	2–2
		28 October 1967	Reading	H	W	1–0
		11 November 1967	Bristol City	H	L	0–2
		18 November 1967	Brighton	A	D	1–1
		25 November 1967	Cardiff City	H	W	1–0
		6 December 1967	Reading	A	W	1–0
		16 December 1967	Bournemouth	A	W	2–1
		23 December 1967	Norwich	H	L	0–1
		26 December 1967	Bristol Rovers	H	W	1–0
		24 January 1968	Bristol Rovers	H	L	3–4
		3 February 1968	Fulham	A	L	1–3
		6 February 1968	Bristol Rovers	A	W	3–2
		10 February 1968	Crystal Palace	A	L	1–4
		17 February 1968	Swansea	H	L	1–2
		24 February 1968	Bristol City	H	L	2–4
		2 March 1968	Brighton	A	L	1–4
		9 March 1968	Fulham	H	D	1–1
		20 March 1968	Bournemouth	H	W	3–0
		27 March 1968	Reading	A	D	1–1
		1 April 1968	Crystal Palace	A	L	0–2
		6 April 1968	Bristol City	A	D	1–1
		15 April 1968	Norwich	H	D	0–0

		16 April 1968	Norwich	A	L	0–1
		20 April 1968	Swansea	A	D	0–0
		24 April 1968	Cardiff City	A	L	0–4
		27 April 1968	Reading	H	L	0–2
		29 April 1968	Brighton	H	L	2–3
		6 May 1968	Fulham	A	D	1–1
		8 May 1968	Cardiff City	H	D	1–1
		11 May 1968	Swansea	A	W	2–1
		16 May 1968	Swansea	H	W	1–0

Football Combination

Season	Comp	Date	Opponents	Venue	Result	Score
1968–69	Combination Cup	10 August 1968	Swindon Town	A	L	0–8
	Combination Cup	17 August 1968	Swindon Town	H	L	0–1
	Combination Cup	21 August 1968	Southampton	A	D	1–1
	Combination Cup	24 August 1968	Arsenal	A	L	1–4
	Combination Cup	28 August 1968	Southampton	H	L	1–2
	Combination Cup	31 August 1968	Arsenal	H	L	0–1
	Combination Cup	11 September 1968	Bournemouth	A	L	2–3
	Combination Cup	14 September 1968	Bournemouth	H	L	1–2
	Combination Cup	25 September 1968	Reading	A	L	0–1
	Combination Cup	28 September 1968	Reading	H	W	4–1
		5 October 1968	Plymouth Argyle	H	W	3–1
		12 October 1968	Chelsea	A	D	1–1
		19 October 1968	Bristol Rovers	H	L	2–4
		26 October 1968	Birmingham	A	W	2–1
		2 November 1968	Northampton	H	W	3–0
		9 November 1968	Tottenham Hotspur	A	L	0–5
		16 November 1968	Peterborough	A	D	0–0
		30 November 1968	Crystal Palace	H	W	2–1
		14 December 1968	Norwich	H	D	1–1
		17 December 1968	Walsall	A	L	1–4
		15 January 1969	Reading	H	W	2–1
		22 January 1969	Fulham	H	L	2–4
		25 January 1969	Ipswich	A	L	0–3
		1 February 1969	Swindon Town	A	L	0–2
		5 February 1969	West Ham	H	L	0–2
		1 March 1969	Southampton	A	L	0–5
		12 March 1969	Luton Town	H	L	1–2
		22 March 1969	Bristol City	A	L	0–3
		26 March 1969	Queen's Park Rangers	H	W	2–0
		2 April 1969	Cardiff City	H	D	2–2
		9 April 1969	Gillingham	H	W	1–0
		19 April 1969	Leicester City	A	L	0–3
		21 April 1969	Bournemouth	A	L	0–1
		24 April 1969	Arsenal	H	L	1–2
		2 May 1969	Swansea	A	L	0–4

Football Combination

Season	Comp	Date	Opponents	Venue	Result	Score
1969–70		9 August 1969	Gillingham	A	W	2–1
		20 August 1969	Crystal Palace	A	W	4–3
	Cup	27 August 1969	Reading	H	D	1–1
		4 September 1969	Swindon	H	L	0–2
		6 September 1969	Norwich	A	L	0–2
		10 September 1969	Tottenham Hotspur	H	L	0–2

Season	Comp	Date	Opponents	Venue	Result	Score
		18 September 1969	Bournemouth	H	W	3–0
		20 September 1969	Bristol Rovers	A	L	0–1
		15 October 1969	Peterborough	H	W	3–0
		18 October 1969	West Ham	A	D	2–2
		3 November 1969	Fulham	A	L	0–3
		12 November 1969	Bristol City	H	L	0–2
		26 November 1969	Birmingham	H	W	3–2
		3 December 1969	Cardiff	A	D	1–1
		10 December 1969	Swansea	H	W	2–1
	Cup	17 December 1969	West Ham	H	L	0–2
	Cup	31 December 1969	Southampton	A	W	2–1
	Cup	3 January 1970	Bournemouth	A	L	2–3
		7 January 1970	Plymouth Argyle	A	D	1–1
		14 January 1970	Walsall	H	W	3–0
		20 January 1970	Northampton	A	D	1–1
		28 January 1970	Ipswich	H	W	1–0
		31 January 1970	Arsenal	A	L	1–3
	Cup	4 February 1970	Bournemouth	H	D	0–0
		11 February 1970	Leicester	H	W	5–1
	Cup	16 February 1970	Fulham	A	L	0–1
	Cup	25 February 1970	Southampton	H	W	2–0
		3 March 1970	Chelsea	H	D	1–1
		10 March 1970	Queen's Park Rangers	A	L	1–4
	Cup	16 March 1970	West Ham	A	W	2–1
		23 March 1970	Reading	A	W	3–1
		25 March 1970	Southampton	H	W	3–0
		1 April 1970	Reading	A	W	4–1
	Cup	6 April 1970	Fulham	H	D	0–0
		15 April 1970	Luton	A	L	0–2

Football Combination

Season	Comp	Date	Opponents	Venue	Result	Score
1970–71		15 August 1970	Birmingham City	H	L	2–3
		18 August 1970	Crystal Palace	H	L	1–2
		22 August 1970	Tottenham Hotspur	A	D	0–0
		26 August 1970	Fulham	A	D	0–0
		29 August 1970	Southampton	H	L	0–2
		2 September 1970	Cardiff City	H	L	1–3
		5 September 1970	Swindon Town	A	W	5–2
		12 September 1970	Leicester City	H	W	2–0
		14 September 1970	West Ham United	A	L	0–3
		26 September 1970	Norwich City	H	W	2–1
		3 October 1970	Birmingham City	A	L	1–3
		10 October 1970	Chelsea	H	L	1–3
		14 October 1970	Plymouth Argyle	H	L	1–2
		17 October 1970	Leicester City	A	L	0–5
		24 October 1970	Ipswich Town	H	L	1–2
		31 October 1970	Queen's Park Rangers	A	L	2–4
		11 November 1970	Reading	H	D	2–2
		14 November 1970	Bristol Rovers	A	L	2–3
		2 December 1970	Bournemouth & Boscombe	H	L	1–3
		5 December 1970	Arsenal	A	L	0–2
		12 December 1970	Plymouth Argyle	A	L	2–4
		19 December 1970	Tottenham Hotspur	H	L	0–2
		28 December 1970	Bristol City	A	W	4–1

		9 January 1971	Crystal Palace	A	L	0–1
		13 January 1971	Fulham	H	L	1–2
		6 February 1971	Arsenal	H	W	3–2
		13 February 1971	Swansea City	A	D	0–0
		24 February 1971	Queen's Park Rangers	H	W	2–1
		3 March 1971	Gillingham	H	W	3–2
		6 March 1971	Ipswich Town	A	L	0–3
		8 March 1971	West Ham United	A	W	3–0
		17 March 1971	Bristol Rovers	H	D	1–1
		24 March 1971	Reading	A	L	1–2
		29 March 1971	Swansea City	H	L	1–2
		3 April 1971	Southampton	A	W	2–0
		5 April 1971	Bournemouth & Boscombe	A	W	1–0
		14 April 1971	Bristol City	H	W	2–1
		17 April 1971	Chelsea	A	L	0–4
		21 April 1971	Cardiff City	A	L	0–1
		26 April 1971	Swindon Town	H	D	2–2
		1 May 1971	Norwich City	A	L	1–3

Football Combination

Season	Comp	Date	Opponents	Venue	Result	Score
1971–72		14 August 1971	Norwich City	A	L	1–2
		18 August 1971	Fulham	A	D	1–1
		25 August 1971	Queen's Park Rangers	H	D	1–1
		28 August 1971	Swansea City	A	W	2–1
		1 September 1971	Cardiff City	A	D	1–1
		8 September 1971	Reading	A	L	0–2
		15 September 1971	Cardiff City	H	W	3–0
		18 September 1971	Plymouth Argyle	H	W	2–0
		22 September 1971	Chelsea	A	D	1–1
		25 September 1971	Tottenham Hotspur	A	L	0–2
		2 October 1971	Norwich City	H	W	2–1
		9 October 1971	Bristol Rovers	A	D	1–1
		13 October 1971	Chelsea	H	W	2–1
		20 October 1971	Fulham	H	W	3–0
		27 October 1971	Bristol City	H	W	1–0
		6 November 1971	Swindon	A	W	2–1
		10 November 1971	Crystal Palace	H	W	1–0
		24 November 1971	Leicester City	H	D	0–0
		27 November 1971	West Ham United	A	W	2–0
		1 December 1971	Bournemouth	H	W	2–1
		11 December 1971	Bristol City	A	W	3–2
		18 December 1971	Birmingham City	A	D	2–2
		29 December 1971	Southampton	H	W	1–0
		5 January 1972	Swansea City	H	L	0–1
		25 January 1972	Leicester City	A	L	0–3
		29 January 1972	Queen's Park Rangers	A	D	1–1
		5 February 1972	Ipswich Town	H	W	3–2
		9 February 1972	Birmingham City	H	D	1–1
		16 February 1972	Bristol Rovers	H	D	2–2
		19 February 1972	Arsenal	A	W	1–0
		23 February 1972	Swindon	H	L	0–2
		4 March 1972	Crystal Palace	A	D	1–1
		8 March 1972	Reading	H	W	6–2
		15 March 1972	Arsenal	H	W	2–0

Season	Comp	Date	Opponents	Venue	Result	Score
		18 March 1972	Plymouth Argyle	A	D	0–0
		22 March 1972	Tottenham Hotspur	H	D	1–1
		1 April 1972	Southampton	A	D	2–2
		8 April 1972	Bournemouth	A	D	0–0
		12 April 1972	West Ham United	H	L	1–2
		22 April 1972	Ipswich Town	A	L	0–2

Football Combination

Season	Comp	Date	Opponents	Venue	Result	Score
1972–73		12 August 1972	Southampton	H	D	3–3
		19 August 1972	Tottenham Hotspur	A	D	1–1
		22 August 1972	Queen's Park Rangers	H	W	1–0
		30 August 1972	Bristol City	H	D	1–1
		2 September 1972	Birmingham City	A	L	0–1
		16 September 1972	Swindon Town	A	D	1–1
		23 September 1972	Norwich City	H	W	2–0
		30 September 1972	Chelsea	A	D	0–0
		4 October 1972	Fulham	H	W	2–0
		11 October 1972	Reading	H	W	2–0
		18 October 1972	Leicester City	A	L	1–3
		25 October 1972	Bournemouth	H	D	1–1
		28 October 1972	Fulham	A	W	1–0
		31 October 1972	Queen's Park Rangers	A	L	1–3
		11 November 1972	Crystal Palace	A	L	0–1
		15 November 1972	Cardiff City	H	W	1–0
		25 November 1972	West Ham United	A	D	0–0
		29 November 1972	Swansea City	H	W	3–2
		13 December 1972	Crystal Palace	H	L	1–2
		20 December 1972	Bristol Rovers	H	W	4–1
		27 December 1972	Southampton	A	W	3–1
		3 January 1973	Tottenham Hotspur	H	D	2–2
		10 January 1973	Birmingham City	H	D	1–1
		13 January 1973	Ipswich Town	H	L	1–2
		24 January 1973	Reading	A	D	0–0
		31 January 1973	Swindon Town	H	W	2–0
		3 February 1973	Bristol Rovers	A	D	1–1
		13 February 1973	Swansea City	A	W	1–0
		17 February 1973	Norwich City	A	W	2–0
		23 February 1973	Chelsea	H	W	2–1
		28 February 1973	Arsenal	H	W	1–0
		6 March 1973	Bournemouth	A	D	2–2
		14 March 1973	Leicester City	H	W	1–0
		21 March 1973	Plymouth Argyle	A	L	1–3
		26 March 1973	West Ham United	H	L	1–2
		2 April 1973	Arsenal	A	D	2–2
		14 April 1973	Plymouth Argyle	H	W	2–0
		17 April 1973	Bristol City	A	L	1–3
		25 April 1973	Ipswich Town	A	L	0–2
		4 May 1973	Cardiff City	A	D	1–1

Football Combination

Season	Comp	Date	Opponents	Venue	Result	Score
1973–74		25 August 1973	Plymouth Argyle	H	D	0–0
		29 August 1973	Bristol Rovers	H	W	2–0
		1 September 1973	Swindon Town	A	L	0–1
		5 September 1973	Cardiff City	A	W	3–1

		12 September 1973	Cardiff City	H	W	1–0
		18 September 1973	Bristol Rovers	A	W	1–0
		29 September 1973	West Ham United	A	W	2–1
		3 October 1973	Queen's Park Rangers	H	W	2–1
		13 October 1973	Ipswich Town	A	L	0–2
		16 September 1973	Southampton	H	D	1–1
		23 October 1973	AFC Bournemouth	A	L	0–1
		30 October 1973	Arsenal	A	D	0–0
		7 November 1973	Reading	H	W	3–0
		10 November 1973	Norwich City	A	L	0–3
		14 November 1973	Arsenal	H	D	1–1
		21 November 1973	Luton Town	A	D	0–0
		5 December 1973	Tottenham Hotspur	H	D	1–1
		11 December 1973	Fulham	A	L	0–1
		19 December 1973	Swansea City	H	W	3–0
		29 December 1973	Plymouth Argyle	A	L	0–1
		2 January 1974	Swindon Town	H	W	1–0
		19 January 1974	Crystal Palace	A	D	1–1
		22 January 1974	Bristol City	A	L	0–1
		30 January 1974	Leicester City	H	L	0–1
		13 February 1974	Birmingham City	H	W	2–1
		16 February 1974	Ipswich Town	H	L	1–2
		23 February 1974	Swansea City	A	W	2–1
		27 February 1974	Bristol City	H	W	2–1
		5 March 1974	AFC Bournemouth	H	D	1–1
		13 March 1974	Luton Town	H	W	1–0
		16 March 1974	Southampton	A	L	1–3
		23 March 1974	Norwich City	H	D	2–2
		27 March 1974	Reading	A	W	3–1
		3 April 1974	Crystal Palace	H	D	0–0
		6 April 1974	Birmingham City	A	W	2–1
		20 April 1974	Tottenham Hotspur	A	L	0–2
		24 April 1974	Chelsea	H	W	1–0

Football Combination

Season	Comp	Date	Opponents	Venue	Result	Score
1974–75		17 August 1974	Chelsea	H	L	1–2
		21 August 1974	Bristol City	H	W	3–1
		24 August 1974	Swindon	A	W	4–0
		27 August 1974	Bristol City	A	L	1–3
		31 August 1974	Cardiff City	H	L	1–2
		4 September 1974	Leicester City	A	W	1–0
		7 September 1974	Luton Town	A	D	1–1
		14 September 1974	Birmingham City	H	W	1–0
		18 September 1974	Swindon	H	L	0–1
		21 September 1974	Norwich City	A	W	1–0
		28 September 1974	Southampton	H	L	0–5
		9 October 1974	Swansea City	H	W	2–1
		12 October 1974	Plymouth Argyle	A	L	0–1
		19 October 1974	Crystal Palace	H	W	3–0
		26 October 1974	QPR	A	L	1–2
		30 October 1974	West Ham	H	W	3–1
		9 November 1974	Arsenal	A	L	0–1
		30 November 1974	Ipswich	H	L	0–2
		3 December 1974	Fulham	A	L	0–5

		7 December 1974	Bournemouth	A	L	0–2
		14 December 1974	Chelsea	A	L	1–2
		21 December 1974	Tottenham Hotspur	H	W	1–0
		1 January 1975	Reading	A	W	2–0
		15 January 1975	Bournemouth	H	W	3–0
		18 January 1975	Ipswich	A	L	3–4
		5 February 1975	Arsenal	H	L	0–1
		8 February 1975	Bristol Rovers	A	D	1–1
		12 February 1975	Fulham	H	D	1–1
		26 February 1975	Cardiff City	A	L	1–2
		8 March 1975	Luton Town	H	W	2–1
		15 March 1975	Tottenham Hotspur	A	L	0–1
		22 March 1975	Norwich City	H	W	3–0
		29 March 1975	Southampton	A	L	0–3
		2 April 1975	Reading	H	W	2–0
		5 April 1975	Plymouth Argyle	H	D	1–1
		12 April 1975	Birmingham City	A	L	0–4
		16 April 1975	QPR	H	D	2–2
		23 April 1975	Bristol Rovers	H	D	1–1

Football Combination

Season	Comp	Date	Opponents	Venue	Result	Score
1975–76		16 August 1975	Crystal Palace	H	W	4–1
		19 August 1975	Bristol Rovers	A	W	3–1
		23 August 1975	Queen's Park Rangers	A	W	1–0
		26 August 1975	Chelsea	H	L	0–2
		3 September 1975	Tottenham H	H	W	1–0
		6 September 1975	Southampton	A	L	0–2
		13 September 1975	Swindon	H	W	1–0
		20 September 1975	Fulham	A	D	3–3
		27 September 1975	Birmingham	H	D	1–1
		4 October 1975	Luton	A	L	0–3
		15 October 1975	West Ham	H	L	1–4
		21 October 1975	Birmingham	A	L	0–1
		1 November 1975	Arsenal	A	L	1–2
		4 November 1975	Bristol City	A	L	0–6
		5 November 1975	Norwich	H	L	1–2
		12 November 1975	Reading	A	W	2–1
		26 November 1975	Bristol City	H	D	1–1
		3 December 1975	Cardiff	H	D	1–1
		6 December 1975	Bournemouth	A	W	2–0
		10 December 1975	Orient	H	L	1–2
		17 December 1975	Queen's Park Rangers	H	D	1–1
		20 December 1975	Crystal Palace	A	L	0–1
		10 January 1976	Swindon	A	D	0–0
		21 January 1976	Southampton	H	W	3–1
		24 January 1976	Tottenham H	A	W	2–1
		7 February 1976	Chelsea	A	L	0–2
		14 February 1976	Norwich	A		
		17 February 1976	Bristol Rovers	H	W	1–0
		23 February 1976	Reading	H	L	0–1
		28 February 1976	Plymouth Argyle	A		
		13 March 1976	West Ham	A	L	1–6
		22 March 1976	Ipswich	A	L	1–4
		24 March 1976	Cardiff	A	D	0–0

	31 March 1976	Bournemouth	H	W	2–1
	3 April 1976	Orient	A	D	0–0
	14 April 1976	Fulham	H	W	1–0
	17 April 1976	Leicester City	A	W	2–0
	21 April 1976	Ipswich	H	L	0–2
	23 April 1976	Leicester C	H	D	0–2
	26 April 1976	Arsenal	H	W	0–0
	28 April 1976	Luton	H	W	2–1

Football Combination

Season	Comp	Date	Opponents	Venue	Result	Score
1976–77		21 August 1976	Luton Town	H	D	1–1
		25 August 1976	Leicester City	A	D	1–1
		28 August 1976	Arsenal	A	L	0–2
		11 September 1976	Bristol Rovers	H	W	2–0
		14 September 1976	Southampton	H	W	2–1
		25 September 1976	West Ham United	H	D	0–0
		2 October 1976	Ipswich Town	A	W	2–1
		9 October 1976	Queen's Park Rangers	H	L	0–3
		13 October 1976	Crystal Palace	A	L	2–4
		23 October 1976	Fulham	H	L	0–1
		30 October 1976	Orient	H	W	3–1
		13 November 1976	Norwich City	H	D	1–1
		20 November 1976	Birmingham City	A	L	0–1
		7 December 1976	Tottenham	H	W	2–1
		1 January 1977	Reading	H	L	0–1
		15 January 1977	Leicester City	H	D	3–3
		22 January 1977	Luton Town	A	W	2–1
		25 January 1977	Bristol City	H	L	0–2
		29 January 1977	Hereford United	A	D	2–2
		2 February 1977	Tottenham	A	L	1–2
		8 February 1977	Arsenal	H	W	1–0
		12 February 1977	Southampton	A	L	0–2
		22 February 1977	Chelsea	H	L	1–3
		26 February 1977	Bristol City	A	W	2–0
		1 March 1977	Plymouth Argyle	A	D	2–2
		5 March 1977	West Ham United	A	L	0–4
		8 March 1977	Queen's Park Rangers	H	W	3–2
		12 March 1977	Ipswich Town	H	D	2–2
		22 March 1977	Cardiff City	H	D	1–1
		26 March 1977	Crystal Palace	H	D	1–1
		2 April 1977	Fulham	A	L	0–2
		11 April 1977	Reading	A	W	2–0
		16 April 1977	Plymouth Argyle	H	D	0–0
		19 April 1977	Swindon Town	A	W	1–0
		23 April 1977	Chelsea	A	D	1–1
		27 April 1977	Norwich City	A	W	4–1
		30 April 1977	Birmingham City	H	D	0–0
		3 May 1977	Orient	A	W	2–1
		11 May 1977	Hereford United	H	W	1–0
		14 May 1977	Swindon Town	H	W	2–1
		18 May 1977	Cardiff City	A	W	1–0

Football Combination

Season	Comp	Date	Opponents	Venue	Result	Score
1977–78		20 August 1977	Crystal Palace	A	L	0–2
		27 August 1977	Leicester City	H	L	0–2
		10 September 1977	West Ham United	H	L	1–3
		14 September 1977	Tottenham	A	D	2–2
		17 September 1977	Southampton	A	L	1–2
		24 September 1977	Swindon Town	A	W	1–0
		1 October 1977	QPR	H	D	0–0
		5 October 1977	Fulham	H	L	1–3
		11 October 1977	Bristol City	A	L	1–2
		15 October 1977	Plymouth Argyle	H	L	1–5
		22 October 1977	Arsenal	A	D	0–0
		29 October 1977	Tottenham	H	W	2–0
		12 November 1977	Birmingham	A	L	0–2
		19 November 1977	Luton Town	H	W	2–1
		23 November 1977	Bristol Rovers	A	L	1–2
		30 November 1977	Reading	A	D	0–0
		10 December 1977	Ipswich Town	H	L	1–5
		13 December 1977	QPR	A	D	1–1
		17 December 1977	Cardiff City	H	D	1–1
		21 December 1977	Chelsea	A	W	1–0
		31 December 1977	Hereford	A	L	1–3
		2 January 1978	Crystal Palace	H	D	2–2
		7 January 1978	Chelsea	H		
		14 January 1978	Leicester City	A	W	4–1
		18 January 1978	Cardiff City	A	W	2–0
		25 January 1978	Norwich City	H	L	0–1
		22 February 1978	Southampton	H	W	1–0
		18 February 1978	Swindon Town	H	W	3–1
		6 March 1978	Bristol City	H	W	3–0
		11 March 1978	Plymouth Argyle	A	L	1–3
		18 March 1978	Arsenal	H	D	0–0
		22 March 1978	Orient	H	W	5–0
		1 April 1978	Orient	A	D	0–0
		5 April 1978	Birmingham	H	D	0–0
		8 April 1978	Bristol Rovers	H	W	2–1
		15 April 1978	Luton Town	A	W	5–3
		18 April 1978	West Ham United	A	L	0–1
		22 April 1978	Reading	H	W	2–0
		25 April 1978	Fulham	A	D	0–0
		29 April 1978	Ipswich Town	A	L	1–2

Football Combination

Season	Comp	Date	Opponents	Venue	Result	Score
1978–79		19 August 1978	Luton Town	H	W	2–0
		23 August 1978	Norwich City	A	W	4–2
		26 August 1978	West Ham United	A	L	1–2
		2 September 1978	Arsenal	H	L	0–1
		9 September 1978	Bristol City	A	L	0–4
		16 September 1978	QPR	A	D	2–2
		20 September 1978	Reading	A	W	3–1
		26 September 1978	Birmingham	A	L	0–1
		30 September 1978	Southampton	H	L	1–3

		14 October 1978	Ipswich Town	H	L	0–1
		21 October 1978	Swindon Town	A	W	3–2
		25 October 1978	Cardiff City	A	L	0–3
		4 November 1978	Fulham	H	L	0–2
		6 November 1978	Crystal Palace	A	D	1–1
		11 November 1978	Luton Town	A	D	0–0
		18 November 1978	West Ham United	H	L	0–3
		25 November 1978	Orient	H	W	6–1
		9 December 1978	Tottenham	H	D	1–1
		13 January 1979	Bristol City	H	W	7–2
		17 January 1979	Hereford	A	L	2–3
		20 January 1979	QPR	H	L	2–3
		31 January 1979	Plymouth Argyle	H	W	4–0
		3 February 1979	Reading	H	W	8–0
		10 February 1979	Southampton	A	L	0–5
		26 February 1979	Ipswich Town	A	L	0–3
		3 March 1979	Swindon Town	H	W	2–1
		10 March 1979	Cardiff City	H	L	0–1
		13 March 1979	Arsenal	A	L	0–2
		21 March 1979	Birmingham	H	L	2–4
		24 March 1979	Norwich City	H	L	0–1
		31 March 1979	Orient	A	L	1–2
		4 April 1979	Crystal Palace	H	L	0–1
		7 April 1979	Leicester	H	W	3–2
		14 April 1979	Hereford	H	D	1–1
		18 April 1979	Bristol Rovers	A	D	1–1
		21 April 1979	Chelsea	H	L	2–3
		23 April 1979	Leicester	A		
		28 April 1979	Tottenham	A	L	1–3
		30 April 1979	Plymouth Argyle	A		
		2 May 1979	Fulham	A	L	0–2
		5 May 1979	Bristol Rovers	H	W	5–1

Football Combination

Season	**Comp**	**Date**	**Opponents**	**Venue**	**Result**	**Score**
1979–80		22 August 1979	Norwich City	H	W	2–1
		25 August 1979	Swindon Town	H	W	4–1
		29 August 1979	Cardiff City	A	W	3–1
		11 September 1979	Bristol City	A	L	0–1
		15 September 1979	Reading	H	D	1–1
		19 September 1979	Chelsea	H	D	1–1
		22 September 1979	Fulham	A	L	1–2
		29 September 1979	Crystal Palace	H	D	0–0
		2 October 1979	QPR	A	L	1–5
		5 October 1979	Bristol Rovers	H	L	0–1
		10 October 1979	Norwich City	A	D	1–1
		13 October 1979	West Ham United	A	D	4–4
		20 October 1979	Arsenal	H	L	0–1
		24 October 1979	Tottenham	H	L	0–1
		3 November 1979	Cardiff City	H	W	2–1
		14 November 1979	Leicester City	A	L	0–1
		17 November 1979	Luton Town	H	W	3–0
		24 November 1979	Birmingham City	A	D	1–1
		1 December 1979	Hereford	A	L	1–3

		8 December 1979	Plymouth	H	W	1–0
		15 December 1979	Southampton	H	W	5–0
		21 December 1979	Orient	A	W	3–1
		29 December 1979	Swindon Town	A	L	0–3
		12 January 1980	Ipswich Town	A	D	1–1
		23 January 1980	Tottenham	A	L	3–4
		26 January 1980	Ipswich Town	H	L	0–1
		6 February 1980	Reading	A	L	1–5
		16 February 1980	Crystal Palace	A	L	2–3
		23 February 1980	West Ham United	H	L	0–4
		26 February 1980	Chelsea	A	D	1–1
		1 March 1980	Arsenal	A	L	0–3
		8 March 1980	QPR	H	L	0–1
		15 March 1980	Bristol Rovers	A	D	0–0
		22 March 1980	Leicester City	H	L	2–4
		24 March 1980	Luton Town	A	D	0–0
		2 April 1980	Bristol City	H	D	0–0
		9 April 1980	Orient	H	W	3–2
		12 April 1980	Plymouth	A	W	2–1
		19 April 1980	Birmingham City	H	D	0–0
		23 April 1980	Fulham	H	L	1–2
		26 April 1980	Southampton	A		
		3 May 1980	Hereford	H	W	3–1

Football Combination

Season	Comp	Date	Opponents	Venue	Result	Score
1980–81		16 August 1980	Arsenal	A	L	0–2
		20 August 1980	Reading	A	L	0–2
		23 August 1980	Bristol City	H	W	3–1
		30 August 1980	Birmingham City	A	L	0–4
		6 September 1980	Swindon Town	A	W	2–1
		13 September 1980	Tottenham	A	L	0–4
		20 September 1980	QPR	A	L	0–4
		27 September 1980	Leicester City	H	L	1–2
		4 October 1980	Fulham	H	D	2–2
		8 October 1980	Cardiff City	A	D	2–2
		11 October 1980	Crystal Palace	A	D	2–2
		18 October 1980	Orient	H	W	2–0
		22 October 1980	Bristol Rovers	H	L	0–2
		25 October 1980	Hereford United	A	D	0–0
		1 November 1980	Luton Town	H	W	1–0
		8 November 1980	Ipswich Town	A	L	1–2
		12 November 1980	Reading	H	D	2–2
		29 November 1980	West Ham	A	W	2–0
		3 December 1980	Chelsea	H	L	1–3
		10 December 1980	Norwich City	A	L	0–2
		20 December 1980	Cardiff City	H	L	1–2
		3 January 1981	Southampton	H	L	2–4
		7 January 1981	Plymouth Argyle	H	D	2–2
		10 January 1981	Southampton	A	L	1–3
		24 January 1981	Birmingham City	H	W	1–0
		30 January 1981	Bristol City	A	W	1–0
		4 February 1981	Tottenham	H	L	0–3
		14 February 1981	Swindon Town	H	W	4–3
		17 February 1981	Bristol Rovers	A	W	2–1

21 February 1981	Leicester City	A	L	0–3
28 February 1981	QPR	H	W	3–1
18 March 1981	Arsenal	H	D	1–1
21 March 1981	Orient	A	L	0–1
28 March 1981	Hereford United	H	W	3–1
4 April 1981	Luton Town	A	L	2–4
8 April 1981	Crystal Palace	H	L	0–2
11 April 1981	Fulham	A	L	0–1
15 April 1981	Ipswich Town	H	D	1–1
22 April 1981	Norwich City	H	D	0–0
25 April 1981	Chelsea	A	L	2–4
29 April 1981	Plymouth Argyle	A	L	0–4
2 May 1981	West Ham	H	L	0–3

Football Combination

Season	Comp	Date	Opponents	Venue	Result	Score
1981–82		29 August 1981	Plymouth Argyle	H	W	3–0
		1 September 1981	Chelsea	A	L	1–4
		5 September 1981	Luton Town	A	L	1–2
		12 September 1981	Arsenal	H	D	0–0
		19 September 1981	Fulham	A	L	0–3
		26 September 1981	Ipswich Town	H	D	1–1
		30 September 1981	Bristol Rovers	H	L	0–2
		3 October 1981	Crystal Palace	A	L	3–4
		10 October 1981	Bristol City	H	L	0–2
		24 October 1981	Queen's Park Rangers	H	L	1–2
		31 October 1981	Orient	A	L	1–2
		7 November 1981	Leicester City	A	L	1–2
		11 November 1981	Hereford United	A	W	3–2*
		21 November 1981	Southampton	H	L	0–2
		28 November 1981	Tottenham	A	L	1–2
		5 December 1981	Norwich City	H	L	0–2
		2 January 1982	Ipswich Town	A	W	3–2
		16 January 1982	Plymouth Argyle	A	W	3–1
		20 January 1982	Queen's Park Rangers	A	L	0–1
		23 January 1982	Swindon Town	A	D	1–1
		30 January 1982	Fulham	H	L	1–3
		6 February 1982	Arsenal	A	L	0–5
		10 February 1982	Leicester City	H	L	1–2
		12 February 1982	Crystal Palace	H	L	1–3
		17 February 1982	West Ham United	A	L	0–1
		24 February 1982	Watford	A	D	1–1
		2 March 1982	Bristol Rovers	A	L	0–1
		6 March 1982	Birmingham City	H	L	1–2
		10 March 1982	Luton Town	H	W	2–1
		20 March 1982	Orient	H	D	1–1
		24 March 1982	Reading	A	W	1–0
		3 April 1982	Reading	H	W	1–0
		10 April 1982	West Ham United	H	L	0–2
		17 April 1982	Southampton	A	L	1–3
		21 April 1982	Swindon Town	H	L	0–1
		28 April 1982	Tottenham	H	W	2–1
		1 May 1982	Norwich City	A	L	0–6
		5 May 1982	Chelsea	H	D	1–1
		8 May 1982	Watford	H	L	0–1
		15 May 1982	Birmingham City	A	D	1–1

Football Combination

Season	Comp	Date	Opponents	Venue	Result	Score
1982–83		1 September 1982	Queen's Park Rangers	H	L	0–1
		8 September 1982	Birmingham City	A	L	0–1
		15 September 1982	Millwall	A	L	0–5
		22 September 1982	Luton Town	H	L	1–3
		6 October 1982	Ipswich Town	H	L	2–3
		12 October 1982	Fulham	A	W	3–1
		19 October 1982	Crystal Palace	A	L	0–6
		26 October 1982	Bristol Rovers	A	D	1–1
		3 November 1982	West Ham United	H	L	0–4
		10 November 1982	Brighton & HA	H	L	0–1
		16 November 1982	Chelsea	A	W	3–2
		27 November 1982	Tottenham Hotspur	A	L	0–1
		1 December 1982	Southampton	H	W	3–2
		8 December 1982	Charlton Athletic	H	W	5–0
		15 December 1982	Norwich City	A	D	2–2
		29 December 1982	Swansea City	H	W	4–1
		12 January 1983	Leicester City	H	L	0–3
		18 January 1983	Queen's Park Rangers	A	W	2–1
		24 January 1983	Luton Town	A	W	1–0
		2 February 1983	Tottenham Hotspur	H	L	0–8
		23 February 1983	Fulham	H	D	3–3
		3 March 1983	Crystal Palace	H	D	2–2
		7 March 1983	Watford	A	L	0–3
		9 March 1983	Bristol Rovers	H	W	2–1
		12 March 1983	West Ham United	A	L	0–1
		15 March 1983	Ipswich Town	A	L	0–1
		28 March 1983	Millwall	H	W	3–1
		30 March 1983	Chelsea	H	L	0–2
		2 April 1983	Swansea City	A	W	2–1
		6 April 1983	Swindon Town	H	W	5–0
		11 April 1983	Reading	H	L	2–4
		13 April 1983	Leicester City	A	L	0–2
		19 April 1983	Southampton	A	D	2–2
		23 April 1983	Swindon Town	A	L	0–1
		26 April 1983	Charlton Athletic	A	W	2–1
		30 April 1983	Watford	H	D	3–3
		4 May 1983	Arsenal	H	W	1–0
		9 May 1983	Arsenal	A	W	1–0
		11 May 1983	Reading	A	W	4–0
		14 May 1983	Birmingham City	H	W	4–0
		16 May 1983	Brighton & HA	A	W	3–1
		18 May 1983	Norwich City	H	W	6–1

Football Combination

Season	Comp	Date	Opponents	Venue	Result	Score
1983–84		1 September 1983	Leicester City	H	D	4–4
		3 September 1983	Swansea City	A	L	1–2
		7 September 1983	Arsenal	H	L	0–4
		13 September 1983	Ipswich Town	A	L	0–3
		20 September 1983	Crystal Palace	A	D	1–1
		1 October 1983	West Ham United	A	D	0–0
		5 October 1983	Watford	H	W	2–1
		12 October 1983	Tottenham Hotspur	H	L	2–4

18 September 1983	Fulham	A	L	1–2
22 September 1983	Birmingham City	H	D	2–2
26 September 1983	Millwall	L	L	0–1
2 November 1983	Southampton	H	W	2–1
16 November 1983	Norwich City	A	D	1–1
22 November 1983	Luton Town	A	W	1–0
29 November 1983	Brighton & HA	A	L	0–2
7 December 1983	Queen's Park Rangers	H	L	0–2
14 December 1983	Bristol Rovers	A	L	0–8
4 January 1984	Chelsea	H	L	2–3
14 January 1984	Reading	H	W	2–1
18 January 1984	Leicester City	A	L	2–7
31 January 1984	Chelsea	A	L	0–4
8 February 1984	Crystal Palace	H	W	2–0
11 February 1984	Watford	A	L	0–4
14 February 1984	Swindon Town	A	D	1–1
27 February 1984	Reading	A	W	3–1
29 February 1984	Millwall	H	L	0–1
5 March 1984	Swindon Town	H	D	0–0
7 March 1984	West Ham United	H	L	0–3
10 March 1984	Southampton	A	L	1–3
17 March 1984	Brighton & HA	H	L	1–2
20 March 1984	Charlton Athletic	A	L	0–1
28 March 1984	Fulham	H	W	2–1
31 March 1984	Arsenal	A	L	0–2
3 April 1984	Birmingham City	A	W	5–3
5 April 1984	Charlton Athletic	H	L	1–2
7 April 1984	Swansea City	H	W	2–1
11 April 1984	Norwich City	H	W	4–1
16 April 1984	Tottenham Hotspur	A	D	2–2
25 April 1984	Ipswich Town	H	L	0–1
28 April 1984	Luton Town	H	D	2–2
30 April 1984	Bristol Rovers	H	W	6–2
8 May 1984	Queen's Park Rangers	A	D	1–1

Football Combination

Season	Comp	Date	Opponents	Venue	Result	Score
1984–85		25 August 1984	Fulham	H	W	2–1
		11 September 1984	Crystal Palace	A	W	2–0
		15 September 1984	Norwich City	A	W	3–1
		22 September 1984	Luton Town	H	L	0–2
		25 September 1984	Swindon Town	A	L	1–2
		29 September 1984	Reading	A	W	1–0
		3 October 1984	Reading	H	W	5–2
		6 October 1984	Southampton	H	D	2–2
		9 October 1984	Brighton & HA	A	L	1–2
		16 October 1984	Chelsea	A	L	0–3
		22 October 1984	Tottenham Hotspur	H	D	3–3
		5 November 1984	Portsmouth	A	W	2–1
		7 November 1984	Swansea City	H	D	1–1
		14 November 1984	Arsenal	H	L	1–2
		20 November 1984	QPR	A	L	1–4
		22 November 1984	West Ham United	A	L	0–7
		28 November 1984	Bristol Rovers	H	D	1–1
		5 December 1984	QPR	H	D	1–1

Season	Comp	Date	Opponents	Venue	Result	Score
		8 December 1984	Watford	A	L	2–3
		12 December 1984	Ipswich Town	H	L	0–2
		18 December 1984	Charlton Athletic	A	L	1–4
		30 January 1985	Norwich City	H	D	2–2
		2 February 1985	Millwall	H	L	0–1
		20 February 1985	Birmingham City	H	L	1–2
		22 February 1985	Swindon Town	H	L	0–1
		26 February 1985	Swansea City	A	D	1–1
		2 March 1985	Tottenham Hotspur	A	D	2–2
		6 March 1985	Chelsea	H	L	2–5
		14 March 1985	Brighton & HA	H	D	1–1
		23 March 1985	Southampton	A	L	2–4
		27 March 1985	Watford	H	L	0–3
		30 March 1985	Bristol Rovers	A	W	4–2
		1 April 1985	Portsmouth	H	L	0–2
		5 April 1985	Luton Town	A	D	1–1
		10 April 1985	West Ham United	H	L	2–3
		12 April 1985	Crystal Palace	H	W	2–0
		17 April 1985	Millwall	A	L	2–7
		23 April 1985	Arsenal	A	L	0–3
		27 April 1985	Fulham	A	W	2–1
		29 April 1985	Birmingham City	A	W	2–1
		1 May 1985	Charlton Athletic	H	W	3–0
		9 May 1985	Ipswich Town	A	W	1–0

Football Combination

Season	Comp	Date	Opponents	Venue	Result	Score
1985–86		17 August 1985	Swansea City	H	W	4–0
		21 August 1985	QPR	A	D	1–1
		27 August 1985	Swindon Town	A	W	4–2
		4 September 1985	Tottenham Hotspur	H	L	1–2
		7 September 1985	Norwich City	H	D	1–1
		10 September 1985	Fulham	A	L	3–5
		17 September 1985	Crystal Palace	A	W	2–1
		2 October 1985	Luton Town	H	D	1–1
		16 October 1985	Southampton	H	L	0–1
		19 October 1985	Chelsea	A	L	0–3
		23 October 1985	Watford	H	W	3–0
		26 October 1985	Portsmouth	A	L	0–1
		2 November 1985	Charlton Athletic	H	W	4–2
		6 November 1985	Brighton & HA	A	L	3–5
		9 November 1985	Reading	A	D	1–1
		13 November 1985	Ipswich Town	H	D	0–0
		16 November 1985	Birmingham City	A	W	2–0
		23 November 1985	Arsenal	A	L	2–4
		27 November 1985	QPR	H	L	0–1
		30 November 1985	West Ham United	H	L	1–3
		7 December 1985	Bristol Rovers	A	W	2–1
		10 December 1985	Charlton Athletic	A	L	1–2
		18 December 1985	Millwall	H	W	1–0
		4 January 1986	Tottenham Hotspur	A	L	0–2
		13 January 1986	Swindon Town	H	W	8–3
		15 January 1986	Fulham	H	W	4–1
		20 January 1986	Norwich City	A	W	3–1
	Oxon Senior Cup	1 March 1986	Morris Motors	A	W	10–1

		8 March 1986	Chelsea	H	L	0–2
		15 March 1986	Reading	H	W	9–1
		22 March 1986	Portsmouth	H	W	2–1
		25 March 1986	Millwall	A	W	3–0
		29 March 1986	Swansea City	A	W	8–1
		2 April 1986	Brighton & HA	H	W	1–0
		4 April 1986	Southampton	A	W	2–1
	Oxon Senior Cup	7 April 1986	Oxford City	A	L	0–2
		12 April 1986	Arsenal	H	D	0–0
		15 April 1986	Ipswich Town	A	D	2–2
		22 April 1986	Watford	A	L	1–3
		23 April 1986	Bristol Rovers	H	W	6–0
		26 April 1986	Crystal Palace	H	W	5–1
		3 May 1986	West Ham United	A	L	3–4

Football Combination

Season	Comp	Date	Opponents	Venue	Result	Score
1986–87		23 August 1986	Reading	H	W	3–0
		27 August 1986	Brighton & HA	A	W	8–0
		3 September 1986	Chelsea	H	W	2–1
		7 September 1986	Swindon Town	A	W	4–3
		10 September 1986	Arsenal	A	L	0–2
		17 September 1986	West Ham United	H	W	3–0
		27 September 1986	Watford	A	D	1–1
		1 October 1986	Ipswich Town	H	L	1–2
		4 October 1986	Crystal Palace	H	W	1–0
		15 October 1986	Fulham	H	D	4–4
		8 November 1986	Southampton	A	D	1–1
		10 November 1986	Millwall	H	W	5–3
		13 November 1986	Charlton Athletic	A	L	1–4
		21 November 1986	Norwich City	A	L	1–2
		29 November 1986	Portsmouth	A	L	0–3
		2 December 1986	Bristol Rovers	A	L	2–5
		10 December 1986	Tottenham Hotspur	H	D	2–2
		16 December 1986	QPR	A	L	2–5
		3 January 1987	Norwich City	H	L	0–2
		24 January 1987	Chelsea	A	L	0–4
		28 January 1987	Arsenal	H	D	0–0
		4 February 1987	Charlton Athletic	H	D	2–2
		14 February 1987	West Ham United	A	D	2–2
		18 February 1987	Watford	H	L	0–4
		21 February 1987	Brighton & HA	H	W	1–0
		23 February 1987	Ipswich Town	A	L	0–3
		18 March 1987	Portsmouth	H	L	1–3
	Oxon Senior Cup	21 March 1987	Morris Motors	A	W	6–0
		1 April 1987	Southampton	H	L	0–1
		4 April 1987	Luton Town	H	L	0–3
		15 April 1987	Bristol Rovers	H	W	6–1
		21 April 1987	Reading	A	D	1–1
	Oxon Senior Cup	27 April 1987	Oxford City	H	W	2–1
		29 April 1987	QPR	H	L	1–3
		2 May 1987	Luton Town	A	L	0–1
		6 May 1987	Millwall	A	D	0–0
		9 May 1987	Tottenham Hotspur	A	L	1–2
		11 May 1987	Crystal Palace	A	W	2–1
	Oxon Senior Cup	13 May 1987	Banbury United	A	W	2–1

Football Combination

Season	Comp	Date	Opponents	Venue	Result	Score
1987–88		19 August 1987	Tottenham Hotspur	H	L	2–4
		26 August 1987	Bristol Rovers	H	W	5–2
		1 September 1987	QPR	A	L	2–4
		9 September 1987	Luton Town	H	L	3–4
		15 September 1987	Portsmouth	A	L	3–8
		3 October 1987	Arsenal	A	L	0–4
		7 October 1987	West Ham United	H	D	1–1
		12 October 1987	Crystal Palace	H	W	4–0
		14 October 1987	Ipswich Town	A	W	3–2
		24 October 1987	Watford	A	L	0–4
		29 October 1987	Charlton Athletic	H	W	3–0
		7 November 1987	Southampton	A	L	0–3
		12 November 1987	Reading	H	W	2–1
		21 November 1987	Chelsea	A	D	1–1
		25 November 1987	Brighton & HA	H	W	2–1
		2 December 1987	Swindon Town	A	W	3–1
		18 December 1987	Norwich City	A	L	0–2
		21 December 1987	Millwall	A	L	1–3
		29 December 1987	Fulham	H	L	3–4
		9 January 1988	Tottenham Hotspur	A	L	0–2
		12 January 1988	Bristol Rovers	A	L	3–5
		25 January 1988	Luton Town	A	L	2–5
		3 February 1988	Portsmouth	H	L	2–3
		17 February 1988	Crystal Palace	A	D	1–1
		23 February 1988	Arsenal	H	L	2–3
		29 February 1988	QPR	H	D	1–1
		2 March 1988	Ipswich Town	H	L	0–3
	Oxon Senior Cup	9 March 1988	Bicester Town	H	D	0–0
		12 March 1988	West Ham United	A	L	1–2
		16 March 1988	Watford	H	L	0–4
	Oxon Senior Cup	20 March 1988	Bicester Town	A	W	2–1
		22 March 1988	Charlton Athletic	A	L	2–3
		26 March 1988	Reading	A	W	1–0
		6 April 1988	Chelsea	H	L	0–1
		13 April 1988	Brighton & HA	A	L	0–8
		18 April 1988	Southampton	H	D	2–2
		20 April 1988	Millwall	H	W	1–0
		27 April 1988	Swindon Town	H	L	1–2
		4 May 1988	Norwich City	H	D	0–0
		6 May 1988	Fulham	A	W	3–0

Football Combination

Season	Comp	Date	Opponents	Venue	Result	Score
1988–89		31 August 1988	Crystal Palace	H	W	3–1
		3 September 1988	Reading	A	W	5–3
		7 September 1988	Watford	H	L	0–2
		14 September 1988	Tottenham Hotspur	H	L	1–2
		21 September 1988	Norwich City	A	L	1–5
		24 September 1988	Luton Town	A	L	1–7
		6 October 1988	Arsenal	A	L	1–4
		8 October 1988	West Ham United	A	L	1–6
		12 October 1988	Swindon Town	H	W	4–1
		19 October 1988	Portsmouth	H	W	3–1
		22 October 1988	Watford	A	L	0–2

		26 October 1988	Brighton & Hove Albion	H	W	4–3
		1 November 1988	Charlton Athletic	A	D	2–2
		9 November 1988	Wimbledon	H	D	1–1
		15 November 1988	Fulham	A	D	3–3
		30 November 1988	Luton Town	H	D	3–3
		5 December 1988	Millwall	A	D	2–2
		8 December 1988	Queen's Park Rangers	H	W	2–0
		14 December 1988	Chelsea	H	W	1–0
		28 December 1988	Ipswich Town	H	W	2–0
		4 January 1989	Charlton Athletic	H	W	5–0
		17 January 1989	Queen's Park Rangers	A	L	3–4
		1 February 1989	Southampton	H	W	5–1
		8 February 1989	Reading	H	W	3–0
		18 February 1989	Southampton	A	L	1–4
		22 February 1989	Norwich City	H	W	3–0
		8 March 1989	Tottenham Hotspur	A	L	0–1
	Oxon Senior Cup	12 March 1989	Carterton	A	W	3–1
		22 March 1989	Arsenal	H	W	3–1
		29 March 1989	Brighton & Hove Albion	A	D	0–0
		8 April 1989	Wimbledon	A	L	0–1
		12 April 1989	Swindon Town	A	D	1–1
		17 April 1989	West Ham United	H	W	5–0
		19 April 1989	Fulham	H	W	4–0
		26 April 1989	Ipswich Town	A	W	2–1
		1 May 1989	Crystal Palace	A	L	1–2
		3 May 1989	Portsmouth	A	W	2–0
	Oxon Senior Cup	8 May 1989	Witney Town	H	W	2–0
		10 May 1989	Millwall	H	L	1–2
		15 May 1989	Chelsea	A	W	3–0
	Oxon Senior Cup	17 May 1989	Banbury United	H	W	3–1

Football Combination

Season	Comp	Date	Opponents	Venue	Result	Score
1989–90		22 August 1989	Charlton Athletic	A	D	3–3
		5 September 1989	Swindon Town	A	W	4–0
		1 September 1989	Watford	A	L	2–3
		11 September 1989	Queen's Park Rangers	H	W	2–0
		20 September 1989	Reading	H	W	4–1
		26 September 1989	Millwall	A	L	0–2
		4 October 1989	Fulham	H	W	4–0
		7 October 1989	Wimbledon	A	L	3–5
		10 October 1989	Portsmouth	A	D	0–0
		18 October 1989	Southampton	H	W	1–0
		25 October 1989	Norwich City	H	L	0–1
		8 November 1989	Crystal Palace	A	W	3–1
		15 November 1989	Wimbledon	H	W	3–2
		22 November 1989	Tottenham Hotspur	H	L	0–2
		24 November 1989	Norwich City	A	L	1–3
		29 November 1989	Fulham	A	L	0–1
		11 December 1989	West Ham United	H	W	3–0
		13 December 1989	Ipswich Town	A	L	3–5
		27 December 1989	Portsmouth	H	W	2–1
		3 January 1990	Arsenal	H	D	1–1
		10 January 1990	Luton Town	H	W	3–0
		17 January 1990	Brighton & Hove Albion	A	D	1–1

Season	Comp	Date	Opponents	Venue	Result	Score
		31 January 1990	Brighton & Hove Albion	H	W	3–1
		10 February 1990	Southampton	A	D	0–0
		14 February 1990	Swindon Town	H	W	3–0
		17 February 1990	Luton Town	A	L	0–3
		21 February 1990	Chelsea	H	D	2–2
		24 February 1990	Arsenal	A	L	0–3
		28 February 1990	Reading	A	D	2–2
		14 March 1990	Watford	H	W	6–1
	Oxon Senior Cup	26 March 1990	Banbury United	A	W	4–3 aet
		28 March 1990	Millwall	H	W	2–0
		2 April 1990	Charlton Athletic	H	D	1–1
		7 April 1990	Tottenham Hotspur	A	L	2–5
		11 April 1990	Crystal Palace	H	D	0–0
	Oxon Senior Cup	19 April 1990	Witney Town	A	W	1–0
		21 April 1990	West Ham United	A	L	2–3
		24 April 1990	Chelsea	A	W	2–1
		30 April 1990	Queen's Park Rangers	A	L	2–3
		2 May 1990	Ipswich Town	H	W	3–1
	Oxon Senior Cup	9 May 1990	Sonning Common–Peppard	H	W	4–0

Football Combination

Season	Comp	Date	Opponents	Venue	Result	Score
1990–91		28 August 1990	Tottenham Hotspur	A	L	1–2
		31 August 1990	Norwich City	A	L	1–5
		12 September 1990	Fulham	A	D	3–3
		19 September 1990	Wimbledon	H	L	2–3
		22 September 1990	Reading	A	W	2–0
		26 September 1990	Swindon Town	H	L	0–1
		3 October 1990	Charlton Athletic	H	W	3–1
		13 October 1990	Southampton	A	L	1–2
		16 October 1990	Watford	A	W	5–1
		23 October 1990	Arsenal	H	D	1–1
		25 October 1990	Ipswich Town	H	D	1–1
		6 November 1990	Wimbledon	A	L	0–1
		14 November 1990	Tottenham Hotspur	H	W	2–1
		29 November 1990	West Ham United	H	L	0–1
		1 December 1990	Luton Town	A	L	0–2
		17 December 1990	Brighton & Hove Albion	H	L	0–2
		18 January 1991	Fulham	H	W	5–0
		21 February 1991	Watford	H	L	1–2
		23 January 1991	Brighton & Hove Albion	A	W	1–0
		30 January 1991	Swindon Town	A	W	3–0
		4 February 1991	Luton Town	H (at Luton)	W	1–0
		18 February 1991	Queen's Park Rangers	A	L	1–2
		20 February 1991	Norwich City	H	D	1–1
		25 February 1991	Millwall	A	L	1–2
		2 March 1991	Portsmouth	A	L	2–4
		6 March 1991	Reading	H	W	3–0
		11 March 1991	Ipswich Town	A	W	2–1
		15 March 1991	Crystal Palace	H	L	1–2
		18 March 1991	Southampton	H	L	0–1
	Oxon Senior Cup	25 March 1991	Watlington	H	W	5–0
		27 March 1991	Chelsea	H	D	2–2
		30 March 1991	West Ham United	A	L	1–5
		3 April 1991	Portsmouth	H	W	4–0

		9 April 1991	Charlton Athletic	A	W	2–1
		11 April 1991	Millwall	H	W	1–0
		15 April 1991	Crystal Palace	A	L	1–4
	Oxon Senior Cup	18 April 1991	Headington Amateurs	Thame	W	4–1 aet
		30 April 1991	Chelsea	A	L	0–2
		4 May 1991	Arsenal	A	W	2–1
		8 May 1991	Queen's Park Rangers	H	D	0–0
	Oxon Senior Cup	10 May 1991	Carterton Town	H	W	5–0

Football Combination

Season	Comp	Date	Opponents	Venue	Result	Score
1991–92		14 August 1991	West Ham United	H	W	2–0
		19 August 1991	Crystal Palace	A	D	1–1
		28 August 1991	Watford	H	L	0–2
		2 September 1991	Chelsea	A	W	2–1
		7 September 1991	Reading	H	L	4–5
	Reserve Team Cup	11 September 1991	Bristol City	H	W	2–1
		16 September 1991	Millwall	A	W	3–2
		25 September 1991	Norwich City	H	L	1–4
		2 October 1991	Southampton	H	L	0–1
		7 October 1991	Luton Town	A	D	2–2
	Reserve Team Cup	14 October 1991	Cardiff City	A	W	3–2
		16 October 1991	Ipswich Town	A	L	0–3
		21 January 1991	Brighton	A	W	2–1
		30 October 1991	Swindon Town	H	W	2–0
		5 November 1991	West Ham United	A	L	0–3
		12 November 1991	Watford	A	L	2–4
	Reserve Team Cup	18 November 1991	Cheltenham Town	A	W	4–3
		20 November 1991	Brighton	H	W	2–1
		23 November 1991	Arsenal	A	W	4–2
		26 November 1991	Charlton Athletic	A	L	2–6
		4 December 1991	Wimbledon	H	L	1–3
		7 December 1991	Portsmouth	A	L	2–3
		18 December 1991	Chelsea	H	L	2–5
		8 January 1992	Fulham	A	L	2–3
		15 January 1992	Charlton Athletic	H	W	2–1
		21 January 1992	Queen's Park Rangers	A	L	1–2
		29 January 1992	Swindon Town	A	L	0–2
		12 February 1992	Luton Town	H	W	1–0
		19 February 1992	Portsmouth	H	L	1–2
		24 February 1992	Arsenal	H	L	1–5
		27 February 1992	Wimbledon	A	D	1–1
	Reserve Team Cup	2 March 1992	Swindon Town	H	L	2–3
		4 March 1992	Tottenham Hotspur	A	W	2–1
		10 March 1992	Reading	A	D	2–2
	Oxon Senior Cup	14 March 1992	Bletchingdon	A	W	5–0
		25 March 1992	Queen's Park Rangers	H	L	0–3
		27 March 1992	Southampton	A	D	1–1
		31 March 1992	Fulham	H	D	1–1
		3 April 1992	Norwich City	A	W	1–0
		8 April 1992	Millwall	H	W	1–0
		10 April 1992	Crystal Palace	H	W	3–2
	Oxon Senior Cup	13 April 1992	Peppard	Thame	W	3–2
		15 April 1992	Ipswich Town	H	D	0–0
		22 April 1992	Tottenham Hotspur	H	L	0–2
	Oxon Senior Cup	28 April 1992	Witney Town	H	W	3–1

Football Combination

Season	Comp	Date	Opponents	Venue	Result	Score
1992–93		19 August 1992	Portsmouth	H	W	2–1
		24 August 1992	Millwall	A	L	0–6
		2 September 1992	Norwich City	H	D	1–1
		9 September 1992	Wimbledon	A	D	1–1
		16 September 1992	West Ham United	H	W	2–0
		21 September 1992	Crystal Palace	A	W	2–1
		30 September 1992	Tottenham Hotspurs	H	D	0–0
		12 October 1992	Luton Town	A	W	3–2
		14 October 1992	Wimbledon	H	L	0–4
		21 October 1992	Fulham	A	D	1–1
		28 October 1992	Crystal Palace	H	D	1–1
		4 November 1992	Brighton & Hove Albion	A	L	2–4
		11 November 1992	Queen's Park Rangers	H	D	1–1
		18 November 1992	Portsmouth	A	L	0–1
		23 November 1992	Norwich City	A	W	3–2
		8 December 1992	Arsenal	H	L	1–2
		15 December 1992	Ipswich Town	A	L	0–3
		6 January 1993	Brighton & Hove Albion	H	W	2–0
		18 January 1993	Bristol City	A	W	3–0
		20 January 1993	Swindon Town	H	L	0–5
		25 January 1993	Charlton Athletic	A	W	3–0
		3 February 1993	Fulham	H	W	2–1
		8 February 1993	Chelsea	A	D	1–1
		17 February 1993	Watford	H	W	2–0
		20 February 1993	Arsenal	A	D	3–3
		24 February 1993	Tottenham Hotspurs	A	D	1–1
		2 March 1993	West Ham United	A	D	1–1
		10 March 1993	Luton Town	H	D	0–0
		16 March 1993	Queen's Park Rangers	A	L	0–1
		24 March 1993	Charlton Athletic	H	W	2–1
		27 March 1993	Chelsea	H	W	1–0
		30 March 1993	Watford	A	D	3–3
		31 March 1993	Southampton	H	W	3–0
		14 April 1993	Millwall	H	W	5–0
		24 April 1993	Southampton	A	L	1–3
		26 April 1993	Bristol City	H	W	2–0
		3 May 1993	Swindon Town	A	W	3–2
		5 May 1993	Ipswich Town	H	L	0–4

Football Combination

Season	Comp	Date	Opponents	Venue	Result	Score
1993–94		18 August 1993	Brighton & Hove Albion	A	W	2–1
		25 August 1993	Crystal Palace	A	W	4–3
		1 September 1993	Bristol City	H	W	7–2
		7 September 1993	Arsenal	A	L	0–3
		13 September 1993	Millwall	A	L	3–4
		23 September 1993	Bristol Rovers	H	W	2–1
		29 September 1993	Luton Town	A	L	3–4
		6 October 1993	Ipswich Town	A	L	1–3
		14 October 1993	Charlton Athletic	H	W	2–1
		19 October 1993	Bristol City	A	L	0–1
		27 October 1993	Chelsea	H	D	1–1
		3 November 1993	Crystal Palace	H	L	1–2

		8 November 1993	Chelsea	A	D	1–1
		15 November 1993	Portsmouth	H	D	0–0
		24 November 1993	Ipswich Town	H	L	0–2
		29 November 1993	Luton Town	H	W	4–0
		8 December 1993	Charlton Athletic	A	D	1–1
		15 December 1992	Millwall	H	L	1–3
		21 December 1993	Bristol Rovers	A	D	0–0
		29 December 1993	Queen's Park Rangers	H	W	3–1
		21 January 1994	Tottenham Hotspur	A	D	0–0
		24 January 1994	Southampton	H	D	1–1
		2 February 1994	Portsmouth	A	D	2–2
		7 February 1994	West Ham United	H	L	0–1
		19 February 1994	Southampton	A	L	1–5
		1 March 1994	West Ham United	A	D	0–0
		7 March 1994	Brighton & Hove Albion	H	L	2–3
		16 March 1994	Tottenham Hotspur	H	L	0–1
	Oxon Senior Cup	20 March 1994	Carterton	A	L	0–1
		21 March 1994	Watford	H	L	0–1
		25 March 1994	Norwich City	A	L	0–3
		30 March 1994	Wimbledon	A	W	3–2
		31 March 1994	Arsenal	A	W	1–0
		6 April 1994	Swindon Town	A	W	2–0
		13 April 1994	Swindon Town	H	W	2–1
		18 April 1994	Norwich City	H	L	1–3
		20 April 1994	Wimbledon	H	L	1–4
		3 May 1994	Watford	A	L	0–4
		7 May 1994	Queen's Park Rangers	A	D	1–1

Football Combination

Season	Comp	Date	Opponents	Venue	Result	Score
1994–95		17 August 1994	Bristol City	A	D	2–2
		23 August 1994	Crystal Palace	A	L	1–2
		31 August 1994	Wimbledon	H	L	0–1
		7 September 1994	Charlton Athletic	H	L	0–1
		14 September 1994	Tottenham Hotspur	A	W	2–1
		21 September 1994	Luton Town	A	L	1–2
		28 September 1994	Ipswich Town	A	L	1–2
		5 October 1994	Bristol Rovers	H	D	3–3
		12 October 1994	Luton Town	H	L	0–1
		17 October 1994	Millwall	A	L	2–4
		26 October 1994	Tottenham Hotspur	H	W	3–2
		2 November 1994	Swindon Town	A	W	1–0
		9 November 1994	Bristol City	H	L	1–4
		14 November 1994	Arsenal	A	W	1–0
		23 November 1994	Ipswich Town	H	D	3–3
		30 November 1994	Charlton Athletic	A	L	2–5
		7 December 1994	Millwall	H	D	0–0
		12 December 1994	Bristol Rovers	A	L	1–2
		19 December 1994	Chelsea	H	W	2–1
		7 January 1995	West Ham United	H	W	1–0
		11 January 1995	Queen's Park Rangers	H	L	0–2
		24 January 1995	Queen's Park Rangers	A	L	1–3
		9 February 1995	Brighton & Hove Albion	H	D	2–2
		15 February 1995	Swindon Town	H	W	5–1

		27 February 1995	Wimbledon	A	D	2–2
		1 March 1995	Watford	H	L	1–3
		6 March 1995	Chelsea	A	L	0–3
		15 March 1995	Arsenal	H	W	2–1
		22 March 1995	Norwich City	A	D	1–1
		29 March 1995	Portsmouth	H	W	4–0
		10 April 1995	West Ham United	A	L	0–3
		12 April 1995	Norwich City	H	D	2–2
		19 April 1995	Southampton	A	L	0–2
		26 April 1995	Crystal Palace	H	L	0–1
		1 May 1995	Portsmouth	A	L	0–1
		3 May 1995	Southampton	H	D	2–2
			Watford	A		

Football Combination

Season	Comp	Date	Opponents	Venue	Result	Score
1995–96		23 August 1995	Millwall	H	D	1–1
		28 August 1995	Swindon Town	A	D	0–0
		6 September 1995	Tottenham Hotspur	H	L	1–2
		13 September 1995	Portsmouth	A	D	1–1
		29 September 1995	Queen's Park Rangers	H	W	2–1
		26 September 1995	Watford	A	L	2–3
		4 October 1995	Crystal Palace	H	D	2–2
		10 October 1995	West Ham United	A	L	2–3
		18 October 1995	Bristol City	A	W	3–1
		25 October 1995	Brighton & HA	A	L	1–2
		1 November 1995	Charlton Athletic	H	L	3–4
		8 November 1995	Ipswich Town	A	W	2–0
		15 November 1995	Luton Town	H	W	3–2
		22 November 1995	Norwich City	A	L	0–1
		29 November 1995	Wimbledon	A	L	1–2
		4 December 1995	Chelsea	A	D	1–1
		6 December 1995	Southampton	H	L	0–3
		12 December 1995	Arsenal	A	L	1–4
		18 December 1995	Bristol Rovers	H	L	1–3
		27 December 1995	Millwall	A	W	4–2
		3 January 1996	Swindon Town	H	W	3–2
		8 January 1996	Tottenham Hotspur	A	W	2–1
		23 January 1996	Queen's Park Rangers	A	L	0–1
		31 January 1996	Portsmouth	H	D	0–0
		7 February 1996	Crystal Palace	A	D	1–1
		21 February 1996	Bristol City	H	D	1–1
		28 February 1996	Brighton & HA	H	W	2–1
		6 March 1996	Charlton Athletic	A	L	1–2
		13 March 1996	Ipswich Town	H	D	2–2
		20 March 1996	Luton Town	A	L	2–3
		25 March 1996	Watford	H	L	0–2
		27 March 1996	Norwich City	H	D	1–1
		3 April 1996	Wimbledon	H	D	1–1
		10 April 1996	Southampton	A	L	0–2
		17 April 1996	Arsenal	H	L	1–4
		22 April 1996	Bristol Rovers	A	L	0–1
		29 April 1996	Chelsea	H	D	1–1
		6 May 1996	West Ham United	H*	L	1–2

*(played at Chadwell Heath)

Football Combination

Season	Comp	Date	Opponents	Venue	Result	Score
1996–97	League Cup	28 August 1996	Bristol City	A	D	2–2
		2 September 1996	Queen's Park Rangers	H	W	4–0
		18 September 1996	Wimbledon	A	D	3–3
		2 October 1996	Portsmouth	H	L	0–2
		9 October 1996	Bristol City	A	L	1–4
		23 October 1996	Millwall	H	W	3–2
	Friendly	30 October 1996	Watford	H	L	0–1
		6 November 1996	Swindon town	H	D	3–3
		11 November 1996	Tottenham Hotspur	A	L	0–5
	League Cup	20 November 1996	Cardiff City	H	W	1–0
		27 November 1996	Charlton Athletic	A	L	1–2
		9 December 1996	Luton Town	A	W	2–0
		15 January 1997	Swansea City	A	W	2–1
		22 January 1997	Bristol Rovers	H	D	1–1
	League Cup	27 January 1997	Swindon town	H	W	2–1
		5 February 1997	Cardiff City	A	L	0–1
		11 February 1997	Ipswich Town	H	L	0–1
		26 February 1997	Brighton & Hove Albion	A	L	3–4
	League Cup	5 March 1997	Bristol Rovers	H	W	2–0
	League Cup	10 March 1997	Swansea City	A	D	1–1
		12 March 1997	Arsenal	H	W	5–0
		19 March 1997	Bournemouth	A	W	2–1
		25 March 1997	Southampton	A	D	1–1
		1 April 1997	Crystal Palace	H	L	2–3
		7 April 1997	Watford	A	L	0–1
	League Cup	9 April 1997	Wimbledon	A	L	1–2
		15 April 1997	Norwich City	H	D	2–2
		21 April 1997	Chelsea	A	L	0–1

Football Combination

Season	Comp	Date	Opponents	Venue	Result	Score
1997–98		13 August 1997	Luton Town	A	D	1–1
		20 August 1997	Brighton & Hove Albion	H	W	2–1
		27 August 1997	Charlton Athletic	A	L	2–5
		3 September 1997	Portsmouth	H	D	0–0
		10 September 1997	Wimbledon	H	D	0–0
		18 September 1997	Norwich City	A	D	1–1
		24 September 1997	Southampton	H	W	4–1
		1 October 1997	Ipswich Town	A	W	3–2
		7 October 1997	Arsenal	A	L	0–5
		15 October 1997	Chelsea	H	W	4–1
		22 October 1997	West Ham United	H	D	1–1
		30 October 1997	Queen's Park Rangers	A	L	1–4
		3 November 1997	Millwall	H	W	1–0
		12 November 1997	Swindon Town	A	L	1–5
		26 November 1997	Tottenham Hotspur	H	L	0–5
		3 December 1997	Charlton Athletic	H	L	0–1
		23 December 1997	West Ham United	A*	L	1–2
		7 January 1998	Wimbledon	A	W	3–1
		13 January 1998	Luton Town	H	W	2–1
		21 January 1998	Southampton	A	D	2–2
		28 January 1998	Arsenal	H	W	3–1

		2 February 1998	Chelsea	A	L	0–4
		10 February 1998	Watford	H	W	3–2
		14 February 1998	Swindon Town	H	D	1–1
		23 February 1998	Brighton & Hove Albion	A	D	1–1
		4 March 1998	Millwall	A	W	1–0
		9 March 1998	Queen's Park Rangers	H	L	1–2
		23 March 1998	Ipswich Town	H	L	0–1
		31 March 1998	Crystal Palace	A	L	0–3
		6 April 1998	Tottenham Hotspur	A	L	0–4
		21 April 1998	Norwich City	H	L	0–2
		23 April 1998	Watford	A	L	0–1
		28 April 1998	Crystal Palace	H	L	0–1
		1 May 1998	Portsmouth	A	W	2–1

* (played at the Manor)

Football Combination

Season	Comp	Date	Opponents	Venue	Result	Score
1998–99		19 August 1998	Peterborough United	H	W	5–2
		24 August 1998	Northampton Town	A	L	0–2
		2 September 1998	Cambridge United	A	L	0–1
		16 September 1998	Brighton & Hove Albion	H	L	0–1
		23 September 1998	Portsmouth	A	L	1–4
		6 October 1998	Reading	H	W	3–1
		14 October 1998	Swindon Town	A	W	1–0
		21 October 1998	Tottenham Hotspur	H	L	1–4
		4 November 1998	Millwall	H	W	2–1
		18 November 1998	Brentford	A	L	2–4
		25 November 1998	Crystal Palace	H	D	0–0
		3 December 1998	Norwich City	A	W	1–0
		9 December 1998	West Ham United	A	L	0–4
		5 January 1999	Arsenal	A	W	1–0
		20 January 1999	Chelsea	A	L	2–3
		10 February 1999	Southampton	A	L	1–7
		15 February 1999	Fulham	A	W	2–0
		22 February 1999	Bournemouth	H	L	0–1
		2 March 1999	Wimbledon	A	L	0–1
		17 March 1999	Barnet	H	W	2–0
		23 March 1999	Queen's Park Rangers	A	W	3–0
		30 March 1999	Wycombe Wanderers	H	W	3–1
		7 April 1999	Luton Town	A	L	0–4
		14 April 1999	Watford	H	D	2–2
		21 April 1999	Colchester United	H	D	0–0
		27 April 1999	Charlton Athletic	H	L	0–2
		4 May 1999	Ipswich Town	H	L	0–4
		5 May 1999	Gillingham	A	L	1–3

Football Combination

Season	Comp	Date	Opponents	Venue	Result	Score
1999–2000		18 August 1999	Peterborough United	A	D	1–1
		1 September 1999	Cambridge United	H	W	2–1
		6 September 1999	Northampton Town	A	D	2–2
		28 September 1999	Luton Town	H	W	4–2
		4 October 1999	Barnet	A	L	1–3
		13 October 1999	Millwall	H	L	0–2
		27 October 1999	Gillingham	H	W	5–0
		3 November 1999	Fulham	A	W	2–1

		16 November 1999	Bristol City	H	L	1–3
		1 December 1999	Portsmouth	A	L	1–2
		8 December 1999	Swindon Town	H	L	0–2
		12 January 2000	Wycombe Wanderers	A	L	2–4
		17 January 2000	Brighton & HA	H	L	3–4
		26 January 2000	QPR	A	L	0–5
		2 February 2000	Bournemouth	A	L	0–2
		9 February 2000	Bristol Rovers	H	D	1–1
		22 February 2000	Norwich City	A	L	0–2
		1 March 2000	Ipswich Town	H	L	0–2
		15 March 2000	Southend United	H	L	0–1
		29 March 2000	Colchester United	A	D	1–1
		5 April 2000	Leyton Orient	A	L	1–4

Football Combination

Season	Comp	Date	Opponents	Venue	Result	Score
2000–01		23 August 2000	Swindon Town	A	L	0–3
		30 August 2000	Wycombe Wanderers	H	D	2–2
		20 September 2000	Bournemouth	H	D	1–1
		26 September 2000	Norwich City	H	L	2–3
		2 October 2000	Brighton	A	L	2–3
		11 October 2000	Cheltenham Town	A	W	1–0
		18 October 2000	Bristol Rovers	A	W	4–1
		31 October 2000	Colchester United	H	W	2–0
		7 November 2000	Southend United	A	W	3–0
		14 November 2000	Peterborough United	H	W	1–0
		29 November 2000	Northampton Town	H	W	2–1
		6 December 2000	Cambridge United	A	L	1–2
		18 December 2000	Luton Town	A	L	0–1
		8 January 2001	Barnet	H	W	1–0
		16 January 2001	Millwall	A	W	1–0
		22 January 2001	Leyton Orient	H	W	2–1
		31 January 2001	Gillingham	A	L	2–4
		6 February 2001	Fulham	H	L	1–5
		28 February 2001	Crystal Palace	H	D	2–2
		14 March 2001	Reading	A	L	0–2
		28 March 2001	Bristol City	A	D	2–2
		4 April 2001	Portsmouth	H	D	2–2
		11 April 2001	Brentford	H	L	1–2
		3 May 2001	QPR	A	L	2–3

Football Combination

Season	Comp	Date	Opponents	Venue	Result	Score
2001–02	Friendly	14 August 2001	Oxford City	A	W	4–2
		29 August 2001	Swindon Town	H	W	1–0
		4 September 2001	Wycombe Wanderers	A	L	0–4
		12 September 2001	Brighton & Hove Albion	H	D	1–1
		19 September 2001	Bournemouth	A	D	1–1
		3 October 2001	Bristol Rovers	H	W	2–1
		10 October 2001	Norwich City	A	W	1–0
		17 October 2001	Cheltenham Town	H	L	1–3
		7 November 2001	Southend United	H	D	1–1
		12 November 2001	Peterborough United	A	D	1–1
		21 November 2001	Colchester United	A	W	1–0
		11 December 2001	Northampton Town	A	W	2–1
		19 December 2001	Cambridge United	H	D	1–1

		9 January 2002	Millwall	H	L	1–2
		16 January 2002	Barnet	A	L	0–2
		30 January 2002	Leyton Orient	A	L	2–3
		13 February 2002	Cardiff City	A	D	0–0
		20 February 2002	Queen's Park Rangers	H	D	2–2
		6 March 2002	Luton Town	H	L	1–3
	Friendly	8 March 2002	Banbury United	A	W	1–0
	Friendly	13 March 2002	Oxford University	A	W	4–0
		20 March 2002	Reading	H	W	2–1
		27 March 2002	Bristol City	H	W	3–1
		6 February 2002	Gillingham	H	W	3–0
		10 April 2002	Portsmouth	A	W	2–0
		13 March 2002	Brentford	A	L	0–2

Football Combination

Season	Comp	Date	Opponents	Venue	Result	Score
2002–03		21 August 2002	Portsmouth	H	L	0–1
		28 August 2002	Cheltenham Town	A	W	2–1
		4 September 2002	Colchester United	H	L	0–1
		18 September 2002	Brentford	A	L	2–3
		25 September 2002	Bristol City	A	W	3–2
		2 October 2002	Wycombe Wanderers	H	L	0–2
		30 October 2002	Bournemouth	A	W	1–0
	Friendly	4 November 2002	Reading	A	L	1–4
		20 November 2002	Cardiff City	A	L	0–1
		27 November 2002	Leyton Orient	A	L	1–2
		2 December 2002	Bristol Rovers	A	L	1–3
	Friendly	9 December 2002	Northampton Town	H	L	0–2
		15 January 2003	Reading	A	W	1–0
		22 January 2003	Cambridge United	H	D	4–4
		30 January 2003	Queen's Park Rangers	H	W	1–0
		3 February 2003	Plymouth Argyle	A	L	0–2
		19 February 2003	Millwall	H	W	3–0
		26 February 2003	Gillingham	A	D	0–0
		5 March 2003	Barnet	H	W	4–1
		10 March 2003	Crystal Palace	A	L	1–3
		19 March 2003	Northampton Town	H	W	4–1
		26 March 2003	Brighton	H	D	1–1
		2 April 2003	Southend United	A	L	1–3
		9 April 2003	Norwich City	H	W	1–0
		16 April 2003	Peterborough United	H	W	3–2
		30 April 2003	Luton Town	H	W	3–1
		6 May 2003	Swindon Town	A	L	1–3

Football Combination

Season	Comp	Date	Opponents	Venue	Result	Score
2003–04		20 August 2003	Bristol City	A	L	0–5
		27 August 2003	Plymouth Argyle	H	W	3–0
		10 September 2003	Bristol Rovers	A	L	1–5
	Friendly	17 September 2003	Wycombe Wanderers	H	W	3–1
		7 October 2003	Cardiff City	H	W	1–0
		29 October 2003	Swansea City	H	W	5–0
		12 November 2003	Yeovil Town	A	L	0–5
	Friendly	18 November 2003	Oxford City	A	W	3–2
		26 November 2003	Bournemouth	A	D	1–1
	Friendly	15 December 2003	Northampton Town	H	L	0–1

		21 February 2004	Northampton Town	H	L	0–1
		28 January 2004	Yeovil Town	H	D	4–4
		18 February 2004	Cheltenham Town	H	L	1–5
	Oxon Senior Cup	23 February 2004	Thame United	H	W	1–0
	Oxon Senior Cup	23 March 2004	North Leigh	Banbury	W	2–0
		21 April 2004	Bournemouth	H	L	0–2
		26 April 2004	Bristol Rovers	H	W	5–3
	Oxon Senior Cup Final	29 April 2004	Banbury United	H	L	0–1
		5 May 2004	Swansea City	A	L	1–3

Football Combination

Season	Comp	Date	Opponents	Venue	Result	Score
2004–05	Friendly	21 September 2004	Luton Town	H	D	2–2
		6 October 2004	Gillingham	A	L	0–4
		26 October 2004	Northampton Town	A	W	2–1
		5 January 2005	Crawley Town	H	L	2–5
		12 January 2005	Reading	H	L	0–4
		1 February 2005	Peterborough United	A	L	0–3
		9 February 2005	Stevenage Borough	H	W	5–2
	Oxon Senior Cup	8 March 2005	Carterton Town	H	W	2–0
	Oxon Senior Cup	15 March 2005	Thame United	H	W	5–2
		12 April 2005	Luton Town	A	L	1–5
	Oxon Senior Cup Final	19 April 2005	Oxford City	H	W	3–1
		27 April 2005	Aldershot Town	H	W	2–0
		2 May 2005	Colchester United	H	D	1–1

Football Combination

Season	Comp	Date	Opponents	Venue	Result	Score
2005–06		17 August 2005	Southend United	H	D	0–0
		7 September 2005	Luton Town	H	L	0–1
		21 September 2005	Stevenage Borough	A	L	0–1
		4 October 2005	Northampton Town	A	L	0–5
		8 November 2005	MK Dons	A	L	0–3
		30 November 2005	Leyton Orient	H	L	1–2
		17 January 2006	Barnet	H	W	4–2
	Oxon Senior Cup	31 January 2006	Thame United	H	L	0–1
		21 February 2006	Luton Town	A	L	1–6
		7 March 2006	Northampton Town	H	L	0–2
		5 April 2006	MK Dons	H	D	1–1
		12 April 2006	Stevenage Borough	H	L	1–2
		19 April 2006	Colchester United	A	L	1–3
		25 April 2006	Leyton Orient	A	D	0–0
		2 May 2006	Barnet	A	L	1–2

Football Combination

Season	Comp	Date	Opponents	Venue	Result	Score
2006–07		14 August 2006	Norwich City	H	L	1–2
		30 August 2006	Stevenage Borough	A	L	0–2
		20 September 2006	Milton Keynes Dons	A	L	1–3
		25 September 2006	Ipswich Town	A	L	0–9
		18 October 2006	Ipswich Town	H	L	2–3
		14 November 2006	Leyton Orient	A	D	1–1
		21 November 2006	Southend United	A	D	2–2
		11 December 2006	Southend United	H	L	1–4
		15 January 2007	Northampton Town	H	L	0–1
		5 February 2007	Luton Town	H	L	0–1
		14 February 2007	Colchester United	H	L	0–4

	Oxon Senior Cup	21 February 2007	Ardley	H	L	2–3
		19 March 2007	Stevenage Borough	H	W	1–0
		28 March 2007	Norwich City	A	D	2–2
		3 April 2004	Colchester United	A	D	0–0
		10 April 2007	Northampton Town	A	L	0–5
		16 April 2007	Milton Keynes Dons	H	L	0–3
		23 April 2007	Leyton Orient	H	L	0–1
		1 May 2007	Luton Town	A	L	2–3

Football Combination

Season	Comp	Date	Opponents	Venue	Result	Score
2007–08	Friendly	2 October 2007	Milton United	A	D	1–1
	Friendly	22 January 2008	North Leigh	A	W	3–1
	Friendly	30 January 2008	Milton United	A	L	1–2
	Oxfordshire Senior Cup	6 February 2008	North Leigh	H	L	0–1

Football Combination

Season	Comp	Date	Opponents	Venue	Result	Score
2008–09	Friendly	9 September 2008	Brentford	A	L	1–2
	Friendly	17 September 2008	Kidlington	A	L	0–3
	Friendly	16 December 2008	Milton United	A	L	2–3
	Friendly	14 January 2009	Didcot Town	A	D	1–1
	Friendly	26 January 2009	Didcot Town	A	L	0–3
	Oxon Senior Cup	24 February 2009	Old Woodstock Town	A	W	3–1
	Oxon Senior Cup	25 March 2009	North Leigh	Oxford City	W	3–0
	Friendly	18 April 2009	Kidlington	A	W	2–0
	Oxon Senior Cup Final	21 April 2009	Banbury United	H	W	2–1

Player Records

Surname	Forename	Season	Total			League			FA Cup			FL Cup			Other			FA Trophy			Setanta Sld			SL Cup			SL Inter Zone		
			app	subs	gls	app	subs	gls	app	subs	gls	app	subs	gls	app	subs	gls	app	subs	gls	app	subs	gls	app	subs	gls	app	subs	gls
Adams	Don	1956–57	6	0	1	5	0	1	1	0	0	0	0	0	0	0	0	0	0	0	0	0	0	0	0	0	0	0	0
Adams	Eddie	1955–56	47	0	14	41	0	13	1	0	1	0	0	0	0	0	0	0	0	0	0	0	0	5	0	0	0	0	0
		1956–57	31	0	6	29	0	5	0	0	0	0	0	0	0	0	0	0	0	0	0	0	0	2	0	1	0	0	0
Adams	Graham	1958–59	17	0	1	15	0	1	0	0	0	0	0	0	0	0	0	0	0	0	0	0	0	0	0	0	2	0	0
		1959–60	42	0	0	37	0	0	2	0	0	0	0	0	0	0	0	0	0	0	0	0	0	3	0	0	0	0	0
		1960–61	26	0	0	20	0	0	5	0	0	0	0	0	0	0	0	0	0	0	0	0	0	1	0	0	0	0	0
Aldous	Stan	1958–59	5	0	0	2	0	0	2	0	0	0	0	0	0	0	0	0	0	0	0	0	0	1	0	0	0	0	0
Aldridge	John	1983–84	5	3	4	5	3	4	0	0	0	0	0	0	0	0	0	0	0	0	0	0	0	0	0	0	0	0	0
		1984–85	50	0	34	42	0	30	2	0	1	6	0	3	0	0	0	0	0	0	0	0	0	0	0	0	0	0	0
		1985–86	53	0	31	39	0	23	2	0	1	7	0	5	5	0	2	0	0	0	0	0	0	0	0	0	0	0	0
		1986–87	30	0	21	25	0	15	1	0	0	4	0	6	0	0	0	0	0	0	0	0	0	0	0	0	0	0	0
Aldridge	Martin	1995–96	16	5	9	15	3	9	1	2	0	0	0	0	0	0	0	0	0	0	0	0	0	0	0	0	0	0	0
		1996–97	24	14	9	18	12	8	1	0	0	5	2	1	0	0	0	0	0	0	0	0	0	0	0	0	0	0	0
		1997–98	16	13	4	13	11	2	0	0	0	3	2	2	0	0	0	0	0	0	0	0	0	0	0	0	0	0	0
Aldridge	Norman	1949–50	48	0	0	45	0	0	2	0	0	0	0	0	0	0	0	0	0	0	0	0	0	1	0	0	0	0	0
		1950–51	34	0	1	34	0	1	0	0	0	0	0	0	0	0	0	0	0	0	0	0	0	0	0	0	0	0	0
		1951–52	4	0	0	4	0	0	0	0	0	0	0	0	0	0	0	0	0	0	0	0	0	0	0	0	0	0	0
Aleksic	Milija	1976–77	2	0	0	0	0	0	0	0	0	2	0	0	0	0	0	0	0	0	0	0	0	0	0	0	0	0	0
Allen	Chrissy	1991–92	13	3	1	13	1	1	0	1	0	0	0	0	0	1	0	0	0	0	0	0	0	0	0	0	0	0	0
		1992–93	21	17	5	18	13	3	2	0	0	1	2	2	0	2	0	0	0	0	0	0	0	0	0	0	0	0	0
		1993–94	40	12	4	34	10	3	2	2	1	2	0	0	2	0	0	0	0	0	0	0	0	0	0	0	0	0	0
		1994–95	38	3	2	32	3	2	0	0	0	4	0	0	2	0	0	0	0	0	0	0	0	0	0	0	0	0	0
		1995–96	19	13	5	13	11	3	1	2	0	4	0	2	1	0	0	0	0	0	0	0	0	0	0	0	0	0	0
Alsop	Julian	2003–04	28	3	5	26	3	5	1	0	0	1	0	0	0	0	0	0	0	0	0	0	0	0	0	0	0	0	0
		2004–05	3	2	0	3	2	0	0	0	0	0	0	0	0	0	0	0	0	0	0	0	0	0	0	0	0	0	0
Amphlett	Ray	1949–50	7	0	0	7	0	0	0	0	0	0	0	0	0	0	0	0	0	0	0	0	0	0	0	0	0	0	0
Andrews	Keith	2000–01	5	0	1	4	0	1	0	0	0	0	0	0	1	0	0	0	0	0	0	0	0	0	0	0	0	0	0
Angel	Mark	1995–96	22	14	2	16	11	1	4	1	0	0	1	0	2	1	1	0	0	0	0	0	0	0	0	0	0	0	0
		1996–97	17	10	2	15	9	2	0	0	0	2	1	0	0	0	0	0	0	0	0	0	0	0	0	0	0	0	0
		1997–98	11	17	1	9	14	1	0	1	0	2	2	0	0	0	0	0	0	0	0	0	0	0	0	0	0	0	0
Ansell	Jack	1952–53	54	0	0	42	0	0	5	0	0	0	0	0	0	0	0	0	0	0	0	0	0	7	0	0	0	0	0
		1953–54	58	0	0	40	0	0	10	0	0	0	0	0	0	0	0	0	0	0	0	0	0	8	0	0	0	0	0
		1954–55	37	0	0	31	0	0	2	0	0	0	0	0	0	0	0	0	0	0	0	0	0	4	0	0	0	0	0
Anthrobus	Steve	1999–2000	34	12	2	25	11	2	3	1	0	3	0	0	3	0	0	0	0	0	0	0	0	0	0	0	0	0	0
		2000–01	16	7	2	13	6	1	1	0	0	2	0	0	0	1	1	0	0	0	0	0	0	0	0	0	0	0	0
Arendse	Andre	1999–2000	18	1	0	13	0	0	1	1	0	3	0	0	1	0	0	0	0	0	0	0	0	0	0	0	0	0	0
Aries	Eddie	1959–60	2	0	0	2	0	0	0	0	0	0	0	0	0	0	0	0	0	0	0	0	0	0	0	0	0	0	0
Ashton	Jon	2003–04	34	4	0	30	4	0	1	0	0	2	0	0	1	0	0	0	0	0	0	0	0	0	0	0	0	0	0
		2004–05	31	0	0	30	0	0	0	0	0	1	0	0	0	0	0	0	0	0	0	0	0	0	0	0	0	0	0

Surname	Forename	Season	Total			League			FA Cup			FL Cup			Other			FA Trophy			Setanta Sld			SL Cup			SL Inter Zone		
			app	subs	gls	app	subs	gls	app	subs	gls	app	subs	gls	app	subs	gls	app	subs	gls	app	subs	gls	app	subs	gls	app	subs	gls
		2005–06	33	1	1	32	1	1	1	0	0	0	0	0	0	0	0	0	0	0	0	0	0	0	0	0	0	0	0
Ashton	Roger	1951–52	31	0	0	31	0	0	0	0	0	0	0	0	0	0	0	0	0	0	0	0	0	0	0	0	0	0	0
Atkinson	Graham	1959–60	5	0	2	4	0	1	0	0	0	0	0	0	0	0	0	0	0	0	0	0	0	1	0	1	0	0	0
		1961–62	33	0	19	32	0	19	0	0	0	0	0	0	0	0	0	0	0	0	0	0	0	1	0	0	0	0	0
		1962–63	21	0	5	18	0	4	2	0	1	1	0	0	0	0	0	0	0	0	0	0	0	0	0	0	0	0	0
		1964–65	18	0	12	18	0	12	0	0	0	0	0	0	0	0	0	0	0	0	0	0	0	0	0	0	0	0	0
		1965–66	47	0	19	45	0	19	1	0	0	1	0	0	0	0	0	0	0	0	0	0	0	0	0	0	0	0	0
		1966–67	35	1	15	32	1	13	3	0	2	0	0	0	0	0	0	0	0	0	0	0	0	0	0	0	0	0	0
		1967–68	43	1	13	38	1	11	3	0	1	2	0	1	0	0	0	0	0	0	0	0	0	0	0	0	0	0	0
		1968–69	39	0	5	36	0	5	2	0	0	1	0	0	0	0	0	0	0	0	0	0	0	0	0	0	0	0	0
		1969–70	45	0	6	37	0	4	2	0	1	6	0	1	0	0	0	0	0	0	0	0	0	0	0	0	0	0	0
		1970–71	47	0	6	40	0	5	5	0	1	2	0	0	0	0	0	0	0	0	0	0	0	0	0	0	0	0	0
		1971–72	26	0	1	24	0	1	0	0	0	2	0	0	0	0	0	0	0	0	0	0	0	0	0	0	0	0	0
		1972–73	6	0	0	5	0	0	0	0	0	0	0	0	1	0	0	0	0	0	0	0	0	0	0	0	0	0	0
		1973–74	29	2	4	28	2	3	1	0	1	0	0	0	0	0	0	0	0	0	0	0	0	0	0	0	0	0	0
Atkinson	Ron	1959–60	45	0	3	39	0	2	2	0	0	0	0	0	0	0	0	0	0	0	0	0	0	4	0	1	0	0	0
		1960–61	47	0	1	40	0	1	5	0	0	0	0	0	0	0	0	0	0	0	0	0	0	2	0	0	0	0	0
		1961–62	42	0	1	38	0	1	2	0	0	0	0	0	0	0	0	0	0	0	0	0	0	2	0	0	0	0	0
		1962–63	49	0	3	45	0	3	3	0	0	1	0	0	0	0	0	0	0	0	0	0	0	0	0	0	0	0	0
		1963–64	47	0	3	41	0	3	5	0	0	1	0	0	0	0	0	0	0	0	0	0	0	0	0	0	0	0	0
		1964–65	50	0	3	46	0	2	1	0	0	3	0	1	0	0	0	0	0	0	0	0	0	0	0	0	0	0	0
		1965–66	49	0	2	46	0	2	2	0	0	1	0	0	0	0	0	0	0	0	0	0	0	0	0	0	0	0	0
		1966–67	43	0	0	41	0	0	1	0	0	1	0	0	0	0	0	0	0	0	0	0	0	0	0	0	0	0	0
		1967–68	37	0	0	34	0	0	3	0	0	0	0	0	0	0	0	0	0	0	0	0	0	0	0	0	0	0	0
		1968–69	45	0	1	42	0	1	2	0	0	1	0	0	0	0	0	0	0	0	0	0	0	0	0	0	0	0	0
		1969–70	48	0	0	40	0	0	2	0	0	6	0	0	0	0	0	0	0	0	0	0	0	0	0	0	0	0	0
		1970–71	44	1	3	37	1	2	5	0	1	2	0	0	0	0	0	0	0	0	0	0	0	0	0	0	0	0	0
		1971–72	13	0	1	11	0	1	0	0	0	2	0	0	0	0	0	0	0	0	0	0	0	0	0	0	0	0	0
Attley	Brian	1982–83	5	0	0	5	0	0	0	0	0	0	0	0	0	0	0	0	0	0	0	0	0	0	0	0	0	0	0
Aylott	Steve	1971–72	30	1	1	28	1	1	1	0	0	1	0	0	0	0	0	0	0	0	0	0	0	0	0	0	0	0	0
		1972–73	32	3	1	28	3	1	0	0	0	3	0	0	1	0	0	0	0	0	0	0	0	0	0	0	0	0	0
		1973–74	23	2	2	22	2	2	1	0	0	0	0	0	0	0	0	0	0	0	0	0	0	0	0	0	0	0	0
		1974–75	38	2	3	37	1	3	1	0	0	0	1	0	0	0	0	0	0	0	0	0	0	0	0	0	0	0	0
		1975–76	32	4	2	28	4	1	1	0	0	3	0	1	0	0	0	0	0	0	0	0	0	0	0	0	0	0	0
Aylott	Trevor	1991–92	38	2	6	35	2	6	2	0	0	0	0	0	1	0	0	0	0	0	0	0	0	0	0	0	0	0	0
Bailey	Stefan	2007–08	6	0	0	4	0	0	2	0	0	0	0	0	0	0	0	0	0	0	0	0	0	0	0	0	0	0	0
Bain	Jimmy	1955–56	35	0	2	33	0	2	1	0	0	0	0	0	0	0	0	0	0	0	0	0	0	1	0	0	0	0	0
		1954–55	45	0	5	39	0	4	2	0	0	0	0	0	0	0	0	0	0	0	0	0	0	4	0	1	0	0	0
Banger	Nicky	1997–98	22	11	4	18	10	3	0	0	0	4	1	1	0	0	0	0	0	0	0	0	0	0	0	0	0	0	0
		1998–99	27	10	5	22	10	5	3	0	0	2	0	0	0	0	0	0	0	0	0	0	0	0	0	0	0	0	0
		1999–2000	1	3	0	1	2	0	0	0	0	0	1	0	0	0	0	0	0	0	0	0	0	0	0	0	0	0	0
Bannister	Gary	1991–92	7	3	2	7	3	2	0	0	0	0	0	0	0	0	0	0	0	0	0	0	0	0	0	0	0	0	0
Bardsley	David	1987–88	46	0	1	34	0	1	2	0	0	8	0	0	2	0	0	0	0	0	0	0	0	0	0	0	0	0	0
		1988–89	43	0	6	37	0	6	3	0	0	2	0	0	1	0	0	0	0	0	0	0	0	0	0	0	0	0	0
		1989–90	5	0	0	3	0	0	0	0	0	2	0	0	0	0	0	0	0	0	0	0	0	0	0	0	0	0	0

Surname	Forename	Season	Total			League			FA Cup			FL Cup			Other			FA Trophy			Setanta Sld			SL Cup			SL Inter Zone		
			app	subs	gls	app	subs	gls	app	subs	gls	app	subs	gls	app	subs	gls	app	subs	gls	app	subs	gls	app	subs	gls	app	subs	gls
Barker	Bobby	1951–52	22	0	5	14	0	2	4	0	3	0	0	0	0	0	0	0	0	0	0	0	0	4	0	0	0	0	0
Barley	Jack	1955–56	14	0	1	10	0	1	1	0	0	0	0	0	0	0	0	0	0	0	0	0	0	3	0	0	0	0	0
Barnes	Ashley	2007–08	4	4	1	1	2	1	2	0	0	0	0	0	0	0	0	1	1	0	0	1	0	0	0	0	0	0	0
Barnett	Gary	1982–83	25	4	3	18	4	2	2	0	0	3	0	1	2	0	0	0	0	0	0	0	0	0	0	0	0	0	0
		1983–84	25	3	7	18	1	7	3	0	0	3	2	0	1	0	0	0	0	0	0	0	0	0	0	0	0	0	0
		1984–85	1	1	0	1	1	0	0	0	0	0	0	0	0	0	0	0	0	0	0	0	0	0	0	0	0	0	0
Barney	Vic	1950–51	46	0	12	43	0	9	2	0	3	0	0	0	0	0	0	0	0	0	0	0	0	1	0	0	0	0	0
		1951–52	47	0	14	39	0	10	4	0	3	0	0	0	0	0	0	0	0	0	0	0	0	4	0	1	0	0	0
Barron	Jim	1965–66	12	0	0	12	0	0	0	0	0	0	0	0	0	0	0	0	0	0	0	0	0	0	0	0	0	0	0
		1966–67	26	0	0	24	0	0	1	0	0	1	0	0	0	0	0	0	0	0	0	0	0	0	0	0	0	0	0
		1967–68	35	0	0	35	0	0	0	0	0	0	0	0	0	0	0	0	0	0	0	0	0	0	0	0	0	0	0
		1968–69	45	0	0	42	0	0	2	0	0	1	0	0	0	0	0	0	0	0	0	0	0	0	0	0	0	0	0
		1969–70	47	0	0	39	0	0	2	0	0	6	0	0	0	0	0	0	0	0	0	0	0	0	0	0	0	0	0
Basham	Steve	2002–03	30	6	8	25	6	8	3	0	0	1	0	0	1	0	0	0	0	0	0	0	0	0	0	0	0	0	0
		2003–04	40	0	15	38	0	14	1	0	0	1	0	1	0	0	0	0	0	0	0	0	0	0	0	0	0	0	0
		2004–05	32	10	9	29	10	9	1	0	0	1	0	0	1	0	0	0	0	0	0	0	0	0	0	0	0	0	0
		2005–06	36	12	13	30	10	8	4	0	5	0	1	0	2	1	0	0	0	0	0	0	0	0	0	0	0	0	0
		2006–07	19	4	4	17	3	4	2	0	0	0	0	0	0	0	0	0	1	0	0	0	0	0	0	0	0	0	0
Batt	Damien	2008–09	16	0	0	16	0	0	0	0	0	0	0	0	0	0	0	0	0	0	0	0	0	0	0	0	0	0	0
Beauchamp	Joey	1989–90	2	1	0	2	1	0	0	0	0	0	0	0	0	0	0	0	0	0	0	0	0	0	0	0	0	0	0
		1990–91	5	1	0	4	0	0	0	0	0	1	0	0	0	1	0	0	0	0	0	0	0	0	0	0	0	0	0
		1991–92	27	4	8	24	3	6	3	0	1	0	1	0	1	0	0	0	0	0	0	0	0	0	0	0	0	0	0
		1992–93	51	0	9	44	0	7	2	0	1	3	0	1	2	0	0	0	0	0	0	0	0	0	0	0	0	0	0
		1993–94	51	2	8	43	2	6	4	0	1	2	0	1	2	0	0	0	0	0	0	0	0	0	0	0	0	0	0
		1995–96	27	11	8	25	7	7	2	2	1	0	0	0	0	2	0	0	0	0	0	0	0	0	0	0	0	0	0
		1996–97	45	9	7	36	9	7	1	0	0	8	0	0	0	0	0	0	0	0	0	0	0	0	0	0	0	0	0
		1997–98	51	0	19	44	0	13	1	0	0	6	0	6	0	0	0	0	0	0	0	0	0	0	0	0	0	0	0
		1998–99	34	7	4	31	6	4	1	1	0	2	0	0	0	0	0	0	0	0	0	0	0	0	0	0	0	0	0
		1999–2000	44	3	6	33	1	4	5	0	0	3	0	2	3	2	0	0	0	0	0	0	0	0	0	0	0	0	0
		2000–01	36	12	7	32	11	7	2	0	0	1	1	0	1	0	0	0	0	0	0	0	0	0	0	0	0	0	0
		2001–02	2	2	1	2	1	1	0	0	0	0	1	0	0	0	0	0	0	0	0	0	0	0	0	0	0	0	0
Beavon	Cyril	1958–59	20	0	1	17	0	1	0	0	0	0	0	0	0	0	0	0	0	0	0	0	0	0	0	0	3	0	0
		1959–60	48	0	0	42	0	0	2	0	0	0	0	0	0	0	0	0	0	0	0	0	0	4	0	0	0	0	0
		1960–61	48	0	1	41	0	1	5	0	0	0	0	0	0	0	0	0	0	0	0	0	0	2	0	0	0	0	0
		1961–62	46	0	2	42	0	2	2	0	0	0	0	0	0	0	0	0	0	0	0	0	0	2	0	0	0	0	0
		1962–63	50	0	1	46	0	1	3	0	0	1	0	0	0	0	0	0	0	0	0	0	0	0	0	0	0	0	0
		1963–64	53	0	0	45	0	0	7	0	0	1	0	0	0	0	0	0	0	0	0	0	0	0	0	0	0	0	0
		1964–65	47	0	3	44	0	3	0	0	0	3	0	0	0	0	0	0	0	0	0	0	0	0	0	0	0	0	0
		1965–66	44	0	1	41	0	1	2	0	0	1	0	0	0	0	0	0	0	0	0	0	0	0	0	0	0	0	0
		1966–67	48	0	2	44	0	2	3	0	0	1	0	0	0	0	0	0	0	0	0	0	0	0	0	0	0	0	0
		1967–68	36	0	0	30	0	0	3	0	0	3	0	0	0	0	0	0	0	0	0	0	0	0	0	0	0	0	0
		1968–69	21	3	0	21	2	0	0	1	0	0	0	0	0	0	0	0	0	0	0	0	0	0	0	0	0	0	0
Beeby	Olly	1961–62	7	0	0	5	0	0	2	0	0	0	0	0	0	0	0	0	0	0	0	0	0	0	0	0	0	0	0
Beechers	Billy	2004–05	0	3	0	0	3	0	0	0	0	0	0	0	0	0	0	0	0	0	0	0	0	0	0	0	0	0	0

Surname	Forename	Season	Total			League			FA Cup			FL Cup			Other			FA Trophy			Setanta Sld			SL Cup			SL Inter Zone		
			app	subs	gls	app	subs	gls	app	subs	gls	app	subs	gls	app	subs	gls	app	subs	gls	app	subs	gls	app	subs	gls	app	subs	gls
		2005–06	0	3	0	0	3	0	0	0	0	0	0	0	0	0	0	0	0	0	0	0	0	0	0	0	0	0	0
		2006–07	0	1	0	0	1	0	0	0	0	0	0	0	0	0	0	0	0	0	0	0	0	0	0	0	0	0	0
Benjamin	Declan	2007–08	0	2	0	0	2	0	0	0	0	0	0	0	0	0	0	0	0	0	0	0	0	0	0	0	0	0	0
Bennett	Ken	1954–55	5	0	0	4	0	0	0	0	0	0	0	0	0	0	0	0	0	0	0	0	0	1	0	0	0	0	0
Berry	Paul	1976–77	5	4	0	5	4	0	0	0	0	0	0	0	0	0	0	0	0	0	0	0	0	0	0	0	0	0	0
		1977–78	9	2	1	7	2	1	1	0	0	1	0	0	0	0	0	0	0	0	0	0	0	0	0	0	0	0	0
		1978–79	16	3	4	16	3	4	0	0	0	0	0	0	0	0	0	0	0	0	0	0	0	0	0	0	0	0	0
		1979–80	42	2	14	39	2	14	1	0	0	2	0	0	0	0	0	0	0	0	0	0	0	0	0	0	0	0	0
		1980–81	30	2	1	27	1	1	1	0	0	2	1	0	0	0	0	0	0	0	0	0	0	0	0	0	0	0	0
		1981–82	6	0	0	4	0	0	2	0	0	0	0	0	0	0	0	0	0	0	0	0	0	0	0	0	0	0	0
Bidois	David	1949–50	1	0	0	1	0	0	0	0	0	0	0	0	0	0	0	0	0	0	0	0	0	0	0	0	0	0	0
		1950–51	13	0	0	13	0	0	0	0	0	0	0	0	0	0	0	0	0	0	0	0	0	0	0	0	0	0	0
		1951–52	4	0	0	3	0	0	0	0	0	0	0	0	0	0	0	0	0	0	0	0	0	1	0	0	0	0	0
		1955–56	1	0	0	1	0	0	0	0	0	0	0	0	0	0	0	0	0	0	0	0	0	0	0	0	0	0	0
		1956–57	7	0	1	7	0	1	0	0	0	0	0	0	0	0	0	0	0	0	0	0	0	0	0	0	0	0	0
		1957–58	3	0	0	3	0	0	0	0	0	0	0	0	0	0	0	0	0	0	0	0	0	0	0	0	0	0	0
Biggins	Steve	1982–83	11	3	2	8	2	1	0	0	0	2	0	1	1	1	0	0	0	0	0	0	0	0	0	0	0	0	0
		1983–84	49	9	24	35	7	19	4	1	2	9	1	3	1	0	0	0	0	0	0	0	0	0	0	0	0	0	0
		1984–85	2	7	2	1	6	2	0	0	0	1	1	0	0	0	0	0	0	0	0	0	0	0	0	0	0	0	0
Biggins	Wayne	1995–96	11	4	2	8	2	1	0	0	0	3	1	1	0	1	0	0	0	0	0	0	0	0	0	0	0	0	0
Billington	Wilf	1958–59	32	0	0	18	0	0	5	0	0	0	0	0	0	0	0	0	0	0	0	0	0	3	0	0	6	0	0
Blackwood	Michael	2007–08	5	2	0	5	2	0	0	0	0	0	0	0	0	0	0	0	0	0	0	0	0	0	0	0	0	0	0
Blake	Henry	1949–50	9	0	1	7	0	1	1	0	0	0	0	0	0	0	0	0	0	0	0	0	0	1	0	0	0	0	0
		1950–51	1	0	0	1	0	0	0	0	0	0	0	0	0	0	0	0	0	0	0	0	0	0	0	0	0	0	0
Blizzard	Les	1956–57	12	0	0	12	0	0	0	0	0	0	0	0	0	0	0	0	0	0	0	0	0	0	0	0	0	0	0
Bodel	Andy	1975–76	4	0	0	3	0	0	0	0	0	1	0	0	0	0	0	0	0	0	0	0	0	0	0	0	0	0	0
		1976–77	50	0	6	46	0	6	2	0	0	2	0	0	0	0	0	0	0	0	0	0	0	0	0	0	0	0	0
		1977–78	42	0	3	37	0	3	1	0	0	4	0	0	0	0	0	0	0	0	0	0	0	0	0	0	0	0	0
		1978–79	42	0	2	40	0	2	1	0	0	1	0	0	0	0	0	0	0	0	0	0	0	0	0	0	0	0	0
		1979–80	3	0	0	2	0	0	0	0	0	1	0	0	0	0	0	0	0	0	0	0	0	0	0	0	0	0	0
Bolland	Phil	2001–02	23	0	1	20	0	1	1	0	0	1	0	0	1	0	0	0	0	0	0	0	0	0	0	0	0	0	0
Booth	Colin	1964–65	48	0	23	45	0	23	0	0	0	3	0	0	0	0	0	0	0	0	0	0	0	0	0	0	0	0	0
		1965–66	4	0	0	3	0	0	1	0	0	0	0	0	0	0	0	0	0	0	0	0	0	0	0	0	0	0	0
Bottoms	Mickey	1961–62	4	0	0	4	0	0	0	0	0	0	0	0	0	0	0	0	0	0	0	0	0	0	0	0	0	0	0
Boulton	John	1958–59	6	0	1	5	0	0	0	0	0	0	0	0	0	0	0	0	0	0	0	0	0	0	0	0	1	0	1
Bound	Matthew	2001–02	22	0	0	22	0	0	0	0	0	0	0	0	0	0	0	0	0	0	0	0	0	0	0	0	0	0	0
		2002–03	48	0	1	41	0	1	3	0	0	3	0	0	1	0	0	0	0	0	0	0	0	0	0	0	0	0	0
		2003–04	37	4	1	33	4	1	1	0	0	2	0	0	1	0	0	0	0	0	0	0	0	0	0	0	0	0	0
Bowie	Jim	1956–57	12	0	1	12	0	1	0	0	0	0	0	0	0	0	0	0	0	0	0	0	0	0	0	0	0	0	0
Bowstead	Peter	1962–63	5	0	2	5	0	2	0	0	0	0	0	0	0	0	0	0	0	0	0	0	0	0	0	0	0	0	0
		1963–64	3	0	0	3	0	0	0	0	0	0	0	0	0	0	0	0	0	0	0	0	0	0	0	0	0	0	0
Bradbury	Lee	2004–05	42	2	5	39	2	4	1	0	1	1	0	0	1	0	0	0	0	0	0	0	0	0	0	0	0	0	0
		2005–06	23	6	5	18	4	5	3	1	0	1	0	0	1	1	0	0	0	0	0	0	0	0	0	0	0	0	0
Bradley	Jimmy	1953–54	12	0	6	10	0	5	1	0	0	0	0	0	0	0	0	0	0	0	0	0	0	1	0	1	0	0	0

Surname	Forename	Season	Total			League			FA Cup			FL Cup			Other			FA Trophy			Setanta Sld			SL Cup			SL Inter Zone		
			app	subs	gls	app	subs	gls	app	subs	gls	app	subs	gls	app	subs	gls	app	subs	gls	app	subs	gls	app	subs	gls	app	subs	gls
Bray	Geoff	1972–73	9	5	5	8	4	4	0	0	0	1	0	1	0	1	0	0	0	0	0	0	0	0	0	0	0	0	0
		1973–74	7	3	0	7	3	0	0	0	0	0	0	0	0	0	0	0	0	0	0	0	0	0	0	0	0	0	0
		1974–75	8	4	2	7	4	2	1	0	0	0	0	0	0	0	0	0	0	0	0	0	0	0	0	0	0	0	0
Brevett	Rufus	2006–07	24	3	0	19	3	0	2	0	0	0	0	0	0	0	0	3	0	0	0	0	0	0	0	0	0	0	0
Briggs	Gary	1977–78	20	0	2	20	0	2	0	0	0	0	0	0	0	0	0	0	0	0	0	0	0	0	0	0	0	0	0
		1978–79	45	0	0	39	0	0	1	0	0	5	0	0	0	0	0	0	0	0	0	0	0	0	0	0	0	0	0
		1979–80	48	0	1	46	0	1	1	0	0	1	0	0	0	0	0	0	0	0	0	0	0	0	0	0	0	0	0
		1980–81	48	0	1	42	0	1	2	0	0	4	0	0	0	0	0	0	0	0	0	0	0	0	0	0	0	0	0
		1981–82	59	0	1	45	0	1	6	0	0	5	0	0	3	0	0	0	0	0	0	0	0	0	0	0	0	0	0
		1982–83	45	0	1	37	0	1	1	0	0	4	0	0	3	0	0	0	0	0	0	0	0	0	0	0	0	0	0
		1983–84	54	2	3	36	2	3	7	0	0	10	0	0	1	0	0	0	0	0	0	0	0	0	0	0	0	0	0
		1984–85	50	0	4	42	0	4	2	0	0	6	0	0	0	0	0	0	0	0	0	0	0	0	0	0	0	0	0
		1985–86	51	0	2	38	0	0	2	0	0	7	0	1	4	0	1	0	0	0	0	0	0	0	0	0	0	0	0
		1986–87	45	0	4	40	0	3	0	0	0	4	0	1	1	0	0	0	0	0	0	0	0	0	0	0	0	0	0
		1987–88	24	0	2	18	0	1	2	0	0	3	0	1	1	0	0	0	0	0	0	0	0	0	0	0	0	0	0
		1988–89	17	0	1	15	0	1	0	0	0	1	0	0	1	0	0	0	0	0	0	0	0	0	0	0	0	0	0
Briggs	Max	1973–74	13	0	0	13	0	0	0	0	0	0	0	0	0	0	0	0	0	0	0	0	0	0	0	0	0	0	0
		1974–75	28	3	0	26	3	0	1	0	0	1	0	0	0	0	0	0	0	0	0	0	0	0	0	0	0	0	0
		1975–76	19	0	1	18	0	1	1	0	0	0	0	0	0	0	0	0	0	0	0	0	0	0	0	0	0	0	0
		1976–77	37	0	0	35	0	0	0	0	0	2	0	0	0	0	0	0	0	0	0	0	0	0	0	0	0	0	0
		1977–78	5	0	0	2	0	0	0	0	0	3	0	0	0	0	0	0	0	0	0	0	0	0	0	0	0	0	0
Brine	Albert	1949–50	19	0	0	16	0	0	2	0	0	0	0	0	0	0	0	0	0	0	0	0	0	1	0	0	0	0	0
Brock	Kevin	1979–80	15	4	2	15	4	2	0	0	0	0	0	0	0	0	0	0	0	0	0	0	0	0	0	0	0	0	0
		1980–81	31	2	6	24	2	5	2	0	0	5	0	1	0	0	0	0	0	0	0	0	0	0	0	0	0	0	0
		1981–82	27	6	5	26	2	5	1	1	0	0	1	0	0	2	0	0	0	0	0	0	0	0	0	0	0	0	0
		1982–83	44	3	4	34	3	4	3	0	0	4	0	0	3	0	0	0	0	0	0	0	0	0	0	0	0	0	0
		1983–84	63	0	7	45	0	3	7	0	1	11	0	3	0	0	0	0	0	0	0	0	0	0	0	0	0	0	0
		1984–85	42	1	7	36	1	6	2	0	0	4	0	1	0	0	0	0	0	0	0	0	0	0	0	0	0	0	0
		1985–86	26	5	0	18	5	0	2	0	0	4	0	0	2	0	0	0	0	0	0	0	0	0	0	0	0	0	0
		1986–87	35	1	1	31	0	1	1	0	0	2	1	0	1	0	0	0	0	0	0	0	0	0	0	0	0	0	0
Brooks	Jamie	2000–01	3	1	1	3	1	1	0	0	0	0	0	0	0	0	0	0	0	0	0	0	0	0	0	0	0	0	0
		2001–02	20	7	10	18	7	10	1	0	0	0	0	0	1	0	0	0	0	0	0	0	0	0	0	0	0	0	0
		2004–05	6	7	2	6	6	2	0	1	0	0	0	0	0	0	0	0	0	0	0	0	0	0	0	0	0	0	0
		2005–06	4	5	0	4	5	0	0	0	0	0	0	0	0	0	0	0	0	0	0	0	0	0	0	0	0	0	0
Brown	Danny	2003–04	14	0	0	12	0	0	0	0	0	1	0	0	1	0	0	0	0	0	0	0	0	0	0	0	0	0	0
		2004–05	4	1	0	3	1	0	0	0	0	1	0	0	0	0	0	0	0	0	0	0	0	0	0	0	0	0	0
Brown	David	1979–80	18	0	0	18	0	0	0	0	0	0	0	0	0	0	0	0	0	0	0	0	0	0	0	0	0	0	0
		1980–81	6	0	0	3	0	0	0	0	0	3	0	0	0	0	0	0	0	0	0	0	0	0	0	0	0	0	0
Brown	Keith	2000–01	6	0	0	3	0	0	2	0	0	0	0	0	1	0	0	0	0	0	0	0	0	0	0	0	0	0	0
Bryan	Peter	1962–63	2	0	0	2	0	0	0	0	0	0	0	0	0	0	0	0	0	0	0	0	0	0	0	0	0	0	0
		1963–64	1	0	0	1	0	0	0	0	0	0	0	0	0	0	0	0	0	0	0	0	0	0	0	0	0	0	0
		1964–65	5	0	0	4	0	0	1	0	0	0	0	0	0	0	0	0	0	0	0	0	0	0	0	0	0	0	0
		1965–66	12	0	0	11	0	0	1	0	0	0	0	0	0	0	0	0	0	0	0	0	0	0	0	0	0	0	0
Buchanan	Peter	1949–50	36	0	14	35	0	13	1	0	1	0	0	0	0	0	0	0	0	0	0	0	0	0	0	0	0	0	0

Surname	Forename	Season	Total			League			FA Cup			FL Cup			Other			FA Trophy			Setanta Sld			SL Cup			SL Inter Zone		
			app	subs	gls	app	subs	gls	app	subs	gls	app	subs	gls	app	subs	gls	app	subs	gls	app	subs	gls	app	subs	gls	app	subs	gls
		1950–51	13	0	4	10	0	3	2	0	1	0	0	0	0	0	0	0	0	0	0	0	0	1	0	0	0	0	0
Buck	Tony	1962–63	3	0	0	3	0	0	0	0	0	0	0	0	0	0	0	0	0	0	0	0	0	0	0	0	0	0	0
		1963–64	1	0	0	1	0	0	0	0	0	0	0	0	0	0	0	0	0	0	0	0	0	0	0	0	0	0	0
		1964–65	2	0	0	1	0	0	1	0	0	0	0	0	0	0	0	0	0	0	0	0	0	0	0	0	0	0	0
		1965–66	12	1	3	12	1	3	0	0	0	0	0	0	0	0	0	0	0	0	0	0	0	0	0	0	0	0	0
		1966–67	13	5	4	12	4	3	1	0	0	0	1	1	0	0	0	0	0	0	0	0	0	0	0	0	0	0	0
		1967–68	1	0	0	1	0	0	0	0	0	0	0	0	0	0	0	0	0	0	0	0	0	0	0	0	0	0	0
Bullock	Mick	1967–68	50	0	16	45	0	13	3	0	1	2	0	2	0	0	0	0	0	0	0	0	0	0	0	0	0	0	0
		1968–69	14	1	2	13	1	2	0	0	0	1	0	0	0	0	0	0	0	0	0	0	0	0	0	0	0	0	0
Burgess	Andy	2005–06	12	3	1	12	3	1	0	0	0	0	0	0	0	0	0	0	0	0	0	0	0	0	0	0	0	0	0
		2006–07	36	8	6	34	7	6	1	0	0	0	0	0	0	0	0	1	1	0	0	0	0	0	0	0	0	0	0
Burnell	Joe	2008–09	24	1	1	21	0	1	1	0	0	0	0	0	0	0	0	1	1	0	1	0	0	0	0	0	0	0	0
Burton	Paul	2004–05	0	2	0	0	1	0	0	0	0	0	1	0	0	0	0	0	0	0	0	0	0	0	0	0	0	0	0
Burton	Ron	1953–54	8	0	1	5	0	1	0	0	0	0	0	0	0	0	0	0	0	0	0	0	0	3	0	0	0	0	0
		1954–55	5	0	0	4	0	0	0	0	0	0	0	0	0	0	0	0	0	0	0	0	0	1	0	0	0	0	0
Burton	Roy	1971–72	20	0	0	20	0	0	0	0	0	0	0	0	0	0	0	0	0	0	0	0	0	0	0	0	0	0	0
		1972–73	45	0	0	37	0	0	2	0	0	3	0	0	3	0	0	0	0	0	0	0	0	0	0	0	0	0	0
		1973–74	45	0	0	42	0	0	1	0	0	2	0	0	0	0	0	0	0	0	0	0	0	0	0	0	0	0	0
		1974–75	15	0	0	14	0	0	1	0	0	0	0	0	0	0	0	0	0	0	0	0	0	0	0	0	0	0	0
		1975–76	42	0	0	39	0	0	1	0	0	2	0	0	0	0	0	0	0	0	0	0	0	0	0	0	0	0	0
		1976–77	39	0	0	39	0	0	0	0	0	0	0	0	0	0	0	0	0	0	0	0	0	0	0	0	0	0	0
		1977–78	43	0	0	38	0	0	1	0	0	4	0	0	0	0	0	0	0	0	0	0	0	0	0	0	0	0	0
		1978–79	45	0	0	39	0	0	1	0	0	5	0	0	0	0	0	0	0	0	0	0	0	0	0	0	0	0	0
		1979–80	31	0	0	28	0	0	1	0	0	2	0	0	0	0	0	0	0	0	0	0	0	0	0	0	0	0	0
		1980–81	47	0	0	43	0	0	2	0	0	2	0	0	0	0	0	0	0	0	0	0	0	0	0	0	0	0	0
		1981–82	60	0	0	46	0	0	6	0	0	5	0	0	3	0	0	0	0	0	0	0	0	0	0	0	0	0	0
		1982–83	17	0	0	12	0	0	0	0	0	3	0	0	2	0	0	0	0	0	0	0	0	0	0	0	0	0	0
Butcher	John	1982–83	22	0	0	16	0	0	4	0	0	1	0	0	1	0	0	0	0	0	0	0	0	0	0	0	0	0	0
		1983–84	1	0	0	0	0	0	0	0	0	0	0	0	1	0	0	0	0	0	0	0	0	0	0	0	0	0	0
Butler	Ray	1951–52	7	0	3	7	0	3	0	0	0	0	0	0	0	0	0	0	0	0	0	0	0	0	0	0	0	0	0
Butters	Guy	1994–95	4	0	1	3	0	1	0	0	0	0	0	0	1	0	0	0	0	0	0	0	0	0	0	0	0	0	0
Byrne	John	1993–94	31	3	9	27	3	7	4	0	2	0	0	0	0	0	0	0	0	0	0	0	0	0	0	0	0	0	0
		1994–95	32	0	10	25	0	10	1	0	0	4	0	0	2	0	0	0	0	0	0	0	0	0	0	0	0	0	0
Byrne	Paul	1989–90	2	1	0	2	1	0	0	0	0	0	0	0	0	0	0	0	0	0	0	0	0	0	0	0	0	0	0
		1990–91	2	0	0	2	0	0	0	0	0	0	0	0	0	0	0	0	0	0	0	0	0	0	0	0	0	0	0
Cairney	Charles	1955–56	2	0	0	2	0	0	0	0	0	0	0	0	0	0	0	0	0	0	0	0	0	0	0	0	0	0	0
Calder	Bill	1963–64	31	0	14	25	0	9	6	0	5	0	0	0	0	0	0	0	0	0	0	0	0	0	0	0	0	0	0
		1964–65	27	0	16	24	0	12	0	0	0	3	0	4	0	0	0	0	0	0	0	0	0	0	0	0	0	0	0
		1965–66	15	1	6	13	1	4	2	0	2	0	0	0	0	0	0	0	0	0	0	0	0	0	0	0	0	0	0
		1966–67	5	0	3	4	0	3	0	0	0	1	0	0	0	0	0	0	0	0	0	0	0	0	0	0	0	0	0
Campbell	Andy	2005–06	3	2	0	3	2	0	0	0	0	0	0	0	0	0	0	0	0	0	0	0	0	0	0	0	0	0	0
Capper	Jack	1955–56	11	0	0	8	0	0	1	0	0	0	0	0	0	0	0	0	0	0	0	0	0	2	0	0	0	0	0
Carpenter	Tom	1951–52	2	0	0	2	0	0	0	0	0	0	0	0	0	0	0	0	0	0	0	0	0	0	0	0	0	0	0
Carr	Hughie	1950–51	3	0	0	3	0	0	0	0	0	0	0	0	0	0	0	0	0	0	0	0	0	0	0	0	0	0	0

Surname	Forename	Season	Total			League			FA Cup			FL Cup			Other			FA Trophy			Setanta Sld			SL Cup			SL Inter Zone		
			app	subs	gls	app	subs	gls	app	subs	gls	app	subs	gls	app	subs	gls	app	subs	gls	app	subs	gls	app	subs	gls	app	subs	gls
Carr	Jack	1949–50	3	0	0	2	0	0	0	0	0	0	0	0	0	0	0	0	0	0	0	0	0	1	0	0	0	0	0
Carruthers	Chris	2008–09	37	5	0	35	4	0	2	0	0	0	0	0	0	0	0	1	1	0	1	0	0	0	0	0	0	0	0
Carter	Jimmy	1993–94	5	0	0	5	0	0	0	0	0	0	0	0	0	0	0	0	0	0	0	0	0	0	0	0	0	0	0
		1994–95	3	1	0	3	1	0	0	0	0	0	0	0	0	0	0	0	0	0	0	0	0	0	0	0	0	0	0
Carter	Tim	1995–96	17	0	0	12	0	0	0	0	0	4	0	0	1	0	0	0	0	0	0	0	0	0	0	0	0	0	0
Casley	Jack	1949–50	17	0	3	16	0	3	1	0	0	0	0	0	0	0	0	0	0	0	0	0	0	0	0	0	0	0	0
		1950–51	2	0	0	2	0	0	0	0	0	0	0	0	0	0	0	0	0	0	0	0	0	0	0	0	0	0	0
Cassells	Keith	1980–81	18	2	3	16	2	3	2	0	0	0	0	0	0	0	0	0	0	0	0	0	0	0	0	0	0	0	0
		1981–82	40	1	22	27	0	10	6	0	7	5	0	4	2	1	1	0	0	0	0	0	0	0	0	0	0	0	0
Cassidy	Jim	1963–64	6	0	0	5	0	0	1	0	0	0	0	0	0	0	0	0	0	0	0	0	0	0	0	0	0	0	0
Cassidy	Nigel	1970–71	24	0	5	19	0	4	5	0	1	0	0	0	0	0	0	0	0	0	0	0	0	0	0	0	0	0	0
		1971–72	42	1	13	39	1	13	1	0	0	2	0	0	0	0	0	0	0	0	0	0	0	0	0	0	0	0	0
		1972–73	41	2	10	33	2	10	2	0	0	3	0	0	3	0	0	0	0	0	0	0	0	0	0	0	0	0	0
		1973–74	25	0	6	22	0	6	1	0	0	2	0	0	0	0	0	0	0	0	0	0	0	0	0	0	0	0	0
Caton	Tommy	1986–87	17	0	2	17	0	2	0	0	0	0	0	0	0	0	0	0	0	0	0	0	0	0	0	0	0	0	0
		1987–88	45	3	1	33	3	1	2	0	0	8	0	0	2	0	0	0	0	0	0	0	0	0	0	0	0	0	0
Chapman	Adam	2008–09	21	0	2	20	0	2	0	0	0	0	0	0	0	0	0	1	0	0	0	0	0	0	0	0	0	0	0
Charles	Jeremy	1984–85	11	0	4	11	0	4	0	0	0	0	0	0	0	0	0	0	0	0	0	0	0	0	0	0	0	0	0
		1985–86	31	6	12	23	5	9	0	0	0	5	0	2	3	1	1	0	0	0	0	0	0	0	0	0	0	0	0
		1986–87	8	0	0	7	0	0	0	0	0	1	0	0	0	0	0	0	0	0	0	0	0	0	0	0	0	0	0
Charles	Ralph	1953–54	6	0	3	6	0	3	0	0	0	0	0	0	0	0	0	0	0	0	0	0	0	0	0	0	0	0	0
Chung	Sammy	1950–51	8	0	3	8	0	3	0	0	0	0	0	0	0	0	0	0	0	0	0	0	0	0	0	0	0	0	0
		1951–52	12	0	6	8	0	7	2	0	2	0	0	0	0	0	0	0	0	0	0	0	0	2	0	0	0	0	0
Clark	Willie	1958–59	2	0	0	1	0	0	0	0	0	0	0	0	0	0	0	0	0	0	0	0	0	0	0	0	1	0	0
Clarke	Bradie	2004–05	3	1	0	3	1	0	0	0	0	0	0	0	0	0	0	0	0	0	0	0	0	0	0	0	0	0	0
Clarke	Colin	1965–66	3	0	0	3	0	0	0	0	0	0	0	0	0	0	0	0	0	0	0	0	0	0	0	0	0	0	0
		1966–67	27	1	0	25	1	0	2	0	0	0	0	0	0	0	0	0	0	0	0	0	0	0	0	0	0	0	0
		1967–68	48	0	9	42	0	8	3	0	1	3	0	0	0	0	0	0	0	0	0	0	0	0	0	0	0	0	0
		1968–69	40	0	2	38	0	2	2	0	0	0	0	0	0	0	0	0	0	0	0	0	0	0	0	0	0	0	0
		1969–70	47	0	1	39	0	1	2	0	0	6	0	0	0	0	0	0	0	0	0	0	0	0	0	0	0	0	0
		1970–71	49	0	2	42	0	1	5	0	1	2	0	0	0	0	0	0	0	0	0	0	0	0	0	0	0	0	0
		1971–72	41	0	3	37	0	3	1	0	0	3	0	0	0	0	0	0	0	0	0	0	0	0	0	0	0	0	0
		1972–73	46	0	1	38	0	0	2	0	0	3	0	1	3	0	0	0	0	0	0	0	0	0	0	0	0	0	0
		1973–74	37	0	1	36	0	1	1	0	0	0	0	0	0	0	0	0	0	0	0	0	0	0	0	0	0	0	0
		1974–75	43	0	2	41	0	2	1	0	0	1	0	0	0	0	0	0	0	0	0	0	0	0	0	0	0	0	0
		1975–76	45	0	2	41	0	2	1	0	0	3	0	0	0	0	0	0	0	0	0	0	0	0	0	0	0	0	0
		1976–77	36	0	3	32	0	3	2	0	0	2	0	0	0	0	0	0	0	0	0	0	0	0	0	0	0	0	0
		1977–78	34	0	0	29	0	0	1	0	0	4	0	0	0	0	0	0	0	0	0	0	0	0	0	0	0	0	0
Clarke	Derek	1970–71	16	1	5	16	1	5	0	0	0	0	0	0	0	0	0	0	0	0	0	0	0	0	0	0	0	0	0
		1971–72	29	2	5	26	2	5	1	0	0	2	0	0	0	0	0	0	0	0	0	0	0	0	0	0	0	0	0
		1972–73	21	3	8	17	2	5	0	1	0	1	0	2	3	0	1	0	0	0	0	0	0	0	0	0	0	0	0
		1973–74	40	0	5	37	0	5	1	0	0	2	0	0	0	0	0	0	0	0	0	0	0	0	0	0	0	0	0
		1974–75	38	1	9	37	1	8	1	0	1	0	0	0	0	0	0	0	0	0	0	0	0	0	0	0	0	0	0
		1975–76	43	0	8	39	0	7	1	0	1	3	0	0	0	0	0	0	0	0	0	0	0	0	0	0	0	0	0

Surname	Forename	Season	Total			League			FA Cup			FL Cup			Other			FA Trophy			Setanta Sld			SL Cup			SL Inter Zone		
			app	subs	gls	app	subs	gls	app	subs	gls	app	subs	gls	app	subs	gls	app	subs	gls	app	subs	gls	app	subs	gls	app	subs	gls
Clarke	James	2007–08	17	5	0	13	5	0	2	0	0	0	0	0	0	0	0	2	0	0	0	0	0	0	0	0	0	0	0
		2008–09	16	2	0	12	2	0	3	0	0	0	0	0	0	0	0	1	0	0	0	0	0	0	0	0	0	0	0
Clarke	Tony	1954–55	1	0	1	1	0	1	0	0	0	0	0	0	0	0	0	0	0	0	0	0	0	0	0	0	0	0	0
Clayton	Roy	1969–70	8	1	2	8	1	2	0	0	0	0	0	0	0	0	0	0	0	0	0	0	0	0	0	0	0	0	0
		1970–71	20	0	4	18	0	3	0	0	0	2	0	1	0	0	0	0	0	0	0	0	0	0	0	0	0	0	0
		1971–72	24	2	3	22	2	3	0	0	0	2	0	0	0	0	0	0	0	0	0	0	0	0	0	0	0	0	0
		1972–73	2	1	1	1	1	0	0	0	0	1	0	1	0	0	0	0	0	0	0	0	0	0	0	0	0	0	0
Clinch	Peter	1969–70	2	0	0	2	0	0	0	0	0	0	0	0	0	0	0	0	0	0	0	0	0	0	0	0	0	0	0
Clinkaberry	Les	1951–52	1	0	0	1	0	0	0	0	0	0	0	0	0	0	0	0	0	0	0	0	0	0	0	0	0	0	0
		1953–54	1	0	0	1	0	0	0	0	0	0	0	0	0	0	0	0	0	0	0	0	0	0	0	0	0	0	0
		1954–55	2	0	0	2	0	0	0	0	0	0	0	0	0	0	0	0	0	0	0	0	0	0	0	0	0	0	0
Clist	Simon	2008–09	14	0	3	14	0	3	0	0	0	0	0	0	0	0	0	1	0	0	0	0	0	0	0	0	0	0	0
Cole	Jake	2008–09	5	0	0	5	0	0	0	0	0	0	0	0	0	0	0	1	0	0	0	0	0	0	0	0	0	0	0
Colfar	Ray	1962–63	19	0	3	17	0	3	2	0	0	0	0	0	0	0	0	0	0	0	0	0	0	0	0	0	0	0	0
		1963–64	1	0	1	1	0	1	0	0	0	0	0	0	0	0	0	0	0	0	0	0	0	0	0	0	0	0	0
Collins	Brian	1955–56	7	0	3	4	0	3	1	0	0	0	0	0	0	0	0	0	0	0	0	0	0	2	0	0	0	0	0
		1956–57	4	0	1	4	0	1	0	0	0	0	0	0	0	0	0	0	0	0	0	0	0	0	0	0	0	0	0
Collins	Dave	1992–93	16	1	0	12	1	0	0	0	0	3	0	0	1	0	0	0	0	0	0	0	0	0	0	0	0	0	0
		1993–94	20	9	0	18	8	0	0	0	0	1	0	0	1	1	0	0	0	0	0	0	0	0	0	0	0	0	0
		1994–95	5	0	0	3	0	0	1	0	0	0	0	0	1	0	0	0	0	0	0	0	0	0	0	0	0	0	0
Collins	Patrick	2007–08	2	0	0	1	0	0	1	0	0	0	0	0	0	0	0	0	0	0	0	0	0	0	0	0	0	0	0
Cominelli	Lucas	2004–05	11	5	1	11	5	1	0	0	0	0	0	0	0	0	0	0	0	0	0	0	0	0	0	0	0	0	0
Constable	James	2008–09	47	2	26	40	2	23	4	0	2	0	0	0	0	0	0	2	0	1	1	0	0	0	0	0	0	0	0
Cook	Jamie	1997–98	9	12	2	9	11	2	0	1	0	0	0	0	0	0	0	0	0	0	0	0	0	0	0	0	0	0	0
		1998–99	11	11	1	9	10	1	2	0	0	0	1	0	0	0	0	0	0	0	0	0	0	0	0	0	0	0	0
		1999–2000	16	25	3	11	19	3	1	3	0	1	1	0	3	2	0	0	0	0	0	0	0	0	0	0	0	0	0
		2000–01	4	5	1	4	5	1	0	0	0	0	0	0	0	0	0	0	0	0	0	0	0	0	0	0	0	0	0
Cooke	Joe	1979–80	42	1	7	41	1	7	1	0	0	0	0	0	0	0	0	0	0	0	0	0	0	0	0	0	0	0	0
		1980–81	36	0	6	30	0	6	1	0	0	5	0	0	0	0	0	0	0	0	0	0	0	0	0	0	0	0	0
Coombes	Gregg	2006–07	1	0	0	1	0	0	0	0	0	0	0	0	0	0	0	0	0	0	0	0	0	0	0	0	0	0	0
Corbo	Mateo	2004–05	13	0	0	13	0	0	0	0	0	0	0	0	0	0	0	0	0	0	0	0	0	0	0	0	0	0	0
Corcoran	Michael	2006–07	16	0	1	16	0	1	0	0	0	0	0	0	0	0	0	0	0	0	0	0	0	0	0	0	0	0	0
		2007–08	17	2	1	15	2	1	1	0	0	0	0	0	0	0	0	0	0	0	1	0	0	0	0	0	0	0	0
Cornwell	Kevin	1961–62	2	0	0	2	0	0	0	0	0	0	0	0	0	0	0	0	0	0	0	0	0	0	0	0	0	0	0
		1962–63	11	0	5	11	0	5	0	0	0	0	0	0	0	0	0	0	0	0	0	0	0	0	0	0	0	0	0
		1963–64	15	0	5	15	0	5	0	0	0	0	0	0	0	0	0	0	0	0	0	0	0	0	0	0	0	0	0
Cotton	Fred	1957–58	27	0	6	22	0	5	3	0	0	0	0	0	0	0	0	0	0	0	0	0	0	2	0	1	0	0	0
Cox	Simon	2003–04	5	0	0	5	0	0	0	0	0	0	0	0	0	0	0	0	0	0	0	0	0	0	0	0	0	0	0
		2004–05	2	1	0	2	1	0	0	0	0	0	0	0	0	0	0	0	0	0	0	0	0	0	0	0	0	0	0
Craig	Bobby	1951–52	47	0	0	41	0	0	3	0	0	0	0	0	0	0	0	0	0	0	0	0	0	3	0	0	0	0	0
		1952–53	46	0	0	37	0	0	4	0	0	0	0	0	0	0	0	0	0	0	0	0	0	5	0	0	0	0	0
		1953–54	54	0	8	37	0	5	10	0	2	0	0	0	0	0	0	0	0	0	0	0	0	7	0	1	0	0	0
		1954–55	44	0	2	38	0	2	2	0	0	0	0	0	0	0	0	0	0	0	0	0	0	4	0	0	0	0	0
Crichton	Johnnie	1950–51	2	0	0	2	0	0	0	0	0	0	0	0	0	0	0	0	0	0	0	0	0	0	0	0	0	0	0

Surname	Forename	Season	Total			League			FA Cup			FL Cup			Other			FA Trophy			Setanta Sld			SL Cup			SL Inter Zone		
			app	subs	gls	app	subs	gls	app	subs	gls	app	subs	gls	app	subs	gls	app	subs	gls	app	subs	gls	app	subs	gls	app	subs	gls
		1951–52	46	0	6	38	0	4	4	0	2	0	0	0	0	0	0	0	0	0	0	0	0	4	0	0	0	0	0
		1952–53	46	0	7	35	0	5	5	0	2	0	0	0	0	0	0	0	0	0	0	0	0	6	0	0	0	0	0
		1953–54	56	0	7	39	0	4	10	0	0	0	0	0	0	0	0	0	0	0	0	0	0	7	0	3	0	0	0
		1954–55	37	0	5	32	0	5	2	0	0	0	0	0	0	0	0	0	0	0	0	0	0	3	0	0	0	0	0
Croker	Ted	1953–54	50	0	0	34	0	0	9	0	0	0	0	0	0	0	0	0	0	0	0	0	0	7	0	0	0	0	0
		1954–55	41	0	0	35	0	0	2	0	0	0	0	0	0	0	0	0	0	0	0	0	0	4	0	0	0	0	0
Crombie	Don	1953–54	3	0	1	2	0	1	0	0	0	0	0	0	0	0	0	0	0	0	0	0	0	1	0	0	0	0	0
Crook	Les	1968–69	1	0	0	1	0	0	0	0	0	0	0	0	0	0	0	0	0	0	0	0	0	0	0	0	0	0	0
Crosby	Andy	2001–02	22	1	1	22	1	1	0	0	0	0	0	0	0	0	0	0	0	0	0	0	0	0	0	0	0	0	0
		2002–03	53	0	7	46	0	6	3	0	0	3	0	0	1	0	1	0	0	0	0	0	0	0	0	0	0	0	0
		2003–04	45	1	5	41	1	5	1	0	0	2	0	0	1	0	0	0	0	0	0	0	0	0	0	0	0	0	0
Cross	Jimmy	1958–59	32	0	0	21	0	0	3	0	0	0	0	0	0	0	0	0	0	0	0	0	0	2	0	0	6	0	0
Cross	Jack	1957–58	40	0	27	32	0	25	5	0	1	0	0	0	0	0	0	0	0	0	0	0	0	3	0	1	0	0	0
Cullen	John	1961–62	9	0	0	9	0	0	0	0	0	0	0	0	0	0	0	0	0	0	0	0	0	0	0	0	0	0	0
Curran	Hugh	1972–73	37	0	17	31	0	15	2	0	0	0	0	0	4	0	2	0	0	0	0	0	0	0	0	0	0	0	0
		1973–74	39	0	14	36	0	12	1	0	1	2	0	1	0	0	0	0	0	0	0	0	0	0	0	0	0	0	0
		1974–75	3	1	1	2	1	1	0	0	0	1	0	0	0	0	0	0	0	0	0	0	0	0	0	0	0	0	0
		1977–78	32	4	11	29	4	11	1	0	0	2	0	0	0	0	0	0	0	0	0	0	0	0	0	0	0	0	0
		1978–79	4	1	0	1	1	0	0	0	0	3	0	0	0	0	0	0	0	0	0	0	0	0	0	0	0	0	0
Cusack	Nick	1992–93	36	10	7	30	9	4	2	0	1	3	0	2	1	1	0	0	0	0	0	0	0	0	0	0	0	0	0
		1993–94	21	4	6	18	2	6	2	2	0	0	0	0	1	0	0	0	0	0	0	0	0	0	0	0	0	0	0
Cutler	Neil	2000–01	11	0	0	11	0	0	0	0	0	0	0	0	0	0	0	0	0	0	0	0	0	0	0	0	0	0	0
Davidson	David	1949–50	7	0	0	7	0	0	0	0	0	0	0	0	0	0	0	0	0	0	0	0	0	0	0	0	0	0	0
		1950–51	8	0	0	6	0	0	1	0	0	0	0	0	0	0	0	0	0	0	0	0	0	1	0	0	0	0	0
Davies	Craig	2004–05	13	16	6	13	15	6	0	0	0	0	0	0	0	1	0	0	0	0	0	0	0	0	0	0	0	0	0
		2005–06	13	13	2	10	10	2	1	2	0	1	0	0	1	1	0	0	0	0	0	0	0	0	0	0	0	0	0
Davies	Rob	2008–09	1	0	0	1	0	0	0	0	0	0	0	0	0	0	0	0	0	0	0	0	0	0	0	0	0	0	0
Davis	Steve	1997–98	15	0	2	15	0	2	0	0	0	0	0	0	0	0	0	0	0	0	0	0	0	0	0	0	0	0	0
		1998–99	3	0	0	3	0	0	0	0	0	0	0	0	0	0	0	0	0	0	0	0	0	0	0	0	0	0	0
		1999–2000	25	5	1	20	4	1	1	0	0	3	0	0	1	1	0	0	0	0	0	0	0	0	0	0	0	0	0
Day	Matt	2006–07	26	18	5	23	16	5	1	1	0	0	0	0	0	0	0	2	1	0	0	0	0	0	0	0	0	0	0
		2007–08	39	4	1	36	3	1	2	0	0	0	0	0	0	0	0	0	1	0	1	0	0	0	0	0	0	0	0
		2008–09	21	3	1	15	3	1	3	0	0	0	0	0	0	0	0	2	0	0	1	0	0	0	0	0	0	0	0
Dean	Brian	1955–56	4	0	0	4	0	0	0	0	0	0	0	0	0	0	0	0	0	0	0	0	0	0	0	0	0	0	0
		1956–57	25	0	8	24	0	8	0	0	0	0	0	0	0	0	0	0	0	0	0	0	0	1	0	0	0	0	0
		1957–58	4	0	3	4	0	3	0	0	0	0	0	0	0	0	0	0	0	0	0	0	0	0	0	0	0	0	0
Deegan	Mark	1994–95	5	0	0	2	0	0	0	0	0	0	0	0	3	0	0	0	0	0	0	0	0	0	0	0	0	0	0
Deering	Sam	2008–09	13	11	2	8	11	2	4	0	0	0	0	0	0	0	0	1	0	0	0	0	0	0	0	0	0	0	0
Dempster	John	2005–06	6	0	0	6	0	0	0	0	0	0	0	0	0	0	0	0	0	0	0	0	0	0	0	0	0	0	0
		2006–07	10	10	0	8	9	0	0	1	0	0	0	0	0	0	0	2	0	0	0	0	0	0	0	0	0	0	0
Denial	Geoff	1956–57	24	0	0	23	0	0	1	0	0	0	0	0	0	0	0	0	0	0	0	0	0	0	0	0	0	0	0
		1957–58	39	0	8	33	0	6	5	0	2	0	0	0	0	0	0	0	0	0	0	0	0	1	0	0	0	0	0
		1958–59	46	0	5	31	0	4	5	0	1	0	0	0	0	0	0	0	0	0	0	0	0	2	0	0	8	0	0
		1959–60	46	0	32	40	0	28	2	0	4	0	0	0	0	0	0	0	0	0	0	0	0	4	0	0	0	0	0

Surname	Forename	Season	Total			League			FA Cup			FL Cup			Other			FA Trophy			Setanta Sld			SL Cup			SL Inter Zone		
			app	subs	gls	app	subs	gls	app	subs	gls	app	subs	gls	app	subs	gls	app	subs	gls	app	subs	gls	app	subs	gls	app	subs	gls
		1960–61	21	0	6	19	0	5	2	0	1	0	0	0	0	0	0	0	0	0	0	0	0	0	0	0	0	0	0
		1961–62	17	0	0	16	0	0	0	0	0	0	0	0	0	0	0	0	0	0	0	0	0	1	0	0	0	0	0
		1962–63	7	0	0	6	0	0	1	0	0	0	0	0	0	0	0	0	0	0	0	0	0	0	0	0	0	0	0
Diaz	Emiliano	2004–05	2	5	0	2	5	0	0	0	0	0	0	0	0	0	0	0	0	0	0	0	0	0	0	0	0	0	0
Dickson	Joe	1958–59	48	0	27	31	0	12	6	0	8	0	0	0	0	0	0	0	0	0	0	0	0	3	0	4	8	0	3
		1959–60	45	0	8	40	0	8	1	0	0	0	0	0	0	0	0	0	0	0	0	0	0	4	0	0	0	0	0
		1960–61	8	0	4	6	0	3	1	0	1	0	0	0	0	0	0	0	0	0	0	0	0	1	0	0	0	0	0
Dobson	James	2008–09	0	2	0	0	0	0	0	2	0	0	0	0	0	0	0	0	0	0	0	0	0	0	0	0	0	0	0
Dobson	Tony	1994–95	5	0	0	5	0	0	0	0	0	0	0	0	0	0	0	0	0	0	0	0	0	0	0	0	0	0	0
Doherty	Sam	1955–56	33	0	2	29	0	2	1	0	0	0	0	0	0	0	0	0	0	0	0	0	0	3	0	0	0	0	0
Donaldson	O'Neill	1997–98	6	0	2	6	0	2	0	0	0	0	0	0	0	0	0	0	0	0	0	0	0	0	0	0	0	0	0
Donnelly	Ron	1959–60	1	0	1	1	0	1	0	0	0	0	0	0	0	0	0	0	0	0	0	0	0	0	0	0	0	0	0
Donovan	Terry	1982–83	3	0	0	3	0	0	0	0	0	0	0	0	0	0	0	0	0	0	0	0	0	0	0	0	0	0	0
Doudou		2004–05	0	1	0	0	1	0	0	0	0	0	0	0	0	0	0	0	0	0	0	0	0	0	0	0	0	0	0
Doughty	Eric	1959–60	1	0	0	1	0	0	0	0	0	0	0	0	0	0	0	0	0	0	0	0	0	0	0	0	0	0	0
Douglas	Stuart	2001–02	1	3	0	1	3	0	0	0	0	0	0	0	0	0	0	0	0	0	0	0	0	0	0	0	0	0	0
Doyle	John	1977–78	3	0	0	3	0	0	0	0	0	0	0	0	0	0	0	0	0	0	0	0	0	0	0	0	0	0	0
		1978–79	7	0	0	5	0	0	0	0	0	2	0	0	0	0	0	0	0	0	0	0	0	0	0	0	0	0	0
		1979–80	10	0	0	10	0	0	0	0	0	0	0	0	0	0	0	0	0	0	0	0	0	0	0	0	0	0	0
		1980–81	18	0	0	18	0	0	0	0	0	0	0	0	0	0	0	0	0	0	0	0	0	0	0	0	0	0	0
		1981–82	42	0	0	30	0	0	6	0	0	5	0	0	1	0	0	0	0	0	0	0	0	0	0	0	0	0	0
Dreyer	John	1986–87	27	3	2	23	2	2	1	0	0	2	1	0	1	0	0	0	0	0	0	0	0	0	0	0	0	0	0
		1987–88	45	1	0	34	1	0	1	0	0	8	0	0	2	0	0	0	0	0	0	0	0	0	0	0	0	0	0
Druce	Mark	1992–93	3	1	1	3	1	1	0	0	0	0	0	0	0	0	0	0	0	0	0	0	0	0	0	0	0	0	0
		1993–94	6	16	0	5	14	0	0	0	0	1	1	0	0	1	0	0	0	0	0	0	0	0	0	0	0	0	0
		1994–95	11	11	3	9	9	3	0	0	0	0	2	0	2	0	0	0	0	0	0	0	0	0	0	0	0	0	0
		1995–96	1	7	0	1	7	0	0	0	0	0	0	0	0	0	0	0	0	0	0	0	0	0	0	0	0	0	0
Drysdale	Brian	1977–78	18	0	0	15	0	0	0	0	0	3	0	0	0	0	0	0	0	0	0	0	0	0	0	0	0	0	0
Duffy	Robert	2006–07	38	5	21	33	5	18	1	0	1	0	0	0	0	0	0	4	0	2	0	0	0	0	0	0	0	0	0
		2007–08	17	7	6	14	6	6	0	1	0	0	0	0	0	0	0	2	0	0	1	0	0	0	0	0	0	0	0
Duncan	Ben	1950–51	26	0	10	26	0	10	0	0	0	0	0	0	0	0	0	0	0	0	0	0	0	0	0	0	0	0	0
		1951–52	45	0	5	39	0	3	4	0	0	0	0	0	0	0	0	0	0	0	0	0	0	2	0	2	0	0	0
		1952–53	48	0	10	39	0	8	5	0	0	0	0	0	0	0	0	0	0	0	0	0	0	4	0	2	0	0	0
		1953–54	46	0	3	34	0	1	8	0	2	0	0	0	0	0	0	0	0	0	0	0	0	4	0	0	0	0	0
		1954–55	21	0	2	16	0	2	1	0	0	0	0	0	0	0	0	0	0	0	0	0	0	4	0	0	0	0	0
Duncan	Colin	1974–75	24	0	0	23	0	0	1	0	0	0	0	0	0	0	0	0	0	0	0	0	0	0	0	0	0	0	0
		1975–76	7	0	0	5	0	0	0	0	0	2	0	0	0	0	0	0	0	0	0	0	0	0	0	0	0	0	0
		1976–77	49	1	0	45	1	0	2	0	0	2	0	0	0	0	0	0	0	0	0	0	0	0	0	0	0	0	0
		1977–78	48	0	3	45	0	3	1	0	0	2	0	0	0	0	0	0	0	0	0	0	0	0	0	0	0	0	0
		1978–79	48	0	4	43	0	3	1	0	0	4	0	1	0	0	0	0	0	0	0	0	0	0	0	0	0	0	0
		1979–80	30	0	0	27	0	0	1	0	0	2	0	0	0	0	0	0	0	0	0	0	0	0	0	0	0	0	0
Durnin	John	1988–89	19	0	3	19	0	3	0	0	0	0	0	0	0	0	0	0	0	0	0	0	0	0	0	0	0	0	0
		1989–90	43	3	15	39	3	13	1	0	0	2	0	1	1	0	1	0	0	0	0	0	0	0	0	0	0	0	0
		1990–91	24	7	10	20	6	9	2	0	1	1	0	0	1	1	0	0	0	0	0	0	0	0	0	0	0	0	0

Surname	Forename	Season	Total			League			FA Cup			FL Cup			Other			FA Trophy			Setanta Sld			SL Cup			SL Inter Zone		
			app	subs	gls	app	subs	gls	app	subs	gls	app	subs	gls	app	subs	gls	app	subs	gls	app	subs	gls	app	subs	gls	app	subs	gls
		1991–92	31	9	8	28	9	8	2	0	0	1	0	0	0	0	0	0	0	0	0	0	0	0	0	0	0	0	0
		1992–93	41	3	11	34	3	11	2	0	0	3	0	0	2	0	0	0	0	0	0	0	0	0	0	0	0	0	0
Dyer	Alex	1993–94	37	8	6	30	8	5	4	0	1	1	0	0	2	0	0	0	0	0	0	0	0	0	0	0	0	0	0
		1994–95	39	6	2	32	6	1	1	0	0	3	0	1	3	0	0	0	0	0	0	0	0	0	0	0	0	0	0
E'Beyer	Mark	2004–05	7	4	1	6	4	1	1	0	0	0	0	0	0	0	0	0	0	0	0	0	0	0	0	0	0	0	0
		2005–06	4	5	1	3	3	1	0	1	0	0	0	0	1	1	0	0	0	0	0	0	0	0	0	0	0	0	0
Edwards	Bill	1949–50	1	0	0	1	0	0	0	0	0	0	0	0	0	0	0	0	0	0	0	0	0	0	0	0	0	0	0
Edwards	Christian	1999–2000	5	0	1	5	0	1	0	0	0	0	0	0	0	0	0	0	0	0	0	0	0	0	0	0	0	0	0
		2002–03	5	1	0	5	1	0	0	0	0	0	0	0	0	0	0	0	0	0	0	0	0	0	0	0	0	0	0
Eele	Ron	1955–56	13	0	4	11	0	3	0	0	0	0	0	0	0	0	0	0	0	0	0	0	0	2	0	1	0	0	0
		1956–57	10	0	2	10	0	2	0	0	0	0	0	0	0	0	0	0	0	0	0	0	0	0	0	0	0	0	0
		1957–58	4	0	2	4	0	2	0	0	0	0	0	0	0	0	0	0	0	0	0	0	0	0	0	0	0	0	0
Elliott	Jack	1950–51	32	0	6	32	0	6	0	0	0	0	0	0	0	0	0	0	0	0	0	0	0	0	0	0	0	0	0
		1951–52	11	0	2	11	0	2	0	0	0	0	0	0	0	0	0	0	0	0	0	0	0	0	0	0	0	0	0
Elliott	Matt	1993–94	36	0	7	32	0	5	4	0	2	0	0	0	0	0	0	0	0	0	0	0	0	0	0	0	0	0	0
		1994–95	53	0	5	45	0	5	1	0	0	4	0	0	3	0	0	0	0	0	0	0	0	0	0	0	0	0	0
		1995–96	58	0	8	45	0	8	6	0	0	4	0	0	3	0	0	0	0	0	0	0	0	0	0	0	0	0	0
		1996–97	34	0	5	26	0	4	0	0	0	8	0	1	0	0	0	0	0	0	0	0	0	0	0	0	0	0	0
Evans	Bernard	1962–63	9	0	1	8	0	1	1	0	0	0	0	0	0	0	0	0	0	0	0	0	0	0	0	0	0	0	0
		1963–64	5	0	2	5	0	2	0	0	0	0	0	0	0	0	0	0	0	0	0	0	0	0	0	0	0	0	0
Evans	Ceri	1988–89	4	0	0	4	0	0	0	0	0	0	0	0	0	0	0	0	0	0	0	0	0	0	0	0	0	0	0
		1989–90	26	0	2	24	0	2	2	0	0	0	0	0	0	0	0	0	0	0	0	0	0	0	0	0	0	0	0
		1990–91	22	1	1	17	1	1	0	0	0	3	0	0	2	0	0	0	0	0	0	0	0	0	0	0	0	0	0
		1991–92	31	2	0	27	2	0	2	0	0	1	0	0	1	0	0	0	0	0	0	0	0	0	0	0	0	0	0
		1992–93	49	0	0	41	0	0	2	0	0	4	0	0	2	0	0	0	0	0	0	0	0	0	0	0	0	0	0
Evans	Paul	2008–09	2	2	0	2	1	0	0	0	0	0	0	0	0	0	0	0	0	0	0	1	0	0	0	0	0	0	0
Evanson	John	1966–67	5	1	0	4	1	0	0	0	0	1	0	0	0	0	0	0	0	0	0	0	0	0	0	0	0	0	0
		1967–68	6	0	2	5	0	2	1	0	0	0	0	0	0	0	0	0	0	0	0	0	0	0	0	0	0	0	0
		1968–69	16	2	1	13	2	1	2	0	0	1	0	0	0	0	0	0	0	0	0	0	0	0	0	0	0	0	0
		1969–70	10	2	0	10	2	0	0	0	0	0	0	0	0	0	0	0	0	0	0	0	0	0	0	0	0	0	0
		1970–71	32	2	2	27	1	2	5	0	0	0	1	0	0	0	0	0	0	0	0	0	0	0	0	0	0	0	0
		1971–72	28	3	3	25	3	2	1	0	0	2	0	1	0	0	0	0	0	0	0	0	0	0	0	0	0	0	0
		1972–73	47	0	3	39	0	3	2	0	0	3	0	0	3	0	0	0	0	0	0	0	0	0	0	0	0	0	0
		1973–74	24	1	0	21	1	0	1	0	0	2	0	0	0	0	0	0	0	0	0	0	0	0	0	0	0	0	0
Fahy	John	1963–64	1	0	0	1	0	0	0	0	0	0	0	0	0	0	0	0	0	0	0	0	0	0	0	0	0	0	0
		1964–65	12	0	10	11	0	10	1	0	0	0	0	0	0	0	0	0	0	0	0	0	0	0	0	0	0	0	0
		1965–66	12	0	4	11	0	4	0	0	0	1	0	0	0	0	0	0	0	0	0	0	0	0	0	0	0	0	0
Farr	Tony	1954–55	4	0	0	4	0	0	0	0	0	0	0	0	0	0	0	0	0	0	0	0	0	0	0	0	0	0	0
Farrell	Craig	2008–09	7	8	2	7	8	2	0	0	0	0	0	0	0	0	0	0	0	0	0	0	0	0	0	0	0	0	0
Fear	Peter	1999–2000	19	7	1	13	6	1	1	1	0	2	0	0	3	0	0	0	0	0	0	0	0	0	0	0	0	0	0
		2000–01	16	5	2	14	5	2	2	0	0	0	0	0	0	0	0	0	0	0	0	0	0	0	0	0	0	0	0
Fearnley	Harry	1963–64	30	0	0	23	0	0	7	0	0	0	0	0	0	0	0	0	0	0	0	0	0	0	0	0	0	0	0
		1964–65	48	0	0	44	0	0	1	0	0	3	0	0	0	0	0	0	0	0	0	0	0	0	0	0	0	0	0
		1965–66	26	0	0	23	0	0	2	0	0	1	0	0	0	0	0	0	0	0	0	0	0	0	0	0	0	0	0

Surname	Forename	Season	Total			League			FA Cup			FL Cup			Other			FA Trophy			Setanta Sld			SL Cup			SL Inter Zone		
			app	subs	gls	app	subs	gls	app	subs	gls	app	subs	gls	app	subs	gls	app	subs	gls	app	subs	gls	app	subs	gls	app	subs	gls
Feehan	Ignatius	1959–60	19	0	0	14	0	0	2	0	0	0	0	0	0	0	0	0	0	0	0	0	0	3	0	0	0	0	0
Fisher	Alex	2007–08	1	13	1	1	9	1	0	3	0	0	0	0	0	0	0	0	1	0	0	0	0	0	0	0	0	0	0
		2008–09	0	4	1	0	4	1	0	0	0	0	0	0	0	0	0	0	0	0	0	0	0	0	0	0	0	0	0
Fitzgerald	Scott	2005–06	2	1	1	2	1	1	0	0	0	0	0	0	0	0	0	0	0	0	0	0	0	0	0	0	0	0	0
Flay	Steve	1973–74	2	0	0	1	0	0	0	0	0	1	0	0	0	0	0	0	0	0	0	0	0	0	0	0	0	0	0
		1974–75	2	0	0	2	0	0	0	0	0	0	0	0	0	0	0	0	0	0	0	0	0	0	0	0	0	0	0
Fleming	John	1971–72	12	1	0	11	1	0	1	0	0	0	0	0	0	0	0	0	0	0	0	0	0	0	0	0	0	0	0
		1972–73	31	2	2	25	2	2	2	0	0	0	0	0	4	0	0	0	0	0	0	0	0	0	0	0	0	0	0
		1973–74	21	2	0	20	2	0	0	0	0	1	0	0	0	0	0	0	0	0	0	0	0	0	0	0	0	0	0
		1974–75	12	3	0	11	3	0	0	0	0	1	0	0	0	0	0	0	0	0	0	0	0	0	0	0	0	0	0
Flood	John	1959–60	1	0	0	1	0	0	0	0	0	0	0	0	0	0	0	0	0	0	0	0	0	0	0	0	0	0	0
Fogg	David	1976–77	40	2	1	37	2	1	2	0	0	1	0	0	0	0	0	0	0	0	0	0	0	0	0	0	0	0	0
		1977–78	51	0	2	46	0	2	1	0	0	4	0	0	0	0	0	0	0	0	0	0	0	0	0	0	0	0	0
		1978–79	50	0	3	44	0	2	1	0	0	5	0	1	0	0	0	0	0	0	0	0	0	0	0	0	0	0	0
		1979–80	38	1	2	35	1	2	1	0	0	2	0	0	0	0	0	0	0	0	0	0	0	0	0	0	0	0	0
		1980–81	46	1	1	44	0	1	1	0	0	1	1	0	0	0	0	0	0	0	0	0	0	0	0	0	0	0	0
		1981–82	57	1	4	45	1	3	4	0	0	5	0	0	3	0	1	0	0	0	0	0	0	0	0	0	0	0	0
		1982–83	43	0	8	33	0	5	4	0	2	4	0	1	2	0	0	0	0	0	0	0	0	0	0	0	0	0	0
		1983–84	4	0	0	3	0	0	0	0	0	1	0	0	0	0	0	0	0	0	0	0	0	0	0	0	0	0	0
		1984–85	2	0	0	2	0	0	0	0	0	0	0	0	0	0	0	0	0	0	0	0	0	0	0	0	0	0	0
Foley	Dominic	2002–03	4	2	0	4	2	0	0	0	0	0	0	0	0	0	0	0	0	0	0	0	0	0	0	0	0	0	0
Foley	Peter	1974–75	2	0	0	2	0	0	0	0	0	0	0	0	0	0	0	0	0	0	0	0	0	0	0	0	0	0	0
		1975–76	30	6	5	27	6	4	0	0	0	3	0	1	0	0	0	0	0	0	0	0	0	0	0	0	0	0	0
		1976–77	50	0	13	46	0	12	2	0	1	2	0	0	0	0	0	0	0	0	0	0	0	0	0	0	0	0	0
		1977–78	48	0	21	43	0	19	1	0	0	4	0	2	0	0	0	0	0	0	0	0	0	0	0	0	0	0	0
		1978–79	37	1	11	31	1	9	1	0	1	5	0	1	0	0	0	0	0	0	0	0	0	0	0	0	0	0	0
		1979–80	28	3	12	26	3	10	0	0	0	2	0	2	0	0	0	0	0	0	0	0	0	0	0	0	0	0	0
		1980–81	44	2	7	38	2	5	1	0	1	5	0	1	0	0	0	0	0	0	0	0	0	0	0	0	0	0	0
		1981–82	48	0	10	37	0	7	4	0	2	5	0	1	2	0	0	0	0	0	0	0	0	0	0	0	0	0	0
		1982–83	19	3	11	12	3	5	4	0	4	1	0	0	2	0	2	0	0	0	0	0	0	0	0	0	0	0	0
Folland	Rob	1999–2000	26	7	2	17	6	1	4	1	1	2	0	0	3	0	0	0	0	0	0	0	0	0	0	0	0	0	0
		2000–01	1	5	1	1	4	1	0	0	0	0	1	0	0	0	0	0	0	0	0	0	0	0	0	0	0	0	0
		2001–02	1	11	0	0	10	0	0	0	0	0	1	0	1	0	0	0	0	0	0	0	0	0	0	0	0	0	0
Foran	Richie	2003–04	3	1	0	3	1	0	0	0	0	0	0	0	0	0	0	0	0	0	0	0	0	0	0	0	0	0	0
Ford	Bobby	1993–94	15	3	0	12	2	0	2	0	0	0	1	0	1	0	0	0	0	0	0	0	0	0	0	0	0	0	0
		1994–95	24	3	3	20	3	2	1	0	0	0	0	0	3	0	1	0	0	0	0	0	0	0	0	0	0	0	0
		1995–96	38	2	5	26	2	3	6	0	2	3	0	0	3	0	0	0	0	0	0	0	0	0	0	0	0	0	0
		1996–97	35	5	1	29	4	0	1	0	0	5	1	1	0	0	0	0	0	0	0	0	0	0	0	0	0	0	0
		1997–98	23	1	2	17	1	2	0	0	0	6	0	0	0	0	0	0	0	0	0	0	0	0	0	0	0	0	0
		2002–03	35	6	1	31	6	1	2	0	0	2	0	0	0	0	0	0	0	0	0	0	0	0	0	0	0	0	0
Ford	Mike	1988–89	6	5	1	6	4	1	0	1	0	0	0	0	0	0	0	0	0	0	0	0	0	0	0	0	0	0	0
		1989–90	27	7	2	25	6	2	0	0	0	1	1	0	1	0	0	0	0	0	0	0	0	0	0	0	0	0	0
		1990–91	30	1	1	27	1	1	0	0	0	3	0	0	0	0	0	0	0	0	0	0	0	0	0	0	0	0	0
		1991–92	9	0	1	9	0	1	0	0	0	0	0	0	0	0	0	0	0	0	0	0	0	0	0	0	0	0	0

Surname	Forename	Season	Total			League			FA Cup			FL Cup			Other			FA Trophy			Setanta Sld			SL Cup			SL Inter Zone		
			app	subs	gls	app	subs	gls	app	subs	gls	app	subs	gls	app	subs	gls	app	subs	gls	app	subs	gls	app	subs	gls	app	subs	gls
		1992–93	48	1	4	43	1	4	1	0	0	3	0	0	1	0	0	0	0	0	0	0	0	0	0	0	0	0	0
		1993–94	49	0	2	41	0	1	4	0	0	2	0	0	2	0	1	0	0	0	0	0	0	0	0	0	0	0	0
		1994–95	20	3	1	15	3	0	0	0	0	4	0	1	1	0	0	0	0	0	0	0	0	0	0	0	0	0	0
		1995–96	55	1	3	43	1	2	5	0	1	4	0	0	3	0	0	0	0	0	0	0	0	0	0	0	0	0	0
		1996–97	51	0	5	42	0	4	1	0	0	8	0	1	0	0	0	0	0	0	0	0	0	0	0	0	0	0	0
		1997–98	25	0	2	22	0	2	1	0	0	2	0	0	0	0	0	0	0	0	0	0	0	0	0	0	0	0	0
		2000–01	1	0	0	1	0	0	0	0	0	0	0	0	0	0	0	0	0	0	0	0	0	0	0	0	0	0	0
Forrester	George	1956–57	6	0	0	6	0	0	0	0	0	0	0	0	0	0	0	0	0	0	0	0	0	0	0	0	0	0	0
Foster	Luke	2006–07	7	2	1	7	2	1	0	0	0	0	0	0	0	0	0	0	0	0	0	0	0	0	0	0	0	0	0
		2007–08	36	2	0	29	2	0	4	0	0	0	0	0	0	0	0	2	0	0	1	0	0	0	0	0	0	0	0
		2008–09	44	0	1	39	0	1	3	0	0	0	0	0	0	0	0	2	0	0	0	0	0	0	0	0	0	0	0
Foster	Martin	2006–07	15	0	0	15	0	0	0	0	0	0	0	0	0	0	0	0	0	0	0	0	0	0	0	0	0	0	0
Foster	Steve	1989–90	40	0	4	35	0	4	2	0	0	2	0	0	1	0	0	0	0	0	0	0	0	0	0	0	0	0	0
		1990–91	47	0	7	38	0	4	2	0	0	5	0	2	2	0	1	0	0	0	0	0	0	0	0	0	0	0	0
		1991–92	25	0	2	22	0	2	1	0	0	2	0	0	0	0	0	0	0	0	0	0	0	0	0	0	0	0	0
Foyle	Martin	1986–87	3	1	0	3	1	0	0	0	0	0	0	0	0	0	0	0	0	0	0	0	0	0	0	0	0	0	0
		1987–88	39	3	11	30	3	10	2	0	1	6	0	0	1	0	0	0	0	0	0	0	0	0	0	0	0	0	0
		1988–89	45	0	15	40	0	14	2	0	0	2	0	0	1	0	1	0	0	0	0	0	0	0	0	0	0	0	0
		1989–90	13	2	3	11	2	2	0	0	0	2	0	1	0	0	0	0	0	0	0	0	0	0	0	0	0	0	0
		1990–91	44	1	15	36	0	11	1	0	1	6	0	3	1	1	0	0	0	0	0	0	0	0	0	0	0	0	0
Francis	Kevin	1997–98	15	0	7	15	0	7	0	0	0	0	0	0	0	0	0	0	0	0	0	0	0	0	0	0	0	0	0
		1998–99	12	8	1	12	6	1	0	2	0	0	0	0	0	0	0	0	0	0	0	0	0	0	0	0	0	0	0
Fraser	John	1956–57	3	0	0	3	0	0	0	0	0	0	0	0	0	0	0	0	0	0	0	0	0	0	0	0	0	0	0
Fursdon	Alan	1967–68	1	1	0	0	1	0	1	0	0	0	0	0	0	0	0	0	0	0	0	0	0	0	0	0	0	0	0
Gabbiadini	Marco	1996–97	5	0	1	5	0	1	0	0	0	0	0	0	0	0	0	0	0	0	0	0	0	0	0	0	0	0	0
Gardner	Lee	1990–91	2	5	0	2	5	0	0	0	0	0	0	0	0	0	0	0	0	0	0	0	0	0	0	0	0	0	0
Gaston	Ray	1968–69	12	1	2	12	0	2	0	1	0	0	0	0	0	0	0	0	0	0	0	0	0	0	0	0	0	0	0
Gemmill	Scot	2005–06	0	1	0	0	1	0	0	0	0	0	0	0	0	0	0	0	0	0	0	0	0	0	0	0	0	0	0
George	Ricky	1966–67	7	0	0	6	0	0	1	0	0	0	0	0	0	0	0	0	0	0	0	0	0	0	0	0	0	0	0
Gerrard	Paul	1998–99	16	0	0	16	0	0	0	0	0	0	0	0	0	0	0	0	0	0	0	0	0	0	0	0	0	0	0
Gibbins	Roger	1975–76	16	3	2	16	3	2	0	0	0	0	0	0	0	0	0	0	0	0	0	0	0	0	0	0	0	0	0
Gibbs	Alan	1957–58	8	0	1	6	0	1	1	0	0	0	0	0	0	0	0	0	0	0	0	0	0	1	0	0	0	0	0
Gibson	Dave	1957–58	39	0	10	33	0	8	4	0	1	0	0	0	0	0	0	0	0	0	0	0	0	2	0	1	0	0	0
		1958–59	44	0	20	30	0	17	6	0	1	0	0	0	0	0	0	0	0	0	0	0	0	1	0	0	7	0	2
		1959–60	14	0	1	13	0	1	0	0	0	0	0	0	0	0	0	0	0	0	0	0	0	1	0	0	0	0	0
Gibson	Stuart	1983–84	0	1	0	0	0	0	0	0	0	0	0	0	0	1	0	0	0	0	0	0	0	0	0	0	0	0	0
Gilchrist	Phil	1994–95	18	0	1	18	0	1	0	0	0	0	0	0	0	0	0	0	0	0	0	0	0	0	0	0	0	0	0
		1995–96	54	0	3	42	0	3	5	0	0	4	0	0	3	0	0	0	0	0	0	0	0	0	0	0	0	0	0
		1996–97	44	0	2	38	0	2	1	0	0	5	0	0	0	0	0	0	0	0	0	0	0	0	0	0	0	0	0
		1997–98	41	4	2	35	4	2	1	0	0	5	0	0	0	0	0	0	0	0	0	0	0	0	0	0	0	0	0
		1998–99	43	0	3	39	0	2	2	0	1	2	0	0	0	0	0	0	0	0	0	0	0	0	0	0	0	0	0
		1999–2000	1	0	0	1	0	0	0	0	0	0	0	0	0	0	0	0	0	0	0	0	0	0	0	0	0	0	0
		2006–07	41	0	1	38	0	1	2	0	0	0	0	0	0	0	0	1	0	0	0	0	0	0	0	0	0	0	0
		2007–08	3	0	0	3	0	0	0	0	0	0	0	0	0	0	0	0	0	0	0	0	0	0	0	0	0	0	0

Surname	Forename	Season	Total			League			FA Cup			FL Cup			Other			FA Trophy			Setanta Sld			SL Cup			SL Inter Zone		
			app	subs	gls	app	subs	gls	app	subs	gls	app	subs	gls	app	subs	gls	app	subs	gls	app	subs	gls	app	subs	gls	app	subs	gls
Gillies	Bill	1955–56	2	0	0	1	0	0	0	0	0	0	0	0	0	0	0	0	0	0	0	0	0	1	0	0	0	0	0
Gladwin	Robin	1968–69	27	0	0	26	0	0	0	0	0	1	0	0	0	0	0	0	0	0	0	0	0	0	0	0	0	0	0
		1969–70	21	0	0	18	0	0	0	0	0	3	0	0	0	0	0	0	0	0	0	0	0	0	0	0	0	0	0
Glass	Jimmy	2000–01	2	0	0	1	0	0	0	0	0	0	0	0	1	0	0	0	0	0	0	0	0	0	0	0	0	0	0
Gnohere	Arthur	2007–08	7	1	0	7	1	0	0	0	0	0	0	0	0	0	0	0	0	0	0	0	0	0	0	0	0	0	0
Goodhind	Warren	2005–06	4	2	0	4	2	0	0	0	0	0	0	0	0	0	0	0	0	0	0	0	0	0	0	0	0	0	0
Gordon	Gavin	2002–03	3	4	1	3	3	1	0	0	0	0	1	0	0	0	0	0	0	0	0	0	0	0	0	0	0	0	0
Gough	Keith	1972–73	18	1	3	14	1	2	2	0	1	0	0	0	2	0	0	0	0	0	0	0	0	0	0	0	0	0	0
		1973–74	15	3	2	14	3	2	0	0	0	1	0	0	0	0	0	0	0	0	0	0	0	0	0	0	0	0	0
		1974–75	4	3	1	4	3	1	0	0	0	0	0	0	0	0	0	0	0	0	0	0	0	0	0	0	0	0	0
Grant	David	1982–83	24	0	1	20	0	1	1	0	0	0	0	0	3	0	0	0	0	0	0	0	0	0	0	0	0	0	0
		1983–84	5	0	0	4	0	0	0	0	0	1	0	0	0	0	0	0	0	0	0	0	0	0	0	0	0	0	0
Gray	Martin	1995–96	6	1	0	6	1	0	0	0	0	0	0	0	0	0	0	0	0	0	0	0	0	0	0	0	0	0	0
		1996–97	49	2	2	41	2	2	1	0	0	7	0	0	0	0	0	0	0	0	0	0	0	0	0	0	0	0	0
		1997–98	30	3	2	28	3	2	1	0	0	1	0	0	0	0	0	0	0	0	0	0	0	0	0	0	0	0	0
		1998–99	43	0	0	40	0	0	2	0	0	1	0	0	0	0	0	0	0	0	0	0	0	0	0	0	0	0	0
		2000–01	1	0	0	1	0	0	0	0	0	0	0	0	0	0	0	0	0	0	0	0	0	0	0	0	0	0	0
Gray	Phil	2000–01	24	2	9	21	2	7	2	0	2	0	0	0	1	0	0	0	0	0	0	0	0	0	0	0	0	0	0
		2001–02	15	7	4	14	7	4	0	0	0	1	0	0	0	0	0	0	0	0	0	0	0	0	0	0	0	0	0
Gray	Stuart	2005–06	11	0	0	10	0	0	0	0	0	1	0	0	0	0	0	0	0	0	0	0	0	0	0	0	0	0	0
Graydon	Ray	1978–79	19	0	5	18	0	5	1	0	0	0	0	0	0	0	0	0	0	0	0	0	0	0	0	0	0	0	0
		1979–80	20	4	5	18	3	5	0	1	0	2	0	0	0	0	0	0	0	0	0	0	0	0	0	0	0	0	0
		1980–81	1	3	0	0	3	0	1	0	0	0	0	0	0	0	0	0	0	0	0	0	0	0	0	0	0	0	0
Grebis	Kristaps	2006–07	3	1	0	3	1	0	0	0	0	0	0	0	0	0	0	0	0	0	0	0	0	0	0	0	0	0	0
Green	Matthew	2007–08	17	4	10	16	4	10	1	0	0	0	0	0	0	0	0	0	0	0	0	0	0	0	0	0	0	0	0
Greenall	Colin	1987–88	12	0	0	12	0	0	0	0	0	0	0	0	0	0	0	0	0	0	0	0	0	0	0	0	0	0	0
		1988–89	44	0	2	40	0	2	1	0	0	2	0	0	1	0	0	0	0	0	0	0	0	0	0	0	0	0	0
		1989–90	18	0	0	15	0	0	0	0	0	2	0	0	1	0	0	0	0	0	0	0	0	0	0	0	0	0	0
Gregory	Pete	1949–50	4	0	0	4	0	0	0	0	0	0	0	0	0	0	0	0	0	0	0	0	0	0	0	0	0	0	0
Grieve	David	1959–60	8	0	4	7	0	4	0	0	0	0	0	0	0	0	0	0	0	0	0	0	0	1	0	0	0	0	0
Griffin	Adam	2005–06	12	1	0	8	1	0	2	0	0	0	0	0	2	0	0	0	0	0	0	0	0	0	0	0	0	0	0
Groves	Richard	2008–09	1	2	0	0	1	0	0	1	0	0	0	0	0	0	0	0	0	0	1	0	0	0	0	0	0	0	0
Guatelli	Andrea	2005–06	4	0	0	4	0	0	0	0	0	0	0	0	0	0	0	0	0	0	0	0	0	0	0	0	0	0	0
Gunn	Andrew	2006–07	1	2	0	1	2	0	0	0	0	0	0	0	0	0	0	0	0	0	0	0	0	0	0	0	0	0	0
Guy	Jamie	2008–09	21	5	5	18	3	2	2	1	1	0	0	0	0	0	0	1	0	2	0	1	0	0	0	0	0	0	0
Guyett	Scott	2001–02	23	2	0	20	2	0	1	0	0	1	0	0	1	0	0	0	0	0	0	0	0	0	0	0	0	0	0
Hackett	Chris	2000–01	11	7	2	10	6	2	1	0	0	0	0	0	0	1	0	0	0	0	0	0	0	0	0	0	0	0	0
		2001–02	5	12	0	5	10	0	0	1	0	0	0	0	0	1	0	0	0	0	0	0	0	0	0	0	0	0	0
		2002–03	2	12	0	1	11	0	0	0	0	0	1	0	1	0	0	0	0	0	0	0	0	0	0	0	0	0	0
		2003–04	7	18	1	6	16	1	0	1	0	0	1	0	1	0	0	0	0	0	0	0	0	0	0	0	0	0	0
		2004–05	31	8	4	31	6	4	0	1	0	0	0	0	0	1	0	0	0	0	0	0	0	0	0	0	0	0	0
		2005–06	23	4	2	19	2	2	2	0	0	0	1	0	2	1	0	0	0	0	0	0	0	0	0	0	0	0	0
Haldane	Lewis	2008–09	40	10	3	34	9	3	4	0	0	0	0	0	0	0	0	1	1	0	1	0	0	0	0	0	0	0	0
Hale	Graham	1949–50	10	0	0	10	0	0	0	0	0	0	0	0	0	0	0	0	0	0	0	0	0	0	0	0	0	0	0

Surname	Forename	Season	Total			League			FA Cup			FL Cup			Other			FA Trophy			Setanta Sld			SL Cup			SL Inter Zone		
			app	subs	gls	app	subs	gls	app	subs	gls	app	subs	gls	app	subs	gls	app	subs	gls	app	subs	gls	app	subs	gls	app	subs	gls
Hale	Ken	1965–66	18	0	3	18	0	3	0	0	0	0	0	0	0	0	0	0	0	0	0	0	0	0	0	0	0	0	0
		1966–67	34	0	5	32	0	5	2	0	0	0	0	0	0	0	0	0	0	0	0	0	0	0	0	0	0	0	0
		1967–68	18	2	5	14	2	5	2	0	0	2	0	0	0	0	0	0	0	0	0	0	0	0	0	0	0	0	0
Hall	Alan	1949–50	1	0	0	1	0	0	0	0	0	0	0	0	0	0	0	0	0	0	0	0	0	0	0	0	0	0	0
		1951–52	11	0	0	8	0	0	1	0	0	0	0	0	0	0	0	0	0	0	0	0	0	2	0	0	0	0	0
		1955–56	1	0	0	1	0	0	0	0	0	0	0	0	0	0	0	0	0	0	0	0	0	0	0	0	0	0	0
		1956–57	17	0	0	15	0	0	0	0	0	0	0	0	0	0	0	0	0	0	0	0	0	2	0	0	0	0	0
Hamilton	Billy	1984–85	31	0	17	23	0	9	2	0	0	6	0	8	0	0	0	0	0	0	0	0	0	0	0	0	0	0	0
		1985–86	8	0	3	8	0	3	0	0	0	0	0	0	0	0	0	0	0	0	0	0	0	0	0	0	0	0	0
		1986–87	2	0	0	1	0	0	0	0	0	1	0	0	0	0	0	0	0	0	0	0	0	0	0	0	0	0	0
Hand	Jamie	2004–05	12	0	2	11	0	1	0	0	0	0	0	0	1	0	1	0	0	0	0	0	0	0	0	0	0	0	0
		2007–08	13	0	0	13	0	0	0	0	0	0	0	0	0	0	0	0	0	0	0	0	0	0	0	0	0	0	0
Hardwick	Steve	1982–83	18	0	0	18	0	0	0	0	0	0	0	0	0	0	0	0	0	0	0	0	0	0	0	0	0	0	0
		1983–84	64	0	0	46	0	0	7	0	0	11	0	0	0	0	0	0	0	0	0	0	0	0	0	0	0	0	0
		1984–85	50	0	0	42	0	0	2	0	0	6	0	0	0	0	0	0	0	0	0	0	0	0	0	0	0	0	0
		1985–86	31	0	0	23	0	0	0	0	0	4	0	0	4	0	0	0	0	0	0	0	0	0	0	0	0	0	0
		1986–87	27	0	0	23	0	0	1	0	0	2	0	0	1	0	0	0	0	0	0	0	0	0	0	0	0	0	0
		1987–88	6	0	0	4	0	0	2	0	0	0	0	0	0	0	0	0	0	0	0	0	0	0	0	0	0	0	0
Hargreaves	Chris	2005–06	38	1	1	34	1	1	3	0	0	0	0	0	1	0	0	0	0	0	0	0	0	0	0	0	0	0	0
		2006–07	36	9	5	32	8	5	2	0	0	0	0	0	0	0	0	2	1	0	0	0	0	0	0	0	0	0	0
Harper	Tony	1955–56	22	0	0	21	0	0	0	0	0	0	0	0	0	0	0	0	0	0	0	0	0	1	0	0	0	0	0
		1956–57	38	0	3	35	0	3	1	0	0	0	0	0	0	0	0	0	0	0	0	0	0	2	0	0	0	0	0
		1957–58	49	0	2	41	0	2	5	0	0	0	0	0	0	0	0	0	0	0	0	0	0	3	0	0	0	0	0
		1958–59	23	0	1	15	0	1	4	0	0	0	0	0	0	0	0	0	0	0	0	0	0	3	0	0	1	0	0
		1959–60	7	0	0	6	0	0	0	0	0	0	0	0	0	0	0	0	0	0	0	0	0	1	0	0	0	0	0
Harrington	Colin	1962–63	6	0	0	6	0	0	0	0	0	0	0	0	0	0	0	0	0	0	0	0	0	0	0	0	0	0	0
		1963–64	51	0	7	43	0	7	7	0	0	1	0	0	0	0	0	0	0	0	0	0	0	0	0	0	0	0	0
		1964–65	43	0	4	40	0	3	0	0	0	3	0	1	0	0	0	0	0	0	0	0	0	0	0	0	0	0	0
		1965–66	39	0	5	36	0	5	2	0	0	1	0	0	0	0	0	0	0	0	0	0	0	0	0	0	0	0	0
		1966–67	43	0	7	39	0	6	3	0	1	1	0	0	0	0	0	0	0	0	0	0	0	0	0	0	0	0	0
		1967–68	19	0	3	18	0	3	0	0	0	1	0	0	0	0	0	0	0	0	0	0	0	0	0	0	0	0	0
		1968–69	38	1	4	35	1	4	2	0	0	1	0	0	0	0	0	0	0	0	0	0	0	0	0	0	0	0	0
		1969–70	13	4	2	11	3	2	2	0	0	0	1	0	0	0	0	0	0	0	0	0	0	0	0	0	0	0	0
		1970–71	2	1	0	2	0	0	0	1	0	0	0	0	0	0	0	0	0	0	0	0	0	0	0	0	0	0	0
Harris	Andy	1991–92	1	0	0	1	0	0	0	0	0	0	0	0	0	0	0	0	0	0	0	0	0	0	0	0	0	0	0
Harris	Bernard	1960–61	4	0	1	4	0	1	0	0	0	0	0	0	0	0	0	0	0	0	0	0	0	0	0	0	0	0	0
Hartland	Mick	1963–64	11	0	3	10	0	3	1	0	0	0	0	0	0	0	0	0	0	0	0	0	0	0	0	0	0	0	0
		1964–65	9	0	3	9	0	3	0	0	0	0	0	0	0	0	0	0	0	0	0	0	0	0	0	0	0	0	0
Hatch	Peter	1968–69	3	2	0	3	2	0	0	0	0	0	0	0	0	0	0	0	0	0	0	0	0	0	0	0	0	0	0
		1969–70	5	1	1	5	1	1	0	0	0	0	0	0	0	0	0	0	0	0	0	0	0	0	0	0	0	0	0
		1971–72	1	0	0	1	0	0	0	0	0	0	0	0	0	0	0	0	0	0	0	0	0	0	0	0	0	0	0
		1972–73	7	0	1	6	0	1	0	0	0	0	0	0	1	0	0	0	0	0	0	0	0	0	0	0	0	0	0
Hatswell	Wayne	2000–01	27	1	0	26	1	0	0	0	0	0	0	0	1	0	0	0	0	0	0	0	0	0	0	0	0	0	0
		2001–02	24	0	0	21	0	0	1	0	0	1	0	0	1	0	0	0	0	0	0	0	0	0	0	0	0	0	0

Surname	Forename	Season	Total			League			FA Cup			FL Cup			Other			FA Trophy			Setanta Sld			SL Cup			SL Inter Zone		
			app	subs	gls	app	subs	gls	app	subs	gls	app	subs	gls	app	subs	gls	app	subs	gls	app	subs	gls	app	subs	gls	app	subs	gls
Havenhand	Keith	1963–64	9	0	1	7	0	1	2	0	0	0	0	0	0	0	0	0	0	0	0	0	0	0	0	0	0	0	0
		1964–65	7	0	3	5	0	2	0	0	0	2	0	1	0	0	0	0	0	0	0	0	0	0	0	0	0	0	0
Haynes	Arthur	1951–52	9	0	2	9	0	2	0	0	0	0	0	0	0	0	0	0	0	0	0	0	0	0	0	0	0	0	0
Heath	Phil	1988–89	10	10	1	8	8	1	0	1	0	1	1	0	1	0	0	0	0	0	0	0	0	0	0	0	0	0	0
		1989–90	19	5	0	16	5	0	2	0	0	0	0	0	1	0	0	0	0	0	0	0	0	0	0	0	0	0	0
Hebberd	Trevor	1981–82	15	0	2	15	0	2	0	0	0	0	0	0	0	0	0	0	0	0	0	0	0	0	0	0	0	0	0
		1982–83	50	0	12	39	0	10	4	0	1	4	0	0	3	0	1	0	0	0	0	0	0	0	0	0	0	0	0
		1983–84	63	0	11	46	0	11	6	0	0	10	0	0	1	0	0	0	0	0	0	0	0	0	0	0	0	0	0
		1984–85	50	0	7	42	0	6	2	0	0	6	0	1	0	0	0	0	0	0	0	0	0	0	0	0	0	0	0
		1985–86	56	0	6	41	0	3	2	0	0	8	0	2	5	0	1	0	0	0	0	0	0	0	0	0	0	0	0
		1986–87	42	0	2	38	0	2	1	0	0	2	0	0	1	0	0	0	0	0	0	0	0	0	0	0	0	0	0
		1987–88	50	0	3	39	0	3	2	0	0	7	0	0	2	0	0	0	0	0	0	0	0	0	0	0	0	0	0
Heron	Brian	1974–75	32	2	7	30	2	7	1	0	0	1	0	0	0	0	0	0	0	0	0	0	0	0	0	0	0	0	0
		1975–76	9	0	2	7	0	1	0	0	0	2	0	1	0	0	0	0	0	0	0	0	0	0	0	0	0	0	0
		1976–77	3	1	0	3	1	0	0	0	0	0	0	0	0	0	0	0	0	0	0	0	0	0	0	0	0	0	0
Higgins	Peter	1962–63	2	0	0	2	0	0	0	0	0	0	0	0	0	0	0	0	0	0	0	0	0	0	0	0	0	0	0
		1963–64	4	0	0	4	0	0	0	0	0	0	0	0	0	0	0	0	0	0	0	0	0	0	0	0	0	0	0
		1965–66	5	0	0	5	0	0	0	0	0	0	0	0	0	0	0	0	0	0	0	0	0	0	0	0	0	0	0
		1966–67	5	0	0	5	0	0	0	0	0	0	0	0	0	0	0	0	0	0	0	0	0	0	0	0	0	0	0
		1967–68	4	0	0	4	0	0	0	0	0	0	0	0	0	0	0	0	0	0	0	0	0	0	0	0	0	0	0
		1968–69	16	5	0	15	5	0	1	0	0	0	0	0	0	0	0	0	0	0	0	0	0	0	0	0	0	0	0
Hill	Charles	1955–56	5	0	0	5	0	0	0	0	0	0	0	0	0	0	0	0	0	0	0	0	0	0	0	0	0	0	0
Hill	Danny	1998–99	1	9	0	1	8	0	0	0	0	0	1	0	0	0	0	0	0	0	0	0	0	0	0	0	0	0	0
Hill	Richard	1987–88	21	12	3	15	9	3	1	1	0	4	1	0	1	1	0	0	0	0	0	0	0	0	0	0	0	0	0
		1988–89	37	8	14	33	6	10	3	0	3	1	1	0	0	1	1	0	0	0	0	0	0	0	0	0	0	0	0
Hinchliffe	Ben	2008–09	4	2	0	4	2	0	0	0	0	0	0	0	0	0	0	0	0	0	0	0	0	0	0	0	0	0	0
Hinshelwood	Paul	1983–84	61	0	1	43	0	0	7	0	0	10	0	1	1	0	0	0	0	0	0	0	0	0	0	0	0	0	0
		1984–85	3	0	0	2	0	0	0	0	0	1	0	0	0	0	0	0	0	0	0	0	0	0	0	0	0	0	0
Hodgson	Gordon	1978–79	32	0	1	31	0	1	1	0	0	0	0	0	0	0	0	0	0	0	0	0	0	0	0	0	0	0	0
		1979–80	38	1	2	35	1	2	1	0	0	2	0	0	0	0	0	0	0	0	0	0	0	0	0	0	0	0	0
Holder	Alan	1958–59	2	0	0	2	0	0	0	0	0	0	0	0	0	0	0	0	0	0	0	0	0	0	0	0	0	0	0
Horsted	Liam	2005–06	1	3	0	1	3	0	0	0	0	0	0	0	0	0	0	0	0	0	0	0	0	0	0	0	0	0	0
Houghton	Bud	1960–61	14	0	13	14	0	13	0	0	0	0	0	0	0	0	0	0	0	0	0	0	0	0	0	0	0	0	0
		1961–62	42	0	43	39	0	39	2	0	3	0	0	0	0	0	0	0	0	0	0	0	0	1	0	1	0	0	0
		1962–63	46	0	18	42	0	16	3	0	2	1	0	0	0	0	0	0	0	0	0	0	0	0	0	0	0	0	0
		1963–64	12	0	1	11	0	1	0	0	0	1	0	0	0	0	0	0	0	0	0	0	0	0	0	0	0	0	0
Houghton	Ray	1985–86	49	0	7	35	0	4	2	0	0	7	0	2	5	0	1	0	0	0	0	0	0	0	0	0	0	0	0
		1986–87	43	0	6	37	0	5	1	0	0	4	0	1	1	0	0	0	0	0	0	0	0	0	0	0	0	0	0
		1987–88	13	0	1	11	0	1	0	0	0	2	0	0	0	0	0	0	0	0	0	0	0	0	0	0	0	0	0
Houseman	Peter	1975–76	40	0	0	37	0	0	1	0	0	2	0	0	0	0	0	0	0	0	0	0	0	0	0	0	0	0	0
		1976–77	32	0	2	28	0	2	2	0	0	2	0	0	0	0	0	0	0	0	0	0	0	0	0	0	0	0	0
Howard	Michael	2007–08	17	0	1	17	0	1	0	0	0	0	0	0	0	0	0	0	0	0	0	0	0	0	0	0	0	0	0
Howlett		1953–54	1	0	0	1	0	0	0	0	0	0	0	0	0	0	0	0	0	0	0	0	0	0	0	0	0	0	0
Howse	Doug	1949–50	7	0	3	7	0	3	0	0	0	0	0	0	0	0	0	0	0	0	0	0	0	0	0	0	0	0	0

Surname	Forename	Season	Total			League			FA Cup			FL Cup			Other			FA Trophy			Setanta Sld			SL Cup			SL Inter Zone		
			app	subs	gls	app	subs	gls	app	subs	gls	app	subs	gls	app	subs	gls	app	subs	gls	app	subs	gls	app	subs	gls	app	subs	gls
Hucker	Peter	1986–87	5	0	0	5	0	0	0	0	0	0	0	0	0	0	0	0	0	0	0	0	0	0	0	0	0	0	0
		1987–88	33	0	0	27	0	0	0	0	0	5	0	0	1	0	0	0	0	0	0	0	0	0	0	0	0	0	0
		1988–89	27	0	0	26	0	0	0	0	0	1	0	0	0	0	0	0	0	0	0	0	0	0	0	0	0	0	0
		1989–90	10	0	0	8	0	0	0	0	0	2	0	0	0	0	0	0	0	0	0	0	0	0	0	0	0	0	0
Hudson	Ernie	1952–53	19	0	0	18	0	0	0	0	0	0	0	0	0	0	0	0	0	0	0	0	0	1	0	0	0	0	0
		1953–54	40	0	1	27	0	1	9	0	0	0	0	0	0	0	0	0	0	0	0	0	0	4	0	0	0	0	0
		1954–55	11	0	0	9	0	0	1	0	0	0	0	0	0	0	0	0	0	0	0	0	0	1	0	0	0	0	0
		1955–56	25	0	0	22	0	0	0	0	0	0	0	0	0	0	0	0	0	0	0	0	0	3	0	0	0	0	0
		1956–57	20	0	0	20	0	0	0	0	0	0	0	0	0	0	0	0	0	0	0	0	0	0	0	0	0	0	0
Hughes	Rob	2005–06	2	3	0	0	3	0	0	0	0	1	0	0	1	0	0	0	0	0	0	0	0	0	0	0	0	0	0
Humpston	Ron	1953–54	1	0	0	1	0	0	0	0	0	0	0	0	0	0	0	0	0	0	0	0	0	0	0	0	0	0	0
		1954–55	4	0	0	4	0	0	0	0	0	0	0	0	0	0	0	0	0	0	0	0	0	0	0	0	0	0	0
Hunt	James	2002–03	44	0	2	39	0	1	2	0	0	3	0	1	0	0	0	0	0	0	0	0	0	0	0	0	0	0	0
		2003–04	38	5	2	36	5	2	1	0	0	1	0	0	0	0	0	0	0	0	0	0	0	0	0	0	0	0	0
Hunter	Roy	2002–03	14	5	1	12	5	1	1	0	0	0	0	0	1	0	0	0	0	0	0	0	0	0	0	0	0	0	0
Husbands	Michael	2008–09	0	2	0	0	2	0	0	0	0	0	0	0	0	0	0	0	0	0	0	0	0	0	0	0	0	0	0
Hutchinson	Eddie	2006–07	10	11	0	8	10	0	1	1	0	0	0	0	0	0	0	1	0	0	0	0	0	0	0	0	0	0	0
		2007–08	26	6	1	22	6	1	2	0	0	0	0	0	0	0	0	2	0	0	0	0	0	0	0	0	0	0	0
		2008–09	18	16	3	12	16	2	2	0	0	0	0	0	0	0	0	2	0	0	1	0	1	0	0	0	0	0	0
Hyde	Steve	1964–65	5	0	0	4	0	0	1	0	0	0	0	0	0	0	0	0	0	0	0	0	0	0	0	0	0	0	0
		1965–66	5	0	0	5	0	0	0	0	0	0	0	0	0	0	0	0	0	0	0	0	0	0	0	0	0	0	0
Hynd	Roger	1975–76	5	0	0	5	0	0	0	0	0	0	0	0	0	0	0	0	0	0	0	0	0	0	0	0	0	0	0
Jackson	Darren	1989–90	1	0	0	1	0	0	0	0	0	0	0	0	0	0	0	0	0	0	0	0	0	0	0	0	0	0	0
		1990–91	6	1	0	4	1	0	0	0	0	2	0	0	0	0	0	0	0	0	0	0	0	0	0	0	0	0	0
		1991–92	6	1	0	4	1	0	2	0	0	0	0	0	0	0	0	0	0	0	0	0	0	0	0	0	0	0	0
		1992–93	1	0	0	1	0	0	0	0	0	0	0	0	0	0	0	0	0	0	0	0	0	0	0	0	0	0	0
		1993–94	1	1	0	1	1	0	0	0	0	0	0	0	0	0	0	0	0	0	0	0	0	0	0	0	0	0	0
Jackson	Elliot	1996–97	3	0	0	3	0	0	0	0	0	0	0	0	0	0	0	0	0	0	0	0	0	0	0	0	0	0	0
		1997–98	6	0	0	3	0	0	0	0	0	3	0	0	0	0	0	0	0	0	0	0	0	0	0	0	0	0	0
		1998–99	4	0	0	1	0	0	3	0	0	0	0	0	0	0	0	0	0	0	0	0	0	0	0	0	0	0	0
Jackson	Fred	1954–55	3	0	0	3	0	0	0	0	0	0	0	0	0	0	0	0	0	0	0	0	0	0	0	0	0	0	0
		1955–56	2	0	0	2	0	0	0	0	0	0	0	0	0	0	0	0	0	0	0	0	0	0	0	0	0	0	0
Jackson	Jimmy	1958–59	43	0	23	28	0	13	6	0	8	0	0	0	0	0	0	0	0	0	0	0	0	3	0	0	6	0	2
Jacques	Tony	1961–62	1	0	0	1	0	0	0	0	0	0	0	0	0	0	0	0	0	0	0	0	0	0	0	0	0	0	0
		1962–63	7	0	0	7	0	0	0	0	0	0	0	0	0	0	0	0	0	0	0	0	0	0	0	0	0	0	0
Jarman	Lee	2000–01	19	5	1	15	5	1	2	0	0	2	0	0	0	0	0	0	0	0	0	0	0	0	0	0	0	0	0
Jeannin	Alex	2007–08	32	1	2	27	1	1	2	0	1	0	0	0	0	0	0	2	0	0	1	0	0	0	0	0	0	0	0
Jefferies	Ray	1951–52	29	0	5	27	0	5	0	0	0	0	0	0	0	0	0	0	0	0	0	0	0	2	0	0	0	0	0
Jeffrey	Billy	1973–74	10	0	1	10	0	1	0	0	0	0	0	0	0	0	0	0	0	0	0	0	0	0	0	0	0	0	0
		1974–75	25	0	1	24	0	1	0	0	0	1	0	0	0	0	0	0	0	0	0	0	0	0	0	0	0	0	0
		1975–76	33	0	4	29	0	2	1	0	0	3	0	2	0	0	0	0	0	0	0	0	0	0	0	0	0	0	0
		1976–77	42	1	8	40	1	8	2	0	0	0	0	0	0	0	0	0	0	0	0	0	0	0	0	0	0	0	0
		1977–78	49	0	3	44	0	3	1	0	0	4	0	0	0	0	0	0	0	0	0	0	0	0	0	0	0	0	0
		1978–79	46	2	1	40	2	1	1	0	0	5	0	0	0	0	0	0	0	0	0	0	0	0	0	0	0	0	0

Surname	Forename	Season	Total app	Total subs	Total gls	League app	League subs	League gls	FA Cup app	FA Cup subs	FA Cup gls	FL Cup app	FL Cup subs	FL Cup gls	Other app	Other subs	Other gls	FA Trophy app	FA Trophy subs	FA Trophy gls	Setanta Sld app	Setanta Sld subs	Setanta Sld gls	SL Cup app	SL Cup subs	SL Cup gls	SL Inter Zone app	SL Inter Zone subs	SL Inter Zone gls
		1979–80	47	0	3	44	0	3	1	0	0	2	0	0	0	0	0	0	0	0	0	0	0	0	0	0	0	0	0
		1980–81	52	0	2	45	0	2	2	0	0	5	0	0	0	0	0	0	0	0	0	0	0	0	0	0	0	0	0
		1981–82	49	0	3	35	0	3	6	0	0	5	0	0	3	0	0	0	0	0	0	0	0	0	0	0	0	0	0
Jemson	Nigel	1996–97	52	0	23	44	0	18	1	0	0	7	0	5	0	0	0	0	0	0	0	0	0	0	0	0	0	0	0
		1997–98	30	0	10	24	0	9	1	0	0	5	0	1	0	0	0	0	0	0	0	0	0	0	0	0	0	0	0
		1999–2000	13	5	0	13	5	0	0	0	0	0	0	0	0	0	0	0	0	0	0	0	0	0	0	0	0	0	0
Jenkins	Alf	1949–50	7	0	1	7	0	1	0	0	0	0	0	0	0	0	0	0	0	0	0	0	0	0	0	0	0	0	0
		1950–51	21	0	0	21	0	0	0	0	0	0	0	0	0	0	0	0	0	0	0	0	0	0	0	0	0	0	0
		1951–52	16	0	1	13	0	1	2	0	0	0	0	0	0	0	0	0	0	0	0	0	0	1	0	0	0	0	0
Johnson	Gavin	2006–07	26	9	2	23	8	1	0	1	1	0	0	0	0	0	0	3	0	0	0	0	0	0	0	0	0	0	0
Johnston	David	1949–50	9	0	1	9	0	1	0	0	0	0	0	0	0	0	0	0	0	0	0	0	0	0	0	0	0	0	0
		1950–51	1	0	1	1	0	1	0	0	0	0	0	0	0	0	0	0	0	0	0	0	0	0	0	0	0	0	0
Johnston	Peter	1953–54	2	0	0	2	0	0	0	0	0	0	0	0	0	0	0	0	0	0	0	0	0	0	0	0	0	0	0
		1954–55	27	0	2	26	0	2	0	0	0	0	0	0	0	0	0	0	0	0	0	0	0	1	0	0	0	0	0
		1955–56	21	0	0	20	0	0	0	0	0	0	0	0	0	0	0	0	0	0	0	0	0	1	0	0	0	0	0
		1956–57	6	0	1	6	0	1	0	0	0	0	0	0	0	0	0	0	0	0	0	0	0	0	0	0	0	0	0
Johnston	Ron	1950–51	13	0	9	10	0	6	2	0	1	0	0	0	0	0	0	0	0	0	0	0	0	1	0	2	0	0	0
Johnstone	Gordon	1961–62	1	0	0	1	0	0	0	0	0	0	0	0	0	0	0	0	0	0	0	0	0	0	0	0	0	0	0
Jones	Davy	1968–69	7	1	0	7	1	0	0	0	0	0	0	0	0	0	0	0	0	0	0	0	0	0	0	0	0	0	0
		1969–70	12	3	1	9	3	0	0	0	0	3	0	1	0	0	0	0	0	0	0	0	0	0	0	0	0	0	0
		1970–71	1	0	0	1	0	0	0	0	0	0	0	0	0	0	0	0	0	0	0	0	0	0	0	0	0	0	0
Jones	GH	1953–54	1	0	0	1	0	0	0	0	0	0	0	0	0	0	0	0	0	0	0	0	0	0	0	0	0	0	0
Jones	Mark	1980–81	37	1	1	35	1	1	0	0	0	2	0	0	0	0	0	0	0	0	0	0	0	0	0	0	0	0	0
		1981–82	33	1	3	20	1	3	5	0	0	5	0	0	3	0	0	0	0	0	0	0	0	0	0	0	0	0	0
		1982–83	21	8	1	19	7	1	0	1	0	1	0	0	1	0	0	0	0	0	0	0	0	0	0	0	0	0	0
		1983–84	14	11	2	13	7	2	0	1	0	1	2	0	0	1	0	0	0	0	0	0	0	0	0	0	0	0	0
		1984–85	11	9	0	10	8	0	0	1	0	1	0	0	0	0	0	0	0	0	0	0	0	0	0	0	0	0	0
		1985–86	4	6	0	4	2	0	0	0	0	0	2	0	0	2	0	0	0	0	0	0	0	0	0	0	0	0	0
Jones	Tony	1959–60	21	0	6	19	0	5	0	0	0	0	0	0	0	0	0	0	0	0	0	0	0	2	0	1	0	0	0
		1960–61	40	0	38	35	0	34	4	0	4	0	0	0	0	0	0	0	0	0	0	0	0	1	0	0	0	0	0
		1961–62	42	0	9	38	0	8	2	0	0	0	0	0	0	0	0	0	0	0	0	0	0	2	0	1	0	0	0
		1962–63	43	0	11	39	0	9	3	0	2	1	0	0	0	0	0	0	0	0	0	0	0	0	0	0	0	0	0
		1963–64	54	0	5	46	0	2	7	0	3	1	0	0	0	0	0	0	0	0	0	0	0	0	0	0	0	0	0
		1964–65	50	0	4	46	0	4	1	0	0	3	0	0	0	0	0	0	0	0	0	0	0	0	0	0	0	0	0
		1965–66	46	0	7	43	0	7	2	0	0	1	0	0	0	0	0	0	0	0	0	0	0	0	0	0	0	0	0
		1966–67	47	0	13	43	0	13	3	0	0	1	0	0	0	0	0	0	0	0	0	0	0	0	0	0	0	0	0
		1967–68	12	1	4	9	0	4	1	1	0	2	0	0	0	0	0	0	0	0	0	0	0	0	0	0	0	0	0
Judge	Alan	1985–86	26	0	0	19	0	0	2	0	0	4	0	0	1	0	0	0	0	0	0	0	0	0	0	0	0	0	0
		1986–87	11	0	0	9	0	0	0	0	0	2	0	0	0	0	0	0	0	0	0	0	0	0	0	0	0	0	0
		1987–88	13	0	0	9	0	0	0	0	0	3	0	0	1	0	0	0	0	0	0	0	0	0	0	0	0	0	0
		1988–89	25	0	0	20	0	0	3	0	0	1	0	0	1	0	0	0	0	0	0	0	0	0	0	0	0	0	0
		1989–90	18	0	0	17	0	0	0	0	0	0	0	0	1	0	0	0	0	0	0	0	0	0	0	0	0	0	0
		1990–91	7	0	0	6	0	0	0	0	0	1	0	0	0	0	0	0	0	0	0	0	0	0	0	0	0	0	0
		2002–03	1	0	0	1	0	0	0	0	0	0	0	0	0	0	0	0	0	0	0	0	0	0	0	0	0	0	0

Surname	Forename	Season	Total			League			FA Cup			FL Cup			Other			FA Trophy			Setanta Sld			SL Cup			SL Inter Zone		
			app	subs	gls	app	subs	gls	app	subs	gls	app	subs	gls	app	subs	gls	app	subs	gls	app	subs	gls	app	subs	gls	app	subs	gls
		2004–05	1	0	0	1	0	0	0	0	0	0	0	0	0	0	0	0	0	0	0	0	0	0	0	0	0	0	0
Karam	Amine	2004–05	0	2	0	0	2	0	0	0	0	0	0	0	0	0	0	0	0	0	0	0	0	0	0	0	0	0	0
Kay	Arthur	1949–50	24	0	8	23	0	6	1	0	2	0	0	0	0	0	0	0	0	0	0	0	0	0	0	0	0	0	0
Kay	Bert	1950–51	20	0	7	17	0	6	2	0	1	0	0	0	0	0	0	0	0	0	0	0	0	1	0	0	0	0	0
Kearns	Mick	1969–70	3	0	0	3	0	0	0	0	0	0	0	0	0	0	0	0	0	0	0	0	0	0	0	0	0	0	0
		1970–71	49	0	0	42	0	0	5	0	0	2	0	0	0	0	0	0	0	0	0	0	0	0	0	0	0	0	0
		1971–72	26	0	0	22	0	0	1	0	0	3	0	0	0	0	0	0	0	0	0	0	0	0	0	0	0	0	0
Kearns	Ollie	1981–82	11	12	4	9	9	4	0	1	0	0	2	0	2	0	0	0	0	0	0	0	0	0	0	0	0	0	0
Kee	Paul	1989–90	23	0	0	21	0	0	2	0	0	0	0	0	0	0	0	0	0	0	0	0	0	0	0	0	0	0	0
		1990–91	16	0	0	13	0	0	0	0	0	3	0	0	0	0	0	0	0	0	0	0	0	0	0	0	0	0	0
		1991–92	9	0	0	8	0	0	0	0	0	1	0	0	0	0	0	0	0	0	0	0	0	0	0	0	0	0	0
		1992–93	16	0	0	11	0	0	0	0	0	3	0	0	2	0	0	0	0	0	0	0	0	0	0	0	0	0	0
		1993–94	4	0	0	3	0	0	0	0	0	0	0	0	1	0	0	0	0	0	0	0	0	0	0	0	0	0	0
Keeble	Matthew	1992–93	1	0	0	1	0	0	0	0	0	0	0	0	0	0	0	0	0	0	0	0	0	0	0	0	0	0	0
Keeley	John	1991–92	6	0	0	6	0	0	0	0	0	0	0	0	0	0	0	0	0	0	0	0	0	0	0	0	0	0	0
Kennett	Josh	2006–07	0	1	0	0	1	0	0	0	0	0	0	0	0	0	0	0	0	0	0	0	0	0	0	0	0	0	0
Kerr	George	1966–67	30	0	5	29	0	4	1	0	1	0	0	0	0	0	0	0	0	0	0	0	0	0	0	0	0	0	0
		1967–68	13	1	1	11	1	1	0	0	0	2	0	0	0	0	0	0	0	0	0	0	0	0	0	0	0	0	0
Key	Lance	1994–95	6	0	0	6	0	0	0	0	0	0	0	0	0	0	0	0	0	0	0	0	0	0	0	0	0	0	0
Killip	John	1955–56	2	0	1	2	0	1	0	0	0	0	0	0	0	0	0	0	0	0	0	0	0	0	0	0	0	0	0
Killock	Shane	2008–09	4	0	0	3	0	0	0	0	0	0	0	0	0	0	0	1	0	0	0	0	0	0	0	0	0	0	0
King	Simon	2000–01	2	0	0	2	0	0	0	0	0	0	0	0	0	0	0	0	0	0	0	0	0	0	0	0	0	0	0
		2001–02	1	1	0	1	1	0	0	0	0	0	0	0	0	0	0	0	0	0	0	0	0	0	0	0	0	0	0
Kingston	Andy	1977–78	26	0	0	26	0	0	0	0	0	0	0	0	0	0	0	0	0	0	0	0	0	0	0	0	0	0	0
		1978–79	4	0	0	3	0	0	0	0	0	1	0	0	0	0	0	0	0	0	0	0	0	0	0	0	0	0	0
		1979–80	8	1	0	6	1	0	0	0	0	2	0	0	0	0	0	0	0	0	0	0	0	0	0	0	0	0	0
		1980–81	10	2	0	8	2	0	1	0	0	1	0	0	0	0	0	0	0	0	0	0	0	0	0	0	0	0	0
		1981–82	3	3	0	1	2	0	0	0	0	0	0	0	2	1	0	0	0	0	0	0	0	0	0	0	0	0	0
Knight	Peter	1960–61	48	0	8	41	0	8	5	0	0	0	0	0	0	0	0	0	0	0	0	0	0	2	0	0	0	0	0
		1961–62	46	0	13	42	0	13	2	0	0	0	0	0	0	0	0	0	0	0	0	0	0	2	0	0	0	0	0
		1962–63	49	0	4	45	0	4	3	0	0	1	0	0	0	0	0	0	0	0	0	0	0	0	0	0	0	0	0
		1963–64	46	0	7	39	0	7	6	0	0	1	0	0	0	0	0	0	0	0	0	0	0	0	0	0	0	0	0
		1964–65	11	0	1	10	0	1	0	0	0	1	0	0	0	0	0	0	0	0	0	0	0	0	0	0	0	0	0
Knight	Richard	1999–2000	12	1	0	12	1	0	0	0	0	0	0	0	0	0	0	0	0	0	0	0	0	0	0	0	0	0	0
		2000–01	37	0	0	33	0	0	2	0	0	2	0	0	0	0	0	0	0	0	0	0	0	0	0	0	0	0	0
		2001–02	3	0	0	3	0	0	0	0	0	0	0	0	0	0	0	0	0	0	0	0	0	0	0	0	0	0	0
Kyle	Maurice	1958–59	17	0	0	15	0	0	0	0	0	0	0	0	0	0	0	0	0	0	0	0	0	0	0	0	2	0	0
		1959–60	37	0	0	33	0	0	2	0	0	0	0	0	0	0	0	0	0	0	0	0	0	2	0	0	0	0	0
		1960–61	44	0	2	37	0	1	5	0	1	0	0	0	0	0	0	0	0	0	0	0	0	2	0	0	0	0	0
		1961–62	44	0	0	41	0	0	2	0	0	0	0	0	0	0	0	0	0	0	0	0	0	1	0	0	0	0	0
		1962–63	49	0	0	45	0	0	3	0	0	1	0	0	0	0	0	0	0	0	0	0	0	0	0	0	0	0	0
		1963–64	53	0	0	45	0	0	7	0	0	1	0	0	0	0	0	0	0	0	0	0	0	0	0	0	0	0	0
		1964–65	50	0	0	46	0	0	1	0	0	3	0	0	0	0	0	0	0	0	0	0	0	0	0	0	0	0	0
		1965–66	34	0	0	33	0	0	0	0	0	1	0	0	0	0	0	0	0	0	0	0	0	0	0	0	0	0	0

Surname	Forename	Season	Total			League			FA Cup			FL Cup			Other			FA Trophy			Setanta Sld			SL Cup			SL Inter Zone		
			app	subs	gls	app	subs	gls	app	subs	gls	app	subs	gls	app	subs	gls	app	subs	gls	app	subs	gls	app	subs	gls	app	subs	gls
		1966–67	46	0	2	42	0	2	3	0	0	1	0	0	0	0	0	0	0	0	0	0	0	0	0	0	0	0	0
		1967–68	44	0	0	40	0	0	1	0	0	3	0	0	0	0	0	0	0	0	0	0	0	0	0	0	0	0	0
		1968–69	15	0	0	13	0	0	2	0	0	0	0	0	0	0	0	0	0	0	0	0	0	0	0	0	0	0	0
		1969–70	15	0	0	11	0	0	0	0	0	4	0	0	0	0	0	0	0	0	0	0	0	0	0	0	0	0	0
Lambert	Jamie	1999–2000	10	6	2	8	5	2	2	1	0	0	0	0	0	0	0	0	0	0	0	0	0	0	0	0	0	0	0
Langan	David	1984–85	47	0	2	39	0	1	2	0	0	6	0	1	0	0	0	0	0	0	0	0	0	0	0	0	0	0	0
		1985–86	40	2	0	32	2	0	0	0	0	5	0	0	3	0	0	0	0	0	0	0	0	0	0	0	0	0	0
		1986–87	45	0	0	39	0	0	1	0	0	4	0	0	1	0	0	0	0	0	0	0	0	0	0	0	0	0	0
		1987–88	2	0	1	2	0	1	0	0	0	0	0	0	0	0	0	0	0	0	0	0	0	0	0	0	0	0	0
Lawrence	George	1981–82	15	0	4	15	0	4	0	0	0	0	0	0	0	0	0	0	0	0	0	0	0	0	0	0	0	0	0
		1982–83	25	0	9	22	0	9	3	0	0	0	0	0	0	0	0	0	0	0	0	0	0	0	0	0	0	0	0
		1983–84	52	0	11	34	0	9	7	0	1	11	0	1	0	0	0	0	0	0	0	0	0	0	0	0	0	0	0
		1984–85	9	0	3	7	0	3	0	0	0	2	0	0	0	0	0	0	0	0	0	0	0	0	0	0	0	0	0
Leach	Brian	1957–58	50	0	7	42	0	7	5	0	0	0	0	0	0	0	0	0	0	0	0	0	0	3	0	0	0	0	0
		1958–59	27	0	3	15	0	1	5	0	2	0	0	0	0	0	0	0	0	0	0	0	0	1	0	0	6	0	0
Ledgister	Joel	2007–08	9	4	0	6	3	0	1	1	0	0	0	0	0	0	0	1	0	0	1	0	0	0	0	0	0	0	0
Lewis	Brian	1969–70	12	0	4	12	0	4	0	0	0	0	0	0	0	0	0	0	0	0	0	0	0	0	0	0	0	0	0
Lewis	Fred	1955–56	19	0	0	16	0	0	0	0	0	0	0	0	0	0	0	0	0	0	0	0	0	3	0	0	0	0	0
Lewis	Mickey	1988–89	40	0	0	36	0	0	3	0	0	0	0	0	1	0	0	0	0	0	0	0	0	0	0	0	0	0	0
		1989–90	50	0	1	45	0	1	2	0	0	2	0	0	1	0	0	0	0	0	0	0	0	0	0	0	0	0	0
		1990–91	40	1	1	34	0	1	0	0	0	5	0	0	1	1	0	0	0	0	0	0	0	0	0	0	0	0	0
		1991–92	45	0	4	40	0	4	2	0	0	2	0	0	1	0	0	0	0	0	0	0	0	0	0	0	0	0	0
		1992–93	47	2	0	40	1	0	2	0	0	3	1	0	2	0	0	0	0	0	0	0	0	0	0	0	0	0	0
		1993–94	53	1	0	46	0	0	3	1	0	2	0	0	2	0	0	0	0	0	0	0	0	0	0	0	0	0	0
		1994–95	34	10	1	30	9	1	0	0	0	1	1	0	3	0	0	0	0	0	0	0	0	0	0	0	0	0	0
		1995–96	5	15	0	5	15	0	0	0	0	0	0	0	0	0	0	0	0	0	0	0	0	0	0	0	0	0	0
		1999–2000	5	3	0	3	2	0	0	0	0	1	0	0	1	1	0	0	0	0	0	0	0	0	0	0	0	0	0
Leworthy	David	1985–86	9	0	4	7	0	4	2	0	0	0	0	0	0	0	0	0	0	0	0	0	0	0	0	0	0	0	0
		1986–87	18	6	4	15	3	3	0	1	0	2	2	0	1	0	1	0	0	0	0	0	0	0	0	0	0	0	0
		1988–89	4	9	1	3	9	1	0	0	0	0	0	0	1	0	0	0	0	0	0	0	0	0	0	0	0	0	0
Light	Jimmy	1972–73	2	0	0	2	0	0	0	0	0	0	0	0	0	0	0	0	0	0	0	0	0	0	0	0	0	0	0
		1973–74	25	0	0	23	0	0	0	0	0	2	0	0	0	0	0	0	0	0	0	0	0	0	0	0	0	0	0
		1974–75	37	0	1	36	0	1	1	0	0	0	0	0	0	0	0	0	0	0	0	0	0	0	0	0	0	0	0
		1975–76	4	0	0	3	0	0	0	0	0	1	0	0	0	0	0	0	0	0	0	0	0	0	0	0	0	0	0
Lilley	Derek	1999–2000	45	10	7	36	8	6	5	0	1	1	2	0	3	0	0	0	0	0	0	0	0	0	0	0	0	0	0
		2000–01	16	5	2	15	4	2	1	0	0	0	1	0	0	0	0	0	0	0	0	0	0	0	0	0	0	0	0
Linighan	Andy	2000–01	14	1	0	12	1	0	2	0	0	0	0	0	0	0	0	0	0	0	0	0	0	0	0	0	0	0	0
Linney	David	1982–83	35	2	0	26	0	0	4	0	0	4	0	0	1	2	0	0	0	0	0	0	0	0	0	0	0	0	0
Lloyd	John	1965–66	12	0	0	12	0	0	0	0	0	0	0	0	0	0	0	0	0	0	0	0	0	0	0	0	0	0	0
		1966–67	19	0	0	19	0	0	0	0	0	0	0	0	0	0	0	0	0	0	0	0	0	0	0	0	0	0	0
		1967–68	28	2	0	27	2	0	0	0	0	1	0	0	0	0	0	0	0	0	0	0	0	0	0	0	0	0	0
		1968–69	11	2	0	10	2	0	0	0	0	1	0	0	0	0	0	0	0	0	0	0	0	0	0	0	0	0	0
Longbottom	Arthur	1963–64	37	0	14	30	0	12	6	0	2	1	0	0	0	0	0	0	0	0	0	0	0	0	0	0	0	0	0
		1964–65	5	0	2	4	0	2	0	0	0	1	0	0	0	0	0	0	0	0	0	0	0	0	0	0	0	0	0

Surname	Forename	Season	Total			League			FA Cup			FL Cup			Other			FA Trophy			Setanta Sld			SL Cup			SL Inter Zone		
			app	subs	gls	app	subs	gls	app	subs	gls	app	subs	gls	app	subs	gls	app	subs	gls	app	subs	gls	app	subs	gls	app	subs	gls
Louis	Jefferson	2002–03	15	24	7	12	21	6	1	2	1	1	1	0	1	0	0	0	0	0	0	0	0	0	0	0	0	0	0
		2003–04	7	16	3	6	14	2	0	1	0	0	1	1	1	0	0	0	0	0	0	0	0	0	0	0	0	0	0
		2004–05	0	1	0	0	1	0	0	0	0	0	0	0	0	0	0	0	0	0	0	0	0	0	0	0	0	0	0
Love	Johnny	1954–55	1	0	0	1	0	0	0	0	0	0	0	0	0	0	0	0	0	0	0	0	0	0	0	0	0	0	0
		1955–56	1	0	1	1	0	1	0	0	0	0	0	0	0	0	0	0	0	0	0	0	0	0	0	0	0	0	0
		1957–58	39	0	7	37	0	7	1	0	0	0	0	0	0	0	0	0	0	0	0	0	0	2	0	0	0	0	0
		1958–59	51	0	9	34	0	6	6	0	1	0	0	0	0	0	0	0	0	0	0	0	0	3	0	0	8	0	2
		1959–60	39	0	6	33	0	6	2	0	0	0	0	0	0	0	0	0	0	0	0	0	0	4	0	0	0	0	0
		1960–61	41	0	8	35	0	6	5	0	2	0	0	0	0	0	0	0	0	0	0	0	0	1	0	0	0	0	0
		1961–62	47	0	9	43	0	9	2	0	0	0	0	0	0	0	0	0	0	0	0	0	0	2	0	0	0	0	0
		1962–63	25	0	5	23	0	5	1	0	0	1	0	0	0	0	0	0	0	0	0	0	0	0	0	0	0	0	0
		1963–64	2	0	0	2	0	0	0	0	0	0	0	0	0	0	0	0	0	0	0	0	0	0	0	0	0	0	0
Lowe	Nick	1972–73	8	1	0	6	0	0	0	0	0	0	0	0	2	1	0	0	0	0	0	0	0	0	0	0	0	0	0
		1973–74	10	0	0	8	0	0	0	0	0	2	0	0	0	0	0	0	0	0	0	0	0	0	0	0	0	0	0
		1974–75	9	0	0	8	0	0	1	0	0	0	0	0	0	0	0	0	0	0	0	0	0	0	0	0	0	0	0
		1975–76	38	0	2	35	0	1	1	0	0	2	0	1	0	0	0	0	0	0	0	0	0	0	0	0	0	0	0
		1976–77	14	0	2	14	0	2	0	0	0	0	0	0	0	0	0	0	0	0	0	0	0	0	0	0	0	0	0
Lucas	Dick	1967–68	2	0	0	2	0	0	0	0	0	0	0	0	0	0	0	0	0	0	0	0	0	0	0	0	0	0	0
		1968–69	8	1	0	8	1	0	0	0	0	0	0	0	0	0	0	0	0	0	0	0	0	0	0	0	0	0	0
		1969–70	49	0	0	41	0	0	2	0	0	6	0	0	0	0	0	0	0	0	0	0	0	0	0	0	0	0	0
		1970–71	49	0	3	42	0	1	5	0	1	2	0	1	0	0	0	0	0	0	0	0	0	0	0	0	0	0	0
		1971–72	35	0	1	33	0	1	0	0	0	2	0	0	0	0	0	0	0	0	0	0	0	0	0	0	0	0	0
		1972–73	49	0	0	40	0	0	2	0	0	3	0	0	4	0	0	0	0	0	0	0	0	0	0	0	0	0	0
		1973–74	20	0	0	19	0	0	1	0	0	0	0	0	0	0	0	0	0	0	0	0	0	0	0	0	0	0	0
		1974–75	6	0	0	5	0	0	0	0	0	1	0	0	0	0	0	0	0	0	0	0	0	0	0	0	0	0	0
Luke	George	1960–61	21	0	9	17	0	8	4	0	1	0	0	0	0	0	0	0	0	0	0	0	0	0	0	0	0	0	0
		1961–62	3	0	0	2	0	0	0	0	0	0	0	0	0	0	0	0	0	0	0	0	0	1	0	0	0	0	0
Lundin	Pål	1998–99	7	0	0	7	0	0	0	0	0	0	0	0	0	0	0	0	0	0	0	0	0	0	0	0	0	0	0
		1999–2000	29	1	0	21	1	0	4	0	0	0	0	0	4	0	0	0	0	0	0	0	0	0	0	0	0	0	0
Lythgoe	Phil	1980–81	26	2	5	21	2	3	2	0	0	3	0	2	0	0	0	0	0	0	0	0	0	0	0	0	0	0	0
		1981–82	5	3	0	2	3	0	2	0	0	1	0	0	0	0	0	0	0	0	0	0	0	0	0	0	0	0	0
Mackay	Dave	2004–05	47	0	0	44	0	0	1	0	0	1	0	0	1	0	0	0	0	0	0	0	0	0	0	0	0	0	0
Maddison	Lee	2001–02	11	0	0	11	0	0	0	0	0	0	0	0	0	0	0	0	0	0	0	0	0	0	0	0	0	0	0
Magilton	Jim	1990–91	45	0	10	37	0	6	2	0	1	3	0	1	3	0	2	0	0	0	0	0	0	0	0	0	0	0	0
		1991–92	48	0	13	44	0	12	1	0	1	2	0	0	1	0	0	0	0	0	0	0	0	0	0	0	0	0	0
		1992–93	45	0	13	40	0	11	2	0	1	2	0	0	1	0	1	0	0	0	0	0	0	0	0	0	0	0	0
		1993–94	35	0	6	29	0	5	3	0	1	2	0	0	1	0	0	0	0	0	0	0	0	0	0	0	0	0	0
Mansell	Lee	2005–06	51	0	2	44	0	1	4	0	0	1	0	0	2	0	1	0	0	0	0	0	0	0	0	0	0	0	0
Mansell	Ray	1949–50	2	0	1	1	0	1	0	0	0	0	0	0	0	0	0	0	0	0	0	0	0	1	0	0	0	0	0
Marsh	Simon	1994–95	13	0	0	8	0	0	1	0	0	2	0	0	2	0	0	0	0	0	0	0	0	0	0	0	0	0	0
		1995–96	3	5	0	2	3	0	1	0	0	0	2	0	0	0	0	0	0	0	0	0	0	0	0	0	0	0	0
		1996–97	6	2	1	6	2	1	0	0	0	0	0	0	0	0	0	0	0	0	0	0	0	0	0	0	0	0	0
		1997–98	15	1	0	13	1	0	0	0	0	2	0	0	0	0	0	0	0	0	0	0	0	0	0	0	0	0	0
		1998–99	22	1	2	20	1	2	0	0	0	2	0	0	0	0	0	0	0	0	0	0	0	0	0	0	0	0	0

Surname	Forename	Season	Total			League			FA Cup			FL Cup			Other			FA Trophy			Setanta Sld			SL Cup			SL Inter Zone		
			app	subs	gls	app	subs	gls	app	subs	gls	app	subs	gls	app	subs	gls	app	subs	gls	app	subs	gls	app	subs	gls	app	subs	gls
Maskell	Dennis	1952–53	19	0	3	12	0	3	3	0	0	0	0	0	0	0	0	0	0	0	0	0	0	4	0	0	0	0	0
		1953–54	28	0	3	17	0	2	8	0	1	0	0	0	0	0	0	0	0	0	0	0	0	3	0	0	0	0	0
Massey	Stuart	1994–95	26	2	1	20	2	0	1	0	0	4	0	1	1	0	0	0	0	0	0	0	0	0	0	0	0	0	0
		1995–96	43	2	8	33	2	4	6	0	4	2	0	0	2	0	0	0	0	0	0	0	0	0	0	0	0	0	0
		1996–97	18	18	3	15	14	3	0	1	0	3	3	0	0	0	0	0	0	0	0	0	0	0	0	0	0	0	0
		1997–98	15	4	1	14	3	1	1	0	0	0	1	0	0	0	0	0	0	0	0	0	0	0	0	0	0	0	0
Mathers	David	1959–60	37	0	1	34	0	0	2	0	1	0	0	0	0	0	0	0	0	0	0	0	0	1	0	0	0	0	0
		1960–61	19	0	0	13	0	0	4	0	0	0	0	0	0	0	0	0	0	0	0	0	0	2	0	0	0	0	0
McAllister	Craig	2007–08	9	8	2	9	8	2	0	0	0	0	0	0	0	0	0	0	0	0	0	0	0	0	0	0	0	0	0
McCaldon	Ian	2001–02	31	0	0	28	0	0	1	0	0	1	0	0	1	0	0	0	0	0	0	0	0	0	0	0	0	0	0
McCall	Tony	1957–58	29	0	9	22	0	7	4	0	2	0	0	0	0	0	0	0	0	0	0	0	0	3	0	0	0	0	0
McCarthy	Paul	2002–03	6	0	1	6	0	1	0	0	0	0	0	0	0	0	0	0	0	0	0	0	0	0	0	0	0	0	0
		2003–04	28	1	2	28	1	2	0	0	0	0	0	0	0	0	0	0	0	0	0	0	0	0	0	0	0	0	0
McClaren	Steve	1989–90	20	6	0	17	5	0	2	0	0	1	0	0	0	1	0	0	0	0	0	0	0	0	0	0	0	0	0
		1990–91	9	1	0	6	1	0	1	0	0	1	0	0	1	0	0	0	0	0	0	0	0	0	0	0	0	0	0
		1991–92	4	0	0	4	0	0	0	0	0	0	0	0	0	0	0	0	0	0	0	0	0	0	0	0	0	0	0
McCulloch	Andy	1974–75	30	0	8	29	0	8	0	0	0	1	0	0	0	0	0	0	0	0	0	0	0	0	0	0	0	0	0
		1975–76	13	0	1	12	0	1	1	0	0	0	0	0	0	0	0	0	0	0	0	0	0	0	0	0	0	0	0
McDermott	Brian	1984–85	16	4	3	14	4	2	2	0	1	0	0	0	0	0	0	0	0	0	0	0	0	0	0	0	0	0	0
		1985–86	2	2	0	2	2	0	0	0	0	0	0	0	0	0	0	0	0	0	0	0	0	0	0	0	0	0	0
McDonagh	James	1987–88	1	0	0	0	0	0	0	0	0	0	0	0	1	0	0	0	0	0	0	0	0	0	0	0	0	0	0
McDonald	Bobby	1983–84	57	0	11	39	0	4	7	0	4	10	0	3	1	0	0	0	0	0	0	0	0	0	0	0	0	0	0
		1984–85	41	0	7	34	0	7	2	0	0	5	0	0	0	0	0	0	0	0	0	0	0	0	0	0	0	0	0
		1985–86	17	1	3	14	0	3	0	0	0	1	0	0	2	1	0	0	0	0	0	0	0	0	0	0	0	0	0
		1986–87	8	1	0	6	1	0	1	0	0	0	0	0	1	0	0	0	0	0	0	0	0	0	0	0	0	0	0
McDonald	Colin	1950–51	23	0	0	23	0	0	0	0	0	0	0	0	0	0	0	0	0	0	0	0	0	0	0	0	0	0	0
		1951–52	14	0	0	7	0	0	4	0	0	0	0	0	0	0	0	0	0	0	0	0	0	3	0	0	0	0	0
McDonald	Gordon	1958–59	25	0	0	14	0	0	4	0	0	0	0	0	0	0	0	0	0	0	0	0	0	2	0	0	5	0	0
		1959–60	5	0	0	4	0	0	0	0	0	0	0	0	0	0	0	0	0	0	0	0	0	1	0	0	0	0	0
McGarrity	Tom	1953–54	13	0	5	11	0	3	2	0	2	0	0	0	0	0	0	0	0	0	0	0	0	0	0	0	0	0	0
McGowan	Neil	1999–2000	19	8	0	15	5	0	2	1	0	0	0	0	2	2	0	0	0	0	0	0	0	0	0	0	0	0	0
		2000–01	12	0	0	11	0	0	0	0	0	1	0	0	0	0	0	0	0	0	0	0	0	0	0	0	0	0	0
McGrogan	Hugh	1974–75	7	2	1	7	2	1	0	0	0	0	0	0	0	0	0	0	0	0	0	0	0	0	0	0	0	0	0
		1975–76	7	6	2	6	6	2	0	0	0	1	0	0	0	0	0	0	0	0	0	0	0	0	0	0	0	0	0
		1976–77	28	6	1	24	6	1	2	0	0	2	0	0	0	0	0	0	0	0	0	0	0	0	0	0	0	0	0
		1977–78	30	6	4	27	5	2	0	1	0	3	0	2	0	0	0	0	0	0	0	0	0	0	0	0	0	0	0
		1978–79	26	3	4	21	3	4	0	0	0	5	0	0	0	0	0	0	0	0	0	0	0	0	0	0	0	0	0
		1979–80	17	3	3	16	3	3	1	0	0	0	0	0	0	0	0	0	0	0	0	0	0	0	0	0	0	0	0
McGuckin	Ian	2000–01	6	1	0	6	1	0	0	0	0	0	0	0	0	0	0	0	0	0	0	0	0	0	0	0	0	0	0
McIlvenny	Eddie	1957–58	23	0	0	21	0	0	1	0	0	0	0	0	0	0	0	0	0	0	0	0	0	1	0	0	0	0	0
		1958–59	16	0	0	8	0	0	3	0	0	0	0	0	0	0	0	0	0	0	0	0	0	3	0	0	2	0	0
McIness	George	1959–60	8	0	2	6	0	2	0	0	0	0	0	0	0	0	0	0	0	0	0	0	0	2	0	0	0	0	0
McIntosh	Ian	1960–61	48	0	18	41	0	17	5	0	1	0	0	0	0	0	0	0	0	0	0	0	0	2	0	0	0	0	0
		1961–62	11	0	1	9	0	1	2	0	0	0	0	0	0	0	0	0	0	0	0	0	0	0	0	0	0	0	0

Surname	Forename	Season	Total			League			FA Cup			FL Cup			Other			FA Trophy			Setanta Sld			SL Cup			SL Inter Zone		
			app	subs	gls	app	subs	gls	app	subs	gls	app	subs	gls	app	subs	gls	app	subs	gls	app	subs	gls	app	subs	gls	app	subs	gls
McIntosh	Malcolm	1978–79	26	0	0	23	0	0	0	0	0	3	0	0	0	0	0	0	0	0	0	0	0	0	0	0	0	0	0
		1979–80	23	4	0	21	3	0	1	0	0	1	1	0	0	0	0	0	0	0	0	0	0	0	0	0	0	0	0
		1980–81	10	0	0	9	0	0	1	0	0	0	0	0	0	0	0	0	0	0	0	0	0	0	0	0	0	0	0
		1982–83	2	0	0	2	0	0	0	0	0	0	0	0	0	0	0	0	0	0	0	0	0	0	0	0	0	0	0
McKeown	Joe	1951–52	13	0	6	13	0	6	0	0	0	0	0	0	0	0	0	0	0	0	0	0	0	0	0	0	0	0	0
McLain	Tom	1956–57	24	0	6	21	0	6	1	0	0	0	0	0	0	0	0	0	0	0	0	0	0	2	0	0	0	0	0
McLaughlin	Bob	1959–60	1	0	0	0	0	0	0	0	0	0	0	0	0	0	0	0	0	0	0	0	0	1	0	0	0	0	0
McNiven	Scott	2002–03	50	0	1	44	0	1	3	0	0	3	0	0	0	0	0	0	0	0	0	0	0	0	0	0	0	0	0
		2003–04	45	0	0	41	0	0	1	0	0	2	0	0	1	0	0	0	0	0	0	0	0	0	0	0	0	0	0
McPhee	Doug	1949–50	20	0	7	20	0	7	0	0	0	0	0	0	0	0	0	0	0	0	0	0	0	0	0	0	0	0	0
Medlock	Owen	1959–60	24	0	0	23	0	0	0	0	0	0	0	0	0	0	0	0	0	0	0	0	0	1	0	0	0	0	0
		1960–61	49	0	0	42	0	0	5	0	0	0	0	0	0	0	0	0	0	0	0	0	0	2	0	0	0	0	0
		1961–62	37	0	0	33	0	0	2	0	0	0	0	0	0	0	0	0	0	0	0	0	0	2	0	0	0	0	0
		1962–63	23	0	0	19	0	0	3	0	0	1	0	0	0	0	0	0	0	0	0	0	0	0	0	0	0	0	0
Melville	Andy	1990–91	57	0	4	46	0	3	2	0	0	6	0	1	3	0	0	0	0	0	0	0	0	0	0	0	0	0	0
		1991–92	50	0	5	45	0	4	2	0	0	2	0	0	1	0	1	0	0	0	0	0	0	0	0	0	0	0	0
		1992–93	52	0	6	44	0	6	2	0	0	4	0	0	2	0	0	0	0	0	0	0	0	0	0	0	0	0	0
Middleton	Jimmy	1953–54	2	0	1	1	0	0	1	0	1	0	0	0	0	0	0	0	0	0	0	0	0	0	0	0	0	0	0
Mike	Leon	2000–01	1	2	0	1	2	0	0	0	0	0	0	0	0	0	0	0	0	0	0	0	0	0	0	0	0	0	0
Milkins	John	1974–75	29	0	0	28	0	0	0	0	0	1	0	0	0	0	0	0	0	0	0	0	0	0	0	0	0	0	0
		1975–76	4	0	0	3	0	0	0	0	0	1	0	0	0	0	0	0	0	0	0	0	0	0	0	0	0	0	0
		1976–77	9	0	0	7	0	0	2	0	0	0	0	0	0	0	0	0	0	0	0	0	0	0	0	0	0	0	0
		1977–78	8	0	0	8	0	0	0	0	0	0	0	0	0	0	0	0	0	0	0	0	0	0	0	0	0	0	0
		1978–79	7	0	0	7	0	0	0	0	0	0	0	0	0	0	0	0	0	0	0	0	0	0	0	0	0	0	0
Milliner	John	1953–54	1	0	0	1	0	0	0	0	0	0	0	0	0	0	0	0	0	0	0	0	0	0	0	0	0	0	0
Mills	Norman	1952–53	50	0	22	39	0	15	5	0	3	0	0	0	0	0	0	0	0	0	0	0	0	6	0	4	0	0	0
		1953–54	23	0	12	18	0	10	1	0	1	0	0	0	0	0	0	0	0	0	0	0	0	4	0	1	0	0	0
Mitchell	Bobbie	1952–53	35	0	17	30	0	14	2	0	3	0	0	0	0	0	0	0	0	0	0	0	0	3	0	0	0	0	0
		1953–54	9	0	4	6	0	3	1	0	0	0	0	0	0	0	0	0	0	0	0	0	0	2	0	1	0	0	0
Molyneaux	Lee	2004–05	7	10	0	6	10	0	0	0	0	0	0	0	1	0	0	0	0	0	0	0	0	0	0	0	0	0	0
Monk	Garry	2000–01	5	0	0	5	0	0	0	0	0	0	0	0	0	0	0	0	0	0	0	0	0	0	0	0	0	0	0
Moody	Paul	1993–94	15	0	8	15	0	8	0	0	0	0	0	0	0	0	0	0	0	0	0	0	0	0	0	0	0	0	0
		1994–95	40	7	24	34	7	21	1	0	0	4	0	1	1	0	2	0	0	0	0	0	0	0	0	0	0	0	0
		1995–96	41	12	24	30	12	17	6	0	5	3	0	1	2	0	1	0	0	0	0	0	0	0	0	0	0	0	0
		1996–97	22	24	6	19	19	4	0	1	0	3	4	2	0	0	0	0	0	0	0	0	0	0	0	0	0	0	0
		2001–02	30	6	13	29	6	13	1	0	0	0	0	0	0	0	0	0	0	0	0	0	0	0	0	0	0	0	0
Mooney	Tommy	2004–05	45	0	15	42	0	15	1	0	0	1	0	0	1	0	0	0	0	0	0	0	0	0	0	0	0	0	0
Morgan	Danny	2004–05	0	4	0	0	3	0	0	0	0	0	1	0	0	0	0	0	0	0	0	0	0	0	0	0	0	0	0
		2005–06	2	2	1	1	2	1	0	0	0	1	0	0	0	0	0	0	0	0	0	0	0	0	0	0	0	0	0
Morley	David	2001–02	16	2	3	16	2	3	0	0	0	0	0	0	0	0	0	0	0	0	0	0	0	0	0	0	0	0	0
Morris	Mike	1964–65	32	0	3	29	0	3	1	0	0	2	0	0	0	0	0	0	0	0	0	0	0	0	0	0	0	0	0
		1965–66	27	0	5	27	0	5	0	0	0	0	0	0	0	0	0	0	0	0	0	0	0	0	0	0	0	0	0
		1966–67	35	1	7	33	1	7	1	0	0	1	0	0	0	0	0	0	0	0	0	0	0	0	0	0	0	0	0
Mulgrew	Andy	1955–56	8	0	1	5	0	1	0	0	0	0	0	0	0	0	0	0	0	0	0	0	0	3	0	0	0	0	0

Surname	Forename	Season	Total			League			FA Cup			FL Cup			Other			FA Trophy			Setanta Sld			SL Cup			SL Inter Zone		
			app	subs	gls	app	subs	gls	app	subs	gls	app	subs	gls	app	subs	gls	app	subs	gls	app	subs	gls	app	subs	gls	app	subs	gls
Mumford	Percy	1954–55	1	0	0	1	0	0	0	0	0	0	0	0	0	0	0	0	0	0	0	0	0	0	0	0	0	0	0
Munro	Kevin	1960–61	1	0	0	1	0	0	0	0	0	0	0	0	0	0	0	0	0	0	0	0	0	0	0	0	0	0	0
Murphy	Matt	1992–93	2	0	0	2	0	0	0	0	0	0	0	0	0	0	0	0	0	0	0	0	0	0	0	0	0	0	0
		1994–95	18	7	8	17	5	7	0	0	0	0	0	0	1	2	1	0	0	0	0	0	0	0	0	0	0	0	0
		1995–96	19	26	8	13	21	5	2	2	0	2	2	1	2	1	2	0	0	0	0	0	0	0	0	0	0	0	0
		1996–97	5	28	3	5	24	3	0	1	0	0	3	0	0	0	0	0	0	0	0	0	0	0	0	0	0	0	0
		1997–98	15	17	3	15	14	2	0	0	0	0	3	1	0	0	0	0	0	0	0	0	0	0	0	0	0	0	0
		1998–99	38	10	8	33	10	4	3	0	2	2	0	2	0	0	0	0	0	0	0	0	0	0	0	0	0	0	0
		1999–2000	58	0	17	46	0	11	5	0	3	3	0	1	4	0	2	0	0	0	0	0	0	0	0	0	0	0	0
		2000–01	41	3	8	37	3	6	2	0	1	1	0	1	1	0	0	0	0	0	0	0	0	0	0	0	0	0	0
Murray	Adam	2007–08	21	0	3	21	0	3	0	0	0	0	0	0	0	0	0	0	0	0	0	0	0	0	0	0	0	0	0
		2008–09	50	1	7	45	1	7	4	0	0	0	0	0	0	0	0	1	0	0	0	0	0	0	0	0	0	0	0
Murray	Tom	1955–56	14	0	2	12	0	1	1	0	1	0	0	0	0	0	0	0	0	0	0	0	0	1	0	0	0	0	0
Mustoe	Robbie	1986–87	2	1	0	2	1	0	0	0	0	0	0	0	0	0	0	0	0	0	0	0	0	0	0	0	0	0	0
		1987–88	13	5	0	12	5	0	0	0	0	0	0	0	1	0	0	0	0	0	0	0	0	0	0	0	0	0	0
		1988–89	33	5	3	28	5	3	2	0	0	2	0	0	1	0	0	0	0	0	0	0	0	0	0	0	0	0	0
		1989–90	37	2	7	36	2	7	0	0	0	0	0	0	1	0	0	0	0	0	0	0	0	0	0	0	0	0	0
Muttock	Jon	1989–90	1	0	0	1	0	0	0	0	0	0	0	0	0	0	0	0	0	0	0	0	0	0	0	0	0	0	0
		1992–93	14	2	0	12	2	0	0	0	0	1	0	0	1	0	0	0	0	0	0	0	0	0	0	0	0	0	0
		1993–94	2	1	0	1	0	0	0	0	0	0	0	0	1	1	0	0	0	0	0	0	0	0	0	0	0	0	0
Nelthorpe	Craig	2008–09	14	2	2	14	2	2	0	0	0	0	0	0	0	0	0	0	0	0	0	0	0	0	0	0	0	0	0
Newton	Eddie	1999–2000	7	0	0	7	0	0	0	0	0	0	0	0	0	0	0	0	0	0	0	0	0	0	0	0	0	0	0
Nicklas	Charlie	1954–55	14	0	4	13	0	4	0	0	0	0	0	0	0	0	0	0	0	0	0	0	0	1	0	0	0	0	0
Nielson	Bill	1955–56	5	0	1	5	0	1	0	0	0	0	0	0	0	0	0	0	0	0	0	0	0	0	0	0	0	0	0
Nogan	Lee	1987–88	2	2	0	2	1	0	0	0	0	0	0	0	0	1	0	0	0	0	0	0	0	0	0	0	0	0	0
		1988–89	2	1	0	2	1	0	0	0	0	0	0	0	0	0	0	0	0	0	0	0	0	0	0	0	0	0	0
		1989–90	2	3	0	2	2	0	0	1	0	0	0	0	0	0	0	0	0	0	0	0	0	0	0	0	0	0	0
		1990–91	36	4	7	29	3	5	2	0	1	2	1	0	3	0	1	0	0	0	0	0	0	0	0	0	0	0	0
		1991–92	25	0	5	22	0	5	0	0	0	2	0	0	1	0	0	0	0	0	0	0	0	0	0	0	0	0	0
Norris	Eddie	1957–58	1	0	0	1	0	0	0	0	0	0	0	0	0	0	0	0	0	0	0	0	0	0	0	0	0	0	0
N'Toya	Tcham	2005–06	7	1	4	7	1	4	0	0	0	0	0	0	0	0	0	0	0	0	0	0	0	0	0	0	0	0	0
Nugent	Cliff	1949–50	36	0	6	36	0	6	0	0	0	0	0	0	0	0	0	0	0	0	0	0	0	0	0	0	0	0	0
		1950–51	32	0	9	29	0	7	2	0	2	0	0	0	0	0	0	0	0	0	0	0	0	1	0	0	0	0	0
Odell	Bob	1956–57	35	0	1	32	0	1	1	0	0	0	0	0	0	0	0	0	0	0	0	0	0	2	0	0	0	0	0
		1957–58	30	0	2	22	0	2	5	0	0	0	0	0	0	0	0	0	0	0	0	0	0	3	0	0	0	0	0
Odhiambo-Anaclet	Eddie	2006–07	48	4	4	43	3	4	2	0	0	0	0	0	0	0	0	3	1	0	0	0	0	0	0	0	0	0	0
		2007–08	31	2	2	30	1	1	1	1	1	0	0	0	0	0	0	0	0	0	0	0	0	0	0	0	0	0	0
O'Dowd	Adrian	1979–80	6	2	1	6	2	1	0	0	0	0	0	0	0	0	0	0	0	0	0	0	0	0	0	0	0	0	0
		1980–81	3	0	0	2	0	0	0	0	0	1	0	0	0	0	0	0	0	0	0	0	0	0	0	0	0	0	0
Odubade	Yemi	2005–06	4	4	1	4	4	1	0	0	0	0	0	0	0	0	0	0	0	0	0	0	0	0	0	0	0	0	0
		2006–07	26	26	12	21	25	12	1	1	0	0	0	0	0	0	0	4	0	0	0	0	0	0	0	0	0	0	0
		2007–08	33	15	11	28	13	10	3	1	1	0	0	0	0	0	0	1	1	0	1	0	0	0	0	0	0	0	0
		2008–09	24	26	7	21	22	6	1	3	1	0	0	0	0	0	0	1	1	0	1	0	0	0	0	0	0	0	0
Oldfield	David	2002–03	23	10	3	19	9	2	2	0	1	2	0	0	0	1	0	0	0	0	0	0	0	0	0	0	0	0	0

Surname	Forename	Season	Total			League			FA Cup			FL Cup			Other			FA Trophy			Setanta Sld			SL Cup			SL Inter Zone		
			app	subs	gls	app	subs	gls	app	subs	gls	app	subs	gls	app	subs	gls	app	subs	gls	app	subs	gls	app	subs	gls	app	subs	gls
		2003–04	1	3	0	1	2	0	0	0	0	0	1	0	0	0	0	0	0	0	0	0	0	0	0	0	0	0	0
Oldham	Eric	1958–59	3	0	0	1	0	0	2	0	0	0	0	0	0	0	0	0	0	0	0	0	0	0	0	0	0	0	0
Omoyinmi	Manny	2000–01	19	9	3	16	8	3	0	1	0	2	0	0	1	0	0	0	0	0	0	0	0	0	0	0	0	0	0
		2001–02	13	12	3	11	12	3	1	0	0	0	0	0	1	0	0	0	0	0	0	0	0	0	0	0	0	0	0
		2002–03	4	16	3	4	13	3	0	1	0	0	2	0	0	0	0	0	0	0	0	0	0	0	0	0	0	0	0
		2003–04	1	3	0	1	2	0	0	0	0	0	0	0	0	1	0	0	0	0	0	0	0	0	0	0	0	0	0
Osbourne	Karleigh	2008–09	6	0	0	6	0	0	0	0	0	0	0	0	0	0	0	0	0	0	0	0	0	0	0	0	0	0	0
O'Sullivan	Cyril	1951–52	2	0	0	1	0	0	0	0	0	0	0	0	0	0	0	0	0	0	0	0	0	1	0	0	0	0	0
Otter	Peter	1954–55	5	0	0	5	0	0	0	0	0	0	0	0	0	0	0	0	0	0	0	0	0	0	0	0	0	0	0
		1955–56	26	0	0	23	0	0	1	0	0	0	0	0	0	0	0	0	0	0	0	0	0	2	0	0	0	0	0
		1956–57	1	0	0	1	0	0	0	0	0	0	0	0	0	0	0	0	0	0	0	0	0	0	0	0	0	0	0
		1957–58	17	0	0	12	0	0	4	0	0	0	0	0	0	0	0	0	0	0	0	0	0	1	0	0	0	0	0
		1958–59	9	0	0	7	0	0	0	0	0	0	0	0	0	0	0	0	0	0	0	0	0	0	0	0	2	0	0
Page	Malcolm	1980–81	7	0	1	7	0	1	0	0	0	0	0	0	0	0	0	0	0	0	0	0	0	0	0	0	0	0	0
		1981–82	11	0	0	7	0	0	0	0	0	1	0	0	3	0	0	0	0	0	0	0	0	0	0	0	0	0	0
Parker	Bernard	1953–54	10	0	0	9	0	0	0	0	0	0	0	0	0	0	0	0	0	0	0	0	0	1	0	0	0	0	0
		1954–55	19	0	0	16	0	0	0	0	0	0	0	0	0	0	0	0	0	0	0	0	0	3	0	0	0	0	0
		1956–57	2	0	0	2	0	0	0	0	0	0	0	0	0	0	0	0	0	0	0	0	0	0	0	0	0	0	0
Parker	Terry	2004–05	6	3	0	6	2	0	0	0	0	0	1	0	0	0	0	0	0	0	0	0	0	0	0	0	0	0	0
Parks	Tony	1986–87	5	0	0	5	0	0	0	0	0	0	0	0	0	0	0	0	0	0	0	0	0	0	0	0	0	0	0
Parsons	Roy	1956–57	9	0	0	9	0	0	0	0	0	0	0	0	0	0	0	0	0	0	0	0	0	0	0	0	0	0	0
Paton	Danny	1964–65	2	0	1	2	0	1	0	0	0	0	0	0	0	0	0	0	0	0	0	0	0	0	0	0	0	0	0
Patterson	Darren	2000–01	18	0	1	18	0	1	0	0	0	0	0	0	0	0	0	0	0	0	0	0	0	0	0	0	0	0	0
		2001–02	2	0	0	2	0	0	0	0	0	0	0	0	0	0	0	0	0	0	0	0	0	0	0	0	0	0	0
Peart	Bob	1952–53	9	0	6	8	0	5	0	0	0	0	0	0	0	0	0	0	0	0	0	0	0	1	0	1	0	0	0
		1953–54	29	0	9	20	0	3	7	0	4	0	0	0	0	0	0	0	0	0	0	0	0	2	0	2	0	0	0
Pembery	Gordan	1957–58	18	0	0	16	0	0	0	0	0	0	0	0	0	0	0	0	0	0	0	0	0	2	0	0	0	0	0
Penney	David	1989–90	23	9	2	20	9	2	1	0	0	2	0	0	0	0	0	0	0	0	0	0	0	0	0	0	0	0	0
		1990–91	4	8	1	3	6	1	0	0	0	1	1	0	0	1	0	0	0	0	0	0	0	0	0	0	0	0	0
		1991–92	20	6	5	17	6	4	1	0	1	1	0	0	1	0	0	0	0	0	0	0	0	0	0	0	0	0	0
		1992–93	29	11	6	23	10	6	0	1	0	4	0	0	2	0	0	0	0	0	0	0	0	0	0	0	0	0	0
		1993–94	15	4	2	13	3	2	0	1	0	2	0	0	0	0	0	0	0	0	0	0	0	0	0	0	0	0	0
Perryman	Steve	1985–86	9	0	0	9	0	0	0	0	0	0	0	0	0	0	0	0	0	0	0	0	0	0	0	0	0	0	0
		1986–87	8	0	0	8	0	0	0	0	0	0	0	0	0	0	0	0	0	0	0	0	0	0	0	0	0	0	0
Peters	Peter	1957–58	7	0	0	7	0	0	0	0	0	0	0	0	0	0	0	0	0	0	0	0	0	0	0	0	0	0	0
		1958–59	10	0	0	9	0	0	1	0	0	0	0	0	0	0	0	0	0	0	0	0	0	0	0	0	0	0	0
		1959–60	5	0	0	5	0	0	0	0	0	0	0	0	0	0	0	0	0	0	0	0	0	0	0	0	0	0	0
Pettefer	Carl	2006–07	39	6	1	34	5	1	2	0	0	0	0	0	0	0	0	3	1	0	0	0	0	0	0	0	0	0	0
		2007–08	19	9	0	15	8	0	1	1	0	0	0	0	0	0	0	2	0	0	1	0	0	0	0	0	0	0	0
Phillips	Jimmy	1988–89	50	0	3	45	0	3	3	0	0	1	0	0	1	0	0	0	0	0	0	0	0	0	0	0	0	0	0
		1989–90	39	0	4	34	0	3	2	0	0	2	0	0	1	0	1	0	0	0	0	0	0	0	0	0	0	0	0
Phillips	Les	1983–84	2	4	0	2	4	0	0	0	0	0	0	0	0	0	0	0	0	0	0	0	0	0	0	0	0	0	0
		1984–85	2	2	0	2	1	0	0	0	0	0	1	0	0	0	0	0	0	0	0	0	0	0	0	0	0	0	0
		1985–86	41	1	5	28	0	2	2	0	0	7	1	3	4	0	0	0	0	0	0	0	0	0	0	0	0	0	0

Surname	Forename	Season	Total			League			FA Cup			FL Cup			Other			FA Trophy			Setanta Sld			SL Cup			SL Inter Zone		
			app	subs	gls	app	subs	gls	app	subs	gls	app	subs	gls	app	subs	gls	app	subs	gls	app	subs	gls	app	subs	gls	app	subs	gls
		1986–87	37	2	0	33	2	0	0	0	0	4	0	0	0	0	0	0	0	0	0	0	0	0	0	0	0	0	0
		1987–88	39	1	5	29	1	4	2	0	0	7	0	1	1	0	0	0	0	0	0	0	0	0	0	0	0	0	0
		1988–89	28	1	4	25	1	4	1	0	0	2	0	0	0	0	0	0	0	0	0	0	0	0	0	0	0	0	0
		1989–90	6	2	0	6	2	0	0	0	0	0	0	0	0	0	0	0	0	0	0	0	0	0	0	0	0	0	0
		1990–91	33	1	1	24	1	1	2	0	0	4	0	0	3	0	0	0	0	0	0	0	0	0	0	0	0	0	0
		1991–92	8	0	0	7	0	0	0	0	0	1	0	0	0	0	0	0	0	0	0	0	0	0	0	0	0	0	0
		1992–93	12	2	0	9	2	0	0	0	0	2	0	0	1	0	0	0	0	0	0	0	0	0	0	0	0	0	0
Phillips	Lionel	1955–56	24	0	12	22	0	10	0	0	0	0	0	0	0	0	0	0	0	0	0	0	0	2	0	2	0	0	0
		1956–57	25	0	11	21	0	11	2	0	0	0	0	0	0	0	0	0	0	0	0	0	0	2	0	0	0	0	0
Pitt	Courtney	2003–04	5	3	0	5	3	0	0	0	0	0	0	0	0	0	0	0	0	0	0	0	0	0	0	0	0	0	0
Potter	Tom	1952–53	22	0	0	19	0	0	0	0	0	0	0	0	0	0	0	0	0	0	0	0	0	3	0	0	0	0	0
		1953–54	5	0	0	4	0	0	1	0	0	0	0	0	0	0	0	0	0	0	0	0	0	0	0	0	0	0	0
Potts	Henry	1949–50	3	0	0	3	0	0	0	0	0	0	0	0	0	0	0	0	0	0	0	0	0	0	0	0	0	0	0
Powell	Paul	1995–96	1	4	0	1	2	0	0	0	0	0	0	0	0	2	0	0	0	0	0	0	0	0	0	0	0	0	0
		1997–98	12	10	1	11	9	1	1	0	0	0	1	0	0	0	0	0	0	0	0	0	0	0	0	0	0	0	0
		1998–99	43	5	3	40	4	3	3	0	0	0	1	0	0	0	0	0	0	0	0	0	0	0	0	0	0	0	0
		1999–2000	49	2	12	39	1	6	3	1	3	3	0	0	4	0	3	0	0	0	0	0	0	0	0	0	0	0	0
		2000–01	16	5	1	15	5	1	0	0	0	1	0	0	0	0	0	0	0	0	0	0	0	0	0	0	0	0	0
		2001–02	34	4	4	33	3	4	1	0	0	0	0	0	0	1	0	0	0	0	0	0	0	0	0	0	0	0	0
		2002–03	5	12	2	4	10	2	0	0	0	0	2	0	1	0	0	0	0	0	0	0	0	0	0	0	0	0	0
Puffett	Geoff	1959–60	1	0	0	1	0	0	0	0	0	0	0	0	0	0	0	0	0	0	0	0	0	0	0	0	0	0	0
Purdie	Jon	1988–89	7	7	0	5	6	0	1	0	0	1	1	0	0	0	0	0	0	0	0	0	0	0	0	0	0	0	0
Purse	Darren	1996–97	30	7	1	25	6	1	1	0	0	4	1	0	0	0	0	0	0	0	0	0	0	0	0	0	0	0	0
		1997–98	34	1	6	27	1	4	1	0	0	6	0	2	0	0	0	0	0	0	0	0	0	0	0	0	0	0	0
Quartermain	Pat	1955–56	35	0	0	32	0	0	1	0	0	0	0	0	0	0	0	0	0	0	0	0	0	2	0	0	0	0	0
		1956–57	6	0	0	6	0	0	0	0	0	0	0	0	0	0	0	0	0	0	0	0	0	0	0	0	0	0	0
		1957–58	21	0	0	19	0	0	1	0	0	0	0	0	0	0	0	0	0	0	0	0	0	1	0	0	0	0	0
		1958–59	2	0	0	2	0	0	0	0	0	0	0	0	0	0	0	0	0	0	0	0	0	0	0	0	0	0	0
		1959–60	1	0	0	1	0	0	0	0	0	0	0	0	0	0	0	0	0	0	0	0	0	0	0	0	0	0	0
		1960–61	3	0	0	3	0	0	0	0	0	0	0	0	0	0	0	0	0	0	0	0	0	0	0	0	0	0	0
		1961–62	31	0	0	30	0	0	0	0	0	0	0	0	0	0	0	0	0	0	0	0	0	1	0	0	0	0	0
		1962–63	50	0	0	46	0	0	3	0	0	1	0	0	0	0	0	0	0	0	0	0	0	0	0	0	0	0	0
		1963–64	46	0	0	39	0	0	6	0	0	1	0	0	0	0	0	0	0	0	0	0	0	0	0	0	0	0	0
		1964–65	48	0	0	44	0	0	1	0	0	3	0	0	0	0	0	0	0	0	0	0	0	0	0	0	0	0	0
		1965–66	37	0	0	34	0	0	2	0	0	1	0	0	0	0	0	0	0	0	0	0	0	0	0	0	0	0	0
		1966–67	25	1	0	21	1	0	3	0	0	1	0	0	0	0	0	0	0	0	0	0	0	0	0	0	0	0	0
Quinlan	Eddie	1949–50	1	0	0	1	0	0	0	0	0	0	0	0	0	0	0	0	0	0	0	0	0	0	0	0	0	0	0
		1950–51	2	0	1	2	0	1	0	0	0	0	0	0	0	0	0	0	0	0	0	0	0	0	0	0	0	0	0
Quinn	Barry	2003–04	5	1	0	5	1	0	0	0	0	0	0	0	0	0	0	0	0	0	0	0	0	0	0	0	0	0	0
		2004–05	35	2	0	34	2	0	1	0	0	0	0	0	0	0	0	0	0	0	0	0	0	0	0	0	0	0	0
		2005–06	52	0	2	44	0	2	4	0	0	1	0	0	3	0	0	0	0	0	0	0	0	0	0	0	0	0	0
		2006–07	48	1	1	42	1	1	2	0	0	0	0	0	0	0	0	4	0	0	0	0	0	0	0	0	0	0	0
		2007–08	49	0	1	42	0	1	4	0	0	0	0	0	0	0	0	2	0	0	1	0	0	0	0	0	0	0	0
		2008–09	15	0	2	15	0	2	0	0	0	0	0	0	0	0	0	0	0	0	0	0	0	0	0	0	0	0	0

Surname	Forename	Season	Total			League			FA Cup			FL Cup			Other			FA Trophy			Setanta Sld			SL Cup			SL Inter Zone		
			app	subs	gls	app	subs	gls	app	subs	gls	app	subs	gls	app	subs	gls	app	subs	gls	app	subs	gls	app	subs	gls	app	subs	gls
Quinn	Robert	2000–01	12	1	2	12	1	2	0	0	0	0	0	0	0	0	0	0	0	0	0	0	0	0	0	0	0	0	0
		2001–02	11	5	0	11	5	0	0	0	0	0	0	0	0	0	0	0	0	0	0	0	0	0	0	0	0	0	0
Ramshaw	Frank	1950–51	46	0	0	43	0	0	2	0	0	0	0	0	0	0	0	0	0	0	0	0	0	1	0	0	0	0	0
		1951–52	48	0	0	41	0	0	4	0	0	0	0	0	0	0	0	0	0	0	0	0	0	3	0	0	0	0	0
		1952–53	53	0	0	41	0	0	5	0	0	0	0	0	0	0	0	0	0	0	0	0	0	7	0	0	0	0	0
		1953–54	51	0	0	35	0	0	8	0	0	0	0	0	0	0	0	0	0	0	0	0	0	8	0	0	0	0	0
		1954–55	37	0	0	34	0	0	2	0	0	0	0	0	0	0	0	0	0	0	0	0	0	1	0	0	0	0	0
		1955–56	47	0	1	41	0	1	1	0	0	0	0	0	0	0	0	0	0	0	0	0	0	5	0	0	0	0	0
		1956–57	45	0	0	42	0	0	1	0	0	0	0	0	0	0	0	0	0	0	0	0	0	2	0	0	0	0	0
		1957–58	34	0	0	28	0	0	3	0	0	0	0	0	0	0	0	0	0	0	0	0	0	3	0	0	0	0	0
Raponi	Juan Pablo	2004–05	5	5	0	5	5	0	0	0	0	0	0	0	0	0	0	0	0	0	0	0	0	0	0	0	0	0	0
Rawle	Mark	2003–04	11	22	8	10	21	8	0	1	0	1	0	0	0	0	0	0	0	0	0	0	0	0	0	0	0	0	0
		2004–05	0	6	0	0	6	0	0	0	0	0	0	0	0	0	0	0	0	0	0	0	0	0	0	0	0	0	0
Reck	Sean	1986–87	6	3	0	4	2	0	1	0	0	1	1	0	0	0	0	0	0	0	0	0	0	0	0	0	0	0	0
		1987–88	1	1	0	1	1	0	0	0	0	0	0	0	0	0	0	0	0	0	0	0	0	0	0	0	0	0	0
		1988–89	6	0	0	6	0	0	0	0	0	0	0	0	0	0	0	0	0	0	0	0	0	0	0	0	0	0	0
Reece	Paul	1992–93	38	0	0	35	0	0	2	0	0	1	0	0	0	0	0	0	0	0	0	0	0	0	0	0	0	0	0
		1993–94	7	0	0	4	0	0	0	0	0	2	0	0	1	0	0	0	0	0	0	0	0	0	0	0	0	0	0
Rees	Billy	1955–56	19	0	16	17	0	15	0	0	0	0	0	0	0	0	0	0	0	0	0	0	0	2	0	1	0	0	0
		1956–57	36	0	10	33	0	10	1	0	0	0	0	0	0	0	0	0	0	0	0	0	0	2	0	0	0	0	0
		1957–58	39	0	15	33	0	13	5	0	1	0	0	0	0	0	0	0	0	0	0	0	0	1	0	1	0	0	0
		1958–59	37	0	19	22	0	14	5	0	2	0	0	0	0	0	0	0	0	0	0	0	0	3	0	0	7	0	2
Reid	Levi	2008–09	6	4	2	6	4	2	0	0	0	0	0	0	0	0	0	0	0	0	0	0	0	0	0	0	0	0	0
Remy	Christophe	1997–98	17	4	0	13	3	0	0	1	0	4	0	0	0	0	0	0	0	0	0	0	0	0	0	0	0	0	0
		1998–99	11	4	1	10	2	1	1	2	0	0	0	0	0	0	0	0	0	0	0	0	0	0	0	0	0	0	0
Rhoades-Brown	Peter	1983–84	22	1	4	19	1	4	2	0	0	0	0	0	1	0	0	0	0	0	0	0	0	0	0	0	0	0	0
		1984–85	27	8	5	23	8	4	0	0	0	4	0	1	0	0	0	0	0	0	0	0	0	0	0	0	0	0	0
		1985–86	20	7	4	12	5	3	0	1	0	5	0	1	3	1	0	0	0	0	0	0	0	0	0	0	0	0	0
		1986–87	3	3	0	3	3	0	0	0	0	0	0	0	0	0	0	0	0	0	0	0	0	0	0	0	0	0	0
		1987–88	34	8	3	25	6	2	2	0	1	5	2	0	2	0	0	0	0	0	0	0	0	0	0	0	0	0	0
		1988–89	7	2	0	5	2	0	0	0	0	2	0	0	0	0	0	0	0	0	0	0	0	0	0	0	0	0	0
Rhodes	Jordan	2007–08	4	1	2	3	1	0	1	0	2	0	0	0	0	0	0	0	0	0	0	0	0	0	0	0	0	0	0
Richards	Justin	2007–08	10	5	1	10	5	1	0	0	0	0	0	0	0	0	0	0	0	0	0	0	0	0	0	0	0	0	0
Richards	Mike	1962–63	27	0	0	27	0	0	0	0	0	0	0	0	0	0	0	0	0	0	0	0	0	0	0	0	0	0	0
		1963–64	3	0	0	3	0	0	0	0	0	0	0	0	0	0	0	0	0	0	0	0	0	0	0	0	0	0	0
Richardson	Jon	2000–01	46	0	2	41	0	2	2	0	0	2	0	0	1	0	0	0	0	0	0	0	0	0	0	0	0	0	0
		2001–02	16	2	0	16	2	0	0	0	0	0	0	0	0	0	0	0	0	0	0	0	0	0	0	0	0	0	0
Ricketts	Sam	2000–01	14	1	0	13	1	0	0	0	0	0	0	0	1	0	0	0	0	0	0	0	0	0	0	0	0	0	0
		2001–02	21	10	1	19	10	1	0	0	0	1	0	0	1	0	0	0	0	0	0	0	0	0	0	0	0	0	0
Rivers	Ron	1959–60	6	0	5	5	0	4	1	0	1	0	0	0	0	0	0	0	0	0	0	0	0	0	0	0	0	0	0
Roach	Neville	2005–06	2	5	0	1	5	0	0	0	0	0	0	0	1	0	0	0	0	0	0	0	0	0	0	0	0	0	0
Roberts	Dave	1970–71	14	1	0	14	1	0	0	0	0	0	0	0	0	0	0	0	0	0	0	0	0	0	0	0	0	0	0
		1971–72	36	0	2	33	0	2	0	0	0	3	0	0	0	0	0	0	0	0	0	0	0	0	0	0	0	0	0
		1972–73	50	0	4	42	0	3	2	0	0	3	0	0	3	0	1	0	0	0	0	0	0	0	0	0	0	0	0

Surname	Forename	Season	Total			League			FA Cup			FL Cup			Other			FA Trophy			Setanta Sld			SL Cup			SL Inter Zone		
			app	subs	gls	app	subs	gls	app	subs	gls	app	subs	gls	app	subs	gls	app	subs	gls	app	subs	gls	app	subs	gls	app	subs	gls
		1973–74	45	0	1	42	0	1	1	0	0	2	0	0	0	0	0	0	0	0	0	0	0	0	0	0	0	0	0
		1974–75	30	0	1	29	0	1	0	0	0	1	0	0	0	0	0	0	0	0	0	0	0	0	0	0	0	0	0
Roberts	Peter	1949–50	24	0	10	21	0	8	2	0	2	0	0	0	0	0	0	0	0	0	0	0	0	1	0	0	0	0	0
Robertson	John	2000–01	41	3	0	37	3	0	1	0	0	2	0	0	1	0	0	0	0	0	0	0	0	0	0	0	0	0	0
Robinson	Les	1989–90	1	0	0	1	0	0	0	0	0	0	0	0	0	0	0	0	0	0	0	0	0	0	0	0	0	0	0
		1990–91	54	0	0	43	0	0	2	0	0	6	0	0	3	0	0	0	0	0	0	0	0	0	0	0	0	0	0
		1991–92	30	0	0	27	0	0	0	0	0	2	0	0	1	0	0	0	0	0	0	0	0	0	0	0	0	0	0
		1992–93	15	2	0	14	2	0	1	0	0	0	0	0	0	0	0	0	0	0	0	0	0	0	0	0	0	0	0
		1993–94	43	0	2	36	0	2	4	0	0	2	0	0	1	0	0	0	0	0	0	0	0	0	0	0	0	0	0
		1994–95	55	0	1	46	0	0	1	0	0	4	0	1	4	0	0	0	0	0	0	0	0	0	0	0	0	0	0
		1995–96	50	1	1	40	1	0	4	0	0	4	0	1	2	0	0	0	0	0	0	0	0	0	0	0	0	0	0
		1996–97	44	2	0	36	2	0	1	0	0	7	0	0	0	0	0	0	0	0	0	0	0	0	0	0	0	0	0
		1997–98	53	0	2	46	0	1	1	0	0	6	0	1	0	0	0	0	0	0	0	0	0	0	0	0	0	0	0
		1998–99	49	0	0	44	0	0	3	0	0	2	0	0	0	0	0	0	0	0	0	0	0	0	0	0	0	0	0
		1999–2000	59	0	0	46	0	0	5	0	0	3	0	0	5	0	0	0	0	0	0	0	0	0	0	0	0	0	0
Robinson	Marvin	2006–07	13	11	4	10	11	3	0	0	0	0	0	0	0	0	0	3	0	1	0	0	0	0	0	0	0	0	0
		2007–08	2	7	0	2	7	0	0	0	0	0	0	0	0	0	0	0	0	0	0	0	0	0	0	0	0	0	0
Robinson	Matthew	2002–03	48	1	1	42	0	1	3	0	0	3	0	0	0	1	0	0	0	0	0	0	0	0	0	0	0	0	0
		2003–04	43	0	1	40	0	1	0	0	0	2	0	0	1	0	0	0	0	0	0	0	0	0	0	0	0	0	0
		2004–05	48	0	2	45	0	2	1	0	0	1	0	0	1	0	0	0	0	0	0	0	0	0	0	0	0	0	0
		2005–06	52	0	0	44	0	0	4	0	0	1	0	0	3	0	0	0	0	0	0	0	0	0	0	0	0	0	0
Rogan	Anton	1993–94	36	0	2	29	0	2	4	0	0	2	0	0	1	0	0	0	0	0	0	0	0	0	0	0	0	0	0
		1994–95	30	2	1	27	2	1	0	0	0	2	0	0	1	0	0	0	0	0	0	0	0	0	0	0	0	0	0
Roget	Leo	2004–05	36	0	2	35	0	2	0	0	0	1	0	0	0	0	0	0	0	0	0	0	0	0	0	0	0	0	0
		2005–06	40	1	3	32	1	2	4	0	0	1	0	0	3	0	1	0	0	0	0	0	0	0	0	0	0	0	0
Rose	Andrew	1998–99	2	3	0	1	3	0	0	0	0	1	0	0	0	0	0	0	0	0	0	0	0	0	0	0	0	0	0
Rose	Daniel	2006–07	23	1	2	21	1	1	0	0	0	0	0	0	0	0	0	2	0	1	0	0	0	0	0	0	0	0	0
		2007–08	6	16	0	4	15	0	1	0	0	0	0	0	0	0	0	0	1	0	1	0	0	0	0	0	0	0	0
Rouse	Vic	1963–64	21	0	0	20	0	0	0	0	0	1	0	0	0	0	0	0	0	0	0	0	0	0	0	0	0	0	0
		1964–65	2	0	0	2	0	0	0	0	0	0	0	0	0	0	0	0	0	0	0	0	0	0	0	0	0	0	0
Rowden	Len	1956–57	1	0	2	1	0	2	0	0	0	0	0	0	0	0	0	0	0	0	0	0	0	0	0	0	0	0	0
Rowstron	Bill	1950–51	28	0	24	28	0	24	0	0	0	0	0	0	0	0	0	0	0	0	0	0	0	0	0	0	0	0	0
		1951–52	20	0	7	16	0	5	2	0	1	0	0	0	0	0	0	0	0	0	0	0	0	2	0	1	0	0	0
Rush	David	1994–95	25	15	9	22	12	9	0	1	0	0	1	0	3	1	0	0	0	0	0	0	0	0	0	0	0	0	0
		1995–96	49	4	14	41	2	11	2	2	1	3	0	0	3	0	2	0	0	0	0	0	0	0	0	0	0	0	0
		1996–97	4	13	1	4	11	1	0	0	0	0	2	0	0	0	0	0	0	0	0	0	0	0	0	0	0	0	0
Russell	Craig	1999–2000	5	1	0	5	1	0	0	0	0	0	0	0	0	0	0	0	0	0	0	0	0	0	0	0	0	0	0
Sabin	Eric	2005–06	34	1	9	28	1	7	4	0	1	0	0	0	2	0	1	0	0	0	0	0	0	0	0	0	0	0	0
Salmon	Mike	1998–99	1	0	0	1	0	0	0	0	0	0	0	0	0	0	0	0	0	0	0	0	0	0	0	0	0	0	0
Sandwith	Kevin	2008–09	9	3	1	9	3	1	0	0	0	0	0	0	0	0	0	0	0	0	0	0	0	0	0	0	0	0	0
Santos	Georges	2006–07	5	0	0	3	0	0	0	0	0	0	0	0	0	0	0	2	0	0	0	0	0	0	0	0	0	0	0
Sappleton	Ricky	2008–09	2	3	1	1	3	1	0	0	0	0	0	0	0	0	0	1	0	0	0	0	0	0	0	0	0	0	0
Saunders	Carl	1993–94	2	3	0	2	3	0	0	0	0	0	0	0	0	0	0	0	0	0	0	0	0	0	0	0	0	0	0
Saunders	Dean	1986–87	12	0	6	12	0	6	0	0	0	0	0	0	0	0	0	0	0	0	0	0	0	0	0	0	0	0	0

Surname	Forename	Season	Total			League			FA Cup			FL Cup			Other			FA Trophy			Setanta Sld			SL Cup			SL Inter Zone		
			app	subs	gls	app	subs	gls	app	subs	gls	app	subs	gls	app	subs	gls	app	subs	gls	app	subs	gls	app	subs	gls	app	subs	gls
		1987–88	46	3	21	35	2	12	2	0	2	7	1	6	2	0	1	0	0	0	0	0	0	0	0	0	0	0	0
		1988–89	12	0	6	10	0	4	0	0	0	2	0	2	0	0	0	0	0	0	0	0	0	0	0	0	0	0	0
Savage	David	2001–02	45	0	1	42	0	1	1	0	0	1	0	0	1	0	0	0	0	0	0	0	0	0	0	0	0	0	0
		2002–03	50	0	4	43	0	4	3	0	0	3	0	0	1	0	0	0	0	0	0	0	0	0	0	0	0	0	0
Scott	Andy	2000–01	21	0	5	21	0	5	0	0	0	0	0	0	0	0	0	0	0	0	0	0	0	0	0	0	0	0	0
		2001–02	26	5	9	25	5	8	0	0	0	1	0	1	0	0	0	0	0	0	0	0	0	0	0	0	0	0	0
		2002–03	31	10	11	29	9	11	0	1	0	2	0	0	0	0	0	0	0	0	0	0	0	0	0	0	0	0	0
		2003–04	2	5	0	2	4	0	0	0	0	0	1	0	0	0	0	0	0	0	0	0	0	0	0	0	0	0	0
Scott	David	1949–50	25	0	0	25	0	0	0	0	0	0	0	0	0	0	0	0	0	0	0	0	0	0	0	0	0	0	0
		1950–51	7	0	0	4	0	0	2	0	0	0	0	0	0	0	0	0	0	0	0	0	0	1	0	0	0	0	0
Seacole	Jason	1976–77	19	5	3	19	5	3	0	0	0	0	0	0	0	0	0	0	0	0	0	0	0	0	0	0	0	0	0
		1977–78	36	7	10	33	5	9	1	0	0	2	2	1	0	0	0	0	0	0	0	0	0	0	0	0	0	0	0
		1978–79	49	2	11	45	1	8	1	0	1	3	1	2	0	0	0	0	0	0	0	0	0	0	0	0	0	0	0
		1980–81	5	5	1	3	5	1	0	0	0	2	0	0	0	0	0	0	0	0	0	0	0	0	0	0	0	0	0
		1981–82	4	2	1	4	0	1	0	0	0	0	0	0	0	2	0	0	0	0	0	0	0	0	0	0	0	0	0
Selby	Peter	1959–60	2	0	0	2	0	0	0	0	0	0	0	0	0	0	0	0	0	0	0	0	0	0	0	0	0	0	0
Semple	Ryan	2007–08	0	1	0	0	1	0	0	0	0	0	0	0	0	0	0	0	0	0	0	0	0	0	0	0	0	0	0
Sharman	Pete	1949–50	25	0	0	22	0	0	2	0	0	0	0	0	0	0	0	0	0	0	0	0	0	1	0	0	0	0	0
Shaw	Paul	2007–08	9	0	2	9	0	2	0	0	0	0	0	0	0	0	0	0	0	0	0	0	0	0	0	0	0	0	0
Shelton	Gary	1987–88	42	1	2	32	0	0	2	0	0	7	1	2	1	0	0	0	0	0	0	0	0	0	0	0	0	0	0
		1988–89	31	5	1	28	5	1	3	0	0	0	0	0	0	0	0	0	0	0	0	0	0	0	0	0	0	0	0
Shepheard	Jon	1999–2000	3	1	0	1	1	0	0	0	0	0	0	0	2	0	0	0	0	0	0	0	0	0	0	0	0	0	0
		2000–01	7	0	1	5	0	0	0	0	0	2	0	1	0	0	0	0	0	0	0	0	0	0	0	0	0	0	0
Shepherd	John	1969–70	14	2	1	9	2	1	2	0	0	3	0	0	0	0	0	0	0	0	0	0	0	0	0	0	0	0	0
Sheridan	Jimmy	1951–52	37	0	4	29	0	2	4	0	2	0	0	0	0	0	0	0	0	0	0	0	0	4	0	0	0	0	0
Sherratt	Brian	1965–66	11	0	0	11	0	0	0	0	0	0	0	0	0	0	0	0	0	0	0	0	0	0	0	0	0	0	0
		1966–67	24	0	0	22	0	0	2	0	0	0	0	0	0	0	0	0	0	0	0	0	0	0	0	0	0	0	0
		1967–68	17	0	0	11	0	0	3	0	0	3	0	0	0	0	0	0	0	0	0	0	0	0	0	0	0	0	0
Shields	Jimmy	1958–59	2	0	1	2	0	1	0	0	0	0	0	0	0	0	0	0	0	0	0	0	0	0	0	0	0	0	0
		1959–60	3	0	0	2	0	0	0	0	0	0	0	0	0	0	0	0	0	0	0	0	0	1	0	0	0	0	0
Shipperley	Keith	1959–60	2	0	0	2	0	0	0	0	0	0	0	0	0	0	0	0	0	0	0	0	0	0	0	0	0	0	0
		1960–61	8	0	3	7	0	3	0	0	0	0	0	0	0	0	0	0	0	0	0	0	0	1	0	0	0	0	0
Shotton	Malcolm	1980–81	44	0	7	38	0	5	1	0	0	5	0	2	0	0	0	0	0	0	0	0	0	0	0	0	0	0	0
		1981–82	53	0	4	40	0	4	5	0	0	5	0	0	3	0	0	0	0	0	0	0	0	0	0	0	0	0	0
		1982–83	57	0	2	46	0	1	4	0	1	4	0	0	3	0	0	0	0	0	0	0	0	0	0	0	0	0	0
		1983–84	62	0	1	43	0	1	7	0	0	11	0	0	1	0	0	0	0	0	0	0	0	0	0	0	0	0	0
		1984–85	50	0	1	42	0	1	2	0	0	6	0	0	0	0	0	0	0	0	0	0	0	0	0	0	0	0	0
		1985–86	57	0	0	42	0	0	2	0	0	8	0	0	5	0	0	0	0	0	0	0	0	0	0	0	0	0	0
		1986–87	13	1	0	11	0	0	0	0	0	2	1	0	0	0	0	0	0	0	0	0	0	0	0	0	0	0	0
Shuker	John	1962–63	18	0	5	18	0	5	0	0	0	0	0	0	0	0	0	0	0	0	0	0	0	0	0	0	0	0	0
		1963–64	16	0	0	12	0	0	4	0	0	0	0	0	0	0	0	0	0	0	0	0	0	0	0	0	0	0	0
		1964–65	11	0	0	11	0	0	0	0	0	0	0	0	0	0	0	0	0	0	0	0	0	0	0	0	0	0	0
		1965–66	36	1	9	33	1	9	2	0	0	1	0	0	0	0	0	0	0	0	0	0	0	0	0	0	0	0	0
		1966–67	28	2	3	24	2	3	3	0	0	1	0	0	0	0	0	0	0	0	0	0	0	0	0	0	0	0	0

Surname	Forename	Season	Total			League			FA Cup			FL Cup			Other			FA Trophy			Setanta Sld			SL Cup			SL Inter Zone		
			app	subs	gls	app	subs	gls	app	subs	gls	app	subs	gls	app	subs	gls	app	subs	gls	app	subs	gls	app	subs	gls	app	subs	gls
		1967–68	41	1	10	36	1	9	3	0	1	2	0	0	0	0	0	0	0	0	0	0	0	0	0	0	0	0	0
		1968–69	37	0	8	34	0	8	2	0	0	1	0	0	0	0	0	0	0	0	0	0	0	0	0	0	0	0	0
		1969–70	41	0	3	34	0	3	2	0	0	5	0	0	0	0	0	0	0	0	0	0	0	0	0	0	0	0	0
		1970–71	49	0	1	42	0	1	5	0	0	2	0	0	0	0	0	0	0	0	0	0	0	0	0	0	0	0	0
		1971–72	45	0	0	41	0	0	1	0	0	3	0	0	0	0	0	0	0	0	0	0	0	0	0	0	0	0	0
		1972–73	44	0	1	36	0	1	2	0	0	3	0	0	3	0	0	0	0	0	0	0	0	0	0	0	0	0	0
		1973–74	43	0	0	41	0	0	1	0	0	1	0	0	0	0	0	0	0	0	0	0	0	0	0	0	0	0	0
		1974–75	44	0	3	42	0	3	1	0	0	1	0	0	0	0	0	0	0	0	0	0	0	0	0	0	0	0	0
		1975–76	44	0	3	40	0	3	1	0	0	3	0	0	0	0	0	0	0	0	0	0	0	0	0	0	0	0	0
		1976–77	32	1	1	29	1	1	2	0	0	1	0	0	0	0	0	0	0	0	0	0	0	0	0	0	0	0	0
Sills	Tim	2005–06	9	4	1	9	4	1	0	0	0	0	0	0	0	0	0	0	0	0	0	0	0	0	0	0	0	0	0
Simpson	Billy	1960–61	11	0	3	9	0	3	0	0	0	0	0	0	0	0	0	0	0	0	0	0	0	2	0	0	0	0	0
Simpson	George	1957–58	3	0	0	1	0	0	2	0	0	0	0	0	0	0	0	0	0	0	0	0	0	0	0	0	0	0	0
Simpson	Paul	1988–89	28	1	8	24	1	8	3	0	0	0	0	0	1	0	0	0	0	0	0	0	0	0	0	0	0	0	0
		1989–90	42	4	12	38	4	9	2	0	2	2	0	1	0	0	0	0	0	0	0	0	0	0	0	0	0	0	0
		1990–91	57	0	18	46	0	17	2	0	0	6	0	1	3	0	0	0	0	0	0	0	0	0	0	0	0	0	0
		1991–92	35	1	12	30	1	9	2	0	1	2	0	0	1	0	2	0	0	0	0	0	0	0	0	0	0	0	0
Sims	John	1974–75	6	1	1	6	1	1	0	0	0	0	0	0	0	0	0	0	0	0	0	0	0	0	0	0	0	0	0
Skeen	Ken	1967–68	43	2	8	37	2	4	3	0	2	3	0	2	0	0	0	0	0	0	0	0	0	0	0	0	0	0	0
		1968–69	26	1	3	24	1	3	2	0	0	0	0	0	0	0	0	0	0	0	0	0	0	0	0	0	0	0	0
		1969–70	50	0	13	42	0	9	2	0	1	6	0	3	0	0	0	0	0	0	0	0	0	0	0	0	0	0	0
		1970–71	46	1	9	39	1	6	5	0	3	2	0	0	0	0	0	0	0	0	0	0	0	0	0	0	0	0	0
		1971–72	29	6	3	26	5	2	1	0	0	2	1	1	0	0	0	0	0	0	0	0	0	0	0	0	0	0	0
		1972–73	33	2	3	27	2	2	2	0	0	3	0	1	1	0	0	0	0	0	0	0	0	0	0	0	0	0	0
		1973–74	21	10	1	19	9	1	0	1	0	2	0	0	0	0	0	0	0	0	0	0	0	0	0	0	0	0	0
Skull	John	1954–55	18	0	8	18	0	8	0	0	0	0	0	0	0	0	0	0	0	0	0	0	0	0	0	0	0	0	0
		1955–56	14	0	6	12	0	2	0	0	0	0	0	0	0	0	0	0	0	0	0	0	0	2	0	4	0	0	0
Slabber	Jamie	2006–07	2	1	0	2	1	0	0	0	0	0	0	0	0	0	0	0	0	0	0	0	0	0	0	0	0	0	0
Slatter	Neil	1985–86	34	0	4	22	0	2	2	0	1	6	0	1	4	0	0	0	0	0	0	0	0	0	0	0	0	0	0
		1986–87	19	3	2	15	3	1	0	0	0	4	0	1	0	0	0	0	0	0	0	0	0	0	0	0	0	0	0
		1987–88	21	0	3	16	0	3	0	0	0	5	0	0	0	0	0	0	0	0	0	0	0	0	0	0	0	0	0
		1988–89	28	0	0	25	0	0	3	0	0	0	0	0	0	0	0	0	0	0	0	0	0	0	0	0	0	0	0
		1989–90	10	0	0	10	0	0	0	0	0	0	0	0	0	0	0	0	0	0	0	0	0	0	0	0	0	0	0
Sloan	David	1967–68	16	0	4	16	0	4	0	0	0	0	0	0	0	0	0	0	0	0	0	0	0	0	0	0	0	0	0
		1968–69	45	0	6	42	0	5	2	0	1	1	0	0	0	0	0	0	0	0	0	0	0	0	0	0	0	0	0
		1969–70	33	3	9	27	1	6	0	2	0	6	0	3	0	0	0	0	0	0	0	0	0	0	0	0	0	0	0
		1970–71	38	4	6	31	4	6	5	0	0	2	0	0	0	0	0	0	0	0	0	0	0	0	0	0	0	0	0
		1971–72	32	3	5	29	2	5	0	1	0	3	0	0	0	0	0	0	0	0	0	0	0	0	0	0	0	0	0
		1972–73	25	1	3	21	1	2	0	0	0	3	0	1	1	0	0	0	0	0	0	0	0	0	0	0	0	0	0
Smart	Gary	1988–89	19	2	0	16	1	0	2	0	0	1	0	0	0	1	0	0	0	0	0	0	0	0	0	0	0	0	0
		1989–90	42	1	0	39	1	0	2	0	0	0	0	0	1	0	0	0	0	0	0	0	0	0	0	0	0	0	0
		1990–91	19	2	0	14	1	0	2	0	0	1	1	0	2	0	0	0	0	0	0	0	0	0	0	0	0	0	0
		1991–92	41	2	0	38	1	0	1	0	0	2	0	0	0	1	0	0	0	0	0	0	0	0	0	0	0	0	0
		1992–93	49	0	0	41	0	0	2	0	0	4	0	0	2	0	0	0	0	0	0	0	0	0	0	0	0	0	0

Surname	Forename	Season	Total			League			FA Cup			FL Cup			Other			FA Trophy			Setanta Sld			SL Cup			SL Inter Zone		
			app	subs	gls	app	subs	gls	app	subs	gls	app	subs	gls	app	subs	gls	app	subs	gls	app	subs	gls	app	subs	gls	app	subs	gls
		1993–94	25	2	0	22	1	0	0	1	0	1	0	0	2	0	0	0	0	0	0	0	0	0	0	0	0	0	0
Smillie	Jimmy	1955–56	43	0	25	37	0	23	1	0	0	0	0	0	0	0	0	0	0	0	0	0	0	5	0	2	0	0	0
		1956–57	31	0	4	30	0	4	0	0	0	0	0	0	0	0	0	0	0	0	0	0	0	1	0	0	0	0	0
Smith	Andy	1957–58	26	0	0	23	0	0	1	0	0	0	0	0	0	0	0	0	0	0	0	0	0	2	0	0	0	0	0
		1956–57	44	0	0	41	0	0	1	0	0	0	0	0	0	0	0	0	0	0	0	0	0	2	0	0	0	0	0
Smith	Barry	1959–60	14	0	5	11	0	4	2	0	0	0	0	0	0	0	0	0	0	0	0	0	0	1	0	1	0	0	0
Smith	Charlie	1958–59	1	0	0	1	0	0	0	0	0	0	0	0	0	0	0	0	0	0	0	0	0	0	0	0	0	0	0
Smith	Dave	1994–95	50	1	0	41	1	0	1	0	0	4	0	0	4	0	0	0	0	0	0	0	0	0	0	0	0	0	0
		1995–96	58	0	2	45	0	1	6	0	0	4	0	1	3	0	0	0	0	0	0	0	0	0	0	0	0	0	0
		1996–97	54	0	0	45	0	0	1	0	0	8	0	0	0	0	0	0	0	0	0	0	0	0	0	0	0	0	0
		1997–98	50	1	1	43	1	1	1	0	0	6	0	0	0	0	0	0	0	0	0	0	0	0	0	0	0	0	0
		1998–99	20	5	0	19	3	0	0	1	0	1	1	0	0	0	0	0	0	0	0	0	0	0	0	0	0	0	0
Smith	Jay	2005–06	5	1	0	5	1	0	0	0	0	0	0	0	0	0	0	0	0	0	0	0	0	0	0	0	0	0	0
Smith	Jim	1949–50	34	0	15	33	0	14	1	0	1	0	0	0	0	0	0	0	0	0	0	0	0	0	0	0	0	0	0
		1950–51	34	0	2	34	0	2	0	0	0	0	0	0	0	0	0	0	0	0	0	0	0	0	0	0	0	0	0
		1951–52	25	0	0	21	0	0	2	0	0	0	0	0	0	0	0	0	0	0	0	0	0	2	0	0	0	0	0
		1952–53	12	0	4	8	0	4	2	0	0	0	0	0	0	0	0	0	0	0	0	0	0	2	0	0	0	0	0
		1953–54	28	0	1	19	0	1	2	0	0	0	0	0	0	0	0	0	0	0	0	0	0	7	0	0	0	0	0
		1954–55	9	0	0	8	0	0	1	0	0	0	0	0	0	0	0	0	0	0	0	0	0	0	0	0	0	0	0
		1955–56	1	0	0	1	0	0	0	0	0	0	0	0	0	0	0	0	0	0	0	0	0	0	0	0	0	0	0
Smith	Ken	1953–54	40	0	17	25	0	12	10	0	5	0	0	0	0	0	0	0	0	0	0	0	0	5	0	0	0	0	0
		1954–55	18	0	15	13	0	13	2	0	1	0	0	0	0	0	0	0	0	0	0	0	0	3	0	1	0	0	0
Smith	Roy	1952–53	26	0	0	19	0	0	4	0	0	0	0	0	0	0	0	0	0	0	0	0	0	3	0	0	0	0	0
Smithers	Tim	1980–81	32	3	3	27	3	3	1	0	0	4	0	0	0	0	0	0	0	0	0	0	0	0	0	0	0	0	0
		1981–82	58	0	2	44	0	1	6	0	1	5	0	0	3	0	0	0	0	0	0	0	0	0	0	0	0	0	0
		1982–83	28	3	2	24	1	2	4	0	0	0	0	0	0	2	0	0	0	0	0	0	0	0	0	0	0	0	0
Smithson	Rodney	1965–66	2	0	0	1	0	0	1	0	0	0	0	0	0	0	0	0	0	0	0	0	0	0	0	0	0	0	0
		1966–67	5	2	0	5	2	0	0	0	0	0	0	0	0	0	0	0	0	0	0	0	0	0	0	0	0	0	0
		1967–68	36	0	1	32	0	1	2	0	0	2	0	0	0	0	0	0	0	0	0	0	0	0	0	0	0	0	0
		1968–69	26	2	0	24	2	0	1	0	0	1	0	0	0	0	0	0	0	0	0	0	0	0	0	0	0	0	0
		1969–70	50	0	0	42	0	0	2	0	0	6	0	0	0	0	0	0	0	0	0	0	0	0	0	0	0	0	0
		1970–71	35	0	5	28	0	5	5	0	0	2	0	0	0	0	0	0	0	0	0	0	0	0	0	0	0	0	0
		1971–72	15	0	0	14	0	0	1	0	0	0	0	0	0	0	0	0	0	0	0	0	0	0	0	0	0	0	0
		1972–73	1	1	0	0	1	0	0	0	0	0	0	0	1	0	0	0	0	0	0	0	0	0	0	0	0	0	0
		1973–74	1	1	0	1	1	0	0	0	0	0	0	0	0	0	0	0	0	0	0	0	0	0	0	0	0	0	0
		1974–75	3	0	0	3	0	0	0	0	0	0	0	0	0	0	0	0	0	0	0	0	0	0	0	0	0	0	0
Spearing	Tony	1984–85	5	0	0	5	0	0	0	0	0	0	0	0	0	0	0	0	0	0	0	0	0	0	0	0	0	0	0
Spelman	Ron	1965–66	18	1	2	15	1	1	2	0	1	1	0	0	0	0	0	0	0	0	0	0	0	0	0	0	0	0	0
St Aimee	Kieron	2007–08	3	0	0	2	0	0	1	0	0	0	0	0	0	0	0	0	0	0	0	0	0	0	0	0	0	0	0
Stables	Ian	1958–59	6	0	0	3	0	0	0	0	0	0	0	0	0	0	0	0	0	0	0	0	0	2	0	0	1	0	0
Standing	Michael	2007–08	3	4	0	3	3	0	0	1	0	0	0	0	0	0	0	0	0	0	0	0	0	0	0	0	0	0	0
Stanton	Sid	1949–50	44	0	1	41	0	1	2	0	0	0	0	0	0	0	0	0	0	0	0	0	0	1	0	0	0	0	0
		1950–51	7	0	0	7	0	0	0	0	0	0	0	0	0	0	0	0	0	0	0	0	0	0	0	0	0	0	0
Steel	Ronnie	1952–53	54	0	15	42	0	11	5	0	3	0	0	0	0	0	0	0	0	0	0	0	0	7	0	1	0	0	0

Surname	Forename	Season	Total			League			FA Cup			FL Cup			Other			FA Trophy			Setanta Sld			SL Cup			SL Inter Zone		
			app	subs	gls	app	subs	gls	app	subs	gls	app	subs	gls	app	subs	gls	app	subs	gls	app	subs	gls	app	subs	gls	app	subs	gls
		1953–54	52	0	13	35	0	7	10	0	3	0	0	0	0	0	0	0	0	0	0	0	0	7	0	3	0	0	0
		1954–55	25	0	4	20	0	3	2	0	0	0	0	0	0	0	0	0	0	0	0	0	0	3	0	1	0	0	0
Steele	Lee	2002–03	3	8	3	3	7	3	0	1	0	0	0	0	0	0	0	0	0	0	0	0	0	0	0	0	0	0	0
		2003–04	3	13	1	3	13	1	0	0	0	0	0	0	0	0	0	0	0	0	0	0	0	0	0	0	0	0	0
Stein	Mark	1989–90	41	3	9	38	3	9	2	0	0	0	0	0	1	0	0	0	0	0	0	0	0	0	0	0	0	0	0
		1990–91	34	7	8	28	6	8	0	1	0	4	0	0	2	0	0	0	0	0	0	0	0	0	0	0	0	0	0
		1991–92	6	1	1	6	1	1	0	0	0	0	0	0	0	0	0	0	0	0	0	0	0	0	0	0	0	0	0
Stephens	Alf	1949–50	7	0	1	6	0	1	1	0	0	0	0	0	0	0	0	0	0	0	0	0	0	0	0	0	0	0	0
Stirling	Jude	2005–06	9	5	0	6	4	0	0	1	0	1	0	0	2	0	0	0	0	0	0	0	0	0	0	0	0	0	0
Stockley	Sam	2001–02	42	2	0	39	2	0	1	0	0	1	0	0	1	0	0	0	0	0	0	0	0	0	0	0	0	0	0
Stott	Ian	1977–78	6	0	2	6	0	2	0	0	0	0	0	0	0	0	0	0	0	0	0	0	0	0	0	0	0	0	0
		1978–79	3	0	0	2	0	0	0	0	0	1	0	0	0	0	0	0	0	0	0	0	0	0	0	0	0	0	0
		1979–80	21	0	1	19	0	1	1	0	0	1	0	0	0	0	0	0	0	0	0	0	0	0	0	0	0	0	0
Styles	Alan	1958–59	5	0	0	4	0	0	0	0	0	0	0	0	0	0	0	0	0	0	0	0	0	0	0	0	1	0	0
Sweetzer	Jimmy	1978–79	1	8	2	0	8	1	0	0	0	1	0	1	0	0	0	0	0	0	0	0	0	0	0	0	0	0	0
Tait	Mick	1974–75	4	0	0	4	0	0	0	0	0	0	0	0	0	0	0	0	0	0	0	0	0	0	0	0	0	0	0
		1975–76	34	4	12	34	3	12	0	0	0	0	1	0	0	0	0	0	0	0	0	0	0	0	0	0	0	0	0
		1976–77	27	0	12	23	0	11	2	0	0	2	0	1	0	0	0	0	0	0	0	0	0	0	0	0	0	0	0
Tait	Paul	1998–99	19	0	0	17	0	0	2	0	0	0	0	0	0	0	0	0	0	0	0	0	0	0	0	0	0	0	0
		1999–2000	43	0	0	34	0	0	2	0	0	3	0	0	4	0	0	0	0	0	0	0	0	0	0	0	0	0	0
		2000–01	24	4	3	22	4	3	0	0	0	2	0	0	0	0	0	0	0	0	0	0	0	0	0	0	0	0	0
		2001–02	14	1	0	13	1	0	0	0	0	1	0	0	0	0	0	0	0	0	0	0	0	0	0	0	0	0	0
Tallant	E	1951–52	2	0	0	2	0	0	0	0	0	0	0	0	0	0	0	0	0	0	0	0	0	0	0	0	0	0	0
Tapping	Fred	1949–50	21	0	6	18	0	1	2	0	4	0	0	0	0	0	0	0	0	0	0	0	0	1	0	1	0	0	0
		1950–51	13	0	1	10	0	1	2	0	0	0	0	0	0	0	0	0	0	0	0	0	0	1	0	0	0	0	0
Tardif	Chris	2004–05	43	0	0	40	0	0	1	0	0	1	0	0	1	0	0	0	0	0	0	0	0	0	0	0	0	0	0
		2005–06	13	1	0	10	1	0	0	0	0	1	0	0	2	0	0	0	0	0	0	0	0	0	0	0	0	0	0
		2006–07	4	1	0	4	1	0	0	0	0	0	0	0	0	0	0	0	0	0	0	0	0	0	0	0	0	0	0
		2007–08	1	1	0	1	1	0	0	0	0	0	0	0	0	0	0	0	0	0	0	0	0	0	0	0	0	0	0
Taylor	Geoff	1956–57	15	0	4	12	0	4	1	0	0	0	0	0	0	0	0	0	0	0	0	0	0	2	0	0	0	0	0
Taylor	Les	1974–75	5	0	0	5	0	0	0	0	0	0	0	0	0	0	0	0	0	0	0	0	0	0	0	0	0	0	0
		1975–76	37	0	0	35	0	0	1	0	0	1	0	0	0	0	0	0	0	0	0	0	0	0	0	0	0	0	0
		1976–77	34	0	2	32	0	2	0	0	0	2	0	0	0	0	0	0	0	0	0	0	0	0	0	0	0	0	0
		1977–78	51	0	6	46	0	6	1	0	0	4	0	0	0	0	0	0	0	0	0	0	0	0	0	0	0	0	0
		1978–79	52	0	2	46	0	1	1	0	0	5	0	1	0	0	0	0	0	0	0	0	0	0	0	0	0	0	0
		1979–80	36	0	6	36	0	6	0	0	0	0	0	0	0	0	0	0	0	0	0	0	0	0	0	0	0	0	0
		1980–81	24	0	0	19	0	0	0	0	0	5	0	0	0	0	0	0	0	0	0	0	0	0	0	0	0	0	0
Taylor	Matt	2007–08	0	4	0	0	3	0	0	0	0	0	0	0	0	0	0	0	0	0	0	1	0	0	0	0	0	0	0
		2008–09	0	7	0	0	4	0	0	2	0	0	0	0	0	0	0	0	0	0	0	1	0	0	0	0	0	0	0
Tether	Colin	1960–61	23	0	0	22	0	0	0	0	0	0	0	0	0	0	0	0	0	0	0	0	0	1	0	0	0	0	0
		1961–62	12	0	0	10	0	0	0	0	0	0	0	0	0	0	0	0	0	0	0	0	0	2	0	0	0	0	0
Thomas	Andy	1980–81	7	2	1	7	2	1	0	0	0	0	0	0	0	0	0	0	0	0	0	0	0	0	0	0	0	0	0
		1981–82	40	8	18	31	8	14	6	0	3	3	0	1	0	0	0	0	0	0	0	0	0	0	0	0	0	0	0
		1982–83	18	12	9	15	9	7	0	0	0	1	2	1	2	1	1	0	0	0	0	0	0	0	0	0	0	0	0

Surname	Forename	Season	Total			League			FA Cup			FL Cup			Other			FA Trophy			Setanta Sld			SL Cup			SL Inter Zone		
			app	subs	gls	app	subs	gls	app	subs	gls	app	subs	gls	app	subs	gls	app	subs	gls	app	subs	gls	app	subs	gls	app	subs	gls
		1983–84	35	0	9	23	0	7	3	0	0	9	0	2	0	0	0	0	0	0	0	0	0	0	0	0	0	0	0
		1984–85	1	3	1	1	3	1	0	0	0	0	0	0	0	0	0	0	0	0	0	0	0	0	0	0	0	0	0
		1985–86	19	5	7	12	5	2	0	0	0	4	0	3	3	0	2	0	0	0	0	0	0	0	0	0	0	0	0
Thomas	Johnnie	1952–53	5	0	0	3	0	0	0	0	0	0	0	0	0	0	0	0	0	0	0	0	0	2	0	0	0	0	0
Thomas	Kevin	1972–73	6	0	0	5	0	0	0	0	0	0	0	0	1	0	0	0	0	0	0	0	0	0	0	0	0	0	0
Thomas	Martin	2001–02	14	1	2	13	1	2	0	0	0	1	0	0	0	0	0	0	0	0	0	0	0	0	0	0	0	0	0
Thompson	Brian	1969–70	22	2	2	20	2	2	2	0	0	0	0	0	0	0	0	0	0	0	0	0	0	0	0	0	0	0	0
		1970–71	22	1	0	20	1	0	0	0	0	2	0	0	0	0	0	0	0	0	0	0	0	0	0	0	0	0	0
		1971–72	11	1	2	11	1	2	0	0	0	0	0	0	0	0	0	0	0	0	0	0	0	0	0	0	0	0	0
		1972–73	1	1	0	1	1	0	0	0	0	0	0	0	0	0	0	0	0	0	0	0	0	0	0	0	0	0	0
Thompson	Harry	1949–50	44	0	0	41	0	0	2	0	0	0	0	0	0	0	0	0	0	0	0	0	0	1	0	0	0	0	0
		1950–51	21	0	1	17	0	1	3	0	0	0	0	0	0	0	0	0	0	0	0	0	0	1	0	0	0	0	0
Thomson	Andy	1998–99	26	14	7	25	13	7	0	1	0	1	0	0	0	0	0	0	0	0	0	0	0	0	0	0	0	0	0
Thomson	Jim	1958–59	9	0	2	9	0	2	0	0	0	0	0	0	0	0	0	0	0	0	0	0	0	0	0	0	0	0	0
		1959–60	38	0	10	35	0	9	2	0	0	0	0	0	0	0	0	0	0	0	0	0	0	1	0	1	0	0	0
Thornley	Barry	1967–68	22	0	3	19	0	3	1	0	0	2	0	0	0	0	0	0	0	0	0	0	0	0	0	0	0	0	0
		1968–69	3	1	1	3	1	1	0	0	0	0	0	0	0	0	0	0	0	0	0	0	0	0	0	0	0	0	0
Titcombe	Ken	1960–61	16	0	0	16	0	0	0	0	0	0	0	0	0	0	0	0	0	0	0	0	0	0	0	0	0	0	0
Todd	Colin	1983–84	12	0	0	12	0	0	0	0	0	0	0	0	0	0	0	0	0	0	0	0	0	0	0	0	0	0	0
Togwell	Sam	2004–05	4	1	0	3	1	0	1	0	0	0	0	0	0	0	0	0	0	0	0	0	0	0	0	0	0	0	0
Toulouse	Cyril	1949–50	13	0	4	13	0	4	0	0	0	0	0	0	0	0	0	0	0	0	0	0	0	0	0	0	0	0	0
		1950–51	44	0	3	41	0	2	2	0	1	0	0	0	0	0	0	0	0	0	0	0	0	1	0	0	0	0	0
		1951–52	45	0	3	37	0	3	4	0	0	0	0	0	0	0	0	0	0	0	0	0	0	4	0	0	0	0	0
		1952–53	34	0	7	25	0	6	3	0	0	0	0	0	0	0	0	0	0	0	0	0	0	6	0	1	0	0	0
		1953–54	17	0	3	14	0	3	2	0	0	0	0	0	0	0	0	0	0	0	0	0	0	1	0	0	0	0	0
Townsley	Derek	2003–04	12	2	0	9	2	0	0	0	0	2	0	0	1	0	0	0	0	0	0	0	0	0	0	0	0	0	0
Train	Ray	1981–82	15	0	0	15	0	0	0	0	0	0	0	0	0	0	0	0	0	0	0	0	0	0	0	0	0	0	0
		1982–83	40	2	0	33	1	0	2	1	0	4	0	0	1	0	0	0	0	0	0	0	0	0	0	0	0	0	0
		1983–84	3	1	0	1	0	0	0	0	0	1	1	0	1	0	0	0	0	0	0	0	0	0	0	0	0	0	0
Trainer	Phil	2007–08	47	0	9	41	0	9	4	0	0	0	0	0	0	0	0	2	0	0	0	0	0	0	0	0	0	0	0
		2008–09	19	3	5	16	1	4	2	1	1	0	0	0	0	0	0	0	1	0	1	0	0	0	0	0	0	0	0
Trewick	John	1983–84	5	0	0	3	0	0	1	0	0	1	0	0	0	0	0	0	0	0	0	0	0	0	0	0	0	0	0
		1984–85	49	1	0	41	1	0	2	0	0	6	0	0	0	0	0	0	0	0	0	0	0	0	0	0	0	0	0
		1985–86	44	4	3	34	1	3	2	0	0	6	1	0	2	2	0	0	0	0	0	0	0	0	0	0	0	0	0
		1986–87	36	0	1	31	0	1	1	0	0	3	0	0	1	0	0	0	0	0	0	0	0	0	0	0	0	0	0
		1987–88	3	0	0	3	0	0	0	0	0	0	0	0	0	0	0	0	0	0	0	0	0	0	0	0	0	0	0
Turley	Billy	2005–06	37	1	0	32	1	0	4	0	0	0	0	0	1	0	0	0	0	0	0	0	0	0	0	0	0	0	0
		2006–07	50	0	0	44	0	0	2	0	0	0	0	0	0	0	0	4	0	0	0	0	0	0	0	0	0	0	0
		2007–08	50	0	0	45	0	0	4	0	0	0	0	0	0	0	0	1	0	0	0	0	0	0	0	0	0	0	0
		2008–09	44	0	0	37	0	0	4	0	0	0	0	0	0	0	0	2	0	0	1	0	0	0	0	0	0	0	0
Turner	Arthur	1952–53	22	0	15	14	0	4	4	0	8	0	0	0	0	0	0	0	0	0	0	0	0	4	0	3	0	0	0
Twigg	Gary	2007–08	8	6	3	5	5	3	2	0	0	0	0	0	0	0	0	1	1	0	0	0	0	0	0	0	0	0	0
Van Heusden	Arjan	1997–98	13	0	0	11	0	0	0	0	0	2	0	0	0	0	0	0	0	0	0	0	0	0	0	0	0	0	0
Varadi	Imre	1992–93	3	2	0	3	2	0	0	0	0	0	0	0	0	0	0	0	0	0	0	0	0	0	0	0	0	0	0

Surname	Forename	Season	Total			League			FA Cup			FL Cup			Other			FA Trophy			Setanta Sld			SL Cup			SL Inter Zone		
			app	subs	gls	app	subs	gls	app	subs	gls	app	subs	gls	app	subs	gls	app	subs	gls	app	subs	gls	app	subs	gls	app	subs	gls
Varney	John	1954–55	11	0	9	11	0	9	0	0	0	0	0	0	0	0	0	0	0	0	0	0	0	0	0	0	0	0	0
		1955–56	6	0	1	5	0	1	0	0	0	0	0	0	0	0	0	0	0	0	0	0	0	1	0	0	0	0	0
Veysey	Ken	1990–91	31	0	0	25	0	0	2	0	0	1	0	0	3	0	0	0	0	0	0	0	0	0	0	0	0	0	0
		1991–92	36	0	0	32	0	0	2	0	0	1	0	0	1	0	0	0	0	0	0	0	0	0	0	0	0	0	0
Vickers	Keith	1958–59	1	0	0	0	0	0	0	0	0	0	0	0	0	0	0	0	0	0	0	0	0	0	0	0	1	0	0
Vinter	Mick	1982–83	53	1	14	42	1	10	4	0	3	4	0	1	3	0	0	0	0	0	0	0	0	0	0	0	0	0	0
		1983–84	40	2	14	25	1	11	7	0	1	8	1	2	0	0	0	0	0	0	0	0	0	0	0	0	0	0	0
Viveash	Adi	2002–03	15	0	0	11	0	0	0	0	0	3	0	0	1	0	0	0	0	0	0	0	0	0	0	0	0	0	0
Walker	Ian	1990–91	3	0	0	2	0	0	0	0	0	1	0	0	0	0	0	0	0	0	0	0	0	0	0	0	0	0	0
Walker	Richard	2003–04	3	1	0	3	1	0	0	0	0	0	0	0	0	0	0	0	0	0	0	0	0	0	0	0	0	0	0
Wanless	Paul	1991–92	3	4	0	3	3	0	0	0	0	0	1	0	0	0	0	0	0	0	0	0	0	0	0	0	0	0	0
		1992–93	5	2	0	5	2	0	0	0	0	0	0	0	0	0	0	0	0	0	0	0	0	0	0	0	0	0	0
		1993–94	2	10	1	1	7	0	0	0	0	0	2	1	1	1	0	0	0	0	0	0	0	0	0	0	0	0	0
		1994–95	4	7	0	3	6	0	0	0	0	0	0	0	1	1	0	0	0	0	0	0	0	0	0	0	0	0	0
		2003–04	40	0	5	38	0	5	1	0	0	1	0	0	0	0	0	0	0	0	0	0	0	0	0	0	0	0	0
		2004–05	20	9	1	18	8	1	1	0	0	1	0	0	0	1	0	0	0	0	0	0	0	0	0	0	0	0	0
Ward	Ron	1955–56	17	0	0	14	0	0	0	0	0	0	0	0	0	0	0	0	0	0	0	0	0	3	0	0	0	0	0
Warrell	Sam	2007–08	2	0	0	0	0	0	0	0	0	0	0	0	0	0	0	1	0	0	1	0	0	0	0	0	0	0	0
Warren	Mark	1998–99	4	0	0	4	0	0	0	0	0	0	0	0	0	0	0	0	0	0	0	0	0	0	0	0	0	0	0
Washington	Lawrie	1949–50	1	0	0	1	0	0	0	0	0	0	0	0	0	0	0	0	0	0	0	0	0	0	0	0	0	0	0
Waterman	David	2001–02	4	1	0	4	1	0	0	0	0	0	0	0	0	0	0	0	0	0	0	0	0	0	0	0	0	0	0
		2002–03	31	2	2	27	2	1	3	0	0	0	0	0	1	0	1	0	0	0	0	0	0	0	0	0	0	0	0
		2003–04	8	7	0	6	7	0	1	0	0	0	0	0	1	0	0	0	0	0	0	0	0	0	0	0	0	0	0
Watson	Gary	1978–79	10	0	0	9	0	0	0	0	0	1	0	0	0	0	0	0	0	0	0	0	0	0	0	0	0	0	0
		1979–80	15	0	0	15	0	0	0	0	0	0	0	0	0	0	0	0	0	0	0	0	0	0	0	0	0	0	0
Watson	Mark	1998–99	26	0	0	23	0	0	3	0	0	0	0	0	0	0	0	0	0	0	0	0	0	0	0	0	0	0	0
		1999–2000	42	1	0	34	1	0	5	0	0	1	0	0	2	0	0	0	0	0	0	0	0	0	0	0	0	0	0
Way	Mick	1969–70	3	1	0	3	1	0	0	0	0	0	0	0	0	0	0	0	0	0	0	0	0	0	0	0	0	0	0
		1970–71	2	1	0	2	1	0	0	0	0	0	0	0	0	0	0	0	0	0	0	0	0	0	0	0	0	0	0
		1971–72	11	0	0	9	0	0	1	0	0	1	0	0	0	0	0	0	0	0	0	0	0	0	0	0	0	0	0
Weatherstone	Ross	1999–2000	6	0	0	3	0	0	1	0	0	0	0	0	2	0	0	0	0	0	0	0	0	0	0	0	0	0	0
		2000–01	1	0	0	1	0	0	0	0	0	0	0	0	0	0	0	0	0	0	0	0	0	0	0	0	0	0	0
Weatherstone	Simon	1997–98	2	9	1	2	9	1	0	0	0	0	0	0	0	0	0	0	0	0	0	0	0	0	0	0	0	0	0
		1998–99	4	10	2	4	8	1	0	0	0	0	2	1	0	0	0	0	0	0	0	0	0	0	0	0	0	0	0
		1999–2000	15	9	1	13	8	1	0	0	0	0	1	0	2	0	0	0	0	0	0	0	0	0	0	0	0	0	0
		2000–01	6	1	0	6	1	0	0	0	0	0	0	0	0	0	0	0	0	0	0	0	0	0	0	0	0	0	0
Weedon	Ben	2005–06	1	1	0	1	1	0	0	0	0	0	0	0	0	0	0	0	0	0	0	0	0	0	0	0	0	0	0
		2007–08	2	2	0	1	1	0	1	1	0	0	0	0	0	0	0	0	0	0	0	0	0	0	0	0	0	0	0
Whatmore	Neil	1982–83	22	1	12	22	1	12	0	0	0	0	0	0	0	0	0	0	0	0	0	0	0	0	0	0	0	0	0
		1983–84	17	5	4	11	2	3	2	2	0	3	1	1	1	0	0	0	0	0	0	0	0	0	0	0	0	0	0
Whelan	Phil	1997–98	7	2	0	6	2	0	0	0	0	1	0	0	0	0	0	0	0	0	0	0	0	0	0	0	0	0	0
		1998–99	15	1	1	14	1	0	0	0	0	1	0	1	0	0	0	0	0	0	0	0	0	0	0	0	0	0	0
		1999–2000	40	0	2	31	0	2	5	0	0	1	0	0	3	0	0	0	0	0	0	0	0	0	0	0	0	0	0
White	Archie	1976–77	2	0	0	2	0	0	0	0	0	0	0	0	0	0	0	0	0	0	0	0	0	0	0	0	0	0	0

Surname	Forename	Season	Total			League			FA Cup			FL Cup			Other			FA Trophy			Setanta Sld			SL Cup			SL Inter Zone		
			app	subs	gls	app	subs	gls	app	subs	gls	app	subs	gls	app	subs	gls	app	subs	gls	app	subs	gls	app	subs	gls	app	subs	gls
		1977–78	2	9	1	2	7	0	0	0	0	0	2	1	0	0	0	0	0	0	0	0	0	0	0	0	0	0	0
		1978–79	3	7	1	3	5	1	0	0	0	0	2	0	0	0	0	0	0	0	0	0	0	0	0	0	0	0	0
		1979–80	3	2	0	3	2	0	0	0	0	0	0	0	0	0	0	0	0	0	0	0	0	0	0	0	0	0	0
Whitehurst	Billy	1986–87	21	1	4	19	1	2	1	0	0	0	0	0	1	0	2	0	0	0	0	0	0	0	0	0	0	0	0
		1987–88	21	6	2	17	3	2	0	1	0	3	2	0	1	0	0	0	0	0	0	0	0	0	0	0	0	0	0
Whitehead	Dean	2000–01	18	5	0	16	4	0	0	1	0	2	0	0	0	0	0	0	0	0	0	0	0	0	0	0	0	0	0
		2001–02	32	11	1	30	10	1	1	0	0	0	1	0	1	0	0	0	0	0	0	0	0	0	0	0	0	0	0
		2002–03	11	11	1	9	9	1	1	1	0	1	0	0	0	1	0	0	0	0	0	0	0	0	0	0	0	0	0
		2003–04	40	7	7	37	7	7	1	0	0	2	0	0	0	0	0	0	0	0	0	0	0	0	0	0	0	0	0
Whitehead	Phil	1993–94	43	0	0	39	0	0	4	0	0	0	0	0	0	0	0	0	0	0	0	0	0	0	0	0	0	0	0
		1994–95	44	0	0	38	0	0	1	0	0	4	0	0	1	0	0	0	0	0	0	0	0	0	0	0	0	0	0
		1995–96	42	0	0	34	0	0	6	0	0	0	0	0	2	0	0	0	0	0	0	0	0	0	0	0	0	0	0
		1996–97	52	0	0	43	0	0	1	0	0	8	0	0	0	0	0	0	0	0	0	0	0	0	0	0	0	0	0
		1997–98	34	0	0	32	0	0	1	0	0	1	0	0	0	0	0	0	0	0	0	0	0	0	0	0	0	0	0
		1998–99	23	0	0	21	0	0	0	0	0	2	0	0	0	0	0	0	0	0	0	0	0	0	0	0	0	0	0
Whittingham	Guy	2000–01	1	0	1	1	0	1	0	0	0	0	0	0	0	0	0	0	0	0	0	0	0	0	0	0	0	0	0
Whyte	Chris	1996–97	10	0	0	10	0	0	0	0	0	0	0	0	0	0	0	0	0	0	0	0	0	0	0	0	0	0	0
Wilkie	Alex	1958–59	20	0	0	12	0	0	3	0	0	0	0	0	0	0	0	0	0	0	0	0	0	1	0	0	4	0	0
Willey	Alan	1960–61	1	0	0	1	0	0	0	0	0	0	0	0	0	0	0	0	0	0	0	0	0	0	0	0	0	0	0
		1961–62	31	0	23	27	0	23	2	0	0	0	0	0	0	0	0	0	0	0	0	0	0	2	0	0	0	0	0
		1962–63	29	0	9	26	0	9	2	0	0	1	0	0	0	0	0	0	0	0	0	0	0	0	0	0	0	0	0
		1963–64	35	0	7	29	0	5	5	0	2	1	0	0	0	0	0	0	0	0	0	0	0	0	0	0	0	0	0
		1964–65	18	0	3	17	0	3	1	0	0	0	0	0	0	0	0	0	0	0	0	0	0	0	0	0	0	0	0
		1965–66	13	1	6	13	1	6	0	0	0	0	0	0	0	0	0	0	0	0	0	0	0	0	0	0	0	0	0
Williams	Brett	1991–92	7	0	0	7	0	0	0	0	0	0	0	0	0	0	0	0	0	0	0	0	0	0	0	0	0	0	0
Willmott	Chris	2005–06	45	3	2	38	3	2	4	0	0	0	0	0	3	0	0	0	0	0	0	0	0	0	0	0	0	0	0
		2006–07	18	0	0	17	0	0	1	0	0	0	0	0	0	0	0	0	0	0	0	0	0	0	0	0	0	0	0
		2007–08	6	2	0	5	2	0	1	0	0	0	0	0	0	0	0	0	0	0	0	0	0	0	0	0	0	0	0
		2008–09	38	3	2	34	3	2	2	0	0	0	0	0	0	0	0	1	0	0	1	0	0	0	0	0	0	0	0
Wilson	Charlie	1949–50	9	0	0	9	0	0	0	0	0	0	0	0	0	0	0	0	0	0	0	0	0	0	0	0	0	0	0
Wilson	Joe	1954–55	33	0	7	30	0	6	1	0	0	0	0	0	0	0	0	0	0	0	0	0	0	2	0	1	0	0	0
Wilson	Phil	2000–01	1	1	0	1	1	0	0	0	0	0	0	0	0	0	0	0	0	0	0	0	0	0	0	0	0	0	0
Wilsterman	Brian	1996–97	1	0	0	1	0	0	0	0	0	0	0	0	0	0	0	0	0	0	0	0	0	0	0	0	0	0	0
		1997–98	16	9	0	15	9	0	0	0	0	1	0	0	0	0	0	0	0	0	0	0	0	0	0	0	0	0	0
		1998–99	14	5	2	12	5	2	1	0	0	1	0	0	0	0	0	0	0	0	0	0	0	0	0	0	0	0	0
Windass	Dean	1998–99	38	0	18	33	0	15	3	0	3	2	0	0	0	0	0	0	0	0	0	0	0	0	0	0	0	0	0
Winters	Tom	2003–04	0	1	0	0	1	0	0	0	0	0	0	0	0	0	0	0	0	0	0	0	0	0	0	0	0	0	0
		2004–05	1	4	1	0	4	0	0	0	0	0	0	0	1	0	1	0	0	0	0	0	0	0	0	0	0	0	0
Wolleaston	Rob	2004–05	16	6	0	14	6	0	0	0	0	1	0	0	1	0	0	0	0	0	0	0	0	0	0	0	0	0	0
Wood	Brian	1954–55	2	0	0	2	0	0	0	0	0	0	0	0	0	0	0	0	0	0	0	0	0	0	0	0	0	0	0
		1955–56	2	0	0	2	0	0	0	0	0	0	0	0	0	0	0	0	0	0	0	0	0	0	0	0	0	0	0
Wood	Steve	1994–95	3	0	0	2	0	0	0	0	0	0	0	0	1	0	0	0	0	0	0	0	0	0	0	0	0	0	0
		1995–96	14	1	2	10	1	0	3	0	2	0	0	0	1	0	0	0	0	0	0	0	0	0	0	0	0	0	0
Woodman	Andy	2001–02	15	0	0	15	0	0	0	0	0	0	0	0	0	0	0	0	0	0	0	0	0	0	0	0	0	0	0

Surname	Forename	Season	Total			League			FA Cup			FL Cup			Other			FA Trophy			Setanta Sld			SL Cup			SL Inter Zone		
			app	subs	gls	app	subs	gls	app	subs	gls	app	subs	gls	app	subs	gls	app	subs	gls	app	subs	gls	app	subs	gls	app	subs	gls
		2002–03	52	0	0	45	0	0	3	0	0	3	0	0	1	0	0	0	0	0	0	0	0	0	0	0	0	0	0
		2003–04	45	0	0	41	0	0	1	0	0	2	0	0	1	0	0	0	0	0	0	0	0	0	0	0	0	0	0
Woodward	Gerry	1949–50	19	0	0	16	0	0	2	0	0	0	0	0	0	0	0	0	0	0	0	0	0	1	0	0	0	0	0
		1950–51	17	0	0	17	0	0	0	0	0	0	0	0	0	0	0	0	0	0	0	0	0	0	0	0	0	0	0
Woozley	David	2004–05	13	2	1	11	2	1	1	0	0	0	0	0	1	0	0	0	0	0	0	0	0	0	0	0	0	0	0
Wright	Anthony	1998–99	5	2	0	4	2	0	1	0	0	0	0	0	0	0	0	0	0	0	0	0	0	0	0	0	0	0	0
Wright	Mark	1980–81	1	0	0	0	0	0	1	0	0	0	0	0	0	0	0	0	0	0	0	0	0	0	0	0	0	0	0
		1981–82	9	2	0	8	2	0	1	0	0	0	0	0	0	0	0	0	0	0	0	0	0	0	0	0	0	0	0
Yates	Harry	1952–53	41	0	22	31	0	16	4	0	2	0	0	0	0	0	0	0	0	0	0	0	0	6	0	4	0	0	0
		1953–54	14	0	7	8	0	3	0	0	0	0	0	0	0	0	0	0	0	0	0	0	0	6	0	4	0	0	0
		1954–55	47	0	25	41	0	21	2	0	2	0	0	0	0	0	0	0	0	0	0	0	0	4	0	2	0	0	0
Young	George	1949–50	1	0	0	1	0	0	0	0	0	0	0	0	0	0	0	0	0	0	0	0	0	0	0	0	0	0	0
Youngman	Brian	1957–58	1	0	0	1	0	0	0	0	0	0	0	0	0	0	0	0	0	0	0	0	0	0	0	0	0	0	0
Zebroski	Chris	2006–07	9	1	2	9	1	2	0	0	0	0	0	0	0	0	0	0	0	0	0	0	0	0	0	0	0	0	0

Printed by Printforce, United Kingdom